General John M. Palmer,
Citizen Soldiers,
and the
Army of a Democracy

Brigadier General John McAuley Palmer, on Active Duty in the Pentagon, 1943
U.S. Army Photograph

General John M. Palmer, Citizen Soldiers, and the Army of a Democracy

I. B. HOLLEY, JR.

Contributions in Military History, Number 28

GREENWOOD PRESS
Westport, Connecticut • London, England

Library of Congress Cataloging in Publication Data

Holley, I. B. (Irving Brinton), 1919-
 General John M. Palmer, citizen soldiers, and the
army of a democracy.

 (Contributions in military history, ISSN 0084-9251 ;
no. 28)
 Bibliography: p.
 Includes index.
 1. Palmer, John McAuley, 1870-1955. 2. United States
—History, Military—20th century. 3. Generals—United
States biography. 4. United States. Army—Biography.
I. Palmer, John McAuley, 1870-1955. II. Title.
III. Series.
E745.P25H64   355'.0092'4 [B]   81-6963
ISBN 0-313-23121-4 (lib. bdg.)   AACR2

Library of Congress Catalog Card Number: 81-6963
ISBN: 0-313-23121-4
ISSN: 0084-9251

First published in 1982

Greenwood Press
A division of Congressional Information Service, Inc.
88 Post Road West
Westport, Connecticut 06881

Printed in the United States of America

10 9 8 7 6 5 4 3 2 1

Copyright Acknowledgment

Permission has been granted for use of an extract from
Army & Navy Journal, 17 July 1948, pp. 1275-82. Copyright
© 1948 by Army & Navy Journal Inc.

To

MARY PALMER ROCKWELL

without whose devotion to her father's
ideals this volume could not have been completed

Contents

Contents   ix

Illustrations

PHOTOGRAPHS

Preface

The volume presented here offers far more than the life story of an officer who graduated from the U. S. Military Academy in 1892 and after serving in the army with distinction in many capacities finally retired, for the second time, in 1946. In a sense, this is not one book but several, for the narrative account can be read on many different levels.

On one plane this is the story of an individual officer's perspectives on the transformation of the small regular army of the Indian frontier into the almost incomprehensibly complex institution it had become by the end of World War II. John M. Palmer's years of service reflect the gradual evolution of the homogeneous officer corps in the "Old Army," built upon the ideal if not always the actuality of the officer and gentleman, into the far more professional but socially heterogeneous force extant at the end of his career. In sharper focus is a second theme, a story of the General Staff and, indeed, the very concept of a military staff. The reforms Elihu Root began as Secretary of War (1899-1904) required at least a generation to implement, and Palmer was an active participant in the process from the days when he scribbled orders with a stub pencil on the pommel of his saddle in the Arizona deserts down to the time when he watched electronic data processors in the Pentagon spewing out information faster than he could read it.

Another theme of this study is the art of command. Palmer exercised command and was an intimate of those at the top for a long generation: civilian secretaries; chiefs of staff; and division, corps, and army commanders in the field. All of them revealed widely differing styles and practices in wielding authority and in coping with the inescapable human equation.

Finally, and most significantly, this volume is a study of the U. S. Army as a political institution. This fourth theme reflects Palmer's lifelong preoccupation with the fundamental issue of manpower for national defense: How can the citizen soldier best be related to the regular forces for the most effective national defense at the least social and financial cost? Here Palmer's substantial contributions may be epitomized by his friend Gen. George C. Marshall, who described him as a "military elder statesman" who provided the "civilian conscience" of the Army.

A few words of explanation concerning the authorship of this volume are in order. General Palmer had completed slightly less than a fifth of the book as it now appears when declining health forced him to give it up. While doing research at the Library of Congress he had come to admire Col. Willard Webb, for many years the chief of the Stack and Reader Division, whose role as a reserve officer in the World War II seemed to exemplify the ideal of the citizen soldier and reservist. When Palmer transferred his papers to the Library of Congress, he appointed Webb his literary executor, asking him to select a suitable scholar to carry on the unfinished work. Webb approached, among others, Prof. Ralph Gabriel of Yale University, who suggested that I, one of his former students and a reserve officer, undertake the task.

The resulting manuscript represents a three-way division of labor. Chapters 1 to 10, written entirely by General Palmer, are untouched save for minor editorial details. They reflect the charm of his late Victorian prose, expansive and anecdotal, with a light sprinkling of classical phrases and Miltonian quotations. Palmer also roughed out drafts or extended notes for Chapters 11 through 24, but all of these had to be reworked in varying degrees. Because these chapters were largely completed while the general was still alive and with his extensive collaboration, it seemed appropriate to use the first person singular down to the point where the narrative switches to the third person in Chapter 25. From that point on, the volume is biography rather than autobiography. Even though I made use of some rather sketchy notes and outlines compiled by Palmer for a few of the subsequent chapters and discussed with him many of the events and issues, the last half of the book can in no sense be called collaboration; I accept full responsibility for the interpretations presented there.

General Palmer's own conception of his memoirs was perhaps best stated in a letter to Grenville Clark, 14 September 1940:

It will tell how a hidebound professional soldier gradually came to see that a government by the people must rest its defense upon Washington's army of the people and not upon Upton's expansible standing army. We must build military strength into the democratic state without creating an exclusive samurai caste. We must have military power without militarism.

As a historian, I confronted two rather troublesome problems: I could not write the book originally planned by the general without surrendering my scholarly independence. To this end I asked for and the general's family generously granted me full freedom of interpretation. Thus reassured, I have attempted to present Palmer's often highly controversial views with such detachment that a reader would be unable to detect my personal position. No less difficult was the problem of how to handle the general's psychological state at several crucial junctures in his career. I have resisted any attempt to write a psychoanalytic history, as I am not a psychoanalyst. Instead, I have endeavored to lay out the evidence as fairly as I could, for readers to interpret as they will. Above all, I have tried to treat my subject in the context of his own times and not to judge him by the rapidly shifting standards and values prevailing in the decades following his death in 1955.

Acknowledgments

Although I am credited on the title page as the author of this book, I am conscious of the many people who shared in the effort with me, generously contributing time, effort, and ingenuity to bring the project to fruition. First among those to whom I am obligated, of course, is Mary Palmer Rockwell, General Palmer's daughter, without whose help it would have been difficult indeed to complete this volume. Her contributions to the final product, too numerous to itemize, are but inadequately recognized in the enumeration of helpful informants recorded in the note on Sources.

At the Library of Congress, Willard Webb, Robert Land, David Mearns, and Katharine Brand assisted me in various ways. Miss Brand, after retiring from the Library of Congress, continued, with her friend and companion Miss Carol Piper, to take a lively interest in the progress of this volume, criticizing chapter drafts and sharing memories of General Palmer.

At the National Archives, Robert W. Krauskopf, John E. Taylor, Jerry Ryan, and Tom Holman were particularly helpful. At the U.S. Army Center for Military History, Kent Roberts Greenfield, Stetson Conn, Maurice Matloff, Charles Romanus, Naomi Allen, and Israel Wice made many resources available, as did George Stansfield at the National War College. At the U.S. Army Military History Institute, Carlisle Barracks, Col. George Pappus, Miss Joyce Eakin, and Richard Sommers uncovered a number of elusive items of value. Similarly, the author received much help at the U.S. Military Academy library from Egon Weiss, Thomas Russell, J. M. O'Donnell, Alan Aimone, Robert Schnare, and Marie T. Capps, as well as from Col. Thomas Griess of the History Department.

For sustained assistance over many years, I am deeply indebted to my many friends and associates in the Duke University Library. Those who merit my gratitude most particularly include Mary Canada and Florence Blakely, outstanding reference librarians, and Gertrude Merritt, Anne and Elvin Strowd, Wilhelmina Lemon, John Waggoner, Shirley Stevens, and Robert Christ. My debts to my colleague in the Department of History, the distinguished military historian, Theodore Ropp, go far beyond gratitude for reading and criticizing the entire manuscript of this book. And to Vivian Jackson, who for many years has headed the departmental secretarial staff, I am deeply indebted for patient efforts in the preparation of manuscript drafts.

Among those elsewhere who assisted in one way or another, I wish to single out the following individuals: John Clifford of the University of Connecticut shared his insights on the Military Training Camps Association; Edward Coffman of the University of Wisconsin generously provided Palmer items turned up in his research on Peyton C. March; Martha Derthick lent me her excellent manuscript study of the National Guard while still a graduate student at Harvard; James Harbison, a member of the New York bar, contributed items on Grenville Clark; Forrest Pogue, Director, Dwight D. Eisenhower Institute for Historical Research, Smithsonian Institution, not only provided a number of Palmer documents from his research in the George C. Marshall papers but also shared his vast knowledge of the U.S. Army; Dr. Samuel R. Spencer, when President of Davidson College, made available the superb manuscript of his unpublished dissertation on the Military Training Camps Association; Prof. Donald Smythe, S. J., of John Carroll University read the entire manuscript and contributed valuable perspectives from his vantage point as biographer of Gen. John J. Pershing; and finally, Col. Eben Swift, U.S. Army, retired, grandson of General Palmer's associate in Italy, Gen. Eben Swift, generously made available a veritable treasure trove of his grandfather's papers. While I am deeply grateful to all of the individuals enumerated above and in the note on Sources, I accept full responsibility for the use made of their contributions.

Institutional debts deserve recognition no less than the help of individuals; I wish to acknowledge financial assistance from the following: the Duke University Research Council and the Carnegie Corporation of New York, for most generous subsidies; the Social Science Research Council, for two separate sabbatical grants; and the American Council of Learned Societies, for support as a Smithsonian Institution fellow.

Finally, I wish to thank my wife, Janet Carlson Holley, not only for her assistance in research and in reading successive drafts critically but also for loyal support throughout the years this book was in the making.

BOOK I

In which John Palmer, after a "Tom Sawyer" boyhood in Abraham Lincoln's Springfield, attends the Military Academy at West Point, where he is trained but scarcely educated, a process he achieves largely on his own by self-directed reading and stimulating associations. The newly commissioned lieutenant joins a regiment in transition from its old Indian fighting army traditions to a modern, professional force, painfully finding new ways in an increasingly technological environment. An expedition to the Orient offers broader horizons but raises moral issues for the young officer. After a decade in the field and two small wars, a return to West Point reveals a fresh outlook there as a rising generation of faculty members reflects the ferment of Progressivism. Palmer writes with grace and humor on political reform for the leading muckraking journals and acquires a circle of literary friends.

1 Abraham Lincoln and My Grandfather

When I was a boy in Springfield, Illinois, many of my grown-up friends and neighbors had known Abraham Lincoln. My grandfather, John M. Palmer, had been closely associated with him at the bar and in politics. In the Lincoln-Douglas debates, Douglas singled my relative out as one of Lincoln's close associates—and with a touch of bitterness too—for Palmer was one of the "anti-Nebraska" Democrats who left Douglas to join Lincoln and the old Whigs in forming the Republican party.

The little prairie city had changed but little since Lincoln left it. My boyhood home on South Seventh Street was near his old home on South Eighth. My grandfather and my father, John Mayo Palmer, practiced law before the Sangamon County Circuit Court in the room where Lincoln had announced that "a house divided against itself cannot stand." Most of the older lawyers had been his associates at the bar. In my grandfather's room at the law office, many old lawyers and veterans used to gather round the big stove and exchange reminiscences of Lincoln and the Civil War. As a small boy I used to hide behind an old secretary and listen to these tales. I have forgotten all of them. If I had been old enough and wise enough to write them down I might have become a Homer of the Lincolniad.

There was a curious phenomenon in the Illinois of those days. When one of the old settlers felt moved to tell a Rabelaisian tale of exceptional coarseness, he would generally save his face by attributing its authorship to Lincoln. "That reminds me of one of Abe Lincoln's stories," he would say. Then he would regale his hearers with some filthy abomination, unredeemed by any trace of wit or wisdom.

One day when I was on my way to my father's office, I saw a group of men lounging in the wide doorway of Little's Livery Stable. There was a burst of laughter as I drew near. Then I heard "Doc" Jones, an old "horse doctor,"

make the usual preface, "That reminds me of a story Abe Lincoln told me."
With the curiosity of a small boy I slipped in behind the group of hostlers and
loafers and listened to one of the coarsest yarns I have ever heard. Though I
scarcely understood it, I listened with gusto and joined in the laughter which
followed.

From the livery stable, I went to the law office. My father was not at his desk
but I could see my grandfather busy in the front room. While I was waiting for
my father a young kinsman came in and I gleefully told him Doc Jones'
story—but in low tones so that my grandfather would not hear me.

As we were laughing at the choice tidbit, my grandfather's deep voice came
booming from the front room:

> "John McAuley!" (I was his namesake. He never called me "John,"
> always "John McAuley.")

> "John McAuley, come in here," he said.

I can see him now as I saw him then when I approached his desk. He was a
big, broad-shouldered, ruddy-faced man. He looked at me over his spectacles
and asked, "What were you telling Louis just now?"

> "I was telling him one of Abe Lincoln's stories."

> "Where did you hear it?", he asked.

> "I heard 'Doc' Jones tell it."

> "Tell it to me."

I was overwhelmed with confusion. I tried to beg off, but his deepset blue
eyes bored into mine and he made me tell the whole filthy story. He verily
burned it out of me. There was nothing in it to laugh at when I got through.

Then as I stood abashed before him, he said, "Come here, John McAuley."
He put his hand on my shoulder and drew me close to him and when I looked
up the steel had gone out of his blue eyes.

"I am going to tell you something, John McAuley, that you will remember
as long as you live. Abraham Lincoln never told that story. He told many
stories but none like that." Then he showed me how Lincoln often spoke in
parables to explain things to simple uneducated men who could not understand abstract principles; how his allegories were frequently broad but always
redeemed by wit and wisdom and always with a meaning back of them. He
made me see that Lincoln could never have told the gratuitously filthy story
that I had received from "Doc" Jones.

No lesson ever sunk into a boy more deeply. I wanted to slip away and take
it with me. But as I moved toward the door he called me back again.

"One thing more, John McAuley. Do not say *Abe* Lincoln. After he left 'Old Salem,' nobody called him Abe except behind his back. He was a friend of mine for years and I always called him Mr. Lincoln. Judge Logan and Major Stuart called him Mr. Lincoln. His closest personal friend, Osias M. Hatch, always called him Mr. Lincoln. He could exchange tales and laughter with plain men on the street corners. But he had a strange dignity all his own. No man slapped him on the back or called him Abe."

My grandfather Palmer could remember his grandfather, Isaac Palmer, who served in the Virginia Militia at Yorktown. The old gentleman always referred to the English commander as Lord *Cob*wallis because, said he, "We shucked the *corn* off of him in Yorktown." After the Revolution, Isaac and his family moved from Virginia to Kentucky. There my grandfather was born in 1817. When he was fourteen years old, his father, Louis D. Palmer, settled with his family in Illinois, about ten miles east of Alton.

Louis D. Palmer was a cabinetmaker by trade. During his seven years' apprenticeship in Lexington, Kentucky, he found access to good books and became an omnivorous reader. He was a skilled cabinetmaker, but he worked at his craft temperately, much as Thoreau worked at the same craft later. As Louis had a large family to support, he was forced to waste more time than Thoreau did in earning a living; but he never allowed his business to interfere unduly with his reading, his philosophic meditation, or his communing with nature—especially when the fish were biting. Isaac Palmer was a devout Baptist who refused to lay up earthly treasures for moths to corrupt—because he was intent upon laying up treasures in heaven. Louis adopted at least the first part of his father's creed and transmitted it to his descendants. As to their accumulations in heaven, I have no means of knowing, but I do know that few moths have been nourished by their earthly leavings.

This freedom from the taint of lucre appears to be characteristic of our branch of the Virginia Palmer family. Whenever I hear of a rich Palmer, I put him down as a member of the Connecticut clan with no valid claim to close kinship with me. There is a family tradition, however, that the first of the Virginia Palmers was a successful pirate from Stonington, Connecticut, who found the Chesapeake a convenient base for the practice of his profession. I have recently declined to submit this pirate progenitor to a genealogist for fear that I might lose him. Many a valued ancestor has been evaporated by historical research.

Though he had little worldly wealth, Louis Palmer made a liberal provision for my grandfather's education. Under the common law of the frontier, a boy's "time" belonged to his father until his twenty-first birthday. The father could use the son's time on his own farm or he could hire him out to a neighbor, just as he could hire out his mule or his ox. When young Abraham Lincoln split rails for a neighbor, the wages paid for splitting them were the property of Thomas Lincoln, his father. Abraham was not free to pursue any enterprise, educational or otherwise, until he came of age. Louis Palmer held precisely the same right to his son's time. One day when John was seventeen years old, his father heard him talking to a younger brother about the blessing of having an education. "Would you like to have an education, John?" he asked. When the boy timidly replied in the affirmative, his father said, "You shall have it. I give you your time." I have heard my grandfather speak gratefully of his father's munificence in endowing him with this scholarship—four years of his own youth. In his old age he wrote: "Next morning after an early breakfast, I left home on foot without money or clothes; both seemed unnecessary for was I not going out into the world a free man, where money and clothes were abundant, and to be had by anyone who would earn them?"

I was born at Carlinville, Illinois, in 1870, but I cannot remember our home there for my parents moved to Springfield early in my third year. Upon our arrival at the capital we were guests at the executive mansion for at that time my Grandfather Palmer was governor of Illinois. But I was not the guest of honor; that distinction was reserved for my new baby brother, Robertson Palmer.

My visit to the "Governor's Mansion" has no proper place in my reminiscences, for I do not remember it. But I do remember when I was an inmate of the Illinois State Penitentiary at Joliet a few months later. If I have no memory picture of my grandfather as governor, I do see two charming gentlemen arrayed in black and white stripes who told me funny stories and made me laugh while they were polishing a shining hardwood floor. I remember skimming over the ice at thrilling speed in a little sled propelled by one of my striped friends on skates. I see other figures flitting and circling over the ice, but whether they wore striped clothes I cannot see for the light has grown too dim. In the background of the skating picture there is a high wall and a man walking on top of it with a gun on his shoulder. I also remember my "Uncle Major" Edwards. He was the king of all my friends in stripes for he was the warden of the penitentiary. No little boy could forget such an uncle. An old newspaper clipping tells me that he weighed 370 pounds at that time. When he sat in his big armchair he looked like Old King Cole on his throne.

There are many early Springfield memories, but the first that I can date approximately is a shopping trip with my mother, Ellen Clark Robertson Palmer. It must have been in the summertime, for I can remember the little flowers on her dress as we rode downtown on the streetcar—well up front so that I could see the horses. We got off at the southwest corner of the square and went into Kimber and Ragsdale's store. There Miss Gillmore showed my mother some material for a dress. Apparently my mother admired it but thought it too girlish for a staid matron with a big boy like me. And now the memory becomes vivid. Miss Gillmore said: "Why, Mrs. Palmer, you are such a young woman!" I resented that as a reflection on my great, wise, wonderful mother, so I shouted: "She is not young. She is twenty-six years old." My mother's age fixes that memory in the summer of 1874, a few months after my fourth birthday.

The first memory picture that I can date exactly is labeled 7 March 1875. Early that morning, my Grandmother Robertson took me into the front room to see a new baby brother who had just arrived. I expected to see another serviceable youngster like my brother Robin, then well on his third year. But though I looked closely there was no other boy in the room. My grandmother led me to the sofa where I saw nothing but a pile of pillows and blankets. Then she lifted a coverlet gently and showed me a tiny, red-faced, bald-headed creature with its eyes tight shut.

That was my first great disillusionment! There had been systematic propaganda for some time about the joy of having a new brother or sister. But when I saw that ugly little runt, I felt that as a brother, he had been greatly overadvertised. My confidence in my grandmother's judgment also was rudely shaken. When she whispered, "Isn't he a lovely boy?" I simply stood mute.

Thus, early in life (about six weeks before my fifth birthday), I learned to be skeptical of propaganda. But I also learned not to be too much discouraged by even the most discouraging first impressions. My baby brother gradually unwrinkled, grew some hair and became more presentable. Though I have never been able to see the beauty that my mother, and later my sister-in-law, found in him, candor compels me to admit that considering his most unpromising start, he attained a very creditable degree of comeliness. In fact, when I last saw him in his well-starched white gown, I was not surprised to hear one of his patients whisper, "Doesn't Dr. Palmer look like a cherub?"

In due time the baby was named George Thomas for my grandfather's friend and hero, Gen. George H. Thomas. Grandfather had served under Thomas in the Army of the Cumberland. He commanded one of the four divisions that held their ground under Thomas at Chicamauga. Later, when Thomas became Commander of the Army of the Cumberland, he gave Palmer his old command, the XIV Army Corps.

Our house faced the east on South Seventh Street. There was a white picket fence in front, and a vine-covered trellis separated the front from the back yard. The house stood at the center of the front yard. There were two pine trees near the fence on either side of the front gate. There was a big "jenneting" apple tree near the southeast corner of the house and a "bellflower" apple tree near Mr. Harpole's fence to the south. There were two other trees between the house and Mr. Clark's fence to the north, but I do not remember what they were. I remember the apple trees because there are no apples in the world today that can compare with those old-time jennetings and bellflowers.

Directly back of the house, flanked on either side by the high board alley fence, was the old red barn. A cinder walk, covered by a grape arbor, extended from the back porch to the barn door and divided the back yard into two equal parts. To the north next to the grape arbor were raspberry bushes. Beyond them the kitchen garden extended to Mr. Clark's fence. All of the back yard south of the grape arbor was our playground. Here we could dig and build as we pleased. Here, too, all the other boys in the neighborhood played. My mother kept her boys at home by maintaining a community playground. The Palmers were noisy neighbors but there were compensations. All the other mothers knew where to find their sons.

We did everything in our back yard that boys ever do. There Bob had his elaborate railroad system. He did not have real tracks and switches and electric locomotives such as children have today. His tracks were shallow little trenches scraped in the hard bare soil—for no grass ever grew in our playground. His trains were strings of corncobs. Each cob was a car and the cars were coupled together with bits of twig inserted in pitch at their ends. A big cob with a nail sticking up in front was a locomotive. A cob with a nail in the middle of its back was a caboose. At every station along the railroad there were extra cars on the side tracks. A train would "choo choo" into a station. The caboose would be uncoupled and left on the main line. Then with puffing and bell ringing the engine would back into a siding and leave three or four cars. In another siding other cars would be coupled on. Then it would return to the main line, back up and recouple with the caboose. The reassembled train would then "choo choo" to the next station, where the switching and coupling and uncoupling would be repeated.

One day Paul Harlan and I made a furnace from some old bricks that lay roughly piled near the grape arbor. When the furnace was finished we decided to build a fire in it. Remarking that corncobs made good fuel, Paul found a supply of them conveniently distributed all over the yard. I forgot to tell him that they were really Robin's freight cars. Just as the fire was well started the railroad magnate appeared on the scene. There was a howl of rage and a burst of epithets—highly sophisticated for a seven-year-old boy. With keen strategic instinct, he rushed to the brick pile and immediately opened fire at close range. Nothing could resist such fury. He was smaller than either of us but we ran for our lives. We finally made peace by borrowing a new lot of freight cars from Mr. Wilms. We couldn't find any ready-made cobs in Mr. Wilm's barn, so we had to manufacture a supply by shelling some of his corn.

We were expected to confine our operations to our playground, but as we and our comrades grew bigger we frequently overflowed into the front yard. A battle that started down by the barn might extend clear to the front picket fence, leaving a wrack of weapons and other spoils of war behind it. Instead of trying to restrict our theater of war too rigidly, Mother solved this problem by employing "Uncle Henry" Douglas to clean up the front yard every Monday. One Monday evening after a hard day's work, Uncle Henry expostulated. "Mis' Palmer," he said, "if you all keep dem boys back yonder where dey belong, dey won't be so much trash all over dis yere yard." "But, Uncle Henry," she replied, "if the boys don't make so much trash, I won't need you every Monday." "Yas'm," said Uncle Henry. He never complained but once again and that was after the battle of the raspberry bushes.

I had never noticed the raspberry bushes particularly until that morning. Uncle Henry had just pruned them. All of the disheveled branches and twigs were gone and each bush stood almost as straight as the stake that supported it. It was Saturday and our whole band was assembled for battle, each warrior armed with his wooden sword. As I peeped through the grape arbor, I suddenly discovered the enemy—a real enemy this time. The raspberry patch had become an army of Saracens drawn up in battle array. I put my finger to my lips and beckoned to the warriors. As they crouched around me they recognized the Saracens at once. We had become an army of Crusaders. I was King Richard. But when I saluted Paul Harlan as Ivanhoe, Bob got mad and cried. Between his sobs, he announced in unmistakable terms that he'd be damned if he'd play unless he could be Ivanhoe. When Bob cried it was no sign of weakness. It was a challenge to mortal combat. In order to avoid a mutiny in our ranks, Paul relinquished Ivanhoe and became Robin Hood.

Our little brother, Georgie, was there too, in his kilts and his long curls. He almost stopped the war when he said, "I'll tell Momma if you fight against Uncle Henry's bushes." But Ivanhoe was always resourceful. He seized George Thomas by the shoulder and muttered fiercely, "Base churl, if you breathe one word of this, I'll—I'll tell on *you*—you know what I mean." George didn't know, but older men than he have been silenced by the threat of blackmail.

Having reconnoitered the enemy, we slipped stealthily through the barn and deployed behind the currant bushes. Then at King Richard's signal, the Crusaders charged right into the hostile phalanx, smiting the Saracens right and left. It was bully fighting, for these raspberry Saracens gave us real targets for our swords. At the first assault we made our way half through the hostile ranks only to be driven back in disorder. Fiercely the battle ebbed and flowed. It was not until the fifth assault that we made our way clear through the hostile position. There the combat suddenly ended. The bedraggled Saracens were reinforced. Uncle Henry, in the role of an enraged giant, charged into the fray. When Mother appeared a moment later, the last of the Crusaders were scrambling over the alley fence. King Richard got the only licking. When George Thomas turned state's evidence, his testimony exonerated Robin, who appeared before the court as an innocent and confiding little brother, always easily led.

There were many truces in our warfare with Uncle Henry. Sometimes after eating his lunch out in the barn, the old man would sing us songs that he learned years ago in Virginia. One of them lingers in my memory:

> Oh young man, young man,
> You is foolin' away yo' time
> When you ought to be out a huntin',

For we've houn's of our own
Just as good as ever was known
An' the houn's in old England
Can't beat 'em, God knows!

As I went out a huntin'
So early in the mornin'
I heard a most beautiful holler.
It was Miss Eliza Jane
She's the leader of the train
An' the houn's in old England
Can't beat her, God knows!

An' it's o'er the highest hill
An' it's down the lowest vale
The ole fox is makin' for the water
An' it's by our runnin' fast
Dat we kotch Br'er Fox at last
And it's Roxy Toxy, September
God Knows!

There was an ole King,
(Or there was supposed to be)
Who was very fond of huntin'
And it's O! Miss Eliza Jane
She's the leader of the train
And it's Roxy Toxy, September
God knows!

My ole mother, she told me,
Once't a long time ago,
O! my son, don't never be a spotesman
For dey'll push you to the front
An' you'll never stand the brunt
An' you'll spote in hard luck,
God knows!

There were many stanzas that I do not remember. Perhaps Uncle Henry improvised some of them. But every stanza ended in the phrase *"God knows!"* in his deep bass voice—so deep and rumbly that it sent delightful shivers running down my back.

When Robin was about eight years old he decided that he needed a "gym-a-nasium." By this he meant a trapeze and horizontal bar to be erected in our back yard. When father announced that he could not afford the expense, Bob decided to consult Grandfather Palmer and asked me to go with him. As we made our way on the streetcar, I was not optimistic. Bob had a deft touch when it came to beguiling an occasional dime or quarter from his grandsire, but fifteen whole dollars for a gym-a-nasium seemed far in the domain of high finance.

Grandfather was not at home when he got to his house. Grandmother told us that he was very busy at the courthouse. When he finally came in, his face was stern and he passed his two grandsons apparently without seeing them. Bob was too experienced a diplomat to approach him then. We waited. Presently the sounds we expected began to come from the library. We could hear Grandfather tuning up his big violincello. Then he began to sing in there all alone. That was his relief after a stressful day. Like King David of old he sought solace of sweet sounds after the heat of the battle. His voice was very deep but very musical as it blended with the tones of the cello. First he sang "Bethany" and several other old hymns. Then as the day's burden slipped from his shoulders we could hear "Old Black Joe" and "Annie Laurie" and "Old Kentucky Home."

When he came out of the library the sternness was gone. He saw us now and welcomed us with his good-natured smile:

"Good afternoon, John McAuley. Good afternoon, Robertson."

I returned his salutation but Bob did not reply. "Good afternoon, Robertson," Grandfather repeated. Again there was no reply. Robin was apparently in revery. By this time his grandfather was becoming interested. "Why don't you answer me, Robertson?"

After a pause, Bob said, "Because I don't like that name."

"You don't like to be called Robertson?"

"No, sir."

"Why? You should be very proud of your name. You were named for your Grandfather Robertson."

"Yes, but it isn't a real name. It's a behind name."

"A behind name? What do you mean by that?"

"Well, it isn't a front name like John or George. Robertson's a behind name like Palmer or Jones. I'd rather have a front name like the other boys."

Grandfather was now thoroughly absorbed in Bob's problem. After a pause he said, "Well, how would you like me to give you a new front name?"

"What name will you give me?"

"Well, you can have either Moses or Aaron."

"I don't like either of those names."

"Which one do you like best?"

"Well, I like Aaron better than Moses, but I don't like either one very much. Couldn't you give me a decent name?"

By this time Grandfather was thoroughly in the spirit of the game. He became very firm. He insisted that Bob must be either Moses or Aaron. Robin was now convinced that his fish was well hooked so he said:

"Well, I'll let you name me Aaron if you'll give me a gym-a-nasium."

That's how we got the trapeze and horizontal bar in our back yard and that's why my early letters from Bob were subscribed, "Yores respectively, Aaron R. Palmer."

When I was born, my Grandfather Palmer was the Republican governor of Illinois. But when I first remember him, a few years later, he was a leader in the Democratic Party. In his old age, while in the U.S. Senate as a Democrat, he bolted the platform of his party and led the "Sound Money" Democrats against Bryan—thus assuring the election of a Republican president. After his death, an old politician said to me, "Your grandfather was the dam'dest turncoat I ever knew." Before I could recover from my surprise, he added, "But he was different from every other turncoat because he always turned away from the fleshpots." As this was a just epitome of his whole career, and as he strongly influenced my own life, a brief outline of his early history may be appropriate here.

When his father gave him his "time" in 1834, he went to Upper Alton to work his way through Shurtleff College. In the summer of 1838, while still struggling to earn an education, he was employed by a Connecticut clock merchant to peddle clocks in western Illinois. During his travels he met Stephen A. Douglas for the first time. In his old age he described their meeting:

One night, after Mr. Sands N. Breed ... and I had retired (we occupied separate beds in the same room), the landlord ... came to our room accompanied by two gentlemen who were introduced to us as Mr. Stuart and Mr. Douglas, opposing candidates for Congress. The landlord called us by name and informed us that we would have to occupy the same bed. Douglas then asked our politics, and Mr. Breed told him that he was a Whig and that I was a Democrat. Douglas replied, "I will sleep with the Democrat, and Stuart may sleep with the Whig." The arrangement suited all parties. I heard Douglas speak next day, and though not quite twenty-one years old, voted for him on the first Monday of August following. He had no more devoted adherent than myself until we separated in 1854 over the Nebraska bill.

In the spring of 1839, my grandfather settled at Carlinville, the county seat of Macoupin County, about forty miles south of Springfield. As to his financial status he wrote:

> My own capital was entirely satisfactory to me; I had twelve dollars in money, a *few* extra clothes, a rifle gun ... and a silver watch which was of uncertain value.... I got excellent board for one dollar and twenty-five cents per week, washing included. The washing involved no great labor, for two extra shirts, made of what we call "domestic" ... left the laundry labor light.

In December of that year he borrowed a horse from a neighbor and rode up to Springfield, where he was admitted to the bar upon the certificate of Stephen A. Douglas. "I ... was then a lawyer, lacking nothing but learning, experience and clients."
In December, 1842, he married Malinda Anne Neely, my grandmother.

> She was ... very young at the time of our marriage.... I had no home for her, but we found a snug, hewed log house, which I rented for four dollars per month.... Her mother gave her the "Illinois fortune", a feather bed and its equipments. I had a bureau ... which I always insisted to her was an equivalent for the bed and its furnishings. A local mechanic made for us a walnut table, and with twenty-five dollars worth of the simple household and kitchen furniture, ... a little sugar and coffee, some flour and ham, I, proud of my new position, the head of a family,
> "Felt that swelling of the heart I ne'er shall feel again."

He rose rapidly at the bar and in politics. He was a member of the state convention which prepared the Illinois Constitution of 1847. He was a close friend and supporter of Douglas until 1854 when they differed on the slavery question. He then left his promising position in the Democratic party and joined Lincoln in forming the Republican party. He was chairman of the first Republican or Anti-slavery Extension Convention at Bloomington in 1856, where Lincoln made his famous "lost speech." That same year he was a delegate to the national convention which nominated Fremont for president. In this convention he contributed to the growth of Lincoln's national reputation by nominating him for vice-president. At the state convention in May, 1860, he opposed instructions for Seward and introduced the resolution instructing the delegates to the national convention to vote for Lincoln. At Chicago, a few days later, he took an active part in securing Lincoln's nomination for the presidency.

Upon the outbreak of the Civil War, he became colonel of the 14th Illinois Infantry and soon thereafter was appointed brigadier general of volunteers. He commanded a division at Stone's River and after the battle was appointed major general. He rose to the command of the XIV Army Corps and at the close of the War was military governor of Kentucky. After the war, Grant offered to recommend him as a brigadier general in the regular army, but he declined because military service in time of peace made no appeal to him.

In 1868, he was elected governor of Illinois as a Republican and served from 1869 to 1873. With his fine political and military record and his strategic position in the northwest, his friends considered him a coming man who might succeed Grant as president. Many ambitious young Republicans took their places on the Palmer "bandwagon." Then, suddenly, to their amazement and horror, their hero threw his political advantage overboard and returned to the Democratic Party. He had left it on the slavery question. With his hostility to the centralizing tendencies in the Republican administration after the war and with his views as to the importance of conserving the legitimate sovereign powers of the states, he felt it his duty to return to his old allegiance. That he might be sacrificing a brilliant political career for himself probably did not enter his head. He was again a turncoat, but as his old political acquaintance expressed it, "he turned away from the fleshpots." He was a strong party man when his party happened to be going in his direction. When it left what he considered the true path, he was quite content to march on alone.

It is probable that his innate hostility to federal encroachment was brought to a head at the time of the great Chicago fire in 1871. He protested vigorously that the dispatch of federal troops to do police duty in Chicago without the application or request of the state authorities and without any federal mission was an unwarranted encroachment upon the sovereignty of the state.

2

Boyhood in Old Carlinville

Many of my childhood memories are staged in Carlinville. There lived my Grandfather and Grandmother Robertson with their two youngest children, Charles and Anna. Uncle Charley was about eighteen and Aunt Annie about fourteen when I first remembered them. There were also many of my father's kin in Carlinville. Grandfather Palmer had his home there until he moved to Springfield shortly before his election as governor. My father and mother were both born there and were sweethearts there from childhood. When I was a small boy it seemed to me that nearly everybody in town was an uncle or aunt or a cousin.

My grandfather, William Addison Robertson, was born at Lynchburg, Virginia, in 1803. Soon after his birth his parents moved to Harrodsburg, Kentucky. In his early thirties, he emigrated to Illinois where he bought cheap land and by holding it became a rich man for his day. There is a family tradition that one of his Scottish forebears was a brother or cousin of William Robertson, the historian. My grandfather's mother was Elizabeth Burton, the daughter of Robert Burton of Bedford County, Virginia. His middle name, Addison, was given him by his Grandfather Burton, who was a great-nephew of Joseph Addison. Robert Burton's copy of the *Spectator*, in eight calf-bound volumes, descended to me through my mother. The title page of each volume bears the autograph "Ro Burton, 1770." He was descended from William Burton, who settled in Accomack County before the middle of the seventeenth century. William was a nephew of Robert Burton, author of *The Anatomy of Melancholy*.

As my Grandfather Robertson died during my early childhood, I have few memories of him. I was not chummy with him as my grandsons are with me. I rarely saw him except at family prayer every morning and at mealtimes. At other times he was generally alone in his library working on a theological book that he never finished. But though I exchanged few pleasantries with him, I was very proud of him. He could sneeze louder than anybody else in the world. When he sneezed upstairs in his library you could hear him downstairs—even way back in the kitchen where Mary Kelly used to let me roll the biscuit dough. He made the whole house tremble. When I first heard an earthquake described I gathered that it was a rather widespread sneeze. His son, my Uncle Charley, told me that Grandfather got his sneezes out of the shiny little black snuff box that he carried in his waistcoat pocket. It was one of my earliest ambitions to grow up and have a snuff box of my own. But like many other youthful aspirations, this one was never realized.

Grandmother Robertson was much younger than Grandfather and survived him many years. Her maiden name was Nancy Halliday. Her grandfather, James Halliday, emigrated from Scotland and settled in Maryland before the Revolution. He was born in Moffat, Dumfrieshire, in 1741 of an old Annandale family. Her father, the Rev. Mr. Charles Halliday, was one of the famous "circuit riders" who preached the gospel of Methodism out on the frontier long before Illinois attained statehood.

She was a remarkable woman, one of the noblest human beings I have ever known. She was nearly six feet tall, slender and erect to the day of her death in her seventy-seventh year. I still see her beautiful old wrinkled face looking out from her white lace cap. She followed her father's stern religious creed. To her, life was a battle against original sin to be won only by constant prayer. But the sternness of her religion was only for herself. Toward others it was a gospel of kindness. She held her wealth in trust for her less fortunate neighbors and did all she could to bring the Kingdom of Heaven into her little corner of the Earth. She had a keen sense of humor, but she struggled against it, for her father had taught her that any amusement or pleasure was a wile of the devil and dangerously akin to sin. So, when she had to laugh, she would cover her mouth with her hand; but we knew that she was laughing because we could see the twinkle in her eye.

One of my earliest memories is a starry night out on the lawn at Grandmother's. Holding me in her arms she pointed out the more brilliant stars and constellations and called them by their names. She had studied astronomy as a girl, but her interest in the skies was something more than scientific. Her contemplation of the heavens was a religious rite, a confirmation of her faith. There she beheld the veritable handiwork of the God that she served and worshipped. There were no doubts and uncertainties in her conception of the universe.

Sunday was a solemn day at Grandmother's. She always called it the Sabbath or the Lord's Day. Family prayer was longer than usual that morning, and when we finally got to the breakfast table there was another long "blessing" before I could get my oatmeal. About nine o'clock we went to church. Grandmother sat very straight in her high old-fashioned surrey as she drove downtown. Matthew, her well-fed sorrel horse, was a dignified animal even on weekdays. On Sundays he marched with exceptional sedateness. He could feel the Sabbath in the air just as I could.

First, we had sunday school for about an hour. There were songs and stories and pictures. And there was a Golden Text to recite. There were other little boys in my class. When the teacher wasn't looking, we pinched each other and giggled and had a pretty good time even if it was Sunday. But the nicest thing was to look across the aisle and see the little girls in their fluffy dresses with pink and blue sashes and curls and hair ribbons. Some of my classmates made faces at them, but they only turned up their noses.

Then came the morning service. It wasn't so bad at first. It was nice to hear the singing and to see cousin Carrie Mayo with the other ladies and gentlemen in the choir. Then there was a long prayer and an anthem while two solemn gentlemen in long black coats took up the collection. Then the preacher told us about the sewing society and the missionary meeting and the midweek prayer meeting and many other "means of grace." After that came another hymn and then the sermon. To a little boy whose legs were too short to touch the floor, it was a very long sermon about things he could not understand. He tried his best to keep awake but finally he leaned against his grandmother and went to sleep.

After the service most of the congregation trooped out, but we real Methodists moved closer to the pulpit and had an "experience meeting." Some old gentleman would tell us how for years he lived in sin and neglected to go to meeting and how finally he got religion. Then Grandmother and I and the other brothers and sisters would say "Praise the Lord!" He would then tell us that even after being saved we must continue to wrestle with Satan and never cease to watch and pray. Then he would sit down and we would all say "Amen!" Then some old lady would be moved to pray and after that other brothers and sisters would tell us how wrestling with the devil was their favorite form of exercise. I got the impression that the surface of the earth was a thin and precarious crust over a sea of boiling fire. Under this crust was Hell and above the sky was Heaven. I was not particularly enthusiastic about going to Heaven for it appeared to be a perpetual Sunday morning in church. But I devoutly wanted to go there for the only alternative was to broil forever in Hell. We Methodists had no middle ground for ordinary folks who were neither saints nor sinners.

After Uncle Charley's marriage we spent most of our holidays with him and our new Aunt Alice. We had other aunts and uncles in Carlinville but most of them were typical grown-ups with little time for other children than their own. Uncle Frank Burton, who married Aunt Annie, was a busy lawyer. "Uncle Doctor" Matthews, who married my father's sister Bettie, was a busy physician. Both of them were imbued with the singular doctrine that small boys should be disciplined. Uncle Charley was different. He was a naturalist. He also was a busy man, but his business took him into the woods and fields, where he loved to take his nephews with him. The woods began just back of his house. There a ravine led down to Burrough's Branch, a small brook that flowed through a wooded valley to Macoupin Creek. When we were little he would find a safe place for us to wade and splash in the brook while he pursued his studies. Later as we grew older he would take us further afield. He gave us our first lessons in swimming and fishing and duck shooting. We got our woodcraft, our woodlore, and our woodlove from him.

Charles Robertson was a pioneer in the study of the relations between flowers and insects. Bob and I were with him one day when he started an important experiment. He took us to an old pasture covered here and there with little clumps of milkweed just about to bloom. He counted all the buds in one of these clumps and then covered it with a sheet of gauze so fine that even the tiniest insects would be unable to visit the flowers. Then he counted another clump and covered it with a slightly coarser gauze. He spent a whole afternoon at this task, covering each successive clump with netting of slightly broader mesh. The last one, for example, would admit the honey bee but exclude the bumblebee. The last clump that he counted he left uncovered.

It was a long afternoon for two small boys. We went down to the creek for a swim, but when we returned Uncle Charley was still busy. While we were waiting for him, two substantial burghers of Carlinville drove by in a buggy. When they saw our naturalist unrolling a sheet of netting in an open field, the driver stopped his horse and exclaimed:

    "Who in Hell is that?

    "Oh!" said the other, "It's that damn fool Charley Robertson."

    "He must be crazy, trying to seine in a meadow."

    "Well, he ain't exactly crazy. He's a damn nice fellow but he ain't practical. I reckon he's catching bugs and bees for his collection."

    "There ain't no money in that, is there?"

    "No, I reckon not."

    "Then if you ask me, I'll say he's crazy."

The wise men of Carlinville didn't think highly of their naturalist. They did not know that he was their only fellow townsman who was doing something of worldwide importance. They did not know that what he was doing in that meadow was the only activity in Macoupin County, that day, that would be known to wise men in London and Berlin and Paris and Rome as a permanent contribution to human knowledge.

Many mornings that summer we returned to that meadow. Uncle Charley kept a record of each insect visitor that he found in each group of flowers. In the autumn he harvested the ripened crop and determined the percentages of fertile seeds in each group. And he studied other plants besides the milkweeds, keeping carefully preserved specimens of each flower and each visitor. On stormy days and throughout the winter, he was busy upstairs in his study. There he kept his ever-growing collection of plants and insects. There, with the aid of his microscope, he made sketches of the correlated mechanism of flowers and their insect visitors. Out of these studies grew important contributions on the processes of evolution—how the insect shaped the flower and the flower shaped the insect. When he began his studies he found that many of his captive bees and other insects had never been named or catalogued. As a result, many species in the Central Mississippi Valley were first described and named by him. Many of these no longer exist except in his collection. They are now extinct with the Illinois prairie flowers that still survived in many sheltered places when he began his researches.

During his early manhood, Uncle Charley taught botany and biology in Blackburn College at Carlinville. Among his pupils was Mary Hunter Austin, who tells of the inspiration she received from him in her autobiography, *Earth Horizon.** He published his observations in strictly scientific journals for the use of other naturalists, but he could never be induced to interrupt his researches in order to do any popular writing. As his father had left him a competency, he was able to devote his entire life to the pursuit of pure science. He was a good man of business and was careful to conserve his property. But as he had enough for his family and for the pursuit of his life work, he was unwilling to waste any of his valuable time in earning more money. He sought no reward nor popular applause. He enjoyed the recognition of a very few co-workers widely scattered throughout the world. He was content to spend his whole life in adding a little to human knowledge. His was the happiest and best rounded life that I have ever known. He was further removed than most of us from our paleolithic ancestors. What a world this will be someday in the far distant future when the mass of mankind has overtaken such pioneers as he!

No boys ever had a more delightful uncle. He awakened our love of nature long before we had any understanding of his scientific work. But we absorbed something of the spirit of science from him. Long before I heard of "evolution" or "natural selection" in school, I had the gist of them from him. He tried

---

*New York, Houghton Mifflin, 1932.

20

to teach me to base my opinions upon evidence. He would listen to my boyish views patiently, but he was always full of scorn for an opinion that was based upon partisanship or personal interest. I learned from him early in life that relatively few people, even among the so-called educated, are capable of forming a sound opinion "if self the wavering balance shake." Early in life, he was forced to reject his mother's rigid, positive theology. But his attitude toward the universe was always reverent. Though he had no orthodox formula, he was essentially religious. Although he could not understand the ways of God, he did not deny His existence. He could no longer accept the Christ of dogma, but his reverence for the authentic Jesus of history was unbounded. He read in his Greek testament every day.

Though our uncle was generally indulgent, he was capable of righteous indignation on occasion. One day he took us fishing at "Old Cameron," a long deep stretch of water in Macoupin Creek. For some time we sat quietly in his canvas boat, but the fish were not biting freely and we became restless. Finally he put us ashore to play and then returned to midstream where he could cast his minnows toward either shore.

On the bank of the creek we found a supply of last year's wild hemp, straight, tapering stalks, five or six feet long. With their sharp-pointed heavy roots they made splendid javelins. If properly balanced they would fly from our hands as straight and true as arrows. We took a supply of spears to a bluff overlooking the creek and for a time we were content with target practice against the tree trunks. Finally, Bob put his finger to his lip and pointed. Just below us was Uncle Charley placidly fishing. I accepted Bob's view, at once, that he was really an Indian chief in his birch bark canoe. We poised our javelins carefully and let fly, intending to surprise our uncle with two loud splashes near his boat. But our aim was better than we expected. Both javelins went through the canvas and anchored the boat to the muddy bottom of Macoupin creek. Uncle Charley exploded into dire threats and his indignation was justified. By the time he could pull up his javelin anchors and get to shore, his boat was rapidly filling with water. We did not wait to go home with him. We took a short cut through the woods and found sanctuary with Aunt Alice.

Uncle Charley died in 1935 at the age of seventy-seven. In deference to his wish, long known to the family, there were no religious exercises at his funeral. Instead, one of his old pupils told of his scientific work and his reverent attitude toward the mystery of life. Some of his orthodox Methodist and Presbyterian neighbors were shocked by the absence of prayer and hymn and sermon and other funeral convention. After his brief talk, the speaker quoted from Tennyson:

> Flower in the crannied wall
> I pluck you out of the crannies;—
> Hold you here, root and all, in my hand,

Little flower—but if I could understand
What you are, root and all, and all in all,
I should know what God and man is.

In conclusion he said: "Scientists will tell you that few men in the world understood the secret of that little flower better than Charles Robertson did. Perhaps, therefore, he knew more about God than any of us here."

My first school was a kindergarten conducted by Mrs. Russell Churchill and her two daughters. It was the first kindergarten in Springfield. When I outgrew it I was sent to the Bettie Stuart Institute. This was a seminary for young women, but small boys were admitted in the primary department. The principal, Mrs. M. McKee Holmes, has been described by one of her alumnae as "a lady of vast size and great dignity." Her school no longer exists but it was an important institution in the central Illinois of that day. There I had my first Latin lessons and there I was spoiled by some of my female teachers. One of them praised some of my childish rhymes and encouraged me to believe that I was destined to be a great poet.

When I was twelve my father wisely decided that I needed a masculine preceptor and sent me to a private school conducted by Prof. Andrew M. Brooks. Mr. Brooks was a robust Scot with the build and activity of a gladiator, deep-set black eyes, and a bristling black moustache. If I needed maculine discipline I soon got it. The first afternoon at recess, Paul Harlan and I with some other youngsters started a bit of roughhouse in the school room. Mr. Brooks rushed in and scattered us. As he hustled us through the door, he charged us with damaging his furniture. Paul and the others beat a hasty retreat to the playground, but I drew myself up and protested against the charge of vandalism. "Don't cuff the chat with me," roared Mr. Brooks. With that he grasped me by the collar and the seat of my pants and propelled me swiftly down the hall and out on the porch.

I was indignant. Budding poets did not suffer such outrages at the Bettie Stuart Institute. I marched downtown to submit my grievance to my father. He was not in his office but Wiley Jones, one of his law students, wrote a note for me informing Mr. Brooks that if he would send in an itemized bill, Mr. Palmer would pay for any damage his son had done to his furniture. When I got back to the school, Mr. Brooks was hearing a grammar class. He had prolonged the recess to finish a football game and his face was still red from strenuous exertion. He stood with one foot on the top of one of the front desks and was glowering down with great ferocity at one of the big boys who was tentatively parsing "horse" as an adverb. Confident in the righteousness of my cause and sure of triumphant vindication, I walked straight down the aisle and presented my note. As Mr. Brooks read it his whole appearance was transformed. He seemed to swell to treble his normal size. For an instant he became a cyclone that wafted me over two rows of desks to my seat on the far side of the last aisle. There he left me with the assurance that he would attend to my case after school.

For more than an hour I had leisure to meditate upon my impending fate. Paul Harlan, screened behind his open geography, informed me by expressive gestures that I was in for corporal punishment of extreme severity. When the schoolroom finally emptied, Mr. Brooks sat down beside me and rested his big hand on my shoulder. "Paamer," said he, (He always pronounced my name to rhyme with "clamor"). "Paamer, those womenfolks have spoiled you. We are menfolks here." But his temper flashed out again for a second as he looked up and caught Paul peeping in through the window; and again when he said: "Paamer, you tell that smart aleck, Wiley Jones, that I'll answer that note of his the next time I catch him on the street."

Football as we played it at the Brooks school bore little resemblance to the modern game. Ours was the ancient kicking game of our British forefathers. The ball was a hand-sewn spheroid of cowhide stuffed with horsehair and had about as much resilience as a bag of cornmeal. We kicked it along the ground toward the hostile goal. It was *foot* ball in the strictest sense. It was against the rules for a player to touch the ball with his hands. To run with it or to "pass" it through the air was an unheard-of illegality. The game started with a "kickoff" from the center of the field. After the ball had skidded along the ground a dozen or so yards, one of the opposing players would collide with it and kick it back again. Presently both teams would gang around it and there would be a violent kicking battle. The players were supposed to confine their kicks to the ball, but they sometimes missed it and landed them on their opponents' shins. Presently the ball would dribble out of the scrimmage and now an alert player would have a free chance to kick it down the field. But before travelling far it would become the center of a second shindig.

Our football teams were pure democracies. One half of the school played against the other, but there was no permanent organization and no limit to the number of players. A fellow arriving at school and finding a game in progress was supposed to join what appeared to be the weaker side. If there was a close shin battle on when Professor Brooks arrived in the morning, he would take off his coat and plunge into the fracas. The players did their best to make it interesting for him. When they succeeded, he would forget to stop at nine o'clock to ring the school bell. It was a rough game, and I didn't particularly enjoy it; but I played because public opinion demanded it. Mr. Brooks made it clear that boys who were afraid to risk their shins were sissies. They had no standing in his school.

One morning after playing hookey for several days, I returned to school with considerable trepidation. There was a shin battle on and Mr. Brooks was in the midst of it. Suddenly the ball dribbled out and Chester Bolles seized the chance to give it a big kick toward his goal. He rushed in pursuit of it in full career to give it one more kick across the goal line. A collision with Chester would be hazardous as he was nearly twice my size. But I couldn't resist the opportunity to divert attention from the hookey question. I dropped my schoolbooks and charged. Chester and I kicked the ball at exactly the same instant. What happened immediately after that I don't know, but when I came to, Mr. Brooks was supporting me and patting me on the back. "That was bully, Paamer," he said. "You stopped that big fellow, Chester Bolles, and saved the goal. That's a lot better than playing hookey."

I went to Mr. Brooks's until after my sixteenth birthday. In my preparation for college he carried me through Caesar's *Commentaries* and the first six books of the *Aeneid*. He also coached me in Greek grammar and started me in the *Anabasis*. But I am indebted to him most for inuring me to mathematics. When he first introduced me to algebra, I made little progress. I did not dig into it because I remembered a statement by one of my aunts to the effect that the Palmers had no talent for mathematics. She implied that we were highly gifted for literature and the fine arts but that our talents did not lie in the direction of the exact sciences. When I submitted this interesting theory to Mr. Brooks as a reason for an unfinished task, he hoisted me over the intervening aisles to my own desk and announced that he would discuss the matter further after school. At that session he performed a successful operation on my inferiority complex. He made me dig in and when I dug in I discovered that I had the makings of a fairly respectable mathematician.

But I got my best education at home. When we were young children, Mother told us stories and read to us every evening at bed time. We knew the story of the children of Israel and the Christ child long before we could read the Bible. To us, Christian's fight with Apollyon was a real battle and no mere allegory. She read *St. Nicholas* to us from its very first number. On nights when Mother and Father were out or had company, Vinie came up from the kitchen and gave us the old folk stories of her race. She told us about Br'er Rabbit and Br'er Fox and the tar baby before Joel Chandler Harris published the same stories in his Uncle Remus. When we grew older, Mother introduced us to the American Indian, first through Hiawatha and then through the *Leather Stocking* tales. She also gave us King Arthur and Robin Hood and Ivanhoe. From the *Tanglewood Tales* she led us into the old Greek myths, the story of the siege of Troy and the wanderings of Ulysses. With Charles and Mary Lamb, she introduced us to Shakespeare. I enjoyed hearing her read to my younger brothers long after I learned to do my own reading. My love of books was first awakened by her voice.

Almost every morning I walked downtown with my father on my way to school. During these walks we talked of everything that can interest a growing boy. He always welcomed my questions and confidences and did all he could to satisfy my boyish curiosity. At first, he made it a point to answer my questions from his own experience and reading. But as I grew older he taught me how to look for and find the information that I sought. He would direct me to some book and later would check up on my researches. One Sunday morning, I asked him one of my questions and he showed me where to find the answer in *Chamber's Encyclopedia.* I wanted the information but not badly enough to go to the trouble of digging it out for myself. When he quizzed me a little later, he found that I had decided that it was not worthwhile to go to the trouble of consulting Mr. Chambers. Thereupon, he sat me down at the library table and required me to copy the whole encyclopedia article *twice.* Twice, because my first copy was hastily written, with many misspelled words and omissions. It was not until late in the afternoon that he read and approved my carefully written second copy. As I recall it, that was the most important single incident in my education.

When spring came Father used to take us fishing. It was a seven-mile drive out to Clear Lake. There we would take a skiff and fish for bass and crappie. Father was a gentle angler of the Isaac Walton type. That was before the days of flies and other artificial lures in central Illinois, and he was content to be a skillful artist with the worm and minnow. He could always catch fish if there were any there, and in fact our old Negro oarsman used to say, "Mr. Palmer kin ketch fish where they ain't." In those days the road to Clear Lake passed through several bits of shady woodland. It was a delightful hour's trip with a horse and buggy over a winding country road. Some years ago I got my brother George to drive me out to Clear Lake in his automobile. It took about ten minutes. The old road had become a slab of concrete, the woods were all gone, and the lake had shrunk to less than half its size. It is a mistake to look again at the scenes of childhood through an old man's eyes. But the glorious woods along Sugar Creek still stand in my imagination because I could not revisit them. The city has built a big dam across the valley and that whole region now lies below the surface of Lake Springfield.

In August, 1885, four months after my fifteenth birthday, I went to Northern Michigan with my father's sisters, Aunt Margaret Jayne and Aunt Jessie Weber. This was a great adventure for an untravelled boy. We went to Chicago by rail and thence by steamer to Petoskey. It was like going to sea, for as we sailed up Lake Michigan we could see no land for a whole day. At Mackinack Island I visited the old fort, then garrisoned by a single company of infantry, and had my first glimpse of our regular army.

When we embarked for our return journey to Chicago, I noticed a young girl among the passengers. She was travelling with a lady and gentleman, ostensibly her parents, and two boys, ostensibly her younger brothers. This young lady made a powerful impression upon me and as a young gentleman of Springfield, Illinois, I was accustomed to the highest standards of feminine grace and beauty. Soon after we sailed, I struck up an acquaintance with the younger of the two ostensible brothers. When I casually inquired, "Is that young lady your sister?" he replied, "Aw she isn't a young lady. She is only fourteen years old." That information rather dampened my growing ardor, "but after all," I reflected, "fourteen is not so distressingly young in a woman as it is in a man."

Later that afternoon, Aunt Jessie introduced me to the ostensible parents, Mr. and Mrs. C. B. Laning of Petersburg, Illinois. A few minutes later, their daughter joined us and I was duly presented to Miss Maude Laning. That night there was a moon, the most brilliant full moon that I had ever seen. I found two deck chairs for Miss Laning and myself. But our tête-à-tête was not to be a duet. Her brothers joined us and favored us with their society until Mrs. Laning assembled her whole brood for the night. After they left me I sat there alone and discovered a melancholy new beauty in moonlit solitude. The more I saw of that girl, the better I liked her. And this progressive growth in my esteem for her has continued even beyond the time we celebrated the fifth anniversary of our golden wedding day.

In the summer after my sixteenth birthday I made a cruise down the Sangamon River with my schoolmate George Anderson. Our craft was a canvas canoe which George had made with his own hands. We put our boat in the river about five miles northwest of Springfield, near the site of the old village of Sangamontown where Abraham Lincoln and John Hanks built the flatboat in which they made their journey to New Orleans in 1831. Our objective was New Salem, where Lincoln spent six years of his young manhood after his return from New Orleans. We took great pride in the fact that we were about to explore a historic river.

It is about twenty miles, as the crow flies, from Springfield to New Salem, but as the river is very crooked we decided to estimate our cruising distance as fifty miles. That should give us an easy voyage of about two days with plenty of time for fishing on the way. But the Sangamon proved to be much crookeder than we expected. As the river was low there was little current to aid us and we had to carry canoe and cargo around several long rafts of tangled driftwood. We had four days of hard labor before we finally landed on the New Salem dam, just where Lincoln's flatboat had landed fifty-five years before.

Our first view of New Salem was therefore from the river, just as Lincoln's had been. He could not see the village because it was behind the crest of the hill. We could not see it even when we climbed the hill, for it had ceased to exist. The mill dam and the stone foundation of the mill, as he knew them, were still there. The mill itself had been destroyed by fire some years before our visit. The State of Illinois has subsequently completed a replica of the mill and dam as a part of its restoration of the whole village of New Salem.

We pitched our tent on the right bank, just across the river from the old mill. After we made camp I walked out on the dam, where a shabby old man was fishing. He proved to be Mr. Peter Hohimer, who had spent his whole life in Menard County near New Salem. He was a boy there when Lincoln was postmaster and clerk in Samuel Hill's store. I got a new Lincoln reaction from Peter Hohimer. Back in Springfield, even in those days, the Lincoln legend was rapidly growing. His apotheosis was well under way. My obvious reverence for Lincoln disgusted Mr. Hohimer. My hero was no hero to him. Peter Hohimer did not disguise the fact that he was himself as common as an old shoe, and he insisted that "Abe" Lincoln was just as common as he was. It disgusted him that anybody should make a trip all the way to New Salem just to see where such a "feller as Abe Lincoln used to live." All this stuff about his being a great man was pure gammon. It was all a question of luck and if luck had come his way, Peter could have done things just as well as Abe did. "Why," said Mr. Hohimer, "Abe was as ornery as hell, when he lived down here. He didn't have an extra pair of britches when I first knowed him. All this talk about him makes me sick to my stummick." Thereupon, Mr. Hohimer anointed his fishing worm liberally with tobacco juice and returned it to the water below the dam. His incantation was successful for immediately thereafter he yanked out a lusty channel catfish.

The next morning we went up the hill and made our first exploration of New Salem with Peter Hohimer as our guide. At that time it was a scrubby, sparsely wooded pasture. There were no traces of the deserted village except a few shallow depressions where cellars had been. Pete knew each one of them, as well as the sites of the less pretentious log cabins which left no cellars to mark them. He had also known the men and women and children who had lived in each log house.

Ever since then, the story of New Salem has appealed to my imagination. Lincoln settled there when the village was new. He lived there six years, and soon after he left to practice law in Springfield, it ceased to exist. The village was the university where he achieved his self-education. It served that purpose and then disappeared from the face of the earth. It did not survive, as did many frontier settlements, to become a shabby little rundown village.

It has never surprised me that Lincoln should make himself a lawyer and statesman. Other presidents have risen from birthplaces in log cabins. But when he left New Salem his literary style was already formed. We recognize him as one of the great masters of English prose with a unique style, peculiarly his own. Where and how did this unschooled man get his artistic awakening? Principally from Jack Kelso, one of his New Salem friends. He went fishing with Kelso because Jack liked to recite passages from Burns and Shakespeare while he fished. Later, after Jack's quotations had aroused his imagination, he borrowed the books and read them. Jack Kelso was Lincoln's professor of *belles lettres*—and a most effective one though (and perhaps because) he knew only two books. I first heard of Jack Kelso from Peter Hohimer. Pete used to dig fishing worms for him. He, too, was one of Kelso's pupils but only in the fine art of catching fish. Here, he was greatly Lincoln's superior. As he expressed it, "Abe was too damn lazy to be a good fisherman."

The State of Illinois has completed the restoration of New Salem as a historical monument. The plan of the village and the details of the log houses have been recovered after years of critical and exhaustive research. I was there with my daughter and my two grandsons during the summer of 1940. We rested for a moment in the shade of Jack Kelso's log house. From there I could see the whole village—but not so vividly as I saw it in my own imagination when I visited it with old Peter Hohimer more than three score years ago.

My interest in the New Salem country was not solely archeological. Two miles down the river lay the city of Petersburg, New Salem's successful rival as the metropolis of the lower Sangamon Valley. It would please my Aunt Jessie Weber if I should go there and call upon Mr. and Mrs. Laning whom we had met so pleasantly last summer on Lake Michigan. I might even have the pleasure of finding their daughter at home. George Anderson finally consented to go calling with me. We looked like tramps, but after our adventure in navigating the Sangamon we considered our garb as a badge of achievement. We had worn our oldest clothes when we left Springfield. Sleeping on sand bars and portaging our canoe through the woods had not rejuvenated them. As a partial protection from mosquitoes, I had slept in my straw hat. This had given its wide brim a permanent upward set on one side which I considered rather rakish. I flattered myself that it made me look like a pirate.

When we got to Thorne Place, the Laning home, Miss Laning was giving a party. The beauty and chivalry of adolescent Petersburg were assembled on the lawn. As the assembly was not a fancy dress party, our costumes were not exactly in keeping with the occasion. Miss Laning apparently took us for tramps, but she finally recognized me and made a brave effort to give us a cordial welcome. She introduced us to her guests. They were polite, but they apparently did not admire us as much as we admired ourselves.

Finally, Mr. Laning came out and invited us to join Mrs. Laning on the porch. This suited us as we had come to make a formal call on sensible people and had no desire to enter into the frivolities of Petersburg society. Mr. Laning was interested in our cruise down the river and apparently admired our costumes—especially my on-the-bias straw hat which he repeatedly requested me to try on for him. After we had enjoyed some of Mrs. Laning's ice cream and angel cake—which I have never seen equalled in the past half century—Mr. Laning hitched old Jim to the surrey and drove us back to our camp.

If I had ever had any romantic inclination toward Maude Laning it completely disappeared that evening. She was evidently a worldly and conventional young person with little capacity to see hearts of gold under rough exteriors. And, in fact, after living with her more than half a century, I have never been able to correct this overconventional view. She still insists that I should always wear my good clothes to a party and that if my good clothes are not accessible, I should not go to the party.

The next day we loaded our canoe on a freight car at Petersburg and returned with it to Springfield.

3 Off to West Point

The September after my sixteenth birthday I entered the senior class at the Springfield High School. After graduating there, I would go away to college. My head was full of dreams of college life, but I could not make up my mind whether to go to Harvard or Yale or Princeton. My father was annoyed at this vacillation but still more at my uncertainty as to my future profession. Most of the time I expected to follow the family tradition and join my grandfather and father at the bar, but there were also frequent hankerings to be a doctor or an engineer or a novelist or an actor. There were other schemes that I did not discuss with my father, such as exploring Central Africa or prospecting for gold and diamonds in South America. After a few years of thrilling adventure it would be fine to return to Springfield as a latter-day Monte Cristo.

One day in the law office, my father said to my grandfather: "This boy can't stick to anything. He is as unstable as water. I've a good notion to put him in the army. Do you think you could get him an appointment to West Point?"

"That's worth considering," Grandfather replied. "When I was seventeen, my father started me in life by giving me my time. But things have changed since then. Apparently, the only show for your youngster is to take his time away from him. How would you like to go to West Point, John McAuley?"

"Oh! That would be fine!" I exclaimed, welcoming a new air castle, for up to that moment, I had never given a thought to the Military Academy.

"All right, John McAuley, I'll write President Cleveland this morning. West Point may be the best place for a scatterbrain like you."

The incident was soon forgotten in the usual procession of boyish activities and air castles. It was therefore a great surprise one morning in the spring of 1887 to read in an Associated Press dispatch that John McAuley Palmer of Springfield, Illinois, had been appointed a cadet at the Military Academy. A few days later, I received notice from the Adjutant General of the Army directing me to report at West Point for examination early in June, 1888.

When I took this exciting news to my chum, Paul Harlan, I found him in bed with a bad cold. When I visited him a few days later he was feeling better and we discussed plans for a long-delayed fishing trip. Next day my mother told me that Paul had typhoid fever. In a few days he was dead and I helped to bear him to his grave. This was my first close contact with death. Hitherto he had taken old people like Grandfather Robertson and Grandmother Palmer. Here he had taken my closest friend in all the vigor of youth. This was my first intimate reminder of our universal mortal lot.

In June 1887 I graduated from the Springfield High School. In July, I made another cruise down the Sangamon. This time there was a squadron of six canoes. As the river was high we made better time than we made the year before. We camped a day or two at New Salem, but I made no social calls in Petersburg. We went on down the river past the mouth of Salt Creek and made our last camp at the railroad bridge northwest of Oakford. From there we returned to Springfield by rail. About this time my father decided to send me to a West Point preparatory school at Sing Sing, New York. In August, I made a farewell visit to Grandmother Robertson and the rest of my Carlinville kin.

About the middle of August, a few days before my departure for the east, I went down to the law office for a farewell talk with Grandfather Palmer. He was not enthusiastic about my going to West Point. Like many other volunteer officers he had come out of the Civil War with a strong feeling of resentment against the Regular Army and what they called the "West Point crowd."

There was some ground for this attitude. After the battle of Chickamauga, when Thomas became commander of the Army of the Cumberland, he placed Palmer at the head of his old command, the XIV Army Corps. This was a high honor and an official recognition of brilliant military service and leadership. But its consequences were unfortunate. Most of the division commanders in the XIV Corps and many of the brigade commanders were graduates of West Point and professional soldiers. It also included the "Regular Army Brigade" of the Army of the Cumberland. All the officers and enlisted men in that brigade were regulars. Most of the numerous contingent of professional officers in the XIV Corps resented the appointment of a nonprofessional or citizen soldier to command them. No doubt the youngest West Point graduate in the regular brigade, though an inexperienced second lieutenant, considered himself the professional superior of his new corps commander.

This attitude produced misunderstanding and friction. Eventually, without doubt, the malcontents got the sympathetic ear of General Sherman, who rarely disguised his contempt for nonprofessional or "politician" generals, as he called them. In the operations near Atlanta, he directed Palmer to place himself and the XIV Army Corps under the orders of General Schofield, a West Point graduate and professional soldier. Palmer obeyed the order but protested that Schofield was his junior in rank. He and Schofield had been appointed major generals at the same time. The Senate confirmed Palmer at once but did not confirm Schofield until more than a year later. During that year Palmer actually served as major general while Schofield was serving in the same army as a brigadier general. Sherman decided that Schofield's rank dated back to his original appointment and that he was now the senior, even though Palmer had served a year longer as major general. Sherman's decision was technically correct under the Army Regulations, but a layman will sympathize with Palmer's point of view. To him, this was the culmination of many humiliations and annoyances. He believed that the situation had been contrived to place him in a position that he could not accept without loss of self-respect. In his indignation, he tendered his resignation, which is probably what his enemies were seeking. President Lincoln refused to accept it and appointed him military governor of Kentucky, where he served until after the end of the war.

He returned to civil life with a strong prejudice against the Regular Army. He believed that the "West Point crowd" had combined against the volunteer leaders. Many other volunteer officers held the same belief. He admired General Grant and was strongly attached to General Thomas, who was always the spirit of fairness and never a partisan. But he resented the supercilious attitude of many professional officers toward all nonprofessionals. He believed that in a republic, military leadership as well as political and economic leadership should be open to able civilians with gifts of leadership. This was the basis of Washington's military philosophy and had been the national tradition since the Revolutionary War.

Sherman held another view. He succeeded Winfield Scott as head of a variant school, which grew up after the War of 1812. He and his followers believed that higher military leadership should be the monopoly of professional officers. Pushed to its logical conclusion, this would result in a highly privileged militarist or samurai caste, which my grandfather believed would be inconsistent with the genius of democratic institutions.

In our farewell conversation, he warned me not to become a narrow Regular Army partisan. He reminded me that Washington and Greene and all the other American officers in the Continental Army were citizen soldiers. He might have reminded me, had he known it, that Washington proposed military academies solely as a means of providing technical instructors for the citizen officers of the future. It was not until many years later that I caught the full significance of what he said to me that day.

The night before my departure, my mother came to my bedside for a last good night talk. I could not understand her emotion as she clung to me. I was going away to a life of excitement and adventure, but only for a time. After a few years I would return to her again. I could not see, as she saw, that this was my last night as a boy in my boyhood home—the end of our close association as mother and son under the same rooftree.

The next day I set out on my journey. There are but few distinct memories of my flight from home. I can see a crowd of my boy and girl friends down at the Chicago and Alton station to see me off. My father and mother and brothers were there too, but I cannot see them now. There was a day in Chicago where I had a fine time with a number of Springfield boys who had jobs in the city. I invited them to luncheon and entertained them *en prince.* We enjoyed our cocktails and Henry Clay cigars and considered ourselves mature men of the world. I remember that luncheon particularly because it made an uncomfortable item in the expense account that I submitted to my father later.

I do not remember my departure from Chicago, but my first glimpse of Niagara Falls remains one of my most vivid memories. From Albany down the east shore of the Hudson there were many unforgettable pictures—a prairie boy's first tastes of mountain scenery. I recognized the Catskills hazy in the distance. There my imagination pictured the awakening of Rip Van Winkle. That picture gave me a twinge of homesickness, for it made me think of my mother. She had read that story to me years ago and only recently she had taken me to see it played by Joe Jefferson.

Soon we passed under the shadow of Storm King and just below "Cro' Nest" I had my first glimpse of West Point. I saw it then as Grant and Lee saw it when they were cadets before the Mexican War. There were glimpses of a few simple buildings hiding modestly among the trees. It was beautiful with the beauty of nature unadorned. The modern traveler does not see that picture as he whirls by on the Twentieth Century Limited. It now lies hidden beneath the splendid architecture of the modern West Point.

That same day I reported to Colonel Symonds at Sing Sing. The Colonel conducted a small school where he coached candidates for West Point and Annapolis. He was a graduate of West Point and during the Civil War he had distinguished himself as the chief commissary of Sherman's army. After the war he had resigned from the army to go into private business. But though he had disbursed millions in the intricate and exacting business of supplying a great army he did not succeed in the business of making money for himself. Finally, he settled down at Sing Sing where he made his living preparing young gentlemen for the two national academies. He was a master in the fine art of cramming. He held us strictly to the requirements for admission. They were simple but within their narrow limits he demanded absolute accuracy. A boy who could pass one of the colonel's examinations would almost certainly pass the similar examination that awaited him at West Point.

That was a busy winter at Sing Sing. We had little more comfort and luxury than were enjoyed by the students at New York's great penal university about a mile down the river. But we did have an occasional holiday. At Thanksgiving time I made my first visit to New York where I joined other Springfield boys who were attending school in the East. Our fellow townsman, Maj. Bluford Wilson, assembled all of the Springfield youngsters and gave us our Thanksgiving dinner at the Fifth Avenue Hotel. His daughter, Jessie, came down from Miss Porter's school at Farmington, Connecticut, and acted as hostess for us. She was always the "belle of the ball," but this time she was more than a belle for she was the only girl at the party. The Fifth Avenue was the elite hotel in those days. But even the Fifth Avenue housed no splendor that equaled the art gallery over the bar at the Hoffman House just a few steps up Broadway.

Our Thanksgiving dinner was the end of a perfect day. In the afternoon we had seen Yale defeat Harvard at football. That was my first glimpse of the modern game. For the first time I saw a halfback rush with the ball. And that ball was not stuffed with horsehair. When the fullback kicked it, it sailed through the air half the length of the field. The players wore knee breeches and jerseys and long hair and some of them wore whiskers and flowing mustaches. The captain of the Yale team was a big fellow named "Pop" Corbin. He wore sideburns and looked like an English country gentleman. But he didn't look like a country gentleman the next morning when he came into the *Eden Musée*, where Jessie and I were admiring the waxworks. On that occasion, he wore two black eyes in addition to his side whiskers and he stole the whole show. Nobody looked at Napoleon or Bismarck or Ivan the Terrible or Queen Victoria while "Pop" Corbin was in the room.

I spent my Christmas holiday at Baltimore as the guest of Mack Barry, one of my schoolmates. Just after New Years Day, 1888, I went to Washington for a few days. Our congressman, the Hon. William M. Springer, took me to the Executive Mansion, as the White House was called in those days. There he presented me to President Cleveland and reminded him that he had appointed me to West Point. The President received this information without enthusiasm. He observed to Mr. Springer that only a few of his appointees "got in" and his glance at me appraised me as a prospect rather below the average. I met him again at Princeton about a dozen years after I graduated. When I gratefully reminded him that he had appointed me to West Point, he inquired, "Did you get in?"

After our visit with the President, Mr. Springer took me to the Navy Department. There we were received by Secretary William C. Whitney, who showed us the model of a cruiser which was launched a little later as the first ship of our modern steel navy.

Just before Easter my father surprised me by sending me money for a trip to Springfield. There I spent my spring vacation at our old home. There were two weeks of parties and other good times. My friend Maude Laning came over from Petersburg for some of the dances. During this visit I attended my Grandfather Palmer's wedding. He was married to an old family friend, Mrs. Hannah Lamb Kimball—or "Aunt Han" as we called her. The bridegroom was nearly seventy-one years old but he looked like a well-preserved man of fifty-five—about the age of the dainty little bride whose head barely reached his shoulder.

One morning in June, 1888, I boarded the old ferry boat at Garrison and ten minutes later disembarked at West Point. As I stepped from the boat I was welcomed by a martial figure who looked to me like a major general but who was really a police sergeant. "Will ye be a can'idate?" he asked. When I replied in the affirmative he directed me up the long hill to the Administration Building. There another son of Mars steered me upstairs, where one of his brethren assigned me a seat on a bench just outside the "adjutant's office." Another "candidate" was already seated on that bench. This proved to be William Ruthven Smith, the first of my future classmates that I had the pleasure of meeting. Neither of us knew then that one day "Smythe" would lead an American division against the German Army and that later he would be the commanding general at West Point—one of the really great superintendents of the Military Academy.

Presently Smythe was ushered into the adjutant's office, and a few minutes later it came my turn. The adjutant, Lt. W. C. Brown of the Cavalry, examined my letter of appointment, asked me a few questions, and directed me to join Smythe, who was waiting in an adjoining room. By this time other candidates had arrived and when there were six of us we were formed into a squad and marched to the hospital. There we stripped and the doctors examined us from our scalps to our toenails. Those of us who passed were then marched over to cadet barracks for assignment to quarters. There was room for all of the candidates there, as the battalion of cadets was now in its summer camp.

Up to this time we had been guided and escorted by blue-clad functionaries of the regular army. But from the moment we reached barracks we came under the command of a group of supermen in grey coats and white duck trousers. These gentlemen were Cadet Lieutenants Hagadorn and Rhodes of the first (senior) class and six cadet corporals of the third (yearling) class. If the second class was not represented on this reception committee it was because all of its members were away on furlough.

Our cadet instructors took a keen interest in our military education. From the very first day they marched us to all of our meals. Before each meal they lined up outside the mess hall, where we stood in admiration while the Corps of Cadets marched briskly by to the music of the drum and fife. It did not seem possible that we could ever attain such martial perfection.

Our grey-clad commanders did not haze us. They simply treated us as veterans have treated raw recruits from time immemorial. They were authorized to give us legitimate military orders and we were too zealous and patriotic to postpone our military education until after the entrance examinations. Those who passed them would be that much ahead of the curriculum and those who failed would return to civil life enriched by valuable military experience.

It might be thought that our six yearling corporals who had just risen from the plebe class would have a tender feeling for those who were about to enter into durance. But they were not guilty of any such weakness. During a long life in the army, I have been the victim of many efforts to educate me, but I have never found more earnest and conscientious instructors than I found in the class of 1891 at the U.S. Military Academy. Some of them were so zealous that they even found time to tutor me when I was not on duty. During my first afternoon in barracks, Cadet Cpl. Hanson E. Ely came to my room and devoted much of his valuable time to correcting what he considered serious defects in my military bearing. First he exhorted me to throw my shoulders back. When he found that I couldn't quite pinch his forefinger with my shoulder blades, he insisted that I should "grind them back." This, I finally did to his satisfaction. But now, to his horror, he found that my effort had so upset my equilibrium that I was standing sway-back with my abdomen protuding. With great patience, he applied a correction to this defect by exhorting me, "lean forward on your hips and suck up your gut." Eventually I learned how to coordinate shoulder, hip, and gut without sticking out my chin—but that took time and continued coaching from Ely and other ardent instructors. I have always been especially grateful to Ely, who later wound up his distinguished pedagogic career as Major General Ely, president of the Army War College. But for his painstaking tutelage, I might never have attained the exalted rank of cadet captain three years later. To paraphrase Sir Joseph Porter, I might have then sung:

I sucked up my gut so carefulee
That now I am Captain of Company 'C'.

In those days all entrance examinations were held at West Point. Each day for about a week we were assembled in the Cadet Mess Hall to write answers to questions. My recollection of these exercises is very dim but I remember our last examination very vividly. We were marched to the grove of trees just across the road from the library. There we were formed in a line facing a row of desks which were occupied by the Academic Board comprising all the professors at the Military Academy. They were magnificent in the old-fashioned professorial uniform, swallowtail coats with brass buttons. It was an impressive picture as they sat there under the trees with the library and the old chapel in the background. They were assembled in all this splendor to examine us in reading. As his name was called each candidate took his place in front of the center and read a passage from a book that was placed in his hands. As he read, each professor observed him carefully and checked off his name on his copy of the list of candidates. It surprised me that while the other examinations were conducted by junior officers, the whole Academic Board should be assembled to determine whether I could read my own language. But the reading examination was much more than that. It gave each professor an opportunity to size us up. A candidate obviously not the makings of an officer and gentleman could be rejected now, even though he had passed his written examinations. On the other hand, some fine manly boy of obvious intelligence, might convince the authorities that he was worth a chance to make up for a low mark in arithmetic or geography. In such cases, after the brief reading, members of the Academic Board would question the candidate as to his opportunities for schooling. In short, the examination in reading was a highly important examination in personality.

In the mess hall that night we were informed that the results of the examinations would be announced next morning. Some of us would be going home tomorrow and the rest of us would enter into the treadmill of cadet life. After one week of it, I felt that I had had enough of the profession of arms. After supper that night "Teddy" Rhodes marched us all to the weekly prayer meeting at Dialectic Hall just over the north sally port of barracks. With a few upperclassmen, already present, we filled up the whole room. The exercises were conducted by Cadet Ogden of the new "yearling" class, a gallant Christian soldier whose noble character shone from his face. After a few songs and a prayer he had a few kind words for us. His Christianity extended even to the poor despised candidates. In conclusion, he asked if any one of us would like to speak or to offer a prayer or to propose a hymn. Almost instantly, one of my comrades, a burly Illinoisan by the name of Leonard Morton Prince, rose to his feet and said, "Please sing a few verses of hymn no. 552." The organist played the accompaniment and soon we were all singing:

> We're going home, we're going home,
> We're going home tomorrow.

As a publicity stunt, Prince had achieved a great success. He was a marked man from that moment. After the doxology we remained standing while the upperclassmen passed out. On the way most of them paid their respects to Prince: "Mister Prince, it will be damn lucky for you if you do go home tomorrow." "Mister Prince, just wait until we get you in camp." "Mister Prince, you are the freshest beast that ever came to the Military Academy."

Such were some of their salutations. Prince fairly beamed. He enjoyed this early token of popularity in his new alma mater. Most of us trembled for him, but his face was wreathed in smiles that grew even broader when a fierce looking yearling, "Gobbo" Upton, growled at him: "Mr. Prince, wipe that grin off your face."

Next morning we stood in line in the "area" of barracks while the adjutant read an alphabetical list of the candidates who had failed to pass the entrance examinations. As each name was called its owner stepped out of ranks and went to his room for his luggage. I almost hoped to hear my name. I had already had enough of military life. But he passed me by and when the last name was called, those of us who remained in ranks were no longer candidates. We were not cadets, though, until later that morning when we took the oath of allegiance to the United States. After that we were officially known as "new cadets." Unofficially we were no longer "beasts" but "plebes" and our quarters now became Plebe Barracks instead of Beast Barracks.

That same day our cadet corporals formed us in squads and marched us to the cadet store, where the tailors measured us for our uniforms. As it would take some days to build and fit these garments, ready-made gray flannel trousers and jackets were issued to us. These military hand-me-downs were known as "plebe skins." When we marched to supper that night in our ill-fitting gray suits and blue forage caps our military metamorphosis had begun. If we were not yet dapper soldiers, we were no longer a nondescript crowd of civilians.

The next morning our military education really began. We were marched out to the parade ground and divided into small squads, each under a brand-new yearling corporal. These young gentlemen tutored us in the "position of the soldier," the "setting up exercises," and the elements of the fine art of marching. They were the most competent instructors in these military minutiae in the world. For a year they had been perfecting themselves for their present mission of imparting these minutiae to a new plebe class. They knew more about them then than they would ever know again. Like all new brooms they swept clean. Three times a day they did their best to sweep away every vestige of our awkwardness. In my case there was plenty to sweep away. At the command "Right face," I generally faced to the left and soon found myself in the awkward squad. They drilled us and exercised us until every bone in our bodies ached. After a week or ten days, rifles were issued to us. Again the task seemed hopeless but we gradually mastered the manual of arms. By the end of a month our new dress coats and white trousers were issued to us and we were marched over to camp and were assigned to companies. Some of my classmates were taken up for full company duty, but I remained in the awkward squad for several more weeks.

There were only four companies in the Corps of Cadets in those days. With a fourth part of my class, I was assigned to A Company. The old cadets, two to a tent, were quartered on the north side of the company street. We plebes were crowded three to a tent just across the way from them. While in Plebe

Barracks, we had had no contact with any upperclassmen except the lieutenants and corporals who were assigned to duty over us. But when we got to camp every upperclassman was free to take part in our military education. I cannot remember that any of them neglected this pedagogic duty. In barracks we had had brief breathing spells between drills. Now, thanks to a numerous corps of private tutors, our instruction was continuous from reveille to taps—with occasional tutoring in "double step" or "second exercises" back of our tents in the wee small hours of the night.

In addition to our numerous volunteer instructors, our tent had many other visitors. This was because Leonard Prince was one of my tentmates. We have seen that Leonard had laid the foundations of wide publicity while we were still in Beast Barracks. His fame extended far beyond the limits of our company and pilgrims came from as far as D Company to hear him sing:

> We're going home, we're going home,
> We're going home tomorrow.

His audience was generally too big for the tent and extended out into the company street. I can see him now in his undershirt and drawers, with his burly chest thrown out and his shoulders "ground" well back. He was proud of his deep baritone, and its volume and range were marvelous for an artist who had to sing in "the position of the soldier" with his hands "finned out" and his "gut sucked up."

My other roommate was Charles Pelot Summerall, an earnest young man from Florida. He also was a songster and his rendering of the "Marseillaise" was greatly admired and frequently encored. He sang the words in French and did it as solemnly and earnestly as everything else he has ever done in the course of his earnest life. He was as dignified singing there in his shirttail as he ever was later when he appeared before the Senate Military Affairs Committee as the Chief of Staff of the Army. I have one memory picture of Pelot as he was singing the "Marseillaise" for a delegation of yearlings from "D" Company. One of them, John L. Hines, was known to his classmates as "Birdie," probably because he was as unbirdlike as six feet of sturdy, rawboned manhood could make him. I see Pelot singing to "Birdie" and then, as in the movies, the picture fades and is replaced by another in which Pelot and Birdie are standing by Pershing in the Meuse-Argonne. They have become corps commanders, each of them commanding a greater number of American soldiers in battle than Grant commanded in the Wilderness. But though the picture has changed, I still hear the strains of *Marchons, marchons!*

By the first of August, even I had graduated from the awkward squad and had taken my place in the rear rank of Company A. In my well-starched white trousers and full dress coat, I marched to dress parade with my company and could even go through the manual of arms without disgrace. One morning I marched to guard mounting for the first time and soon found myself on duty as a sentinel. I had committed all the Guard Orders to memory and was able to recite them glibly to the cadet officer of the guard. When the officer of the day crossed my post, I saluted him with a smashing "Present arms." On the whole I was a very snappy sentinel—and knew it.

After dark I was required to challenge every one who approached my post. If several approached from different directions at the same time, the Guard Orders required me to halt them all, to ascertain who they were and then direct them to advance, one by one, in the order of their rank. It would be a tremendous breach of etiquette to keep a captain waiting for a sergeant. Soon after taps, the officer of the day approached from the front, the officer of the guard from the left, and the corporal of the guard from the right. I could not think fast enough and allowed the two juniors to continue their advance while I was receiving their senior. The officer of the day, Cadet Lt. "Duke" Stockham, bawled me out and reminded me that in war I might have been disarmed and captured. He then had the same situation restaged. This time I challenged each one as he emerged from the darkness, ordered him to halt and then advanced them one by one in their proper order.

After this bit of coaching I felt equal to any emergency. But now my unofficial tutors had their chance. Some emerged from the A Company tents on my right, others from the moat of old Fort Clinton on my left. I cannot remember all who replied to my challenges, but among them were President Harrison, the Secretary of War, Rip Van Winkle, General Putnam, and Benny Havens. One figure who raced back and forth across my post in his shirttail and astride a broomstick, informed me that he was General Sheridan on his way to Winchester. The general was followed by a cavalry escort of lusty yearlings who galloped by on all fours, rearing and snorting and giving other manifestations of equine high spirits. There were also awesome figures dressed in white, among them the ghosts of Washington, Napoleon, and Benedict Arnold. It was impossible for me to determine the precedence of these visitors in the limited time at my disposal. There were still too many coming from too many directions. They wouldn't stand still when I ordered "Halt!" And when I said "Please halt," they all laughed. Just then somebody said "Sh-h-h!" And they all withdrew into the darkness. A moment later the officer in charge, Lieutenant Galbraith of the 5th Artillery, arrived to inspect my post. I was so glad to see him that I forgot to challenge him. I wanted to shake hands with him; but for his walrus moustache, I might have kissed him.

Every morning at Guard Mounting the cadet adjutant selected three sentinels to guard the national and corps colors during the ensuing day. This honor went to the three men whose uniforms, arms, and equipment were neatest, who were snappiest in the manual of arms, and who presented the most soldierly appearance. During the summer this competition was open only to upperclassmen, but on the last day of camp, the color sentinels were selected from the fourth class. Each cadet captain detailed his likeliest plebes for this contest and there was a keen competition between the companies. Why I was selected as one of the aspirants from "A" Company I never knew, unless it was my success in attaining Corporal Ely's ideal of soldierly bearing. For at that time, my back was as straight as a ramrod and I could suck up my gut to the vanishing point. In those days, I didn't need "galluses" to hold up my trousers.

No bride was ever dressed for her wedding with more care than I was dressed for Guard Mounting that morning, and no bride ever had so many or such distinguished bridesmaids. Cadet Lt. Stockham pinned my collar on my dress coat. Cadet Corporal Ely put the final polish on my brass waist plate. Another upper classman rubbed in a last touch of linseed oil on my gun stock. Cadet Lt. Rhodes brought me his finest pair of duck trousers. For duck trousers, like wine, improve with age. No new trousers will stiffen and glisten with starch like a pair that has been in the corps of cadets for several generations. Every graduate leaves his best duck trousers to some friend in the new first class. They pass from class to class as cherished heirlooms. The laundry marks on the inside of the pair that I wore that morning made quite an autograph album.

But if old duck will shine it will also wrinkle easily, so I was not permitted to put on my own trousers. Ely and another husky yearling, "Sep" Adams, lifted me up the ridge pole of the tent, where I clung while Teddy and another cadet officer drew the precious white raiment over my legs. Just before first call, Cadet Captain Flagler came in to inspect. "Great God!" he roared, "You're not going to let that plebe go to guard mounting with that flowing beard!" This was a high compliment to the down that was just beginning to appear on my cheek. When the captain found that I had not yet acquired a razor he got his own and gave me my first shave. Then came first call and I stood stiff-legged in the company street. At assembly we marched to the parade ground. What an ordeal it was while that demigod, Bill Harts, the cadet adjutant, inspected us. Finally he tapped Dickson, then Rutherford, and then Palmer with his sword point. A Company had won two of the three "colors," first and third.

On the twenty-eighth of August, the battalion struck camp and we marched over to Barracks. The academic year began on the first day of September. That morning the plebe class was assembled for a preliminary lecture by "Papa" Bass, the professor of mathematics. He spoke in gentle tones and as he spoke he held a lead pencil vertically between the palms of his hands and gently rotated it back and forth. There was something hypnotic in his blue eyes, the tones of his voice, the reciprocating motion of his hands, and the rotation of the lead pencil. He gave me the shivers. I remember only one passage of his lecture but it contained his whole theme: "This institution is like the car of Juggernaut. It moves slowly and steadily on its way." (Here his hands barely moved and the pencil barely rotated.) "If you climb on board it will carry you with it." (Here the pencil rotated more briskly.) "But if you fall under its wheels" (here he paused for a moment and the rotation stopped) "it will crush you."

That was a true description of old West Point. We were over a hundred strong that morning. But when we graduated four years later, only sixty-two had escaped the wheels of Juggernaut.

Just thirty years later I went up the headquarters of the French army with General Pershing. There we were the guests of its new commander, General Pétain. As we sat down at the luncheon table, I had a feeling that I had seen our host before. There was something familiar in his keen eyes, his professorial poise, and his softly modulated voice. Suddenly it dawned upon me that he looked and spoke like "Papa" Bass.

Prince was my first roommate. Our room was on the first floor of the second division of barracks. In those days there was only one barrack building. It was constructed ten years before the Civil War and contained sixteen rooms in each of its ten divisions. It thus had accommodations for the entire Corps of Cadets, which never numbered more than three hundred in those days. This old barrack still stands but has been supplemented by others. For the corps is eight times as big as it was when I was a cadet. There is now a brigade of two big regiments while we had a single small battalion. My grandson's class in 1949 was twice as big as the whole corps when I graduated.

The old Cadet Barracks formed the north and west sides of a quadrangle known as the Area of Barracks. East of the Area was the Academic Building, a fine old structure of red sandstone that was replaced by a larger building before the Spanish-American War. On its northeast corner was a clock tower, with a clock that sounded the hours and could be seen from the parade ground. It was an accurate timepiece but its minute hand seemed to move very slowly when we were counting the minutes until recall from drill. The old Academic Building contained our recitation and lecture rooms. The dancing academy and gymnasium were on its ground floor. About the time I graduated, a new gymnasium was contructed near the northwest corner of Barracks. It was one of the finest and largest school gymnasiums in the country then but was outgrown in a few years. One of its titles to fame was an indoor swimming pool. Many old graduates were shocked and grieved when they first heard of this highly sybaritic innovation. They had had to march more than a mile to the river north of the post when they took their swimming lessons. The service would certainly go to the devil if future cadets should have an easier time than they had.

From the northwest corner of Barracks, the Officer's Line extended to the north. In those days there were a half-dozen sets of officers' quarters between the corner and the superintendent's mansion. These were the most attractive quarters in the post. From their verandas you could look out over the plain and see Guard Mounting and Dress Parade. All of these cozy army homes have disappeared. Their sites are now covered by massive modern buildings.

Across the street from the Academic Building and to the east of the clock tower was the Cadet Chapel. This was a beautiful old building of granite trimmed in red sandstone. It was built in 1836, ten years before the Mexican War. When it was proposed after the Spanish-American War to demolish it to make room for an additional academic building, there was an indignant protest form the whole army. The old chapel was enshrined in the memory of every graduate then living. They all remembered the allegorical painting by Robert Walter Weir over the altar with the legend "Righteousness exhalteth a nation: but sin is a reproach to any people." They all remembered the black marble shields on the walls, one for each general of the Revolutionary War and bearing his name in gold letters. They all remembered one of these shields where the name had been gouged out with a chisel. This was Benedict Arnold's shield. This building, more than any other, embodied the spirit of old West Point. As a compromise, the building was finally removed, stone by stone, and re-erected in the Cadet Cemetery. There we old graduates still find one relic of the West Point that we knew.

Small as it was, the old chapel had plenty of room for the cadets and for the professors and instructors and their families in my day. There was also room for our mothers and sisters and sweethearts when they came to West Point. But it would not hold a tenth of the present Corps of Cadets. For them a magnificant Gothic cathedral has been erected high on a hill where it stands as the architectural crown of the new West Point. There you will hear the voices of the great cadet choir which the radio now bears from ocean to ocean. But even when I listen to these magnificent tones, I still hear our little choir in the old chapel. No cadet chorister today had a more beautiful voice than our sweet singer, "Ike" Jenks of the Class of 1891. There were only about a dozen members of the old choir because the organ loft was to small for any more. The privilege of membership was highly sought, not solely because the candidates were lovers of music but because when the choristers were seated, they were invisible from below. They were, therefore, the only members of the corps who really enjoyed the sermon. When old "Possy" rose to preach, they took off their belts and dress coats and reverently went to sleep.

On the site of the old Mess Hall there is now a modern building where the cadets of today have the facilities of a modern club, with comfortable reception rooms where they can entertain their families and friends. There is also a bar where they can treat their sweethearts to ice cream and Coca-Cola. They can even buy cigarettes and smoke them without blowing the smoke up the chimney or making unnecessary trips to the water closet. We old timers were shocked when we first heard of these departures from the old Spartan discipline. But we are beginning to realize that a young soldier is none the worse for being treated like a young gentleman with normal tastes and interests. In fact, there are not so many serious breaches of discipline in the big corps of today as there used to be in the little corps of sixty years ago. Where there are normal outlets for the escape of animal spirits they are not stored up until they explode.

This reminds me of a party that "Mary" Powell gave when I was a plebe. "Mary" drew a substantial prize in the Louisiana State Lottery and invested the proceeds in a variegated stock of liquor. On the night of the New Years Hop he opened a free bar in a vacant "tower room" in the Eighth Division. "Mary" and two of his classmates garbed themselves as bartenders and dispensed free refreshment to all comers. Three other members of his class acted as bouncers and policemen, and two others acted as patrols in observation of the commandant's office. Everybody not at the hop, including the whole plebe class, was invited to attend. Nearly everybody got more or less tight except "Mary" and his assistants, who refrained from taking a drink until the next day when they had a more exclusive little New Years party of their own. Such a celebration would be unthinkable today. When the authorities are doing their best to give you a good time, what's the use of going to the trouble of contriving a hell of a good time just to spite them.

The present Cadet Mess Hall is in the mass of new buildings south of the superintendent's quarters. It has table room for the whole modern Corps of Cadets. There we old graduates get our meals when we come back for class reunions during graduation week in June. The academy gives a hearty welcome to its alumni. Each class is assigned to a section in Cadet Barracks. Each old-timer rooms with his old cadet roommate if he happens to be present. But there are always some absentees. Leonard Prince, my plebe roommate, died before the Spanish-American War. My last roommate was killed by a German shell in France where he commanded a regiment. Fort William D. Davis down by the Panama Canal is named for him. But the absentees are all present when we sit on the barrack porch after taps and talk over old times. It is a comfort to sleep in a cadet bed and not have to get up when we hear the drums and fifes playing reveille.

The old Cadet Hospital stood just south of Grant Hall. It was an oasis in our desert, a sanctuary of escape from the everlasting grind of drills and parades and recitations. When I hurt my foot in plebe camp, the doctor excused me from drills for a week. That gave me a spell of luxurious loafing much to the envy of my classmates. We didn't condole with our sick friends; we congratulated them. Tom Sawyer never enjoyed his sore toe half as much as I enjoyed mine.

Of course when you were seriously ill being in the hospital was not much fun. But a mild case of the mumps with five or six classmates suffering from the same ailment could be made the basis for a delightful house party—just the right number for a quiet little game of poker—for it was one of the amenities of the hospital that tactical officers didn't come nosing around there to inspect. One of my most cherished memories is an attack of the hives which gave me my first opportunity to meet Mr. Pickwick and Sam Weller. I lost two weeks of conic sections during this illness, but I have never missed them particularly. As a permanent educational acquisition, I'd rather have Sam and his father than any of them.

Some of my classmates were geniuses at getting cosy little vacations "on sick report." I could go to "sick call" with a most promising bellyache, but instead of marking me "hospital" or "sick in quarters" the doctor would give me a dose of salts and send me back to duty. Prince would know how to exploit a heaven-sent opportunity like that. He had been to medical school for a while before he came to West Point. He could therefore describe and locate those abdominal symptoms with such technical accuracy that the doctor would generally keep him under observation for a week. Fortunately, that was before the vermiform appendix was invented. If a modern cadet should emulate Prince he would be lucky to escape the operating table.

At our final physical examination, just before graduation, one of the doctors took up Prince's clinical record while the others were finishing my examination. He shook his head ominously when he saw the long list of Prince's physical disabilities. I shall never forget the surprise on his face when the invalid, in the garb of Adam before the fall, pranced into the room. Except that he was a bit muscle-bound about the shoulders, he might have posed as an exceptionally healthy Adonis.

When a graduate of the eighteen-nineties comes back for the first time, he hardly knows his alma mater. The old West Point lies buried under the new. The few landmarks that survive are almost hidden by new architectural splendors. At dress parade, a full brigade replaces the little battalion of the old days. Cadet life has changed even more than its background. We lived a narrow, monastic life in our day. There were no organized sports and no contacts with the outer world. Today, college teams come to West Point almost every weekend for athletic games and competitions. The annual football game with the Navy is but the crowning event of a zestful year. The old-timer is shocked to find that his West Point is gone never to return. At first, he feels that the changes are all for the worse. But if he has any vision he soon sees that this broader life is better than the narrow life of the old days. Graduates of today have a wider knowledge of the country they are to serve than we had. But the old West Point had one charm that has gone forever. Our classes were small and classmates knew each other intimately. The very narrowness of our lives brought us close together like brothers in the same family. My class was a large one for its day but there were only sixty-two of us when we graduated. My grandson cannot know a tenth of his classmates as I knew all of mine.

In those days the veterans of the Civil War were beginning to pass away and many distinguished generals received their final honors in the West Point Cemetery. On such occasions the Battalion of Cadets acted as escort. This included a march from the chapel to the grave side, where we formed in line and fired the customary salutes by battalion. One afternoon while we were standing at "Aim" waiting for the command "Fire," the commandant of cadets, Colonel Hawkins, waited a bit too long and some cadet in A Company pulled his trigger too soon. This resulted in a most disgraceful fusillade which extended like a burst of rapid skirmish fire from the right to the center of the battalion. After this fiasco we fired the two remaining volleys with our customary precision. When we formed line upon our return to barracks, Colonel Hawkins shouted: "I hope you young gentlemen in A Company are damned well pleased with yourselves. The rest of us are not. Dismiss your companies."

We rather enjoyed the military funerals because they were held during the afternoon drill hour. After the ceremony, the tactical officer in charge generally called off dress parade, which gave us a release from quarters until suppertime. But one afternoon as we were setting out from barracks on pleasure bent we were surprised to find that no "recall" followed first call for dress parade. Thereupon Cadet Bookmiller exclaimed: "That is a hell of a note." This same remark was being made by almost everybody else in the corps just at that time, but Bookmiller made it within the hearing of the officer in charge, Lieut. John A. Johnston of the Cavalry. Bookmiller might have escaped with a report for "an improper expression," but when the lieutenant asked him whether he was aware that he, as officer in charge, had ordered the drummer not to beat the "recall," Bookmiller stood by his guns and made it clear that he considered a dress parade under such circumstances "a hell of a note" no matter who ordered it. Thereupon he was placed in arrest and a few days later was tried by court martial under charges prepared by Lieutenant Johnston.

After the court martial, its proceedings were read out by the cadet adjutant at parade. It was the first of these ominous documents that I ever heard. The charge was "conduct to the prejudice of good order of military discipline in violation of the 62d article of war." There were at least a half-dozen specifications, each in highly technical legal language and each ending in the phrase "hell of a note or words to that effect." Then, in due course, followed the court's finding of "guilty" and the sentence, under which Cadet Bookmiller was confined to Barracks and the Area of Barracks until just before his graduation about eight months later.

Bookmiller gave me the sequel to this incident many years later. When he graduated he was determined never to forgive Lieutenant Johnston. Should he meet him in the army, he would salute him as a military senior but he would never shake hands with him and never know him socially. Soon after he joined his regiment, he learned that Johnston, by that time a captain, was about to visit his post as inspector. Bookmiller did his best to avoid him, but one morning he met the inspector just in front of post headquarters. The lieutenant drew himself up and was prepared to pass with a formal salute when Johnston recognized him and advanced toward him with both hands extended and his face wreathed in smiles. "Why! Here's old Hell-of-a-Note," he cried. Bookmiller capitulated at once. Their hands met in the beginning of a lifelong friendship. Thus does army blue forget the resentments of cadet gray.

The first half of the plebe year culminated in January examinations. After that ordeal I found myself in the upper fourth of the class, a comfortable position—high enough to be safe from the wheels of Juggernaut but not so high that I could not spare a bit of time to get acquainted with *Tom Jones* and *Peregrine Pickle*. I recall few incidents that winter, but on the 30th of April we had an unprecedented adventure. That morning, the whole Corps of Cadets embarked for New York to take part in the centennial of Washington's first inauguration. We landed at the Battery and marched up Broadway and Fifth Avenue to Central Park. There we executed column left and marched to the North River, where we reembarked for West Point. That was an unusual outing in those days. But there was little fun in it for we never broke ranks. Nor was there much sightseeing, especially for a plebe. Whenever I peeped to the right or left, a file closer would roar: "Keep your eyes to the front, Mister Palmer. Draw in your chin. Throw your shoulders back." Being a plebe I marched in the rear rank close up to my front rank file. It was tough going up Broadway, for I had my left foot on a slippery street car rail and my right foot on the cobblestones. Every two or three blocks, my front rank file, a tall first classman, would relieve the monotony by taking a step with his feet crossed. At this I would stumble and butt him in the small of the back. This brought encomiums on my marching ability from all of the file closers. Until then I had hoped to be made a corporal in June. But my disgraceful marching in New York blasted all my hopes.

June finally came, but we did not become yearlings until after the graduation of the class of 1889 on the twelfth. Although we were still plebes we were permitted to attend our first hop—the Graduation Ball—the night of the eleventh. This indulgence enabled some of us to perform an important service for members of the graduating class. After arranging for his best girl to come down from Vassar to attend his farewell hop, a fellow might receive a belated and unexpected acceptance from some hometown girl out in Ohio or Colorado. If he could not find a classmate who was free to escort girl number two, it was customary to confer the honor upon some likely plebe.

This is why William Ruthven Smith stood in front of Grant Hall that evening. He was waiting for Miss Lutetia Johnston to disembark from one of the buses from Cranston's Hotel. "Smythe's" company commander had told him that Miss Lutetia would wear a blue dress with a white rose in her hair.

But dusk had fallen and though several buses had unloaded their lovely passengers, Smythe had been unable to identify the lady to whom he owed his devoirs. As the last bus was unloading a cargo of dowagers and old maids, Smythe's company commander came charging out of the ballroom to find him. When the knight pleaded complete ignorance as to the lady's whereabouts, his company commander exclaimed, "She is waiting for you in the hop room now. She's the girl in blue under Grant's picture." Smythe hurried through the crowded lobby and into the ballroom. The band was playing a waltz but three girls in blue were sitting on the divan under General Grant. Smythe beat it back to barracks swearing that he would never go to another hop.

4 Cadet

Graduation Day was a day of revolution for the whole corps. The class of '89 received their diplomas and became full-fledged army officers. The class of '90 became First Classmen. The class of '91 donned civilian clothes and went off on their two month's furlough. We of '92 became yearlings and twenty of us received bright new corporal's chevrons.

The next day we marched over to camp leaving barracks vacant for the new crop of "beasts" that would soon become the class of 1893. A year ago when we were plebes we had resolved to do no hazing when we became yearlings. We would establish a new era of kindliness at West Point. Instead of "bawling out" the new plebes we would lead them gently into the mysteries of the profession of arms. But when we first saw that motley mob, lined up by the Academic Building as we marched behind the drums and fifes to the Mess Hall, we saw that we must sacrifice our humanity to our patriotism. We must reluctantly lay our kindly aspirations upon the altar of our country. If these new beasts had been the promising material that we were a year ago, gentle methods might suffice. But from our first glimpse of the class of '93, it was obvious that only the sternest measures could ever make soldiers of them. And we did our duty by them. No doubt, as they look back over a half-century of brilliant military service, the men of '93 are as grateful to '92 as we were to '91. And they, too, passed on the torch. A year later they started '94 upon the path to military glory.

In a few days we were at squad drill again but this time as drill masters. In due time I was given the important duty of drilling the awkward squad. In my new corporal's chevrons I forgot that I had ever been a member of that clumsy organization. Presently the new plebes came over to camp and before long they took their places in the battalion.

Among my many friends in the class of '93, one of them stands preeminent in my memory. This was Henri Le Comte of Switzerland. "Frenchy," as we called him, was the son of a Swiss officer who had served as an honorary member of McClellan's staff during the Civil War. Through the influence of his father's friends, he was admitted to West Point by a special act of Congress. He was one of the most popular men of his time, not only in his own class but in the whole Corps of Cadets. After his graduation at West Point he attended our Infantry and Cavalry School at Fort Leavenworth and served in one or more U.S. Army posts. After his return to Switzerland, he became a distinguished Colonel of Engineers in the Swiss army. He was therefore probably the only man in the world who knew both the American and the Swiss military systems intimately. When in 1938 his American classmates celebrated the forty-fifth anniversary of their graduation, Frenchy joined them at West Point as their guest of honor. In his Swiss uniform he was the most conspicuous figure in the alumni parade.

One plebe of that summer stands out as a historic figure. This was Butler Ames of Massachusetts. He was famous because he was the grandson of Ben Butler, but he was even more famous in his own right for he was the first cadet to bring pajamas to West Point. We still wore nightshirts in those days. So, when we heard that one of the plebes was clad in the exotic night garb, we all went to see him. *Mister* Ames wore his pajamas day and night all that summer, except when he was on military duty, and there was always an admiring group of upperclassmen at his tent door. As he posed and postured for us, the beauty and utility of his garments appealed to us. But most of us had misgivings. There was something un-American about them. If Uncle Sam should swap shirttails for pajamas, would he still retain his sturdy, antique virtue?

Our ten weeks of "Yearling Camp" were full of active life but they have shrunk to a few days in my memory. We danced with pretty girls at the hops and strolled with them on Flirtation Walk. In August, Mother and George came to see me and spent a week or so at the old West Point Hotel, just a few steps from Cadet Camp. Our old Springfield home had been sold and from West Point they would go to Tacoma, Washington, where Father had decided to stake his fortunes. Mother was leaving our Illinois home and our many friends with serious misgivings. But Father's health seemed to demand the change and he was confident that great opportunities awaited him in the Puget Sound country, then in full boom. George looked forward to the change with delight. To his fourteen years it was a great adventure. And it gave a new aspect to my own plans for next summer. My furlough would take me clear across the continent.

Soon after Mother left, we broke camp and marched back to Barracks to begin our second academic year. Few memories stand out that winter. There was the usual grind of study and military duty. After the January examinations, we counted the days to June more eagerly than ever, for after graduation this year we would go away on our ten weeks of furlough. We arranged to have a class dinner in New York and a class meeting was held down at Battery Knox to discuss whether we should have wine on the menu. Some of us sat astride the big guns, and the others on the grassy parapet between them. The controversy was bitter as controversies on this subject usually are. Finally, Johnnie Woodward spoke in the role of a peacemaker. He announced that while he would enjoy a bit of wine with his dinner, he was loath to offend the scruples of so many classmates. He therefore proposed in a spirit of compromise, that we drop wine from the menu and content ourselves with brandy and soda. After taking a brief recess to bump Johnnie against the muzzle of the biggest gun, we adopted Prince's suggestion that those who wanted wine should have it and those who didn't want it should preserve their virtue by the simple device of turning down their glasses.

When spring came, tailors and other tradesmen were permitted to display their samples and wares in the Dancing Academy on Saturday afternoons. As I had an expensive trip across the continent before me, I had little money for clothes and it was hard for me to choose between a blue sample displayed by Mr. Magnus of New York and a gray offered by Mr. Cohen of the same city. In the course of my negotiations, Mr. Cohen called me aside and whispered: "Mr. Magnus is a fine chentleman and vun of my best friends, but I think I ought to tell you confidential, that, in a business vay, he is cott-tam son of a bitch." A few minutes later, Mr. Magnus found an opportunity to express his affectionate regard for Mr. Cohen in substantially the same terms. After that, Mr. Magnus and Mr. Cohen got together and jointly evolved a practical solution of my financial difficulty. Under this arrangement I purchased both the blue and the gray to be paid for after my graduation. In this way I had two furlough suits instead of one and had saved fifty dollars to add to my limited stock of pocket money.

During the brief "release from quarters" between supper and study hour we assembled each evening to practice our furlough yells and class songs. Among them, of course, was "Benny Havens Oh!" to which we added our class verse:

> Come sing of ties forever green,
> Of friendships strong and true
> The fellowship of common toils
> That binds old "Ninety Two."
> Fill high each glass with sparkling wine
> And as the red drops glow
> We'll drink again to West Point days
> And Benny Havens, Oh.

I might add that this verse is the only surviving relic of my boyish muse.

I have no clear recollection of the commencement exercises that year. Some great man made a speech to the class of 1890 and some other great man gave them their diplomas. Before we broke ranks, the adjutant read the "new makes" and I found myself promoted to senior line sergeant of the Corps of Cadets. When he dismissed us we hurried into our civilian clothes and took the first train for New York where we assembled at the Murray Hill Hotel— at that time a fashionable new hostelry away uptown at Forty-first Street. We had our class dinner there that night. There were jokes and toasts, none of which I remember. Next morning a lot of us Westerners took the Pennsylvania Limited and continued our class celebration as far as Chicago, where we separated.

Before continuing my journey to Tacoma, I went down to Springfield for a short visit. There were many old friends to see but with the family gone it was a melancholy place. It saddened me to go by the old house on South Seventh Street and find that it no longer welcomed me as home. There were several happy days in Carlinville and several trips over to Petersburg. There Mr. and Mrs. Laning made me welcome and I resumed my acquaintance with their daughter. Before I left she gave me her promise to go into permanent partnership with me the summer after graduation.

My trip from Illinois over the prairies and mountains to Puget Sound was a thrilling experience at the time, but it left me no memories worth recording now. Father and Mother and the boys met me at Tacoma and took me to their temporary home in the Hotel Florence. The hotel, like most of the other buildings in the city, was a frame structure, for the town was growing too fast for brick and mortar to keep up with it. Its population that summer of 1890 was thirty-six thousand. It had grown from five thousand in the past three years. My father and his business associates considered it the city of destiny, soon to grow into the great metropolis of the Pacific Coast. It had almost overtaken Seattle and just then was growing more rapidly. After carefully weighing the prospects of the rival cities, Father had confidently staked his fortunes on Tacoma. If he had bet the other way I might be a rich man now.

The evening after my arrival my mother took me to the roof of the hotel for my first view of Mount Tacoma. After a foggy day the air had cleared, and there to the southeast the old volcano stood out in all its snow-clad majesty. Back of us, to the northwest, the sun was setting behind the jagged peaks of the Olympics. But after he disappeared from our sight his rays still shone on top of the great mountain, turning its snow-white dome into a great opal. In those days the name of the mountain was still in dispute between the rival cities. Seattleites called it Mount Rainier, but we called it Mount Tacoma (snow-covered mountain), as the Indians had called it for ages before Vancouver dubbed it for a long-forgotten rear admiral in the British navy.

While it grew dark I told my mother about my engagement and my plan to be married the summer after my graduation. She knew and admired my sweetheart, but she felt that the responsibilities of married life should not be undertaken so young. "You are only twenty now and you will be only twenty-two when you graduate."

But she, herself had given me the best reply to this argument. "You and father were only twenty-one when you were married and you were only twenty-two when I was born."

She smiled at this argument but did not attempt to answer it. As to my ability to support my wife, I pointed out that as a second lieutenant my monthly pay would be $116.67. In addition to this goodly sum I would be entitled to a rent-free dwelling and many practical perquisites such as commissary privileges and free medical attendance for myself and family. She was probably not convinced, but she was too wise to contend against the tide of youth. From that moment she accepted the plan as hers.

My mother had looked forward to my furlough for the past three years. At first, she counted on having me back in our old Springfield home. When she closed the old Seventh Street home and moved to Tacoma she looked forward to my joining her there. My coming would gladden her loneliness in strange new surroundings. So, she busied herself filling her hotel rooms with the spirit of home. An old letter tells me that she was expecting me about the twentieth of June. In a later one she agrees that I should stop a week in Illinois to see the kinsfolk in Springfield and Carlinville. The one week's delay had grown into more than two when I finally got to Tacoma, and now in her first long talk with her boy she found that his boyhood was over and that his heart was full of another woman. She gave no sign of her feeling. The summer was still young and she told me of her plans for my outing. Among other things, she had planned a cruise up Puget Sound and to British Columbia with her three boys.

A few days after my arrival, Bob and I went over to Springfield, one of the several town sites on Puget Sound that my father and his business associates were developing. It was to be one of the rural satellites of Tacoma, the metropolis. Its name would attract immigrants from Illinois. At that time a country store and the storekeeper's log dwelling were the only buildings in the town. But streets and avenues and public squares had been surveyed through the woods, and town lots were all ready for the settlers who would soon come on the crest of the boom. The site for a sawmill had been duly located and before long the big trees would be transformed into beams and joists and shingles. In the meantime Bob and I caught brook trout and shot ruffed grouse without having to leave the city limits. The fir trees were so tall that partridges perched on their lower branches were beyond the range of Bob's shotgun.

But we did not make that journey to British Columbia. Mother knew before I did what would happen. In a few weeks, mountains and forests lost their charm for me and my thoughts went back to the Illinois prairie. About the end of July, I started back eastward. Mother was full of interest in my journey. If she was disappointed in her shrunken summer with her boy she gave no sign of it, and I was too young and selfish to understand. But as I recall the eager letters she wrote me that spring, my heart is full of sadness. I would give anything if that journey to Vancouver could be included in these memoirs.

And how that summer sped by. Even those weeks in Illinois have shrunk to brief memories. Before I knew it I was back with my classmates at the Murray

Hill Hotel. Then we were on the day boat sailing up the Hudson and before we knew it furlough was over and we were back in ranks.

In September, 1890, shortly after our return from furlough, the monotony of our lives was broken by a revolutionary event. Annapolis challenged West Point to play a game of football. At first, it seemed almost certain that this challenge must be rejected. We had no football team and very few cadets had ever handled a modern football. The Academic Board would have vetoed such a distracting innovation during the academic year even if the cadets were prepared for such a contest, but in the actual circumstances the odds were at least a thousand to one against it.

But these odds were trifling to my classmate, Dennis Mahan Michie. Dennis had played football at Lawrenceville for several years and was one of the few in the Corps with any real knowledge of the game. But even more important, he was also the only cadet with any power to influence the academic authorities. He was born at West Point and had spent his childhood there. He knew all the professors and their families intimately. Most of the instructors had chummed and jollied with him when they were cadets and he was an attractive small boy about the post. In fact, Michie's position in the Corps of Cadets was absolutely unique. I was walking with him one day when we met that superb cavalier, Lt. Daniel L. Tate of the U.S. Cavalry. As the lieutenant returned our salutes, he said, "Good morning, Dennis." When Dennis replied, "Good morning, Danny," I almost expected the skies to fall.

It was something to have friends among the officers on the post. But in those days West Point was dominated by the Academic Board and the Academic Board was dominated by Peter S. Michie, "Old Pete," the professor of natural and experimental philosophy. As the senior professor, Old Pete was known as the dean of the board and presided over its meetings. And his official position was fortified by his dominating personality. As a rule, Pete was highly conservative and could be counted on to lead the resistance against innovation. But when the football challenge came before the Board, his position was weakened by the fact that Cadet Michie was his favorite son. When Dennis first told me about the challenge, I inquired, "But how about your father?"

To this he replied with a grin. "Old Pete is dead against it now, but I will bring him around." Old Pete finally came around but even he was hard pressed to secure a majority of the board and the final approval of Col. John M. Wilson, the superintendent of the Military Academy.

Dennis now had his hands full. He was captain, coach, trainer, and business manager of a nonexistent team that must play a championship game at the end of eight weeks. There was plenty of promising material in the corps, but among those cadets who were physically qualified very few had had any experience. As I recall it, only Michie, Prince, and Butler Ames had ever played on an organized team. On the other hand, the midshipmen had been playing for several years. Last year, they had defeated Virginia 26 to 6 and this year they were playing a full schedule of games. Dennis had scant time to teach the simplest fundamentals to his raw recruits. They had no team practice except for a few riotous scrimmages against an even more inexperienced second team. And there was no time for coaching except in the brief intervals between military duties. It was only on Saturday afternoons and when the weather was too bad for drills and parades that Dennis could count on any time for continuous practice. On rainy afternoons he had almost two hours on the tanbark in the riding hall. But that rarely happened. The weather gods up there in the Hudson Highlands are highly militarized. Even after an all-day rain they generally turn off the spigot about 3:50 p.m.—just before the first call for drill.

The great day, Saturday, 29 November 1890, finally arrived. A gridiron was laid out at the southeast corner of the Parade Ground. There was plenty of room for the officers and their families and there were a few visitors from outside the post. There was no grandstand and no seats except chairs for some of the ladies, borrowed by their escorts from the nearby Academic Building. We cadets had plenty of standing room along the sidelines. There were so few of us that we could shift freely with the ball from one end of the field to the other. The West Point band played but we had no football songs. Presently our team ran out on the field and we yelled a welcome, each man yelling for himself. When the Navy team trotted out it was welcomed by an organized cheer from a small group of young naval officers from some ship down in New York Harbor. This was a new one on us. We were surprised to find that a dozen regimented voices could make more effective noise than our whole vocal democracy.

I have no recollections of the details of the game. I do recall that the Navy started off with a V and made fifteen or twenty yards before Prince brought down the runner. It speaks volumes for the individual strength and prowess of our raw players that an experienced Navy team made only three touchdowns in the first half and two in the second. In those days a touchdown counted four points and a conversion two. The Navy made five touchdowns and two conversions, a total of 24 points. No West Point player crossed the goal line, but several times Michie's raw recruits carried the ball in a series of first downs half the length of the field. Considering its opportunities for training and the odds against it, no Army team ever made a braver showing.

One feature of the game stands out in my memory. The Navy quarterback gave out his signals in the form of nautical commands. We could hear him sing out "Helms a lee" or "Clear decks for action" or "Reef top sails" or "Man the spanker trails." Then there would be a tangle of bodies in which a husky soldier would block every sailor except the one who happened to be carrying the ball.

Kirby Walker, our quarterback, gave military commands such as "In battery, heave" or "As skirmishers" or "Forward guide center" or "Left wheel" or "Right forward fours right." At our last class reunion, Kirby told me that these were merely premonitory commands and that the words right and left had no significance. He said that for the real command of execution he pressed his thumb against "Sep" Adam's leg. Whereupon Sep would pass the ball and the play would be on.

One of the Navy plays was especially effective. Their fullback dropped back to kick, and when he got the ball, instead of kicking it as he had clearly promised to do, he ran the whole length of the field with it and made a touchdown. We greenhorns on the sidelines were indignant. We expected that the officials would recall the play. It was clearly a false official statement for an officer and gentleman to announce that he was going to kick a ball and then do something else with it. To our surprise and disgust, the officials let the play stand. Instead of protesting the decision, Dennis merely slapped Emrich, the Navy captain, on the shoulder and grinned.

Another play stands out in my memory. One of our players grabbed Emrich while he was running with the ball and held him fast. It was a brilliant tackle and was hailed by vociferous cheers and yells from the side lines. But when the tackler heard this demonstration he thought he had made a mistake and that the spectators were voicing their disapproval. He therefore released his captive who immediately resumed his gallop to another touchdown. My memory leaves me uncertain as to the identity of the hero of this play, but my impression is that it was "Taurus" Murphy of the Class of 1891.

The final score was twenty-four to nothing. Dennis had lost his game but he had won the strategic objective of his campaign. He had established the game of football at West Point and he, alone, could have done it at that time. The Army could not stomach that defeat and there would be at least one more game. In fact, as I recall it, though the challenge came from the Navy, the initiative really came from Michie. There was a slim enough chance that he might be permitted to organize a team to defend a challenge from Annapolis. But even with the influence of Old Pete behind him he would not be permitted to extend a challenge before he had even organized his team. My memory is not clear but my impression is that he talked it over with some midshipman friend while he was on furlough. As an informal Ways and Means Committee, they decided that in order to start the ball a-rolling, the Navy must send the first challenge.

One of the spectators at the game was my friend and brother-in-law to be, Harris Laning. Harris came up from Peekskill where he was attending school that year. He was a strong rooter for the Army and felt our defeat almost as keenly as I did. But his Army partisanship was short-lived. Next June he became a midshipman at Annapolis. After that Admiral Laning always rooted for the Navy.

During this winter there was interesting news from Illinois. Early in January, 1891, the legislature convened and proceeded to the election of a U.S. Senator. There were 101 Democrats who were pledged to vote for John M.

Palmer, 100 Republicans who generally voted for Governor Oglesby, and three Populists who held the balance of power. This situation continued for weeks until the deadlock broke on the 154th ballot and my grandfather became a senator from Illinois. A few months later my father left Tacoma and resumed his place in the old law firm at Springfield, Illinois. His Puget Sound adventure had not been fortunate. The boom had collapsed. Tacoma would not become the great metropolis of the Northwest. All of his speculations had failed.

In mid-February, the Corps of Cadets went to New York to serve as the escort at General Sherman's funeral. This time I marched as the right guide of a platoon and not as a plebe private in the rear rank. In May, I was promoted to be first sergeant of Company C. In June, after the men of 1891 had received their diplomas, I was appointed cadet captain and assigned to command the same company. My captain's chevrons were official tokens of success, but my most cherished honor that summer was conferred upon me by my classmates. They elected me to make the annual Fourth of July address. The ceremony was held in the grove in front of the Library. A flag-decked rostrum was erected under the trees and seats were provided for the Corps of Cadets, the officers and their families, and all of the weekend visitors including hundreds of pretty girls and their chaperones. There was patriotic music by the band and then our class president, Howard H. "B. S." Whitney introduced the orator of the day. I have forgotten my speech, but I shall never forget the sea of friendly faces that looked up at me. I remember Old Pete particularly. There was to be a facetious and not too respectful allusion to him in my speech. As I approached this questionable passage, I looked down at him with misgivings. But a twinkle in his eye encouraged me to go on. Whatever the joke was, Old Pete led the laughter that welcomed it.

That summer the Corps of Cadets went on a trip to Bennington, Vermont. Nowadays the cadets make several trips a year to sing and cheer at the big football games. But in those days the corps never left West Point except on some momentous occasion, such as a national centennial, or the funeral of General Sherman. We were invited to attend the dedication of the Battle Monument at Bennington and the invitation was accepted because it came from the Hon. Redfield Proctor, a distinguished citizen of Vermont, who happened at that time to be Secretary of War. We embarked in sleeping cars at West Point and the next morning we found ourselves on the outskirts of a beautiful town in the Green Mountains. On my two trips to New York with the corps we had spent the day either marching or shivering in ranks, but this beautiful day in Bennington was one continuous picnic. Our military duties were light and we spent most of the day enjoying the scenery and mingling with an interesting crowd of visitors. Among these I found some old friends from Springfield, Illinois.

We were not the only soldiers that day at Bennington. The Organized Militia of Vermont was assembled there and there were a number of organizations from adjoining states. Among the latter was a brilliant company known as the Amoskeag Veterans from Manchester, New Hampshire. These warriors wore gorgeous raiment of many colors with the tall "bearskins" of British guardsmen on their heads. Late in the afternoon, the militia gave a dress parade. This performance struck us as very ragged. We looked upon it as the military Pharisees that we were, thanking God that we were not like these publicans and sinners or "tin soldiers," as we called them. After the militia ceremony, our first call sounded and we were assembled for dress parade. We showed the militia how to do it and did our best to rub in the fact that we were models of military perfection and they were a military joke.

Many years were to pass before I understood the real significance of that display. It was not surprising that the Organized Militia of Vermont was poorly drilled. It was surprising that it was drilled at all. Here were hundreds of patriotic young men who were giving freely of their limited leisure to prepare themselves to serve their country in time of war. This they did largely at their own expense with meager appropriations from their states and practically no financial aid or other encouragement from the nation they proposed to defend. In fact, they were giving the American nation a very liberal return when we consider that they were costing the federal government less than one cent per man per day.

I did not realize it then but no group of men in our country has performed a greater public service than the officers and men of the National Guard. In spite of every discouragement, they have kept alive the tradition of the peacetime citizen army that Washington considered the true foundation of our national defense. Unfortunately for us and for our country, the true history of our military institutions was not included in the curriculum at West Point. If it had been, we might have had a sound national defense system long before I became a cadet. As we laughed at the Vermont militia we did not know that they were awkward and ill-trained because the graduates of West Point were not carrying out their historic mission. We did not know that Washington and his generals had proposed military academies in order to train leaders for the organized citizen army which he considered "the palladium of our security." From his point of view, the training of second lieutenants for a standing army was a purely secondary mission.

And strange to say, I did not consider what a few weeks of competent instruction might do for these lusty Green Mountain Boys. I forgot that even that accomplished soldier, Cadet Captain Palmer, had passed from the awkward squad to the color guard in little more than a month.

When we returned to Barracks that September of 1891 we found ourselves in a new West Point. The first real football season was on. Even the most hidebound conservative conceded that the army must play at least one more game. It must settle its score with the navy. Contributions came from every regiment in the army. Dr. H. H. Williams, a former Yale player and future creator of great Minnesota teams, was employed as coach and we had our first series of games with outside teams. We defeated St. John's, Stevens, and Schuylkill and tied Princeton's second team, but Rutgers beat us 27 to 6. As the team learned the game, we learned our duties on the sidelines. We were regimented to practice football yells and to sing paeans of victory in unison with the band. Never had old "Cro' Nest" echoed such sounds before. After the first game even the worst conservatives on the Academic Board were converted. The day Rutgers licked us, "Sammie" Tillman, the professor of chemistry, charged up and down the sidelines, waving his arms, and whenever an enemy player made first down, he shouted the exhortation, "Kill him, kill him." When we made our lone touchdown, somebody slapped me on the back, and I was amazed to find that my exuberant neighbor was no other than "Papa" Bass. A little later, Professor Bass became the first president of the Army Athletic Association. In one of the games, Colonel Hawkins, the commandant of cadets, was outraged because most of the enemy found it necessary to jump on Dennis after he was tackled. As the colonel was new to the amenities of the game, he marched out on the field with his white goatee protruding belligerently. As Dennis and the umpire soothed him and escorted him back to the sidelines, the hostile center inquired of "Sep" Adams, "Who is your white-haired chaperone?" The only conservative who was immune from the excitement and preserved his dignity was Col. Sylvanus Thayer, the Father of the Military Academy. But he was out of earshot over on the far side of the parade ground. If his pedestal had been nearer the sidelines, he might have stepped down to join his recreant disciples, "Sammie" Tillman and "Papa" Bass.

The Army-Navy game was played at Annapolis and, of course, we did not see it. That the whole Corps of Cadets should make such a journey to see a football game was unthinkable in those days. In fact, when it first leaked out that the team itself would be allowed to go away on such a junket, there were misgivings throughout the army and the superintendent's mail was filled with Jeremiads from virtuous old Levites who were convinced that all of the virtue was about to go out of Zion. Just think of it! A party of cadets was to go away on a pleasure junket just a month before the January examinations. They would miss their recitations, drill and dress parade Friday afternoon, and their study hour Friday night. They would miss Saturday morning inspection and Saturday afternoon dress parade. They would miss chapel on Sunday morning and would not have to "call to quarters" for two hours Sunday afternoon in order to throttle down the dangerous surplus of animal spirits that might flow from too much liberty. In all probability they would miss the two-hour study period Sunday night, and, if so, bad marks Monday morning would be on the heads of the authorities. The nation would pay for such idle indulgence on some future battlefield. The point of view of these Jeremiads was not unnatural. We must remember that "Sammie" Tillman and "Papa"

Bass were leaders among them until they were seduced from the path of virtue by lingering too long on the sidelines. Evil communications certainly corrupt good manners.

Notwithstanding the protests from the elder alumni, the superintendent, Col. Wilson, had the moral courage to authorize the pilgrimage of eleven cadets to Annapolis. But when he learned that Dennis wanted to include six substitutes in his squad, his gray goatee shot out to the horizontal and he determined to call the whole thing off. It was finally explained to him that if Navy should break Michie's neck, Army should have an understudy as fullback. When he saw that it was merely an application of the classical military problem of "replacements," so sadly neglected during our Civil War, he approved the "permit" for seventeen cadets to make the journey. And while he was in this yielding mood he was induced to make several other concessions to be described later and which no doubt he bitterly repented. He was to learn too late, that conservatism should beware of the first concession. Give innovation an ell and it will surely take a mile.

And so when the squad set off for Annapolis, the whole Corps of Cadets, headed by the band, marched down the hill to the railroad station to see them off. We were not permitted to break ranks, but while waiting for the train, we were allowed to stand "at ease." This gave us a chance to sing our football songs, and to give the new Corps yell eighteen times, once for each player and an extra one for Captain Michie. If some old graduate had been a passenger on that train as it stopped at the West Point Station, he would surely have died of apoplexy. After the train left, "Battalion atten-shun!" from Pelot Summerall, the senior captain, reconditioned us as soldiers and we marched up the hill again.

There was no radio to give us play by play in those days, but Johnnie Woodward, one of the substitutes, was to send us a telegram after each score. The first one came a few minutes after the game began when E. W. Clark of '93 scored a touchdown—Army's first score against Navy. A minute later Dennis kicked the goal and the score was six to nothing in our favor. At this rate Army would more than cancel last year's defeat. But our optimism sagged a few minutes later when Navy tied the score and revived a bit when the first half closed, Army 10, Navy 6.

During the second half, Navy took a brace and began to score. And just then our special telegraph service stopped. This, we learned later, was because Johnnie got too excited to send any more reports. For this he was soundly bumped upon his return. Dusk came and we marched to the Mess Hall for supper. There we heard a report from a New York evening paper that the Navy had won the game. Jim Jervey left the Mess Hall early and hurried to the telegraph office. As cadet quartermaster, Jim was excused from marching to meals with the battalion. There was still no news when we formed line in the Area of Barracks. Just before we broke ranks, Jim came running through the sally port waving a telegram. Pelot examined it and then announced with his customary solemnity: "Final score, Army 32, Navy 16, dismiss your companies."

By special permission of the superintendent, the band was playing under the trees north of barracks. We charged through the sally port and followed it across the plain to the north where we had been authorized to light a bonfire in the event of victory. We danced around it like Indians and drowned out the music of the band with our songs and cheers. There was never such a night at West Point since its garrison of ragged Continentals got news of another victory down on the Chesapeake—Cornwallis's surrender at Yorktown.

And what did Col. Thayer think of such wit and license as he stood there on his pedestal? No doubt he found comfort in the thought that "tattoo" would soon sound and call us all to Barracks. As for the "supe," he probably reflected that now since we were square with the Navy it would be a good thing to put that football jinni back in the box from which Alladin Michie had released it.

Long before tattoo, the bonfire died down and we sought other worlds to conquer. Someone, I think it was Julian Lindsey, took command of the band and its attendant mob. He seized the drum major's baton and led us to the Officers Line. First, we stopped in front of the supe's house and sang our paeans of victory. The colonel's goatee seemed rather wilted when he finally stepped out on his veranda and bowed a very reluctant acknowledgment to our cheers. Somebody in the crowd, I think it was Bill Davis, had the impudence to call out "Speech," but the colonel did not accept the invitation. After another bow and a somewhat sickly smile, he retreated into his castle. What should a successor of Sylvanus Thayer do to uphold the dignity of his office in such a situation? What would William Tecumseh Sherman think if his ghost should behold his alma mater in this bacchantic mood? And suppose that damned jinni should refuse to go back into its box? What then would posterity think of John M. Wilson?

From the supe's we danced behind the band down the Professors' Row. "Papa" Bass and "Sammie" Tillman made no response to our cheers. They were probably over at the Club where the officers were celebrating the victory with ardent as well as animal spirits. But at Old Pete's house we would not be denied. He had at last reached the pinnacle of fame. He was Captain Michie's father. He didn't look exactly happy when he came out on the porch, but he was a good sport and made a pleasant little speech of thanks for our appreciation of his reflected glory. At tattoo, the band left us and we returned to Barracks. Lights were out and we were all in bed by taps. But there were many nightshirt seances in Barracks that night. Nobody "skinned," however, for the "tacs" made no inspections. They were all too busy at the Club.

The football jinni did not return to the magic box but has grown to mighty proportions. Dennis graduated the following June, but his handiwork and influence still endure. Michie Stadium perpetuates his memory as the father of

West Point football. But he was much more than that. In a very real sense he was the father of the new West Point. His statue as well as Sylvanus Thayer's should look out over the Parade Ground. Our football songs and cheers sounded the knell of the old monastic days and brought the academy into a broader contact with the modern world. Dennis was the only cadet who could have started that sequence of events. He did not live to see the full fruition of his work. Six years later they brought him home to the old West Point Cemetery. He was killed by a Spanish bullet at Santiago.

When the team returned from Annapolis, we settled back into our normal routine. After the January examinations, we again began to count the days till June. They seemed many and almost unending then, but now they seem but a few fleeting hours. On the 11th of June we assembled under the trees in front of the Library and received our diplomas from the secretary of war. That night we had our graduation dinner at the Murray Hill Hotel. And for the last time all of our voices joined in "Benny Havens Oh!"

5   Fort Sheridan, Illinois

The morning after our class dinner I set out for Springfield, where Mother had reestablished our home after her return from Tacoma. But just before my graduation, Father had entered a law firm in Chicago. This was a great disappointment for her. It meant another breakup and another move in a few months. But she found some consolation in the fact that her new Chicago home would be near my first army station. For at the end of the summer I would join the 15th Infantry at Fort Sheridan, the newly built post on Lake Michigan about thirty miles north of the city. Meanwhile, she would have her three boys together for one more summer in central Illinois. It was indeed a happy summer with many renewals of ties with old friends in Springfield and Carlinville—not to speak of Petersburg.

In fact, I went over to Petersburg the morning after my arrival at Spring-field. There, I called upon Mr. and Mrs. Laning and happened to find their daughter at home. I proposed to that young lady that we should get married that summer. But with Maude, as always, romance was tempered with com-mon sense. She therefore proceeded to lay down the law to me. She finally convinced me that it would be wiser to postpone the wedding until I had paid for my new army uniforms which I had purchased on credit. A year's savings would extinguish that debt. Besides, there would be a substantial increase in income on the first anniversary of my graduation. My second lieutenant's pay amounted to only $116.67 per month. Next June I would draw my first "fogey" and my monthly stipend would rise to the princely figure of $128.33.

A few weeks later, I went to Chicago to attend the Democratic National Convention. At that time Grover Cleveland was the principal candidate for the presidency. But there was a strong movement in the Illinois delegation to cast its vote for my Grandfather Palmer. As this interested me greatly, I went immediately to the Illinois headquarters. There, very much to my disappointment, my father told me that Senator Palmer had just refused to be a candidate and had insisted that the Illinois delegation should cast its vote for Cleveland. This was highly to my grandfather's credit. He was seventy-five years old, and though still a vigorous, active man, he realized he was too old to assume the burdens of so great a responsibility. As he expressed it, "Young men for action; old men for counsel."

His decision was a momentous one. There was strong opposition to Cleveland in the state of New York, and its delegation was instructed to support New York Governor David Bennett Hill. It was generally conceded by Cleveland's supporters that he must be nominated on the first ballot or not at all. He did win on the first ballot but by a margin of only six and a half votes. If Illinois had cast her vote for Palmer, Cleveland might have lost the nomination which gave him his second term as President.

On the last day of September, with my classmates Jamieson and Weeks, I reported for duty at Fort Sheridan. The garrison comprised my regiment, the 15th Infantry, and Capron's Light Battery of the 1st Artillery. The 15th was the first regiment to be stationed at Fort Sheridan. Until assembled there it had been scattered in small posts on the western frontier for more than twenty years.

Upon my arrival at the post, I reported to my regimental commander, Colonel R. E. A. Crofton, who also commanded the garrison. He received me kindly and informed me that he had served as a captain in the Regular Army brigade of the XIV Army Corps when my grandfather was corps commander. While he was talking to me, a handsome officer of Herculean figure entered the room and the colonel said, "Captain McGunnegle, this is Mr. Palmer, your new Second Lieutenant." My new captain received me graciously. I was greatly impressed by his splendid physique but even more by his youth, for he was a captain at the early age of forty-one—a rare phenomenon in the regular army of that day. When my classmate Alex Davis graduated as a second lieutenant of cavalry, his father was still a first lieutenant of artillery. Our old army song, "Army Blue," was at least 50 percent accurate in its opening stanza:

> In the Army there's sobriety,
> Promotion's very slow.

There may have been a bit of poetic license in its first line, but its second was a statement of literal fact.

As the Bachelors Building was not yet finished, I was assigned to a room on the third floor of a senior officer's quarters. As no general mess had been established, my classmate George McD. "Mac" Weeks and I were invited by Captain G. A. Cornish, class of 1873, to join his bachelor mess. The captain had a comfortable house and a good cook, and my membership in his family was one of the most delightful experiences in my short career as an army bachelor. He was a great lover of Thackeray and through him I made my first acquaintance with Colonel Newcome. Ever since then, Cornish remains in my memory as a typical officer and gentleman—close kin to his beloved colonel. He was one of the most devoted friends that I ever had.

A few weeks after my arrival at Fort Sheridan, two troops of the 7th Cavalry joined the garrison. The Second Lieutenant of one of these troops was Bob Fleming of the class of '91, one of my closest West Point friends. Bob's first lieutenant was Selah R. H. "Tommy" Tompkins, a famous figure in the old army. Tommy was a cavalryman who would have been a worthy comrade for Charles O'Malley. His appearance was striking. His cheeks were round and ruddy and he was very proud of the most enormous mustachios that I have ever seen. At that time they were golden in color. Tommy was indeed a *beau sabreur*. In fact, he rather overemphasized his cavalry stigmata. The yellow stripes on his blue trousers were quite a bit broader than the regulations prescribed. When he went into the field, he wore a yellow silk handkerchief about his neck. At one time he affected Mexican spurs with little tinkling silver bells attached to them. But this practice an unsympathetic troop commander forced him to abandon. Before the end of the year, my classmates F. E. Harris, W. R. Smith, and J. A. Shipton joined Capron's Battery and we now had six '92 men in the garrison.

One day in browsing through Cornish's library, I found a book on the Franco-Prussian war which gave me the peacetime organization of the Prussian Army. I was impressed by the fact that Prussia's speedy victory was largely because the Kaiser's war army was fully organized in peacetime. He did not extemporize his fighting team on the eve of the war as both the North and the South had done in our Civil War. This led me to read the article on army organization in Cornish's *Encyclopaedia Britannica*. After descriptions of the principal armies of Europe and Asia, there was a very brief concluding paragraph on the army of the United States. There I read with indignation that the "so-called" American army was not an army at all. It was described as nothing more than a constabulary for the Indian frontier—totally devoid of the team organization required in the modern army. When I mentioned this British slander to Cornish, he said: "The *Britannica* is absolutely right. We have no modern military team and none of our officers has had any practice in training or leading such a team."

After a little reflection, I could see that Cornish was right. What we called the army was really not an army. It comprised 2,156 officers headed by three major generals and six brigadier generals. Its authorized enlisted strength was only 25,000. It included 25 regiments of infantry, 5 artillery regiments (with 10 coast artillery companies and two light batteries in each) and 10 regiments of cavalry—all at greatly reduced strength. It had no permanent brigade or divisional organization and there was no battalion organization in the infantry. There was practically no team play among the three arms. Each arm drilled separately and, in fact, each played "solitaire" all by itself. Each branch of the service had its separate line of promotion and there was great rivalry among them.

Although I served four years at Fort Sheridan where there was a regiment of infantry, two troops of cavalry, and a battery of light artillery, I never saw one single tactical exercise in which the three arms acted together. But the individual company units were magnificent. In those days the men enlisted for a five-year period. In my company, no man ever became a corporal until after his first enlistment. The noncommissioned officers were superb and were capable of handling all the administration of the company. We had a drill in the morning and a dress parade in the afternoon. After the morning drill, except for an occasional tour of guard duty or service on a court-martial, our time was our own.

One of the charms of the old army was this abundant leisure. This was fine for the few men who knew how to utilize that priceless gift. It was a wonderful place for a young officer who wanted to read and study, but for those who had no tastes of that kind, leisure frequently became idleness which often required the stimulation of too much whiskey. I once knew a major of infantry who had no duty in the post except to conduct the summary court each morning. For a day or two after payday, he was busy until noon, but on ordinary days his labors were light enough for him to go to the club for a first drink and a game of cards at half past nine. He was generally comfortably tight by noon. Then, after lunch and a nap at home, he was back at the club in time to get tight again before dinner.

In those days, as there were no typewriters and carbon paper, the triplicate reports of boards of survey were written out in longhand on legal-cap paper. The recorder of the board, always its junior member, had to do the writing. After the papers were completed, the three members assembled and the three copies were carefully compared as the recorder read one of them aloud. If the junior member happened to be a new second lieutenant, it was a time-honored custom for the senior members to require him to rewrite the whole document if a single error was discovered. A few years later when the typewriter came into use and we were able to make three copies at once by the use of carbon paper, many old timers thought that this luxury would send the army to the devil. Certainly, new second lieutenants would miss one of the most valuable elements in their education. I knew one old captain who required that all three copies be checked even after the advent of carbon paper. The mere fact that all three copies were now exactly alike was no sufficient reason for abandoning a good old army custom that dated back to the War of 1812.

In a statement before a joint congressional committee shortly after World War I, General Pershing said that when he entered the army, like every other lieutenant, he carried an army organization bill in his vest pocket. He said that he did not recall the details of his bill, but he felt sure that its passage would not have retarded promotion in the cavalry. General Pershing's testimony is substantiated by my own experience. Shortly after I joined the 15th Infantry, I, too, prepared an army organization bill. My bill proposed to increase the strength of the regular army from 25,000 to 65,000. How it would have affected the cavalry I do not recall, but it would have promoted every second lieutenant of infantry to the grade of captain. When I submitted my plan to Captain Cornish he was most enthusiastic. It would have made him a lieutenant-colonel at once. He advised me to polish it up and show it to my grandfather Palmer who was then a member of the Senate Military Affairs Committee.

While polishing up my plan, I found an unanswerable argument for national military organization in one of Cornish's books. This was an English translation of Karl von Clausewitz's famous treatise on war. In browsing through it I found the striking statement that "war is not a separate thing in itself but is merely a special violent phase of human politics." This truth was so startlingly simple that I could not grasp it at first. But it gradually dawned upon me that here was a fundamental military concept which I had never heard about in my four years at West Point. I had read and studied about war, but none of my professors or textbooks had ever told me what war really is. There had been no trace of this fundamental thought in the whole curriculum. We had thought of peaceful international intercourse as one separate entity and of war as another separate entity. We had never been told that they are simply transitory aspects of the same thing, international politics—both governed by the same fundamental laws and neither of them understandable without an understanding of the other.

Here was indeed new food for thought. If war is a phase of politics, then every *complete* political system should include machinery for dealing with this specific phase of political action. My grandfather would grasp this at once and would agree with me that the American political system had been incomplete in this essential respect since the founding of our government. I would submit this to him at our next meeting. It would prepare him to welcome my plan. I would thus enable him to round out his long career with constructive legislation of the highest national importance. He would be very grateful to his grandson.

While waiting for an opportunity to see my grandfather, my studies in military statesmanship were interrupted by a matter of more immediate importance. On the 14th day of June, 1893, Maude and I were married in Trinity Church at Petersburg. The bride was never more charming. She was escorted by seven bridesmaids while six of my classmates and Maude's brother, Midshipman Harris Laning of the Naval Academy, formed my suite. The little church was filled with friends and kinfolks. As we left the church, we marched under a pointed arch of crossed swords in the hands of my groomsmen.

It was one of the hottest days that I have ever known, and the fact that the bridegroom and his faithful attendants wore heavily padded full dress uniforms added little to their comfort. After the ceremony was over and I marched out of the church with my bride, she looked forward with keen interest, as she told me later, to treasure my first words to my new wife. She was therefore somewhat disappointed when I exclaimed, "My God, wasn't it hot in there!"

At the wedding reception, my father said to me, "John, I can assure you that the fact that you are now a married man has been established beyond the shadow of a doubt from a legal standpoint. Since the rite was performed by a bishop and two priests of the Episcopal Church, there can be no question but that you are not a Benedict." He also said, "The whole service was most beautiful, but I was especially touched by your princely liberality when you announced to Maude: 'With all my worldly goods I thee endow.'"

There was dancing at the wedding reception, and the dancing began with a quadrille in which the bride and bridegroom and their attendants took part. This ceremony had been carefully rehearsed, and I had gotten through the rehearsal tolerably well. But in the formal ceremony I was greatly embarrassed by the fact that the bride now wore a long train, which she had not worn at the rehearsal. In spite of all my agility and dancing experience, it was impossible to keep off it and the repetition of this misfortune must have shown in my face, for the bride finally whispered to me, "If you are not happy, John, at least try to look happy." After the reception, we tried to elude our friends by taking the southbound train from Petersburg. We went as far as Jacksonville and there took a northbound train to Chicago. But this ruse was not successful, for when we left the train, on our arrival in that city, the six classmates who had acted as my groomsmen were lined up as a reception committee.

When I left Fort Sheridan to go to the wedding, a set of married officer's quarters had been assigned to me. But before we returned from our wedding journey, a senior officer arrived at the post and when we got there, there was no place for us. It was therefore necessary to assign us one of the two-room suites in the new Bachelor Building. We lived there for several weeks, taking our meals at the bachelor officers' mess, but we were not entirely welcome. Today, ladies are welcome at clubs and enjoy all their privileges, but in those days the presence of women was not appreciated by clubmen. My efforts to get separate quarters were therefore cordially seconded by my friends in the mess, and we were finally given a small vacant house that had been built for the senior noncommissioned officer of the Post Hospital.

Our tenure of our new quarters was brief. The house had been vacant because an unmarried hospital steward preferred to live in the Hospital

Building. But now a married steward arrived and demanded the quarters to which he was entitled. This sent us back to the Bachelors' Building. We were received very graciously, but our bachelor friends saw to it that we should have news of the first officer's quarters that became vacant. When an officer was ordered away from the post, this gave us a brief tenure of a house on the "Third Loop." We moved six times during our four years at Fort Sheridan. Whenever a new officer came to the post, he ranked out one of his juniors, and then that junior ranked out one of his juniors. It was like tipping over a line of dominoes set on end. As Lieutenant Palmer was the junior married officer in the post, whenever anybody else moved, he always had to move.

But moving in the old army was not a difficult matter. After drill the day of the move, the whole company would turn out to assist, and with a column of forty or fifty men, each carrying a lamp or a picture or some other household article in his hand, the transfer was soon made. An escort wagon was sent up from the corral to move the heavier furniture, but the whole move was accomplished in a few hours.

This reminds me of an old army story about Captain Maddox of the cavalry. Whenever he had to move, he directed his first sergeant to report to Mrs. Maddox for instructions. Then he went hunting or fishing for two or three days and did not return until Mrs. Maddox was settled in her new quarters. On one occasion when he returned from one of these expeditions he forgot that he had moved and went back to his old quarters. He walked in and sat down by the fire and made himself at home. Presently, Mrs. Smith, the wife of the new tenant of the house, entered the room in some surprise. But before she could say anything, Captain Maddox rose with great politeness and said, "Sit down, Mrs. Smith, Mrs. Maddox will be down in a minute."

During the summer of 1893, the junior officers at Fort Sheridan were given an exceptional opportunity to visit the World's Columbian Exposition at a minimum of expense. At the request of the Spanish government, a guard was placed over the beautiful replica of the Convent of La Rabida, well known in the history of Columbus. The guard detail was taken from my regiment. It comprised twenty enlisted men under an officer and was changed each two weeks. Eventually I had my turn to take one of these detachments down to the fair. We were encamped inside the fair grounds, near the convent. We had comfortable cots in our tents and got our meals from the detachment mess. During the first week of my stay, Maude shared my tent with me and then went down for a visit to Petersburg. After she left, my father came out from Chicago and visited me for a few days.

That year we had our first Christmas in our new home. Our army quarters were comfortably settled and beautified with Christmas evergreens. Father and Mother and my two brothers came out to spend the holiday with us. In response to their request, we allowed them to bring the Christmas turkey and all of the other materials for the Christmas dinner. On Christmas Eve, we all hung up our stockings and after that ceremony, Father read Dickens's *Christmas Carol*. He knew just how to read the story with full effect, because as a young man, he had heard it read by Charles Dickens himself.

In the summer of 1894, the great Debs Railroad Strike occurred. This was in sympathy with a strike started by the employees of the Pullman Car Company. Traffic throughout the country was upset and the militia of the several states were unable to preserve order. Finally, upon President Cleveland's order, our regiment among other army organizations was ordered to Chicago. Our first station was at Grand Crossing, some miles south of the city. After being there a day or two, we were ordered to entrain for a large camp on Lake Front Park. As we moved north on the Illinois Central, shortly after sundown, we passed near the World's Fair Grounds where most of the beautiful exposition buildings were still standing. Just as the train passed the Exposition Grounds, flames broke forth from several of these buildings, and by the time we got to the lake front, just after dusk, the whole southern horizon was in flames. We knew where the fire started, but it seemed then that all of the southern and southwestern suburbs were on fire. With the rumors that filled the air, the outlook seemed serious. Finally, the troops began to control the situation. The 15th Infantry remained on the lake front for several days; and my company under Capt. George K. McGunnegle and G Company under Captain Cornish went into camp on LaSalle Street to guard the Federal Building.

There were many exciting incidents during the strike, but I have space for only one of them. F Troop of the 7th Cavalry had been ordered out to the stockyards, where there was much disorder. On one occasion a crowd gathered in front of one of the main entrances, and Tommy Tompkins with his platoon of cavalry was ordered to move them and guard the gateway. The crowd at this particular place was under the leadership of a very aggressive woman identified with the foreign Anarchist Party that existed in Chicago at that time. Tommy rode to the gate and gave his instructions, whereupon the leader of the crowd placed her hands on her hips and cried out to him, "What is the matter with you, you ginger-whiskered son of a bitch?" Thereupon Tommy responded with the spirit of a true cavalier. He removed his campaign hat from his head and bowed so low that its brim swept the ground. As he came up again in his saddle, he said, "Madam, you have the advantage of me." This quick action caught the spirit of the crowd, many of whom were merely good-natured spectators. They burst into applause, and Tommy had no further difficulty in controlling the situation.

On September 4th our son was born. The day after his birth, my father, then assistant corporation counsel of the city of Chicago, came out to make the acquaintance of his new grandson. He received the honor with great joy, although he did not particularly relish being a grandfather at the age of forty-six. He looked at the boy with great interest, and the boy looked at him with the solemnity that goes with the age of two days. Whereupon my father said, "He looks like a judge." And thereafter Judge or Judgy was the youngster's family name. A few months later, he was christened John McAuley after his father and his great grandfather. With his grandfather, John Mayo Palmer, he was thus John M. Palmer IV.

Sometime during the summer we heard that there was to be a public test of "horseless carriages" in a continuous run all the way from Waukegan to Chicago. The road over which these vehicles were to pass ran just west of the post. So all of us, men, women, and children, moved over to see them go by, for few of us had ever seen an automobile at that time. As I remember it, there were about a dozen cars. The leaders made as much as eight or ten miles an hour when they were able to run at all, but most of them had to stop every mile or so while the chauffeur crawled under the car to make necessary repairs and adjustments. Next morning our newspapers informed us that the winner had made the whole distance of about forty miles in something less than ten hours.

In April, 1896, our two troops of the 7th Cavalry left Fort Sheridan for Arizona. This was a personal sorrow for Maude and me as it meant saying goodbye to our closest army friends, Bob Fleming and his wife, Augusta. It is difficult to understand today how far away Arizona seemed at that time. Of course, we had military posts out in California and Oregon, but as they were located near centers of population, we did not consider them so remote as Arizona, which seemed at the very end of the world. Most of the country there was a sparsely settled desert where we were still having trouble with the Apache Indians. In fact, shortly after Fleming arrived at Fort Grant, he went out with an expedition in pursuit of a band of Indians which had left the White Mountain Reservation on a raid down into Mexico. It must be remembered that this was before the Spanish-American War—before most of us had ever heard of the Philippines. Today, when an officer and his family are ordered to North China it does not seem anything like so far away as Arizona did then.

Later that summer, Bryan stampeded the Democratic National Convention and was nominated for the presidency on the free silver issue. This caused great dissatisfaction among the old-line conservative Democrats, who accordingly called a sound money convention at Indianapolis. In this convention my grandfather Palmer was nominated for the presidency, and Gen. Simon Bolivar Buckner of Kentucky was nominated for the vice-presidency.

A few weeks later when the two candidates came to Chicago to attend a political meeting, I went to town to pay my respects to them. I also hoped to find an opportunity to present my views on military legislation to my grandfather. As a member of the Senate Military Affairs Committee, he would be glad to have the conclusions of an educated military expert on this important question.

It was very hot that morning. When I got to my grandfather's room in his hotel, he was sitting by an open window in his shirt sleeves with a palm leaf fan in his hand and a big cigar in his mouth. When I asked to be presented to General Buckner, he took me to an adjoining suite where the candidate for Vice President was sitting at another open window. He was garbed exactly like the candidate for President except that he wore a corncob pipe instead of a cigar. In presenting me, my grandfather said, "General Buckner, this is my grandson, Second Lieutenant John McAuley Palmer of the 15th Infantry. As one of your brother West Point graduates he wants to meet you." Then, declining to accept a chair, he drew himself up and said, "No sir, I will now withdraw. I am aware that there is a free-masonry between you West Pointers, upon which I will not venture to intrude."

Like many other volunteer officers, my grandfather had come out of the Civil War with something less than love for my alma mater. Among her sons, he worshipped Thomas and admired Grant, but he did not see eye to eye with all of them. He had known some of them who could not conceal their conviction that all graduates of West Point are necessarily military geniuses and all citizen officers necessarily nincompoops. It had been his experience that both of these generalizations were a bit too broad.

Lieutenant General Buckner, West Point 1844, was very gracious to Second Lieutenant Palmer, West Point, 1892. There was indeed a fraternal bond between us—the bond of love that binds together all sons of the stern old mother. He told me about his plebe year when among the yearlings who hazed Cadet Buckner of Kentucky was Cadet Ulysses S. Grant of Ohio. They soon became close friends, were friends together in the old army, and remained close friends even after one of them surrendered to the other at Fort Donelson. The West Point that I knew was the same West Point that General Buckner had known, the same course of study, the same little four-company battalion, the same secluded monastic life, the same simple architecture.

When I returned to my grandfather's room, I told him that I wanted to submit something for his serious consideration as a member of the Military Affairs Committee of the U.S. Senate. Thereupon I produced my plan for a national military organization based upon a substantial increase of the Regular Army. I was very proud of this document. It was the result of profound study ever since my first discussion of our defective military system with Captain Cornish. Before accepting my screed for formal reference to the Senate Military Affairs Committee, my grandsire asked me to read it to him. As he heard my preamble outlining our military weakness and our need for sound military institutions, he nodded his approval. But he gave no sign of approval for my remedy. When I got through, he lit a fresh cigar and proceeded to give me his opinion. Though more than half a century has passed since then, I remember the gist of our conversation vividly. It was in substance as follows:

"Well, John McAuley, what effect will that plan have on your own fortunes?"

"It will make me a captain, but..."

"That's fine, John McAuley—second lieutenant to captain in one jump. I approve of that. But it seems to me that you suggest a rather expensive method of accomplishing your purpose. Your proposed increase of the Regular Army will cost about $40 million a year as I figure it. I might possibly justify your promotion from the standpoint of the public interest, but I question whether it would be worth $40 million a year to your country. A cheaper method occurs to me. Of course Congress has no power under the Constitution to appoint you a captain. But we might pass a joint resolution authorizing the President to promote a second lieutenant from a limited group answering your general description, to the grade of captain. I might get that resolution through, and then if I get to President Cleveland quick enough, I might get him to give you the appointment. It would be a cheaper method than yours. It would cost Uncle Sam less than $500 a year instead of $40 million."

This idea of becoming a captain by joint resolution appealed to me at first. But the twinkle in my grandfather's eyes made me see that he had been speaking in a purely Pickwickian sense. He then terminated our interview as follows:

"Now, John McAuley, let *me* give *you* a bit of expert opinion. Of course, I am not an educated *military* expert as your West Point diploma proves you to be, but even my worst enemies give me credit for being something of a *political* expert. And as a *political* expert I can assure you of one thing. The American people will never adopt a national defense system based on that expansible standing army scheme of yours. If you tell me that that is the best system from a purely military standpoint, I'll simply reply, 'Then, John McAuley, you'd better forget it, because you'll never get it.' If that is your best solution, you had better figure out a second-best solution that will have some chance of acceptance by the American people and their Congress. And one thing more, John McAuley, if you want to solve our national defense problem, forget about your own promotion and take your motto from Bobby Burns:

If self the wavering balance shake
It's rarely right adjusted."

A few days after my visit to Chicago, my father and grandfather paid us a visit at Fort Sheridan. This was the only time that the four John M. Palmers were ever together. John M. IV was approaching his second birthday and his great-grandfather was approaching his seventy-ninth.

In spite of his age, the old gentleman made a vigorous fight in the political campaign that year. He went to the polls early on election day, but as there was not a single vote cast for Palmer and Buckner in his precinct, his friends wondered whether he had voted for Bryan or McKinley.

When they questioned him on this subject, he declined to incriminate himself. When he left the Senate at the age of eighty, an old friend who had voted for Bryan said to him, "General, this is probably the end of your political career." To this the octogenarian replied optimistically, "Oh, I don't know about that. I come into fashion in Illinois at least once every ten years."

6   Fort Grant, Arizona

Early in the autumn of 1896, our regiment was ordered to New Mexico and Arizona. The regimental headquarters and four companies were to go to Fort Bayard, New Mexico; two companies to Fort Grant, Arizona; and two companies to Fort Huachuca, Arizona. My company was to go to Fort Bayard, a sufficiently remote post, but we congratulated ourselves that we were not among those to go to Arizona.

In those days, when a regiment moved, everybody was included—enlisted men, officers, enlisted men's families, and officers' families. This meant that in addition to passenger cars for the personnel there would be many freight cars for our personal baggage and furniture as well as for the regimental baggage. My own transportation, of course, was paid for by the government, but as there was no travel allowance for families at that time, I had to pay Maude's fare. We had a baggage allowance paid by the government, but not enough to cover all of our household effects. It was therefore quite a problem for a married second lieutenant with his limited pay to finance such a journey. With two other officers who were going to Fort Bayard, I engaged a freight car to take care of some of my excess property. For this we were given a low rate by the Santa Fe Railroad, whose officials were always very liberal in matters of this kind. There was also a custom in those days which was reprehensible but almost universal. We married officers had excess baggage and our bachelor friends did not. So we followed the practice of presenting them with some of our personal effects which they packed in their luggage—the understanding being that they would return these gifts to us upon arrival at our destination. As a result, some of my impedimenta were turned over to the quartermaster to be shipped to Fort Bayard at government expense; some were placed in the chartered car; and some were presented to my bachelor friends.

One morning in October we entrained at Fort Sheridan. The train was formed in three sections, each composed of freight cars for the baggage, coaches for the men, and a sleeping car for the women and children. In due time our section left the siding and finally reached a freight yard in Chicago where the trains were to be transferred to the Santa Fe Railroad. There my father and mother and brothers came to tell us goodby. They brought us a big basket of provisions for the journey including a roasted turkey and many other delicacies for we might be at least a week on the road. We left Chicago that night and arrived at Kansas City the following morning, stopping at the Old Union Depot. There we had a reunion with Maude's family. Her father and mother had come down from Petersburg and were joined by aunts and uncles and cousins who lived in Kansas City. There we took on another basket of provisions and now felt equipped to feed the whole regiment. It was an interesting journey for all of us and especially for our two-year-old son. As it was his first long railroad trip, he enjoyed every minute of it.

When we arrived at Hutchinson, Kansas, that night, Colonel Crofton received a telegram from the War Department changing the destination of nearly every company in the regiment. As a result there were few men, women, or children on the troop train whose plans were not completely upset. The Palmers, for example, were now destined for Fort Grant, Arizona, with all of their household goods still en route to Fort Bayard, New Mexico—except the temporary gifts to their bachelor friends, none of whom were scheduled to Fort Grant. I have never known so much confusion in my life and have never heard more artistic and eloquent profanity. We learned later, that one of our captains who did not like the station assigned to his company, had had enough pull through a senatorial kinsman to have the schedule changed. It is fortunate for this enterprising gentleman that he remained incognito until some time later.

By practicing the greatest economy and skill, I had barely been able to finance our journey to Fort Bayard, even with the Santa Fe's reduced rates. And now we must pay full rates on the Southern Pacific from Deming, New Mexico, to Willcox, Arizona.

When we finally got to Deming it was necessary to stop there and have almost every freight car repacked. As the junior officer in Company "F," it was my job to stay and do the repacking for my company which meant that Maude and John must go into the Indian country without me. But fortunately for us, my first lieutenant asked for the assignment so that he could look out for his two private horses. While I was wondering how it would be possible for me to pay Maude's railroad fare and the freight charges for the rest of the journey and was wondering whether I would have time to make a telegraphic draft upon my father, dear old Captain Cornish came up to me and whispered: "I want a little private conversation with you." We were standing alone on the depot platform, but as that was not sufficiently private, he took me upstairs to an empty room on the upper floor of the railroad station. After taking care to close the door, he frowned at me, put his hand in his pocket and pulled out a big roll of bills. Then he whispered: "Young man, don't you need some money?" When I admitted that I did and indicated that seventy-five dollars would probably see me through, he said, "You better take a hundred and fifty." This was typical of the old army, where all the officers of a regiment were really members of one big family.

Finally we got on a special train and started across the desert toward the Arizona boundary. With the resiliency of youth, we had forgotten our troubles and were delighted to feel that we would soon rejoin the Flemings at Fort Grant. When we arrived at Willcox we were welcomed by Tommy Tompkins, who had ridden the thirty miles from Fort Grant to meet us. After his six months in Arizona, Tommy was superb. He had embellished his uniform with some of the ornaments of a classy cowboy. His campaign hat was really a sombrero. He wore a brilliant yellow silk handkerchief around his neck. He had resumed his big Mexican spurs with their tinkling silver bells. By tickling his horse gently on the offside with one of these musical instruments, he had taught him to rear up, cavort, snort, and emit other sounds that marked him as the highly spirited charger of a true dragoon.

At Willcox we also met two companies of the 25th Infantry which our two companies were to replace at Fort Grant. The 25th was a Negro regiment with white officers. This was the first time I had ever come in contact with any of our fine colored troops. They were big husky men and were delighted to leave Arizona for another station. They took great pleasure in telling our white soldiers what they might expect on their march across the desert. I heard one of them say, "Yes suh, it's hot here, but just wait till you press yo' foot in that hot sand." These cordial amenities were soon interrupted by two gorgeous first sergeants who proceeded to form their companies in ranks alongside the troop train. In aligning his company to the right, one of these officials exclaimed: "Dress back there, you George Washington, Thomas Jefferson, Andrew Jackson and the rest of you presidential sons of bitches."

We were busy unloading our freight cars for some hours and before that was finished, Maude and John with Captain McGunnegle's mother and daughter were sent ahead to the post in a dougherty wagon. This was an old-fashioned stage coach drawn by four mules. I learned later that they had quite an exciting journey. As they approached Fort Grant, Mrs. McGunnegle looked out and saw a band of mounted Indians approaching with their horses at a gallop. She was greatly relieved when she found that the Indians were really a detachment of Apache scouts from Fort Grant who were taking this occasion to welcome the ladies to their new post.

Our two companies finally got under way and marched to Six Mile Ranch where there was a well and facilities for camping. There we passed the night and early next morning took up our twenty-four miles to Fort Grant. It was typical desert country. We were in the Sulphur Springs Valley, a tract of land from thirty to forty miles wide, bounded on the north and east by the Graham and the Chiricahua Mountains and on the west by the Galiuro Range. Mount Graham itself was directly ahead of us and as we approached it, under the hot sun, it seemed to grow farther and farther away. The whole region was new to me. There was a little sparse grass with patches of mesquite brush, cactus, and yucca. The country did not seem attractive to me then, but after I became accustomed to those mountains and valleys, it seemed to me the most beautiful region in the world. The valley was about 5,000 feet above the sea and the climate was perfect. The air was dry with practically no humidity. It would be intensely hot while the sun was shining, but almost immediately after sundown it became cold. In our field operations there, we rarely used tents but slept out under the sky. But it was neccessary to have plenty of blankets.

Finally in the afternoon, we arrived at Fort Grant and marched in through a gate in the rubble stone wall. Near the gate was the house where the Flemings lived. In front of this house as we marched by were Maude and John IV and Augusta and Bob. In Bob's arms was his son and heir, who had joined their family since they left Fort Sheridan.

The greatest concern of the Palmer family was the question of quarters. Would there be quarters for us and what would they be? Until this was settled, we stopped with the Flemings. They were comfortably located in an old adobe building which had formerly been a post hospital. Its walls were thick and like all adobe houses it was cool in summer and warm in winter. Maude had been unable to get any information about our quarters and was told to wait until I arrived. After dinner we went out on the porch and then Bob told us we would live under the same roof with him. Our quarters would be two rooms in a wing of the old hospital.

The outlook was not very encouraging. There was a door leading from the porch into each of these rooms and when we went inside, to our surprise we found that there were no windows. So when we closed the doors we were in utter darkness. But we were informed that the quartermaster had been ordered to cut windows and to add a little frame wing which would contain a kitchen for us. Maude could not understand why it was that these two rooms should be built without any windows, and when she went to see the workmen cut through the thick walls, she expressed her surprise. Upon this, the quartermaster sergeant in charge of the work turned to her and said, "Why, lady, don't you know what this house used to be?" When she replied in the negative, he said, "Why this was the dead house of the old hospital!" This was not a particularly pleasant prospect, but after the windows were cut and our little kitchen shack was built, we found ourselves very comfortable. People can stand most anything when they are still in their twenties. We were soon able to employ a capable maid of all work. As she came from the Gila Valley, Augusta referred to her as the Palmers' "gila monster." After several months' residence in our renovated morgue, we were assigned a regular set of quarters in the officers' line.

Fort Grant was a typical post of the old frontier. It was built in the form of a quadrangle. On the north side of this quadrangle was the officers' line, with cottonwood trees on either side of the road. On the south side were the barracks for the soldiers. On the east was the hospital, the officers' mess, and a building which was used both as chapel and schoolhouse. Here we had our weekly dances. On the west side of the quadrangle were the regimental offices, the commissary, the quartermaster, and beyond them, the post exchange. Off at a little distance were the cavalry and quartermaster stables. The post was just at the foot of Mt. Graham, which rose to an elevation of more than 11,000 feet. It was possible to ride horseback up to the top of the mountain in three or four hours and the change of scene was marvelous. At the post we were in the desert surrounded by cactus and mesquite. On the plateau at the top of the mountain we were in a forest of evergreens like those of Wisconsin or Maine. Up on this plateau there was running water in the brooks. These streams ran down from the mountainside. But in the dry season the water disappeared in the sand long before it got down into the valley.

Our garrison consisted of the headquarters and six troops of the 7th Cavalry and our two companies of infantry. Colonel E. V. Sumner of the 7th commanded the post. There must have been twenty-five or thirty officers in the garrison and most of them had their families with them. We were thirty miles from the railway and two days from Los Angeles, the nearest large city, but our life was full of activity and gaiety of every kind.

Life in the old army was most delightful. Each regiment was one great united family. In the old days of regimental promotion, officers might spend a lifetime in the same regiment. Young men and women would grow from childhood in this same family. Troops out on the frontier had no access to cities but enjoyed a social life of their own. The women and children of the post would assemble to hear the band at guard mounting and again at dress parade. Once a week we would have a garrison hop or dance. An orchestra from the regimental band gave us our music.

There was good hunting in the Fort Grant country. There were deer in the mountains and antelope in the more distant plains. There were wild turkeys and several varieties of western quail. Strange to say, the best duck shooting I ever saw was in Aravaipa Valley about twenty miles from Fort Grant. Running down the valley from south to north was a string of small ponds which formed part of a duck run from Canada and the Northern Rockies to Mexico. The birds were always in perfect condition for they had little fish diet in their long migration.

I was so fascinated with the Arizona country that, although I was an Infantry officer, I got Colonel Sumner to place me on the Cavalry scouting roster. These little expeditions covered the whole country between the White Mountain Indian Reservation and the Mexican border. We were still taking all the precautions that had been followed for many years on account of the Indians, for Indian trouble might occur again. We did not know then that the last Indian campaign in Arizona had already been fought. On my first trip, I had a sergeant, six cavalry soldiers, and four Apache scouts. As our trip would take us far from any wagon road, I had a packer and six pack mules. After the detachment was formed, I lined it up in front of the colonel's quarters and, according to the custom of the frontier, he came out and inspected each man and each animal.

After the inspection, I started eastward for Stockton Pass, as I was ordered to go to Duncan, a little town near the border of New Mexico. Small as my command was, it was a proud experience for I was an independent commander out on my own on a two weeks' scouting trip. We crossed the San Simon Valley, making one or two camps before we reached the mountains to the east. After patrolling a day or two at Duncan, we started back toward Ash Peak. It was beautiful, hilly desert country. I shall never forget a hot afternoon when we approached the Gila Valley near Solomonville. We had been in the bare desert for days. So when we suddenly came to the crest of the valley and looked down on the brilliant green fields of irrigated alfalfa, the sight was a glorious one. From Solomonville, after a trip down the Gila to old Fort Thomas, we went southward to old Fort Bowie and thence back home through Willcox.

These journeys were interesting in the daytime but very lonely in the evening as I was the only officer with the detachment. Sometimes at night I would slip out of my tent and then circle around and come in behind a mesquite bush near the campfire where I could not be seen, and listen to the picturesque conversation between the soldiers and the Apache scouts. The show would have been spoiled if they had known that there was an officer listening to them. One type of man would not talk at all under such circumstances. Another type would show off.

Our rations on these journeys were very compact: bacon, beans, hardtack, coffee. This was eked out with game occasionally and sometimes we would swap bacon for fresh beef with the cowboys. The boxes of hardtack, of course, were jostled continually on the pack mules, and in the course of time the crackers became cracker crumbs. The soldiers solved this by frying the cracker fragments in bacon grease. This made a very solid ration and would probably have been indigestible for men who were taking less exercise. The soldiers' name for this item on their menu was "son-of-a-bitch." When the menu got down to a steady diet of son-of-a-bitch and coffee we were all ready to go back to Fort Grant.

While on this trip I had my first opportunity to observe the skill of the Apache Indians in following a desert trail. While the men were making camp one afternoon, I took "Mike," one of the Apache scouts, deer hunting with me. While we were moving along at a brisk trot, Mike pointed to the gravelly soil and said, "A deer go along here." As I was a bit skeptical, I made him dismount with me. After looking closely at the ground, I said, "Mike, I can't see any trail. You show me." With his forefinger he pointed out where, here and there, the deer's foot had displaced a grain or two of gravel. When he showed me each of the successive prints, I could recognize it. But Mike could follow such a trail with his horse at a lope. This skill was marvelously developed among the Apaches. With them it was almost a sixth sense.

Shortly after we got to Fort Grant, Lieutenant May's thoroughbred horse jumped the corral fence and ran away. Like most horses just arrived from the East, he had become highly nervous and was afraid of the cactus, yucca, and other unfamiliar desert vegetation. After breaking out of the corral, there were thousands of square miles of desert open to him and yet two of the Apache scouts followed him for more than fifty miles and brought him back from the neighborhood of old Fort Bowie. The remarkable thing is that on one occasion, this horse joined a herd of half-wild cow ponies. There were now hundreds of hoofprints besides his own, and yet these Apaches were able to follow his trail into the track of the herd and then out of it when he left it.

As a matter of fact, as I learned later, each horse writes an autograph with his hoofs that is just as distinct and characteristic as the fingerprints of a man. I, myself, learned to recognize the track of my own horse, but the Apaches never failed to recognize the track of one they had once seen. To them it was not a question as to whether a horse was black or sorrel or brown. What they recognized was the trace of his hooves. Many of the old frontiersmen acquired the art from the Indians, but they were never so perfect. Old Monty, a hunter near Fort Grant, who had been a scout for many years, told me that he could tell from the tracks whether a horse had a man on his back or not. I accepted this without difficulty. But when he told me that he could tell from the horse's trail whether it was mounted by a white man, or a Mexican, or an Indian, I had my doubts—even though Monty assured me, "I'm a son-of-a-bitch if it ain't so."

This insight I got in trailing that day came in good stead a few weeks later. One day our little John ran away from home and was lost. Somebody saw him near the entrance gate to the post, but when we went for him, there was no trace of him. Beyond the gate was a desert of sand and gravel with dense thickets of mesquite and cactus. Maude was greatly alarmed, but when I took Mike to the gate, he followed the youngster's almost invisible footprints and soon brought him home.

In the spring of 1897, Ed King of the 7th Cavalry and I were ordered on mapmaking duty. Sections of the so-called "progressive map" were sent down from department headquarters at Denver, and it would be our task to ride over the country and work in topographical details. As our territory covered most of southeastern Arizona south of the Gila, we would both be in the field most of the time for an indefinite period. It was therefore decided that Maude and John should go back to Illinois for a prolonged visit.

As the daily train for the East left Willcox early in the morning, we had to spend the night in a nondescript hotel. Our room was immediately over the barroom. As a cattle roundup was on, the town was full of cowboys who were busy drinking whiskey, yelling, and firing their pistols. Every now and then we could hear a shot fired in the barroom below. Fortunately, the weapons must have been aimed at the barroom floor for none of the bullets passed through the ceiling and into our room. In these circumstances, John was the only member of the Palmer family who had much sleep. I shall never forget his tense excitement when I put him on the train the next morning. He was approaching three years old, and at that time he was so entranced by locomotives and cars that he had no eye or thought for anything else. As the train pulled out he was so absorbed in an engine on a neighboring side track that he could barely spare time to kiss his father goodbye. And oh! the loneliness when I got back to Fort Grant and went into our empty quarters. No Maude, no John, but everything in every room a reminder of them.

Soon after my family's departure, King and I started out on our first mapmaking trip. We took the Osborne Trail from Fort Grant to the top of Mt. Graham. As we approached the plateau at the top of the mountain, we entered a heavy forest of tall evergreens with a thick growth of fern in between the trees. In a little valley near a running brook, we came upon old Monty's camp. At that time, he was trapping bear and mountain lions. He made good wages at this because he received a bounty from the cattlemen for each animal that he killed and, in addition, was able to sell bearskins and other furs. As we paused, we saw two new bearskins nailed against the front of his cabin to dry.

A little beyond Monty's camp, we found a beautiful spring near the southeastern high spur of Mt. Graham. There we camped several days, making a careful study of the ground that lay beneath us. This was an excellent preliminary for our mapmaking trip. As a matter of fact, much of the region that we were to map lay within sight beneath us. Fifty miles to the east we could see Stein's Peak. Eighty miles to the south we could see the mountains near Fort Huachucua. I happened to be on this observation point late one afternoon and could see the shadow of the peak upon which I stood, stretching twenty miles away in the San Simon Valley. As the sun gradually went down, the shadow moved eastward until, just before sunset, it was seventy-five miles long. It is difficult for one who has never been in the desert to appreciate how far we could see in that region. Before we left our camp near the spring, we rode up to the very top of the mountain, which is some 11,000 feet above the sea. There the spruce and pine gave way to tamarack.

The spring near our camp was the finest I have ever seen. The mountain was covered with snow until June with the result that the water was icy cold. It was also highly aerated, with a distinct taste of carbonic acid gas. One night, when Bob Fleming came up to spend the night with us, he brought a bottle of Scotch with him. We were able to make sparkling highballs with water dipped from our spring.

After our return from the top of Mt. Graham, we made a long trip down the Sulphur Spring Valley to the Mexican border. King, with his detachment, went down along the Dragoon and Galiuro Mountains on the western edge of the valley and was to wait for me at Bisbee. With my part, I went down the eastern, or Chiracahua, side of the valley. First, I visited old Fort Bowie and then circled around to the west and made camp about ten miles south of the Dos Cabezos Peaks. We found a most attractive camping place. On one side of a dry stream bed was a tight corral where we put up our animals, and on the other side was a growth of trees where we pitched our own camp. After we got settled and supper was being cooked, I noticed a heavy storm cloud in the north. I could tell from its motion that it would pass to the east and miss us, but I could see that there was heavy rain up in the Dos Cabezos Peaks. There were flashes of lightning, and I could hear the crash and rumble of thunder. A little later I heard a dull roar and saw a wall of water pouring down the dry river bed. In a few minutes, there was a wide stream flowing between our camp and our animals. But in a little while, all but a trickle of the water ran out and we were able to cross again. The stream beds from the mountains were like the gutters of a house. After a rain, the water would pour down in a torrent and, in a little while, the stream bed would be dry again.

In order to reduce the transportation required for our trip, the quartermaster and commissary had furnished us cash for the purpose of buying provisions on the road. We would buy vegetables or eggs and take a receipt as a voucher for settlement after our return to the post. Strange to say, it was almost always possible to get fresh beef from the ranchmen. As we had bacon and they did not, we could always trade with them to advantage. In the course of this trip, I went up into Rucker Canyon in the Chiracahua Mountains. There Camp Rucker used to be in the old days during the campaigns against the Apaches. As we gradually left the desert and went up into the hills, we left the mesquite and cactus and were surrounded by forest trees. After we got into the pine woods, we found a clearing where there was a beautiful peach orchard with trees covered with fruit. At the edge of this orchard was an occupied house where I decided to make a call, telling the men to wait on the road until my return. I was graciously received by an old gentleman who had lived there for many years. He served some delicious peach brandy which he made himself. As I was about to go, he said "Tell your men to take just as many peaches as they want. I have no market for them and can't use half of them myself." When I rejoined the detachment, I transmitted this invitation to the men, and they made some halfhearted efforts to gather peaches. I had never seen a group of soldiers so indifferent to so wonderful an opportunity. But when we made camp that night, I found that every hole and crevice in the escort wagon had been filled with peaches while I was making my call.

By the time we left Rucker Canyon I was getting short of money. I had spent all that the quartermaster had given me and had exhausted my own supply, except a single twenty-five-cent piece. It was therefore with relief that I turned across the valley to Bisbee. There I would meet King who would be in funds. There we would stop a day or two, get a much-needed bath, take a rest, and get something good to eat and drink. When I finally rode into Bisbee Canyon, I found King in camp with his detachment. He was evidently on the lookout for me and welcomed me with the question, "Have you any money?" "Just one quarter, how about you?" He replied, "I haven't a penny." We therefore decided that as we were not able to enjoy the delights of Bisbee, we would ride up to the town and use my quarter to split a bottle of beer. But as we got into the business district, we found a commodious gambling parlor on a street corner. As was customary on the frontier, this place was wide open with the roulette tables and all of the machinery of fortune exposed. King said, "Let's be sports. Let's go in to the roulette table. Put your quarter on a color and if we win, we'll have a bottle of beer apiece, and if we lose we won't be much worse off than we are now." I placed my quarter on the red and won, Then I placed my fifty cents on the black and won. Then I placed my dollar on another color and won. As I started to make a new investment, King exclaimed, "Oh! no, wait a minute! You have never played roulette before and are having a beginner's streak of luck. Let me coach you." Under King's supervision, I played numbers and soon had ten or fifteen dollars and wanted to quit. But he was so confident in the combination of my luck and his skill that we lingered too long, and when we left the wheel we didn't have a cent. As we left the roulette table, rather disconsolately, two well-dressed young men approached us. They were officials of the Copper Queen Mine who had heard that two army officers had arrived. They had come down to meet us and put us up at their club. When they saw us at the wheel and heard our conversation, they watched the drama until we were broke. Then they met us with outstretched hands and took us with them. We each had a comfortable room, a bath, and every luxury in life. At their own suggestion, our hosts even cashed checks for us.

The smelter of the great Copper Queen Mine was up in the canyon in those days. The smoke and fumes from the smelter made it a very uncomfortable place. Since then, the smelters have concentrated down at the prosperous city of Douglas, Arizona. At that time, Douglas did not exist.

After several pleasant days at Bisbee, we went down to the Mexican border and then followed it eastward to San Bernardino where Col. John Slaughter had his famous ranch. Slaughter owned a Mexican land grant, which extended well within the limits of the United States. He was a famous man in that region. He had been the sheriff of Cochise County in the lawless days that

Alfred Henry Lewis described in his "Wolfville" stories. At that time, the region was infected with outlaws. Finally Slaughter accepted the office of sheriff and cleaned up the country. His fame extended through the whole Southwest. I do not know exactly how many bandits he killed, but according to tradition, they numbered fifteen or twenty. I had heard many stories about him and was anxious to see him. When we got to his house, I rang the front doorbell, and a little brown-eyed man came to the door. I announced who I was and asked to see Colonel Slaughter. Said he, "I am Colonel Slaughter." It was almost impossible to believe that this gentle-eyed little man had been the scourge of Cochise County. He received us hospitably, and gave us a camping place for our detachment with its horses and pack mules.

In the course of conversation with him, I explained that we were out of fresh meat. He smiled and said, "I am glad to hear it, for I am out of bacon. I have no meat already killed but let's go out in the pasture and pick out a yearling." While we were walking toward the pasture, I noticed for the first time that Slaughter wore a belt with two pistols and holsters. Since his days as sheriff, as the relatives of some of his victims still lived in Cochise County, it had always been necessary for him to go armed. We walked toward the yearlings and finally approached a likely one. Slaughter asked, "How would that one do?" As I answered, "That's a good one," there was a pistol shot and the yearling fell dead. When I looked at the colonel in surprise, his pistol was already back in its holster.

From Slaughter's we moved northward along the trough of the San Simon Valley. We made several camps before we got to the Southern Pacific railroad. There we turned westward on our return journey to Grant. The distance to Willcox was fifty or sixty miles, and with our tired horses and mules, it took us two or three days. Our road ran alongside the Southern Pacific. It was thrilling to see how fast even slow freight trains travelled as they passed us frequently on our journey.

I had little time for the study of military policy during those busy days at Fort Grant. But among my papers I find an essay which I read at a meeting of the Post Lyceum. As at Fort Sheridan, I proposed to treble the strength of the regular army as a nucleus for expansion in time of war. But apparently it did not occur to me to explain just how I proposed to expand it.

7 At the University of Chicago

Late in August, 1897, after five months in the field, I was granted leave of absence and joined Maude and John at Petersburg. While at Thorne Place, we celebrated our son's third birthday. As he was rapidly passing from babyhood to boyhood, he was now old enough to enter into the spirit of the day. From Petersburg we took the youngster to see his great-grandfather Palmer at Springfield and his great-grandmother Robertson at Carlinville. This was my last visit with my grandmother, as she died the following spring. Toward the end of the month we went to Chicago for a final visit with my parents and brothers before our return to Arizona.

While in Chicago, I had several talks with Maj. Edgar B. Tolman, my father's law associate. Tolman was an officer in the 1st Infantry, Illinois National Guard. He was one of those patriotic citizens who, though a busy lawyer and man of affairs, found time to prepare himself to serve his country as a citizen soldier if war should come. During one of our talks, he told me about a recent conversation with Dr. William R. Harper, president of the then new University of Chicago, in which they had discussed a proposal to establish a military department in the university.

Through Major Tolman, I had the pleasure of meeting President Harper. While he did not want compulsory military training in the university, he had been interested in a suggestion that it might be a good idea to establish a university battalion of cadets, composed solely of volunteers. When he asked for my views, I suggested that while such an organization might be an attractive feature of undergraduate life, there was a much more important military mission for a great American university. It would make little difference to the welfare of the country whether or not a few of his students should be drilled as soldiers. But it would make a great difference if, among the University's graduates, a few should enter public life with some scientific knowledge of the interrelations between war and peace. These would be pioneers in an undeveloped field of American scholarship. One of them might even become a constructive military statesman and thus fill a great void in American public life, which had never been refilled since Washington was gathered to his fathers. We had a tradition that in a republic the civil authority must be superior to the military authority. But the first step toward this supremacy had never been taken because our citizenry knew nothing about the proper place of military institutions in the modern democratic state.

This was a rather brash statement from a youngster still in his twenties to a distinguished scholar and educator. But as President Harper encouraged me to develop my views, I ventured to remind him that effective government by the people depends upon the education of the people. Where the people and their political leaders are informed, government by the people can be the best government on earth. Where they are uninformed or misinformed it can be one of the worst, if not *the* worst. In the field of military affairs the leaders of the American people were not only ignorant but indifferent. In fact, most of them were indifferent because they were too ill-informed to know that they were ignorant. Although most of our burdens of national debt were chargeable to wasteful and unintelligent military expenditure in the past, there was no public interest in providing sound and economical military institutions for the future. But if the American people and their political leaders were ignorant in this field, it was because of a fundamental defect in American education. They were ignorant because their educators, their publicists, and their historians were almost unanimously uninformed in the same field. Government by the people had managed to squeeze by for a century in spite of this handicap. But sometime in the future it might lead us to national disaster. Obviously, here was an undeveloped educational field where the University of Chicago could become a pioneer. I, therefore, ventured to suggest that, since war is simply a special phase of politics, a start might be made through a short course of lectures on military policy and institutions in the university's department of political science. Such a course of lectures might suggest to some professor of political science that he and his colleagues were completely overlooking a rather important branch of their special field. It might at least remind them, in their future studies of national debt and taxation, that since the founding of our government, the lack of sound military institutions had always been the most fruitful source of both.

When Dr. Harper suggested that such a subject might better be considered in the department of history, I replied that there was a practical reason for an approach to public education through a faculty dealing with political institutions as a whole. In support of this view, I told him about my discussions with Captain Cornish on the Clausewitzian dictum that war is simply a special violent phase of politics and not a detached and separate thing in itself. If this be true, I urged, then every complete political system should include the machinery for dealing with that special violent form of political action.

Although Washington died before Clausewitz published *Vom Krieg* (On War), he understood this fundamental fact in international relations. This was the principal thought in his "Farewell Address" and his other political writings from the close of the revolution to the end of his life. In the light of his recognition of the fact of war and its great significance in human affairs, he continually urged his countrymen to maintain themselves in a "respectably defensive posture" lest some other nation be tempted to substitute war for peaceful political action in its dealings with them. He sought to make this "respectably defensive posture" the cornerstone of the new American political structure. But his countrymen refused and were still refusing to follow his guidance. In this way, while very properly hating war, they continued to invite it through contributory negligence. If this outstanding fact could first be exploited by one teacher of political science, it might encourage some future historian to study the history of our military institutions.

When I left his office, President Harper said that he had made no decision as to a military department, but that he was glad to have my reaction.

Some time in October we got back to Fort Grant and settled down in our army home. Upon my return from a scouting trip a few days before Christmas, Maude came running to meet me as I crossed the parade ground. She was waving a newspaper in her hand and was evidently the bearer of exciting news. When she reached me, quite out of breath, she showed me the following news item in the *Chicago Chronicle:*

> President Harper of the University of Chicago has been informed by the War Department of the appointment of Lieutenant John M. Palmer of the Fifteenth Infantry as professor of military science and tactics at the Midway School.
>
> The establishment of a department of military science at the University of Chicago is the outcome of a proposition made to the students by Dr. Harper several weeks ago in which he laid before them a plan of having a volunteer "university guard." The proposition was eagerly indorsed by a majority of the students, and as the government was desirous of furnishing the instruction the idea was adopted by the university authorities.

A few days later I received my travel orders. After a busy week packing our household goods and bidding our friends goodbye, we set out for the East. In the excitement of our new adventure we did not realize that we were closing one of the happiest chapters in our army life. We both loved Arizona and we were both young. For more than a half century we dreamed that we might go back there some day.

We got to Chicago in time for a ceremony at the university as announced in the *Chicago Times* of January 3, 1898:

MARS IN THE FACULTY
LIEUTENANT PALMER'S ADVENT

UNIVERSITY OF CHICAGO'S CONVOCATION TODAY
MARKED BY THE ARMY MAN'S PRESENCE....

A new department in the University of Chicago will claim honors at the twenty-first convocation at the Auditorium tonight. This adjunct to the university will not materially increase the number of the faculty staff but for all that the average under-graduate will perhaps see more that is attractive in the head of the department than in all the rest combined. The new head is John McAuley Palmer, lieutenant in the United States Army, and incidentally detailed by Secretary Alger to form a military company of the students of the University of Chicago.

Lieutenant Palmer, who is the son of John Mayo Palmer of this city, and a grandson of Senator Palmer, will not turn the whole campus into a military camp, but he is expected to teach a goodly number of the maroons how they do things at West Point. Lieutenant Palmer will be by tonight a full fledged member of the faculty.

BRIGHT FOIL TO CAP AND GOWN

Besides representing the majesty and power of Uncle Sam he will have the distinction of being the only one of the faculty who will not be garbed in the conventional cap and gown. He will be in the front rank of the procession clad in the full regimentals of the United States Army. It will be a novelty such as the convocation of the university has never seen before. An oasis of gold lace and braid in a desert of black....

An old clipping from the *Chicago Evening Post* reminds me that on the morning of January 11, I accompanied President Harper to the chapel at the head of the "faculty procession." After the president introduced me, I explained my mission to the student body and outlined tentative plans for the formation of a small battalion of infantry to be composed of volunteers. It was also announced that I was preparing a course of lectures on national military policy. But before my progress was well under way, it became apparent that my tour of duty at the university would be brief. On February 15th, the Battleship *Maine* was blown up in Havana Harbor. As we were now headed toward war in the near future, the actual organization of the university battalion was suspended for the present.

I was relieved from duty at the university shortly after the outbreak of war, but before I left I delivered a lecture on "the War Power of the United States" in the auditorium of Haskell Museum. After the lapse of half a century, it is gratifying to read in a contemporary newspaper that "the lecture was listened to with profound attention and appeared to make a deep impression on the large audience present."

The excerpts quoted in the old newspaper give me no cause to be ashamed. Even after a half-century of experience and reflection, it would be difficult for me to write a better argument for the proposition that every nation should include a sound and economical military system among its political institutions. The lecture fully confirmed my thesis that in this field, the American people, their political leaders, their historians, their scholars, and their educators were almost completely uneducated. Having thus established the need for a sound military system, I announced that in a second lecture I would describe the characteristics of such an institution.

Fortunately for me, I was ordered to other duty before I could finish my second lecture. It gives me the shivers when I realize how close I came to making a fool of myself. In my first lecture I presented a sound diagnosis. In the second I would have presented an unsound remedy. I had pointed out the mote in the eye of my civilian brethren without being conscious of the beam in my own eye. They were indeed uneducated in this important field. But I was worse than uneducated. I was miseducated.

I had indeed grasped the first corollary of the Clausewitzian dictum that "every sound political system must include effective military institutions," but I had not yet discovered the second corollary that a "nation's military institutions should be in harmony with its political traditions." Like practically all army officers since the War of 1812, I favored an expansible standing army to be dominated in peace and war by a corps of professional army officers. None of us were conscious militarists, but since we favored a system which (if developed to include the whole national manpower) would form the full machinery of militarism, we might well have been called *cryptomilitarists.* I had not yet learned that such a military system could have no congenial place among the political institutions of a self-governing free people. My grandfather had tried to make me see that the American people would risk unpreparedness rather than embrace a system so alien to the genius of the modern democratic state. But here, as usual, miseducation was a more refractory bar to wisdom than mere ignorance could have been. As yet, the beam in my own eye completely distorted my vision.

8 The Spanish-American War

Some time before my relief from duty at the University of Chicago, I found that my interest in military affairs was no longer purely academic. War was approaching and I would soon be on active duty—but where? As my own regiment was slated to remain in Arizona, I assisted John A. Logan, Jr., in the organization of a regiment of Illinois Volunteer Cavalry. As Logan was the son of the late Gen. John A. Logan, it was expected that his distinguished Republican antecedents would induce the Republican governor of Illinois to accept our regiment. If so, Logan was to be its colonel and I was to be its lieutenant colonel. Here we followed the time-honored tradition of mobilization by political influence which had descended to us from the Civil War.

We enrolled our prospective captains and each of them enrolled the lieutenants and enlisted men for his troop of cavalry. But we had our labor for our pains, as Governor Tanner rejected our regiment and accepted another offered by one of our competitors. Then, as if to add insult to injury, the War Department made me quartermaster of a horse board with orders to go to the Chicago Stockyards to buy 980 horses for our successful rival.

My unsuccessful effort to form a volunteer regiment was not an isolated incident. All over the country men were being enrolled in volunteer regiments which were never called into service. Until this phase of the politico-military mobilization ended, it was difficult to find volunteers for the new organizations which Congress had recently authorized for the Regular Army. As a result, many of these new units went into the Santiago campaign at reduced strength or overburdened with ill-trained recruits.

While I was still busy at the stockyards, an order came formally relieving me from duty at the University of Chicago and directing me to proceed to Mobile, Alabama, for assignment to the 20th U.S. Infantry, one of the regular regiments assembling there for active service in Cuba. This order was to take effect immediately upon the completion of the stockyards job. After my unfortunate experience with politico-military mobilization I was delighted to have this prospect of active service in a famous regular regiment.

But before the horse-buying job was done, I received another War Department order directing me, upon the completion of my present duties, to act as mustering officer for the 8th U.S. Volunteer Infantry. As this was one of the ten "yellow fever immune" regiments recently authorized by act of Congress, I expected to go eventually to the Gulf Coast where yellow fever immunes were supposed to be procurable. But the order directed that I should first report to Col. E. L. Huggins, the regimental commander in Washington, for detailed instructions. As I was authorized to employ two clerks, I first engaged First Sergeant Maynard, an experienced retired soldier, who had demonstrated, while acting as the clerk of the horse board, that he was familiar with Army Regulations and every phase of military administration. While I was looking for a second clerk, my brother Robertson Palmer applied for the job. Bob had just been admitted to the bar, but as he was not yet burdened with clients, he concluded that a trip to Washington and thence to the Gulf Coast at Uncle Sam's expense would be an agreeable adventure.

So on the 18th of June, I set out for Washington with my two clerks. When I reported to Colonel Huggins, the regimental commander, I supposed that we would soon start southward to the yellow fever region. But to my surprise, he informed me that his first company was already assembled for muster at Newark, New Jersey. No doubt there were genuine yellow fever immunes in some of the ten immune regiments, but I am quite sure there were none in the regiment that I mustered into the service. Political as well as sanitary factors appeared to influence the distribution of these regiments. If they had all been recruited down in the yellow fever belt, the privilege of appointing the captains would have been restricted to a limited number of congressmen. By spreading them out, one company to a congressional district, there would be a little slice of patronage for a much greater number of congressmen. This was a factor of some importance in the mobilization of 1898. But for this, under the general volunteer act, only the governors of the states could have had any slices of the "volunteer" watermelon. I also learned from Colonel Huggins that all of the enlisted men of his regiment would be Negroes, with white captains and colored lieutenants.

We set out for Newark that night. Upon our arrival we were escorted to the Essex Troop Armory, where the newly appointed captain had two or three hundred Negroes ready for examination. It took several days for the new regimental surgeon to give them their physical examinations and to weed out many of them who were physically unfit. Meanwhile, under my orders from the War Department, I acted as quartermaster, providing shelter and subsistence for the candidates and meeting all other expenses. After a sufficient number of men had been accepted, I assembled them and explained their new military obligations to them. After that I swore them into the service and dispatched them in special railroad cars, under their new captain, to the regimental rendezvous at Fort Thomas, Kentucky.

When we got back to Washington a temporary office was assigned to me on the second floor of the old Center Market at the corner of Pennsylvania Avenue and 7th Street. There I found two companies of Washington Negroes ready for muster. While the members of the first company were undergoing their physical examinations, for some reason or other I was instructed not to muster in the second company. There seemed to be some hitch in the normal process of mobilization by political influence because of some rivalry between several candidates for the captaincy of the company. This so crossed the wires between the Adjutant General's office and the offices of several competing statesmen up at the Capitol that it was decided not to accept this company.

While we were waiting for this snarl to untangle, Bob and I went to call on our old friend and neighbor, Sen. Shelby M. Cullom of Illinois. Since I could not be a lieutenant colonel of volunteers and could not join a regular regiment en route to Cuba, another aspect of politico-military mobilization had occurred to me. Two of my classmates had recently been appointed temporary captains in the Commissary Department. As I had been an officer for six years since my graduation at West Point, I felt that the senator would welcome this opportunity to give a bit of temporary promotion to a trained constituent. But that was not his reaction. He said: "Why, John you already have a life job. Now if Bob here wanted something, it would be a different matter."

After mustering the Washington Company into the service, we set out for Greenville, Tennessee, a charming little town under the shadow of the Great Smoky Mountains. Here we found another white captain with a bunch of colored men waiting to be mustered in. After dispatching this Greenville company to Fort Thomas, I went down to Chattanooga en route to my next assignment at Harriman, Tennessee.

While I was at Chattanooga, news of the fighting in Cuba began to come in. I stood before a bulletin board in front of a newspaper office and read the news dispatches as they were posted. Among the regiments mentioned was the 20th Infantry, which I had hoped to join at Mobile. Finally lists of casualties began to come in. Among the dead and wounded were several of my old West Point comrades. At last came news that my dear friend and classmate, Dennis Michie, was among those who had been mortally wounded. It seemed to me that my being up in Tennessee mustering in fake yellow fever immunes while my friends were in battle down in Cuba was a disgrace and humiliation from which I could never recover.

The next morning, when Bob joined me at the breakfast table, he showed me a telegram from Senator Cullom informing him that he had been appointed captain of the Washington Company which I had been instructed not to accept while there. I was now able to account for Bob's frequent visits to the Senator while he was in our capital city. As the new captain took his seat beside me he grinned and said, "Well, Lieutenant, I think I'll have to borrow enough money from you to buy a railroad ticket back to Washington."

This incident shows how the War Department personnel problem was solved in those good old days. Here I was, a first lieutenant of infantry who had served six years in the Regular Army since graduation at West Point, and here, as my breakfast guest, was a full-fledged captain of infantry whose only military education had been a few months in a "tin soldier" school in his teens, and whose sole military experience had been three weeks as my clerk. But as it turned out, Bob's military education and experience were little, if any, below the average of the captains of the 8th U.S. Volunteer Infantry. In fact, Capt. Robertson Palmer had had as much of both as Col. William Jennings Bryan, who was given the command of a regiment of infantry by the Governor of Nebraska. Those were the days of fiat military leaders as well as fiat money.

After Captain Palmer's departure to assume command of his company, Lieutenant Palmer was unable to employ another clerk. As a result, he had to act as Sergeant Maynard's assistant in addition to his other duties. And when notification of his promotion to first lieutenant in the Regular Army arrived a few days later, it did very little to assuage his rankling sense of injustice.

After mustering in the company at Harriman, I was ordered to Murfreesboro, Tennessee, where another company awaited me. Its captain, Charles O. Thomas, Jr., was an accomplished young gentleman who later entered the Regular Army, where he served with distinction until he retired as a colonel after thirty-seven years service.

Unfortunately, Captain Thomas had not been able to collect enough recruits to meet the minimum legal requirements for muster as a company. When I reported this fact to Colonel Huggins, he procured a telegraphic order from the War Department directing me to act as recruiting officer for the Murfreesboro Company until I could legally function as its mustering officer. The Adjutant General's plan of mobilization required that Uncle Sam should pick up a company of yellow fever immunes at Murfreesboro, Tennessee. So, obviously, if its captain did not have enough immunes to form a company, it was up to Uncle Sam to get them for him.

This resulted in a pleasant sojourn of about two weeks in a delightful town where I enjoyed true southern hospitality. One of my fellow guests at the hotel was the Judge of the Circuit Court. His Honor was greatly interested in Captain Thomas's company and gave me substantial aid in my efforts to procure recruits for it. In order to facilitate my operations he placed his main courtroom at my disposal and held court temporarily in a smaller room on an upper floor of the court house. He even instructed his bailiffs to assist me in procuring recruits.

My relations with His Honor were most delightful. He had commanded a Confederate regiment at the Battle of Murfreesboro, or Stone River. When he learned that my grandfather had commanded a division on the other side, he acted as my guide on the battlefield. We spent several pleasant afternoons tracing out the positions of the troops on both sides. After each of these historical surveys we returned to the hotel, where the judge brewed a marvelous mint julep for our philosophic delectation while we waited for a supper which always included little fried chicken—not much bigger than quail.

One morning when our quota of recruits was just about filled, the chief bailiff came into the main courtroom and told me that the judge would like to see me in his temporary courtroom upstairs. When I entered the courtroom, His Honor recessed a lawsuit that was in progress and invited me to take a seat beside his on the bench. While the bar and witnesses rested, the judge turned to me and inquired:

> "Lieutenant, just when does the federal government assume jurisdiction over these boys that you are taking into the army?"

> "They become soldiers just as soon as I swear them in—probably tomorrow morning."

> "Would it be convenient for you to fix ten o'clock tomorrow morning as the precise time? The exact time is a matter of importance from a legal standpoint as I have given some of these boys the option of joining the company or going to the penitentiary."

> This situation required some quick thinking on my part. I was determined not to accept these convicts and I was equally determined, if possible, not to offend this charming old gentleman. So I said, "Your Honor, I am not a lawyer. I must have legal advice and unless I can get it from you I am helpless. Under the law, the soldiers of this Murfreesboro company are to be volunteers—and though I know little or no law, I wonder whether the option you mention would not amount to duress. You are my only lawyer friend down here. Won't you advise me?"

> His Honor stroked his gray goatee a moment and said, "Lieutenant, I will take this matter under advisement and will give you my opinion at suppertime." Then, as I left the room, he resumed his conduct of the lawsuit.

That evening, over the most delectable mint julep that mortal ever brewed, the judge turned toward me and said: "Lieutenant, I must advise you not to accept those boys." This decision produced vacancies in the company which took at least another week to fill even with the continued assistance of the bailiffs. I have always been grateful for the delay. For after more than half a century, my sojourn in Murfreesboro stands out as one of my most treasured memories.

Murfreesboro was as near the yellow fever belt as I ever got in my quest for yellow fever immunes. From there I turned northward and mustered in several companies in the Ohio and Kanawha valleys. About the middle of August, after procuring a company at Parkersburg, West Virginia, I was relieved from further mustering duty and directed to rejoin my regiment, the 15th Infantry, which had recently been ordered from Arizona and New Mexico to Fort Logan, Colorado. Permission was given me to stop off for a week at Petersburg, where Maude and John awaited me.

While at Petersburg I went over to Springfield for a day's visit with my Grandfather Palmer. Though approaching his eighty-first birthday, he was still hale and hearty and was busy every day in his law office. Although no longer a member of the Senate Military Affairs Committee, he was still interested in military affairs and heard me patiently when I urged that we should have at least 50,000 more regulars. This led to a conversation, in substance, as follows:

"Why do you want 50,000 more regulars, John McAuley?"

"In order to check any invader while we are expanding our army for war."

"If that's what you want, John McAuley, why don't you organize and train a citizen army in time of peace? That will cost less money and will give you many more soldiers ready for defense. Your 50,000 extra regulars won't help much in a big war unless you have a citizen army to put behind them. And if you have a citizen army to put behind them, you won't need 50,000 extra regulars."

I did not like to have a mere civilian talk to me, an educated military expert, in that way, even if he had commanded troops in battle and had served on the Senate Military Affairs Committee, so I said, "But such troops as you describe would not be fit for anything in war."

"Why not, John McAuley? With such an army, Washington won our independence. He did not have any troops like our regular army. He and all the rest of his Continental Army were citizen soldiers. We finally did pretty well with citizen soldiers during our Civil War. But the North didn't go at it as promptly or as intelligently as the South did. From the first, the Southern graduates of West Point concentrated on creating a good citizen army, while their Northern brethren wasted time and energy and opportunity in an increase of the regular army. The Confederacy almost won the war because the North *did* have and the South *did not have* what you call a regular army."

That was too much. "Where did you ever get an idea like that?", I asked.

"I got it from one of your fellow West Point graduates, John McAuley, a gentleman by the name of Ulysses S. Grant. He tells about it in his *Memoirs*.* I would commend it to you and to other military experts as a book well worth careful reading."

Of course I could not accept this view at first. For though he had commanded one of Thomas's divisions at Chickamauga, he was only an amateur in the profession of arms, while my West Point diploma and my recent commission as first lieutenant certified me as an educated professional expert. So, after I left him, I decided to confute him by working out the expansible standing army scheme in detail.

But the results were discouraging. When I assumed a peacetime nucleus big enough to make a real foundation for effective expansion for a great war, I found that the American people would be saddled with an excessively costly standing army in time of peace. When I assumed a peacetime nucleus small enough to give any chance of acceptance by Congress, it would result in too small a war army—unless I also assumed a rate of expansion that would be obviously absurd. And how to get the men for expansion in a great war? Volunteering would certainly fail on so vast a scale, and to propose conscription solely for the expansion of a big standing army would be asking the American people to adopt a militaristic system like that of Germany.

So, in my last conversation with my grandfather, several months later, I brought him a plan that he could approve. If American citizen armies, extemporized after the outbreak of war, could do as well as the citizen armies of Lee and Stonewall Jackson, what might they not do if organized and partially trained in time of peace? This, then, should be the basis of our military policy. Instead of expanding a standing army we would simply give final training to a pre-existing citizen army. As for professional officers and soldiers, we would need them only to do those things that citizen soldiers cannot do effectively and in time. We should therefore have enough professionals for these special purposes and no more. When I said goodbye to my grandfather this last time, I was no longer a cryptomilitarist. There was no longer a beam in my eye.

Our trip from Petersburg to my new post in Colorado was a great adventure to our son. He was approaching his fourth birthday and every incident of railroad travel thrilled him. Shortly after I joined my regiment at Fort Logan,

---

*U.S. Grant, *Personal Memoirs*, (New York, 1885-86), vol. 1, p. 283.

our old friend, Gen. E. V. Sumner, commanding general of the Department of the Colorado, ordered me to Denver to act as his aide-de-camp and as acting chief signal officer and chief engineer officer of the department.

As General Sumner commanded the Department of the Missouri as well as the Department of the Colorado, I made several official trips to Omaha with him. On one of these visits I had the honor to act as aide-de-camp to President McKinley who had come to Omaha as the honor guest of the Trans-Mississippi Exposition. When General Sumner was relieved from the command of the Department of the Colorado some time in January, the Palmers moved to Omaha with him. Finally, about the middle of March, I was ordered to Puerto Principe, Cuba, to join the 15th Infantry, which had been sent there as part of the Cuban army of occupation. After escorting Maude and John to Petersburg, I set out for the port of embarkation in New York.

On April Fool's Day, 1899, I sailed for Nuevitas, Cuba, on the "Ella," a banana freighter of about 2,000 tons burden. It was my first trip at sea, and as I did not suffer from seasickness, I enjoyed every minute of it. The second day out we entered the Gulf Stream and I had my first glimpse of flying fish and of phosphorescent seas. We passed within hailing distance of Columbus's San Salvador and later skirted several Bahama islets where turquoise waves broke clean and white on coral beaches.

As we entered the bay of Nuevitas, the morning of the seventh, we passed the cruiser *Nashville* on her way out. She was famous because she had fired the navy's first shot in the recent war with Spain. On reaching the wharf at Nuevitas, I was welcomed by the quartermaster of the port, who happened to be my classmate Samuel V. Ham. He took me to his quarters where his wife had established a comfortable army home. After lunch he drove me out to the hills where two companies of my regiment were in camp. After inspecting I boarded the train for Puerto Principe.

And what a train it was! An engine of the old wood-burning type with a tender full of blocks of mahogany, then two water tanks, some boxcars, and three coaches. The coaches were much like the boxcars—no backs to the seats except in the first-class car, where I paid an extra fare for the luxury of having something to lean my back against. The area between Nuevitas and Puerto Principe was not what I expected to see in the tropics. It was a cattle-grazing country and looked much like the plains in Arizona. The palmettos were so much like the yucca that the near outlook might have been in the Sulphur Springs Valley. But when we crossed a swampy watercourse, the difference was startling. Tall royal palms and cocoanut palms made a new landscape.

Late in the afternoon, I left the train at Camp Allyn Capron about three miles short of Puerto Principe. There the 15th Infantry was tented to the right of the railroad tracks, and the 8th Cavalry was tented to the left. It was expected that the troops would move into Spanish barracks in Puerto Principe as soon as the fine old city could be put in sanitary condition. But it took time to clean up the filth of the Spanish regime, which had been accumulating ever since the first cesspools were dug shortly after the days of Columbus. Our sanitary programs were unduly expensive, complicated, and aimless because we had not yet learned that soldiers can be healthy anywhere in the tropics if they are protected from flies and mosquitoes.

I was glad to rejoin the regiment. My old friends Edmund Wittenmyer, W. H. Bertsch, John Cotter, J. A. Maney, and J. A. Lynch were there. Col. Edward Moale commanded the regiment. Lt. Col. Constant Williams had recently joined. Arthur Cowan, a recent graduate from West Point, had arrived a few days before I reported. My old friend George Cornish, now a major, was about seventy miles away in command of a battalion at Ciego de Avila. As my company was under his command, I had hoped to join him there. But as there was a shortage of officers at regimental headquarters, Colonel Moale assigned me to duty in the Puerto Principe Garrison.

I had a talk with Major Cornish, however, when he paid a short visit to regimental headquarters on official business. As he had encouraged my early studies in military policy, I hoped he would welcome my new doctrine in favor of a peacetime citizen army instead of an expansible standing army. But I was disappointed. Perhaps, I was not eloquent enough to present my case convincingly in so short a time. But on looking back on it I feel the major's old army miseducation had finally hardened into a permanent cryptomilitarist set.

As I had no more success with my own contemporaries, it gradually dawned upon me that the new doctrine would have to be imposed upon the army from the outside. This idea gradually developed into a resolution to write a book on the subject—not to persuade my brother officers but to awaken the interest of my civilian brethren. As this would require a thorough review of our military history, and that would be impossible down in Cuba, I determined to wait until things settled back into the old garrison routine. Before long we would return to the abundant leisure of the old army and then it would be possible to write my book in a short time. But I was over optimistic. A half-century has passed since then and my book remains unfinished. We still have cryptomilitarism supported by miseducation.

About the first of May the troops moved into Puerto Principe. We were assigned to the Spanish Infantry Barracks near the railroad station. The 8th Cavalry moved into another Spanish barrack about a quarter of a mile away. Our quarters were superb, comprising a great quadrangle surrounding a spacious court. At the center of the front facade of the quadrangle was the sally port—with the regimental offices on either side of the entrance. To the right and left were quarters for the junior officers. The other three sides of the quadrangle contained spacious squadrooms and offices for the companies of the regiment. The inner court was a thing of beauty—there were palm trees at each of the four corners with a formal garden of tropical plants surrounding a fountain at the center. The whole building had been carefully cleaned by the sanitary squads. It appeared to be an ideal health resort for our men. We did not know then that our lovely inner garden, moistened by gentle showers as well as by the central fountain, was an ideal breeding place for the yellow fever mosquito. Uncle Sam had spent thousands of dollars cleaning up the ancient city of Puerto Principe for his soldiers. If he had invested one percent of that money in mosquito bars and crude petroleum he might have accomplished something.

We junior officers were comfortably housed in the front section of the Infantry Barracks. In his spacious room opening onto the inner court, Jerry Lynch established the 15th Infantry Club on a self-service basis. In one corner of his room was a barrel of bottled beer. Next to it was a tub of water with a chunk of ice floating in it. At the bottom of the tub were usually about a dozen bottles of cold beer. When a member of the club was thirsty, he went to Jerry's room, took a cold bottle from the tub and replaced it by a warm bottle from the barrel. He then signed his name to a cigarette paper and deposited it in a cigar box receptacle tacked to the wall just above the tub. After depositing his chit, the member was free to drink his beer from the bottle.

At the end of each month, Jerry counted the chits and gave each member his bill. We wanted to elect Jerry president of the club, but he suggested another solution. At each monthly settlement, the signer of the greatest number of chits would be president for the next month. When we adopted this rule it never occurred to us that no officer of the 15th Infantry would ever be president of the 15th Infantry Club. The officers of the 8th Cavalry had been made honorary members of our club. One of them, Captain K, called at the Infantry Barracks every morning on his way to the Cavalry Barracks and again every afternoon on his way back to his quarters. Somehow or other, and without any special effort on his part, Captain K was elected president every month by a substantial majority.

In the latter part of July, I was taken ill and was in the brigade hospital for about a month. Whether I had malaria or a light case of typhoid or yellow fever was undetermined. Toward the end of August, soon after my return to duty, yellow fever broke out in the city and the regiment was moved back into camp. A few weeks later I was detailed on temporary duty as quartermaster and disbursing officer of civil funds, with my office in Puerto Principe and my living quarters on the top floor of a fine old Spanish mansion.

Early in November, Maude with her mother and John arrived in Puerto Principe. The ladies had a new experience in their efforts to keep house in my old Spanish quarters. They were comfortable enough in quartermaster beds but they were not enthusiastic about their servants. The morning after her arrival Mrs. Laning looked across the inner court and was surprised to see our buxom black cook preparing breakfast with a big cigar in her mouth.

My apartment was regarded as a most delightful domicile by my Cuban neighbors, but it had shortcomings from the standpoint of an Illinois housekeeper. As all of the rooms were floored in brick, the ladies of my household suffered sadly from flea-bitten ankles. Fortunately, I was relieved from my temporary assignment a few weeks later and we joined the little colony of officers' families in the regimental camp. There we were housed in two hospital tents with an awning between them and our meals were brought in from the officers' mess. Five-year-old John was delighted with camp life. His mother was somewhat less enthusiastic, but his grandmother emphatically did not like it. Soon after a tropical tornado blew down our tents, we escorted her down to Neuvitas where she embarked for God's Country.

Toward the end of December, 1899, the 15th Infantry was ordered back to the United States. The regiment, with the officers' families, embarked on a transport at Nuevitas. As my company with the regimental headquarters was headed for Plattsburg Barracks, New York, we encountered a radical change in climate. As we approached New York just before New Years, it turned bitterly cold. Few of the children in the regiment were equipped with winter clothing, so on our arrival Maude, with a number of other ladies, went into the city and made purchases for everybody. Finally we got on the troop train and arrived at Plattsburg in the midst of one of the worst blizzards I have ever known. As the post had been ungarrisoned for some time, most of the families had to move into unheated houses. Fortunately, we happened to draw a house that had only recently been vacated.

We were greatly concerned for our men in making this sudden change of climate but there was only one loss of life. One old soldier slipped into Plattsburg and got tight. When he got back to the post he decided to take a little nap before entering barracks, as he might have done a few weeks before in Cuba. He never awakened from his sleep.

After two years of unsettled life since we left Fort Grant we were pleased to be in army quarters again. Our house faced toward the parade ground, and beyond it John was delighted to see the ice yachts racing on Lake Champlain. But he took even greater delight in watching the passing trains on the railway along the lake shore. As he was approaching his sixth birthday, his interest in railroading had become highly technical. One morning while we were at breakfast, Private Jones, my orderly, came in and told us how, in the blinding snow, he had just missed being run down by a passing train. John was greatly excited. While his mother was congratulating Jones on his narrow escape, John broke in with the purely technical inquiry: "Jones, was it a freight or passenger?"

Spring finally came to the Lake Champlain region, but with it came rumors of changes of station. At first, it was reported that our regiment would go to the Philippines before the end of the summer. With this prospect in view, my mother came to pay me a goodbye visit. Before her arrival news came of the Boxer Rebellion in China and the hurried efforts to relieve the foreigners in Peking. The Taku forts were seized on June 17. Soon after these events, news came that the 9th and 14th Infantry regiments had been ordered from the Philippines to China. Early in July the headquarters and first battalion of my regiment were ordered to San Francisco to embark for China. As my captain was away on detached service, this gave me the honor of commanding Company D.

While we were hurriedly packing our household goods, John left with his grandmother for Illinois. It was decided that Maude would go on the troop train with me as far as Chicago and from there would go with our son to Petersburg. We arrived in Chicago late in the afternoon. That night while the train was awaiting routing orders, my father and mother brought John down to the railroad yards to tell me goodbye. As it grew very late before the train started, my parents took the boy home with them. He was almost too sleepy to say goodbye to his father, even though our separation was to be a long one.

9 The Boxer Rebellion

When we arrived in San Francisco the newspapers were filled with lurid news from China. On 17 July 1900 we set sail on the transport *Sumner*. We had hoped that we would touch at Honolulu, but the chart in the captain's cabin showed our route as a curve far into the North Pacific. Most of us were landlubbers and did not realize that the direct great circle route across the Pacific would be portrayed as a curve on a Mercator projection map. When I tried to explain this to one of my brother officers he yawned and said, "John, I don't give a damn how big a circle we travel on. I am in no hurry to get to China."

Another interesting incident for landlubbers on their first voyage across the Pacific was the loss of a day when we crossed the 180th meridian. The lost day happened to be the Sabbath, as the chaplain discovered when he came into the main saloon prepared to conduct the usual Sunday morning service. At first, he was pleased to see more officers than usual. But he was shocked to find that his prospective worshippers were busy at poker, cribbage, and other occupations not in keeping with the Sabbath spirit. When they explained that it was Monday and not Sunday, he complained to Colonel Moale that he had been deprived of a means of grace to which he was entitled under the Army Regulations. The Old Man replied, "You might make it a little longer next Sunday, Padre."

One morning as we sailed into the Japan Current, we saw great numbers of whales rising to the surface and spouting as far as we could see. There must have been thousands of them, for we enjoyed this spectacle until sunset. Long before we could see the coast of Japan, we beheld the great dome of Fujiyama rising above a bank of cloud on the horizon. After dark on August 7th we anchored off the port of Kobe.

The next morning we could see the city in the distance. We were not allowed to go ashore, but we had our first glimpse of the Japanese people. Our transport was soon surrounded by bumboats. Each little sampan carried a crew of two or three half-naked men and women, one at the stern with the sculling oar and the others in the cockpit where they had their wares for sale. And what an assortment of merchandise—shoes and shoemakers' tools; silks and laces; and postage stamps, flowers, watermelons, photographs, albums, everything.

One member of each crew carried a long bamboo pole. A basket attached to its upper end served as an elevator for passing goods up to the deck of the ship. If you wanted anything on one of the boats you would gesture, grimace, and point until you attracted the merchant's attention. He would then place the article in the basket and pass it up to you. If you liked it you would keep it and send the purchase money down in the basket.

From Kobe we passed through the Inland Sea. The following excerpts from a letter to Maude give my contemporary impressions, 8 August 1900:

This is the most beautiful body of water in the world. We are passing between Honshu on our right and Shukoku on our left. The channel is studded with tiny islets of which 3600 are said to be inhabited. They are all mountainous and all of them are covered with verdure. Most of them, steep as they are, are terraced from the water's edge to the crest.

The Japanese are probably the most laborious farmers in the world. On the slopes of the steeper hills the terraces are frequently less than forty feet in width and as they are all retained by stone walls they represent a vast expenditure of labor.

Most of these little hillside plots are irrigated and those that are in rice are kept under the water most of the time. The most picturesque crop is the Japanese potato. It looks like the "elephant ear" plants in your garden at Thorne Place.

Frequently the channels between the mountain islands are narrow, giving us close views of the native villages—and what picturesque little villages they are.

One of the most surprising things to me is the constant indication of military strength. I have never seen so many modern guns. The narrow channels are commanded by modern forts. The Inland Sea is so firmly held in the Mikado's hands that I doubt if all the fleets in the world could force a passage against his will.

I had expected to see great development in Japan. I had expected to see a barbarous nation with a thin veneer of civilization. But a closer view shows that in military and naval might she is already a world power and one of the greatest.

It is interesting, however, to observe that she has borrowed what she needs from Occidental civilization without losing her individuality. She has borrowed the torpedo boat, the breechloader and the locomotive, but she has retained her national costumes and her national art and culture. We westerners have little to teach the Japs in the way of appreciating and delineating the beautiful.

From the Inland Sea we sailed into the China Sea and thence down to Nagasaki. We anchored in the narrow harbor and were there for several days. Here was our first experience on dry land in Japan. The beauty of the country, the entirely novel architecture, and the charm of the friendly people appealed to us strongly. As we came to anchor we witnessed the skill and energy of Japanese labor in coaling a great ocean liner. From the barges alongside, eight streams of coal flowed up to the ship's bunkers. The eight conveyor belts were bamboo ladders with half-clad Japanese women on the rungs. From one to the other there passed a steady stream of baskets full of coal. As each basket was poured into the ship, it was thrown back to be refilled again at the bottom of the human conveyor.

While in Nagasaki we got fresh news from China. The world was on fire up there and we were headed toward the conflagration. Some American officers had come down from Tientsin with valuable loot. This had been captured by undisciplined foreign soldiers and had been sold by them to eager speculators. To seize private property was against all of our traditions, but to buy what others had stolen in a black market of plunder seemed to be quite another thing.

At Nagasaki, the *Sumner* was ordered to Manila and we were transferred to the *Indiana*, a chartered transport. This ship had been remodeled a few years before for the Klondike trade and was fixed so as to exclude every possible breath of fresh air. This was a poor fitting for an August cruise to the broiling coast of North China. Finally we got under way and set out to cross the Yellow Sea. Surely there has seldom been a more uncomfortable journey. There was no ventilation down below, and when we gathered on the upper deck we found little relief. The speed of the ship was just about the speed of a steady breeze from astern. As a result, the smoke from the funnel formed a black cloud above us and the deck was soon covered by a snow of black soot.

Nevertheless, it was a fascinating journey. We found a romance that none of our much-travelled army officers can feel today. The doors of the wide world had just come ajar. It seemed unbelievable that we home-keeping Americans were on our way to battlefields in Cathay. Jerry Lynch was in his element. One evening just before sunset a lot of us youngsters gathered on the upper deck. There Jerry strummed his mandolin as an accompaniment to Kipling's songs of the Far East. His beautiful rendering of "On the Road to Mandalay" was most effective, for as he sang, "the sun went down like thunder" into China just across the Yellow Sea. Then he gave us Kipling's "Loot, Loot, Loot." This led us to a discussion of the ethics of loot. Just then one of our seniors, Capt. William N. Blow, a Virginia Military Academy graduate of 1876, came up and scolded us for discussing such things. He reminded us that looting was forbidden by our Army Regulations. When somebody said, "But, Captain, suppose you were out walking and some coolie should offer to sell you a fine piece of jade, wouldn't you buy it?" "No," he replied, "we are paid by our government as officers and gentlemen. Our pay should be our only compensation." Then as he started on, he paused and said: "Of course, if I should find a likely setter dog out there, I might be tempted to keep him until his lawful owner claimed him."

The night of August 16 we anchored twelve miles off the mouth of the Hai Ho, which is to say, the River Hai. When morning broke we found ourselves in the midst of a great international fleet which included the American cruisers *Brooklyn* and *Yorktown*. The water offshore was so shallow that it was necessary to transfer troops and baggage to a river steamer, the *Foo-chow*. This laborious operation kept us busy all day. That night news came that the international forces had captured Peking. So we had come halfway round the world only to be too late for anything more glorious than service on the line of communications.

The morning of the 18th the *Foo-chow* bore us between the Taku forts and into the Hai Ho. As we wound our way up the narrow, crooked stream, the surrounding country was very low and flat. Along the shore were supply bases each under the flag of some European power. In these establishments we saw great gangs of Chinese coolies working under foreign foremen who treated them with great brutality. In one case an impatient supply sergeant seized a coolie by his long queue and twirled him off the dock. As the tide was low the poor devil splashed in the deep mud. From there he crawled slowly shoreward like a fly entrapped in sticky fly paper. No wonder the Chinese considered us "foreign devils." Finally we tied up to a pier near the U.S.S. *Monocacy*, an ancient side-wheel gunboat which our navy maintained in North China at that time. As we had no place to pitch our tents, we slept that night in our blankets on the dock near the berth of the *Monocacy*. We officers were the dinner guests of our navy brethren that evening. But as we rolled into our blankets later, we reflected on the contrast between army and navy service. Even on the eve of battle, the sailor has shelter, a comfortable bed, well-cooked food, shower baths, and clean clothes, while the doughboy struggles on in the mud.

Early on the morning of 19 August 1900, we marched to the railroad station and were packed close together on flatcars. At about six o'clock our train moved northward at a creeping pace toward Tientsin. The railroad was in the hands of the Russians and every few miles we passed Russian sentinels. The country was flat, with marshes at intervals covered with ducks and other waterfowl. Scattered over the flat country clear to the horizon there were beehive-shaped mounds of earth. These were the family tombs where the Chinese had buried their ancestors for thousands of years. In ordinary summers, these ancestral tombs would have been hidden by thick crops of kaóliang, beans, and Indian corn. But in this Boxer year there had been no crops planted in the Tientsin region. The country was therefore as bare as it was after last year's harvest. For the Chinese harvest is a total harvest. After the grain and beans are garnered, the stubble and roots are collected and stored for winter fuel. In a normal summer, North China is a fertile garden. In the winter it is a desert, more naked and lifeless than the Sahara.

About noon we came to the suburbs of Tientsin. First there were some castellated buildings which belonged to a Chinese arsenal now occupied by foreign troops. We saw Russian carts and finally were delighted to see American six-mule army wagons. We left the train at the Tientsin railroad station and marched to our campground. The bridge over the river had been destroyed during the recent fighting in Tientsin, so we crossed on foundered junks with planks thrown between. We pitched our tents on the west bank of the Hai Ho just south of the European quarter of Tientsin. The regimental headquarters and storehouses were established in brick warehouses which had been looted when the international troops invested Tientsin. From the top of a mud wall near our camp we had a view of the open country to the west. With our field glasses we could make out small detachments of troops of many nationalities. Off to the northwest we could see the high walls of the ancient Chinese city recently occupied by the allied forces. The old walled city of Tientsin, at the confluence of the Grand Canal and the Hai Ho, had been a great center of commerce for centuries.

A few days after we were settled in camp, I went with Captain Blow and Jerry Lynch on a hike to the walled city. We followed the Taku Road which, at that time, marked the western limit of the foreign concessions. Our progress was slow, for the road was full of traffic moving in both directions. There were detachments of troops, Russians, French, Italians, and British from Europe; Bengal Lancers, Sikhs, and Rajputs from India. There were gangs of coolies carrying heavy burdens under ruthless foreign taskmasters, and there was every kind of military transportation, including a column of Mongolian camels which had been commandeered by the Russians. We were proud of our American army wagons with their well-groomed six-mule teams. We were to learn that though they made a fine showing on Taku Road, they were worthless as field transportation in a country where there were no roads outside the cities. There, pack mules were the only effective military transportation.

As we left the foreign concessions and approached the Chinese city we went into a small building, apparently a shrine, where looters had torn open the grave of some ancient Chinese saint. Strange to say, they had neglected to take a beautiful jade vase which lay by the ransacked tomb. Captain Blow took it in his hands and looked at it. Then he looked at Jerry and me and grinned. He apparently remembered his lecture on loot that night on the *Indiana,* for as he put the treasure in his pocket he said: "This is pretty near the setter-dog that I mentioned. But I am prepared to return it to its rightful owner when he claims it."

While we were in the old shrine a coolie came in and opened a bag of loot which he had for sale. There were a few pieces of European glassware mingled with American cigarette holders, cheap mirrors, corkscrews and other worthless junk. There were a few pieces of Chinese porcelain but whether they had any value none of us knew. The black market had evidently degenerated. Most of the valuable items garnered in the rape of the ancient city had been bought up by speculators before we arrived in China.

From the shrine we made our way through a ruined suburb and thence through a demolished city gate into the walled city. In its narrow streets we found ourselves back in the Middle Ages. In narrow little shops we saw artisans of every craft working with hand tools that were in use in Europe for hundreds of years before the invention of modern machinery. We were back in the China of Marco Polo. The streets were crowded with peddlers, beggars, and coolies bearing burdens. The dense multitude of filthy, half-naked human beings was almost nauseating. There was no modern sanitation. Once while we were passing a doorway a mother opened a door and held out a naked child while he defecated in the street. There were many poor devils afflicted with unsightly skin diseases—some of them with disgusting running sores. We thought of leprosy and other Asiatic curses.

When we left the walled city we were fortunate enough to find rickshaws. In these we returned to camp by way of the main highway through the foreign concessions. This fine street is known as Rue de France as it passes through the French Concession and becomes Victoria Road when it enters the British Concession. This main highway, with the Taku Road to the west and the Bund along the Hai Ho to the east, were the only highways through the European quarter of Tientsin in those days. When I returned to North China just before World War I, the European city had grown far to the west of Taku Road. South of the British Concession, a splendid new German municipality covered the bare ground where we had camped during the Boxer campaign. There Victoria Road had become Wilhelmstrasse.

Although we of the 15th Infantry were too late to have a part in the glory that the 9th and 14th regiments won in the Boxer Campaign, we were given a highly important duty. When it was decided that American troops should form part of the international garrison at Peking, General Chaffee, the commanding general of the American Expedition Force, was hard pressed to solve his supply problem. As the railroad from Tientsin to Peking had been destroyed by the Boxers, it became necessary to return to the water transportation of ancient China. Hundreds of small river and canal junks must be assembled, laden with rations and other military supplies, and dispatched up the Hai Ho to T'ung Hsien, the head of navigation about fifteen miles from Peking, and this must be done in a few weeks. It was already past mid-August; the river was running low and by the first of December it would be frozen solid.

Tientsin was the base for this operation. Temporary warehouses roofed with Chinese matting were established on the Bund. There lighters from the ships off Taku were unloaded. There the military freight was sorted, transferred to river junks, and dispatched up the river in small fleets of from ten to twenty boats. As each junk carried a crew of five or six coolies to tow it against the swift current of the upper river, its net freight capacity was little more than five or six tons. And since it took at least ten days to make the round trip by the crooked river to Peking, a distance of more than one hundred miles, the ten-mile-per-day capacity of our junks was very low. If General Chaffee's troops in Peking were to be supplied before winter, there must be a continuous flow of junks up the river.

Our battalion of the 15th Infantry played a principal part in this supply operation. We not only furnished guards for the Supply Depot on the Bund, but acted as military police for the whole Tientsin area. Our most demanding duty, however, was to guard the supply junks on their way up the river. The crowded Hai Ho was the supply route for Russia, Germany, Italy, and Japan as well as the United States. Each of these powers had a contingent in the international garrison at Peking that had to be supplied before winter. In these circumstances, an unguarded junk moving up the river with military supplies could easily have been appropriated by one of our allies. It was therefore necessary to assemble our supply junks in fleets of about twenty, each guarded by a detachment of soldiers under an officer.

On the second of September we moved from our camp to more comfortable quarters in the buildings of the American Methodist Mission, which had been vacant since the allied occupation of Tientsin. This establishment occupied two large walled enclosures or "compounds" on the opposite sides of Taku Road. In the eastern compound there were office rooms and quarters for the regimental headquarters and band. Here there was a well-furnished dwelling house for Colonel Moale and a larger house with bedrooms for the regimental staff officers and a well-appointed dining room and kitchen for their mess.

Across Taku Road the western compound had room for A, B, and D companies. Company C was on guard duty at the arsenal in the walled city. Each of the three companies had a well-drained subcompound with ample room for conical wall tents. In brick outbuildings along the compound walls there were offices and storerooms for each company. In the main mission house, there was a well-furnished bedroom for each of the captains and one for each two of the lieutenants. I took one of these rooms with my West Point classmate, George McD. ("Mac") Weeks, as my roommate. On the first floor there was a large dining room and kitchen. Here we established the battalion mess with Lieut. Arthur Cowan, better known as "Frenchy" Cowan, as mess officer. As the cooks and houseboys formerly employed by the missionaries immediately applied to him for employment, he was able to serve us a good dinner the night of our arrival.

Early in September 1900, General Dorward, commander of the British troops in Tientsin and provisional governor of the Tientsin Military District, learned that Boxer troops were assembled at the walled town of Tiu-liu, about thirty miles up the Grand Canal. After a conference with the American, Japanese, Russian, and, Italian commanders, it was decided to send a joint expedition to capture or destroy this hostile detachment or, in the event of its escape, to destroy the town in order to prevent its use as a hostile rendezvous on the flank of the allied line of communications during the winter. It was also decided that the total strength of the expedition should be 3,600 men and that each of the five powers should furnish a quota proportioned to the strength of its garrison in Tientsin. On this basis, the American contingent was fixed at two companies of the 15th Infantry—C Company under the command of Capt. James A. Maney and D Company under the command of First Lieut. John McA. Palmer. These two companies were to form a provisional battalion under the command of Maj. Edgar B. Robertson.

The expedition under the command of General Dorward was to march toward Tiu-liu in three columns the morning of September 9th. We were assigned to the right, or Canal Column, a force about 900 strong, which was to follow a great bend in the Grand Canal. It was ordered to march as follows:

Advance Guard

A detachment of Bengal Lancers
A company of the First Madras Pioneers

Main Body

A company of the First Sikhs
Two companies, 15th U.S. Infantry
Three companies of Italian infantry (Bersaglieri)

Rear Guard

A company of Punjab infantry.

The center column, 1,200 strong, and the left column, 1,500 strong, were to cut across the great bend of the canal so as to attack Tiu-liu from the left and rear. They comprised Japanese, Russian, Italian, and British infantry supported by artillery.

General Dorward with his staff was to accompany the Canal Column using a cabin boat as headquarters. The supplies for the Canal Column, with a Japanese detachment of heavy artillery, were to follow in canal boats.

Early on the morning of September 9, with Cowan, my second lieutenant, I marched at the head of D Company for the rendezvous of the Canal Column west of the walled city. We were escorted by a Bengal Lancer who had been detailed by General Dorward as our guide. This picturesque warrior should have led us straight through the walled city, but he lost his way and took us across the canal to the north rampart of Tientsin. From there Cowan replaced our lancer as guide and finally conducted us to the canal, where we saw the Canal Column forming on the *opposite* bank. This unexpected development did not delay us long, however. Cowan, with the effective aid of a platoon of doughboys under Sergeant Sullivan, located a number of junks which were tied up at the bank and compelled their crews to ferry us across. Thanks to our early start from our quarters, we all got over the canal in time to take our proper place between the Sikhs and the Bersaglieri.

To march in such a column was a marvelous experience for the American doughboy of that day. His younger brothers of this generation who have served in every part of the globe can have no conception of the dreamlike quality of that experience. After generations of isolation, the doors of the wide world had at last begun to open. It then seemed unbelievable to boys bred in Illinois and Kansas and New Hampshire that they were carrying the American flag along the Grand Canal of China with Sikhs from India marching ahead of them and Italians with rooster feathers in their hats behind them. Off to the right Japanese soldiers in the artillery junks hailed us with the friendly cry, "Merikee, Merikee." Off to the left a flanking detachment of Bengal Lancers picked its way through the swampy ground. The stately Sikhs with their long and slender bare legs made a great impression upon our men. In the ranks just behind me I heard Private Wendling say: "I bet them Sikhs can sing." When Private Flaherty asked, "Why?" he replied, "Coz' they have legs like mocking birds."

We marched on the dike or levee along the bank of the canal. For the first four miles the trail was wide enough for a column of twos. After that the path narrowed, and it was necessary to march in a column of files. This caused a considerable elongation of the column and added greatly to the fatigue of the men, who were already oppressed by the intense heat of the day.

Such narrow trails in most countries would indicate a sparse population, but this was not the case along the Grand Canal of China. There, most heavy burdens were carried by coolies bearing shoulder yokes or by Chinese wheelbarrows equipped with great wheels which can follow the narrowest trails.

At about noon the main body of the Canal Column reached the outskirts of a village where it was expected to halt for the night. While we were waiting assignment to a campsite, the men were instructed to remove their packs and to rest by the side of the trail. Finally, one of General Dorward's staff officers led us to a large compound which surrounded the village joss house, or pagoda. The pagoda itself was occupied by General Dorward and his staff. Here, as everywhere else, we were given the best campsite and every other consideration by our British commander. Soon we had shelter tents up and the company kitchens established. Near us were the Bengal Lancers, the Sikhs and the Madras Pioneers. The Bersaglieri were encamped on the opposite side of the central pagoda. The compound presented a lively picture. American doughboys, English tommies, Sikhs from India and Italian Bersaglieri soon found that they were brothers under the skin.

After the men were settled in camp, Major Robertson with his adjutant, Jerry Lynch, and his two company commanders went to call upon General Dorward. He received us in the pagoda. He had no chairs for his guests but found seats for us between the joss house idols which occupied a bench against one of the walls. There was just room for one of his visitors between each two of the Chinese gods. In such celestial company, conversation was a bit stiff until a tall turbaned Hindu orderly came in with Scotch and cigarettes.

The morning of September 10 we broke camp at daybreak and crossed the canal on a bridge of boats. My company acted as rear guard that day. Since the canal was really a crooked canalized river, to save a long march around a great bend we followed a trail straight across country for about three miles. The country was fertile and intensely cultivated. It astonished me, a native of the Illinois corn belt, to march for more than a mile between two of the finest fields of Indian corn that I ever saw. We passed several Chinese villages and here we learned the secret of the soil's fertility. Each village is surrounded by compost heaps where every bit of organic refuse is kept throughout the year to fertilize next year's crop. As the principal ingredient of each compost heap was the village's carefully conserved night soil, we were able to smell each settlement long before its mud huts came into view.

During this cross-country march, "D" Company did a bit of foraging. Near each village there were fruitful gardens and Mess Sergeant Flanagan with his kitchen police and their coolie assistants harvested a rich crop of melons, radishes, lettuce, plums, and persimmons. When the sergeant displayed his spoils at one of our halts, Maj. W. H. Corbusier, our medical officer, interfered. He pointed out that fresh fruits and vegetables growing in or immediately on the Chinese soil might well be infected with cholera or other Asiatic scourges. When he pointed out that these gardens were located so as to catch the drainage from the noisome village compost heaps, even Sergeant Flanagan saw the point. After throwing his melons, radishes, and lettuce into the canal, he turned to the doctor and said: "But how about the plums and persimmons?" To this Corbusier replied: "They're probably safe, Sergeant. I don't see how even a Chinaman could infect the branches of a plum tree even if he tried—unless he happened to be nine or ten feet tall."

During our first halt after getting back to the bank of the Grand Canal, the Center Column marched by on the opposite side of the stream. There they were: English Tommies, British-Indians, Russians, Japanese, and Italians. It was a marvelous moving picture of foreign soldiery for us untravelled American doughboys. We saw this picture from the front seats, for the canal was narrow here and the pageant was less than fifty yards away. In fact, we were within hailing distance and there was a continued exchange of pleasantries between the two columns. As the Japanese passed us, they again hailed us with a friendly "Merikee! Merikee!" Our Sikhs exchanged battle cries with their Rajput and Baluchi friends. Our Bersaglieri exchanged excited Latin greetings with their countrymen. Between us and this military pageant was the ever-shifting commerce of the Grand Canal. Junks and barges floating downstream toward the Hai Ho; strings of coolies towing other vessels upstream toward the Hwang Ho.

At this halt, rumors came from the front. The Boxers were ready to give us a hard fight at Tiu-liu. They had mounted cannon on the walls of the town. Our allied artillery which had marched with the Left Column was said to be hopelessly stuck in the mud too far to the rear to do any good. We were ordered to proceed to a bend in the Grand Canal two miles ahead. From there we would be able to see the walls of Tiu-liu and there receive our orders for the attack in support of the Center Column. As we approached the bend, we were eager for the fight; perhaps the 15th Infantry would win a little glory to match that of the 9th and 14th. We expected to hear artillery fire any moment but there was not a sound. When we arrived at the bend and closed up our ranks we could see Tiu-liu scarcely three miles away. What appeared to the naked eye as Boxer banners, however, when studied through our field glasses proved to be four British flags which the Bengal Lancers had hoisted when they found that the Boxers had pulled out without a fight. With our glasses we could also make out crowds of people fleeing from the town to escape us foreign devils. Later we learned that the Bengal Lancers had hoisted British flags on all the Tiu-liu pawnshops. From their wide experience in Oriental warfare they knew that (except portable valuables that could be carried by the refugees on their persons) all valuable loot would be stored behind the barred doors of the pawnshops.

That a formidable force of Boxers had retreated without a fight was the official story. But it is my private opinion that there were never any Boxers there at all. From all that I could see in my humble position as a company commander, Tiu-liu was simply a Chinese trading town whose peaceful inhabitants were frightened almost to death by a savage horde of foreign devils, which included Company D, 15th U.S. Infantry, commanded by First Lieutenant John McA. Palmer.

While we were awaiting orders at the bend, it began to rain. Finally one of General Dorward's staff officers came with the information that we were to be quartered in Tiu-liu for the night and that he would guide us to our billets. Under his guidance we had the good fortune to enter the town before the troops of the Center and Left Columns poured in. C and D Companies were each assigned a large compound on one side of the street with a smaller compound for Major Robertson and his officers in between. We were glad to find that the Anglo-Indian troops of the Canal Column had already moved into several similar compounds across the way. Apparently we were to have a quiet little Anglo-American neighborhood of our own.

When I marched D Company into its compound we were delighted with our billet. There was a great warehouse big enough for the whole company, and several roomy outbuildings along the compound walls. After stacking arms where the men were sheltered from the rain and assigning one of the outbuildings as the company kitchen, I left the men under the senior line sergeant with instructions to keep them near their weapons until Cowan and I and the first sergeant could make an inspection of our whole billet.

First we went into the big warehouse and found it dry, well-ventilated, and big enough to form a comfortable dormitory for the whole company. Along one of the walls were smaller rooms. Two of these I set off as the first sergeant's quarters and orderly room and assigned the others as quarters for the other sergeants. While I was making these arrangements, Cowan called my attention to some great piles of jute matting against one of the walls of the main room. I authorized the first sergeant to issue enough of these to the men so that each man could have a mattress between his blankets and the brick floor and instructed him to collect them all and replace them in a pile against the wall immediately after reveille the next morning.

After these arrangements were made I went out and called the men to attention. It occurred to me that when the Japanese and Russian contingents entered the town there would be the usual orgy of loot and destruction. So I reminded the men that they were American citizens, as well as soldiers, and that it was against our principles as well as our Army Regulations for any officer or man in the American uniform to appropriate any private property to his own use. We were authorized to take what was strictly needed for military purposes, but that whatever we took, we took for the military service of the United States and not for ourselves. The men were then turned over to the first sergeant, who marched them into their temporary barracks. By this time the kitchens were established and D Company's compound was filled with the fragrance of coffee and sizzling bacon.

As Cowan and I were about to leave the D Company compound to seek our own billets, he went into one of the small outbuildings, where a number of large masonry jars were ranged along the wall. When he removed the cover of one of these jars, he beckoned to me and I was surprised to find that these innocent vessels contained enough villainous Chinese gin to give every man in D Company a glorious jag. Cowan solved this problem by applying a Chinese sledgehammer to the bottom of each jar, with the result that all the fragrant liquor disappeared in the gravel of the compound. This operation was unobserved by the men of the company, for they were all busy fixing their jute bed mattresses for the night. The behavior of the men of D Company was exemplary throughout the whole Tiu-liu campaign. So far as I know (except for a few chickens and ducks which they borrowed on occasions) they all respected their company commander's injunction in regard to the looting of private property. It probably is just as well, though, that Lieutenant Cowan discovered that Chinese gin before Private Wendling and his brethren happened upon it.

When we finally left the company compound we found that we were not to have the quiet Anglo-American neighborhood that we expected. Our narrow street happened to be one of the main thoroughfares through the town. And now a Russian column was marching through in one direction and a column of Italians and Japanese in another. Outrages were already beginning. Except at the compounds covered by the American and British flags, fatigue parties were tearing down houses and breaking captured furniture to get fuel. Dignified soldiers from the northwest frontier of India were exercising the traditional rights of Mohammedan warriors. Here were all the evils of an international military force with no effective international command to control it.

All this time it was raining and there was cursing in every language. Once a polyglot crowd of hungry soldiers chased a Chinese pig through the crowd. Every available bayonet gave him a thrust as he went by. Finally he was killed by a warrior who did not start the chase. That created a small but serious international incident. Before blood began to flow, and before Cowan and I could intervene, a Russian officer and an Italian officer broke in to restore order, but not until the Russian had laid about him with his knout and the Italian with the flat of his sword.

Just as we were about to enter our billets we heard ear-piercing shrieks from two coolies who were being dragged along by their queues. According to their captors, three Chinese soldiers of the British Hong Kong regiment, they were to be executed as Boxer spies. On closer scrutiny, we found that the two alleged spies were our private servants. We rescued them with great difficulty with the assistance of three Sikhs who recognized us as their comrades in the Canal Column. No doubt many of the alleged Boxers who were executed in North China were as innocent as these poor devils.

Late in the afternoon, Jerry Lynch and I took a walk to the part of the town we had marched through earlier in the day. We found it entirely gutted. Everything valuable had been taken out of the houses and what was not looted was broken in pieces. Some of the foreign soldiers, drunk with Chinese liquor, had been very brutal. Our medical officer, Corbusier, did what he could to treat a number of Chinamen who were brought to our billets with broken arms and legs and one with a bayonet wound in his abdomen. Another part of the town was already in flames and crowds of poor homeless wretches were finding their way into the country. They set out with heavy bundles of household goods on their backs. But in most cases, these were seized by foreign soldiers who after taking out what they wanted trampled the rest of the bundle in the mud. With the looting once started, the Chinese lower classes began to loot the homes of their former masters.

In the course of our walk we met our friend, Major Monocle of General Dorward's staff, who exclaimed: "Oh, I say Jerry, we are well met. I have been looking for you all over this blasted town. General Dorward has appointed a board to divide up the loot that we found in the pawnshops. He thinks that you American chaps should have your share so he wants Major Robertson to detail two officers to represent the American contingent.

To this Jerry replied: "As Major Robertson's adjutant, I hereby detail Lieutenant Palmer and Lieutenant Lynch as the American members of the board."

Major Monocle was delighted with this prompt action and suggested that we should go with him at once to one of the captured pawnshops, where the board was already in session. It was with great reluctance that I protested, "But, Jerry, we cannot do that. Our regulations do not recognize any appropriation of private property except for strictly military purposes."

When Major Monocle finally grasped the point he smiled and said: "Oh I see, but I will fix that. I am a member of the board. When I explain this technical defect in your Army Regulations to the other fellows, they will accept me informally as the American representative. I will see that you chaps get your share when we get back to Tientsin."

And Major Monocle kept his word. When we got back to Tientsin each American officer who took part in the Tiu-liu campaign received a bundle from the major. This was the only loot that I acquired in the Boxer campaign. It was not very valuable, for Tiu-liu was not a rich city and the treasures found in the pawnshops proved to be disappointing. In fact, they were hardly worth the initiative of the Bengal Lancers in giving them the protection of the British flag. When Maude finally saw my spoils of war she disposed of most of them by filing them in the wastepaper basket. But she retained a small bolt of pink silk with the imperial seal woven in it. With this she upholstered and cushioned some antique chairs which for many years graced her living room. There were also one or two pitiful bits of embroidery which were converted into doilies. She also kept a dress which had probably been worn on a gala occasion by some Chinese peasant woman. This Maude kept for a daughter she might one day have. Some eighteen years after that daughter finally arrived, she wore that peasant woman's dress as the hit of a fancy dress party. And there was one real curio. It was a cheap print showing the interior of an humble Chinese dining room. It was made when Chinese artists were just beginning to put perspective in their pictures. In the middle of the picture there was a foreshortened dining table. But the foreshortening was in reverse. Instead of narrowing from front to rear, this table widened.

During the night of September 10th orders were issued for most of the allied troops, including the American contingent, to return to Tientsin. Early the following morning we left Tiu-liu with instructions to pass the night in the vicinity of Ho-chang about nine miles away near the east bank of the Grand Canal. As the weather was hot, we were ordered to march light and to put all baggage, including the men's packs, on canal boats which should reach Ho-chang in advance of the troops. The mess sergeants of C and D Companies each established his company kitchen, with his "kitchen police" and their attendant coolies, on a roomy canal boat. So we expected to have a hot dinner awaiting us on our arrival at Ho-chang.

Our column was under the command of Lieutenant Colonel Cooke-Collis of the British Army. It comprised, in their order of march, Anglo-Indian, American, Russian, and Japanese troops (except the Japanese artillery, which was ordered to march with the Italian troops in another column further to the right). Another detachment under the command of Brigadier General Richardson of the British Army was left behind "to destroy the village of Tiu-liu except the two pawn shops." General Richardson's detachment was to comprise British troops only and included units of Bengal Lancers, Royal Horse Artillery, Mounted Sappers, the 34th Punjab Pioneers, the First Madras Pioneers, and the First Chinese Regiment (Hong Kong). In the column ahead of us were companies of the 24th Punjab Infantry, the 26th Baluchistan Regiment, and the 7th Rajputs. Behind us came the Russian and the Japanese infantries. When we finally got under way, clouds of smoke were already rising above the doomed town.

When we got to Ho-chang about noon we were assigned a camping place with the Baluchis in a fine grove of shade trees surrounded by a brick wall. In the center of the grove was a well of cold water. While the Baluchis were pitching camp and preparing to cook their dinner, we poor Americans stood around without tents, rations, or blankets. Everything we had, including our dinner, was on canal boats and our canal boats had failed to arrive. The Baluchi canal boats also had failed to arrive, but they, like all the other troops except the Americans, had a little train of pack mules to meet emergencies.

When I went down to the canal to check up on our boats, I found the water very low. The natives had cut a dike upstream from Ho-chang, with the result that the water that should have borne our canal boats was flooding the country. Many British canal boats had come through Ho-chang before the water gave out, but many others, including all of the American boats, had run aground several miles upstream. Later, I learned that the mess sergeants of C and D Companies might have brought the American supply fleet through if they had not overdone their plans to give us a good dinner. In order to surprise us with a record-breaking menu including ducks, fresh pork, and fruit, they had stopped off to do a bit of foraging. When they got back to the canal with their prizes they found their whole fleet in dry dock on the muddy banks of a stream which had dwindled to a little trickle a few yards wide and a few inches deep.

If our men were hungry they were even more humiliated. Why shouldn't we Americans have a train of pack mules like the Baluchis? In the streets of Tientsin our army wagons with their four- and six-mule teams were fine transportation but they were of no use at all on the narrow trails of the Chinese countryside. No doubt American pack mules had come to China from the Philippines but, if so, they were all with General Chaffee's command up at Peking.

But if the men of D Company were humiliated, their company commander was even more so. He now realized that he might have formed a crew of Chinese carriers even more effective than the Baluchis' pack mules. Ever since our first night's camp at the pagoda, Chinese peasants had come to us for protection. My mess sergeant had enrolled enough of them to relieve the company of kitchen police and fatigue duty. I might easily have formed a corps of porters from these people. If I had paid them current agricultural wages, about five cents per man per day, it would have been a small drain on the company fund. But it would not have been necessary to pay them. The poor devils were half-starved and would have been glad to serve for their "chow." A sufficient crew of Chinese carriers would have subsisted in luxury on the refuse of the D Company kitchen. In fact the scrapings from Private Wendling's mess tin would have been a banquet for any one of them. But they wanted the protection of Uncle Sam more than they wanted wages or food. When we turned them away at the pagoda most of them were drafted by less indulgent masters.

So when I saw the men of D Company lounging around that compound without food or shelter tents or blankets, I felt that I had let them down when a little forethought on my part would have made them comfortable. I heard no word of complaint, but their very patience and silence was the most severe reprimand in my whole military career. An officer can forget a reprimand from a superior officer, but the memory of a failure to serve the men who rely upon him will never leave him.

Meanwhile we looked on hungrily while the Baluchis prepared their midday meal. Their mess equipment and emergency ration were marvels of simplicity and mobility. Their kitchen range was a single sheet of steel plate about three feet long and two feet wide. Each of these steel plates was supported about a foot above the ground by earth and stones. A small fire under it kept it hot enough to cook two of their big pancakes at a time. Each of these pancakes was a circle about a foot in diameter. When it was brown on both sides it was rolled and each of these rolls was a good square meal for one soldier. There must have been a dozen of these ranges in operation throughout the grove and in a little while there were enough rolled pancakes for every officer and man in this battalion of the 26th Baluchistan Infantry.

But these Baluchi pancakes were not for the Baluchis. When they were done a detachment under a turbaned sergeant came over and issued a hot rolled pancake to every officer and man in the American contingent. We were surprised only because we did not realize that these warriors were followers of Mohammed and that no true believer can dine when there are hungry guests within his gates. And were those pancakes good! If any survivor of the Tiu-liu campaign should read this he will agree with me that the Baluchis gave him the best meal that he ever ate.

The Baluchi kitchens were busy all afternoon. After providing for their guests, the cooks made another batch of pancakes for their own battalion. They cooked another double round for the evening meal and still another for breakfast next morning. But during the afternoon they had eager assistants. The doughboys of C and D Companies served as volunteer kitchen police for their Baluchi friends. They rustled firewood and kept the fires going. They even spelled the cooks. I can still see Private Wendling pouring batter and rolling pancakes while his Mohammedan mentor took time off to enjoy some American cigarettes. There was never a gayer afternoon. Toward sunset, we observed a dramatic rite performed by the Baluchis. In the center of the camp a priest stood up and in a loud musical voice chanted something that we could not understand. Then all over the camp the others joined in the refrain, turned their faces toward Mecca, and prostrated themselves for an instant. Then there was another shrill cry and they resumed their tasks.

But the hospitality of our Anglo-Indian friends had only begun. As the boats of a field hospital had reached Ho-chang before the water gave out, the chief of the British medical staff was able to lend us enough tents and blankets for both companies. This was a great comfort for our half-clad, blanketless men, as it grew quite cold after the sun went down. I slept that night in the tent of Captain Poor of the Baluchis. As my blanket roll was on one of the missing boats and as I had issued all of the British hospital blankets to my men before I thought of one for myself, I prepared myself for a cold night. But as I lay there shivering, Captain Poor covered me with his military greatcoat. So, for one night, I wore the insignia of Victoria, Queen of Great Britain and Ireland and Empress of India. Thus, without any formal alliance, and forty-four years before Ike Eisenhower landed an Anglo-American army in France, I learned that these British soldiers were our brethren in arms.

When morning came, Major Robertson authorized me to stay at Ho-chang with D Company long enough to return the British blankets and tents to the hospital boats. This enabled the Baluchis and C Company to march off on time. When I got down to the canal with the first load of hospital supplies, I found that the stream was again in full flow. The Anglo-Indian Sappers left at

Tiu-liu had mended the dike during the night. While I was standing there our company mess boats arrived. As C Company had already marched, I stopped the boats only long enough to supplement D Company's Baluchi pancake breakfast with hot coffee and to give each man a noonday sandwich and a canteen of boiled water. By hard marching we would be back to our quarters in Tientsin in the early afternoon.

After loading the British boats and finishing our other Ho-chang chores, D Company took up its march for home with the British medical staff riding just ahead of us. As we passed along the cobbled street of a small village, I heard cries and shouts from the rear. Looking back I saw the men of D Company breaking to either side of the road while a jackass in pursuit of a jenny came charging down the center of the highway. As Cowan and I hastily got out of the way, I was amazed to see that Private Wendling was mounted precariously on the jackass with his arms around the amorous creature's neck. Having routed D Company, the jack and jenny kept on their way and charged the group of mounted Britishers just ahead of us. These cavaliers got out of the way just in time and a moment later Private Wendling was thrown to the ground while his mount disappeared in a kaoliang field in pursuit of his ladylove.

No doubt the chief of the medical staff was surprised at this manifestation of unconventional American initiative. But if so, his first reaction was that of a good surgeon in the presence of a prospective patient. He immediately dismounted and went to Wendling, who still lay on the ground. Fortunately he found no bones broken. When Wendling finally came to and scrambled to his feet, the surgeon assured me that my soldier would be able to get back to Tientsin under his own power. He then remounted and said, "If you don't mind, Palmer, we will trot on and gain a bit of road space ahead of you and your astonishing Americans." Thereupon, I placed Wendling in arrest in the custody of the first sergeant and announced that I would investigate his case at the first halt.

When we finally halted, I found a drove of thirty or forty mules, jacks, jennies, and gelt-asses carefully herded just in rear of my company. They were of every size and color. There were one or two proud stud jacks such as the one that Private Wendling had recently ridden and these were little grey ones about the size of the burros down on the Mexican border. They were all in good voice and, as I had learned in my Arizona days, the little fellows of the genus *asinus* could outbray any of their larger brethren. It took me some time and the examination of several witnesses before I could arrive at an explanation of how this collection of animals came to be in our rear.

Here is the story in a nutshell. When the men of D Company got to Ho-chang without blankets or rations and learned that their canal boats were stuck in the mud away up the Grand Canal, they were hungry but they were even more humiliated. When they saw that the Baluchis, with the aid of a few pack mules, could be comfortable even under such conditions, they were ashamed that soldiers of Uncle Sam should be so helpless.

Then Private Wendling or some other ingenious soul proposed a practical remedy. He reminded them of my lecture on looting that night at Tiu-liu. They had played the game with me and had taken no private property. But they remembered what I said about seizing things that were needed for the military service. And didn't their experience at Ho-chang prove that Uncle Sam's 15th Infantry needed pack mules? Accordingly, while we were guests of the Baluchis, and while detachments were reloading the British hospital boats, other self-appointed detachments had scoured the country and gathered in every long-eared brayer they could find.

They did not take me or Lieutenant Cowan or the first sergeant into their confidence. I suspect that they wanted to keep their enterprise from the knowledge of their company commander until they brought their herd of future pack animals back to Tientsin as a *fait accompli*. In order to herd their jackasses on the march without noticeably depleting the ranks of the company, they also drafted enough coolies to act as herders under the capable supervision of Private Wendling and one or two other kindred spirits. This, of course, was a mere incident in their general plan of procuring much-needed field transportation for the American military service. In fact, they might have kept the enterprise from me if Wendling had not tried to use one of his prospective pack animals as a private mount. Even then, everything might have gone well if that fascinating little jenny had not pranced coquettishly in front of him.

Here was a delicate problem for the commander of D Company to solve. The first solution that occurred to me was restitution. I would return the captured jackasses to their owners. But this would require D Company to march back to Ho-chang instead of obeying existing orders to return to Tientsin. And even if we marched back to Ho-chang, how would it be possible to find the owners? Then it occurred to me that we might send the jackasses back in the custody of the coolies who had been drafted as herdsmen. When this idea was finally interpreted to the coolies, there were loud cries of protest. They did not want to go back to the short rations and insecurity of Ho-chang. They wanted to go to Tientsin where they would have ample chow and light labor under the protection of their friends, the doughty warriors of D Company. In fact, the world never saw such contented captives. Freedom was the last thing that they wanted. They did not agree with Patrick Henry in preferring death to life without liberty.

As restitution was out of the question, it was evidently a case for military justice. Private Wendling and his associates had raided a whole countryside. It was evidently their company commander's duty to prefer charges against them and bring them before a court-martial. But that solution also presented difficulties. When brought before the court, the culprits would plead their company commander's lecture on looting at Tiu-liu. He had told them that they could not take private property for their own use, but it was lawful to take what was needed in the military service. And God knows that their regiment needed pack animals. In these circumstances, Private Wendling et al., would be acquitted, but the proceedings would reveal that the culprit was their company commander. In his hurried lecture on looting, he had neglected to explain that the right of seizure could be lawfully exercised only under the orders of superior military authority. In ignorance of this highly pertinent limitation, the men of D Company had simply exercised the initiative of practical soldiers.

When I submitted this difficulty to my second in command, Frenchy Cowan, he simply doubled up with laughter. When he finally recovered his composure, he endorsed my final solution. We agreed that even if they had exceeded their lawful powers, Private Wendling and his associates had acted in good faith in what they conceived to be the public interest. So we would simply march on to Tientsin with our asinine captives and let the regimental quartermaster take them up on his returns as government property. As it took some time to march through the crowded streets of the walled city with our four-legged impedimenta, we did not get back to the Methodist compound until after dark. Then, remembering the biblical injunction that "sufficient unto the day is the evil thereof," I decided not to report to the quartermaster until morning. So we tied our jacks to one end of the regimental picket line and our jennies to the other, "borrowed" a bit of quartermaster hay for them, and called it a day.

The notes of reveille next morning were followed by a sonorous refrain from our picket line. This music awakened everybody in the foreign concession from Taku Road to the Bund. When Capt. W. F. Blauvelt hurried to the picket line, he was the maddest regimental quartermaster in the U.S. Army. When I explained the situation to him, he said he'd "be damned if he would take up a lot of worthless jackasses on his return." He also threatened to prefer charges, not against Private Wendling, but against me. Just then Colonel Moale, who had been awakened from his beauty sleep, came down to the picket line with Edmund Wittenmyer, his adjutant. As the colonel was a gouty old gentleman that morning, he was a bit testy at first. But when he finally got the whole story out of me, it appealed to his sense of humor. Blauvelt never did take up my jackasses on his property returns. When I visited the corral a few days later, they had disappeared. How he got rid of them, I never knew. As to Private Wendling, a few days after our return I promoted him to the grade of corporal. He had proved himself to be a natural leader, and as natural leaders are sure to lead either "for" or "agin" the government, I decided to take him up in the official hierarchy of command. This proved to be a sound decision. When I last heard of him, some years later, he was serving as a sergeant in the Philippines.

On the 27th of September, 1900, it became my turn to escort a fleet of supply junks up the Hai Ho. It would be a long tedious journey, but I welcomed the assignment because from T'ung-Hsien, the head of navigation, I would have a chance to visit Peking. My fleet comprised twelve river junks, each one thirty or forty feet long. The military freight was packed in a hold amidships. At the stern of each boat was a tiny cockpit where the Chinese crew, a pilot and six coolies, had their crowded quarters. As admiral of the fleet, I established my headquarters in a shelter tent, amidships, on the deck of the leading junk. Two of my soldiers occupied a single shelter tent ahead of the mast near the bow. The detachment cook with his coolie kitchen police and two soldiers were assigned to the second junk. Each of the others carried two soldiers as guards. Each ship in the fleet flew a small American flag at the top of its mast. This was to warn the "Rooshians," the "Prooshians," and our other allies that this ship had been duly preempted by Uncle Sam.

Early in the morning we sailed from the Tientsin Bund. Two tugboats towed my flotilla until we passed the walled city. There the tugboats dropped us and we proceeded upstream under our own power. From a towpath along shore, six coolies towed each junk by means of a long rope attached to the top of the mast, while the pilot manned the rudder and kept the bow of his vessel off shore. Presently the river widened and as a breeze blew up from the south, each junk hoisted its big square sail and its coolies came aboard from the towpath. So we went on up the Hai Ho, towing where the river was swift and narrow and sailing when it widened into long, lake-like stretches. The view back from the flagship when the whole fleet was under sail presented a most vivid picture.

After sundown we tied up our junks for the night. The cook built his fire on the shore and prepared our supper. But while our bacon and beans and coffee were cooking, the pilot and the six coolies squatted on the deck near my shelter tent and filled their bellies with rice which had been simmering all day on a little charcoal burner near the stern. As their chopsticks propelled their food from their bowls into their mouths there was a continued chorus of the hisses and belches with which a courteous and grateful Chinese coolie expresses satisfaction with his food. I had intended to dine alone in my quarters on deck, but the eloquent gustatory noises of the crew and the odor of their unwashed bodies were too close to my shelter tent. So I took my cup and mess tin ashore and dined with my fellow Christians of D Company near the detachment's kitchen fire.

Next morning after an early breakfast we resumed our journey and soon arrived at Yang-ts'un. Here a bridge of boats replaced the steel railroad bridge which had been destroyed by the Boxer army on its retreat from Tientsin to Peking. It took some time for the Russian guards to pass my fleet through the bridge and while waiting, I visited the camp of a detachment of the 6th U.S. Cavalry, which was stationed at Yang-ts'un as a guard post on General Chaffee's line of communications.

After leaving Yang-ts'un, instead of returning to the crowded quarters of my flagship, I walked ahead of my fleet along the towpath. Every mile or two I passed a crowded village of mud huts where the stench of the municipal compost heap was overwhelming. How the Chinese peasants could live and thrive in such surroundings seemed incomprehensible—especially as with more than a million of their countrymen, they used the river both as a source of drinking water and a sewer. After a walk of several hours the river again grew wide enough for sailing, so I reembarked. About sunset that evening as we tied up at the bank for the night, an immense flight of wild ducks passed high above us. For at least an hour, it extended from horizon to horizon. I did not realize that there were so many ducks in the whole world.

Early the next morning we passed Ho-Hsi-Wu, where Company C of the 9th U.S. Infantry was in camp. There we saw a long file of Cossacks riding along on the opposite side of the river. That afternoon I walked across a great bend with a sergeant and another soldier. As we approached each village all the inhabitants fled. They were in great terror, as they had learned to dread all foreign soldiers. That evening we had our first glimpse of the distant mountains which lie to the north of Peking.

At about noon on the 30th of September we tied up at Ma-tou-chen where a company of the 14th U.S. Infantry was in camp. There I had lunch with Capt. Frank F. Eastman, the commanding officer. By this time we were not far from T'ung-Hsien. But the water was now so low and there were so many tortuous channels that it was not until late in the morning of October 2nd that we tied up at the U.S. Army supply base. It had taken us almost a week, by the winding river, to cover an air-line distance of less than one hundred miles from Tientsin.

After reporting my arrival to Capt. Thomas Franklin, the base quartermaster, I asked him for transportation to Peking. To this he replied: "Nothing doing, old man. General Chaffee is here now. He is mad as hell because his winter supplies are arriving so slowly. He knows you are here and has just issued orders for you to take your junks back to Tientsin just as soon as I can unload them. You will just about have time to take lunch with me before you start back." Just then General Chaffee's aide-de-camp entered Franklin's office. As he happened to be my classmate, former roommate, and close friend Julian R. Lindsey, I asked him to intercede for me. If the general would let me go to Peking just for the afternoon, I would start back down the river early the next morning. Julian did his best for me but the commanding general of the American Expeditionary Force was adamant and my fleet started back down the Hai Ho that afternoon. So after I had traveled halfway round the world to within ten miles of Peking, that hardboiled old warrior Chaffee sent me back to Tientsin without a glimpse of the ancient city.

With our unladen junks we made good time going downstream. As there was moonlight we did not tie up until about eight o'clock. The next day we reached Ma-tou-chen before noon. There I picked up three Japanese infantry soldiers as passengers. As we went down the river I saw a pig standing on a sand bar about four hundred yards ahead. One of my Japanese passengers asked me if he could take a shot at it. To my surprise, his bullet caught the beast just back of its head and killed it instantly. We then halted long enough to take our supply of meat on board. One of my D company men had been a farmer and understood the art of dressing pork. He hung the pig over the side of the boat so that the intestines could fall into the river. Our Chinese coolies howled with despair when that catastrophe occurred and one of them jumped into the river to recover the offal. The coolies rarely had meat with their rice and to them, pig guts were a rare luxury. That night each of my eighty-four coolies had bits of animal food in his rice bowl.

We passed Ho-Hsi-Wu about sunset. After tying up for the night, just at dusk, I hailed a boat manned by American artillary soldiers on its way upstream. They told me that their commanding officer, Lieutenant Summerall, was on a boat behind them. I kept on the lookout for him and when it became too dark to see, I challenged every passing boat by crying out, "Summerall!" Finally somebody cried from the darkness, "Who is that?" to which I replied: "Palmer of the Class of '92." Thereupon, Pelot moored his boat alongside mine and we had a class reunion for two or three hours until he resumed his journey upstream. Summerall was already a distinguished soldier. He had fought at Tientsin and Peking with Reilly's famous light battery and had taken command when Reilly was killed.

Except for my unexpected visit with Summerall, my river trip was very lonely. For the first time in weeks I had had time to think of the future. A letter written to Maude, on the way down the river, lies before me as I write and brings those lonely hours back to me. In the first place I was homesick for her and our boy. While at T'ung Hsien, Lindsay had told me that the headquarters of the 15th Infantry and our 1st Battalion would go to the Philippines in the near future. The 3rd Battalion was already there. The 2nd Battalion was still in the States and would come to the Philippines before too long. As some officers' families were already in Manila, I suggested to her that in a little while she and John might join me there. There was also the thought that I would like to leave the army when things quieted down in the Philippines. Perhaps I might get a job as a professor of mathematics in some small college. There I would have time to study the history of our military institutions. As I expressed it in my letter, "Indeed, I think I can repay the government better for my education by writing a book on a sound American military system than I can by escorting junks on the Hai Ho and sleeping under a shelter tent within ten feet of a half dozen lousy Chinese coolies." I was beginning to grasp the full import of my Grandfather Palmer's belief that a *government by the people* should rest its defense upon an *army of the people.*

Below Ho-Hsi-Wu my fleet made good speed toward Tientsin. As the river widened, our sails reinforced the speed of the current. We passed through the

Russian bridge at Yang-ts'un the afternoon of October 4th. As we sailed by the walled city the afternoon of the 5th we saw the handsome houseboat of the Imperial Chinese Viceroy, Li Hung Chang, moored near the eastern gate of the city. We tied up at the Tientsin Bund a little later and by sunset we were back at our quarters in the Methodist compound. There I found several letters from Maude filled with news of John, the last one written a few days before his sixth birthday.

Early the morning of October 25 I was ordered to make another journey up the Hai Ho, but this time I would travel in state and would have a chance to visit Peking. With six enlisted men of my company I was to escort the Chinese general, Tin, who was making an official visit to General Chaffee in Peking. The general, his military suite, and his escort would travel in a luxurious houseboat. Upon receipt of my orders I called upon General Tin and found that he desired to leave Tientsin on the 27th. During the day, I exchanged several signal corps telegrams with the headquarters at Peking and by supper-time I had made all necessary arrangements and had received a telegram of approval from General Chaffee's headquarters.

After supper, Mac Weeks, Jakie Moore, and Frenchy Cowan went to my room with me for a postprandial smoke. There were three telegrams and a letter on my desk. When I opened the first two telegrams and found that they were duplicates of others that had been acted on during the day, I postponed opening the third until later. When I announced that the letter was from Maude, my guests urged me to read it at once. It was written on John's sixth birthday and contained a snapshot of the youngster the morning of his first day in school. There was a grin on his face as he proudly carried his school-books and slate under his arm. My guests were almost as delighted with the picture as I was. They were all good friends of John's and had known him since we all had served together at Puerto Principe and later at Plattsburg Barracks. After reading portions of Maude's letter aloud, I opened the third telegram. It was a copy of a cablegram to General Chaffee from the War Department and read as follows:

Chaffee: Peking
Inform Palmer, 15th Infantry, his son died twenty-first, diphtheria. Wife well.

I did not accompany General Tin to Peking. When Colonel Moale learned about John's death, he felt that I should remain in Tientsin where Maude could reach me by cable. He therefore arranged for Cowan to make the trip up the river in my stead. A few days after he left, I received a delayed cable from Maude: "Do nothing until you hear from me."

It was impossible for me to grasp what the situation called for. My first impulse was to cable Maude to get ready to join me in the Philippines. But I found that the War Department had recently ordered that no more officers' families should go there. It is difficult to conceive my distress. For the next six weeks, I kept receiving letters written before the boy's illness, letters full of his boyish activities and his interest in school. Finally came one with an account of his illness and death. Then I realized, more than ever, how much harder Maude's lot was than mine. In my memory John was a merry little boy whom I should never see again. I had never gone through the losing battle of fighting for his life as she had. In the circumstances, I was inclined to resign from the army and find something to do in civil life. Meanwhile, the regiment's departure for the Philippines was delayed. Finally, on November 22, I received an order from General Chaffee's headquarters directing me, pursuant to cable instructions from the War Department, to report to the commanding officer, Fort Porter, New York, for duty. Fort Porter was the station of one of the companies of our 2d Battalion, which had recently been designated as the "home battalion" of the regiment. This meant that Maude could be with me for a while.

On November 27, 1900, I sailed from Taku for Nagasaki on the *California*, a chartered freighter which was returning empty after delivering military stores in China. After several days in Nagasaki, I boarded the transport *Grant*, en route to San Francisco. We had a stormy voyage across the North Pacific and passed through the Golden Gate the night before New Year's Day, 1901. As it was very late when we docked, I remained in my stateroom for the night. Early the next morning I was awakened by unusual and unnecessary noises as the deckhands shifted the steamer chairs and scrubbed down the deck. When I went to my stateroom door to protest, the leader of the working party turned to me and said; "We are not longer at sea, Lieutenant, we are in the U.S.A. where every son of a bitch is equal." As I pondered this comprehensive statement of democracy, I gently closed the door and returned to my berth. That afternoon, New Year's Day, I boarded the Overland Limited for Chicago. There my father and mother met me at the station. After a few hours with them, I went on down to Petersburg.

After a few days in Petersburg we proceeded to Buffalo, New York, where I reported to Lt. Benjamin H. Watkins, the commanding officer at Fort Porter. As Watkins was a second lieutenant and therefore my junior in rank, I automatically superseded him as commander of the post and of Company H of the 15th Infantry. A few weeks later I was promoted to the grade of captain and was formally assigned to H Company. As a portion of the company was on duty as a caretaking detachment at Fort Niagara, I commanded that post as well as Fort Porter. As neither post was fully garrisoned, many of its officers' quarters were occupied by the families of officers who were on duty in the Philippines. Maude and I moved into a small set of quarters where we resumed our lonely housekeeping. But lonely as we were, it was a comfort to be together again, if only for a little while. But our domestic outlook was most uncertain. In all probability I would go to the Philippines in the near future. It was doubtful if Maude's health would permit her to go with me.

A month or two after my arrival at Fort Porter, I published an illustrated article in the *New York Sunday Herald* under the title "Why Pan-America Must Be." Pan-America was pictured as a great commercial city at the western end of the ship canal which would one day connect the Atlantic and Pacific Oceans. In my prophecy, beautifully illustrated by the *Herald's* artist, the city stood at the western end of the canal just west of Lake Nicaragua. The prophecy as to the building of the canal was realized a few years later, but it was to be a Panama Canal and not a Nicaragua Canal and my Pan-America would bear the name of Balboa.

While at Fort Porter, I became acquainted with Louis L. Babcock, a prominent young lawyer of Buffalo. This was the beginning of a close and valued friendship. Babcock was greatly interested in military history and subsequently published a history of the War of 1812 on the Niagara frontier. For many years he served as president of the Buffalo Historical Society. He was an officer of the New York National Guard and was greatly interested in our military institutions. His advice as a lawyer, a historian, and a citizen soldier were invaluable to me in my effort to work out a military organization consistent with the needs of a modern democratic state.

On the 21st of May, 1901, with Louis Babcock and his wife, Maude and I attended the opening exercises of the great Pan American Exposition in Buffalo. The orator of the day was our new Vice President, Theodore Roosevelt. It was my first glimpse of him, and I was greatly impressed by his vital personality. He made an eloquent speech in which, while acclaiming our great material prosperity, he stressed the need for equally great moral reforms, a need which would soon confront him as President McKinley's successor. Conspicuous among the distinguished men on the platform was Sen. Mark Hanna. It struck me that the senator from Ohio received Teddy's address and the applause that followed it with singular imperturbability.

In July, my little command assembled at Fort Niagara for target practice. I marched from Fort Porter with the company while Maude went by train. We camped out in a vacant set of officers' quarters and took our meals with Lt. Gustave A. Wieser who commanded the Fort Niagara detachment of H Company. Our sojourn there was a real outing for Maude. She frequently accompanied me to the target range and we took long walks about the post. She was especially interested in old Fort Niagara, a stout masonry fortress which the British had built at the mouth of the Niagara River before the Revolutionary War. She accompanied me often to the wharf at the mouth of the river near the old fort. There I would fish for black bass while she would sit in a camp chair with a book. As the water was very deep, I used a heavy sinker to carry my crawfish bait down through the swift current. The fishing was good, but I could never induce Maude to try her hand at it. One day when I was suddenly called to the telephone in the wharf house, she very reluctantly dropped her book and held my rod for me. On my return she had become an ardent angler and refused to return my rod to me. Just after my departure, she had felt a tug on the line and suddenly found herself fighting a big bass. With the strong current to aid him, her prey almost pulled her off the dock, but she finally landed it with the aid of the sergeant in charge of the wharf. A few moments later, she landed another trophy unaided. Thereafter, I carried two rods when we visited the old fort, and thereafter she carried the crawfish can and left her book at home.

A few days after our return to Fort Porter, a War Department order directed me to report to the superintendent of the U.S. Military Academy, for assignment to duty as an instructor in the Department of Chemistry.

10

Instructor at West Point

On the morning of August 28th, 1901, I reported to Col. Albert L. Mills, the superintendent of the Military Academy, and to my new chief, Col. Samuel E. Tillman, the professor of chemistry. With these official visits out of the way, Maude pressed for a solution of our paramount domestic problem: where were we to live? We therefore visited the post quartermaster's office where we learned that quarters had been assigned me in one of the newly built double houses at the south end of the post. Armed with the front door key we immediately went to inspect our new home. It stood high above the main road to Highland Falls with its front windows looking across the Hudson toward the highland east of the river. The south half of the house was assigned to my classmate, Jim Jervey. Two other classmates, C. C. Jamieson and W. R. Smith, had quarters on the same row. Maude was delighted with her brand-new house. In a few days her curtains were up, her rugs down, and her furniture in place. In old Ellen, a tall, dignified West Indian mulatto, we had an excellent cook. Lonely as we were, for the first time since we left Fort Grant, we felt the security of a settled home. West Point would probably be my station for the next four years.

On the first day of September as my cadets marched into the recitation room, I was deeply conscious of my limitations as an instructor. I had stood fairly well in chemistry while a cadet, but with no postgraduate training I was ill prepared to teach that interesting science. Before the recitation, as prescribed by regulations, I asked my cadets if they had any questions for me. This gave one of them an opportunity to put a scientific poser to me—a time-honored trick to play on a new instructor. I did not have the slightest idea as to the answer, but I took the wind out of his sails by saying: "I don't know, Mr. Brown, but I'll look it up and let you know tomorrow morning." During the whole of my first year, I was hard put to it to keep ahead of my cadets. At the end of my tour of duty as an instructor I had obtained some knowledge of elementary chemistry. But the whole science has changed since those days when the atom was an indivisible unit. If one of my cadets had told me then that an atom is really a solar system with planets revolving about a central sun, he would have been "found deficient" in chemistry and could never have been a graduate of West Point. What a pity it is that our scientists could not let well enough alone. If they had stuck to the unfissionable atom, there would be no atom bomb today to threaten civilization.

I owe a great deal to my four years at West Point as a cadet, but I got much more education from my five years as an instructor. I had reached the age of thirty-one when, like most officers in the "old army," I was beginning to go to seed. During those five years I had to work harder than any of my cadets and was required to check my knowledge by passing it on to others. This gave me a new intellectual awakening. Also, among my cadets I found some of the most valued friends in my whole army career. They were all young then but now they have all passed the retiring age. Among the chemistry students of that time were Douglas MacArthur, "Vinegar Joe" Stilwell, "Skinny" Wainwright, and "Hap" Arnold. There was a wide difference in our ages then, but in later years it seemed to be very little.

During my days as an instructor at West Point, I was much interested in football. There had been a great development since my classmate Dennis Michie organized the first team. With players like E. L. Daley '06, Ernest "Pop" Graves '05, and R. E. Boyers '03 we now had one of the nation's great teams. There were games with Harvard, Yale, Princeton, and others at West Point. But the final game with Annapolis was played at Franklin Field in Philadelphia. There Maude had the pleasure of meeting her brother, Harris Laning, who was then an instructor at the Naval Academy. By mutual consent we had our social visits with Harris and his wife before the game. After the game our feelings were too intense for the free interchange of family amenities.

I fear that my interest in football sometimes disturbed my impartiality as an instructor. During my first year, one of the pupils in my lower section, the thirteenth, played on the football team. He was more distinguished as a lineman than as a chemist. He was so near the foot of the thirteenth section that he was threatened with transfer to the fourteenth, which happened to be the bottom section in the class—or "the goats" as it was designated in cadet parlance. Now if the varsity center got to the "goats," he might fall clear through the bottom of the class at the January examination and so be lost to next year's football team. Here was a great responsibility which his instructor felt keenly the morning before the Yale game. As the harrowing ordeal of a "front-board" recitation might upset his morale in the pending battle, I decided to question him on the subject matter of the last few lessons. When I asked for the formula for alcohol he gave me the proper letters of the alphabet but was vague as to the accompanying numerals. When I made another approach and asked how to make alcohol, he was distinctly noncommital. But when I hinted, "Don't you know what whiskey is made of?" he promptly informed me that they made it from corn out West where he came from. That was his only useful contribution on the chemistry of alcohol. But early in the afternoon's game, when I saw him press the visage of the Yale center fimly into the turf, I knew that the morning's ordeal had not affected his morale.

During graduation week, 1902, the Military Academy celebrated the centennial of her birth. Among her distinguished guests were President Theodore Roosevelt, Secretary of War Elihu Root, and a representative from each of our great universities and colleges. The alumni, including General Longstreet and other veterans of the Civil War, were quartered in the Cadet Barracks. So far as practicable, each of these old timers occupied his old cadet room and, in a few cases, his old cadet roommate was present to share it with him. As a full account of the centennial was published as a contemporary government document, only a few striking incidents need be described here.

The centennial exercises opened with the alumni meeting on Monday, June 9th. The program included addresses by Gen. Thomas J. Wood, class of 1845, a veteran of the Mexican War; General Thomas H. Ruger, class of 1854, a Union veteran of the Civil War, and General Edward P. Alexander, class of 1857, a Confederate veteran who had served as Longstreet's Chief of Artillery at Gettysburg and as Lee's Chief of Artillery in the closing campaign of the war.

General Alexander's address was the most effective speech that I ever heard. When he rose to speak, his fellow Confederate veterans welcomed him with a lusty "rebel yell." This was taken up first by the cadets from the Southern states and then by the whole audience. The orator was so overwhelmed by emotion that he would scarcely recite the following verses he had selected to open his address:

> Once more the light of Jackson's sword
> Far flashes through the gloom.
> There Hampton rides and there once more
> The toss of Stuart's plume.
>
> Oh, life goes back through years to-day
> And we are men once more,
> And that old hill is Arlington
> And there the alien shore.
>
> And over yonder on the heights
> The hostile campfires quiver,
> And sullenly twixt us and them
> Flows by Potomac's river.

Then after further applause and more "rebel yells" he resumed:

> The Confederate Veteran! With these words does there not rise in
> every mind the thought of a meteoric army which over forty years ago
> sprang into existence, as it would seem out of space and nothingness,
> and after a career of four years, unsustained by treasury or arsenal, but
> unsurpassed for brilliant fighting and lavish outpour of blood, vanished
> from earth as utterly as if it had been a phantom of imagination....
>
> And the whole people who had created the annihilated army ... with
> one consent gave to the cause for which they had striven vainly but so
> well, the title The Lost Cause....
>
> And this people mourned over their lost cause as the captive Israelites
> mourned over Zion:
>
> "If I forget Thee, O Jerusalem! let my right hand forget its cunning,
> and my tongue cleave to the roof of my mouth...."
>
> And now a generation has passed away.... Whose vision is now so
> dull that he does not recognize what it is to himself and his children to
> live in an undivided country?
>
> Who would, today, relegate his own state to the position it would hold
> in the world if it were declared as a sovereign, as are the States of Central
> and South America? To ask these questions is to answer them. *And the
> answer is the acknowledgment that it was best for the South that the
> Cause was Lost!*
>
> The right to secede, the stake for which we fought so desperately, were
> it now offered as a gift, we would reject as we would a proposition of
> suicide....

Those were brave words to be uttered in those days when the sufferings of
the South were still fresh in many living memories. At first, the response of the
audience was subdued. Then, once more, after a thrilling pause, there was an
explosion of "rebel yells" from the orator's fellow veterans, from the Southern
cadets, and finally from the whole audience. And this explosion came again
after the address when the West Point Band played "Dixie."

The centennial exercises also included addresses by our Commander in
Chief, President Theodore Roosevelt, and his Secretary of War, Elihu Root.
But for me the most significant part of the program was the address given at
the centennial banquet by President Harper of the University of Chicago, who
spoke as the representative of the American universities and colleges. He
expressed great interest in the opportunity which had been given him to
examine the system of instruction at West Point; its concentration of effort, its
thoroughness and especially "the spirit of subordination, of obedience, engendered in the student." In this connection he said:

I appreciate the fact that the question I am raising touches vitally the most sacred articles in the creed of the modern educator. I understand that it is today a piece of pedagogical heterodoxy to look with any favor on an educational institution which is not based upon the idea that the student must be allowed to follow his own sweet will in selecting his courses of study and his methods of work. At the same time, I venture to inquire whether in the application of this modern educational policy we have not gone too far; . . . whether, for example, it would not be well for every boy to have at one stage or another of his development, a period of discipline at all events similar to that which is called military.

Here a great American educator was proposing some sort of universal military training—as an essential feature of general education—a dozen years before World War I made us see that such a scheme might well be essential to our national secutiry. Here, also, whether consciously or not, President Harper echoed John Milton's famous precept: "I call, therefore, a complete and generous education, that which fits a man to perform justly, skillfully and magnanimously, all the offices, both private and public, of peace and war." I did not know that Switzerland was then the one and only country in the world where the Miltonian education was universal—the only country in which every able-bodied young man was trained to perform the duties as well as to enjoy the rights and privileges of democratic citizenship. Nor did I know then that when President Washington submitted an American adaptation of the Swiss system to the First Congress he was really proposing the Miltonian education for every young American.

My most treasured personal memory of the West Point centennial is the opportunity it gave me to renew my acquaintance with Dr. Harper. I acted as his guide in his visits to the recitation rooms, the cadet barracks, and other places that interested him. He was especially impressed by General Alexander's speech and together we visited the orator on the sunny porch of the old West Point Hotel. Before he left West Point he invited me to return to the University of Chicago because, he was good enough to say, "You have organizing genius." But I declined an opportunity to renew my lectures there because I was not so cocksure at thirty-two as I had been at twenty-seven. I had escaped from some of the toils of *mis*education which hampered me when I delivered my first lecture on military policy at the University of Chicago but was still too *un*educated to deliver the second.

My memories of those years as an instructor at West Point are happy ones. There I was part of a lively group of alert young contemporaries, officers who took their professional calling seriously, endlessly discussing the military issues of the day. I remember on one occasion Maude's father came up to see us while on a business trip to New York. He took great pleasure in visiting the officers' mess with me. It was, he said, the only club he ever knew where the members did not talk shop. He didn't realize that while we were not talking his kind of shop, we were all very busily talking our kind of "army shop."

Some of my fellow instructors were truly remarkable individuals. There was, for example, my classmate George Blakely. One day we hiked to the top of Cro' Nest where from the summit of the mountain we looked down upon the Hudson. The air was virtually still and the schooners in the river were motionless. When I tried to quote Coleridge's lines about "a painted ship upon a painted ocean," George corrected me and recited long passages from the "Ancient Mariner." At another time when I referred to Lincoln, he recited Walt Whitman's "Captain, My Captain." At first I thought his capacity to quote in this way was a mere coincidence, but I soon found that he had an absolutely photographic memory, such as Macaulay was said to have had. Whenever he read anything that interested him, he could quote whole pages of it.

While we were at the academy our daughter Mary was born and our home life once again underwent a great change. Not long afterward we moved from the hill to a vacant set of officers' quarters on "the plain." In those days there were five or six sets of quarters on a line extending northward from the Cadet Barracks to the superintendent's quarters. All of them were torn down years ago to make room for magnificent modern buildings. They were the most delightful quarters on the post. As they faced the parade ground, we could see dress parade from our front porches.

During my tour at West Point, I published an article, "Railroad Building as a Mode of Warfare," in the *North American Review* for December, 1903. In this article I presented the view that a system of railroads in the Philippines would expedite the pacification of the islands and that their cost would be justified from a purely military standpoint without any reference to their ultimate commercial value. This article was received with considerable interest in Congress and throughout the country. In a response to an official inquiry by a member of the Senate, the Secretary of War, Mr. Root, fully confirmed my thesis.

While my purpose in writing this article was purely military, its preparation took me far afield. In order to write it, I had to learn something about the cost of railroads and their equipment. This led me to an examination of *Poor's Manual of Railroads of the United States*. There I found the balance sheet of every American railroad with the "cost of road and equipment" on the assets side of the account, and the par value of its stock and bonds on the liabilities side. At first I accepted these statements of cost as gospel truth, but I soon encountered discrepancies. This induced me to compare the balance sheets of two railroads which I happened to know, the Wabash and the Chicago and Alton. They both passed through Springfield, Illinois, where I had known them since my boyhood. As the Alton was one of the best-built railroads in the state, and as the Wabash was one of the worst, I was surprised to find that the Wabash had cost about three times as much per mile as the Alton.

I was surprised because I was unsophisticated and had never studied anything about railroad finance. It was therefore some time before it dawned upon me that the Wabash statement of "cost of road and equipment" was simply a lie. The Alton had stocks and bonds based upon actual cost while the watered securities of the Wabash covered more than treble the actual cost. It therefore had to falsify the asset side of its balance sheet. And why should such a lie be necessary? Then it dawned on me that railroads lied in watered securities in order to conceal the relation between earnings and investment. The Alton with its honest capitalization could pay dividends with low freight and passenger rates. This, the watered Wabash could not do.

In fact, the Alton had its turn a little later. If it remained honest, public opinion must eventually compel a reduction of rates. Evidently, if the watered stocks of the Wabash and other inflated railways were ever to have any real value they must prostitute the Alton also.This soon led to a reorganization of that corporation. Within twenty-four hours its "cost of road and equipment" was trebled although the only physical change was a change of name from "Railroad Company" to "Railway Company." As I pursued this theme I found even more startling falsification in our public utility finances. A New York state report informed me that one of New York City's crosstown street railways had cost more per mile than the Panama Canal. As its tracks lay on a right of way graded by the taxpayers of New York, how could it cost so much money even if its rails were sterling silver and all of its cars were golden chariots?

This came to me with all the force of an original discovery. For the first time, I realized that much of our public utility finance was really fraudulent and that many large fortunes in the country had been made by robbing the public and then deliberately lying about it. This struggle for loot explained a great deal about the corruption in municipal politics at that time. The whole theme impressed me so much that I wrote a short story about it.

The hero of my story was Col. Timothy Lumpkin, who had made a fortune in manipulating gas and street railway franchises in Westport, his native city. In due time, for some reason or other, the Colonel happened to get honest; this completely changed his point of view. After his reformation, having a sense of humor, he thought it would be a good joke to tell his fellow citizens just how he had robbed them. With this in view, he ran for mayor as a reformed captain of industry, and in his campaign speeches he frankly confessed his robberies and how he had made them. This story was published in *McClure's Magazine* for August 1903 under the title "Colonel Lumpkin's Campaign." As my story was not exactly military, I published it under the name John McAuley Palmer. This proved to be an effective nom de plume for Capt. John McA. Palmer—so effective that Professor Tillman, my superior in the department of chemistry, called my attention to the article without realizing that he was speaking to its author.

"Colonel Lumpkin's Campaign" made quite a hit. Shortly after its publication, Lincoln Steffens, the editor of *McClure's,* invited me to New York for a conference. He congratulated me on my story and assured me that, in his confessions, Colonel Lumpkin had made an almost impossible subject intelligible to the average reader. "But," said he, "we have a broader interest in the Colonel. In him you have invented a real character. You should therefore make him the hero of a novel to run serially in our magazine before publication in book form." This, however, did not appeal to me. I might write an occasional Lumpkin confession for the magazine in addition to my duties as an instructor at West Point, but my academic schedule was too tight to squeeze a novel into it. Later, Mr. McClure wrote me a letter urging me to reconsider. He assured me that Colonel Lumpkin might be made as great a character as Mark Twain's Colonel Sellers.

If my visit to Steffens did not make me a novelist, it was one of the most interesting experiences in my life; I learned that my Colonel Lumpkin was helping to popularize the gospel Steffens was preaching in his *The Shame of the Cities.* After discussing the Colonel's future, he introduced me to three other members of the McClure staff—Ida M. Tarbell, Ray Stannard Baker, and Albert A. Boyden, who later relieved Steffens as editor. From that day they were all close friends of mine.

A few weeks after my visit to *McClure's,* I submitted another story giving another installment of Colonel Lumpkin's confessions. After reading the manuscript, Miss Tarbell asked me to come and see her on my next visit to New York. When I called a few days later, she told me the magazine wanted to exploit a theme that might be a little over the heads of the readers of a popular magazine. She therefore asked me whether I could not induce Colonel Lumpkin to make it the subject of one of his confessions. This the colonel did and thereafter, in his capacity as confessor, he became a sort of honorary member of the staff of *McClure's Magazine..*

On one of my visits to New York, I asked Steffens why the magazine had delayed publishing his article, "The A B C of Politics," which had been advertised for some time. To this he replied in perfect good humor, "Oh! Mr. McClure threw that article in the wastepaper basket after he read Colonel Lumpkin's 'The Man in the Pigeon Hole.'" In that article, which appeared in March, 1905, the colonel had told how he had controlled the election of aldermen in the city of Westport. He explained that 49.5 percent of Westport's honest voters were always locked up in the Republican pigeon hole and that another 49.5 percent were locked up in the Democratic pigeon hole. This simplified his political problem. So long as he could round up a shade more than half of one percent of the total voters in sixteen of the thirty-one wards, he could always control the city council. Of course, he explained, a larger margin was safer and he generally had it. In order to keep a majority of his fellow citizens safely pigeon-holed, the colonel owned a controlling interest in the city's leading Democratic newspaper and in the leading Republican newspaper. In each of these competing newspapers the same editorial writer extolled the virtue of party loyalty.

During my tour of duty at West Point, I wrote several other stories for *McClure's*. In one of them, "The Innoculation of Mr. Skads," which came out in June, 1904, I told how that great captain of industry and philanthropist, Maecenas V. Skads, had financed Dr. Agar in his epoch-making researches in bacteriology. In his examination of blood specimens from pickpockets and other inmates of the state penitentiary, Dr. Agar had discovered a specific organism which he published to the scienfitic world as the "crimino-coccus." Later, when he sought to develop a corresponding antitoxin, Mr. Skads was glad to give him the fullest financial assitance. Here, at last, was a philanthropy worthy the aid of Maecenas V. Skads. It would not only reduce the cost of our penal institutions, but would raise the general level of honesty in the lower classes. Shortly after Dr. Agar's investigations were crowned with success, there happened to be a smallpox scare in the city. When Mr. Skads went to Dr. Agar to be vaccinated he was given the crimino-coccus antitoxin by mistake. This made him quite ill for a few days, but he recovered just in time to preside over a meeting of the Westport Consolidated Gas Company to consider a great increase in its capitalization which he had recently proposed. When Mr. Skads open the meeting he said: "Gentlemen, I am surprised that I ever proposed such a solution. That increase that I proposed at our last meeting is quite unnecessary. All we have to do is to lower the price of gas."

But one of my stories was a little too hot for *McClure's*. In this story I presented the view that Jacob, the son of Isaac, was the first great financier and capitalist in recorded history. His sale of a mess of pottage to Esau showed distinct genius for salesmanship. Later in his cattle-breeding contract with Laban, he taught future generations that more than an equitable share of profits may be garnered when stock is properly watered. Steffens wanted to publish this story but Miss Tarbell vetoed it. Later, in 1906, it was published by a small Chicago magazine known as *The Voter*.

My informal contact with *McClure's* continued until early in the spring of 1906 when I was ordered to leave West Point in June and to sail for the Philippines early in September. When I went to New York for a goodbye visit with my good friends, Mr. McClure received me in his office with Miss Tarbell, Mr. Baker, and Mr. Boyden. During this visit, Mr. McClure turned to me and said, "Captain Palmer, we would like to have you as a staff writer on the magazine. There is a place for you here right now if you are willing to leave the army." I was flattered of course, but felt that I must consult Maude before giving an answer.

After the meeting, Baker took me to lunch at the Players in Gramercy Park. Over the dessert, he said: "We would all be very happy if you should join us. But you should consider Mr. McClure's offer very carefully before you accept it. If you have any literary plans of your own, the worst thing you can do is to earn your living writing what somebody else tells you to write."

That is what Ray Stannard Baker had been doing for years. Nobody could clarify a complex theme better than he. But I can see now that his very success was keeping him from the *Adventures in Contentment* which already filled the heart of David Grayson, the peudonym Baker used.

Baker's hint brought me to an important decision in my own life. For four years I had been coquetting with popular literature, and with some promise of success. Already I was planning a novel to be written in the Philippines. But a man cannot serve two masters. Before I got back to West Point that night, my way became clear to me. I would remain in the army, and thereafter such literary gift as I might have would be devoted to the search for a sound military policy. Perhaps I might be able to invent a military Colonel Lumpkin who would be able to awaken popular interest in the problem of preparedness.

About the middle of June we said goodbye to our friends at West Point and set out for Maude's family home in Petersburg where we spent our vacation. There were the usual visits with relatives and friends in Springfield and Carlinville, but only one experience of this summer seems to stand out in memory: this was an automobile trip we took with Horace and Mary Wiggins. The summer of 1906 was long before the day of good roads in Illinois and we had our trials. Our vehicle was a two-cylinder Rambler. It had no top and the girls on the back seat wore veils and goggles. Horace and I, garbed in overalls, occupied the front seat where we would be ready for tire or engine trouble any minute. Between Bloomington and Joliet on what is now the main highway from Chicago to St. Louis, the mud was so deep we had to leave the car at Dwight and go on by rail. After a few days Horace and I recovered the car and picked up the girls in Chicago. We visited Waukesha and Madison. Fortunately, on our return the dirt road was dry enough for us to get to Springfield without further delay. Toward the end of August, I said goodbye to Maude and my daughter, Mary, who was then not quite three, and set out for San Francisco to take the September transport for the Philippines.

United States Military Academy Cadet John M. Palmer, 1889
Courtesy of the U.S. Military Academy

"The Four Johns"
Left to right: John Mayo Palmer (father), John McAuley Palmer (son), Lieutenant John McAuley Palmer, Governor (Major General) John McAuley Palmer (grandfather).
Family Photograph

Lieutenant John M. Palmer, 15th Infantry, 1896
Family Photograph

Maneuver Division, Leon Springs, Texas, 1911
Staff of the 1st Brigade. *Left to right*: Captain J. M. Palmer, Lieutenant E. M. Watson, Brigadier General F. A. Smith (*seated*), Lieutenant R. D. Smith.
Courtesy of the Manuscripts Division, Library of Congress

1st Brigade Encampment, Leon Springs, Texas, 1911
Courtesy of the Manuscripts Division, Library of Congress

BOOK II

In which Capt. John Palmer is ordered to the Philippines, where he becomes governor of the Lanao District in Mindanao and must cope with the burdens of empire. Returning to the United States, he attends the Line School and Staff College at Fort Leavenworth, where he acquires the skills of a professional staff officer and finds a fast friend in 1st. Lt. George C. Marshall. Duty on the General Staff in Washington involves exposure to a wide range of politico-military problems and brings a promising young officer to the attention of the high command. A return to China offers experience with the international community, until promotion and the coming of World War I send Palmer back to the General Staff, where he helps shape the Draft Act of 1917 and is selected by General Pershing to be chief of Operations in the newly formed American Expeditionary Force setting off for France to fight the German empire.

11   To the Philippines

The most important fruit of my experiences in the army thus far was a set of convictions about the proper role of the military in a republic and the relationship of the civilian components to the regular forces. So it seemed only logical that I should write a book on military policy. My assignment to the Philippines was to divert me from this avowed purpose for a considerable period, but, as so often in the past, I was to return to my writing enriched with many new experiences and far wider horizons.

At San Francisco I met Claude Miller of the 29th Infantry and J. K. "Jakie" Moore, both of the class of '97. Jakie and I had served in China together and we had been fellow instructors at West Point. We set sail 4 September 1906 for Manila in the transport *Thomas*. Among those on board I found Brig. Gen. Tasker Bliss, who was going out to be governor of the Moro Province in the Philippines, along with Mrs. Bliss and their daughter, as well as my classmate Capt. J. P. Jervey, also of the 15th Infantry, who would later become deputy to Bliss.

Our trip across the Pacific afforded us a relaxing cruise with delightful interludes ashore when we stopped for two days at Honolulu and a day at Guam. Finally on 1 October 1906 we disembarked at Manila. We found many interesting sights to take in during our two-week layover in the city, and one of these I described in a letter to Maude.

Just about dark this evening Miller and I were going out to the Luneta, the big grassy plaza around which much of the life of the city centers. We found the streetcars were stopped by a religious procession.... We could see at once that it was a wonderful spectacle, so we went up on the porch of the Grand Hotel to view it.

The long narrow street was brilliantly lighted, but all of the light came from the candles carried by the thousands in the procession. On either side of the street was a file of men, women and children, each bearing a taper, while within the two files came the procession of saints. There must have been 20,000 people in the procession escorting the sacred images from the archbishop's palace to the church of San Domingo.

The saints were life-sized figures, each borne on the shoulders of a dozen men. They were covered with candles in little glass globes and were decked with beautiful flowers. Each image had its escort of priests and friars followed by hundreds of lay worshippers, and each was preceded by an embroidered banner displaying the name of the saint. After every two or three images came a band, generally of stringed instruments.

In the diffused light of the candles, the otherwise tawdry splendor was beautiful. The saintly images passed by for a long time until finally down the street we saw the most sacred of all, the Virgin of San Domingo. This famous image represents the Queen of Heaven in regal robes. For generations rich natives have bequeathed gems to the figure until it is said that its robes and jewels are worth several hundred thousand dollars.

My account ran on for several more paragraphs full of similar details, but this should be enough to convey something of the impression made by my exposure to an alien culture. And this was only one of the many episodes which introduced the urban, Christian aspect of life in the Philippines to a young captain who was to spend the next phase of his career among vastly different rural Mohammedans in a remote province.

We left Manila at last on the transport *Seward* bound for Iligan on the north coast of Mindanao. Upon our arrival at nearby Camp Overton on the afternoon of 20 October, Jakie and I put up for the night with Lt. Charles L. Sampson, the acting quartermaster of the 15th Infantry. The following morning we set out for Camp Keithley in a four-mule dougherty wagon such as we used to have in Arizona. Our route followed the right bank of the Agus River, a torrent which falls 2,400 feet from Lake Lanao to the sea in about 30 miles.

At Pantar we crossed to the left bank, where an Engineer unit was garrisoned. Among its officers we found Lt. Robert S. Thomas and Lt. Arthur R. Ehrnbeck, both of '05, who had been cadets under me at the academy. We finally reached Camp Keithley near the village of Marahui late in the afternoon having come nearly twenty miles from the coast. The post was laid out on high ground from which beautiful Lake Lanao could be seen about a mile to the south surrounded by volcanic mountains and lesser lakes.

After reporting to Col. William S. Scott, the regimental commander, Jakie and I went to our quarters. Like all others at Camp Keithley, our new home

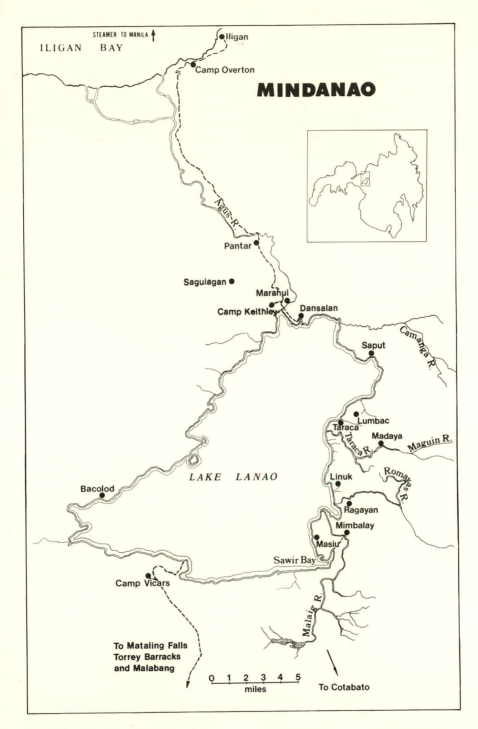

Lake Lanao District, Mindanao

was built entirely of cogan grass and bamboo. There was not a nail in the whole structure. The bamboo and cogan grass matting were bound together with rattan, known in the Philippines as *bejuca*. However primitive, the structure proved to be very comfortable. We had a large living room, two bedrooms, and a kitchen, and when we walked in we found a Chinese cook and two Filipino boys prepared to look out for us. The next morning we visited our companies and tried to settle into the routines of life in our new garrison.

At the nearby village of Marahui where the Agus River flows out of Lanao, a word which means simply "lake" but has come to be applied to the surrounding region as well, was a Moro market. Here also were the headquarters of the district governor, Maj. E. W. Griffith, who was a career officer in the Philippine Constabulary. When we went to call upon him, he received us on the front porch of his quarters, where he was holding a session of the Tribal Ward Court. On a concrete floor surmounted by a corrugated iron roof a group of Moro dignitaries were squatted in a semicircle facing him. Three of the four ruling sultans of the lake region were present. Most of the others were fierce-looking datos, which is to say, lesser chieftains.

I was greatly impressed by the district governor's skill and dignity in dealing with the native officials before him. Major Griffith was an Englishman, a true son of Devonshire, an adventurer of the stamp of Drake. I was also glad that I did not have the responsibility that rested on his shoulders. As he explained it, the Maranao, or "people of the lake" as they called themselves, had a complex political system something like feudalism. All about the lake were fortified communal houses called *cottas*. A number of cottas made up a community under a dato. Groups of datos owed allegiance to one or another of the four reigning sultans of the lake district. Since, according to tradition, all stemmed from a common ancestor, each property holder had a number of choices as to which ancestral line and thus which dato or sultan he would support. The resulting shifts in allegiance made conflict endemic, and as a consequence the Tribal Ward Court was more important to the Moros politically than as a vehicle of either civil or criminal justice.

I had been on duty in Lanao only a week when a note arrived from Major Griffith inviting me to take lunch with him and General Tasker Bliss, who had taken up his office as governor of the Moro Province and had come up to the lake for a visit. After our meal together Griffith went out to preside over his Tribal Ward Court, leaving me alone with the governor. General Bliss got right to the point: Griffith was going home to England for a long leave of absence, and he had decided to appoint me district governor during his absence.

I assured the general that he could not possibly make a worse appointment. I reminded him that I had been away from my regiment for five years, that I knew nothing of the country, and that unlike himself I had no knowledge of the Moro language and practically none of Spanish. The general listened to me patiently, then said, "Captain Palmer, your objections are very well stated; nevertheless you are now appointed governor of Lanao to take effect a week from today." With this, he led me out to the Tribal Court, where Griffith presented some of the leading datos to their prospective governor.

Upon my return to camp Keithley that afternoon I explained to Jakie Moore that we would not be sharing a house after all, since in a few days I would be moving into the district governor's headquarters at Marahui. Following dinner that evening as we sat smoking on the veranda, I said, "Jakie, I've been wondering if any governor in human history was less equipped than I to handle his job, and at last I've thought of one—Don Quixote's Sancho Panza." "I don't know," Jakie replied, "Sancho could at least speak the language of his subjects."

I had good reason to flinch at the task before me. The Moros were the most warlike and ungovernable people in the entire Philippine Islands, and of all the Moro people, the Maranao tribe which inhabited Lanao were the most spirited, bellicose, and unruly. Griffith explained to me that the Moros, or Moors, the general name the Spanish gave all Mohammedans they found in the Philippines, were the predominant inhabitants of Mindanao and the southern group of islands. They had been converted to the faith of the Prophet by an influx of Arab and Malay people in the fourteenth century. These people presented a sharp contrast to the Filipinos in the north, to whom civilization came later with Christian missionaries followed by the Spanish conquest. As a consequence the people of the northern islands had benefited from continuing contact with the Western world and were therefore readier than the Moros for self-government.

General Bliss had assigned me the task of controlling the Moros of the Lanao district, an enterprise in which seasoned Spanish officers with three hundred years of national experience behind them had not succeeded. Well-meaning officers such as myself charged with the subjugation and government of the Moros could have profited greatly from a detailed study of Spanish experience if their records had been available to us, but they were not. We simply blundered forward as best we could. Minor uprisings and civil disturbances continued in Mindanao long after the rest of the Philippines had been pacified. As a consequence, until 1913 when on the eve of World War I mounting demands for troops elsewhere led to a withdrawal, only in the Moro country did the provincial governor and the district governors under him continue to play a dual role as military commanders and civil governors.

After the departure of General Bliss I turned over command of my company, which I had held for less than a week, and reported to Governor Griffith for further orientation. He pointed out that the sultanates were very small, the largest claiming to rule an area little larger than the District of Columbia back home. What is more, he observed, the task of governing here was more difficult than it was for the British, for example, in their Malay States, close as the superficial similarity might be. There, a few powerful rulers dominated extensive and well-defined territories. All the British had to do was to control the existing administrative system. They assigned a resident "adviser" at the court of each ruling prince or sultan, who generally accepted the guidance he was given. In Lanao, however, there were no such powerful leaders. The several sultans held small and ill-defined territories and lived in perpetual jealousy of one another. The district governor himself had to assume command. His legal authority came by virtue of his role as a justice of the peace, but in dealing with the warlike Moros he often had to play the role of autocrat.

Although the dominions of the Moro sultans were small, these leaders had all the dignity of Mohammedan potentates. Each had his entourage of armed retainers, his harem, and all the pomp and appurtenances that go with such high estate. Among those present at Griffith's Tribal Ward Court were the Sultans of Bacolod, Babayan, and Madaya. The Sultan of Madaya impressed me especially. The following extract from one of my letters to Maude written at the time will convey some idea of the figure he cut.

> His head dress was a Mohommedan turban of yellow silk with a brilliant green stripe running through it. He wore a tight-fitting jacket of green brocade silk with silver buttons that looked like small sleigh bells. He also wore a brilliant yellow sarong about his waist. Tied up in its folds was a handsome box of brass and inlaid silver from which His Majesty occasionally abstracted a chew of betel nut. He was a handsome man when his mouth was shut, but when he smiled, like all the betel nut chewers, he exposed two sets of jet-black teeth. His Majesty's trousers were made of yellow silk (yellow being the royal color), so tight that it must have been impossible for him to take them off. In fact they were absolutely skin tight, and as the Sultan had thin ankles and very large bare feet, I could see that once on, he must wear his pants until they wore out. The Sultan informed me, through Governor Griffith, that he was my friend and brother and that he was an awfully good Moro.

The Moros are of medium height with fairly dark skin and small dark eyes set close together. Slight traces of the blood of the Arab traders and missionaries who brought Islam to the Philippines remain in the faces of some individuals, who regard this as a mark of aristocracy. The Moros filed their teeth to points. The betel nut they chewed not only blackened these teeth but stained their lips and tongues vermillion. Single men shaved their heads, but after marriage they let their hair grow like a woman's. Proud, fierce, cunning, and often cruel, the Moro was armed everywhere he went. His customary hand weapons were the war club; the barong, or long knife; and the *campilan*, or kris, a two-handed sword with either a straight or wavy blade.

As to Moro character, one of the most striking examples was Amai-Puingan, who came into Keithley for the first time, shortly after my arrival, to pay his respects to the American government. Amai-Puingan's fame had preceded him, as he was known among the Moros as a man of extreme bravery. In his travels his only attendants were two slaves, one of whom carried his bundle and the other his *buya* box, or betel nut. But he himself always carried his pet gamecock under his own arm. Like most Moros he was an inveterate gambler, and many stories were told about him in this connection. On one occasion when visiting a powerful dato, he discovered his host trying to cheat him in the game they were playing. Amai-Puingan rose, put his hand on the hilt of his kris, and said: "You are the Dato of Saloon, and you are surrounded by your *secopes*. You are trying to cheat me. I am alone, but I, Amai-Puingan, will make you and your secopes run." And run they did.

After meeting many of the visiting magnates I began to wonder if my predecessors had been as unfamiliar with the character of their charges as I was. My lack of knowledge was unfortunate, but even more so was my inability to communicate directly with my subjects. Baltazar Diaz, my newly acquired interpreter, spoke Spanish and the Maranao dialect but he did not speak English, so our medium was my very meager Spanish.

In view of my obvious inexperience as a governor, Major Griffith felt that before leaving Lanao he must visit the potentate Nurul Hakim, meaning "noble judge," of Romayas and secure his oath to support the new American regime. This Moro was a *pandita*, or scholarly interpreter of the Koran. He and his son, Radia Bagandali, were unquestionably the two most powerful leaders in Lanao. Thus far he had refused to obey the district governor's summons to come in and tender his allegiance to the U.S. government. So, on 4 November 1906 I set out with Griffith to capture this troublesome man, the Dato of Romayas, in his cotta on the eastern side of Lake Lanao.

Late in the afternoon we boarded the largest of the government steamboats along with a company of the Philippine Constabulary under the command of Lt. James L. Wood and without lights sailed slowly to the middle of the lake. A little after midnight we took to the whaleboats and rowed ashore on the east side of the lake. There, under the guidance of another of our interpreters, Tomas Torres, and two husky natives familiar with the terrain, we took up our march in total darkness just before dawn.

Tomas Torres was a most remarkable man. I first met him when he accompanied Maj. Gen. Leonard Wood on a visit to Marahui. He was the bravest human being I have ever known, repeatedly confirming this impression of him by acts of outstanding courage. He would go through the whole Moro region armed with nothing but a carbine and accompanied by a single native boy carrying his personal effects. In those days when I had no inkling of the crowded life that lay before me I planned to write a story about Tomas Torres. He was a real hero, brave, wise, and just in his dealing with the Moros.

Our plan for capturing Nurul Hakim was very simple. The Moros were highly superstitious about walking abroad by night. If we could slip up quietly in the night and surround the cotta before daybreak, then we could surprise the renegade dato along with his followers in the morning and make our arrests.

The Moros were also superstitious about firearms. Their guns were crude affairs, smoothbore muskets of rather large caliber. As they had little lead, they would fill the muzzles of their weapons with old screws, nails, or even small pieces of rock, in fact, almost anything they could find. Before our troops came to the Philippines, the Moros had virtually no modern weapons. When General Pershing pushed his pacification column into the Moro Province the natives attributed his success to the repeating rifles, or Krags, the troops employed. For this reason the Moros would take almost any risk to steal a Krag. Because of this, we regularly mounted our sentries in pairs so as to reduce the chance of surprise, but even then many soldiers lost their lives. Not unnaturally our men soon took to protecting themselves by firing at anything or anybody approaching their posts.

Just before Governor Griffith went away he gave me two boxes of dummy cartridges which had been filled with high explosives. One of these, fired in a Krag, would blow to pieces the man who held the rifle. These devilish pieces had been prepared so they could be dropped on a trail in the hope that some Moro would pick one up and try to use it, making one less captured weapon— and one less Moro—to worry about. Griffith said he had never permitted these booby traps to be used as they did not appear to be quite sporting. A few days after he left I took the two boxes out in a boat on Lake Lanao and dropped them overboard.

The Moros evidently regarded the virtues of our rifles as a species of magic. They did not really understand how to use the sights to take aim. If they had forgotten about guns and relied upon their own native weapons, the kris or the barong, they would have been much more formidable to us. Frequently our trail through the cogan grass, which grew taller than our heads, was so narrow we had to advance in single file. Had the natives broken in upon us from our flanks when we were all strung out, they could have cut us to pieces, but fortunately for us they never made such an attempt. The natives of Samar killed many Americans by this tactic, but the Moros, who were individually braver and more formidable, never seem to have thought of such a stratagem.

Our night march to Nurul Hakim's hideout was a terrible ordeal. Several times we were literally up to our necks in muddy water. Finally we managed to surround the dato's big bamboo house before any alarm could be given. Presently, in response to a loud summons from Tomas Torres, Nurul Hakim himself came to the door. I have never seen such ferocity on a human face. But he prudently yielded to the superior force confronting him and with two of his retainers returned with us to our steamboat. There he sat on the deck fingering his beads, a veritable Arabian prophet, with a rapt look upon his face. When we got back to Marahui, he and his two retainers were placed under guard on the concrete floor of the Tribal Ward Court, where mats and cushions were provided for them.

While Griffith and I were at breakfast Baltazar Diaz came in to say that as this was a great Mohammedan feast day, the neighboring datos would like to bring their rice bowls to Nurul Hakim to be blessed according to the rites prescribed in the Koran. Griffith assented, and soon after we beheld a remarkable procession. First came my friend the Sultan of Madaya followed by one of his retainers carrying the sultan's rice bowl on his head. When the Sultan of Madaya disappeared in the direction of the Tribal Ward Court, Amai Sankakala came into view escorting a gorgeous yellow rice bowl and after him came the Sultan of Babayan. His rice bowl had pink flowers on it and looked to me like genuine Royal Worcester. Similar delegations waited upon Nurul Hakim throughout the day. Later Governor Griffith explained to me that for many years the merchants at Malabang and Iligan had been importing these *pots de chambre* for the Moro trade. In spite of what these vessels were designed for originally, the Moros treasured them as highly utilitarian rice bowls.

Most of the following day I spent in conversation with Nurul Hakim. After assuring him that we had no aims against his religion and no desire to interfere with Mohammedan customs, I found he became increasingly amenable. He promised to be amicable in the future and to come in when needed.

While I was still engaged with Nurul Hakim, yet another Moro came in to visit the Tribal Ward Court. Griffith received him cordially and introduced him to me as Nusca Alim, which translates as "religious authority," a Mohammedan priest of considerable sanctity. He became one of my most trusted friends. I certainly needed such associates, for I soon discovered that the principal role of the civil governor in Lanao was to function as the head of a miniature League of Nations.

For hundreds of years there had been petty wars amongst the various Moro sultans and datos, and it was now up to the district governor to resolve their differences if he hoped to keep the peace. By far the greatest portion of my juridical activity consisted of arbitrating questions according to local custom without resorting to formal legal procedure. Nearly a third of the tribal cases had to do with relations between datos and their secopes, or lower-class Moro tenants and retainers, although slaves, peasants in hereditary bondage or sharecroppers might be more appropriate terms for these individuals.

With several gratifying exceptions, the datos had not yet learned how to handle their secopes under the new conditions brought about by the American presence. Many cases that at first appeared to be violations of the antislavery law newly promulgated by the American authorities, upon investigation called for nothing more than a tactful adjustment of the relationship between a dato and his secope.

Governor Griffith arranged for me to accompany him on a series of tours over the entire district before he left. For the most part our expeditions to the outlying reaches of the jurisdiction involved trips on Lake Lanao. Since much of the surrounding countryside was unmapped and all but impassable jungle, the lake was our best highway. The quartermaster at Camp Keithley had at his disposal four steamboats, along with a number of steel lighters or barges, in which two companies of infantry and all their equipment could be towed. In a matter of hours we were able to move a considerable force of men to remote points which would have required days to reach with a column marching through the lush semitropical verdure which grew around the lake shores and lower mountain slopes. In the wider valleys between the mountains with their pine-clad peaks, the natives cultivated corn and other vegetables as well as cotton, tobacco, and sugar cane. But wet rice, grown in the marshy flats along the lake, was the staple of the Maranao diet and economy.

Governor Griffith and I made one of our most interesting expeditions in a dougherty wagon drawn by mule teams following the road built by our troops north to Camp Overton and thence over the old Spanish road to Iligan, the leading costal town on the north shore of Mindanao. With its population of about 5,000, including both Christian Filipinos and Moros, Iligan was the largest municipality in the district of Lanao, so we spent several days meeting local datos and visiting the surrounding district in company with Capt. William Green, whose Constabulary company was located in the town. Settlers from the United States were already beginning to move in, and I was greatly interested in a hemp plantation recently established by an American named Shepherd. He was making good progress employing Moro laborers under the wage system.

In Iligan I first encountered Allen Gard, who was serving as district secretary there. He was a most remarkable individual. A recent Yale graduate, from the class of 1901, Gard had an unusual gift for languages. He was rapidly mastering the Maranao dialect and was thus able to get very close to the Moros.

I had planned to return to my district headquarters at Marahui as soon as Griffith sailed in order to reflect at leisure on all I had learned about my new responsibilities before plunging into action. But soon after the *Seward* departed, into the harbor sailed General Bliss on his private yacht, the *Sabah*, and summoned me aboard for an interview. As if I did not already have more than enough to keep a greenhorn busy, he told me that he wanted me to move the settlement of Marahui to some new site located outside the military reservation of Camp Keithley. The existing town had all the unfortunate characteristics of the villages that almost invariably spring up around military posts. A number of civilian employees lived there, to be sure, but so too did camp followers of all kinds. There were bootleggers, opium dealers, and prostitutes as well as Japanese merchants, loan sharks, and petty traders who dealt with the Moros. Just as he was leaving he gave me an order addressed to Capt. Alfred B. Putnam, who commanded the Engineer unit at Pantar, directing him to have the new townsite surveyed when I selected it.

As it was too late to make the long journey up to Marahui that day, I rode back into Iligan to look up Allen Gard, whom I ordered to join me at the district governor's headquarters at Camp Keithley as soon as practicable. If I were to be moving whole towns and building new ones in addition to my other duties, it was obvious that I needed an able assistant. Gard arrived promptly and commenced serving me with great efficiency. Because of his gift for languages, he was able to handle the Tribal Ward Court better than I, leaving me free for my other duties.

To continue my education into Moro affairs and to inspect the further reaches of my district, I decided to visit Malabang, a town on the coast some twenty miles southwest of Camp Vicars, which lay high above the southern end of the lake. To get there, I set out by steam launch down the lake, climbed up to Vicars, and secured a spring wagon to ride down the trail cut through the jungle to Malabang and its adjacent port by Pershing's men during the 1903 pacification.

About midway between Camp Vicars and Malabang, I stopped long enough to inspect the Constabulary post at Mataling Falls. This station was commanded by Lt. James L. Wood, an officer of the 19th Infantry, but at the time of my visit Wood and most of his troops were out in the field on some mission and only a few soldiers under a sergeant remained on guard at the camp. Looking back now from our era of good roads and easy communication with radio and telephone, it is difficult to recall just how painfully isolated these little outposts in the jungle could be. That the troops who served there fared as well as they did speaks well out not only of their courage but their patience in adversity.

When my wagon at last bumped and jounced its way down the trail into Malabang I was delighted to be greeted by my old friends Lt. Col. Charles A. Varnum and his wife. Varnum had his headquarters in the Torrey Barracks, on the site of the old Spanish fort named after General Corcuera. His command consisted of a single squadron from his own regiment, the 4th Cavalry, and four companies from the 19th Infantry, making this outpost by far the strongest force in the southern islands.

Malabang proved to be a thriving port. The town itself had a population of about 600, but with the hinterland included in the municipality there were about 4,000 souls in all. Chinese merchants had been settled here for years trading with the Moros. The principal export was coffee of a rather inferior quality, but some really good coffee was to be found growing half wild in various locations about the lake. Lt. William P. Screws of the 19th Infantry was serving as a judge in the Tribal Ward Court as well as *presidente*, or mayor, of the town. The treasurer was a Filipino, one Pantalion Ramos, and the municipal council consisted of two merchants, one Filipino and one American. The chief of police was an American, Otto Willie, but his sergeant was a Filipino. Under him I found two Filipino and one Malabang, or native Moro, serving as corporals along with five Filipino and four Malabang privates. I mention this mixture because it appeared to indicate the extent to which our policies and our presence had helped to mute ethnic conflicts and tribal animosities.

Less than three months after my visit to Malabang a large part of the town was destroyed by fire in February, 1907. When the place was rebuilt under the direction of Lt. Karl D. Klemm of the 4th Cavalry, who was by then serving as the municipal *presidente*, it was decided that no building could be erected unless it had a hardwood frame, board sides, and a galvanized iron roof in place of the highly flammable nipa palm huts and thatched roofs formerly utilized. The new town was less picturesque, but it was decidedly safer and more efficient, a transformation which could be said to characterize both the good and the bad of the American presence in the Philippines.

Upon my return to Marahui from my expedition down to Malabang, I had scarcely begun to catch up on the routine matters of administration which had accumulated in my absence when once again Nurul Hakim began to give trouble. This time it started with a series of *reclamos* presented against him by less powerful Moros charging debt and fraud. Although we made repeated attempts to establish better relations with him, his friendship always remained doubtful. Indeed, it is entirely possible that the consideration we extended only led him to exaggerate his importance and encouraged his spirit of independence.

In March, 1907, our difficulties with Nurul Hakim came to a head. I learned that the Sultan Dimabara, who was wanted for murdering one of our soldiers in Parang, a town in the adjacent district of Cotabato, had taken refuge in my district and was hiding in the neighborhood of Romayas. A force under Lieutenant Wood set out to arrest him in the home of Paramanis, a kinswoman of Nurul Hakim, who was known to be sheltering him. Unfortunately Dimabara escaped, but the other occupants of the house were arrested and brought into Marahui. Nurul Hakim promptly arrived to secure their release, but he was informed that sheltering a criminal was a serious offense and if he wished his kinsfolk released he should assist in the capture of Dimabara. Soon afterward a report came in of the renegade's arrest in Cotabato, so we released our prisoners. Nonetheless the incident seems to have goaded Nurul Hakim into active disaffection.

A few weeks later he sent the following letter to the district headquarters:

Praise be to God, ruler of the Universe. Letter of Nurul Hakim, Kadarunain of Bayabao, Maciu, and Unayan, to the Civil Governor.

I could not go to Mecca on account of a letter which I received from Akhmad Basa which was brought by a black steamboat that arrived in Zamboanga during the Fair. This letter was delivered to me by an agent of the Radia Nuda of Suranayan [the defunct Dato Ali].

All that Akhmad says in this letter is in regard to the rule of the Sultan of Istambul and on account of that I beg you not to change the customs adopted by the said sultan which are the customs of all the datos of Lanao.

You should take into account the agreement of the Sultan of Istambul with the government, including the President, the Secretary of War, and the generals, that the government established in Lanao . . . should not injure the inhabitants nor change their customs: the sale of slaves, except people of the upper classes, should be free and without objection; also the arms of the people of Lanao should be free for their use and should not be confiscated by the government. Akhmad Basa has understood that all this agreement has been annulled. The Sultan of Istambul has ordered me to oppose the orders of the district governor, and if you are not satisfied with this, you should communicate with the sultan direct. And if you do not do this, you can judge my rancheria in whatever way you care to, since all this matter is the special charge of Akhmad and is in his hands. He will arrive here the latter part of next month (Saribulan).

I shall oppose your orders since I have an order from the Sultan of Istambul which, if I disobey will bring punishment.

The Sultan of Istambul desires that I beg of you not to let the Americans come to my rancheria without giving me notice beforehand, and if the Americans come by night, the people of the rancheria ought to offer resistance since the Americans do not conform to the proper formalities.

Despite the tone of defiance in the letter I resolved to do nothing until Nurul Hakim had had time to respond voluntarily to the letter I had sent a few days earlier directing him to present himself to the district governor in Marahui. Instead of complying, four days later he sent a second letter:

Praise be to God, Lord of the Universe. Letter from Rajah Nurul Hakim, Kadarunain of Bayabao, Maciu, and Unayan, to the District Governor.

I have learned that you were displeased on account of the letter that I received from Akhmad Basa sent by order of the Sultan of Istambul, on which letter I based the one which I wrote to you. If I had failed to write that letter to you, the sultan would have sentenced me to be punished, and at the same time I should have been lacking in my duty toward you.

If you intend to punish my rancheria, I beg you to wait until Akhmad Basa comes, for he is the representative of the Sultan of Istambul. If the law provides that my rancheria should be punished, I acquiesce because I am wrong, but I cannot obey your orders because Romayas is part of the domain of the Sultan of Istambul, and I have no power there apart from that delegated to me by him. If you attack Romayas, the United States will also be attacked. If you punish me the heads of the president, of the secretary of war, . . . of the general, of the colonels, and of the governors will be cut off.

I advise you that it will be better to pay me tribute because by so doing all the Americans in Lanao will be left in peace, but if I revolt, be assured that not a single American will be left in the district of Lanao.

I desire that you be less pressing with your orders. The Americans have got along well here since their arrival, and it would be a pity for them to have to repent afterward. It would be better for you to treat me with consideration and not change our laws and customs, since by no manner of means can you vanquish the Sultan of Istambul. Do not heed the words of those datos who deny the power of the sultan. If these suggestions do not appeal to you, it would be better for you to consider evacuating Lanao, which would be the best course for the Americans to follow.

In regard to the notification that you sent to me and my relatives that if we do not come in to be heard, we would afterwards have no voice in the matter, I will put you a question: if I fail to present myself at your headquarters after being notified, still is there no justice in my position?

In this case you are the one who is in the wrong because you do not do that which is proper.

I desire that this conference be put off until Akhmad Basa says that we ought to present ourselves at your headquarters, then we will come. Today I cannot do more than what I am ordered to do by Akhmad Basa and the Sultan of Istambul.

As far as your interpreters are concerned, be very careful as to how you act because the day will soon come when your mouth will be cut along with your feet and your hands with your ears and your eyes. I desire that you, the district governor, have the district secretary act as interpreter because he is a true American, and the reason I have become an enemy is because of the interpreters who have taken from what the district governor has wished to say to me.
God knows the right.

The very same day this curiously cajoling and threatening letter arrived, one of the friendly datos, Amai Corut of Saguiaran, reported that some of his followers had met Nurul Hakim and his retainers in Maguing and found them armed with four Krags and about forty Remingtons. This was reason enough to be greatly concerned. Even though we knew the Moros were seldom very skillful in using modern firearms, any such number of weapons represented a formidable threat.

I recognized at once that no time should be lost in launching an expedition against Nurul Hakim and his supporters in Romayas, but the situation was an exceedingly delicate one. President Theodore Roosevelt had recently announced to Congress that the Philippines had been fully pacified. It would therefore be politically embarrasing if word were to get out that violent fighting was still going on in Lanao.

My occasional requests for Regulars to support the Constabulary pointed up one of the anomalies of my new position, especially in regard to my relations with Colonel Scott, my regimental commander. As district governor, I was a civil officer, and for the time being he had no jurisdiction over me. We worked out an arrangement which met the situation nicely: if I had to make an arrest in the Taraca country, for example, and concluded that the available Constabulary troops were not strong enough, I would call upon the regimental commander and say, "Colonel Scott, that Taraca country looks most interesting. It would make a beautiful place for a practice march of about a battalion of infantry."

Thus it turned out that one morning early in the year 1907, two companies of the 15th Infantry under Capt. Harry A. Smith left Marahui on a "practice march" to Romayas. The preceding night I had set out myself for Romayas via Linuk with eighty-six Constabulary under Capt. William Green along with a reinforcement led by Capt. Bertram P. Johnson in company with Allen Gard. When the Constabulary force arrived at Nurul Hakim's rancheria about two in the morning, having ignored his distaste for nocturnal operations, we found the place abandoned. The next morning, however, when Captain Smith's infantry companies joined us, they reported being fired upon from a cotta about a mile away. The captain had turned aside to capture these snipers, killing in the process one Moro armed with a musket and five armed with krises, *armas blancas*. Because I had to get back to my duties at Marahui, I left Tomas Torres with Captain Green and the Constabulary with instructions to arrest Nurul Hakim and his son Radia Bagandali, if they showed up. Meanwhile they were to inspect all the rancherias in Romayas to find and punish any known lawbreakers among the Moros.

Captain Green's sweep of the region was thorough, and, I believe, largely successful. Which is to say, I agreed with his report that the expedition discouraged any general uprising of disaffected Moros around Nurul Hakim and his son, both of whom continued to escape capture by hiding in the mountains back of Romayas. Even if our quarry eluded us, it was evident that our expedition and others like it subsequently sent out were decidedly beneficial because they gave a sense of security to friendly Moros and discouraged the doubtful ones who might otherwise have been tempted to join Nurul Hakim. These armed sorties also facilitated the gathering of information from friendly natives. And sure enough, some months later, reports began to drift in suggesting that Nurul Hakim was getting tired of living as a fugitive in the mountains and was now willing to come in and present himself.

Nurul Hakim was, of course, only one of the many troublesome individuals with whom we had to deal in our efforts to abolish slavery and bring peace and good order to the Lanao District. For example, on one occasion when General Bliss was engaged in one of his frequent inspection trips, on returning from Camp Vicars, instead of steaming directly across Lake Lanao to Marahui, he cruised along the Maciu coast in the southeastern reaches of the lake. There, not far from the mouth of the Malaig River, he was fired upon by hostile natives in a rough, unsettled area not yet pacified and known to be a refuge for many of the renegades and criminals from the whole lake region. Needless to say, General Bliss was hot under the collar when he arrived at district headquarters and promptly ordered Colonel Scott to assemble a suitable force to clean out the miscreants.

After some hurried preparations, we began to embark a substantial force in our flotilla of three steamboats and their tows. The expedition, led by Colonel Scott with several units from the 15th Infantry along with forty or more Constabulary as my excort, was still getting ready when up sailed a Moro chieftain, Amai Binanning of Taraca, in his gorgeously decorated *casco*. This worthy declared that he had heard of the dastardly firing on General Bliss and as a loyal subject he was offering his services in helping to arrest the offenders. I interpreted this gesture, somewhat naively as it later turned out, as evidence that we were making progress in winning over the Moro tribesmen.

When our flotilla reached Maciu, on the advice of Tomas Torres I located our base camp on the left bank of the Malaig River about two miles from its mouth. As the river itself was too shallow for navigation by the steamboats, we landed at Sauir Bay in the southeast corner of the lake and, with the help of Moro carriers, carried our supplies overland to the riverbank campsite. The local Moros gave us but slight resistance when we landed and then took to their heels. And before I was aware of what was happening and could take steps to prevent it, the troops had set fire to the Moro dwellings and crops.

Our reconnaissance in the region soon convinced us that there was no need to maintain such a large body of troops at Maciu so Colonel Scott determined to return to Camp Keithley. But I decided to remain on the banks of the Malaig, so I could study at first hand the complex social and political relationships of the local Moros. With Allen Gard at Marahui to handle the routine business and conduct the Tribal Ward Court, there was no reason why I could not remain at Maciu indefinitely, so long as two companies of the 15th Infantry under Capt. W. A. Cavanaugh could be spared to guard my field headquarters.

I wanted to find out just why it was that there was always so much trouble in the southeastern lake region. To my way of thinking, going down there with troops to burn crops and houses and chasing the poor devils into the hills was no way to get a permanent solution to the problem.

The more deeply I investigated the situation at Maciu the more it puzzled me. Our self-professed friend, Amai Binanning, claimed that all our troubles were caused by the outlaw Moro by the name of Gundauali, but as I pursued the case I became suspicious of this accusation. Amai Binanning's announced friendship for the United States seemed to have increased the hostility of the Gundauali faction, and there was no doubt that Amai Binanning did everything in his power to use his friendly ties with the government for his own advantage.

After a long conference with several prominent datos, I sent a message to Gundauali through Nusca Alim, who was much revered as a priest throughout the region, inviting him to come in and see me. I gave him my word of honor that if he came in to parley, he would be permitted to depart without reference to any of the charges pending against him. At the same time I sent similar messages to Gundauali's subordinate chiefs, among them one known as Magum Para, the Kabugatan of Mimbalay.

Two days later Nusca Alim brought in several datos who had not heretofore submitted to the American authorities. This was a most encouraging beginning. Then Magum Para, who was a far more prominent leader, came in for a long talk, and true to my promise I let him depart freely even though there were serious charges outstanding against him. Among other things he told me that his coming had been strongly opposed by several of the other datos and somehow or other I got the impression that our professed friend, Amai Binanning, was not at all happy over the prospect that Gundauali, too, might come in.

Our long and careful examination of the datos who came in of their own volition finally brought out the following story. Even before the Spanish penetrated the Lanao region there had long been a rivalry between Gundauali and Amai Binanning for the sultanate of Puna-Maciu. In the course of this factional struggle, Amai Binanning had attacked and captured Magum Para's cotta, but the latter had escaped to the hills. Then when General Pershing established his first camp at Lanao during the initial pacification, Amai Binanning gave him great help, all the while directing the Americans against Gundauali and his supporters such as Magum Para.

I sent for Amai Binanning and examined him closely on his hereditary claims to the Puna-Maciu region. I told him that I had learned about his former relations with Gundauali and that I expected to bring Gundauali to my camp and arbitrate between them, inviting Nurul Hakim and other prominent Moros to sit with me as assistants. Shortly after this, ominous rumors reached us indicating Gundauali and his followers had gone on the warpath. Sure enough, very early the next morning, around two o'clock, shots were fired into our camp from across the Malaig River. At dawn I sent Lt. Ned M. Green and a small detachment of 15th Infantry troops over to scout the ground, but they could find no trace of an enemy.

Both Baltazar and Tomas Torres, who had recently joined us at the camp, predicted from their knowledge of Moro customs and character that the attackers would come again. Therefore, shortly after dusk, we sent Lieutenant Green and some troops to the hills behind our camp. Then, to set a trap, we posted a group of Amai Binanning's men along the edge of the trail to intercept anyone driven down the path by the troops on the hilltop. Sure enough, once again at about two in the morning those of us in ambush heard brisk firing from Ned Green's position. Then we heard screams as the Moro troublemakers retreated. Green's fire had caught the Moros by surprise, killing their leader. When the dead man was brought into our camp we identified him at once, and greatly to our surprise, as Amai Binanning's right-hand man.

I thereupon sent Lt. James L. Wood with a detachment to arrest Amai Binanning. This action created a great sensation throughout the whole lake region. When I conferred with my trusted advisers and friends among the Moros as to the disposition of my prisoner, Nusca Alim advised me to release Amai Binanning on his own promise of good behavior in the future. I was reluctant to do this in view of his outragous conduct and manifest duplicity, but both Torres and Baltazar joined in Nusca Alim's recommendation, pointing out that he was a leader with many and influential connections throughout the region and to treat him generously would make a great impression.

Releasing Amai Binanning on his own recognizance turned out to be a wise move, for the very next day he came in to report a hostile band in Ragayan. And soon afterward the Constabulary acted on the information and captured fourteen prisoners we had been trying to arrest for a long time. With Amai Binanning exposed and subdued, I daily expected Gundauali to come in. Then, abruptly, the entire situation changed. All communication with the outlying Moros seemed to dry up. We were at a loss to explain this sudden change of temper. Finally one small piece of intelligence came to hand and gave us a clue.

We learned that Manalao, one of the Maciu datos, had visited the cotta of the well-known prophet Uti. This gave us reason to believe that the sudden breakdown in our negotiations with the renegades might have come about because of the Uti's influence over the highly superstitious datos. A day or two later when I returned to Marahui to confer with Colonel Scott, my worst fears were confirmed when I found an elaborately initialed letter from Uti addressed to me as district governor.

This fanatical priest had proclaimed a holy war against the Americans. Because he was said to have a charmed life and to be armed with a magic kris, he held a considerable appeal for the people of Maciu. The letter, when translated, read as follows:

> The Lion of God to the District Governor, and to Tomas and Baltazar; Pigs, do not come in the night. If you do, I crush you. Come in the daytime so the Maciu can see the dead Americans. Assigned by God. All of you who come I will give as a sungud. Durum Pacal, the kris that cuts first, is ready.*

The following day I learned that Uti was holding a cotta on the lake shore at Lumbac, east of the mouth of the Taraca River at a location scarcely nine miles across the water from Marahui. Colonel Scott and I had no difficulty in locating the strongly fortified cotta close to the shore. Brilliant red banners were flying above the breastworks, and Moros armed with krises were dancing about. They fired three or four shots at us without effect as we approached, but we had already seen all we needed to see; Uti's cotta was far too strong for the limited forces we had immediately available.

Upon our return to Marahui Colonel Scott and I composed a joint telegram to General Bliss seeking authority to undertake an assault on Uti's cotta. Our plan was to send a full battalion of the 15th Infantry, but because a frontal attack upon the walls of the cotta would almost certainly cost many lives, we also asked for Capt. Leroy S. Lyon's battery of mountain artillery so we could bombard the fort before making our assault.

Our expedition against Uti landed with but slight opposition and the troops began to work their way into position at the edge of the cleared space surrounding the cotta. There they could cut down any Moros who attempted to rush across the bare ground toward us. Apparently the methodical, deliberate movement of our troops as they took their time in preparing to attack got on the nerves of the defenders. At any rate, a tall Moro came out in front of the cotta and walked up and down waving his sword and shouting epithets at us in a display of bravery to encourage his followers.

I suspected that this exhorter was Uti, the prophet himself, with his magic kris. One of the officers standing near me asked permission to have his men fire at the shouting figure. I said, "No, but you can have one or two expert riflemen shoot close to him." When the first shot struck near his feet, he waved his blade defiantly. When another hit just behind him he wilted perceptibly.

---

*Sungud means dowry or bride price. Durum Pacal, a corruption of Juru Pakal, means the legendary sword of the mythic Rajah or Radia, Indarapatra, hero of the Moros. This sword was supposedly handed down through Dato Ali of Cotobato who held out against both the Spanish and the Americans, attributing his success to his magic sword.

Then as he waved his kris above his head one of our riflemen had the skill or good luck to hit the blade and break it in two. After this demostration he evidently felt that his life was not so charmed after all, for he suddenly broke and ran off into the cogan grass and disappeared, following the other defenders who had already fled.

In the pursuit that followed one of the Moros who was killed turned out to be Uti's father. He was armed with a kris but nothing else. Our troops pursued the fleeing Moros into the hills near Maguin. Here and in a number of other rancherias as soon as we threw in a few shells from our mountain batteries the inhabitants fled before the infantry could close with them. This was frustrating, but as it afterwards appeared, not entirely without utility, for we soon learned from Moro informants that the pretentions of the prophet Uti had been entirely discredited by his ignominious flight from the Lumbac cotta and the subsequent dispersal of his followers.

My whole effort at achieving pacification since establishing an outlying base at Puna-Maciu had proved to be a disappointment, but at least we had acquired a great deal of valuable information and we most certainly had come to understand the nature of our problem better than we had before. I now believed that more enduring results would come about if we allowed matters to settle and sought solutions by negotiation rather than armed forays.

If my own appraisal of our accomplishments was inclined to be critical, General Bliss apparently thought otherwise, for the provincial secretary informed me that the general was highly pleased with the progress being made in my district. In this he was perhaps a better judge than I, for a few days later Gundauali sent word that at long last he was coming in to present himself. He arrived with a considerable retinue in several cascos decked with flags. A most impressive looking man of fine physique and truly regal bearing, Gundauali presented a Krag rifle as evidence of good faith and his desire to submit to the government. He declared that he had no other wish than to return to Puna-Maciu and settle among his people there. I told him that if he were to return there his old enmity with Amai Binanning must first be accommodated, whereupon he said he would be glad to place the adjustment of their difficulties in my hands.

Here at last was evidence that the kind of solution I had been seeking was now in sight. It seemed to me all wrong to expect armed expeditions to produce any kind of lasting pacification of the Moros. If the American presence were to bring law and order of an enduring kind to Lanao, it would be through patient negotiation, through understanding and the accommodation or adjustment of ancient feuds and petty local grievances. I was repelled by the needless use of force, which only treated the squabbling Moros on their own terms. If we ever hoped to make peaceful citizens out of these warring people we had to show them a better way to reconcile their differences. With this objective in mind I now firmly resolved to be indeed a *civil* governor; one who would lead his tribal wards to a true understanding of the ways of peace.

12 District Governor

To carry out my resolve to stress my civil role as pacifier, I sent word to Gundauali and Amai Binanning of my desire to have them come in and present their controversy over the sultanship of Puna-Maciu for my decision. My various native advisers indicated that Mamantum, the Sultan of Maciu, of which Puna-Maciu was a subdivision, should also be present for any such adjudication, but almost immediately difficulties began to crop up.

Mamantum let it be known that he would come in providing his jurisdiction over the sultanate of Maciu were explicitly recognized. He also insisted on coming in with an escort of sixty retainers armed with krises and demanded that a salute be fired in his honor when he sailed up in his *vinta*, one of the outrigger vessels with brilliantly colored patchwork sails used by the natives of Mindanao. To this demand I returned word that as district governor I would be responsible for Mamantum's security in Marahui and would grant him the courteous reception befitting a sultan. He was given to understand, however, that the hearing was to be held to provide him an opportunity to state his claims to the overlordship of Puna-Maciu; if he did not come, he would be ignored in the matter. Thus firmly forewarned, he agreed to drop his conditions and to appear on the appointed day.

On the date set, the three grandees presented themselves. Much of the first day of our deliberations was consumed in gathering information on the history of Maciu. By patiently eliciting the legendary background of the area, I eventually learned that at some time in the distant past there had been an effective government over all of Maciu. The last ruler of this line was one Balundung. When he died the various datos of the sultanate simply agreed among themselves not to recognize a successor or to pay further taxes. Whereupon Balundung's seven sons divided up among them his dignities and titles. The story of the division of titles among seven sons was merely a symbolic way of indicating that the unified government had degenerated into the multiplicity of rulers and political anarchy which characterized the area when the Americans arrived.

Although the various datos were entirely unwilling to concede any political powers to the sultan, they nonetheless regarded the hereditary line of the sultan of Maciu as a very sacred matter and were quite ready to treat him with great reverence as the head of the family of Balundung, which is to say the highest dato among the Maciu Moros. Thus, on the occasion when Mamantum was elevated to be sultan, Gundauali, who was not invited to the ceremonies by Amai Binanning, bitterly resented this affront to a descendent of one of the hereditary seven sons. To avenge this slight, Gundauali's immediate kinsmen proclaimed him Sultan of Puna-Maciu.

Gundauali's pretensions as Sultan of Puna-Maciu had been taken as a casus belli by Sultan Mamantum, Amai Binanning, and their lesser datos. But when they attempted to drive him out by force of arms, they were unsuccessful. In my view, the strongest argument in Gundauali's favor was that in spite of all opposition he had managed to sustain himself as the de facto Sultan of Puna-Maciu.

Although drawing out the vital details of the tribal history of Maciu consumed a great deal of time, I was greatly encouraged. The parties involved appeared to be in a conciliatory mood and agreed to suspend all further hostilities, leaving the case in my hands as district governor. Both Mamantum and Amai Binanning said that they would renounce any claim to rule in Puna-Maciu and were willing to concede almost anything to Gundauali except the title of sultan. For his part Gundauali said he was willing to make any concession to the other side except the title of Sultan of Puna-Maciu!

At this stage in the negotiations I drew aside Sultan Mamantum for a private talk, pointing out that inasmuch as Bacolod, Oato, Tugaya, Linuk, and other parts of Maciu had sultans who admitted his superior rank, there could be no loss of dignity for him if he would settle the difficulty by proclaiming Gundauali Sultan of Puna-Maciu. But Mamantum would have none of it. I must understand, he said, that long years ago when the first Moslem to visit Lanao came up from Cotabato he had carried with him some of the sacred white earth of Paradise which had been deposited at Mecca. When a sultan performed the ritual of stepping on the white soil he assured not only the legitimacy of his authority but also fertility and prosperity for his people. When the first Moslem came to Lanao he stood on the shore of Puna-Maciu, and there he planted the white earth. The people of Maciu, Mamantum assured me, sprang from this white earth. Indeed, the very words Puna-Maciu, mean "the origin of Maciu." For this reason, Mamantum declared, the title "Sultan of Puna-Maciu" would mean far more than a simple territorial title.

As Mamantum went on to expound the legendary significance of the white earth, I began to realize why my predecessors had turned to the relatively simple expedient of settling tribal grievances by sending out a body of soldiers.

Until I could get to the bottom of the problem, weighing the legendary accounts more deliberately against the entirely practical consideration that Gundauali was in possession and had the power to enforce his claims, I resolved to grant a continuance in the case.

As neither side was disposed to yield in regard to the title, it seemed prudent not to interfere one way or the other for the moment, especially since all parties had accepted the supremacy of the government and were not likely to cause any further hostility. Unfortunately, my auspicious beginning to an equitable solution was soon shattered. Scarcely two months later a Constabulary force operating under Lt. Leonard Furlong in the Taraca River valley was fired upon from a nearby cotta. Furlong's men returned the fire, and upon entering the fort subsequently they discovered Mamantum, the Sultan of Maciu, among the dead. Whether or not the sultan was responsible for the initial firing upon the Constabulary or what provoked the incident I was unable to determine. Nonetheless, I remained unshaken in my belief that only by peaceful negotiation would it ever be possible to bring civic order to the Lanao District.

Meanwhile my personal life had taken a distinct turn for the better. Early in March, 1907, I received a telegram informing me that Maude, her cousin Luranah Harris, and our daughter Polly had reached Manila. Nine days later the interisland steamer dropped them at Iligan, where I drove down to meet them with a dougherty wagon.

Worn out from her prolonged seasickness, Maude was none too happy as we bounced along the trail in the dougherty wagon on our day-long journey up to Lanao. Upon reaching the lake, we stopped just long enough at Camp Keithley to pay our respects to Colonel and Mrs. Scott and then drove on to Marahui. There we found Allen Gard holding a Tribal Ward Court out in front of the governor's "mansion" with a dozen or more fierce-looking Moros squatting on the ground before him. To avoid disturbing this serious session we had to enter the back door, a move which struck poor Maude as an affront to her dignity.

After a brief survey of her new home Maude made it quite clear that she did not think highly of my housekeeping arrangements. She was particularly annoyed to find that the best room at the front of the house was occupied by my office and pointedly remarked that it would make a most attractive living room. To compound my problems, Maude also let it be known that she was not very favorably impressed with my bathroom. There was no hot water, and she was not in the least charmed with our temporary shower bath. I was quite proud of it. There was a ten-gallon tin can with a spray underneath which Prudencio, the houseboy, could hoist to the ceiling with a pulley arrangement. Then, by pulling a string and tipping the can one could get a very fair shower.

In at least one respect our new home pleased Maude greatly. After I pointed out to her that there was a large garden, she sallied out and inspected her plantation at great length. She had had the foresight to bring out packets of seeds from the States, and I arranged with the Moros who worked the garden to sell for their own account all the vegetables which we did not need for our household. To carry them over until the crop matured, I paid the gardeners wages of seventy-five cents per man per month, actually a substantial sum in those days.

As the season progressed Maude's garden produced a bumper crop. Because we were so far above sea level it was possible to raise such northern vegetables as American green peas and lima beans which brought no end of pleasure to our guests. All in all, Maude's garden demonstrated the feasibility of the program introduced by the U.S. Department of Agriculture, which distributed thousands of free packets of seeds to encourage the natives to raise a wider range of nutritious foodstuffs.

Shortly after Maude's arrival we got up one morning to discover an array of Moros squatting in a semicircle before our house awaiting the opening of the Tribal Ward Court. I told Maude that she and Luranah could peep out and look at the Moros if they cared to do so but should not make themselves conspicuous. I tried to explain that from the point of view of the Moros she and cousin Luranah constituted the District Governor's harem and it was not considered good taste for the ladies of the harem to expose themselves unduly.

As I left the ladies to go out and open the deliberations of the Tribal Ward Court I told them that I was to conduct an important murder trial that day. Then I got down to the business of the day with Baltazar as translator. One of the local sultans was charged with killing the retainer of a neighboring sultan. All the principal datos of both sultans were present and following the proceedings with intense concentration.

By this time, notwithstanding my crude Spanish, I was able to communicate rather effectively with Baltazar and soon found that this was no ordinary murder but an episode in a long-standing feud between the two sultans. The defendant had killed in the course of a raid to recover a carabao stolen in an earlier raid conducted by the plaintiff's retainers. Further inquiry revealed that the plaintiff's men had taken the carabao to compensate for the theft of a slave girl by the defendant's men. Clearly this was not one of your run-of-the-mill homicides but a tribal squabble extending back over many years. I could bind over the defendent to the Court of First Instance for murder, but that would afford no cure for the situation. What was needed here was a settlement satisfactory to all parties.

Sensing what lay ahead, before proceeding further I turned to Nusca Alim and Amai Corut, who were present, and asked them to serve as amici curiae, friends of the court. Then with great patience and Baltazar's skillful assistance, I traced the feud back for many years, tit for tat, blow for blow, until at last we emerged with something like the score of a football game in which the defendant was ahead 47 to 46. It took all morning to reach this conclusion, but having done so, I addressed the seated assemblage. The evidence showed, I told them, that in the long sequence of reprisals and counterreprisals the time had come to bring the whole transaction to an end, once and for all. The defendant, I pointed out, seemed to be just a little bit ahead in acts of retaliation, so if he would agree to pay the plaintiff one carabao, the score would be even.

Finally Nusca Alim informed me that both the plaintiff and the defendant accepted my solution to achieve permanent peace between their two sultanates. He went on, moreover, to suggest that it would be well to clinch the matter by calling upon the defendant to marry one of the princesses of the plaintiff sultan. Upon this happy suggestion I decided to release the defendant on his good behavior. The offending sultan was so happy on hearing of this decision that he promised to bring in the outlaw Ampuanagaus, a most elusive troublemaker, if I would but lend him a revolver and some cartridges. To this I agreed.

In the course of the morning investigation, to make my score between the plaintiff and defendant come out even I had to have some knowledge of pecuniary values from the Moro point of view. I knew the approximate value of a carabao but not the value of a slave girl. It appeared, after much questioning, that a carabao was worth a little more than a slave girl. Apparently the drift of my inquiry was misunderstood by the assembled datos, for after our deliberations were concluded Baltazar came to me with considerable glee to report that if the District Governor would like to have a slave girl, the two sultans would be glad to present him with one as a further addition to his harem.

Despite my reluctance to use force when dealing with the Moros, Ampuanagaus, the strongest and most hostile leader on the eastern side of the lake, left me little alternative. Therefore, late in April, 1907, when we received word from a friendly dato, Amai Puingan of Lineg, that Ampuanagaus planned to assemble with his people in the foothills above the Camanga River to celebrate a fiesta, we determined to move against him. Because Ampuanagaus was known to possess ten Krag rifles and an unknown number of other firearms, we obtained authority to take a substantial force consisting of "C" Company, 15th Infantry, under Lt. Guy E. Bucker, accompanied by Lt. Alfred A. Hickox and Assistant Surgeon Henry S. Greenleaf and two corpsmen, along with Constabulary Captain William Green and fifty-two of his men accompanied by Lt. James L. Wood.

Our party left Marahui at dusk on 26 April in the steam launch, and sailed eastward to Saput where we disembarked about midnight. From there we followed a most difficult trail to the site of Ampuanagaus' celebration, a stockade made of logs or poles extending some six feet above the earth. Unfortunately, our approach was perceived: we drew fire before we could surround the stockade, and our quarry made off into the sheltering jungle after an exchange of rifle fire. We subsequently learned from local informants that a number of Ampuanagaus' men, including one of his principal subordinates, Tubasan, had been wounded, but there was no satisfaction in this. What is more, we ourselves suffered four casualties, with an officer, two enlisted men, and a guide wounded.

Our launch did not reach Marahui until late the following afternoon because of the delays we encountered in getting our wounded down the trail to Saput on the lake shore. By that time Maude was concerned not only about herself and the girls but also about me. She saw the launch steam up and watched the stretchers being carried ashore. When I failed to come up to the house her concern turned to alarm. Try as they might to put up a brave front, there was no denying that it was a strain for our womenfolk to live in the wilds of Moroland. Of this I was once again rudely reminded a day or two later when working in the office; I heard Maude call Mary several times and then she came to me in great alarm saying that Mary was lost. Gard and Lt. Owen Seaman took up the search as did several of the Constabulary. Finally, after a considerable period of frantic searching, Maude found her daughter, then about three and a half years old, in our spare bedroom where she had taken her dolls to play house under the bed and had fallen asleep, blissfully unaware of the consternation she was causing. This scare was alarming to Maude, but even more so to me, for I knew, as she did not, of Americans in Lanao before us who had been stabbed to death in their homes by hostile Moros bent on vengence.

That afternoon Colonel Scott came down from Camp Keithley. He had heard from the Smiths how upset Maude was when she thought Mary was lost. He came into my office and addressed me firmly: "Mr. District Governor, I have a crow to pick with you. As your regimental commander, I have played the game with you and have subordinated myself to you as a representative of the civil authority. But now I am Colonel Scott, your commanding officer. I cannot tolerate this situation any more! I have a vacant set of quarters for you and your family up at Camp Keithley, and you must move there at once. Wagons will be here to move your personal effects tomorrow morning. You will arrange to have your house properly guarded tonight. If not, I will send down sentinels myself."

The next day we moved up to Camp Keithley, and as Maude had not been consulted she was somewhat upset when she found she would be living in a thatched house. Little Mary liked it at once. She found it convenient when playing out in the yard to poke her dolls through the wall without having to go around and come in the door. But safe as the house might be from attacks by Moro outlaws, I must confess it did have certain disadvantages. When the rain fell, the thatch leaked, so we had to place umbrellas over our pillows. We eventually began to save the tin from kerosene cans, so when the roof leaked too badly the houseboy could climb up and insert a tin patch in an effort to stop the drips.

With my family secure in the midst of the 15th Infantry station, I was free once again to take up the problem of the troublesome Ampuanagaus. I had reported to General Bliss, the provincial governor, my conviction that ordinary military expeditions would be unable to deal effectually with this elusive bandit. The only solution, in my opinion, was to train a special Constabulary force to go out into the mountains with Tomas Torres and slowly encircle the renegades until they had no way to escape deeper into the jungle.

With just such a plan in mind, on 1 June 1907 a force of Constabulary under Inspector Leonard Furlong set out for the Taraca Valley on a reconnaissance to determine if it might not be possible to operate against Ampuanagaus from the mountains to the south of his lair. Four days later this force received rifle fire from a cotta in Galawan which killed one Constabulary soldier and wounded another. In the ensuing engagement seventeen Moros were killed, but Ampuanagaus, who participated in the fight, slipped off into the jungle before the troops closed in. Some days later Furlong and his Constabulary force located a cotta in the Camanga river valley containing a large store of rice used by Ampuanagaus to replenish his supplies before he and his men faded into the jungle. This was destroyed, but still Furlong and his men were unable to flush their quarry. They were repeatedly fired upon but were never able to pin down Ampuanagaus himself.

The frequency with which the Constabulary force drew fire showed how important it was for us to bring in Ampuanagaus. As long as he remained at large he could stir up disaffection among the datos. Fortunately for us, while these datos may have sympathized with Ampuanagaus and sheltered him as a kind of folk hero for eluding the Americans, they showed no disposition to yield their independence by joining forces with him in a concerted effort against us. Although I was reluctant to use force as the principal instrument of policy, I was compelled to admit that our frequent patrols with strong Constabulary forces into the river valleys to the east of Lanao did seem to dissuade the datos there from forming any significant combinations against us.

I was not only disappointed but humiliated by my failure to bring in Ampuanagaus. So long as he remained at large, it was clear that the peaceful and constructive administration I aspired to would in large measure elude my grasp. The annual report of the director of Constabulary gave my efforts a fine accolade in reporting on "the energetic policy of Governor Palmer, which allows the outlaw element no rest," predicting that we soon would eliminate the renegades. This was generous but sadly off the mark, for not one of my army successors as district governor during the next six years ever succeeded in bagging Ampuanagaus, a veritable Moro Robin Hood.

If my inability to capture Ampuanagaus left me with a sense of failure, I could take some consolation and no little pride in my success in founding the

new settlement of Dansalan. My role in this reminds me of the delightful
opportunity for a throwaway line it afforded me at a dinner party in Washington not long before World War II. One of the guests, Woodrow Wilson's
son-in-law the Honorable Francis B. Sayre, who was the High Commissioner
to the Philippines, on learning that I had served in Lanao, asked if I had ever
seen the beautiful little city of Dansalan on the lake. To this I replied
nonchalantly, "Yes, but not since I laid it out in 1907."

Laying out the future city of Dansalan proved to be a far more challenging
task than I had suspected when General Bliss gave me the assignment. The
purely technical problems, such as selecting an attractive site above the lake
shore and getting Captain Putnam's engineers to survey it, caused me few
difficulties. The real problem came in devising ways of putting the new
municipal government into operation without the resort to outside funding
and without incurring the hostility of the native population.

My first move was to call in Martin Geary, an enterprising American
merchant in Iligan, who had expressed an interest in developing the interior.
Geary and several other traders and businessmen in Marahui agreed to raise a
sum of money sufficient to purchase a tract of land large enough for the
proposed town. My only stipulation was that the actual negotiation and
purchase had to be conducted through me as governor. If I were satisfied that
the transaction was sound from the standpoint of the natives, I would then pay
them the money and see to its distribution among them. After that, Captain
Putnam's engineers could make detailed plats of the chosen site and the
promoters would deed their land over to the municipality. They would be
reimbursed to the extent of their original investment by the sale of lots, and
any income above their original investment would go into the municipal
treasury. It was clearly understood, however, that I was at liberty to stop the
whole operation if at any time I felt the Moros were not receiving a fair deal.

A few days later my old students, Lt. Robert Thomas and Lt. Arthur
Ehrnbeck, Putnam's engineers, came up from Pantar and together we crossed
the Agus River where it runs out of the lake and hiked all over the acreage
Baltazar had pointed out as singularly well suited to the needs of the new
town. When fully satisfied that this was just what was wanted, I then went to
call on Amai Sankakala, the sultan in whose region the site lay. At first he
objected strongly to any encroachment on his side of the river. He was
somewhat mollified when I explained that I would not allow the new municipality to go there unless the Moros were paid full value for the land, but still he
had doubts about the whole enterprise. He came around promptly, however,
when I mentioned that we had another site under consideration, and he
realized that he might lose out entirely.

Armed with Amai Sankakala's approval, I returned to Martin Geary and
his group of promoters, who were delighted with the site we had picked out.

"Do you think 2,000 pesos (about $1,000 in U.S. currency) would be a fair price?" they asked. To this I replied, "Yes, but nonetheless, I feel it my duty to advise the Moros not to accept it." I was determined to show the natives that I had their interest at heart. After much discussion the promoters finally agreed to put up 3,000 pesos, to be paid in shining silver coins which, seen all together, made the sum appear much larger than it actually was.

Even though there were a number of settlers who were most anxious to move into the new municipality, I gave orders that no one was to enter the area before all the lots were properly surveyed and staked, and the purchase price had been accepted as fully satisfactory by the Moro owners. This prudent delay proved to be a decidedly wise move, for it turned out that Amai Sankakala, while quite willing to accept the proffered silver, had, with exquisite skill, steered me to a plot of land actually belonging not to him but to a pair of neighboring sultans, one of whom resolutely refused to sell his half of the proposed townsite.

After several weeks of ineffectual dickering, we finally had to settle for half the desired plot, an area comprising about 75 acres. For this we paid the Sultan of Dansalan the 3,000 pesos raised by the promoters. On the day appointed for the official transfer, the sultan and his principal supporters announced that they would indeed accept the 3,000 pesos as a fair price but only on the condition that I personally would agree to divide the sum among them. At this conference we also settled upon the name of the town. I had originally proposed to call it New Marahui, but Nusca Alim informed me, through Baltazar, that Marahui was the name of a particular place and would therefore not be appropriate. Since the area had been known to the Moros for many generations as Dansalan, I resolved to give the town this name, a decision approved by all present.

In agreeing to divide the purchase price among the Moros, I took on far more than I bargained for. The task consumed three whole days. Because the Moros had led a communal life for generations, they had little or no conception of individual holdings or real estate. Moreover, as word leaked out that 3,000 pesos in silver were to be divided among the natives of Dansalan, all their kinsmen and creditors in the whole Lanao basin came pouring in with claims. Because I wanted the Moros to regard me as their loyal friend and protector, and because I wanted to establish a precedent of absolute good faith in my dealings, I heard every claim proffered, no matter how small and at what sacrifice in time and patience.

The task would most certainly have tried the wisdom of Solomon, and I doubt whether I could have met the challenge were it not for the wise advice given me by Nusca Alim and Amai Corut. In the end there were about 100 claimants for that 3,000 pesos. The average amount ran about 30 pesos per claim, though I do recall some as low as 5 pesos, each such representing a fourth interest in a single coconut palm. My decisions must have been fairly sound for after the division was all over I never had a Moro complain that he was not satisfied with his share.

In view of the prevailing system of communal ownership and the absence of clear titles to real estate in the Western tradition, I arranged to have each Moro claimant give a quit-claim to the committee which had raised the 3,000 pesos. My hope was that these quit-claims would provide the basis for a clear title to the purchasers should the matter ever come before a court for determination. When all the transactions with the Moros were completed, I then had the committee quit-claim the whole tract to the municipality of Dansalan. With Lt. Owen Seaman, my designee, as acting presidente, the town was ready for business.

A few days later I authorized the sale of 42 lots, with bids open only to members of the committee who had subscribed the original 3,000 pesos. These lots brought in 3,120 pesos, more than enough to reimburse the committee members for their investment. And there were still 142 surveyed lots to be sold to the public at large, the income providing a nest egg for the municipal treasury. This would constitute a useful capital for various civic improvements but, of course, the town would need a regular income to meet current operating costs.

My scheme for raising funds to meet current running expenses was predicated upon the idea that under the laws of the Moro province there would be a liquor zone in Dansalan just as there was in Malabang and Iligan. In this liquor zone there would be liquor licenses issued and the money thus raised in license fees would pay the salaries of the police and other municipal officers.

When I announced that the sale of the remaining 142 lots would be held on the first Sunday in March to give time for bidders to come up from the coastal towns, the original purchasers immediately set to work improving their property. Those who had buildings in Marahui made plans to remove them to the new town. The Moros showed themselves quick to take advantage of this opportunity, for by lashing together cascos to make a stable platform, they were able to charge fees for floating structures to the new location.

This commercial enterprise on the part of the Moros pleased me, for I hoped that Dansalan would become the center of trade for the whole lake region. It was my conviction that the pacification would never be successfully completed until the Moros became engaged in a thriving commerce. As I envisioned it, Dansalan would become a commercial center. Here outsiders, traders like Martin Geary, would make money, but they could never achieve real success without promoting the prosperity of the natives also.

There was ample opportunity in the Lanao region for native enterprise in commerce and industry as well as in agriculture, and some of the datos were beginning to appreciate this. The Lanao Moros were obviously a hard-working people capable of considerable development. Their skill in working metals and weaving beautiful sarongs and other cloth has long been known. What is more, I observed that they were careful and successful farmers. At the time, however, they were cultivating only small subsistence plots of rice, vegetables, and fruit. The only export crop of any importance was coffee, which grew on the southern shore of the lake.

General Bliss had convinced me that the key to increased production for export was the provision of better marketing facilities. To this end we both saw the town of Dansalan as ideally situated to become the central market for a substantial import and export trade. With a strong center there for well-financed, large-scale traders, the system of native markets already operating in the villages surrounding the lake would provide a means for local distribution and collection perfectly complementary to the wholesale trading center at Dansalan.

A copy of a letter in my files addressed to Martin Geary clearly reflects my conviction that developing commerce would have a powerful civilizing effect upon the Moros:

> There are some thirty-two native markets about the lake where the Moros do their trading among themselves. And in some cases native traders make a business of traveling from market to market. Most of this commerce, of course, is local and small, but the mechanism of trade is there, and I believe that an importer can gradually develop these native traders as a means of distribution for imported goods....
>
> So much for imports. The purchasing power of the Moros is perhaps limited now, but they have an industrial capacity that can be developed. Their sarongs and other cloths are already well known,... and I believe an export market could be found for them. The Moros are also skillful metal workers. There is a demand for their krises and other weapons as curios. Their brass work is also capable of development.... Here, too, by importing cheap raw materials, [one] could foster the trade.
>
> Then there is the coffee trade.... The coffee is grown half wild, each producer having only a few trees. When he gathers his crop, he has to pack it on his head to Malabang or Iligan. If somebody were on the ground to buy it here, by offering a fair price he could enormously develop the trade....
>
> This is the proposition: The government believes that better commercial facilities will civilize the Moros and make them a prosperous and industrious people. We want to accomplish this end even if we have to take it up as a government measure, but it will be better done in every way if the merchant who enters the field is able to see that nobody has a greater interest than he in developing a liberal policy with the natives.

This letter implicitly summarized my conviction that there was room for businessmen to make money in legitimate trade and in so doing they would make the Moros more prosperous and civilized.

With the official approval of the Provincial Governor, General Bliss, Dansalan began to function as a legal entity on 24 May 1907, when I appointed Lt. Jesse Gaston of the 15th Infantry as presidente and G. W. Earl, J. Cook, C. Michael, Francisco Ibol, and Anastasio Ramon as city councilmen. Of these, the first three had served on the committee making the original land purchase from the Moros. The prompt official inauguration of the municipal government was a matter of no small importance because without legal status there was no authority to spend municipal funds. And, without the civic improvements made possible by such expenditures, there was little inducement for merchants and traders to buy lots. With the funds now legally available, the municipal officials built a dock on the lake front, improved streets, and, most important of all, appropriated 300 pesos and a plot of land for the construction of a Constabulary barrack and blockhouse.

The security of Dansalan was a problem which had given me no little concern. Isolated as it was along the right bank of the Agus, on the far side from the 15th Infantry garrison at Camp Keithley, the town was vulnerable to attack by outlaws from the east shore of the lake ill-disposed to the government. As the provincial secretary put it in a letter to me, "they might show their enmity by making a concerted attack . . . where they could secure some considerable booty and deprive a few Christians of their lives to the Glory of Allah."

By the end of June, scarcely a month after the municipality began functioning, there were thirty houses under construction in Dansalan. Once assured that a Constabulary force would be garrisoned there, settlers overcame their timidity about investing, and the building boom began. I was especially proud of the bustling little community when our signal detachment added a most up-to-date refinement by installing a telephone line between Dansalan and Camp Keithley.

Everything seemed to be working out splendidly for my experiment when all at once I encountered an unexpected snag. The occasion of this setback was a visit from General Bliss, who telegraphed that he would visit me about the middle of June. Maude made arrangements to put him up in our thatched house and prayed for good weather. Fortunately, her garden was just beginning to flourish, so she was able to set a meal of fresh vegetables before the general. He was delighted; such delicacies could not be grown in the tropical heat down on the coast where he spent most of his time at Zamboanga. In fact, Maude's tender young lima beans made such a hit that he virtually made a whole meal of them.

When dinner was over the general and I withdrew for some serious conversation. On such occasions he always liked to sip a little Scotch and *tan san.*

Our discussion went on for several hours, so Maude grew increasingly concerned when she heard me make repeated trips to the icebox. What she did not know was that early in the evening I had switched to drinking tan san without the Scotch. I knew better than to try to keep up with General Bliss. He was a great man and an even greater drinker. But unlike any other man I've ever known, his mind grew clearer and clearer as one sip of Scotch followed another.

We talked at great length about various aspects of Moro affairs and then finally got around to Dansalan. To my chagrin he then launched into a tirade on the iniquity of having liquor licenses in towns near our military posts. Drunkenness amongst the soldiers and offenses triable by court martial, he pointed out, increased in proportion to the number of legalized saloons and their proximity to the garrison. Then came his peroration: "We are financing towns on the drinking habits of American soldiers! Captain Palmer, if the American people ever hear about this there will be a terrible scandal. I have given this matter serious thought and there will be no liquor licenses authorized in the town of Dansalan."

I reminded the general that he had told me that I would have to finance the town myself without any aid from the provincial government. This I had proceeded to do according to law, and now his decision was going to wreck the whole arrangement. The upshot was that he agreed to permit liquor sales providing I limited the licensing to no more than two or three saloons and insisted upon a minimum annual license fee of no less than 4,800 pesos.

My success in founding the city of Dansalan provided a convenient occasion to terminate my role as district governor. I had received word that Major Griffith, my predecessor, was returning from his long home leave and would soon be ready to take up his burdens again, so I wrote to General Bliss requesting leave for myself. He replied most graciously, expressing a desire to have me serve his administration in Zamboanga if I were willing to remain in the Philippines after the 15th Infantry was routinely rotated home. With this flattering encouragement in hand, I set out with Maude and Mary for a visit to General Bliss's headquarters.

We reached Zamboanga late in July, 1907, and were delighted to be taken in by Lt. Col. Harry Otis Perley, chief surgeon of the Department of Mindanao, and his wife, old friends of ours during my years as an instructor at West Point. Most of my days down on the coast were spent in lengthy conferences with General Bliss and various members of the Legislative Council, discussing such subjects as reform of the Tribal Ward Courts by gradual conversion to native judges and the need for placing the Constabulary on a more permanent footing. It was evident that the army with its frequent rotation of personnel could never provide the continuity of service necessary to a satisfactory development of the Moro Province or any province for that matter. On the other hand, the Constabulary, if given satisfactory assurances as to pay, promotion and pensions, held high promise as a suitable instrument. The Constabulary appealed to me for other reasons, most particularly because of the opportunity it afforded to develop the use of citizen soldiers, who would be less costly and politically more acceptable locally than our Regulars, inevitably regarded as threatening strangers from a foreign land.

During my visit to Zamboanga I was able to make a side trip to Jolo. To my surprise, the Moros there proved to be quite different from those we knew in Lanao. Among other things, in Jolo there were juramentados, fanatics unknown, happily for us, in Lanao. We had heard of Moros who ran amok, that is, became crazed and frenzied, killing all bystanders, Moros and Christians alike, until they themselves were killed. But the juramentados were different. Here the Moro dresses in a white ceremonial robe and after making meticulous preparations of a religious character rushes out to behead and disembowel every Christian he meets—all to the greater glory of Allah and in the belief that when he himself is finally killed, he will enter directly into Paradise.

Shortly after my return to Zamboanga from Jolo I fell seriously ill. Our host, Dr. Perley, did what he could for me but made it clear that the real difficulty was my poor adjustment to the tropics. I had been driving myself far too hard, he said, in my inexperience demanding more of myself than a white man should reasonably expect in the tropics. When I continued to do poorly, Dr. Perley reported to General Bliss that in his opinion I should take sick leave in Japan or some such cooler place. If my condition then did not improve, he said he would recommend that I rejoin my regiment when it returned to the United States. So I took the next steamer for Japan.

As my health returned, my spirits rose. What really restored my old zeal, however, was a splendid letter from General Bliss praising my work as governor of Lanao. He described the district as "the most turbulent of any in the Province" and my work most successful in bringing "order, observance of law, and a recognition of American authority." He urged me to return to continue working with him, saying all I had to do was cable one word, "Yes," and he would issue the necessary orders. I was strongly motivated to accept General Bliss's offer, but Maude, reinforced by my many friends in the 15th Infantry crowd who had begun to arrive in Japan, finally persuaded me that it would be far wiser not to jeopardize my health by a return to the Philippines.

The only memento of the long trip home I seem to have retained is a copy of the regimental newspaper published on board. In it is a poem I contributed as a gentle spoof of Maude and some of the other ladies in our party:

A Tourist a la Mode

"And did you see the Chinese Wall
When you traveled in Cathay?"
I hung upon her words

To hear what she might say.
"I had no time for crumbling walls,"
Replied the charming maid,
"But I have bought, as you may see,
Some lovely Chinese jade."

"And did you see the Yamen grand
Where reigns the mandarin?"
"Oh, no," she said in accents mild,
"But I bought a peacock pin.
And as for your old mandarin,
I'd have you well to note,
I had no time to think of him
For I bought the old sport's coat."

I won't inflict the other stanzas on my readers; these two should be sufficient to demonstrate how in those now long departed days we whiled away a Pacific voyage of three weeks to San Francisco before continuing on to our new regimental post, Fort Douglas, Utah.

13　Line School and Staff College

We were delighted with the prospect of garrison life at Fort Douglas, but our sojourn there was very brief. Early in the spring of 1908, Lt. Col. Arthur Williams, in temporary command of the regiment, told me he had been ordered to nominate an officer to attend the army School of the Line at Fort Leavenworth and had decided to select me. As I was nearly twenty-eight years old and well up in the list of captains, the thought of returning to school again did not particularly appeal to me.

Fortunately, the colonel persisted. He advised me as a friend to accept this opportunity, pointing out that under a new War Department policy a tour at Fort Leavenworth would become almost essential to a successful army career. After a year there in the new School of the Line, the upper half of the class would be detailed for an additional year in the Staff College. Successful graduates of the Staff College would then be eligible for a year of study at the Army War College recently established in Washington as a result of Secretary Root's efforts. Assignment to the War College would eventually lead to duty on the newly organized General Staff and future opportunities for high command.

In view of the colonel's advice—which was probably as good as any I ever received—I gladly accepted the nomination and a few weeks later received War Department orders directing me to report at Fort Leavenworth on 15 August. Again following Colonel Williams's sound advice, I immediately applied for a leave of absence to prepare by intensive study for my new school duties.

We left Fort Douglas in June, 1908, stopping off in Kansas City on our way East for a brief visit with some of Maude's relatives. While there I spent a day at Fort Leavenworth with my old friend Capt. Arthur S. Cowan—"Frenchy" Cowan of the 20th Infantry—who was just finishing a course in the Army

Signal School. Frenchy escorted me about the buildings and showed me the various points of interest around the post.

Among other places we visited a conference room where the Staff Class was attending one of its final sessions before graduation. My escort pointed out various members of the group, among them my old friend C. D. "Teddy" Rhodes of the 6th Cavalry. Then, after indicating several other contemporaries of mine, he said, "But the wizard of this class is that rangy youngster down there in the front row. He is a brand new first lieutenant by the name of George C. Marshall." There was nothing particularly remarkable in the young man's appearance. I thought it a bit unusual for an old army captain to boost a junior so emphatically, but it was not until several months later that I really began to appreciate this comment.

Just as I was leaving the post, Cowan gave me a copy of Otto Griepenkerl's *Tactical Exercises* and advised me to study it with care. He told me particularly to work out each problem thoroughly before reading the "approved solution" at the end of the book.

We arrived at Petersburg in due time and after dutiful visits with our family and friends in Springfield and Carlinville, I took up the book Cowan had given me. It was a translation of a German text written to assist young officers who were preparing to attend the *Kriegs Akademie*. Here was a book ideally suited to an officer in my position.

I looked over the first problem and the accompanying maps and immediately commenced to write my solution. It seemed almost too easy. After finishing it I turned to the "approved solution" with great satisfaction. But after reading it I experienced a sense of acute humiliation. My answer was an essay whereas the real solution was a tactical decision and a field order to carry that decision into effect. With this order the commander of every subordinate unit in a small force should have known exactly what he was expected to do.

I now saw for the first time that though I was a studious officer I had never had any practice in my profession. Here was a definite solution of a practical problem in troop leading such as we had never had in our service before. My approach to the remaining problems was with a good deal more humility, and during the three or four weeks before I returned to Fort Leavenworth, I learned that it was possible to get practice in the profession of arms in time of peace. If we had had this method of study before the Civil War our commanders would have had an opportunity to write their Bull Runs and Shilohs in ink during peacetime instead of having to write them in blood after the outbreak of war.

The introduction of this practical method of teaching tactics at Fort Leavenworth marked a substantial revolution in our military system. There had been a service school for some years, but not until after the Spanish-American War was a curriculum developed by which the essence of German staff technique could be taught. Here, for the first time in our national history, we had a system of instruction suited to the needs of general staff officers.

Previously, the training offered at Fort Leavenworth was little more than a service course for junior officers. In fact, when the Infantry and Cavalry School, as it was called, was first established in the 1880s, General Sherman regarded it as something of a substitute for those officers who had not had the benefit of a West Point education. Now, however, the course had been entirely reorganized into a School of the Line and a Staff College, each with a term lasting one year. And while other subjects including law, languages, and engineering found a place in the curriculum, it was the course in applied tactics using the so-called applicatory or case method of instruction which offered the most important training for general staff officers.

When Gen. J. Franklin Bell, the school commandant, sensed the significance of this revolution in staff training, he wrote to the War Department and recommended that older officers should be sent to Fort Leavenworth instead of young lieutenants as in the past. This recommendation was unfavorably received by his military superiors, who probably resented the suggestion that there was something new in military education that they knew nothing about. A little later Bell himself became Chief of Staff, so he was able to effect the change he had suggested earlier. Mine was one of the first classes under the new system.

When the school finally opened in the fall of 1908, it faced a rather novel pedagogical problem. The students were to be senior officers, but the only people who could teach them were the lieutenants who had graduated in recent years. Among these young instructors was Lt. Walter Krueger, who was to lead the U.S. Sixth Army in the Pacific during World War II. Along with him there was a stripling lieutenant of engineers named Douglas MacArthur. The very idea of being subordinate to such youngsters came as something of a shock to senior officers as conscious of their dignity and position as we were. The arrangement might have been uncomfortable in almost any profession; it was particularly so in the military where, normally, all seniors are teachers and all juniors are pupils.

While it was awkward enough in an ordinary classroom to have junior instructors, it was even more so in the department of topography, where the work was out in the open field and whoever taught the class frequently had to act as our commander. The instructor in this department was Lt. George Catlett Marshall, the officer who had been pointed out to me by Frenchy Cowan during my visit the previous spring.

After Lieutenant Marshall had marched his platoon of captains and field-grade officers through the evolutions required by the map problem, his aged pupils came to understand somewhat better why he was so clearly a man marked for the future: he was ever mindful of the respect due his superiors, yet he always made it clear that he knew his job and that he was in charge of the work at hand. Happily, my association with young Marshall was not confined to the class in topography. In those days it was customary for the service school branch of the Infantry Association to choose a member of the Staff Class as its president and a member of the Line Class as vice-president. Upon my arrival, I became vice-president. Since Marshall was the secretary, we were brought together frequently, and although there was a considerable difference of years between us, we became close friends. From that time on my attitude toward him was that of an elder to a younger brother.

Map problems were the main feature of the course in the School of the Line. In addition to individual set piece exercises of the type found in Griepenkerl, we also engaged in two-sided map maneuvers. In these the commanders appointed for each side gave whatever orders they thought appropriate for the situation, and the umpires then worked out the results. Perhaps more than anything else these map maneuvers showed how much we needed systematic training in the techniques of staff work. At the beginning of the Line Class a student might take from a half to three-quarters of an hour to make his estimate of the situation, reach a decision, and issue his order, but after a year of practice two or three minutes would usually suffice. The order form became second nature to us. Moreover, we all learned to speak the same language. This kind of drill, which had been so lacking in the old army, was to be invaluable when we later faced the test of war.

If map problems were the backbone of the course work at Fort Leavenworth, it was the introduction of German order forms which brought the real revolution in staff training. The revised curriculum, while revolutionary in its implications, was not fundamentally new. It was actually nothing more than a realistic adaptation of the well-known *Kriegsspiel* or sham battle methods, themselves as old as the lawyers' moot court and the doctors' clinic. Although no one officer wrought this change single-handedly, a few names stand out as significant innovators. One of these was Maj. Eben Swift, a cavalry officer who served as an instructor at Leavenworth in 1893-1897 and again from 1904 to 1906. He put his students to work on command problems using such classics of European military practice as Verdy du Vernois's *War Game*. And in the absence of an English translation of Griepenkerl's *Tactical Exercises*, he set about preparing one himself, working with a French edition because he knew no German.

Swift's work made a profound impression on General Bell, the commandant. And when Bell became Chief of Staff, he arranged to have Swift ordered to Washington to help organize the curriculum of the new Army War College. Fortunately, the beginnings wrought during Swift's years at Leavenworth were not allowed to lapse after his departure. His work was taken up in 1907 by Maj. John F. Morrison, who became assistant commandant and senior instructor in the department of military art.

Major Morrison not only continued to use the applicatory method which required students to draft orders for concrete cases but arranged to devote a substantially larger portion of the course to this kind of discipline. In doing so, he built the foundations of doctrine upon which our whole modern system of command and staff rests. Many officers who served with Morrison shared my high opinion of his work. Among them was Lt. Col. Hunter Liggett of the 13th Infantry Regiment, which was stationed at Fort Leavenworth when I was going through the course there. Since many of his younger officers were keenly interested in the new tactical training being given in the school, Liggett arranged a special class meeting one or two evenings a week at which Morrison and some of his assistants served as instructors. After this had been going on for some time I happened to overhear Colonel Liggett discussing the question of army promotion; he was urging with evident sincerity that Major Morrison ought to be promoted to brigadier general immediately for the good of the service. To say the least, this was a most unusual compliment for a senior officer to pay his junior.

Although there were many keen instructors at Fort Leavenworth, the most interesting I met there was Capt. Arthur L. Conger of the 29th Infantry. He was a man of brilliant, if sometimes eccentric, genius. I frequently differed with him, but I think he inspired me to more real thought than any other teacher at the school.

Whether it was Captain Conger or another who led me to read Count von Moltke's *Tactical Problems* I cannot remember, but the experience was stimulating. This work gave me a lasting impression of the German system of general staff education and suggested the possibility of using the applicatory method as a practical means of measuring a staff's capacity during the years of peace. This idea so intrigued me I subsequently wrote an article on the subject. It appeared in the *National Service Magazine* for April, 1917, under the title "A Tactical Measuring Rod."

To reach a large audience, the faculty at Fort Leavenworth established a correspondence course for officers anywhere in the service. General Pershing was only one of the many who had availed themselves of this opportunity. He had been jumped from the grade of captain to that of brigadier general in 1906 before the new course had been established. Under the circumstances he obviously could not attend the school as a student.

Whether one took the course by mail or in person, every class suffered from one serious defect. We had no real military maps of any part of North America. We groused bitterly because we had to use German maps of the Franco-German frontier in the area around Metz. This appeared totally unrealistic; it would have been far more meaningful, we believed, had we been issued maps of Canada or Mexico.

Among those who protested at having to use European maps for staff problems was Capt. Fox Conner of the 1st Field Artillery. Yet only a few years later as General Pershing's Chief of Operations in the American Expeditionary Force (AEF) he was called upon to prepare for an American attack on Metz. And the maps he used were the very ones he had complained about in his student days. Thus it turned out because of an inability to supply the maps we wanted, American officers knew the topography of the theater of war in Europe better than any part of their own country.

Before I left the school, our engineers had begun to develop a satisfactory map of the region around Fort Leavenworth. And later on they turned out serviceable maps of the battle area at Gettysburg and other historic locations for use in executing tactical problems. We never even dreamed of the elaborate maps and reproduction services now available to students taking the course.

My class at the School of the Line graduated in June, 1909. Capt. A. W. Bjornstad, 28th Infantry, stood first; Capt. Paul B. Malone, 27th Infantry, second; and I placed third. We three along with the rest of the twenty-one officers with the highest standing in the line class were promptly detailed to take the Staff College course the following fall.

During the summer I spent much of my time with Maude and Mary at Fort Leavenworth in our pleasant home overlooking the river, but there were military occupations as well. My free hours were filled with professional reading on subjects which my recent studies induced me to pursue. And for a brief spell I was detailed as an instructor at the annual encampment of the Missouri National Guard near Joplin, Missouri. This assignment was far from unwanted since it gave me a further opportunity to follow my interest in the civilian components of the army. Although it was customary among Regular officers to take a patronizing view of these summer soldiers, I was gradually coming to realize that an interested and alert National Guardsman might know more about the profession of arms than an uninterested professional.

Shortly after the Staff College opened in the autumn of 1909, I was elected president of the service school branch of the Infantry Association. My young friend Lt. George Marshall was again elected secretary.

A new attitude was beginning to appear in the Infantry Association at that time. Hitherto it had operated almost exclusively to promote an increase in the number of Infantry regiments authorized for the army. Its members indulged in the idea that by proper organization they could lobby successfully in Congress. Under Capt. George H. Shelton, national secretary of the association and editor of the *Infantry Journal*, we began to take a broader view. Shelton, who was a member of the newly sanctioned General Staff Corps, advocated a well-balanced army and maintained that the Infantry had more to gain by seeking no more than its fair share in whatever establishment might be authorized.

Shelton's policy had appealed to me even before I was ordered to Fort Leavenworth. I had done whatever I could to advocate his measures, but it was clear to me now that the most effective support for this new and more disinterested role for the association would come from the service schools.

After serving there as student officers, we began to have a much broader conception of military organization. Above all, we came to appreciate the importance of teamwork among the several arms. Certainly our course work in tactical training had fostered this awareness.

Soon after I became president of the service school branch of the Infantry Association, I discussed this subject with my brother infantrymen. Many of them were in strong sympathy with the point of view presented by Shelton in the *Infantry Journal*. We therefore decided that our branch should start a crusade for a better organization of the army. To this end we undertook to confer with our brother officers in the other arms with a view to finding a mutually acceptable program. Our zeal for sweeping reforms was soon cooled by the reception we met.

Throughout the fall of 1909 we held meeting after meeting without reaching any agreement whatsoever. By December we were at an impasse. Each of the four arms (Infantry, Cavalry, Field Artillery, and Coast Artillery) still struggled for its own advantage. At that time each branch of the service had its own separate promotion list and each fought jealously to preserve it.

One afternoon toward the end of December I sat discussing our difficulties with Capt. Jens Bugge of the 28th Infantry, who had been my predecessor as president of the local branch of the association. I maintained that with sentiment in the army what it was at the time, anything like agreement would be impossible. To this Bugge replied, "What we need is a single list." When I asked him what he meant he explained that the officers of all arms should be placed on the same promotion list. This was an entirely novel idea to me although I learned later that Bugge had heard of the scheme from Capt. E. E. Booth of the 7th Cavalry, who had studied the question at some length during the preceding year.

The proposal to establish a single promotion list throughout the army was certainly radical, but it struck me as a solution to one of the major ills of the establishment—providing it was feasible in practice. Of this there seemed to be some doubt. When I took the single list idea up with the other members of the local Infantry Association branch, they showed little enthusiasm. Most of them thought the idea impractical. Almost to a man they said, "It won't work."

The single list scheme seemed beaten from the start. The only way to get past this barrier was to prove that it could work by a practical trial of the idea on its merits. During our Christmas vacation, I asked some of my comrades to work on this subject while we were free from our school duties. Several, including A. W. Bjornstad and George Marshall, agreed to help. We divided all the officers of the army into several lists of equal length. Each of us then took one of these lists and began to break it down on separate cards showing the length of service, time in grade, and other data for each individual officer.

In this way we could arrange the cards to try out various combinations or systems of promotion. In those days there were only about 3,000 officers of the line in the whole Regular Army, but they were scattered over the different lists maintained by the separate arms. So the task we had set for ourselves involved a good deal of highly detailed work. Nevertheless, by surrendering our holiday and working late each evening we completed the project, a workable single list including every officer of the line in the army. The 500 or more officers in the various services such as the Ordnance Department, the Signal Corps, and the Medical Corps were not included in our proposal.

Early in January, 1910, we transmitted the results of our vacation effort to Major Morrison who was then the assistant commandant. The finished product was in the form of a sixty-five-page bill to place before Congress. Major Morrison was most favorably impressed with our work, but to test it thoroughly, he referred it to a joint committee representing the other arms of the service as well as the Infantry.

Soon afterward Major Morrison forwarded the finished proposal with a strong endorsement through official channels to the War Department. I need hardly add that it was coolly received there and soon pigeonholed. Even so, the publicity given our scheme undoubtedly helped to develop sentiment for the single list although it was many years before this concept was finally made into law.

In retrospect it is difficult to recall how narrowly partisan were our loyalties in those days before World War I. We looked first to our regiment and then to our branch. We tended to think of ourselves as 15th Infantry or 6th Cavalry rather than as officers of the U.S. Army. Two years in close association with the officers of other arms at Fort Leavenworth did much to broaden my outlook in this respect. My work on the single list study went even further. I became persuaded that a drastic change in the attitudes of the officer corps as well as in the prevailing organization was absolutely necessary if the army were to meet the new responsibilities thrust upon it after 1898.

During the spring of 1910 a West Point alumni dinner held in Kansas City afforded me an excellent opportunity to vent some of the ideas which had been shaping in my mind. A toast "to the army" offered a perfect foil for my purposes. The substance of my reply was as follows:

> Fellow graduates, what is our proper and peculiar relation to the army? It is not a monopoly of military ability or training, for armies were trained before West Point was ever heard of and many of the most efficient officers in our service are not of the brotherhood of Benny Havens. If, then, good officers can be obtained without educating them at public expense, what is the justification for the military academy? Why is it an indispensable part of our army?

The answer is to be found in the mind of the creative genius whom we revere as the father of our country. If we read Washington's letters written during the Revolution, we find him overwhelmed not by the enemy but by misguided friends. He could reckon with Howe and Burgoyne and Cornwallis, but he could not reckon with unenlightened patriotism. He could surmount an obstacle like the ice-filled Delaware, but he never gained an inch through the partisan blindness of the Continental Congress.

The absence of military statesmanship was regarded by Washington as the greatest danger to the new republic, and as statesmanship must rest upon enlightened public opinion, it was the aim of his policy to establish a vital nucleus for such an opinion. It did not exist in his day, but he sought to plant the seed of its future growth. This was the conception of a military academy as it developed in his constructive mind.

West Point was founded not merely to train soldiers but to educate the nation, for victory must be organized in time of peace and there can be no constructive statesmanship without an enlightened opinion. This is what Secretary Root meant when he spoke at our centennial about the "informing genius" of West Point.

And now after the lapse of a century we may estimate the progress of Washington's ideal. How has West Point performed its higher functions? Have we a public opinion upon which we can hope to build an enlightened statesmanship of war?

It has been said that our army is suffering from too much introspection. This is a serious indictment if it is true. It means that the nucleus designed to expand into the nation's war force is not looking outward but is contemplating its own digestive apparatus. It means that the sons of Sylvanus Thayer are repudiating his whole system of education by degenerating into mere infantrymen, cavalrymen, artillerymen and engineers; that the chosen priesthood of the spirit of Washington are satisfying the country's demand for constructive military legislation by proposing self-serving promotion bills.

There is a great opportunity before us, but we must return to our old ideals, if we would embrace it. We must not be partisans of corps or arm, nor can we even be partisans of the regular establishment. For the army of Washington is the larger army of Regulars, National Guard, and volunteers, the American ideal of the nation in arms. If we would succeed, we must raise army legislation from the field of politics to the field of statesmanship. Herein lies the peculiar relation of West Point to the army.

And so, gentlemen, ... the army!

If my remarks at the alumni dinner failed to produce an immediate reformation of attitudes throughout the officer corps, at least the occasion gave me an incentive for gathering my wits and formulating a consistent view of this important problem. The Staff College regulation requiring each student to prepare a thesis on some military subject provided an almost identical spur. And soon after the alumni gathering I found myself once again before my classmates presenting an elaborate paper on the subject of army organization. My thesis was entitled "Changes in Law and Regulations Necessary to Reorganize the Army of the United States on a Tactical Basis."

In my thesis I called for a sweeping change in the existing organization. My proposal envisioned an army formed into brigades and divisions even though the units composing them were left widely scattered at camps or posts. A scattered division needs the tactical supervision of a competent commander even more than an assembled division does, yet under the prevailing territorial organization most if not all of the energies and abilities of the higher commanders were absorbed in the mechanics of administration to the detriment of training in the essentials of the military art.

Just how my proposed reorganization would obviate all this I tried to point out graphically in the final paragraphs of my paper:

> The great gain would not be in the economies of administration, important as these might become. With all of the details of supply, property and money accountability, as well as military justice cared for at division headquarters, there would be a new field of usefulness for the brigade commander. For the first time in the history of the American Army we would have general officers who were not too busy to practice their profession in time of peace. Every infantry brigade would have an infantry brigadier general to instruct and inspect it, and each of the other arms would enjoy a similar trained supervision.

> The brigadier general in his capacity as inspector would not be concerned with the details of administration but he would exert a most important influence on administrative activities by not permitting them to interfere with the military efficiency of his command. He would not check the commissary's vouchers, but he would see that the commissary performed his functions in the field. He would not count the number of chipped soup plates in the quartermaster's storehouse, but he would note how the quartermaster handled his field train during the maneuver. In short, in order to make his inspection of a regiment at the end of the season, the brigade commander would put it in the field for a week or two and make it solve every phase of a progressive war problem. If he found an inefficient tactical unit he would not have to write an inspection report. He would simply relieve the inefficient commander from the

responsibilities of command and give him an interval of leisure to be employed in the study of his profession.

My proposal could be accomplished without elaborate legislative changes. An executive order from the President would do the trick.

The editor of the *Infantry Journal* was sufficiently interested in my thesis to publish it in the November, 1910, issue where it attracted a gratifying amount of attention and provoked a lively discussion throughout the service. Nonetheless, as might be expected, my whole scheme was strongly opposed by most of the general officers then in command of the departments. If these general officers were ordered to lead brigades or divisions, they would have to learn something about tactics. Obviously this did not appeal to many of them.

The final exercise in our Staff College course was a historical ride over the route of Sherman's campaign of 1864 to Atlanta. This excursion, which had been introduced as an annual feature of the course four or five years before my time, was highly popular. The whole class went on a volunteer basis after graduation even though no mileage was authorized.

From Fort Oglethorpe, Georgia, some twenty-six of us set out southward on horseback toward Atlanta in a series of day-long rides. The itinerary for this expedition had been fixed the preceding autumn when the whole campaign was divided into twenty-one phases with a student officer assigned to each one. When the class arrived in a new territory, the officer who had made a detailed study of that portion of the campaign took charge and became our guide. Since the class had studied the campaign as a whole in a general way over a period of four or five months, we had some lively critiques.

All told, the historical ride lasted for twelve days. While we spent most of each day in the saddle, we passed the evenings in comfortable camps prepared for us by a cavalry detachment consisting of an officer and ten men who had been sent out for this purpose from the station complement at Fort Leavenworth.

14 From Fort Douglas to the Mexican Border

Although the Academic Board at Fort Leavenworth had recommended me especially for detail to the War College, the orders I received from the War Department sent me back to duty with troops. It was a pleasure to be returning to my old regiment, the 15th Infantry. But if I thought this would mean picking up where I left off when detailed to special duty, I was sadly mistaken. The old army life we had known was already fast becoming a thing of the past. And in some measure this was partly my own doing. Many of the reforms I had worked for—the single list, organization on tactical lines, frequent exercises and maneuvers employing large formations of all arms, and the use of reserve components as well as regulars—were part of the ferment against the traditional life and restricted loyalties of the small units on isolated posts which had characterized the old army.

From our farewell dinner in Atlanta after the historical ride, my orders sent me directly to Peoria for duty as an instructor at the summer encampment of the Illinois National Guard. From Peoria I went to Pine Camp, New York, to serve as an umpire at the annual encampment of the Department of the East under Maj. Gen. Fred D. Grant, the son of President Ulysses S. Grant. Among the many I encountered that summer, I remember in particular Pvt. James Shine. He had been devoted to Maude after she had befriended him during our stay at Fort Grant in Arizona many years before. So on seeing his unit listed among those present at Pine Camp, I made a point of looking him up.

After the conclusion of the summer exercises I applied for two weeks' leave and hurried out to Petersburg to join Maude and Mary. While visiting there and in Springfield I tried to improve the occasion by drawing my old friends and relations into discussions about the desperate need for a better military establishment. It was uphill work. There was no public interest at all in this subject at that time, and my neighbors were no exception to the general rule. The whole country was thoroughly isolationist in outlook, and almost nobody believed we should ever have much need for soldiers again.

One evening at a small social gathering at the country club in Springfield I suggested that it would be a fine thing to have a military post established nearby. This proposal was received with immense enthusiasm; my friends favored millions for a military post at Springfield but not one cent for a regiment to occupy it.

When my leave ran out we resumed our journey to Fort Douglas where once again I found myself a company commander. My experience in the service schools had given me a new interest in the responsibilities of this position, and now I was determined to apply the Leavenworth methods of tactical instruction to the men in my company. Instead of the monotonous old infantry drills I conducted maneuvers, pitting one platoon against another. And in the noncommissioned officer schools I gave them on a small scale some of the problems I had studied on a large scale. The whole experience was an eye-opener to me. The men responded to these practical methods of instruction with genuine enthusiasm.

When the regimental commander placed me in charge of the officer's school at the post, I was able to test the new techniques even further. Instead of the routine recitations of former years I gave the class map problems. After working up through increasingly complex problems to a series of two-sided map maneuvers, we moved outside for terrain exercises conducted in the area about the fort. The introduction of Leavenworth methods in the training program certainly gave the young officers of the regiment an insight into their profession which was completely lacking when I was a lieutenant. By means of these exercises I found I could pick out the young men of real tactical ability long before we actually went out into the field to maneuver with troops.

Although my duties as a training officer absorbed much of my time and energy, life as a company commander at Fort Douglas did not entirely curtail my interest in the larger issues of military policy. During the month of November, 1910, my fellow officers in the 15th Infantry elected me to serve as their delegate to the annual meeting of the Infantry Association held at the Great Northern Hotel in Chicago. The Chicago meeting developed into a hot fight between the old-timers and the Young Turks. As usual, the old-timers wanted to support a lobby to work for an increase in the Infantry. As it turned out, a majority of the delegates present were men who had recently taken the course at Leavenworth, so we carried the day.

I now realized that most of the army reforms I looked for would be accomplished only after more officers went through the Line School and the Staff College. Few who were exposed to the Leavenworth curriculum could continue to maintain the narrow loyalties and branch prejudices which characterized the old army, but the pace of time was slow indeed.

Just how slowly the Leavenworth influence permeated the upper echelons of the army may be seen from the composition of the General Staff at that time. The *Army Register* for 1910 showed four officers in the Staff Corps who had graduated at Leavenworth, seven who had been through the War College, and only three who had completed Secretary Root's ideal of staff training by graduating from both schools. This left thirty-one out of a total of forty-five who had had no General Staff education at all, and this majority included the Chief of Staff and all his senior officers. In fact, not until twenty-five years later when Gen. Malin Craig became Chief of Staff did the army come under the command of an officer who had had a complete General Staff education.

Shortly after my return to Fort Douglas from the Infantry Association meeting in Chicago, word reached us that the 15th Infantry would soon be going out to the Philippines. Maude and little Mary hurried home to Illinois for one last visit with the grandparents before going out to San Francisco where they were to meet me and board the transport for the long voyage across the Pacific. Their eastbound train was hardly over the horizon when a new set of orders arrived at regimental headquarters. Instead of going to the Philippines, the 15th Infantry was to proceed to San Antonio, Texas, to form part of a so-called Maneuver Division which was being assembled at Fort Sam Houston.

This last-minute change of plans, so typical of army life, called for some rapid readjustments in the arrangements we had made for our household effects. As I went out of the headquarters building I grumbled to one of my fellow officers, Capt. Charles H. "Duke" Bridges, about the awful job of packing ahead of me. He said he had the same chore to do. A little later as I bustled by on some errand I was surprised to see him sitting on his front porch doing nothing. Somewhat incredulously I asked him about his packing. "It's done," he replied. "All I ever do is pack my trunk and bedding roll. I never pack the other things; I just leave them in the house and buy a new supply at my next station."

In due time the 15th Infantry arrived at San Antonio and marched out to its campsite on the reservation at Fort Sam Houston. The Maneuver Division which we joined comprised eight regiments of infantry assembled from all over the United States, a regiment of cavalry, a regiment of artillery, a battalion of engineers, a signal battalion, a hospital unit, and some other service contingents. Somewhat naively, we thought all these troops made a truly impressive concentration of force.

In point of fact the Maneuver Division was a rather sorry affair. Its eight infantry regiments—all at half-strength—were grouped into three improvised brigades under three brigadier generals of whom not one had ever held such a command before. For that matter, the major general who was to lead the division itself had never previously commanded a force of all arms.

Indeed, few of those present in San Antonio during the spring of 1911 had ever seen so many soldiers all in one place let alone commanded them with competence. And now, when a larger organization became available, we hardly knew what to do with it. We knew so little that we did not know how little we knew.

The 15th Infantry, along with the 11th and the 18th formed the First Brigade of the Maneuver Division. A few days after we reached San Antonio, I was directed to report to Brig. Gen. F. A. Smith, our brigade commander. He told me he wanted me to serve on his staff for two reasons. First, I had been highly recommended by my old friend Col. Arthur Williams, who was now in command of the 11th Infantry. And second, since he himself had never had any tactical education, he felt the need of a trained staff officer, a recent graduate of the Staff College, who could develop the tactical instruction of the brigade.

After I had thanked the general for honoring me with the position of brigade adjutant, he directed me to make an estimate of our needs at headquarters. To get started, he suggested, we would need a sergeant major, an assistant sergeant major, and several clerks, as well as typewriters, office supplies, and various other facilities for a large headquarters office. To his surprise I replied that we would need only one sergeant and one clerk and a single hospital tent. A few days later, however, he admitted good-humoredly that I was right. He had just returned from visiting one of the other brigade commanders, who had surrounded himself with a big staff and was already swamped with paper work.

For the first time in my army career I found myself engaged in the delicate business of educating a general officer. This was a matter requiring great tact. Fortunately I hit upon a scheme which worked beautifully, and in no time General Smith and I got along famously. Every night after dinner I smoked an evening cigar with him in his tent. Somehow, on leaving, I would contrive to leave my book of tactical instructions lying forgotten on his table. I never told the general that it contained the lesson he should study; instead I accidentally left a bookmark in the right place. Later as I passed by his open tent I would see the old gentleman deeply engrossed in the appropriate passages. Then next day when the brigade officers were assembled he would give them a learned lecture on some phase of brigade tactics.

The assembly of so many troops at San Antonio might have served a most useful purpose if we had made it an occasion for much-needed tactical instruction for large formations. Instead, while waiting in the rain, we seemed very much in danger of being carried away by our own newspaper headlines which hailed our troop concentration as a "mobilization on the Mexican border."

For all its ineptitude, the Maneuver Division was a matter of great interest to the newspapers. Photographers and correspondents were soon crowding into San Antonio looking for colorful news stories.

Not long after the 15th Infantry reached Fort Sam Houston, a group of newsmen banded together to give what they called a beefsteak dinner for all the senior officers of the division. In addition to the beefsteak there was an abundant supply of very excellent barleycorn. Some of our senior officers became a bit indiscreet and made references to Mexico and Japan which may have delighted the newsmen but gave me the shivers. Finally the toastmaster called on young Capt. Aldebert de Chambrun, the military attaché from the French embassy, who had come down to watch our maneuvers. Captain de Chambrun rose and said, "In my country we have a tradition that diplomats should rarely speak and soldiers never, so I will simply say that I hope we may see less rain in San Antonio."

I have always considered de Chambrun's remarks the fittest short speech that I ever heard; among other things, it put an end to the indiscretions of my military superiors. Perhaps one should have expected no less from such a distinguished officer, for the captain was the Count de Chambrun, a descendent of the Marquis de Lafayette. Because of this lineage he enjoyed the unusual privilege of holding citizenship in the United States as well as in France. He had other ties with this country as well; he was married to the gifted Clara Longworth, sister of Nicholas Longworth, longtime Speaker of the House of Representatives.

So far as I can recall, the principle characteristic of the Maneuver Division was that it never maneuvered—at least while I was in it. Every morning our troops would turn out for a session of close order drill just as they had been doing for years past at their little home stations all over the country. The War Department provided something of a climax to this whole operation by inviting the various foreign military attaches in Washington to travel down to Texas to see our wonderful army in action. We were so ignorant of what an army should be that we saw nothing absurd in the invitation. Along with Captain de Chambrun of the French Army these official guests included a Major Hans Wolfgang von Herwarth of the Great General Staff in Berlin.

I was curious to see how our military display would impress Herwarth, but if he saw any difference between our hastily contrived Maneuver Division and a Prussian Guards division he made no sign of it. He did not show me his official report to his superiors at Potsdam, but the gist of it must have been: "These Americans have absolutely no tactical organization even in their little Regular Army and no settled plans for war expansion. It will be impossible for them to extemporize a war army in a reasonable time because even their professional officers, and especially their seniors, have little or no conception of what a modern army is." When a number of the junior officers complained that they were doing no maneuvering, some of us suggested to General Smith that he might wish to take the brigade up to the Leon Spring campgrounds about twenty miles from San Antonio. There at least he could hold brigade maneuvers if nothing better. The jovial old gentleman embraced this suggestion with enthusiasm.

We prepared a program of one-sided maneuvers for the brigade before leaving San Antonio, so on the morning after our arrival at Leon Spring the general directed me to ride out and select a site for the first of these exercises. This was to be a deployment of the brigade in a defensive position. As I mounted my horse the general said, "Captain Palmer, go out there and find us a position with a front of two or three miles." Now a two- or three-mile front was manifestly too much for a single brigade to defend, but I couldn't very well contradict my superior to his face. Instead I simply failed to find the site he asked for. The only defensive position I could find had a front of about one-half mile with well-protected flanks, a front narrow enough to form the brigade in depth.

When I returned from reconnoitering I said, "General, I couldn't find a good position near camp with a front as broad as you directed, but I did find one where it will be possible to deploy the brigade in depth with supports, reserves, and a field hospital all in their proper places." Then once again I conveniently left my book of tactical instructions in the general's tent with the proper lesson duly marked. The next day he assembled all the officers and gave them a critique. "Gentlemen," he said, "I have occupied this position to give you an opportunity to understand the importance of depth in military formation. The usual trouble with the American Army is that we are inclined to disperse all over the country, and I desire to call this defect to your attention."

While we were still out at Leon Spring I received a letter bearing exciting news. It was from Capt. William S. Graves, the secretary of the General Staff, who wrote to forewarn me that orders would soon arrive for me to proceed to Washington for duty on the General Staff.

Apparently my initial effort in the education of a general officer was not entirely a failure, for in relieving me from duty as brigade adjutant, General Smith presented me with a most complimentary letter. In particular he expressed appreciation for the "efficient, capable and zealous manner" in which I made available my professional knowledge acquired at Fort Leavenworth.

But the congratulatory letter which pleased me most came from my good friend Maj. James W. McAndrew of the 8th Infantry who was then serving as an instructor at Fort Leavenworth.

> Nothing that I have seen for some time in the way of Army news pleased me more than the notice of your selection for the General Staff. Although we knew for some time it was coming, it was good to see it in

black and white in an official order. As infantrymen we need you in Washington, and the Army as a whole needs you there.

McAndrew was an able officer who was to go on and become General Pershing's Chief of Staff in France. He had been one of the most active leaders in the Chicago meeting of the Infantry Association during the previous year, when we maneuvered the Old Guard into supporting a less partisan policy. And now as I was about to go off to join the General Staff, McAndrew's letter made me realize that I went not alone, but with the support of all the Young Turks in the Infantry Association behind me.

15 General Staff Duty

In 1911 the War Department was still located in that bewildering pile of pillars and porches just west of the White House, so my path to work led me down Connecticut Avenue. And what a beautiful old Connecticut Avenue it was then. There were large trees on either side of the street and another double row down the center flanking the streetcar tracks. And instead of the bustling business establishments of today, fine old private residences lined the avenue almost all the way down to where a convent occupied the site of the present Mayflower Hotel.

On reaching the War Department, I reported directly to Maj. Gen. Leonard Wood, who was then the Chief of Staff. With many other officers in the old army I shared a prejudice against him because he seemed to be the beneficiary of presidential favoritism, but when I went into his office I came immediately under the charm of his personality. On his desk he had a marked copy of the *Infantry Journal* containing my Leavenworth thesis proposing a tactical organization for the army, and he gave me the impression that I would soon have an opportunity to carry its doctrine into effect. Although I didn't know it at the moment, I was soon to be deflated.

Before World War I the General Staff was organized into three major divisions. Two of these, the Mobile Army Division and the Coast Artillery Division, were located in the War Department building proper with offices adjacent to the Chief of Staff. The third, or War College Division, was situated in the new War College building down on Greenleaf Point at what is now called Fort Lesley J. McNair. Most of the important current decisions were handled by the two staff divisions in the War Department building. Memoranda that these officers near the throne did not care to act upon and problems requiring the preparation of exhaustive staff studies were sent on down for consideration at the War College or "W.C." Division. The inferior status of the "W.C." Division inevitably led army wags to apply this abbreviation in its least flattering sense, to the discomfiture of officers on duty there. I was therefore grievously disappointed to receive orders assigning me to the War College Division. For some little time my duties involved nothing more than keeping the General Staff map of the Mexican border up to date by shifting colored pins from day to day as news arrived from that quarter.

While still smarting at having been relegated, so it seemed, to the War College Division, I received orders sending me off for a week of detached service as an umpire at the annual maneuvers being held by the Massachusetts Militia of Essex and Middlesex counties. On reaching Boston I discovered that the maneuvers were to be conducted by my friends Capt. Matthew E. Hanna and Lt. George C. Marshall, my instructors at Fort Leavenworth. The exercise which they had prepared was an interesting one. The Massachusetts troops were divided into two parts. One was to represent an invading force which, after landing at Newburyport, was to move up the Merrimack valley. The other force, stationed between Lawrence and Haverhill, was to advance against the invaders.

In setting up this mock invasion, Marshall, who had carried out most of the detailed planning, had done a remarkable job. He had worked for several months preparing every phase of the action and securing permission from landowners for our troops to cross their property. The government did not then own extensive maneuver areas in the East, and every large military exercise ran the risk of incurring a whole string of damage and trespass suits. But Marshall had contrived this operation so cleverly that there was no need for deployments or troop contacts except on land owned by people who had given permission for its use. In all other places the problem was so arranged that the troops moved only along the public ways. And surprisingly enough all this was accomplished without producing a situation too utterly farfetched or unrealistic.

Back at the War College Division, while marking time over the Mexican frontier maps, I decided to employ my energies in an attempt to revive interest in the Single List or Consolidated Promotion Bill which we had drafted out at Leavenworth in 1910. Because I was an infantry officer, my advocacy was open to the suspicion that the proposal smacked of branch preference. To forestall this criticism, my friends Capt. Fox Conner of the Field Artillery and Capt. Matthew E. Hanna of the Cavalry prepared brief statements of concurrence and all three items were published in full by the *Army and Navy Journal* in July, 1911.

As we saw the problem it came down to this: the army, as currently organized, was no army at all; lacking in tactical organization, it was entirely unsuited either to peacetime training or to operations in war. Each of the arms and services, with its separate promotion list, presented Congress with a different view of what the army needed. Each too often tended to see the national interest only in terms of more regiments of infantry or cavalry—and hence more openings for promotions. The hope of the single list advocates was that it would remove entirely the question of organization from the question of promotion. Once assured that promotion was in no way affected by proposed reorganizations, the officer corps as a whole would desist from lobbying, and the General Staff would be free to prepare rational plans for the nation's defense.

The single list scheme drawn up at Fort Leavenworth placed every officer of the three arms on one roster according to seniority. Thereafter promotions would go to the first eligible officer in each grade without regard to the arm in which the vacancy appeared. To avoid the inconveniences of transfers between arms in which, for example, a lieutenant colonel of Infantry would move up into the command of a colonel of Cavalry, we hoped to get Congress to authorize an extra list or reservoir of officers for whom command assignments were not immediately available. By this means we expected to equalize promotions in the three arms and at the same time save officers from having to assume commands outside their range of training. Unfortunately Congress subsequently failed to establish an extra list as large as we had hoped for, so our original Leavenworth bill had to be revised.

As soon as it was published, our single list article stirred up a veritable hornet's nest. Letters for and against the plan filled the pages of the *Army and Navy Journal* for months thereafter. Although most of the letter writers opposing our idea hid behind pseudonyms, it was perfectly clear that the major resistance came from the Field Artillery, where a substantial increase in the number of authorized regiments was expected in the near future.

The critics solemnly pointed out how terrible it would be for half-educated infantrymen and cavalrymen to go into a highly scientific arm like the Field Artillery. This point was stressed to me in a conversation with Lieutenant P., an excellent young artilleryman. When he expounded the scientific and abstruse character of the Field Artillery and the impossibility that it would be for an outsider to acquire the necessary skills, I suddenly remembered that this very lieutenant had been one of my cadets when I was an instructor in chemistry at West Point. It amused me to recall that his scientific attainments at that time were not quite high enough to keep him out of the lowest section in chemistry. So in reply to his allegations regarding the unusual abilities demanded of artillerymen I reminded him of his marginal performance, and then concluded by saying, "But I see, Lieutenant P., that you have finally made good at it."

After I had served an apprenticeship of two months or more as a General Staff officer at the War College Division, General Wood finally gave me an opportunity to prove myself. He directed me to prepare a staff paper looking to a major reorganization of the land forces of the United States. Why he selected a humble captain for this important duty would be hard to say.

Presumably my advocacy of the single list had marked me out as an officer who was working for the service as a whole and not merely for his own branch. Doubtlessly my article in the *Infantry Journal* on a tactical organization for the army played some part in bringing me to the attention of the Chief of Staff.

Early in the autumn of 1911, I reported back to General Wood that I was prepared to submit some preliminary conclusions on the broad lines of policy which should serve as a basis for my future work. Instead of hearing my proposals then, however, the general told me that in a few days he intended to inspect Fort Leavenworth and Fort Riley with the new Secretary of War, the Hon. Henry L. Stimson, and he wanted me to go along too.

Soon after our train left Washington, General Wood took me to the Secretary's drawing room. When asked for my views I pointed out that the problem before us was much more than a matter of determining the total strength of the army, the location of its units, or the particular organization applied to them; what we needed was nothing less than a comprehensive military policy for the United States. Until such a policy was formulated none of the problems of detail could be resolved effectively.

Of one thing I was certain: Whatever the particulars of that policy, in principle it must be in complete harmony with the social and political institutions of a democratic people. With this in mind, it had been apparent to me for some time that the old army doctrine of an expansible standing army could have no congenial place on the American scene. It was my grandfather, the "politician general" of Civil War days, who had first opened my eyes to this realization, when I was a brand-new second lieutenant.

When I set out to prove my grandfather wrong by working out an expansible army scheme in detail, the wisdom of his remarks became increasingly apparent. If I assumed a peacetime nucleus big enough to make a real foundation for effective expansion for a great war, I found the taxpayers would be saddled with a big standing army in time of peace. If I assumed a peacetime nucleus small enough to give any chance of acceptance by Congress, it would result in too small a war army, unless I presupposed a rate of expansion that would be obviously absurd.

After much reading and a good deal of experience as a leader of typical American soldiers, the truth of my grandfather's contentions was brought home to me. This led me off on another track. If American citizen armies, extemporized after the outbreak of war, could do as well as the citizen armies of Grant and Lee, what might they not do if organized and trained in time of peace? This then should be the basis of our wartime military force. Instead of expanding a standing army we should simply mobilize a preexisting citizen reserve and give it further training after mobilization.

The traditional policy of the United States, I pointed out, has been to rely upon a small Regular Army in time of peace and upon a great army of citizen soldiers in time of war. Such a policy has been and will be in harmony with the national spirit. It follows therefore that our most important military problem is to devise means of preparing great armies of citizen soldiers to meet the emergency of modern war. The organization of the Regular Army is but a smaller phase of this problem.

Secretary Stimson and General Wood listened to my exposition with interest and after some little discussion they agreed that it should be accepted as the cornerstone of our subsequent efforts to formulate the details of a general military policy for the United States. In effect, their decision moved the center of gravity or central focus of our national military policy away from the Regular Army where it had generally rested and placed it instead on the citizen army and its relation to the permanent establishment.

Once this fundamental principle was agreed upon, I felt free to go on to a consideration of the details. Our long rail journey gave me numerous occasions to express my ideas on the need for consolidated promotion and a tactical rather than a geographical organization for the army. Here too the principles expounded in my published articles on these subjects were approved as a basis for future planning. Thus, long before we returned to Washington, my work as a staff officer for months to come was cut out for me.

Once back at my desk in the War College, it should have been clear sailing, but there were many interruptions and delays. For example, hardly had I settled down when a directive arrived placing me on a committee to consider garrisoning the department of Hawaii.

The Hawaiian garrison problem was typical of the grist being ground through the newly erected General Staff mill. We took great pains to prepare objective and factual studies although we were often expected to reach conclusions regarding vital tactical matters with no more information than we could derive from the maps and papers already in the files at the War College. Subsequently the Chief of Staff wisely decided to send a board of officers out to Honolulu to inspect the ground in person. At my suggestion he selected Lt. Col. John F. Morrison, the assistant commandant at the Army Staff College as a member of the group. In recommending him I knew the job would be done well. What is more, it pleased me to be able to reward in some small way the service Morrison had rendered me at Leavenworth, where he did so much to direct my thinking and shape my career.

The first draft of my policy study amounted to a small book of some 200 typescript pages entitled "The Organization of the Land Forces of the United States." Each of its eleven chapters constituted a separate staff paper on some important aspect of army organization: the relation of the home forces to foreign garrisons, the necessity of a reserve system, tactical organization for mobile troops, the relation of promotion to organization, and so on.

I knew from my experience with the single list article and the reaction it stirred up in the *Army and Navy Journal* that it would be well to subject my work to the scrutiny of other minds and other points of view before seeking final approval by the Chief of Staff and the Secretary of War. General Wood agreed, and at my request detailed Lt. Col. R. P. Davis of the Coast Artillery, Maj. William Lassiter of the Field Artillery, and Capt. George V. H. Moseley of the Cavalry as a committee to work with me. After our committee reached agreement, copies of the study were referred to the various agencies of the War Department for consideration. Typical of the branch prejudices and partisan attitudes we met were the objections raised against our plans for the overseas forces.

In order to have a stable tactical organization at home it was necessary to reorganize the military garrison in the Philippines. At that time a regiment stationed, say, in Texas would be sent to the Pacific for two years. At the end of this tour it would be relieved by another regiment from the states and sent home to a new station, say, in northern New York. There was no serious objection to this so long as the army at home was merely a scattered constabulary, a series of regimental posts for the most part in Indian country. But this continual shifting of whole regiments to and from the Philippines would interfere with the stability of the proposed new organization into tactical brigades and divisions. And this evil would grow worse in the future, for enlarged garrisons would soon be required in Oahu and the Panama Canal Zone. The only practical solution was to assign certain regiments permanently to foreign stations.

In 1912 there were eight half-strength Infantry regiments and four half-strength Cavalry regiments in the Philippines. We therefore recommended that all the infantry soldiers should be concentrated in four full-strength regiments and all the cavalry in two. This would make it possible to bring home all the officers and overhead of four Infantry regiments and two Cavalry regiments and make them available to fill some of the gaps in the proposed tactical brigades and division. There would be no reduction in the number of effective combat soldiers in the Philippines, but the net cost of the garrison would be materially reduced. Since the existing field service regulations were concocted to give the maximum possible number of professional officers in any given number of troops, our full-strength regiments—which meant more men and fewer officers—brought down a frightful clamor upon us.

If our proposed reorganization met with a chilly reception among junior line officers, who saw it as a threat to their hopes of promotion, it was attacked even more bitterly by many of the senior officers of the army. Those who saw their accustomed routines in the geographic departments threatened by our scheme of tactical organization into divisions and brigades were particularly critical. One of the most outspoken of these opponents was Maj. Gen. Arthur Murray, an old army artilleryman who at that time commanded the three Western departments. What was the basis of his opposition? "Why," he replied, "you are a captain and I a major general." Then he added, "There are two stars on my shoulder and only two bars on yours," as if that settled the matter once and for all without further explanation or justification. And so long as senior officers persisted in this kind of attitude, the very principle of a General Staff as conceived by Secretary of War Elihu Root was endangered. If the staff had to bow to superior rank merely because it was superior without an opportunity to weigh objections on their merits, then the army could never hope to formulate an objective military policy to present to the nation.

Of course, as Chief of Staff, Gen. Leonard Wood could accept our report, which pleased him, and send it to the Hill, but to do so without wide support from within the department would only insure the defeat of every reform we hoped for. General Wood, always a controversial figure, had many enemies in Congress. At the very time we were working on our studies of army reorganization, the long-smoldering dispute between the Chief of Staff and his Adjutant General, the notorious Maj. Gen. Fred C. Ainsworth, came to a head with the latter's dismissal. I need not recount that dramatic quarrel here; it has been adequately told by others. But while General Wood emerged the victor in his contest with Ainsworth, he was left with a considerable residue of hostility among the congressional friends of the former Adjutant General.

Just how vindictive the Ainsworth clique could be may be suggested by the rider tacked on the army appropriations bill for 1912. It was baldly contrived to legislate General Wood from office. This was hardly an atmosphere in which one could expect favorable treatment of a measure from the War Department proposing sweeping reforms and bearing the enthusiastic endorsement of General Wood himself. Confronted with widespread opposition from within the army and heading for a hostile Congress, the plan seemed doomed almost from the start. But we reckoned without the astute political skills and administrative talents of Secretary of War Henry L. Stimson.

My journey to Fort Leavenworth and Fort Riley with General Wood and Secretary Stimson had given me a wonderful opportunity to know them both rather more intimately than I ever expected before being detailed to General Staff duty. It was not until sometime later, however, that I first came to appreciate Secretary Stimson's very real abilities as a leader. One day in July, 1912, General Wood and I went to see the Secretary in his home about some feature of the appropriation measure then before Congress. We arrived to find Maj. Gen. W. H. Carter, the Assistant Chief of Staff, there before us. He and Mr. Stimson were discussing the formation of a supply corps consolidating the subsistence, quartermaster, and other related departments into a single organization. To my disgust, as they concluded their conversation, the secretary asked General Carter to draw up a bill for the kind of supply corps he thought we ought to have.

I knew that General Carter ought not to be working independently on what was really one facet of the whole larger problem being considered by our committee on reorganization. What is more, I was convinced that General Carter's old-fashioned ideas would turn out to be entirely unsuitable.

When General Wood and I had completed our business and were about to go, Secretary Stimson asked me to remain behind a while to explain something about the staff organizations of the French and German armies. This gave me an opportunity to get around to the subject of the supply corps.

After General Carter had departed, I said "Mr. Secretary, I was a little disappointed that you should give the job to General Carter." He smiled and I continued. "To be perfectly frank, I don't think General Carter is familiar with the data upon which the solution should be based." The secretary came over to me then and said, "Well, to be perfectly frank with you, Captain Palmer, I gave it to General Carter just to keep him occupied." Much relieved at this revelation, I again moved to depart, whereupon Mr. Stimson sat me down and began explaining in detail what his plans were for dealing with our reorganization proposals.

Instead of publishing the report and then letting the army critics fire away at it as originally intended, Secretary Stimson decided to reverse the order. He had copies of our draft furnished to every division of the General Staff, all the bureau chiefs, and interested army commands. And all officers were then informed that they would be given an opportunity to submit their criticisms and objections in an open court over which the Secretary of War would preside in person. This was a masterful stroke, for in this way he forced the opposition to deal with the proposed reforms openly and on their merits.

Secretary Stimson's plan of procedure had decided advantages, too, when dealing with Congress. If our whole reorganization study were hammered out, section by section, in public, before going to the Hill, then there could be no claim in Congress that the measure did not truly reflect the desires of the army. And to make sure that there was no slip-up in this respect, Mr. Stimson invited the chairmen of both the Senate and House Military Affairs Committees to sit on the bench with him if they cared to. This was nothing less than brilliant strategy inasmuch as Representative Hay, chairman of the latter committee, was the leader of the House cabal against General Wood. Senator Root, as the father of the General Staff, was also invited to sit in on the policy sessions.

The Secretary of War lost no time in getting under way. Hardly an hour after I left he issued the orders establishing the open court he had just outlined to me. And a day or two later we commenced the first session. Mr. Stimson's procedure was simplicity itself: he had the report read section by section, then, after each section, he invited frank criticism from any officer present. After each criticism he called upon our committee to reply.

As the author of the original plan, the burden of the rebuttal generally fell upon me. Like a young lawyer arguing a case before a very distinguished court, I was fully aware of the responsibility resting upon me. I knew I was making the fight of my life. Success here would have a crucial effect upon my subsequent career, so I worked furiously to prepare myself by mastering all the myriad details which lay behind the text of our study. By and large, most of the objections were withdrawn when the reasons for a provision were fully explained. In other instances, the secretary made a decision, sometimes sustaining the committee and sometimes directing us to revise the provision at issue.

We had to devote many long, hot summer afternoons to the hearings, but the experience was well worth the effort. To begin with, the secretary's open court marched a whole gallery of leading army personalities upon the stage to demonstrate their skills and foibles.

Take old General Aleshire, for example. Maj. Gen. J. B. Aleshire was the Quartermaster General of the Army. As a bureau chief he was much disturbed over the consolidated supply corps we proposed to establish. Following one afternoon session in which we had had quite a tilt, he invited me to his office where he asked me just what I was after. To this I replied, "General, we have no bias in this matter. Your point of view is the departmental point of view; ours is the view of the war army, the fighting army in the field. In the settlement of this matter there must be a compromise. All we insist is that your point of view be presented as ably and as objectively as you can give it and that our point of view be presented too. Then the secretary can make the necessary compromise with a full appreciation of the facts." This spirit of fair play immediately appealed to the fine old gentleman, and thereafter he was one of us.

On the other hand Brig. Gen. E. M. Weaver, the chief of the Coast Artillery, was much perturbed over the plan we presented for recruiting our volunteer reserve or civilian component. When we concluded the open session which revealed our differences, he buttonholed me and smilingly declared he wanted to have a talk. We were no sooner seated in his office when be began, "Little man (I didn't like that very much), you have done the finest piece of work that has ever been done in the United States Army. True, you are only one of a committee, but we all know you are the wheelhorse." Then, believing he had softened me up with appropriate blarney, he proceeded to tell me how he differed with us in regard to the problems at hand and to put out advice on what course we should take in the next day's session.

By the time we were halfway through the hearings, it became evident that our reorganization was going to carry. Although we accepted many modifications along the way, we did not have to yield on one material point. The only real opponent we had on a serious matter of principle was General Carter, the assistant chief of staff. He stood for the old idea taught by Emory Upton in his *Military Policy of the United States* which called for an expansible Regular Army and therefore he deprecated our emphasis on the organized civilian reserves. It grew apparent at the hearings that what he stood for would soon be discarded. His little speeches in opposition aroused little interest. At last, he too came over and joined the majority in favor of the reorganization.

It was most diverting to see how people crawled up on the bandwagon as we made our case. From the very beginning I had good reason to believe that General Carter was trying to soft-pedal our report. Just before the open hearings began he called me into his office and said, "Palmer, you have a very ingenious pen. Don't be discouraged if that report doesn't go all at once. At any rate it will be a good book, and the service should read it." Then, somewhat later, when he saw how we had begun to roll, he called me in again to tell me he had changed his mind. "When I first read that report, he said, I must confess I read it hurriedly. I thought it was only an essay. During these conferences I've read it line by line, and I want to say this now. I wrote the bill creating the General Staff. Since then it has sometimes appeared to be a mistake. But the work you four junior officers have done in writing a harmonious policy for the army is vindication enough for the whole General Staff idea. It demonstrates that the conception of Secretary Root was not a mistake." Coming from General Carter, this capitulation was most generous indeed.

While Secretary Stimson's open hearings afforded a most interesting spectacle of the human relations behind a staff at work, they were even more significant as an example of effective leadership at the top. As a trained lawyer, Mr. Stimson reduced all ex parte views to clear issues for decision. In the United States, where it is a settled principle of government that the civil authority is superior to the military, he really maintained his position of superiority. Only by weighing the conflicting opinions of experts and specialists, as he did, can civilian secretaries definitely settle those questions of military policy which rest upon technical considerations. Too often Mr. Stimson's predecessors made decisions on complex questions without realizing that only one of several ex parte views had been presented to them. If any of his successors have repeated the error, it has not been from lack of a sound precedent.

In its final form the revised staff study, "The Organization of the Land Forces of the United States" was published as an annex to Secretary Stimson's annual report for 1912. The mobile land forces were to include three distinct elements:

1. The Regular Army organized into full divisions and into brigades of cavalry both to be ready for immediate use—as an expeditionary force if need be—while the citizen soldiery mobilized. The formation of divisions, effective tactical units of all arms trained to function together, would make it possible for the War Department to set a striking force in motion during an emergency by sending a single telegram. Under the prevailing organization of the army the concentration of such a force consumed days on end as orders went out to small detachments all over the country. And even when finally assembled these elements could

hardly be called a true division. As our experience with the Maneuver Division on the Mexican border had shown us, not until the officers and men of the several arms learned to function as a single team did a division become a significant tactical force. To wait until after an emergency arrived to begin this team training was nothing less than reckless negligence—yet this is precisely what the nation had done in every previous crisis.

2. A reserve army of citizen soldiers organized during peace into complete divisions and prepared to reinforce the Regular Army in time of war. The first line of this reserve army already existed in the National Guard, but to make it fully available Congress would have to pass legislation to permit the Guard to be absorbed into the Regular Army with the coming of war. So long as state troops continued to be organized under the militia clause of the Constitution, they could never be employed to maximum effectiveness by the federal government.

3. An army of volunteers, citizen soldiers, to be organized under prearranged plans when an emergency arose which required forces greater than those furnished by the Regular Army and the organized reserve. Strange as it may seem, in 1912 there was no standing legislation on the statute books providing a system by which the Regular Army and the National Guard could be reinforced in time of need. True, the law did hold all able-bodied citizens theoretically liable for militia duty, but no machinery existed to transform this obligation into tactical units. Every other modern army in the world had built up an elaborate system by which the standing army could be expanded and fed with replacements from the national manpower pool in time of need. In the United States such a system would have to be extemporized after the crisis arrived. Since the resulting delay might well prove fatal to the nation's defense, and inasmuch as it would cost nothing to provide a legal framework for an army of citizen soldiers, the legislations we expected of Congress appeared to us as nothing more than common sense.

The threefold organization described above would never provide an effective military force unless it were to be administered in the spirit of the report as a whole. This spirit or underlying philosophy was summed up in two brief paragraphs:

It is the traditional policy of the United States that the military establishment in time of peace is to be a small Regular Army, and that the ultimate war force of the nation is to be a great army of citizen soldiers. This fundamental theory of military organization is sound economically and politically....

It is therefore our most important military problem to devise means for preparing great armies of citizen soldiers to meet the emergency of modern war. The organization of the regular army is but a smaller phase of this problem. It is simply the peace nucleus of the greater war army and its strength and organization should always be considered with reference to its relation to the greater war force which cannot be placed in the field till war is imminent....

Secretary Stimson saw to it that the final plan of reorganization reached a wide audience. It was published in pamphlet form and copies were sent to every member of Congress, to every officer of the army and the National Guard, as well as to a large number of educational institutions. In a covering letter he commended the report—one of the most important fruits of the General Staff, he said—to every citizen interested in the development of a sound military policy for the nation. Meanwhile, he directed the staff to undertake a study of the legislative and executive action which would be required to implement the report.

As a matter of fact I had already given a good deal of thought to the problem of implementation. My modest success in writing magazine articles on reform subjects in *McClure's* and elsewhere led me to believe I might make myself most useful by acting as literary agent for the scheme of reorganization we had just prepared. So one night after a dinner party at the home of Brig. Gen. William Crozier, who was then chief of Ordnance, when Secretary Stimson offered me a ride home in his carriage, I seized the opportunity to ask his opinion. To my delight he took up the idea with enthusiasm. He had read my most recent article, "The Insurance of Peace," in *Scribner's Magazine* for February, 1912, and was convinced I could do a most useful service by writing others like it to publicize our new national military policy.

Magazine articles might prove highly useful to the cause of army reform if they reached a wide audience across the nation. But this kind of publicity worked only for the long-run interest. Congress, I realized, should be our immediate target. But how should we approach the Hill?

One dreadfully hot evening during that summer of 1912 I left my office at the War Department utterly worn out from my day's effort. My two girls, Maude and little Mary, had fled the city to escape the heat, so I was temporarily keeping bachelor quarters. Tired and lonely, I decided to walk over to the Raleigh Hotel where I could go up to the roof and cool off. My conscience told me it would be wiser to take supper at a lunch counter, for it was difficult making ends meet when living in Washington on a captain's pay.

Quite by chance I drew a chair next to Congressman H. T. Rainey, who represented a district in my home state of Illinois. He served with such distinction that his Democratic colleagues later elected him Speaker of the House. In no time at all we were deeply engaged in conversation on army matters. As we talked it suddenly occurred to me that this was just the opportunity I had been waiting for. The Democrats, I explained to him, were in grave danger of making a serious tactical error. They were committing a political blunder, I said, in tying up with the discarded reactionaries, the old army of independent bureau chiefs so beloved by the Ainsworth clique. Congressman Rainey admitted that Chairman Hay of the Military Affairs Committee had for some time occupied "the old army pew," so I went on with my exposition: "The time has arrived for a fundamental reorganization of the army. If properly done, large economies will be possible. And should Wilson be elected, the Democrats will have a splendid opportunity to score with a program of positive legislation." By the time Congressman Rainey departed late that evening I was sure I had planted an idea which would bear important political fruit.

Whatever hopes I may have entertained of pushing the army reorganization through Congress were doomed to disappointment. A few days after Secretary Stimson issued our published report, I was legislated out of the General Staff. With several other graduates of the Staff College I was disqualified by an act of Congress known in army parlance as the "Manchu law." It prescribed that all officers who had had less than two years' service with troops during the past six years should be ordered back to their regiments. Those of us affected by the measure were dubbed "Manchus" by our brother officers since our exile from Washington paralleled that of the Manchu Dynasty which had then recently been ousted from Peking.

There were sound reasons for the passage of the "Manchu" law, for excessive detached service had become a crying abuse. Subsequently the act was amended to credit attendance at the Staff College and other schools of application as "service with troops." But all efforts to get that proviso into the original act were unsuccessful. In fact, some of us, as members of the "Leavenworth crowd," were regarded as the most pernicious of all the Manchus by those who objected to the changes we were threatening to effect in the army. So, in effect, I was dismissed from the General Staff because I had taken the trouble to qualify for staff duty during my two years of hard work at Fort Leavenworth. And not long afterward I was ordered to join my regiment which was then at Tientsin, North China—as near Manchuria and as far from Washington as it was possible to send me.

To make matters worse, not only were Stimson's disciples scattered far afield, but he himself was soon afterward relieved by the Hon. Lindley M. Garrison, newly elected President Wilson's first Secretary of War. The consequences of this turn of events were tragic. Had the reorganization Mr.

Stimson sponsored gone into effect, we should have had at least four Regular Army divisions and at least twelve National Guard divisions fully organized when we entered the war in 1917. In addition to this, we should have had approved plans all ready for the prompt formation of a first wave of at least twelve National Army divisions of citizen soldiers. In the event, no such preparedness was achieved, and the nation blundered toward war woefully unready.

16 Military Observer and Aide

Just as the Manchu measure was about to terminate my stay in Washington, General Wood informed me he had one more duty for me to discharge before rejoining my regiment. The French and German governments had each invited the Chief of Staff to attend their fall maneuvers. Would I care to go along with one or two other young officers as an aide and observer?

A trip to Europe would be great fun, but it would leave my brave little wife at home struggling to make ends meet. General Wood said the trip would cost about two hundred dollars over and above the travel charges that the War Department would eventually reimburse with the usual mileage allowance. "Eventually,"—that was the rub. I would have to suffer the embarassment of asking my father-in-law for a loan to tide me over until my claims were repaid. We cursed the rules and regulations that made such inconveniences necessary, yet somehow managed to raise the funds required.

The officers selected by the Chief of Staff were, besides myself, Capt. Paul B. Malone and Capt. George V. H. Moseley, both colleagues of mine on the General Staff. Our orders directed us to proceed to Europe immediately. There we would be joined by General Wood in time to attend the maneuvers.

We sailed from New York on 29 August 1912 in the old French Line steamship *La France*. There were very few passengers aboard, since we were eastbound at the end of August, when the traffic was all the other way. But among those present I remember Col. E. St. J. Greble, a Field Artillery officer, who was on his way to study the new system of artillery organization devised by the French army. Another interesting passenger was Melville E. Stone, then head of the Associated Press. He had a world of information about Europe, and it was richly rewarding to talk with him.

At Le Havre we missed the boat train, so we decided to explore the city as tourists. There were all sorts of novelties to take our interest, but we saw few of them. Instead, in that overworked phrase, we took a busman's holiday and spent most of our brief stay inspecting a *caserne*, the barracks of a French infantry unit, which we found not far from the docks. In an hour or so there we learned more about French infantry equipment and practices than we could have absorbed in months from books back home.

When we finally did reach Paris and cleared the customs house, we took a taxi to the Hôtel de Londres near the Place Vendôme. The next morning, still thrilled with the very idea of being in Paris, we walked down toward the Rue Rivoli and breakfasted at the Continental, where, being tourists, we were outrageously stung. Some of our joy with Paris began to wear off. Thereafter we patronized the sidewalk cafes, where the natives dined, and retained our affection for the city undiminished.

We were utterly worn out when we finally got back to the hotel after a day of sightseeing. It was nearly midnight, and we were ready to sleep for hours, but alas, the concierge had a message for us from the embassy. We were to proceed immediately to Germany to attend the army maneuvers, which would be held there before those in France began.

In Berlin the military attaché informed us that there had been another change in plans. General Wood was unable to attend the maneuvers, so we would not be official guests. Instead we were given a *carte de circulation*. This amounted to a press pass, which would allow us to go into the areas occupied by the troops. There was one serious drawback in our new status as unofficial guests at the German maneuvers. Since we could not go in uniform, the Imperial Army would not furnish us with transportation. We managed to hire a Berlin taxicab for three days. The price seemed exorbitant; we had to pay thirty-two cents a mile for its services, while we could only claim reimbursement from the U.S. government at seven cents a mile each. We went ahead anyhow, feeling rather lordly, and as it turned out, we had struck more of a bargain than we realized. The garage manager himself showed up as our chauffeur. He had lived for some time in St. Louis, so he spoke excellent English. And even more important, at one time he had served in the German army and was thoroughly familiar with the maneuver area, a circumstance that proved decidedly advantageous to us during the next few days.

We set out southward from Berlin, going on up the Elbe valley. On every hand were the battlefields of Gustavus Adolphus, Frederick the Great, and Napoleon. In fact, most of the area where the maneuver took place lay in the theater of the battle of Leipzig. Although we had never been there before, the whole region was familiar to us from our intensive map studies at Fort Leavenworth. On the other hand, nothing in our schooling had prepared us for some of the other things we saw. The roads, for example, were wonderful. At that time, when there were very few good surfaced roads in the United States, we found the German auto highways impressive. The forests, too, were interesting. At home, under Teddy Roosevelt's prodding, the people were only just beginning to be interested in conservation. In Germany scientific forestry had been practiced for more than a century, and we passed through large sections where the timber grew in rows as in an orchard.

The general plan of the maneuver was for a red army to cross the Elbe from the east against the defense of a blue army advancing from the west. The first day's action was a collision of cavalry divisions. This was a most impressive operation to officers from the United States. In our professional careers we had seen only one division fully assembled, and it had done nothing but parade in review. Here were not one but several tactical divisions maneuvering against one another across the countryside, and we were in the midst of it.

Much of the time during the maneuvers was spent racing along back country roads in our taxi trying to keep up with the rapidly advancing troops. Fortunately there were occasional respites. As the situation required, young general staff officers held briefings to explain the military evolutions to the attachés and other visitors. At best, however, the pace was rigorous; after pursuing cavalry units all day we stayed up most of the night watching columns of the red or attacking army cross the Elbe on pontoon bridges.

When the maneuvers finally ended after four days of nearly continuous action, we attended a grand critique conducted by the Kaiser himself. This ritual was held outdoors in a natural theater of rolling fields. The Emperor, surrounded by magnificently uniformed officers, stood on slightly rising ground just in front of the assembled crowd of German officers and visiting observers. The whole panorama looked as if it had been especially posed for effect. The Kaiser, a perfect picture of human grandeur, certainly looked like the almightiest as he skillfully handled his beautiful black stallion without the slightest regard for his withered hand.

As men who had spent a good part of our adult lives in the saddle, we fancied ourselves as rather fair judges of horsemanship. We were quite ready to admire the display, and would have, had we not been aware of a little episode which had taken place a short time before. A few minutes previously, when driving toward the scene of the critique in our weary taxi, we had learned something of how the Kaiser's stallion was educated before his imperial master appeared. In a heavily plowed field beside the road we had seen a groom patiently riding the spirited animal back and forth over the broken ground. This wore him out and soothed him, so he was really quite docile when the all-highest finally mounted him.

Another interesting personality we saw during the maneuvers was Count Zeppelin, the great builder of lighter-than-air military dirigibles. Throughout most of the exercise, one of his great cigar-shaped airships had been floating in the air over the Elbe, demonstrating the newest form of military power. The count himself was definitely not the latest thing in military power. He had been a dashing hussar in the Franco-Prussian war; when we saw him he was a pot-bellied old man visiting the encampment of his former regiment. When a horse was led up for him to ride to the Emperor's critique, the old boy was quite unable to heave himself into the saddle until a young aide-de-camp came to his rescue.

With the conclusion of the German maneuvers, we had to hurry to get back before the French army began to move. The general plan of the French maneuver was very similar to that of the German exercise just completed. Once again we saw an invader, consisting of two army corps and a cavalry division, force the crossing of a river against two army corps and a cavalry division on the defensive. And once again the magnitude of the assembled tactical units impressed us deeply.

Coming as we did from a country that had no organized army corps and divisions in time of peace, we marveled at the high degree of teamwork each of the field armies achieved in handling their larger tactical formations. Both were highly efficient, but there was an extra precision in the German army which the French seemed to lack. What it was I did not understand at the time; two years later it became apparent. Then I realized that while the French army was preparing for a war that might come some day, the Germans were engaged in a final practice for the war they knew would come in a year or two.

After the maneuvers were completed, our orders routed us through London for the journey home. It would have been faster to sail directly from France, but the Secretary of War had instructed us to dig up some information for him at the British War Office. No doubt we felt very important in attending to such a mission at the time, yet now as I look back it is evident that we were sent to England as a part of our education. We learned our way around London, became familiar with the War Office, and met a number of interesting people there. In general we acquired a good deal of experience, which was to prove useful a few years later when we joined the British as comrades in arms.

When we went down to Aldershot as guests of the 11th Regiment of Hussars (which had charged with the Light Brigade at Balaclava), we had occasion once again to see how far the British could push the matter of tradition. The young hussar charged with our entertainment described with the utmost gravity how his regiment had as its honorary colonel-in-chief no less a personage than His Imperial and Royal Highness, Frederick William, Crown Prince of the German Empire and of Prussia. In view of the expressions concerning the German state then appearing in the British press, this honorary patronage seemed to us a bit outworn. Nonetheless, to understand these oddities was to know the British better. And the money our government paid out to send us through a round of seemingly empty social calls was probably wisely spent. This was certainly true insofar as we became more understanding allies when the war broke out; only in understanding is there successful cooperation.

Back in Washington after six weeks of most interesting duty, I was more than ever convinced that the reforms we had drafted for the army were absolutely essential. Everything we had seen in the armies we inspected abroad confirmed this impression. But if I had hoped for a reprieve from the operation of the "Manchu law" to carry on the unfinished task of army reorganization, I was sadly mistaken. Shortly after my return from Europe, orders were issued directing me to take the army transport when it sailed from the West Coast in February, 1913.

The day after my sailing orders came in, Secretary Stimson asked me if I would accompany him on an inspection trip to Panama as his military aide. Whether the secretary extended this invitation as a reward for my hard work on the reorganization plan during the previous summer or to round out my education in preparation for future responsibilities, I do not know. At any rate I accepted with pleasure, and the very next day we set out for the Canal Zone.

There were six of us in the secretary's party. In addition to his military aide Mr. Stimson had a legal aide, a brilliant young lawyer named Felix Frankfurter. The others were personal guests; besides Mrs. Stimson we were accompanied by Miss Helen Taft, the President's daughter, and Dr. Louis Atterbury Stimson, the secretary's father, a distinguished surgeon and man of letters.

Our first night at sea I went out on deck and stood looking over the horizon at the evening star. Venus was in one of her closest conjunctions to the earth, larger and more brilliant than she had been for years. Just then a voice behind me recited,

> Fair as a star when only one
> Is shining in the sky....

Turning around, I found Frankfurter standing there. Clearly he was adept at citations, literary as well as legal.

When we reached Panama the canal was nearing completion. They were still excavating the lower levels of the Culebra cut, and as Gatun Lake was full, a large temporary dam had been built to hold back the waters. The Engineer officer engaged in building the massive Gatun locks below this dam was none other than my old classmate, Maj. Jim Jervey, who had been so helpful to me in the Philippines. Not far away another classmate, Maj. Tracy C. Dickson, who had become an Ordnance officer, was in charge of the elaborate machine shops that kept the railroad cars and heavy construction equipment in repair. These two old friends showed me all over the miles of excavations, then still teeming with tens of thousands of workmen.

We had a delightful reunion, but I could not help reflecting on how much faster promotion had come to them. Both of them had attained the rank of major several years before, although we were all from the same class. In contrast with the Infantry and Cavalry, advancement in the Corps of Engineers and the Ordnance Department seemed rapid indeed—and, incidentally, was specific evidence of the crying need for some sort of equitable solution to the whole problem of army promotions.

On one occasion during our visit, Secretary Stimson took me out to inspect the site of a new military post, which later became Fort Clayton. We were accompanied by the two most outstanding personalities of the canal project, Col. George W. Goethals, the Engineer officer in charge, and Col. William Gorgas, the Medical Corps officer who had done so much to free the area from disease. Precariously perched on a crude observation car, we rode out on an extemporized railway track to the edge of a tailing slope where the cars from the Culebra cut dumped their fill.

When we arrived at the end of the line and stood looking out over the swamp that covered the floor of the valley below, Colonel Goethals spoke up. "Mr. Secretary," he began, "we propose to build the new army post here." For some time before this the two colonels had been at loggerheads with one another. In his zeal to banish the fevers that had plagued every effort to build the canal, Gorgas was inclined to spend funds lavishly on preventive measures. Goethals, on the other hand, had a passion for economy. Secretary Stimson knew all about the differences that separated these two men, so in answer to the engineer's remark he turned to the doctor. "And what," he asked, "does Colonel Gorgas think about a post in a swamp like this?" To which Gorgas replied, "Mr. Secretary, if you finally decide to locate it here, Colonel Goethals will turn out Culebra fill until in a few days there isn't any swamp left." Clearly the pest killer and the mountain mover had learned to appreciate one another's abilities. And once again Secretary Stimson demonstrated that he knew how to handle men.

My fears for the modernization of the army were confirmed soon after I left Washington. Just before he went out of office, Secretary Stimson held a conference of all the general officers in the army on ways and means of implementing our reorganization plan. Far from suggesting how it might be put into operation expeditiously, the gathering revealed that most of these senior officers were openly hostile to the whole idea. One hard-bitten old major general told the Secretary of War in no uncertain terms that if he wanted to know anything about military policy in the future, he would do better if he referred the matter to his generals. No wonder I was being sent to China.

17 China Again

We sailed from San Francisco for China on the transport *Sherman* early in February 1913. There was the usual stop at Honolulu, and a week or so afterward we put in at Guam long enough for us to drive up to the capital to visit my friend Capt. Robert E. Coontz, USN, who was then governor of the island as well as commandant of the naval station. When we stopped at Manila, who should we find on the dock to greet us but our old friends C. H. "Duke" Bridges and E. E. Booth, both of whom were serving as aides-de-camp for Maj. Gen. J. Franklin Bell, who was then the army commander in the Philippines. In old army fashion they insisted that we come up and share their quarters.

Although we did spend a good deal of time visiting, our stay in the Philippines was not entirely devoted to social activities. My mind was still very much filled with the schemes of reorganization and modernization that had absorbed my attention for so long. And the trip to China afforded an opportunity too good to neglect for preaching the gospel of army reform. In passing through Fort Leavenworth on my way west from Washington, I had taken the trouble to arrange a lecture before the officer complement to publicize the character and objectives of the General Staff reorganization plan. And here in the Philippines the occasion seemed appropriate again, so I made a trip out to Camp Stotsenburg to address the officers of the Field Artillery regiment stationed there. It was uphill work. They were ready enough to accept the citizen-army doctrine expressed in the Stimson report, but the proposed promotion list left them cold. They feared it would slow their advancement, so they wanted no part of it.

My self-imposed role of publicist for the Stimson reform was not entirely without result, even if few artillerymen were won over. General Bell was greatly interested in hearing all about it, and I made several visits to his quarters to discuss the details. By the time we sailed from Manila he seemed to be generally in favor of the changes we had proposed. Of course, General Bell may not have been typical, but it seemed to me that much of the opposition we had encountered from so many of the senior officers of the army could have been dissipated if they had been approached personally by someone thoroughly familiar with the subject.

Great changes had taken place since my first visit to Tientsin during the Boxer campaign in 1900. Revolution had swept through the land; Dr. Sun Yat Sen was now a magic name, and the Dowager Empress had given way to the Republic of China. Of course, the Republic was more impressive on paper than in fact. The war lords of rival factions kept the country in turmoil, and sheer anarchy prevailed. By international agreement after the Boxer Rebellion, most of the great powers maintained detachments in North China to protect their diplomatic and commercial interests there. The American contingent, the North China Command as it was called, was comprised of the regimental headquarters and two battalions of the 15th Infantry. Six companies of this force were normally retained in Tientsin, while two companies were out on guard duty at stations along the Peking-Mukden railway. Up in Peking a detachment of U.S. Marines was the legation guard.

In the thirteen years that had elapsed since the rebellion, Tientsin had become a great city, with a population of nearly 100,000 Chinese. In addition to the natives, it had a foreign population of several thousand people, not counting the military garrisons living in the foreign concessions. I doubt if many American boom towns exceeded Tientsin's rate of growth. During the rebellion Taku Road had been the eastern limit; now the city was built up for two miles or more beyond. The ancient wall about the city was gone, and in its place a wide modern boulevard had been constructed. To the south, the British and German Concessions had grown into large suburbs filled with beautiful homes and public buildings. And here, in due course, the quartermaster found us a house.

We probably never lived more comfortably in all our lives. With the aid of our indispensible No. 1 boy, Li, we recruited a suitable retinue of servants. What then constituted a suitable retinue gives one pause in retrospect. The full staff, in addition to Li, included a No. 2 boy, Mo; a cook; a cook's understudy coolie, or makey-learn; the amah, or nursemaid; a stove coolie; and a hot water coolie. The whole establishment cost us about $35.00 U.S., a month. Li, as No. 1 boy, received the largest salary, $15.00 Mex., which amounted to about $6.00 in our money. To top it all off, on these wages the whole lot turned out to be truly splendid servants.

Living in Tientsin, as one can readily see, was a housekeeper's paradise. Almost everything we had to buy for the household could be had inexpensively and in good quality. For example, Maude kept the house perpetually filled with blooming plants. As soon as any dropped their blossoms, they were replaced immediately with fresh stock. The total cost of this luxury came to about $2.00 Mex., or less than $1.00 U.S., a month.

Maude found a Chinese craftsman with a hand loom right in our own neighborhood and commissioned him to make several rugs for her. She selected the patterns and colors she wanted, and to get just the desired result, she herself bought raw wool in the market and had it dyed under her own supervision. Then later, as the rugmaker worked away at his loom, she visited his shop every day to observe his progress. The rugs we procured in this way were unusually beautiful, treasures that ornamented our successive homes ever afterward. An investment of $50 produced a rug worth upward of $1,000 in the United States.

A military garrison in peacetime is almost always a pleasant place to live, but Tientsin was a garrison town par excellence. In addition to our own regiment, there were usually two or three British regiments, a battalion of Germans, a whole brigade of Japanese, as well as an assortment of Russian, Italian, Austrian, and French units of various strengths. Altogether we made up a most cosmopolitan community, in which our officers and their families mingled with the foreign officers and their families, enjoying the gay social life of what was perhaps the most interesting and picturesque military garrison in the world. Apart from occasional stints at guard out on the rail lines, there was little to do.

Our military duties were certainly not oppressive. Indeed, our primary purpose in China was to show the flag. Our mere presence there was expected to act as a deterrent to those lawless forces that had disrupted the country for so long. As a consequence, all the foreign detachments made a great point of parading their forces on the slightest pretext. If the American minister passed through Tientsin on his way down from Peking, he received an honor guard and review. If the French contigent celebrated Bastille Day, all the other nationalities would join the parade in their full-dress uniforms.

While the troops of the several nationalities continued to play their own favorite games among themselves, they vied in open competition at meets featuring the various Olympic sports. In a succession of field days, first at the British Recreation Grounds and then at the French East Arsenal, the star contenders from each garrison would vie for honors. These were truly international events, with Chinese, Italian, British, and French troops all mingled in with our own in the 100-meter dash, the high jump, or the relay. The British excelled in these sports and often carried off first place, but the 15th Infantry contestants performed creditably.

The friendliness that characterized the troops of the various nationalities was typical also of the foreign civilian groups living in the concessions. A little island of Westerners in a turbulent sea of Orientals, we were drawn toward one another by the civilization we shared. And yet, even in this sharpened sense of community, the little differences in our various cultures kept cropping up. There were, for example, three foreign schools in the Concessions, one French, one British, and one German. Children from the families of the 15th Infantry attended any of the three, with a cosmopolitan disregard for national lines. Unfortunately, the subjects they studied were not always so freed from provincialism. My daughter Mary attended the excellent English school, and there, along with all the other children, she studied geography. She was taught to bound and locate all the counties of England, but she learned nothing about her own or other countries. She learned all about Yorkshire and Cornwall, though she never heard of Kansas or Colorado. Obviously, even when they live in China some people never leave home.

Peking, a short train ride away, was a fascinating city to explore. At street level everything was bleak and grey, as one walked through miles of narrow lanes lined with houses surrounded by high stone walls. From the top of the wide city wall one had an entirely different view. When I took little Mary up there, we could look down into all the beautiful gardens and courtyards that were invisible from the streets below. Would Mary remember this entrancing scene when she grew up? I reminded her of reading how on a similar occasion Cellini's father had slapped him full across the face so he would be sure to remember some particular occasion and offered to perform the same service for her. She assured me this was quite unnecessary. And true enough, years later in talking with her I found she recalled vididly many details of our walk along the wall, details that I had long since forgotten.

If one were to read only what I have recorded here, the Tientsin force, or China Expedition, as it was sometimes called, must seem to have been more social than military. This is not surprising; we remember the highlights, the good times, and the unusual adventures and forget the routine. For this reason it may be useful to point out that we were not always idle. In fact, when not out guarding the railroad lines, we kept the men rather fully occupied with a rigorous training schedule. Yet, insofar as my junior officers relieved me from this kind of work, I was free to pursue my military studies.

When I left Washington to rejoin my regiment, I looked forward to a good deal of leisure in which to write a book on military policy. Such a book, I hoped, would make me a recognized authority on the subject and win adherents for the cause of army reform. Once out in China, however, the book never seemed to get written. True, with a house full of servants, my days were longer, since my usual domestic chores were done for me. It wasn't time that stopped me, but distance. We were far from the people and issues with which my book would have to deal, and none of the necessary sources of information were at hand. For some time after we first arrived in China I tried to continue my interest in the General Staff reorganization plan by writing long letters reporting on some of the reactions I had encountered during my trip out, but these proved disheartening. The mail took so long coming out and going back that issues were dead before I heard of them.

On one occasion, for example, I was officially directed by the Adjutant General to prepare a paper on the education of army officers. This was a challenging subject that interested me greatly. Unfortunately, the Adjutant General indicated that the finished paper would be required by the beginning of February, 1914, but his directive did not even reach me until the middle of that month. Feeling thoroughly frustrated, I went ahead and prepared the paper anyhow. The effort wasn't entirely wasted, for many of the ideas I toyed with then proved highly useful in an important staff study I wrote more than two years later.

While we were in China my name finally moved up to the top of the list and I became the senior captain in the 15th Infantry. To qualify for the next grade I had to submit to an examination conducted by my friend Maj. Palmer Pierce. This involved a careful study of my 201 file, which he had the War Department send out to him. Some of its contents proved highly amusing. Among other things he found that on my graduation from the Staff College I had been recommended as qualified to command a division in the event of war. Pierce seemed to regard this as a great joke. "If you are already so qualified," he asked, "why should we bother to examine you for promotion to the rank of major?" The truth was, of course, I had never actually commanded anything larger than a company in more than twenty years of army service.

Soon after my examination Pierce saw to it that I had an opportunity to take temporary command of a battalion comprising C and D Companies of the 15th Infantry. We set out on a practice march up the Grand Canal toward Peking, percisely the same route our column had followed in 1900. By chance we stopped at the very same place where we had camped during the Boxer expedition, and to make the coincidence even greater, once again the same two companies, C and D, of the 15th Infantry were present. When I assembled the men to recall the circumstances of our earlier expedition, it came to me as something of a surprise to discover that I was the only member of the 1900 campaign still present. The stability and continuity of service that had so characterized the old army was already becoming a thing of the past.

During the winter of 1914 military duties began to absorb more and more of my attention. When it came time for C Company to take its turn guarding the railway lines, we turned our backs on the pleasant life in Tientsin and moved out to Tongshan. Our principal task there was to guard the great repair shops of the Peking-Mukden railroad located in that city.

Tongshan was rapidly becoming an important strategic center in the growing industrial economy of North China. In addition to the railway shops it was the location of the Kailan Mining Administration, a giant coal-mining concern that produced vast quantities of fuel for export. From Tongshan the railroad ran on about a hundred miles to Chinwangtao, where the mining company had constructed a modern seaport in the only location on the Gulf of Liaotung that remained ice-free all year around.

Although virtually all of this industrialization was recent, for the most part new since 1901, and the equipment in use was the very lastest design, here and there the primitive methods of ancient China continued in operation right along with the most modern machinery. For example, when General Bell came over from the Philippines to inspect the army units in North China, I was ordered down to Chinwangtao to meet him. The president of the Kailan Mining Administration generously took me along in his private railroad car, and when General Bell arrived showed us all over the wharves constructed by the company.

We were amazed to find great seagoing steamers being laden with coal entirely by hand. Long lines of coolies passed up thousands of tons of coal bit by bit in tiny baskets. General Bell asked why labor-saving machinery wasn't used, and the mining company president replied, "Why should we? We can hire coolies at fourteen cents a day, so there's no use tying up capital in machinery to save cost." Although this sounded like callous indifference at first, on reflection we realized that it rested on economic fact. Whatever long-term benefit modern labor-saving machinery might produce, at the moment it would only impoverish the community by reducing employment. The savings effected would simply accrue to the outside investors and not the native population. As it was, the fourteen-cent daily wage was so far above the prevailing level of coolie earnings that it attracted labor from hundreds of miles away into the new industrial cities such as Tongshan and Chinwangtao.

Against the background of impoverishment typified by coolie coal heavers, it should not be difficult to understand why the mushrooming city at Tongshan was a veritable den of iniquity. As a consequence, my company had an excessively heavy demand for guard details. Not only were sentries required around the railway shops to keep rioters and pilferers out, but in addition they had to be posted around their own barracks to keep the men in.

Needless to say, with the men confined to their barrack areas during off-duty hours, morale became a serious problem. To cope with this situation, one of my predecessors at Tongshan had established an illicit canteen. This was entirely contrary to regulations, but he believed the men would be far better off if they had regulated beer at home. By the time my company's turn for duty at Tongshan rolled around, it had become the regular practice of the company commander to give the canteen concession to a trusted noncommissioned officer. I followed the custom and allowed one of my sergeants to buy out the canteen sergeant of the unit we relieved. But then, after thinking the matter over for some time, I began to doubt whether it was really a wise thing to do. Was this really good for the men, I asked myself? I was willing to risk my commission by allowing the illicit canteen, but the whole arrangement seemed wrong in principle.

I had no intention of closing the canteen solely for my own peace of mind. My objective was far more significant. Assembling the company, I explained my purpose briefly: "I'm going to treat you men like mature American citizens. Beginning tonight all sentinels will be taken off the barracks. Any one of you, when off duty, can go into Tongshan whenever you feel like it and without accounting to me. All I insist upon is that you return on time and in proper condition for duty. Failing this you shall face a court martial. I do not expect to penalize 150 men for the few who cannot be trusted."

My experiment was highly successful. The men responded to my trust. When I went into Tongshan and met soldiers coming out of a saloon, they would salute me and I would return their salutes. There was no need for furtive evasion. They were responsible citizens. Of course, there were two or three soldiers who couldn't stand prosperity. After the first week, however, they were permanent inmates of the guardhouse while the majority of their comrades were free men.

Guard duty is never very exciting, and after the lively life in the cosmopolitan foreign concessions in Tientsin we found Tongshan dull indeed. Only a few incidents of our stay there linger in my memory, but one of these is worth recording for the light it sheds on the character of our military training at that time—early 1914. This was the annual field firing, which each company had to perform under the eyes of an inspector. The observer in this instance turned out to be an old friend of mine, Maj. Fred W. Sladen, who had just joined the 15th Infantry after a tour of duty as the commandant of cadets at West Point.

On the appointed day I marched C Company out to the firing area. The men were in high spirits. They were confident of their ability, for we had practiced diligently at the rifle butts throughout the year. I had taken great pride in this work myself and had trained a number of men to estimate range with remarkable accuracy. If our first shots were over or short, we made the proper corrections from the puffs of dust they kicked up. This technique was all very well for daily target practice at our usual range, but field firing presented an entirely different situation. For our test Major Sladen selected a site where we had to fire at distant targets over a field of alfalfa. There was no dust, so we could make no correction. As a result, when the hits were counted they added up to very few, and C Company received an abominable rating.

As we marched back to camp at route step, I could tell how disgusted the men were from their conversation, so just before dismissing the company I explained to them that the bad shooting was not their fault. I had been estimating the range and the failure was entirely mine. "In fact," I continued, "It was only because some of you were bad shots that the company made any hits at all, for with incorrect ranging only the wild shots chanced to hit the targets."

Fortunately C Company's miserable performance was not without its brighter side. At that time field firing for record was a comparatively new idea in the army. We had been strong on target practice for many years, and while this resulted in many excellent match-shooters firing under carefully controlled conditions, we were entirely without practice in the distribution of fire on battle targets over typical terrain. Thanks to the efforts of the school of musketry at the Presidio in Monterey, field firing eventually became a regular part of our Infantry training. Chastened by failure, my company took pains to develop skill at firing under realistic conditions.

My mind was full of schemes to perfect the men of my company in field firing, when a communication from the War Department brought everything to a halt. On the fifth of June, 1914, after serving more than thirteen years as a captain of Infantry, I received my promotion to the grade of major. I was then forty-four years old. The young officers of today's army would undoubtedly regard this as a most venerable age to attain such a rank, but at the time I received many letters congratulating me on making the grade while still so young. Of course my promotion pleased me immensely, yet it was not without its bleaker side. There were no vacancies at the moment in the 15th Infantry, so I was assigned to another regiment, the 24th, then in the Philippines, where an opening did exist.

When we sailed from China late in July, 1914, we carried with us a great many happy memories, not only of our comrades in the regiment but also of our many friends in the other foreign garrisons at Tientsin—French, British, German, Russian, and all the rest. To be sure, just as we embarked there was a war scare in Europe, but we gave it scant attention. Before our transport reached Manila, however, we learned by wireless that the Germans had invaded Belgium, the Russians were mobilizing, and a general European war had already broken out.

For me at least, the war did not seem entirely real until we approached Corregidor. There, just outside the three-mile limit, we passed some British warships relentlessly cruising back and forth across the entrance to Manila Bay. Inside, a considerable fleet of German merchant ships rode at anchor, where they had taken refuge in the neutral harbor. They were destined to remain at anchor longer than any of us then realized.

18 Corregidor

The 24th Infantry, to which I was assigned as a battalion commander, was a Negro regiment with white officers stationed on Corregidor Island in Manila Bay. The men in the ranks were splendid physical specimens, the cream of our colored population. The average colored man in the 24th was actually taller and stronger than the average white soldier on the island. This physical superiority was fully evident when our men played baseball against the Coast Artillery soldiers who were also stationed on the Rock. By the third inning our colored players usually had the game sewn up, and from then on they just teased their opponents, catching with one hand and pulling all sorts of monkeyshines until the game was over.

The colored boys were big, strong, and healthy, yet in many respects they were still children. The very first morning after my arrival I had to look into a serious breach of discipline; one of the soldiers had tried to kill another with a kitchen knife. Investigation revealed that the assault—happily unsuccessful— had grown out of a quarrel on the drill field. When the company broke ranks, the rear rank man said to the front rank man, "You better take back that son-of-a-bitch you called me." To which the other replied, "I didn't call you no S.O.B., but if I did I wouldn't take it back." It was this trivial exchange of pleasantries that had almost led to murder.

In sharp contrast to the easy routine I had enjoyed in Tientsin, military activities on Corregidor drove me at a furious pace. While still learning the ropes as a battalion commander, I was directed to serve on a board to make recommendations concerning the defense of Manila and the surrounding area. This threw me in with a most interesting group of men. Among them were several who were soon to distinguish themselves: my old friend Brig. Gen. Hunter Liggett, who would rise to command the First Army, AEF; Lt. Col. Ernest Hinds, who would become Pershing's chief of Artillery; and Maj.

Frank K. Fergusson, a Coast Artillery officer who would win a name for himself and a general's stars in the AEF.

The department commander, Maj. Gen. T. H. Barry, lent us his official steamboat, and for weeks we cruised up and down the coast of Luzon visiting points of strategic interest. While we actually did hold many of our board meetings on the steamer, this was no pleasure junket. We hiked across the Bataan Peninsula, along jungle trails and over every inch of Corregidor, sketching and studying the terrain at first hand while planning defenses for Wheeler Point, Malinta Hill, and a dozen other places with names that have since been rendered famous by their heroic defenders in World War II.

In light of what took place in 1941, some of the recommendations we made way back in 1914 make interesting reading. We correctly anticipated that an enemy would select the Lingayen Gulf area for his main landings aimed at capturing Manila. On the other hand, we rejected a proposal to concentrate the main body of the defense forces in Bataan to prevent the enemy from shelling Corregidor from the shore. After careful study, we concluded that there was no natural line of defense in the peninsula that could be held with the limited number of troops at our disposal against superior forces. We also recognized that if any considerable defensive force were placed on Bataan the problem of supply would become critical in view of the almost complete lack of transportation in the area.

The outbreak of war during the summer of 1914 gave a new and terrible urgency to the problem of army organization, which had been left unsettled when the Manchu law dismissed so many of us from the General Staff two years earlier. Our country was almost totally unprepared for the part it would eventually take in the struggle. True, in the Stimson report we had a military policy for the United States, but little or nothing had been done to put that policy into effect. As it was, when the war arrived our plans for a modern army were for the most part still on paper. And by our very weakness we invited contempt.

In his annual address to Congress early in December 1914, President Wilson laid out a clear statement of the military policy he intended to pursue. Not until weeks later, in January 1915, did a copy of this message reach me in the Philippines, but when it finally did arrive I was highly pleased to find that he had adopted, at least in general terms, the underlying philosophy of the Stimson report. He favored building the nation's defense, not upon a large standing army, but upon "a citizenry trained and accustomed to arms." That he believed this as a matter of principle seemed clear. He urged the training of citizens not because the immediate occasion made it expedient but because he regarded such an approach to our national safety as a matter of "permanent and settled policy."

Mr. Wilson's pronouncement for a citizen army appealed to my imagination. Of course it would meet with resistance. The opposition stirred up by our army reorganization plan only two years before was still too vivid a memory for me to forget. Inevitably there would be some old army Regulars who would pull out Emory Upton's *Military Policy of the United States* to quote chapter and verse on the virtues of an expansible Regular Army and the evils of relying upon civilian components. These objections I could not meet personally so long as I remained stuck on the Rock outside Manila. On the other hand, it might be possible to build up public understanding for the presidential theme with a short, nontechnical book aimed at the largest possible audience. I immediately resolved to write such a book if I could.

Of course I realized that even a full-perspective rendering of the citizen army scheme would attract few readers if it consisted of a dry-as-dust description of the proposed organization. To get reader appeal I concocted a cast of characters who acted out their parts as if the legislation I desired had already been passed. There were speeches on the Hill by Senator Straightedge—clearly a high-minded type with the best interest of the nation at heart—and some shortsighted maneuvering by Senator Skimp, who threatened to pare the arms budget unwisely for partisan advantage. And finally a series of extracts from the diary of a typical young reserve officer in the citizen army reflected the way the mobilization worked out.

Although my general purpose in writing *An Army of the People* was to explain the citizen army idea in popular terms, there was another or secondary thesis running through the book. The main obstacle to the creation of an effective citizen army was the ineffective militia, or National Guard, that we already had in existence. These state troops comprised a really splendid body of men, with potentialities of a high order. But I was convinced that these potentialities could never be exploited to the utmost so long as the National Guard was formed entirely under the militia clause of the Constitution. This clause restricted its use as a federal force and subjected it to a political influence from the states that seemed to make operations in the field with the Regular Army all but intolerable. The most obvious solution to this difficulty was to establish a completely new force under the clause in the Constitution authorizing Congress to "raise and support" armies directly and without reference to the states. From long experience, however, I realized that any national administration would hesitate to run the risk of antagonizing the politically powerful National Guard lobby by proposing to do away entirely with federal reliance on the militia in favor of a citizenry organized under the army clause. While virtually every serious student of military reform would admit that such a move was theoretically desirable, only an unusually courageous administration would propose the change in the face of active opposition from the Guard lobbies in all the forty-eight states.

There was good reason to believe that a substantial number of influential guardsmen were willing and anxious to secure legislation that would provide a citizen army along the lines suggested in my book. The *National Guard*

Magazine advocated a similar scheme editorially, and some high-ranking Guard officials had already endorsed the idea publicly. Moreover, the highly favorable response stirred up by an article on this subject which I had written in December, 1914, for the *Infantry Journal* convinced me—too easily, perhaps—that the guardsmen would accept my thesis and help push an appropriate measure through Congress.

Writing my book was something of an ordeal physically, but getting permission to publish it brought even greater anguish. As soon as the manuscript was completed, I sent off a copy to former Secretary of War Henry L. Stimson, who had returned to private law practice but continued to take an active interest in the problems of national defense. He read the book carefully and sent me an enthusiastic endorsement that could be used by the publisher. And then the roof fell in. The War Department issued an order prohibiting military personnel from publishing articles dealing with the current defense situation. Since my book concerned a domestic rather than a diplomatic problem, and made no reference to events in Europe or the Mexican border, I was confident that it did not fall under the ban. Nonetheless, to be scrupulously correct I sent the manuscript to my old West Point friend, Capt. Frank S. Cocheu, who was then serving on the General Staff, and asked him to get official permission for publication. As it turned out this was a serious tactical error.

Weeks passed and nothing happened. Finally, late in August, 1915, a good five months after I had finished the book, word came that permission to publish was denied. The grounds stated for withholding publication were utterly fatuous. On the premise that the War Department's ban on writing had "probably prevented the publication of similar articles by other officers," permission was denied to avoid making an exception in my case. The real reason for the refusal, of course, was something entirely different.

To put the matter bluntly, there were a number on the General Staff who were unwilling to build any significant portion of the nation's defense around civilian components. Some of the objections that the General Staff raised against the National Guard were admittedly valid. So long as the appointment and promotion of officers, the enforcement of discipline, and the details of organization were left entirely to the states, the efficiency of the Guard as a national military force was certain to suffer. In this I agreed with the General Staff. Where we parted company was on the question of a remedy. Almost no one on the General Staff believed that it would be possible to overcome the inherent weakness of the National Guard by congressional action. As a consequence, in making formal recommendations on defense policy to the Secretary of War, the General Staff asked for no new legislation strengthening the Guard. On the contrary, utterly ignoring the political potency of the National Guard, the General Staff actually went so far as to ask for the repeal of existing provisions in the law that required the President to muster the Guard into service ahead of any volunteer force newly organized in time of war. In effect, they would relegate the existing Guard units to the role of local constabularies. Needless to say, since they had committed themselves to such a plan, they were not at all anxious to let me publish a book that advanced the merits of the organization they proposed to abandon.

Although the official ban on the publication of my book irritated me profoundly—it seemed to be nothing less than a restraint on constructive discussion—there was little time for vain regrets. The 24th Infantry was scheduled for transfer to the United States, and to prepare for departure we moved from Corregidor into Manila.

19   My First Book

We arrived in San Francisco about the middle of October, 1915, and marched the regiment directly to the Presidio. This was to be our station only temporarily, so we did not bother to unpack. Then, as now, army life was filled with domestic inconveniences. Nonetheless, it did have its compensations. We learned to take our pleasures in small things, enjoying them whenever we could. As ever before, there was the delight of renewing old acquaintances that one invariably met on reaching a new post. And after the heats and fevers of the tropics, the glorious California climate was decidedly something for which we could be thankful.

One of the highlights of our stay at the Presidio was the Panama-Pacific Exposition, which had been erected right on our own military reservation. As we had a family pass, we went over to the grounds nearly every day. Naturally the Illinois building was particularly interesting to us. Among other things, the state exhibit contained a display of Lincoln letters under glass, and on our first visit my daughter Mary discovered that one of them held a very personal appeal. This was a letter from Abraham Lincoln to her great-grandfather Palmer concerning his political relations with her great-grandfather Harris. Through the courtesy of my aunt Jessie Palmer, who was at that time secretary of the Illinois Historical Society, we had a photographic copy of the letter made for Mary to keep.

While we remained at the Presidio I was directed to serve as garrison fire marshal in addition to performing my routine duties as a battalion commander. This assignment carried with it something more than a nominal responsibility, since many of the old frame buildings around the post were frightful firetraps. Scarcely more than a month before our arrival this had been demonstrated in most tragic fashion, when General Pershing's quarters were struck by a fire that took the lives of Mrs. Pershing and her three daughters. At the time the general himself was absent on duty with the troops along the Mexican border. With this sad loss in mind, I took particular pains to drill the men of my unit in their duties as firemen.

Since we were only transients at the Presidio with no regular schedule, my responsibilities with the troops were not very burdensome. This gave me plenty of time to reflect on the fate of my book. During the long voyage home on the transport, my good friend Maj. Johnson Hagood had read over the manuscript for me, and we had discussed it at length. I had seen a good deal of Hagood, who was a Coast Artillery officer, in connection with my work planning the defenses around Manila. I respected his opinions, even though this was several years before he won his stars and made a name for himself in his work with SOS, the Service of Supply, in the AEF. Although he was inclined to take issue with some of the ideas presented in my book, he encouraged me to keep on trying to get it published.

While I was still pondering Hagood's advice, encouragement came to me from an entirely different quarter. This time it was from my friend Louis Babcock of Buffalo, New York. Babcock was a successful lawyer who had been active in the National Guard ever since the war in Cuba. We had been drawn together by our mutual interest in the role of the militia after a chance meeting at a West Point house party years before, and as I valued his judgment on such matters I had sent him a copy of my manuscript for criticism. He was enthusiastic over the thesis I presented but told me frankly that it had been a mistake to give the General Staff an opportunity to raise objections to it. He felt I should have tried to place the book before Secretary Garrison personally and offered to ask Sen. James W. Wadsworth of New York to do this for me if I wished.

This approach, Babcock realized, was not without risk. When a department head is asked a favor by a congressman, he is inclined to see a political motivation behind the request. And since it would be highly undesirable to let my book become involved in partisan politics, he recommended against such a course. It would be far better, he urged, to take the matter up personally by getting leave and traveling to Washington myself.

As it turned out, the trip to Washington proved unnecessary, for Washington, or the next thing to it, came to me. While I was still at the Presidio, who should turn up but my good friend Brig. Gen. Albert L. Mills, the chief of the Division of Militia Affairs on the General Staff. I had seen a good deal of General Mills, socially as well as officially, first as an instructor at West Point and then again while working on the Stimson report during my first tour on the General Staff. And now our association was to prove highly advantageous. General Mills had come out to visit the Panama-Pacific Exposition in company with the assistant secretary of war, Henry S. Breckinridge, and this, I realized, provided me with an unparalleled opportunity. At the general's request, Mr. Breckinridge promised to read my manuscript with an eye to authorizing publication.

To my delight, General Mills went even further. Without waiting for the assistant secretary to act, he began building fires in my behalf as soon as he returned to Washington. Recalling my close association with Gen. Tasker Bliss when he was governor of the Moro Province in the Philippines, General Mills went to see Bliss, who was now a major general and serving as assistant chief of staff, and put in a good word for my book. He even managed to say something on the subject to Secretary Garrison. What is more, besides advancing the merits of my manuscript, General Mills wrote out a most flattering report recommending me for immediate assignment to General Staff duty.

Long after General Mills' death, his widow gave me a copy of this report that she found among his papers. He seemed to think that I would be most useful if detailed to serve with the Secretary of War as a special adviser on legislative matters.

Since Mr. Garrison had an entirely open mind on the subject of defense policy when he first requested a report on the subject from the General Staff, it is not entirely inconceivable that the whole subsequent preparedness controversy that led to his resignation might well have been avoided had I been given the post General Mills suggested. As it turned out, the officer who was the secretary's right hand man on these matters during the crucial months of 1915 came to the job from extended service with the Engineers. He was a charming person and unquestionably able, but there was good reason to doubt whether his background fitted him for the role of legislative adviser.

Looking back now, long after the event, it seems clear that Mr. Garrison was the victim of his own failure to provide himself with the best professional advice on military preparedness. This is not to suggest that my advice or that of any other individual officer would have been in itself superior to what he got, but the fact remains, Mr. Garrison did not insist upon a fully rounded exposition of the defense problem. Ignoring the precedent set by Secretary Stimson's open court procedure, he requested a general staff study on the proper composition of the army and then gave only one of the parties at interest a role in preparing this paper. The professional soldiers had their day in court, but the representatives of the citizen soldiers were not consulted. As a consequence, when the professionals came up with a plan that President Wilson would not accept, Secretary Garrison was driven into the untenable position that subsequently led to his resignation.

Whatever merits my book may or may not have possessed, the machinations that lay behind my efforts to have it approved reveal a good deal about how ideas were put before those in the seats of authority in the War Department at that time. And although these events took place a long time ago, I strongly suspect that the pattern of happenings described here sheds not a little light on the relationship of the staff and the civilian authorities in the Defense Department today.

Not long after General Mills intervened in my behalf, General Bliss sent me a telegram authorizing publication. Later he wrote that he had read the manuscript with enthusiasm and had gone in to see Secretary Garrison to recommend approval only to discover that the Secretary himself was already reading a copy that Assistant Secretary Breckinridge had given him. Under these circumstances, Bliss said, it was an easy matter to get official sanction. He admonished me to get the book into print without delay.

To understand why the officials who had rejected my request in August, 1915, should turn about and urge me to publish with all haste only four months later, one must recall something of the political situation that prevailed at the time. In August the officers of the General Staff still had high hopes that the plan they had concocted for a large standing army would be accepted by the Secretary and sent to Congress. These men did not realize that the central problem of military policy in a democracy such as ours is to determine the proper relationship of the professional and nonprofessional soldiers. Their plan was just what one might have expected from a group of men who had not used the Stimson report as their point of departure. They called for an expansible Regular Army of more than half a million men, backed by a secondary force of a million reservists to be trained by serving a full twelve months on active duty. The National Guard they all but ignored, virtually relegating it to the status of a state police force.

One scarcely need say that the Wilson administration would have none of the General Staff scheme. In October, Secretary Garrison came out with an alternative, the so-called Continental Army plan, which contemplated only modest increases in the Regular Army, relying instead upon a volunteer force of 400,000 reservists to be trained in annual increments, two months at a time for a total of six months in a three-year period. Mr Garrison had been inclined to go along with the views of his military advisers, but the President was far too astute for that. He realized that compromise would be necessary; the estimated cost of the General Staff proposal was enough in itself to frighten off Congress without adding the obvious objection that a twelve-month training period for volunteer reservists would find few takers so long as the nation remained out of the war. The Continental Army of volunteer reservists entirely under federal control was Mr. Garrison's attempt to please the General Staff by avoiding all reliance on the militia while satisfying President Wilson's reluctance to approve large increases in the standing army.

President Wilson showed a great deal of political sagacity in the way he handled the difficult problem of military legislation confronting him. In his third annual address before Congress, he gave his qualified assent to Mr. Garrison's Continental Army plan. Then, to strengthen this position, he refused to release the General Staff proposal to the newspapers, as Mr. Garrison requested, until the far more moderate Continental Army compromise scheme had received the fullest publicity for a period of several weeks. As an experienced politician, the President understood how important it was to avoid a multiplicity of plans. Too many conflicting alternatives only confuse the public, and confusion leads to apathy.

Thus it turned out that by December, 1915, the officers on the General Staff who had rejected my manuscript in August as contrary to their proposals, now welcomed my help. During the intervening months they had come face to face with some political realities. Not only was their big army plan shelved, but it began to look as if even Secretary Garrison's watered-down alternative would meet formidable opposition in Congress. In these circumstances any propaganda, including mine urging prompt revision of the defense statutes, must have appeared welcome. Naturally I was grateful to General Mills for doing what he could to get my book before the Secretary. But in the light of what had transpired on the political front between August and December, 1915, it now appeared that his personal intervention was not nearly so instrumental in pushing the manuscript toward publication as it may at first have appeared. Clearly there is great danger in reasoning *post hoc, ergo propter hoc* to reach historical conclusions.

While the fate of my manuscript was still undecided, George Moseley telegraphed to say that orders would soon come out detailing me once again for duty on the General Staff. But when the official orders finally did come through, they directed me to report for duty at the end of January, 1916. That was nearly two months from the day General Bliss had wired official War Department approval of my manuscript. How could I find a publisher and take care of all the details of proofreading and the like while still out on the West Coast? I was still pondering this difficulty when a solution to my problem turned up quite suddenly and unexpectedly.

My lawyer friend, Louis Babcock, wrote from Buffalo to say that he had found a sponsor or patron for the book. Among his many business associates there was one, Anson Conger Goodyear, who was an unusually enthusiastic proponent of military preparedness. This patriotic young businessman had caught the contagion from Gen. Leonard Wood, and after attending the Plattsburg training encampment during the previous summer, he was taking action wherever he could to arouse public opinion in favor of preparedness. Besides serving on the Plattsburg camp committee, Goodyear was engaged in a number of similarly patriotic projects. Among others, for example, he had pledged himself to raise funds to buy an artillery battery to use in training the students at Yale.

Aware of all this, Babcock had placed a copy of my manuscript in Goodyear's hands to enlist his support. To his surprise and delight, Goodyear came back the very next day offering to underwrite the whole cost of publication.

Subsequently Goodyear wrote me himself, saying that he was eager to do anything he could to get my ideas before the public. True to his word, he carried the manuscript to New York and persuaded the firm of G. P. Putnam's Sons to publish it.

To say that Goodyear persuaded Putnam is something of a misrepresentation, which vanity leads me to explain. He presented the manuscript to Mr. George Haven Putnam, who was decidedly cool to the whole proposition. As a courtesy, however, he did agree to look over the manuscript. The following day he wrote back reversing his original stand completely. After reading the book for himself, he was sufficiently impressed by its unusual treatment to feel that it warranted publication after all. As the author, I was flattered to learn that my first book had literally won its way to publication on its own merits.

My benefactor, Anson Conger Goodyear, was an interesting example of the product turned out by the so-called "Plattsburg movement." In fact, my association with him gave me my first contact with that patriotic phenomenon General Wood and his friends had launched during the two years I was out of the country. Here was something new in American life; in a series of summer camps at Plattsburg, New York, and elsewhere, hundreds of young business and professional men volunteered to undergo military training at their own expense to prepare themselves for responsible roles in the nation's defense. These men were to have a far greater influence than any of them probably realized at the time. The vast majority of those who attended the early series of encampments were successful men of affairs; they were the educated, able, and aggressive young leaders in the communities from which they came. Returning home, they carried with them the gospel of preparedness and the doctrine of the citizen army. And this they preached with an effectiveness out of all proportion to their numbers.

If my book was to have any influence at all on the subsequent course of legislation, it was obviously imperative to get it out at the earliest possible moment. The President had already addressed the new session of Congress that met in December, 1915, and a number of military measures had gone before the appropriate committees—even before we settled on a publisher. Under Goodyear's prodding, however, Putnam's performed remarkably. In less than a month the firm had turned out page proofs and was getting ready for the final binding. To be sure, the manuscript was a brief one, not more than 30,000 words or about 160 printed pages, but with all the delays from having to mail proofs back and forth and sending telegrams to me on the West Coast querying this or that particular, it was February, 1916, before the book finally came out.

Although I was certainly not unwilling to accept a flood of royalty money if the book became a best seller, I had not written it as a moneymaking proposition. My whole concern was to secure the largest possible audience in order to bring a significant influence to bear on public policy. With this end in view, I instructed the publisher to use my royalties for advertising to push sales of the book. To increase distribution still further, review copies were sent to as many interested publications as we could think of. This secured us an unusually large number of reviews and notices, in England as well as in this country, almost all of them highly favorable.

It would be a pleasure to record that my book was as well received by the public as it was by the reviewers. Unfortunately, this was not the case; the book was a dismal failure. Only a few hundred copies were sold, the majority of them in New England. And most discouraging of all, the publisher reported that the sales in the national capital were inconsiderable. The financial loss to my generous patron was not serious; the publisher's bill for the initial printing of 1,000 copies, clothbound and gilt stamped, was only $437.00, and most of this was recovered from the limited number of copies sold. As a piece of timely propaganda, however, the book was a complete dud.

Bad timing seems to have been the root of the fiasco. Had the book come out soon after it was written, early in 1915, it would have appeared in a clear field. By offering a concrete proposal where none yet existed officially, it might well have stirred up constructive discussion and perhaps even legislative action along the lines I suggested. As it turned out, the General Staff ban delayed publication until after the lines of controversy had been formed, with Secretary Garrison obdurately on one side supporting the General Staff, the Military Affairs Committee of the House on the other side, and President Wilson in the middle. In short, the book was planned to initiate discussion, yet when it appeared the subject had gone far beyond that stage to the point of climax. The week the book was published, Secretary Garrison and Assistant Secretary Breckinridge resigned in protest against what they regarded as President Wilson's inadequate concern for preparedness.

No doubt I was unduly optimistic to believe, as I labored away night after night out on Corregidor, that I could influence the course of preparedness legislation by writing *An Army of the People* for popular consumption. The problems posed by the need for military legislation are not only complex but elusive. Proposals that are sound today may become obsolete tomorrow, as rapid developments on the diplomatic front revise the nation's needs and alter public opinion. Writing in early 1915, I had premised my entire conception of a citizen army upon the principle of voluntary service. At the time the book came out, however, a great deal of history had rushed past, and compulsory service was a subject for serious political discussion. As a consequence, my book was something of an anachronism when it appeared. I sent copies to all the important members of the House and Senate military committees, but there was an element of absurdity in this. While I as an army officer was advocating a rather mild form of voluntary service, Democratic Sen. G. E. Chamberlain of Oregon, one of those to whom I had sent a copy, had already presented a bill calling for universal compulsory military training.

My venture in publishing *An Army of the People* was not all lost motion. If nothing else, I at least learned this: a book may be useful as legislative propaganda if it deals with general principles, but the delays of publication and distribution militate against it as a vehicle advocating the specific details of legislation. To do this, one must work directly with the Congress from day to day, sensing every successive change in the nation's needs or the nation's mood and responding to each appropriately. It was my good fortune that orders detailing me to General Staff duty gave me an opportunity to do just this during a crucial period of our country's history.

20 Return to the General Staff

When I reported for duty to the Chief of Staff, Maj. Gen. Hugh Scott, at the end of January, 1916, I did so with the confidence of an old hand. Although Scott himself, a Cavalry officer and Indian fighter, was virtually a stranger to me, his assistant chief, Maj. Gen. Tasker H. Bliss, was a close friend. What is more, my work on the Stimson report four years earlier had been such that I had met and knew most of the departmental officials at headquarters.

Once again my orders placed me in the War College Division of the General Staff, with a primary assignment to the Committee on War Plans. Where else could a trained General Staff officer wish to be on the eve of a great war than precisely where I was—on the War Plans Committee? In another, later war a young officer named Eisenhower moved from just such an assignment to a considerable command in a matter of months.

Shortly after my arrival in Washington a letter from General Wood confirmed my suspicion that he had been active in engineering my return. As he well knew, the composition of the General Staff determined the character of the advice fed up to the Secretary of War and went a long way in shaping the policies formulated in consequence. Although I was inclined to see the central problem facing the General Staff as a contest between the advocates of a big standing army and those who favored a greater reliance upon the civilian components, General Wood saw the main issue in terms of his fight with old General Ainsworth, the former Adjutant General whom he had driven from office. He still feared that the General Staff principle itself was endangered by the entrenched bureau chiefs:

I sincerely hope, [he wrote] that you will be able to reestablish a normal balance which should exist between a grasping group of permanent staff officers interested at least to the full extent of the law with their own affairs, and a General Staff having at heart the real interests of the Army.

Time was to show how right General Wood was; the opponents of the General Staff principle made one last attempt to cripple the organization before the war demonstrated its utility beyond all question.

For several months after joining the General Staff I was occupied with more or less routine legislative duties. Although my primary assignment was supposedly in war planning, a substantial proportion of my work consisted of grinding out staff studies in response to bills referred to the department for official comment.

Almost without exception, the staff papers I prepared followed the classic pattern taught at Leavenworth: research to gather the facts, discussion to weigh the question on its merits pro and con, followed by a conclusion recommending a decision for the signature of the Chief of Staff. My Staff College training served me well. Nevertheless, I felt that the really significant legislation, the long-promised revision of the organic statutes of the army, was going on without me. The formal hearings for this major legislative change had been completed before my return to Washington, and all during the winter and spring of 1916, while I dutifully turned out small-bore staff papers, the Senate and House were struggling over the terms of a defense law that could spell the difference between adequate preparedness and an almost criminal neglect in a world at war.

During the early months of 1916, as our relations with Germany and Mexico continued to deteriorate, the need for a major overhaul of the military establishment became even more acute. The legislators were not unwilling to act, if only they could agree upon a common course. In practice the choices open to them narrowed down to four, each representing an entirely different principle or military policy. The first alternative was the volunteer reserve force or Continental Army suggested by Secretary Garrison. Failing this, Congress could adopt the official proposal of the General Staff and vote for large increases in the Regular Army itself. As a third possible solution, Congress could pass the militia pay bill sponsored by Rep. James Hay of Virginia, the chairman of the House Committee on Military Affairs. The Hay bill, as this measure was called, would strengthen national defense largely by strengthening the National Guard. And finally, if they wished, the legislators could rest the nation's defense on a program of universal and compulsory military service such as that proposed by the chairman of the Senate Committee on Military Affairs, Sen. G. E. Chamberlain of Oregon.

Needless to say, there were advantages and disadvantages to each of the four alternatives before Congress. A vastly enlarged Regular Army would ensure a higher standard of professionalism than any other form of defense. On the other hand, a big standing army was certain to cost the taxpayers far more than they were willing to pay, and its very existence was foreign to the democratic political institutions of the nation.

Mr. Garrison's Continental Army plan was an attempt to secure the advantages of the Regular Army without its more evident drawbacks. As a reserve force with a total of six months of training, the Continental Army would cost less than a large standing army, while in being formed under the army clause of the Constitution it would enjoy the same advantages of centralized control and unified command as the Regular Army. But it depended entirely upon volunteers, and because it would add a competitor in the open market for volunteers, the Continental Army plan almost automatically led the National Guard lobby into opposition.

On the other hand, one of the most outstanding advantages of Mr. Hay's militia pay bill was that it commanded the political support of the National Guard lobby. Unlike the Continental Army, the Guard was already a force in being. And even if its training was far below the standard desired, as a going organization built around a relatively large number of experienced officers, it was the only force in the country that by any stretch of the imagination could be designated a ready reserve.

In a sense, it was precisely those characteristics of the National Guard cited as advantages that counted also as disadvantages. The same fierce state loyalties that brought governors and senators to support the Guard against every political threat, made it exceedingly difficult to use militia divisions as an integral part of a national defense force under the Chief of Staff. While the Hay bill did propose to "federalize" the Guard far more than any previous legislation, it still left the vital power to appoint and promote officers in the hands of the several state governors, a circumstance that could scarcely fail to operate to the detriment of efficient, unified command.

The case for compulsory universal training as proposed by Senator Chamberlain was a good one. Most significantly, it would make the manpower of the country freely available to the requirements of national security. At the same time, being universal in its application, it would meet the political test of equity. Surely no one could deny the obvious advantage in having a large body of men well trained before the outbreak of war. Quite apart from the powerful leverage a system of universal military training would give to the President in his diplomatic negotiations, such training would save lives. History has repeatedly shown the folly of throwing untrained levies directly into battle, yet repeatedly our nation had done just this in the past, waiting until a crisis arrived before attempting to raise the necessary manpower. The high cost of this course has been spelled out in the agonizing roll of casualties that had followed every attempt to train men on the field of battle.

However sound the argument for universal and compulsory military training may have been, at the beginning of 1916 there was very little support for this particular alternative in Congress. The legislators probably reflected the attitudes of their constituents on this subject more or less accurately, since there was a deep-seated public prejudice against universal military training. Memories of the Civil War draft still rankled, and no doubt many confused universal training with the militaristic conscription practiced by so many Old World powers.

Since the nation was still overwhelmingly isolationist in early 1916, it was politically dangerous to talk about emergency legislation for raising large armies. Instead, most legislators indulged, understandably enough, in a polite fiction: they conducted the entire debate in terms of permanent legislation for national defense. As a consequence, precious months slipped by and still no constructive military legislation emerged.

The high-ranking military officers directly charged with the nation's security were well aware of the need for constructive legislation, but they were loath to enter the political arena to get what they wanted. They remembered only too well the political mobilization of the Spanish-American War and were anxious to avoid any repetition of that fiasco. Ever since Secretary Root's day, a succession of conscientious leaders had been struggling to take the army out of politics, and the incumbent officials had no intention of reversing this growing tradition. Even if they had wished to lobby furiously for one or another of the bills before Congress, they were, for the most part, ill-equipped to do so by training and experience. And besides, officers who ventured into the territory of politics did so at the risk of their careers, as Gen. Leonard Wood was soon to discover.

To assume that Mr. Wilson understood all the intricacies of the preparedness problem from the moment he turned his attention in that direction would be a serious mistake. Only slowly did he come to a full grasp of the issues involved. From his early predisposition to oppose warlike preparations, the events of 1915-16 gradually led him to appreciate the broader implications of national defense. Yet even when he was finally persuaded in his own mind, he found it difficult to go all-out for preparedness at once. He had to be sure at every step of the way that he carried the people—voters—along with him. For it wasn't enough to ram through a new statute reorganizing the army. Adequate defense would require vast appropriations, which in turn meant new and heavier taxes. The President's task was to pursuade the voters to accept these burdens. To move too fast would be to lose their support, and 1916 was an election year.

While one may sympathize with President Wilson and appreciate the considerations that induced him to play such a limited role in shaping the defense legislation of 1916, the consequences of this course cannot be ignored. To begin with, for want of realistic political guidance, the General Staff marched headlong into a serious tactical blunder. Convinced that the National Guard could never be developed into a suitable reserve force to supplement the Regular Army, the General Staff proceeded to publish a study urging Congress to replace the Guard with a proper federal force as soon as possible. Certainly it was true that so long as the Guard was raised under the militia clause, there would be difficulties in any attempt to use it as a federal force, but instead of trying to adjust the constitutional harness, the General Staff set out to kill the horse. With signal absence of tact, the General Staff study flatly asserted that it would be the wisest policy to place no dependence upon such a "questionable asset" as the National Guard.

Just as any experienced Capitol hand could have predicted, the guardsmen reacted violently to this threat to their existence as the nation's principal ready reserve. The National Guard Association moved into open and active opposition. This was dangerous if not catastrophic from the point of view of the War Department, for the association was strongest where it could hurt most—in the lobbies of Congress.

Thus it turned out that by February, 1916, President Wilson found himself in the decidedly embarrassing position he had foreseen when he refused to give more than a somewhat qualified support to Secretary Garrison's Continental Army scheme, which embodied the General Staff's desire for a reserve entirely under federal control. Congressman Hay made a careful canvass and then reported to the president that the Continental Army measure would not carry. On the contrary, he declared, nine-tenths of the representatives would vote instead to strengthen the National Guard.

When President Wilson saw how the political winds were blowing, he trimmed sail to meet them and agreed to accept an improved National Guard rather than insist upon Mr. Garrison's Continental Army scheme. For Secretary Garrison this was the last straw. To continue longer in office, he decided, would be to sanction what he regarded as the President's willingness to settle for defense legislation which he as secretary believed to be totally inadequate to the nation's needs.

Events in the next few months were to prove Mr. Garrison was mistaken in taking the word of his General Staff advisers so literally. The Constitution turned out to be far more flexible than they believed. Scarcely more than a year later the National Guard found a way to send a large number of divisions across the Atlantic to fight with the AEF in France without violating the Constitution. In at least one respect, however, Secretary Garrison was correct. Because of the Administration's inability to give positive direction to every aspect of the legislation shaping up on the Hill, the Defense Act of 3 June 1916, as it was finally passed by Congress, contained a number of features that were detrimental to the cause of national defense, to say the very least.

Probably the most obnoxious provision in the Defense Act was that contained in Section 5, which not only reduced the number of General Staff officers immediately available for duty in Washington to a mere handful but also threatened to make the various bureaus within the War Department independent of the Chief of Staff.

That a majority of the legislators had no such intention seems clear from the history of the act. As originally offered, the House bill did not contain any provisions that threatened the existence of the General Staff. The objectionable provisions had been quietly slipped into the text when the bill was being adjusted by conference committees in the final stages of its progress toward enactment. Although the allegation cannot be proved, it now seems clear that Representative Hay inserted the offensive provisions at the suggestion of Gen. Fred Ainsworth, who continued to exercise his baleful influence on Congress long after he was forced into retirement by Secretary Stimson.

General Scott, the Chief of Staff, immediately perceived the menacing character of Section 5. If this section were to be interpreted literally as it stood on the statute books, the army would revert to the chaotic conditions that had prevailed during the war in Cuba; the Chief of Staff would lose much if not most of his authority, and the bureaus would once again become virtually independent satrapies responsible only to Congress.

The backdoor approach by which Section 5 had been introduced gave some hope that the legislators would not insist on a literal execution of its terms if a broader construction could somehow be contrived. To this end, General Scott referred the problem to the War College Division for study and report. Here at last was the opportunity for which I had been waiting. From personal observation as well as from extensive reading, I knew a good deal about how the theory of a general staff was applied or misapplied, not only in the United States but in Germany, in France, and in Great Britain as well. Most important of all, I was thoroughly familiar with the history of our own General Staff; the details of Secretary Root's struggles were fresh in my mind; and I could put my hands on all the various statutes, amendments, and pertinent staff studies that had marked its evolution.

Less than three weeks after the problem was referred to me, I was ready to present the Chief of Staff with a report on the organization and functions of the General Staff that went back into the history since 1903. Soon afterwards General Scott presented the problem to the new Secretary of War, Newton D. Baker, for decision and provided him with the relevant papers. Mr. Baker's ruling, when it finally appeared, was a masterpiece of legal reasoning. Although he could find no way to get around the clauses in the Defense Act that reduced the size of the General Staff on duty in Washington to fewer officers than at any time since its inception, he completely circumvented the stipulations that would have stripped the Chief of Staff of his control over the departmental bureaus.

By his own admission Mr. Baker knew nothing whatever about the War Department and its problems when he accepted the secretaryship. For this reason I have always felt sure that my study must have played some part, however small, in helping to provide him with the background necessary to an understanding of the crucial decision he was called upon to make so soon after he took office. And it was a truly crucial decision; General Scott always said this was probably the most important decision Secretary Baker ever had to face.

If Mr. Baker showed himself a worthy successor in the tradition of Secretaries Root and Stimson, he did so not alone by the talent he displayed for legal reasoning. Equally shrewd was his sense of political timing. He was careful not to publish his decision circumventing the most harmful features of the Defense Act until after Congress adjourned. There were some grumbles of protest from the Ainsworth clique when his handiwork appeared, but since Congress was not in session there was little that faction could do about it.

There was a sequel to my modest role in working to save the General Staff principle from destruction. While preparing my study on the background of the Root reforms, I became convinced that the opposition encountered by the General Staff was engendered as much by the officers comprising the Staff Corps as by any other cause. It appeared to me that few indeed of those assigned to duty on the General Staff really understood what their proper function should be. Accordingly, I recommended the formation of a special committee to draft a revision of the Army Regulations pertaining to the General Staff Corps and its operations. This suggestion was approved, and I was deeply engaged in the work of this committee for several months thereafter, during much of the summer and fall of 1916, in addition to my many other duties.

Section 5 was by no means the only adverse feature in the Defense Act of 1916. Important as this might be to the future of efficient army command, it was, after all, only incidental to the avowed purpose of the act—to strengthen the nation's defenses. To this end the new law offered a hodgepodge of two mutually antagonistic systems. All the apparatus of the General Staff's misguided scheme for an expansible Regular Army was retained, but now it was hastily wedded to a reserve force to be made up by the newly federalized National Guard. The resulting union was far from compatible. Worse yet, it failed to provide a military establishment adequate to the needs of the hour. Under the terms of the act, the nation would have at its disposal a force of no more than 700,000 men by the fall of 1920—a full two years after the armistice, as it turned out—and then only if a sufficient number of volunteers turned up. But would they? The answer to that question leads me to the story of the Plattsburg movement and my relation to it.

21

The Plattsburg Movement

The shortcomings of the Defense Act of 1916 forcibly demonstrated the desperate need for some agency capable of educating the public to the realities of the crisis that was rapidly moving upon the nation. Somehow public opinion had to be led to the point where congressmen could face up squarely to the nation's military needs without fearing reprisals from their constituencies. The problem was a difficult one. To do the job well required prestige enough to attract attention and a sufficient grasp of the technical aspects of the military questions involved to simplify them for public consumption. The President had the prestige to command attention, but at least until after his election in November, he was under tremendous political pressure to soft-pedal his full interest in military matters. On the other hand, the army officers who understood the technicalities and had enough rank to find an audience, knew they risked executive displeasure if they trespassed too far in seeking to mold public opinion. General Scott gave excellent evidence of this in the guarded way he handled the subject of compulsory training when testifying on the Hill in early 1916.

Fortunately for the cause of preparedness, there was an agency at hand that was surprisingly well suited to the task of educating the public on the military needs of the time. This was the Plattsburg movement, to which I alluded in a previous chapter. The first contingent of business and professional men who attended the encampment at Plattsburg during the summer of 1915 were quick to recognize the need for some sort of continuing organization to urge further preparedness upon the nation. Therefore, while the regiment was out on bivouac with enthusiasm running high, they held a meeting and took the first steps toward forming what came to be known as the Military Training Camps Association.

A number of individuals must share the credit for establishing the association. The presiding officers at the organizational meeting out in the field were John Purroy Mitchell, who was then mayor of New York City, and former Secretary of State, Robert Bacon, both company officers in the first businessmen's camp. But the man who offered the resolutions that started the association on its way was a private in Company G named Grenville Clark. Without in the least detracting from the contributions of all the others involved, it is probably fair to say that Clark's genius and personality were the mainsprings of the whole organization.

Grenville Clark was a brilliant young New York lawyer with an impressive tradition of public service behind him. As a cofounder of Root, Clark, Buckner and Ballantine, in its day one of the nation's most distinguished law firms, he had come into the orbit of Elihu Root. That great Secretary of War must have made an indelible impression on him, for Clark became a lifelong advocate of military preparedness, stressing, as did Secretary Root, the tremendous importance of civilian participation in this undertaking.

In many ways the Military Training Camps Association that Clark and his Plattsburg friends formed was an ideal apparatus for spreading the gospel on preparedness. It had a number of active committees, manned by a roster of well-known personalities whose very names would attract public interest. And although the main offices of the organization were in New York, there were branches in leading cities all over the United States. Moreover, the association could rightly claim that its entire membership ardently advocated preparedness. This was demonstrated by the willingness of all its members, not just the association's leaders but the rank and file as well, to participate in summer camps at their own expense. In this respect the association was decidedly unlike the National Guard lobby, which not infrequently supported policies that did not fully reflect the opinion of the men in the ranks.

In short, the Plattsburg movement was a going concern; it was national in scope, and it could count on the enthusiastic support of many prominent and respected figures in public life. What is more, these men had demonstrated a willingness to inform themselves on the technicalities of the military problem, both by attending summer camps and by pursuing all sorts of correspondence courses and other types of voluntary training. These considerations alone would have made the Plattsburg movement—or, more precisely, the Military Training Camps Association—a useful instrument in forming public opinion. But it enjoyed yet another advantage that was of the first importance.

The Plattsburg movement was bipartisan. Although it is true that ex-President Theodore Roosevelt had played a vigorous role in fostering the Military Training Camps Association, the movement drew its leaders from the ranks of both political parties. This fact was of inestimable value in lifting the association above the charge of partisan motivation. Nevertheless, to call the movement bipartisan is not to say that it was nonpolitical. Indeed, the Plattsburg crowd was exceedingly politically minded.

If not all the association's leaders enjoyed the reputation and public record of ex-Secretary Henry L. Stimson, who was actively behind the movement, still, in the main, they were men with a good deal of experience in local, state, or national politics. They demonstrated their sagacity in this respect from the very start by the extreme care they took not to alienate the National Guard Association. Unlike so many of the officers on the General Staff, they had a healthy respect for the power, if not the policies, of the Guard lobby in Washington.

Even more significant was the political sensitivity the Plattsburg leaders displayed when dealing with the issue of compulsory training. Many individuals in the association favored some form of obligatory duty. Mr. Stimson, for example, came out for the principle as early as 1915. Nonetheless, when Congress first began to debate military legislation in 1916, the association's official stand was in favor of the volunteer principle.

By the time Congress passed the Defense Act in June 1916, however, the futility of building any system of national defense on volunteers was already fast becoming apparent. But the men who determined the association's policies were far too shrewd to come out all at once for some scheme of universal compulsory training. No matter how desirable or essential compulsory training might be in the national interest, they knew it would be unwise to thrust this idea suddenly upon the public as a sine qua non. To do so would risk branding the organization as extremist and thereby discounting its influence. First there must be a campaign of gradual education, to lead the public to accept the idea of compulsion when the time was ripe.

Two problems, then, confronted the Military Training Camps Association. The organization must somehow wage an appropriate campaign of education—over and above what was already being done—and then decide the question of timing. In both of these matters I was to play a part.

During that summer of 1916, former Secretary Stimson and his wife invited me up to spend the weekend with them at their home out on Long Island. Justice Charles Evans Hughes had recently been nominated for the presidency and was already embarked on his campaign. The question Mr. Stimson wanted to discuss with me was whether or not Hughes should come out in favor of compulsory military training. Such a move required the utmost care. If it came too soon it might kill off the candidate; if it came too late it would do nothing to serve the cause of preparedness.

We canvassed the problem at great length over the weekend. Then, Monday morning, on our way back to the city, Mr. Stimson suggested that it might be useful to stop in at Sagamore Hill to ask ex-President Roosevelt for his opinion. We arrived there while the family was still at breakfast. "The Colonel" himself came to the door, and when Mr. Stimson started to apologize for our early call he literally yanked us both into the house and showed us into his library, where he soon rejoined us.

Colonel Roosevelt was a superb host; he was one of the most attractive personalities I have ever known. Mr. Stimson actually found difficulty in broaching his subject because the Colonel was so busy making us feel at home. Among other things he showed us an autographed photo taken of the Kaiser and himself on horseback while watching a sham battle during his visit to Germany in 1910. The Kaiser must have had a real sense of humor, even though the headlines then appearing in our daily newspapers would seem to belie the suggestion. On the back of the photograph he had written: "The Colonel of the Rough Riders instructing the German Emperor in field tactics."

When Mr. Stimson finally managed to divert the talk to politics, I felt impelled to interrupt, asking him to remind Colonel Roosevelt that I was a Democrat and not a Republican. Mr. Stimson then explained that I was the grandson of John M. Palmer of Illinois. At this the Colonel slapped me on the back and declared, "There is nothing I can say that cannot be said in the presence of a grandson and namesake of John McAuley Palmer."

At last, when the conversation turned to the reason for our visit, whether Hughes should come out for universal training, Roosevelt instantly demurred. "You know," he said, "that I am for universal training, but after all the only issue in this campaign is to defeat Woodrow Wilson, and even so meritorious a cause as universal training might not help at this time." Here was evidence, indirect and unintended to be sure, but from the highest sort of political authority, that President Wilson's reluctance to take a firm line on the army question reflected not personal weakness but the plight of every party leader in the political climate prevailing at that time.

The Colonel's reply to the question we posed shows how thoroughly antipathy for President Wilson had taken possession of him. Just as we were about to leave Sagamore Hill, Mr. Stimson told the Colonel about my book. At Roosevelt's request I mailed him a copy. A few days later he sent me the following reply, which is worth quoting in full for two different reasons. It reveals the excesses into which his feeling against Mr. Wilson led him, and at the same time it shows how acutely sensitive he was to the political symbolism of the Roosevelt name.

Sagamore Hill
July 20th 1916

My dear Major Palmer,

I think that there are capital features in your book; but I am sure it would be misunderstood, and would cause harm, if I should sanction or praise any system that is not based on universal obligatory training and service. The President's message of Dec. 6th 1914 I regard as one of the most thoroly and inexcuseably mischievous messages ever written by a President of the United States.

I know that *you* believe in obligatory universal training and service; but I fear your book, especially in view of the quotation from the President's message, would be regarded as an argument against such training and service.

Sincerely yours,

Theodore Roosevelt

Mr. Roosevelt's opinion of my book came as no surprise. He only reiterated what I already knew. The volume was published stillborn; it had been lapped by the rush of events long before it appeared. When I wrote again telling him that I was considering a revised version of *An Army of the People* based on compulsory training, he supported the idea. With characteristic exuberance, he sent me a note saying that a new edition along the lines I proposed would be "of really capital value."

My scheme to rewrite *An Army of the People* to incorporate the principle of compulsory training requires explanation. I hardly need say that I had no intention of publishing another book. The total failure of the first edition had cured me of all enthusiasm for that approach to constructive military legislation. This new venture was to appear in serial form in a magazine established by the Military Training Camps Association to advocate preparedness and gradually build up public support for universal and compulsory military training.

The idea of founding a national magazine for propaganda purposes occurred to the leaders of the Plattsburg crowd at about the time they organized the Military Training Camps Association. But it was no easy matter to launch such an undertaking. First they had to raise funds by soliciting donations, and then they had to round up a suitable staff. The original editorial and managing board of *National Service*, as the magazine came to be called, comprised the following: Grenville Clark, Nelson Doubleday, Anson Conger Goodyear, DeLancey K. Jay, Theodore Roosevelt, Jr., Willard Straight, E. F. Strother, and J. Lloyd Derby, who was to be the editor. All were hard-working lawyers or businessmen in the New York area who found time and energy for the cause of military preparedness only by adding countless hours to their regular working days. Under the circumstances it is not surprising that more than a year slipped by before the first issue of *National Service* came out.

My association with *National Service* came through Anson Goodyear, the ardent preparationist and charter member of the Plattsburg crowd who had so generously sponsored the publication of my book. It was at his suggestion that I undertook to rewrite the text as a serial in the new magazine. The whole idea of a journal to plead the cause of preparedness excited me enormously. Here indeed was vindication for the thesis I had so long advanced. The Regular Army makes a great mistake when it fails to recognize and make full use of the widespread interest in national security that exists in so many segments of society. I privately resolved that these conscientious citizen soldiers would not waste their time and effort from want of cooperation from the military—not if I could help it. And to carry my resolve into effect I sat right down and wrote a long letter to the editorial board suggesting a variety of topics for possible articles and offering my services in a number of ways.

My offer of assistance brought an immediate reply from Grenville Clark, who welcomed my proposals with enthusiasm. That letter marked the beginning of a lifelong friendship, one I came to value increasingly as the succeeding years revealed Grenny Clark's delightful personality and his extraordinary capacity for public service. In fact, as I look back now, it is clear to me that my association with the Plattsburg crowd as a whole has been among the most rewarding of my life. As conspirators in behalf of better national defense for more than thirty years, we were drawn together by the common ties of a high purpose. We did not always achieve the objectives we sought, but that has in no way diminished the pleasure of the relationship.

Without vanity I think I can safely say that my help—or that of someone in my position—was exactly what the editors of *National Service* needed. To begin with, I was able to line up a number of Regular Army officers as contributors. They could write with the authority of recognized professionals. What is more, they had something to offer that many of the big, popular national periodicals would have been glad to print—eyewitness accounts of operations at the front in Europe. There was, for example, the amazing development of aviation, which had already begun to show its revolutionary influence on strategy and tactics. Was anyone better equipped to write on this subject than Lt. Col. George O. Squier, the officer who had been so kind to me during my stay in London in 1912? He had only just returned from his long tour as an attaché in Great Britain to become chief of the army's aviation section in the Signal Corps and should be able to speak from intimate knowledge. And among my other associates in Washington, I knew I could line up a dozen more like Squier who would write for the new magazine, not because it would pay, but simply because they were genuinely dedicated in their professional calling.

My usefulness to the editors of *National Service* was by no means confined to lining up writers among my military colleagues. Far more significant was the role I played as an informal liaison officer between the General Staff and the magazine's editors and, through them, the Military Training Camps movement at large. With my knowledge of the plans and proposals being formulated by the General Staff, on several occasions I was able to give the editors a judicious steer on matters of policy to keep them from working at cross-purposes with the army.

All sorts of policy questions cropped up to plague the editors of *National Service*. As soon as the association came out officially for universal compulsory training at its national convention in November 1916, the editors were free to advocate this policy. But how long should the training period be? On such a question there could be no absolutely objective answers. When I queried my colleagues on the General Staff, I encountered a surprising variety of opinions. Some favored twelve months of training, others six.

If even amongst the professionals there was no agreement on the proper period of service under a scheme of universal compulsory training, surely the citizen-soldiers who edited the magazine could not be expected to come up unerringly with the right solution. And by "right" I mean a period of training long enough to do the job adequately by army standards and short enough to be politically acceptable. Until opinion on this subject crystallized, I counseled an open-minded course, inviting writers holding all shades of opinion on the subject to express themselves freely in the columns of the magazine until some sort of consensus emerged.

Although my own inclination was to regard six months as adequate, I knew that in the long run the term of service would have to be settled by compromise. In our democratic state, the policy decided upon would inevitably fall somewhat short of the extremes represented by the contending interests at stake—military, political, and economic. But who should make the necessary compromise? Was this the proper function of the General Staff? When I first tackled this issue I believed it was. Then, after hearing from my colleague George V. H. Moseley, who had been serving as a colonel with the 7th National Guard Division at El Paso, Texas, I was not so sure.

Moseley told me that while he was at El Paso he had received a visit from Congressman A. P. Gardner of Massachusetts, who was down on the border studying the needs of the military establishment at first hand. Gardner, son-in-law of Sen. Henry Cabot Lodge, was well known as an ardent advocate of preparedness. His address in 1914, "Wake Up America," was one of the first to arouse public concern for national security. Would six months of training be adequate, the congressman wanted to know, if a program of compulsory service were to be adopted? Moseley replied that in his opinion the many technical demands of modern war necessitated a somewhat longer period of training, but he believed that six months was about all the army could hope to get from the legislators. Congressman Gardner then told Moseley in no uncertain terms that this was not a proper answer for a military expert to make. The military specialist should state without equivocation what his best professional judgment indicated to be necessary. It was for Congress and the people, he declared, to make such compromise as might prove necessary.

Congressman Gardner's exposition of the proper relationship between the General Staff and the legislature made a profound impression on me even though it came at second hand. Unfortunately, I was never able to express my appreciation personally. When the war came, Gardner resigned his seat in Congress and, although he was well over the age limit, wangled himself a commission as a line officer in an Infantry regiment, where he died of pneumonia while still in training. His services to the nation were notable; he deserves to be remembered.

The need for a decision on whether to advocate twelve or six months of training was by no means the only question of policy that vexed the editors of *National Service*. In their enthusiasm for the cause of compulsory service, they had to take care not to be used by apparent allies. There were, for example, a number of individuals in National Guard circles who vigorously advocated universal and compulsory training but did so only as a means of perpetuating the existing Guard. There was a very real danger that these people would ride along with the movement for universal service and then at the last moment lobby a measure through Congress requiring that service to be taken in the ranks of the National Guard. Obviously it was of the utmost importance for the editors of *National Service* to avoid playing into the hands of this or any other group. From years of experience with the militia, I could see this danger before it developed and forewarned my friends accordingly.

For those of us who regarded universal training as essential to national security, the period was a most discouraging one. Anson Goodyear wrote from Buffalo to report on a conference with Sen. James W. Wadsworth. Although the Senator himself favored obligatory training, he warned that nothing could be expected from Congress along this line before the close of the current session. There was little to do but continue our campaign of education at every opportunity. For me this meant even greater extracurricular exertions. In addition to working with my friends on *National Service*, I began to make speeches before patriotic societies and to carry on a large correspondence with interested individuals all over the country, doing what I could to explain just why it was so necessary to establish a democratic system of universal training before the country stumbled into war.

Week after week throughout the fall of 1916, I tried to crowd two lives into one. After working all day at my regular duties on the General Staff, I went home and sat up most of the night working for universal military training. My friend Llewellyn P. Williamson, a captain in the Medical Corps who was then serving on the War College faculty, saw what I was doing and warned me against overworking. "If you do," he said, "you'll have to pay for it." Of course I ignored his advice. Thoroughly persuaded as to the importance of all my jobs, I hadn't the least intention of slackening off.

Even if I had wished to ease up in my work during the fall of 1916, it would not really have been feasible to do so, at least insofar as my official duties were concerned. The mobilization of the National Guard on the Mexican border and the expansion of the army voted by Congress enormously increased the number of problems referred to the General Staff for study. At the same time, Congress had cut the size of the organization almost in half, so the few remaining on duty in Washington had to work harder than ever. Thus, at the very moment when all our energies should have been devoted to the preparation of plans for our possible involvement in the European war, we were swamped with the details of routine administration.

In one sense the overburdening of the staff was fortunate; it gave me a great many illustrations of what was wrong with the existing organization. As a consequence, when the Chief of Staff took up my earlier suggestion and ordered me to recommend changes in the Army Regulations governing the Staff Corps, I was well equipped for the job. Now I was armed with concrete examples and not just abstract notions of what needed correcting.

Ever since I first began to study the problems of general staff organization at Fort Leavenworth, I had been sure that the true nature of the institution was not generally understood in the United States. Moreover, although my instructions only called for recommendations as to changes in the existing regulations, I knew that without a most convincing rationale, any changes that might be suggested, especially if they were of a radical character, would have little chance of official acceptance. With this in mind I set out to prepare a comprehensive historical survey explaining the nature of the general staff idea as it had evolved in Germany and elsewhere. Then, tracing the growth of the institution after its importation by Secretary Root, I tried to show why and where our own General Staff was improperly organized.

Late in November 1916, after several weeks of the most gruelling effort, I completed the study and sent it forward for approval. To the best of my knowledge this report in mimeographed form was the first comprehensive analysis of the General Staff and its functions to appear in the United States. It looked innocuous enough and even dull—some twenty-five legal-sized pages addressed to the Chief of Staff and ponderously captioned "War College Division memo report 639-136, 20 November 1916." But it was more significant than it looked; in fact, it turned out to be something of a bombshell.

To say the very least, my study was no whitewash. Three serious charges were implicit in its historical account of our General Staff: first, that it had not been performing the proper duties of a General Staff; second, that it had been used to carry out tasks properly belonging to other agencies; and third, that it was not composed of General Staff officers in the historically appropriate sense of the term.

The first difficulty, as I saw it, lay in the simple fact that the existing General Staff organization was required to perform two rather different functions. It was expected to prepare plans for war, and at the same time it had to assist the Chief of Staff to perform his duties as a supervisory and coordinating agent under the Secretary of War. These two functions made entirely different demands on the officers assigned to perform them. Where one required careful, deliberate, and continuous study, the other related almost exclusively to ephemeral problems demanding immediate attention. Under pressure for answers to problems connected with the routine peacetime administration of the army, the officers involved repeatedly pushed aside their work of long-range planning. And every such interruption not only delayed the preparation of war plans but seriously impaired the quality of the work done.

The solution I proposed was simple enough. Let the staff be divided into two distinct groups: one to prepare plans for war, the other to assist the Chief of Staff in carrying out his supervisory duties. To officers trained since World War I, this functional organization may seem more or less obvious, but it is well to recall that the conventional staff organization, now so familiar, was something borrowed from the French by the AEF. The "G's," G-1, G-2, etc., and the War Plans Division (WPD) were all innovations introduced during and after the war.

By itself the proposed reorganization of the General Staff along functional lines would undoubtedly have aroused little comment or protest. It was my suggestions pertaining to the staff officers as individuals that raised the biggest opposition. My initial premise was that the defects in the existing structure stemmed from the prevailing ignorance in our army as to the nature of the general staff principle. Since this criticism applied to the officers currently comprising the Staff Corps, and inasmuch as few of us care to admit ignorance where our professional careers are at stake, it is perhaps not at all surprising that my suggestions were not greeted with enthusiasm.

The source of the problem was etymological, or so my historical research led me to believe. When Secretary Root adopted the General Staff from Germany as an institution, many officers failed to understand the terminology employed. The German word *generalstab* is not accurately translated into English by the phrase "general staff." In English the word "general" has connotations implying universal, or widespread, and over all. For this reason it was assumed that the General Staff newly created in our army was to be an agency with a universal supervisory relation to all other military activities, a sort of busybody group of general managers to ride herd on the bureaus and tactical organizations. Actually, nothing could be further from the truth.

The correct English equivalent of *generalstab* is "the general's staff," which is to say, a group of specialists trained in troop leading, or "generalship."

When the British took over the German staff structure they recognized this etymological problem and carefully defined their new organization as an operations staff. In the United States this nicety of language went unnoticed. And since the very men who comprised the Staff Corps regarded themselves as "generalists" rather than "specialists," they tended to perpetuate the misconception.

The problem, then, was twofold: first, we would have to teach the army just what a General Staff officer really should be—a highly trained specialist in troop leading who has been assigned to assist his commanding officer in this duty, preparing plans in peace and operational orders in war. And second, we would have to insist that only properly trained staff officers be accepted for duty with the General Staff Corps. To this end I proposed to limit service on the staff in the future to those officers who had successfully completed the Staff College course and then moved on for a year at the War College, where they would have served a probationary tour before being placed on a list of "General Staff eligibles" to await assignment.

The need for some such device as an "eligible list," to insure that only trained officers came to duty on the staff, should be readily apparent from a glance at the record. Since 1905, when the Root reforms began to take hold, some 230 officers had graduated from the Staff College. Over a hundred of them were specifically recommended as well fitted for higher responsibilities. Yet so little did the majority of senior officers in our army appreciate the importance of training before General Staff duty that only a relatively small proportion of these graduates had actually been assigned to the General Staff. At the time I was writing in 1916, there were thirty-four officers in the Staff Corps, exclusive of general officers. Of these, only eight had graduated from the Staff College. Some of the others had attended the War College, but there were fifteen who had been to neither of these two schools. Obviously, if my recommendations were accepted, there would be a considerable exodus from Washington.

Needless to say, my plan to establish an "eligible list" drew a good deal of fire from the officers in the division who would be excluded under its terms. They voted to reject the paragraphs they found objectionable, while approving all the rest of the study. Since the "eligible list" was the very essence of my paper, I was thoroughly disgusted at this emasculation. At it turned out, however, the idea was not entirely lost.

My old friend Palmer Pierce, who had received his assignment to the General Staff shortly after I did, heartily agreed with my insistence upon a highly trained Staff Corps. As a former instructor at Fort Leavenworth, he understood the value of the Staff College course and was as anxious as I to see it adopted as a prerequisite to service on the General Staff. With the canny skill of an old and experienced soldier, he found a way to put the offensive sections of my report into the official record. Although we were outvoted by our colleagues in the War College Division, there was nothing to prevent Pierce from entering a minority report. This he did, attaching it to the excised paragraphs describing the "eligible list."

Of course Pierce's dissent had no immediate effect. But though it was filed away, it was not entirely forgotten. Some time later Major Ulysses S. Grant III found it in its pigeonhole and, liking the idea, sent a copy along to his father-in-law, Elihu Root. The former Secretary of War was favorably impressed with the proposal and wrote to tell me that he would push it when an opportunity to do so appeared. His letter gave more than an inkling of that charm that made him so effective throughout his long and useful life.

> One of the distressing things [he wrote] about the former system before the passage of the General Staff law was to see a lot of fine able officers who wanted to work over military questions, but had absolutely no way in which to get anybody to pay the slightest attention to the work they did. No one can tell how many Heaven-born generals have been smothered in that way. Gray's Country Churchyard with its mute inglorious Miltons would be quite out of the competition.

An occasion to push my "eligible list" scheme eventually did crop up, and I was able to put it over with complete success—but that is another story. It did not take place until several years later and can best be told in its proper place. At the time, the completion of my report on the General Staff brought no release from the pressure of work upon me. Almost immediately I was plunged into another highly interesting and important project.

22   Drafting the Draft Act

Even though many of us on the General Staff had been urging the principle of obligatory training for a long while, the Chief of Staff, Gen. Hugh Scott, was far too shrewd to commit the army to this policy until the time was ripe. General Scott believed in the idea personally, but he felt that, by attracting the charge of militarism, it would do more harm than good if he were to commit the army to a campaign for universal training before the nation had become accustomed to the idea. Finally, after much deliberation and with the support of his assistant chief, Gen. Tasker Bliss, he took the plunge. His annual report to the Secretary of War published in the fall of 1916 came out vigorously for universal military training. But no one knew better than General Scott that the army was not the administration.

If compulsory training were to be adopted, it would require the whole-hearted support of President Wilson in mustering the approval of Congress. And absolutely nothing could be expected along this line until Secretary Newton D. Baker, the alleged pacifist, was brought into camp.

General Scott sensed the danger of trying to convert his man by frontal assault. Open debate might well lead to acrimony. This would accomplish nothing helpful and almost certainly would poison all subsequent dealings between the Secretary and his chief of staff, a relationship that by its very nature had to be intimate to be effective. Instead, General Scott resorted to a campaign of gradual attrition. Having sent out his annual report with its plea for universal training as a trial balloon, he sat back and waited. Each day, as editorials favoring the report were sent in from newspapers all over the country, he would refer them to Mr. Baker without comment. He knew the Secretary would eventually make up his own mind, as indeed he did—after more than 800 editorials favoring compulsory duty had crossed his desk. And once persuaded of his own volition that the principle was sound, Mr. Baker himself took the initiative in winning over President Wilson.

Newspapers, then, played an important part in shaping the policy of the War Department. Without their support even the diplomatic skill of General Scott might well have proved inadequate. Secretary Baker may not have realized just how much he himself was influenced by General Scott's barrage of editorials, but he was certainly not blind to their impact on the country at large. In reviewing his experiences after the war, he was at pains to point out the crucial part the papers had played in conditioning public attitudes before Congress finally passed the Draft Act. I must confess I found this gratifying, for it represented the ultimate accolade for the splendid work being done by the Military Training Camps Association in forming public opinion. And, quite incidentally, this in turn suggested that all my labor, all the midnight oil I burned working with the Plattsburg crowd, had been far more significant than I had dared to hope at the time.

Of course, General Scott knew perfectly well that winning over the Administration was only a part of his problem. If the War Department intended to push a program of universal military training, a great deal of detailed planning would first be needed. To this end, on 9 December 1916 he directed the War College Division of the General Staff to draw up an appropriate bill to place before Congress. Specifically, he wanted a measure that would resolve all the problems of organization and at the same time provide the necessary administrative mechanisms to draft the military manpower of the nation for training.

At the War College the tasks outlined in the Chief of Staff's directive were referred to a committee comprising Lt. Col. P. D. Lochridge, Maj. Andrew Moses, Capt. Tenney Ross, and myself. In view of the extended thought I had given to the problem of organizing a civilian reserve in writing *An Army of the People*, Colonel Lochridge gave this portion of the assignment to me. To Tenney Ross, who for some time had been studying the history of the unpopular draft measures employed during the Civil War, he gave the job of proposing suitable methods for registering and inducting the citizen force.

On Wednesday, 24 January 1917, the Chief of Staff directed Colonel Lochridge to submit a completed study by the following Saturday. The colonel replied that this was impossible but was rebuffed with a peremptory order. There was nothing to do but comply, using the materials we had already assembled. Since Ross's section of the bill was substantially complete, I believed I could put mine into acceptable shape in short order if the other members of the committee would come to a decision on three or four unsettled points of policy. This they did immediately, and the following morning I set out to dictate the unfinished text of the bill. I very much doubt if it is entirely conventional to draw up complicated statutes in this fashion, but the urgency of the occasion left no other out.

Whether conventional or not, my attempt succeeded; the necessary text was ready on time. But to accomplish this was something of a tour de force and involved the help of several stenographers. I dictated to one for an hour and then had her relieved by another for an hour and so on through the day. When we finished at about five in the afternoon, I had turned out some 18,000 words, the equivalent of 18 newspaper columns, or enough to fill a small book.

Our proposed bill and the various studies in support of it were sent up to the War Department 27 January 1917. There they were circulated for comment and finally returned with suggested revisions. A final version incorporating these criticisms was put out in the form of a mimeographed booklet of nearly a hundred legal-sized pages. This went up to the Chief of Staff 14 February 1917. I mention these exact dates only because subsequent events were to make chronology a matter of considerable importance.

The bill our committee drew up at the War College was far more than just a suggested statute to authorize universal military training. In it we contemplated nothing less than a radical reorganization of the whole military establishment. Generally speaking, the reforms we proposed rested on the principles laid down in the Stimson report of 1912. As we visualized it, the army would consist of two main elements, the Regular Army and a reserve force that we designated the National Army. The latter was to be raised by a program of universal obligatory military training, which would draft for twelve months of duty each successive crop of nineteen-year-olds as they came of age.

Our committee believed that the bill we proposed offered a number of decided advantages. To begin with, it would provide a maximum of defense at a minimum cost. By building up a large organized reserve, we could hold down the size of the standing army and reduce the tax burden accordingly. Apart from such duties as garrisoning the overseas possessions, the Regular Army would be used primarily for training the new reserves in the National Army. But economy was only one feature in our scheme. More significantly, the continuing obligation to train each annual intake of reservists would provide the officers and men of the permanent force with a challenging responsibility. Never again could they slip back into the dreary routine and professional lethargy of garrison life that had characterized so much of the military establishment in the years following the Civil War.

Although the concept of universal compulsory training was undoubtedly the most radical feature of the legislation we proposed, it is probably no exaggeration to say that the real cornerstone of our bill lay in our plan to form the men so trained into organized units as an integral part of the nation's system of defense. It was not enough, we felt, to train individuals. Even if highly trained individual soldiers became available in large numbers, they would constitute little more than an armed mob until they learned to function within the framework of the higher tactical units. Only by organizing trained individuals into the brigades, divisions, and corps of a National Army, fully staffed and trained to cooperate effectively in the field, could we really hope to cut down on the size of the Regular Army.

Our plan for the National Army was to divide the country into sixteen areas of substantially the same military population. In each of these areas a cadre of Regular Army troops would train the men brought in by the draft and organize them into a corps comprising three full-strength divisions. Taking the sixteen areas together, the available reserve force would soon make up a fully equipped National Army of sixteen corps, or forty-eight divisions. Each summer these units were to be mobilized for a brief period of training and inspection. The draftees of the current year, fresh from their individual and small-unit training, would then take their places beside the men of previous classes as first-line reservists. Individual trainees were to remain in this first-line reserve of organized units for three years after their initial period of training. Thereafter they would drop back into a secondary reserve, which carried with it no further obligation in time of peace but provided a valuable pool of trained manpower for use in time of war.

One feature of our plan posed a peculiarly knotty question: What was to become of the National Guard? Since the National Army, as we developed it, would shortly provide an entirely adequate ready reserve by means of universal, compulsory training, there would soon be no further need for the existing National Guard in federal service. For this reason we proposed to withdraw the federal subsidy to the Guard, which had just been provided by the Defense Act of 1916. Within five years this would reduce the Guard, as such, to a collection of state constabularies without any federal function.

One might well ask how I could possibly be a party to any proposal to eliminate the politically powerful Guard, when only a few months before I had vigorously criticized the General Staff for suggesting something of the same sort. The answer is simply this: between June 1916, when the Defense Act passed, and February 1917, when we sent our War College bill to Congress, the National Guard had had occasion to demonstrate a great many rather serious shortcomings as the nation's principal ready reserve. Barely two weeks after he signed the Defense Act, President Wilson had made use of the powers it gave him to call out the Guard for duty on the Mexican border. Large numbers of individual guardsmen were found to be physically unfit; others proved unwilling to take the oath required of them before entering federal service. And many of those who did go to the border chafed at remaining there for an indefinite period. Some feared they would lose their jobs; others complained that extended duty imposed unfair hardships. In a few cases their families at home were left in actual want.

At a time when so many guardsmen in the ranks were obviously and vociferously disgruntled with the existing arrangement, the occasion seemed most opportune to propose a major transformation in the character of the

National Guard. I say transformation advisedly. We recognized that the National Guard, for all its faults, contained a large number of really splendid men with a great deal of valuable experience. Insofar as we could persuade them to accept, we hoped to offer them positions as charter members in our new National Army.

When the chief of staff carried our War College bill up to the Secretary of War for approval, he urged Mr. Baker to work for its passage on the Hill. But Secretary Baker was too gifted a political leader to move—even for a measure he believed in—without the most careful preparation. He assured the congressmen with the utmost tact that he did not really expect them to pass such an important piece of legislation, coming as it did at the very end of the current session. Instead he offered it, he said, in the hope that it would provoke discussion, first on the need for universal compulsory training and then on the mode by which such a program could be effected if required.

Secretary Baker certainly leaned over backwards not to offend congressional sensibilities, but he might just as well have spared himself the effort. The Kaiser's ambassador, Count von Bernstorff, had been handed his passport and sent home on February 3, and on April 6 President Wilson called for a declaration of war. What the nation actually needed was not a long-range program of universal training but an immediate draft to provide manpower to fill the ranks of a mighty army bound for the battlefields of Europe.

As it turned out, our work on the War College bill was not all lost motion, even though it did not meet the requirements of a nation at war. To begin with, it was the first truly comprehensive study undertaken by the General Staff on the problems to be faced in a large-scale draft. Our research on the distribution of military population and other such technical details proved useful in the mobilization that was soon to follow. In particular I was gratified when the plan which I had drawn up for sixteen training areas across the country was subsequently utilized as the basis for the sixteen National Army divisions raised from the men who were called into the service by the draft.

Probably the most useful feature of the work accomplished by our War College Committee was that done by Capt. Tenney Ross on the administration of the draft. From his intensive study of the federal government's experience with compulsory service during the Civil War, he knew that there were certain blunders that ought not be repeated. As a consequence, in working out the mechanics of our bill for universal training he took great care to include two vital principles: responsibility for registration was to rest upon the individual rather than the government, and the administration of the act was left to civil rather than military authorities.

The entire enrollment or registration was to be done by local postmasters. This precluded the need for new office space and minimized the cost of clerical help. At the same time, the very familiarity of the local post office with its unthreatening and nonmilitary character would go far to allay public fears that the draft would bring in squads of uniformed and armed provost marshal soldiers, to manhandle the local citizens after the manner of eighteenth-century press gangs.

Another facet of Ross's civilian administration was the system he devised to handle appeals for exemption. He proposed to set up appeal boards composed of three individuals: a U.S. commissioner, an assistant U.S. district attorney, and an army officer. Their unanimous decisions were to be final. All others could be appealed in the U.S. District Court. Clearly, Ross visualized a predominantly civilian and more or less judicial administration for the draft. Apart from the single army officer on the appeals board, the appeal boards would be civilian, but for all of this, they would still be decidedly federal in composition. In this respect his proposal differed markedly from the draft measure that was finally enacted.

The draft bill that President Wilson sent to the Hill with his blessing when he asked Congress for a declaration of war against Germany was not the one we produced at the War College. It was quite another bill, one drawn up by the army's judge advocate general, Enoch Crowder, and his legal staff. To what extent our preliminary work at the War College influenced Crowder I cannot say. But this I do know: the text of our bill, with its elaborate description of the administrative machinery we proposed for the draft, had been circulating in the War Department for more than a week when Secretary Baker first asked General Crowder to draw a bill for the President's use.

After the Armistice—after the draft had proved to be a great success—a number of people came forward to claim authorship of this important statute. I shall not pretend to weigh the merits of their contentions, but it may be that I can shed some light on what happened at the time. During the period when General Crowder was at work on the bill requested by Mr. Baker, my colleague Tenney Ross was temporarily assigned to duty in the judge advocate's office, to put his first-hand knowledge and historical research at the general's disposal. When I asked him about this episode after the war, Ross told me that the real draftsman of the Selective Service Act of 1917 was Capt. J. J. Mayes, an officer on Crowder's staff. Captain Mayes, Ross insisted, wrote the original text of the measure in Ross's presence. Perhaps it doesn't really matter who drew up the original bill that General Crowder carried to the Secretary of War, for like our War College effort it was defective; it lacked the cardinal feature that was to convert the measure into a practical success, into a truly great monument of constructive democratic statesmanship. For this achievement Secretary Baker himself deserves the credit; it was he who conceived the idea of making the draft a local institution, with selection by "friends and neighbors" rather than by external federal authorities. With autonomous local boards deciding which of their own sons to send to war, the draft lost every taint of militarism and became a remarkable example of popular self-government.

Apart from the officers on General Crowder's staff, there were a number of political figures, among them Senator Chamberlain of Oregon, who sat in on the conferences that hammered out the final version of the text. Perhaps the forgotten heros of the 1917 act were U.S. Army Provost Marshal J. B. Fry and Acting Provost Marshal James Oakes of Illinois, whose long and meticulously detailed accounts of their trials and tribulations while administering the draft during the Civil War gave Tenney Ross and his fellow workers some idea of what *not* to do. In the final analysis, however, the predominating genius behind the Selective Service Act was Secretary Baker. Others contributed details; he added the vital principle of local control.

To persuade the government to do its part even indifferently well in April 1917 was not easy. Although President Wilson asked Congress for a draft act when he called for a declaration of war against Germany, the legislators were agonizingly slow to give him the statute he needed. They preferred instead to rely upon the traditional method of voluntary enlistments. Despite William Jennings Bryan's claim that a million men would spring to arms overnight, weeks of intensive recruiting after the declaration of war turned up only 86,000 men.

Since a draft act was absolutely essential to our national war effort, the administration sought to mobilize every available resource to assure its passage. To this grand political drive I was able to make a few small contributions, in the form of staff studies supplying Secretary Baker with ammunition for use when testifying in behalf of the bill before Congress. The first of these was a statement on the failure of the volunteer system in England; the second was a statistical study to show that the total number of men required by the army was greatly in excess of the numbers actually on the front at any one time because of the need for replacements to make good the many casualties sustained in battle.

Although Secretary Baker used my paper on the failure of volunteering, he ignored the other one entirely. Years later I had occasion to ask him why. He said that my calculation of the casualties we could expect, approximately 10 percent per month, was so high that he simply dared not publish the figure at the time. The experience of the AEF when actually engaged in operations, 9.9 percent per month during the Meuse-Argonne offensive, was soon to show that my estimate had been surprisingly accurate.

While it was gratifying to help put over the Selective Service Act by drawing up official staff studies, my unofficial activities in this direction with the Plattsburg crowd brought me a greater satisfaction. By April 1917 the Military Training Camps Association had well-informed representatives in nearly every congressional district. These gentlemen built fires under all the pussyfooting congressmen they could find, and thus produced a good many votes that even the most logical of studies by the General Staff would never have won over.

23 Origins of the American Expeditionary Force

In the years following the Armistice, it became fashionable to blame the General Staff for the military unpreparedness that confronted the nation in April 1917. Even General Pershing joined in. In his memoirs he, too, arraigned the General Staff for its inertia, its lack of foresight, and its failure to draw plans for sending more than a single division to France up to the moment he arrived in Washington to take command. The duly assigned function of the General Staff is to plan for war, yet in the months leading up to the diplomatic break with Germany, this kind of planning was by no means easy to carry out. In the Defense Act of 1916, Congress had reduced the authorized strength of the organization to a point far below that required to perform even a small portion of the routine work of the army in peacetime, let alone take on the extra burdens imposed by the imminence of war. In addition President Wilson, in his efforts to preserve the nation's neutrality, had instructed the General Staff to avoid every overt indication of warlike activity. To say the least, this further restriction did little to hasten our preparation. Nonetheless, despite these serious handicaps, the General Staff did undertake studies looking toward a possible war with Germany.

Less than a week after Mr. Wilson broke off diplomatic relations with Germany, the staff officers began studying the possibility of launching attacks against the Central Powers through such widely separated theaters as Holland in the north and the Balkans in the south. And what is more, these studies were decidedly realistic. The officers who compiled them were fully aware of the many tedious months of preparation and large numbers of men that would be required. For example, the plan for an attack on the German rear through Holland called for no less than a million men, a figure utterly refuting those who subsequently charged the General Staff with failing to "think big." Moreover, the time estimated as necessary to launch such an assault—fourteen months—compared favorably with the later experience of the AEF.

If they did nothing else, the several war plans we drew up in the General Staff indicated the need for closer coordination with the Entente Powers. We recognized that ill-considered or independent planning on our part for operations against Germany might aid the enemy by embarrassing the Allied armies already in the field. With this in mind, we urged the Administration to take steps, without waiting for a declaration of war, to establish a basis of cooperation between our government and the governments then at war with the Central Powers. In particular, we suggested that the existing diplomatic agencies be supplemented by a commission of officers from the army and navy empowered to confer with the military authorities of the Entente nations. To this the French and British governments both responded favorably, but before they could send their representatives to Washington, the United States declared war upon Germany. Thus it turned out that what we had intended as a scheme of technical liaison to improve the quality of our preliminary planning became instead the first stage of that military collaboration that was to continue for the duration of the war.

About a fortnight after we entered the war, the two foreign delegations finally reached Washington. With the British mission, headed by Foreign Secretary Arthur Balfour, came Gen. Sir Tom Bridges and a military staff. The official head of the French mission was René Viviani, like Lord Balfour a former prime minister. But in the hearts and minds of the American people it was Marshal Joffre, the principal French military representative accompanying the mission, who held first honors. To them he was Papa Joffre, the hero of the Marne, and wherever he went the crowds received him with wild enthusiasm. Few, if any, then realized how completely the old soldier had been removed from power by his own government. For the moment, at least, his prestige was still enormous, and because of this his advice in military matters carried far more weight than it would a few months hence.

To appreciate the profound influence the foreign missions and especially Marshal Joffre were to have on the character of our intervention, it may be useful to hark back for a moment to the staff studies we were drawing up at the War College before the French and British officers arrived. We were at great pains to warn against the danger of premature operations against Germany. Far better, we argued, to wait until we could muster a force sufficient to influence the issue decisively than to rush into battle half-prepared. In particular, we urged the War Department to resist every popular demand that one or two divisions be sent off immediately. This was sound advice, based on the experience of the British army, as reported to us by our military attaché in London. Nonetheless, a few days later we found ourselves recommending a course of action diametrically opposite. We had reckoned without Marshal Joffre.

I can still vividly remember Marshal Joffre's first visit. Just before he came we had a considerable flurry of preparation. To avoid giving offense to our French guests, someone thought it necessary to remove the big bronze statue of that renowned student of war, Frederick the Great of Prussia, from its accustomed place on the front steps of the college building. Poor Frederick served out the remainder of the war in the cellar. He was reprieved after the Armistice, but during World War II once again I found him in disgrace. He was standing out behind the lecture hall with his face turned to a corner like a naughty schoolboy, as if he personally were responsible for the outrages of the Nazis.

Old Marshal Joffre made quite a picture as he presented his views on the military contribution expected from the United States. Above his head, as he sat there hunched over the conference table, loomed a bust of Napoleon. But this bit of symbolism was quite unnecessary. The old marshal needed no stage props. He was himself the living embodiment of the strength of France, the enduring peasant: hulking frame, drooping mustache, slow speech, yet withal a shrewd and calculating mind.

The marshal's insight was evident in the way he presented his case. When the two missions reached Washington, both the French and British governments were in desperate straits. They had virtually exhausted their resources in manpower. And while they welcomed the prospect of fresh armies from the United States, they were by no means certain they could hang on until these armies were formed. They understood, perhaps even better than we, that more than a year would be consumed in recruiting troops and training them, first as individuals and then in larger tactical units. What the Allies needed most at the moment was manpower, individual soldiers to feed into the line to make good the daily losses incurred on the front. Replacements of this sort could be whipped into shape in a matter of weeks. They would learn quickly from the veterans around them, and since they would be fitted into existing tactical units, there need be no delay while training the staff officers required to organize brigades, divisions, and corps. With this in mind, both missions had been instructed to emphasize the need for manpower in the immediate future rather than fully equipped armies after many months of delay.

In his canny way, Marshal Joffre sensed the weakness of the official Allied schemes for using our manpower. He realized at once that national pride would make the course they proposed quite unthinkable; no great power could ever willingly accept such a subordinate role. If the United States wished to send soldiers to France, Marshal Joffre declared, they must be led by an American commander and must fight as an entirely separate force under the Stars and Stripes.

At one stroke the old Frenchman completely disarmed us. By taking our part, by grasping the compulsions of our national psychology on the major issue so readily, he won our respect and induced us to weigh his other proposals with the utmost care.

Some of my fellow officers have been inclined to regard Joffre as a senile old man, a superannuated officer who was little more than a figurehead. Their judgment, I suspect, had been colored by subsequent events. The old man may have been retired, but it was evident from our conference at the War College that he still retained much of the talent that had made him a Marshal of France. Before he arrived we were determined not to send troops to the front until we were ready to do so in decisive force. Against our contention that dispatching a Regular Army division to France at once would strip us of the men we needed for training, he argued that such a force was absolutely indispensable. A single division from the United States now, he said, would produce a tremendous effect upon the morale of the French army and the French people.

Although the old marshal kept talking about the wonderful lift a few of our troops would give the French, it gradually dawned on us that he had a far more subtle purpose in mind. His real concern was with morale in the United States. For all the enthusiasm with which the crowds had greeted him, he knew that the people of this country were not yet deeply and emotionally committed to the war. They would not be so committed, he realized, until they began to suffer. For this reason he wanted us to send a division abroad at once. And the sooner it shed blood the better. Long before Pearl Harbor, Marshal Joffre understood how useful it could be for a nation to lose heavily in its first battle.

General Bliss was somewhat disturbed when he began to appreciate what the wily old Marshal really had in mind. It would be foolish, the general believed, for us to repeat the mistake of the British and burn up the best of our Regulars as an exercise in applied psychology. General Bliss explained all this to Secretary Baker, but it was too late. Mr. Baker had already adopted Marshal Joffre's plan to send an expedition to France as soon as possible.

I do not know whether or not Secretary Baker perceived the subtle purpose of Marshal Joffre's advice. As an experienced political leader he was certainly not unaware of the practical advantages to be derived from the national unity that casualty lists from the front would certainly produce. In any event, he decided to send a division overseas immediately. And on 10 May 1917, President Wilson approved both Mr. Baker's plan and his selection of Maj. Gen. J. J. Pershing to command the division.

Once the decision was made, the Chief of Staff directed the War College to work out the details for assembling a division to ship abroad. It was characteristic of our army at the time that we did not have any such unit currently organized and ready to order into the field in an emergency. Instead, we had to extemporize a provisional division as best we could. This task fell to a committee of three comprising Maj. Briant Wells, Capt. Dan T. Moore, and myself.

As a preliminary step, our committee decided to confer with the staff officers who accompanied Marshal Joffre to Washington. In our first conference with them we discovered that the regulation infantry division prescribed in the Defense Act of 1916 would have to be abandoned. The organization authorized by statute simply would not fit into the system of trenches and supporting network of railroads found along the western front. Indeed, we were mortified to learn that virtually all of the larger tactical units provided for in our Regulations were totally unsuited to the requirements of modern warfare.

Our committee had no alternative but to sit down and draw up entirely new tables of organization, at best a tedious and time-consuming chore. Fortunately, we did not have to wait for Congress to approve our work. A most useful provision in the 1916 act authorized the President in wartime to alter at will the higher organizations prescribed by statute whenever the exigencies of the service required. On such trivial legislative footholds great events depend.

The revised division our committee worked out with the help of Marshal Joffre's staff consisted of two infantry brigades (each of two regiments) and a brigade of field artillery (of three regiments), along with appropriate auxiliary units of engineers, signal troops, and so on. With some slight modification, this division became the prototype for the army we later sent to France. In all, the revised organization numbered 600 officers and 17,000 enlisted men. And as a reminder of how long ago this took place, I must not forget to mention that we also provided in the table of organization for 8,600 horses and mules. Except for a few motorcycles and staff cars, our division was animal powered.

With a total of nearly 18,000 men, our provisional force was substantially smaller than the infantry division of 28,000 prescribed in the Defense Act. Nonetheless, the committee was decidedly unhappy about removing even this number of regulars from the all-important work of training. Our answer to this dilemma was a compromise. We suggested that the units of the advance division be given the same proportions of untrained men and reserve or temporary officers that the entire establishment would have after the increments authorized by the drafts were added. This would minimize the drain on our slender resources in trained men, yet still make it possible to send off a full-strength division at once. We recognized that a division diluted with so many recruits would require a considerable period of training in France before it would be ready for the front. On the other hand, its mere presence abroad would show the flag for morale purposes, and by training in France it would acquire first-hand experience of great value in guiding the program at home.

Although the instructions originally issued to our committee were limited to the formation of one division, Briant Wells, Dan Moore, and I decided to include some additional recommendations in the report we submitted. During our numerous conferences with Marshal Joffre's staff, one of his officers, a Major Requin, had suggested that in addition to a division with its commander, we might find it advisable to appoint a commander in chief for all the American forces in Europe. This officer, if sent abroad at once with a staff, could establish relations with the French high command and prepare for the arrival of troops in large numbers from the United States.

The wisdom of Major Requin's proposal immediately appealed to us, so we urged its adoption. Until a theater commander with plenary powers set up his headquarters in France, a full machinery of military cooperation simply would not function. The first division to go abroad would actually be only an advance element of the immense force ultimately intended. Obviously the commander in chief should not concern himself with the immediate details of command or administration in this preliminary division. His energies would better be spent, we believed, in maintaining liaison with the French and in preparing bases, developing lines of communication, and arranging those "services of the rear" required by a large army. With this in mind, we urged that consideration be given to the selection of a commander in chief and appropriate subordinate commanders to assist him, quite apart from the question of who was to lead the preliminary division.

Our recommendation was to have far-reaching effects. When General Pershing arrived in Washington on 10 May 1917, Secretary Baker told him he was to lead the advance division to France. That very same day our committee report went up to the Chief of Staff. Two or three days later Secretary Baker called in General Pershing once again and told him the President had decided not to send him abroad with the initial division; instead he was to go as Commander in Chief of all the American forces in the European theater. Between these two visits, our committee's staff paper had met with official favor in the War Department. Thus, in a modest way, we seem to have assisted at the birth of the American Expeditionary Force, or AEF.

Soon after the President designated him to command the AEF, General Pershing established an office in Room 223 of the old War Department building and began to look about for a suitable staff. His first selection was Maj. James G. Harbord, whom he invited to serve as his chief of staff. I knew Harbord rather well. His wife was the daughter of Brig. Gen. Samuel Ovenshine, who had served for many years in my old regiment, the 15th Infantry. I had worked with Harbord during my first tour in the Philippines in 1906-1907 and again during the past year, when he had come to Washington as a student in the War College.

Like most of Harbord's friends and admirers, I felt somewhat envious in my congratulations on his good fortune, for I should very much have liked to go on the expedition to France. The prospects seemed remote, however, for up to that time I had never so much as met General Pershing. Then, on my return home one evening a few days after Harbord received his appointment, Maude told me he had telephoned requesting me to come to his house as soon after dark as convenient. One can readily imagine my anticipation as I set out in response to this mysterious invitation.

Scarcely had I arrived when in came my friend, Maj. Dennis E. Nolan, equally anxious to learn why he had been summoned. Maj. Harbord broke the news to us at once. He and General Pershing had selected us as the two General Staff officers on duty in Washington who were authorized to accompany the Commander in Chief to France. Nolan was to head up intelligence, and I was to be in charge of military operations; each of us would bear the title, Assistant Chief of Staff, AEF.

Those last two weeks in Washington were utterly hectic. There were far too many things to take care of in the short time remaining even if one worked all day and half the night. I was so busy I scarcely had time to take note of my selection for promotion to the rank of lieutenant colonel, which came at this juncture. As chief of the nascent Operations Section of the AEF, I was instructed to select a suitable staff of stenographers and clerks, along with the stationery and office equipment we would require for several months. On top of these petty details there were all sorts of personal matters requiring attention.

Not the least of my burdens was the necessity of doing business as chief of Operations while still trying to assemble a proper staff. A great many questions of policy required decision before our departure, but for want of a staff accustomed to working effectively as a team, it was difficult to prepare the necessary background studies, without which the Commander in Chief would be seriously handicapped. As a consequence, busy as I was getting ready to go, I spent most of my last three or four days in Washington trying to deal with several complicated matters of policy more or less single-handedly.

Of these many problems I remember one in particular. My brother-in-law, Capt. Harris Laning, who was then in the navy's Bureau of Navigation, called me in some agitation one afternoon shortly before we left; he informed me that a serious conflict had developed between the army and the navy as to which service should control the transports carrying our troops to France. The army, it seems, wished to retain its transports as in time of peace; the navy, confronted with all the technical difficulties arising from the need for convoys, wished to assume jurisdiction. After getting the facts from Captain Laning I presented the matter to General Pershing, who immediately accepted the navy's point of view. The general's decision settled the issue at hand, but the episode clearly revealed how desperately the army needed additional staff officers.

Unless we secured a large number of competent staff officers, we would court almost certain disaster in the field. With a million or more men to supply and train and move to the front in a distant theater of operations, we would need staff work of a scope and caliber far beyond anything the army had yet seen if we expected to keep from becoming snarled in our own confusion.

Anticipating all this, I recommended the prompt inauguration of a scheme for training staff officers by the apprentice system. Although I was fully aware of the tremendous pressure in the War Department to put every available Regular officer directly into the work of training the new army to be raised by the draft, I felt that we would make no mistake if we rounded up all the young Staff College graduates we could get and sent them to France immediately. There they could be attached to French and British units as understudies, and after a suitable period of training they could return to the United States and join the divisions ready to move overseas. To make my scheme effective, I urged the General Staff to begin work immediately on a manual prescribing the organization and functions of staff officers in the field. That a publication of this sort was not already available is perhaps the most telling evidence of how imperfectly the role of the staff was understood by many of the senior officers then on duty in the War Department.

The failure of those in authority to appreciate the importance of a fully trained staff to an army in the field was to impede us seriously in the months to come. Despite Major Harbord's most urgent pleas for additional officers, Nolan and I were the only men he was permitted to select from the General Staff in Washington. The authorities did relent, however, to the extent of letting him call in three other qualified members of the staff corps who were then on duty with troops. By this means he added Maj. Arthur L. Conger, Maj. Hugh A. Drum, and Capt. William O. Reed to the small group bound for France with General Pershing. But even with these reinforcements we were woefully short-handed.

On 26 May 1917, barely two weeks after learning he was to be the Commander in Chief of our armies in Europe, General Pershing officially activated the American Expeditionary Force and assumed command. This was a mere formality, of course, for some of us had already been hard at work in the new organization for several days. But the publication of AEF General Order No. 1 did signify that the selection of staff was now complete and that we could expect to leave in short order. Sure enough, that same day those of us who had been fortunate enough to be chosen to accompany the advance party to Europe received verbal orders concerning our departure. To conceal our movements we were instructed to don civilian attire and proceed individually to Governors Island in New York Harbor. There we were to meet General Pershing two days later and receive further instructions.

In New York the next day I spent most of the morning buying French books and making arrangements with the American Express Company for some traveler's checks. Then I took the ferry out to our appointed rendezvous on Governors Island, the headquarters of the Eastern Department of the army. To my delight, who should meet me at the dock but my old friend George C. Marshall. He was there on the island as a staff officer with Maj. Gen. J. Franklin Bell, the department commander. Marshall took me in to call on the general and then drew me aside for a hurried word in private. Like every other officer in the Regular Army, Marshall was terribly anxious to join the AEF. Knowing his unusual capacities as I did, I was equally anxious to have his wish fulfilled. I assured him that if it could be arranged, I would like very much to have him join me on the Operations staff in Paris as soon as possible.

When General Pershing reached Governors Island, he learned to his horror that all our baggage, which had been gathered surreptitiously, was sitting on the White Star Line dock with large stenciled lettering proclaiming its owners and its destination. While we had all been busy avoiding spies by various masquerades, every railroad employee, dock worker, or casual idler on the waterfront could read the labels on our belongings and learn what ship we were taking and to what port in England we were sailing. The general was furious at this careless breach and dashed off a red-hot letter to the Quartermaster General, which I had the pleasure of reading before it was mailed.

We boarded the lighter at high noon on 28 May 1917, and there for the first time saw our party assembled all in one place. There were almost two hundred of us: fifty or more officers and seventy clerks and other civilian employees, as well as about the same number of enlisted men, forming a headquarters company, with a strong detachment of Signal Corps troops to handle communications. In later years the survivors of this group became charter members of the Baltic Society, formed to commemorate the crossing of this first contingent of the AEF. At the time, however, our thoughts were far from post war reunions. We were headed for the wars, and who could tell what fate?

24   With Pershing to Paris

Although I had been looking forward to the ocean voyage as an opportunity to recuperate from the strain of long-continued overwork, our crossing in the *Baltic* turned out to be no pleasure cruise. On the first morning out, General Pershing assembled the whole group and assigned a regular routine of duties. In effect my work continued at much the same pace as in Washington. To make matters worse, when the medics gave us all a second round of immunization shots, my reaction was painfully severe.

At first I was much annoyed to learn that we were to have recitations in French at fixed hours. This threatened to interrupt our regular staff work most inconveniently. In time, however, I came to realize that the arrangement was a sensible one. For all our good intentions, we were so busy we would probably have put off studying French until too late, had any other course been adopted.

Along with Nolan and Harbord, it was my good fortune to be in a class taught by Maj. Robert Bacon, one of the most remarkable men in our party. He had been in Teddy Roosevelt's class at Harvard; as a Morgan partner he had participated in the formation of the U.S. Steel Corporation, and then at Elihu Root's request he had entered the State Department, where he had served successively as assistant secretary and secretary under Roosevelt and as ambassador to France during William Howard Taft's administration. He returned to France as a volunteer ambulance driver in 1914 but came home the following year to take part in the preparedness campaign. Although he was active in the Plattsburg movement, I had never met him until he turned up on the *Baltic* with a commission as a major in the Army Reserve.

In the Operations Section we had problems enough to busy a staff of twenty or more, yet I remained single handed save for the clerical help Harbord had authorized me to assemble before leaving Washington. What I needed most of all was one or more trained staff officers capable of working up policy studies without my immediate supervision. On paper, at least, I did have an assistant in the Operations Section. He was Maj. Hugh Drum, an officer already recognized as one of the ablest in the army, although still a very young man. Drum would have been of tremendous help to me had he not received a special assignment shortly after we sailed. General Pershing asked him to make an investigation of the port facilities of France to prepare for the coming of the AEF, a project that kept him busy throughout the voyage and for several days thereafter. Happily, the selection of someone to replace Drum did not take too many hours from my work.

One of the very real advantages of the old army was its limited size. The officer corps was so small that one was almost sure to know something of the capabilities and limitations of more or less everyone in it. My table companions on the *Baltic* offer a case in point. There were five officers besides myself. Of these only one, an intelligent young reserve officer, Capt. S. T. Hubbard, was a stranger to me. Each of the others I knew at first hand. Dennis Nolan and I had worked together most recently on the General Staff; Hugh Drum was my erstwhile assistant; Arthur Conger had been one of my instructors at Fort Leavenworth; and Fox Conner had served with me at the War College during my first tour in Washington back in 1911-12.

Fox Conner was my man; I needed no prolonged period of trial to determine this. I had seen him at work on the General Staff and well knew what substantial abilities he possessed. Since then he had served a tour of duty with the French army. This experience and his knowledge of the French language made him exceptionally well qualified to serve in the Operations Section. He had joined the expedition as an assistant to Col. A. W. Brewster, the inspector general, but I was sure that Operations carried a higher priority than Inspection and determined to pry him loose.

When I presented my case to Harbord, he was impressed with my reasons for wishing Conner's transfer and promised to take the matter up with General Pershing. A few hours later he called me to his stateroom and pointed out that there was one substantial objection to my proposal. In the forthcoming expansion of the army, Fox Conner, as a Field Artillery officer, might well receive his promotion before I did. And as the senior officer he would have to displace me as the chief of Operations. To this objection I replied, "If that should happen, I would be very glad to change desks with Conner. I recommended him for the job because I believe that nobody else is so well fitted to serve in that capacity, and I certainly would not revoke the recommendation even if it should prove prejudicial to my own fortunes." Harbord smiled somewhat at my highminded speech but agreed to let me have the man I wanted. His decision made a great deal of difference in Conner's subsequent career.

Fox Conner soon proved his worth many times over in the Operations Section. While we were still on the Atlantic he prepared an excellent paper on the problem of artillery for the AEF. Later, along with my West Point classmate Maj. J. H. Parker, he helped me deal with endless difficulties in planning the organization and training of machine gun units at the regimental level. We had been forced to consider this subject anew, largely as a result of what we had learned during the conference we had held with the French and British missions during our last few days in Washington. Since the Allied officers had behind them years of experience on the Western Front, in this as in most other purely technical questions we were inclined to attach great weight to their opinions.

I had been particularly interested in what our visitors had to say about the organization of a theater commander's staff. Our deficiencies in this respect had been appallingly evident, to me at least, even before the foreign missions arrived in the United States. Sure enough, in the course of one of his visits to the War College, Gen. Sir Tom Bridges had made a special point of emphasizing the tremendous importance of a properly constituted staff in modern warfare. Mounting a battle on the front, he said, was now a vast, impersonal affair. Men and supplies had to move toward the front in endless procession on a clockwork schedule. Coordinating such an operation, he assured us, required the services of an elaborate and highly trained staff, which gave generalship a new dimension.

The points General Bridges made about the role of field commander's staff received confirmation from an unexpected source. Among the few passengers sailing for Europe on the *Baltic*, apart from the Pershing group, was a British colonel by the name of Puckle. At Harbord's request Colonel Puckle agreed to give us a series of lectures on the problems of maintaining an expeditionary force in France. These talks, which proved to be highly interesting, reinforced the impression left on me earlier by General Bridges that success in contemporary warfare is less a matter of dash than of mass—millions of men and tons of supplies—subject to the closest possible control by top command.

The more I reflected on the comments of our British friends, the more I came to appreciate how rudimentary and inadequate our existing staff organization really was. If we were to handle the enormous volume of detailed planning required to send armies of a million men and more into battle, we would have to revamp the scheme of organization we had planned before leaving Washington. Back in Washington, before the AEF as such had even been conceived, Harbord and I together had drawn up a plan outlining the duties and relationships of a field commander's staff. Figure 1 indicates the gist of our ideas.

One can see at a glance that our objective was to free the commander's operating staff, insofar as possible, from administrative burdens.

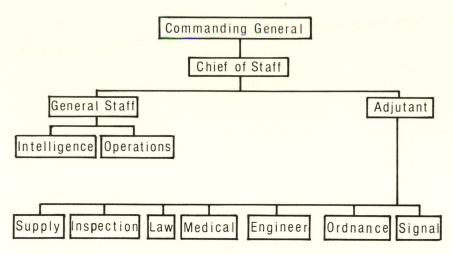

Figure 1

When our more experienced British friends finally led us to see the need for a substantial modification in our conception of the staff we would soon require, Harbord and I spent many hours trying to find a workable substitute for what we already had. We met complications at every turn. For one thing General Pershing wanted us to create an executive section in the General Staff "to give it responsibility." The implications of this required the most careful study. Yet even if it proved feasible to carry out the general's desires, we knew we would be hard put to find the necessary personnel, for our roster of talent was sharply limited. Above all, we realized only too well how seriously handicapped we were from lack of actual experience with staff operations on a grand scale.

After many long and exhausting sessions in Harbord's stateroom office, some of them lasting far into the small hours of the morning, we finally gave up revising the form of our staff organization. Until we could learn something more about how the Allied armies handled this problem, we concluded, our efforts might better be spent elsewhere. And so it was decided that my principal mission during our stay in London would be to haunt the Operations Division of the British General Staff to learn whatever I could of how it functioned.

The *Baltic* entered the Mersey on the evening of 7 June, and the following morning we warped up at the dock in Liverpool. We spent six days in England, six eventful days filled with a curious mixture of contrasting impressions. We rushed about in breathless haste on military missions and then attended leisurely state dinners in the grand manner. And set against the pomp and ceremony of the formal receptions tendered us, we saw everywhere the austerity and agony of war.

While we moved steadily toward the scene of action in a physical sense, from Washington to New York to London and soon to Paris, we also moved there emotionally, step by step. To dine on fish instead of beef is not war, but like the darkened ship our first night at sea, little evidences of austerity like this helped to push one closer toward understanding what it meant. Perhaps the biggest single step I took toward war was outside Charing Cross Station. There, long lines of ambulances were loading wounded soldiers just back from the fierce engagement going on in Flanders. Old Joffre was right, I mused; a skillful general planning for battle must know his troops, and the people back home for that matter, in spirit as well as flesh. In building the AEF, I now perceived, we would do well not to let our concern about external and material factors blind us to the significance of this subjective feature of our task.

Without a doubt, the high point of our visit in London was the great state dinner given in behalf of General Pershing by the British government. It was held at Lancaster House, the historic mansion that houses the London Museum. Prime Minister David Lloyd George himself presided, and the roster of guests included some of the most distinguished statesmen and military leaders of the day. There were brief toasts to the King and the President, but we were spared the usual speeches from the head table; in fact, there was no head table. The guests were distributed around six tables for eight, with four British and four Americans at each. Moreover, every table had about the same proportion of junior to senior officers and civilian to military guests.

As I looked about the room, it occurred to me that this was no empty ceremonial but a dinner with a purpose. Whoever arranged the seating had carefully contrived to mix us all into congenial groups representing a wide cross-section of interests. Here were the people who would be working to make a success of coalition warfare for months to come; the better we knew one another as individuals, the easier it would be to collaborate harmoniously.

Among those present at the table to which I was assigned were Admiral Sims, Sir Alfred Mond, a successful industrialist and Liberal member of Parliament who was serving in Lloyd George's coalition ministry, and my longtime friend Col. William S. Graves. I was particularly delighted to find myself seated next to Maj. Bertie Spender-Clay, Lord Astor's brother-in-law, whom I had come to know quite well when he was in Washington a few weeks earlier with Gen. Sir Tom Bridges and the British mission.

After the meal the Prime Minister took the trouble to greet the members of General Pershing's staff individually and hold a few moments of private conversation with each. However much one might disagree with him on particular issues, one could not help but admire his technique. Mr. Lloyd George was certainly one of the greatest in that long line of great men that every national crisis brings forward in England.

In the next few days we spent many hours at the War Office, where our opposite numbers in the British army did all they could to explain how their organizations functioned. The more we learned, the more discouraged we became. In Operations my guides led me through an elaborate establishment where hundreds of officers and a thousand clerks were engaged in the work I was to do in the near future. Talking it over afterward with Nolan, I voiced my dismay at the contrast. The whole Operations office for the AEF, officers, clerks, and all, could ride comfortably in a single one of those funny little London taxis. Dennis shook his head miserably in agreement. He reported that the British Intelligence Section was even larger than what I had seen in Operations.

Ever since the visit of the French and British missions to Washington, we had understood that the staff of the AEF was too small; now, after seeing the War Office in action, we realized that our problem was something more than merely quantitative. Large numbers of additional staff officers would help, but our real task would be to perfect the necessary procedures and routines for an elaborate and far-flung organization. We would have to devise a host of new forms and master intricate systems of statistical reporting before we could even begin to operate on a scale comparable to that of the French and British. When I asked Nolan what he thought about all this, he looked at me wryly and said, "Well, Palmer, we're simply plain boobs, aren't we."

The next morning Fox Conner and I got up at 5:30 and set out by auto for the army training center at Colchester. There we spent a busy day watching demonstrations of trench warfare. First we saw a training camp for drafts, as the British call raw recruits, then in succession we visited a bayonet school and a gas school and had our first glimpse of grenade fighting in a highly realistic mock trench raid.

Before six o'clock on the morning of 13 June, we boarded a little Channel steamer at Folkestone and set out on the twenty-eight-mile journey to Boulogne. In many ways our landing in France more or less paralleled our arrival in Liverpool less than a week before. There was the same sort of honor guard drawn up on the wharf, bands playing the Star Spangled Banner, and the inevitable delegation of notables. Conspicuous among them was Brigadier General Peltier, a veteran campaigner, whose loss of an arm had done nothing to detract from his prodigious energy and vivacious spirit. The general spoke excellent English, having lived in the United States as a boy. He subsequently became a useful liaison officer at General Pershing's headquarters.

Of the many dignitaries who met us in Boulogne, one at least was no stranger to me. This was Lt. Col. the Count de Chambrun, whom I had first met in San Antonio when he came down to see our Maneuver Division as an observer for the French Army back in 1911. He, too, spoke English like a native and was soon to prove his worth as an aide to General Pershing.

With a grasp of practical psychology that would surely have evoked the admiration of an experienced campaign manager back home, the French authorities had deliberately arranged for us to reach Paris at the evening rush hour, when the shops and offices had just closed and the streets were filled with people. In the station a delegation of distinguished officials, including our ambassador, several members of the French cabinet, and the grand old Marshal Joffre, welcomed General Pershing in a brief ceremony and then ushered us out to a line of autos waiting in the street.

I was utterly unprepared for what followed. A cheering mob surged forward the moment the general appeared and all but swept him off his feet as he climbed into his auto at the head of the line. Just then Marshal Joffre's staff officers, Fabry, Remond, Requin, and the others whom we had met in Washington, rushed up and embraced me like a long-lost brother. All the while, a huge military band was pounding out the Star Spangled Banner and the Marseillaise, working everybody up to a feverish pitch of excitement. Nolan and I piled into one of the waiting cars with a French officer, and after some delay, the procession started off.

Procession is hardly the word; the streets were so jammed with people who pressed upon us from all sides that our autos had to stop repeatedly to keep from injuring someone. Flowers pelted in upon us as hysterical men and women, sobbing and laughing, flung themselves forward to reach out and touch us, shouting "Vive l' Amérique" again and again as they danced about in an orgy of delight. It was a strange and wonderful sight, a vivid manifestation of that emotionalism one always hears attributed to the French people. Throughout the rest of my life I doubt if I have ever experienced anything quite like it. Even the celebrations of Armistice Day fell short of the ovation touched off by General Pershing's arrival in Paris that June evening in 1917.

"Walking Companions"
Headquarters, AEF, Paris, 1917. *Left to right*: Lieutenant Colonel J. M. Palmer, Captain Menot,
Major D. E. Nolan.
Courtesy of the Manuscripts Division, Library of Congress

Lieutenant Colonel J. M. Palmer, Assistant Chief of Staff for Operations, Temporary Headquarters, AEF, Paris, 1917
Courtesy of the Manuscripts Division, Library of Congress

General Pershing and His Staff on the Steps of the State, War, and Navy Building, Washington, D.C., 1919
Left to right: Colonel Aristides Moreno, Lieutenant Colonel Albert S. Kuegle, Major General Fox Conner, Colonel George C. Marshall, General John J. Pershing, Colonel John Quekemeyer, Major General Andre Brewster, Major Robert C. Davis.
Courtesy of George C. Marshall Foundation; Army Photograph 63939, SC91374

286

Colonel J. M. Palmer, General J. J. Pershing, and Mary Laning Palmer, about 1921
Family Photograph

Portrait of Brigadier General J. M. Palmer by Baron Robert Doblhoff, 1931
Family Photograph

Maude Laning Palmer (Tiss) and John McAuley Palmer in Retirement at "Edgewild," 1940
Family Photograph

Brigadier General John McAuley Palmer with Chief of Staff General George Catlett Marshall, The Pentagon, 1944
U.S. Army Photograph, Signal Corps Photo # APS-44-992

BOOK III

In which Palmer goes to Paris and begins planning for the millions of Americans to follow. There he seriously overworks himself, falls ill, recovers, is sent to Italy on a military diplomatic mission, suffers a relapse and is invalided home, recovers and returns to lead a brigade at the front, breaking through the German lines before Verdun. Returning to the United States as Pershing's representative on postwar legislation for the army, Palmer is appointed special adviser on Capitol Hill, where he plays a major role in drafting the landmark Defense Act of 1920. As peacetime retrenchment dangerously weakens the U.S. Army, General Palmer retires to write books on military policy, hoping to awaken an apathetic public to the need for peacetime training of citizen soldiers, to save lives and insure an adequate defense for the nation without sacrificing democratic values. The outbreak of World War II in Europe draws the general into a new and successful effort to secure legislation for a peacetime draft. Recalled to active duty, he serves throughout the war as a military elder statesman and adviser to the Chief of Staff, Gen. George C. Marshall, on the citizen components and postwar planning. When the postwar effort to enact universal military training is defeated, Palmer retires a second time, having been the oldest officer on active duty. He resolves to write a book about his struggles to establish a truly democratic army as his final contribution to the cause to which he has devoted his life.

25   Assistant Chief of Staff

General Pershing and his staff set out the very next morning after their tumultuous reception, to transform Headquarters, AEF, from a paper organization to an operating reality. Long before the *Baltic* party arrived, the army observers working with the U.S. military attaché in Paris had been instructed to find accommodations for this purpose. Conventional office space was unobtainable in wartime Paris, but they had been able to secure some private dwellings directly opposite the Esplanade des Invalides on the corner of the Rue de Grenelle and the Rue de Constantine to house the staff until a suitable place could be located nearer the front. Needless to say, converted residences were far from ideal as military headquarters; nearly a hundred officers and clerks had to find space in the few available rooms. But hardly had they begun on this when Marshal Joffre sent word that he wished to receive the Americans at the Hotel des Invalides, just across the street from their new quarters.[1]

As General Pershing walked over the esplanade with his entourage at his heels, there was a good deal of grumbling amongst the American officers over this needless diversion from the important tasks at hand. In the hour that followed, however, many of those who had complained came to realize that the French understood very well indeed what they were doing. Years later Palmer recorded his impressions with a vividness that clearly indicated that the significance of the occasion had not been lost upon him.

> General Pershing was received by Marshal Joffre at the Hotel des Invalides. Each general was accompanied by the officers of his staff. We were thus given an opportunity to become acquainted with some of our new comrades in arms.
> After the formalities of introduction, the Governor of the Invalides, an aged veteran of the Crimean War, conducted his two distinguished

guests through the precincts of the historic temple. The staff officers, Frenchmen and Americans, intermingling informally, followed their chiefs.

Finally we passed through the Church of St. Louis, and came out under the great Dome of the Invalides. A mysterious bluish light streamed down upon us from above. It fell upon the hero of the Marne and upon the new and untried American commander. Below us its beams fell upon the red porphyry sarcophagus of the great Emperor and tinged it purple.

Then the Governor of the Invalides whispered something to Marshal Joffre who bowed his head in assent. We followed the old Crimean general until we came to a massive doorway. This he unlocked with a great key. From this doorway he led us to a flight of marble steps that brought us down to the level of the sarcophagus. We marched past it silently and passed into a crypt dimly lighted by funeral lamps.

Here we stood in the very holy of holies of the French soldier. In the center of the chamber there was an antique altar surmounted by a cabinet of glass and gold. Within the cabinet lay a cushion of white satin. Upon this rested the golden chain or collar that Napoleon wore when he was crowned Emperor of the French. Upon this lay the sword of Austerlitz. And upon these two relics reposed the famous Bonaparte chapeau, the one the Emperor had worn at the Battle of Eylau.

We all stood at attention. Then Marshal Joffre faced toward the sarcophagus. As he raised his hand to his visor we all joined in the salute to the imperial soldier.

Then the aged Crimean general left his place between Marshal Joffre and General Pershing and walked with feeble steps toward the altar. As he approached it, he drew a golden key from the bosom of his uniform coat. With trembling fingers he unlocked the door and slowly opened it. He placed his hands under the chapeau and laid it aside. Then he took the sword of Austerlitz in his hands. He faced about and holding it before him he walked with slow steps toward General Pershing and offered him Napoleon's sword.

I cannot recall a tenser moment in all my life. What a magnificent gesture! Here was France presenting her most sacred military symbol to the new American General. What would he do with it? Would he take it in his hands? Many things flash through one's mind in such a crucial instant—more thoughts in a fraction of a second than one can express in an hour. What enormous possibilities for the wrong thing!

But if those who surrounded him stood in suspense, there was no hesitation in the American soldier. He was standing at attention. He did not move his hands from his sides. As the sword was presented to him, he bent forward and kissed its hilt. Then he straightened up and resumed the position of a soldier at attention.

Two elderly French officers were standing just behind me. One of them exclaimed, "Magnificent!" The other whispered, "This will be told at every dinner table in Paris tonight."

This incident [was] characteristic of General Pershing. In many years of close association with him, I never knew him to do a tactless thing. From the beginning, this unfailing sense of propriety had a powerful influence upon his relations with our allies.[2]

The temporary headquarters on the Rue de Constantine was not easily set in motion. The entire Operations Section, clerks, officers, and equipment, was still confined to a single room and the floor was still littered with great boxes of yet unpacked supplies, large rolls of maps, and piles of French and British training manuals, when in walked a delegation of French staff officers to discuss questions of policy.

From the visitors' point of view it was of the utmost importance to impose a French imprint upon the as yet unformed AEF. If the American army in France were to accept French training doctrine and conform to French tables of organization, it would vastly facilitate their scheme to employ units from the AEF as integral elements of the French army. If they waited until General Pershing's staff had settled all questions of organization without suggestions from the French, there was good reason to believe that the resulting units would be difficult if not impossible to employ efficiently under French command.

From the point of view of Lt. Col. John M. Palmer, the new and untried assistant chief of staff for Operations, AEF, who didn't even have a desk to sit at, the arrival of the French officers for a discussion of policy was profoundly distressing. To cap the difficulty, none of the visitors crowding into the littered office could speak English. Lieutenant Colonel de Chambrun was a tremendous help, but he couldn't be everywhere at once.[3] There was nothing to do but put the French off with hasty excuses.

Fortunately at least some measure of relief was at hand. As soon as he established himself in Paris, General Pershing added to his staff the members of the U.S. Military Mission, who had been serving for some months as observers with the French army. Two of these men, Maj. Frank Parker and Maj. John W. Barker, were promptly assigned to the Operations Section, where they soon proved invaluable. Barker and Palmer had been friends and classmates at Fort Leavenworth, so they worked together easily from the start. Barker was married to a French woman, and Parker had gone through the French cavalry school at Saumur. Both knew the French intimately, and their insights helped save the staff from many a diplomatic blunder at a time when it was imperative to avoid treading upon French toes. The recent failure of the Nivelle offensive, on which the French had placed so many hopes, had left them abnormally sensitive to seeming affronts against their dignity.

Another interesting member of the U.S. Military Mission in Paris who joined the AEF was Lt. Col. William Mitchell. Already a zealous advocate for air power, Billy Mitchell had been ordered to France during the previous winter as an observer, and by the time the Pershing party arrived, he was overflowing with schemes for hurling an American air force against the Germans in the early fall of 1917. Palmer and Mitchell had been at Fort Leavenworth together in 1909. That was before Mitchell had become an air power partisan, and Palmer remembered him only as an exuberant Signal Corps officer who was habitually at the center of some madcap adventure.

When Mitchell ran into Palmer at a luncheon proffered by the French at the Cercle National, he promptly buttonholed his old friend and began to pour out his plans for aviation in the AEF. Perhaps to his surprise, he found a willing listener. To be sure, Palmer was a General Staff officer, and Mitchell was already persuaded that most General Staff officers did not—or would not—appreciate the potentialities of the airplane. But if Palmer did not grasp the full implications of aviation for military operations, he was by no means blind to the problems involved. As early as November 1916, in planning articles for the magazine *National Service,* he had called attention to the "amazing development" of aviation and had urged the publication to secure an article by a qualified officer to show its "revolutionary influence upon strategy and tactics."[4]

With such a receptive individual as Palmer serving as assistant chief of staff for Operations, Mitchell had reason to feel considerably encouraged. With characteristic enthusiasm he insisted on driving Palmer the seven miles out to Le Bourget Aerodrome to show him the impressive array of aircraft in the Grand Aviation Reserve maintained by the French army. This was a fine beginning, and Palmer was suitably impressed. Instead of hammering his points home, however, Mitchell, in a change of mood entirely typical of him, climbed into a French plane and flew off toward the front, leaving his guest to make his way back to AEF headquarters alone.[5]

Looking back afterward, Palmer saw the incident as highly significant. Mitchell was an attractive personality, filled with good humor and obvious sincerity. Nevertheless, he was inclined to be impulsive, relying on dash and colorful aerial exploits to prove his points. As one French officer put it, his was "une ardeur juvenile."[6] It seemed that he had not yet learned what Palmer and Nolan had sensed after their visits to the War Office in London, that this was a war of mass armies in which meticulous staff planning was to play a crucial part. If Mitchell had immediately returned with Palmer to the make-shift headquarters to begin a campaign of tactful persuasion and detailed planning, he might have accomplished far more for air power than he ever could by aerial acrobatics.

Back in his crowded office on the Rue de Constantine, Palmer began to map out the major tasks confronting the Operations Section. As he saw it, the week ahead was to be the most critical period. Decisions would have to be made that, once reached, would commit the AEF for months to come if not permanently. In effect, the Operations shop would have to produce a master blueprint for the AEF. First this required some fundamental decisions on organization, to determine the size and composition of the corps, divisions, brigades, and lesser units that would comprise the expeditionary force. Once these points were settled, it would be possible to work for agreement with the French and British on general strategy. This in turn would influence the character of the training and equipment to be given the troops already mobilizing in the United States.

Unfortunately, other problems intruded to upset the timetable. As is so often the case in war, matters of immediate urgency shouldered aside those of greater significance. In this instance the important issue of the moment was the imminent arrival of the 1st Division, the advance guard of the AEF, sent to France with all possible dispatch to bolster French morale.

Planning for the reception of the 1st Division was greatly facilitated by a suggestion offered by the French. The British were already dug in on the western end of the front, where they had the shortest possible lines of communication across the Channel. In the central sector, the French could scarcely be expected to trust the defense of Paris to the untried Americans. The eastern sector, therefore, was the only one left for the AEF. With the arrival of the 1st Division only days away, a prompt decision was imperative, for until the American front was decided upon, the Operations staff could not begin working on such details as the selection of supply lines and depots and the location of rear area cantonments, training grounds, and the like.[7] Impelled by these considerations, General Pershing directed Palmer to drop everything and proceed to the front with his staff to make a thorough reconnaissance of the eastern sector as a potential theater of action for the AEF.

As with all the officers in the Paris headquarters, Palmer's spirit of adventure was fired by the prospect of seeing the war at close range. More significantly, such a trip afforded an occasion to learn at first hand something of the conditions prevailing in those areas where much of the planning by the Operations Section would soon fall. A realistic view of the zone of advance would go far to minimize the necessity for planning done in a vacuum, which is ever the bane of staff officers.

The small party of officers leaving the Gare de l'Est on 21 June 1917 had one major objective: they were to study the eastern sector of the existing

combat zone to see if it offered a suitable field of operations for the AEF. Did
the terrain offer possibilities for a war of maneuver such as General Pershing
envisioned, or would it inexorably dictate a continuation of the stalemate of
trench warfare that now absorbed the French so thoroughly? In theory—
according to the staff manuals—such a reconnaissance should have been
carried out by independent observers, trained staff officers entirely free to
make objective judgments on the facts as they found them. In actual practice,
when they left Paris they joined a guided tour from which the French manage-
ment allowed few if any deviations.

The guided tour began with a four-hour train journey to Bar-le-Duc. In
addition to Palmer the party included four officers of the AEF: Lt. Col. Fox
Conner, Maj. Hugh Drum, Maj. Frank Parker, and Maj. Sanford Wadhams,
a medical officer, as well as two French liaison officers, Lt. Col. de Chambrun
and a Major Rozet. At Bar-le-Duc the whole group climbed into staff cars
provided by the local French authorities and hustled off to the nearby town of
Gondrecourt.[8] Ostensibly the visit was to survey one of the cantonments the
French proposed to turn over to the AEF, but the military authorities may also
have had quite another purpose in mind. They were at great pains to get the
American visitors to mingle with the officers and men of the crack regiment of
chasseurs billeted there. Discontent, if not sedition and mutiny, had been
evident back in Paris, so the French had good reason to do what they could to
counteract any unfavorable impressions the AEF officers might have formed.
Palmer duly noted in his journal at the time that he was "greatly impressed"
with the morale of the French troops and remarked on the contrast in this
respect between Paris and the front.[9]

From Gondrecourt the party drove on toward Neufchâteau to inspect a vast
maneuver ground stretching back from the left bank of the Meuse. On the way
the convoy of cars stopped in a little village to take lunch at a tiny sidewalk
cafe. While strolling after the meal, Palmer came upon a small châsselle
marking the birthplace of Joan of Arc; quite by accident they had dropped in
on the famous village of Domrémy. Minutes later the staff cars dashed off to
yet another appointment.

The whirlwind tour continued as far south as the ancient fortified city of
Besançon on the river Doubs, where the visitors inspected the artillery
grounds at Valdahon and then returned northward again through Epinal in
the Vosges mountains to Nancy. Just beyond that city they visited the headquarters of the French Eighth Army. Here they were given a brief opportunity
to visit the Intelligence and Operations sections to learn something of French
staff procedure.[10] Finally a young officer was told off to escort the party on the
customary "trip to the front." In this instance the tour consisted of little more
than a hike out to a bit of high ground just behind the trenches facing Metz.

Before returning to Paris, Palmer gathered his colleagues in a hotel room to
discuss the report they would submit on their return. Insofar as a captive

audience could be expected to determine, the area they had just toured seemed to offer a suitable theater of action for AEF. Certainly their French hosts had been most accommodating in offering to withdraw their troops to make cantonments and training grounds available. But that was just the point; everywhere they visited, they had been confronted with a *fait accompli*. At Gondrecourt, for example, the French had gone ahead with extensive preparations just as if it had long since been decided that the AEF would definitely move in.

The situation required sensitive diplomacy, for the line between freedom of action and subservience was unusually difficult to draw. When the French offered Palmer an elaborate course of instruction for use in training the AEF, he faced a typical dilemma. To take over the whole curriculum would commit the American forces to a slavish imitation of French doctrine; to reject it entirely would be to give offense and at the same time to ignore many hard-won lessons from the experience of battle. Not ten days had elapsed since Headquarters, AEF, had begun to function in Paris, yet it was already evident that the full range of activities calling for decisions by the high command involved a great deal more than the lecturers at Fort Leavenworth had led Staff College graduates to believe.

For better or worse, the Operations conference decided that it was wise to go along with the French plans. As a practical matter, the Gondrecourt-Neufchateau region was prepared to receive the first 50,000 troops to arrive from the United States; a few ready-made French cantonments in hand were certainly more desirable by far than an indefinite number of demountable accommodations yet to be procured and transported across the Atlantic. To be sure, there were still some few difficulties to resolve before the American troops could actually move in. Not the least of these was the presence of some 15,000 Russian troops who had been stranded in France, where they had been in training when the Revolution and collapse of the Russian front during the previous winter had converted them into a ticklish diplomatic problem. But that was for the French to worry about. The Operations staff had more than enough cares in trying to compute how many additional structures would be required in Gondrecourt for hospitals, stables, and all the other facilities the French did not intend to provide.[11]

When the travelers finally returned to Paris on 25 June, Palmer presented his report to General Pershing, who promptly decided to go ahead with the plan outlined.[12] He had little choice in the matter, for the very next day word arrived that the first convoy from the United States had landed at Saint-Nazaire and that the troops of the 1st Division would soon be moving up.

Even before leaving Paris on his trip to the front, Palmer had decided he would have to make some change in his domestic arrangements. He felt he could not continue living at the Hotel Crillon, where the *Baltic* group had put up on the day of their arrival. Quite apart from the question of expense, which was by no means inconsiderable, the hotel was inconveniently situated across the river from the headquarters. Moreover, since the place was teeming with Americans, it offered little or no opportunity for repose.

A little searching turned up just the sort of place the situation called for: a quiet pension run by a Mme. Bassieul at 38 Rue de Varenne, only three or four blocks from the headquarters. A day or two later General Pershing himself left the Crillon for accommodations on the Rue de Varrene, where the residence of Ogden Mills, the prominent American financier, was placed at his disposal. This magnificent town house was laden with historic associations. Among other notables, it had once been occupied by Marshal Lannes, the illustrious Napoleonic officer—occupied, that is, until Marshal Lannes was killed in battle, a circumstance that Palmer, the student of history, wryly noted. General Pershing, whose interests lay elsewhere, doubtlessly never gave this unhappy precedent a second thought.

Mme. Bassieul's pension may have been less elegant than the Ogden Mills residence, but what it lacked in splendor it made up in atmosphere. It was a typical Parisian pension, located on the edge of the Latin Quarter and patronized by French officers and their families. When Palmer and his friend Dennis Nolan moved in, they were followed by two other officers in Nolan's Intelligence Section, the young reservist Capt. S. T. Hubbard, and Palmer's friend from Leavenworth days, Maj. Arthur L. Conger. Conger was one of the few officers at Headquarters, AEF, who had managed to bring his wife over to Paris before the authorities clamped down on the practice.

The American officers—and Mrs. Conger—enjoyed their life at the pension. The French families living there were delightful people who made every effort to be congenial. Especially they seemed to enjoy helping the new arrivals in their stumbling efforts at conversation in French. Nolan and Conger manfully continued to take formal lessons, but Palmer found himself too exhausted to pursue such a rigorous course. He did make it a point to take his lunch at the pension. This not only permitted him to escape the pressures of the office but also helped him acquire the French he so urgently needed.

Constant practice certainly improved the French spoken by the Americans at Mme. Bassieul's, but it was slow going at best, as Palmer implied in a letter to his wife:

Tell Mrs. Nolan she should have *seen* Dennis tackling French.... before he had gotten his vocabulary focussed. I said she should have *seen* him talk French because most of it was in his smile and his gestures. He was so engaging and persuasive that they just had to understand him even if he couldn't find the word. Nobody could resist him. Like most of the rest of us, much of his French was mixed with Spanish at first. When we first came over a lot of us went to lunch one day at a restaurant in the Latin Quarter. Dennis and I sat at one end of the table and [Col.] J. L. Hines, who is very tall, sat at the other end. In due course the waiter tried to give us a dish that Hines had ordered.... With the utmost gravity Dennis said to the waiter, pointing at Hines, "Cet hombre grand lá."... And the finest thing about Nolan is that when I told this joke on him a few days later, his laugh was the loudest and most appreciative of all.[13]

Congenial company, an excellent table, and the brisk walk to and from the office made the pension an ideal lodging for Palmer. Nevertheless, he found himself approaching exhaustion as he struggled to meet the torrent of demands placed upon him.

Short-handed to begin with, Palmer found that the problems confronting him could not be resolved without a great deal more detailed information than he had at the Paris headquarters. How many men should be assigned to the newly formed trench mortar companies? Should mortar units be assigned to each infantry battalion, or should they be treated as artillery and brigaded separately? Unless the AEF was going to accept the recommendations of the French staff, on these and a hundred other questions, uncritically and at face value, which Palmer was reluctant to do, there was no alternative to sending Operations officers out to the British and French units in the field where they could see for themselves.[14] But every time he sent two or three officers out fact gathering, he denuded his office and the work of detailed planning nearly came to a standstill.

Palmer felt a peculiarly personal sense of responsibility for the work of his staff, and criticisms, real or imagined, served only to goad him into greater physical effort—as if working later and later into the night would somehow compensate for the lack of essential information that accounted for so many of the delays. As a matter of fact, his colleagues throughout the headquarters were remarkably understanding. Unfortunately, as it turned out, the demand for results from the Operations Section was not to be paced by understanding colleagues within the headquarters. Instead, an entirely extraneous circumstance compelled the members of the staff to complete their organizational studies before they were really satisfied with all the premises upon which the studies were based.

The event that forced the Operations staff to come up with a master plan for the AEF, ready or not, was the arrival in Paris of Col. Chauncey B. Baker.[15] Colonel Baker headed an independent mission of a dozen officers sent over to France by the War Department to study the organization and equipment of the Allied commands. That no effort had been made to coordinate this roving mission with the newly created AEF is vivid evidence of the prevailing confusion in Washington. Colonel Baker might make recommendations directly contrary to those drafted by Headquarters, AEF. And since he was returning to the United States immediately, he could advocate his recommendations in person to the Chief of Staff and all others in authority. If the War

Department accepted Baker's suggestions, then General Pershing might end up having to fight with an instrument not of his own choosing.

General Pershing rose to the challenge successfully. With infinite tact he suggested that Colonel Baker and the members of his mission might find it useful to attend a conference with the officers of the AEF to coordinate their recommendations for the War Department. To his credit, Colonel Baker accepted the invitation of his old classmate. He must have known that in cooperating with Pershing he was virtually assuring the eclipse of his own mission, but he agreed to cooperate anyway.[16]

Colonel Baker's willingness to cooperate saved the AEF no end of future trouble, but it precipitated an immediate crisis for the Operations Section. With the Baker-Pershing conference set for 5 July, only a day or two away, prompt completion of the tables of organization and equipment became imperative. What organizational structure did the AEF require? To a generation of officers trained at Leavenworth, the classic triad had the virtue of familiarity; the three-brigade division and the three-regiment brigade each provided the essential ingredients for maneuver: one on the line, one to flank, and one in reserve. But trench warfare along a stabilized front gave little scope for maneuver and at the same time put a heavy premium on any form of organization assuring an effective method of providing replacement units to the front lines.

There seemed to be general agreement among the Allies on the desirability of introducing a four-division corps, with two divisions in the line and two in reserve. This would give a front wide enough to utilize corps artillery effectively and at the same time permit the line and reserve divisions to be rotated without having to pull the whole corps out of position every time the troops on the front needed to be relieved. Since the AEF would be desperately short of experienced senior officers capable of manning the various corps headquarters, there would also be an advantage in limiting the number of corps formed.

All this seemed reasonable enough, but once the officers of the Operations Section accepted the logic of the four-division corps, they found themselves caught in a chain reaction that required seemingly endless hours of detailed planning to disentangle.[17] If the four-division corps, with all its corollary modifications down through brigade and regiment to the company level, seemed to facilitate the tactical problem of replacements on the front, it would also create a host of difficulties in other directions.

Long before coming to Paris, while working on the provisional show-the-flag division, Palmer had come to appreciate the important relationship between the size of a division and the peculiar character of the French railroad system. A rough calculation indicated that the proposed Infantry division of 28,000 men would occupy some thirty miles of road space. When on the march with full equipment and accompanying supply trains, such a combat division presented a formidable array: 72 pieces of artillery, some 16,000 riflemen, more than 600 trucks, 100 motorcycles, and 30-odd staff cars, with 6,000 horses and 2,500 mules hauling reel carts, baggage wagons, ammunition carts, and caissons. When moved by rail, a division required over 1,700 cars for animals and men alone. For inexperienced leaders, such a division could become a nightmare.[18]

Back in the United States, cantonment construction had been started on the basis of the division in the latest issue of *Field Service Regulations*, but now virtually every unit from corps to company was to be of a different size. All of which may explain to veterans of the training camps during the winter of 1917-18 just why it was that they occupied brand-new 150-man company barracks that bore no relation to the 250-man company established by the planners in the AEF.

Officers commissioned in the newly raised National Army could readily be reassigned according to the revised AEF tables of organization, but officers in National Guard units were quite another matter. Palmer was keenly aware of the political sensitivity of the Guard. Any change in organization affecting the number and allocation of officers required was certain to call forth a violent reaction in many state capitals.[19]

Palmer's letters home during this trying period were few and far apart, but brief as they were, they revealed the growing intensity of his anxiety. Although customarily oblivious of his physical surroundings when on duty, he now complained that his crowded office was becoming more and more uncomfortable. His genial disposition gave way to a curt hypersensitivity. When his wife in one of her letters innocently remarked on the newspaper reports of the many gay festivities arranged for General Pershing and his party, he wrote back in some irritation, forgetting that the censored press in the United States had little else to tell about the AEF. More significantly, his letters began to mention the heavy burden of responsibility he felt. He repeatedly described the tasks before him as "overwhelming."[20]

The day set for the meeting of the AEF staff with Col. Chauncey Baker's roving mission finally arrived, and ready or not, the Operations Section had to submit its organizational papers as they stood. The conference was held in the garden of General Pershing's residence, where in a series of sessions extending over several days the two groups of officers hammered out substantial agreement on the form and organization they believed the AEF should take.

On one point in particular the discussion grew acrimonious. Col. C. P. Summerall, Palmer's friend and classmate who was serving as the artillery expert of the Baker mission, disagreed violently with the recommendations regarding the artillery complement to be provided for each thousand yards of front. Where Colonel Summerall urged 256 guns, the Operations Section called for but 118, a spread far too great to compromise. Since each side adduced French and British experience as the grounds for its position, the debate turned to opinion, each questioning the soundness of the other's judgment.[21]

Good staff papers rest on fact, not on opinion, and Palmer was painfully aware of the factual deficiencies in the papers he had brought to the discussion. Had they been complete, they would have provided enough data to reveal the faulty assumptions on which Colonel Summerall rested his case. Subsequent staff work did just this, revealing that the colonel's abnormally large artillery complement was based on erroneous information as to the ratio between troops and guns employed by the British in the operations at Messines Ridge.[22]

On the final day of the conference Palmer suddenly felt unable to concentrate. Exhaustion from overwork and the gnawing sense of inadequacy that his own high standards induced him to feel had at last caught up with him. Confused and somewhat alarmed, he adjourned the discussion as soon as he could and went to find Col. Merritte W. Ireland, the senior medical officer in the Paris headquarters.

Colonel Ireland had no trouble diagnosing the case before him. When recalling the episode years later, he told Palmer that the symptoms he described added up to a classic account of a nervous breakdown, utter mental exhaustion from sustained overwork and worry. There was, he declared, no alternative to an immediate rest. Ireland promised to explain the situation to Harbord and took full responsibility for ordering his patient away without the least delay.[23]

For Palmer, on the very eve of great things in his chosen profession, here was the ultimate disaster; he was failing before he had fairly begun.

26   Personal Disaster

Palmer's agony of spirit when he learned the medical officer's verdict may be readily appreciated. He was chief of Operations in the greatest military expedition the nation had ever mounted. This year he was to plan the action of a million men and next year of two million more. Rapid promotion was sure to follow, promotion that would symbolize all the rewards of the military calling: power, prestige and the sheer pleasure of exercising the arts of one's profession, not in make-believe maneuvers but in an epic world war.[1]

If Palmer dreaded being invalided home, to fritter out the war in one of the inconsequential jobs reserved for convalescents, he reckoned without his friends. Early the next morning before he left his lodgings, a messenger brought him the following hastily penned note from headquarters:

My dear Palmer:

I am satisfied we have, or better said I have been piling too much on you. I wish you would go down to the [Army] zone around the general region of Neufchateau—visit the various cities in that region—learn a little French, or rather brush up on your own, and come back with a suggestion as to where we had better locate our Headqrs when [we] leave Paris. Inside the Army zone but not close enough to Gondrecourt to get us drawn into the division business. Take all the time you need—ten days or two weeks. I will get the order out tomorrow. Leave an address with Nolan.

Yours,

Harbord[2]

Although Harbord's face-saving suggestion was most considerate, the medical officers insisted it was too late for such a trip to be of any use. Only by a complete rest could any sort of recovery be effected. Colonel Ireland prescribed at least two weeks with no responsibilities whatever and suggested that a stay at Versailles would be ideal. An hour or two later the colonel was on his way in a staff car, accompanied by Maj. Robert Bacon. As a former U.S. ambassador to France, Major Bacon was well known about the capital, and his prestige no less than his fluency proved most helpful in locating suitable accommodations. He soon had his sick friend comfortably ensconced only a stone's throw from the palace in a small hotel, where Palmer was treated with all the ceremony generally reserved for a visiting dignitary of state.

Had Palmer been left to his own resources, his convalescence would have been far from restful. Fortunately he was not left alone. Whenever his friends at the Paris headquarters could manage to do so, one or another of them would drive out to visit him. The colonel found the loyalty and thoughtfulness of his fellow officers most encouraging. And one of his visitors brought what turned out to be an ideal medicine.

Maj. Nelson Margetts, one of General Pershing's two aides-de-camp, drove out to Versailles one afternoon to carry Palmer his chief's assurances that he would be wanted back at headquarters as soon as he was thoroughly rested. He also took his friend to a stately chateau in the ancient forest of St. Cloud not far from Versailles and there introduced him to three elderly ladies, the Misses Newhouse, expatriate Americans and old friends of his family, who had lived in France for more than twenty-five years. These charming people immediately took the convalescent colonel in charge, extending him their hospitality and introducing him to their circle of friends.

Other invitations helped hasten the cure. Especially welcome were those from French officers, whose hospitality afforded a glimpse of French family life not normally enjoyed by American visitors. Of all the dinners the colonel attended during his leave, however, he remembered best a delightful evening spent with Harbord and Col. Benjamin Alvord, the Adjutant General of the AEF, in the home of Lt. Col. the Count Aldebert de Chambrun, the French liaison officer in General Pershing's organization. With the de Chambrun family the visitors felt thoroughly at home. The count's good humor, as well as his wide acquaintance among Americans, had long since made him a great favorite at AEF headquarters. But no less popular was his charming wife. Because Mme. de Chambrun was a native-born American, a sister of Nicholas Longworth and a sister-in-law of Alice Roosevelt, she knew intimately those circles in Washington most frequented by her guests, and her table conversation transported them easily, if all too briefly, back to familiar surroundings.

In writing of the event to his teenage daughter Mary, who was then a student at Miss Madeira's School in Washington, Palmer may have unconsciously revealed why the visit had meant so much to him. He had met the de

Chambruns' daughter, he wrote—somewhat pretentiously—"a great grand-daughter of the Marquis de Lafayette." Then he went on to add, "She is about your age and what gave me an immediate bond of sympathy was that she had braces on her teeth and she made me think very much of my little girl."[3] His reaction to an evening spent in a friendly household with warmhearted people so very much like his own family circle only tends to confirm the many hints scattered through his letters: he missed his family acutely and desperately needed the kind of encouragement and confidence their affectionate interest had afforded him at home.

After two weeks of convalescence at Versailles, Palmer returned to Paris to resume his duties as chief of Operations. He resolved to get more exercise, if possible a long walk before work each morning and another after supper each evening, with the whole of Sunday devoted to sightseeing.

He knew that what he really needed was strenuous exercise to keep himself in trim. When the headquarters went out into the field, horses would be provided as a matter of course, and like so many officers of his generation he had learned early in his career that horseback riding offered an ideal compromise between relaxation and vigorous exercise.[4] His friend George Marshall had learned this lesson too, and throughout World War II as Chief of Staff in Washington, he found time for a periodic canter about the reservation at Fort Myer. All of which may suggest to some that the army may have suffered a great loss when its horses were permanently retired to pasture after World War II. And surely it is not without some significance that the Pentagon was originally built without any gymnasium or other provision for relaxation through exercise.

So long as the headquarters remained in Paris, Palmer made a determined effort to do at least some walking each day, and soon he was proudly writing home that he was beginning to know Paris intimately. His pleasure in these expeditions was considerably enhanced when he struck up an acquaintance with a friendly native who proved to be a most enjoyable guide and companion. His letter home reflected almost as much of his own personality as it did of his subject.

> Several times a week I take my afterdinner walk with a dear old French officer who lives here at the pension. He was a retired captain who was called back to duty in the War Ministry when the war began. He is simply delightful, like some wonderful character out of the best French literature. As we walk out you should see him in his red cap with its embroidered top, his light blue tunic and his loose red military trousers with a wide black stripe. He is a gentle, sweet old soldier who served twenty-eight years in Algeria where he won the *Croix de Guerre* that he wears on his bosom. He is typically French of the good Abbé Constantin kind. It rests me to walk with him and his French is made so simple and

slow that I am able to talk with him and understand him. He knows old
Paris well. We live here just outside the Latin Quarter and he takes me
through the queerest old streets. Of course, every evening when we walk
we cross one of the boulevards and have a little cup of coffee at some cafe
where the little tables and chairs are all out on the sidewalk. At times like
this when I look out at my little comrade with his merry eyes and his
sharply turned gray moustache, I feel that I am in a really pleasant
France that is not all work and worry.[5]

The light tone at the end of the letter was intended entirely for home
consumption, for in reality the colonel was far from merry. Despite his good
intentions about taking Sundays off, it was nearly a month after his return
from Versailles before he managed to do so, and the cumulative effect of
worry and overwork were continuing to tell on him. In one letter home he
described himself as a "tired old man"—he was then only 48—and in another
he confessed that he fell into bed each night "hoping that the next day would
be a better one," hardly the language of a carefree boulevardier.[6]

There were, to be sure, some factors working to make life easier for those
who carried the heaviest responsibilities at the American headquarters. When
Nolan's Intelligence Section moved to a new building, the Operations staff at
last had room enough to move around. More significantly, the larger quarters
were soon filled with reinforcements. Each new arrival was welcomed with
unaffected enthusiasm—and then immediately piled with work.

Palmer was delighted with the caliber of men assigned to help him in
Operations. Almost all of them were old friends or acquaintances whose
capabilities and range of experience were more or less familiar to him. In
addition to Barker, Parker, Drum, and Conner, who were already in the
section, were new arrivals including Lt. Col. Kirby Walker, Lt. Col. Paul B.
Malone, Maj. LeRoy Eltinge, and Maj. Stuart Heintzelman. All four had
studied at Leavenworth. Malone and Eltinge had been there during the period
Palmer attended, so they were well known to him. And since Malone had
attended the French and German maneuvers with Palmer in the summer of
1912, he was peculiarly well fitted to take on responsibilities in the Operations
Section without a long period of preliminary training. That Palmer was
substantially sound in his appraisal of these men is suggested by the fact that
three of the four were promoted to the rank of brigadier general before the
Armistice and all three subsequently received the Distinguished Service
Medal. Each time the section was unable to produce results on schedule, the
section chief saw the episode as a personal failure and began to worry about
his capacity to perform the role assigned to him.

From the record it is clear that Palmer was a poorer judge of his own
capacities than were his superiors. Harbord, in particular, showed unusual
sensitivity in his role as a leader of men. Correctly perceiving that Palmer's

undeniable gifts were exploited best when his needlessly wavering self-confidence was bolstered, the Chief of Staff made a point of demonstrating his high regard overtly and officially. When General Pershing left Paris for a two- or three-day visit on the front, Harbord went with him, ostentatiously designating Palmer as acting chief of staff. Whether or not Palmer actually caught the message at the time would be impossible to say.[7]

Even with the most pointed reassurances from above, the burden of directing the Operations Section remained staggeringly heavy. In the first place, the staff was expected to draw up elaborate plans for an army of a million and more men before learning the exact nature of many of the problems to be faced. In August 1917, at the very time when Palmer had hoped to see his officers finish up some of their most important studies, he was still obliged to send out teams to visit French and British installations to study hitherto neglected phases of the war.

The scope of the problems to be reported on was almost limitless. Tanks, rifle grenades, Stokes mortars, and many other weapons or items of equipment had to be studied at first hand. For example, someone in Operations had to be told off to investigate the relative merits of French and British sound-ranging and flash-detection instruments for adjusting artillery fire.[8] If their use required highly skilled specialists, then such men would have to be trained and the existing tables of organization adjusted. Such a problem could easily absorb the full time of an experienced staff officer for several days. With hundreds of similar matters crying for attention by the beginning of August 1917, only nine officers were available in Operations to shoulder the work.[9]

Throughout the summer Palmer did his best to enlarge the staff, though with scant success. Experienced staff school graduates were as much in demand in Washington as they were in Paris, so the flow of talent was agonizingly slow. While waiting for reinforcements from home, Palmer undertook to borrow manpower from some of the other offices not yet at peak load. That such raiding expeditions were largely unsuccessful hardly needs saying, but the attempt in itself suggests something of the desperate situation in the Operations Section.

Ever since the arrival of the 1st Division in the Gondrecourt area, the French authorities had been pushing for a number of decisions regarding the precise character of the training to be given the troops arriving from the United States. Since the French were to supply most of the special facilities and many of the weapons to be employed, not to mention the specialist-instructors, this impatience was entirely understandable. Their interest, however, was not limited to purely logistical considerations.

One day early in August, Palmer received a phone call from his friend Maj. George Marshall, who was then at Gondrecourt serving as divisional operations officer. The French, Marshall reported, were moving ahead in the matter of training facilities without waiting for an official decision on policy from

General Pershing.[10] To delay action any longer was clearly impossible, yet to proceed without first perfecting the studies on training being prepared by Operations was to surrender entirely to French leadership in the matter of doctrine.

Much as the AEF might welcome French assistance in the form of facilities or technical instructors, on questions of doctrine General Pershing insisted that French aid was largely unacceptable. After years of bloody stalemate, the French had acquired a defensive outlook, which permeated virtually every feature of their training program. Moreover, the French high command seemed to have accepted the idea that modern weapons had made large-scale wars of maneuver a thing of the past. As a consequence, their schemes of training concentrated on trench or siege warfare. And within this context the emphasis was on defensive action. General Pershing was absolutely determined to shape the AEF into an independent command, aggressive in spirit and carefully trained in the problems of a war of movement. He wanted troops who would be ready to break the stalemate and end the war in a single sweeping campaign.[11]

As chief of Operations, Palmer clearly understood that his task was to interpret General Pershing's desires in the form of training doctrines that could be converted into manuals for every conceivable kind of tactical instruction. A squad leader may throw away the book and convey his ideas by personal demonstration, but the tone or spirit of an army depends upon how well it manages to convey the will of the commander to every last man, including the most recently arrived replacement.

There were many facets to the problem, but a description of one will illustrate its general nature. In selecting training areas for the American troops, the French conceived the task largely in terms of finding enough billets for the troops concerned. The training program, as they visualized it, could be carried out in a relatively limited space. A few assembly areas, drill grounds, model trenches for sham battles, and a number of sheds or classrooms for use by technical instructors seemed to fill the bill.

To the Americans these facilities were entirely inadequate. If the 1st Division and the others soon to follow were to receive any real training in open warfare, large-scale operations involving the movement of whole corps in combat, vast maneuver grounds would be absolutely necessary. And with the French transportation system already burdened to the breaking point, unless such training grounds were located adjacent to the divisional billeting areas, the possibility of holding corps-wide maneuvers would be sharply limited.

Since Palmer could not present a finished statement of policy to the French, he had to find some substitute. As a stopgap, he arranged for a joint committee of French and American officers to consider the problem anew. Joint study by its very nature was almost certain to consume a great deal of time, and time above all else was what the AEF Operations staff needed. To make sure that the joint undertaking ran smoothly, Palmer referred the whole matter to his friend, the Count de Chambrun, in whose unfailing good humor and high diplomatic skills he had the utmost confidence.

The crisis helped bring to a head the whole question of a proper organization for Headquarters, AEF. Ever since the Pershing party had visited the British staff organizations in London on the journey to France, it had been evident to virtually every officer in the group that the staff structure drawn up for the AEF during the *Baltic* voyage was inadequate. Although the *Baltic* plan was based upon one of Palmer's War College studies, pride of authorship did not blind him to the need for drastic revisions. In retrospect he was inclined to believe that it might have been better had his whole energies been devoted to contriving an adequate staff instrument as soon as the Pershing group reached Paris. As it was, he had allowed himself to be drawn off into various functional or substantive questions, and the problem of forging a suitable organization had been put aside for days and even weeks.

The delay in reconstituting Headquarters, AEF, retarded the development of the American forces in France and almost proved fatal to Palmer's military career. The heart of the difficulty lay in the character of the responsibilities laid upon the Operations Section. By the terms of reference drawn up on the *Baltic*, there were only two General Staff sections: Intelligence and Operations. Each was headed by an assistant chief of staff. The Adjutant General was expected to function as an office of record, coordinating the activities of the Special Staff, including the Inspector General, along with the Quartermaster. Engineer, Ordnance, Signal, and Medical officers. In practice, however, the problems of all these technical services were in one way or another directly dependent upon decisions or policies formulated in Operations. Almost inevitably the Operations staff became a center of coordination, although no one had clearly anticipated this during the discussions held on board the *Baltic*.[12]

Of the many organizational changes finally introduced in the AEF headquarters during August, only those affecting the General Staff need be mentioned here. In place of the two original sections, Intelligence and Operations, a five-section staff was created to subdivide the several functions hitherto grouped within Operations. An Administrative Policy Section took over all problems of transportation and supply in the line of communications; a Training Section absorbed the whole task of promulgating doctrine, preparing manuals, and organizing schools; while a Coordination Section took over some of the functions performed in Operations, along with still others formerly handled by the Adjutant General. Even the bare mention of this subdivision of responsibilities is enough to suggest why Palmer had been working himself into a state of collapse before the work load was spread out.

Although the formation of a Training Section in particular promised to afford great relief in time, the actual parturition was not painless. At no time to the very end of the war did Operations ever have enough men to carry out its assigned functions. Because of the acute shortage of trained staff officers, the section never even received the limited quota it was authorized to employ. And by the end of 1917 the official manning tables called for a complement of twenty-four officers and seventy-one enlisted men.

Among the many duties retained by Operations after the reshuffling, none was more important than the proper composition of the forces to comprise the AEF. In their haste to publish the original organization project before Col. Chauncey Baker and his party returned to Washington, the staff in Paris had left many details unsettled. Especially vexatious were the perplexities raised by recent technical advances. Should regimental machine guns, for example, be assigned to each of the component battalions, or should they be grouped in a separate, specialized battalion of their own and treated somewhat akin to artillery? Should the standard infantry brigade have a separate machine gun unit of its own, or should it rely entirely upon the weapons allocated to its component regiments and battalions? And what, precisely, was the optimum composition of a machine gun battalion? Questions such as these, whether asked about machine guns, mortars, airplanes, or any other item of equipment, could only be resolved after the most thorough study of French and British practice by staff officers with sufficient experience to profit from their observations.[13]

When he first tackled the duties of Operations chief, Palmer was inclined to see the problem of organization in somewhat static terms. Gradually, however, he realized that the stress of war would result in an almost continuous evolution of ideas about organizational structure and functions. So he encouraged Maj. Frank Parker to explore the possibility of establishing permanent military missions at the French and British army headquarters. Permanent missions, he believed, would provide a flow of operational, administrative, and technical information far more effective than a succession of brief visits. Such missions would cultivate sources of information and soon provide insights far beyond those of occasional visitors. For this reason Palmer laid great emphasis on selecting individuals who were in genuine sympathy with the nations to the headquarters of which they were assigned.

As it turned out, the staff paper suggesting permanent missions to the Allied headquarters was among the last significant contributions Palmer made as chief of Operations. Toward the middle of August the entries he made in a brief diary he kept at the time took an ominous tone: 13 August 1917, "not feeling very well"; 14 August, "Usual heavy work.... Beginning to think I may have to go on sick leave." Two days later he added, "Tired out at noon. Left after lunch."[14] The implications of this last entry were not lost on Palmer's colleagues. The following day he received orders directing him to accompany General Pershing on a visit to the field headquarters of a French army on the front.

For the Commanding General to take his chief of Operations on a tour of inspection was an entirely appropriate action and seemed so at the time. But in looking back on the event, Palmer realized that Pershing's ostensible reason for taking him was probably not the real reason behind the order. Palmer was obviously on probation in the minds of his superiors, and a trip to the front would afford an excellent opportunity for the Commanding General to study his man intimately.

On the afternoon of 18 August General Pershing, his aide Capt. Carl Boyd, and Palmer left Paris in a staff car bound for the French general headquarters at Compiègne.[15] After some two hours the party reached the chateau in which General Pétain had made his headquarters. The dinner with the general that followed was no ordinary occasion, for among the civilian guests present was Albert Thomas, who was then minister of munitions in the French government. As the wine went around, Palmer was able to observe at first hand something of the difficult relationship that always exists between generals and politicians. For the insights the occasion offered, he sensed that he was indebted to his persistent efforts at mastering conversational French. An officer without effective training in foreign languages, he realized, suffers a decided handicap.[16]

The following day, at Gondrecourt, they reviewed the resident French troops, the 47th Infantry Division, a superb organization of hardened veterans, before going on to inspect the 16th U.S. Infantry, one of the regiments in the newly arrived 1st Division. The contrast between the French veterans and the Americans was painful to behold. Apart from the Marine units present, the Americans presented a decidedly unsoldierly appearance. If General Pershing was humiliated by the disparity between the French and American troops, Palmer observed that he gave no sign of his displeasure. Criticism and correction General Pershing would leave to others; for his part he must do nothing to impair the loyalty the units in training were even then coming to feel for him.[17]

Even if he appeared never to concern himself with minutiae, General Pershing was well aware of the circumstances under which the 1st Division had been shipped to France. Although nominally a Regular Army unit, the division had been so extensively filled up with raw recruits that it was for all practical purposes a green organization when it arrived behind the front. It was the measure of Pershing's stature, Palmer believed, that he remained sensitive to the implications of such details as this without becoming lost in them and without losing sight of his main objective. That Pershing was less than successful in conveying something of this skill to all of his subordinate commanders was evident during his visit of inspection. Maj. Gen. William L. Sibert, the commander of the 1st Division, plagued Pershing throughout his brief stay with protests against the number of officers he had been forced to relinquish at the request of Headquarters, AEF.[18] General Pershing was going to build an army of more than twenty divisions, and as the unit longest in France, the 1st Division would be expected to spawn far more officers than any other organization in the AEF. Soon afterwards General Sibert was replaced.

After completing their inspection of the divisions near Gondrecourt, the party drove to Souilly, where the French Second Army of General Guillaumat had its headquarters in the mairie, or local municipal building. They arrived to find the Chief of Staff giving his final orders for the offensive that General Pershing had come to see, the first major French effort since the disastrous Nivelle campaign the previous spring.

What impressed Palmer most was the simplicity of the whole affair. Although this offensive was a major undertaking covering a dozen miles of front on both banks of the Meuse, the army commander found plenty of time to chat casually with his guests. The reports of the various corps commanders were received by the Chief of Staff, "a runty little Frenchman," as Palmer described him, who was "as simple and business-like as if he were a clerk in a dry goods store selling ribbons over the counter." All this only confirmed the visitors' respect for the months of elaborate staff work by hundreds of trained specialists that lay behind this big offensive.

At dinner that evening Palmer's observations were underlined by General Pétain, who had come from his headquarters to attend General Pershing on his visit to the front. For at least a year more, the French commander declared, the American contribution to victory would amount to little beyond moral support. This year of grace he believed should be used to establish schools for training General Staff officers in numbers sufficient to man the divisions and corps being created in the United States. Pétain's remarks, coupled with the demonstration they had just witnessed, precipitated General Pershing's determination to set up a "get-rich-quick" staff school in France along the lines suggested by the French.[19]

After dinner that evening the visitors retired to General Pétain's private railroad car. Long before daylight Palmer was awakened by the rumble of artillery; the barrage had begun. Just then the train began to move; he assumed that the train was moving up closer. Sometime later, after a fitful sleep, he was startled by sunlight streaming into his compartment. The direction of the sun indicated that the train was moving away and not toward the battlefield. Only then did it dawn on him what had happened. The battle was to be under the command of General Guillaumat of the Second Army. General Pétain was drawing away deliberately so as not to interfere with his subordinate's freedom of action. Whether or not General Pershing perceived this significant lesson in leadership, Palmer couldn't be sure, but he did resolve to make it a part of his own growing store of military experience.

While the battle was going on, General Pétain's train carried the visitors to St. Dizier, nearly forty miles south of Verdun, where they spent a good part of the day inspecting one of the big distributing centers maintained by the French army. Here bulk cargoes coming in on standard-gauge railroads were transferred to warehouses, where they were parceled out to wagon trains, truck convoys, and narrow-gauge lines that fed supplies forward to the units scattered along the front. Ordnance repair shops, an evacuation hospital, and quartermaster depots for refurbishing materiel and re-equipping troops returning from leave completed the picture.

What fascinated the American visitors was the orderly dispatch with which the St. Dizier center operated. Although their tour coincided with a major offensive on the front, they found no evidence of frenetic activity. The whole logistical system was so well organized that it functioned normally even at peak loads. And peak loads involved as many as 2,000 trucks pouring in and out of the center each day, not to mention an equal number of narrow-gauge railway cars hauling as many as 100,000 rounds of 75-mm ammunition to the front every twenty-four hours.[20]

The visit to St. Dizier made a profound impression upon Palmer. To begin with, it enlarged his understanding of the complex organizations, as yet unformed, that would be necessary to cope with the logistical problems soon to appear in the AEF. But more than anything else, the day spent tramping around the trackage and warehouses at the French depot made him appreciate the scope and scale of modern warfare. Only a few days earlier in a letter home, he had indicated his growing awareness of the effort expected of the United States. "The magnitude of this war," he said, "is beyond anything I ever dreamed of."[21] Now, immense as his previous estimates had appeared, they were far too small. Palmer resolved that in all his future planning he would escape the shackles of the past and think big.

One of the cardinal attributes of effective command is imagination—to escape the limitations of outlook well-nigh inevitable in peacetime training, with its emphasis on economy, make-do, and do without. If Palmer reached this conclusion by conscious reflection, General Pershing appears to have arrived at the same end intuitively. Only a few days after visiting St. Dizier, he unhesitatingly entered into a $60 million contract with the French to procure some 5,000 aircraft over the succeeding ten months.[22] Whether or not his powers as Commanding General of the AEF authorized such an expenditure, he left for others to dispute. For his part he knew only that the aircraft were needed. He had learned to think big and act boldly.

Late in the afternoon General Pétain returned with his American visitors to the scene of the battle beyond Verdun. From an observation post on high ground somewhat northwest of the fortified city, they had a magnificent view of virtually the entire area of assault. This included hills "304" and "Mort homme," soon to be notorious in the annals of the AEF, for the line reached by the French in this single day of action was to become the jumping-off point of the Americans a year later in the Meuse-Argonne offensive. Palmer's official report of the trip described the French attack as a "distinct success." It had penetrated only two or three miles, but this had become the characteristic French conception of a major operation. In Palmer's words it was "an excellent example" of careful preparation for "a conservative advance on certain specified objectives."[23]

The more Palmer reflected on this "victory," the more dejected he became. Millions of dollars worth of artillery shells and hundreds of thousands of rounds had gone into the preparatory barrage. Thousands of trucks, railroad cars, and wagons were needed to support even this limited assault. If it required this staggering scale of logistical backing for shallow penetration along a dozen miles of front, how then could the AEF ever execute the grand war of maneuver General Pershing talked about? As chief of Operations Palmer was expected to work out the details of the thrusts Pershing planned to hurl against the Germans to end the war in a single overwhelming campaign. But the contrast between Pershing's boldness of conception and the poverty of the means at his disposal plunged the colonel into a profound depression.

Upon returning to Paris, Palmer sat down in his office to draw up his official report. Try as he would, he found it almost impossible to concentrate. What should have consumed an hour or two of dictating time required several days to complete. What he wrote was acceptable enough, but his pace was hardly adequate. Looking back later the colonel himself described his condition vividly: "My mind had become like an engine working effectively but very slowly because there was little steam left in the boiler."[24]

After struggling along for five days, he realized he simply was not fit for duty. Despairingly, he turned himself over to the doctors. A physical examination showed he was suffering from greatly reduced blood pressure, dilation of the heart, and loss of weight but was otherwise physically sound. If he wished to forestall a more serious breakdown, his medical friends warned, he would have to give up all work immediately and go away from the turmoil at headquarters for a month or two of complete rest. This advice, though unquestionably wise, struck Palmer as a sentence of execution. After a second breakdown on duty, he felt sure he would be dismissed from his post and invalided home as a hopeless failure. The prospect was crushing.

27

Convalescing in Wartime

Palmer's fears of immediate dismissal proved groundless. When General Pershing was apprised of the situation, he immediately authorized two months of sick leave for his chief of Operations, explicitly directing him to return to his post when the leave expired. That he did not immediately dismiss Palmer was a positive indication of General Pershing's confidence.[1]

Since the headquarters was under enormous pressure to prepare for the millions of troops soon to flesh out the paper armies of the AEF, the amount of time, effort, and personal consideration that many members of the staff devoted to Palmer in his hour of need is particularly noteworthy. As virtually all the officers who served with Palmer have testified, to know him was to love him. His good humor, his quiet charm, his ability to tell a good story, and his innocence of manner all combined to win him lasting friendships wherever he served. Even those who disagreed with him on questions of policy found his personality hard to resist. For this reason it should probably occasion no surprise that the whole of Headquarters, AEF, seems to have engaged in a conspiracy to shield him from the worst consequences of his breakdown.

To leave one's post in wartime, even when ordered to do so by competent medical authority, is never easy, especially for the dedicated and ambitious regular officer; and Palmer was no exception. Fortunately, however, both Col. Merritte W. Ireland and Maj. Henry Beeuwkes were shrewd and sensitive observers of the human animal. Though they may have lacked formal training in psychiatric techniques, they had acquired in practice a fund of insight that served them well. Both gave Palmer the hand he so desperately needed. You must go now, they told him, so you will be ready to shoulder the far heavier responsibilities that will be yours later when the troops arrive. Seizing this cue, Palmer wrote to his wife: "My condition is simply this: I am tired and have low blood pressure and the hours are too long to make it possible to rest up as I should, so I am going to lay off for awhile, rest up, accumulate some energy and then go back to work again."[2] Gratefully, Palmer clung to the notion given him by the doctors—I must go now when I can be spared better than later. He repeated this formula again and again in his subsequent letters home, as if to persuade himself that what the doctors had said would come true if reiterated often enough.

By an unhappy coincidence, Palmer's departure for Cannes, the site selected for his rest cure, fell in the same week as the shift of Headquarters, AEF, from Paris to Chaumont. As his friends packed their records and moved off to the new field headquarters, he felt more than ever dejected. They were off to the wars, the culminating adventure after a lifetime of training, and he was remaining behind. Palmer's loyal classmate Dennis Nolan sought to bolster his sick friend's morale by organizing a farewell dinner party at the Hotel Lutetia with Palmer and his walking companion, the retired French captain, Menot. The gathering was something less than festive.

If Nolan's farewell dinner turned out badly, Palmer's journey south was even worse. He had to make the twenty-hour journey from Paris to Lyon, down the Rhone to Marseilles and then east to Cannes, sitting up in a crowded compartment. On arriving at his destination he learned that the resort hotels were not yet open for the season. In desperation he found temporary accommodations in an unspeakably filthy railroad hotel, where he collapsed, utterly worn out, to sleep for sixteen hours.

When he finally did awaken, he faced an agony of indecision. What should he do? Where should he stay? The necessity of deciding anything, no matter how trivial, plunged him into a spiral of despair. Terrified by his own panic, he rushed from his room and out into the street if only to escape the loneliness that seemed to oppress him.

Down on the seafront he approached a passing French officer. But hardly had he begun to speak when a lady walking by stopped and said, "You're an American officer, aren't you?" She introduced herself as Mrs. E. Braden Kyle, the widow of a Philadelphia surgeon, who was doing volunteer nursing in one of the local military hospitals. After a few moments she sensed Palmer's predicament and suggested he accompany her back to her own pension-hotel, where a number of other Americans were staying. It was a great relief not to have to struggle with French for a while, and as they walked along in conversation, it soon developed that they had mutual friends at West Point. On reaching Mrs. Kyle's pension, the Hotel des Orangers, Palmer was introduced to a number of Americans, who promptly persuaded the weary officer that his recovery would be hastened by a circle of compatriots, and arrangements were soon made to transfer his belongings from his previous lodgings.

Soon after moving to the Hotel des Orangers, Palmer wrote to his wife saying, "I can rest here and get back in shape now that I am relieved from the dread of loneliness. It means a great deal," he added, "... when one's self-reliance is temporarily gone, to know that there are some sympathetic people within call."[3] For a professional soldier, this was a remarkably candid revelation, but in many ways it was typical of the man, utterly frank, open, and artless.

In a sense it was Palmer's innocence that contributed so largely to his charm. At that time an American uniform was a novelty in the south of France, and an officer from General Pershing's staff was a prize for any hostess to capture for her dinner table. Blissfully unaware of all this, Palmer wrote home of each new encounter as a happy coincidence.

Once he felt secure in his new-found circle of friends, he began to enjoy his enforced idleness, although to be sure, he did suffer from pangs of conscience. This made it hard to write home about a wonderful morning spent swimming in the blue Mediterranean. "I feel like a pig going off on a lark all alone," he confessed, yet quite certain that his family would understand the medical necessity for his relaxation.[4]

The thought of leaving his post in wartime continued to rankle until he finally evolved a rationalization that went even further than the one suggested to him by the doctors. "It is hard to leave important work like mine," he wrote his wife, "but it is better now than later." To this old justification he added a new refinement: "I feel that it is my duty to rest and not worry."[5] Having persuaded himself that duty required it, he conscientiously threw himself into the hard work of relaxing. At first he confined himself to walking, reading, and sunning on the beach, with an occasional "seabath before breakfast," as he described it. Some of his friends suggested golf, and soon he was out on the links taking instructions from the local professional, a well-known English golfer. When the pro observed that his American pupil played much the same kind of game as one of his former clients, the late King of England Edward VII, Palmer observed that this was not in the least complimentary to His Royal Highness.

In the sheltered harbor at Cannes one could procure a small sailboat and the services of an old sailor for the ridiculously small sum of three dollars a day. To a lifelong fisherman this opportunity was too good to miss, and soon Palmer was writing enthusiastically to his wife reporting on the success of his first fishing expedition. "I got up this morning feeling more like myself than I have for months." "I am afraid," he wrote almost wistfully, "all my life I have underestimated the value of little social recreations."[6]

Thereafter, sailing trips in the *Jeune Louis* with her grizzled French master became Palmer's favorite relaxation. He particularly enjoyed visiting the historic islands lying off the coast south of Cannes. Ile Ste-Honorat, a mile-long strip of pine-studded outcroppings, he found peculiarly intriguing. Here was the foundation, dating back to the fifth century, of the monastery where St. Patrick supposedly studied before journeying to the British Isles. Here too one could clamber about the ruins of an eleventh-century castle and recall the raids of pirates who had habitually plundered this tempting bit of coast.

All those hours of reading during Palmer's early years on dreary western outposts now brought their rich reward. With his back against a gnarled pine and a picnic lunch of bread and cheese spread in his lap, he dreamed of the Odyssey as he gazed out over the bright blue sea.

One reason Palmer enjoyed his sailing expeditions so much was that they afforded him an opportunity to repay some of his many social obligations. At Ile Ste-Marguerite, for example, he could show his guests the old castle where German prisoners of war were confined. And there too he could entertain them with stories of the days when Louis XIV used the same fortress to dispose of obnoxious noblemen, including, according to legend, the mysterious Man in the Iron Mask. Palmer's sense of mastery over the limited challenges these "recreations" thrust upon him bolstered his self-confidence— at least until he heard from his wife.

After weeks of delay a letter from home finally reached Cannes. Under any other circumstances what Mrs. Palmer wrote would have seemed conventional enough: some family business matters, the difficulties of packing up the household on moving into an apartment, and so on. Then, almost casually, she added her congratulations on her husband's promotion to full colonel, which she had seen reported in the *Army-Navy Journal*, concluding with a passing query as to when his promotion to brigadier general would come through. Whatever momentary pleasure Palmer may have felt on learning of his advance to full colonel—his wife's letter was the first word he had received of the promotion—upon reflection apparently gave way to acute distress. It had not been easy to serve on Pershing's staff without advancing in grade while back home one's juniors were securing exalted rank as unit commanders in the National Army.

Palmer was actually right in step with all the other officers around him. Even Harbord, as Chief of Staff, AEF, did not go up to brigadier until October 1917, when Pershing was made a full general. In commenting on Pershing's promotion, Harbord had written, "I think it is a very encouraging sign that our country gives him the grade at this time realizing that it is an instrumentality for winning the war." Promotion in the AEF was one thing; promotion for those back home was quite another. Surely there was more than a hint of envy in Harbord's remarks about the division commanders sent over to view the war at first hand before their troops arrived: "The British front," he observed, "is infested with American major generals, a dozen of them, with each a chief of staff and the inevitable Aide-de-Camp."[7]

Harbord's fling reflected something of the misgivings that had beset all of Pershing's staff officers. Both Nolan and Palmer had agreed that continued service on the staff would interfere with their immediate prospects of promotion no matter how impressive their assignments might look. But this was a price worth paying. Palmer flatly declared he wouldn't trade his role as chief of Operations for a brigadier generalship.[8] Did he really mean this? The evidence suggests that he did, and more significantly, it also reveals something of the internal chemistry of General Pershing's staff.

Throughout his military career Palmer had been inclined to let promotion take care of itself. Unlike some of his contemporaries, he never wrote self-serving appeals to each new Chief of Staff in Washington. However slow promotion might be, it would inevitably come to the officer who poured his energies into doing the job before him.

Palmer's trusting attitude is reflected in a letter he wrote in response to several queries from his wife about his prospects. General Pershing had given assurances, he told her, that if General Staff officers in the AEF failed to keep pace with their contemporaries who received National Army commissions, the disparity would be made up by promotions in the Regular Army after the war. "Frankly," continued Palmer, "I have no particular worry about it because I feel sure that our general is going to make good and that he is going to protect the interests of those who make good under him."[9] That his general, his patron, might die before this occurred or that a postwar Congress might prove reluctant to comply with the general's wishes, seems never to have crossed Palmer's mind.

Unhappily, Mrs. Palmer's repeated inquiries only served to plunge her husband further into his depression. Far from expecting immediate promotion, he considered himself fortunate not to have been shipped home in disgrace. That he had been given an opportunity to recuperate with the expectation of returning to duty he regarded as an act of sheer benevolence on the part of his superiors. He expressed his gratitude to Harbord, saying "If I were your own brother I could not have received more thoughtful consideration."[10]

Palmer's experience clearly suggests that to understand the inner workings of the high command in the AEF one must know something of the warm personal relationships that bound its members. Unlike many of his colleagues, Harbord not only recognized this but articulated his observations effectively. Years after the war he reminded an audience at the War College that "personal relationships" played a dominant part in "America's greatest adventure:"

The student of the military art who seeks to deduce principles from the story of the AEF must constantly take them into account. Personalities really govern the world, and personal relationships are, in my judgment, more potent in politics, professional and business life than any other single factor. To the extent that they influenced the course of events in the American Expeditionary Forces, it is important that someone shall make a record of them. Memories of the Great War are already fading and will die with our generation. The bare record of administration, the tactical studies, the official reports and rosters, will no longer glow with life when the last survivor of the events of which they treat has joined his comrades in the beyond. The future historians and biographers of our time, if of the "debunking" type so obnoxious in recent years, will undertake to supply the human interest by synthetic process if those of us who knew and lived have left behind no record.[11]

The strong personal devotion Harbord attracted is not difficult to explain. His letters alone give ample evidence of his sensitive consideration in dealing with the staff. His friends were inclined to believe that this quality in him had been accentuated by his devotion to his wife, a tiny, frail woman who for many years was a semi-invalid. But General Pershing's personality presents another problem altogether. While several of his wartime associates have turned out voluminous accounts of their days in the AEF, none, not even the gifted Harbord, has managed to explain just what it was about Pershing that attracted such fierce loyalties. In the absence of more explicit testimony explaining General Pershing's ability to command the utmost from his immediate subordinates, it might be surmised that the most important fact may have been the general's attitude on promotions.

General Pershing was inclined to place responsibility for slow promotion in the AEF squarely on the authorities in Washington. This was especially true after Peyton C. March, his former subordinate, became Chief of Staff. The details of the March-Pershing quarrels need not be repeated here except to note the General Pershing's officers tended to adopt their chief's antipathies as their own, but it should be evident that the whole question of wartime promotion was far too complex to permit full responsibility to be pinned on any single individual.[12]

Undoubtedly General Pershing found it highly expedient to blame the War Department for all delays in promotion. By doing so he could continue to command the loyalty of his subordinates as the champion of their interests against the authorities back in Washington. The general himself was always careful to present his criticisms in the most moderate terms, but from his lead it was an easy step for others to make unflattering contrasts between officers with field experience in France and those entrenched in their swivel chairs at the War Department. In practice, then, loyalty to General Pershing came to be more or less synonymous with acceptance of his implied explanation of the reasons behind the slow pace of promotion in the AEF.

In retrospect it seems clear that the memoir writers who sided with General Pershing were somewhat less than just. To begin with, when the army began to reorganize under the Defense Act of 1916, colonels who had made a fine showing as regimental commanders sometimes turned out to be poor leaders when promoted to the grade of brigadier, and effective brigadiers when moved up to the rank of major general frequently made inferior division commanders. From bitter experience the Chief of Staff turned to the expedient of withholding promotions for a few months until officers had actually demonstrated in practice their fitness to occupy positions calling for the next-higher grade.[13]

Officers in the AEF were inclined to blame the authorities in Washington collectively for slow promotions without making fine distinctions, but in the General Staff there was actually a strong inclination to make all of Pershing's principal staff officers brigadiers, if for no other reason than to bolster their prestige in dealing with the representatives of the Allied armies. Such opposition as there was to this step came not from envious staff officers within the department but rather from the Secretary of War, Newton D. Baker.[14]

Baker was not blind to the importance of rank as an element of prestige in negotiating with the Allies, but during the summer and fall of 1917 his relations with Congress were in a most difficult stage. When the mobilization touched off by the declaration of war in April 1917 failed to produce armies overnight, the secretary became the target of a considerable criticism. Not a few legislators, it appears, were quite content to see Baker made a scapegoat. Then, too, the residual antagonisms between the old supply bureaus and the General Staff undoubtedly contributed to the secretary's discomfiture. And no matter how many openings or slots were authorized for general officers, no appointments could take effect until confirmed by the Senate.[15]

If General Pershing and his fellow officers tended to underestimate the intricacies of the promotion problem, almost the same might be said of those in Washington who saw the AEF only at a distance. The assistant chief of staff, Lt. Gen. Tasker H. Bliss, believed that at least part of the difficulty lay with Pershing himself. After studying the proposed organization of the AEF, Bliss pointed out that Pershing appeared to be holding the number of generals to a minimum.

The normal practice was to have a brigade led by a brigadier, a division by a major general, and a corps by a lieutenant general. This would leave only the rank of full general for the commander of a field army. When General Pershing cabled his recommendations for a six-division corps in the AEF, General Bliss was inclined to suspect that this move reflected his desire not to create any army commanders who would be his peers with the rank of full general. As Bliss saw it, Pershing was planning to call his field armies corps and leave them under the command of lieutenant generals.

Evidence to support General Bliss's surmise can indeed be found. Throughout the entire Saint-Mihiel offensive and even down to the beginning of the Argonne operations, General Pershing retained personal command, directing the movements of every corps and even those of many of the divisions. Not until well over a million men were engaged and less than a month before the end of the war did he relinquish this personal control to his two army commanders, Gen. Hunter Liggett and Gen. Robert L. Bullard. But it can be argued with equal weight that Pershing retained direct control because his subordinates had yet to demonstrate beyond a doubt that they had acquired sufficient experience to command a field army. Finally, although a six-division corps may have suggested the commander's vanity to those who studied the AEF cables in Washington, the record now available shows that it was Palmer and his Operations staff who concocted that particular structure in response to tactical needs, the problem of replacements, and the available transportation in France.[16]

Since the evidence is inconclusive, the enduring loyalties General Pershing inspired in the officers around him remain as enigmatic as ever. But it may still be possible to identify some of those practices that helped make his gift for command so effective. In selecting James Guthrie Harbord as his Chief of Staff, the general may simply have stumbled into a fortunate choice. But surely it was no accident that the two worked together so successfully. Harbord was more than a mere coordinator of staff papers; he was a perceptive student of human nature who supplemented the general's personality in precisely those areas needing it most. Consciously or unconsciously, he served in the role of mediator between the general and the officers around him. At the very least, Harbord's kindly and continuing services as intermediary between Palmer and Pershing seem to confirm this conjecture.[17]

Throughout his stay at Cannes, Palmer was buoyed up by a string of encouraging letters from Harbord. Most significant was Harbord's repeated assurance of his continued trust and high regard. How could the convalescent colonel feel other than flattered when he received the following from his Chief of Staff:

> If General Pershing desires it, would you be willing to undertake a mission to the United States while you are on sick leave?
> It is possible that he may wish an officer fully in his confidence to ... deliver a message to the Secretary of War. It occurred to me that the trip might do you good and at the same time you would be of great service to the General. It would, of course, be understood that he would insist on your returning to France.[18]

Palmer rushed off to the local hospital, where a British army surgeon was keeping tabs on his health. That worthy advised aginst the trip on the grounds that it would be foolish to risk a relapse now that a cure was so well advanced. This disappointment might have plunged Palmer into the depths once again had he not learned soon afterward from Harbord that the trip would not be necessary after all, since General Pershing had been able to resolve the problem by mail.

As Palmer's vigor rose he became increasingly impatient. Quite unwittingly Harbord contributed to this mounting anxiety. One of his letters chanced to mention that Fox Conner had been operated on for appendicitis. Then he added, "I think that things are very much in need of a leader in your Section, and wish you were back. To lose you and Fox Conner at the same time is a severe blow."[19] Though obviously well intended, this sent the colonel into a state of nervous agitation. He was needed back on duty; how could he continue to relax at a resort on the Riviera at such a time? To make matters worse, the weather suddenly turned foul. Cooped up indoors for a succession of rainy days, Palmer waited for the earliest moment when the surgeon would certify him fit for duty.

Toward the end of October he could contain his impatience no longer. The disasters at Caporetto on the Italian front proved to be the last straw. To shore up the battered Italian armies along the Piave, the French and British had been forced to send into Italy some eleven divisions of their own desperately needed troops. As the colonel watched trainload after trainload of men pouring eastward through Cannes, he had no need to be told that a crisis confronted the Allies. He hurried off to the British hospital, where the doctor finally agreed it would be safe for him to undertake the journey north.

Back in Paris, he reported to the American hospital at Neuilly. There for two days he submitted to a thorough medical examination by a whole team of physicians. To his delight, they came up with a favorable verdict. His elation, however, was short lived. The doctors all agreed that he should not return immediately to full duty as chief of Operations. What he needed was a job where he could control at will the amount of work involved, preferably one with opportunities for exercise.

The doctors' decision was a painful disappointment, but even this frustration was considerably lessened by the chance presence in Paris of General Pershing, who graciously found time for a long talk with Palmer about his immediate future. He was to have a temporary job helping to organize staff school courses for the officers who would soon be manning the divisions arriving from the United States. It was hard not to go directly back to Operations, but as he wrote home to his wife, "everybody assures me that this will not affect my future usefulness."[20]

28   AEF Staff School Duty

Before setting out on his temporary assignment to the staff schools, Palmer took the first available train for Chaumont to pick up orders confirming the verbal arrangements General Pershing had just made. With characteristic graciousness, Harbord met him at the station and drove him to the new headquarters. There the officers of the Operations staff welcomed him warmly and led him off to their mess for a dinner celebrating his return. With utmost respect, they insisted that he preside at the head of the table. This gesture, though trivial in itself, touched the colonel deeply. In a sense, it accurately reflected the character of the leadership prevailing at Headquarters, AEF, where both Pershing and Harbord by their example made personal loyalty a significant tool of command.[1] As he looked at the faces of the men about the table—Fox Conner, Hugh Drum, Stuart Heintzelman, LeRoy Eltinge, and the rest—he was filled with pride at their accomplishments. By his evident pleasure in the work of these men, Palmer showed that he, too, no less than Pershing and Harbord, understood that loyalty, based on mutual respect, runs down the chain of command as well as up.[2]

After dinner Harbord drew the colonel into a long conversation. In doing this the Chief of Staff was simply following a practice that General Pershing almost invariably followed when high-ranking officers reported for duty within the AEF, trying to communicate something of his philosophy of command to give an added dimension to the written orders he would subsequently issue. After an interview of this sort, General Pershing habitually urged the new arrival to remain at headquarters for several days, or even a week or two if possible, to become thoroughly acquainted with the several staff sections and how they functioned. The time spent on these orientation visits paid high dividends later in the form of vastly improved relations between the staff at headquarters and the unit commanders in the field. In addition, these visits could do much to reinforce the personal relationships that were so clearly a significant factor in General Pershing's conception of command.

The most serious difficulty confronting the AEF, Harbord believed, was the lack of trained men for the top positions in the currently forming corps and divisions. Even those officers fortunate enough to have received schooling at Leavenworth were decidedly chastened after brief exposure to the elaborate staff work they found going on in the French and British headquarters they visited. The simple format for order writing they had learned from Griepenkerl and some of the other manuals used at Leavenworth had been replaced by order forms and annexes as complex as the new weapons they were intended to control.[3]

The need for broader staff training was nowhere more evident than in Headquarters, AEF. If this was a difficulty at headquarters after several months of operation, how much more was it the case with divisions only recently formed and newly arrived in France?[4]

Nor was the problem of staff training confined to corps and division officers. Equally necessary were the staff officers absorbed by the various technical services behind the lines. The AEF could not live off the land; for all practical purposes its operations in France might almost as well have been conducted in a desert. Every item used or consumed by the American troops, whether purchased in Europe or shipped from the United States, had to be transported, stored, issued, and accounted for by elaborate supply services, which threatened at times to require as many staff officers as the divisions on the front.[5]

The problem, as Harbord saw it, was to expand the complex of staff schools around Langres and elsewhere as rapidly as possible. Here officers from a variety of backgrounds would receive not only the most recent lessons derived from experience on the front but also exposure to a uniform or standardized doctrine. They would all then "speak the same language." The importance of this common ground was something Harbord was to insist upon for the rest of his career. In most cases, he argued, men so trained will draw the same inferences from the same circumstances, and they will report their conclusions—whether as recommendations or orders—in language that will convey similar conclusions to others who have been subjected to the same schooling. Harbord was under no illusion that this ideal could be accomplished by any course, no matter how excellent, lasting only weeks or months. But in the absence of years of close personal association, a staff course of no more than a few weeks duration was not to be scorned. Yet there were a great many officers in the AEF, particularly senior officers, who did not appreciate the need for staff training at all.[6]

Many of those who objected to staff training failed to distinguish between the simple designation "staff officer" and the rather more narrowly defined term "general staff officer." The former applied to any officer working on a staff, whether at army, corps, or division level. Many jobs calling for highly technical qualifications could be performed by civilians in uniform or by specialists without prior military experience. Traffic dispatchers drawn from the railroads were typical of this group. But "general staff officers," in the distinctive sense, applied only to those men whose broad military experience and staff school training qualified them for the general staff eligible list. They were presumed to be capable of rising above branch interests or narrow professional prejudices. They were supposedly capable of taking a general view of all problems, in the same sense that a newly promoted general officer is expected to leave behind the partisan interests of his arm or service. To qualify as a general staff officer thus raised a presumption that one was of the timber from which general officers are hewn.[7]

Some officers resented the "Leavenworth clique," as they called the eligibles, simply because they envied their superior opportunities for promotion. Many others opposed any elaborate scheme of training for staff officers because they honestly believed experience to be the only valid kind of schooling. The way to train young officers, they contended, was to put them up on the front and let them fight. For old-guard types of this persuasion, a week or two at headquarters sometimes proved highly beneficial. Once they saw the staggering complexity of the logistics involved, their hostility to paperwork generally abated somewhat. But of course only a relatively few officers could be spared from their units for an orientation tour at Chaumont.[8]

Some division commanders accepted the idea of staff school training in principle but were reluctant to send their most promising young officers away for two or three months of schooling. If a commander sent his best men off to school, the division would have to make do with their less experienced replacements in precisely that period when it was most important to make a good showing. Moreover, there was always some danger that outstanding officers detached for training at the staff schools would be kept there as instructors to replace the French and British instructors temporarily assigned to get courses under way.[9]

Harbord's appraisal was a realistic summary of what was already taking place. In the 1st Division, nine out of twelve battalion commanders were already off at schools. Their posts were filled with inexperienced replacements, who could scarcely be expected to excel until they had acquired a good deal of service. Meanwhile the division was being judged on its performance. Under such circumstances there was a real danger that division commanders would protect themselves by sending only their culls to staff school while retaining their best men.[10]

Although there were many reasons why it was proving difficult to get the best-qualified officers into the schools, this was by no means the most vexing problem in the training program. Far more troublesome was the matter of the assistance being rendered by French and British instructors. The AEF lacked officers with the specialized skills required. For example, there were few if any fully qualified to plan the moves of corps and divisions through the French rail network behind the front. Nor were there anywhere near enough officers in the AEF with sufficient experience in coordinating artillery fire for an American division working as a part of a French corps. Much the same could also be said for a host of other skills, ranging from instruction in the authorized procedure for purchasing supplies from the local authorities to the proper method for billeting troops in French villages.[11]

Even those officers who had been fortunate enough to go through the courses at Leavenworth and the War College recognized their various shortcomings when confronted with new weapons and a foreign environment. But to employ foreign officers was to open the door to all sorts of difficulties. Quite apart from such obvious obstacles as language and differences in national customs, especially in the matter of relations between officers and enlisted men, the use of foreigners in the staff schools raised fundamental questions of doctrine.

The French and British often brought with them an atmosphere of gloom and defeatism. After three years of reverses, they were usually lacking in that aggressive spirit General Pershing was trying so hard to instill in every one of his officers. These Allied instructors were excellently qualified to explain the mysteries of trench warfare, but trench warfare was essentially defensive. The general's high hopes for a single decisive offensive, winning the war in one great maneuver beyond the line of trenches, could never be fulfilled by men indoctrinated by defense-minded instructors. But obviously the AEF could not dispense with these Allied officers. Their technical skills were essential. The only solution was to employ them where necessary and bend every effort to minimize or offset the defeatism in their doctrine. This was not easy to do. The officers coming to the staff schools arrived almost as soon as their units reached France; virtually all of them lacked any kind of experience under fire, and they were inclined to attach an exaggerated importance to the opinions expressed by the Allied veterans in their lectures, while at the same time discounting the remarks of the less-experienced AEF officers serving as instructors.

The dangers of defeatism and a defensive tactical doctrine were not the only objections to the use of Allied instructors. No less threatening was the well-founded suspicion that the Allies, the French in particular, were deliberately trying to discourage or at least to retard the training of officers for the higher corps and army positions. The longer they could delay the formation of competent staffs for these larger tactical units, the easier it would be for them to use AEF regiments as fillers in existing Allied divisions. Needless to say, the general did not agree. In fact, he was busy casting about for suitable means to check the French designs when he ran into Palmer in Paris.[12]

The doctors' decision not to permit Palmer to return immediately to full duty as chief of Operations thrust him into General Pershing's hands at just the right moment. Here was an officer fully in his confidence who was thoroughly imbued with the General Staff point of view. He could be counted upon to sense even the slightest French threat to the training program. And through his intimate associates at headquarters, he could readily communicate his observations where they would do the greatest service. Were it not for Pershing's intense concern for the General Staff idea, why would he retain an officer who had twice suffered serious breakdowns, incapacitating him for long periods of time?

In effect, General Pershing was waging three separate battles in France: on the fighting front he was pitted against the Germans for military victory; on the diplomatic front he was wrangling with the Allies to preserve the AEF as a unified force under its own officers; and within the American forces in France he was struggling to establish the general staff idea, once and for all, as a tool of command. The means employed were to prove far more enduring than the victory itself, for the experience of the AEF in France made the general staff idea an integral part of the nation's military tradition. For this reason Palmer's relations with his commanding general take on more than a purely personal interest.[13]

When Pershing had arrived in Washington to take command, he had never met his future chief of Operations. He had selected Palmer entirely on his record, which revealed an able officer and a vigorous advocate of the general staff system. Yet Palmer was known to be in the confidence of the former Chief of Staff, Leonard Wood, whose bitter feud with General Pershing is too well known to require elaboration. In this context, Pershing's continued confidence in Palmer after the disintegration of his health only serves to underline the signal importance he attached to the general staff concept. Its success or failure would in large measure be determined by the performance of the staff at Headquarters, AEF, and no one of his principal officers would play a greater role in this trial than his chief of Operations.

With mixed emotions the colonel set out from headquarters to catch the Paris-Lyons express on its way south. It was a bitter disappointment not to take up the burdens of Operations immediately, but he was intrigued by the problems Harbord had just described. In a sense Palmer's mood as he rode toward Lyons reflected Harbord's superb skill as a leader of men. He knew how much anguish it brought Palmer not to return directly to Operations, so he had gone out of his way to play up the interesting and challenging questions raised by the training program. Yet he understood that it would never do to tell the convalescent colonel all about his new responsibilities. To have done so might have touched off a new round of doubt, indecision, and total loss of self-confidence.

When Palmer's train pulled into the station at Lyons, Brig. Gen. Robert L. Bullard's aide was there to greet him. This courtesy he found doubly pleasing on discovering that the young officer was an old friend from the 15th Infantry, Capt. Walter R. Wheeler, who had served with him in China. In short order Wheeler had him comfortably established in a luxurious room at the Grand Nouvel-Hôtel, where General Bullard had set up his headquarters. This arrangement was expensive, but as Palmer explained to his wife, having plenty of hot water was a rare treat he had not enjoyed for months.[14]

The colonel's relations with General Bullard proved to be most cordial. They had worked together at the Army War College in 1911, so the general already knew a good deal about him. With characteristic shrewdness he put his finger right on the colonel's difficulty. "Palmer," he said, "the trouble with you is that you never stop gnawing on the bone."[15]

The headquarters at Lyons, Bullard pointed out, had been created to operate two schools just outside the city at La Valbonne and at Valréas, where some 700 young officers freshly arrived from the United States were in training. Although these men were graduates of officer candidate schools, they had been found woefully untrained in tactics, in field fortifications, and in the use of the several new weapons, such as mortars and 37 mm guns, recently added to the armament of the AEF. Until these skills had been mastered at the level of company commanders and platoon leaders, there was no use in attempting any kind of staff training for positions in the higher corps and divisional organizations.

The schools around Lyons, Bullard explained, were nominally under the AEF with an American commandant, but the entire instructional staff was made up of French and British officers. For lack of qualified instructors in the AEF, it had been decided in the Training Section at Chaumont to discontinue the schools at Lyons and transfer the whole program to Langres. There the foreign officers not only would be under an American commandant, Brig. Gen. James W. McAndrew, but in addition would be intermingled with the few American instructors who were available. Only a month remained before the transfer would take place, but meanwhile General Pershing had tapped Bullard to take command of the 1st Division as soon as he could break in Palmer as his replacement.

Gradually it dawned on Palmer that his temporary assignment as commandant of schools was precisely what the doctors in Paris had ordered. Bullard had borne the brunt of the difficulties encountered in setting up the establishment, getting courses organized and supply lines open. The new commandant could virtually coast to the end of the course, his only real problem being to maintain harmonious relations with the local French authorities. "I am obeying orders," he assured his wife when writing home, "—and taking life easy."[16] Although he had an auto and chauffeur at his disposal, he found it far more refreshing to make his daily inspection of the training camps on horseback, enjoying to the utmost the backdrop of snow-clad Alps looming up in the distance.[17]

One of the more enjoyable of the commandant's duties was the exchange of courtesies with various French officials. The Americans had to maintain friendly relations with the French because they were dependent upon French sources not only for facilities but for virtually all their supplies and equipment. And since the commandant had to take a rather hard line in resisting repeated attempts by the French to force their officers and their methods upon the school, it became more than ever important to establish the warmest personal friendships with the French officials.[18] In this, duty coincided with pleasure, and on frequent occasions Palmer found himself sharing a box at the opera with the French general who commanded the local military district.

Soon after he took over as commandant, the colonel was invited to the local conservatory to attend an elaborate ceremony. This affair, so characteristic-ally French and so typical of the generation, could only be described as a patriotic folkrite. The guests of honor, including the American consul, a Dr. John E. Jones, occupied boxes elaborately draped with the Stars and Stripes. The program began with an impassioned address entitled "America," deliv-ered by the Mayor of Lyons, and ended very much later with a rendition of "The Star Spangled Banner" in French by a chorus of school girls. And if the long-winded hands-across-the-sea oration was somewhat tedious, the speaker himself was quite otherwise.[19] In 1917 the Mayor of Lyons was none other than Edouard Herriot. This distinguished French political leader, who was later to cap his long public career with a heroic refusal to collaborate with the Vichy regime in World War II, proved to be a most gracious host, and Palmer enjoyed dining at the Herriot home on several occasions.[20]

Dining with the French was often a considerable adventure. There was, for example, a notable meal at the 200-year-old restaurant said to be the place where lyonnaise potatoes were first concocted. The successive courses of this meal, a gastronomic triumph, included such exotic delicacies as fish wrapped in soufflé and boiled capon with truffles tucked under the skin. Yet after recording a long list of culinary wonders such as these in a letter home, Palmer ended on a characteristic note. "I wish I could have some American spoon bread and a cup of our kind of coffee."[21]

Of the many Frenchmen Palmer met in his round of official duties at Lyons, none proved more interesting than the young man assigned as his aide and liaison officer, Lt. Henri Scheresse. In private life the lieutenant was a restau-rateur, who after the war achieved distinction as the proprietor of the Restau-rant Laurent on the Champs Elysées in Paris. In appearance he was almost a caricature of the American conception of a Frenchman, complete even to the gigantic handlebar mustachio with ends sweeping up in the most approved fashion. He had fought at the Marne and again at Verdun, where he had been critically wounded while leading troops in an assault. Decorated for bravery, he had been assigned to liaison duty during his convalescence.[22] "How different they all are from us," Palmer exclaimed in a letter to his wife after one particularly long session with his new French friend.[23]

In many ways Lieutenant Scheresse was the perfect embodiment of the type of reserve officer on whom Palmer built his whole conception of the properly expanded wartime army. He was energetic and imaginative, yet wise enough to know that resourcefulness is most telling when applied with tact. In the nimble-witted Lieutenant Scheresse, Palmer discovered for himself what Marshal Foch professed to have learned from long years of professional services: to be successful, officers must be men of broad cultivation, and a reservist of wide experience and far-ranging outlook may prove more effective when war comes than a highly trained but narrow regular who has confined his interests to petty military politics or a preoccupation with promotion.[24]

The splendid quality of the American officers in training at La Valbonne and Valréas tended to reinforce Palmer's confidence in the potentialities of citizen soldiers. When the time came to close the school, he singled out some of the most promising for assignments in the Operations Section at General Headquarters. Nearly half of the group selected subsequently proved to be recent graduates of Yale, while the remainder included men from several other well-known colleges.[25]

In some ways the excellence of the young student officers made Palmer all the more conscious of his own shortcomings. During the first few days after his arrival at Lyons, he was much buoyed up by the marked return of physical vigor he experienced as he made his regular rounds of the camps on horseback. But gradually it dawned on him that his return to bodily health had not restored his zest for sustained intellectual effort. "I had been ill so long and had been so blue because I had broken down, that the truth is... my self-confidence was shaken a little."[26] After three weeks of vigorous activity at Lyons, the disparity between his bodily vigor and his mental torpor could no longer be ignored.

Anxious as he was to return to his role as chief of Operations, in all honesty Palmer knew he was not yet ready to take on any such responsibility. He was still struggling with this dilemma when Harbord, recently promoted to brigadier, came to his rescue with a letter from Chaumont. The Chief of Staff suggested that the end of the program at Lyons would afford an occasion for another medical checkup. If the doctors found that it was still unwise to return to Operations, there was plenty of work to be done at Langres. "Just now," Harbord concluded, "there is no more important duty than that connected with the Staff College."[27]

Palmer reached Chaumont 15 December 1917. There, following a thorough physical examination, he sat down with the presiding medical officer, his friend Maj. Henry Beeuwkes, to learn his fate. Beeuwkes was a model of humane concern. He encouraged his patient by complimenting his splendid physical improvement, then went on to warn him not to spoil his chances of full recovery by returning too soon to long hours and heavy responsibilities. The position Harbord had lined up for him as adviser to the commandant at Langres, Beeuwkes assured him, was perfectly suited to his needs.[28]

Before leaving GHQ, Palmer went to Harbord and insisted that Fox Conner be made chief of Operations in name as well as in fact. For months Palmer had been carried on orders as assistant chief of staff, with Conner in an acting capacity. Now in simple fairness to Conner he knew he would have to relinquish his role as one of Pershing's principal staff officers. This was a step not easily taken.

Throughout his sickness Palmer had rationalized his extended leave on the cues provided by his medical friends. The moral support afforded by this line of reasoning now disappeared, and he was in danger of plunging back into a new depression, overwhelmed by his own sense of failure. From this fate he was happily saved, however, by the skill and consideration of his friends.

Beeuwkes, for example, refused to take the easy course and simply order his patient home to the United States. This, he knew, would only confirm Palmer's sense of failure. Fox Conner, too, did his bit to encourage his friend. "Palmer," he said, "the trouble with you is that for the last ten years you have been doing twice as much for the Army as the Army has done for you, and everybody knows it." Only a few months before, when Pershing first singled Palmer out as chief of Operations, success had seemed certain. Surely he was the most fortunate officer of his grade in the whole army. Then all this was swept away almost overnight. In this context Conner's bluff assertion that "everybody" in the army knew his real worth provided a good deal of solace.[29]

The assurances of various colleagues were important, but it was Harbord who gave the most meaningful assist. Palmer was being assigned for a rest cure and knew it, but Harbord did hold out the attractive future prospect of a brigade command on the front. This was a far cry from being the principal planner of the AEF, but it meant a great deal to one whose self-confidence had been so thoroughly shattered. The fact that command of a brigade would virtually assure promotion to the grade of brigadier served only to enhance the medicinal effect of Harbord's suggestion.

Happily there was little time for brooding on the past. The twenty-two-mile journey to Langres was soon over, and Palmer found himself treading the narrow streets of the old hill town that had once been Julius Caesar's head-quarters. At the school headquarters he was greeted by the commandant, Brig. Gen. James W. McAndrew, whom he had known for years. The general was already well aware of his friend's problems and put him at ease imme-diately. He insisted that the colonel become a member of his personal mess, along with the two or three ranking officers at Langres. "Your main job," said McAndrew, "is to get well," adding bluntly that Palmer was "important enough to be looked out for," since great things were expected of him later on. Vastly reinforced by this kind of assurance, the colonel set off with one of the general's aides to find a suitable billet.[30]

They soon located a promising accommodation on the *place* opposite the 700-year-old cathedral in the center of town. Madame the landlady, who gloried in the name of Pflub, was a typical bourgeois. Bustling along ahead of *le colonel américain,* she explained that the tiny three-room apartment she had for let belonged to her bachelor brother, then, alas, a prisoner of war in Germany. She was sure he would find everything precisely to his desire: the plump feather bed, the porcelain stove, the interesting prints adorning the room. The exotic portrait on the wall was of her own grandfather, a captain of artillery who had served in Egypt with Napoleon.

At $30 a month the colonel was convinced he had found a real bargain, but as soon as he moved in he began to have second thoughts. As he wryly noted, the winter climate in France is cold, but not so cold as the inside of a French house. Wood was the only fuel available, and one had to pay thirty dollars a cord for that. Moreover the stove was so small it required stoking every hour in the day, so one paid an enlisted orderly or striker an additional $7 a month to keep up a fire. But the billet had much to commend it. Madame Pflub insisted on grandmothering her lodger, sending in a tin hot water bottle on cold nights and in dozens of similar kindnesses transferring her attentions from her absent brother to the American visitor.[31] After moving in Palmer discovered that his Military Academy classmate James A. Shipton, now a brigadier, already had rooms under the same roof. And only a few doors away lived another West Point contemporary and friend from the 15th Infantry, Col. Harry A. Smith, who enjoyed dropping in for an occasional meal or afterdinner chat. [32]

To give the convalescent colonel some sort of official status, General McAndrew appointed him secretary of the Staff College. In thus removing any sense of pressure, General McAndrew filled Beeuwkes's prescription to perfection, and the patient made substantial strides toward recovery. As all who knew him might have predicted, Palmer used his new-found freedom to embark on a vigorous program to learn all he could about the Staff College and the whole complex of schools directed from Langres. He attended classes, hiked up and down in all kinds of weather to watch demonstrations, discussed problems of policy with his brother officers, and soon felt thoroughly at home in his new role.

Although the Staff College had been in operation for less than a month, the overall dimensions of the training program were already evident. The Training Section at headquarters had evidently caught the conception of magnitude that the French and British had been at such pains to convey when General Pershing first reached Paris. Modest though the beginnings might be, McAndrew had laid out the AEF schools for an eventual output of some 10,000 officers a month, representing the whole gamut of skills from platoon leader to corps commander.

General McAndrew understood perfectly well that truly effective staff officers are produced only by extended schooling and years of practical experience. But GHQ had directed him to establish a course with a term of three months and to begin turning out staff officers in classes of 200 each as soon as he could. For this all but impossible task, the general selected Lt. Col. A. W. Bjornstad, Palmer's Leavenworth classmate and companion at the French and German maneuvers of 1912.

The easiest part of Bjornstad's job was to locate a campus for his college at Langres in the Carteret-Trecourt barracks of the French army. For a faculty he was forced to rely upon eight instructors rather too willingly provided by the French and British. A student body proved even more difficult to muster. Since the entire Regular Army could boast of but 4,000 officers with a year or more of service, and only a fraction of these had reached France, it was all Bjornstad could do to scrape together a class of 75. So pressing was the demand for officers throughout the AEF that nearly half of this scanty class was sent directly to assignments without time to finish the course to qualify officially for General Staff duty.[33]

The curriculum of the Staff College was modeled closely upon the course at Leavenworth. The core of the training offered consisted of some twenty map problems, each involving one or more principles of staff operations. Student officers were required not only to master these principles but also to learn the technique of communicating their decisions to subordinates in orders drawn according to standard army form.

The pattern of instruction was substantially the same for each problem: first there were two days in which the mornings were devoted to a series of lectures on theory by French or British officers. These were followed by lectures by an American officer, who attempted to reconcile the sometimes conflicting views of the French and British instructors and to translate those views into terms applicable to the organization of the AEF, which differed from Allied practice. During these two days the students had their afternoons free for study. On the third day each student was assigned a map problem calling for a specific application of the theory presented by the lecturers. Individual solutions were then exchanged, and students were provided with copies of the approved "school solution" and instructed to write critiques of their classmates' papers. Student solutions and critiques were turned in for grading by the faculty. Finally, on the fourth day, all papers were returned and the instructors discussed their merits and defects in conferences with small groups of students.[34]

With each problem on a four-day cycle, twenty problems consumed virtually the full three months allowed for the course. The most significant sacrifice was the exercise with troops, by which the individual student officer at

Leavenworth was afforded an opportunity to test his grasp of theory with a practical field problem. Even though abbreviated, Palmer was inclined to believe that the training offered at the Staff College was better suited to the needs of the AEF than the curriculum proffered by the French. The paper exercises conducted at Langres did give student officers an opportunity to participate as individuals, to learn by doing and by making mistakes. The French practice of relying upon demonstrations by crack troops left the student officers to learn what they could by looking on at the unfolding of a set-piece exercise.[35]

Palmer soon began to look about seriously for ways to make himself useful. An opportunity presented itself almost immediately in the horde of foreign officers who appeared each week to inspect the various AEF schools around Langres. Some came to learn what they could about American training methods; some came hoping to shape the training according to their own national doctrines; while others came to pay courtesy calls. All had to be shown every attention, for no opportunity should be lost to encourage the friendliest of relations with Allied officers. Palmer was ideally suited to this duty. Because he was one of General Pershing's intimates and was thoroughly familiar with GHQ, visitors could not feel they were being fobbed off on an underling. After a day or two spent touring the schools with the genial little colonel, they seemed to depart in high spirits no matter what their motives for coming.

Palmer delighted in preaching the gospel of staff training according to the rubrics of Leavenworth. In return he was rewarded with comments from visiting officers who had a wealth of experience far richer than any he could hope to find in the AEF. Among the guests none was more colorful and interesting than Capt. Roald Amundsen, the Norwegian polar explorer, who regaled the general's mess far into the night with tales of Arctic and Antarctic discovery.[36]

Probably the most interesting guest, professionally speaking, was Brig. Sir Charles Bonham-Carter, the principle staff officer for training at the British GHQ. Sir Charles's interests closely paralleled those of his American host. Indeed, after the war, when Palmer was actively engaged in defining the role of the reserve forces in their relation to the Regulars, Bonham-Carter went on to become director general of the Territorial Army, the British equivalent of local militia. The brigadier also exemplified much of what Palmer regarded as the ideal for staff officers: he was not only a shrewd student of human nature but in addition possessed a lively imagination reflecting both the catholic scope of his reading and the wide range of his acquaintances beyond the confines of his professional circle.[37]

Fortunately for Palmer's hypersensitive conscience, his job as General McAndrew's informal chief of protocol led him directly into the work that made his stay at Langres thoroughly worthwhile. Foreign officers constituted only a small portion of the total number of high-ranking visitors who poured through the training center; the great majority were American major generals—division commanders with their staffs, who were touring the AEF for a hasty preview before their units finished training back in the United States. Although it might appear that there was little to choose between escorting one or the other group about the schools, there was in fact a highly significant difference. The visits of the American division commanders had been part of General Pershing's scheme of familiarization for all senior officers, but with Palmer as a guide the visitors received far more than had been officially intended. General McAndrew had in his subordinate a highly proficient propagandist for the whole concept of staff school training.[38]

In many respects Palmer was the ideal man for putting over the staff school message. His personal charm was disarming; more significantly, since he was known to have General Pershing's confidence, division commanders listened to him with respect. The general had already demonstrated by his policy of ruthless removals that no one who failed to measure up to his standard could expect to command a division, so the major generals who came to Langres had good reason to listen attentively when Palmer expounded the staff doctrine of which the general approved.

For nearly two months the convalescent colonel continued his absorbing role as special advocate for staff training. Good company, plenty of outdoor exercise, freedom from pressure, and a sense of genuine usefulness all combined imperceptibly to restore Palmer to something like his customary physical vigor. When a thorough medical examination at Chaumont confirmed his impressions, the colonel could expect to be given command of a brigade on the front. And beyond that, who could predict what opportunity would open up?

Opportunity did appear, and almost immediately, but not in the form he expected. In the first week of February 1918, only a few days after his encouraging medical examination, the colonel received an official dispatch from Chaumont. "By direction of the President," he read, a military mission would soon be sent to Italy; Col. John McAuley Palmer was ordered to wind up his affairs at Langres and report to headquarters for further instructions as a member of this mission.[39]

29 Mission to Italy

When Palmer reached Chaumont, he sought out the Chief of Staff for a thorough briefing on the forthcoming mission to Italy. Although General Pershing regarded the Western Front as the proper theater of operations for the AEF, he was well aware that German divisions such as those used to spearhead the Austrian breakthrough at Caporetto might be redirected against the eastern end of the line in France, where the main effort of the AEF would soon be made. It was vitally important to learn as much as possible about the Italian forces and their capacity to maintain pressure on the enemy.[1]

The formal directive Harbord was drawing up made it clear that General Pershing was primarily interested in the morale of the Italian army. The mission was to submit reports on its supplies and equipment, training, and defensive dispositions. In addition to these more or less tangible components of that imponderable, military morale, the mission was to do what it could to appraise the attitude of the Italians toward the other Allies, and especially toward the French and British troops that had been sent into Italy after Caporetto.[2]

Although Harbord's directive did not say so, the mission was also to have a significant diplomatic function. By their mere presence on the Italian front, American uniforms would serve to hearten the Italians, yet unavoidably they would also be regarded as harbingers of the aid the Italians had looked for ever since the United States declared war on the Austro-Hungarian Empire in December 1917. And it was precisely these expectations that made the mission so delicate.

To bolster Italian morale was one thing; to send any considerable number of American troops to Italy was quite another. General Pershing was already struggling to preserve the integrity of the AEF in the face of demands from the French and British, who wished to use his manpower as replacements in their dwindling divisions; he had no desire to add a third suppliant. Unfortunately from his point of view, the Italians had interpreted President Wilson's message to Congress before the declaration of war as a pledge that American troops would be sent to Italy. In pressing General Pershing to fulfill this expectation, no one had been more insistent than Thomas Nelson Page, the U.S. ambassador to the Kingdom of Italy.

The general had scarcely established his headquarters in Paris during the summer of 1917 before Ambassador Page came up from Rome to urge a major intervention by the AEF on the Italian front. Since the United States had then not yet declared war on the Austro-Hungarian empire, this proposal was easily deflected. But the ambassador's arguments could not be entirely ignored. A few AEF units would indeed go far to boost Italian morale, and American intervention in Italy during the war might well strengthen President Wilson's postwar diplomatic position when the troublesome question of national boundaries came up for settlement. Even if General Pershing accepted the doubtful assumption, implicit in Ambassador Page's contentions, that nations act from gratitude, he was more concerned with present military problems. But he was not insensitive to political realities; he knew that Ambassador Page had direct access to President Wilson. For this reason if for no other, the ambassador's proposals had to be accorded respectful attention.[3]

As anyone at the Chaumont headquarters could have predicted, as soon as Congress voted to wage war against the Austrians as well as the Germans, Ambassador Page repeated his request for American troops, "even a single division," as he blandly expressed it.[4] Obviously the ambassador had not the slightest understanding of the meager resources then available to the American command in France. On the day that he asked for "a single division," the combat forces of the AEF consisted of two divisions, neither of which had completed its scheduled training.

Two months later, in February 1918, Ambassador Page repeated his appeal, but now he was better informed and therefore somewhat more realistic. In place of combat troops for offensive operations, he asked only for small units to be used for propaganda purposes on the home front. Two or three regiments, he believed, would make a far greater impact than all the food, fuel, and cash the U.S. government was currently pouring into Italy. To clinch his argument the ambassador recounted an anecdote from the summer of 1914, when the French government had desperately begged London to send troops across the Channel. On receiving the reply that none were yet ready to depart, the French wired back, "Send the flag and the Guards' band if nothing more."[5]

General Pershing had already determined to "show the flag" in Italy. He had no intention of sending any large body of troops, but he was quite willing to take up the ambassador's suggestion that a military mission would be welcomed by the Italians. At the moment a major general was easier to find than a regiment. In fact, he had several such high-ranking officers to choose from, all elderly gentlemen close to retirement, individuals for whom he was delighted to find honorable employment as an alternative to field commands.[6]

As General Harbord explained the problem to Palmer, the mission to Italy was to play a difficult hand. A considerable part of the job performed by the AEF staff consisted of "tactful semidiplomatic jollying" of the various allies. Had General Pershing been interested only in gathering information on conditions in the Italian army, he could readily have arranged to reinforce Col. M. C. Buckey, the military attaché assigned to the embassy in Rome. Instead he expected the members of the mission to do all they could to show the flag and lend encouragement without creating false expectations.[7]

The resulting assortment of officers clearly reflected the double role Pershing expected of them. As chief of the mission he selected Maj. Gen. Eben Swift, Commanding General of the 82nd Division, who along with several other division commanders had come to Europe in advance of his troops to study operations on the French and British fronts before taking his unit into battle. His rank was high enough to satisfy the requirements of Italian pride, and as a one-time director of the Army War College, he had helped to flesh out Secretary Root's conception of an army general staff. Swift could be counted upon for a professional evaluation of the Italian staff organization.

Colonel Palmer, the second ranking member of the mission, as Pershing's choice for his chief of Operations would impress the Italians as an officer enjoying a close personal relationship with the Commander in Chief. Palmer himself, however, understood that it was his experience and his availability because of ill-health, rather than any considerations of prestige, that dictated his selection.

The other members of the mission were Lt. Col. Robert U. Patterson and Capt. Fiorello H. LaGuardia. The former was a medical officer who had won a DSM for gallantry in the Philippines and had led the Harvard Medical Unit to France to take over a base hospital from the British. Patterson's courage and efficiency under fire had singled him out as a resourceful officer who could be relied upon to appraise the medical facilities on the Italian front with a realistic eye. LaGuardia, who had left his seat in Congress to become an Air Service officer, had gone to Italy in October 1917 with a detachment of aviation cadets who were to be trained by the Italians at Foggia. After the disaster at Caporetto, Ambassador Page had called upon him to help revive Italian morale by speaking before a huge gathering at Genoa. His success had been instantaneous. An American officer who could use the native tongue to harangue vast crowds, whipping up waves of emotion for Italian-American friendship and cooperation, was a propaganda resource too valuable to ignore. As it turned out, however, the ebullient captain never did join the mission, except on paper, but continued to operate, characteristically, as a one-man show.

Since nearly a week remained before 20 February 1918, the day the members of the mission were ordered to rendezvous in Paris, Harbord suggested that Palmer might find it highly rewarding to go up to the front for a visit. The 1st Division had recently taken over a sector from the French First Army and was still busy digging in, so he could be sure of some practical suggestions from his friends at Le Mésnil-St.-Firmin, the small town where the 1st Division headquarters had been established.

The American position lay about midway along the south face of the Saint-Mihiel salient, stretching east and west from the village of Seicheprey. On the way up, Palmer's escort explained that the division had only one brigade in the line, but since a single AEF brigade was the equivalent in manpower of a full French division, it had been decided to set up divisional as well as brigade headquarters. With only two regiments and a machine gun battalion at the front, this provided a rather top-heavy command structure, but the arrangement afforded the fullest possible range of experience for the higher staffs.[8] As the visiting party trudged further into the labyrinth of communication trenches, Palmer found that each step of the way involved a contest to see if he could recover his feet from the mud. It was a distinct relief when his guide finally turned him over to his old friend, Col. John L. Hines, the commanding officer of the 16th Infantry.

Hines, who was soon to become a corps commander and after the war would rise to be Chief of Staff, had a dinner laid out. It was, he admitted, not quite up to the meal they had shared at Simpson's in London. Meanwhile, the enemy proved uncooperative and kept interrupting the conversation with heavy shelling up and down the trench system.

After dinner Hines took his visitor out to observe the difficulties in moving up troops and supplies during the night. The eerie darkness was broken only by occasional outbursts of enemy shelling; Yet all around them working parties were busy digging in and stringing wire, and not far behind them they could hear men at work constructing gun emplacements as the 3rd Field Artillery battalion moved into position. Only careful staff planning and the most meticulous map work kept units from bumping into one another or becoming totally lost in the treacherous terrain.

The next morning Hines took his guest through his front line trenches. For the most part the lines ran along low-lying and swampy ground, so the trenches were little more than shallow excavations. Had they been any deeper they would simply have filled up with water. German observers high up on Montsec, which loomed up above the level of the plain, seemed to peer right down into the American position. After observing such conditions, now more than ever Palmer realized that Pershing's desire to avoid dissipating the manpower of the AEF in the demoralizing small-scale local operations of trench warfare made sense.

When the colonel finally got back to Le Mésnil-St.-Firmin, Brig. Gen. R. L. Bullard invited him to dinner with his several friends on the division staff. This gave Palmer an opportunity to catch up on the news with George Marshall, who was serving as division operations officer. Marshall regaled the company with an anecdote. Like everyone else in the AEF he found it irksome to wear his gas mask for any length of time. To accustom himself to the bulky apparatus he had made it a practice to slip on his mask whenever he hiked along the highway to the trenches. He had just donned his mask and was so preoccupied with breathing correctly that he scarcely noticed a long oncoming mule train. A wizened old mule skinner sat huddled on the wagon seat with almost nothing but his pipe showing beyond his turned up collar. Suddenly discovering the masked officer, the figure on the wagon fairly exploded—hat, pipe, arms and legs seeming to fly in every direction—as the mule skinner whipped up his team, bellowing "Gaaazzzz"! When last seen the whole column, mules, wagons, and drivers, was careening down the road at a pace that threatened to carry them deep into Germany.[9]

Marshall was about to give point to his story by observing how green the troops were, when the whole room shuddered and lights went out. A German airplane had flown over and laid a stick of bombs across the town. Although Le Mésnil was some eight miles behind the front, it had become a favorite target for enemy air attacks. Just outside, Marshall found the cook running a big wooden spoon up and down the slats of a louvered door. To the major's query the cook replied while keeping up the racket, "I'm trying to make the Germans think we've got a machine gun here."[10]

When the mission to Italy finally set out, it had grown to be a considerable party. In addition to the three principles who with the absent Captain LaGuardia constituted the mission proper, there were thirteen enlisted men to act as orderlies, drivers, communications specialists, and the like. And in addition, both Swift and Palmer were accompanied by young reserve officers serving as aides. General Swift had selected as his aide Capt. E. Ormonde Hunter, a young lawyer from Savannah, Georgia. Palmer chose another young lawyer, Lt. Eugene C. Pomeroy, whom he had first met in Lyons while closing out the schools there. Pomeroy had won his respect while serving as the local provost marshal. The assignment was by no means an easy one, especially on weekends, when hundreds of wild young Americans poured into the city, apparently bent on living up to the reputation of the French Foreign Legion, which was normally based in the barracks at La Valbonne. The lieutenant had performed so tactfully that Palmer knew he was just the man for a quasi-diplomatic mission.[11]

In Rome the members of the party were greeted by crowds of cheering people, by newsreel cameramen, and by public dignitaries, since it was obviously in the interests of the Italian government to capitalize on the

Americans' propoganda value. Almost immediately the group was swept up in a round of official entertainments.[12] Ambassador Page led the way with a formal dinner and reception at his official residence, the Palazzo del Drago, a magnificent Renaissance structure almost next door to the Quirinal, or royal palace. The next day the members of the mission were tendered a luncheon by General Alfieri, the Minister of War, and introduced to the leading officials of the ministry.[13] Palmer tried to squeeze in a little sightseeing, but it was almost impossible to escape the attentions of Roman officialdom.

Pleasant as it was, the mission's stay in Rome was not without its disturbing side. Ambassador Page had talked about sending no more than a "corporal's guard" to show the flag, but his corporal's guard grew to a demand for at least two or three regiments. When it was pointed out that this was roughly equivalent to the force General Bullard then had on the front, Mr. Page shifted his ground. If no troops could be committed to the Italian front at the moment, would it not be possible to send one or two American brigades to Italy for training? Where such troops would be used could be decided later, he suggested. But the mission knew that once large numbers of American troops were sent into Italy, it would be virtually impossible to withdraw them without touching off a diplomatic crisis.

Looking back afterward, Palmer realized that much of the difficulty stemmed from the mission's efforts to talk to a man who did not understand military terms. Did the ambassador know that his "brigade or two" would involve some ten to twenty thousand men? Perhaps he was still thinking in terms of Civil War units. They had no doubt of Page's sincerity, but his refusal to see the problem from General Pershing's perspective soon led to difficulties.

Understandably enough, the Italians were inclined to take Ambassador Page's statements at face value. He was saying what they wanted to hear. As a consequence it was hardly surprising when an American newspaper correspondent filed a story asserting that General Swift and his missions were the vanguard of the troops Wilson had promised months before.[14] The Italian censors were only too glad to pass and disseminate this kind of report.

While Ambassador Page seemed to be at cross-purposes with the mission in the matter of troops for Italy, he was able to alert the visiting officers to other diplomatic pitfalls. Among these was the ambiguous attitude of the Vatican toward the American war effort. At least some highly placed Vatican officials, the ambassador reported, were virulently anti-American or antiwar. One important cardinal, according to an embassy informant, had gone so far as to accuse the Protestants of letting the Roman Catholics do the fighting, claiming that Catholics numbered only 20 percent of the population in the United States but constituted 60 percent of the AEF.[15] These statistics were too absurd to require refutation, but they did serve to point up the subtlety and complexity of the diplomatic task confronting the military mission. Indeed, it was becoming increasingly evident to the members of the mission that their assignment was going to be far more difficult than it had appeared from France.

The high command for the whole Italian front, extending from Switzerland to the Adriatic, was centered on the ancient walled city of Padua, where the mission arrived on the last day of February 1918. The communications network and many important staff functions were located within the old city, but the *Comando Supremo,* or general staff proper, had been moved to the village of Abano to escape the air raids that repeatedly harassed the city. The members of the mission were cordially greeted by the chief of the General Staff, Lt. Gen. Armando Diaz, who in turn presented them to his immediate subordinates, Lt. Gen. Pietro Badoglio and Maj. Gen. Scipione Scipioni.[16]

Col. Aldo Aymonino, as chief of the Allied Missions Mess, presided over the elaborate arrangements made by the Italian government to provide for the host of Allied visitors then swarming on the Italian front. In addition to British, French, and American officers, the mess catered to an assortment of Belgian, Russian, Romanian, and Serbian visitors, not to mention occasional representatives from Japan, China, and even Siam. Normally French was spoken in the mess, but the real common denominator was the superb cuisine. With shrewd foresight the Italian government not only provided a talented chef but also paid the mess bills of the guests.

Swift and Palmer, as the senior members, drew quarters in the Treves Palace, a beautiful marble pile made available by Baronessa Treves dei Bonfili d'Alembert. The colonel's enthusiasm at the regal splendor of his rooms soon waned; during a midwinter coal famine the palace was cold and damp. "Others may dream of dwelling in marble halls," he wrote his wife, "but frankly I much prefer good American central heating."[17]

Frequent bombing raids added to the discomfort of life in marble halls. During the first few raids the American officers rushed down into their designated bomb shelters. Gradually, however, they gave up this practice. It was far easier to take a fatalistic attitude and stay warm in bed.[18]

Soon after the AEF mission reached Padua, the King, Victor Emmanuel III, asked the members of the mission and their aides to dinner. After a good deal of conferring about protocol, the American officers drove to a villa in Battaglia, a mile or two beyond the headquarters in Abano. They were quite unprepared for the entirely delightful reception they encountered. The King put them at ease immediately, drawing out his visitors in fluent English and making them feel that he was genuinely interested in their work.[19]

The tiny King, as all his visitors had been repeatedly forewarned, was painfully sensitive about his stature. In his efforts to make conversation with Palmer's aide, Lieutenant Pomeroy, he had asked him a question about the insignia he wore on his collar, walking over to inspect the device more closely. Unfortunately, to do so, the King had to stand on tiptoe and even then he had to look up, for Pomeroy was a man well over six feet tall. At this juncture

Palmer, who was only slightly taller than the King, stepped up beside him, also on tiptoe, to identify the insignia. This entirely unconscious gesture seemed to charm the King, who was impressed that an officer as short as Palmer had chosen an aide who towered over him as Pomeroy did. So he seated the colonel next to him during the meal and addressed most of his remarks to him.[20]

History has dealt harshly with King Victor Emmanuel III. Nonetheless, it may be worth recalling that until the Fascist era, his contemporaries thought highly of him. In 1918 Ambassador Page believed he was "the ablest and wisest King on a throne," or off one for that matter.[21] Page was a highly partisan witness, but Theodore Roosevelt, who was no sycophantic respecter of royalty, had found King Victor Emmanuel one of the strongest men in Europe.[22] Part of the King's charm derived from his unaffected simplicity. When Palmer commented on some cottage cheese served at the meal, the King replied in a matter of fact way, "Yes, it *is* good; my wife made it and sent it up to me." Somehow the image of Queen Helene, the Montenegrian princess, busy in her palace kitchen straining curds, did not seem at all incongruous.[23]

When the meal was over, the King had cigars handed around. Since he disliked tobacco himself, he said he would withdraw while his guests enjoyed themselves. As the little monarch walked out, General Swift lighted up one of the proffered stogies, a wicked-looking, long, black, oddly-shaped affair, which gave off great clouds of acrid smoke. Then, puffing like a woodburning locomotive, he stalked after the King, whom he soon cornered in conversation, enveloping the unhappy man with noxious fumes. The others were soon writhing in embarrassment as they watched their royal host torn between his desire to be gracious and his obvious distress at being fumigated.[24]

General Swift's inconsiderate treatment of the King was not in the least typical. He was an officer and a gentleman of the old school, courtly in manner and highly literate. He could quote Shakespeare and Walter Scott by the hour. At the same time he had been a doughty Indian fighter and was a thoroughly capable military organizer. But he was also a man of colorful prejudices, not least among which was his thinly veiled contempt for the Italians, whom he rated in military capacity on a par with the Mexicans he had known along the border. Swift had come to Italy a somewhat embittered man. Furious at having been removed from command of his division, solely because of his age, before he had been given an opportunity to prove his capacity in battle, he was scarcely in a mood for military diplomacy. Nonetheless, as a good soldier, he swallowed his disappointment and labored to the best of his ability for the success of the mission until the day of his retirement in 1918.[25]

Once the requirements of diplomatic protocol had been satisfied, the next item in the order of business for the members of the mission was to arrange a tour of the entire front. Since their objective was to be seen as well as to see, they had to visit as many units as possible, showing the flag all the way from the Adriatic to the Swiss border.

While working out the details of the proposed tour, Palmer was invited to take a flight over the front in a Caproni bomber. He had never flown in an airplane of any kind, let alone a bomber over hostile territory, but this gave him an unparalleled opportunity to see the opposing systems of entrenchments he was soon to study on the ground.[26] The flight turned out to be thrilling, in fact far more than he had bargained for. After a period of straight and level flying to facilitate observation, the pilot suddenly dropped a wing and sideslipped toward the earth. If he hoped to enjoy his passenger's discomfort, he was not in the least disappointed; Palmer found himself clutching a strut for dear life as his familiar world showed a distressing tendency to stand up on end. When it subsided, the plane was skimming directly over the Austrian trenches. The pilot seemed to be insolently thumbing his nose at the ground troops, deliberately trying to provoke them into firing their rifles at the passing interloper. Although the colonel was much relieved to escape from the custody of his wild young pilot, he was greatly impressed with the possibilities of the airplane as a military weapon—in mature and responsible hands!

The members of the AEF mission arrived in Venice on 4 March 1918, just in time to be caught by a ferocious air attack, which the Austrians kept up for nearly eight hours. The main purpose of the trip was to confer with the Italian naval command, but the American officers also expected to get in a little sightseeing. They were largely disappointed, however. The famous horses at San Marco had been shipped to a place of safety, and most of the other historic landmarks were piled high with sandbags. All these precautions gave the historic city a desolate air, which along with the raw, overcast skies left the visitors with no heart for tourism. In writing home to his wife, Palmer explained that an overcast at least guaranteed them a night free from enemy air raids. Only a few days before the mission arrived in Venice, two American Red Cross volunteers killed by an Austrian air raid, had been buried by the Italians with full military honors as "martyrs" to the common cause and welcome symbols for the official propagandists.[27]

Writing wartime letters presented a number of problems, apart from those imposed by the military censor. The colonel wished not to worry his wife with unduly lurid accounts of the dangers to which he was exposed. If, on the other hand, he wrote of nothing but his most sedentary activities, his wife would never be able to hold her own in her circle of Army friends who were reporting what their husbands were doing on the front. To strike a proper balance called for a sense of humor.

The colonel's delightful humor continually cropped up in his letters. Knowing her decided views on the subject of total abstinence, he told her he was now regularly taking wine with his meals. Just a little claret, he assured her, and this only on the doctor's orders. Two weeks later he contritely assured her that he was once more "on the wagon."[28]

From Venice the mission went on a dozen or more miles to Cavezuccherina, the small town on the mud flats just below the mouth of the Piave that marked the extreme right of the Italian front. This visit established a pattern for virtually all the other visits made by the American officers. First came the call upon a rear area corps headquarters with its inevitable ceremonial luncheon. The party was then passed on through division headquarters, where a bright young English-speaking officer escorted the Americans up to a regimental command post. From there they pushed forward along an underground tunnel, coming up at last through the ruins of an old church. Here they found themselves in a lookout built from the remains of a marble vault that once graced the cemetery surrounding the church. From this macabre vantage point they could peer out at the Austrian lines a couple of hundred yards away. The sentinel on duty had once lived in New York and could explain the significant features of the crater-marred terrain.[29] By the time they had completed their tour of the whole northern front, they were fully convinced that every other soldier in the Italian army had been to New York or at the very least had a brother there.

For Palmer these trips proved highly interesting, but writing up his military reports afterward was a dreadful burden. He realized that he had by no means fully recovered from his breakdown. The few papers he did turn out made matters worse because he knew how far short they fell by his own standards.

While visiting the defenses beyond Treviso, the American party stumbled into an artillery barrage that proved a good deal less than pleasurable, but for the most part the succession of visits to the forward areas were both professionally interesting and scenically rewarding. One of the most dramatic was the mission's tour of inspection along the lines above Bassano at the edge of the Alps. A young officer from one of the crack alpine regiments led them up a tortuous road through deep snow to the top of Mount Grappa. Climbing through a maze of tunnels or galleries cut from solid rock, they came to a lookout in the sheer face of a cliff. Below them the whole Piave front lay stretched out like a map.[30]

The vista from Mount Grappa was more than awe-inspiring; it provided a military education. The tremendous tactical advantage accruing to the forces controlling the peaks was immediately evident. So too were the difficulties of conducting warfare in this alpine terrain. The achievement of the Italians in seizing and defending the mountain heights was all the more impressive in view of the acute shortage of equipment that beset their armies. Not only were they wanting in trucks, guns, and other heavy items but also in such essentials as food and fuel. Many even lacked adequate uniforms for winter operations. To make matters worse, soldiers in the ranks had to endure all these hardships knowing that their families were receiving from the government food allotments of no more than eight cents a day![31]

In contrast with the ill-accoutred Italians were the French and British units sent in after Caporetto. To the visiting Americans they seemed to be perfect models of what the well-dressed army should wear—and carry. Understandably enough, the Italians found this perfection intensely irritating; they resented having to be rescued after Caporetto, and they felt it was unfair to be compared as to military performance with troops so much better equipped.

The most vivid impression of shortages the Americans carried away came from a visit to an Italian field hospital. While inspecting the unit in connection with Colonel Patterson's medical survey, they were invited in to watch an Italian surgical team amputate the shattered leg of an Austrian officer who had fallen into Italian hands during a night raid. To the horror of the visitors, the entire operation was performed without anesthetics.[32]

Although Palmer was conscientious to a fault in pursuing his military duties, he never missed an opportunity to do what sightseeing he could. When, for example, the party passed through Asolo en route to the alpine front, he insisted on a brief stop at the house where Robert Browning wrote "Pippa Passes." There, even though it was March and the snow lay deep upon the mountains, he found yellow primroses in bloom in the walled garden. Carefully plucking a blossom to send his teenage daughter, Mary, he returned to the staff car and his waiting companions, who were charmed but not a little puzzled by this unusual man. Here was a professional army officer who quoted Browning at length and then, as if recalling that all was not right with the world, abruptly returned to the technical questions confronting the mission.[33]

In many ways the most interesting trip was the expedition to study the front to the west of Lake Garda. As the party set out in a caravan of automobiles, Palmer felt an exhilarating sense of well-being that made him quite forget his convalescent condition. Here he was being driven through a beautiful countryside in an Italian army vehicle manned by a driver, a mechanic, and a liaison officer, just as if he were personage of great importance. The crew might seem a bit excessive, but the staff car had already shown an alarming tendency to break down on the highway. The wild driving of the Italian chauffeurs was hard on the cars; it was also hard on the passengers. To the American visitors the auto drivers seemed to have something of the same psychology as the Italian aviators; they acted as if under some inner compulsion to prove how fearless they were, taking a positive delight in speeding at breakneck pace up and down winding mountain roads while teetering along the edge of sheer precipices.

If Palmer found that his drivers often left something to be desired, he was more than delighted with the liaison officer assigned to him. In Capt. Prospero Colonna he discovered a kindred soul. As the party drove past Verona and then beyond Lakes Garda and Iseo to reach the alpine front, the colonel learned that his companion was directly descended from one of the leading aristocratic families of Rome. His father's family, the Italian assured his

American friend, was really quite new, going back only five or six hundred years; on the other hand, his wife's family, the Massimo connection, was truly ancient, claiming to date all the way back to the Fabius Maximus of Roman antiquity. The captain carried all this lineage lightly although entitled to style himself Prince Colonna, but what charmed Palmer most was his escort's sense of humor. Far from putting on airs because of his noble ancestors, he regarded them as a frightful collection of brigands. To prove that he meant what he said, he told endless stories about their villainous exploits in many of the medieval towns through which the party passed.

Much to the colonel's distress, he had scarcely begun to enjoy his friendship with Prince Colonna when the liaison officer was threatened with removal. There was a young captain at the Italian headquarters who occupied a most unfortunate and ambiguous position. Son of an American mother married to an Italian prince, the young man held a commission in the Italian army but found himself unable to secure any position of trust since his step-father had strong family connections in Germany.

With the skill of an experienced diplomat, the aspiring captain launched a campaign to take over Colonna's job. First he sought to sweeten up the members of the mission with gifts of fresh butter, a wartime rarity, which he brought in from his family's country estate several times a week. Then he secured a strong letter of commendation from Ambassador Page, who was glad to help the unhappy young man. There would have been no objection to the Italian captain if he had merely offered his services, but when he urged the dismissal of Colonna to make way for himself, he forfeited his opportunity. Lieutenant Pomeroy knew how much pleasure his colonel derived from their association with Colonna, and having studied General Swift at close range, he knew his man well. Carrying in Ambassador Page's letter, he deplored it as a typical example of political meddling. The old general responded according to prediction and denounced the ambassador and all his suggestions. So Colonna remained with the mission, but the gifts of fresh butter stopped coming.[34]

Palmer was amazed at the way the Italian army had recovered its morale since the disaster at Caporetto and was inclined to believe that the position on the Piave could be held. But some of the American officers in Italy felt he was entirely too optimistic.

Among those who had some doubts about the Italian capacity to hold was the colonel's own aide, Pomeroy. It was his duty to secure the daily ration of gasoline allowed by the Italian army for use in the three AEF staff cars that had finally arrived from France for the use of the mission. Lieutenant Pomeroy suggested to General Swift that it might be a good idea to secure a substantial supply of gasoline just in case the Austrians did break through. It would be most awkward, he pointed out, if they were all caught up in a great retreat without gasoline and had to hike south.[35]

General Swift indignantly refused to allow any such request to the Italian authorities; it would undermine that very morale the mission had come into Italy to bolster. So Pomeroy instructed his sergeant to siphon one gallon from the ration provided each day by the Italians and thus accumulate a reserve against a time of disaster. Undoubtedly it was a good thing that the colonel was unaware of the many measures, legitimate or otherwise, his imaginative aide undertook in his behalf.

Even though Palmer believed the Italians would be able to hold along the Piave, he was not at all impressed with their staff work. Most appalling of all was the faulty coordination between the infantry units and their supporting artillery. Again and again he noted instances of excessively long delays between the time the infantry called for artillery support and the time they actually received fire on designated targets. At best the Italian performance made a sorry contrast to the almost mathematical precision demonstrated by the French in laying down rolling box barrages to carefully prescribed specifications.

The American observers were also surprised and even shocked to discover the vast gulf that seemed to separate the officers at the higher headquarters from the troops in the front-line trenches. This overt display of caste was acutely offensive to the visiting Americans, with their deeply ingrained democratic values. It seemed particularly inappropriate for soldiers who had repeatedly shown themselves to be incredibly brave. If the Italian forces had been defeated, it was largely attributable, the American observers believed, to faulty leadership and defective staff work on the part of the very officers who held their men in such contempt.[36]

There were, of course, wide differences in attitude and outlook among American officers, even among the handful comprising the party in Italy, but all these men operated within the democratic presuppositions of the society from which they came. To understand the reaction of the mission to the class consciousness displayed by so many of the Italian officers, one had only to look at the relations of the officers and men comprising the American party at Padua. When, for example, a travelling YMCA unit organized a party for the enlisted men of the American mission, it was taken as a matter of course that the officers would be invited also. As Lieutenant Pomeroy brought in the invitation to this affair, he started to tell General Swift that "the boys" wanted him to attend, but the stiff-backed old regular cut him off sharply, saying "They are men, Lieutenant, not boys." To this Pomeroy replied with a lawyer's deft sense of the appropriate citation that Napoleon had called his troopers "mes enfants."[37] Clearly in the AEF the distance that separated officers and enlisted men was not nearly so great as the distance between an elderly senior officer of the Regular Army and a brash young reservist.

With their survey of the front completed, the AEF mission next visited the more important rear area training installations, gas schools, machine gun schools, and similar centers. For the most part the training was rudimentary at best. On the other hand, when the mission visited a training installation maintained by the British forces in Italy, Palmer found that the British were brimming with ideas and busily experimenting with all manner of advanced techniques for improving staff operations. With unfeigned admiration, he asked for copies of the curriculum and training directives to send off to Langres. To the discerning observer, the contrast between the British and Italian schools was painful indeed.

Although the Italian schools had disappointingly little to offer, Palmer always felt better after a day of driving in an open car through beautiful countryside. But much as he enjoyed these trips, he would have preferred to make them on horseback. He enjoyed this form of exercise immensely and was fully in sympathy with General Pershing's insistence that all officers should be prepared to take to the saddle where necessary.[38] Not every officer shared this enthusiasm. Indeed, there were a number of corpulent generals who regarded Pershing's views on the subject as scarcely less than catastrophic. Nevertheless, if they hoped to command divisions in France, they knew they would have to come to terms with the horse no less than with the adamant general. One unfortunate brigadier discovered that no saddle could be found large enough to accommodate him, so he had to parade before his troops mounted in most unmilitary fashion upon a folded blanket.[39]

For Palmer it was Prince Colonna who made his trips behind the northern front especially rewarding. The captain always managed to find something or someone of interest. On one occasion he had his American friend introduced to one of Garibaldi's many grandsons; another time he organized a memorable dinner party at the famous Cafe Pedrocchi in Padua with the notorious Gabriele d'Annunzio as the guest of honor. Like so many others before and since, Palmer found the poet-politician heady company. But unlike so many, he was not in the least overwhelmed by the fiery Italian patriot. In fact, quite the contrary; as often happened to him in the presence of interesting strangers, something in his makeup induced him to rise to the occasion and appear at his best as a raconteur and generally engaging personality.[40]

This trait of Palmer's was perhaps nowhere better illustrated than on a trip he took with a group of British officers to visit the headquarters of Gen. Sir Herbert Plumer, who then commanded the British forces in Italy. Along the way the party passed through the village of Arquà Petrarca, famous as the home of the poet Petrarch. Palmer insisted that they all stop and visit the house where the great man died. As they strolled through the tiny garden of the poet's house, he carefully plucked a laurel leaf, saying he would send it to his daughter, Mary, as a memento. At this his companions teased him, saying he surely must already have provided his daughter with an impressive collection of botanical specimens.[41] The colonel scarcely seemed to recognize the teasing as such. Part of his indefinable charm was an innocence that apparently extended to the belief that all military officers, as educated men, just naturally shared his enormous enthusiasm for anything remotely concerned with history or literature.

When one of the British officers present remarked on the apparently endless range of Palmer's knowledge, he hastened to disclaim any particular erudition. It was all very simple, he confided. Each night before setting out on an expedition, he did his homework, studying everything he could lay hands upon that would enlarge his understanding of the people and places he expected to visit on the morrow. Much of what he had just told them he admitted, quite guilelessly, that he had learned only recently from Captain Colonna, whose ancestors had been patrons of Petrarch, even providing the very house before which they were then standing.

In the episode at Arquà Petrarca Palmer revealed a great deal about himself. Clearly he was a man without pretense or sham. It is evident, too, that much of the charm that made him such an effective personality came from the catholicity of his tastes and the impressive scope of his intellectual curiosity. But he drove himself relentlessly, filling every off-duty moment with study. Even when avowedly relaxing, he kept up his endless questioning. Little wonder that his mission to Italy turned out to be something less than the rest cure General Harbord had envisioned.

Palmer's first few weeks in Italy were highly beneficial. His frequent letters home became increasingly more confident as his sense of well-being returned. The vigorous outdoor exercise involved in his tour of the front had proved to be an excellent tonic. But when it came time to prepare reports, his progress toward recovery was abruptly checked.[42]

The turning point came early in April 1918; the occasion was the visit Secretary of War Baker paid to the Italian headquarters. When Baker set out on this trip from Chaumont, General Pershing had assigned Col. T. B. Mott, Palmer's friend of long standing, to accompany him. Mott was an exceptionally able officer who, after years of service as a military attaché in Paris, enjoyed a uniquely intimate relation with the French military authorities. He had accompanied the French forces sent into Italy after Caporetto and remained with them as an observer for several months, so he was peculiarly well equipped to advise the Secretary on the military diplomacy of the Italian front.

From his friend "Tibbie" Mott, Palmer heard the latest word on many issues that he had only sensed imperfectly while touring with the mission in Italy. Not least among the matters coming to a boil was one affecting the mission itself. Soon after the American party set out for Rome, there had been some maneuvering by the friends of Gen. Leonard Wood to secure his appointment as head of the AEF mission. But Pershing had no intention of replacing Swift with a man who had already become an acute embarrassment to him. As the ranking officer of the army, Wood had fully expected to be given command of the AEF, so his relations with his erstwhile junior were almost inevitably somewhat strained. Then, when he subsequently reached France as a division commander, the papers gave his exploits and ambitions such play as to leave General Pershing little choice but to ship Wood home.

Ambassador Page, ever anxious to seize an opportunity to present his case for the use of American troops in Italy, invited Wood to come to Italy, but General Pershing flatly refused permission. Such a visit, he declared, was liable to "embarrass General Swift." He might have added, but did not, that such a visit, with all its opportunities for sounding off in public and capturing headlines, was almost certain to embarrass the Commanding General, who was doing everything he could to keep Ambassador Page and the Italians from running off with AEF. General Wood, quite ready to suspect Pershing's motives, believed Swift had been given the job in the first place simply to exclude him.[43]

Palmer counted himself among Wood's friends, yet he enjoyed a close relationship with Pershing, to whom he was completely loyal.[44] As an honorable officer serving under Swift, he wished to be entirely correct in his relations with the head of the mission. Whatever might be his personal opinion of Swift as a diplomat, he entertained a good deal of respect for him as an officer and as a friend. Palmer knew that the easiest course, and in fact the only course open to him, was to maintain a discreet silence. He had worked in the upper echelons of command long enough to realize that his problem was as nothing compared with that of General Pershing.

The episode led Palmer to observe, as he frequently did on subsequent occasions, that a commanding general will be damned no matter what he does. In the postwar years those who sought to fathom the inscrutable Pershing often neglected this truism; they have gathered evidence from men hurt by Pershing's rulings without seeing that hard decisions almost inevitably satisfy none of the parties involved. What appears to be selfish egotism in the commanding general from the perspective of the aggrieved, may look like inescapable necessity when seen from the vantage of the commander himself.[45]

Mott also reported that the Italian drive for large numbers of American troops was far from dead. In fact, as increasing numbers of American divisions arrived in France, the Italians became more exigent in their demands, and Ambassador Page still continued to plead their cause.

General Pershing's response to these continuing pressures sheds a good deal of light on his diplomatic tactics. His first step had been to send an expendable major general and a mission. This effort had been aimed primarily at shaping opinion in command circles of the Italian army. His next step, taking Ambassador Page's advice almost literally in at least one respect, was to send a regimental band. This move, aimed primarily at the civilian population, turned out to be highly efficacious. The band held concerts before large and enthusiastic crowds, giving the impression that vast numbers of American soldiers were swarming up the peninsula.[46] Many Italians were amazed to learn after the Armistice that no more than a single show-the-flag regiment of Americans actually reached the Italian trenches, and these had not arrived until midsummer, 1918, by which time more than a million men had joined the AEF in France.[47]

General Pershing also stalled for time. After letting a month elapse before answering one of Ambassador Page's urgent requests, the general blandly wrote that the ambassador's letter seemed to have been "somewhat delayed in transmission." He had also deferred any decision, he explained, until he could consult with the Secretary of War, who was soon to visit Chaumont. This was literally true, for Pershing had every reason to want Baker to hear his version of the problem before the secretary heard a very different account from the ambassador.[48]

The official AEF position rested upon both principle and expediency.[49] Any dispersion of force that weakened the AEF in the presence of its main enemy ran counter to one of the most ancient of military axioms. At the same time, General Pershing's desire to preserve the integrity of the AEF represented far more than selfish personal ambition. The commanding general was without doubt intensely ambitious, but he also wanted to build up the instrument of command, not only the General Staff but the whole hierarchy of leaders for army, corps, and division. Unless the AEF were preserved as an integral organization, American officers would never acquire the experience in handling those large formations of troops virtually unknown in the peacetime army. While General Pershing will remain an enigmatic figure, many of his actions take on a fuller meaning if it is recognized that the long-range development of the American army and its command structure was one of his conscious objectives, scarcely less pressing than victory itself.

If he gave way to the Italians, Pershing would open the door to similar concessions to other nations. His appraisal was certainly sound, but events did not yield gracefully to reason. During the week before Baker and Mott came to Padua, the long awaited spring offensive of the German forces had burst upon the French and British armies in France to send them reeling back in a major retreat. In this crisis Pershing abandoned his principles and offered American manpower to help stem the tide, even if it meant employing units as small as regiments or companies within the Allied armies.[50]

Now the mission in Italy could no longer argue from principle that diversions of strength were impossible. The Italians now had reason to feel that if their demands were importunate enough, American troops could be secured. In this context the decision was reached to send an American regiment to Italy. Because General Pershing had diplomatically suggested that this token might eventually be built up to a division, it became the task of the AEF mission to see that the Italians did not convert this suggestion into a pledge.

The real solution of the Italian problem as Colonel Mott saw it was not to send in large numbers of American troops but to get more effective use of the

Italian forces.[51] Palmer's observations along the front had only confirmed what Mott had reported earlier. Army commanders in Italy seemed to think largely in terms of infantry rather than in terms of teams in which the several arms functioned together in coordinated operations. They customarily massed large numbers of men in hideously exposed positions on the front, in sharp contrast to the prevailing practice in France, where thinly held forward trenches masked the main line of resistance.

The Italians' reliance on infantry was reflected in the absence of any really effective staff organization to insure cooperation among the various arms. Such essential technical skills as photo interpretation and aerial spotting for artillery fire seemed to be left largely to chance. What is more, the Italians appeared to have little or no conception of counterbattery fire, which had been developed to a high art if not an exact science on the Western Front.

Training, Mott and Palmer agreed, was the obvious remedy for the Italian army. But the Italians would bitterly resent the slightest suggestion that their officers were in any way inferior to the officers in the other Allied armies. Even after the disaster at Caporetto—perhaps because of it—the Italians were reluctant to admit their defects. The members of the AEF mission had attended a lecture by an officer at the Italian Supreme Command who assured them that the collapse had resulted from a chance Austrian shell burst that had destroyed the communications network of a field headquarters. The ensuing absence of orders, he declared, had touched off a panic at the front.[52]

Colonel Mott proposed a single Allied command for all the forces in Italy. By putting the King or his noble cousin, the popular Duke of Aosta, in command, the arrangement would be acceptable to the Italians; a mixed staff of Allied officers would represent all the nations present. Allied officers could thus infiltrate the Italian Supreme Command and put over whatever program of staff training seemed desirable. If only they could get a majority of the officers to take three or four months of training along the lines of the American staff college at Langres, it should be possible, he believed, to convert Italy's fifty divisions into a formidable striking force.[53]

Unfortunately, Mott's scheme threatened to raise political difficulties. Far more feasible was a plan he had picked up from the French forces in Italy. They established a staff school of their own at Verona and then offered to accept Italian officers as students if their own officers were accorded the privilege of attending Italian schools. The French authorities knew perfectly well that there were no such schools but that from sheer pride the Italians would soon establish some rather than admit as much. If all the Allies played this game, Mott believed, it might be possible to achieve a remarkable reform in the character of Italian staff training.

Even if they tricked the Italians into setting up schools, the French had no assurance that the training given conformed to the best available, so they resorted to another sly maneuver. Gen. Marie Emile Fayolle prepared elaborate operations orders, far more elaborate than his own highly trained troops actually required, and sent coordination copies to the Italian high command in the hope that they would be sufficiently impressed to copy the format for general use. To make this game of charades more effective, even the Americans played along. Colonel Fox Conner, Palmer's successor as chief of Operations, received a copy of General Fayolle's order at Chaumont. There, well primed by Mott, he grandly announced that it was so good he was having it reproduced and distributed to all headquarters officers as an instructive model. The Italians were left to draw the obvious inference that officers of the AEF were not too vain to learn from the French.[54]

Probably no argument on the need for staff training was more persuasive than the success of the Allied units serving in Italy. The remarkable advances—and low casualties—of the French at Mount Tomba, in contrast with repeated Italian failures, led many Italian officers to take notice of Allied methods. Even before the Italians had been induced to set up staff schools, at least two division commanders admitted that they were using General Fayolle's operational orders as models.[55]

A few isolated instances, of course, did not spell success for the French scheme. True, the Italians had set up some staff schools, but they had not ordered any significant number of staff officers to attend. The real problem, as Mott and Palmer saw it, was how to influence the Italian high command without seeming to do so. A good example might help, so General Swift gamely volunteered to attend one of the Italian courses for whatever favorable impression this might create. But somehow the visiting officers must not only persuade the Italians to send more of their officers to school, but also find ways to insure that the instruction offered was the best available.[56]

Palmer greatly admired Col. T. B. Mott as an able and gifted officer. Without Mott's insights he would have understood far less of what he saw in Italy. But precisely because Mott could focus the issues so clearly, he started Palmer worrying again.

The depression that soon engulfed him descended with remarkable speed. On the very day Secretary Baker arrived in Italy with his party, Dr. Patterson, as the medical member of the mission, had sent General Pershing a most hopeful report on Palmer's progress toward recovery. Almost immediately after Patterson wrote, however, Palmer began to show alarming symptoms. He fretted about his loss of memory and avoided making even the most trivial decisions until at last it became evident that nothing short of drastic action would restore the patient to health.[57]

After many consultations between Patterson and Swift, it was finally decided that the colonel would only respond to several months of sick leave in the United States. Swift wrote explaining the situation to Pershing, concluding with the observation that he regarded Palmer as one of the army's best men and would consider his departure a distinct loss.[58] The colonel had no choice but to accept the decision made for him; he would have to go home. He was a failure.

30 Maine Woods Rest Cure

The decision to send Palmer back to the United States filled him with a crushing sense of defeat. His career was finished. Yet somehow he couldn't just quit; he was far too much of a soldier to do that. He would take Patterson's advice and get away from it all. He would go back to the States, not to Washington but to the Maine woods, where he could forget the war and his worries and try to make himself over again.

During the last few days the colonel spent in Padua, his friends rallied about with a round of farewell dinners at Stoppato's, one of the more famous restaurants of the city, where they sat beneath an Austrian cannon ball imbedded in a wall, symbolic reminder from an earlier war of the continuing Italian struggle against invaders from beyond the Alps. The officers of the Italian headquarters were no less thoughtful; just before the colonel's departure they arranged a little ceremony to present him with an official theater ribbon to show that he had been under fire on the Piave front.

The next ten days were a memory he ever afterward wished to forget. There was the bleak train journey back to France, a hurried visit to Chaumont for a series of examinations at the army hospital, a brief conference with General Pershing, and then the long ride across France to Brest, where he boarded the army transport *Great Northern* on 11 May 1918. Whatever shred of comfort he may have found on the voyage home came from a letter delivered to him just before the transport sailed. It was from the ever-thoughtful Harbord, who had just stepped down from his position as Chief of Staff to take command of a Marine brigade in the 2nd Division. The letter concluded in characteristic fashion:

> I wish to say at parting that it has been one of the very great regrets of all
> of us that your health has given way. I had high hopes that you were to

be identified with the best of our activities. I know that General Pershing feels the same way and that if you can get back in good condition and get to France, command and opportunity await you. Command, opportunity and health are all you need.[1]

It was characteristic of Harbord that he also voiced a word of encouragement from General Pershing. Although no longer officially his chief's alter ego, the habit had become ingrained for him to articulate those thoughts the general himself found it so difficult to express, even to his most trusted subordinates.

When the *Great Northern* reached Hoboken, New Jersey, Palmer was suffering from a profound depression. As he stood there, fighting unsuccessfully to keep down the wave of awful despair sweeping over him, a quiet voice from the gloom beside him asked, "Is it Colonel Palmer?"

Up stepped one of the sentries. It was Sgt. James Shine, who remembered him from his Fort Grant days out in Arizona more than twenty years before. Gratefully he let the sergeant take him in charge, and in short order he was comfortably ensconced in a Pullman bound for Washington. In looking back later he was inclined to regard Sergeant Shine's providential appearance as a fine illustration of that spirit of community that so typified the old army. The gulf that then separated officers and men was wide indeed, yet from prolonged association on isolated posts came individual ties of deep and genuine friendship. It pleased the colonel to recall that it was Sergeant Shine, of all people, who had rescued him in his distress. Twenty odd years before at Fort Grant, the sergeant had been in difficulties and the Palmers had befriended him with a good deal of kindly attention, which won his lifelong devotion.[2]

In Washington the colonel remained only long enough to pick up his wife and daughter, Polly, and to secure suitable fishing tackle before setting off for Maine. The presence of his family did much to revive his spirits, but it wasn't until they traveled north from Portland, up the Androscoggin River, and took the narrow-guage railroad to the Rangeley Lake district that the magic of the Maine woods really began to take effect.[3]

At Loon Lake, just north of Rangeley on the headwaters of the Dead River, the family rented a rough cabin at York's Camps. The days that followed were almost perfectly suited to fulfill Dr. Patterson's prescription. There were no deadlines to meet, no hard decisions to make, no tensions, nothing that *had* to be done. Yet each day brought its measure of adventure and excitement, the lake trout fighting hard for life, the red fox suddenly confronted at a turn in the trail, or the unexpected discovery of a gull's nest on a rocky outcrop in the lake far inland from the sea. Such episodes as these made each day memorable in its own way.

Not least among the colonel's joys was the delight he found in sharing his fisherman's lore with his daughter Polly. It flattered him immensely that she proved a willing and apt pupil, for he had seriously doubted whether a sixteen-year-old girl would take kindly to a summer in the Maine woods. His doubt vanished the first time they went trolling; she hooked a big trout and then played him skillfully for nearly two hours. To his pleasure as a teacher was added the still greater pride of a parent.

When trolling on Loon Lake began to pall, the colonel ventured out on expeditions to nearby streams and ponds. On one occasion he joined a fellow vacationer, a Dr. L. A. Van Kleeck of Manhasset, Long Island. As it turned out their morning's association proved momentous. The doctor was a fly fisherman who urged the merits of this exacting sport upon his new-found friend. As an old-fashioned bait fisherman from the cornbelt, the colonel looked upon the fly as something of an affectation. Sensing his indifference, the doctor undertook to prescribe as a physician. "Your illness," he said, "simply means that some of your brain cells are tired out. If you will get a fly rod and learn to use it, I assure you another set of brain cells will soon be so busy the old ones will have a complete rest."[4]

Palmer's best teacher proved to be a grizzled old native guide named Ben Gile. After a lifetime in the Maine woods, he was a man of few words and deliberate habits. Nothing seemed to worry him, and he couldn't be hurried. He and the colonel would rise before dawn and set off to hike for miles through the forest to try their luck with the brook trout in a choice stream known only to Ben. And if along the way they stirred up a ruffed grouse and her brood, the pleasure each felt in watching only drew them closer without the necessity for words. Ben knew where whole fields of wild strawberries could be found, and if the morning's catch was good, he knew how to cook trout over an open fire to provide a succulent lunch miles from camp. Best of all, he knew that fly fishing is a discipline that can never be fully mastered. With infinite patience for hours at a stretch, he coached Dr. Van Kleeck's new convert in the rudiments of this fine art.

For the colonel the climax of his leave came with a five-day expedition he and his guide took to the headwaters of the Kennebago River. Alternating hiking and canoeing, they fished their way up to the northwest corner of the state just below the Canadian border, trying virtually every promising stream and pond as they went. It was a wonderful trip. It was while out on this expedition that Palmer suddenly realized he had regained his health. After hiking five miles along a rough trail over broken ground carrying a heavy canoe, he was surprised to find himself not in the least tired. But what was infinitely more important, he had not a care in the world. Scarcely six weeks had passed since he had stumbled down the gangplank in Hoboken a beaten man, yet now he was sure he had recovered.

Once convinced that he was indeed in sturdy good health, the colonel threw himself into the task of getting back to France and into a position of responsibility. True, he was still technically a member of the AEF, though on leave in the United States. This had been General Pershing's parting kindness. But he understood perfectly well that the general had little reason at the time to expect anything in the way of a recovery on his part. Now the problem was how best to convey the word back to Chaumont that he really had recovered and was anxious to return to duty. To General Pershing he wrote simply to report his recovery. To Harbord, who had just been promoted to major general, he wrote with more candor, frankly revealing his fear that the Commander in Chief would have forgotten all about his erstwhile officer now lost in the Maine woods. As it turned out, he was on his way back to France by the time his friends could reply, but their answers would have gratified him. Busy as they were, they found time to write reassuringly that with his restoration to health, opportunity lay ahead for him.[5]

When the colonel realized he was fit for duty, nothing would do but a hurried return to Washington, where he could settle the family before sailing for France. If he had any question about how thoroughly he had recovered, an encounter he had during his brief stay in the capital should have put his doubts at rest. Shortly before he was scheduled to sail, he was striding down Connecticut Avenue, full of a sense of his own vigor and well-being, when he chanced upon the Chief of Staff, General P. C. March. Saluting smartly, he greeted the general pleasantly, only to be rebuffed with the acid rejoinder, "Palmer, you're out of uniform!" The censure, he understood, was aimed at his Sam Browne belt and shoulder strap, the hallmark of an officer in the AEF but specifically forbidden to those in General March's jurisdiction. The colonel found himself blandly replying without hesitation, "General March, I am wearing the uniform prescribed for a member of General Pershing's command."[6] Hearing this, the general stalked off without another word. Only later, when he learned of the rift that had developed between March and Pershing during the summer, did Palmer understand the meaning of General March's odd behavior. But then, armored with his newly restored self-confidence, he refused to be disturbed by the episode.

On 19 September 1918 the colonel went to a military pier at the port of embarkation in Hoboken. There he bid farewell to his family at a heavily guarded gate and went directly on board his transport, the former *Kaiser Wilhelm IV*. He was ready for the wars, but the transport wasn't; nearly two days were to pass before the vessel finally cleared the harbor. Meanwhile the colonel was left to think about his family, so near at hand and yet so unapproachably far away. As he thought back over the summer just past, he realized that it had been in many ways the most rewarding leave he had ever taken. He had regained his health, but more than that, he saw the summer as one of the happiest times of his life. The long unhurried days in the wilderness had drawn him closer in understanding companionship with his wife, while endowing his daughter with a love of nature she would never lose.

Although the crossing was uneventful, it was a busy one. With a new resolve to keep fit and avoid overwork, the colonel joined a group of fellow officers in daily sessions of vigorous exercise on deck and even went so far as to allow himself time for a rubber of bridge after dinner. But for the most part, and far more typically, he laid out a schedule of hard study. There had been a more or less continual refinement in the divisional tables of organization and equipment in the AEF ever since Operations staff had first grappled with this problem on the *Baltic* during the previous summer, and as Palmer knew from his work with the staff schools, effective command at the level of brigade, division, and corps rested upon an intimate knowledge of every component in a formation. In battle one had to know without query such details as whether the brigade machine gun battalion had three or four companies and at precisely what echelon one found a mortar platoon; a good leader must visualize almost without effort the uttermost implications of the orders he issued.[7]

As the convoy neared Brest a new misfortune struck. The transport had scarcely reached port when the colonel was beset with a burning fever. A flu epidemic had broken out, and several ships in the convoy had suffered considerable loss of life. When Palmer finally reached shore he was running a high temperature and feeling desperately ill, but he was determined to let nothing, nothing at all, stop him this time. So he dragged himself to the train and set out across France for Chaumont, where he reported for duty miserably sick but still on his feet.[8]

31   In Action on the Front

Although both Pershing and McAndrew were absent from Chaumont when Palmer arrived, he was elated to find that they had not forgotten him. The Chief of Staff had left word that he was to be given command of a brigade when he reported for duty. But would McAndrew's instructions be honored if he entered the hospital, where he belonged? Since this seemed hardly likely, he persuaded his old friend Henry Beeuwkes of the Medical Corps to mark him down simply as "sick in quarters." He could only hope that his fever would subside and he would be back on his feet before this final opportunity slipped from his grasp.

When at last a long "make list" of brigadiers appeared, Palmer was chagrined to discover that his name was not included. The best he could look for now was command of a regiment. Then his fortune changed; on the morning of 11 October 1918 an officer called from headquarters to ask how soon he could be ready to take command of a brigade on the front. He was still in bed with a fever, but he knew it was now or never. Soon afterward he was speeding northward in a staff car toward First Army headquarters at Souilly, his illness entirely forgotten.[1]

The ancient *mairie* where General Pershing received him when he reached Souilly was already familiar. Here only a year earlier they had come to observe General Guillaumat's French Second Army in its successful push in the "Mort Homme" area beyond Verdun. Then they had been visitors from a headquarters without an army; now General Pershing had at his disposal not one but two armies, each comprising several corps. The big difference in Palmer's eyes, however, was not just a matter of size—more than a million men were engaged in the First Army offensive along the Meuse-Argonne front—but a matter of control.

A year ago they had all been struggling to pull together a rudimentary staff; now General Pershing presided over a hierarchy of staffs well enough organized to coordinate five corps and twenty divisions in a single operation along some thirty miles of front. As if to demonstrate this progress, Pershing's First Army Chief of Staff, Brig. Gen. Hugh Drum, invited his erstwhile superior to attend a briefing he was about to conduct for Malin Craig, A. W. Bjornstad, and W. B. Burtt, each a brigadier and each the chief of staff of an army corps.

Here was evidence that General Pershing understood the functions of a staff as no American commander ever had before; here was the triumph of all those dedicated officers—Arthur L. Wagner, John F. Morrison, James Franklin Bell, Eben Swift Jr. and others—who had worked for a generation to perfect the conception of the general staff as an instrument of command. Except for an ominous rumble to the north, they might have thought they were back at Leavenworth. The technique and the talk were the same—only now Drum spoke for General Pershing and not for General "A," and the umpire this time would be the god of battles.[2]

General Drum's briefing gave Palmer his first inkling of the part he was to play. He had been told that he would command the 58th Brigade in the 29th Division, but just where these fitted into the picture, he had only the vaguest idea. The First Army, Drum explained, lay astride the Meuse with three U.S. corps on the west bank and two French corps on the east bank some eight or ten miles above Verdun. The army's strategic objective was the main lateral German supply line, a railroad running through Sedan. Although the major American advances were planned for the west bank of the Meuse, an elaborate feint had been staged in the Belfort area, and immediately east of the river, a heavy attack had been unleashed at the hinge or pivot of the enemy's defenses north of Verdun. The Germans would feel compelled to concentrate their artillery and mobile reserves there rather than in the area where First Army expected to make its greatest gains.[3]

When Palmer saw where his brigade was to operate, he felt a certain grim satisfaction. The 29th Division was assigned as an element of the French XVII Corps on the right bank of the Meuse, in the very area where the enemy could least afford to give ground. It was flattering to be entrusted with such an obviously difficult assignment; on the other hand, the considerable scope for failure that the situation afforded was not to be ignored. General Drum described the enemy's successive lines of entrenchments and strong points, the *Brabanter Stellung,* the *Hagen,* the *Volker,* the *Etzel* and the *Kriemhild Stellung.* As he considered these obstacles, Palmer reflected that it was not going to be easy to make his reputation as a combat commander.

Before retiring Palmer gathered all the information he could about the 29th Division. The mere fact that it was a National Guard division suggested many questions he would want to ask before he could feel at home in his assignment. The 29th was called the Blue and Gray Division because it had originally been organized from Guard units on both sides of the Mason and Dixon line. Of its two infantry brigades, the 57th was made up of guardsmen from New Jersey and Delaware, while the 58th which he would command came from Virginia and Maryland. Although the division had been assembled in August 1917, its training had been seriously hampered by repeated reorganizations and replacements. Some of the latter, including many draftees from New York who spoke no English, had reached the division only a few days before it sailed for France.

The most distressing information about the 29th Division had to do with its fire power. Very little if any real training had been accomplished in the United States with grenades, automatic rifles, and trench mortars. And although the troops had trained with Springfield rifles, just before sailing they had been issued Enfields.[4] Some of these deficiencies had been partially corrected by a vigorous training program in France, but the division had never had any extended exercises with its organic artillery. Palmer learned that the 29th had entered the current offensive accompanied by artillery from the 83rd Division; there had been no opportunity whatsoever to perfect a team in which the individuals concerned knew one another personally.[5]

The next morning the colonel arrived at Vacherauville, a village on the right bank of the Meuse. There, in a heavily sandbagged structure so well camouflaged that it seemed to be a part of the bleak hills along the river, he was cordially received by Maj. Gen. Charles G. Morton, the division commander.[6] Although the division commander was one of the senior officers of the Regular Army, Palmer knew him only slightly; their paths had crossed briefly years before out in Utah, when Morton had turned up at Fort Douglas while serving as Inspector General. Pershing had described him as an able, austere officer who was exceedingly strict in military discipline. Since Pershing himself had a reputation for strictness that was something of a byword, this appraisal had an ominous sound. Palmer discovered that Morton was thoroughly disliked by many of the Guard officers in the 29th Division. While they were willing to concede that strict discipline was necessary, they resented the apparent relish with which the general castigated both officers and men serving under him.[7]

There were a great many factors contributing to the somewhat strained relations existing in the organization. General Morton and many if not most of the Guard officers in the division had approached the task of building a division from entirely different points of view. For the general, a Regular deeply imbued with the ideal of unquestioning obedience, the goal was an impersonal machine, an organization of superb staying power, capable of continued aggressive action even while sustaining the heaviest casualties. From the very beginning he had inaugurated a regime of training that pushed men to the limits of their endurance—and beyond—spiritually as well as physically. Most of the guardsmen, on the other hand, came to the division with a civilian point of view. When General Morton announced that he intended to impose "discipline such as the Regular Army has never known and the National Guard has never dreamed of," many guardsmen were inclined to see this threat as clear evidence of a sadistic fanaticism.[8]

In time both officers and men in the 29th came to appreciate Morton's rigorous discipline. He made soldiers out of them; this they demonstrated in battle. Until then, however, there were many who believed that the general was an utterly ruthless professional officer motivated at least in part by a desire to "smash the Guard" once and for all. A long procession of officers had already been relieved of their commands. While it was true that the general was entirely relentless in dismissing officers who failed to measure up to his exacting standards, much of his alleged hostility toward the National Guard stemmed from considerations quite beyond his control. This was certainly the case when the War Department issued new tables of organization during the summer of 1917 in response to General Pershing's recommendations calling for square divisions to replace the existing triangular divisions. The revised tables consolidated many famous National Guard units without regard to their state origins, and a large number of officers were left without commands. This was none of General Morton's doing, but as the individual at the summit of the divisional pyramid of authority, he took the blame.[9]

If General Morton was merciless in his treatment of Guard officers, it was only too true that there were many elements in the Guard inviting his anti-pathy. He was understandably incensed when a few disgruntled individuals had him subjected to severe political pressure when the division was in the process of reorganization. Even more unfortunate was the political influence that made it difficult for him to dismiss Guard officers, especially those of high rank, when they had proved to be thoroughly incompetent. As Palmer heard the story, one of General Morton's senior commanders, an intimate friend and protégé of the governor who had appointed him, had presented a most vexatious case. This soldier-politician surrounded himself with cronies who were sadly inefficient in the field. Not until the division reached France did General Morton feel sufficiently free from political pressure to clean house, so he was still weeding out ineffectual officers when the division was committed to battle.[10]

Because most of those dismissed were guardsmen, it was easy to infer that the general was hostile to such officers. This was simply not so. Indeed, when Palmer asked about the regimental commanders who would be his principal subordinates, the general declared that one of them, Col. Milton A. Reckord, a National Guard officer commanding the 115th Infantry, was the finest colonel he had ever known in all his army experience. As subsequent events were to reveal, this flattering opinion was fully justified; Colonel Reckord was the only regimental commander in the division who went through the entire war without being replaced.[11]

General Morton was no less exacting in his treatment of regulars. In fact, the brigade commander Palmer replaced was a regular who had proved lamentably deficient when it came to leading a large formation into battle. When his brigade was thrown against the German lines across the Meuse, he had shown a complete lack of appreciation of the need for detailed operational orders to coordinate the movement of his assault battalions, their supporting fire, their supply lines, and so on. In short, he had demonstrated little comprehension of the complex staff work that had become an inherent part of modern command. He had been, as General Morton declared, unfit in every respect.[12]

While Palmer listened, it occurred to him that there was something ironic in the general's condemnation of faulty staff work. It had been intimated at First Army that Morton was a remarkable disciplinarian but knew next to nothing about the use of a staff. He was of that older generation of officers who had not gone to Leavenworth, so he lacked technical training in this area. However, since GHQ was well aware of this, he had been provided with a well-trained chief of staff, Col. Sydney A. Cloman. An officer of wide experience, Cloman had served on the War Department General Staff, had put in a tour as a military attaché in Russia, and just before joining the 29th Division had taken the course at Langres, so he was well equipped to complement the general's aptitudes and limitations.[13]

Colonel Cloman led Palmer to the division operations office, where he tried to explain in the few minutes at his disposal the role of the 29th in the battle then in progress. When First Army called for an advance up the east bank of the Meuse, the job fell to the French XVII Corps, which included the U.S. 33rd and 29th Divisions, as well as the French 18th, 26th and 10th Colonial Divisions, deployed in that order from west to east, each with a front of one or two miles. In the initial river crossing of 8 October, the 58th Brigade of the 29th had distinguished itself, Cloman said, by advancing further than any of the other units, French or American, participating in the assault.

In spite of faulty staff work at brigade, the troops had overrun the first two lines of enemy entrenchments and swept on at some points as much as a mile beyond. But formidable difficulties lay ahead: this was more than evident when Cloman handed his visitor a map of the sector in which he was to operate. This splendid example of French cartography from the mobile print shops of the XVII Corps had entered upon it every detail of the enemy's defenses that could be detected by aerial photography.[14] A cursory inspection of the map revealed that the enemy occupied a series of heavily wooded ridges, broken by numerous steep-sided ravines and interspersed here and there with large farms surrounded by cleared fields. The position was ideally suited to defense; the woods gave ample concealment, while the open farm land afforded a clear field of fire especially suited to automatic weapons. Moreover, the whole area was provided with a system of narrow-gauge tracks that made it possible for the Germans to bring heavy loads of supplies and ammunition all the way up to their front line. The attacking forces had left their railhead far behind. Their very success in the first three days of battle had pushed them so far into enemy territory that the problem of supply was becoming increasingly acute.

Only one road led to the front in the division sector, and for much of its length even this was swept by shell fire directed by enemy observers on the hills ahead. When Palmer remarked that it might prove difficult to push down this single road with a division of 28,000 men or even the 20,000 men comprising the rifle companies and machine gun battalions of its forward elements, Colonel Cloman reminded him that he was using paper figures. The 29th had entered the October offensive with a total strength somewhat under 24,000, and casualties since than had cut the total still further.[15] With this admonishment, the division staff chief wished his visitor good luck and excused himself.

As Palmer climbed into his staff car for the last leg of his journey, he suddenly realized that he was on his own. Even though his brigade had been reduced by casualties to less than 7,000 men, as Cloman had warned, that still gave him a force fully half the size of the army Winfield Scott had led into Mexico. Would he make good with such a brigade? His reflections were interrupted by the sound of shell bursts unpleasantly close. His driver had turned away from the river at the village of Brabant-sur-Meuse and was now moving north along the narrow road that led toward the division front. Since it was evident that the Germans were searching this highway with accurate artillery fire, speculations on his new command seemed distinctly out of place. Only a few days before, one of his contemporaries, a brigadier who had set out confidently from First Army, had been killed by shell fire before he even reached his new assignment.[16]

Palmer's arrival at the headquarters of the 58th Brigade was something less than the formal transfer of authority he had anticipated. He had moved only a short distance from his car toward the abandoned German dugout that served as a command post, when an approaching shell came screaming toward him. With an instinct nourished by frequent practice on the Italian front, he dove headlong into the yawning entrance. He landed inside sprawling face down at the feet of a somewhat startled brigade staff, as the explosion demolished the auto he had just quit.[17]

The first task was to take stock of his resources at hand. The brigade staff was a makeshift group of willing but largely untrained men. Even the position of brigade adjutant, his principal subordinate, was filled by an untrained and inexperienced battalion officer hastily drafted to substitute for a casualty. If the capabilities and limitations of his immediate staff were unknown, his two regiments lying somewhere up front were all the more so. Except in a general way, he really had no idea just how his troops were deployed. How had his regimental commanders placed the three battalions each had at his disposal? His map showed him the approximate location of his two machine gun battalions, but were they really well sited to meet a counterattack? Where were the sixteen rolling field kitchens of each regiment; were the men on the front getting hot food? Nearly 400 horses and mules were authorized for each regiment; how many of these animals were still fit for use after five days of battle?

Palmer knew he could find answers to most of his questions, but there was no time for leisurely education. The brigade had stalled in the middle of an engagement. He had been sent in to get things moving again; the division commander wanted action. Since it was already dark he couldn't survey the front for himself, but he could do the next best thing and summon his regimental and battalion commanders for a conference.[18]

When the unit commanders were finally assembled around the map table in the brigade command post, Palmer asked each one in turn to indicate the position of his troops and comment on their condition. Muddy, wet, and weary after five days of continued strain, the officers were hollow-eyed from want of sleep. It was easy to imagine the state of the riflemen lying in rain-filled shell craters. Fatigue alone had been a major factor in slowing down the advance; moreover, all the assault companies had suffered heavy casualties. One company in the 115th Infantry had lost all its officers and was presently commanded by the first sergeant. Ammunition had become a serious problem. One officer reported that during the previous day the machine gun company supporting his battalion had been limited to a total of 800 rounds, scarcely enough for a single gun. By way of contrast he recalled finding some 20,000 rounds in one of the German machine gun positions the division had taken a day or two earlier. Some of the other officers present mentioned the need for a larger supply of grenades. These had proved extremely valuable in cleaning out strong points in the enemy line and, the two issued to each trained grenadier were nowhere near enough.[19]

The enemy positions encountered in the division attack toward the Bois de la Grande Montagne were far more strongly organized than had been anticipated. Aerial photographs had failed to reveal a large number of machine gun positions of reinforced concrete that had remained undamaged even after a lengthy barrage by divisional artillery. Heavier guns would be needed to knock out these centers of resistance, but Palmer warned them not to expect help from Corps. All Corps artillery was being used to assist the divisions to the right of the 29th where little or no progress had been made since the beginning of the offensive.[20]

An immediate continuation of the assault was out of the question. It would require another day or two to build up an adequate supply of ammunition and to arrange for the right kind of artillery support. There was little need for a brigade order beyond suggesting a consolidation of the present line against whatever counterattacks the enemy might launch. Just before dismissing the assembled group, however, Palmer made an effort to remedy a serious defect he had inherited when he took command: there was no brigade reserve. If the enemy counterattacked anywhere along the front, there would be nothing to bring up to plug any breaks that might develop. Fortunately Colonel Reckord of the 115th had prudently withheld a regimental reserve, and this Palmer borrowed for the time being, apologizing for seeming to penalize the colonel's foresight by taking temporary control of his reserve.[21]

Colonel Reckord made an excellent impression on Palmer, and everything he subsequently learned about him served only to confirm this initial judgment. Here was a thoroughly competent citizen officer. He had been seasoned by extensive experience with the Guard on the Mexican Border in 1916, and later, before joining the 29th Division in the summer of 1917, he had gone to Fort Sill to attend a special infantry officer's course not unlike the basic course later taught at Fort Benning. Then, after the division reached France he had been sent to take the staff course at Langres. As a consequence he knew how to handle a regiment and understood what staff work was all about. But more than this, he was a gifted leader. As one of his junior officers observed, he could censure a man without making him feel like a whipped dog. It was easy to see why General Morton held him in such high regard.[22]

The next morning Palmer was awakened by the sickening thuds of heavy shells exploding nearby. The air in his dugout was foul and his bedroll uncomfortable, but he experienced an almost overwhelming desire to stay right where he was, deep underground and surrounded by a thick layer of reinforced concrete. Appealing as this notion was, he knew that he must reconnoiter his entire front. Even the most thoughtful perusal of the map was no substitute for personal observation. Only the night before one of his officers had reported the difficulties his battalion had run into in attempting to infiltrate some dense woods shown on the map, and the woods had turned out to be a sparse growth in nearly open ground. Then, too, it was important for a new commander to show himself to his forward units. From his conversations with front-line troops in Italy, he knew how easy it was for men lying in the mud out near the enemy to feel entirely forgotten by the high command. Above all, he had to get the feel of the terrain; he had to get some sense of where and how his orders would be carried forward, how long it would take to go from brigade to regiment and from regiment to battalion.[23]

Escorted by each of his regimental commanders in turn, Palmer set out to inspect the positions of his whole brigade. Not content with visiting every battalion and company command post, he toured the entire front, even crawling out to see the men stationed as pickets in shell holes well beyond the main line of resistance. As one of his officers subsequently remarked, what impressed the troops most was Palmer's modesty; instead of trying to cover up his ignorance by issuing a lot of arbitrary and impossible orders, he asked questions. This modesty and his obvious willingness to share the dangers and discomforts of the front won him their lasting respect, the essential foundation of effective leadership.[24]

That Palmer's concern for his men was genuine and not just a pose consciously assumed for effect is evident from the letters he hastily penciled from his dugout. Repeatedly he agonized over their sufferings as they crouched in the rain and mud, continually harassed by shell-fire. Of the dead he wrote, "It is sad enough to see the poor Fritzes lying out with their faces to the sky, and it is sadder still to see our own men." After finding one of his troopers dead upon the road, he told of having an orderly search for some identification. He found it on a recent letter—Private Harry Sunshine. "What a pathetic name for such a boy."[25]

The colonel's orientation tour was not confined to his own front; getting to know the units on either flank was also important. Each had exchanged liaison officers with the 58th Brigade, but this was no substitute for personal contact. So Palmer set out on foot to visit his neighboring brigades. By coincidence both turned out to be led by old friends, on the left Brig. Gen. Edward L. King with a brigade in the 33rd Division and on the right Brig. Gen. Leroy S. Upton, a contemporary at the Military Academy, who had been given command of the 57th, or New Jersey and Delaware, Brigade of the 29th Division only a few weeks earlier. Since both were friends of long standing, the briefest sort of visits sufficed.[26]

Back again at his own command post, the colonel was delighted to find that a replacement had arrived to take over as brigade adjutant. The newcomer was Capt. L. G. Thomas, the son of Augustus Thomas the dramatist, whose plays were then popular in the States. The colonel had first met this capable young officer at Langres, where he had been one of General McAndrew's aides. Since then he had taken the Staff College course, where he had been trained in the duties he was about to assume. Thomas's assignment may have been only a coincidence, but Palmer was inclined to regard it as another example of McAndrew's solicitous concern, for both of them. A well-trained adjutant would free the brigade commander from a welter of paper work, allowing the commander to exert his personal leadership where it was most needed.[27]

The new adjutant had hardly been introduced when a runner brought in a divisional order calling for an attack the following morning, 15 October 1918, on the German positions along the ridge of Grande Montagne. Little or no time remained to shape up proper brigade assault orders if the subordinate units down the line were to make the dispositions required before the jump-off hour. When the order was at last sent forward, Palmer was acutely conscious of its imperfections. A multitude of details and refinements had been omitted, but he could scarcely do otherwise. So he turned in for a few hours of sleep against the inevitable strains of the morrow.[28]

The assault planned for the next day was almost entirely dictated by the nature of the terrain and the positions already held by the two regiments of the brigade. Each occupied a front of about three quarters of a mile, running along an east-west axis, but unfortunately the two units were not aligned. On the left the 115th, operating almost entirely in dense woods, had pushed half a mile further than the 116th on the right, which had been brought to a standstill when it emerged from the woods at the edge of an immense clearing, Molleville Farm, which afforded an unobstructed field of fire for the many enemy machine guns concealed in the heavily forested hills beyond. As a consequence, each regiment had been forced to extend a flank through a right-angle turn to cover the gap, and the north-south link where the two units joined was completely enfiladed, since it lay perpendicular to the enemy's line of entrenchments.[29]

The first order of business was to bring the two regiments into alignment. But since the 116th had already been stopped by the murderous fire laid down across the fields of Molleville Farm, it would first be necessary to neutralize the enemy's guns in the woods beyond. There were no heavy-caliber guns available from the Corps. Division artillery, over two miles to the rear, had just enough ammunition to provide a thirty-minute concentration before the assault, but experience had shown that indirect fire of such limited duration seldom if ever knocked out the heavily reinforced emplacements protecting most of the enemy machine guns. Therefore during the night ten six-inch mortars were moved up close behind the front, to work over the enemy strong points at close range as soon as it became light enough to see. Finally, as an additional and somewhat desperate expedient, it was decided to bring up a battery of 75's directly behind the 116th Infantry, to provide observed fire at point-blank range across the open fields of Molleville Farm.

When the preparatory barrage opened on the morning of 15 October, it was the single battery firing up on the front that attracted all the attention. From the high ground behind, the brigade officers could see a Napoleonic battle that had somehow become misplaced. There were field pieces firing in the open right up with the infantry. And then, at the hour appointed for the assault, the battery commander called "cease fire," limbered his guns, and galloped off to the rear before the enemy artillery could respond. Few who witnessed the sight would ever forget it.[30]

Although the action at Molleville Farm began dramatically, it soon reverted to type.[31] The assault waves moved off on schedule and promptly disappeared in the early morning fog. Soon afterward, enemy shelling cut the phone lines from the forward area. For several hours only the most fragmentary reports came back, first from the walking wounded and then from an occasional runner. Not until nearly dark did the multitude of messages reveal that on the whole the assault had been highly successful. On the left the 115th had pushed well ahead, while on the right the 116th had crossed the Molleville Farm clearing and established a foothold at the edge of the woods, more or less abreast of the line from which the 115th had jumped off in the morning. In a sense the assault had been too successful. Since both regiments had made substantial gains, their odd alignment of the morning was in some degree mirrored in the positions they held at nightfall. Reluctantly Palmer pulled back the advanced elements of the 115th, until the two regiments were aligned on a common front far better suited to resist the counterattacks the enemy could and did underake during the coming night.

The scheme combining six-inch mortars with the regimental battery was less successful than had been anticipated. A heavy fog blanketing the fields of Molleville Farm had virtually nullified the advantages expected from direct fire at short range. But the fog had been most helpful in concealing the advancing infantry crossing the open ground. This advantage, however, was purchased at the cost of a good deal of confusion. One battalion commander in the 116th, for example, had moved his command post across Molleville Farm believing he was well behind his assault wave, only to discover that he had actually taken a position ahead of his own front line, where much to his surprise, he was fired upon by an enemy machine gun in his rear. Before this troublesome gun was knocked out with grenades, a forward observer from the artillery brigade had been killed and several members of the battalion staff wounded.[32]

The fog not only made it difficult for battalion officers to keep in touch with their men, but also compounded the problem of maintaining liaison with flanking units. The successful advance across the fields of Molleville Farm had opened a wide gap between the right flank of the 116th and its neighbor to the east, the 113th Infantry in General Upton's 57th Brigade, where no advance had been undertaken. To plug this gap a company from the 116th reserve was sent forward. It deployed just in time to parry two separate night attacks by enemy units probing in search of just such weak spots in the line. The commotion raised by these thrusts induced a defensive response in the 57th Brigade on the right, where the 113th had also ordered a company into the gap formed during the day's advance. This unit, blundering in the darkness, took up positions to the *left* of the company from the 116th already positioned in the area. This simple and entirely understandable mistake laid the base for a whole train of misunderstandings perfectly illustrating the problems of liaison confronting the commanders of large formations in battle. One company commander believed himself to be the extreme left of his regiment and the other thought he was on the extreme right of his regiment. But the two regiments involved happened to come from different brigades, so the error was not immediately detected. Erroneous coordinates on the operations map at Brigade were an open invitation to tragedy if they chanced to be employed in laying an artillery barrage. This danger was averted when the misplaced company of the 113th was temporarily transferred to the tactical control of the 58th Brigade on the following day.[33]

If the action on 15 October taught the brigade commander some useful lessons about the difficulties of tactical liaison, he also had occasion to learn from hard experience something about the problems inherent in the chain of command. While he himself had fretted until well on toward evening about his inability to find out what was happening at the front, how much greater was the uncertainty back at division and corps headquarters? Not until 7:30 p.m. did the French staff at XVII Corps have enough information to justify a decision to resume the attack on the following morning. By the time this order reached the 58th Brigade it was already too late to begin making any significant changes in the disposition of the units on the front. Palmer hurried out a brigade order at midnight that did little more than indicate the next day's objectives and confirm the existing arrangements. Next time, he vowed, he would remember the inevitable time lag and try to anticipate the intentions of Corps and Division.[34]

On the morning of 16 October, once again the attack was preceded by a thirty-minute barrage, but this time the jump-off hour was moved up to 9:30 a.m. Since both regiments of the brigade would be operating for the most part in thick woods, the need for concealment was far outweighed by the difficulties of coordinating movements in a fog. But even without the blanket of fog, which had complicated the problems of command on the previous day, the attack quickly moved beyond the control of the officers at regiment and Brigade, as one company after another disappeared into the underbrush. Even the battalion commanders were unable to exercise much control when the attack devolved into a series of squad and platoon actions, each bent on reducing one or another of the numerous enemy strong points that covered the wooded slopes of Grande Montagne.[35] The real problems of leadership were now those of the junior officers and the noncoms. Unless they had been wisely chosen and well trained, nothing in the way of orders from the upper echelons was going to do much to improve on the job they were doing.

The action on the 16th proved to be quite different from that of the previous day. In the first place, there was a noticeable diminution in the enemy's shelling. In part this was attributable to the nature of the struggle going on in the woods, where it was impossible to lay down a protective barrage that would distinguish friend from foe. But even the approach road running up the center of the division sector from the Meuse valley suffered only from desultory and scanty fire. This suggested that the Germans too were having their troubles. Apart from the usual difficulties of ammunition supply, the continuing Allied advance beyond the Meuse forced them to pull back their batteries to new positions.

The reduction in enemy shelling was more than offset, however, by a marked stiffening in the defense put up by the enemy troops scattered through the woods. Snipers high up in the trees and automatic riflemen cleverly concealed in shell holes covered with piles of brush made the attackers pay in heavy casualties for every position they took. In contrast to the previous day, very few prisoners were bagged. When at last a number were finally cornered, they revealed why the defense had become so tenacious: the regiments of Austrian troops that had occupied the sector ever since the initial push across the Meuse eight days before had been stiffened with units of tough, experienced Saxons, storm troops, whose morale showed no signs of being shaken by the peace rumors then circulating in the enemy army.

By 7:00 p.m. both regiments of the 58th had reached the heights of Grande Montagne and held the entire line designated as the brigade objective except at the extreme right. Here the front curved back nearly a mile to conform with the divisions on the right, which had not advanced during the day. Because further gains in the sector would only accentuate this difficulty until comparable progress was made by the neighboring units on the right, XVII Corps ordered the position to be consolidated. So the brigade dug in on the line it occupied.[36]

32 Battle Command

The order to go on the defensive was more than welcome; the 58th Brigade had sustained severe casualties during the attack. One assault battalion of 24 officers and 790 men was down to 9 officers and 257 men by the morning of 17 October. Palmer's companies were reduced to an average of 75 rifles; some could barely muster 50. The brigade losses were by no means confined to assault companies. Gas attacks claimed victims for days afterward, and enemy artillery knocked out supply dumps and rolling kitchens with painful regularity. For troops exposed in cold, rainy weather for more than a week while subjected to continuing shell fire, exhaustion conspired with epidemic flu to produce still more casualties.[1]

There was a noticeable lift in morale on the morning of 17 October; after a week of rain the sun came out. For the brigade commander, however, it was a message from the division commander that sent his spirits soaring.

Headquarters 29th Division
17 Oct. 18

From: The Commanding General
To: Colonel John Palmer, Commanding 58th Brigade
Subject: Commendation

The Division Commander desires to express to you and your gallant officers and men his warmest thanks and congratulations for the wonderful work your brigade has performed.... Seasoned veterans could not have done better. Your advance places you in the very front line of the Corps and has been gained after overcoming the most stubborn resistance....

C. G. Morton
Major General, U.S. Army
Commanding[2]

These words gave Palmer an almost child-like sense of elation. He quoted the commendation in full when writing to his wife, as if quite unaware that such letters were almost a matter of routine for the general—or, it might better be said, for his Chief of Staff, since this particular letter reflected more of the urbanity of Colonel Cloman than his commander's Inspector General style of official prose. Scarcely a month before Palmer had been a failure; now he had made good: here was the evidence in black and white. No matter what happened, this would stand in his record. Even if promotion to high rank eluded him, he had worked his way back from disaster to success.

As Palmer later looked back upon the whole business more objectively, it raised some interesting questions about the attributes of a good leader. This, or any other letter of commendation, could be considered an important instrument of command. A division of more than 28,000 men was too big for personal leadership in the heroic mold. The conditions of modern war were scarcely conducive to battlefield showmanship by generals on prancing horses. The contemporary officer of high rank had to project himself in other ways. Skillful letter writing, if less glamorous, was obviously one of the more potentially effective devices of command. This was not to suggest, however, that General Morton's leadership was confined to letter writing; his technique of generalship, when not shaped by his staff, was decidedly in the traditional pattern. Whatever his limitations, and they were many, the division commander seemed to understand that men hunger for appreciation. When inspecting a unit in the field, he made it a point to recall some particularly meritorious conduct on its part that had come to his attention. Especially when speaking to the men of the various auxiliary units, sanitary troops, ammunition train, signalmen, and the like, he went out of his way to make them feel that their contributions were significant.

Although General Morton was confined to his quarters with flu during much of the fighting, he spent a good deal of time later roving about the division sector, where his coolness under fire made a highly favorable impression. The line between foolhardy exposure and exemplary steadiness is always difficult to draw, but the men in at least one company later recalled with a certain awe the impression made by their captain, Peter Stone, as he led an assault smoking a cigar and swinging his cane.[3]

While the division commander's personal courage won him sincere respect, down to the day the division went into action he had been thoroughly and openly hated by virtually every individual in his command. They were annoyed by his almost fanatical concern over trivia; every last man in the division had to lace his shoes in the unusual pattern the general prescribed; every chin-strap had to be cocked—most uncomfortably—on the point of the chin; and so on and on. These things were galling, but they seemed relatively insignificant next to the General's bullying and hectoring of his officers. One of his own aides finally told him to his face that he was nothing but a "sublimated first sergeant." At this the general chuckled and walked off. He liked men who would stand up to him.[4] And there was more than a grain of truth in the charge; his methods *were* those of many an old army first sergeant. He seemed to know no other means of getting what he wanted—troops capable of unquestioning obedience. Bully that he was, General Morton did build a highly disciplined division. In time the men on the 29th seemed to glory in his reputation as a martinet, at least in retrospect. If the division was known as a rough outfit, it followed that one had to be tough to thrive there.

The nature of command had held Palmer's interest throughout his professional career, but the recent days of fighting had put the problem into sharper focus than ever before. Ultimately it came down to a single question: What is it that induces men to climb out of their trenches and advance at a walk over open ground swept by hostile fire? Part of the answer lay with the example of good leaders; part of it came from the habit of obedience inculcated by months of training. But it was equally evident that there were various roads to the same results. Palmer's regimental commander, Colonel Reckord, also won the respect of his troops by his seeming contempt for danger. He was, for example, observed on at least one occasion sitting on the summit of an exposed hill in full view of the enemy, calmly studying his map and relating it to the terrain before him. But where General Morton secured obedience with a bludgeon, Colonel Reckord employed more subtle means. His discipline was based on genuine personal respect, more elusive and more difficult to isolate and identify. He was a leader who would bear close study.

For several days after the division went over to the defensive, the front remained relatively quiet; yet in contrast to the frustrating idleness forced upon him when his troops were actually engaged, the brigade commander was occupied virtually every minute of the day. Brigade housekeeping involved such duties as supervising the relief or rotation of battalions on the front to positions affording some measure of comfort, even though still under shell fire. Then there was the matter of feeding. Palmer's two Infantry regiments alone still had some 3,000 men to serve each day, a task greatly complicated by the loss of rolling kitchens to enemy shell fire. Despite careful sitting in ravines and wooded areas, German observation airplanes had repeatedly directed enemy fire on these hidden mess units. Every time a rolling kitchen was destroyed, companies had to double up, and there was an obvious limit to the number a single kitchen could serve. Was it better to deliver at least two hot meals a day to the men on the front and take the inevitable losses in kitchen units, or to pull them back to a safer area? Palmer concluded that hot meals were worth the cost but decided to ask the division engineers about camouflage.[5]

Equally mundane was the question of replacement underwear. Lice in their underclothing—"cooties" the troops called them—disturbed their sleep and helped to lower their resistance to diseases that threatened to produce as many casualties as enemy action. Still other details that called for the brigade commander's scrutiny were the running inventories of the supply dumps in the brigade area. Faulty information as to the number of mortar shells at a given point could spell the difference between success and failure in battle. Fortunately for Palmer his newly acquired adjutant, Captain Thomas, shouldered a great many burdens of this sort, leaving him free to devote his energies to his other major responsibility, planning for the next thrust forward.[6]

While awaiting the order from the division that would start his brigade staff planning, Palmer tried to garner every lesson he could from the experience of the days just past by visiting each of his subordinate units. With their men's lives at stake, his unit commanders could be counted on to take an intense interest in learning from their mistakes. Later there would be less interest in doctrine and more in efforts to make the record look good. Such a round of visits also gave Palmer an opportunity to learn his officers' wants and needs as well as their opinions. There was a decided psychological advantage in this. The brigade commander attached enough significance to the officers' views to solicit them. That he did so in person could scarcely fail to enhance the effect.

Almost all of the officers the colonel talked to admitted that battle had shown how much they had to learn about the weapons available to them. The automatic rifle was a remarkable firearm; they wanted more of them and more ammunition. Many officers complained that the difficulties encountered in lugging up shells had limited the use of their mortars; only a few had discovered how to use rifle grenades as a substitute. Others distrusted their rifle launchers after trying them in thick woods where the grenades exploded prematurely in the trees above their heads. But the least understood, and certainly the least used, weapon was the 37-mm one-pounder gun. Since there had been no effective training with this weapon in the United States, few if any of the unit commanders had any clear idea of its employment. Almost the same thing could be said of the machine gun. Even some of the ablest company and battalion commanders were decidedly hazy on just how this revolutionary weapon might best help their units.

The experience of Palmer's brigade clearly showed the need for a careful formulation of tactical doctrine, not just in the use of individual weapons but in the disposition of the units employing them. Colonel Reckord called his attention to the need for training company and battalion officers to organize in depth for defense against counterattacks. The colonel was but one of many who suggested instruction in the use of captured weapons. Even if retreating enemy gunners carried off the sights of their machine guns, these weapons and the ammunition found near them had repeatedly proved valuable in organizing defensive positions before American guns and ammunition could be lugged up from the rear.[7]

Every officer in the brigade seemed to agree on the need for better coordination between infantry and artillery. Though careful inquiry produced only one or two instances of friendly fire falling short, there was ample evidence of defective artillery support in other respects. Sometimes the artillerymen dropped their initial bursts behind the enemy line. When the barrage rolled back, the assault waves were confronted with an undamaged line of defense. Sometimes the artillerymen rolled their fire back too fast, allowing the enemy gunners to scramble from their deep shelters and man their guns before the assault waves came up.

Improved coordination would obviously require better communications. The division signal battalion had laid nearly 100 miles of wire in the sector, and the telephone system had proved highly effective where it was available. But circuits were frequently cut by enemy shelling, and a few breaks had also occurred when some of Palmer's men tried to dry out their sodden blankets on the telephone lines.[8]

Persistent questioning failed to reveal that other signaling devices had been much used. Virtually no one seemed to have resorted to visual signals. And while the forward units were supplied with pigeons, these too were seldom employed. The brigade commander had the distinct impression that at least some birds had been converted into rations.

The few available radios had been useful mainly in keeping the front-line troops informed about other parts of the front. Since the reports of operations west of the Meuse were most encouraging, radios had produced an entirely unanticipated lift in morale. But radios had not been as helpful as anticipated, especially in adjusting artillery fire. Several unit commanders found them valuable in emergencies, when calling for fire on previously registered targets, but the delays of encoding and decoding messages had largely offset any other advantages radios might have.

Until the officers and men of the brigade were trained to make full use of their signal equipment, Palmer was going to find it difficult to solve the universal complaints about coordination. Understandably enough, several officers urged an increase in the number of runners or messengers for company, battalion, and regimental commanders. Since there was scarcely time before the next attack to accomplish any significant training in signal techniques, they had to look for any immediate improvement to this most primative, most costly, and probably slowest form of communication.

Upon returning to his command post after a full day of gleaning ideas, Palmer found a note from the commander of one of the field artillery regiments supporting his brigade, a note that epitomized the whole problem of coordination. The artilleryman complained that during the day he had received four different maps of the front from four different sources within the 58th Brigade. "I am not criticizing," wrote the officer, "but I am sure you can understand my difficulties when I receive such varying information which should be definite. I am really at a loss to know just where to lay down a barrage."[9]

Palmer seized a phone and lost no time in telling the hapless artilleryman that his message was highly impertinent. How could his men prepare accurate maps from their shallow trenches out in the woods? Every time they poked their heads up an enemy machine gun let loose a burst. "I know," he said, "I was up there this morning reconnoitering, and as I got shot at every time I moved I really can't tell whether my front line was 800 or 1,000 meters north of the railway shown on the map." Under the circumstances no two maps would be exactly alike. The artillery officer expressed his regret and declared that in view of the facts he could not lay down an accurate barrage. Although infuriated, Palmer managed to respond with icy correctness, reminding his listener that map-firing except for initial ranging was prohibited by regulations. He concluded with a lecture on the merits of forward observers by saying, "I am going out again tomorrow, and I would be glad to have you come with me; if I haven't the guts to go out as far as you want to go, I have plenty of young men who can accommodate you."

The brigade staff was somewhat startled at this outburst by their normally soft-spoken and mild-mannered colonel. Palmer sensed this, and made a point of going to the artillery command post the next day to settle the matter in person. While the regulations did call for adjustment of fire by forward observers, Palmer's imputations had been somewhat less than just. Only two days before an artillery liaison officer had been killed while serving in the most advanced line of the brigade, and others had performed with credit. The colonel also discovered that the officer he had so recently excoriated had been one of his cadets at West Point. So he made amends and settled the matter graciously.[10]

The real need was for an agreed-upon procedure, a standardized staff doctrine. Staff procedures should be hammered out so well in peacetime training that officers completely unknown to one another could function harmoniously on short notice, just as if their brigades, regiments, or other units were interchangeable building blocks. Yet the men involved would still confront differing personalities, so it seemed logical to extend the training of staffs to instruction in the art of liaison. This could never be standardized, but a beginning might sensitize individual officers to the need for perfecting methods of liaison best suited to their own requirements.

While still mulling over ways for improving liaison, Palmer received word that the U.S. 33rd Division on his left was to be relieved by the French 15th

Colonial Infantry Division. His friend King would be replaced by a stranger, and a whole new set of subordinate relationships would have to be established. A short time later the newly arrived French brigade commander invited him and some of his staff to dinner. The colonel's first reaction was one of annoyance; battlefield was scarcely the place for dinner parties. The visit was a huge success however. The French commander's mess sergeant, a skillful chef, served his callers a superb meal, complete even to the point of linen. The American officers were tremendously impressed, and thereafter each of them whenever possible found urgent military reasons to visit the French command post just at dinner time.[11]

The French technique for cultivating good relations hardly lent itself to emulation, so long as the cuisine remained what it was in the AEF. And the language barrier confirmed the wisdom of General Pershing's determination to avoid using American troops in French formations except as divisions. Quite apart from national pride and the need for leverage at the peace conference, Palmer had seen so many misunderstandings crop up within his own brigade that it was easy for him to imagine how much more serious these troubles would have been had his battalions and companies found themselves working within the framework of French regiments and supported by French artillery. But there was much to be learned by observing the French military organization at close range, and the presence of the 29th Division in the French XVII Corps afforded some excellent opportunities to do just this.

The corps commander, Gen. Henri Edmond Claudel, offered a prime example of French leadership. In his dealings with the 29th Division he displayed a real grasp of practical psychology. Palmer first came to appreciate General Claudel's gifts while planning for the Bois d'Etrayes operation, the next big attack to be mounted by the 29th. While briefing the division officers on the main outlines of the coming engagement, the general managed to weave into his remarks a whole series of comments shrewdly calculated to put his listeners—and through them the troops—in precisely the right mood. First he emphasized the extensive artillery preparation specified in the corps plan. This he followed with the suggestion, but not the promise, that the coming attack would be the last assigned to the 29th before the division was relieved. Then he explained how the coming attack had been planned to take the enemy in the flank to make the operation an easy one. Having held out this bait, he recalled the splendid record already achieved by the men of the 29th. The general concluded by urging the officers to see to it that his remarks reached every last private.[12] The formula was adroit: instill confidence, provide an incentive, minimize the risks, praise past performance, and set a standard of achievement by involving the ego.

The very next day, 21 October, a letter from General Morton to the officers and men of the division suggested that Claudel's fine performance had by no means been wasted. It was just what the corps commander had asked for.

You have pushed 7 kilometers into the enemy's lines in the face of stubborn resistance, and you are now further to the front than any element of the XVII Corps. You have captured well over 2,000 prisoners, ... 15 pieces of artillery and 250 ... machine guns. ... The worst is well over but somewhat still remains to be done. Fortunately what is ahead is not so serious or trying as what is already behind.[13]

The division commander—or his chief of staff—had caught Claudel's message and something of his technique. Or was this simply a direct translation from one of the French general's letters? It mattered little; to the officer bent on learning the arts of command, the episode had already furnished its lesson.

An observant officer could learn much from even a very few days of battle. The experience he acquired here would largely shape his views for the years to come. Palmer's consciousness of this made him doubly alert to activities about him. And the more he looked back over these days later, the more he realized that with few exceptions the difficulties encountered could have been minimized by better training. Ever since his tour at Leavenworth he had felt that realistic peacetime training was entirely feasible. Imaginative officers ought not to find it too difficult to devise programs that would profit directly from AEF experience. The big problem was to record and distill this experience. The 29th Division was generating reams of records, but would these reflect the essential lessons of experience and in particular the all-important human factors? If one looked no further than the brigade staff, it was clear that something more than updated manuals along the lines of Griepenkerl or Verdy du Vernois would be required. If young officers were to be given useful insights on the web of human relationships even in this limited arena, an enormous amount of effort would have to be put into the undertaking before a realistic training program could be devised.

Peacetime training was not at the moment an entirely academic question; it had a direct bearing on the immediate problems of the coming attack. Palmer was far from satisfied with his brigade staff; he expected his officers to learn by doing just as he himself was learning, but in many instances they were still acquiring the rudiments. The ideal to which he aspired was General Bullard's: a staff so well trained it becomes a machine that will work independently of the quality of the man who turns the crank. Unfortunately, the one trained man on whom he counted most heavily, Captain Thomas, had succumbed to a bad case of flu. Without this officer, the brigade commander himself had to take care of a great many administrative details at a time when he should have been freed to cope with the unexpected and the unusual—the primary function of command in battle. Given enough time, Palmer was certain that the temporary officers he observed around him would make excellent staff men. If only a peacetime system of training for reserve officers could be devised along the lines already laid down at Langres, each echelon in a division would be assured of replacements to meet the kinds of problems now confronting his brigade.[14]

In dealing with his sick adjutant, Palmer revealed a good deal about himself. The young captain tried to keep on working but eventually collapsed with a raging fever. He insisted on sticking it out at the brigade dugout. The enemy laid down an unusually heavy gas barrage, and the brigade commander spent the whole night nursing the captain, who was delirious, trying to keep on his gas mask. An orderly could easily have been assigned to this job, but characteristically Palmer assumed the burden himself. His interest in his officers was genuinely paternal; they were his boys. Not once but several times he described one or another of them in his letters home as "just the age our son, John, would be."[15]

When the division order for the Bois d'Etrayes attack finally arrived at the 58th command post the short-handed brigade staff plunged into a flurry of activity. The operation was to assure the collapse of the enemy's defensive system by capturing the last remaining ridges dominating the Meuse. In the 29th Division sector, this would center upon a wooded ridge, Hill 361, surmounted by an enemy lookout tower, or pylon. With this high ground taken, the broad valleys and strategic rail lines beyond would lie open, and all the advantages of terrain enjoyed by the defenders would pass to the attackers. But to achieve this goal a most intricate operation was required. The corps plan called for a shift in the axis of attack from due north to due east. Instead of continuing to advance directly into the enemy lines, the 29th, with two brigades abreast, was to orient its attack to the right. By this maneuver the corps commander expected to take the enemy line end on, at right angles to the interlocking fields of fire from its reinforced strongpoints.[16]

The corps scheme posed a difficult problem for Palmer's brigade. Although the axis of the attack was to be to the east, the northern front still had to be maintained. Thus as the attackers pushed further toward the east, they would open a progressively wider gap between themselves and the troops holding the line facing north. The obvious solution was to arrange for a reserve force to feed in units to fill the gap as it developed, but this solution posed serious problems in planning and execution. It would be extremely difficult to know where the attackers would be at any given moment. Units sent forward to fill in the gap were liable to become lost and fail to make contact with the elements on either flank of the gap. Some help could be expected from fabric display panels marking the location of ground troops to observers in the air, but thick woods in much of the assault area were almost certain to limit the use of this device.

The officers of the brigade staff had to coordinate a three-ring circus: on the right, a major attack eastward to capture the ridge; on the left, a display of fire northward to pin down the enemy forces there; and in the middle, a covering attack to fill in the gap and prevent hostile counterattacks from slipping through. All this was to take place over ground broken by deep-sided ravines and largely covered by heavy woods. If it had proved difficult to satisfy the divisional artillery with sufficiently precise information on the whereabouts of the front-line troops in the simpler operations undertaken previously, it was going to be far harder to do so in this intricate assault. And this time not only division but corps artillery would be engaged. Even some of the heavy guns in the permanent fortifications around Verdun were to join in pounding the enemy lines.[17] Only by a continuous flow of information from the front to the rear would it be possible to exploit all this fire power. It wasn't enough to write orders; the brigade commander and his staff had to see that the men of every subordinate unit understood what was expected of them.

Up to the very eve of the attack, the men of the brigade were subjected to a continual process of instruction, while unit commanders struggled to improve their methods of liaison, weapon specialists demonstrated the use of rifle grenades, and a machine gun battalion in reserve but within range of enemy shell bursts set up a school for NCO's on the techniques of indirect fire. A stream of admonishments came down from the division. One in particular epitomized General Morton's approach to discipline: "The matter of straggling and shirking is a shame to the good soldiers of this division.... The shirking of front line duties by these few culprits simply means added work and losses to the other soldiers, and all men should take an active and individual interest in spotting them and forcing them to do their duty. The most rigid and forceful means of dealing with these cases are authorized, short of actual maiming." The handling of skulkers and shirkers was a serious challenge, but one wonders whether any soldier, let alone a slacker, could ever have been *forced* to do his duty.[18]

The attack on the Bois d'Etrayes was finally launched at 6:15 a.m. on 23 October. After the attackers disappeared into the morning mists, Palmer knew he could expect little significant information for at least two or three hours. As usual the forward telephone lines were shot out, and the only news came from runners. The couriers with unfavorable news seemed to make their way back promptly, while those bearing reports of success were pinned down by hostile fire and delayed, sometimes for hours.[19]

The first really encouraging message to reach the 58th command post arrived about midmorning; an aerial observer reported seeing display panels on the objective designated for the 116th Infantry, which was making the major attack on the right. But any enthusiasm for aerial observation that this initial report may have kindled was soon dampened. The enemy too had airplanes, and the advancing ground troops soon learned not to display marking panels because they led hostile airmen to direct shell fire into the area.[20]

The initial report of success turned out to be only partially correct. The first wave of attackers had reached their objective on the heights of the Bois d'Etrayes without stopping to mop up pockets of resistance. They had rushed ahead before the enemy could organize an artillery barrage in the threatened area. Before the second wave could move up, however, a hostile barrage had been laid across the threatened front. The assault troops in the first wave, while on the designated objective, were actually in grave danger. Exposed in the rear to fire from the strongpoints bypassed in the initial dash, they lacked the heavy machine guns to organize their position against the counterattacks they could expect almost immediately.

Any modification of the plan of attack was out of the question. By the time Brigade and the higher echelons of command could sense the situation, the occasion for changes would have passed. So the successive assault waves worked their way through the hostile barrage at the cost of heavy casualties. On the high ground, the isolated troops already on the objective fell back only enough to take advantage of the terrain, and dug in on the crown of the hill they had captured. Only a genuinely disciplined organization could have weathered such a test. Instead of finding excuses for not advancing through the unexpectedly intense and accurate enemy barrage, the troops pushed ahead according to plan. This feat was the more remarkable at a time when rumors of a coming armistice had already begun to affect the troops. At least one nearby American division had recently suffered a serious loss of discipline when some of its elements were found parlaying with the enemy: "We won't shoot you if you don't shoot us."

Early in the afternoon the signal teams managed to restore the telephone lines from Brigade forward; by then the operation was over. The day had been a success, but why? Palmer was again acutely conscious of how little control he had exercised after the attack had begun. He recalled with new understanding General Guillaumat's studied nonchalance during the visit of Pershing's party to the Souilly during the Verdun offensive a year before. Once started, the outcome had rested largely upon the subordinate officers, for the most part platoon leaders and company commanders. If these imperfectly trained young men—these citizen soldiers—were capable of such discipline, such courage, how much more could they have accomplished if properly trained!

The performance of the brigade in storming the Bois d'Etrayes heights made a profound impression upon Palmer. He saw there unequivocal confirmation of his longstanding faith in the capacity of citizen soldiers. No one could deny their courage or their ability to accept discipline. All they needed was a greater technical proficiency and thoroughly trained leaders. But trained leaders were hard to produce. Such leaders had to have a thorough knowledge of the weapons at their disposal, and to handle their commands with tactical skill, they would need wide-ranging experience in extended maneuvers. This was the most compelling argument imaginable for peacetime military training of citizen soldiers.

For several days after the successful action in the Bois d'Etrayes, the brigade was entirely occupied in securing its position. The enemy counterattacks were ill-coordinated and relatively feeble; German resistance was crumbling fast. But any further advance by the division was out of the question. The push to the eastward had so elongated the line to be defended that virtually every available unit had to be employed just to maintain a continuous front. Nearly three weeks of exposure had begun to tell heavily. Almost one-fourth of the division had already been evacuated as casualties, and the cumulative effect of gas threatened to incapacitate as many more. It was time to be relieved.[21]

The eagerly awaited disengagement order from Division arrived 27 October, and Palmer promptly set his staff to work on detailed instructions for withdrawal the following night. Only the day before he had learned what can happen when a unit commander fails to execute a proper relief. One of his companies had failed to provide either experienced guides or map coordinates for the incoming troops and had neglected to report the location of a nearby enemy machine gun, which immediately cost the newcomers several casualties. Slipshod staff work could lead to wide gaps in the front line, an open invitation to disaster. Even veteran troops, released after many days under stress, could dissolve into a mob.[22]

The need for infinitely careful staff work was also dictated by the peculiar character of the front occupied by the brigade. The front resembled nothing so much as a meandering stream, as it circled around the wooded flanks of hills, now and again looping back sharply to avoid dipping into gullies or ravines. Since the troops available were far too few to cover the front of nearly three miles, in many places only roving patrols guarded against enemy penetrations. Under such conditions it would be fatally easy for incoming units to become lost in the woods at night and fail to take up the positions assigned to them. Not once but several times in the previous few days, enemy reinforcements had unwittingly wandered into the brigade lines. On one occasion Colonel Reckord's men had ambushed a whole platoon marching in close order with rifles slung. On another occasion a company of the 115th, cut off from its kitchen by shell fire, dined on sausage, black bread, good butter, and hot coffee captured from a ration-carrying party of eight Saxons, who had been unaware that their lines had been altered during the previous day.[23]

Palmer's staff officers were now beginning to work effectively with a minimum of supervision. Their growing craftsmanship gave him a new sense of confidence, and he was delighted when General Morton directed him to transfer his command post back to the town of Verdun to take charge of moving all four regiments in the division to their assigned billeting areas. The operation would involve some eighty different organizations, rifle companies, supply companies, and headquarters troops, accounting for more than 8,000 men, all that remained in the depleted infantry regiments of the 29th Di-

vision.[24] During the next twenty-four hours the staff drew up marching sched-
ules carefully scaled to the exhausted troops, made arrangements for transient
billets in the French fortresses and elsewhere around Verdun, and coordinated
every step to avoid entangling the troops of the 79th Division, who were
moving in as replacements.

When Palmer finally ordered his driver to head south toward Souilly in the
wake of his troops, it was nearly midnight. Although he had been working
furiously for nearly 24 hours, he was conscious of a real sense of exhilaration.
This stemmed in part, no doubt, from a mounting sense of security; he was at
last out of range of the enemy's guns; even in Verdun, more than a dozen miles
behind the front, there had been shell bursts every few minutes. But his feeling
of well-being also reflected in the pride he felt in the success of his brigade, the
work of his staff, and his own long pull back from despair.

At Souilly he stopped to call on his old friend Maj. Gen. Hunter Liggett, to
extend his congratulations on the recent successes of the First Army, which
Liggett now commanded. He fully expected to overtake his troops at the next
town, but when he arrived they were not there. At each succeeding checkpoint
no one seemed to know where his brigade had gone. For the moment, at any
rate, he had no control over the troops supposedly in his charge. What if First
Army issued an unexpected change of orders? Would he be forced to confess
he was not in a position to comply? Filled with forebodings of failure, he
continued his journey southward.[25]

Not until nearly noon of the following day, 30 October, did he at last
overtake his command. He could only be thankful that this mischance had
happened on the way out of action and not on the way in. For the next several
days he was so busy that the whole episode dropped completely out of his
mind—until recalled by an official communication. Instead of a rebuke this
proved to be a commendation from the division commander for the excellent
march discipline displayed by the 58th Brigade in its retirement.[26] The irony in
all this appealed to Palmer, who saw at once that military reputation is based
as much on what is not known about a commander as on the facts officially
recorded.

33 End of the War

The rest area assigned to the 29th Division lay southeast of Bar-le-Duc. Here the men had to be billeted wherever shelter could be found. This meant scattering them by squads and platoons for eight or ten miles over the countryside in parish crossroad hamlets and towns. In one of these, the village of Trémont, Palmer set up his brigade headquarters and then spent the next forty-eight hours trying to cope with the thousands of men who came swarming hungry, dirty, and exhausted back from the front. He needed no orders from the division; his primary mission was to restore these men to fighting trim as fast as possible.

Locating billets for nearly 5,000 men was a difficult job. In one of the villages assigned to the 58th French troops still occupied the alloted quarters. The brigade commander leaned over backwards to keep a simple misunderstanding from burgeoning into an acrimonious inter-Allied dispute. A captain who had just marched the remnants of his weary company seven miles to an outlying village, only to find he had to march back to where he started and double up with a company already in the available billets, was scarcely to be blamed if he cursed the selfish French and grumbled about his own muddle-headed staff officers.[1]

When every man in the brigade finally had shelter of some sort, though often no more than a hayloft, the brigade commander's work was only begun. A great many soldiers had no blankets. Most of these had shed their packs deliberately on going into battle; sixty pounds or more of blankets, overcoat, extra hobnail boots, rain slicker as well as mess kit, rifle, ammunition, and all the rest made up a staggering load. A few officers, disobeying orders, had instructed their men to deposit their packs in the rear to be picked up on the way out. Their men were rewarded with some degree of comfort, while the troops of other more obedient but less imaginative officers shivered and lost sleep. The real veterans among the latter had scrounged blankets—with or without lice—from captured enemy dugouts. Being a veteran, Palmer came to realize, was more a state of mind that a matter of chronology.[2]

Several thousand additional blankets for a single brigade could never have been found without vigorous salvage operations by division supply troops directly behind the front during the recent fighting. But processing salvage took time, and it was several days before fresh supplies of blankets were available. Even then, issuing small lots in widely scattered villages took time. Much the same thing occurred with respect to clothing and other items. Enemy barbed wire had left many of the men literally in rags. Few had changed their clothing in nearly a month. A good washing, even when limited to cold water, would do wonders. But a large supply of fresh clothing was highly desirable. To be ideally effective it should be ready for issue as soon as the men emerged from bathing and delousing.[3]

The business of arranging hot baths for the troops was typical of the many problems confronting the brigade commander. Someone had to take the initiative in securing a mobile bath unit from Division and scheduling its use through the brigade. Wood for the boilers was scarce and could only be procured after extended negotiations with the local authorities. Duties of this sort could be assigned to junior staff officers, but most of them were woefully inexperienced. Palmer realized that it would have been easier to do the work himself, but that would defeat the training he hoped to accomplish. His difficulties were compounded by the prevailing shortage of officers in the brigade. Many had been lost in battle, and still others were succumbing to the delayed effects of gas. Even among those ostensibly fit for duty, many were listless and inert after the prolonged strain of battle.[4]

Palmer plunged in with the zeal of a newly commissioned second lieutenant. He wasted no time complaining that he who had so recently been General Pershing's chief of Operations should now be doing work better suited to a junior staff officer; in fact, he seemed to relish the opportunity. His personal example could demonstrate an officer's responsibility to his men. Too many young officers seemed to think their jobs were done when they obeyed orders. He wanted to show them no task was too trivial, even for a brigade commander, if it contributed to the primary mission of getting the men back in shape.

Of all the tasks Palmer had to carry out, none was more onerous than the work of distributing the remaining manpower in every echelon where it would do the most good. Where a company commander had fallen, sometimes a first lieutenant could take over; in other situations it seemed best to bring in an officer from a neighboring unit. When neither of these alternatives appeared feasible, a complete stranger, an officer from the replacement depot, was given command of the company. The process was sure to be painful to someone.

Those passed over were inclined to be resentful, and the outsider could almost inevitably count on a certain amount of hostility, especially if he had had no battle experience and his men regarded themselves as veterans.[5]

Palmer learned a great deal from the experience of regrouping. As never before, he came to understand how intensely men dislike being uprooted from units to which they have become accustomed and in which they feel at home. Officers moved from one company or battalion to another were frequently slow to identify themselves with their new commands. This was true even of some who had been enthusiastic leaders. When dealing with their own troops, fellow townsmen in the Guard, they excelled, but when transferred to a group of strangers they were often painfully slow to adjust. Replacements from the depot division suffered from a similar malady. Many of them were deeply embittered because their division, the 41st, made up of National Guard troops from the Rocky Mountain area, had been broken up and used as fillers. Bitterest of all were the men who had recovered from wounds and returned from the hospital only to find themselves assigned to units other than their own. The whole experience left an indelible impression on Palmer. For the rest of his life he was an ardent advocate of every possible measure that would offer men secure membership in an organization whose traditions, practices, and leaders were familiar.[6]

While the brigade was still regrouping, the division commander let it be known that he expected an immediate return to his old uncompromising standards of personal appearance. He directed his officers to hold drills and formal inspections.[7] It need hardly be said that the troops resented this return to spit and polish. They had fought well and knew it; now they wanted to rest. Why was the general annoying them with his everlasting concern for superficial details? Many of the temporary officers tended to agree with the men, but the more experienced officers understood what the division commander was doing. General Morton was determined to scotch any letdown in morale before it got started, and to do so he acted in the only way he knew—by exacting of his men more than they believed it possible to give.

Palmer's own morale had never been better. He too was exhausted and suffering from the aftereffects of gas; nonetheless, he enjoyed an unusual sense of exhilaration. Letters from home, his first since his return to France, did much to bolster his spirits.[8] But the greatest lift came from the realization that he had been successful as a commander in battle. General Morton recommended him for immediate promotion to the rank of brigadier general.[9] A few days later General McAndrew wrote from Chaumont that the commander in chief had approved the recommendation. "We are sure to find your name on the next list," he said. "Your friends all hope this star is only a beginning."[10] This was no more than he had expected from his friends at headquarters. He was immensely pleased, however, that his promotion would come not on the initiative of well-wishers at Chaumont but at the recommendation of a notoriously hard-bitten officer who had judged him entirely on his performance in combat.

Along with everyone else in the division, Palmer needed every encouragement he could get. The 29th was scheduled for an immediate return to the front to participate in the scheduled Second Army attack on Metz. During the morning of 10 November, rumors of a coming armistice circulated among the troops, but Division promptly branded these as false and ordered them to start the four-day march to the front as planned. It was after midnight when the first elements of the 58th set out on the highway, heavy-hearted at the prospect of a return to battle. Palmer returned to his room but not, as it turned out, to sleep. Years afterward he recorded his impressions:

> While I was sitting in my billet in the little village of Trémont, I heard the notes of a trumpet and the sound of women's voices. As I could not see from my window what was passing in the unlighted street, I went down to the front door. Just then the notes of a trumpet stopped, and I could hear the quavering voice of an old town-crier, though I could not see the insignia of his office—his tri-color sash and his old Bonaparte chapeau. He was reciting a proclamation in which *La France* announced to her children that an armistice had been signed and that the long war was over. Then he resumed his slow march down the street, blowing his trumpet for a hundred paces or so when he stopped again and announced his official message.
>
> There were few men in the village, but the women had gathered before their doorways. There were no loud cheers and there seemed to be more of sadness than of gladness in their voices. I asked the woman who kept the Tabac next door to my billet if she was not happy that the war was over. "Yes, yes, Monsieur," she said, "but my three brothers will not return."[11]

The reception accorded the news of the Armistice by the peasants of Trémont was in marked contrast to the reaction of the Americans. The units that had set out for the front were hurriedly recalled to their billets, where they joined in wild celebrations; the war was over and it was time to go home.[12] Even Palmer was inclined to see the victory somewhat too simply as "a great triumph of right over wrong," but he understood that the war was not quite over. Divisions in fighting trim would be needed to make the Armistice stick, and others would be required for the occupation of Germany.[13] So he began planning a practice maneuver for his two regiments, just as if the Armistice had never happened.[14]

After several days of uncertainty, the men of the 29th learned that while they were not to join the army of occupation in Germany, their horses would! The 29th was to turn over the best of its animals and automobiles to the 3rd Division, which was headed for occupation duty and desperately short of transportation. Palmer saw at once that this was the sort of order veteran troops were sure to sabotage unless specifically dissuaded. He ostentatiously surrendered his staff car, a Winton-six limousine of which he was immensely proud. The division commander subsequently received a commendation for the fair-minded way in which his organization had complied with the orders, but this was scant consolation for the loss. The troops also felt this way, especially when the virtually immobilized division soon afterward received orders to move more than seventy miles southward to a training area around Bourbonne-les-Bains, just east of Chaumont.[15]

General Morton ordered Palmer to take charge of loading the entire division on railroad cars while General Upton of the 57th Brigade supervised unloading at the other end. The division filled twenty-five separate trains, each of approximately eight cars. These trains had to be summoned through the appropriate French authorities, and then spotted at convenient towns along the line. Where no sidings were available, the troops had to be loaded in the shortest possible time to avoid tying up the line. Where units were quartered more than a day's march from the railway, it was difficult to time the march precisely, but unless accurate timetables were laid down, road congestion near the railhead was almost certain to cause difficulties.

In spite of meticulous planning, the division entrainment did not go off without a hitch. The French railroad authorities could not always produce the promised trains at a given hour. Troops in full pack, who had been hurried along for a dozen miles to arrive on time, were forced to wait for hours before their cars arrived. And then, after loading and moving a few miles, they had to wait hours longer at insignificant rail junctions. Of course the discomfited men grumbled about their bumbling superiors, but when the last train load of troops finally departed for Bourbonne-les-Bains, Palmer was pleased with the work his staff had accomplished under his able acting adjutant, Capt. George Henderson, a Guard officer from Cumberland, Maryland. Most of the snags encountered were inevitable in such a large-scale operation. His officers still had much to learn, but they were beginning to function as a team. If they could show this much improvement in the few weeks he had been training them, what might they have done had they received previous instruction in the rudiments of staff work?[16]

Although Bourbonne-les-Bains was a considerable town, only General Morton, his staff, and a few elements of the division were accommodated there. The rest of the troops were scattered about the neighboring countryside for several miles in every direction. The 58th Brigade alone occupied a dozen communities in the foothills of the Vosges, with headquarters at Serqueux, a tiny village three or four miles north of the divisional center. When Palmer finally arrived, the advance party had already set up an office and prepared comfortable quarters for him. After all the tensions of the past few weeks, he was quite content to rest for a while in agreeable surroundings.[17]

For at least a week the colonel's letters reflected a mood of contentment. He enjoyed visiting his troops in picturesque villages that reminded him at every turn of paintings by Millet. After the never-ending noise of shell fire and the tragically war-scarred billets in the area around Trémont, he found the peaceful silences of untouched Serqueux a source of profound pleasure. His pride was further bolstered when he heard that he was the only colonel left in command of a brigade now that the fighting was over.[18] He enjoyed his role as country squire, riding his horse over the beautiful countryside day after day to inspect a command once again grown to nearly 8,000 men. But most of all he enjoyed his billet in the house of the village priest. There he occupied an enormous room with a beautiful view. It had only one drawback; his chamber was "as cold as Greenland" except just in front of the fireplace, and the big four-poster bed was in a far corner of the room where no heat ever penetrated. However, the curé's housekeeper, a gray-haired, rosy-cheeked old lady, took great delight in mothering her American visitor. Every evening, just about the time the colonel's guests were bundling on their trench coats and saying good night, the dear old lady would enter with a huge warming pan. As she thrust it between the icy sheets, she always explained: "Camarade du lit pour le colonel."[19]

Palmer soon discovered that he was an object of rivalry between the curé's housekeeper and his own orderly, or striker, a private named Van Horn. Both saw at once that the way to his heart was through his family. When the housekeeper noticed the pair of photographs he kept on his bedroom table, she insisted he must bring his wife and daughter to Serqueux for a visit. Sensing that the colonel was pleased to talk about his loved ones, the canny old peasant woman led him on, encouraging him to confuse anticipation with reality in a conversation he subsequently recorded with great delight. "I asked her if I could have this room. She said yes.... this would do for me and 'madame' but that 'mademoiselle' should have another room. She took me to see Mary's room and 'Voila! La chambre pour mademoiselle.'" But Van Horn, the orderly, was also blessed with a considerable grasp of practical psychology. When he saw the photograph of Mrs. Palmer, he assured the colonel that he remembered seeing her when she made shopping trips to the market in Washington, D.C., where he was employed. That Van Horn soon had his commanding officer well in hand was evident from the colonel's letters. "Van Horn is a splendid orderly and is taking fine care of me. And incidently I am taking good care of him."[20]

As for taking care of the men in his charge, no detail escaped Palmer's attention. One day at lunch, as he sipped at a glass of water, he suddenly turned to an officer at the end of the table, Lieutenant Thomas Blow, the son of his old colleague in the 15th Infantry, Capt. William N. Blow. "Tom," he asked pointedly, "are you making sure our drinking water is being properly chlorinated?"

"Oh, yes indeed, sir, that's always done out in the kitchen."

"Tom, look out there." Everyone craned about to peer through the door to the kitchen, to see their French waitress vigorously pumping water from the well into the pitcher she had just removed from the table. Thereafter the drinking water always tasted of chlorine.[21]

After dining with the French on the front, Palmer knew that something could be done to improve the cuisine of his headquarters. He turned the whole matter over to Lt. Pierre La Rochelle, the French interpreter attached to the brigade, who immediately procured a civilian chef, and the 58th soon acquired a local reputation for good living. Thanksgiving dinner marked a high point, when the staff sat down before neatly lettered menus promising Consommé au Bully Beef, Wilson Turkey, Pershing Peas, Foch Corn, and Apple Pie `a la Palmer.[22]

The brigade commander's unusual preoccupation with creature comforts reflected his desperate need for emotional as well as physical recuperation after the demands of battle. Necessary though this rest period was, it tended to obscure a profound shift in outlook brought about by the Armistice. With occupation duty apparently out of the question, the brigade had lost its purpose. The men in the ranks were afflicted first. Unlike the colonel in the curé's guest chamber, many of them were lodged in unheated and unlighted barns on straw ticks, where physical discomfort accelerated their declining morale.[23] To meet this inevitable slump, General Morton called for training exercises, inspections, and reviews at every echelon. Palmer used all the devices he could think of to insure enthusiastic participation. Whenever possible, for maximum effect he held his inspections when high-ranking visitors from Corps or Army happened by.

The most useful morale builder was the time-honored one—the ceremonial presentation of decorations and awards. On 9 December, Palmer assembled the entire brigade at Serqueux; there, under the watchful eye of his classmate C. P. Summerall, now a major general commanding V Corps, who had been invited to preside over the ceremony, he pinned the Distinguished Service Cross on thirteen enlisted men and one officer from his command. In some respects this episode marked the high point in the life of the 58th Brigade. The field was muddy, and a bitterly cold rain poured down all through the presentation, but the men had never looked better. They were veterans. For the moment they seemed deeply awed by the ceremony of which they were a part.[24]

The longer Palmer studied the subject, the more he came to see that decorations, if properly handled, could be made into a significant tool of command. If passed out too freely medals rapidly depreciated in value, especially where division staff officers received the same awards granted to front-line riflemen. Moreover, where awards were made by quotas, assigning a given number of medals to each organization, the men quickly sensed the sham and dismissed the whole game. General Morton invited every unit commander to select candidates and write up justifications for screening by a divisional board. This method did much to preserve the mystique of the awards but put a heavy premium on the initiative of individual commanders. Unlike many of the other officers in the 29th Division, Colonel Reckord of the 115th Infantry treated seriously his responsibility for recommending awards. As a consequence his regiment received far more citations than any other in the division.[25]

Although Colonel Reckord's success in looking out for his men was entirely characteristic, he was subjected to a considerable amount of ragging by his fellow officers. Not long afterwards General Morton decided to assemble a division band as a morale builder. He therefore called on all of his regimental commanders to comb their ranks for musicians. Colonel Reckord was reluctant to part with any of the musicians serving his regiment, so he declared he was unable to find any. General Morton replied, "Well, Colonel Reckord, if you look for musicians as carefully as you did for Distinguished Service Medals, you will find that you can comply my request."[26]

While presentation ceremonies and inspections had a considerable effect, they could not check the slow erosion of morale. For Palmer, however, the pattern was quite different. Then abruptly his whole outlook changed with the arrival of a note from General Pershing:

> American Expeditionary Forces
> Office of the Commander-in-Chief
> France   29 November 1918
>
> My dear Colonel Palmer:
>
> It gives me great pleasure to inform you that on October 17th I recommended you for promotion to the grade of Brigadier General, basing my recommendation upon the efficiency of your service with the American Expeditionary Forces.
>
> The War Department discontinued all promotions to the grade of General Officer after the signing of the Armistice, and I regret that

you will not therefore receive the deserved recognition of your excellent services.

Sincerely yours,

John J. Pershing[27]

In several respects this letter was a curious one. However infelicitously phrased, it left no doubt that Pershing wished to show that full responsibility for denial of the promotion rested not on him but in the War Department. Then, too, the date of his recommendation, 17 October, was before the 58th Brigade had won its unquestioned success in battle and nearly two weeks before General Morton had sent forward his recommendation from Division. Apparently Palmer never noticed this discrepancy. He never alluded to it subsequently, although the obvious inference was that Pershing had thought enough of him as a staff officer to put in his promotion even before he had proved himself as a combat commander. If he did read this inference he may well have forgotten it in his disappointment.

The blow was a painful one, but he wasted no time on self-defeating bitterness. He put the best possible face on the matter, suggesting hopefully but none too convincingly to his wife that his future grandchildren would value the fine letters of commendation from Morton and Pershing more than "any mere promotion." As if trying to persuade himself, he went on: "There are lots of generals who have not been in battle at all, and I regard it as a wonderful stroke of good fortune that I should have had this experience at the very end of the war and after a year of discouragement and ill health."[28]

Palmer was realistic enough to see that all the top assignments in the postwar army would go to those who had reached advanced rank in the AEF. The best he could hope for was a staff position, subordinate to many of his former juniors. He was 48 years old; that would leave 16 years before retirement at 64, always with the knowledge that the choice positions would go to others. But there was an attractive alternative. With nearly thirty years of service behind him, he could now retire "with dignity and self-respect" to take up a life of serious writing. He outlined the prospects for his wife: they could live abroad, go fishing in Maine, or live wherever they pleased, while he turned out half a dozen articles a year and finished one or two really good books on military history.[29]

The present was something else again. Having convinced himself that he had no further career in the army, the colonel found little to sustain his morale. By the middle of December, when the winter rains began to make life still more difficult, a long letter to his wife clearly reflected his discouragement:

> I suppose if I should take the time to examine my symptoms tonight I would find out that I am homesick. You are reading in the papers of a beautiful radiant France, Paris welcoming the President, bands playing, troops marching, the President's wife receiving bouquets, everything beautiful and romantic. But this France that I am in is another kind of France. I am in a stinking little country village where the people and the cattle and the pigs all live together and where every peasant keeps a manure pile at his front door as his biggest index of wealth. I have my troops in this and a half dozen other towns like it, and it rains everyday and the mud and the manure get mixed together. . . . There aren't any more Bosche to fight, and it is pretty stiff keeping everybody drilling and maneuvering all day in a cheerful manner when they are just doing it to keep occupied.

> Yesterday was Sunday and I was going to write you a long letter-. . . but at eight o'clock I hurried out on a call and motored thirty-five miles to Corre to sit on an examining board. . . . I got back about noon still thinking of an early lunch and an afternoon by myself when in came some inspection reports. One said the horses in the supply company of the 116th were not properly groomed, another said that my machine-gun companies had to change station this week and that I must submit a plan for new stationing of the brigade. Another said that the men in the battalion at Parnot were too crowded and another that the delousing at La Rivière was not being done properly. Another inspector wanted to know why we didn't have a maneuver on a certain rainy day and another from a medico wanted to know why so many men in the ...regiments had colds. Then there was a note from ...Corps saying that we would have a divisional maneuver Friday, unless we were called up for the President to review and that we had better make plans and march tables for both so that we could be sure to do either.[30]

Although everything seemed to go wrong at once, Palmer managed to see his plight with a considerable degree of detachment.

> When I write up this period of the war I'll be glad I've had this experience in a manure town. It's so easy to do it all if you're writing orders up in Chaumont, but down here where we have to execute the orders, it's grind, grind, grind.[31]

Coming from an officer whose career had been largely spent as a staff man, this was a remarkable revelation. Further reflection on the wide gulf between order and execution led him to contrast his own condition with that of his troops, the poor devils who had to tramp through boggy woods day after day with no prospect of dry boots and a blazing fire when they retired at sunset, often to unlighted lofts over the cow parlors of a manure factory, as he expressed it. Their plight restored his sense of balance.

> How cheerily and bravely they do their duty, these youngsters of Maryland and Virginia. I marvelled at them when they were suffering in the fighting line. I marvel more as I see them go through the grind here and I feel ashamed of myself when I talk about being tired of it.[32]

General Morton's prescription of hard work as a means of maintaining morale applied to his officers as well as his men. Palmer was no exception. Confronted with the prospect of a divisional maneuver, he was soon absorbed in preliminary planning.

The colonel's enthusiasm mounted as he convinced himself that the forth-coming exercise was not just another drill to keep the troops busy but an important step toward the creation of a peacetime national military reserve. Brave as the troops had been in battle, they needed a good deal more training. They had thoroughly mauled the enemy beyond Verdun, but this success was achieved with heavy numerical odds against an enemy already reeling from four years of war. The 58th and presumably other elements in the division had made tactical errors that would never have been allowed to pass unnoticed by a fresh and unshaken enemy. A vigorous program of tactical training now, before the troops returned home, would lay the foundations of an effective citizen army, one that would give substance to Mr. Wilson's sanctions for peace. For this training to be fully effective, however, the troops would have to understand the reason behind the maneuvers.

Wherever he went in his daily tours of inspecting, Palmer stopped to discuss the problem with the young officers of his command. He told them of the scheme for a citizen army he had drawn up for Secretary Stimson in 1912 and how his faith had been confirmed by their performance in battle. Later he recalled these conversations and their significance to him.

> As I talked to my young comrades, my vision of the citizen army took on a new form in my mind. It was no longer a question of creating such a force; it was the simpler question of preserving the one now in existence. These young soldiers would soon return to civil life and the army of the World War would cease to exist. But why not preserve its organization

as a permanent national institution? A few of these veterans could then serve for a time as charter members in the new peace establishment— long enough to pass on their traditions, their skill and their discipline to their younger brothers and, through them, to their sons. In this way their war effort would not be wasted but would be funded as a permanent national investment. At the beginning of the next war, our traditional army of the people would stand ready for service. For the first time in our history it would not be necessary to jury-rig a new and untried military system after the outbreak of war.[33]

Many of the young officers with whom Palmer spoke were quite willing to discuss the problems of postwar military policy. Several of them were already started on political careers; a few subsequently achieved success. Maj. Millard Tydings was to serve Maryland with distinction in the U.S. Senate. Maj. William P. Lane later became governor of Maryland. Palmer's own adjutant at Serqueux, Capt. George Henderson, became a federal judge; numerous others rose to positions of distinction in their communities. Such men needed no prodding to make them see the role they might play in shaping legislation. They willingly agreed that the nation should never again be unprepared for war, as it had been in 1917.[34]

Palmer was convinced that once his young friends understood him they agreed with him. That their assent might be other than complete acceptance seems never to have occurred to him. He was so utterly willing to listen to the opinions of even the lowest-ranking privates, that reticence on their part was almost inconceivable to him. This capacity for self-delusion when appraising the reaction of others to the views he put forward was to plague him for years to come.

By 20 December, the day appointed for the divisional maneuver, Palmer was determined to turn in a truly professional performance. Before the division broke up he wanted every officer in his brigade to participate at least once in a perfectly administered large-scale exercise; each could then carry away a clear appreciation of all that was involved in maneuvering large bodies of troops and coordinating the fire of many weapons. Then too, he had an additional reason for wishing perfection. His classmate Maj. Gen. C. P. Summerall had come down from V Corps Headquarters to observe the operation.[35]

The maneuver took place in the rolling countryside east of Bourbonne-les-Bains. The troops, who had been concentrated in the area during the previous day, were carefully deployed in the designated assault area, while division, brigade, and regimental command posts were duly established in nearby villages from one to five miles to the rear. Much to Palmer's disgust, the men had no heart for instruction. That was evident when an advancing platoon flushed a large sow and her brood from the underbrush. In an instant the men set off in high glee to capture some fresh pork.[36] Summerall was left to draw his own conclusions about civilian soldiers who had made up their minds that the war was over.

As the operation developed, one of Palmer's regiments moved off on a false bearing and opened a wide gap in the brigade front. At the critique following the maneuver, Summerall called particular attention to this mistake and reproved the colonel involved. Much to Palmer's chagrin, a careful check revealed that the misguided regiment had followed orders precisely. The error was one made by his own brigade operations officer. Characteristically, Palmer himself accepted full responsibility. Equally characteristically, he immediately resolved to send to Langres for a qualified staff school graduate. He was still working on this project when a telephone call from the chief of staff, General McAndrew, in Chaumont once again abruptly changed the course of his army career.[37]

34   Pershing's Emissary

The sum and substance of General McAndrew's call from Chaumont was that General Pershing wanted Palmer to go to the United Stated to represent him in the preparation of legislation for a permanent military establishment. Work on a proposed bill was already under way in the War Department, and the Chief of Staff had cabled from Washington asking for Palmer's services to assist in the effort. It was flattering to learn that the Chief of Staff, Gen. Peyton C. March, had asked for him and that General Pershing was willing to trust him as a spokesman for the AEF point of view. But what pleased him most was the realization that he was at last recognized as a specialist in the problems of army organization. Time was already short, however. March's cable had arrived more than three weeks before, but General Pershing, anxious not to jeopardize Palmer's health, had hesitated to send him back to the relentless grind of staff work in Washington. McAndrew finally persuaded the general to go ahead with the assignment, and he directed Palmer to report to Chaumont the following day, 25 December 1918.[1]

Although Palmer had been with the 29th Division less than three months, his departure was genuinely regretted. The enlisted men at his brigade headquarters demonstrated this when they invited him to share their Christmas dinner and then presented him with a fine carving set made from hand-forged steel by a local craftsman. Even crusty old General Morton, the division commander, recognized the sincerity of the gift. Palmer's men, the general declared, not only respected but loved him.[2] The same sentiment was echoed by most of the officers of the brigade. A farewell letter written by the French liaison officer, Lieutenant La Rochelle, suggests one possible clue: after expressing his great regret at losing a chief "si aimable et si bon," the lieutenant indicated that he especially appreciated the delicacy with which the colonel had always manifested his "sympathie clairvoyante pour la France."[3] This came close to the mark; clairvoyant or not, Palmer's inherent sensitivity to others was ever a notable ingredient of his remarkable personal charm.

When the colonel reached Chaumont, General McAndrew laid down his schedule. For two weeks while General Pershing was away on the Riviera, he was to study the various papers on reorganization being prepared in the AEF. When the general returned, there would be an opportunity to confer with him and get his specific instructions. Since the staff at GHQ had been struggling for nearly a month to work up a suitable statement of postwar military policy, a great many papers and a wide variety of views had already been accumulated. Brig. Gen. H. B. Fiske, the assistant chief of staff for training, and his G-5 staff had done much of the work, but their statement represented an amalgam of views from many sources throughout the AEF.[4]

The military policy proposed in the G-5 paper had three essential features. First, the planners expected to build the nation's defense on a manpower base furnished by universal military training. They were keenly aware of the lack of preparedness in 1917 and the fourteen months of frenzied effort that had slipped by before the first American offensive. Another time there might be no allies to hold the enemy at bay while the nation armed. Universal military training would assure a continuing supply of manpower always ready to meet the demands of defense. Second, the planners envisioned an army in which the regulars, the militia or National Guard of the several states, the marines, and the men of the wartime National Army would be combined into a single whole, with one set of regulations, customs, and traditions. Third, the G-5 paper insisted upon the need for full recognition of the General Staff as a necessary instrument of command. The war in Europe had demonstrated beyond all question, the planners believed, that the mass armies of modern war could never be efficiently handled unless the high command coordinated and controlled every activity and agency of the army through the mechanism of the General Staff, an agency to be manned only by officers drawn from an eligible list of carefully selected and highly trained individuals.

At best the G-5 paper was a crude product. It made little or no distinction between broad outlines of policy and the details of administration. In a sense the paper mirrored the staff procedures still being employed at Headquarters, AEF. The authors of the original draft had circularized the staff sections and a number of other interested individuals, inviting comments. The replies received had been used to prepare a revised statement that was again circulated, and so on through several revisions. Some of the criticisms received were most constructive, but virtually all represented little more than the unsupported opinions of the individuals consulted.[5]

The G-5 planners lacked studies in depth, case histories to supply carefully documented factual accounts of the problems encountered and the solutions found workable by experience in the AEF, to help them decide questions of policy or to support their conclusions. They proposed, for example, to abolish the Signal Corps and transfer its functions to the Corps of Engineers, allegedly to simplify an increasingly complex staff organization. Yet little or no factual evidence was adduced to justify such a drastic step, nor were possible alternatives considered. The planners lost themselves in trivia—should the training period for cavalry be three months longer to provide time for instruction in horse care? Highly subjective rhetoric supported questionable points. Universal training, they argued, would keep the people in closer touch with the military. "Public opinion on questions of war or peace will not be so liable to be influenced by newspapers, as the people will be educated by service as to what war means."[6]

General Pershing was wise indeed in wanting a specialist in organization to represent him in Washington. Palmer's stature as such a specialist was manifest in his response to the very first draft of the G-5 paper, which he had received while still serving with his brigade. In that version the planners had called for a universal military training period of seven months, but they made no provision for any further training. The colonel was quick to point out that this created no organized reserves ready to respond on call, only a reservoir of manpower with a certain amount of previous training. To be effective, a program of universal military training should feed men into fully organized units with provision for annual maneuvers to test the functioning of these units and train their leaders. To this end he urged the addition of a two-week refresher session in the year following the obligatory training period of seven months. One such recall to service was absolutely essential, but more, he believed, would be even better.[7]

Palmer's suggestion was not just a minor detail but a change in fundamental conception. In advocating an organized reserve in place of a mere pool of manpower, he was making the case for a true citizen army as opposed to an expansible regular army. In the former the companies, regiments, and divisions of the organized reserves would be officered by reservists, individuals who knew and understood the character and outlook of citizen soldiers; in the latter, the graduates of universal military training would be partially trained recruits used to fill up the ranks of skeletonized units in the permanent establishment under regular officers. In fact, Brig. Gen. Hugh Drum suggested precisely this. When he learned of Palmer's coming journey to Washington he wrote at length from First Army headquarters offering a number of ideas, proposing, among other things, a reserve organization in which all officers above the rank of captain would be drawn from the Regular Army.[8]

There was nothing new in Palmer's proposal; he did little more than restate the plan he had helped to prepare while serving on the War Department General Staff back in 1916 and 1917. But while many of his contemporaries in the AEF accepted the idea of one or more two-week follow-up sessions, he saw the annual recall period as vital to the whole conception of a citizen army. While every individual participating in a two-week maneuver might learn a great deal from the experience, the main purpose of the repeat session, as he saw it, was not individual but unit training. Without such unit training it would be difficult if not impossible to turn out an adequate number of reserve officers to command the larger units, and without a supply of reservists trained to meet these responsibilities, a true citizen army was out of the question.

In its final form the much-revised G-5 policy paper appeared on 23 December 1918 as a document of some forty pages. It proposed a program of universal military training for young men reaching the age of twenty. The period of training was set at seven months, running from April to October, with two weeks spent in mobilizing, six months in progressive training, and two weeks in demobilizing. September of each year was set apart for a two-week maneuver, with the graduates of the previous year's seven-month training session recalled to the colors. The period from November to March was designated as the school period for training noncommissioned officers and commissioned officers of all grades in their technical specialties. Members of the year's draftee class could, if they wished, remain in service on a voluntary basis for the rest of the year to continue their military training, or they could attend special classes providing vocational instruction for those anxious to improve their earning capacity, physical training for those with bodily defects, and educational work for illiterates.

Although the G-5 planners attempted to sweeten the pill of universal training by emphasizing its value as a giant social service agency, they were convinced that the best case for the program rested squarely on the necessity of a ready reserve for adequate national defense. They proposed to divide the country into four corps areas and, making use of the cantonments already available, to subdivide these into a total of sixteen divisional areas, adding four cavalry divisions "at large," one within each corps area. After training in one of these divisions for seven months and two weeks and attending a two-week refresher session during the following year, a reservist would pass into a second-line reserve, remaining there as a member of his local reserve division until discharged at age 31. Once the scheme became fully operative and a sufficient backlog of reservists accumulated, the planners envisioned a potential force of nearly 100 divisions, a formidable deterrent to any would-be aggressor.

Palmer was fully persuaded that the public would no longer oppose universal military training. The war, he believed, had created "a new public opinion entirely in favor of the principle," and he expected Congress to respond accordingly.[9] Time was to prove this opinion thoroughly wrong, although it probably did no more than mirror the stand taken by a majority of the officers at GHQ.

One obvious weakness of the G-5 paper was in the vital matter of costs. The planners had calculated the annual expense of their universal training program as only slightly more than the amount required under the Defense Act of

1916, the governing statute if no new legislation were passed. They had based their estimates on costs calculated in early 1917, but since then inflationary pressures had driven prices wildly upward. If Palmer's letters from his wife are any index, no officer at GHQ could have been entirely unaware of this inflation. After branding the G-5 figures inaccurate, Palmer bluntly warned, "The system is not a cheap one and it cannot be made to appear so."[10]

Palmer's knowledge of the prewar General Staff studies repeatedly proved of value to his analysis of the G-5 paper. For example, he noted that while he personally favored a seven-month training period, a majority of the General Staff committee studying the question in 1917 had come out for twelve months. They argued that men undergoing training in peacetime would be less highly motivated and thus require a longer period than the minimum found workable in wartime. Palmer believed Congress might balk at a full year of training in peace, and a seven-month session looked like an attractive compromise. But, recalling Congressman A. P. Gardner's admonishment back in 1916, he declared "it is a question whether this compromise should be anticipated in an official recommendation aiming at the highest military efficiency." For this reason he formally recommended a twelve-month training period as official AEF policy.[11] In arriving at this conclusion, he unwittingly demonstrated his value to General Pershing: here was an officer not only widely familiar with the issues involved but also entirely capable of urging a stand contrary to his own preferences.

There were decided limitations to Palmer's technical competence, and even in those areas where he was broadly informed he did not always see problems he did not wish to see.[12] This was clearly revealed in his comments upon the planners' "one army" concept. Their scheme would abolish the National Guard. "Officers of militia," said the G-5 paper, "have consistently been below standard, because of deficient military education, political and local affiliations, and consequent unwillingness to enforce discipline.... Their faults are absolutely inherent in a militia system and cannot be eradicated."[13] This was straight out of the pages of Emory Upton, against which Palmer had inveighed for years, yet in his official report he let the passage pass without comment. He had already come out in favor of offering the Guard an opportunity to accept charter membership in the organized reserve, and he was fully aware of the political power the Guard could muster in Congress. He understood clearly that no scheme for merging the nation's forces into "one army" could succeed without broad support on the Hill.

That Palmer could be sensitive to political reality is evident from his treatment of another aspect of the "one army" scheme. He agreed with the planners that the Marine Corps probably should be absorbed by the army, but rather than divert attention from the main reforms sought by injecting such a highly controversial issue, he recommended that the proposal be dropped. His willingness to see the marines merged with the army was based on a good deal of reflection including study of Japanese and German experience in the use of army troops as marines. His impartiality was demonstrated by his parallel suggestion that the harbor defense duties of the Coast Artillery might well be transferred to the navy. His argument in support of this idea offers an excellent illustration both of his working methods and his imagination in dealing with questions of organization.

> General Arthur Murray told me a number of years ago that the transfer of the harbor defense to the Navy Department was seriously considered, but that he opposed it because he thought it would hurt coast artillery interests inasmuch as the Navy Department would naturally concentrate their attention on their major problem which is mobile defense. He felt that the Navy Department would reduce the fixed harbor defenses to a minimum at the expense of the fleet. In other words, General Murray's argument for keeping the Coast Artillery out of the Navy was the best possible argument for making it a part of the Navy....
> For two years just before the war I had occasion to go over a great many of the coast artillery projects, and I felt satisfied that they were frequently proposing to put in expensive batteries and other emplacements where a scientific study of the problem might lead to a better solution by submarines and destroyers.[14]

Although Palmer's willingness to consider the use of submarines and destroyers as substitutes for coastal batteries showed an open-minded approach to the question of weapons, he was not always so imaginative. He appears to have given no special attention to the problems of postwar training raised by the new and highly complex weapons introduced during the war. Since no tanks had operated with the 29th Division during the Meuse-Argonne offensive, he had no experience whatever with the potentialities of armored warfare. His neglect of the airplane, however, is surprising, for as early as 1916 he had predicted that this new weapon would have a revolutionary impact on tactics. When he spoke of training divisions he seems to have envisioned infantry divisions organized and equipped largely as they had been during the war.

In sum, Palmer's analysis was for the most part penetrating in those areas where he was well informed and superficial or even misleading in those areas where he was poorly informed. Nor did he always know the precise limits of his understanding. He seems to have sensed his lack of first-hand experience with supply and urged the advisability of sending an AEF specialist in this field to help the War Department, but he appeared quite willing to accept a G-5 proposal to divest the Corps of Engineers of all civil functions, as if entirely unaware of the corps's potential political leverage when seeking military appropriations as well as peacetime training for military engineers. These strengths and limitations are doubly meaningful; not only do they help delineate the abilities of Palmer as an individual officer, but they also shed a good deal of light on the character of the staff work performed at Headquarters, AEF.

When Palmer finally submitted his findings to General McAndrews, he suggested that it would be well to rewrite the G-5 study, confining it to a convincing statement of the broad principles of policy desired, leaving the details to be worked out later. In this he was shrewdly capitalizing on the unanimity of opinion in the AEF on the major questions of policy while minimizing the wide differences he had encountered when discussing details. Furthermore, he proposed to drop controversial proposals, if this could be accomplished without sacrificing the major policy changes sought—universal training, the "one army" concept, and the principle of general staff coordination. Thus, for example, while he regarded the introduction of promotion by single list in place of the prevailing system by arms and services as a highly desirable innovation, he was willing to defer the matter for further study. Along with this politically prudent proposal, however, he coupled another that revealed a certain lack of guile if not a total innocence.[15]

The approved AEF policy statement, the colonel declared, should be sent to the Chief of Staff in Washington, leaving all questions of detail to be resolved there in the War Department General Staff by committees "representing different points of view." Palmer confidently assumed the chief of staff would select committees reflecting the whole spectrum of opinions and would be guided by their findings. Soon after coming to Chaumont from his command at Serqueux, he had learned of the gulf that had been developing between Pershing and March and more particularly some of their subordinates. But he was unwilling to attribute anything but the most disinterested intentions to any of his professional colleagues. Though the course of action he recommended would transfer the whole initiative for shaping postwar policy from the AEF to the War Department, which is to say from Pershing to March, he apparently saw no objection to the move.[16]

After completing his critique of the G-5 policy paper, Palmer was impatient to sail for the United States, since he knew that the postwar policies would be formulated in the War Department without reference to opinion in the AEF. At McAndrew's suggestion, he went up to Paris to discuss the permanent establishment with a number of officers whose opinions he respected. Some years afterward he wrote out a nostalgic account of his visit.

> On my way down on the train, I made a budget for my four days. My expenses had been light up at the front so I had an unaccustomed roll of one hundred franc notes in my wallet. I decided to get a big warm room in a first class hotel and to dine at four of the best restaurants during my four days in the city. I found an ideal room at the *Continental* with a

great big bath room and plenty of hot water. That had been an unaccustomed luxury for some time. After weeks of sponge baths in a cold room, it was glorious to sit in a big porcelain tub and let the warm water run in until it submerged my Adam's apple. The first night I dined at *Foyot's*, the second at *Lapérouse*, the third at the *Cafe de Paris*. The fourth night, as my hunger was a bit assuaged, I contented myself with a snack of duck and pommes soufflets at the *Tour d'Argent*.[17]

Between times he did finally manage to visit some of the officers he had come to see, among them General Tasker H. Bliss at the Supreme War Council. Bliss invited him to accept a place on his personal staff during the coming peace conference, but Palmer's assignment as Pershing's emissary seemed paramount—though he was honest enough to admit privately that his decision was somewhat colored by his desire to hurry home to his wife.[18]

When Pershing returned, Palmer reported to his office with a long list of points for the general to clarify. While he did not say as much, even to himself, his letters made it quite clear that he expected some sort of grand pronouncement on policy, a clear and forceful statement by the Commander in Chief that he could carry back to the United States, sweeping all dissidence before him with the enormous prestige of the Pershing name. To his utter astonishment, when he entered the room he found he had come not to a conference but to a ceremony. General Pershing gravely pinned a Distinguished Service Medal to his breast, while off to one side, Brig. Gen. Robert C. Davis, the Adjutant General, read the citation. It was immensely satisfying to be one of the very first officers in the AEF to receive the DSM. In spite of his long illness, in spite of his failure to attain high rank, he had proved himself in the test of war.[19]

As soon as the brief ceremony was concluded he expectantly turned to the Commander in Chief. But the general put him off, saying he had been so occupied with other matters he had been unable to give adequate attention to the problem of postwar policy.[20] After several days the general again postponed their discussion, suggesting that it might be more convenient if they conferred in Paris, where there would be fewer demands on his attention than at Chaumont.

This meant a second pilgrimage to the city. But the conditions had changed. After my four days as a sybarite, I must now return as an anchorite. My roll of hundred franc notes had grown thin. There were barely enough of them left to pay my travel expenses to Washington. So, I took a little room at a Y.M.C.A. hotel and dined at a little *brasserie* well off the Boulevards.[21]

In Paris, however, the general seemed to be busier than ever. As more than a month had elapsed since the War Department had solicited the AEF point of view on the postwar establishment, Pershing directed Palmer to sail for Washington immediately without waiting for detailed instructions.

In his retrospective account the colonel recalled Pershing's final words.

> "Palmer, I have decided not to give you any instructions. The problem of our future military organization is too big for snap judgment. There have been several proposals under discussion at headquarters, but I have never been able to give them the serious consideration that the subject deserves. Furthermore, the Secretary of War has not asked me for my views. So use your own judgment. Good-by and good luck."[22]

Palmer was led to believe that the Commander in Chief held his professional qualifications in sufficient esteem to trust his judgment implicitly as an emissary on a most difficult mission.

In describing the episode in later years, Palmer never gave the slightest indication that he attached any but the most literal interpretation to the general's remarks. There are indications in the record, however, that the Commander in Chief was quite willing to find an excuse for not formulating a position paper to set before the War Department and the Congress.[23]

Not all of Pershing's advisors were persuaded that it was wise for the general to declare himself immediately on postwar policy. Among these was Brig. Gen. Fox Conner, the assistant chief of staff for Operations, G-3. He questioned whether one could assume that Congress would accept universal training on any terms. The President and the Secretary of War were clearly opposed. Discussions of the League of Nations certainly suggested that military preparedness might find precious little congressional support. It was foolish, he believed, to spend time working up the details of military policy before the broad outlines had been determined. The organization, training, and equipping of a hundred thousand or more men "for the protection of national parks" was an entirely different proposition from the problem the army would encounter if universal training were adopted.[24]

Conner pointed out that the Commander in Chief would be in a much stronger position if he refused to identify, at least for the time being, with any particular school of thought. Moreover, since the War Department was reported to have formulated a policy without waiting for word from the AEF, the necessity for a statement from Pershing seemed no longer pressing.[25] The general apparently agreed with Conner, for not long after Palmer's departure he ordered the G-5 paper withdrawn from circulation. "To spring the thing here as our scheme would involve us ... in a good deal of discussion ... entirely out of place."[26] Clearly Pershing had no intention of allowing his luster to tarnish by involvement in premature controversy.

The danger of damaging controversies was by no means imaginary. While Pershing and March, Pershing's nominal superior as Chief of Staff, continued to correspond without overt acrimony, signs of mounting tension between the two leaders became more frequent. Brig. Gen. Hugh S. Johnson wrote to his friend Maj. Gen. J. B. Harbord from his vantage point on the War Industries Board in Washington describing one side of the rivalry.

> I doubt . . . if the army was ever a prey to more implacable, ambitious, and self-seeking control than it is at present. In my opinion a conscious effort is being made to build up against the return of the army from France a powerful and partisan General Staff headed by classmates and men in intimate relationship with the Chief of Staff. There is every indication of this and I believe it is the general opinion. On the other hand the almost meglomaniacal tendencies of the Chief of Staff have created such bitter animosities, such smarting and resentment, as I, at least, have never seen.[27]

While March's request for Palmer's services in formulating postwar policy partly contradicted Johnson's charges of partisanship, the mere fact that such a letter was written tells something of the atmosphere around the principals involved. Significantly, Harbord picked up the theme and passed it along to his chief.

When Harbord gave up his position as Chief of Staff at Chaumont, first for a combat command and later as head of the Services of Supply at Tours, he continued the confidential relationship he had established with Pershing during the formative period of the AEF. Though many miles separated the two headquarters, and their personal encounters were far less frequent than formerly, he had not lost his almost intuitive knack for approaching the general in just the right terms. He went to the heart of the problem, the preservation of Pershing's prestige, his power to shape policy and to secure promotions for his loyal lieutenants in the years to come. Harbord suggested that those who hoped to undermine the general might follow either of two courses. They could recall most of his troops but leave him in France, an empty figurehead, or they could bring him to the United States for a hero's welcome, to be followed by an assignment to duty carefully chosen to insure oblivion. Harbord foresaw many pitfalls along the triumphal route of a returning hero. When daily beset by clamoring newsmen and importunate politicians it would be painfully easy to say something unwise. Then there were the inevitable congressional investigations. Since all wars end with the search for scape-goats, Harbord observed that the prudent course would be to organize the voluminous records of the AEF while the manpower was still available, sorting, classifying, and indexing to provide ammunition for a ready defense against the day when it might be needed.[28]

While Harbord no less than Johnson may have exaggerated the dangers of the alleged cabal against the Commander in Chief and all who bore "the

Pershing brand," his warning suggests how far suspicion could foster animosity. The point is worth making not only for its own sake but also for the contrast it affords to the character of John M. Palmer. He was well aware of the transatlantic tension, but he simply refused to see what he did not wish to see. His innocence of manner was his armor. He saw himself, as he subsequently expressed it, as an "uninstructed delegate," combining authority with broad discretion, the bearer of a blank check. It would be more accurate, however, to say he carried an unsigned check; indeed, the cautious Commander in Chief had sent him off with a nonnegotiable piece of paper.

35   In Search of a Policy

Once back in Washington, Palmer presented himself to the Chief of Staff with some misgivings. General March had asked for his services, but there was always the possibility that he might still resent their tart exchange over the Sam Browne belt during the previous summer. If the general recalled the episode, he gave no sign of it, for his reception was most cordial. Not long afterward at his weekly press conference he described Palmer as "a very able officer," an opinion he confirmed by assigning him to the War Plans Division. When the colonel reported for duty on 31 January 1919, however, he discovered that his role as emissary for General Pershing had been cut out from under him. General March had already carried a War Department bill to Capitol Hill calling for a sweeping reorganization of the Army.[1]

The Chief of Staff's bill proposed a large standing army of over half a million men, the very opposite of everything Palmer had urged for many years. Moreover, since the bill, HR 14560, had been sent to the Hill on 14 January, it must have been prepared even before Pershing decided not to spell out his views on postwar policy.[2] Had March never intended to make use of Pershing's opinions? And why had he asked for Palmer's services, if he favored a standing army nearly as large as that of prewar Germany, supposedly the epitome of autocratic militarism? If March knew the colonel well enough to ask for him personally, surely he must have known of his pronounced views on the subject.

After reading the testimony presented by the Secretary of War and the Chief of Staff in defense of the War Department bill, Palmer was more puzzled than ever.[3] It was evident to the most superficial observer that the two men had markedly different conceptions of the legislation before them. Baker regarded much of the measure as an emergency move. Virtually all enlistments, he explained, would expire four months after the declaration of peace.

Unless the existing statutes were revised, the nation might find itself without an army to meet its obligations in the occupation of Germany and elsewhere. As to the total of 509,909 men specified in the bill, the secretary felt no special commitment. That figure represented only a transient requirement, to be voted away by Congress when the need had passed.

There was nothing in Baker's testimony to suggest that he was not entirely sincere in his belief, but the bill as drawn proposed nothing less than a major reorganization of the army. To begin with, it would perpetuate the new arms and services created during the war by adding an air service, a tank corps, a transportation corps, and several other agencies to the permanent establishment. In addition, the bill called for a number of major procedural changes. These included a section on promotion by selection rather than seniority and another giving the President wide discretion in prescribing the internal organization of the army.

Palmer saw many meritorious features in the War Department bill. The section providing executive latitude on internal organization promised to obviate the difficulties he had experienced back in 1917, when his efforts to devise a suitable table of organization for the AEF were blocked by the rigidity of the prevailing statutes. But the measure as a whole marked a radical departure from tradition. Virtually all of its provisions were highly debatable, and some of them were almost certain to offend congressional sensibilities.

After reading the testimony it was difficult not to suspect that the Chief of Staff was trying to slip through a major reform of the military establishment under the guise of an emergency measure to be passed in haste before Congress adjourned. If this were not his intention, why had he sat blandly by while Baker told the members of the House Military Affairs Committee that the half-million-man army requested was only an estimate of temporary need. General March knew perfectly well that this was not the case. The total of 509,909 men had been carefully computed by the General Staff as a minimum cadre upon which an army of 1,250,000 men or twenty-one divisions could be mobilized without excessive dilution of the regulars.[4]

If General March seriously expected to slip a major reform measure through Congress, he miscalculated badly. The House committeemen were quite ready to recommend a half-million men if the Army of Occupation and other current demands so required, but they were entirely unwilling to be rushed into any sweeping reform of the army without careful scrutiny. One member, Rep. Rollin Sanford of New York, suggested that the War Department bill evaded the central issue. The bill implicitly accepted the principle of a large standing army as the foundation of national defense, while ignoring entirely both the National Guard and the principle of universal military training. The House, Sanford declared, would insist upon considering the fundamental question of "whether the country is going to rely upon a professional army or upon citizens trained as soldiers" as the main element of national defense.[5]

Representative Sanford observed that no member of Congress had the technical proficiency to draft a military bill. If the legislators were to weigh the merits of a large professional army against a system of defense built around the National Guard, universal training, or a combination of these, bills embracing various alternatives would have to be prepared in the War Department and sent to the Hill. But this was precisely what Mr. Baker did not wish to do. He admitted that several bills dealing with universal training had been prepared by the General Staff, but these he declined to send the Congress. The fourth of President Wilson's Fourteen Points looked to a reduction in armament throughout the world. It would never do to urge disarmament abroad while supporting the principle of compulsion at home.[6]

The problem, as Palmer saw it, was how to get a professionally drafted bill for universal training before Congress. With a Chief of Staff who believed in a large standing army and a Secretary of War who apparently regarded universal training as synonymous with autocratic militarism, the task seemed almost hopeless. The colonel discovered, however, that there were a number of legislators who were determined to give universal training a thorough airing. Their approach was clearly revealed in the following letter received by Mr. Baker:

12 February 1919

My dear Mr. Secretary:

The Senate Committee on Military Affairs have directed me to transmit a copy of a bill (S. 5485) providing for a system of universal training, recently introduced by Senator New, with the request that the same be referred to the General Staff, and that they make a study of the bill and of the subject of universal military training generally, and report their recommendations to this committee at their earliest convenience.

Respectfully,

D. W. McIntosh
Assistant Clerk[7]

The Senate committee was obviously trying to smoke out the real views of the General Staff. As it turned out, the Chief of Staff was absent from Washington when the matter came up, and the War Plans Division readily secured approval from the acting chief for the preparation of an elaborate study in response to the Senate request. Soon afterwards, a large task force consisting of some twenty officers was engaged in this project under Palmer's supervision. The full resources of the War Plans Division were deployed on the project to make certain that the final product would stand up under the most penetrating congressional scrutiny.[8]

Palmer went to great lengths to be sure that the end result of his committee's labors enjoyed the broadest possible support within the War Department. He arranged to have copies of the work in progress widely circulated not only in the General Staff but among the arms and services as well, inviting criticism of anything that appeared unsound or ambiguous. His explanation of this departure from the normal staff procedure revealed one of the major defects in the existing practice.

> I do not think that valuable results will come from continuing the method heretofore followed in developing this study entirely within the War Plans Division. The difficulty lies in the fact that busy members of other divisions and bureaus are invited to act on a crystalized system complete in every detail when there may be and are fundamental differences as to the foundations of the plan. If these officers dissent, their comments are treated in further appendices resulting in a continued pyramiding of the appendices pro and con. The study of the project is now very formidable for busy officers of high rank and a continuance of the method simply tends to complicate the problem of presentation to the Chief of Staff and through him to the Secretary of War.[9]

By inviting criticism at the earliest stages of planning and by displaying endless patience in answering the objections raised, Palmer assured himself of wide agreement on principles. When the final report was ready, he solicited formal concurrences from every officer in the War Plans Division. The replies clearly demonstrated that General March was not correct when he testified that the big standing army he advocated more or less accurately reflected prevailing military thought on the subject. By putting the evidence in the record, the congressmen could see the facts for themselves and draw their own conclusions.[10]

The finished paper, "Outline of a National Military Policy Based on Universal Military Training," which was sent to the Chief of Staff 1 April 1919, was little more than a modified version of the ideas Palmer had worked up while still in France.[11] Its fundamental principle was an organized reserve, formed initially from the veterans of the recent war and perpetuated by a new class annually produced through universal military training. The units of this reserve army would be called up for short periods each year to perfect the process of mobilization and afford an opportunity for maneuvering large formations. After an initial period of training, no reservist would be required to attend more than two maneuvers or test mobilizations. On the other hand, officers and noncoms who desired to earn promotions in the reserve would continue to attend annual maneuvers as well as their local unit drills and training meetings.

There were many advantages to the plan, Palmer believed. To the charge of militarism, so often leveled at schemes of universal training, he replied that only 10 percent of the officers engaged in the work of training would be drawn from the Regular Army. The organized reserve forces would be entirely civilian, officers as well as men. For Palmer the plan met the need for organized military strength by means of institutions essentially democratic in character. A significant example of this democratic character was the means by which the plan would "solve the National Guard problem." Officers and noncoms were to be enrolled as volunteers in the newly organized reserve army at their present grades, "subject to liberally interpretated specifications as to qualifications." This arrangement, he believed, would prove acceptable to the greater part of the veteran guardsmen.

Palmer was entirely unprepared for the response his plan received from the Chief of Staff on his return to Washington. General March scarcely had time to read the paper before rejecting it out of hand. Palmer was stunned. He and his colleagues on the staff had prepared a thoroughly rational plan, a "scientific solution" to the problem. For the Chief of Staff to veto the whole thing solely on the basis of his rank and authority seemed unthinkable. So Palmer went to the office of the Chief of Staff in the hopes of achieving a reversal by personal persuasion.[12]

He never got beyond the chief's outer officer. He poured out his case to the deputy chief, but the effort was largely wasted. His message combined arguments in favor of universal training and political insight. From correspondence with his numerous friends who were citizen soldiers—guardsmen, National Army officers, and the like—Palmer was convinced that March's bill had not the slightest chance of becoming law. Both political expediency and sound policy suggested abandoning the "big army" concept of national defense in favor of a more popular "citizen army" approach.[13]

Much to Palmer's chagrin, General March directed the staff to abstain from action on any proposal inconsistent with the "big army" bill he had sent to Congress. If Congress wanted a citizen army, he would give them a bill providing just that—his bill, calling for a standing army of 509,909 men, with a new section to establish a program of universal training.[14] That he had no genuine faith in universal training or in the concept of a citizen army was evident from the character of his proposal. The universal training he approved was limited to three months. He had no intention of creating an organized reserve; once a trainee completed his three months, no further demand would be made upon him, short of a declaration of war. In General March's view, universal service was only a device to give advanced basic training to the draftees who would bring his professional cadres up to full strength in time of emergency.

General March's rejection of the General Staff plan was made doubly galling for Palmer when he was ordered to prepare a draft of the new bill. But worse was to come. He was further instructed to prepare a letter of transmittal in which the measure was presented as the official response of the War Department to the Senate request for a General Staff study of Senator New's bill.[15] Palmer and his friends had been outsmarted; the general was beating them at their own game. He was using the Senate request to fob off his big army bill with its bogus universal training amendment as if it were the product of the General Staff.

General March's tactics plunged Palmer into dark discouragement. The general could outmaneuver his staff, but in so doing, was he really providing the leadership the times required? Congress was desperately in need of careful education on the complex military issues currently requiring action. For want of careful preparation, the whole question of mustering-out pay—so essential in bridging the gap between discharge and civilian employment—had been botched in Congress. Almost the same could be said about the handling of special appropriations for the U.S. Employment Service to help discharged soldiers find jobs. And the question of army pay was a crying scandal. Even with the wartime base pay of $30 per month, a private had little enough left in his pocket after his deductions were subtracted. Nonetheless, economy-minded Congressmen were talking of a return to the old prewar base pay of $15, and one could scarcely condemn them for this when the chief of staff himself had suggested such a course in defending his "big army" bill.[16]

The absence of effective leadership from the War Department was nowhere more evident than in the congressional debates on army manpower for the coming year. The members of the House Committee on Military Affairs took Mr. Baker at his word. While rejecting all thought of authorizing a permanent army of 509,909 men, they recommended an appropriation for this number on a temporary basis.[17] On the floor of the House, however, many congressmen apparently agreed with the representatives who saw the measure as an entering wedge for a large standing army. Although this was precisely what the Military Affairs Committee did not favor, the publicity given to the 509,909 figure in the big army proposal sponsored by General March made the confusion entirely understandable.

In this mood of suspicion and misunderstanding, Congress finally passed an appropriation act in July 1919 cutting army manpower back to the levels authorized by the Defense Act of 1916. The effect was catastrophic. Although the act authorized the War Department to retain temporarily the various new arms and services such as the Air Service, the Tank Corps, the Transportation Corps, and the several others created during the war, the legislators made no provision for commissioned personnel to operate the new organizations. With no permanent commissions authorized for the Air Service, large numbers of temporary officers who would have made excellent career men returned to civilian life. Between the Armistice and July 1919, the Air Service dropped from 11,425 to 148 officers, and even this handful had to be carried under the quotas of the traditional arms and services.[18]

Palmer began to wonder whether he was right to remain in the service after all. Since he had little hope of making much impression in the War Department, at least while General March remained as chief of staff, the idea of retiring to embark on a literary career began to look increasingly attractive. So he drafted a letter to his old friend Arthur Ruhl, the writer for *Collier's* magazine whom he had first met in 1911 on the Mexican border.

> It has seemed to me that there is a field here as important and as interesting as the Naval field traversed by Admiral Mahan, and ... if I could make a contribution in this direction I would be doing a better service than I could possibly do on the active list. ...
>
> I think I have exerted a little influence in guiding the activities of the War Department, but the trouble is ... the scientific solution is generally so modified by purely political influences before it is published that the resultant is generally of little value. I do not believe that the problem of national military organization can be solved in Congress or in the War Department until it is solved in public opinion. ... On the other hand if a sound and reasonable solution could be published in popular form it soon would be reflected in official action.[19]

Palmer's idea of devoting his energies to molding public opinion appealed to his many friends in the Military Training Camps Association. Soon after his return from France he had renewed his ties with the various members of the "Plattsburg crowd" who had worked so zealously for preparedness in 1916 and 1917. Among others Grenville Clark responded, bringing him up to date on the fate of their propaganda organ, *National Service*.[20] The magazine had somehow struggled through the war. Clark's casual suggestion that Palmer might contribute some articles eventually ripened into a proposal for full-time employment. Tompkins McIlvaine, the New York lawyer who was doing his best to keep *National Service* alive as its part-time editor, was delighted at the prospect but anticipated trouble in raising enough money to pay a suitable salary.[21]

In the meantime Palmer continued to do what he could within the General Staff to advance the idea of a citizen army. Most of his working hours were absorbed in papers on the various technical problems assigned to the War Plans staff, but this did not prevent him from devoting a great deal of thought to the subject that interested him most. The great difficulty was to find the right kind of leadership to give direction to the popular will. Even with the best of intentions, congressmen are not in a position to initiate solutions to technical questions; their role is to adjudicate claims, to choose among alternatives. But who would propose the alternatives? The Administration— the President, the Secretary of War, the Chief of Staff? If not these, the initiative would pass to special-interest groups—the National Guard, the Military Training Camps Association, or any one of the many other voices clamoring to be heard.

Very little constructive guidance, it seemed, was to be expected from the Administration. Secretary Baker had already made it quite clear that he was unwilling to embarrass President Wilson's efforts to foster disarmament by coming out for any realistic program of compulsory training.[22] He refused to entertain such a program while the League of Nations was still a possibility. Baker was undoubtedly sincere, but it was not without a certain significance that his coolness to universal training found strong support in Congress, especially among members from southern states, where the issue was entangled with the race question.[23]

Baker had repeatedly shown that he did not really understand the nature of the problem. While testifying on the "big army" bill in January, he had indicated that he saw no relationship between the size of the army and the introduction of universal training. Yet one of Palmer's major arguments for universal training was that it would permit a major reduction in the size of the Regular Army. Even more disturbing, however, was the way Baker put his prestige behind a big army plan that ignored the National Guard, yet continued to assert compliance with the spirit of the Defense Act of 1916, assigning the Guard a central role.

The contradictions and confusions of Baker's views on military policy were nowhere more evident than in his enthusiasm for academic and vocational training throughout the army. This played directly into General March's hand.[24] Making the army into a great educational institution would popularize voluntary enlistment and thus make possible the large standing army General March wished to recruit. Palmer was not opposed to improving army education, but he was highly dubious of the motives behind the scheme. So, too, was Grenville Clark, who reported his reactions to Palmer after a visit with Third Assistant Secretary F. P. Keppel.

> I had quite a long talk with him in the effort to discover whether these recreational and educational ideas are a species of camouflage to bolster up a permanent volunteer army policy with a view to getting away from a universal training scheme. He assured me that there was no such motive and that Mr. Baker's mind was entirely open on universal training but that Baker would not commit himself until the peace treaty situation had cleared up. Keppel is entirely sincere and an honest, nice fellow, but he didn't entirely convince me. In view of past history I would

have to be shown conclusively before I would believe that Baker will ever really support universal training in peace time.

My general point of view on all this is that I have no faith at all in the present War Department administration advocating what we want and believe that the big results are to be achieved only by outside and probably political action. Nevertheless, it is worth while getting all we can out of the present administration and then as long as we do not fool ourselves it is well to work with them instead of giving them up as absolutely hopeless enemies, according to the General Wood policy.[25]

Palmer's reply showed he placed even less confidence in Baker's program.

I think your suspicions are completely justified that the policy here is predicated not only on the idea that we are not to have universal military training, but that it is deliberately aimed at killing the issue if practicable. . . .

The proposition is very adroit. If we assume that we cannot have universal military training, then no doubt we must have special incentives to get recruits if we are to have a large regular force. This makes a great educational feature legitimate, but to assume in advance that we are not to have a sound policy and to tempt the educational interests in this way, is calculated in my opinion to seduce them into an interested opposition to universal training. . . .

I agree with you that the fight must be from the outside and I cannot help feeling that if I am to help I should get at it very soon. . . .

I hope you do not think I am opposed to the ROTC. I would use it to the fullest limit as an integral part of a universal training policy. But I think the present tendency is to use it to camouflage an attack on universal training.[26]

Palmer was thoroughly disillusioned with General March. It was difficult for him to believe that any responsible leader could willfully reject a proposed line of policy without a discussion of its merits. His initial confidence in March's fairmindedness had been such that he had urged Pershing to transfer the whole job of working up postwar military policy to March's staff in Washington. Now he could only feel that his confidence had been thoroughly misplaced. Not surprisingly, he developed a hostility toward March that persisted for the rest of their lives.[27]

As a close student of Elihu Root's great reforms, Palmer was convinced that General March was misusing his authority. March seemed to regard his office as that of a commanding general, entirely free to use his staff as the instrument of his will. For Palmer, who vividly recalled Secretary Stimson's "open court" procedure for dealing with controversial issues, the proper relationship between the chief and his staff was something quite different. His quarrel with March was not with his refusal to support universal training but with his method of doing so. While the general was temperamentally inclined to command rather than preside as a Chief of Staff, when it suited his purpose he was only too willing to assert that he was not at liberty to pursue a line of policy at variance with that laid down by his civilian superiors. He demonstrated this in his reply to a congressman who urged him to release the studies on universal training prepared by the General Staff.

> Universal military training is a question of national policy . . . that is determined, of course, by the responsible civil officers. Whatever I may say about it or think about it, or whatever recommendations the General Staff may make, go to the Secretary of War, and he has told you that he has those recommendations on his desk. When such recommendations do not get by the Secretary, they stop.[28]

The obvious inference was that civil authority had made a selection from among alternative courses; yet in view of the highhanded manner in which General March had treated the latest General Staff plan for universal training, Palmer had reason to doubt whether the secretary had ever really had an opportunity to judge the issue on its merits.

If March's conception of his office was such that he felt under no obligation to make available the full spectrum of professional thought on a controversial issue, then his pose as a loyal subordinate could become dangerously misleading. When he presented the civil authorities his own views and represented— or misrepresented—them as the work of the General Staff, that danger was compounded. But even if General March had exercised his authority in the manner prescribed by Root and Stimson, his insensitivity to political realities suggested that he was ill-equipped to offer constructive guidance for Congress. Nowhere was this more evident than in his handling of the National Guard question.[29]

Palmer knew that any attempt to formulate long-term military policy without full consideration of the National Guard was egregious folly. Not only was a considerable amount of congressional patronage involved— payrolls, armories, and various other occasions for expenditure—but by its very nature the Guard was a question of concern in the home district of every single legislator. In 1919 the sensibilities of Congress had been aroused more than ever about the Guard. A certain amount of friction between regulars and reservists, professionals and citizen soldiers, had been inevitable in the wild scramble to mobilize an army of millions in a matter of months. While the war lasted, however, many of these conflicts had been held in check. After the Armistice, pent-up frustrations compounded by misunderstanding unleashed a wave of charges and countercharges about every aspect of the army and its administration.[30] The same thing had happened after every war in the past and could be expected to recur in the future; demagogues were soon in full cry in Congress, mirroring the complaints of their disgruntled constituents.

The regulars were for the most part apolitical professionals; many were not even registered voters. On the other hand, even if most guardsmen normally abstained from political activity as individuals, the Guard organization in any given state comprised an articulate constituency. Moreover, sheer local pride on the part of the citizens in each state operated to benefit the Guard in any political contest. Palmer was reminded of this by his old friend Louis L. Babcock, the Buffalo lawyer and guardsman, one of those whose opinions he had solicited shortly after his return from France.

> I look to see the Army and the National Guard line up for an old fashioned fight as soon as Congress convenes [Babcock wrote] for all New York Officers seem to be especially sore on the treatment accorded the National Guard by the Regulars. The National Guard has a tremendous advantage in such a fight for it has the backing of the locality. Take, for instance, the 27th Division. The papers have been full of news pertaining to it for months and most people believe it practically broke the German line and turned the tide. Contrast this with the 1st, 2nd, and 3rd Division. Not one person in ten thousand ever heard of . . . them or knew what they did or where they were. . . . Now, when it comes down to a fight in Congress the National Guard has the upper hand and believe me there will be some stirring times over the question of reorganization if the two elements line up. If I were the Regulars, I should say, compromise.[31]

While relatively few congressmen were willing to accept the charge that the army had been grossly mishandled by the "Leavenworth clique," many if not a majority developed a genuine suspicion of the army's intentions. The resulting congressional animus was most often expressed not against General March but against "the Regular Army" as a whole. From Palmer's point of view this obscured the fact that many regulars wished to preserve the Guard, and it complicated the question by pitting the regulars and the guardsmen against one another.[32] The drift of opinion on the Hill was evident from the applause that greeted those congressmen who came out in favor of retaining the National Guard as a basic element of national defense. The difficulty lay in finding out exactly what the guardsmen wanted. The National Guard was an exceedingly complex entity; no one individual or agency could speak for the whole.[33]

Among the several groups lobbying for the militia, the National Guard Association was the largest and probably the best organized. With more than forty years of experience, it should have been in a position to play a constructive role in postwar discussions. Unfortunately, in 1919 the association fell into the hands of extremists. The annual convention elected one of these, Lt. Col. Bennett Clark, son of the former Speaker of the House, Champ Clark of Missouri, as president. The aim of the association, Clark declared, was "to build up the National Guard and smash the Regular Army." Such irresponsible talk brought a prompt denial from many individuals within the association and a wave of highly critical editorials across the nation.[34]

Another lobby was the Adjutants General Association, weak in numbers but with political ties in every state capital. The Adjutants General were particularly interested in legislation giving them a larger part in formulating the regulations laid down for the Guard by the War Department. One recurring complaint leveled against the Militia Bureau of the General Staff was that the regular officers in the bureau were seldom adequately familiar with the practical problems confronting citizen soldiers. By securing the appointment of a Guard officer as chief of the Militia Bureau, some members of the association hoped to remedy this defect. Others even urged that the Militia Bureau be removed completely from General Staff supervision.[35]

Both of the associations could claim a powerful influence, but neither could claim to speak for the rank and file of the Guard at all times. Some Guard officers believed that militia organizations were a thing of the past; others felt that only drastic modifications in structure would make the Guard truly effective.[36] Among the latter, the most distinguished was Maj. Gen. John F. O'Ryan, commanding general of the famous 27th National Guard Division of New York.

Early in June 1919, General O'Ryan prepared a memo for the Chief of Staff to reverse the line of policy then sponsored by the War Department. Instead of dropping the Guard, as General March seemed to be doing, O'Ryan wished to go in the other direction, strengthening and improving the Guard to make it an essential cornerstone of national defense. He was willing to accept the brief three-month period of universal training but would strengthen that training by requiring an additional three-year period of service in the National Guard. By this combination of full-time and part-time soldiering, he expected to preserve the concept of an army based on citizen soldiers, while at the same time winning support for universal training. To be efficient, the plan would require a high degree of centralized control. This would involve removing the organization from the control of the several states and placing it under a single, central federal authority.[37]

General O'Ryan based his appeal on the political premise that any reorganization plan ignoring the National Guard was "fatally defective." Previous plans emanating from the War Department had foundered because they failed to recognize this bit of political wisdom. "This time," he declared, "we must all unite." To this end he urged the professionals to rough out a plan and then call in all the interested parties before presenting a completed bill to Congress. But in stressing the need for cooperation, O'Ryan all but ignored the crucial issue. Federalizing the Guard would virtually hand over control to the professional soldiers in the War Department, a proposition not likely to win widespread support in view of the mood of hostility toward the Regular Army that seemed to prevail in many quarters of the Guard.

General O'Ryan was well aware of the problem. On the one hand he was wooing the War Department—the Chief of Staff, the General Staff, the professional soldiers—and on the other the rank and file of the National Guard. He had to persuade the former to use citizen soldiers rather than a large standing army as the basis for national defense, and he had to persuade the latter that federal or centralized control was essential to an efficient system of defense. In addressing General March he emphasized the need for cooperation and minimized the difficulty of breaking away from state control. In addressing the Guard, he disparaged the Regular Army as a mercenary force and emphasized the special arrangements by which centralized control could be achieved with a staff largely composed of citizen soldiers.[38]

However patriotic his motives, General O'Ryan promptly discovered the difficulty of talking from two sides of one's mouth. Copies of the letter he had addressed to the Guard leaders soon found their way to the War Department. There his slighting remarks about mercenary professionals and the need for freeing citizen soldiers from "the arbitrary dominion of the Regular Army" did little to win support for his proposals. Palmer was quite willing to ignore the implied insults because he thought the document contained a number of constructive suggestions, but the director of the War Plans Division, Brig. Gen. Lytle Brown, apparently felt otherwise. After discussing the matter with the Chief of Staff, Brown instructed his staff to "leave it strictly alone."[39]

Whether or not General O'Ryan could have brought the War Department and the Guard into agreement remains open to question. Although a committee of officers continued to study his formal proposal, the decision to remain strictly aloof from his negotiations with the Guard organizations effectively nullified his role as a matchmaker. With Secretary Baker and General March already disqualified, the decision not to work with General O'Ryan eliminated the last of the symbolic personalities who might have provided the leadership for army reform. More by default than by conscious decision, Palmer looked increasingly toward the Military Training Camps Association as a rallying point.

As a potential source of leadership the Military Training Camps Association suffered from several notable defects. One was the absence of a single well-known personality capable of galvanizing diverse groups into a united effort. On the other hand, probably no other patriotic lobby could boast of such a large number of high-minded, disinterested individuals in its ranks. Yet this asset was also a serious drawback; unlike the National Guard, the Military Training Camps Association had no large body of members with an immediate and highly personal stake in the policies advocated. With more than 1,500 local officers; a magazine, *National Service*; and some 18,000 of its members returning as veterans, the association had all the conventional apparatus to support a major political move, but most of its former enthusiasm was gone. It proved impossible to arouse the same sense of urgency and personal commitment that had animated the young men who flocked to the association's standard during the preparedness movement before the war.[40]

The postwar objective of the Military Training Camps Association remained largely what it had been prior to 1917: the adoption of an adequate, permanent military policy. The association remained unalterably opposed to a large standing army as undemocratic and to a volunteer army as both prohibitively expensive and inadequate in numbers. Instead, on the assumption that "equality of opportunity implies equality of obligation," the goal sought was a citizen army based on universal training.

> We believe that the only sound practicable and democratic method by which the United States can maintain an adequate military force is through a carefully selected training cadre of regular and reserve officers, non-commissioned officers and specialists, supplemented by successive classes of citizens in training and a reserve, selected under the obligatory system.[41]

The program of the Military Training Camps Association was clear and unequivocal, but not ideally suited to attract support. Secretary Baker's unwillingness to sponsor any scheme of compulsory training necessarily kept him from collaborating closely with an organization dedicated to just such a program. When representatives from the association approached him for permission to cooperate with the General Staff in preparing an army reorganization bill, he put them off.[42] In much the same fashion the organization's opposition to a large standing army was not likely to win the enthusiastic cooperation of the incumbent Chief of Staff. Moreover, while the association had always recognized the need to avoid alienating the National Guard—indeed, many of its members were guardsmen—there were substantial differences separating the two groups. The association had little faith in the ability of the Guard to win the confidence of the nation as the proper instrument for training citizens. If for no other reason, the hostility of organized labor toward the Guard for its role in policing strikes promised to alienate an important segment of the population. And at least some members of the association were led to mistrust the Guard as a whole by the selfishness of some of the lobbyists representing Guard interests.[43]

For six months after the Armistice a committee of the Military Training Camps Association headed by Palmer's friend Tompkins McIlvaine labored to draw up a suitable reorganization bill. McIlvaine was a man of prodigious energy, zeal, and imagination. To illustrate this his friends liked to recall one episode in particular about his wartime service as a National Army officer. Always immaculate in dress and a rather vain man, when commissioned he became, if possible, even more impeccable in appearance and self-confident in manner. One day when a whole convoy of fully laden transports was delayed in New York harbor for want of an official release, the self-assured reservist unhesitatingly wrote out the necessary document and signed it grandly:

by order of Woodrow Wilson, President

per Tompkins McIlvaine,
Captain, QMC

McIlvaine returned to civil life to serve as a member of the executive committee of the National Security League, as chairman of the executive committee of the Military Training Camps Association, and for a considerable period as editor of *National Service*. In addition to all this, he maintained an active law practice in New York. He and his committee consulted the widest possible range of opinion, civilian and military, but they made no determined effort to form alliances with interested parties whose support might prove helpful. They were idealists and political amateurs.[44]

Toward the end of July 1919, the Military Training Camps Association finally had a "national service" measure ready for the Hill.[45] To publicize the occasion the leaders of the association organized a large formal dinner at the Willard Hotel in Washington. Sen. James W. Wadsworth of New York, the chairman of the Senate Military Affairs Committee, was asked to preside; Sen. George E. Chamberlain of Oregon and Rep. Julius Kahn of California, who had sponsored parallel versions of the association's bill in Congress, were invited as guests of honor. In addition, a large number of invitations were extended to interested individuals, legislators, reserve officers, regulars, and others. The plan was entirely characteristic of the patriots who sparked the association. They would present their bill and have speakers expound its merits in a straightforward, fair-minded appeal to reason.

Palmer accepted the association invitation with pleasure but was somewhat dubious about further speechmaking. He was beginning to understand the dangers of presenting Congress with too many widely conflicting schemes, each backed by more or less powerful interests. Almost inevitably such a course would lead to irrational compromises and faulty or undesirable legislation. From a careful study of the ideas presented by General O'Ryan along with those submitted by McIlvaine for the Military Training Camps Association, he was convinced that effective compromises could be worked out behind the scenes before going to Congress. With this in mind, he drafted a memo for his immediate superior, echoing a similar suggestion by General O'Ryan.

> The two plans are essentially the same in their broad outline—I say this recognizing that there are decided differences in detail between them. These two plans, insofar as they are based on a national territorial army composed initially of war veterans and ultimately of young men compulsorily trained, are essentially the same in principle as the War Plans Division plan prepared early this spring.
>
> It seems to me that this fact of substantial agreement among men who have approached this problem from quite different points of view, is very important at this time. I am quite convinced that if two or three National Guard officers, including General O'Ryan, and two or three former National Army officers, including Major McIlvaine, could be invited to come down for a conference with officers of the General Staff who have worked on this problem, the results would probably be a recommendation on national military policy that would be fundamentally correct from our point of view and would be assured from the start of the support of the various civilian groups interested in military organization. With such a substantial agreement as to the broad outlines of policy, I am convinced that a little mutual education would bring us together in every essential detail.[46]

It hardly need be said that no action was taken on this suggestion. The climate established in the General Staff by General March's arbitrary way of conducting business was scarcely conducive to a process of give and take for "mutual education." Palmer may have been unduly optimistic, but the idea of a mixed committee had merit.

Palmer set off for the Military Training Camps Association dinner filled with misgivings. The Kahn-Chamberlain bill, whatever its advantages, added just one more complication to an already impossible situation. But the evening proved unexpectedly rewarding; at any rate the colonel was deeply moved by the remarks of Senator Wadsworth. Looking back years later he could still recall the occasion in vivid detail.

> I had never seen the Senator before and was greatly impressed by him—at first by his youthful vigor, for he was barely forty-two years old, a very young man to lead one of the great Senatorial Committees. But I was even more impressed by what he said. He spoke with great earnestness. He explained what his committee was doing. It was determined to erect a sound and permanent military system upon our costly experience in the recent war. With this in view, a special sub-committee had been set apart to obtain the frank views of all sorts and conditions of men who

could contribute to the solution of our military problem. It would question enlisted men as well as officers, junior officers as well as senior officers, officers of the National Guard and National Army as well as regular army officers. "Some of you," he said, "may be called before us. If so, you should remember that the American people, through their Congress, have a right to your frank and honest personal opinions, without reference to the opinions of any other persons." Perhaps it was only the effect of his earnest eloquence, but I forgot that I was one of many hearers and felt that he was speaking directly to me. As Chief of one of the branches of the General Staff, he would probably summon me as a witness. If so, my opinion would be ready for him.

Senator Wadsworth had given Palmer his cue. When the time came, he was resolved to speak out fearlessly, no matter what it might cost him professionally.[47]

36 Called to the Hill

Palmer's resolve to denounce General March's bill if called upon to testify was not made without a great deal of anguish. For months past the papers had been filled with stories about what happened to officers who spoke too freely. Most of these accounts were an outgrowth of the celebrated case of Brig. Gen. Samuel T. Ansell. Soon after he had roundly criticized the administration of justice in the wartime army, Ansell had been demoted to his permanent rank of lieutenant colonel. The Secretary of War denied that the reduction was anything more than a normal consequence of the postwar cutback, but the Ansell case left a widespread impression in army circles, as well as on the Hill, that it was unhealthy for a military man's professional career to criticize duly constituted authority.[1]

Palmer had other reasons to waver in his resolve. To speak out boldly before an investigating committee might inform Congress, but one could also serve the public interest by retaining the confidence of the Chief of Staff. By remaining an insider, one could work for reform from within. And by coincidence, on the very day of the Military Training Camps Association dinner at the Willard Hotel, Palmer was made chief of the War Plans Branch. A few days later the Chief of Staff appointed him to head a committee to consider a reorganization of the General Staff.[2] Both assignments placed him in a position to do constructive work. Both seemed to indicate the confidence of General March, although Palmer was inclined to doubt whether he could achieve any significant reform while serving under a chief who refused to discuss issues on their merits.

Whether he realized it or not, Palmer's position afforded him a considerable leverage for reform. This was evident when his Training Camps Association friend, Tompkins McIlvaine, wrote from New York asking for a list of topics and the names of officers qualified to speak on them to be supplied to Senator

Wadsworth. With his intimate knowledge of the officers around him, Palmer was able to compile a list of individuals whose testimony could be counted on to create the desired impression. And his grasp of the technicalities in General March's official War Department bill made it an easy matter to suggest questions for Wadsworth's use that would bring out the measure's weakness. McIlvaine was optimistic about the results to be obtained if a few officers were "brave enough to come out and tell the truth." Some days later, in passing on Palmer's suggestions to Wadsworth, he left no doubt that he expected the colonel to be one of the brave. After urging the senator to call Palmer, he added, "he has probably made more of a study of the questions in which you are interested than any other officer, and is one of the most broad-minded, fair, and disinterested men I know."[3]

When Wadsworth's special subcommittee of the Senate Committee on Military Affairs began holding hearings early in August, it soon became apparent that Palmer's dilemma was by no means unique. As one distinguished witness after another trooped to the stand, with few exceptions they voiced a considerable reluctance to speak out in opposition to the army reorganization measure sponsored by General March.[4] The senators were inclined to regard this hesitation as evidence that the officers feared to risk official disfavor, but the problem involved considerations far more fundamental than personal relationships with General March or the career prospects of individual officers.

The deeper issue was epitomized by Maj. Gen. James W. McAndrew, who had returned from his assignment as chief of staff, AEF, to serve as commandant of the newly established Staff College in Washington. At the peak of his career, laden with honors and public esteem, even he prefaced his remarks by observing that he was loath to disagree with the Chief of Staff. Like many another high-minded officer since the era of Elihu Root's reforms, McAndrew was acutely aware of the evils resulting from the machinations of political generals. The activities of the bureau chiefs of the Ainsworth mold were still fresh in his memory; he knew the disastrous results to be expected when subordinates attempted to circumvent their superiors by individual end-runs to Capitol Hill. Not long after he appeared before the committee, he spelled out his code of political conduct for the newly assembled class at the Staff College.

Please do not become politically active during your stay in Washington. It is not for us to seek independently and individually legislation from Congress on military matters. We must leave that to the proper officials of the War Department. Even though we may entirely disagree with the policies adopted, we must remember that there can be no efficient team-work on the part of the Army if individual players are to act independent of the captain. When our superiors come to a decision as to military matters, it is for us, as good soldiers, to loyally accept and support that decision. The same rule of conduct applies to the action of Congress. We Army officers may, as authorities on military matters, advise and counsel the Military Committees of Congress when properly called upon to do so. But the decision as to the laws ultimately enacted is theirs and not ours.[5]

The difficulty, of course, lay in determining just where loyalty to one's superiors should begin. One officer asked the Chief of Staff for a statement of policy—the party line—on the War Department bill, to "fortify" himself before going to the Hill. General March replied that all officers should feel "perfectly free" to express themselves "without the slightest fear of any consequences" if they differed from the "views advanced by the War Department."[6] There is no reason to believe that the Chief of Staff was not entirely sincere, but his advice was not really helpful to the prospective witness. March, no less than McAndrew, failed to come to grips with one of the most vexing and unresolved problems of defense in a democracy: How can Congress secure the technical advice it requires on highly controversial issues without compromising the witnesses? Or, expressed the other way around: How can a patriotic and technically informed officer give Congress the benefit of his knowledge and still maintain a professionally acceptable relationship with his legally constituted superiors?

As it turned out, neither fear of personal recrimination nor a desire to avoid political involvement were the sole obstacles to expert testimony. Many of the witnesses were unprepared to testify; several major generals admitted that they had not even read the War Department bill until summoned by the committee. One had been too busy to do more than look the bill over on his way to the Hill. A few witnesses, such as the Surgeon General and the chief of Ordnance, came well prepared but only to attack features in the War Department bill that seemed to threaten their particular branches.[7]

Even though many witnesses were ill-prepared, several made a lasting impression. One of these was Maj. Gen. Leonard Wood, whose experience as a former chief of staff gave weight to his scathing criticism of March's measure. Another was Maj. Gen. John F. O'Ryan of the New York National Guard. In a carefully prepared statement, General O'Ryan outlined the scheme he had already presented to the War Department for federalizing the National Guard. He would organize the Guard under the army clause rather than the militia clause of the Constitution and thus centralize control for efficiency in federal hands. Constitutional objections he brushed aside as needless worries; a nation that could authorize General Foch, a French citizen, to give binding orders to the AEF could, he felt certain, find some way to authorize state governors to make use of a federalized Guard in lieu of the traditional local militia. The existing National Guard was primarily a state force and only secondarily a federal force. His objective was to reverse this relationship.[8]

O'Ryan's impact on the Senate committee stemmed in part from his careful preparation and his Gaelic eloquence. But he also displayed a good deal of political insight, a quality notably lacking in the testimony by most of the major generals. He showed the committee just how a federalized Guard would create a powerful political leverage for national defense.

> Only by the creation of the great citizen force ... can you hope in years to come to maintain up-to-date armament and equipment sufficient for war. For the personnel of such an army will know whether or not they have these things, and ... they will tell you of it. If, however, you rely on an extension of the old expensive regular army system, the people in a few years, as they have after all other wars, will cry out against the expense of maintaining so large a force and will insist upon material reduction in ... military appropriations. These reductions will not be made at the expense of established grades and of promotion where it can be avoided. The saving will be at the expense of maintaining up-to-date war material. Plans for the upkeep of such property will be thrown over in order to salvage the personnel and the old condition of unreadiness in material things will result.[9]

Although the committee was much interested, O'Ryan's proposal was a general proposition, not a concrete piece of legislation. When asked, he declared he could convert his idea into a full-fledged bill in a week's time. Significantly, however, he failed to do so.

Tompkins McIlvaine, who appeared before the committee as official spokesman for the Military Training Camps Association, enjoyed the distinct advantage of defending a bill, the Kahn-Chamberlain measure, already before Congress. Moreover, he, too, was well prepared with a carefully drafted presentation. But the Kahn-Chamberlain bill did not, strictly speaking, provide for a reorganization of the army; it was a military manpower bill dealing with universal military training and the creation of an elaborate organized reserve or citizen army. At no point did it attempt to define the duties of the General Staff or provide permanent organization for the Air Service, Tank Corps, Chemical Warfare Service, or any of the other newly established services.

Unfortunately for the success of McIlvaine's plea, he allowed himself to be drawn into a discussion that nullified much of his effectiveness. Although there were many points of similarity between the federalized National Guard O'Ryan suggested and the federal reserve put forward in the Kahn-

Chamberlain bill, McIlvaine flatly declared that O'Ryan's idea was unconstitutional. The Kahn-Chamberlain measure had already alienated the National Guard by including clauses to limit the Guard in each state to a total of 250 men for each representative in Congress—in lieu of the 800 per representative specified in the Defense Act of 1916—and confining its employment to the territorial limits of the United States for periods of not more than three months.[10] Since the Guard, or at least its spokesmen in the National Guard Association, aspired to keep the militia in its status as the nation's first-line reserve, as provided in the 1916 act, the Kahn-Chamberlain or Military Training Camps Association bill became anathema to the guardsmen. So McIlvaine destroyed the most promising bridge by which the Guard might have been induced to support an organized reserve under direct federal control.[11]

The only thoroughgoing reorganization bill placed before the committee was the official War Department proposal, but General March's testimony did little to persuade the senators of its merits. If anything, the general seemed to go out of his way to make the bill unpalatable. Despite the violent reaction to his original proposal in January calling for a standing army of 509,909, his revised August version raised this figure to 576,000. It was an easy matter for the senators to picture the increase as little more than a device for justifying a large number of promotions, since the bill called for 32 major generals where only nine had been authorized under the 1916 Defense Act.[12]

General March's big army bill was probably doomed from the start because of its enormous costs. He estimated that the Regular Army and the truncated three-month universal training program provided for in his bill would require an annual expenditure of approximately $900 million, exclusive of any federal appropriation for the National Guard. By way of contrast, prewar military appropriations had run somewhat less than $200 million a year.[13]

If high costs were not sufficient to scuttle the War Department bill, Senator Wadsworth's skillful questioning brought out more than enough damaging information on its technical deficiencies. To begin with, he led General March to declare "without qualification" that the fundamental principles underlying his bill truly represented the thinking of the War Department. Since the senator already knew from the fate of Palmer's General Staff study of the previous April that this simply was not true, it was not difficult to elicit evidence from subsequent witnesses to undermine General March's contention. Well primed in advance, Wadsworth and his colleagues were able to spread testimony on the record to show that March's bill failed to remedy the serious shortcomings revealed by the mobilization of 1917-18 and evaded entirely the critical problem of clarifying the relationship between the Regular Army and the National Guard. To the evident confusion of several witnesses, Wadsworth's close questioning clearly revealed how a slight change in the wording of the 1916 Act proposed by General March would open the door to a drastic change in the function of the General Staff. His amended version would have permitted the General Staff to move from supervision to administration, a role entirely foreign to the statute implementing Secretary Root's reforms.[14]

Not surprisingly, the committee hearings proved more effective at uncovering weaknesses than in concocting constructive alternatives. After listening to testimony for nearly six sweltering weeks in the late summer and early fall of 1919, the committee members agreed on only one thing: the War Department bill was *not* acceptable. But where to turn beyond that, none seemed to know. Swamped with masses of information in thousands of pages of published testimony, some members of the committee suggested that the time had come to close the hearings.[15]

Just at this juncture Senator Wadsworth began to receive a number of visitors, army officers, for the most part relatively junior majors and lieutenant colonels. Sometimes they came to his office on the Hill; sometimes they telephoned him, almost furtively, at home. As Wadsworth later recalled, all had one message: "Senator, there is a man named Palmer on the General Staff who, if sent for, will talk. More than that, he has studied this thing for years, much more so than any other officer, and knows what he is talking about. If you will send for him and give him a chance you will hear something." Wadsworth told the other members of the committee about this mysterious man named Palmer, whom none could recall having met, although all of them had been influenced by him indirectly, whether they knew it or not, through Tompkins McIlvaine and the Military Training Camps Association. So they agreed to call the colonel; he couldn't do any harm and he might have something constructive to say.[16]

When Palmer learned that he was to testify, he renewed his earlier resolve to tell the committee what he really believed. Only half facetiously he told his wife she might just as well begin to dismantle the apartment and pack up for a move to Siberia. Such a fate was not entirely out of the question, as an American contingent under Maj. Gen. W. S. Graves was at that time still stationed in Siberia.[17]

As soon as Surgeon General Merritte W. Ireland heard that his friend Palmer had been called, he offered to introduce him to Senator Wadsworth,[18] but Palmer concluded that it would be better to let his testimony stand entirely on its own merits with no hint of personal influence. This proved to be a wise decision.

At the appointed day, 9 October 1919, Palmer presented himself at the appropriate room in the Capitol. To the chairman's surprise, the usually half-empty chamber was already filled, mostly with officers. As they continued to pour in, Wadsworth ordered more chairs and observed to his colleagues that there must be a lot of men AWOL from the department. After many weeks of tedious listening, the committeemen were prepared for the worst when the witness took his seat at the table and arranged a stack of documents about twelve inches high before him. One senator mumbled, "Oh Gawd," while another slumped in his chair expecting to sleep through one more dreary day.[19]

But the senators were not bored. Unlike virtually all of the witnesses who had preceded him, Palmer did not allow himself to become bogged down with detailed criticism; instead he endeavored to state the problem of a proper military policy for the nation in broad, general terms.

> The first question is: what is the measure of the war strength. The next question is: what should be the size of the peace establishment, and the next is: what should be the form of institution...to have a peace establishment that will develop the necessary war strength. I think this war has demonstrated that so long as war is a possible contingency, there is no measure of ultimate war strength other than the total manpower of a nation; and that the military policy should be so constructed as to develop all or any necessary part of the manpower in time to meet any given emergency.
>
> There have been attempts in the past to compute a nation's war establishment from a consideration of other powers that might possibly be enemies, but this is fallacious in principle. The very first requirement of strategy is superior numbers, and the only way of being assured of approaching that as soon as possible is to be prepared to develop the total manpower if necessary.[20]

To illustrate his point Palmer cited an example from the recent past. The British, after preparing elaborate prewar plans to throw six divisions across the Channel to protect the French left flank, belatedly discovered that not just six divisions but their total manpower would be required. By the time this became apparent, the divisions in France had already consumed the greater part of the trained personnel necessary to develop their total manpower. With historical allusions to several similar examples, Palmer hammered the lesson further and then returned to his central theme.

> When we come to the measure of peace strength, the time factor comes in. Economy demands the minimum peace establishment through which the war establishment will develop in sufficient time.... Two nations having the same total manpower might have very different peace establishments, depending on the difference in time allowed for development in the two cases. I believe that complete preparedness

implies capacity to develop all or any necessary part of the manpower of the nation in time to meet any given emergency, and that this can be assured only through universal military training.

When we come ... to the form of military institutions, ... that is very largely a political question and depends upon a consideration of the general system of national institutions. There are two types of armies through which the total manpower may be developed. One is the professional or standing-army type. In this the manpower is drawn into the army very largely in the lower grades. The function of the citizen is ordinarily to be a private in war. Reserve officers are to be used but generally in the lower grades and in subordinate capacities. Under this system leadership in war and conduct of preparation in peace are concentrated very largely and necessarily in a professional class.

This is the system of continental Europe.... It produces a highly efficient military system, but it is open to certain serious political objections. In such a country intelligent opinion as to military policy is largely concentrated in a professional class. Under such a system the people themselves are competent to exert only a limited intelligent influence on the issues of war and peace. As military leadership and control are largely concentrated in the personnel of the professional military establishment, that establishment must be relatively expensive and of relatively large dimensions in time of peace. Under such a system only the brawn of the people is prepared for war, there being no adequate provision for developing the latent military genius of the people as a whole. The evils under this system may be summarized under the term militarism. For militarism is a characteristic of a particular type of military institution, and is not necessarily inherent in all forms of preparedness.

The second type of military institution is a citizen army formed and organized in peace, with full opportunity for competent citizen soldiers to rise by successive steps to any rank for which they can definitely qualify, and with specific facilities for such qualification and advancement as an essential and predominating characteristic of the peace establishment.

An army of this type has, among others, the following advantages:

First. Military leadership is not exclusively concentrated in the professional soldier class. All citizen soldiers after their initial training are encouraged to develop their capacity for leadership to such an extent as may be consistent with their abilities, their tastes, and their civil obligations.

Second, as the war army in this system is identical with the organized citizen army in time of peace, and as the bulk of the officers and noncommissioned officers required for war are assigned in peace to their proper places in the citizen army, the peace establishment of professional personnel is logically reduced to a determinable minimum....

Third. As the bulk of the leaders of the citizen army are included in the civil population as a whole, an intelligent and widespread public opinion is provided as the basis for the determination of all public questions relating to military affairs.

Again, as the war army is identical with the organized citizen army, all plans for national preparedness are simplified into dispositions for the employment of a specific force, always organized, always at war strength, and always prepared to function under tested mobilization plans.

Again, as the war army is identical with the organized citizen army, all plans for equipment and armament, all fiscal arrangements, and all plans for the development and control of war industries and the predetermined provision of the necessary personnel therefore, are definitely associated with the obvious requirements of a specific force of definite size and organization.

Again, as with an organized citizen army, the minimum number of soldiers is maintained on active service in time of peace, the cost of an effective war establishment under such a system is necessarily reduced to a minimum.

And finally, as our great wars have been fought in the main by citizen armies, the proposal for an organized citizen army in time of peace is merely a proposal for perfecting a traditional national institution to meet modern requirements which no longer permit extemporization after the outbreak of war.[21]

As Palmer continued his orderly exposition, the senators about him began to sit up and take notice. Here was a man who evidently knew what he was talking about. Sensing their interest and attention, he switched abruptly, from even-tenored description to vigorous denunciation.

In studying the three plans of military policy before the committee, I consider that the War Department bill proposes a military institution of the first or standing army type. It relies essentially on a large regular army and proposes universal military training primarily as a means of providing men to fill its lower ranks on the outbreak of war. It does not provide for an organized citizen army and does not provide sufficient training to prepare the young men of the country for membership in such a force, nor does it provide the adequate facilities nor the organization essential to the full development of efficient citizen officers. In my opinion, the War Department bill proposes incomplete preparedness at excessive cost and under forms that are not in harmony with the genius of American institutions.[22]

This appraisal of General March's bill made a tremendous impression upon the committee members. From that moment they were eating out of Palmer's hand. He had won their confidence as an officer who was not afraid to speak out. To be sure, he voiced opinions, but his opinions were obviously founded in an impressive depth of experience and presented in a coherent and logical form. Moreover, he was telling the senators what they wanted to hear.

In a sense, what followed was an anticlimax. Having dismissed General March's large standing army as unsuitable, Palmer proceeded to discuss his conception of the citizen army as an alternative. But first he laid the broadest possible base for subsequent political cooperation. The O'Ryan plan and the Kahn-Chamberlain bill he praised as "highly constructive," while minimizing his objections to "certain details" that needed correction. Then, skillfully avoiding the minutiae of administration, where disagreements were most liable to crop up, he presented a panoramic sketch of the citizen army as it had evolved in his mind. The main feature of the military establishment would be a citizen reserve organized territorially into divisions, corps, and armies. The charter members of this force would be those veterans of the National Army and the National Guard who volunteered for such service. If these veterans were assured of fair treatment in the matter of rank, they would, he believed, join with enthusiasm. As the veterans grew older, the organized reserve would be perpetuated by younger men brought in through universal military training.[23]

If the senators were impressed with Palmer's grasp of military organization, they were even more impressed with his fairness and freedom from professional bias. It was evident to all that one of the most critical problems before them was to establish the proper relationships between the professional and the citizen soldiers. The War Department bill had bluntly abandoned the nation's traditional citizen army, and in doing so had aroused indignation and resentment among the veteran citizen soldiers who had so recently served in the National Guard and the National Army. The witness before them took an entirely different tack. He pointed out that wars in the future, as in the past, must be fought mainly by citizen soldiers and that a sound peacetime organization must rest squarely on that fundamental fact. While he readily admitted that a regular army must be provided to do certain tasks that citizen soldiers obviously could not do, such as garrisoning the overseas possessions, he refused to believe that military leadership was the exclusive prerogative of regular officers. To be sure, organizing and training an army of the people in time of peace would require highly trained officers. But, he insisted, the solution lay in opening the pathway of promotion to men of tested ability and capacity, whether they happened to be professionals or nonprofessionals; in any fair system, he contended, there should be no blind presumption *in favor* of the regular officer and equally none *against* the citizen officers.[24]

In answer to a senator's question, Palmer explained that universal military training was not the same thing as compulsory military service. Under a scheme of universal training, young men did not join the army; they remained civilian trainees. When they returned home and entered a local reserve unit, they could not be called unwillingly into military service without an act of Congress. The distinction hinged on the words "service" and "training." While all young men were obliged to train, only volunteers were required to serve, except in time of war. Compulsory service, on the other hand, the traditional conscription practiced by most continental nations, obliged young men to become fillers in the Regular Army, serving wherever the military authorities wished to assign them, in time of peace no less than in war.[25] The key to the whole problem, Palmer explained, was to be found in the qualifications of the reserve officers.

> The primary thing is that they must be efficient, and I believe that the determination of efficiency is purely a question of fact. If a man alleges he is a major of infantry you can determine it in precisely the same way that you can determine whether an alleged chauffeur is really a chauffeur. Let him try it in the presence of competent judges. That has been the practice abroad, and it is thoroughly feasible....
>
> Whether a man is a regular officer or a citizen officer he should not be assigned to command any unit until his capacity to command it has been demonstrated, then he should not be restricted to any particular rank merely because he is a reserve officer or a citizen officer.... There is nothing in our history that justifies the presumption that no citizen officers are capable of rising to high command.[26]

After citing several historical examples of natural leaders who emerged under the stress of war, he returned to his central theme. "With the organized citizen army you would discover such men in time of peace, and put them in their proper places, and multiply their number as much as you can.... In a complete scheme of national preparedness, that feature above all others should be developed." Such testimony, coming from a Regular Army colonel, a West Point graduate, undoubtedly struck the committee as refreshing. At the very least it indicated that not everyone on the General Staff was out to "smash the Guard." As Palmer continued, it became increasingly evident to the senators that they were dealing with an unusually disinterested officer, who wished to reduce the number of professional soldiers in the standing army to the lowest number consistent with preparedness. Moreover, he offered a formula for doing so. Instead of starting with the permanent establishment, as so many of his fellow regulars had done in the past, he proposed to start with the citizen army to be mobilized in time of war and then work back to the regular component needed to generate that citizen force. And finally, when he suggested that the citizen army he proposed would mobilize twice the number of men at half the cost of General March's scheme, he was speaking a language his listeners understood.[27]

The more Palmer talked, the clearer it became that he was acutely aware of the essentially political character of national defense. For example, while opposing a separate agency for giving the citizen forces an entirely separate chain of command below the Secretary of War, as some guardsmen seemed to demand, he gave his enthusiastic backing to any arrangement that would make it possible for citizen officers to serve on the General Staff in conjunction with the Regulars. Indeed, he recalled making a similar suggestion as far back as 1912 during his first tour on the General Staff under Secretary Stimson. Citizen representatives were essential, he argued, if the staff hoped to make a success of any proposal for a great reserve army. At the same time, citizen officers serving on the General Staff could scarcely fail to develop a better understanding of the difficulties confronting the Regulars. As Palmer saw it, this process of mutual education would alleviate political tensions by helping to get the Reserves and the Regulars pulling together in the same direction.[28]

Palmer's sensitivity to politics,—both army and congressional, was nowhere better illustrated than in his proposals for reforming the army's method of promotion. First he outlined the mechanics of a single-list system substantially similar to the scheme he and his classmates had concocted at Leavenworth years before. Then he illustrated the need for such a reform by a few selected examples of the individual inequities growing out of the existing method of promotion by arm or service, where officers in fast growing branches enjoyed opportunities for advancement out of all proportion to that of their equally meritorious brethren in less-favored organizations. But, having made the conventional case for the single list, he suggested far more important grounds than individual equity for adopting the scheme. Some such reform was essential, he declared, because without it Congress could never hope to get an honest computation of the army's requirements. So long as promotion by arm or service remained, the officers in each branch had special incentives to agitate for changes in organization that would maximize promotion. By adopting the single list, Congress would remove these incentives and assure itself a statement of requirements freed from branch interest.[29]

After nearly three hours at the witness table, Palmer realized that he still had some important points to make but was reluctant to tax his listeners further. In the shy and hesitant manner that was so much a part of his charm, he inquired after the committee's wishes. A chorus of approval reassured him that the senators were very much with him, and it was arranged for him to continue on the following day.[30]

Virtually the whole of his second session with the committee was devoted to the vexing subject of the General Staff. And once again his years of careful study afforded him a mastery of the subject. When he described the historic evolution of the General Staff from the time of Frederick the Great onward, the senators were impressed with his grasp of detail and easy flow of language. They did not know that nearly everything he said paraphrased the staff paper he had prepared in 1916. But more than knowledge made his testimony effective. He also enjoyed a happy faculty for making complex problems appear simple—sometimes too simple—with a well-turned phrase or metaphor.[31]

The trouble with the General Staff, he explained, was that few people grasped its true function. Even the officers assigned to duty on the staff frequently misunderstood their duties; instead of confining themselves to coordinating, they tended to operate or administer, encroaching unwittingly upon the proper sphere of the arms and services. To this Senator Chamberlain responded immediately. As one of the authors of the Defense Act of 1916, he reminded the committee that the act had specifically endeavored to check this tendency.[32] Palmer agreed, but suggested that the appropriate solution might well be found elsewhere.

I believe a General Staff is an absolutely indispensable agency, and I believe if it is composed of properly trained General Staff officers that it will necessarily function. I do not believe that any amount of prohibition or injunction will make it function unless that preliminary condition is fulfilled. I know of many cases where General Staff officers have gone beyond their proper sphere in dealing with troop commanders and services; but I do not know of any instance where it ever occurred that it could not be traced back to the fact that the man who did it was not a trained General Staff officer.[33]

The difficulty in the past, he continued, arose from the large number of untrained men assigned to the staff. Recalling his own experience just before the war, he pointed out that only one of the fifty one officers on the General Staff at that time qualified as fully trained by virtue of completing both the Staff College at Leavenworth and the War College in Washington.[34] If Congress wished the General Staff to confine itself to the role envisioned by Elihu Root, the obvious solution was to see that none but properly trained officers were assigned to duty there. By restricting appointments to graduates of the prescribed training schools, Palmer believed, the problem would solve itself. Well-trained staff officers would no more want to perform the duties of the arms and services than well-trained surgeons in a hospital want to trench upon the duties of nurses and apothecaries.[35]

Palmer was convinced that the tensions that blighted the relations of the staff and the bureaus would be substantially eliminated if the officers assigned to staff duty would adhere to the spirit of Secretary Root's great statute.

> The 1903 act is a brilliant and beautifully worded law, ideally adapted to accomplish its intent. In that law the phrase "informing and coordinating" is used. It has been my experience that if the informing part is properly done, the coordination part generally takes care of itself. And that is the great function of the General Staff.[36]

In this revealing insight he had managed to shed more light on the external or operating function of the staff than some of his colleagues had done in dozens of pages of published testimony. The contrast was not lost—at least on some of the members of the committee.

From a consideration of the external relations of the General Staff, Palmer turned finally to a discussion of its internal organization and operation. First he pointed out that the 1903 statute provided for two entirely different types of activity: a policy-forming, or planning, agency and an executive agency to supervise the execution of policy, the former to be performed by the General Staff, the latter by the Chief of Staff. When dealing with questions of policy to be presented to the civilian authorities for decision, the staff is a deliberative body and the Chief of Staff is merely its presiding officer. Once a policy has been settled by the civilian authorities, the Chief of Staff assumes his executive role and issues orders in the conventional fashion of military command, but even these he issues only as an agent in the name of the Secretary of War.[37]

To make perfectly sure that the committee saw the point of this indirect rebuke of General March's very different interpretation of the office, Palmer spelled out his message in detail.

> For example, if I am in command of a regiment of infantry, so long as I act according to regulations and orders of higher authority, the policy of that regiment is my policy and that is proper and right; but if I am the senior officer of a deliberative scientific body, instructed to prepare a recommendation for a higher authority, I am not the commanding officer in that sense. In other words, you cannot apply the principles of command to both processes. . . . I will take my own branch of the General Staff, dealing with national defense plans; if a project is brought to me that I do not agree with, I call the members of the branch together and talk it over with them. Frequently that will result in a correction or amendment. Perhaps there will continue to be a difference of opinion between me and the officers who prepared the plan. In that event I do

not believe I have any right to order them to accept my view. I do not believe I have any right to forward my own opinion and suppress theirs, but I do have the right and duty to forward their view of such adverse comments as I choose to make. I do not think you can arrive at a scientific determination of policy in any other way.[38]

Senator Wadsworth immediately caught the point and related it to the official War Department bill then before the committee. This gave Palmer an opening to comment on what he regarded as an exceedingly dangerous change in the law proposed by General March. Where the act of 1903 made the General Staff the responsible planning agency, General March proposed new language that placed this burden directly upon the Chief of Staff, leaving the General Staff only the ministerial function of working out the details along lines laid down by the chief. This crucial change, Palmer explained, would destroy the institution created by Secretary Root and replace it with another, entirely different in kind. The wisest course, he declared, would be to retain the old language assigning the Chief of Staff his dual task as presiding officer of the General Staff and as an executive agent for the Secretary of War.[39]

Secretary Root had selected the title "Chief of Staff" for a specific purpose. The incumbent was to be Chief of Staff to the Secretary of War and *not* Commanding General. That March had behaved at times very much like a Commanding General rather than a Chief of Staff, Palmer had no doubt. But in urging the proper subordination of the Chief of Staff, he had no intention of transferring the power to muzzle the General Staff from the Chief of Staff to the Secretary or the President. Insofar as the General Staff functioned as a deliberative body, its professional findings should be made available to Congress; the order of authority should never stand in the way of a free discussion of ideas.

> When it comes to ... determining a policy, the whole situation is different from a question of command. Whether a national policy is sound or not, is a question of its intrinsic merit and not a question of authority. It is a good deal like a theorem in geometry, in that it does not make much difference whether the best solution is made by a lance corporal or a field marshal. When it comes to the test it has to be determined on its merits. No question of national policy is ever settled until it is settled right.[40]

When Palmer stepped down from the witness stand, he was conscious of having performed ably. What he could not know was that this had been his finest hour. He had thrown himself into the balance without regard for his career or hopes for promotion, and he had left his mark on the course of events. This was the culmination of a lifetime of effort. All the years of study, the endless hours preparing staff papers, the repeated frustrations in seeing them rejected and misunderstood, now had come to fruition. Above everything else, he had provided a conceptual framework.

As he walked out of the committee room it suddenly dawned on him that he must now pay the piper for the luxury of expressing his views. Somewhat appalled by this prospect, he had started down the Capitol steps when a messenger stepped up to say that Senator Wadsworth wished to see him in his office. When he got there, the senator went directly to the point.

> Colonel Palmer, a very remarkable thing has happened. Night before last, the subcommittee met at my house where we finally disposed of the War Department bill by throwing it in the waste paper basket. We then decided to write a bill of our own. We wrote down a few paragraphs outlining what we considered to be the basis of a sound military organization for the United States. And there we stopped. We didn't know how to expand those principles into a complete bill, and we didn't think we were likely to get much help from the War Department. And now, to our amazement, you have been before us two afternoons and have given us all the details of our own plan. The Committee has therefore instructed me unanimously, to write to the Secretary of War to ask for your assignment as our military advisor. We are going to write our own bill, and we want you to help us.[41]

The prospect of playing such a direct part in writing the army reorganization bill was decidedly pleasing, but it immediately occurred to Palmer that the proposed bill must include far more than the mere enunciation of a military policy. There would be a mass of detail involving the amendment or revision of existing military legislation. If he undertook this task, he might soon become swamped with detail and lose sight of the broader issues. He therefore asked the senator to have Col. John W. Gulick detailed to serve with the committee also. He had worked closely with Gulick for several months and knew that his wide grasp of the military system would make him the best possible partner. Senator Wadsworth assented and wrote to Mr. Baker asking for the two officers.

Almost overnight Palmer discovered he had become something of a public figure. "No one else," the *New York Times* editorialized, "has given the subject so much study or has been so tremendously earnest." Many other papers played up the dramatic character of the evidence he had presented. The *Washington Star* declared that his testimony added a military classic to the literature of warfare.[42] But most gratifying of all were the many letters of congratulation he received from fellow officers, some of them friends, some mere acquaintances. The opinion of Brig. Gen. Amos Fries, the former chief of the Chemical Warfare Service, AEF, who found the testimony "the most comprehensive and valuable" yet put before Congress, was typical.⁴³ Since the Chief of Staff and many of the nation's most distinguished military leaders had also presented evidence on the Hill, this was a significant compliment. Another correspondent suggested that "any new legislation might properly be called by your name."⁴⁴ Such praise was far less rewarding than the realization that his message was actually making an impression in precisely those quarters where it would count most. Friends wrote from Leavenworth, from the Naval War College at Newport, from the Staff College in Washington, and elsewhere. "You have done a tremendous service to the army and to the General Staff," said one characteristic response, "more for the latter than any one has done since Mr. Root's time."⁴⁵

Many of Palmer's well-wishers were determined to see that his message was not confined to military circles. Tompkins McIlvaine wrote from New York to say he was obtaining copies of the published testimony in large quantities from the Government Printing Office for distribution to editors throughout the country. The *Infantry Journal* put out a pamphlet containing the highlights of his remarks, inviting newspaper editors to reprint freely. And Grenville Clark considered raising funds to publish a pamphlet for the Military Training Camps Association, until someone came up with the idea of having Palmer condense his testimony into a form suitable for publication as a book.⁴⁶

The public response was highly gratifying. Besides flattering notices in the press and a flood of them from well-wishers, he received an invitation to testify before the Military Affairs Committee of the House and thus enlarge the scope of his influence. But success was not without its drawbacks; while waiting for Secretary Baker's reply to Senator Wadsworth's request, Palmer found his position in the War Department increasingly uncomfortable. Indeed, he thought it decidedly precarious when he learned from a fellow officer that the Inspector General had been instructed to go over his testimony with a fine-toothed comb.⁴⁷ Happily, nothing that could possibly call for disciplinary action was to be found there. Meanwhile, a week slipped by and no reply to Senator Wadsworth's letter arrived from Secretary Baker. Certain that his days of useful service were numbered, Palmer again turned his thoughts to early retirement.⁴⁸

The problem, of course, was primarily financial. He wanted to write, but he knew well enough that he couldn't rely upon occasional royalties if he hoped to maintain any reasonable standard of living. The most interesting alternative came as an outgrowth of his correspondence with McIlvaine during the previous spring. McIlvaine's scheme was to recruit a group of men interested in the work of the Military Training Camps Association to form a syndicate to put up the difference between Palmer's retired pay and the pay and allowances of a colonel on the active list. Thus subsidized, he would be free to devote his full time and energy to writing serious works on military policy.

Somewhat to Palmer's surprise, McIlvaine managed to enlist the support of seven patriotic businessmen willing and able to join in raising the sum of $2,000 a year for several years. Included in the group were C. C. Jamieson, H. B. Clark, Frank Weld, G. G. Brown, R. Mayo-Smith, W. M. Chadbourne, and C. E. Richardson, nearly all of whom had been temporary officers in the AEF. Jamieson, one of Palmer's classmates at the Military Academy, had retired before the war to become a highly successful engineering consultant with the firm of George W. Goethals of Panama Canal fame. Grenville Clark helped draw up a contract to put the agreement with the seven on a sound business basis, but he himself believed what the colonel really needed was an endowed chair at some university. He persuaded his friend Langdon P. Marvin to include a recommendation for such a position in his annual report as chairman of the Overseers Committee on Military Affairs at Harvard. Nothing came of the proposal, but Palmer found it comforting to discover that he had so many friends genuinely concerned with the progress of his literary propaganda for a sound military policy.[49]

Negotiations with the seven underwriters were still afoot when Secretary Baker replied to Wadsworth's request. He was, he declared, more than willing to assist the Senate committee, but in place of the two officers asked for, he suggested Maj. Gen. Frank McIntyre, General March's assistant, "who ... has devoted his fine mind for years to the study of such questions."[50] The senators knew that General McIntyre was one of the principal authors of the War Department bill they had so recently consigned to the trash heap. Senator Chamberlain, who had been chairman of the Military Affairs Committee during the recent Democratic majority in the Senate, then said to Wadsworth, "By God, Jim, you write to Secretary Baker and tell him that the Senate of the United States *insists* upon the assignment of Colonel Palmer."[51]

Wadsworth did insist, and shortly afterward the secretary telephoned, asking him to come in for a visit. Years later the senator recalled their conversation.

> He said, "Wadsworth, you have put me in a bad mess." I said, "How?" He said, "By writing that letter asking me to assign Colonel Palmer to your Committee." I said, "What's wrong with that?" He said, "There's nothing wrong with it, but General March will tear this building down," or words to that effect. "There will be an awful row around here. I don't know what to do about it. Can't you ask for some other officer?" I said, "No, Mr. Secretary, the Committee will not ask for any other officer. It insists upon having Colonel Palmer."[52]

Secretary Baker finally agreed to let the committee have their man if the request could be made verbally and unofficially. Wadsworth assented and symbolically tore up the letter. Thereupon the secretary wrote a letter granting the committee's desire but was careful to remove any official coloration in the assignment.

> As the views which these officers have expressed in their testimony before the Senate Military Affairs Committee are their individual and personal views, and have not the approval of their superiors in the War Department or my approval as Secretary of War, I would prefer not to have them considered as in any sense detailed by the War Department to advise the Committee in the matter of Army reorganization.[53]

Wadsworth sensed that Mr. Baker had begun to doubt the wisdom of lending further backing to General March's War Department bill. At any rate, thereafter his attitude toward the work of the committee became increasingly sympathetic.[54]

Secretary Baker may have been converted, but General March was not. Wadsworth found hm furious over the committee's action. Not long thereafter, Palmer was dropped from the General Staff and demoted to his permanent rank of lieutenant colonel, a move that cost him approximately one-eighth of his salary.[55] Ever afterwards he attributed this misfortune to the personal antipathy of General March, and so did his friends in the Military Training Camps Association. Tompkins McIlvaine spoke for the group when he wrote:

> We have all decided it won't do as a matter of principle to let pass March's action in dropping you from the G.S.
> It means that when an officer tells the truth he is canned and no one else ever will again if we let it pass. You don't care as you will retire but the principle must be defended.
> This is not the first instance of March's spite. I have some but want the whole history so that it can be used by the press and Congress to whom it will be supplied. Who can give me the details?[56]

In fairness to the Chief of Staff it must be observed that there is nothing in the record to sustain this charge. Palmer was dropped from the staff under the Manchu law because his four years were up. March was dogmatic and he may have been a martinet, but none of the available evidence indicates that he was personally vindictive. And the demotion was entirely in line with those suffered by Palmer's contemporaries. His friend and classmate Dennis Nolan, for example, had been moved down from his position as chief of Intelligence, G-2, in the AEF, with the rank of brigadier general, to resume his permanent grade as a major.

When news of Palmer's demotion reached the Capitol, some members of the subcommittee considered it an affront to the Senate. Senator Chamberlain announced that he was going to "raise hell about it" even if he had to carry the issue to the floor. The colonel urged him to ignore the matter. When he finally consented, he said, "All right, Palmer, if you think best. But I'm getting damned tired of having the War Department spit in my eyes and then tell me it's raining."[57]

37   Adviser to the Senate

By the time Palmer was officially installed as adviser to the subcommittee of the Military Affairs Committee of the Senate, he found himself on the most friendly terms with its members. Besides the chairman, there were three Republicans, Howard Sutherland of West Virginia, Harry S. New of Indiana, and Joseph S. Frelinghuysen of New Jersey. The three Democrats were George E. Chamberlain of Oregon, Duncan Fletcher of Florida, and Charles S. Thomas of Colorado. Several had served as officers in the Spanish-American War, and all had enjoyed—or suffered—a wide range of political experience. Because they trusted the colonel completely, he saw them from a vantage seldom available to outsiders. As one accustomed to reading newspaper accounts of pitched battles between the rival parties, he was particularly entranced by the nonpartisan relations they so obviously maintained. Years later when writing to Wadsworth, this aspect of the subcommittee's behavior still struck him as noteworthy.[1]

> On the eve of an important meeting of the subcommittee, dear old Chamberlain said, "Jim, I will have to attend a caucus, but you vote for me. Whereupon Thomas and Fletcher gave you their proxies also. Is it not an unusual parliamentary order for an entire minority to ask the majority leader to vote for it?[1]

In time the colonel came to realize that the high degree of cooperation within the committee was a direct result of the character and personality of its chairman, James W. Wadsworth, Jr. Famous son of a notable family, Wadsworth was an authentic aristocrat. His broad acres and considerable wealth in the valley of the Genesee in upstate New York helped him to be both fearless and disinterested. But it was his energy, his humor, and his boundless zeal for the public welfare that made him the effective lawmaker he was. Palmer subsequently counted it one of the blessings of his career that this great American had become his lifelong friend.

At least one reason why the senators enjoyed working for Wadsworth was his hospitality. The committee members frequently met for evening sessions at the chairman's home, the old John Hay house on Sixteenth Street, where they discovered a welcome oasis in those arid Prohibition days. Nearly twenty years afterward, Palmer reminded Wadsworth of his reputation as a connoisseur.

> Late one afternoon I entered your office and had the pleasure of meeting your father—"The Boss," I think you called him. You were just starting home and invited me to drive with you. As we approached the corner of Pennsylvania and Fourteenth Street, you pointed out a famous old saloon which had recently succumbed to the Prohibition Crusade. "There," you remarked, "they made the finest whiskey sour in the world." To this your father replied, "I think you are mistaken about that, Jim, and if you and Colonel Palmer will stop at my house on K Street, I will endeavor to prove it to you."
>
> Of course we stopped on K Street, and the first one convinced me that "The Boss" had you. I think you were really convinced, too, but I was glad that you reserved judgment until we sipped the second.[2]

Palmer's first and probably most important contribution to the work of the Senate committee was to draw up the major outlines of a bill along the general plan laid down in his testimony. Section by section, he submitted his handiwork to the committee. It was slow work. Although the senators accepted most of the major features he proposed, all sorts of difficulties cropped up.[3] Even with Colonel Gulick's help, there were literally hundreds of technicalities on which Palmer required the assistance of specialists from one branch or another within the War Department. When he turned to officers on the General Staff or in the arms and services for answers, they frequently responded with pet projects of their own that they wished to see included in the new legislation. Many of these suggestions proved highly constructive. For example, it was in this fashion that Col. C. McK. Saltzman and Assistant Secretary of War Benedict Crowell proposed what later became the famous Section 5a placing procurement under the assistant secretary. And Gen. "Billy" Mitchell wanted to be sure the new law would provide extra flying pay, while limiting command in the Air Service to those who actually flew in airplanes.[4]

On at least one occasion a friend from the General Staff turned up a proposal that obviously came straight out of General March's official War Department bill. With no little relish Palmer looked it over and declined to transmit it to the chairman. Since Secretary Baker had explicitly denied him any official standing as a representative of the War Department, he was free to do as he pleased. He reported his visitor's reaction in the following conversation:

> "But hell, John!" my friend exclaimed, "the War Department wants this in the bill."
> "But you know, that by direction of the Secretary of War, I do not represent the War Department."
> "That's a hell of a note, John; do you mean to tell me that the Secretary of War has no access to the Senate Military Committee?"
> "By no means, all the Secretary has to do is write a letter to the Chairman."
> "And he'll probably refer the letter to you, won't he, John?"
> "Quite likely."
> "And what'll you say then?"
> "I'll tell him what I've just told you, that I don't believe in it."
> "And what will he do then, John?"
> "I don't know. That's up to him. All he expects of me is my frank personal opinion. What he does with it after he gets it is none of my business."[5]

Palmer saw that the two most important questions of policy were also going to be the most difficult to resolve. The senators were quite willing to accept his proposals for a General Staff eligible list, a single promotion list, and other internal reforms, but on universal military training they became wary and hesitant. While most of them were ready to admit, at least privately, both the logic and the equity of universal training, they were reluctant to act officially until they explored the question further. None knew for a certainty the sentiment at the grassroots—among the "folks back home," as they called their constituents. Palmer believed that compulsory training was essential to truly effective preparedness, but he also knew that public sentiment might not accept his view. He resolved, therefore, to draw up the bill in such a way that the structure of the proposed organization would remain intact even if Congress rejected compulsory training.

The second major question of policy could not be deferred so readily. Most of the committeemen backed away from defining the ideal relation between the professional and the citizen soldier. Here, too, they recognized the merit in Palmer's conception of a citizen reserve force organized territorially in time of peace, but they were entirely undecided on its precise form. Broadly speaking, there were three main alternatives. They could establish a federal reserve under the army clause of the Constitution, absorbing National Guard veterans as charter members, as Palmer advocated. Or they could retain the existing National Guard, as General O'Ryan proposed, using the army clause of the Constitution to assure a thorough federalization and centralization of control. Or, following the wishes of the National Guard Association and the Association of Adjutants General, they could retain the Guard in its existing form, organized by the several states under the militia clause of the Constitution.

The senators' reluctance was entirely understandable. Since Amendment II of the U.S. Constitution declares the existence of a "well regulated militia," essential to the security of a free state, there was some feeling that any attempt to organize a federal reserve under the army clause might prove unconstitutional. They also were political realists. Their choice would ultimately have to win approval from a majority in Congress, which is to say, the policy they decided upon, ideal or otherwise, would require wide popular support.

Palmer recalled General O'Ryan's admonishment that the various military factions had better resolve their differences before going to the Hill. It was too late for that, but he could work for some sort of agreement before the reorganization bill came up for a vote. When he first came to the committee he had assumed that his duties would be those of a technical adviser. Now, it appeared, he was becoming a behind-the-scenes political negotiator, actively seeking to accommodate differences and to recruit support for his version of the ideal reorganization measure.

Little or nothing was to be expected from the Chief of Staff, but that did not automatically exclude everyone else in the War Department. Maj. Gen. Enoch Crowder, for example, was an officer with a large circle of powerful friends in Congress who was currently at odds with the Chief of Staff. Palmer suggested to Wadsworth that "it might lead to useful results" to tap this officer's experience as judge advocate and provost marshal in drawing up the clauses pertaining to the induction of draftees for universal training. If Crowder could be personally involved in the effort, he was almost certain to back the bill instead of fighting it.[6]

Enlisting the support of the Military Training Camps Association and one or two of the other patriotic pressure groups posed relatively few difficulties, but the National Guard presented quite another problem. Although the guardsmen had a great many legitimate complaints, their most articulate spokesmen seemed to have an unhappy faculty for putting themselves before the public in a most unflattering light. For instance, when the Kahn-Chamberlain bill was first published, the National Guard Association rushed into print, denouncing the measure as a "ruthless abandonment" of the citizen soldier that would establish a "detestable Prussian system" and "seize from their homes the youth of America for service in the Regular Army." The bill, according to the association, was the "swan song" of the General Staff, a "diabolical scheme" to create high-ranking jobs for regular officers. Since the citizen soldiers of the Military Training Camps Association and not the

General Staff had prepared the Kahn-Chamberlain bill, the Guard attack was easily parried, but the episode made it more than ever difficult to get the members of the two associations to work together thereafter.[7]

Although Senator Wadsworth was a former guardsman, he regarded the key leaders of the National Guard as "fifty percent political and about ninety percent selfish."[8] Palmer, too, deplored their excesses, yet at the same time he realized that many of those who supported the association's charges believed they were fighting for the very existence of the Guard. Instead of taking offense at their attacks on the General Staff and the Regular Army, Palmer recognized the attacks for what they were—ill-informed and inaccurate but nonetheless sincere attempts to frustrate General March's militaristic scheme to transfer the main burden of national defense from the citizen army to a large standing army of professionals. The most rabid attacks on the Regular Army seemed to come from a few individuals; in at least two or three instances, those involved were officers who had been removed from their commands in the AEF by General Pershing. But just because these individuals seemed bent on relieving their bitterness by political action, this was no reason to write off the entire membership of the National Guard Association as incurably selfish.

The problem, as Palmer saw it, was to reach past the disgruntled few and tap the support of the vast majority of guardsmen. He was convinced that these patriotic men would accept his citizen army scheme if assured of a square deal in rank and subsequent right to promotion. Much of their irritation, he realized, was a reaction to the way they had been treated by the War Department at the end of the war. Under General March's policies, Guard units in the federal service had not been transferred as units to the control of their respective states. Instead, they had been stripped of their equipment and demobilized as individuals. The veteran guardsmen woke up to find themselves out in the cold. The organizations of which they had been so intensely proud, many of historic lineage dating far into the nation's past, had ceased to exist, and their commissions had become little more than paper. The guardsmen suspected the army of seizing the occasion to dismantle the Guard once and for all.[9]

One approach to winning the support of the rank and file in the Guard was to offer the proposed legislation in terms of amendments to the Defense Act of 1916. That statute had established the Guard as the main reserve force of the nation. Even if it proved necessary to rewrite most of the act, there was a decided advantage, Palmer believed, in retaining the measure for symbolic reasons. But still more positive steps would be required to reassure the guardsmen that the committee was fully alive to their problems.

Palmer suggested holding a series of informal conferences with representative groups of guardsmen. Before the committee could act on this proposal, however, he sent out a large number of copies of his own testimony, which had been published as a separate pamphlet. It was a shrewd move. He knew from his wide correspondence that the vast majority of Guard officers had not thought out any systematic scheme of reorganization. Preoccupied as they were with rejuvenating their businesses after prolonged absences, he suspected that they would welcome his proposed solution no less than his plea for a fair shake to Guard veterans.[10]

The replies confirmed his expectations. His dramatic rejection of General March's big standing army and frank emphasis upon the primary importance of the citizen forces not only allayed suspicion and won friends but also provided a coherent line of argument for would-be witnesses. The reaction of a former subordinate in the 29th Division, an officer who later became a brigadier general in the Guard, was typical.

> I believe you are right in not urging the reorganization of the National Guard. The Reserve formed as you describe would take the place of the National Guard and there is no reason for having the two systems side by side. On the other hand, if you form a National Guard and limit its duties to service within the country and strike duty, I think few would care to join. I should not, at least. The Guard can afford to pass into history. Those who know will not forget its services in the past. Its traditions could be kept alive by applying the names of its old organizations to those corresponding units of the National Reserve.
>
> I only hope Congress can be brought to see the wisdom of this plan before the lessons of the last war have passed from the memories of the people and before such progress had been made in reorganizing the National Guard that opposition will come strongly from it supporters. Excepting the adjutant generals, ... most of us believe this the prime time to agree upon the best military policy—the best for the country—subordinating every other consideration.[11]

This kind of disinterested patriotism served to underline Palmer's repeated contention that "the better element" in the Guard did not really see eye to eye with the extremists currently in control of the National Guard Association. But in every case the replies came from officers who knew him personally, men who had the utmost confidence in his fair-mindedness toward citizen soldiers. It was gratifying to hear, as he did from one officer, "I am for any general plan you may have thought out, so thoroughly do I trust your judgment."[12] Even if a few individuals of this sort managed to shape opinions favorably in Guard circles, there still remained the larger problem of winning broadly based popular support. For this task, it appeared, General Pershing's help would be required.

Just when Palmer first thought of making use of General Pershing's enormous prestige for the cause of army reform is not clear. The general was then at the peak of his popularity. Ever since his recent return to the United States, he had moved from one triumphant reception to another. Secretary Baker had solved the embarrassing problem of finding suitable employment for his newly created General of the Armies by leaving him nominally in command of the AEF, with headquarters in the old Federal Land Office building in Washington. There he busied himself winding up his final report while adroitly fielding questions about his political intentions.[13]

Palmer was fortunate in having a convenient pipeline to the general through his old friend Col. George Marshall, who was then serving as the general's aide. From time to time Palmer sent down informal reports through Marshall to keep Pershing informed on the committee's progress in drafting a reorganization bill.[14] On several occasions the general discussed the subject with Palmer at some length, but he was not one who could be coached to present a particular view, at least not with any assurance that he would support the desired position. He was very much a man with a mind of his own. Although he was slow and cautious in taking a stand on significant questions of policy, he had a definite method for arriving at his opinions. When, for example, he learned that he was to testify before a joint session of the Senate and House Military Committees, he called in most of his senior colleagues, one by one, and elicited their views, while a stenographer recorded the interviews for subsequent study.[15]

When General Pershing finally appeared on the Hill, he gratified Palmer by coming out in support of every one of the major reforms the colonel advocated: single list promotion, a General Staff eligible list, an organized territorial reserve, six months of universal training, and all the rest. Moreover, his stand on the National Guard was perfectly suited to Palmer's objectives. After complimenting the excellent service of the Guard during the war, the general declared, "They never received, in my opinion, the wholehearted support of the Regular Army. There was always a prejudice against them." A new bond of sympathy would have to be developed between the Regular Army and the veteran guardsmen who entered the Organized Reserve. And, as if to show that he really meant what he said, Pershing assured his listeners that he favored opening promotions up through the grade of division commander to the officers who volunteered for service in the Reserve.[16]

On the whole, General Pershing's testimony was a remarkably skillful performance. He took a positive stand on a number of controversial issues, but in such a way as to give the least possible offense. His views carried great weight in the minds of many congressmen. But, useful as this important accession of support was certain to be, Palmer saw at once that it was still insufficient to assure passage of the reform legislation he sought. Still needed, he realized, was an organized approach to public sentiment throughout the country. For help in this direction, he looked hopefully to the newly formed American Legion.

In the fall of 1919 that organization was something of an unknown quantity. Its character was largely unformed and its purpose imperfectly stated, but there was no question whatever about its enormous potential. Since its formation in Paris during the previous March, nearly a million members had been recruited. Nearly 4 million others were eligible. Although its founders repeatedly protested that the Legion was going to be "absolutely non-political," as the organization approached its first annual convention on the anniversary of the Armistice, many observers, with memories of the Grand Army of the Republic, (GAR) found this difficult to believe. The prospect of a tightly organized national institution of several million individuals still regarded as "our heros" in their local communities was decidedly tempting to those with political purposes. And Palmer was one of those tempted.[17]

If he could get the endorsement of the Legion convention for his proposed reforms, the cause he served would have an incalculable political advantage. The difficulty, of course, lay in salting the bird's tail. The official delegates included a large number of National Guard officers and among them was Col. Bennett C. Clark of Missouri, the president of the National Guard Association.

Although Palmer himself was unable to go to Minneapolis, where the Legion convention was held, several of his friends were delegates. One of these was Lt. Col. D. John Markey, a businessman from Frederick, Maryland, who had served in his brigade during the war. Markey was precisely the kind of patriotic and public-spirited reservist Palmer had in mind as the typical citizen soldier. He was a lieutenant colonel in the Guard and an active member of the National Guard Association, but he was no rubber stamp for the extremist leaders of that organization.

At Minneapolis Markey more than justified the confidence placed in him by his former brigade commander. When the Military Policy Committee of the Legion began to hammer out the planks of a statement for the convention's endorsement, Bennett Clark and several of his friends made a determined effort to get a series of National Guard Association resolutions adopted. But Markey appealed to the larger national interest. Quoting appropriate passages from Palmer's published testimony, he argued that any sound policy would have to consider the interest of the professional soldiers and National Army veterans as well as those of the National Guard. This broader view prevailed, and the committee rejected the Guard planks in favor of a policy statement very much along the lines advocated by Palmer and his friends in the Military Training Camps Association.[18]

The similarity between the statement adopted and the views of the Military Training Camps Association was not a matter of sheer chance. Before the committee met in Minneapolis, Tompkins McIlvaine had taken the trouble to send each member of the committee a concise declaration of his association's objectives. This letter highlighted the legislative goals of the association in such a way as to provide convenient language when the committee began to prepare the wording of its resolutions.[19] But the officers of the National Guard faction did not give up without a fight. McIlvaine described their tactics in a letter to Palmer: "Reason was absolutely thrown away on them; nor could they produce anything concrete. They relied simply on cheap oratory and demagogic appeals." One of them, he said, who had been detailed to present the proposed resolutions of the Military Policy Committee on the floor of the convention, went so far as to absent himself at the time appointed in an effort to quash the report. But a Training Camps Association representative, Arthur F. Cosby, got wind of the situation and hastily lined up another member of the committee to make the presentation. "It went through with a whoop and an attempt to put in a minority report was squelched by the Convention. The Convention itself was absolutely sound for our ideas. The only man who tried to speak against universal training was hooted down.[20]

When he learned what had happened at Minneapolis, Palmer was jubilant. In addition to approving most of the goals sought by the Military Training Camps Association, the convention voted to establish a seven-man committee to work with both houses of Congress, using the Legion's resolutions on military policy as general guidelines. The Senate committee was favorably disposed; General Pershing's prestige had been employed to good effect; and now the backing of the Legion gave promise of widespread popular support. The seven-man committee was yet another asset; it would be useful in harmonizing any difficulties over details that cropped up during the final drafting of the bill.

Confident that the tide was running in his direction, Palmer was inclined to minimize if not to ignore whatever suggested the contrary. When Senator Wadsworth's committee began to call in witnesses to consider the merits of a rival bill proposed by the National Guard Association, Palmer seemed to think that this situation could be met by a few simple tactical dispositions. Still convinced that "the best element of the old National Guard" would gladly flock to a citizen reserve force organized under the army clause of the constitution, he invited McIlvaine and others to suggest the names of two or three "progressive" Guard officers to Wadsworth to give testimony to this effect. His object, he explained, was "to establish the fact that the official National Guard [Association] program does not represent the National Guard point of view."[21]

The heavy reliance Palmer placed upon the Legion endorsement of what he called "our constructive program" suggests that he still had much to learn in the world of practical politics. In the first place, the ability of the Legion to influence public sentiment on broad questions of national policy was by no means manifest. Mushrooming membership may have spelled strength in one sense, but it also indicated that the Legion was becoming unwieldy and difficult to hold to a consistent path of policy. Moreover, in focusing attention upon the Legion's high-minded resolve to "inculcate a sense of individual obligation to the community, state, and nation," Palmer seemed to forget that the veterans had also voted in favor of "mutual helpfulness."[22] The drive on Congress for veterans' benefits that followed soon after the Minneapolis convention might have given him some clue as to which objective would command the most interest, but his attention was elsewhere.[23]

If Palmer overestimated the significance of the Legion endorsement, he seriously underestimated the persistence of the National Guard lobby. The guardsmen knew, as he apparently did not, that political victories seldom if ever stay won. This painful truth rather quickly became evident when the Legion committee finally arrived in Washington early in December 1919. Not all the committeemen showed up, and those who did failed to agree among themselves as to the exact purport of the resolutions they carried.[24] None of them had served on the Military Policy Committee at Minneapolis. Since they had not shared in the discussion that took place when the resolutions were being drawn up, they were inclined to make their own interpretations of the document. The National Guard representatives on the Legion committee were highly suspicious of Palmer's proposed federal reserve organized under the army clause of the Constitution. They seemed determined to continue the existing Guard as the major reserve component of the nation. Instead of having massive Legion support to offset the influence of the National Guard Association and the adjutants general, Palmer now found he would have to fight hard to derive any sort of advantage from the Minneapolis endorsement.[25]

As Palmer sized up the situation, the only course open to him was to start a new campaign of education. He was not without allies: his old chief, former Secretary of War Henry Stimson, was a member of the Legion committee as a representative of the National Army veterans. Stimson's support could be taken for granted; he had demonstrated this only a few weeks earlier while testifying on the Hill. Asked to comment on one feature of Palmer's proposals, he replied that he was unfamiliar with the scheme in question but would "look with predisposition to favor any plan which Colonel Palmer had worked out."[26] Although Stimson's heart may have been in the right place, he himself was not. Along with another National Army veteran on the committee, Franklin D'Olier, the Legion commander, he had many commitments that drew him away from the day-to-day work of the committee. In practice the committee of seven dwindled to three, with the two National Guard representatives constituting a majority.

Palmer made some progress in putting over his point of view in the committee.[27] But, as he himself had always contended, education is a process that cuts two ways. While he was patiently setting forth the merits of his proposed federal reserve, the guardsmen were equally busy propagating their own views on Capitol Hill. It was easy for them to get a hearing; only a singularly inept member of Congress would fail to weigh the Guard interest in his home state. And between the Legion representatives and the various Guard officers who backed the National Guard Association bill, the legislators were learning a great deal about the desires of the Guard. Where the earlier propaganda efforts of the National Guard Association had been emotional, the case now set before Congress was for the most part soberly factual.

Instead of invective, the guardsmen used specific examples to explain why they were unwilling to trust the future of the citizen forces to Regular Army. Wherever the interests of the full-time soldiers abutted those of the part-time soldiers, the professionals in charge almost invariably decided the issue without reference to the interests of the part-time soldiers and, for that matter, without any genuine understanding the problems confronting them. A case in point, one illustration among many, was the Militia Bureau ruling that no state militia company of less than 100 men would receive federal recognition. The rationale was perfectly straightforward: unless Guard companies were maintained at a minimum of 100 in peace, the hard core of trained men would be hopelessly diluted by the addition of the recruits required to bring the unit up to full war strength of 250 men. There was merit in this contention, but as the guardsmen pointed out, it showed little or no appreciation of the practical realities confronting those attempting to organize militia companies in the several states. Numerous communities with armories built to accommodate the 65-man companies authorized before the war found it difficult to take care of the new 100-man requirement. A great many small communities simply did not have the available men to recruit a full complement of 100. Attempts to solve the problem by locating platoons in adjacent communities led to local factions squabbling to capture the company headquarters. The troops enlisted in other communities suffered the double disadvantage of being out from under the eye of the captain to whom they looked for promotion and away from the personnel records on which they depended for routine administration.[28]

The guardsmen seem to have carried great weight with Senator Wadsworth's committee. Belatedly Palmer awoke to the realization that the senators were veering sharply in the direction of major concessions. He had been willing all along to make tactical concessions, such as calling the proposed federal reserve force the "National Guard," but now the senators were talking about the possibility of a dual reserve, preserving the existing National Guard more or less parallel to the proposed federal reserve, an arrangement that threatened to undermine the whole structure of the reorganization.[29]

The real significance—and the danger—of the compromise toward which Senator Wadsworth's committee seemed to be moving lay in its bearing upon the basic principle of universal training. At first the senators considered retaining the Guard organization, but only as state militia without federal aid of any sort. This arrangement was rejected out of hand by the Guard spokesmen; as realists, the guardsmen understood perfectly that state troops without federal appropriations would soon wither and disappear. So the senators hastily shifted to a second alternative along the lines previously suggested by Gen. John F. O'Ryan, giving the Guard federal status parallel to that of the contemplated territorial reserve. But this, the guardsmen promptly pointed out, deprived them of their major source of manpower. If all able-bodied nineteen-year-olds were taken up by universal training and then assigned to units in the Organized Reserve, the only recruits available to the Guard would be older men who had completed their obligatory reserve tours. To enable the Guard to survive, the guardsmen insisted on receiving a share of the young men subject to universal training.

The Guard representatives on the Legion committee were in a good position to get what they demanded; unless their senators complied, they could withdraw their support from the principle of universal military training. Almost without hesitation the senators capitulated, agreeing to insert a provision in the bill authorizing a certain percentage of each year's inductees to elect training with the National Guard. This concession may have appeared to the members of Wadsworth's committee as just another necessary political compromise, but it was far more. When McIlvaine learned of it he immediately warned Palmer of the pitfalls involved.

McIlvaine pointed out the grave political danger in allowing too many young men to enter the Guard in preference to the federal reserve. As a hometown alternative to universal training at an army cantonment, enlistment in the Guard was certain to prove highly attractive, so the Guard would have no trouble in keeping up to full strength. If the Guard quota was set at a total strength of 425,000, as the guardsmen suggested, it was entirely possible, McIlvaine warned, that the public would soon think the National Guard was the "whole show." Given the ability of the Guard lobby to extract appropriations from Congress, McIlvaine feared that a Guard of 425,000 would soon absorb so many tax dollars as to crowd universal training and the federal reserve entirely out of the picture. Unless the Guard was held down to the currently authorized strength of approximately 125,000, he concluded, the citizen army dog would soon be wagged by the National Guard tail.[30]

McIlvaine's prognosis proved to be not far from the mark, but apparently it was too late to turn back. A few days later, Palmer reported to him that "the present view of the committee" was to see the Guard as a first-line ready reserve between the full-time professionals in the Regular Army and the citizen soldiers in the federal reserve, who were liable for duty only in the event of war. This solution appealed to the senators for a number of reasons. A Guard trained and equipped by the federal government was certain to get the political support of the state governors, especially those who had no state police force to call upon in emergencies. In addition, as a force composed entirely of volunteers, the Guard promised to be far more suitable as a first reinforcement for the regulars than would a federal reserve based on compulsion. Moreover, the Guard would provide a ready force for backing up the regulars in situations that did not justify mobilization of the full citizen army in the Organized Reserve. This, Palmer conceded, warranted a larger authorized strength than McIlvaine wished to allow. In any event he wrote again to McIlvaine, pointing out, as if resigned to the inevitable, that the senators would undoubtedly "feel called upon" to adopt a solution agreeable to the National Guard.[31]

Toward the end of December 1919, Wadsworth and his fellow committeemen were about ready to prepare a final draft for presentation in the Senate. Palmer was apparently still hopeful that his major objectives might yet be salvaged without excessive yielding on the Guard issue; he urged the chairman to hold one final conference at which representatives from a wide variety of interests could study advance copies of the committee print and suggest amendments to improve the text. It was a characteristic gesture; Palmer had almost boundless faith in face-to-face negotiation as a means for bringing reasonable men to sound conclusions. Utterly fair-minded and reasonable in conference himself, he found it difficult if not impossible to believe that other men would not behave in the same fashion. In pressing his notion of a meeting upon Wadsworth, he articulated this faith explicitly. "Being mutually informed as to the different points of view involved, they would all be more disposed to accept such compromises as might be necessary and to exert their organized influence for the bill."[32]

Although Palmer did not appear to recognize it at the time, the bill turned out by Wadsworth's subcommittee was the living embodiment of his own philosophy. In his disappointment at seeing the Legion endorsement erode away under continuing pressure from the Guard interests, he lost sight of the fact that he was witnessing a characteristic example of representative government in action. He had condemned General March's big army bill because it was "not in harmony with the genius of American institutions." The Senate subcommittee had met his complaint by tossing March's bill in the wastebasket and opening the gate to the widest possible range of alternatives. In the process the guardsmen had demonstrated—entirely "in harmony with the genius of American institutions"—that they knew how to exert pressure where it would prove most effective. If the resulting bill was something quite different from the one Palmer had hoped for, he could console himself with a highly significant lesson in practical politics. Ironically, the lesson he had acquired the hard way—by experience—had been suggested to him some time earlier by one of his many correspondents, Maj. Richard Stockton, a highly perceptive Guard officer who had taken a permanent commission in the army at the end of the war.

> The Regular [Stockton had written]... must remember that for his own welfare he must have public support, and that the citizen soldier is closer to the public ... and can influence public opinion to a greater extent than the Regular.

Therefore, the Army must adopt a military policy that can both give preparedness and command support of the citizen soldier. . . . It cannot merely determine what is best from a strict Regular viewpoint . . . but must secure public and citizen soldier support for a policy which, though sound, may mean some sacrifice in Regular Army theories.

When the Army does that, it will gain vastly more through public support, than it loses through concessions.[33]

38 Defense Act of 1920

During the first week of January 1920, Senator Wadsworth and his fellow committeemen were at last ready to put the final touches upon their army reorganization bill. The senator welcomed the idea of a last-minute conference of representatives from all of the many groups interested in the reorganization measure; it would provide an opportunity to iron out minor kinks, and by giving a genuine sense of participation it might help to win enthusiastic support for the finished bill.[1] Unfortunately, a single conference for all parties could not be conveniently arranged, and without the face-to-face discussions on which Palmer had banked so heavily for mutual enlightenment, much of the value of the idea was lost. Nonetheless, during the first week of January 1920, the senators did hold a series of meetings, most of them in Wadsworth's home, with those who could come to Washington.[2]

Some of the visitors had no particular technical competence on any single phase of the bill but were invited in an obvious bid for support. Among these were the spokesmen for the Universal Military Training League. This was a typical "letterhead" organization, with national headquarters in Chicago. Its character may be inferred from the endorsement given to Palmer's citizen army proposals by the league's president. "This training," he wrote, "will drive out the red flag spirit from the hearts of the people, unify our citizenship and stabilize civilization."[3] One the league's directors, Wright A. Patterson, controlled a news agency serving a large number of papers in the Midwest, where favorable propaganda for universal training was much needed. In addition, the president of the league had promised that if a suitable bill were reported out, his organization would undertake to flood Washington with "from home" letters demanding its passage.

Of quite another character was the backing drawn from the Military Training Camps Association. Tompkins McIlvaine, as official spokesman, in an open letter to Wadsworth pledged support for the measure from the organization's 1,200 branches. Widely reprinted, the letter afforded a good deal of highly desirable publicity, but it also produced difficulties.[4] The leaders of the association had become convinced that the only hope for universal training in an election year was to link the program with dramatic cuts in the federal budget. Grenville Clark believed that to save funds for universal training it might prove necessary to cut the Regular Army down toward 100,000 men.[5] While McIlvaine's open letter did not go quite this far, it helped persuade the senators to amend their bill by providing for a gradual cutback in the total professional force from the 300,000 they had originally proposed to a new ceiling of 210,000.

The proposal drew cries of anguish from the regulars. Some argued that the slower promotions implicit in a smaller army would only accelerate the flight of talent by resignation that already plagued the service. The editors of the *Army and Navy Journal* saw the proposed cuts as a form of "antagonism to the professional soldier" that had become a congressional habit of mind. After studying the provisions in the Senate measure relating to the National Guard, they were even more incensed, branding the bill a pitiful concession to the Guard lobby. At best this was an oversimplification; as Palmer had come to see from his vantage point on Capitol Hill, it was foolish to talk about any single habit of mind as typical of Congress and even more so to think of the Guard as a monolithic entity.[6]

The National Guard, he now realized, comprised many factions. Wadsworth's committee had made an honest effort to see that all were consulted before the reorganization bill went to the Senate, but by no means all responded cooperatively. Conspicuously absent were the adjutants general of the various state militia organizations. Inconvenience and distance were not significant factors, for only a few days later adjutants from twenty-five states turned up in Washington to attend a meeting of their own in connection with the National Guard Association proposals they were pushing in Congress. This left discussion of the National Guard sections in Wadsworth's bill to those who had agreed to federalize the Guard by organizing it under the army clause of the Constitution along the lines advocated by General O'Ryan.[7]

After several days of working with the representatives coming to Washington, Palmer confessed that he was much discouraged. In his mind's eye he envisioned the task at hand as a noble one; he was searching for a law that would promote the general interest while yet assuring a square deal to every individual who entered the service. In practice, however, he encountered something quite different. "I find," he wrote somewhat sadly, "that there are very few people who take this view of the matter, and nearly everybody that I talk to or correspond with is interested in some minor point affecting his own interest."[8] He was gradually being led to the realization that about the best reform he could look for was a least common denominator among the rival interests concerned.

The colonel believed that the bill as finally presented to the Senate managed to preserve a fair balance between principle and necessary political compromise.[9] Even the National Guard clauses began to look better. He had accepted them only as a matter of political necessity, but now, after considerable reflection, he embraced them with genuine enthusiasm. They offered "a real solution," he told General O'Ryan, to "the great enigma of our military policy since the founding of the government."[10] The enigma was the practical problem of utilizing the militia of forty-eight separate sovereignties as an efficient national force without encroaching upon the constitutional prerogatives of the state governors.

General O'Ryan shared Palmer's mounting enthusiasm for the Senate bill. Both the National Guard and the Regular Army, he had suggested, would support the measure if its provisions were promptly explained. As a politician he saw how important it was to organize sentiment in favor of the measure. The proper tactic, he suggested, was to emphasize the practical advantages the bill would bring to each of the component forces involved. This should be done, he added, before those opposed to the bill had an opportunity to create a prejudice against it. And he left no doubt that he expected the state adjutants general to lead the opposition.[11]

Palmer's reply to this political advice suggests something of his capacity for wishful thinking. Although he readily admitted that he did not understand why the adjutants general had not accepted Wadsworth's invitation to confer on the committee bill, he was inclined to minimize the importance of their opposition. He seemed to feel that if O'Ryan could but arrange to explain its merits to the state adjutants, their resistance would melt. In short, what O'Ryan had pointed out as crucial, Palmer regarded as peripheral. Indeed, he seemed to feel that the battle had moved to another theater of operations. After listing the various groups such as the Military Training Camps Association and the Universal Military Training League who were now lined up behind the Senate bill, he suggested that an entirely new situation had emerged. "Heretofore," he wrote O'Ryan, "it has been a question of a balance between conflicting interests in the Regular Army and the National Guard. For the first time, I believe we have a legislative proposal which makes its appeal primarily to public opinion at large."[12]

Seen in retrospect, Palmer's decision to devote his energies to winning the support of "public opinion at large" appears to have been a tactical mistake. He was probably correct that the adjutants general did not truly represent the entire rank and file of the Guard, but to infer from this that they lacked political strength was a blunder. By the very nature of their jobs, the adjutants were significant political figures with a good deal of patronage to administer. Working in conjunction with their governors, they were often in a position to hold a legislator's feet to the fire if he showed too much independence. To a very real degree the adjutants had a direct interest in retaining the Guard as it was, that is, as a state institution organized under the militia clause of the Constitution. In a federalized Guard under the army clause, their whole power in state politics might well disappear. What Palmer apparently failed to realize was that "public opinion at large" would have at best only a vague and general interest in army reorganization. But the adjutants had a vested interest at stake.

Once he decided that "public opinion at large" was his main target, Palmer turned to the task with vigor and imagination. His first effort was to draft a brief synopsis of the bill. He reduced its hundred-odd pages of cumbersome statutory language to a readable form that would appeal to magazine and newspaper editors about the country. His friends in the Military Training Camps Association wished to get a copy of this digest into the hands of every last member of the American Legion, but shied away from the "stupendous printing" involved. The backers of the association had been annually contributing many thousands of dollars to the causes of universal training, but there was a practical limit to their munificence. On the other hand, the million-odd membership of the Legion offered a most alluring prospect of effective persuasion at the local level.[13]

Palmer was convinced, as he had been all along, that Legion support was vital to the success of the reorganization measure, and at the first opportunity he did what he could to help bring the Legion into line. As soon as the bill was published, the Legion headquarters at Indianapolis had sent out a call for a committee of representatives from every state to decide whether or not it deserved Legion endorsement. Among those selected to attend was Palmer's friend Lt. Col. D. John Markey, who once again was to represent the state of Maryland. Forewarned by Markey as to the nature of the objections to be expected, he prepared a long and careful letter explaining in detail just how the bill protected the rights of citizen soldiers and guardsmen from possible abuse by the regulars. "The real danger," he concluded, "is from prejudice on the other side, ... hostility to the regular officer as such."[14]

True to Markey's prediction, virtually all of the opposition that developed at Indianapolis grew out of the fears of the guardsmen that the bill would not adequately protect them from high-handed treatment by the professional soldiers. Eventually, however, the conference decided to back the bill with minor amendments and authorized a committee to present the Legion endorsement to Congress.[15] Just what part Palmer's arguments played in this result is unclear, but it is significant that guardsmen made up a majority of the committee dispatched to Washington, and among them was Lt. Col. H. L. Opie, who had been one of Palmer's battalion commanders in the 29th during the war. But this success was by no means obtained single-handedly. The Military Training Camps Association had been equally active in plugging for

Legion support, and Palmer's friend Horace C. Stebbins, the chairman of the association's finance committee, was also a member of the Legion deputation.[16]

Palmer subsequently believed that the visit of the Legion representatives was helpful in winning over some of those senators of the full Military Affairs Committee whom he had previously counted as wavering. But he knew he could not let the matter rest there. His earlier experience with the Legion after the Minneapolis convention during the previous November had taught him a bitter lesson. The only way to be sure the Legion would stay put was to build up an overwhelming sentiment for the bill among the rank-and-file members of the organization. To this end, with the help of Horace Stebbins and his friends in the Military Training Camps Association, he undertook to place a series of expository articles in the newly founded *American Legion Weekly*.[17]

His plan was to undermine the opposition by exposing the fallacies behind the stock arguments against the bill. Using a *nom de plume* to avoid the prejudice that many readers might attach to anything by a regular, he cast his first article in the form of a letter from a disgruntled veteran to his backsliding congressman. Written in a style reminiscent of his muckraking articles for *McClure's* back in 1903, it was an ingenious bit of propaganda. His imaginary veteran's complaint was levelled against those congressmen who opposed universal training on the grounds that the nation already had an ample reserve in the millions of veterans from World War I. Palmer had learned that this argument was decidedly unpopular with large numbers of the veterans themselves, who felt they had already done their share. Capitalizing on this sentiment, he used it as a point of departure to argue the wisdom of universal training as a means of gradually replacing the veterans with their younger brothers.[18]

This choice of a subject for a leading article was not just a matter of chance. The views attacked had been put forward by Palmer's two main opponents in the Military Affairs Committee, Sen. Kenneth McKellar of Tennessee and Sen. Morris Sheppard of Texas. They had refused to heed his arguments in committee and had insisted upon entering a minority report when the bill was filed. The nature of the opposition they offered may be inferred from the criticisms they levelled against the measure. Among many other ills, they claimed that it would introduce "militarism along German lines," that it would bestow "virtually unlimited power" on the Chief of Staff, and that it would "destroy the National Guard."[19]

The hollowness of these charges made them easy to refute, but the colonel's efforts were not ideally suited to publication in the Legion *Weekly*. The editors complained that his articles were too long for the limited space available in the periodical, which was desperately fighting for enough advertising to keep solvent. There was, however, insufficient time to publish in the more substantial monthly magazines for which his writing was better adapted.

The monthlies required a considerable lead time before publication, and Palmer expected the fate of the bill to be settled before the first of his articles could possibly appear in their pages.[20]

The only practical thing to do was to make the best possible use of the weekly magazines and news syndicates. For access to these media Palmer relied almost entirely upon his friends in the Military Training Camps Association. The main organ of the association was, of course, the magazine *National Service*, but it suffered from the same drawback as the commercial monthlies. Moreover, while its circulation of 12,000 copies, distributed all over the United States, gave the association a certain influence, its backers recognized that the magazine preached largely to those already converted. To reach the larger public they relied upon the association's reprint service, which regularly fed articles to a select list of 2,500 newspaper editors throughout the country, many of whom made gratifying use of the materials received.[21]

While grinding out articles for the Military Training Camps staff to place wherever they could, Palmer was busy mending fences closer to home. He was distressed by the persistent hostility toward the Senate bill shown by the *Army and Navy Journal*. To correct the misconceptions held by the editors, who championed the cause of the regulars, he wrote a long letter to explain that the bill was not the work of laymen and amateurs, as the editors feared, but a revised version of the General Staff plan of March 1917. This comment, intended to reassure the regulars, played directly into the hands of the National Guard adjutants. In labeling the bill with the General Staff tag, he seemed to confirm what the adjutants had been saying all along. Then, in another unhappy phrase, he referred to the proposed National Guard as a "strictly Federal force," and this, too, was like waving a red flag before the adjutants general.[22] As a consequence, this attempt at internal propaganda appears to have been somewhat less than successful. In any event, the editors of the *Journal* remained unconverted. They continued to attack the bill, which they described as a "Roman holiday in military experimentation" at the expense of the Regular Army.[23]

Apparently unchastened by his initial lack of success, Palmer returned to the attack. He prepared a long article to dispel the many misunderstandings of the Senate bill that kept cropping up in the pages of the *Journal* and made arrangements for his Legion friends to send marked copies to every member of Congress.[24] The editors of the *Journal* published his article in full, but along with it they ran an extended editorial attempting to refute his arguments. Some of their shots were well placed, but for the most part they seemed perversely determined to misrepresent his clear intention, as when they declared that his proposed reductions in the number of regulars would logically lead to the "elimination of the professional soldier in our army."[25]

Palmer continued to write articles for syndication and at the same time conducted a wide correspondence pushing the merits of the Senate bill. He wrote to friends throughout the country to ask them to build fires under their congressmen; he drafted arguments for friendly senators to use in replying to the attacks of opponents; he sent congressmen newspaper clippings that would provide ammunition for debate; and he fed a stream of ideas and arguments to Senator Wadsworth for use in presenting the bill on the floor. Although the army reorganization bill was introduced early in January 1920, because the Senate was occupied in debating the terms of the peace treaty, it was not brought to the floor until the 5th of April.[26]

Wadsworth's opening speech was a masterpiece of exposition. He made a clear and vigorous statement of the general purposes of the bill and then for nearly three hours explained its provisions in answer to questions from all sides. It was a brilliant performance.[27] The senator demonstrated by his ready command of the facts and figures that he had thoroughly mastered the complexities of this highly technical piece of military legislation, but a sure grasp of the facts gave no advantage whatever in dealing with some opponents of the measure.

Before going out on the floor, Wadsworth told Palmer that he expected to be opposed by Sen. James A. Reed of Missouri. The colonel later described the incident at some length.

"Is that a matter of serious concern?" I asked.

"It is a matter of most serious concern. There is not a member of the Senate who is not concerned when he knows that Senator Reed is to oppose him on the floor."

"But does he know anything of this subject?" I asked. I cannot recall Senator Wadsworth's reply exactly, but he implied that limited knowledge of his subject never handicapped Jim Reed as a debater.

Then the Senator from Missouri took the floor. He opened by complimenting the Senator from New York upon his splendid work. He pointed out that the War Department had recently insisted upon a regular army of 560,000 men. He praised the Senator from New York for cutting this number down to 280,000. He was grateful for this much, but he would be compelled to withhold his future approval unless the Senator from New York would consent to apply another fifty percent cut. He was to be praised for reducing the original number to 280,000, but he should make it 140,000. An army of that size, according to the Senator from Missouri, would meet all our national requirements.

At this point another Senator got the floor and reproached the Senator from Missouri upon his recent part in rejecting the League of Nations. He had deprived his country of the means of preventing war entirely, and now he proposed to deprive her of the means of waging war, if war should come.

I was greatly impressed by Senator Reed's reply and repeat it from memory:

"But, Mr. President, the record is the other way. When the Covenant of the League of Nations was brought to us, to be accepted without dotting an *i* or crossing a *t*, we were to have 400,000 men in the Navy and 600,000 men in the Regular Army. In other words, Mr. President, at the very moment when Christ was to begin to reign, we were to have a million men to police the Millennium."[28]

Senator Reed apparently had some sober second thoughts about this final oratorical gem, for he edited it out of the published *Congressional Record*.

Even without the kind of opposition represented by the Missouri senator, it soon became apparent that the universal training feature of Wadsworth's bill was doomed to defeat. Early in February Secretary Baker learned that Champ Clark and some of his colleagues were arranging a caucus of House Democrats to commit them against any form of compulsory training. Baker saw this move as a partisan appeal to southern sentiment against training colored men in the use of arms.[29] At his request President Wilson urged the party leaders to desist, but they went ahead anyhow, voting overwhelmingly to oppose universal training.[30]

As soon as Wadsworth learned that the Democrats intended to make a party issue of the training clauses, he called a conference on strategy. To the senator's surprise, Palmer unhesitatingly recommended that the bill be amended to drop the compulsory feature and to offer instead a program of voluntary training to all young men who might be willing to take it. When Wadsworth pointed out that it would require a great deal of time to prepare amendments in almost every section and to rewrite some parts of the bill entirely, Palmer handed over a printed copy with the necessary changes already inserted. Some weeks before he had suggested to Colonel Gulick that it would be well to prepare for just such a contingency, and with characteristic dispatch Gulick had the revised copy ready and waiting when the need arose.[31]

Palmer's forehandedness and willingness to compromise was to have important consequences in the Senate, where the issue of compulsory training had become inextricably entangled with the party politics of an election year. A private canvass convinced Wadsworth that a majority of the senators were personally in favor of universal training, but among these, several were candidates for the Republican nomination for President and some of the others were unwilling to give their votes if in doing so they conveyed the appearance of supporting Gen. Leonard Wood's candidacy.[32] Under the circumstances, few felt entirely free to vote their convictions.[33] Well aware of this difficulty, Senator McKellar introduced a motion to strike from the bill all reference to universal training. Palmer interpreted this as a move to make political capital by causing compulsory training to appear as a discredited party measure supported by a limited number of Republicans. However, armed with Gulick's amended copy of the bill, Senator Frelinghuysen stepped in and offered a substitute motion calling for voluntary rather than compulsory training. McKellar and his friends delayed for time to rally their forces, but when the substitute came up for a vote on 9 April it carried by a wide margin, even though Wadsworth and several other friends of universal training voted against it as a matter of principle. Three days later McKellar brought in a motion to eliminate even this substitute, but it, too, was roundly defeated.[34]

Was Palmer mistaken in advising Wadsworth to drop universal training? The preponderance of evidence suggests that no other course was open; faced with a groundswell of popular opposition, even the most ardent backers of compulsory training were certain that the time was not opportune. Indeed, some argued that the wisest possible course was to avoid a showdown, since defeat for the principle of universal training in a clear vote by Congress would "set back the cause for several years."[35]

The action of the Senate in dropping compulsory training brought confusion to the ranks of the Military Training Camps Association. The *raison d'être* of the organization was to secure enactment of a universal training statute. A crucial policy decision confronted the leaders of the association: should they continue to support the truncated Senate bill as a practical first step, or should they fight it with all their resources in the hope of salvaging universal training.[36] Some argued that any form of compulsion was now out of the question. Others scoffed that voluntary training would be no more effective than voluntary taxation.[37]

Palmer was aghast when he learned of the debate going on within the ranks of the Training Camps Association.[38] To rally their support he wrote pleading with them to back the watered-down voluntary program, however distasteful it might appear on the surface. Systematically he listed the reasons for such a course. The issue of universal training was not dead, he argued, only deferred until after the election. Moreover, even without universal training, the Senate bill offered substantial advantages; above all, it established a full-fledged citizen army organized on territorial lines and officered by civilian reservists, in sharp contrast to the skeletonized cadres of General March's expansible army, in which the citizen soldiers were destined to be fillers in the rear rank under professional officers. In addition, he urged, by supporting volunteer training now, it would be possible to organize all the essential machinery; when compulsory training was eventually enacted, it would then be a simple matter of enlarging the scale of an existing organization.[39]

Palmer was manifestly beginning to acquire a degree of political insight. The bill as it stood provided for an Organized Reserve and voluntary training; if the members of the Training Camps Association would busy themselves encouraging war veterans to enroll in the Organized Reserve, they would help create a vast number of local organizations with a direct interest in filling up their ranks. In short, the citizen soldiers in the Organized Reserve would become interested workers for compulsory training, or at the very least they would help make voluntary training a measurable success.

To illustrate his point, Palmer offered the example of a hypothetical reserve battalion in his own home community in Illinois.

> I believe that a considerable number of officers and non-commissioned officers of the World War who reside in Sangamon County would enroll in this battalion because, under the terms of the proposed law, they would be permitted to enroll for one year and to secure a discharge upon ninety days notice. Now, if it were understood that any young man in Sangamon County could go the next year for training, I take it that the officers and non-commissioned officers of this battalion ... would encourage their younger brothers in considerable numbers to go to the training camp with the idea of having them enroll in the county battalion after the training.... It seems to me that this would be a very important preparedness measure even if we should never get compulsory training, and that the machinery established ... would furnish the best means for an organized propaganda for training.[40]

As evidence that his argument had merit, Palmer pointed to the remarks of Senator McKellar and others, who frankly declared they opposed even the watered-down voluntary training program because it would lead ultimately to compulsory training.

The more Palmer argued for the Organized Reserve as a vehicle to bring in universal training, the more reason he had to be apprehensive about the army bill recently passed by the House. That measure was almost identical with the Senate bill in its provisions affecting the regulars, but contained no provision whatever for the Organized Reserve, or citizen army, that was the chief feature of the Senate bill.

Behind this important difference lay a whole train of circumstances.[41] During the preceding summer Wadsworth had suggested that the two committees on Military Affairs might save time and reach agreement sooner if they held joint hearings. The invitation had been declined, and the two committees had gone their separate ways in framing bills. Well aware of the technical difficulties confronting congressional attempts at drafting military legislation, Chairman Julius Kahn of the House committee had invited the General Staff to draw up a bill along lines determined by his committee. The General Staff had complied, but the resulting bill proved to be so objectionable that the members of the committee decided to start all over again and do the job themselves. The only feasible course, they had concluded, was to build on the known foundations of the 1916 Defense Act.[42] By preserving the features of that act that had stood the test of time and experience, they hoped to minimize the amount of new legislation required. To assist in this work, Col. Thomas W. Hammond was detailed by the War Department as its representative with the House committee. It so happened that Hammond and his co-worker, Col. Thomas M. Spaulding, were both well-known to Palmer, who had been one of their instructors at West Point when they were cadets. As a consequence there was a good deal of highly fruitful exchange between the two committees, making for uniformity in the measures they drafted. For example, Colonel Spaulding did much of the work underlying the provisions in the two bills establishing a consolidated promotion list. But on one point this helpful collaboration broke down. Unlike Palmer, Colonel Hammond was the official representative of the War Department. As General March's deputy he was very definitely *not* free to urge the merits of a citizen army of the sort Palmer advocated. Little inclined to heed General March's pleas for a big army, the House committee turned elsewhere for advice.[43]

The committee members did not have far to look, since the friends of the National Guard had been busy cultivating a large number of ardent supporters throughout the House. Chief among these was Daniel R. Anthony, Jr., of Kansas, the second-ranking member of the Committee on Military Affairs. Representative Anthony worked closely with Col. Bennett C. Clark, the President of the National Guard Association. But Clark, son of the former Speaker of the House, Champ Clark, and himself at one time parliamentarian in the House, had many other connections on the Hill. Under the circumstances it was hardly surprising when the House Committee on Military Affairs decided to "rehabilitate" the Guard, rather than create a territorial reserve along the lines Palmer had suggested to the Senate. The bill they drafted, which received overwhelming support in the House as a whole, was essentially a National Guard bill. It continued the 1916 act in force and left the Guard under the militia clause of the Constitution. Under liberal terms its strength was to be built up to a ceiling of 400,000 men as the major military reserve of the nation.[44]

When the dissimilar House and Senate bills were sent to a conference committee for reconciliation, it soon became apparent that the main point at issue was the composition of the citizen army.[45] Was it to be a rejuvenated Guard under the militia clause as the House insisted, or would the Senate prevail with its dual arrangement of the Guard and the Organized Reserve, both under the army clause of the Constitution?[46] The meetings of the committee were secret, but Senator Wadsworth kept Palmer informed, frequently sought his advice, and from time to time called him into the conference room to explain some technical point to the rival conferees.

For nearly four weeks neither side was willing to concede the issue that seemed vital. At last the Senate managers decided they would have to make major concessions if they wished to salvage anything from their year-long effort. Any other course would see the session end with no new army legislation and leave the Defense Act of 1916 on the statute books just as if nothing at all had been learned from the painful experience of the war.[47] Wadsworth offered to abandon the Senate bill entirely if in return the House would agree to let the National Guard in each state have the option of deciding whether it wished to organize under the army clause or the militia clause. But the House rejected his proposition decisively in a two-to-one vote. Responsibility for this result, Wadsworth told his colleagues in the Senate, rested with the various adjutants general of the states, who had blocked the bill in defiance of the wishes of the rank and file of the Guard and the American Legion. His fellow committeeman, Senator Thomas of Colorado, even declared that the political power of the state adjutants was such that they were able to "dictate" to the House on army legislation.

But the lopsided House vote made it obvious that any further attempt to get a National Guard under the army clause was out of the question. Assured of this, the House managers were quite willing to listen to the Senate proposals for a dual reserve, with one part of the citizen army, the Guard, under the militia clause and the other part, the Organized Reserve, under the army clause. However, with the date fixed for the adjournment of Congress only a short while off, there was too little time left for a campaign of education to get the House as a whole to accept this unless it could be presented as an amendment to the 1916 Act.[48]

What followed, Palmer described some years later.

> I was waiting in the ante-room when Senator Wadsworth entered from the Committee room and instructed me to make a draft of the proposed amendments. Fortunately, Tom Spaulding was there to help me. The task before us was difficult at best, but when I learned that the House insisted that our summary of the Senate plan must be written in the form of amendments to the National Defense Act of 1916 I was non-plussed. From a purely literary standpoint, the task seemed to be impossible.
>
> When the Senator returned to the Committee room, I said to Spaulding:
>
> "It can't be done. It would be like asking Thomas Jefferson to write the Declaration of Independence in the form of amendments to the Book of Job."
>
> To this Spaulding replied by asking me to let him try his hand at it. I went out to lunch, and when I returned, Tom had performed the miracle. He had squeezed the gist of the Senate's plan into a new

enacting clause and two sections which now stand as Section 3 and 3a of the National Defense Act.[49]

Although Spaulding had indeed performed a remarkable job of compression, the conferees were not too happy with the result. His amendments sanctioned the citizen army organization desired by the Senate but did not spell out all the details. In the space available, all he could do was to outline the organization in general terms and leave the details to the discretion of the President. In practice, of course, the President would delegate his discretion to the Secretary of War, who in turn would pass the task on to the Chief of Staff. This would place the fate of the citizen components directly in the hands of the principal author of the plan for a big standing army that has been so emphatically rejected by both houses of Congress. Alarmed at this prospect, the conferees wanted assurance that the spirit and intent of the bill would be carried out.

At Wadsworth's request, Palmer was called in to reassure the doubters. He pointed out that one of the new amendments rigidly circumscribed the discretionary powers of the executive. While the War Department would indeed be authorized to form the new Army of the United States, all plans for the citizen components of this army would have to be made by a joint committee comprising citizen soldiers as well as professional soldiers. In short, the friends of the National Guard need have no fears. By the terms of the proposed law they were guaranteed an equal voice in the organization of the citizen forces. In determining the location and designation of units within each state, the measure went even further; it placed the decision with boards on which reserve officers appointed by the governor comprised a majority.

In expounding the merits of Section 5, Palmer could speak with the eloquence of conviction. This section was his own handiwork, based on his thirty years of experience as a regular in dealing with citizen soldiers. As he later wrote, "The principle that regular army officers and citizen army officers should work together frankly and equally in the development of our national military policy is the keystone of the National Defense Act." He was convinced that in working together at the same table the two groups would educate each other. Apparently the conferees were moved by Palmer's presentation; at any rate, they promptly agreed to accept the proposed changes, and a few days later the amended bill passed both houses of Congress.[50]

But the hurdle of presidential approval still remained before the much-amended bill could become law. Secretary Baker urged President Wilson to affix his signature to the bill, even while conceding that in its final form it was less desirable than the original Senate version. Despite this recommendation, however, the President decided to veto the measure, whereupon Mr. Baker again pressed him to give his consent. The Secretary noted that its gravest defects were omissions, and critics of a veto would be quick to point out that omissions could easily be remedied by subsequent legislation. In addition, while tactfully observing that he knew that the President would be little swayed by considerations of political expediency, a veto would thrust universal training and the controversy between the National Guard and the Regular Army into the forthcoming political campaign. At least some of the state adjutants, he suggested, would be tempted to use the Guard question for political purposes and thus divert public attention from the League of Nations as the central issue. This appeal apparently struck home, for the President reversed himself and on 4 June signed the Defense Act of 1920.[51]

Secretary Baker's role in rescuing the Defense Act from last-minute disaster marked a significant shift in his outlook. Scarcely more than a year before he had put the prestige of his name and high office behind General March's scheme for a large standing army dominated by professional soldiers. Now he was urging the merits of a measure that stood at the opposite pole of military thought. Undoubtedly a variety of considerations lay behind this conversion, but Palmer's influence loomed large among them. At the time Palmer was unaware of this, but six years later he received a visit from Arthur Page of Doubleday, Page and Company, who invited him to undertake the task of editing a volume of confidential wartime correspondence between Baker and Pershing. Page told him that Baker himself had recommended his name. "In my opinion," Baker said, "Palmer knows more than anybody else about the true place of military institutions in a modern democracy."[52]

Although in later years Palmer was pleased to accept the judgment of Secretary Baker and his own professional colleagues that the Defense Act of 1920 was a triumph of constructive statesmanship, at the time he felt quite otherwise. All he could see while struggling to get the measure passed was a seemingly endless series of concessions and compromises.[53] He had been forced to give up not only such major reforms as universal training and the army clause as the basis for organizing the Guard, but many other features as well. Among these concessions and omissions, at least one was to be of the utmost significance, although it went almost unnoticed at the time. This was the section in the Senate bill providing for an automatic revival of the selective service system upon the declaration of a national emergency by Congress.[54] Palmer found this virtually unbroken succession of retreats painfully hard to bear, but even in defeat he managed to maintain his sense of humor. He told McIlvaine that he felt like the pin boy in a bowling alley. "I get the pins nicely set up only to have them knocked down by a well directed ball, and every now and then a ball not only makes a strike but glances off and hits me."[55]

Soon after the bill passed, Palmer's old mentor and friend Maj. Gen. William H. Carter penned an encouraging note from his retirement home in the Blue Ridge Mountains. As a scarred veteran of many legislative battles, the general spoke with authority and insight. "I felt sure you would be disappointed at the loss of some things from your bill," he wrote, "but I long ago learned that it is too much to expect any great reforms in our methods; if you can compromise and get *some* worthwhile legislation each time, it is all you can hope for."[56]

By General Carter's standard, the new statute was a major success, for in spite of its defects and omissions, it contained a large number of worthwhile innovations in military organization and procedure. And for many of these Palmer could rightfully claim a leading role as midwife, if not as parent. He had helped sell Congress on the merits of the single list for promotion, the General Staff eligible list, and a dozen other administrative provisions, most notably those improving the status and enlarging the role of reservists in relation to the professional forces. He took particular pride in the provisions of the act that defined the Chief of Staff as the presiding officer of the General Staff and required him to submit to Congress on request even those staff studies of which he disapproved. But Palmer's greatest contribution to the Defense Act of 1920 was the underlying philosophy that gave the statute its unique character.[57]

For Palmer, "the great principle of military policy" behind the act was the simple fact that modern wars must be fought, in the main, by citizen forces. To assure the efficiency and timely mobilization of such forces in the nation's hour of need, their organization must be settled and defined in time of peace. By getting Congress to accept this fact and build upon it, he believed he had helped to bring the army a giant step forward. The act gave the General Staff at least some conception of the lines along which the problem of national defense should be solved. In particular, it embodied the idea that the Regular Army was but the professional component of a larger national force and not a cadre or skeleton to be expanded in time of war. By the terms of the act, the Army of the United States was a single comprehensive military force, with the National Guard, the Organized Reserves, and the Regular Army integral parts of the whole. The details of this organization were, as Palmer believed, "wisely and properly" left to the War Department, but the general military policy and the broad outlines of the military institution were for the first time in the nation's history fixed by Congress.[58]

Unfortunately the underlying philosophy of the statute was not immediately evident. Because of the legislative accident by which the Senate bill had had to be compressed into amendments to the Act of 1916, its inherent logic was obscured. If the initial execution of the new statute were left to men unfamiliar with the philosophy on which it rested, it would be entirely possible for much of the measure's intrinsic merit to be lost.[59] Palmer had lived through just such a situation once before in his life. He still recalled his sense of helpless frustration back in 1912 as he watched unfamiliar hands in the War Department first misunderstand and then ignore entirely the statement of military policy he had drawn up for Secretary of War Henry Stimson.[60] Determined to prevent a repetition of this tragedy, he gave up his earlier intention to retire as soon as the bill was passed. Instead he asked Senator Wadsworth if he might continue in his role as adviser so as to be in a strategic position to guide the work of the General Staff on the new statute.[61]

Secretary Baker refused Wadsworth's request and assigned Palmer to duty as a regimental commander at Fort Jay, on Governor's Island in New York Harbor. After four years in the General Staff, he was required by law to return to duty with troops. He had been granted a stay of nearly six months at Wadsworth's request, but the secretary was unwilling to make any further exception. Although Palmer didn't know it at the time, Baker's reply to the senator was actually written by the secretary of the General Staff. Had Palmer realized this, he might better have understood why its author was at such pains to disapprove of detailing an officer directly under a congressional committee "without reference to the views of the War Department." He would also have appreciated somewhat better just why the secretary was so careful to explain that he would be perfectly free at Fort Jay to supply Wadsworth's committee with studies and suggestions, providing these were sent "through the prescribed channels."[62]

Behind the assignment to Fort Jay lay an interesting story. When Palmer first learned he would not remain on the Hill, he was informed that his next assignment was in the Philippines. He accepted this with resignation, but Mrs. Palmer was unwilling to give up so easily. As a veteran army wife, she was well posted on such topics and wasted no time in pointing out several officers in their circle of friends who were still on duty in the United States even though they had far less overseas service than he. The colonel checked with the personnel officer and discovered that none of his service in France had been posted to his credit on the foreign service roster. When offered his choice of several posts in the United States, he chose Fort Jay.[63]

In all probability the mix-up was nothing more than a bureaucratic error, but under the circumstances it was easy to attribute the difficulty to the ill-will of General March. And again, scarcely three weeks later, there occurred another episode that could easily be construed by one so minded as deliberate malice. Thoroughly fagged from his disappointing labor, Palmer applied for a month's leave. He planned to spend it fishing in Maine as he had in the summer of 1918. But just as he was about to set out, a telegram arrived from the War Department assigning him to duty as a member of a special court to hear classification cases arising under the provisions of the new Defense Act governing promotions. Thoroughly disgusted, he set out for New York and Fort Jay.

39 With Pershing Again

In army circles Governors Island was generally regarded as a highly desirable duty assignment. New York City was only fifteen minutes away by ferry, and the commanding officer of the 22nd Infantry occupied a spacious home amidst lawns doubling as greens for the post golf course. Mary, the colonel's teenage daughter, could scarcely wait for the term to end at boarding school. She was no longer the child they had sent away to Miss Madeira's, but a young lady who was elated at the prospect of a summer with dozens of dashing young officers dancing attendance.

The colonel, however, found his new command much disorganized; it was under strength, inexperienced, and untrained, and therefore time consuming. Fort Jay offered only the endless round of petty problems incident to garrison life, not demanding enough to be interesting but sufficiently so to leave little or no time for study and writing.[1] Wadsworth had suggested that the post might prove attractive because it was in easy reach of the New York publishers, but this was a dubious asset if one was too busy to write anything worth publishing.[2]

There were many other annoyances. Secretary Baker's grand scheme for making the army into a vast educational institution complicated the life of a commanding officer immeasurably. With some bitterness the colonel complained that he couldn't so much as put a soldier on guard without first checking to see that it wouldn't conflict with a ukelele lesson or a course in bookkeeping. To make matters worse, the headquarters of the Eastern Department was also located on Governors Island, and the Commanding General's staff officers repeatedly meddled in the affairs of the 22nd Infantry. Fortunately the commander, Lt. Gen. Robert L. Bullard, was a friend of long standing; when Palmer explained the situation, the general ordered his staff to treat the post as if it were just another element of the department a thousand miles away.[3]

The real roots of Palmer's frustration lay in being forced to leave Washington just when the new Defense Act was to be put into practice. He could count on appreciative and sympathetic cooperation from Colonel Gulick and from Maj. Gen. W. G. Haan, the current director of the War Plans Division, both of whom shared his own conception of what the act should accomplish. But so long as General March remained Chief of Staff, Palmer feared that their best efforts would be nullified, and March still had a full year of his official tour to serve.

A letter from Wadsworth reporting on developments did nothing to relieve the colonel's fears.

> I am still disturbed, very much so, about the tactical organization of the regular army. General [W. M.] Wright told me that some committee of the General Staff or someone ... had drawn up a tentative plan involving 21 divisions, each division, at war strength, to be 16,000 ... but ... the attempt ... is utterly ridiculous. I can hardly believe it will be taken seriously by the Secretary of War. Our bill assigns about 100,000 men to the infantry on a basis of 280,000 in the whole army.... Assuming that half the men in a 16,000-man division are infantrymen ... twenty one divisions would mean 168,000 infantry, ... so the 16,000-man division will have to be 50% skeletonized if we are to have 21 of them.
>
> I am afraid that General March and those close to him are still clinging to their dream of a great big regular army which they hope to start with highly skeletonized units and fill up later. As you know, it is a wild dream.... I have warned General Wright repeatedly against this mistake and yet I am not sure that he sees the danger. Secretary Baker admitted the danger to me and told me that General March was wrong.[4]

As it turned out Wadsworth's worst fears were not realized, but the mere fact that a board of professional officers could so much as consider such a "wild dream" was profoundly disturbing.

Compounding Palmer's frustration was his disappointment at failing to win the promotion that all his colleagues assured him he richly deserved. Even before he had left Washington his friends in the Military Training Camps Association, the senators on Wadsworth's subcommittee, and many of his fellow officers declared that his performance in wartime, coupled with his signal services on the Hill, certainly warranted a star.[5] Apparently convinced that he could not expect a fair evaluation on his merits, he did something he had never approved of before; he allowed some of his friends to commend him to Secretary Baker for the next vacancy in the list of brigadiers. The decision to do so indicates how thoroughly he believed what his friends had been telling him: he had to expect punishment for daring to present his personal views in opposition to the official War Department line.[6]

Along with a number of other senators and representatives, Wadsworth wrote the Secretary of War suggesting Palmer's preferment. In doing so, as he later observed, he deviated from his uniform rule never to intrude in such matters.[7] In Palmer's case the senator made an exception, since he believed himself to be the only person in a position to know the full extent of the colonel's services on the Hill. Although Wadsworth needed no prompting, a number of officers called or wrote to him in Palmer's behalf. Doubtlessly many of these were motivated by sincere respect for the merits of their fellow professional, but such intervention was not without overtones of self-interest. Since the colonel was widely known to have the senator's confidence, to advance his cause was to advance a friend with the ear of the chairman of the Senate Military Affairs Committee.[8] A bureau chief would sometimes find it highly advantageous to present his case indirectly through one in the chairman's favor rather than officially through departmental channels. As a matter of fact, at least one of the service chiefs made just such a plea only a short time after commending the colonel for promotion.[9]

Although Palmer had prepared himself to be left out, he was keenly disappointed when the newspapers reported the make list of brigadiers on 23 July 1920. There were 22 names, all of them old friends and associates—his crowd in the AEF—Fox Conner, W. D. Connor, Dennis Nolan, George Van Horn Moseley, Hugh Drum, Malin Craig, and the rest, many of them six to eight years junior to him at the academy.[10] It was particularly galling because he had it on good authority that his name had been on the list of those especially recommended to the Chief of Staff for promotion. Surgeon General Ireland wrote his regrets, suggesting that it was too much to expect anything different "from the two people who really made the selection." George Moseley, writing from his artillery post in Texas, left no doubt where he placed the blame. "You have had to pay dearly for your honesty and nerve in sticking up for what you knew was right." George Marshall added, "Of course we all suspect the reason why, but it is a crime and a shame that you are not now a major general. Few men have done so much for the army, and therefore the country, as you, and whether or not you are accorded your just dues, this fact will remain."[11]

The promotion Palmer did receive—a return to his wartime rank of full colonel—was scant consolation, although the increase in pay did help somewhat in dealing with the high cost of living. But disappointment, coupled with distress over the mishandling, as he saw it, of the opportunity to make the Defense Act of 1920 a landmark of army reform plunged him into a profound depression. To his acute distress, he began to notice a return of all those symptoms that had marked his illness during the war. General Bullard understood his difficulty and encouraged him to take a full two months of leave to go fishing in Maine. Palmer's experience in the summer of 1918 gave him great confidence in the efficacy of the fish cure.[12]

This time he travelled alone. Much as his daughter Mary had enjoyed the lure of the great woods on the previous occasion, she now found life on Governors Island even more alluring, especially the presence of one particularly attractive young infantry officer.

On the way north the colonel struck up a conversation with a fellow passenger, quite obviously a fisherman. The stranger turned out to be Charles Zibeon Southard of Groton, Massachussets, author of the well-known book *Trout Fly-Fishing in America*. Their friendship was to continue for many years. Zibeon Southard was overflowing with energy, which he expended lavishly on the friends he enrolled in his select company of fishermen, known as the Kennebago Tribe. No one could be a chief in the tribe until he had caught a two-and-a-half-pound square-tail trout on the fly in Kennebago waters. Tribal members in good standing enjoyed midwinter dinners at Delmonico's. Palmer never did manage to qualify as a chief, but he attended the annual powwow in New York as a "paleface captive."[13]

Zibeon Southard was a distinguished artist when it came to trout fishing, and he could cook them even better than he could catch them. He also manufactured delectable drinks, in an out-sized cocktail shaker that accompanied him everywhere. The high point of the colonel's trip was a week-long expedition up through the Megantic preserve, with no one but a taciturn local guide for company. They cast in every likely haunt from the Meadow Grounds to Arnold Pond and crossed into Canada to pick up a rucksack full of Scotch for their friends at Kennebago.[14]

When the Colonel returned to Fort Jay he was ready to do battle for the cause into which he had poured so much of his life. He soon learned that at least one of the features he had struggled to incorporate in the Defense Act had proven to be a great success. This was the provision requiring matters relating to the National Guard and the Organized Reserves to be submitted first to joint committees of citizen officers and Regulars.[15] The territorial organization of Guard and Reserve divisions in nine "Corps Areas" involved delicate and perplexing local problems, each, as Wadsworth had warned, "loaded with political dynamite." State militia units, often of distinguished lineage dating back as much as a hundred years, had to be reconstituted to meet the needs of a modern army. For example, many of the infantry companies that had made up the bulk of the Guard in earlier generations had to be converted to antiaircraft and other specialized functions. But in the hands of the joint committees the whole reorganization was carried off with remarkably little friction or dissatisfaction. The citizen soldiers brought to the committees an awareness and a profound understanding of local issues and rivalries that regulars never could.[16]

Although the colonel was fishing in Maine during much of the time the joint committees were at work, he exercised a considerable influence on their deliberations. Quite apart from his role in establishing their statutory mandate, it was he who had drawn up the preliminary instructions directing their discussions. These guidelines were a summation of the political wisdom he had acquired while serving on the Hill. To begin with, he recognized that any solution worked out would meet with objections by National Guardsmen "until they fully understand it." There would be rivalry between the Guard and the Organized Reserve, he predicted, but "this rivalry will disappear when the distinct missions of the two forces are thoroughly understood." The Guard would initially be disposed to recommend an excessive number of skeletonized Guard divisions to retain all the veterans of the war, but the guardsmen would gradually come to see that only those ready and willing to return to active duty on short notice should join the Guard; those who desired to serve only in the event of a serious national emergency should enter the Organized Reserve. Finally, he stressed the importance of keeping the mixed committees in session "for sufficient time to indoctrinate their civilian members in regard to correct military policy." The time required would be well spent, since the committees would "probably have a potent influence on our future military policy."[17]

In predicting a potent influence for the joint committees, Palmer was forecasting the future with considerable accuracy, but he was dead wrong in his opinion that the Guard itself would "demand complete federalization in the next two or three years." Indeed, the committees did their work so effectively that they achieved many of the advantages of federalization desired by the War Department, while retaining the Guard in the states under the militia clause of the Constitution.[18] There was a double irony in this result.

In the first place, among the officers comprising the first of the committees assembled was Col. Milton A. Reckord, the extremely capable Maryland guardsman who had served as a regimental commander in the Fifty-eighth Brigade during the war. Thus one of Palmer's own officers, a man thoroughly inbued with Palmer's outlook and attitudes, helped to make a success of his joint committee idea. But the very success of this idea delayed to an indefinite future his dream of federalizing the Guard under the army clause of the Constitution.

If Palmer's morale rose with the report of the work accomplished by the joint committees in September and October, his spirits soared even further after the elections in November. An avowed Democrat, he nonetheless expected a change of personal fortune from a change of administrations. And with speculation running to Pershing, Wood, and Wadsworth as possible candidates for Secretary of War, it appeared that his interest would be served no matter which one secured the appointment. Although President Harding selected Sen. John W. Weeks to fill the office, this news was soon followed by an announcement that General Pershing would be the next Chief of Staff, taking office 1 July 1921 when General March stepped down.[19]

The real turning point in the colonel's fortune came in April 1921, when his friend George Marshall paid a chance visit to Governors Island. After patiently listening to his host's tale of frustration, he suggested that a letter to General Pershing might be of some help. Marshall's handling of this proposal showed that he was no less skilled in the tactics of human relations than he was in moving armies. While serving as aide to the General of the Armies, he had learned precisely how to handle him.[20] The correct procedure, he explained, was to write a letter outlining the assignment desired and send it to Marshall, who would undertake to place it before his chief at the psychological moment when it would have the maximum effect. Ever since the Armistice the general had been inundated with mail begging his personal intervention. Some wished him to reverse the findings of military courts, some sought his favor in behalf of promotion, and others offered him sure-fire remedies and patent schemes for all the ills of the army. In such a welter, one more letter might easily be missed unless personally handled.[21]

Somewhat earlier Palmer's friends on the General Staff had suggested that he might find it useful to take his next duty assignment as chief of staff with a division of the Organized Reserve.[22] There he could set up a model for all the other divisions to follow. But the possibility of intervention by Pershing opened up an even more tempting opportunity. Following Marshall's instructions, Palmer laid his cards before the general. What he wanted was an assignment in Washington, where he would have ready access to the War College library. With a year or two free from administrative duties, he hoped to take a long step toward clarifying the national military policy. After turning out some popular articles explaining the Act of 1920, he proposed to write a brief history of the army as a political institution. As he saw it, the great difficulty in solving the military problems of the nation was the confusion of ideas on the subject both in the army and in the country at large. His contribution would be to develop a philosophy of military organization "at once satisfactory to the practical soldier and in harmony with our traditional political ideals." There was ample precedent for such an assignment. General Sherman had done as much for Emory Upton back in the 1880s. But whereas Upton's unfinished chapters had largely been confined to destructive criticism of the nation's military institutions, the time now seemed ripe for a more constuctive undertaking.[23]

After sending off his letter, Palmer continued to think about his immediate future: if Marshall could procure Pershing's intervention on his behalf, why should he limit this opportunity to a literary role? Why not get himself assigned to the general's immediate staff? There he might well be able to wield a far wider influence by serving as an adviser directly behind the seat of power. With this thought in mind he again wrote to Marshall, outlining the job he visualized for himself.

In the General Staff there must always be compromises between the scientific point of view and certain ingrained, selfish ideas of the old army. But I take it that before such plans are finally approved the General will be consulted about them, and that his influence will determine the entire future policy and history of the United States. It therefore seems to me that he will have another title to enduring fame only second to that he now holds as America's battle leader in the World War.

In this connection it has occurred to me that my familiarity with the policy as it originally developed ... may be of real service to the General.

Of course it would not be proper for me to make such a suggestion to him, and perhaps I have passed the bounds of modesty and propriety in broaching it to you. But if you think I would be useful along more practical lines in the near future you might feel justified in recommending that I be ordered to regular duty first, leaving the transition to purely literary work to the future.[24]

Under Marshall's skillful prodding, Pershing readily agreed to the proposal, and on 5 May, Palmer received orders to report in person to the General of the Armies for duty. The rest of his family was far from pleased. His daughter Mary had spent a whole year at school looking forward to her return to the delights of Governors Island. For his wife, going back to the capital meant giving up the spacious quarters of a commanding officer for a small apartment in the sweltering city. In time both were to discover that duty with Pershing's staff was to have its social compensations, but at the moment all they could do was swallow their chagrin and follow the colonel, in loyal army fashion.[25]

As soon as Palmer reported for duty in Washington, he found himself caught up in a seemingly endless whirl of administration. General Pershing kept him close at hand, consulted him frequently, and gave him numerous assignments on boards and committees.[26] While it was highly flattering to enjoy the chief's confidence in such obvious fashion, this was scarcely what he had bargained for. On the other hand, it was the pressure of current events that inspired him to constructive thinking on long-range policy. And the most pressing topic of concern in army circles was the rage for economy sweeping Congress.[27]

General Pershing understood perfectly well that after four years of wartime extravagance, Congress was under exceedingly heavy pressure to reduce taxes. As Chief of Staff he stood ready to make drastic cuts in military expenditures, wherever this could be done without harm to the essential machinery of national defense.[28] In Congress, however, military preparedness no longer held any popular appeal. The cry was now all for vote-getting tax cuts. The first big step had come in February 1921, when the legislators had lowered the strength of the army from the 17,000 officers and 280,000 men authorized by the Defense Act to 16,000 and 175,000 men. On 30 June 1921, the day before Pershing took office as Chief of Staff, they further decreased the enlisted strength of the army, to a total of 157,000.[29]

To Palmer, the conduct of Congress served as a catalytic agent. He thought the action ill advised, but instead of blaming the legislators, he was led to ask what the military services could do to present a more effective statement of their budgetary needs. He still maintained a buoyant confidence that the legislators would do right by the military services if only they could be shown the true nature of the problem. After some weeks of playing with the subject, he came up with a formal paper for consideration by the Secretary of War.

The difficulty, as Palmer analyzed it, was readily defined. In the existing governmental structure there was no agency designed to weigh conflicting views as to what the "functions, dimension and proportions" of the various elements in the system of national defense should be.

> Congress appropriates for the Navy and the Army separately without any prior settlement as to the proper joint relations and missions of the land forces and sea forces. One committee prepares legislation based more or less on the Navy's *ex parte* view as to what these relations and missions should be and another committee prepares legislation based more or less upon the Army's *ex parte* view...[and] in due time Congress adopts uncorrelated fragments of both systems, appropriates millions of dollars and calls it a National Defense System.
>
> Now, how can these *ex parte* views be reconciled and the truth determined? The answer is very simple. It is only necessary to bring both experts together in open court, receive their pleadings and join their issues. Any competent judicial mind, after ample time for enlightenment and investigation can weigh these issues and make a reasonable decision. This is the method applied in reconciling conflicting expert views in our courts and by this method issues just as complicated and technical as the issues between military and naval experts are decided daily. The essential thing is to have each expert present his case in the presence of his opponent and indeed this process, through mutual education, will have a decided effect in narrowing the issues themselves.[30]

The practical problem, he concluded, was to devise an agency capable of determining a total plan of national defense, assigning missions to the army and navy, and deducing therefrom the foundations of a joint budget.

> Perhaps the simplest and most complete solution of this problem would be the establishment of a Ministry of National Defense having control over both the Army and the Navy. If such a department should be

formed it should not go the length of consolidating the two services. It should confine itself solely to determining the army program and the naval program as coordinated parts of the general program of national defense. It should also determine the joint army and navy budget, basing the estimate for each service upon its assigned mission. It should have only the limited personnel necessary to perform these two specific tasks. Having fixed the missions and the money allowances for the two services, the Minister of National Defense should allow them to function as they do now. It would not be necessary or desirable . . . to interfere with the command or administration of either service.[31]

Palmer was convinced that an immediate application of his ministry of national defense scheme would result in substantial savings without impairing the nation's security. He was equally certain that such a ministry would soon recognize that small sums invested in training citizen soldiers would increase the defensive power of the nation to such an extent as to justify major reductions in other positions of the military budget.

As it turned out, nothing came of the paper. Secretary Weeks praised and then pigeonholed the document. Probably no other fate was to be expected, since few in Congress were in a mood to reopen the question of military organization. This was just as well, perhaps, for it had already deflected Palmer from the pressing tasks immediately at hand. Nonetheless the effort is an excellent illustration of its author's creative imagination and at the same time earns him a certain priority in grappling with problems that were to be of the greatest interest a generation hence.[32]

The immediate task confronting General Pershing and his newly assembled staff was the all but impossible one of maintaining an effective army with the 157,000-man ceiling imposed by Congress. Although Palmer believed the cuts to be excessive, he was inclined to feel they might turn out to be a blessing in disguise. The smaller the number of enlisted men authorized for the Regular Army, the larger the number of professional officers released to devote their time to the civilian components. Unfortunately, many in Congress had no appreciation of this role for the Regulars. Senator W. E. Borah, the Idaho isolationist, in offering a resolution to reduce the army still further to 100,000 men, argued vehemently for a proportional cut in officers.[33] But less than half of the professional officers actually served with units of the Regular Army. The rest were assigned to the General Staff, to school duty, or duty with the civilian components. Indeed, it was the deliberate intent of those who framed the 1920 legislation to provide a large overhead of professional officers for this very purpose. And in cutting 1,000 officers below the number authorized in 1920, Congress had already seriously hindered the all-important instructional work of the army. Some Regular Army units had been forced to assign officers to regular duty in two different companies at the same time. Many regimental commanders were unable to send officers to Benning and Leavenworth or other similar schools, and they became increasingly reluctant to see any more Regulars drawn off as instructors with the citizen forces.[34]

For Palmer the solution to this problem appeared obvious: the War Department should deactivate still more tactical units of the Regular Army. Officers of the Regular Army, he argued, should regard the development of citizen soldiers as their primary mission; this had been the intent of Congress in the 1920 act. The increasing strength of these relatively inexpensive troops would go far to offset the declining strength of the regulars.[35] The army's unpopularity with the legislators he attributed to "the impression in Congress that the War Department has been frequently disposed to ignore the congressional intent." So the army should release the largest possible number of professionals to train the Guard, the Officers Reserve Corps, and the various forms of popular training provided in the law. Such a course would "strike a popular note in Congress" and demonstrate that the army was loyally carrying out the letter and the spirit of the 1920 statute.[36]

Very few of Palmer's fellow professionals were ready to accept his line of argument. Among the few who did was Col. John Henry Parker, one of his classmates at the academy. Like most of his contemporaries, Parker had been thoroughly indoctrinated with Upton's animadversions on the militia. But wartime service in France with a Guard division engaged in fierce fighting on the front had made Parker a passionate believer in the splendid potential of "trained citizen soldiers." There were, however, very few officers like Parker proffering their services to help convert the Regulars.[37]

Even among his close friends, Palmer found many officers who favored retaining as many Regular Army tactical units as possible. With the limited manpower available, this meant skeletonizing to the point where each unit was little more than a bare shell, a partial complement of officers and sometimes scarcely more than a corporal's guard of enlisted men.[38] Long experience had demonstrated that it was easier to get Congress to authorize a given commissioned strength when it could be shown that the officers requested were needed to man a designated regiment in a particular post—in a particular Congressional District. Officers assigned to overhead were much more difficult to justify. A large number of units, even if highly skeletonized, provided the maximum number of command positions. And aggressive officers quite understandably sought commands in preference to duty as instructors assigned to the civilian components. Such positions required the attributes of a diplomat far more than a flair for command.

On the other hand, there were substantial objections to maintaining a large number of skeletonized units, as Palmer had endlessly reiterated in denouncing General March's proposals. In an emergency, understrength units would have to be filled up at the last minute with untrained recruits. Bare cadres also offered very poor possibilities for realistic training. It would be wiser, he argued, to concentrate all the available enlisted strength into two or three regular divisions. This would afford real opportunities for leadership and at the same time demonstrate in a dramatic way how few units were actually available for the nation's defense. Skeleton units were Potemkin villages that tended to give Congress a false impression of military might. But the main objection was that a great number of skeletonized regular units locked up too large a proportion of the professional officers and kept them from the important business of training the citizen forces. "To absorb more officers than absolutely necessary in the Regular Army," Palmer warned, "is to sell a great birthright for a mess of pottage."[39]

Although he believed that some of the regulars who disagreed with him were motivated by selfish concern for promotion, Palmer continued to affirm his faith in the majority. The regulars simply did not understand what Congress intended in the Defense Act of 1920. If only the act could be explained, they would come around. The difficulty was in knowing how to do the explaining.

A possible solution to this problem had been shaping up in Palmer's mind even before his return to Washington. What was needed, he had confided to Wadsworth, was an authoritative declaration of policy by the President. Such a statement would, as he rather naively put it, settle the national military policy "once and for all." The Secretary of War should issue an official directive to the Chief of Staff making clear to all that the President, as the Commander in Chief, intended to carry out the mandate of Congress; which is to say, the President would base the national defense not upon an expansible army of regulars but upon the Army of the United States, in which units of citizen soldiers, organized territorially, were the most numerous component. From this it would logically follow that the Regular Army should be organized into the minimum number of units at full strength, to release the maximum number of professional officers for duty with the citizen forces. The regulars, whatever their personal preferences, when given such a directive would see that alternative courses were no longer open and would support the official policy.[40]

With Wadsworth's blessing he prepared a draft of the proposed directive and submitted it to Pershing to carry to the civilian authorities. The document, he suggested with characteristic optimism, represented a "final" definition of policy that would "put an end to further controversies and uncertainties within the War Department" and at the same time form the basis for a "harmonious accord between the executive and legislative branches."[41] Pershing approved the ends sought but was inclined to question the means employed. "I don't see the point, Palmer," he declared. "Why in hell shouldn't I just issue the order myself?" But the colonel finally persuaded him that the statement would have far more effect if it came from the civilian authorities. Once convinced, Pershing helped persuade the Administration to adopt the declaration. Soon afterwards Secretary Weeks affixed his signature on what was now officially "the President's desire."[42] To make certain that this significant development was not lost on his fellow professionals, Palmer persuaded Pershing to issue the secretary's letter as a War Department general order, to give it the widest possible circulation.[43]

In retrospect the whole maneuver appears as an ingenious and imaginative effort on Palmer's part. By insisting upon the presidential cachet for his interpretation of the 1920 legislation, he acquired substantial leverage, which he was quick to exploit. Thereafter, especially when addressing unconvinced or unbelieving regulars, he usually included a bland allusion to "the President's policy," as if he himself had had nothing whatever to do with its formulation. He may even have felt that an executive declaration would be useful in dealing with General Pershing. From long experience he knew what powerful pressures could be brought to bear upon the Chief of Staff, so it would certainly be helpful to have such an authoritative statement in hand if the general showed signs of backsliding from his commitment to a central role for the citizen forces.[44]

One of General Pershing's first acts on becoming Chief of Staff had been to set up a board to consider a reorganization of the General Staff. To head this study group he selected Maj. Gen. James G. Harbord, whom he had recalled to Washington as his principal assistant.[45] Inevitably, Palmer, too, was asked to serve. Predictably enough, General March's conception of the staff as an operating agency was scrapped in favor of a return to the "informing and coordinating" role originally envisioned by Secretary Root. In addition, the board recommended adoption of a modified version of the staff structure developed in the AEF. The five staff divisions decided upon, G-1 (Personnel), G-2 (Intelligence), G-3 (Operations), G-4 (Supply), and WPD (War Plans Division), laid the basis for an organization that was to remain substantially intact for more than a generation.[46]

Palmer was highly gratified. He saw the new structure as the culmination of a far-reaching military reform that had begun with the Defense Act of 1920. With presidential backing for his interpretation of the act now reinforced by a General Staff organized along the lines he had advocated when testifying before Congress, he had every reason to feel pleased. His actual influence on military policy had never seemed greater, and his position at the elbow of a chief of staff who reposed the highest trust in him held promise of still larger influence in the immediate future.

Just before the new staff organization was to go into effect, Pershing offered to let the colonel head up the reconstituted War Plans Division.[47] There was considerable appeal in such an assignment, for the job had been specifically designed to free the incumbent to concentrate on planning. Moreover, since the War Plans Division also supervised the various schools of the army, the position would permit him to exercise a large measure of control over the training and indoctrination of the rising generation of staff officers. He was sorely tempted, but after a long talk with George Marshall, he decided it would be wise not to accept. His forte was policy formulation. What he really needed more than anything else was freedom—time to think and time to write without the interruption of daily affairs. The ideal solution, Marshall suggested, was to accept an assignment as one of Pershing's military aides. This would give the freedom he desired while still leaving him in a strategic position at the general's elbow.

Pershing readily assented to the suggested arrangement; and on 15 August 1921 he formally announced to the press that he had appointed Palmer as one of his aides.[48] However, the colonel's transition to the new position was not so easily accomplished. For Marshall, who had engineered the move, and for Pershing, who had agreed to it, the title of aide was merely a convenient vehicle to provide some sort of official status. The colonel, however, presented himself for duty as if expecting to receive orders. On those days when he planned to work for an extended period at the Army War College library, he asked permission, almost apologetically. Finally the general burst out, "Palmer, I don't give a damn where you work. You are an absolutely free agent."[49]

With his relationship to the general thus emphatically clarified, the colonel settled down to what he later described as the most satisfactory assignment of his entire professional life. Although officially without duties, he devoted much of his time to the preparation of speeches and articles, as well as policy papers, for the Chief of Staff. The arrangement seemed to afford a perfect opportunity to exploit the enormous prestige of the Pershing name to publicize his own views on military policy. And time after time he had the satisfaction of seeing his ideas become those of his chief as Pershing used his work without modification or amendment.

A characteristically far-reaching opportunity cropped up when the commandant of the General Staff College invited Palmer to lecture before the incoming class on the evolution of the General Staff. Ordinarily he would have leaped at the chance, but he had resolved not to allow himself to be deflected further from his self-imposed task of interpreting the Defense Act for the army. So he offered to talk on "The Military Policies of the United States as Settled by Recent Law and Executive Orders." Such a lecture, he argued, was an essential preliminary to the work of the staff course, since the law itself was "so complicated and so burdened with unimportant detail" that few officers had grasped its "great underlying principles."[50]

The many compliments he afterwards received led him to believe that his lecture might be published as a means of popularizing the new military policy of the nation. He sent a copy to Tompkins McIlvaine, whose literary judgment as editor of *National Service* he valued highly, but McIlvaine gave him no encouragement whatever. No one short of Bernard Shaw, McIlvaine declared, could make military policy a popular subject. He excepted Shaw because of his scholarly essay on the Dempsey-Beckett ring battle—"if he can classicize a prize fight I think he should be able to popularize a national fight." Get rid of military prose; stop writing for an encyclopedia, McIlvaine warned: if the reader has to weigh every word, he won't stay with it. This must have hurt, for ever since the success of his muckraking articles in *McClure's* Palmer had prided himself on his knack for popularization. Nonetheless, he was grateful. "It is good physic," he admitted, "and like all good physic, is much more agreeable in its ultimate effect than in its first taste."[51]

While the lecture was not in any sense popular, it was skillfully contrived for a military audience. The Defense Act, Palmer explained, was the basic blueprint for a great national institution. But this blueprint was hard to read. His task was to help his listeners go beyond the blueprint stage and visualize the completed structure.

> It has been the practice of the United States upon the outbreak of war to expand a small professional peace establishment into a great nonprofessional war Army.... With a vast expenditure of treasure and human energy we have erected a great war organization and then have demolished that organization after the emergency without any provision for making that expenditure a permanent national investment. After being forced to militarize a whole generation, we have taken no precaution to make the sacrifices of that generation a heritage of experience for the next generation that may be called upon to bear the stress of war. It is primarily the object of our new law to perpetuate the framework of the organization developed in the world war, so that its tremendous cost can be funded as a permanent investment for all time.....
>
> . . . .
>
> Our present national defense law establishes an economical and democratic military policy thoroughly consistent with our national traditions. It provides for a small Regular Army, to be augmented by great citizen forces in the event of national emergency. That is our traditional military policy. But whereas in the past these larger war forces have been extemporized after the occurrence of an emergency, the new law wisely provides that the framework of their organization shall be established and developed in time of peace, insofar as this is practicable through the voluntary service of our patriotic young men. The Army of the United States as defined in the new law comprises the Regular Army, the National Guard, and the Organized Reserves. Every patriotic citizen should encourage the development of these forces, each within its proper sphere.[52]

As Palmer saw it, the proper sphere of the Regular Army definitely embraced among its major functions the task of developing the civilian components. Indeed, in his view the whole structure of national defense depended upon a successful linking of the professional and citizen forces. To make his point, he drew on a series of historical examples to illustrate the tragedy that had occurred after every previous war. The professionals of the Regular Army had stepped down from their wartime role as leaders of the people to become "an isolated caste without vital contact with the body of the nation." But the new law, as authoritatively interpreted by the President, changed all this. The professionals were now confronted with a new challenge and a new opportunity.

Popular or not, some such exposition of the new law was definitely needed. By Palmer's reckoning a majority of the regular officers currently at work implementing the statute had no real understanding of either its spirit or its goals.

> It may surprise you to know [he wrote to a friend in Congress] that very few officers even in the War Department have a clear idea of the new policy. This ignorance is even more wide spread in the Army at large, in the Reserve Corps and the National Guard.... We still have foolish and wasteful conflicts...[between the Regular Army, the National Guard and the Reserves] because individual officers in these several branches have not yet learned that the new law establishes genuine, harmonious relations between the several components of the Army of the United States, on the scientific basis of assigning a definite and logical mission to each.[53]

Still fully convinced that his fellow officers would promptly recognize the "scientific basis" of their new "harmonious" relations if it were explained to them, the colonel persuaded General Pershing to authorize official publication of the lecture. Soon afterward it came out as a War Department bulletin, a format that guaranteed wide distribution.[54] One corps area went so far as to requisition a supply of 8,000 to place a copy in the hands of every officer, regular or reservist, on the corps roster.[55]

Only one dissenting voice was raised officially in criticism of the Staff College lecture. Maj. Gen. G. C. Rickards, the Guard officer recently appointed as chief of the Militia Bureau, protested against Palmer's contention that the 1920 act incorporated "practically all the constructive features" of the original Wadsworth bill except the provision for universal military training. After all, the sharpest fight in Congress had taken place over the provision in the Wadsworth bill organizing the National Guard under the army clause of the Constitution, and this feature had been rejected after a vigorous campaign of opposition by Guard interests. The lecture had glossed over the army clause issue, but it is highly doubtful that Palmer did this consciously. On the other hand, it was entirely characteristic for the colonel to turn his back on inconvenient facts and simply ignore them. He preferred to dwell on the "great constructive intent" of the new law, and by this he meant Section 3, which established the relationship of the Regular Army, the National Guard, and the Organized Reserves within one Army of the United States.[56]

As word of Palmer's abilities spread in army circles, he was asked to speak with increasing frequency by groups of veterans and reservists, and various officials in the War Department began to rely upon him for help.[57] On one occasion, when the Secretary of War asked him to get up a statement for presentation before Congress, it later developed that Pershing would also be called upon to testify. When he, too, asked for assistance, the colonel declined since he was committed to Secretary Weeks. Later, on returning from the Hill, Pershing asked his aide what he thought of his presentation. Palmer replied with a twinkle. "Just fine, General, but I liked the Secretary's statement better."[58]

It was just such sallies of gentle humor that endeared the colonel to so many of his associates. But while he was quite willing to have a little fun at the general's expense, he scrupulously maintained a proper sense of subordination. Even after years of close, even intimate association, their relations were marked by an old-fashioned reserve. Palmer never forgot that it was the general and not he who spoke with authority, although the ideas and even the phraseology were his. Even in his private correspondence he tried to maintain this loyalty, as an exchange with his friend Ida Tarbell clearly reveals. Miss Tarbell had written for permission to publish an extract from one of his letters in which he had used some quotations from Abraham Lincoln. He replied, suggesting that it might prove far more effective if she quoted the Lincoln passages in the context of the speech where General Pershing had employed them. And while he did admit that he had dug up the quotations, he carefully refrained from adding that he had written the speech as well.[59]

Sometimes it proved exceedingly difficult to remain discreetly in the general's shadow. On at least one occasion his efforts failed altogether. Ordinarily the colonel did not accompany Pershing on his official inspections and ceremonial trips about the country, but when the general set off for Palmer's home county in Illinois, he graciously asked the colonel to join him. It proved to be an exceedingly pleasant excursion. Palmer delighted in sharing his fund of anecdotes and local lore as he led his chief from one Lincoln shrine to another. But to his acute distress, at every stop they were accosted by an assortment of family friends, maiden aunts, and boyhood companions. For them the hero of the occasion was the hometown boy, John M. Palmer; the general was a distinctly secondary attraction. To add to the colonel's mortification, at one stop several elderly ladies—doubtlessly kissin' kin—insisted on bussing "the Governor's grandson." As they drove to the next stop Pershing grumbled, "My God, Palmer, you're not going to kiss all the women in this town too, are you?"[60]

One of the rewards of the Illinois trip was the occasion it afforded to observe the general in an informal setting. Despite Pershing's reputation as a martinet, he seemed to find a natural footing of equality with everyone he met. As Palmer subsequently wrote, "He is at ease and at home with the highest on earth, and with the plainest of the plain." But above all Palmer discovered anew the deep human understanding so often missed behind the general's facade. While Pershing was visiting the Anne Rutledge grave, someone mentioned that Palmer's only son and namesake lay buried but a short distance away. Without a word Pershing took him by the arm and led him to the tiny monument, where they stood apart from the crowd for a few moments in silence. Deeply touched, Palmer later wrote, "I have never known any man with more genuine human sympathy."[61]

Membership in Pershing's inner circle brought many compensations, but after several months Palmer began to realize he was far from achieving everything he expected from his favored position. He had anticipated little difficulty in putting over his conception of the Defense Act to his fellow professionals; yet somehow success had eluded him. One after another he had seen his various devices fail: the presidential fiat, enlarged and put into context by his own lecture and scattered broadcast; countless press releases; no end of speech-making; Pershing's explicit instructions to the Corps Area commanders—all, he sadly concluded, had failed to win over a majority of the professionals to his point of view.

That few officers in the Regular Army embraced his ideas with enthusiasm is perhaps hardly surprising. At the very time he was asking them to recast their thinking and dedicate themselves to building a great army of the people, they were recoiling in shock before a series of economy waves from Congress. Morale was at a low ebb; General Harbord declared he had never seen it worse in all his years with the colors.[62] To begin with, army pay was becoming scandalously inadequate as inflation escalated; a lieutenant actually earned less than a plasterer. Cuts in funds for administrative purposes had reached the point were army messengers in the District of Columbia were no longer issued motorcycles but told to ride the trolleys instead.[63] The biggest blow to morale came as a result of the manpower reductions. The legislators had insisted on eliminating more than a thousand officers—bringing the complement far below the necessary minimal force Palmer had fought for in the Defense Act—and within a year they would lop off some 4,000 more, forcing hundreds to go into early retirement or accept reductions in rank. And by limiting enlisted strength to 157,000, Congress touched off acrimonious interbranch disputes, as each of the arms and services fought tooth and claw to preserve an essential nucleus of professionals.[64]

Under such circumstances it is not difficult to see why so many regulars failed to appreciate Palmer's enthusiasm for a citizen army. They were fighting for their professional existence; he was asking them to treat each cut as one more opportunity to encourage the citizen soldiers. And not long since many of these citizen soldiers, or at least some of their more articulate spokesmen in the National Guard Association and in Congress, had been vehemently damning the Regular Army.

Gradually it began to dawn on the colonel that official explanations of the Defense Act of 1920 would never do the trick. At long last he saw the problem, in a flash of insight that every staff officer may well ponder. As he expressed it to his friend George Marshall, "Authority alone is not enough to make it go." The President, the Secretary of War, and the Chief of Staff may promulgate a policy, but when nine-tenths of the officers involved don't understand it or are out of sympathy, "the result is inertia." When those in highest authority have definitely committed themselves to a popular military policy, why, he asked, does G-3 continue twisting the military organization in another direction?[65]

The reason of course was obvious: the men involved could never hope to work out the details unless they understood the basic philosophy of the 1920 act. And what with the continual rotation of officers throughout the service, no sooner did one key individual become indoctrinated than he gave place to a new man ignorant of "the many complicated political issues" so delicately balanced in the new law. To comprehend the act, one had to see it in its broadest historical context and become intimately familiar with the long tradition of conflict between militia and federal forces, not to mention the involved story that lay behind the evolution of the General Staff. The only way to get officers to carry out the act was to help them understand it, thoroughly and fully. Once they grasped the meaning of the law, they could be counted upon to execute it wholeheartedly and with conviction. What was needed, Palmer concluded, was a book, a concise volume that would put the Defense Act in full perspective and illuminate the philosophy behind it. Filled with excitement at the prospect of success, he began to lay plans for writing the volume, which he had already sketched out in his mind.

40

In Search of
Popular Support

Although Palmer intended to begin work on his book at once, he again allowed himself to be diverted by a problem of more immediate concern. This time it was the Conference on the Limitation of Armament that met in Washington during November 1921. Long before the delegates arrived, he had urged Pershing to put the War Plans Division to work studying the questions that were sure to arise. Soon thereafter the staff began turning out a series of papers on the implications for the defensive posture of the United States of conscription, gas warfare, aviation, and the like. Foresight such as this made Palmer a logical choice as one of the "expert assistants" designated by Secretary of State Charles Evans Hughes to aid the U.S. commissioners.

The colonel vastly enjoyed his participation in the conference, but the real return on his investment came from the effort he put into preparing for the sessions. While he was so engaged, General Harbord asked him to comment on a proposal submitted by Thomas F. Millard, an old China hand and Shanghai journalist Palmer had known ever since the Boxer Rebellion. What started out as an interest in the author soon became an intense interest in the subject, and eventually the colonel turned out a full-fledged staff paper that advanced his own thinking about national defense.

"I believe," he wrote to Harbord, "that our policy of maintaining the Open Door and the integrity of China is sound"; however, he added, the present policy of Japan is "diametrically opposed," and that nation will resist our aims "to the extent of war if necessary." In this situation he found the gravest danger confronting the nation in the tendency of public opinion to insist on the integrity of China "without reckoning upon its military consequences." For the United States alone to enforce this policy against Japan would be an undertaking of enormous magnitude, including the possibility of an offensive war across thousands of miles of ocean.

In reading current... articles and official documents bearing upon ... the approaching Conference, I am greatly impressed by the fact that very few people seem to realize the practical significance of the fundamental definition of war as given by Clausewitz:... "War is a continuation of policy by other means."... It is practically certain that the statesmen who represent Japan in the Conference will... understand the inter-relation of national policies and the military preparations necessary to enforce them ... With us, there is a possibility at least that our representatives will continue to regard policy and war as entirely distinct and separate things.[1]

In Palmer's view, since the people of the United States gave no evidence of any willingness to provide the armament necessary to enforce the Open Door Policy, the only feasible alternative was to seek a treaty of alliance.

If we should succeed in reaching a practical understanding with Great Britain, in which France and Italy should join, our armament program would immediately be affected in a most favorable way. The potential military strength of this combination would be so great that Japan would probably be forced to acquiesce ... because ... the maintenance of her own policy to extremity would result in a hopeless war .... This is another illustration ... that intelligent national policies depend upon capacity to enforce them and not solely upon their intrinsic merits or disadvantages.[2]

Part of the difficulty, he realized, lay in the prevailing lack of coordination between the State Department and the two military services. But behind this shortcoming he detected a still more fundamental cause.

In the past we have developed our principal national policy without considering its military corollaries, because ... the Monroe Doctrine ... would require our enemies to attack us in our own strategic area. Our potential strength to meet the requirements of this defensive attitude is so great that is has been unnecessary to consider any detailed development of our military resources.

With reference to the Far East... the conditions are reversed. The favorable position in this case is occupied by Japan .... Our policy of the Open Door is an aggressive attack against Japan in her own theater of war. Therefore we might say that for the first time in our history we have arrived in a situation where it is necessary to understand the definition of Clausewitz if our policy is to rest upon sound grounds.[3]

The effort involved in thinking his way to these conclusions led Palmer to a new perspective on the whole question of national military policy. Hitherto he had been primarily concerned with interpreting the Defense Act for those who had to work under its provisions. Now, however, he could see that this would be relatively meaningless if the Congress and, ultimately, the public failed to provide the necessary support.

The time seemed hardly propitious to approach the public on the question of military policy. The Conference on the Limitation of Arms had stirred up a considerable agitation among pacifist groups, some of which seemed to advocate total abolition of the army and navy. Few went quite this far, but during 1921, a year of depression and deficit spending, Congress was abnormally responsive to any promised reduction in federal expense. And any discussion of cutting army expenditures in Congress led inevitably to Rep. Daniel R. Anthony, Jr., of Kansas.

As chairman of the Subcommittee on Military Appropriations, Anthony exercised a powerful influence. Just how powerful he appeared to his contemporaries may be seen from a comment made by Maj. Gen. W. M. Wright of the IX Corps Area. "When I left Washington last June the future of the Regular Army was in the hands of Dan Anthony, and as far as I can see, it still is."[4] Anthony's conduct also suggested that he was far more interested in patronage than he was in the future of the army. Harbord scathingly dismissed him as the type of legislator who was "unfriendly to everything that does not contribute to the welfare of Fort Leavenworth"—his home district.[5] General March dismissed him as "the unspeakable Anthony."[6]

As Palmer reflected on the problem, it dawned on him that the obstacles imposed by Mr. Anthony might actually be turned to advantage. He must frame his message in terms of its manifest economy, as Grenville Clark had been suggesting in their exchange of correspondence over the past several months. And what could be more economical than a military policy calling for the smallest feasible regular army, backed by a large reserve of citizen soldiers?

After some weeks Palmer drew up an elaborate memorandum for the Chief of Staff.[7] His study of "the national financial situation," he explained, had led him to the conclusion that "certain fundamental economic and political principles have not hitherto received full consideration by the War Department." The doctrines he presented were not really new, only the package. He simply reiterated the ideas he had been trying to popularize all along, in terms of their essential economy. Taking the Defense Act of 1920 as his point of departure, he noted that the law established three different kinds of building blocks to meet the demands of mobilization: the Regular Army, the National Guard, and the Organized Reserve.

The army's problem was to determine the ideal form of organization, one that would meet the political and economic needs of the nation no less than its military requirements. In particular, he drew attention to the widely different costs associated with the three different building blocks available to do the job: regulars at a very high per capita cost; guardsmen at a much lower cost but still relatively high per capita; and the Organized Reserve, with its relatively low per capita costs in peacetime. A Regular Army division, he found, cost some $12 million a year. At the other extreme, a cadre of officers and NCOs comprising a skeleton division of the Organized Reserve cost only about $300,000. And between these two came the National Guard, with a cost somewhat under $3 million a year for each division. If one assumed that twenty-four divisions would be required to defend the United States against invasion, then the problem became a simple task of balancing ends and means. A full complement of twenty-four Regular divisions might be highly desirable, but a total cost of $288 million was far more than the public was willing to pay. By using twenty-four divisions of the Organized Reserve, the cost could be cut to approximately half that of a single Regular division, but divisions in the Organized Reserves were far from combat ready on the eve of a general mobilization.

The obvious solution was to use a mix, balancing the elements of cost and military necessity. From this conclusion came the colonel's first principle: "In forming the peace establishment . . . no organization should be maintained in a higher-priced category if it can be safely maintained in a lower-priced category and mobilized therefrom in time to meet the requirements of an emergency." Given this, it was not difficult to deduce all the other features of the military policy he so fervently believed in. The primary mission of the Regular Army was to train the citizen forces. The Regulars should be organized accordingly, with special training forces set apart from the tactical units designed to serve as ready forces in an emergency. Yet, insofar as possible, reservists should be employed as training instructors, to give them the maximum opportunity for development. Each of these dependent principles he buttressed with elaborate justifications, leaning heavily upon the example of the Swiss, who mobilized a defensive army of 200,000 men in 1914 from a professional cadre of no more than 300 officers by the simple expedient of relying upon an intensive program of reserve training.

A few days later Palmer sent General Pershing another paper amplifying his initial effort. In it he was at pains to meet the arguments of those regulars who were inclined to minimize the effectiveness of divisions made up of reservists.

> There is a natural tendency for regular army officers to underestimate the strategic value of large numbers of partially trained divisions. *Number* is in itself one of the greatest strategic assets. . . . In a military situation where 20 good divisions are required, 30 partially trained divisions may fill the bill whereas 4 or 5 or 6 of the most highly trained divisions in the world would be entirely inadequate.[9]

Neither the divisions of the National Guard nor those of the Organized Reserve would be ready immediately for an offensive action, such as an assault on the Hindenburg line. Such a standard was entirely unnecessary. The initial mission conceived for the citizen forces required a much lesser degree of training. Once again Swiss experience pointed the way.

> Each division of the Swiss army is prepared in peace to occupy a predetermined position covering one of the possible lines of invasion through Switzerland. It is conceded that... this division is only a partially trained division. But it is practicable to prepare it fully for this initial tactical mission with the assurance that after mobilization and while in continued active service its training can be advanced to any desired extent.

In short, Palmer was contending for a peacetime organization that would avoid the confusion of 1917 and provide—on short notice—a defensive force sufficiently strong to win time for further training. He defined his goal as a "national position of readiness," an expedient compromise between the ideal and the possible.

> If we could count on large numbers of highly trained troops at the start it would of course be desirable to take the initiative at once. But we cannot get political support for a peace-time organization permitting an immediate offensive, while on the other hand a bona-fide defensive organization will always receive popular support. The cost of a peace-time organization based on the idea of an adequate initial defensive is well within the limits of our present military budget. A peace-time organization based on the idea of large offensive forces immediately available on mobilization would involve prohibitive cost.

The peculiar appeal of this "national position of readiness" lay in its price tag.

> If we should invest all our military budget in regular troops we should have only a handful upon mobilization for a great war. The same amount of money uniformly and consistently applied to the development of a Citizen Army of adequate size will result in an economical and impregnable system of national defense.

By no means all of the professionals on the General Staff accepted Palmer's proposition. His case was open to attack at a number of points. Certainly his cost figures were subject to challenge. At no point did he give thoroughgoing consideration to the costs of arming and equipping the citizen soldiers of whom he expected so much. Surprisingly enough, the regulars who disagreed with him did not strike at this point. At least some of them chose to argue that his "national position of readiness" amounted to a dangerous abandonment of the spirit of the offensive.[10]

To meet this criticism Palmer concocted a parable, which he related the next time he was invited to lecture at the Army War College. The parable is worth quoting at some length; this characteristic passage goes far to explain not only the colonel's simple charm but also his effectiveness as a speaker.

This reminds me of an unpublished chapter from Don Quixote which a Spanish friend sent me a few days ago. Whether this chapter is genuine or a forgery, it contains a rather interesting story which has some bearing on this subject. According to this questionable document, it appears that after their heretofore published adventures, Don Quixote and Sancho Panza returned to La Mancha. Don Quixote went back to his own home and Sancho Panza established a sheep ranch in the neighborhood.... As was customary, Sancho Panza's farmstead consisted of a stone wall surrounding ... his dwelling house.... One day Don Quixote went on a visit to his former esquire. When he arrived he found Sancho Panza ... upon a rude platform ... over the gateway ... busily engaged in piling bricks, rocks, old fragments of iron and bits of other material....

"What are you doing, friend Sancho?" quoth Don Quixote.

"I'm getting ready for robbers," said Sancho Panza. "As you know, there are many of these villains in this neighborhood. As my shepherds are scattered all over the country ... my plan is to blow this horn for help and then throw rocks at the robbers until the boys come to help me trounce them and drive them away."

Sancho Panza was very proud of his arrangements for defense, and looked to his former chief for approval. But instead of giving him a smile of sympathy ... the melancholy knight looked more melancholy than ever.

"What is the matter?" asked Sancho Panza. "Alas, my friend," said Don Quixote, "you have sacrificed the spirit of the offensive. No true knight like the Cid ... or Lancelot of the Lake would assume so undignified a position. If the enemy should come, they would attack at once."

Sancho Panza was very much crest-fallen. He had always looked up to Don Quixote.... In the Middle Ages a Knight Errant was regarded as a sort of embryonic anticipation of a General Staff officer. He stood at the top of the military profession.... When Sancho Panza saw that his position in readiness had failed to meet the approval of this high authority, he was humiliated indeed. Just then there was a clatter of hooves and a band of robbers was seen approaching. Sancho Panza saw his opportunity to redeem himself. He rushed down the steps, opened the gate and attacked at once. But unfortunately the robbers were too many for him. Don Quixote was unable to go to his rescue on account of his gout. But he did blow the horn; and the shepherds and neighbors came just in time to save Sancho Panza's life and drive the robbers away.

As Sancho Panza...finally reached the platform again, rubbing his head and his rump and the other bruised portions of his anatomy, he came up to Don Quixote and said, "The offensive may be very fine for you, but hereafter I don't take it until the boys come."[11]

Whatever the majority of General Staff officers may have thought about Palmer's "principles," General Pershing recognized their political utility at once. Indeed, he quoted the colonel's paper almost verbatim when he testified before the House Appropriations Committee on 23 February 1922. Nor was this simply a gesture to identify himself as an advocate of economy; not long afterward he appointed a board of officers to plan a suitable organization for the Regular Army "in connection with its primary mission of training the Army of the United States, especially that portion consisting of the citizen soldiery." Palmer, of course, was designated as a member and helped draft the final report. Following the line of the colonel's memos to Pershing, the board favored the establishment of special Training Centers by the Regular Army for the instruction of reservists. These centers were to be manned by carefully selected professionals, men particularly qualified to work with citizen soldiers.[12]

Many signs appeared to suggest that Palmer's policies were at last going to take effect, but he had been disappointed too many times to be unduly hopeful. There was a very great distance between giving an order and actually having it carried out, even an order issued by the Chief of Staff. The only policy that would survive was a policy Congress and the people clearly understood and sincerely believed. Palmer hoped to reach that audience with the book he proposed to write, but Congress was now in session. If he waited for the distant future, the legislators might now act in such a way as to make an enduring system of national defense infinitely harder to achieve.

As Palmer cast about for suitable means to carry his message to Congress, his task began to emerge more clearly. He must find ways to foster pressure on the members of Congress from their constituents back home. Legislators of Wadsworth's caliber might be won over by direct appeals on the merits of the case, but for many others, agitation by groups of voters in their home districts seemed more likely to get results. The problem was to decide which of the agencies at hand were best suited and what tactics to use in each instance. He knew something of the potentialities, and the difficulties, of working with the various National Guard organizations, the American Legion, and the Military Training Camps Association. All held out distinctly interesting possibilities; but so did several others, such as the newly formed Association of the Army of the United States.

When Palmer first learned about the association, it appeared to be an organization ideally suited to his needs. Formed on the West Coast in 1921, its avowed purpose was to unite all the components of the Army of the United

States for the common good. An association in which regulars, guardsmen, and reservists could meet on the same footing promised to be highly useful in fostering the "one army" idea. Far more important, it would unite a large block of individuals with a personal interest at stake, just the sort whose spokesmen commanded respectful attention from congressmen.[13]

The idea of exploiting the association first occurred to Palmer when Sen. William H. King of Utah unleashed a savage attack on the excessive number of high-ranking officers in the Regular Army—68 generals and 599 colonels—to command a force of 142,000 enlisted men. The charge completely overlooked the deliberate intention of the Defense Act to provide a large overhead of professional officers to train the reserves as well as lead the regulars, not to mention the extra officers required for the technical services. But unfair or not, the regulars, lacking both numbers and political organization, were totally unequipped to cope with the charge. With a strong Association of the Army of the United States, however, the situation might be different. The members who were guardsmen and reservists could supply spokesmen out in the congressional districts, where their voices would count most. Nonetheless, when Palmer proposed using the association to stir up opposition in Senator King's bailiwick, he met with immediate resistance.[14]

Maj. Gen. William N. Wright, one of the officers who had been most active in promoting the association on the West Coast, protested that the time was not ripe for any such action. The organization was still actively recruiting. To lobby at this juncture would almost certainly create a suspicion among potential members that they were being sought only to be used by the regulars. The wisdom of this view was evident; the association was clearly not yet in any condition to perform the role the colonel expected of it. For immediate action, Palmer decided, he would have to look elsewhere.[15]

The Military Training Camps Association, with its network of local chapters, its press bureau, and its magazine, seemed to offer an excellent medium for the work of propaganda he had in mind. Unfortunately, the apparatus was no longer what it once had been. A marked decline of interest in many of the local chapters was probably inevitable in the general postwar reaction against all things military; subscriptions to *National Service* had fallen off sharply. The wealthy backers of the organization loyally made good mounting annual deficits, but there was a limit to their generosity.

The association was by no means moribund; its members had taken an active part in arousing interest in the Citizens Military Training Camps (CMTC) program authorized by the Defense Act. Whatever success the program enjoyed, the association deserved a large share of the credit. But the campaign to recruit candidates for the summer training program had been costly; with considerable justice, those who had been making good on the bills began to question whether it was wise to continue underwriting recruiting expenses that should be shouldered by the War Department.[16]

Persistent financial difficulties finally induced the leaders of the Military Training Camps Association to merge their magaizine, *National Service,* with the *Army and Navy Journal.* The *Journal* had recently changed hands and was now being edited by Brig. Gen. Henry J. Reilly, Jr., a son of the colorful commander of "Reilly's Battery" who had been killed in the siege of Peking during the Boxer Rebellion. The younger Reilly, though a West Point graduate, had served in the AEF as an officer in the Illinois National Guard and was highly sympathetic to the views of the association on the importance of citizen soldiers. Nonetheless, the association lost direct control over its most important instrument, and thereafter its effectiveness as a lobby was increasingly doubtful. Palmer apparently sensed the trend, for he made no effort to push the association into a new campaign. Instead, he turned once again to the American Legion.[17]

From long experience the colonel should have known that it would be a grave mistake to expect too much from the Legion. The frustrations and disappointments he had encountered in working with the Legion during the legislative battles on the reorganization bill ought to have forewarned him. But circumstances had altered substantially. His friend and wartime subordinate D. John Markey, the Maryland guardsman, was now chairman of the Legion's Military Policy Committee, and he himself had been asked to serve as a member of that body. What is more, almost half of the veterans on the committee were also members of the Military Training Camps Association or friendly to its aims.[18]

In some respects Palmer's expectations were more than fulfilled. He was repeatedly invited to address large gatherings of veterans at Legion posts up and down the country, and this gave him opportunities to preach the "one army" gospel in ever-wider circles. An even more significant opportunity came his way when National Commander Hanford MacNider invited General Pershing to address a policy-making conference of departmental commanders and others at Indianapolis. Unable to attend, the general sent his aide, saying "I rely greatly on Colonel Palmer's knowledge and judgment with reference to military policy."[19] Occasions of this sort were made to order for the colonel's purpose, for his words carried far beyond his immediate audience. The Legion magazine gave such meetings good coverage, and departmental commanders across the nation saw to it that the word was passed down to the local posts in their jurisdictions.

The line between disseminating ideas and operating a lobby is often hard to distinguish. As the colonel was to discover, using the Legion as a pressure group could have its disadvantages. If the Legion supported a larger appropriation or some other piece of legislation much sought after by the regulars, the legionnaires, or some of them, expected a return for their effort. As the editors of *Stars and Stripes* put it: "it would seem to be a fair proposition if the contact between the Legion and the Army worked both ways. If the staff is anxious for its Army program, the Legion might suggest in return a little General Staff support for the Legion program."

The colonel had long since recognized that "certain elements" of the Legion were drifting away from their original high ideals and turning instead to what he tactfully described as "special service legislation." But he shrank from the prospect of bargaining for army reform. If the legionnaires worked to secure the passage of an army bill, he wanted them to do so because they believed in it, not because they expected help in getting some favored bit of veterans' legislation through Congress.[20]

Thoroughly disillusioned after several months of trying, he summarized his results for General Pershing: "While I was able to accomplish something in developing support from the American Legion, I find the possibilities of effective support . . . are limited by its very large membership." Many legionnaires, he ruefully concluded, were "not interested in the matter of preparedness." Belatedly he was driven to the realization that, with minor exceptions, few indeed were the voters who could be counted upon to maintain an active interest in national defense. For sustained support of a systematic character the Army of the United States would have to look to its own, the organized interest groups numbered among its components. Among these, undoubtedly the best organized and most powerful was the National Guard.[21]

Not long after Palmer began his flirtation with the Legion, an unusually favorable opportunity for working with the Guard presented itself when he received an invitation to attend the annual convention of the National Guard Association in New Orleans during February 1922. General Pershing was asked to give the principal address, but since he could not attend he again gave the assignment to his aide. The burden of Palmer's message was epitomized in his opening remarks: he greeted the assembled delegates as "brother officers of the Army of the United States." Then, after recalling the "one army" conception that underlay the Defense Act of 1920, he went on to explain the principle of economy governing the apportionment of funds, and therefore strength, to the regulars, the guardsmen, and the Organized Reserves.[22]

Although the Guard delegates applauded the colonel's speech and seemed to give tacit approval to his "one army" views, in practice they took quite another stand. They were perfectly willing to bury the hatchet with the Regular Army. This was evident in the invitations to Pershing and Palmer extended by the president of the association, Bennett Champ Clark, whose "smash the army" speech three years earlier had done so much to poison relations between guardsmen and regulars. Now the hostility of the guardsmen was directed toward the Organized Reserve, which they regarded as a dangerous competitor not only for funds but also for recruits.[23]

The fears of the guardsmen were not entirely unfounded. Although authorized a total strength of 425,000 by the act of 1920, a most aggressive campaign of recruitment had brought in somewhat fewer that 150,000 men. The guards-

men were inclined to place the blame upon the Organized Reserve. Some
overly zealous reserve commanders had indeed recruited men for their units
who might more suitably have gone into the Guard, but these were isolated
instances. Nonetheless, it took only a few such episodes—one of them, unfortunately, in Bennett Champ Clark's home state of Missouri—to persuade
many of the guardsmen that the Organized Reserve was simply a reincarnation of Secretary of War Lindley M. Garrison's 1916 scheme for a Continental
Army Reserve, a reserve force organized by the Regular Army under the army
clause of the Constitution. Palmer himself was not entirely above suspicion.
He had fought long and hard before the passage of the act of 1920 to have the
Guard brought under the army clause and thus under control of the Regular
Army.[24]

In retrospect it appears that the fears of the guardsmen were probably
exaggerated. Palmer was entirely sincere in his support of the National Guard
as a first-line reserve of the citizen army. As such, he fully expected it to receive
by far the larger share of the funds available for the citizen components. In any
case, events since the passage of the Defense Act had persuaded him that the
existing solution, the dual status of the Guard, was the proper one. As he told
his friend Col. John Henry Parker, "the position of the National Guard is not
only fixed by law but also by logic." In other words, even if Congress had acted
otherwise and established the entire reserve under the army clause of the
Constitution, it would still have been necessary to divide the force into two
parts, a first-line or ready reserve such as the National Guard and a back-up
echelon, such as the Organized Reserve, to be called out only in the event of a
great national emergency.[25]

As a potential political force the Organized Reserve presented but a slight
threat to the Guard. Largely a paper organization, it held no weekly drills to
build up esprit de corps. It had no functional ties to the local courthouse
crowd or the state legislature and, most significantly, no patronage, no
armories, no drill pay. Nonetheless, many of the delegates at the National
Guard Association convention continued to articulate their opposition, some
of them vehemently.[26]

Palmer returned to his hotel in New Orleans and poured out his views in a
long letter to General Pershing. "The institution as it stands," he wrote, "is
very far from our ideal as to what the first line of the citizen army should be."
As he saw it, the problem was not one of organization. There were some
splendid leaders in the Guard, he admitted, but "the old type of National
Guard politician" was still very much in evidence. If the Guard were led by
high-grade men in every state, all questions of status and the relationship of
the Guard to the other components would easily be resolved.[27]

The "only solution" to the National Guard question, Palmer declared, was
to educate. He was realistic enough to know that little could be done with most
of the guardsmen already involved in politics, but he had great hopes for the

young. "The Citizens' Training Camp should be developed as far as practicable as a direct feeder for the National Guard. Officers of the Regular Army on duty with the ROTC and Organized Reserves should be fully imbued with the idea that the best citizen soldier personnel should be encouraged to enter the Guard." Hitherto, the colonel admitted, quite the opposite practice had prevailed; regular officers had more or less unconsciously favored the Organized Reserves over the Guard. To continue this practice was to perpetuate the problem and justify political activity by the Guard against the third component. By directing the very best of the ROTC and CMTC into the Guard, he concluded, a "new and finer type of personnel" would begin to replace the political soldier. "He is still holding his own as an agitator because he is able to allege that we are really trying to kill the National Guard by indirection through the development of the Organized Reserves."

At the very least Palmer's proposal would require nearly a generation to take effect. But the need for cooperation among the three elements of the Army of the United States was immediate; a strong bloc of economy-minded congressional leaders was doing its best to cut the army back to little more than the Indian frontier garrison it had been in the years before the war.

The army appropriation measure that emerged from the Capitol in June 1922 clearly illustrated the utility of grassroots political support. Even the most determined efforts of Senator Wadsworth and a few other conscientious and well-informed legislators had proved insufficient to prevent Congress from undermining the basic concept of the National Defense Act, a small standing army backed by a mass of citizen soldiers partially trained and organized for rapid mobilization in time of war. To this end the act specified a minimum Regular Army of some 18,000 officers and 280,000 men, but the appropriation of June 1922 provided only 12,000 officers and 125,000 men, a force totally inadequate to train the citizen soldiers on whom the 1920 act placed the ultimate defense of the country.[28]

If the fate of the Regular Army demonstrated the importance of political support at the grass roots, the same could be said with even greater validity for the citizen forces. In fact, the sharp contrast between the experience of the National Guard and that of the Organized Reserve provided an object lesson almost made to order for the campaign Palmer was waging. The army had requested approximately $30 million for the National Guard and just under $5 million for the Organized Reserve. These requests, each affording a rough index of the performance and state of readiness expected of the two components, were referred to the House subcommittee on army appropriations.[29]

In due time Representative Anthony and his economy bloc reported out a bill calling for $21 million for the National Guard and a mere $250,000 for the Organized Reserve. As soon as these figures reached the floor, one representative after another protested the cuts made in National Guard funds. Representative Anthony charged that the members were responding to pressure from local National Guard organizations. A great many congressmen had indeed heard from the guardsmen in their constituencies, and a rash of inspired editorials had appeared in defense of the Guard budget, so the National Guard appropriation was increased to a total of $25.5 million.[30]

The Organized Reserve suffered a different fate. Since no highly coordinated grassroots group fought in its behalf, few congressmen gave it more than passing attention. Its appropriation was partially restored, largely by the efforts of Senator Wadsworth, to $1 million, but this amount was ridiculously inadequate for the training required. The National Guard, with its numerous and well-established elements of local support, had suffered a cut of 15 percent, while the Organized Reserve had to accept a cut of approximately 70 percent.[31]

Hitherto Palmer had been seeking broad popular support for the army as a whole; experience demonstrated that such support materialized only where it sprang from a carefully organized special interest group. This was good Hamiltonian doctrine, but it took a practical demonstration to drive the lesson home.

The obvious solution was to rally the officers of the Organized Reserve. Palmer explained this in a long letter to a fellow officer from his Fifteenth Infantry days.

> During the last session of Congress, a number of Reserve Officers went before Committees of Congress to advocate adequate appropriations for the Reserve Corps.... It was found that these individuals had very little weight as compared with members of the National Guard Association. Members of the committee ... frankly asked them if they represented any Association, and when they said "No," it was quite apparent that their arguments did not carry any immediate weight. These officers felt, and indeed were assured by members of Congress, that they ought to form an Association.[32]

Understandably enough, a number of reserve officers reached the same conclusion at about the same time. Early in the summer of 1922 a call went out to delegates from local reserve associations, "alumni" organizations of AEF divisions, and other similar groups of reservists to attend a national convention in Washington during October. The colonel used his access to General Pershing to seek support in Regular Army circles. The general agreed to address a convention scheduled for October, and not long afterward the Adjutant General not only officially endorsed the gathering but also urged all Corps Area commanders to allow time during reserve training sessions for the organization of local chapters and the election of delegates.[33]

Palmer devoted a good deal of time and effort to the election of a suitable leader. He canvassed his friends in the Military Training Camps Association, mentioning among other possible candidates William J. Donovan and Charles G. Dawes. Although Dawes was one of Pershing's closest friends, the general rejected his name out of hand. "Why, Palmer," he snorted, "Charles Dawes is the most unmilitary human being that ever lived." Whether or not this should have disqualified him as the president of a reserve lobby, the general preferred Henry J. Reilly, Jr., the editor of the *Army and Navy Journal*. This choice was approved by the reservists themselves when they officially established the Reserve Officers Association and elected Reilly as their first president.[34]

A certain amount of suspicion and rivalry was to be expected from the National Guard, but even some regulars had their doubts. Palmer's friend Colonel Willis Uline, for example, feared that the new lobby would tend to work against the "one army" unity that the Association of the Army of the United States had been formed to promote. Palmer suggested that the Association of the Army of the United States would itself be stronger if each of its component groups, the regulars, the guardsmen, and the reserves, were powerfully organized. Within the association, he pointed out, the Organized Reserve would then stand a far better chance of receiving appropriate recognition.[35]

Palmer had come to recognize that men drive hardest when they know the corn is headed to their own cribs. Subsequent events confirmed his judgment. As a lobby serving a special interest, the Reserve Officers Association has continued to flourish; the Association of the Army of the United States, formed to defend an ideal, ultimately disappeared.

Shrewd as Palmer was in sensing the importance of self-interest in generating political support, he was far from omniscient in devising tactics for the defense of the citizen components. In what may have been the crucial blunder of his entire campaign, he completely ignored a suggestion proffered by Uline, who was then on duty in the Eighth Corps Area. Why not establish in the War Department, Uline asked, a chief of Organized Reserves comparable to the chief of the Militia Bureau already in existence? Such an arrangement would afford the reserve with a full-time spokesman at headquarters. Even if the incumbent were a regular, he would be inclined to strive for the aggrandizement of the reserve component reporting to him. Once institutionalized, such a bureau would acquire survival value; even a succession of weak or inept chiefs would scarcely nullify its influence.[36]

Whether Palmer's neglect of Uline's interesting proposal was an oversight or a conscious choice based on anticipated opposition from the National Guard is unknown. Perhaps the best measure of the intrinsic worth of the idea is reflected in the vigorous opposition by the Guard when the same scheme was advanced some years later.[37]

In retrospect, Palmer seems to have largely ignored the weapon nearest at hand—military administration. To be sure, he kept a stream of memos moving into General Pershing's office. And some of these revealed true leadership, shrewdly aligning the call of military duty with the tendency of human nature, as for example when he proposed to hold all Organized Reserve exercises at or near resorts, so the citizen soldiers called up for short summer tours could combine training with vacations. But virtually all of his suggestions aimed at little more than creating a favorable climate for the Reserve. The real problem lay elsewhere.[38]

By Palmer's own analysis, the solution lay in perfecting the relationship between the National Guard and the Organized Reserves. He had sensed this while attending the Guard convention in New Orleans during February. But he allowed himself to become involved in the move to establish the Reserve Officers Association and never returned to follow up the obvious implications of his own ideas, a failure the more surprising because his influence in organizing a lobby was certain to be far less immediate than his influence on military administration, in view of his intimate access to the Chief of Staff.

Had he but cast about for examples of the problems arising under the existing regulations, Palmer would have discovered that a few relatively simple changes in procedure promised to resolve much of the conflict of interest between the two citizen components. For example, if a limited number of qualified Guard officers were permitted to hold higher commissions in the Organized Reserve than they could attain under the more limited tables of organization for the Guard, some of them might have seen the Reserve as a highly useful adjunct of the Guard rather than as a dangerous competitor.

Similarly, a study revealed that many enlisted guardsmen frequently did not sign up for active duty tours at Citizens Military Training Camps because they were unable to obtain additional leave from their employers to attend the summer encampments of their Guard units. If attendance at these Guard camps fell below a specified minimum, none of the officers present received pay. Enlisted guardsmen were thus under pressure from their officers not to apply for CMTC tours. Whether or not a simple change in regulations would have solved this particular problem is of relatively minor significance here, but this and other minor changes within the Chief of Staff's authority gave promise of binding the Guard and the Reserve into a harmonious team such as Palmer had long envisioned.[39]

Palmer's resort to sources of strength outside the army may have resulted from a conscious decision. During 1922 he suffered a crushing defeat on a major question of policy within the General Staff. The details are worth recording, since they illustrate the interplay of factors affecting a major change in military policy. Moreover, as Palmer expressed it later, "it is easier to obtain clarity of vision when our views are not obscured by the mists of self-interest."[40]

The Defense Act provided two prinicipal areas of activity for the Regular Army in the United States: one was to provide a field force to cover the mobilization of the citizen components; the other was to provide troops for training in various specialized schools and Training Centers in the nine Corps Areas.

Each of the nine was to have assigned to it one Regular Army division and five divisions of citizen soldiers, two made up of National Guard troops and three "paper" divisions of the Organized Reserves. To prepare these divisions, each Corps Area was to have a training center staffed with both regular and reserve personnel. The most notable feature of this arrangement was the distinction made between the regulars assigned to divisions and those assigned to the training centers. The regular divisions could, on occasion, serve as demonstration troops for the centers, but this in no way affected their tactical availability. In the event of war they would not have to extricate individual officers and men from the training organization. The professionals assigned to the training centers would, in the event of war, remain there as the centers became replacement depots when the initial mobilization had been completed.

Separation of the tactical and training units would save the Army, Palmer felt, from the disintegration it had suffered on the outbreak of virtually every previous war. That was the theory behind the legislation of 1920, but practice was to be otherwise. Many regular officers were not prepared to accept the implications of this arrangement.[41]

The fundamental cause of opposition was the congressional economy drive. As long as there was enough manpower to meet all needs, no one seriously opposed the Training Centers. Secretary of War John W. Weeks, no less than Chief of Staff Pershing, believed that the primary mission of the Regular Army was to train the citizen components. In listing the duties of the professionals, he gave priority to this task, earmarking more than 50 percent of the regular officers in the combat arms to carry it out.[42] But as budget cuts imposed one reduction in manpower after another, administration and house-keeping, overseas garrisons, coast defense forces, and the like required a virtually irreducible number of men, so further cuts had to be absorbed entirely from the nine regular divisions in the Corps Areas or from the troops assigned to operate the training centers. It was an unequal contest. The General Staff planners favored scrapping the centers entirely to preserve the largest possible number of tactical units.[43]

As far as Palmer could see, the officers of the Operations Division, G-3, displayed little or no appreciation for the basic conception underlying the act of 1920. To "save" manpower, they proposed to have the troops assigned to the tactical units take over all the functions originally contemplated for the professionals with the centers. In Palmer's eyes this was heresy; they were reverting to the very structure found seriously defective in the past. The colonel dashed off a scathing memo to Brig. Gen. William Lassiter, Assistant Chief of Staff for Operations, opposing this stripping of all the professionals from the machinery for mobilization and training at the very time they would be most needed. To do this, he observed, was to repeat an error denounced by General Grant who saw the same mistake made during the Civil War.[44]

Just why the officers in G-3 were so adamant in favoring the tactical units at the expense of the training centers is a question that can never be answered definitively; mens' motives are largely beyond the reach of history. But in looking back on the problem years later, George Marshall, who had sided with Palmer in the discussion, recalled an episode that he believed shed a good deal of light on the matter. It seemed obvious to Marshall at the time that many regulars wanted to retain tactical units rather than training centers because the former offered far greater opportunities for promotion and command, although officers arguing in favor of scrapping the centers almost invariably claimed to be moved by principle. When one such officer, a senior colonel, was informed by Marshall that if the Training Centers were retained he was slated to receive command of the center in his area, assuring him the one-star promotion he coveted before retirement, the man became an outspoken convert to retaining the centers.[45]

The preference shown by so many professional officers for tactical commands extended well beyond hostility to the retention of Training Centers at the expense of regular divisions. When the economies imposed by Congress made it impossible to maintain nine regular divisions, the G-3 planners concocted a scheme to keep three at full strength in those Corps Areas with the best permanent posts, while providing the other six Corps Areas with skeletonized divisions comprising nothing but small, reinforced brigades. Palmer recognized the need to cut back to three divisions if Congress and the public refused to support more, but the proposal to expand the six brigades into full divisions in an emergency he regarded as nothing less than a reincarnation of Emory Upton's "expansible army," undoing some of the most constructive provisions of the 1920 statute.[46]

The colonel prepared a long memo for General Pershing on the fallacy of the G-3 action. Six brigades that required expansion, he declared, were not at all the same thing as six divisions ready to take the field. Indeed, the colonel argued, regular units that had to be fleshed out from the Organized Reserve would actually be less ready and slower to mobilize than National Guard divisions at full strength. How could the army justify the high per capita cost of regular units if those units were less ready for initial defense than Guard divisions? Would it not be wiser to break up the proposed brigades of regulars and use the professional troops in the training centers, where they would get a far greater return on the nation's defense dollar? "It would be difficult," he concluded, "to refute the imputation that the plan is an effort of the Regular

Army to develop itself at the expense of the citizen components." And he added an even more pointed barb: "This apparently is one of those cases where personal interest tends unconsciously to interfere with intellectual honesty."[47]

The last word rested with the Chief of Staff. He could accept the advice of his aide, Colonel Palmer, or the official recommendation of his G-3, General Lassiter. After some delay he chose the latter. For Palmer the decision was a stunning blow. For weeks after the decision was made, he could not bring himself to believe that the general to whom he had been so loyal and admired so much could favor such an unsound course.

Conscious of his earlier success in using a literary touch to put over otherwise dreary military subjects, the colonel cast about for an effective device, to woo not only the Chief of Staff but all those regulars whose advice the general had apparently accepted. Not long afterwards, while browsing in Carlyle's *Past and Present*, it occurred to him that the Abbot of St. Edmundsbury afforded an appropriate foil for an address Marshall was just then stitching together for the general. So he sat down and dictated the following parable:

> Not long after the death of St. Edmund, a question of policy arose in the councils of the Abbey. It was a question of the best use to make of the funds that were beginning to pour in as gifts from pious pilgrims to the Shrine. The new Abbot believed that these funds should be expended largely upon the Shrine itself and upon a suitable chapel for the use of future pilgrims and for lodgings where they could rest and receive hospitable treatment during the period of the pilgrimage. This policy was accepted by most of the monks in a half-hearted way. They could not deny that it rested upon the strongest grounds of Christian piety, but still they were disposed to think that a little less money expended on the Shrine and for the welfare of the pilgrims, with a little more expended upon the refectory and the gardens of the monks themselves would really be a wise provision for the future welfare of the Abbey. It would produce a more contented body of monks and a more comfortable life for all concerned. The Abbot resisted this idea with all of his eloquence. He had no difficulty in finding the Gospels full of texts to justify his position, but he felt that while the soundness of his policy could not be disputed, still if it were supported in a half-hearted way by agents who really lacked faith in it, it would not lead to the great things he had in mind. And so, being a very wise old Abbot, he recognized that the flesh is weak and that few men are dynamic unless they have a selfish motive. He called in his principal advisors to have a little chat with them. He said, "Heretofore I have given you reasons of a more spiritual nature and have perhaps overlooked the interests of our own community. This would, of course, be a very great mistake, because we must have a

prosperous community of monks to serve St. Edmund's Shrine. So now let us consider our own interests in the matter. If we forget ourselves and devote all of our time and all of our resources glorifying the Shrine and the Chapel, and if we make this a haven of refuge for pilgrims throughout the extent of England, then the glory of St. Edmund's will be nation-wide, and the gratitude of all England will extend itself to the monks who serve him. As the Chapel and our pious hospitality gain fame, there will be a greater stream of pilgrims who come here. There will be a greater pious gratitude that will express itself in gifts to our Patron Saint. The Abbey as a whole will grow into a great institution, and we can safely trust that a worthy refectory and suitable gardens and fish ponds will be erected for us. If we stop now and take a larger portion of our present treasures for ourselves, the treasure will not grow. But if we forget ourselves and extend St. Edmund's fame throughout the Kingdom, then the treasure will grow, and only a tithe of that greater treasure will be more for us than the moiety of that which we now have.[48]

This fable, it need scarcely be added, proved no more successful than Palmer's more conventional staff studies. If General Pershing ever identified himself with the medieval abbot or his regulars with the greedy monks, he gave no sign of it. That the colonel had believed such a reversal was in any way probable is vivid evidence of his almost unassailable innocence. The same may be said of his attitude toward Pershing; although he believed his chief woefully wrong, his conception of loyalty was such that he never uttered or wrote a word of personal criticism against the general.

In retrospect Marshall was certain that the Chief of Staff was personally in favor of Palmer's solution; he simply felt that the shortsightedness of Congress left him little or no choice.[49] Palmer's proposed alternative would cut the number of regulars in tactical units to a precariously low level if one did not believe in the capacity of the citizen components, especially the National Guard, to provide an effective supplementary emergency defense force. On the other hand, the general may not have wanted to face up to those outraged regulars who would be affected by the adoption of Palmer's plan. An episode in connection with a possible promotion for Palmer at least hints at some such motive.

As long as Palmer continued to believe that his work with Pershing was constructive and important, he professed to be quite willing to let future promotion take care of itself. But an even dozen of his juniors had received their stars. If a patron as highly placed as the Chief of Staff failed to get him promoted, what could he expect from some less friendly successor? When one of the colonel's wartime comrades in the 58th Brigade wrote offering to organize some sort of political demonstration in his behalf, he demurred; in view of his position on Pershing's staff, any such move would be "very improper." Nonetheless, he frankly admitted that he would like to be promoted and would welcome representations in his favor by National Guard officers and other veterans, but only if they came spontaneously and reflected "public reasons" rather than mere personal interest.[50]

As a consequence, on 18 November 1922, when the colonel received notification of his nomination as brigadier, he could accept with a clear conscience. But the sequence of events leading to his promotion had been far more involved than he ever realized. To begin with, his dossier had long been bulging with unsolicited commendations from men who knew his work. General Pershing rated him "an officer of exceptional ability." So, too, did his wartime division leader, Maj. Gen. C. G. Morton, who added, perhaps more tellingly, "the officers and men of the brigade not only respected ... but loved him. He proved to be a natural leader of men under the most trying circumstances." Maj. Gen. John F. O'Ryan of the 27th Division concluded by saying, "I do not know of any officer whose promotion would win such universal commendation." This was a shrewd thrust, adroitly calculated to touch Secretary Weeks's well-known sensitivity to criticism by officers within the service. But testimonials by high-ranking officers were only a part of the story.[51]

Entirely unbeknown to Palmer, his devoted wife, Maude, and his dearest friend, George Marshall, also took a hand in the affair. Unlike the colonel himself, Mrs. Palmer was frankly ambitious. As successive make lists appeared, she was repeatedly disappointed. At last she sought out Marshall. As he later described the scene, the tiny little lady sat opposite him, bolt upright and obviously furious, her "Queen Mary" hat fairly shaking on top of her head. Pounding the point of her parasol indignantly upon the floor, she came directly to the point: "Drat it, George Marshall, why hasn't General Pershing promoted John?"[52]

Shortly after Mrs. Palmer's visit, Marshall called the Secretary of War and asked for an interview. Weeks, thinking he had come on official business from the Chief of Staff, had him ushered in ahead of several political figures in the outer office. Offered a chair, Marshall declined. ("You can be more forceful when you look down from above.") "I've come on personal business," he said, and then, before any reply was possible, he reminded the Secretary that a recent speech for which he had been so warmly applauded in the newspapers had been written by Palmer. "He has been recommended for brigadier general," said Marshall, "and merits your selection." Without another word, he turned and walked out. Two weeks later the promotion came through.

Unfortunately for Marshall, General Pershing was highly annoyed. He was of course pleased with the promotion of his subordinate, but the general rather resented being shown up by his junior aide, whose appeal pointedly indicated what he himself should have done long before.[53]

Looking back years later, Marshall was inclined to be somewhat less critical of Pershing. After exercising vast powers himself, he had a far better understanding of the burdens involved. He had promoted well over 1,600 generals, and knew from bitter experience the criticism that follows each make list, as many of those denied advancement seek scapegoats. Pershing had been ruthless in wartime, relieving his own academy roommate from command when the occasion demanded. With the war over, Marshall believed, Pershing simply refused to face up to the unpleasant task of discriminating among meritorious candidates for promotion. He would commend them all and leave the hard choice to the Secretary.

41 Unsuccessful Advocate

Palmer's promotion brought congratulatory messages from friends all over the world. Dozens of those who had served with him—master sergeants as well as major generals, senators, and citizen soldiers—in all, nearly two hundred individuals, expressed their gratification. But promotion also forced him to take a fresh look at his future. After the Training Center matter, it was evident that nothing much in the way of effective support could be expected from his chief; moreover, his tour of duty was rapidly drawing to a close. To be sure, the door to the chief's office was not yet entirely shut. Since Secretary Weeks had indicated his intention of moving General Harbord up from deputy to Chief of Staff, it was not unreasonable to look for cooperation in that quarter. In some respects he enjoyed a closer relationship with Harbord than with Pershing. But when Harbord resigned at the end of 1922 to accept the presidency of Radio Corporation of America, the last shred of hope for reform from within seemed to vanish irretrievably.[1]

That Harbord's departure was at least in part prompted by public apathy toward defense is suggested in a letter Harbord wrote former Secretary Baker soon afterwards. The plight of the army reminded him of an inscription he once saw scribbled on one of the gun galleries at Gibraltar:

God and the soldier all people adore
During the war but not before.
When the war is over and all things righted,
God is neglected and the soldier slighted.[2]

Palmer had received his star, but ironically, it was only too obvious that his influence now seemed less rather than more. If reform from within was no longer feasible, he had better turn back to the plan he had projected before coming to Washington and write the book he had thought about for so long, to lay a broad base of public understanding for the army. But what kind of book?

With the public interested only in peace, how could one ever hope to write a book that would attract attention to the need for an adequate army? Tompkins McIlvaine, Palmer's friend in the Military Training Camps Association, described the situation nicely. The nation's army and its military policy reminded him of old-fashioned well buckets on either end of a rope: when one went up the other went down. During the war, he wrote, "we had an army and no policy; now we have a policy and no army." Palmer's participation in the Washington Conference on the limitation of armaments had shown him that the United States would continue to enjoy prestige and influence as a world power only so long as her vast armies of the recent war could be promptly reassembled. With each passing year this potential was declining. But military might was highly unpopular. For this reason Palmer was convinced that his "army of the people" afforded an ideal solution. It would mobilize great power on short notice yet remain nonaggressive in character.[3]

What was needed, he realized, was a book that would somehow persuade the public to recognize the link between world peace and a potentially powerful deterrent force. As he pondered this problem, he became convinced that the example of Switzerland offered an ideal solution: the Swiss defense rested on an ability to mobilize a major portion of the country's manpower, yet at the same time Switzerland as a nation remained the classic neutral, her red and white flag a symbol of peace in a warring world. Here was the perfect blend of elements for the book.[4]

For more than a dozen years past, the Swiss principle of a citizen army had had a number of advocates, among them such influential leaders as Leonard Wood and Theodore Roosevelt.[5] But Palmer went further and undertook to study Swiss methods in minute detail. In this he was favored by a happy coincidence; one of the few full-time professional officers in the Swiss army, Col. Henri Le Comte, had taken his military training at West Point, graduating in the Class of 1893, only a year behind Palmer. Since then the two had kept up a correspondence, from which Palmer had acquired a genuine respect for Swiss military organization.[6] When the question of training centers was being debated by the staff, he urged General Pershing to invite Colonel Le Comte to the United States to explain how the Swiss trained their citizen-soldiers. Although the Chief of Staff rejected this suggestion, Palmer's intensive study of LeComte's papers persuaded him that the Swiss example might also point the way toward training for effective democracy and the organization of world peace. He must somehow describe the nonmilitaristic defense system of the Swiss in an appealing literary form.[7]

After casting about, Palmer finally decided to employ a fictional dialogue. Several of his friends criticized this approach, but he justified his decision by his success with this device when writing for *McClure's* magazine some twenty years earlier.

> I gave my material in the form of the confessions of a reformed financial pirate and political boss, whom I called "Colonel Timothy Lumpkin." The papers were so successful that on several occasions when Mr. McClure or one of his staff had some rather heavy subject to present, they would call upon me to have Colonel Lumpkin include it in one of his confessions. There seemed to be something about the illusion of personality that carried the thing over better than could be done in the direct form.[8]

Although several other individuals, among them Charles Eliot, former president of Harvard, were then advocating the Swiss system for the United States, it seemed to Palmer that they were less favorably situated than he to make the case.

> Dr. Eliot stressed the Swiss system as a means of defense without militarism, and therefore, as a solution of one of the vexed problems of world peace. Dr. Eliot is right, but it would be difficult for even so accomplished a layman as he to maintain this thesis against the practical militarist who will simply deny that the Swiss system is applicable to American conditions. I have the advantage of Dr. Eliot in this—I am not a layman; I know all of the arguments of the militarist, because at one time or another I have used them all myself. In dealing with this subject I am somewhat in the position of the "Col. Lumpkin" of my McClure papers—I am a reformed militarist.[9]

As a reformed militarist he could write as an insider. All that remained was to give his ideas a fictional garb.

The book was set a decade in the future, in 1933, on the eve of a second great Washington arms conference. After explaining how an Americanized Swiss system had gradually evolved from the Defense Act of 1920, the narrative went on to describe how the President of the United States with an "army of the people" at his back had been able to prevent the outbreak of World War II in 1930. The book concluded with an "impregnable but peaceful" United States finally resolving the knotty Far Eastern question. By helping China become a self-governing, self-defending state instead of an area of barometric low pressure, a perennial breeding ground of cyclonic political storms, the American army of the people had at last assumed its ultimate role as the keystone of world peace.[10]

The book cost no end of agony; the writing had to be done at night after working a full day for the Chief of Staff. The fault was probably Palmer's, since Pershing repeatedly told him he was free to think and write as he pleased. But he could never quite bring himself to tell the general he would rather not represent the army at a committee hearing on the Hill or prepare the text of a speech the chief wanted. When the manuscript was completed, he sent it off to George Haven Putnam, who had produced his earlier book back in 1916.[11]

The publisher's reply was utterly discouraging; the market was glutted with military books having little or no sale, so he declined to take the risk. It was no consolation that he offered to publish at the author's expense.[12] What had motivated Palmer was not profit but the expected opportunity to broadcast his ideas. If the volume were to have no sale and thus no influence, one might assume there was little point in pursuing the matter further. But Palmer was a man with an obsession. Rejection by a publisher was only a tactical defeat; he would turn elsewhere for an opening to carry on his long fight. And, strangely enough, just such an opportunity arose in a most unlikely quarter.

During the summer of 1923, Edward William Bok, the well known publisher of the *Ladies' Home Journal*, offered a $100,000 prize for the most practicable peace plan submitted in an essay contest. Palmer promptly extracted the chapters describing the Americanized Swiss system and rewrote them in essay form. He had no hope of winning the prize, but the potential publicity was too good to miss. As his contribution toward world peace, he wanted to show that there was a practical middle way between militarism and pacificism, one avoiding both the overpreparedness of militarism that provokes aggression and the underpreparedness of pacifism that invites attack.[13]

The $100,000 Bok Peace Prize was eventually awarded to an advocate of strengthening the nation's ties with both the World Court and the League of Nations. This was more or less what Palmer had anticipated. But from the 22,000 essays submitted, his had been one of the twenty selected for inclusion as a chapter in a book, *Ways to Peace*, publicizing the winning plan.[14]

Although the editor of the volume rather than the prize jurors selected the essays for publication, it is not irrelevant to observe that at least three of the seven jurors were Palmer's personal friends. Brand Whitlock, the nation's wartime ambassador to Belgium, was a distant relative. Elihu Root and General Harbord were not only friends but had worked closely with him.[14]

Palmer's contribution was epitomized in its title, "Preparedness for Peace—An American Adaptation, on the Volunteer Principle, of the Swiss Citizen Army." He argued that it was possible for the Swiss to live in peace because they were able to mobilize a defensive army suited to their need. With a total population in 1914 about equal to that of Massachusetts, they were able to call up within four days some 300,000 men fully organized and equipped.

Two principles, Palmer observed, underlay this remarkable demonstration; all male Swiss citizens had to undergo training as privates in the national army, and any private who so desired was eligible to rise step by step to the highest command, providing he was willing to volunteer for further training and could meet the qualifications. Such a system, he believed, could be applied in the United States without resort to compulsion because of the vastly larger population. Where the Swiss had to get one soldier from every 13 persons to mobilize a total of 300,000, in the States only one in every 220 would be needed to produce an army of 500,000. This number, he felt certain, could be obtained entirely from volunteers if adequate training funds were forthcoming.

The extensive publicity accorded *Ways to Peace* encouraged Palmer to think once again of publishing his book.[16] In fact, one of the reviewers of the Bok prize volume, Hamilton Holt, the editor of the magazine *Independent,* suggested that Palmer's essay be expanded into a full-length book. He also encouraged the author to approach the Carnegie Endowment for International Peace as a sponsor.[17] Much encouraged by Holt's support, Palmer once again determined to revise the manuscript. Before doing so, however, he invited a number of his friends to read what he had written.

Among his professional associates who were equipped to evaluate his ideas, opinions varied widely. General Harbord wrote a fine tribute to the book, but this was admittedly a literary puff to aid publication. Neither he nor General Pershing who contributed a word of encouragement after reading several chapters of the manuscript, ever undertook any detailed analysis of its arguments. Some of the officers who did so came up with substantial criticisms. Among these, probably the most penetrating was the critique by Palmer's friend, Col. LeRoy Eltinge, who observed that the author's Americanized Swiss system, like its European model, made little or no provision for the development of weapons. Nor did it consider the related changes in organization and training doctrine made necessary by such developments. Palmer's conception of the ideal military organization may have been far too static; certainly development and supply of weapons generally constituted by far the greatest portion of the defense budget.[18]

Characteristically, the colonel did not attempt to revise his manuscript to take account of these criticisms; he simply filed them. It was typical of him that he almost never allowed himself to become genuinely involved in an argument. This avoided a good deal of personal acrimony, but insofar as he failed to heed constructive suggestions, he impaired the effectiveness of his work. There is every reason to believe this was an entirely unconscious reaction. Part of his charm was his innocence. Far from wilfully outmaneuvering his critics, he filed their objections unanswered because, to his way of thinking, ideas that failed to square with his preconceptions were simply not worth rebutting. Entirely capable of self-delusion, he believed what he wanted to believe and frequently behaved as if ideas to the contrary simply did not exist.

This capacity for evading obstacles by ignoring them was nowhere more clearly demonstrated than in the manuscript for the colonel's new book. Any serious proposal looking to an army of citizen soldiers had to face up to one fundamental issue: Are the troops to be organized under the army clause or the militia clause of the Constitution? In framing the original Wadsworth bill back in 1919, Palmer had rested his case on the former. The opposition raised at the time to this use of the army clause, by partisans of the National Guard, he considered as entirely selfish and unprogressive. Events since then had put the matter in a different light. The officers of the Regular Army had proved to be nowhere near as disinterested and unselfish as he had anticipated, and the political activity of the Guard had proved to be far more constructive. A Guard organization frankly cultivating the strongest kind of ties with home state political establishments had demonstrated effective leverage in Congress.

When choosing between the army clause and the militia clause, it was impossible to ignore political considerations. The Defense Act of 1920 had been a compromise measure, in that it established the National Guard under the militia clause and the Organized Reserve under the army clause. Three years of operation had demonstrated that the Guard, with its political orientation, had flourished while the Organized Reserve languished. Admittedly, if carried too far, a political outlook could utterly corrupt the spirit of an organization, influencing appointments, promotions, and the like, as it had in many Guard units before the war. But without its political side the Guard would almost certainly lose much of the support that nourished it. The problem was to draw the line between essential and excessive political activity. Palmer was not blind to these issues; he had lived through them. Yet his blueprint for an ideal system of defense based upon citizen soldiers blandly ignored the whole question.

During the spring of 1923 Palmer was painfully conscious that time was running out. His tour of duty was soon to end, and his name was once again near the top of the foreign service roster. If he expected to turn out a persuasive book, he must do it while he still had the opportunity. Once he returned to duty with troops, leisure for reflection and writing would be difficult to find. So he pushed himself even harder, working longer hours and immersing himself in the subject until the book became an obsession. At the time of his promotion his old friend Gen. Johnson Hagood had warned him against doing just this. "Quit burning the candle at both ends," he wrote, "and you will have a fine future. If you don't, we shall put up a fine monument."[19]

Telling a man of Palmer's temperament to relax was, of course, an exercise in futility. George Marshall discovered this anew when, concerned for his friend's health, he resolved to help him unwind. Knowing the success of the colonel's wartime sojourn in Maine, he suggested a day-long expedition up the Potomac to Black Pond.

Early one idyllic summer morning they set off in Marshall's Model T Ford like a pair of truant schoolboys. At the swimming hole Marshall discovered that his guest had absent-mindedly forgotten to bring his bathing suit.

Undaunted, they decided to swim in the nude. They were splashing about gaily when the unexpected appearance of a young couple strolling hand in hand along the river bank sent them into hiding among the reeds until the coast was clear. After cooking their lunch over an open fire, they broke out their rods for a serious session of fly casting. This occupied them until nearly dusk, when a farm boy came along and amused them by demonstrating the prowess of his collie in recovering sticks tossed into the river.

All in all it had been a banner day. Only one touch more, Marshall felt, was needed to make it a complete success. So he drove his friend back to his quarters at Fort Myer and proceeded to mix some tall drinks. The setting was perfect for absolute relaxation; he was about to congratulate himself on accomplishing just what he had set out to do, when Palmer suddenly turned serious. "Now George," he began, "about my book on military policy...."[20]

If one thought dominated Palmer's professional life, it was his conviction that the future security of the nation and its democratic institutions hinged upon devising adequate means to utilize citizen soldiers. And after 1920 this meant fulfilling the provisions of the Defense Act. Though in every external manifestation a modest man, the colonel behaved as if the success or failure of the entire army and its long-run future turned on his personal effort. While still hopeful for the future, he could look back on an almost unbroken series of defeats over the past three years. His time had run out, and much of the task remained yet to do.

In one quarter at least he had reason to feel thoroughly content. His beloved daughter Mary was engaged to be married to a splendid young man. Indeed, Mary's seemingly endless social engagements had afforded one of the brighter features of the entire Washington tour. Through her father's friendship with the President's military aide, Col. Clarence O. Sherrill—"Shaggy" Sherrill to his friends—Mary had been invited repeatedly to White House tea dances and receptions. In this setting she was introduced to such visiting notables as Queen Marie of Romania and the King and Queen of Belgium. And as each such royal visitor touched off a round of parties attended by most of the eligible young bachelors in town, life had been delightful indeed. But Mary's interest never strayed very far from the young Infantry officer who had caught her fancy at Governors Island nearly three years earlier. At Easter 1923 her parents formally announced her engagement to Capt. Norman B. Chandler of Medford, Massachusetts.[21]

Mary Palmer and Norman Chandler were married 9 June 1923 at St. John's Episcopal Church, across the park from the White House. The service and the reception that followed went off without a hitch, although only a short time before a fire at the Hotel Willard had imposed a last-minute change of plans in the reception. But with General Pershing's intervention, the Officer's Club at the War College was secured on short notice, and the affair proceeded without interruption.

General Pershing was always gallant, but Polly Palmer was a particular favorite. Through her he revealed something of the affection he felt but could not always express for her father; he treated her much as he would have treated one of his own lost daughters. As one last kindness, he offered his car and driver, to speed the young couple from the wedding reception in the traditional shower of rice. Few of Palmer's army contemporaries owned automobiles; they normally walked or rode the street cars.[22]

If Pershing's kindly interest in Polly Palmer affords something of a clue to that all-but-inscrutable man, much the same may be said of George Marshall. To Mary he was always "Uncle George," and for almost the same reasons that seem to have moved Pershing, he lavished kindnesses upon her. Childless himself, he took a paternal interest in her welfare. Though she had never wanted for attentive beaux, he saw to it that she was escorted by none save thoroughgoing gentlemen. He had held high office in the past and would climb far higher in the future, but it was characteristic of him that this never distorted his self-esteem. On the morning of Mary's wedding, when he saw that the church was badly in need of sweeping, he seized a broom and did the job himself.

General Pershing gave Palmer his pick of all the overseas openings suited to his new rank, and Palmer chose Panama. By no means the least of his reasons for doing so was the wonderful fishing his friends promised him there.[23]

Leaving Washington was not easy. The imprint of his thinking was unmistakable, not only in the Defense Act of 1920 but also in many of the policies inaugurated by Pershing to implement the act. Yet in Palmer's own eyes he had fallen short in two significant respects. He had failed to persuade Congress that universal military training in peacetime was essential, and he had failed to persuade the Regular Army that its first obligation was to create an effective reserve of citizen soldiers.

Despite repeated setbacks, the new brigadier remained convinced that the drift of public opinion would eventually insist upon an army on the lines he proposed. To hasten that day he pinned his hopes on the manuscript of his new book, which he was still polishing when he left Washington.

42 Panama Command

A leisurely voyage from New York to Colon on the army transport *Château-Thierry* afforded Palmer ample occasion to reflect on the recent past. In many ways the previous four years had been a succession of lost opportunities. When he compared the actual state of national defense with his vision of what might have been achieved, he was inclined to feel depressed. On the other hand, he could take pride in the role he had played in some of the most constructive features of the Defense Act. He had also enjoyed an intimate association with one of the foremost figures of his generation. In retrospect he realized how clearly the General of the Armies had understood that effective command calls for the liberation of creative imagination in one's subordinates.

That Palmer, too, had learned this lesson was evident in a farewell letter from his colleague, Col. John W. Gulick. "I learned much from you in these years," Gulick wrote, "and I am grateful to you for the many evidences of confidence and consideration shown me." Then he added, "I . . . will work to the end for a superior who holds a light rein, and I always thought you one of those exceptional men who knew how to drive."[1]

When Palmer took over the 19th Infantry Brigade at Gatun in September 1923, he acquired a considerable satrapy. Every one of his units was dangerously under strength, but as senior officer on the Atlantic side of the Canal Zone, he enjoyed an unusual freedom of action and numerous perquisites. Not least among these was the services of a personal aide. To fill this position he asked the department commander, Maj. Gen. Samuel D. Sturgis, to assign a promising young Infantry officer, Lt. Thomas D. White, whose father, Bishop John Chanler White, was an old family friend back in Illinois. The lieutenant proved to be a tall and extraordinarily handsome young man, impeccably turned out in a stiffly starched uniform that seemed to defy the tropical heat. Well aware of his own rather casual approach to sartorial matters, Palmer groaned, "Good God, Maude, am I expected to live up to that?"[2]

The general and the lieutenant achieved a father and son relationship that was to endure for some thirty years. Only once were they seriously at odds; when the younger man became enamored of flying, the general urged him not to leave the Infantry, but the lieutenant went on to a career that culminated in his appointment as Chief of Staff of the U.S. Air Force.[3]

As an officer who had long sought to improve cooperation among the several arms, Palmer particularly delighted in visiting nearby France Field, where Maj. Follet Bradley was struggling to demonstrate the unproved potential of the Air Service. From time to time the general even participated in long-distance cross-country flights in open-cockpit Martin bombers.

Even garrison duties afforded novel or unorthodox adventures; certainly this was true of the general's supervisory role over the sector military police, a responsibility requiring periodic visits to such well-known soldier haunts as Bill Gray's Tropic Bar and Mamie Kelly's. To the general's concern, both of these establishments were much frequented by the younger officers of his command. Only much later did he learn that the cabaret girls were an endless source of garrison rumor, since a convenient curfew sent all the enlisted men home at eleven o'clock and left a clear field for their superiors.[4]

As old hands at garrison life the Palmers found no difficulty in settling down to the local social routine. The quarters assigned to the brigade commander, of a period and style known locally as "commission," were spacious and comfortable. From broad verandas just above Gatun Locks, one could watch the endless procession of ships from the far corners of the world, a dozen or more a day, as they passed through the canal.

At nearby Fort William P. Davis, the tactical units drilled from seven to eleven each morning, and after a midday siesta, spent the hours from one to three on administrative duties. The working day at brigade headquarters was even shorter, running from seven to one. Afternoons were left free for exercise, so necessary for keeping fit in the tropics.

In the first few weeks after their arrival, the Palmers were fairly overwhelmed with social engagements. A later generation may sometimes scoff at the ritual duty call, but in some respects it was every bit as important as an equal number of hours spent in more obvious military activities. The same was true when the officers of the 14th Infantry Regiment honored their new brigadier and his lady at a reception and dance, an occasion that allowed the new chief to begin assessing the men upon whom he had to rely for the success of his mission. Who among them could hold liquor? Which ones were the born diplomats and which the natural leaders? In a command where military success hinged inescapably upon maintaining the most harmonious relations with the Panamanians—as well as with the Navy—an alert leader would seize upon every possible occasion, military or social, to extend his observations.

So it turned out that the weeks after the Palmers first arrived were very delightful indeed. Not only did they attend all manner of functions staged by the families of the 19th Brigade, but in addition their friends on the Pacific side also extended numerous invitations. The general was amused to observe that when he finally had an official automobile with an orderly to drive it, he found himself stationed in a country with almost no highways. As a consequence, invitations from the Pacific side frequently involved a wild last-minute after-work rush to reach the railroad station. Inevitably social life in the Canal Zone took on many of the characteristics familiar to the American commuting public; it was often hectic, but those who participated in the game developed a high degree of camaraderie.

Of many commuting parties to the Pacific side, one in particular was to remain memorable for years afterward. Not long after their arrival in the Zone, the Palmers received a dinner invitation from Col. and Mrs. E. D. Peek, old friends from their days at Leavenworth. Not until Mrs. Palmer was standing in the receiving line as a guest of honor did she discover that her dress was on backwards. Her jovial husband assured her that current fashions being what they were, nobody would notice. But when the assembled guests sat down to dinner, a brass button from the center of the general's military blouse suddenly popped off and flew across the table. When two more buttons popped loose and went skittering across the floor, everyone present, including the victim, fairly whooped for glee. After a few more such casualties, the general suggested that it was time for the Palmers to fall back and regroup.

In a country with more than 150 inches of rainfall annually, life was bound to be trying at times, but it had its compensations. The commodious quarters made it possible to entertain on a lavish scale, while a highly trained staff from the West Indies took over all the burdens. These servants, Jamaican Negros set apart not only by their race but by their brittle English accents, were a remarkable lot; by their pride in craftsmanship they raised domestic service to a fine art. The general illustrated this when he recalled overhearing an elderly servitor instructing his young understudy in the need for tact if one blundered into a W. C. and found a lady there. "You look down," he admonished, "and you should back out saying, 'Excuse me, SIR!'"[5]

Among the many amenities of the brigadier's quarters was a first-floor guestroom with a private bath. This drew all sorts of unexpected guests, especially from ships coming through the canal. On one occasion it was occupied by the well-known Patten sisters, whose spirited ways led their home in Washington to be known locally as the "Irish Embassy." These three ladies had arrived in Panama only to discover that the one hotel willing to accept their dogs was a rather dubious establishment in the native section of Colon.

Mrs. Palmer invited the whole group, guests, servants, dogs, and all, into her home. It was a wild visit, not least for the general's aide, on whom fell the duty of escorting the ladies. But neither he nor the Palmers ever regretted their exertions; the Misses Patten reciprocated with invitations to their famous "at homes" in Washington for many years afterward.[6]

On another occasion the guest room was briefly occupied by a young naval officer long a friend of the family. Since the Zone was under Prohibition, he had secured a satchel full of liquor in Colon.When one of the servants discovered this, Mrs. Palmer was much distressed. Ever since her days at Fort Grant, where she had seen the wretchedness and misery spread among the troops by alcohol, she had been opposed to drinking on principle. It irritated her that her husband by no means shared her views, but she was determined not to let him get into trouble by even a most peripheral breach of the law. So she hastily summoned one of the young officers and told him to return the visitor's bottled property to his ship. Just as he was about to complete his mission, his foot slipped on the gangplank and one of the precious bottles shattered. Unable to retreat gracefully, he handed over a dripping satchel that smelled suspiciously like a distillery.

In Panama during the 1920s, many of the social traditions of the old army seemed to persist, even though they were changing rapidly at many other posts. The officers and their wives still had to look to themselves for entertainment. In many instances they had shared a common past and could reasonably expect to meet again in the future. In a sense they never lost touch with that past or that future, no matter how distant their current assignments. Many, if not most, of the officers were inveterate letter writers. By this means they supplied one another with a continuous stream of shop talk and unwittingly helped preserve a remarkable degree of unity in a widely dispersed army.

Until George Marshall left Washington to join his regiment, Palmer's old 15th Infantry, still in Tientsin, he kept his friend informed of changes at headquarters. General Pershing had left for Paris to work on his memoirs. He had departed, Marshall confided, without giving thought to his annual report; the general had long since learned that "leave it to George" was an easy solution to many of his problems.[7]

Marshall also noted that Brig. Gen. Hugh Drum was to come in as the new G-3, replacing General Lassiter, who would go to Panama. That Marshall already had the better of the man he would one day outstride for the highest office in the army is suggested by one of his subsequent letters.

> I am riding every day for longer periods than heretofore, so I have
> kept in very good physical trim. This afternoon I'm taking Drum out for
> a ride. He was in a few minutes ago to say that the weather was rather
> threatening, it certainly would be muddy, and he had not ridden for two

months; but I gave him no satisfaction and he is in for about fifteen or twenty miles. However, there will be several ladies in the party, which should divert his thoughts from the seat of his breeches.[8]

Not long after Palmer arrived in Panama, he had to turn his full attention to the upcoming winter maneuvers. Every time the dry season rolled around the navy would send down a fleet, throw an assault force of marines on the beaches, and attempt to seize the canal. Planning for this operation had begun months earlier, but by the time Palmer settled down, barely six weeks remained before the mock invasion.

The newly assigned brigade commander knew nothing of the local terrain and very little about the working relationships of the units that would participate. It was soon painfully evident that many of his troops were not fully trained. A considerable number of his officers were even unfamiliar with the weapons employed by their units.

While still engaged in planning, Palmer learned from his old friend Brig. Gen. Briant H. Wells, the commandant of the Infantry School at Fort Benning, that the authorities had been gravely disappointed in the 1923 maneuver. The 1924 maneuver was to be run under the direct supervision of the Joint Board, and a more exacting standard was to be imposed. So Palmer drove himself to perform two years of staff work, as he appraised it, in a scant six weeks.[9]

Whatever the official statements may claim, there are always at least two different objectives for an army-navy maneuver. Such exercises afford an excellent opportunity for interservice coordination, but maneuvers have another objective—to persuade Congress and the public of the need for further support. As it turned out, this political goal was very nearly frustrated before the 1924 maneuvers had fairly begun.

On the day before the war games were scheduled to begin, a young lieutenant named Odas Moon, an Air Service pilot with an epic sense of humor, was flying down the Atlantic coastline from Costa Rica in a bomber loaded with mail. On emerging from a cloud, he discovered the navy's "enemy," or Black, invasion fleet sheltering in the Chiriqui Lagoon off the Panamanian province of Bocas del Toro—four battleships, three submarines, twenty-one destroyers, and more small escort craft than he could count.

By happy chance he had on board some wonderful ammunition, a case of ripe tomatoes he had purchased in Costa Rica for his wife. Without hesitation he selected his victim and dived to attack, scoring three direct hits on the makeshift aircraft carrier *Langley.*

When word of Lieutenant Moon's exploit spread among the troops in the Canal Zone, for a brief while he was the toast of the command. But on sober second thought his superiors decided they were not so pleased. One of the undeclared purposes of the maneuver was to demonstrate that the army desperately needed a $10 million appropriation to mount sixteen-inch coastal defense batteries. After Lieutenant Moon's tomato bombing, there was no little danger that Congress might get the idea that coastal defense guns were no longer needed. The umpires announced that the maneuvers would be delayed one day, and the Black fleet was permitted to take up a new secret position, just as if the airplane had never been invented.[10]

With or without air power, the army's defense mission was a formidable one. Had all the assigned units been at full strength, some 17,000 men would have been available, but the total came closer to 9,000. Half the coastal defense and two-thirds of the antiaircraft guns had to be left unmanned. As Commanding General of the Atlantic sector, Palmer was fortunate to have even such inadequate reserves as a mule-packed mountain battery and two meager machine gun companies, comprising two officers, thirty-six men, and sixteen guns, to supplement the defenses around France Field. Out on the coast he had to stretch his limited manpower to cover a forty-five-mile front, from the Indio River to Las Minas Bay. His only hope was to keep his limited strength concentrated and as mobile as possible, to counterattack whenever the enemy attempted to develop a beachhead.[11]

When the mock war finally began on 17 January 1924, the Black invaders had little difficulty in throwing ashore twenty-five boatloads of marines under the guns of Fort Randolph at the mouth of the canal. A unit from the 19th Brigade was expected to counterattack immediately, but the regimental commander declined to do so. Although Palmer's brigade staff urged him to issue an unequivocal order for an immediate counterattack, he was reluctant to act. As one who had himself held a command on the front during a major engagement, he knew how difficult it was for higher headquarters to appreciate all the factors of the local situation. Moreover, there was another factor, a matter of personalities.[12]

The regimental commander was a man of unusual vanity who had repeatedly made himself a thorn in the side of his brigade leader. A spellbinding lecturer at Fort Leavenworth, he seemed to regard himself as an authority on tactics and gave every evidence of resisting the views of others, including those of his superior. Determined to be perfectly fair, Palmer decided to go forward personally and confer with his subordinate at the front. In his desire to avoid an open break with the difficult colonel, he allowed himself to be talked out of insisting upon an immediate counterattack. The result was disastrous.[13]

The newspaper headlines in the United States trumpeted "Failure At Panama Canal," but there was every reason for the army authorities to welcome "failure" if they wished to demonstrate that the strength available was utterly inadequate for the defense of the canal. Even so, Palmer, a natural worrier, seemed to feel the whole burden of responsibility for the army's less than impressive showing.[14]

The postmaneuver critique held in the YMCA at Colon only served to confirm the general's poor opinion of his recent performance. In the presence of some 400 officers of the army and navy, he was severely criticized by the official umpires for his failure to move decisively against the initial landings. For those who charge that the WPPA—the West Point Protective Association—always shelters its own, it may be worth noting that the senior umpire was none other than Maj. Gen. John L. Hines, a friend of Palmer's ever since their Academy days, and that the umpire who censured the performance most savagely was none other than his lifelong friend and colleague, Brig. Gen. Stuart Heintzelman.[15]

Some of the junior officers of the 19th Brigade urged Palmer to make a full disclosure of the facts and let the blame fall where they felt it belonged. He would have none of this, pointing out that responsibility was properly his, and he leaned over backwards in his formal report to praise the offending regimental commander for those aspects of his mission successfully executed, tactfully omitting anything else.[16]

To many of Palmer's friends and fellow officers his conduct was but another illustration of the reason he attracted such personal devotion. He simply refused to put his own feelings ahead of the call of duty. This capacity for detachment was perhaps never more clearly demonstrated than in his relations with Maj. Gen. William Lassiter. In Lassiter's previous assignment as assistant Chief of Staff for Operations, he had played a leading role in scuttling the Training Center program when the problem came before G-3 in 1922. Nevertheless, when Palmer learned that the commander of the Canal Department was about to retire, he wrote to General Pershing urging the appointment of Lassiter, even if doing so meant ignoring the strict order of seniority. Along with a great many others in the army, he regarded Lassiter as an ideal officer, able, alert, and aristocratic in bearing, the very model of a modern major general.[17]

In a sense the appealing qualities of Palmer's makeup can best be seen in contrast: where Lassiter was respected, Palmer was loved; where Lassiter was aloof, Palmer was kindly. A trivial episode occurring sometime after Lassiter became department commander neatly illustrates this difference. The army was about to take over some quarters from the Canal Commission, and Lassiter, accompanied by Palmer and his brigade quartermaster, went out to inspect the buildings. "Palmer," asked the general sharply, "are the underpinnings free of termites?" Unable to answer, the brigadier passed the question along to his quartermaster, but Lassiter would have none of this. "My questions were directed to you and not your subordinate; I observe that you have not prepared for this inspection. When you have done so, I shall return. Good day, sir." He strode off without another word.[18]

Lassiter, of course, was in the right, but it was somewhat unusual to admonish a fellow general officer so tartly before a subordinate. Nonetheless,

Palmer refused to take offense even though he himself would have behaved quite differently had their roles been reversed.

The kindliness that was a dominant feature of Palmer's personality also involved an element of simplicity, of unaffectedness, that went far to win the loyalty of those around him. On one occasion some of his junior officers discovered him in full uniform stretched out on his stomach upon a low wharf near the Gatun Locks; he explained without the least embarrassment that he had been experimenting to see if he could catch one of those lazy tropical fish in his hand. Such a man, protected as he was by the armor of innocence, was proof against the slings and arrows of all critics. Against all, that is, save one, for his own implacable conscience set impossible standards.[19]

Palmer's conscience was but another face of his simple honesty in his dealings with individuals. Something of this trait was evident in his reply to a fellow veteran of the 15th Infantry who had urged him to use his influence "aggressively" by writing to Pershing, Marshall, Wadsworth, and others in behalf of their mutual friend Col. Alfred W. Bjornstad for appointment as chief of Infantry in preference to another officer also highly esteemed by Palmer. It would have been perfectly easy to ignore the letter or to answer it in some noncommittal fashion, but Palmer deliberated at length over the two rival candidates and then wrote the petitioner that he had concluded not to support either. Bjornstad would make an excellent chief of Infantry; the other aspirant was likewise "peculiarly fitted" for the assignment. "I would be delighted," he declared, "if either one of them should get the appointment, but as an endorsement of either, if it had any influence, would work against the other, I believe the best solution for me is not to make any recommendations at all." Neither candidate received the nod from General Pershing. Palmer, characteristically, had ended up by nullifying the constructive influence he would otherwise have had.[20]

The occasional baleful effects of Palmer's inordinate sensitivity to individual feelings may be illustrated by an episode within his own command. In October 1924 the Adjutant General in Washington ordered the department commander to investigate a report of "unsatisfactory conditions" in one of the regiments of the 19th Brigade. Normally such an inquiry would be entrusted to the inspector general of the command, but for some reason General Lassiter handed the task to the brigade commander. Investigating one's immediate subordinate is awkward under any circumstances; it was especially so in this situation, for the officer complained of was the very one who had caused so much difficulty during the winter maneuvers.[21]

Reluctantly Palmer set out to conduct the inquest. He examined some thirty officers whose testimony indicated that the "unexpected, unusual and unreasonable attitude" of the regimental commander had made their lives "unnecessarily hard and exacting in small matters not affecting the real welfare of the service." The offending officer conceded that he had been unable to achieve a "happy command." He suggested that he be allowed to retire, since he already had over thirty years of service. Palmer eagerly accepted this solution and expected that matter to end there.

The regimental commander's friends and relatives, unaware of all the circumstances, were unwilling to let him retire. Moreover, they apparently enjoyed some influence in Washington. Early in 1925 the Adjutant General returned the whole case with an endorsement demanding a statement of the facts on which the brigade commander based his recommendation, noting a discrepancy between the views stated in the report of the investigation and the rather generous evaluation in the brigade commander's most recent efficiency report on the officer in question.[22]

The curt query from Washington threw Palmer into an agony of doubt and self-accusation. Oblivious of the interests at work behind the scenes in behalf of the unfortunate officer, he saw only the possibility of some neglect or shortcoming of his own. And turning these thoughts over and over, he worried himself sick.

Those close to the general began to sense that something was wrong. This was particularly true of his aide. Lieutenant White had left to join the Air Service, but his successor, Lt. Herbert M. Jones, had become equally attached to the general and his family. His devotion was to continue for more than thirty years. Even after he himself became Adjutant General of the Army, he continued to wait on his old chief with touching loyalty. But never were his services more welcome than during Palmer's time of troubles in Panama.

To help the general shake off his depression, Jones lured him as often as possible into vigorous outdoor exercise. He organized swimming parties in the saltwater pool at the railroad hotel in Colon, and then saw to it that there was a round of relaxing tall drinks afterwards—even though this sometimes led to difficulties with the general's lady. More frequently he arranged an afternoon on the links. Since the general loved golf, this proved highly beneficial. On one occasion, when Palmer sliced a drive, his ball soared over the canal and dropped into the open hold of a passing steamer. It was, he afterward claimed, the only time one of his drives went clear around the world! His greatest delight, however, came on the day his ball struck a rail in the roadbed along the canal and bounced back on the green to give him a hole in one.

What really caused the general's depression and why it persisted is impossible to determine. He had always found life in the tropics trying, but this was a minor aggravation. His self-assessed "failure" in the winter maneuvers caused him much agony, but scarcely enough to undermine his whole self-confidence. Another factor may have been his inability to find a publisher for the book on which he had labored so long. One after another had kept the manuscript interminably, only to reject it in the end. His agent in New York observed that Boni and Liveright had kept it so long he told them the author expected to be asked to pay storage charges. But the cruelest blow came when Scribner's, Palmer's last hope among the major publishers, found the book's fictional treatment entirely unsuitable.[23]

Mrs. Palmer's alarm over her husband's condition led her to write to General Lassiter, who immediately crossed the isthmus to see for himself. One look was enough to persuade him that he had a sick man on his hands, and not long afterwards the Palmers were on a northbound transport headed for home on sickleave. In Washington Merritte Ireland, Palmer's old friend from the Paris headquarters, now the Surgeon General, prescribed a fishing trip for a month or two in the wilderness. In a matter of days Mrs. Palmer was off to visit relatives in Kansas while the general headed for the Canadian wilds.[24]

43 Wilderness Interlude

The site selected for the general's cure was Algonquin Park, a wilderness preserve embracing nearly 3,000 square miles of primeval forest in the heart of Ontario. His friends thought it would be an ideal setting; the only trouble was, he had to get there first, and on the way everything seemed to go wrong. All the little details and decisions he anticipated in choosing a guide and renting equipment seemed to overwhelm him. And the more he recognized these symptoms, the more distressed he became. The crowning disaster, or so it seemed at the moment, was the news that only bass could be found locally; to a fly-rod fisherman and trout buff, this was simply appalling.[1]

Worry, as Washington Irving once said, is the interest we pay on things that seldom happen. The bass did rise to a fly after all, and a helpful park superintendent secured the services of a splendid guide who resolved most of the general's other problems. Already the cure was beginning to take effect.

The French Canadian woodsman, Joe DuBrieul, combined an impressive knowledge of woodlore with an intense personal loyalty. They had been gone scarcely a day when the former infantryman was humiliated by a bad set of blisters from his still-new boots. DuBrieul promptly removed his own boots, soft and pliable from years of wear, and insisted that the general wear them, while he tramped back to the railhead in his stocking feet.

Although DuBrieul spoke English, his visitor rather enjoyed practicing French with him. It was some time, however, before Palmer began to catch the nuances that separated French from Canadian French. For several days he had been discussing the merits of the fishing in LeMob Creek, as Joe called it, when he discovered the stream on his map clearly marked L'Aimable.

With practice the general gradually became quite competent in Canadian French, enough so to enjoy a little foray when he and Joe encountered a wedding party at a tiny railroad hotel. A flashing-eyed young lady seated next to him declared that she spoke two languages. And to this the general replied, "Mais non, mademoiselle; vous parlez trois; l'anglais, la française, et la langue des yeux."

After a day or two spent purchasing supplies and perfecting equipment, the party finally set off to establish a permanent camp in the McDougall Lake area. DuBrieul found the ideal location, an unused loggers' camp on Bridal Creek, an easy canoe journey above Booth's Landing on the Opeongo River. It consisted of a large log cabin in a clearing on a bend in the creek; a fringe of white birch trees shaded the structure itself, and heavily laden blueberry bushes reached back to the virgin forest behind. Although the sun was already setting when they arrived, they pitched camp in short order and dined luxuriously on a meal of "beans à la can and milk à la Klim." Joe constructed a reflector oven, while the general set up a writing desk. With the meticulous care of a trained military cartographer, he prepared a sketch map of the site for his wife. Each feature was labeled for some member of the family: Polly's Bay, Maude's Bay, while the camp itself was proudly named after his newborn grandson.

DuBrieul was initially skeptical of fly fishing. The general, for his part, was determined to live up to the standards of his redoubtable master, Zibeon Southard. The impressive range of his very first cast evoked mild expressions of approval from the guide, but then when a two-and-one-half-pound bass leaped to the hook, he won an instant convert.

Occasionally this summer idyll was broken by visitors. For the most part army friends, they would stop by for a day or two of fishing and then leave. Maj. Hugh Walthall was an old friend from 15th Infantry days in Tientsin. Col. Warren T. Hannum came and brought his eight-year-old son. And Col. Ernest D. Peek—called Pike's Peek by his friends because of his height—came and brought his wife.

The charm of the wilderness, however, was most fully savored in solitude. Only then, Palmer declared, could one truly enjoy the "air of sovereignty." Happily, the two campers were blessed with a great deal of this kind of sovereignty. For one twelve-day stretch they saw no other human save a passing fire ranger. Since firearms were banned from the preserve, wildlife was everywhere. Deer, bear, muskrat, porcupine, and beaver were commonplace, and at night as they lay in their sleeping bags they could hear the "melancholy and bloodcurdling" cry of timber wolves prowling near them.

In such a setting even domestic chores were a pleasure. With an eye to probable shock effect the general described for his wife the process of Luxing his socks and shirt in the dishpan, followed by an effortless rinsing while they dragged behind a canoe. There had been some initial casualties. On his first try he had left his tobacco in his shirt pocket, so his khakis had emerged several shades darker than regulation. But his greatest discovery was that fishing worms relished coffee grounds, and that worms so fed lasted longer and kept fresher. This, he believed, was information of value to anglers everywhere.

Why shouldn't he write a series of articles on fishing? There was sure to be a good market for this sort of thing among tired businessmen, and the Canadian National Railways might even subsidize the articles. While the idea was still fresh in his mind, he began to outline some tales, thinly masking the realities. A central character, of course, was DuBrieul, now become Henri LeBoeuf, an expert woodsman who knew intuitively where to find deer runs and muskrat holes. Algonquin Park became Hiawatha Park, Egan Estate on the Canadian National Railway became Regan Station, and so on.[2]

By the middle of August the general was himself again, but with a difference. When his friends in Panama wrote of planning for the coming winter maneuvers, he showed no interest. He explained to his wife: "More and more I feel that health, happiness, success and prosperity are jeopardized by continuing on active service." Knowing that she would resist the suggestion of retirement, he went on to make a case for himself. "I feel," he wrote, "that I am well enough to lead a life of fullest intellectual activity in my present or other congenial surroundings, but I believe some of my other cells have been strained beyond the elastic limit and are not likely to go back."

In his mind's eye the general pictured the good life he would live in the future. He would busy himself with writing, and there would be a woodland retreat. Ideally it should stand within a day's journey of Boston so he could visit his beloved daughter and her growing family in Cambridge. The cabin would be accessible only by canoe. A hundred yards from the doorstep would be a trout stream, water from which could be led into the cabin by gravity to provide an inexpensive bathroom.[3]

When the time arrived to break camp, the general found it harder to face the departure than he had anticipated. This was the way he wanted to live—or thought he did. The exhaustion of heavy portages offset by the exhilaration of shooting rapids; lazy, sunny days spent trolling in a silent, tree-ringed pond; these were the touches he enjoyed. Standing alone in the empty cabin, he cast one last look about him. Filled with emotion, he felt an overwhelming desire to give thanks for his safe return to health.

Although an Episcopalian, he had never been particularly concerned with formal religious practices. But basic to his creed was a reverence for God in nature. As he often said, "A glorious day is a gift from the Lord." On this particular day, however, he felt a need to go further, a need to express himself in some more emphatic manner. Inspired, perhaps, by the nightly example of his guide, the general knelt down on the cabin floor and "thanked the good Lord for health and healing through close communion with His beautiful handiwork."[4]

Out in the wilderness it had been an easy matter to decide on retirement, but on the long train journey back to Cambridge the whole question seemed infinitely difficult. His ambitious wife was determined to see him a major general and would never leave him in peace if he suggested otherwise. His retirement pay, which was tax free, was ample enough for a simple rural existence, but would his wife accept such Spartan fare? A modest inheritance, characteristically invested in "good conservative bonds," would help, and so would the sums he might expect to earn from writing; yet when he added all these possible sources of income together, they still fell short. Unless, that is, he were to retire with the higher pay of a major general.[5]

Whatever hopes of promotion Palmer may have maintained were vastly whetted by an unexpected article in the *Army and Navy Journal* of 3 October 1925. Under a new policy, the editors reported, the War Department was giving serious attention to retirement dates when considering promotions. "Officers will not be advanced simply to give them an opportunity to retire for age in a higher grade, but when an officer with a notable career is approaching the age retirement limit, he is very apt to be jumped over younger officers as a recognition of exceptionally distinguished service."[6] Although this did not exactly fit his case, since he was not yet actually at the compulsory retirement age, the practice of recognizing distinguished service might very well apply.

In passing through Washington on his way to Canada, Palmer had discussed the subject of promotion with the Adjutant General, Robert C. "Corky" Davis, who proved highly discouraging. A promotion to major general, Davis assured him, did not appear to be justified by his record. After mulling over this opinion for several weeks, the general finally composed a long letter of rebuttal. He wrote, he said, not to urge his promotion, since "matters of expediency and policy" must determine that, but to protest that such a promotion upon retirement was justified by his service record. Now that the War Department was going to reward distinguished service, his own lifelong dedication to the cause of Army reform was apparently to be overlooked. To make matters worse, General Pershing's retirement had left him with no assurance that anyone in the department would take steps to remedy the situation. Unless he was willing to stand by and see the work of his lifetime ignored, the only alternative was the distasteful one of asking his friends to help set the record straight for him.[7]

Men such as Senator Wadsworth and Brig. Gen. Milton Reckord, who had become president of the National Guard Association, needed no urging to certify the distinguished character of the general's career. Even though these and other friends rallied to his support, the effort proved unsuccessful. The whole episode left Palmer embittered. It wasn't the failure to win a terminal promotion that hurt; some of his friends who had been temporary brigadiers and major generals during the war had been retired in their regular rank as colonels or even lieutenant colonels. What really rankled was the way the Adjutant General had written off his career as one not warranting promotion even if an opening were available.[8]

In the estimation of Palmer's friends, his services in connection with the Defense Act of 1920 merited recognition and reward quite apart from all his other accomplishments. Unfortunately, the act of 1920 did not seem very important just then. Indeed, the Coolidge Administration, under the slogan "Peace through reason," seemed bent on scuttling that piece of legislation. The nine Regular Army divisions of the act had long since been cut to three, and the Administration was reducing these to a single full-strength unit and filling up the vacancies with paper units from the Organized Reserve.

According to the *Army and Navy Journal,* officials of the Budget Bureau were informing the regulars that if they wished to retain their current strength, they would have to cooperate in advocating reductions for the National Guard. Guard leaders were being told the same thing with regard to the regulars, playing one group off against the other.[9]

Sometimes the Administration's actions seemed to border on the malicious; bureau chiefs in Washington reportedly fired employees for being absent when they were on duty with the National Guard.[10] Other restrictions, allegedly in the name of economy, made it virtually impossible to carry out the terms of the act. One such ruling denied commutation of rations to noncommissioned officers on duty as instructors with Guard and reserve units. Though the commutation of $1.20 a day was scarcely opulent living, a return to the garrison ration of 30 cents meant that most of the Regular Army NCO instructors would have to be withdrawn from their assignments unless they could be financed locally.[11]

So the Defense Act of 1920 was not a victory but a goal, something that would have to be "won" over and over again. To the man who regarded himself as the chief architect of the act, this realization raised an appalling dilemma. Should he remain on duty to fight for the fulfillment of the act, or would it be better to retire and carry on his campaign as a private citizen? There were advantages and disadvantages to either course.

When the general returned to Washington to keep his appointment with the medical board at Walter Reed Hospital, he was still undecided. Physically and emotionally he wanted to retire, but a nagging sense of duty and his wife's desires induced him to leave the matter to his medical friends. When they found him fit only for limited duty, the issue was settled; he had no desire to stay on unless qualified for full field service. The date of his retirement was officially set for January 1926, when his terminal leave expired.[12]

After thirty-seven years with the army, the thought of leaving once and for all came with something of a shock. As the day of separation approached, the pangs grew more pronounced. These symptoms were mitigated, however, by a flood of heartwarming letters. "In honor and preferment," wrote one such well-wisher, "the Army has little left to bestow upon you. In... the genuine admiration and respect of your fellows, there is nothing left to offer you. You have it in full measure."[13] A number of contemporaries bespoke their irritation with the War Department authorities who had denied him a terminal promotion. The effect of this was unfortunate; it helped the general build up a sense of injustice that scarcely would have persisted had only Mrs. Palmer encouraged the idea.

Of the many letters the general received in connection with his departure from the army, one in particular gave him a wistful satisfaction. It was from his friend George Marshall, out in North China where he was serving with the 15th Infantry, still posted in Tientsin. Because it tells so much of the man who wrote it, as well as of his relationship with his elder colleague, the letter is worth quoting at length.

Tientsin, China
Dec. 31, 1925

My dear Old John:

Your letter of two days ago brought me the first news of your retirement, and while I think it decidedly the wise thing to do, it makes me very sad to feel that you and I are not to serve together again. I never expect to enjoy another relationship like ours—official and personal; but while the chance of a renewal of the former is gone, I propose, with your consent, to look forward to much more of the latter in the future.

I am assuming that all you need to put you back in good shape is a philosophic calm, much fishing and proper contemplation of the duties and responsibilities of a grandfather. What I am particularly interested to know, is where Mrs. Palmer and you propose to locate. I hope in Washington.

Time out here has flown of late, with the sounds of battle in our ears for more than a week and the final confusion incident to the capture of Tientsin by the Peoples Army on Xmas day. Early that morning on the great plain seven miles south of the ex-German Concession, I witnessed a tragic sight. Galloping across country with three mounted men, I encountered hundreds of women and children fleeing from villages further south which had been pillaged and ravaged during the night by the retreating soldiery of Li Ching Lin.

The usual refugee who had congested the roads leading into the foreign lines during the past three weeks, is a sad spectacle, but the donkies [*sic*], carts and household belongings are usually with him. But these little groups had nothing. The thermometer was only a few degrees above zero, the wind keen and piercing and the ground hard with frost. Overhead the sky was a brilliant blue and the sun shone; but to those pathetic little groups it must have been a black, calamitous day. Their heavy clothing was gone, shoes often missing, babies crying. None would look at me or listen to my attempts at reassurance. They resembled animals hunted to exhaustion and paralyzed by fear. And this was Xmas morning in the year of our Lord 1925!

The long camel trains of artillery and supplies, which accompanied the troops from Outer Mongolia, and the troops of cavalry on shaggy Mongolian ponies, made very picturesque sights. We had many difficult contacts with the victors, but came through without precipitating a crisis. I had command of the regiment during this period, as Naylor was sick, so it gave me an interesting problem until two days ago. I did about 25 miles a day on my pony, making early morning and late evening surveys of the daily situations. It was good fun and instructive.

. . .

Today is my 45th birthday. I am no longer of the "Young Turk" party. Isn't that sad after the bombast and assurance of our Leavenworth days of army reformation. With every wish for your contentment, health and happiness in the New Year and my love to Mrs. Palmer and you.

> Affectionately,
> Marshall[14]

Marshall's letter helped the general to realize that retirement did not mean that he would leave the army. His friends, his associations, and his all-consuming interests would remain for the rest of his days. Lassiter, when writing a generous letter of farewell from Panama, had suggested the obvious course by urging him to condense his wide-ranging experiences into studies of value to the service.[15] Palmer was still a young man of fifty-six; thirty interesting and busy years still lay before him.

44

A Reformer in Retirement

Impending retirement raised the problem of where to settle, arousing in the general a long-dormant but persistent idyll that he would one day have a piece of land he could call his own. This primordial urge commonly afflicts rootless army officers in a peculiarly intense form, but Palmer could see his obsession with urbane detachment. Much earlier he had expounded his views on the subject to his old friend, Henry Jervey, newly established on his retirement farm in California.

> I was most delighted to have...your report on the progress of *our* farm. I say our farm advisedly, because you no doubt remember that on entering the agricultural business I was to have an incorporeal interest. It was understood that this interest was not to affect the title or the profits or the expense account. I think I explained to you that ever since I read the Georgics and the Bucolics as a boy I had made up my mind that before I died I was going to have a vine and fig-tree of my own, where I could practice agriculture in a purely Virgilian sense. For many years I had hoped that I might hold this farm in a more literal, mundane sense, but as I became convinced that this was impractical it dawned on me that I might practice poetic agriculture just as well on your farm as on mine.[1]

Unfortunately, the reality of retirement turned out to be somewhat less idyllic. The easiest thing to do was to take a small apartment in Washington. This pleased Mrs. Palmer because she could move into their ready-made circle of friends almost as if they had never gone off to Panama. Moreover, in the capital they would be near enough to visit Mary and the grandsons in Cambridge during the hot summers.

Whatever they decided upon, Palmer would never be content to vegetate. For some time he toyed with the idea of writing a definitive biography of his grandfather and namesake, John McAuley Palmer. A major general in the Civil War, a governor of Illinois, and a presidential candidate would make an intriguing topic. What he took up instead, he had to take up—there was no escaping that inner fire, that driving concern for army reform.[2]

The first task was to rewrite the book that had already cost him so many hours of labor. That he could even bear to face the work involved is eloquent testimony both to his dedication and to his optimism. He was as certain as a man can be that the kind of army he sought was ideally suited to a democracy. As such, it deserved whatever sacrifice might be required to get the message across. He began to convert his fictional narrative, "The Organization of Peace," into a polemical essay pleading the alternatives of statesmanship or war.[3] In short order the general had settled into a routine. His mornings he devoted almost exclusively to writing. Afternoons went to exercise, usually golf at the Soldiers Home, and social calls.

The social circle to which the Palmers returned in 1926 was in many respects a survival from another age. The upheavals of the war had brought new faces and new ways to Washington, but the Palmers' set, by contrast, was largely made up of older officers and their wives. Many of the men had won high rank and distinction during the war. It was something more than age and rank that set them apart, however. While they mingled freely with the newer arrivals at various army social events, the perceptive observer could detect some fundamental differences separating them.

The contrast might best be characterized by a single word—formality. In their dealings with one another, the old army set typically observed an ordered pattern of ritual. This was not a stiff, uncomfortable, or imposed formality, but it was nonetheless conscious. Even within their immediate circle of contemporaries, the general and his friends almost invariably addressed one another by their last names.

Although the Palmers' set attended a great many social functions, especially at the Army-Navy Club, the associations they enjoyed most were within their own circle. They had learned to rely upon themselves for entertainment during long years spent on isolated army posts. There they had learned the importance of maintaining personal dignity and a proper self-respect amidst the slackness, the hardships, and sometimes even the dangers of the surrounding community. The kind of entertainment they seemed to prefer for this purpose was the formal dinner party. The wives lavished endless attention on these affairs. What did it matter that few could provide silver of their own for a dinner party of twenty-four? They could help one another in Washington just as they had in Mindanao. It was almost as if they were staging a rear guard action, albeit unconsciously, against the mounting pace that increasingly threatened their ways of gracious living. On one occasion, at least, this emphasis on lavish formality backfired dangerously. A congressman was so bedazzled by the display of borrowed finery, he went away convinced that all army officers were privately wealthy, and when the next pay bill came up he voted against it, much to the chagrin of his hostess.

There was, perhaps, no better symbol for the vanishing age than the formal dinner dances that the old army set put on several times a year throughout the 1920s. Usually these affairs were staged at Rauscher's, the restaurant of a Connecticut Avenue caterer much favored by the military and diplomatic circles of the day. Invariably there would be a receiving line, and often as not it would include General Pershing. Almost certain to be found were Surgeon General and Mrs. Merritte Ireland, the Stanley Embicks, the John Hineses, the Arthur Cowans, the W. D. Conners, the Fox Conners, and a dozen other couples who had served together and lived together for over thirty years.[4]

At the dinner dances Mrs. Palmer was in her element. She delighted in the cultivation of elegance; indeed, she excelled at it. Young officers who served under her husband recalled years later how "Aunt Maude" had drilled into them the kinship between the simple word "courtesy" and formal "court" manners. Those who experienced her tutelage would never afterward need dread the demands of protocol; she helped men from all sorts of social backgrounds to confidence as senior officers and military diplomats.[5]

As a man utterly without side or pretense, General Palmer was ordinarily oblivious to the problems of protocol; he simply acted naturally. And what came naturally to him was an old-fashioned courtliness. He was the kind of man who would quite un-self-consciously rise and offer his seat on a crowded streetcar to a young lady not yet turned twelve. His age, his grey head, his rank, and most certainly his uniform he took lightly. In fact, to his wife's perpetual distress, he never seemed to give half enough thought to the minor details of appearance. When it came time to turn out in full dress uniform, he would stand with the patience of a display-window mannequin, looking on with amused tolerance as his beloved wife fluttered about adjusting his accoutrements.

While it is true that the general was normally inclined to accept his wife's efforts at improving him with good humor, there were times when she pushed him too far. This was especially so when she threatened to encroach unduly upon the private sanctum where he carried on his all-important writing. After putting up with her "artistic" arrangement of the furniture for several months, he finally insisted upon a utilitarian floor plan. With evident relish he wrote to his young friend and former aide Tom White in China, giving a full account of this domestic uprising. As if reporting a significant political episode, he quoted himself at length, ending with: "'Maudame,' last year I worked in the corner of a bedroom. From now on I'm going to sleep in the corner of a workroom." Then he added, with mock bravado, "The only way is to treat 'em rough once in a while, Tom."[6]

The general's momentary irritation was a reaction typical of many another officer on stepping down from the responsibilities and prerogatives of high command to find himself confined to close quarters with his wife. When she disapproved of even so modest a dissipation as a single highball before dinner, the general sometimes let his fancy roam. On one such occasion he wrote to Tom White telling him how he wished he had his services as a chaperone for one last glorious escapade.

> I want to do that just once before I cash in—not just a hurried spree but an artistic, aesthetic one duly tapered on, duly maintained, and then duly tapered off—with no distracting engagements, obligations, objections or inhibitions, all under the personal direction of a sympathetic Thomas who would be my aide-de-camp again for a few days.[7]

This was a delightful example of Palmer's ability to live in his imagination, a trait that applied as much to his professional as to his private occasions. For example, the book on which he was spending so much effort reflected in full measure his frequent tendency to see what he wanted to see.

The revised manuscript, now formally entitled *Statesmanship or War*, he again sent off to Scribner's, where it was rejected as emphatically as before. This reply was based on a realistic appraisal of the market. "People are . . . accustomed to find all they wish about such matters in newspapers and periodicals." But any reflections the author may have had on the wisdom of the evaluation were promptly lost in his joy on learning that Doubleday, Page & Co. had decided to publish the manuscript.[8]

Doubleday's action was directly attributable to the personal interest of Arthur W. Page, who had taken over the editorial tasks relinquished by his father, Walter Hines Page, when the latter became Wilson's ambassador in London. The younger Page was genuinely interested in the problems of national defense. He had written magazine articles on the subject and a book on the AEF. But it was as a veteran of the historic 7th Regiment of the N.Y. National Guard that he had good reason to be attracted by Palmer's manuscript with its plea for greater reliance on an enlarged and improved National Guard.

The next problem was to see the book effectively promoted. From painful experience Palmer understood that getting published was by no means the same thing as getting read. Even a book winning highly favorable reviews would almost certainly have abysmal sales unless launched with attention-catching fanfare. His first step was to persuade his friend Sen. James Wadsworth to write an introduction. As chairman of the Senate Committee on Military Affairs, Wadsworth would speak with authority; his approval would insure a certain amount of interest. But the general was after bigger game; he hoped to corral Charles Evans Hughes, just then near his peak in popular esteem. Long in the public eye as governor of New York, as a justice of the Supreme Court, as a presidential candidate and as Secretary of State in two administrations, this remarkable man even looked the part of a great statesman.

When President Coolidge appointed Hughes to the Permanent Court of International Justice at the Hague in September 1926, it occurred to Palmer that here was just the kind of figure he was looking for. Here was a man of international stature who was accessible to him personally. He could have appealed to Hughes directly, recalling their association in 1921 when he had served as military adviser to the Washington disarmament conference, but he preferred to employ an indirect approach. He drafted a long letter to his publisher, pointing out the constructive use he had made of Hughes's thought in the manuscript of his book. The general knew perfectly well that Arthur Page was personally acquainted with Judge Hughes and would pass along those complimentary remarks, which would have been discounted by the judge had they been said directly to him. Page picked up the cue without further prompting and arranged an interview.[9]

Although the general's pretext for calling on the elder statesman was to clarify one or two of his interpretations, he actually hoped to persuade Judge Hughes to accept the central thesis of his book. With all the skill of a highly trained staff officer, he proceeded to lay out a campaign. His first step was to employ their exchange of correspondence arranging time and place for the interview to help prepare his attack.

> I hope [he wrote] in my book to present a new point of view that will emphasize the importance of the Washington Conference, not only as to results but as to methods. My study of the more or less confused and abortive efforts at Geneva convinces me that the League authorities have an important lesson to learn from you.[10]

Just what he thought that lesson was, Palmer explained at length in the course of the interview, which turned out to be most cordial. Then he drove the point home again in his letter of thanks. "What you told me," he declared, "only confirmed my thesis that statesmen must make the formula if the world is to escape the burden of war-provocative armaments."[11]

The general's tactic was simplicity itself: by careful iteration he would establish an identity between Hughes' role as a statesman and his own interpretation of that role; he would praise Hughes's imposition of a naval formula at the Washington conference; and then he would insert his own views, expressed in *Statesmanship or War*, as a logical concomitant applying to the land forces. Since it was unreasonable to suppose he could persuade Hughes to accept his thesis in its entirety after a single encounter, he cast about for excuses to continue their association. For example, not long afterward, when he read in his *New York Times* that Adm. Bradley Fiske had denounced the Washington conference in a speech before the National Republican Club, he seized the occasion to get off a long letter to Hughes rebutting the views of this "orthodox militarist."

From their earlier conversations Palmer knew that the judge was extremely sensitive to criticism of his naval policy; a rejoinder to Admiral Fiske, especially if it came from a professional military man, would be most welcome to one who could not with dignity reply directly to such attacks. In his defense of the Washington conference, however, the general adroitly injected a statement of his own thesis.

> The admiral's reasoning assumes there is going to be a war; he then proposes a machinery for waging that war, so effective that it would engender the war if no other cause for it existed. For example, in his reference to the defense of the Philippines, he fails to see that a military and naval establishment based on America and strong enough to assure the defense of the Philippines against Japan, would be strong enough to *attack* Japan. It is natural and proper for the military and naval commanders to want to take the offensive as the best means of defense, but when he proposes an armament through which his nation could assume the political offensive, he is a little beyond his depth. This is a question for the statesman and not the warrior. We must have warriors, but it isn't necessary to create wars for the sole purpose of using them.[12]

As Palmer explained it, the object of the statesman should be to impose upon the land forces neither disarmament at one extreme nor war-provocative armament at the other. The proper political formula, he contended, was one that insisted upon a defensive or peace-conserving armament, which is to say, a small cadre of regulars backed by a large reserve of citizen soldiers on the pattern established by the Swiss. Unfortunately, as the general complained to Arthur Page, the professional military officers advising the League of Nations "have been wearing the same blinders that my associates... have generally worn," thinking in terms of quantities instead of types. "The only army they have in mind is an army dominated in peace and led in war by professional soldiers. The only national mobilization they can conceive is one in which the national manpower is absorbed under a controlling professional caste."[13]

After nearly six months of exchanging letters and visits, the general's campaign finally achieved success. Initially Hughes had declined, on grounds of delicacy, to write a promotional blurb for the dust jacket of *Statesmanship or War*, since the book praised both his policy and himself.[14] But as the criticisms of his naval formula grew more acrimonious, he finally went to the other extreme and volunteered to do what Palmer had hoped for all along: he offered to make use of the book in an important address he was scheduled to present before the American Association of International Law. True to his word, he gave the volume and its author a most flattering boost. The book pointed the way, Hughes declared, toward a solution of the disarmament question, and the general he praised as "one of our foremost military experts, with technical knowledge, absolute candor, and a vision which has not been blurred by professional prejudice."[15]

Hughes's speech, coming as it did two days after the publication of *Statesmanship or War*, provided the kind of send-off publishers dream of. And once his interest had been aroused, the statesman went out of his way to see that the book received the widest possible publicity. He even took the trouble to write to his friends on the *New York Times* to secure a serious review of the volume, sending along appropriate extracts from his own address to indicate the points he wished to see emphasized.[16]

The response of the press was most gratifying. The *New York Times* led the way with page-one news coverage of Hughes' appearance, the full text of his address, and an editorial, all capitalizing on the need for an end to war-provoking armaments. Soon afterward came a flood of book reviews in newspapers throughout the country, nearly all of them highly favorable. A close observer might have noticed that a suprising number of the more flattering accounts had been written by articulate guardsmen for their local newspapers, but the general was far too elated to study the reviews objectively. Nor was he alone in this. His publishers, too, seemed quite ready to equate glowing reviews with the prospect of heavy book sales. While this optimistic mood prevailed, the general conducted final negotiations for a second book.[17]

Several months before the appearance of *Statesmanship or War*, Arthur Page had approached former Secretary of War Newton D. Baker with a scheme to publish the Baker-Pershing correspondence of the wartime years. Baker was receptive and suggested Palmer as a suitable editor. Vastly pleased at the prospect, the general promptly arranged for a conference. Since Baker was coming to Washington early in January 1927 in connection with the famous Chicago Drainage Canal case he was then pushing through the federal courts, they were able to discuss the project at length. Palmer had previously read through the whole file of correspondence, so he had a clear idea of the book he hoped to produce. An appropriate theme, he suggested, might involve "an exposition of the relations that should subsist between the civil and the military authorities in a democratic state." Baker accepted this view and promised to help however he could.[18]

While the negotiations with Baker were afoot, word came that Arthur Page was resigning from the publishing firm to accept a vice presidency with the American Telephone and Telegraph Company. Palmer clearly understood that his tie with the firm rested almost exclusively on Page's personal interest, so he hastily sent off a letter of felicitation and regret. Its tone was lighthearted and bantering; among other things he proposed a joint trout-fishing expedition to Quebec, "a Province where you can practice temperance without encouraging bootlegging." But along with this levity, he voiced his genuine concern. "It is quite natural that a youngster my age just beginning a new profession should not relish losing his publisher so soon after capturing him." Arthur Page put his fears at rest and turned him over to Beecher Stowe, grandson of the famous Harriet and one of the firm's editors, to negotiate a contract for the Baker-Pershing correspondence.[19]

As it turned out, the contract offered by Doubleday, Doran, the newly reorganized company, was by far the most generous the general ever signed. It provided an advance of $5,000 to be paid in monthly installments; the publishers were obviously convinced that the volume was going to be a sellout.[20] Unfortunately, the parties involved had not reckoned fully on the difficulty of securing General Pershing's cooperation.

When first approached concerning the project, Pershing had agreed to think it over. Weeks passed with no word from him. In some exasperation the publisher asked Palmer to try a little personal prodding: "As vigorous as the general is in action," Page lamented, "in writing he is the soul of delay and vacillation." When pressed, Pershing confessed that he feared the proposed volume of correspondence would compete with the memoirs on which he himself was working. On being assured that the Baker-Pershing letters would not appear before his memoirs came out, he finally agreed to let Palmer begin the job of editing. But after allowing work on the project to proceed for about six weeks, he abruptly changed his mind. He now indicated that he planned to use the letters so extensively in his own book that separate publication was out of the question.[21]

If Palmer was annoyed, he tactfully gave no sign of it. In fact, he wrote to Baker, "In losing me as the editor, you obtain a much better one." This was characteristically self-effacing but quite untrue. General Pershing's memoirs made only limited use of his wartime correspondence with Secretary Baker, certainly not enough to justify cancelling the projected volume.[22]

Although Palmer was inclined to be philosophical, the publishers were acutely distressed. Not only had they lost a popular and historically significant book, but they were left with a sense of obligation to their would-be editor, who had invested so much effort in the undertaking. To make amends, Doubleday, Doran agreed to transfer the existing contract to another book, insisting only on cutting the advance to $2,500. Even this reduced amount was exceedingly generous, for the book the general proposed to write could scarcely be expected to sell as well as the Baker-Pershing correspondence.[23]

The new book, as Palmer outlined it initially, was to be another volume of propaganda for a revised national military policy. It would contrast the administrations of Lincoln and Wilson as wartime presidents. Where the former acquired an effective system of command only after two years of bloody fighting, the latter did so in a matter of months. The difference, of course, the general attributed to the institutional reforms set in train by Secretary Root. In 1917, he argued, Baker had been able to find a Pershing because the system was ready to produce a Pershing. And Pershing could cope with the staggering tasks of planning for an army of millions because that same system had produced a trained staff to cope with the necessary details. The book, tentatively entitled *Two War Presidents*, would seek to show "the danger that democracies run when they lack defensive institutions appropriate to the democratic state."[24]

Delighted at the opportunity to continue his work, the general wrote to Beecher Stowe of his high hopes for the future. Without the advance, he confessed, he would have been forced to accept some sort of administrative job in Washington, but now he could go on with his literary career. "With fair luck on these first two books," he wrote, "I ought to be able to carry my own operating costs in the future."[25]

The general's optimism was scarcely justified. Despite the favorable tone in most of the early reviews, *Statesmanship or War* simply did not sell. Even a vigorous promotional campaign failed to bring results. When the author somewhat naively suggested sending out presentation copies to 298 prominent individuals, the publishers had balked, observing that this was more than the traffic would bear. Nonetheless, they did agree to distribute 175 copies, far more than the usual allotment for publicity purposes. In addition, when the National Guard convention passed a resolution endorsing the book, Doubleday, Doran tried sending out a thousand direct mail advertisements to a selected list of Guard officers. Not one of the mailings resulted in a direct sale. Palmer was inclined to place the blame on poorly written advertising copy. To test his contention he offered to pay the cost of mailings to another thousand Guard officers, whose names he himself would hand pick from the rosters. But the publishers were unwilling to waste further effort on the project. Soon afterward they withdrew the edition from their catalogue.[26]

Although *Statesmanship or War* was a total failure financially, its effectiveness as propaganda is somewhat more difficult to appraise. Col. George Marshall, again back in Washington to teach at the Army War College, called the volume "the ablest presentation ever put forth" by any army officer. He accepted the author's major thesis wholeheartedly, both the proposed department of national defense and the suggested plan for an army built on a citizen soldier. These remarks might readily be discounted as coming from a close friend and well-wisher, but the fact remains that nearly twenty years later Marshall, as Chief of Staff, actually pursued a similar line of policy.[27]

Another backer was former Secretary of War Henry L. Stimson. Because Stimson would one day again preside over the department as a wartime secretary, his approval, too, was not without significance. Elihu Root also read the book, but as an elder statesman he knew that reach is usually wider than grasp. "The great problem," he explained, is "to educate the people of the country to an active acceptance of the principle to be followed." With far more realism than Palmer ever mustered, he suggested that at best the book would prove useful in promoting this education for the long-run future.[28]

To get immediate results, Palmer turned his attention toward Europe. From his friend of academy days, Colonel Henri Le Comte of the Swiss army, he learned that the French Socialists were advocating the adoption of a militia army for France. To exploit the occasion, the general persuaded the publishers to authorize a royalty-free translation in French by Colonel Le Comte. Nothing came of this venture, for by the time the arrangements were completed, the Socialists had decided not to press the issue. Le Comte did, however, write long reviews of the book for the *Revue Militaire Suisse* and the *Brugger Tagblatt*, which provoked no little attention in both French and German circles.[29]

In Germany even the professional officer caste was receptive. Confined as they were by the Treaty of Versailles to an army of 100,000 men, Reichswehr officers eagerly explored the militia arrangements of other nations as a possible means of circumventing the imposed ceiling. At least two German military journals reviewed *Statesmanship or War*, but since Palmer was unable to read the language, he was scarcely in a position to pursue the subject effectively; indeed, there is no evidence that he was even aware of the German reviews. If he was to have any significant influence, it was far more likely to be found at home.

To begin with, there was always the possibility that the enduring prestige of General Pershing could be used to advantage. Although Palmer was a modest man, he knew the value of personal recognition. This he revealed when reporting to George Marshall on an extended conversation with their old leader.

The idea occurred to me that perhaps after our next war, the big chief—in all probability George Marshall, if war comes in time—will look back over the evolution of our military system and give me some posthumous credit for my part in putting the modern Army of the United States on the map.

Then, abruptly turning from the future to the present, he continued.

If this were merely an air castle of posthumous recognition I would not record it. Posthumous recognition will take care of itself. But as the air castle grew on me it suddenly dawned on me that a little "antehumous" recognition could do no harm and would be very helpful to me—not as a retired army officer but as a publicist and man of letters, who thinks he still sees possibilities for useful public service.[30]

If Marshall were to encourage Pershing to give public recognition to the author's contributions to military policy, it would "make a good deal of practical difference," Palmer declared.

From most of his professional colleagues Palmer expected little but opposition, or worse yet, apathy. There were exceptions of course. Sherman Miles wrote him an enthusiastic letter, and as one raised in the Uptonian "damn-the-militia" school of the old army, Miles's willingness to experiment with an army of citizen soldiers was not without importance. But such reactions were few and far between. When Nannie Barndollar, the librarian at the Army War College, reported that several copies of the book always had long waiting lists, Palmer wrote to Tom White, "the book seems to be read by a considerable public which is too intelligent and discriminating to pay $2.50 for it." And to this he added, "I am reminded of the ancient maxim that talk is cheap but it takes money to buy whiskey."[31]

If most of the author's fellow officers ignored his book, it might equally be said that the author largely ignored those who gave him a careful reading. He usually acknowledged their letters, but he never really faced up to the criticisms they raised. A former colleague, Maj. T. W. Hammond, suggested that there was a considerable difference between asking militia forces to defend their homes, as in Switzerland, and requiring such citizen soldiers to defend overseas territories of the United States, westward "to Jolo," as he put it. But the general was so bemused by the example of the AEF in World War I that he gave no thought to other situations, such as the Mexican border in 1916, where militia units on extended duty had developed rather serious problems of morale. Instead of dealing with the question on its merits, he resorted to assertion.

> The policy laid down in that book is not my policy. It is the traditional policy of the American people.... I have simply stated the peoples' policy for them.... You can help delay its adoption if it does not convince you. But you cannot prevent the ultimate adoption of its essential principles—that is just as certain as sunrise... It is the bandwagon of the future. I hope you will decide to ride it. You are just the young man to become its driver someday.[32]

Statesmanship or War appears to have had its greatest appeal on Capitol Hill. Congressman J. J. McSwain of South Carolina, a leading member of the House Military Affairs Committee, offered to buy a copy for every member of the committee who promised to read it. Another representative told the author that Congress was "completely bluffed by 'big navy' propaganda" and that he was relying upon the book to reinforce more moderate views. Palmer accepted such statements at face value. That the congressmen might be less concerned with theories of national defense than in further cuts in military spending seems not to have crossed his mind.[33]

Understandably enough, since the book favored substantial reductions in naval expenditures, it provoked a hostile reaction from Capt. Dudley W. Knox, the well-known naval historian who reviewed it in the *Proceedings* of the United States Naval Institute. Scrupulously avoiding a discussion of the citizen army scheme, Knox concentrated on the author's total inadequacy as an historian when dealing with naval matters. Palmer's outline of naval strategy he found "too amateurish to warrant serious consideration." And in the large section devoted to seapower, he found "scarcely a page ... but what is open to grave criticism of fact or logic."[34]

The truth of the matter was that Palmer wrote as a propagandist rather than as an historian. His Swiss friend, Colonel Le Comte, saw this clearly when he suggested that it was just as well the general had never come to Switzerland to study the militia system at first hand. A closer view would almost certainly have curbed his enthusiasm.[35]

Palmer was not a trained historian. He was reminded of this fact by his old friend Col. Arthur L. Conger, who wrote to him from his post as military attaché in Berlin not long after *Statesmanship or War* appeared. Conger admired Palmer's literary flair but questioned the historical validity of his arguments. He also recalled that nineteen years earlier the commandant at Leavenworth had excused Palmer from the required course in methods of historical research to free him to join the group engaged in drafting a single list promotion bill. "It turned out to be precisely you," Conger lamented, "who in the future was to need a knowledge of such work, its methods, and principles. ... Thus do we tamper with fate when we set aside rules."[36]

Although Palmer was not a professional historian, he was soon to acquire a considerable reputation in that capacity as a result of his research on the military policies of Lincoln and Wilson. As originally planned, his new book was to show how the difficulties besetting these war presidents stemmed in large measure from their failure to heed the advice of George Washington concerning the role of citizen soldiers. And because he was dissatisfied with what he found in the editions of Washington's writings edited by Sparks and Ford,[37] the general set out to explore the original manuscripts in the Library of Congress.

The fading pages unfolded an exciting tale. In 1783, when the revolutionary army was about to be disbanded, Congress had called upon Washington for his "sentiments on a peace establishment." In conventional military fashion, that commander had invited opinions from his principal subordinates. To Palmer's delight, their replies were all there, filling several large volumes of manuscript. Some, of course, were perfunctory, but those of Generals Knox, Lincoln, Pickering and Steuben proved most interesting, especially the last.

Although an experienced professional, reared in the hard school of Frederick the Great, Steuben advocated a major reliance upon citizen soldiers. Equally important, in his report to Congress, Washington had borrowed most heavily from Steuben's paper. Moreover, Washington had specifically referred Congress to the Swiss system as a model for democracies. Palmer was elated; here was historical authority of the highest kind for the very ideas he himself had so long advocated.[38]

Not long afterward Thomas B. Wells, the editor of *Harpers*, learned of Palmer's finds from Arthur Page and asked for an article for the magazine. Pleased at the prospect of an immediate cash return, the general set to work. But the task turned out to be more difficult than he had anticipated; "The editor and I have different views on what ought to be stressed," he told Tom White. "However, I'm bowing to him as after all it's his magazine."[39] Although he consumed nearly a month in writing and revising, his investment was to prove highly rewarding. The finished article, "America's Debt to a German Soldier: Baron Von Steuben and What He Taught Us," brought only $400, but it did serve to help convince the general's lady that historical research could pay. Far more realistic than her husband in money matters, she had been continually urging him to give up trying to reform the army and turn his hand to potboilers.[40]

Time and again the general seemed to be on the verge of giving in. When Tom White wrote from China suggesting a book on the Manchurian situation, he replied that hereafter he wanted to do only profitable writing that required no "ponderous" research. "Of course a wise book on the Far East that only the elect would read might be the most important thing to write, but the question is: which is the most apt to buy Aunt Maude a Dodge Sedan while she is still young and pretty?" But his conscience invariably drew him back to army reform.[41]

The cash payment for the Steuben article, besides bringing Palmer peace on the home front, also put his ideas before a wider audience. After it appeared he received more invitations than ever before to lecture to Guard groups, and his faithful friend Colonel Le Comte translated the article for the *Revue Militaire Suisse*.[42] More significantly, the article helped win him admission to a circle of professional scholars.

Recognition from the scholars came in a variety of ways, among them an official appointment as Library of Congress consultant in military history and institutions. This position brought him into frequent association with Herbert Putnam, the colorful librarian with over thirty years of service, who found the general such a genial companion he promptly invited him to become a regular member of his famous Round Table luncheon group. Palmer's charm, his remarkable gifts as a raconteur, and his evident enthusiasms when telling of his adventures in historical research, promptly made him a great favorite. Some months afterward, when the George Washington Bicentennial Commission assembled a committee to advise on the publication of a definitive edition of the first president's papers, the general was included among the eight experts so honored.[43]

Appreciation by literary men greatly strengthened Palmer's self-confidence. Neither of his earlier books had sold, but they had been military propaganda; now he began to think of himself as an historian. When he learned that the Lincoln Centennial Association planned to complete the life of Lincoln, which had been left unfinished on the death of Albert J. Beveridge, he promptly offered his services as a successor. Although his proposal was declined[44], it was not for want of any artistic or literary skill on his part; the very people who rejected his military philosophy freely conceded that he was an unusually gifted stylist.

Even in his letters Palmer had a happy knack for compressing a great deal of meaning into a single sentence. Those who knew him well could detect something of his self-deprecating modesty and humor in his prose. But he did not write easily. His most casual personal letters were often polished compositions, because he worked at them, usually writing a first draft in pencil, revising and editing extensively. "I can't think on a typewriter," he told his friends; "all my ideas come out at the point of a pencil."[45]

Palmer was quite ready to admit that he knew very little indeed about the techniques of research. But what he lacked in method he tried to make up with enthusiasm, imagination, and no end of diligence. Having discovered the source of the true faith, as he saw it, in the words of George Washington, he wanted to learn just how it was that Maj. Gen. Emory Upton came to deviate from that faith when writing about the military policy of the United States. When Upton's publisher, Appleton, could produce no leads, he turned to James R. Garfield, son of the former President, who located a number of letters from Upton and Sherman in his father's papers.[46] Or again, in tracking down the sources of Lincoln's knowledge of Clausewitz, he carried on an illuminating correspondence with two British officers, Col. Frederick N. Maude, the translator of *Vom Krieg*, and Gen. Colin R. Ballard, who had recently published his volume on *The Military Genius of Abraham Lincoln*.[47] For details on the development of military policy in Wilson's administration, Palmer took the trouble to visit the once-powerful leader of the House Military Affairs Committee, James Hay, at his retirement home in Madison, Virginia.[48]

The general's difficulty, however, was not in finding evidence but in using it. His real problem was the attitude with which he approached his task. Was he a historian? Was he a propagandist for army reform? Or was he out to make money?

Although vaguely aware of the often conflicting character of his objectives, the general never really attempted to sort them out or assign them any kind of relative priority. He delighted in his role of historian: the recognition it brought was highly gratifying. But professional prestige did not pay the rent. Unfortunately, potboiling, however profitable, was entirely incompatible with his interests as a propagandist. The serious business of the nation's military policy required closely reasoned prose ill-suited to a popular audience. Yet without a large readership, what hope was there of influencing Congress? On this point he had no illusions whatever. "My impression is that publicity calculated to attract the informed military reader...will repel the general reader. If you get the attention of the general reader you will compel the attention of the military reader. But it will not work the other way around."[49]

In retrospect the general's primary attachment to the role of reformer is obvious; at the time it was not. He allowed himself to be drawn now this way, now that, as pedant, as potboiler, and as publicist. Each shift lessened his chance of achieving genuine success in even one of his several roles.

Because he could never quite make up his mind when he finished the manuscript in July 1929, his new book emerged as something of a compromise. Entitled, in its final form. *Washington, Lincoln, Wilson: Three War Statesmen*, the volume was a restatement of the thesis of *Statesmanship or War*. But this time he let history carry the burden of his argument. He rested his case on the recommendations he had found in Washington papers. As he himself put it, he could now "pass the buck to George."[50]

That not all of his readers would accept the validity of George's counsel for the twentieth century seems never to have troubled the author. Some of our friends may "regard me as a nut," he confided to Henri Le Comte, but "it will jolt them a little to find I am simply following Washington and Steuben." Fully convinced that he had turned out a "sensational" book containing numerous "reversals of accepted history" he awaited the verdict of his readers.[51] The publishers, too, were confident of success. Beecher Stowe pronounced it "that rare combination," a work of scholarship that would also be a sensation. He was especially pleased with the title; Washington, Lincoln, and Wilson seemed to be the ideal formula for success, appealing to three distinct types of buyers.[52]

Copies of the manuscript distributed to outside readers met with enthusiastic response. George Marshall, vacationing in the Big Horn Mountains of Wyoming, had severely criticized the individual chapters sent to him previously, but now, taking the book as a whole, he was well pleased. "With all conceit and no modesty," he wrote Palmer, "I am an expert on military brains—and you most decidedly have 'em."[53]

Several weeks later Marshall sent along a more impressive testimonial. Mary Roberts Rinehart, the novelist, then near the crest of her fame, happened to visit the ranch where Marshall was staying. Without mentioning the author's name, he seated his guest before a blazing fire in his cabin and began to read from Palmer's manuscript. "When I finished, she jumped to her feet and exclaimed, 'That is magnificent; that is one of the most interesting things I've ever heard. I'm thrilled with it.'" This was not just the reaction of a well-known woman novelist, Marshall pointed out. Mary Roberts Rinehart was also a skilled publicist, who had played an important role during World War I in lining up public opinion behind the Wilson administration's Selective Service Act. A favorable review from her would provide truly significant publicity. Gratefully Palmer wrote back, paraphrasing Shakespeare, "I have been advertised by a loving friend."[54]

When Ida Tarbell reacted no less enthusiastically than Mary Roberts Rinehart, the publishers were thoroughly convinced that this time they had a winner. Fully persuaded of the book's intrinsic merit, they determined to launch an elaborate advertising campaign.[55]

As a first promotional step, Stowe urged the author to solicit a statement from General Pershing for use as a jacket blurb. The general said he would be delighted but was too busy at the moment. Palmer, who knew his man well, called on the general in person and repeated his request. General Pershing surrendered, but instead of a blurb for the jacket he insisted on writing the preface, saying he would rather be in the book than on it. Then he instructed his former staff officer to rough out a draft for his signature.

Since Pershing had made it a general rule never to allow his name to be exploited, this exception was highly flattering. Palmer could detect the influence of his friend George Marshall behind this cooperative attitude and expressed his thanks accordingly. But the bird was not yet in hand. While the author was composing a suitable introduction, Pershing went to Wyoming to attend the funeral of his father-in-law, Senator Warren. So Doubleday, Doran hastily decided to set back the date of publication to await his return.[56]

Delaying publication appeared to offer several advantages. When shown Ida Tarbell's enthusiastic appraisal, the editor of the *New York Herald Tribune Magazine*, Marie Mattingly Meloney, invited Palmer to do a special article for the Washington's birthday issue in February 1930. The article, which eventually appeared as a page-one feature under the title "Washington's Lost Legacy," afforded the author a fine opportunity to present his thesis in concise form. And because the *Tribune Magazine* was nationally syndicated, this opened up a potential readership of well over a million. No less important, Stowe believed, was the opportunity to reach the ear of Marie Meloney; from her work with Belgian relief the editor was on intimate terms with President Hoover.[57]

Stowe saw his task as twofold. He hoped to sell the book to the public at large as a history with sensational new interpretations; to that special segment of the reading public interested in national defense, he hoped to sell the book as a first step toward practical or limited disarmament. If he could get President Hoover to see that the book offered a formula to reduce the cost of defense, there was no telling how far sales might soar. The idea was by no means preposterous; the newspapers all during the summer of 1929 were full of Mr. Hoover's proposals to curtail defense costs, so the time was ripe.[58]

By sheer chance the firm of Doubleday, Doran, happened to have a direct line into the White House. One of President Hoover's administrative assistants was French Strother, who for many years had been an editor of the Doubleday magazine, *World's Work*. Strother agreed to study the manuscript. If it warranted such action, he promised to place a resumé of Palmer's ideas before the President. When this news reached the general while he was vacationing in New England, he scarcely dared believe his good fortune. He had written *Three War Statesmen* as a literary effort, looking at most to an influential audience of opinion makers. Now, suddenly, here was an opportunity to have his ideas applied directly at the very heart of the political process.[59]

The more the general reflected, however, the more disturbed he became. It was too good to be true. He began to brood on all the things that might go wrong. Unable to talk out the problem with those around him, he wrote a long letter pouring out his fears to Stowe.

> Unless the matter is carefully handled, this approach to the White House might lead to embarrassment. The President, has little time for reading, and, under the usual routine, would be disposed to refer a military book to the Secretary of War. If my book were referred to Secretary Good, he would not be able, as Stimson would, to pass on its merits himself. He would probably refer it to my dear friend and classmate, the Chief of Staff, [C. P. Summerall] and we would then be in the unpleasant position of having our Washington plan of battle in the hands of the Uptonian enemy before the date set for our attack. We would thus lose the most important of all military assets—surprise— and the author's friends in the War Department would be able, at least, to damn him with faint praise adroitly placed.[60]

The general suggested that it might be better to back off; however, the game had gone too far to turn back. Strother not only agreed to read *Three War Statesmen* but asked for a copy of *Statesmanship or War* as well. The general could only sit back and hope that Strother would grasp his thesis and get it across to Hoover.[61]

The general's message was simply this: A Washingtonian army provides more defense at less cost than an Uptonian army. Which is to say, a minimal Regular Army backed by a well-ordered citizen force will cost less and be better prepared for emergencies than an expansible Regular Army that must be hastily fleshed out with untrained conscripts in time of emergency. Under the terms of the Defense Act of 1920, it was fully within the President's power to adopt a Washingtonian policy by executive action alone. The nation had been moving toward such an army when the catastrophic manpower cuts imposed by Congress had induced Pershing to abandon the attempt. For sheer economy, if for no other reason, Palmer believed, his policy ought to appeal to President Hoover.

Strother made a conscientious effort to grasp Palmer's essential points before submitting them to the President. But as the general never seemed to realize, there was one serious weakness in his case. Although he boldly asserted that a Washingtonian army would be cheaper than an Uptonian one, nowhere had he offered specific figures.

President Hoover immediately questioned the premises. He was inclined to doubt that a citizen force would prove inexpensive to train. On this the general received a direct personal report from Page. Since Page was to be an official adviser to the delegation from the United States at the forthcoming London Naval Conference, he had been to Washington to confer with the president, and they had discussed the military budget at some length.[62]

Even though Page was inclined to agree with the President on the economics of Palmer's formula, he was an enthusiastic proponent of the general's overall plan for army reform. Whether or not all of the promised savings materialized, he believed the plan should be adopted and offered his help in selling the general's book and in publicizing his ideas.

To discuss this promotional campaign, Page invited the general to drive up to the Page summer home in Chocorua, New Hampshire. The expedition, in August 1929, was a great success. Page was full of ideas for getting *Three War Statesmen* before the public. It was a fascinating book, but for the "99-1/2 per cent of the population" who have never thought on military subjects, it would have to be introduced "with authority and controversy." As a start, he suggested an elaborate strategy for getting the book reviewed. Viscount Haldane should be enlisted to do a review article on "preparedness in a democracy" for a British journal. Senator Wadsworth would certainly be willing to do the same at home. Gen. Albert Cox might be persuaded to do a review for the *Raleigh News and Observer*, General O'Ryan for the *New York World*, and Nicholas Roosevelt for the *New York Times*. Page ticked off a long list of distinguished friends and acquaintances who could serve the cause.[63]

If Palmer was distressed over his failure to convert the President, he was immensely pleased over the outcome of his visit to Chocorua. As the general explained to his wife, Page and Grenville Clark "understand my gospel better than anybody." After an enjoyable dinner with the elder Mrs. Page, widow of the ambassador, Arthur Page had led his visitor on a tour of the estate, where three generations of the family enjoyed their vacations. The general was entranced. The separate cottages for the older and younger families, and

Page's long-range plans for improving the property for his children and grandchildren, appealed to him greatly. This was precisely the kind of country place he wished for his own family.[64]

The immediate task was to line up outstanding public figures to whom to present the volume. Through the good offices of Charles Merz, who was a Doubleday author, Stowe secured a promise from Walter Lippmann that he would read and comment on the galley proofs.[65] Elihu Root was readily approached through Grenville Clark, who was one of his law partners. Newton D. Baker seemed to pose no problem, though Baker's known respect for the author did not yield quite the endorsement hoped for.

While expressing admiration for the way the author fought for his beliefs, Baker disclaimed any special competence to judge the issues. This was simply a tactful evasion. In his letter to Stowe he spelled out his objections at some length. War, Baker declared, had become an "industrial art"; the application of science to this art now demands a high degree of professionalism for any scheme of preparedness to be effective. Whether an Uptonian or a Washingtonian organization would give the better solution might be moot, but to quote Washington as an authority was no better than to quote Pericles, perhaps worse, since the emotion engendered might lead people to overlook the great changes in the situation since the Revolution.[66]

Baker did make one highly useful contribution. To Stowe's request for the name of a reviewer who could be counted upon to stir up a violent controversy, Baker suggested General March, saying, "It's sure to make him furious." It did. The acidulous general fired back a vigorous protest against Palmer's views, while admitting that he had rather enjoyed reading the book. This was grist for the publisher's advertising mill, though there were some misgivings in the editorial department. Controversy might be good for sales, but it could also scare away a prized author.[67]

Doubleday had already agreed to publish General March's memoirs, which were certain to prove highly polemical; now Stowe asked Palmer whether this would kill the firm's chances of publishing Pershing. Palmer's response gave scant comfort. If March wrote a hostile book, then Pershing, "a good hater like most strong men," would undoubtedly take offense. But whether or not this resentment would extend to the publisher, he declined to predict.[68]

With authoritative endorsement and a heated controversy both seemingly assured, even the tedious chore of preparing the index failed to dampen Palmer's cheer. On submitting it to the publishers, he playfully declared it the best part of the book, recalling Mark Twain's dictum that every author should write the index of his own book—even if it is the only part he writes.[69]

So certain was the general that *Washington, Lincoln, Wilson: Three War Statesmen* would be a best seller, he even turned down a job offer that reached him shortly before publication day. His friend of long standing, Louis Babcock, wrote as a trustee of the historical society in Buffalo, New York, offering him a position as secretary to the organization. It was a position of dignity, no little local importance, a generous salary, and a comfortable pension. But Palmer rejected all this out of hand. He would be reluctant, he confessed, to leave the vicinity of the Library of Congress. And as to the question of income, he fully expected the sale of his book to "put me on a dividend-paying basis."[70]

Palmer had no way of knowing, of course, that the break in the stock market over the previous few months would soon develop into a catastrophic depression. Certainly nothing in his training had equipped him to grasp the wider implications of the onrushing economic collapse; otherwise he might have gratefully accepted the Buffalo position as a snug place to weather out the lean years ahead.

If the general misjudged the sale of his book, the officials at Doubleday, Doran & Company were no less far from the mark. So impressed were they with the distinguished names and flattering endorsements already secured, they decided to more than double the initial printing.[71] Palmer's lead article in the *Herald Tribune Magazine*, syndicated around the country under a half-page tinted portrait of George Washington, was an almost ideal form of publicity.[72] And with excellent timing, Congressman J. J. McSwain of the House Military Affairs Committee filled three whole columns of the *Congressional Record* praising the author's "monumental contribution to the literature of national defense." There was, he declared, "not a dull page in it." While predicting that the book would soon find its place as a classic on war, McSwain did concede that some misguided critics would undoubtedly contrive ways to put a false construction on the work and try to "nail General Palmer upon the cross." These remarks the author forwarded to the publishers, wryly commenting that they would undoubtedly be quite willing to see him nailed for the helpful controversy. But if the author looked for a journalistic battle of words to boom sales, he was sadly mistaken.[73]

From the very outset sales were disappointing. Neither General Pershing's introductory endorsement nor the free publicity on Capital Hill managed to generate any momentum. What was worse, even the reviewers were for the most part lukewarm.

On receiving his copy in Switzerland, the ever-faithful Colonel Le Comte wrote to enquire whether he should review the book as history or propaganda. It was history, the general assured him, but it should prove effective as propaganda. Ignoring this evasion, Le Comte wrote back assuring his friend that he himself was convinced—but questioned whether those in authority in the United States would be too. "I dare not hope too much from a people who invented the Kellogg Pact and utopias of that kind."[74]

If the general had expected to have his work treated as history, he was soon disabused. As one reviewer put it, the book was a "well-argued tract." Among the hostile critics, several could be dismissed as pacifists. No matter what the author advocated, they would be against it, preferring "no militia" to a "well-regulated militia." This kind of wishful thinking was painful to Palmer, but not nearly so painful as the barbs of the critics who accused him of being a blatant militarist.[75]

The unkindest cut came from the *American Historical Review*. There the journalist, T. H. Thomas, not only dismissed the book as a tract for universal military service but also belabored the author for "the inverted professional spirit" he supposedly turned upon "the long-suffering Regular Army."[76] The first charge was patently false. Although Palmer had repeatedly advocated various peacetime schemes for universal military *training*, he was opposed in principle to universal military *service*, a significant distinction the reviewer ignored. Where universal training would require peacetime preparation for membership in a citizen army to be called up by Congress in time of emergency, universal service involved a selective draft of citizens as fillers for the Regular Army, where they would serve under professional officers in peace or war after the fashion of conscripts. The difference, as Palmer saw it, was the difference between a Washingtonian policy and an Uptonian one. To attribute to the author a hostility to the Regular Army, as such, merely because he advocated a large role for the citizen forces was to misunderstand the tenor of his whole career.

Long before the book appeared, George Marshall had urged his friend to tone down his arguments. Flagrant advocacy, he warned, would only afford "the cast iron regular" too conspicuous a target. Moreover, in Palmer's imaginative constructions of what might have happened if Washington's advice had been followed, he laid himself open to the reviewers' most scathing criticisms.[77]

Criticism, however scathing, meant that the book was engaging readers; infinitely harder to take was the almost complete silence with which the army greeted the work.[78] There were exceptions, but these were the author's friends. George Marshall pronounced the book his best yet, a serious reflection on military policy by a retired officer, in a remarkable contrast to some of the brigadiers on active duty who busied themselves "overseeing the cutting of the grass and whitewashing the corral fence."[79] Col. T. B. Mott wrote appreciatively from his attaché post in Paris, as did old Gen. Eben Swift, Palmer's wartime colleague in Italy. Gen. Hunter Liggett, who had commanded the First Army, AEF, wrote a mutual friend praising the book, adding, "I always knew Palmer was one of the ablest officers we have ever had in the service."[80] But the audience the author most needed to reach, the rising young officers of middle rank, did not respond at all.

The apathy of the army should not have surprised Palmer. Some months before, he had presented the substance of his book to the Army War College class. The discernible impact was nil: nobody disagreed with what he had to say. With only one exception, no one even bothered to debate his thesis.[81]

The one officer who had reacted to the War College lecture was Maj. T. W. Hammond, the young man who had honored Palmer with a constructive criticism of *Statesmanship or War*. Once again his comments went to the heart of the issue. Had Palmer and his associates made a mistake back in 1920, he asked, when they encouraged Congress to establish an Organized Reserve in addition to the National Guard? If the whole citizen reserve had been concentrated in the National Guard, congressional retrenchment would have forced the Regulars to accept the training of the guardsmen as a primary mission. By making Citizen Military Training Camps and college ROTC units into feeders for the Guard, the quality of the Guard might be substantially improved. But the general made no real effort to follow up Hammond's ideas. Apparently he was oblivious to the need for young disciples, especially Regulars who could work for his doctrine from within.[82]

Hammond had also suggested that if other men on the retired list continued to devote as much effort to professional questions, Congress would be led to a better appreciation of the money spent on retirement pay. He might well have added that more sustained thought about military doctrine by officers still on active duty should also impress Congress. Certainly the woeful lack of systematic and critical analysis of military doctrine that characterized the army in the between-war years stands in sharp contrast to the pattern of intellectual activity in army circles following World War II.

Whether Palmer was right or wrong in the course he advocated, he was one of the very few officers attempting to think through the problems of civil-military relations in the between-war decades.

> I am, of course, a partisan and do not expect any of my friends to agree with me in every particular, but I do feel that it is important to realize that there is an issue here that should be settled by the civil authorities. Uncle Sam is spending millions on the Washingtonian system with his right hand and other millions on an anti-Washingtonian system with his left. This is not good business. I may be wrong in my preference for the Washingtonian system, but I am not wrong in the contention that the civil authorities should get busy and decide on one system or the other.[83]

The civilian authorities, however, showed little interest in making a decision on military policy. On Capital Hill Palmer's plea found few takers. Even the pacifism-disarmament bloc, from whom the publishers had expected at least some kind of reaction, good or bad, failed to respond. Perhaps the most fitting epitaph came from Sen. Duncan Fletcher of Florida. On receiving a copy of *Washington, Lincoln, and Wilson*, he wrote a polite note to the author reminding him of Disraeli's ambiguous reply in like circumstances. "I will lose no time reading it."[84]

If the book failed to arouse much interest in military and political circles, it was even less of a success financially. Instead of paying the author after publication, it actually cost him money out of pocket. His page proof corrections ran over the allowable limit, so Doubleday billed his royalty account for $30. Unfortunately, there were no royalties. Sales ran so far below expectations that they failed by more than $2,000 to cover the advances already made to the author.[85]

The final humiliation came when a Washington department store remaindered the edition. Characteristically, the general refused to conceal even this blow to his pride. When one of his old comrades in the 29th Division belatedly asked if one might still secure a copy of the book, he conscientiously steered him to the store's marked-down supply.[86]

Looking back three years later, the general believed he could profit from the whole experience.

> I now see that there was a serious fault in my treatment of the material. It was really a thesis in support of certain views on national military policy. I did not know then what I know now: ... there is no subject of less interest to the general reading public. The historical material was new and interesting, but I put too big a didactic burden upon it. For me it was a rather expensive way of learning that most people are interested in other people and not in theoretical principles.[87]

Was this candid self-appraisal, most unusual for Palmer, still wide of the mark? Was he writing for the "general reading public," or was he working for army reform? And it was certainly an open question whether a book alone, no matter how well written, would ever produce significant reform in the army. Gifted with a prose style that might readily have netted him a high return had he taken up potboiling, he could not bring himself to abandon his role as crusader in an era little interested in crusades. Moreover, it may have been his literary flair that was his undoing insofar as modifying army doctrine was concerned.

The many plaudits Palmer received for his prose only strengthened his belief that his pen could accomplish the reforms he desired. What might he have achieved had he devoted his energies to cultivating disciples among a rising generation of younger officers? But there is not a particle of evidence that he ever seriously considered such an alternative. Indeed, long before he finished *Washington, Lincoln and Wilson*, he was already committed to another book. This was to be a biography of General Von Steuben, which would combine worthwhile historical scholarship with a solid contribution to army reform.

45 In Quest of Baron Von Steuben

Just why Palmer undertook to write a life of General von Steuben is impossible to say. Despite his disclaimers there was undoubtedly a large didactic element in his thinking, but the hope of financial return seems to have played a considerable part in his calculations. As he explained it to his former aide Tom White, the *Harper's* article had led to inquiries from some interested German-Americans about a possible biography. In an effort to rehabilitate the German image, they found in Steuben the ideal symbol, a German who was also an American patriot. What appealed to the general was the prospect of a market among the members of the German-American societies who had adopted the baron as their patron saint. "Altruistic as I am," he confided, "I don't think I should turn down an interesting subject just because it may pay."[1]

Among those who pressed the general to go on with the project, none was more enthusiastic than Dr. Otto L. Schmidt of Chicago. Generous, energetic, and urbane, Schmidt crammed several lives into one. As a physician he pioneered in the use of X-ray in his native Illinois, but his large medical practice absorbed only a small portion of his vitality, which he poured into civic causes ranging from the Chicago Board of Education to the local yacht club. But history was his passion. At one time or another he was president of virtually every historical association in the Chicago area. And none dearer to him than the German-American Historical Society of Illinois, over which he presided from 1911 until his death in 1935.[2]

Schmidt and Palmer first met in May 1927, on the occasion of the latter's address, "President Lincoln's War Problem" before the Illinois State Historical Society.[3] With Schmidt's encouragement the general submitted a budget covering one full year of research toward a biography of Steuben. When an initial solicitation for funds from wealthy German-Americans failed to bring immediate results, the doctor provided a subsidy of $125 a month from his own pocket for four months during the summer of 1929. He was anxious to get started; the following year was to be the 200th anniversary of Baron Von Steuben's birth, an ideal opening for a program of German-American reconciliation.[4]

Palmer gratefully accepted the proffered sum. It would relieve his "current monthly deficit" and permit him to devote full time to research without having to write potboilers.[5] After soliciting nearly $2,000 from his friends, Dr. Schmidt raised the monthly stipend to $200, although he continued to contribute most of this himself.[6] Elated, the general suggested that half of all profits should be earmarked for the underwriters, but the doctor had little interest in a return on his investment; what he wanted was a completed manuscript. The general's timetable of six months for research and four months for writing would produce a book before the end of 1930.[7]

A more unrealistic enterprise would be difficult to imagine. Even by the author's highly optimistic calculations of the time required, it would take a sale of 6,000 to 12,000 copies to repay his monthly cost-of-living stipend. Because the general knew no German, he soon discovered that it was essential to secure the services of a translator. Although he managed to find a woman who agreed to do research in the German sources while serving as his secretary for a salary of $25 a week, this created a new burden. Dr. Schmidt agreed to pick up the added cost, but this was only the beginning of their difficulties.[8]

For the main facts Palmer expected to rely on a biography written by Friedrich Kapp in 1859 and thus confine his own research largely to the military aspects of the baron's career. This would capitalize on Palmer's special assets as an experienced soldier. Kapp had lacked any particular military competence, and had been unable to inspect the military archives to which Palmer had ready access.[9]

From the outset Palmer found the baron a most colorful and engaging figure. "Every glimpse that I get of him brings new delight in his personality- ....His very weaknesses and vanities endear him to me as a very human inhabitant of his century."[10]

Through the good offices of Dr. Schmidt the general was introduced to a number of individuals who were delighted to assist in his patriotic project. One of the most helpful was Julius Goebel, editor of the *German-American Historical Review* and emeritus professor of Germanic languages at the University of Illinois. Goebel, then in the East visiting one of his daughters, who was married to the well-known architectural historian Fiske Kimball, invited Palmer to call upon him at her home, Lemon Hill, in Fairmont Park, Philadelphia. The Kimballs proved most charming and the Lemon Hill mansion a showplace. More significantly, Professor Goebel was convinced that Palmer was precisely the man to turn out "an authoritative life of the great general."[11]

To introduce the author to the German-American community and thus facilitate his search for Steuben items in private hands, Goebel arranged to have Palmer publish an article, "Steuben as a Military Statesman" in the *German-American Historical Review* for 1930.[12] He also dug up numerous leads to obscure sources, notably articles in German language newspapers, and while engaged on his own research in the collections of the New York Historical Society, he compiled an index to the Steuben materials he uncovered there.[13]

Goebel's finds were almost too helpful. When they were combined with Palmer's own discoveries in the Library of Congress and the files of the War Department, the flood of information threatened to get out of hand. So the general set up an elaborate chronological file covering each day of the baron's life. This compounded his troubles; filling in the blank spaces gave Palmer such a sense of gratification that it spurred him to ever greater efforts in tracking down elusive Steuben documents.[14]

Palmer's original program of limited research, largely in connection with military matters, had ballooned into the pursuit of every last scrap of evidence known to exist. Just when he believed he had exhausted the War Department files, some new body of records would turn up with a liberal scattering of Steuben items. As the chronological file thickened, new and intriguing questions sent the author off for further evidence.

With the arrival of each new letter reporting the generosity of yet another German-American donor, Palmer's view of the undertaking took on larger dimensions. In a scarcely veiled hint, he suggested to Schmidt that it would be a great inspiration to the biography if the two of them could travel to Magdeburg, Germany, for the Steuben bicentennial, to be held there in 1930.[15]

The general began to discover a variety of reasons, quite apart from a trip abroad, why his initial timetable was impossible. His research was seriously hampered by the lack of a good history of the American Revolution. Everything available was the work of propagandists or nonprofessionals who knew little or nothing about military problems. Then, too, the baron had obviously been regarded by his contemporaries as a highly colorful character: those who came in contact with him invariably recorded their impressions in diaries, letters, or official reports. The baron himself was a prolific writer; his promissory notes he scattered widely over two continents, in many instances stirring up a subsequent train of letters from irate creditors.[16]

Every additional delay brought pangs to Palmer's conscience. He began to regret ever having suggested the trip to Germany. He even offered to forego all further subsidies, since it was now evident that he would never be able to meet the deadline. Dr. Schmidt, as enthusiastic as ever, generously approved the author's thorough research even if it required far longer than anticipated.[17]

One of Professor Goebel's leads turned up information of a most distressing sort. That the baron was financially profligate, Palmer was quite willing to recognize. "Prodigality, impulsiveness, and whimsicality," as he put it, were evident in Steuben's fading letters. But when systematically analyzed, Steuben's correspondence gave substantial grounds for charging him with a want of candor if not outright prevarication, and even put the validity of his noble title in doubt.[18]

How could Palmer expect a subsidy, let alone a large sale to his German-American friends, if his book turned out to be a debunking study? He wrote to Dr. Schmidt to prepare him for what might come later; "the real Steuben," he confided, "was much less a demi-god than Kapp presents him. He had many weaknesses." Schmidt refused to be deterred; an educated man of humane sympathies, he not only continued the subsidy but agreed to make a large additional contribution toward the purchase of an important collection of privately held Steuben materials, which Palmer was anxious to secure.[19]

This action came at a time when Schmidt was facing grave financial difficulties. By the end of 1930 the bite of the depression was painfully evident. Almost apologetically the doctor explained that his payments in the future might arrive at irregular intervals, for in addition to his other charitable obligations, he was helping to put the children of some friends through college.[20]

The private collection secured through Dr. Schmidt's help consisted of the papers and articles of a German-American journalist, Anton B. C. Kalkhorst, a one-time editor of the *Erie Tageblatt* who had devoted most of his free time to research on Steuben. In German archives Kalkhorst had uncovered a great deal of fresh evidence. A few of his findings had been published in obscure German-language publications in the United States, although the bulk of his work had not reached print at the time of his early death. Palmer expected these materials to be a gold mine; to his horror, Kalkhorst's work not only seemed to confirm his previous suspicions but raised new and even graver scandals. There was evidence that the baron had been dismissed from his position at court when charged with homosexuality.[21]

As an officer whose whole life had been spent working with earthy men of action all around the world, the general liked to think of himself as too sophisticated to be shocked by anything, but in reality the revelations about the baron's personal life shocked him profoundly. This was evident when he informed Dr. Schmidt with Victorian nicety that the Kalkhorst papers had introduced "problems of serious delicacy affecting Steuben's character."[22]

At first he tried to treat the baron's difficulty as one of the "foibles of a very eccentric but lovable human being." He did his best to persuade himself that the charges of immorality were maliciously propagated by the baron's enemies at court. But finally he admitted that the contradictions in the baron's life were beginning to get on his nerves. He speculated that perhaps Kalkhorst had never finished his work because he too had been baffled by the baron's character. Yet even in distress Palmer was ever mindful to play on the sensibilities of his patron. "It would take a Goethe," he wrote Dr. Schmidt, "to do full justice to such a problem."[23]

Somewhat to Palmer's amazement, the subject of his biography had suddenly become an international issue. According to the *New York Times*, the hypersensitive French were developing "considerable pique" over the elaborate German buildup for the Steuben bicentenary celebrations. Two well-known Parisian journals had suggested that the whole affair was the work of German propagandists out to dim the fame of Lafayette, an absurd idea that disturbed Palmer greatly.

He would have been even more upset had he realized that the *Times* reports, it turned out, were only part of the story. Where these reports denounced the Steuben cult in generalized terms as German propaganda, in Paris a pamphleteering zealot, convinced that the Steuben Society, founded in 1919, was endeavoring to "lower the prestige of France," had singled out for particular disparagement "the pro-German bias of the American author, John M. Palmer."[25]

Ironically, at about this time Palmer himself was writing to Schmidt deploring the needless competition between the partisans of Steuben and Lafayette. The problem had been aggravated, he observed, by the tendency of the Steuben Society to inflate the baron's role. But if he released the scandalous imputations in his files, they might be exploited by the sensation-seeking press. Despite this danger, he urged the necessity of telling the truth. Better the Baron's alleged deviations be considered by a fair-minded biographer than exploited by those only too anxious to offer a twisted account. When Dr. Schmidt, with his customary breadth of outlook, concurred, the general had good reason to feel much relieved. But there were still shoals ahead, one of them a rival biographer.[26]

The general first learned of his potential competitor from the mayor of Steuben, New York. Dr. Karl F. von Frank of Vienna had written the mayor for materials on the baron's American career for use in a proposed biography. Thoroughly alarmed at the prospect of being scooped, Palmer planned a vigorous offensive. It would never do to reply in person. Instead he drafted a letter for Schmidt to dispatch in his capacity as president of the Illinois German-American Historical Society. This indicated that General Palmer already had his manuscript approaching completion, that he was a highly competent military man, and that only a military expert could cope with the military facets of Steuben's career.[27]

Von Frank then proposed a division of labor: he could write of the baron in Europe, while the general took the American years. Palmer rejected this suggestion as artistically impossible; it was, he observed, as if one asked two unrelated portrait painters to produce a character study in which each executed a side of the subject's face. A scheme of mutual assistance seemed in order, however. Hitherto the general had secured information from various official archives in Europe by the cumbersome and decidedly unorthodox method of directing specific questions to the German ambassador to the United States, Friedrich Wilhelm von Prittwitz, who passed them on through official channels. It would be far more effective to deal with someone who was actually engaged in research on Steuben. As the correspondence developed, it became clear that Dr. von Frank was primarily interested in genealogy and was scarcely to be regarded as a direct competitor. So the general offered to send copies of his chapters in manuscript and to provide information freely from his files in return for help on archival sources. Confident that his own volume would appear first, he spoke deprecatingly of it as "a brief popular biography" that would help prepare the way for the Austrian's more elaborate study. Dr. von Frank accepted this compromise with a graciousness that belied the strictures of the French critics.[28]

Although little of significance to the biography emerged from the arrangement, it did lead to an interesting friendship. In fact, two friendships grew from the association, for it was at von Frank's suggestion that the distinguished Viennese portrait painter, Baron Robert Doblhoff, called on the general in Washington. Baron Doblhoff had come to the United States to do an official congressional portrait of Nicholas Longworth, the Speaker of the House. His work was so well received that he was soon busy on likenesses of other figures on the Hill. Between sittings he often strolled over to chat with Palmer in his study at the Library of Congress. Thoroughly charmed, he invited his host to sit for a portrait. The general's protest that such luxuries were beyond his reach Doblhoff brushed aside as irrelevant. It would be a favor to him, he declared, to see if he could capture the sensitive face of a soldier-scholar.[29]

As the painting progressed, the two men spent many pleasant hours reminiscing about their experiences as wartime rivals. When the baron finally left Washington, he took the finished portrait with him. Several months later, however, Palmer was delighted to receive the painting with a message from the artist, who presented it as a souvenir of their friendship.

The picture immediately took an honored place among the family treasures. Many years later, when some minor flaking developed, it was taken to the Museum of Fine Arts in Boston for repairs. There, a routine X-ray photograph clearly revealed the portrait of a woman below the surface. Might it be one of the Longworth ladies Baron Doblhoff had been asked to paint? Or was it a likeness of someone no longer able to pay when the Depression struck?

The little mystery delighted the general; a hidden lady in his portrait was far more intriguing than a skeleton in the family closet!

Sitting for a portrait was diverting but did not diminish the anguish Palmer began to feel over his writing. The book he had begun with such high expectations seemed to bring endless troubles. The task was becoming a great deal bigger than he had anticipated. And it annoyed him greatly to be caught up, however unwittingly, in a Franco-German squabble. But these were minor annoyances compared with the distress he experienced each time he grappled with the problem of Steuben's alleged immorality.

Most of the difficulty, of course, lay not with Baron von Steuben but within the general himself. An essentially warmhearted and generous man, he hated to have his hero besmirched. He knew he had to tell the truth, but the prospect pained him. "If I can make the reader know and sympathize with the Baron as I do," he wrote Dr. Schmidt, "the rest will be plain sailing." At last, thoroughly discouraged, he reached a point where he began to think he could no longer go on.[30]

Periodic bouts of discouragement were certainly nothing new to the general; this time, however, they were accompanied by rather alarming physical symptoms. His weight dropped twenty pounds below normal. Many of the signs of a diabetic condition began to multiply, but whether it was the disease that produced the worry or the worry that aggravated the illness would be impossible to say.[31]

Undoubtedly the steady erosion of the family finances contributed something to the general's difficulties. Not only had his small private income dried up, but now there were rumors that even his modest retirement pay would soon be cut by Congress. Palmer could no longer afford to live in Washington.

Moving from Washington might save money, but it would put the Library of Congress and the War Department archives beyond reach. Yet unless his research continued, how could the biographer accept any further subsidy from his long-suffering sponsor? Palmer wrote a full account of his situation to Schmidt. With Job-like patience, that understanding man reaffffirmed his faith in the author and tried to bolster his courage for the trials ahead.[32]

To move from Washington was to leave the large circle of friends who meant so much to the family; yet it was precisely because of these many friends that the move was necessary. Enjoying their company, entertaining them, and participating in the social life of the Army-Navy Club involved commitments that were no longer possible. Only by a drastic change in their whole way of life could the Palmers ever hope to stay within their sharply falling income. So, after weeks of agonized debate, they resolved to take their household goods and depart; they would make a new home in the country and live in idyllic simplicity.[33]

The community to which the Palmers retreated was situated in the rural township of Hill, New Hampshire, where their daughter Mary and her husband had a summer home. They felt they knew the area well enough to settle there without further investigation. The neighborhood into which they moved, known as Murray Hill, was in many respects a rather remarkable colony. It consisted of ten or a dozen families of summer folk, each occupying an abandoned farmstead along somewhat more than a mile of road. At one time these had been prosperous dairy farms, and the houses were large and handsome, virtually all of them dating back well over a hundred years. The forest was already reclaiming the hard-won pastures when the influx of summer people gave a new lift to the community.[34]

The founder of the colony was Harold Murdock, a Boston bank president who since 1920 had managed the Harvard University Press. His father had discovered Murray Hill, but it was he who first thought of building up a community of interesting people there. Among those he had attracted to the neighborhood were his brother, a retired admiral, and his son, Kenneth Murdock, professor of English and master of Leverett House at Harvard. Also in the community was Zenas Nieumeister, a master at Phillips Exeter; André Morize, a one-time colonel in the French army and a professor of French literature at Harvard; James Bryant Conant, who later became president of the university; and the distinguished historian, Perry Miller.

Most of the families had some kind of Harvard connection. They saw each other socially in Cambridge during the winter and simply transferred the relationship to the countryside during the summer. The children had the run of one another's houses. Their elders, especially those at work on literary projects, as most of them seemed to be, found the arrangement no less appealing, providing an informal but useful summer seminar in which to try out their ideas.

The general first visited the New Hampshire colony in the summer of 1929, and from the day he arrived it appealed to his deeply felt need for roots in the soil. No less important than the setting, however, was the friendship he soon established with the patriarchal Harold Murdock. Many a day they spent enjoying each other's company while picking blueberries in overgrown pastures or strolling along country lanes. As Murdock had recently written some books on the American Revolution, they never lacked for subjects of mutual interest. Thus, when a handsome old farmhouse built in 1800 came on the market just as the Palmers decided to leave Washington, the move to Hill seemed almost inevitable.

Judged by any objective standard, the decision to buy a farm at Hill was the utmost folly. It was one thing to summer there, and quite another for a retired couple in poor health to face a New Hampshire winter. The farm was on a dirt road several miles from the nearest village and far beyond commuting range to any considerable city or library. Since the general neither owned an automobile nor knew how to drive one, he would have to cope with these problems before moving.

Although it seemed reasonable enough to pay $3,000 for a farmhouse, a sturdy barn, and 160 acres of land, in a sense this was only a down payment. The house was a good, solid eight-room structure with several fireplaces and hand-hewn beams. But there were no bathrooms, no running water, and no furnace. What is more, there was no electric power in the community.

To persuade his somewhat reluctant wife, the general's table of expenses showing how much cheaper it would be to live in the country was a characteristic display of his tendency to put heart before head. He deluded himself about the real costs of renovation.[35]

Although the Palmers decided to leave Washington in the summer of 1931, negotiations on the purchase of the farm were so protracted that they had to put off their departure until the following spring. This gave the general ample time to reflect on the wisdom of their choice. During the winter the family income continued to shrink, and the estimates on repairs and refurbishing prepared by the local carpenter were far higher than expected. The letters from his new friend, Harold Murdock, plunged the general into the tribulations of country living before he got there. The winter, Murdock reported, had been a mild one, and little or no ice had been cut, certainly not enough to supply two families from the ice house.

Each of the old patriarch's letters introduced some new hazard of country living. He had visited the community in April, he wrote, adding almost as an afterthought that he had had to leave his car at the bridge near the foot of the hill because the road was washed out and impassably muddy. Another letter rather casually mentioned hearing that the Palmer place had been broken into. As if to suggest that this was a more or less annual phenomenon, he concluded, "You are now properly initiated into the summer colony."[36]

The general refused to be frightened off and replied in good humor that he had rather hoped the burglars would carry off some of the dilapidated Victorian furniture left by the previous owners. He did concede that Mrs. Palmer had been quite right in accusing him of building "too many air castles." Ever-mounting costs had forced him to lower his sights; "the chrysalis of our house beautiful will... not open until later." With funds barely sufficient to make the farmhouse weathertight, central heating and electric lighting would have to wait.[37]

On the question of electricity the general and Harold Murdock differed fundamentally; yet their exchange of letters managed to reveal those qualities of gentlemanly courtesy and good humor that made the two men such durable companions. Of the proposal to run a power line to Murray Hill, Murdock wrote: "As an enlightened reactionary I protest against that and every other convenience." But then he concluded, "If I found myself opposed to the general sentiment, I certainly would cooperate with the majority." Palmer replied that he had taken the objection seriously. "I felt that it would almost amount to outrage to bring such an abomination into the simple elysium you have enjoyed so much since your childhood. I understand your feeling and sympathize with it fully, and I therefore think it very generous of you to say that you would be disposed to waive your objection."[38]

Improvident as the move to Hill may have been, it proved to be excellent medicine. Mrs. Palmer's objections to country living were soon dispelled by her pleasure in having a home of her own, after a lifetime of converting drab quarters into attractive places to live. Now at last she was building something permanent, and she intended to make it a work of art. There were, of course, certain obstacles between reality and her vision of perfection. One of these was lack of money; another was the independence of the Yankee carpenters who were the necessary agents of her artistic creation.

By early fall the house was sufficiently renovated to be livable. In the general's eyes that old farm was endowed with a very special glow; it was home, the only property he had ever held in his own name. Admittedly this overlooked the mortgage and ignored the distressing fact that the costs had so far outstripped his estimates that he had been forced to borrow on his life insurance and sell off his few remaining securities at the bottom of the market. Yet none of these liabilities seemed to distress him unduly. Once the dream of a home in the country became firmly entrenched in his mind, the difficulties and burdens virtually ceased to exist. He was a man who could believe in his own dreams, a trait that won him many friends.

With the departure of the summer colony in September the Palmers settled down to country living. They were no longer just summer folk but permanent residents. Or were they? From Cambridge, Murdock wrote one of his gentle, teasing letters. "If you stay through the winter," he declared, "you will have a good subject for entertaining your neighbors next year." Then, with studied nonchalance, he added, "If you have a succession of heavy snow storms, I don't know whether you would be marooned or not."[39]

Whether it was pride or poverty that kept them, the Palmers did spend the winter at Hill. They were snowbound on several occasions and had other adventures to regale their friends with the following summer. One was the mysterious arrival of an automobile in the dead of night at one of the empty and shuttered homes in the neighborhood. The hastily summoned sherriff's men subsequently discovered that the visitor had stolen some valuable furnishings from the unoccupied house. Tire tracks in the snow helped them apprehend the offender almost immediately; apparently unaware that anyone was wintering on the hill, he had made no effort at concealment. The thief turned out to be the antiques dealer who had sold the stolen items to his victims, and apparently planned to sell them over again. Murdock took the matter in stride, writing the general to say how sorry he was to learn that "our friends the burglars opened their season so promptly."[40]

Another nocturnal visitor concerned the Palmers more personally. While seated before a blazing fire one snowy night, the general suddenly felt uneasy. Glancing up from his book he found himself looking into a pair of eyes peering at him from outside the window. When he opened the front door and shouted, a voice cried out "I'm hungry." Further shouts brought no response, so Mrs. Palmer put a tray of hot food on the doorstep. Next morning the food was gone, but there were bloody footprints in the snow leading from window to window. It later developed that the intruder was a dangerous convict who had been wounded by a guard while escaping from the prison at Concord.

For the general the greatest adventure of all was the sheer delight of presiding over Christmas in his own home. Mary and her husband came up from Cambridge with the grandsons, and they all enjoyed a never-to-be-forgotten winter holiday. With their grandfather the boys gathered running pine, and after much searching they finally discovered an absolutely perfect Christmas tree, which they cut and hauled home in triumph. For the general the long days of solitude were bliss. By alternating light reading and long walks in the dry mountain air with an hour or two each day chopping firewood, he gradually recovered his health. An hour of chopping, he discovered, was the equivalent of twice that time spent on the links, but as he confessed to Harold Murdock, no matter how primitive the local plumbing, chopping certainly made the daily bath "a necessity rather than a mere gesture of gentility."[41]

An inveterate record keeper, the general maintained a careful day-by-day account of the advancing season. His entries, though laconic, offer revealing glimpses of a man who found a peaceful refuge in a troubled world: 13 April, 33 inches of snow; 17 April, first robin; 19 April, Smith's river rising; 23 April, arbutus buds; 29 April, frog chorus began; 5 May, dogtooth violets in bloom. But it was the return of the grandsons that afforded greatest pleasure.[42]

Like many another grandparent, he adored the two boys and gave his friends his "absolutely unbiased opinion" of their superlative qualities.[43] Above all, he sought to teach them the "companionship of the woods" that he himself understood so well.[44] In winter he perused handbooks on the trees and flowers. And with his fisherman friend Zibeon Southard, he took an active interest in pressing for conservation statutes to make the fly fishing "better for coming generations."[45]

Best of all, he enjoyed the days spent with his grandsons in the woods and on the river. If they wore him out building a dam to improve the swimming hole, he would recuperate with a tranquil session instructing them in the finer points of fly casting. The nearby Smith River was promptly dubbed the Smithissippi by the boys, who found its boulder-strewn banks an endless source of adventures. Simply by being himself in such a setting, the general helped instill the values he most treasured for his grandsons. As his friend Southard said of him, "I have never known anyone who had such a keenly developed spirit and finely apportioned appreciation of nature."[46]

Although there were many compensations in country living, the prolonged isolation of the winter months was hard to take. There was virtually no one with whom the general could engage in a stimulating conversation. One notable exception was Dr. Frederick McNaughton Robertson, an old-fashioned practitioner in the nearby village of Bristol. The doctor was excellent company, but seldom had time for sociability because of the demands made upon him by a large rural practice. Only a few days before his death he fought his way over a mile on foot through deep drifts to reach a snowbound patient.[47]

Only by letter writing was it possible to keep in touch with the outside world. Fortunately the mail service was excellent; not uncommonly a letter to New York or Washington would bring a reply in forty-eight hours. Typical of the responses Palmer received was one from Herbert Putnam, who wrote from the Library of Congress to assure him that he was much missed at the Round Table, where the conversations were all about the new president, Franklin D. Roosevelt, who, he reported, left the members of the circle "breathless but buoyant." Somewhat later, when the general offered to resign as consultant in military history to the Library of Congress, Putnam assured him "we are entirely unwilling to part with you."[48]

Whatever the occasion for receiving mail, Palmer took advantage of the opportunity offered. For example, when General Pershing wrote inviting him to come to France to attend the dedicatory ceremonies marking the completion of the work of the American Battle Monuments Commission, it was obvious that the family finances made any such trip unthinkable. But instead of writing a perfunctory letter of regrets, Palmer suggested a line of thought for Pershing when drafting the address he would almost certainly be called upon to make the dedication. "One of the essential factors that made the World War possible was the assumption of the warmongers that the reaction of the American people could be ignored. Henceforth your monuments will remind political adventurers that this was a serious miscalculation."[49] That Hitler was already making this a poor prophecy in no way detracts from Palmer's effort to continue a creative role despite retirement.

For the general, letter writing was a fine art. Just how successful his efforts could be is evident from the comment of his daughter in apologizing for her failure to answer one of his letters: "I write *things* to most people ... to you it is much more apt to be *thoughts* which really takes a long time to get down in black and white...." [50] And in writing to his wife on one of her rare trips away from the farm without him, he displayed a real gift for diplomacy. Suddenly remembering that her birthday had come and gone, he assured her that he had remembered her birthday and had even composed a long and loving letter in his mind. But he had become absorbed in other things and never committed it to writing. To make amends he pleaded, "As the letter was already written in my mind on your birthday, won't you be a good girl and let me write it on paper now?"[51]

Actually both Palmers found the long winters a considerable strain. For example, the general could never understand why cooking held no joys for his lady. He described the problem in one of his long letters to Harold Murdock.

She is one of those rare artists who achieve perfection in poached eggs, buttered toast and coffee. But she is an exception to most artists, who, so I am informed, take a delight in the practice of their artistry. How anyone can achieve such a breakfast and not thrill with joy of creative achievement has always been a marvel to me. If I could do anything half so well, I could never delegate it to a mere hireling, but there is no accounting for artistic temperament.[52]

That Mrs. Palmer insisted upon employing household help despite the serious financial reverses suffered by the family is revealing testimony of the marked difference in outlook that separated her and so many of her contemporaries in army circles from the following generation. She had always had domestic servants. It mattered not that the Filipino house boy had given way to the daughter of a neighboring farmer; she would keep on giving formal dinner parties in rural New Hampshire as she had in many another out-of-the-way corner of the world. And the general continued to indulge her with amused forbearance.

On one point of disagreement, however, Palmer found it almost impossible to be good natured with his wife; her refusal to believe that he would ever earn any substantial sums with his pen riled him painfully. It was disturbing enough to contemplate the financial failure of his earlier books but infinitely more so to think about the biography he had been forced to abandon. His doctor had been adamant in ordering him not to pick it up until he was thoroughly recovered. Having borrowed heavily against his life insurance to buy the farm, the general knew he had to find some way to supplement his income to protect his wife if he should die first. He was determined to prove to her that his faith in his literary powers was not mistaken.

This self-confidence was not entirely unwarranted. After all, the article on Steuben in *Harper's* had been a success. And as a byproduct of his research he had placed another article, this time in the *North American Review*, not long before that venerable journal folded in the Depression.[53] There was a limit, however, to the number of marketable items he could mine from the Steuben materials without impairing the prospects of the book. Moreover, fiction seemed to offer promise of a far higher return for the effort expended. In a matter of weeks he prepared several short stories, all thinly disguised experiences from life, and sent them off to his literary agents, Brandt & Brandt, in New York.

The editors who read the pieces readily conceded that they were well written but rejected them nonetheless. One after another, *the Saturday Evening Post, Harper's, Scribner's, the Atlantic,* and several other magazines turned down the manuscripts. Sentimental tales were out of fashion. At last the general decided to abandon fiction altogether.[54]

In response to Palmer's letter throwing in the sponge on fiction, his literary agent wrote that a university press was planning to bring out a biography of

Steuben.[55] Here was a crisis. If he ever expected to recoup his investment of time and energy or repay his moral obligation to the German-Americans who had so patiently subsidized him, he must return to the baron without delay. Had the report of a competitor arrived only a few months earlier, its effect might have been catastrophic; now a challenge was precisely what he needed to galvanize him into action.

In retrospect it seems clear that the long layoff was a positive advantage, not merely to the general's health but to the biography he was trying to write. While the project lay fallow, several things reshaped his whole conception of the book he hoped to write. The editors of the *Dictionary of American Biography* had invited him to write the article on Steuben.[56] This had forced him to select the significant highlights, the irreducible minimum of the baron's career. The intellectual discipline required was painful, but it gave him a perspective on his subject hitherto lacking. And by ruminating on his research at a time when he was not directly involved in the writing, he managed to achieve a larger and more detached point of view of his subject than ever before. Most significantly, he finally thought out a good way to cope with the defects in the baron's character. Since the archival evidence made it abundantly clear that George Washington and many other contemporaries of the highest personal rectitude were well aware of the baron's flaws and forgave and worked with him, why should he as a biographer do anything different?[57]

Now he could write almost indulgently about matters that had troubled him deeply. As he wrote to Murdock, "I can't escape revealing that my hero is a liar, but I am trying to take the curse off by calling him one with a smile."[58] From amused toleration, he gradually came to believe that the baron's indiscretions were almost a virtue. "My hero," he told Dr. Schmidt, "was a deliberate, systematic and comprehensive liar, but when you know why you will forgive and even applaud him. As a patriotic American, you will thank God that, in His inscrutable wisdom, He did not hamper Steuben with the congenital inhibition that checked the flow of Washington's imagination."[59]

Once Palmer realized that the best way to treat Steuben was as a visionary and a fortune hunter in the same tradition as Mark Twain's Colonel Sellers, his misgivings vanished. He returned to his desk with renewed zeal, working four hours at a stretch every morning. In a matter of weeks the book was more than half-finished, and he eagerly looked forward to completing the manuscript before the end of the year. In this mood he sent off a bundle of draft chapters for his agent to read and criticize.

The response from New York was downright exciting. His agent, much impressed by the quality of the manuscript, had carried it to the Yale University Press, where it was received with enthusiasm. The editors had previously commissioned a biography of Steuben, but since the author who took the assignment had done nothing on it, they gladly transferred the project to Palmer. Moreover, to bind the transaction, they offered an advance of $500 against future royalties. This amount would do little to solve the general's financial difficulties, but the approval of a distinguished university press made a new man of him. Here was vindication for his efforts.[60]

Once again filled with enthusiasm, Palmer began enjoying every minute of his work on the biography. It was still brutally hard work, especially the painful business of cutting out page after page to bring the manuscript down to the length prescribed by the editors. But now his whole approach was different. Even the baron's alleged immorality no longer held any terrors for him. "There are only two alternatives for an honest man. He must tell the truth or decide not to write the book."[61]

Much of the pleasure the general now derived from his work came from the host of interesting people he encountered as he followed the leads turned up by his research. When, for example, he visited Steuben, New York, to explore the site of "Sixty," the baron's estate, he was most graciously received by Augustus L. Richards, the current owner. Richards, who happened to be a law partner of Justice Charles Evans Hughes, took a lively interest in the biography, helping him turn up new sources and escorting his visitor over the scenes of the baron's last years. And it was at his suggestion that the New York State historian, Alexander C. Flick, invited Palmer to compose the inscription on the plaque that now marks the memorial at the Steuben state park.[62]

Whether he was tramping through the fields seeking Steuben's burial place or negotiating with Millicent (Mrs. William Randolph) Hearst for permission to use the Steuben portrait by Ralph Earle, the general thoroughly enjoyed the adventures into which his book led him.[63] Archivists, scholars, librarians, and collectors all seemed to find his charm irresistable. So too did the staff at the Yale Press. Before long the editor, Eugene A. Davidson, and the business manager, Norman V. Donaldson, were on the friendliest terms with him, visiting him in his rural retreat and doing everything in their power to sustain his efforts.

Palmer's friends from Yale were determined to help him turn out a best seller. The author already had an engaging subject and a remarkably felicitous prose style. To reach the broadest popular market, they urged cutting the manuscript ruthlessly. This hurt, but he was in no position to resist. As he wrote to his benefactor, Schmidt, "unless we get a little dividend from the Baron we will be on the verge of bankruptcy and will have to sell our home at a sacrifice." Cutting a 12,000-word chapter down to 3,000 words was indeed painful, but the results in fitting the book for the general reader seemed well worth the effort.[64]

Although convinced that the labors of his editors would make a far more readable product, the general was somewhat disturbed at the new direction his book seemed to be taking. As he explained to George Marshall, he had set out to write a military study and now he found himself confronting a puzzling problem of psychology, trying to portray a romantic figure who was "a mixture of Ananias, Colonel Sellers, and Don Quixote." "Strange to say," he added, "my publishers are rather pleased....They seem to think that my amiable crook is much more interesting than the purely military figure I expected to find."[65]

The more he brooded on what was happening, the more disturbed he became. What if he actually did turn out a best seller? Would it contribute anything substantial to an understanding of the military policy required by a democratic nation—the ideal to which he had devoted so much of himself for so many years? In this mood of doubt and self-reproach, sharpened by the pinch of hard times, it was an easy step beyond to a sense of resentment and betrayal, as he reflected that even the reforms he had helped enact into law were now "completely ignored, unrecognized and forgotten." In an exchange of letters with Marshall he spelled out in embarrassing detail the injustice he felt. Marshall tried to bolster his spirits with some good advice. "What you have always needed was a manager and publicity agent, and then a trifling operation in amputation of conscience," concluding drily, "Most people do not require this."[66]

Almost as if in answer to Marshall's prescription, a telegram from James W. Wadsworth invited the general to make the major address at the forthcoming annual convention of the ROTC Association of the United States. Palmer not only accepted with alacrity but agreed to the "trifling amputation" of his reticence that Marshall had advised. He would make his address an account of just how it happened that Washington's long-lost military policy had come at last to fruition in the Defense Act of 1920. Since his friend Wadsworth was to organize the program, it was an easy matter to arrange for an introduction that would spell out his personal contribution in drafting the epoch-making statute. "I hope," he wrote Wadsworth, "you will not think that I am influenced only by *amour propre*. It never hurts the currency of a political ideal if its champions are given a bit of personal prestige in connection with it." When the convention assembled in New York at the end of April 1935, Wadsworth played his part to perfection.[67]

For the general the occasion was an exciting adventure. He had addressed larger and more important audiences before, but this was different. Coming down from his isolated retreat in the country gave him an exhilarating sense of being in the swim again. His speech was a success, or so his friends assured him, but the spoken word evaporates, and the newspapers all but ignored his remarks.

The ideal solution, he realized, was to have his remarks made up as a pamphlet. There was, as he explained the problem to the officials of the ROTC Association, no concise account of the act to be found anywhere. The text of the measure itself was largely incomprehensible to laymen because of the way it had had to be passed in the form of amendments to existing legislation. "This involved a very serious literary handicap, such as must have confronted James Madison if he had had to write the new Constitution of the United States as amendments to the Articles of Confederation. You can imagine what a literary and legislative mess that would have been." For want of a clear exposition, he declared, the intent of the law had never been understood by the public at large and only imperfectly understood by the army itself. "If the real intent [of the Defense Act] were generally understood," he concluded, "it would be hazardous to attempt to evade it."[68]

To Palmer's delight his friends in the ROTC Association not only agreed with him but carried his scheme further than he himself had dared to hope. With the cooperation of Congressman McSwain of the Military Affairs Committee, the association secured an initial order of 20,000 copies of the general's address in the form of reprints from the *Congressional Record.* The executive secretary of the association wrote that he expected to secure 100,000 more, so he could send a copy to every officer in the army and the National Guard, as well as to leading reserve officers and the heads of all appropriate patriotic societies. To top it all off, he sent the general a thousand copies of the pamphlet to distribute where they would do the most good.[69]

The success of Palmer's sally away from the farm did wonders for his battered ego. It pleased him immensely to be fighting another battle in his long campaign for a sound military policy. At the same time, the compliments of his friends in the ROTC Association persuaded him that there might even be an outside chance of securing a promotion on the retired list to major general, a jump in grade that would ease his financial stringency considerably. He explored the possibility with Marshall, pointing out the obvious truth that in writing his books on military policy, he had been working just as hard in the public interest after retirement as he had on active duty. Marshall took up the idea and secured an enthusiastic endorsement from Wadsworth, but a promotion on the retired list required a special act of Congress. It began to appear that financial salvation must come from publishing his *Steuben.*[70]

There were the usual delays and last-minute revisions, so the volume did not actually appear in print until November 1937. In the preceding weeks, however, advance orders from bookstores proved to be so good that the publishers tacked another thousand copies on the initial press order. Although the Book-of-the-Month Club failed to adopt *Steuben,* a favorable endorsement in the club newsletter gave promise of encouraging sales. So did the flattering reviews that began to appear across the country and in Germany as well, after an enterprising publisher in Berlin picked up the translation rights for a European edition.[71]

Hard pressed for Christmas cash, yet anxious not to appear too desperate, Palmer wrote to his friends at the Yale Press. "I will be able to hold the fort for the present. But if the Baron should penetrate the hostile front line during the holidays, it would be a comfort to count on a reenforcement about the first of February."[72] Sales were brisk, cleaning out the whole first printing of 1,500 copies and beginning on the second in less than two months' time. Yet even this highly creditable showing was barely enough to earn the $500 advance received four years earlier. To make matters worse, the publishers reported that the author actually owed the press $47.75, to pay for the excessive number of last-minuted changes he,had made when the book was in page proofs.

Hurt and baffled by the disparity between glowing reviews and lagging sales, he cast about for some explanation. The recession of 1938 had, he learned, cut book buying well below the level of the previous year. The big disappointment, however, was the failure of the German-Americans to show any appreciable interest. They may have felt, the publishers suggested, that the author was too frank in dealing with their hero.[73] In retrospect another explanation seems more reasonable. By 1938 the rise of the Nazis and the activities of Fritz Kuhn and his Bundists in the United States may have persuaded loyal German-Americans that their best course was to have little or nothing to do with things German for the time being.

The actual record was nowhere near as dismal as Palmer painted it. Eventually the biography sold out the entire second printing, a thoroughly respectable performance for a book of its sort. What is more, the book proved sufficiently durable to induce a reprint house to bring out a new edition some years later. The Berlin edition enjoyed a considerable circulation. After the collapse of Hitler's Reich, an American reporter even found a copy in the library of Goebbels's castle in Munich. On learning of this, the general wryly observed that "whatever his deficiencies," Herr Goebbels "seems to be a man of discriminating literary taste." Nevertheless, the royalties received over and above the author's advance amounted to scarcely more than enough to pay the cost of typing the manuscript.[74]

The true measure of failure lay with the general and his utterly unrealistic expectations. He had assumed all along that somehow his book would prove to be that rare exception among historical studies that becomes a runaway best seller. When that failed to materialize, he felt doubly undone. Having shifted his aim from a military tract to a psychological study in the hope of financial success, he now had neither. Only one small ray of hope penetrated his depression; his friends at the Yale Press expressed such a lively interest in publishing his memoirs that he felt more than half inclined to write them.

46

A Grandfather
in Action

When the general's friends at the Yale Press first discussed the possibility of an autobiography, he displayed little enthusiasm. As he wrote to his friend George Marshall, "There are many interesting things in my memory, but most of them lie behind a fog of ill-health and failure that I do not like to penetrate."[1] Because the crucial reform of his entire professional career had miscarried, he was inclined to write off his life's work as unsuccessful.

The general's family and friends were not looking for a serious study of army reform but for a volume of recollections on a colorful life. Charmed by the old gentleman's undeniable gifts as a raconteur, they urged him to share his adventures. Don't be too exact, admonished his brother, Dr. George Palmer, a prominent physician in Springfield, Illinois. Better "some embroidery," George suggested, than "too much citation." Stretching the point, he continued, "I'm willing to swear to anything you say about your early life and experiences, even if it didn't happen or happened to someone else."[2]

When the general expressed qualms about the propriety of rather too candid disclosures concerning public figures, his old friend Jim Wadsworth reassured him. At the most, he suggested, "General March might be a little peeved—but what of it?" So, after many delays and hesitations, Palmer decided to go ahead with his memoirs.[3]

In a sense the decision seemed to indicate that the general regarded his public life as over. He continued to accept occasional invitations to speak on Memorial Day or at other such ceremonials, but he did this as an inescapable burden of good citizenship. Sometimes he accepted invitations to lecture from purely economic motives. As he once had explained it to Tom White after such a request, "I was going to turn them down until I learned of the $150 honorarium. It is astonishing how soon I changed my mind."[4]

More and more the general was content to stay upon his retirement farm. After recovering from a painful and debilitating operation, he found life increasingly circumscribed by the limitations imposed by advancing years. Even the outbreak of war in Europe failed to alter the general's belief that his days of usefulness were over. He did engage in a brief exchange of correspondence with Wadsworth concerning the defense budget, but there was no sense of urgency or deep personal involvement.[5] He prepared a brief article for the *Army and Navy Register* on the evolution of the army's mobilization plans, but this was so short on particulars that it only underlined his lack of touch with current planning.[6] In short, Palmer gave every indication that he was now a full-time grandfather, content to live out his days writing his memoirs for the amusement of his friends, looking forward to his fiftieth reunion at West Point, and devoting his attention to his grandsons. If there were battles to be fought in the future, the boys would have to fight them.

Life in retirement had much to commend it. Despite the financial strains of the Depression, the old, abandoned farm with its overgrown pastures had gradually been made into a country home of distinction. Under Mrs. Palmer's skillful ministrations, Edgewild, as the family called the place, had become a most gracious and hospitable retreat. The general was inclined to grumble at the endless expenses his beloved wife found so necessary, but he was noticeably delighted that visitors never failed to remark on the effect she achieved.

An inveterate auction-goer, the general's lady had many a trophy: fireplace panelings, fine old pine doors, and interesting wrought iron. Once she showed up with a complete circular staircase she had bid on at $50. So for years afterwards the Palmer barn was graced with a spiral stairway to nowhere.[7]

Ordinarily the general was quite content to let his good wife indulge her fancy, so long as she left him alone in his study. But there came a day when even this sacred precinct attracted her attention. It was the last room in the house that remained unimproved. Getting her husband's consent for the construction of some new book shelves was not too difficult, and he scarcely noticed the insertion of one or two comfortable chairs. Not until she came home from an auction bearing a splendid Governor Winthrop desk did the general finally realize that he was confronted with a full-scale invasion. After nearly fifty years of married life, she still did not understand that the only way he could write was seated in a stiff-backed chair at a rickety old card table!

The prudence of years dictated retreat. So while Mrs. Palmer set about converting his upstairs room into an elegant formal study, he fixed up a workroom in an old farm shed across the road, several rods from the house. Here he could spill cigar ashes to his heart's content and leave his papers in convenient disarray without the slightest danger of admonishment. And here, in the intervals when he was not gardening or chopping wood, he enjoyed many happy hours writing his memoirs.[8]

The only interruptions that the general actually welcomed were the visits of his two grandsons, Norman and John Chandler, now teenagers. Even the younger of the two boys towered over him; at fifteen he stood nearly six feet. The boys still enjoyed hikes on the mountains with their grandfather, but their big summer project was rebuilding a vintage Model T they had purchased from a junk dealer. The old soldier knew next to nothing about automobiles, but he was consulted at every step. And when funds for replacement parts ran short, he developed a seemingly insatiable appetite for the wild berries the boys could pick on the hillsides for his table, at twenty-five cents a basket.[9]

Rather suddenly it dawned upon the fond grandfather that the boys were growing up. Dared he hope that one or the other would go to West Point? The boys' father was a Harvard man, and growing up in Cambridge with a wide circle of faculty friends, there was every indication that they would drift into Harvard as a matter of course. If he expected any success at all in winning converts, he would have to excite their enthusiasm and then let nature take its course.

What could be more appropriate than a series of historical tours? The boys had always enjoyed expeditions to such local places as Lexington and Concord; why not go further afield to Fort Ticonderoga or to Gettysburg? Of course there was a trip to West Point, with all its traditional panoply and martial display. This contributed to the desired effect, although it took heroic restraint for the zealous grandfather not to overplay his hand.[10]

At least one of the historical tours turned out to offer somewhat more excitement than the general had bargained for. During the school holiday in the spring of 1939 he took the boys to pay a long-deferred call on General Pershing in Washington. If he could once get the old warrior reminiscing, the result was certain to be most beneficial. Just as he had anticipated, his former chief received them cordially and was chatting with the boys in most satisfactory fashion, when a telephone call interrupted them.

"The White House is calling," a secretary announced. At this, the visitors politely started to withdraw. But the General of the Armies put his hand over the phone and barked an order to his longtime subordinate: "Relax, Palmer, and sit down," before continuing, "Yes, Mr. President...." When he finally put the phone down, he turned to the youngsters and asked, "Can you boys keep a state secret—at least until next week? The President has just decided to appoint your 'uncle,' George Marshall, Chief of Staff."[11]

The news came as a total surprise to Palmer, underscoring how completely out of touch he was in his retirement. But any pangs this reflection may have cost were immediately overwhelmed by his delight in learning that his old commander was apparently still influential enough to help make a Chief of Staff. And that his close friend George Marshall should be the new appointee was a prospect too promising for words. Immediately at hand, however, was the education of grandsons.

A visit to Plattsburg, New York, during the army summer maneuvers proved to be one of the more effective features in the general's campaign of persuasion. When the visitors arrived at the field headquarters, they paid a call on the commanding officer, Lt. Gen. Hugh Drum, Palmer's colleague and friend of many years, to whom the fond grandfather introduced the boys as his aides, "Sergeant" Norry and "Corporal" John. General Drum rose to the occasion immediately. Assigning the visitors a "mission of inspection," he equipped their automobile with the one-star pennon of a brigadier, which gave them ready access to the entire maneuver area. Palmer was immensely pleased and proud. Under the red pennon he was able to visit some of the regiments that had at one time been part of his brigade in the AEF.[12]

Although the maneuver was billed as the largest ever held in peacetime, it was immediately evident to a professional eye that the units engaged were woefully below authorized strength. Virtually none of them had a full complement of equipment. Even more disturbing, the troops involved in the exercise were still little more than a collection of separate units—companies, battalions, and regiments—all too evidently they were not yet welded into smoothly functioning brigades and divisions, let alone into corps or into an army. Their staffs were far below strength and manifestly inexperienced. With the headlines daily screaming new disasters in Europe, this evidence of military unreadiness accentuated the sense of failure that had plagued Palmer for so many years.[13]

Now that the nation's hour of peril was at hand, the machinery of defense was still agonizingly unprepared. True, the country was in better posture than in 1917, and he could take some personal satisfaction from having contributed to this. But there was scant comfort in observing how much remained to be done. If only he were twenty years younger! With George Marshall as Chief of Staff, surely the time was never more propitious. But the general's work was behind him. If he hoped for future success, he had better concentrate on making worthy soldiers of his grandsons.

The more the old general reflected on his hopes, the more he realized he had neglected their indoctrination. In talking with the youngsters he began to sense how little they appreciated his side of the family heritage. He wanted them to know something of their maternal ancestry; most of all, he wanted them to feel just what it meant to be a Midwesterner, a son of Illinois and the Lincoln country. He wanted them to understand, as his brother Dr. George Palmer put it, just how "rooted and re-rooted in the rich soil of Illinois" it was possible to become. "Hot as the summers may be and cold as the winters," his brother had written, " . . . the place is home to me and I could not be tempted to leave it even for the climate of Hawaii or the wealth of a Morgan."[14]

But the grandsons were growing up to be thoroughgoing New Englanders. Through their father, Norman Bemis Chandler, they were related to the two Bemis boys of Watertown, Massachusetts, who had left their plowing and rushed to Concord as Minutemen in 1775. On their way the Bemis brothers had armed themselves with muskets and the accoutrements of two British troopers killed in the running fight along the highroad from Lexington. Those muskets were still to be seen in the local historical society museum, where they made the past very much alive for two awed and impressionable youngsters and reinforced Grandmother Chandler's tireless reminders that they were the heirs of heros.

Turning the problem over in his mind for some weeks, the old gentleman finally decided to conduct the boys on a historic pilgrimage tracing the westward migration of their Palmer forebears. They would visit the places where their ancestors had settled in successive stages, from their first landing at Accomac in Virginia during the seventeenth century to their own grandfather's boyhood home in Carlinville, Illinois.[15]

Something of the general's excitement over the undertaking must have reached his brother George, for the doctor responded with enthusiasm.

> As a guide you would have a bully time of it, and it would be worth a year of schooling to the boys and wouldn't do any harm to my onliest niece. I am a little afraid that, when the time comes for it, if there has been no financial return from your writing, you will be inclined to defer it. I am consequently enclosing a check for two hundred dollars as my part of the enterprise. If you are on the square in the matter, keep the check and put it away in your sock ear-marked for the trip. If you are not on the square, send it back to me. If you keep the check and don't make the trip—you will be guilty of larceny as bailee and I shall turn the matter over to J. Edgar Hoover.[16]

Doctor Palmer's generous check was precisely what was needed to make the expedition a reality. The general began to schedule an itinerary, allowing at least one full day for each generation of the family in its westering. For each of these removes he assembled all the historical evidence he could; the trip would mean far more if he could actually people the places visited by telling stories of their ancestors' lives, loves, and adventures.

One of the byproducts was the closer relationship it brought the general and his brother George. The doctor was just then engaged in completing a biography, *Conscientious Turncoat*, of their famous grandfather, the general's namesake, John McAuley Palmer. But their exchange of letters yielded far more than such things as notes on the ancestral journey through the Cumberland Gap; it helped tighten the bonds of affection that had long existed between the two men, an affection evident in this contrite note from the doctor. "It is a hell of a brother who forgets the day that his big brother passes over the equator of three score years and ten; but I feel that in the end it is better to admit it than to have sent you a note written with a dull pencil saying that . . . I had been suffering from cholera morbus."[17]

As the scheduled time of departure approached, the war in Europe, the stalemate, or sitzkrieg, of many months past, turned into a horrifying blitzkrieg. After an overnight invasion of Norway, on 10 May 1940 the German forces began the massive assault that was to end with the fall of France. While still stunned by the awful news, the general received a long-distance phone call from Grenville Clark. The old crowd in the Military Training Camps Association was planning a big meeting in New York; would he come? There was important work afoot for national defense, and his services would be needed.

The general's immediate reaction was to decline. He was old and tired and sick. He had fought his battles and lost—at least most of them. But, as an able lawyer, Clark knew how to apply just the right pressure. The general's presence was required to do a job no one else could do. There would be plenty of famous names and high-ranking officers at the meeting, but none of them could speak about citizen soldiers with such personal knowledge and authority as John M. Palmer. He must come and help launch a great national movement to secure the passage of legislation calling for a peacetime draft. Such a law, Clark reminded him, would put teeth into the Defense Act of 1920, just as he had always wished to do.[18]

As Clark had intended, the reference to the Defense Act did the trick. To be sure there was no backsliding, Clark took care of all the details. He arranged to have his own chauffeur meet the general at the train and drive him to the Clark family home on Long Island, from which he himself would escort his visitor to the gathering in the city. Palmer greatly appreciated these solicitous attentions from his friend, but it is doubtful whether he yet realized exactly what role Clark expected him to play.[19]

The whole project had begun on 8 May 1940, when ten friends had gathered at the Harvard Club in New York to commemorate the twenty-fifth anniversary of the Plattsburg Movement. Among those present were the members of the executive committee of the Military Training Camps Association (MTCA) in the Second Corps Area. These included Julius Ochs Adler, colonel of the Seventy-seventh Regiment of the N.Y. National Guard and general manager of the *New York Times*; Philip A. Carroll, a New York lawyer of the famous Maryland family; Dr. A. L. Boyce, chairman of the local MTCA organization; Grenville Clark; Arthur F. Cosby, who had done yeoman service with the MTCA in helping to secure the passage of the Defense Act of 1920; J. Lloyd Derby, son-in-law of Theodore Roosevelt; Langdon P. Marvin, a one-time law partner of Franklin D. Roosevelt; Alfred Roelker, the current secretary of the MTCA; along with William D. Stiger and James D. Williams, both lawyers long interested in the work of the association.

At Clark's instigation the group decided that once again the time had come to act in the national interest, as its members had a quarter-century earlier. Never had the need for trained men in the armed forces been more acute, yet both the administration and Congress seemed paralyzed. In an election year neither wanted to take the initiative in calling for a peacetime draft. So the ten friends decided to act; what they had done once they could do again. They would launch a great national movement to arouse public opinion. They would seek legislation fulfilling the traditions of their association: "universal military training in peace and universal service in war." With this in mind they had issued their call for a ceremonial dinner at the Harvard Club in New York City. A hundred distinguished citizens were to begin their campaign, with a burst of publicity that would make headlines across the nation.

The dinner proved to be a great success. Palmer's remarks were well received, although he said nothing he had not presented a hundred times before.

> We dilate upon Washington's aversion to foreign entanglement, but we forget that he proposed to avoid entanglement by maintaining what he called a respectably defensive posture. If modern democracy had armed itself in the beginning,... could an antidemocratic blitzkrieg be raging in Europe today? It is because our forefathers rejected a few ounces of prevention that we must now buy many tons of cure.[20]

The tons of cure, of course, would involve an immediate draft. It was not, however, the resolutions the assemblage voted upon, but the distinguished roster of guests that virtually assured national attention, even without the unusual advantage the group enjoyed in having one of their own members, Julius Ochs Adler, at the *New York Times*.

Leading the list of notables was Palmer's long-time friend Henry Stimson, a cabinet officer in two previous administrations and soon to be appointed Secretary of War by President Roosevelt. Also present was Judge Robert P. Patterson of the U.S. Second Court, who was to follow Stimson to Washington as assistant secretary. Colorful personalities were numerous: Maj. Gen. John F. O'Ryan, who had commanded the 27th Division, N.Y. National Guard, in the AEF; Maj. George G. McMurtry, Congressional Medal of Honor winner in the famous Lost Battalion of 1918; and Col. William J. Donovan, another Medal of Honor winner from the famous old "Fighting 69th" Infantry, shortly to return to the national arena as head of a cloak-and-dagger organization, forerunner to the future Central Intelligence Agency. With bearers of such famous names as Archibald Roosevelt and Elihu Root, Jr., attention from the press could be counted upon. But headlines were only a part of what was needed.[21]

Grenville Clark and his friends understood from the start that their campaign for a peacetime draft of manpower would succeed only if they maintained the closest possible coordination with the War Department. This threatened to be difficult. In an election year the President was manifestly reluctant to push vigorously for a compulsory training bill, which was almost certain to arouse violent opposition. And so long as the Commander in Chief declined to urge such a measure, the Chief of Staff felt constrained to follow suit. As a consequence the army was currently relying upon a voluntary program. At the current rate of volunteering, it would require nearly a year to do no more than bring the army up to authorized strength. Clark interpreted the failure of the War Department to advocate an immediate draft as an indication of some want of conviction on the part of General Marshall. Clark believed it was imperative to establish an understanding with the Chief of Staff as soon as possible, and for this purpose General Palmer was the ideal instrument.[22]

The ceremonial dinner at the Harvard Club was scarcely over when Clark revealed to his house guest the next role he was to play, and soon afterward Palmer was on the train to Washington. But Clark was not one to sit idle. Knowing that a written message can often usefully supplement a discussion, he dashed off a four-page telegram to Palmer, addressing it for delivery at the office of the Chief of Staff. His intention was evident.

> I fear from 1917 experience that staff plans may be inadequate and too careful of supposed Congressional attitude and public opinion.... Earnestly trust this experience will not be repeated and from what you say of the character and abilities of General Marshall have great hope it will not be.[23]

Along with this mixture of flattery and admonishment to think big, so obviously intended for Marshall's eyes, Clark urged Palmer to arrange for a conference between qualified officers from the General Staff and representatives of a hastily organized National Emergency Committee drawn from the ranks of Military Training Camps Association in New York, to work out the text of a suitable bill. Marshall readily agreed to this, although he still felt unable to commit the War Department overtly until the President declared his policy.[24]

During the next few days the amateurs from the MTCA group and the officers designated by the Chief of Staff managed to agree upon the provisions of a mutually satisfactory bill. The two officers assigned to the task, Lt. Col. Victor J. O'Kelliher and Maj. Lewis B. Hershey, had for some time previously been members of a joint army-navy committee established to consider the problems of selective service and were thoroughly familiar with the issues. At the end of three days, on 28 May, they were ready with a workable text. And General Palmer, pleased at having been able to play a useful part, returned to his farm in New Hampshire thoroughly exhausted.[25]

Once back home, he began to feel his years and limitations painfully. His friends in New York wanted him to continue his active role, sharing the day-to-day work of their National Emergency Committee, but he was convinced that this would be impossible. His most useful contribution, he suggested, would be to write articles in support of the proposed legislation. Yet even this effort would have to wait. The long-anticipated day of departure for his family pilgrimage with his grandsons had finally arrived, and he was determined that nothing whatever was going to detain this important expedition.[26]

If pleasures in anticipation are often more delicious than those found in reality, the general's historic pilgrimage proved somewhat an exception, at least at first. The June weather was idyllic, and the general rose to every occasion. Jamestown settlement? With a twinkle in his eye he would show the boys where one of their Palmer ancestors had landed long before their father's kin ever set foot in New England. How he enjoyed being one up at long last on Grandmother Chandler! A visit to Washington's birthplace at Wakefield plantation set him off on a long account of the first President's military policy. Stratford, the seat of the Lees, was the point of departure for a discussion of General Lee as a tactician. And after visiting Monticello and the university, the party continued on to Bedford, Virginia, where Jefferson had fled during the Revolution to Poplar Forest, the estate of a Palmer ancestor.

For a few wonderful days the travelers were almost able to forget that their world was falling apart. Seldom seeing a newspaper and lacking a radio, for the moment at least they could ignore the relentless advance of Hitler's armies, as they relived the westward march of their forefathers. Crossing the Great Smokies they were deeply stirred, as generations before them had been, by the spring wonderland of whole ranges freshly clad in the delicate tints of mountain laurel. And beyond the hills they visited Robertson College, founded by an ancestor in Harrodsburg, Kentucky. From there, with many stops and digressions to points of interest or family association, they followed the Lincoln Trail to Illinois, until at last they reached the general's boyhood haunts in and around Springfield.

Somehow the final homecoming seemed a little flat. Brother George was his usual good-humored self, and all the other relatives were hospitable to a fault. Nevertheless, this part of the adventure wasn't turning out quite as the general had expected. It had been one thing to re-create the ancestral trek westward; that was history. But his own boyhood—that was something else again. Recalling, with nostalgia, fishing for "channel cat" during his boyhood, he had expounded at length on the delights to be expected from this freshly caught delicacy. For an expert fly fisherman who had worked some of the best trout streams in all of North America, however, baiting a hook for bottom fish in the muddy creek proved dull sport indeed. And at supper that night, while his grandsons managed to down the portions of fish set before them, both firmly declined a second helping.[27]

Every morning following the party's arrival in Illinois, Clark had been calling by long-distance telephone to confer on the latest developments. Clark and his friends on the self-appointed National Emergency Committee had already raised nearly $50,000 in contributions and were projecting a budget of more than $250,000 to finance an elaborate press campaign. They had secured the services of Perley Boone, a highly successful public relations man with the New York World's Fair, who was already at work recruiting a staff. But Clark's main purpose was to secure Palmer's help.[28]

After days of delicate negotiation, the committee was finally ready to introduce a bill in Congress. Clark wanted to secure the approval of General Pershing. Since the General of the Armies had declared he wished to have Palmer's judgment "above all others" before making up his mind on the measure, it was imperative to act immediately.[29]

Just as if he were once again Pershing's devoted staff officer, Palmer sat down to compose a carefully worded telegram urging endorsement of the proposed bill. The argument he used echoed, perhaps unwittingly, the tactics "Grenny" Clark had employed to secure his own participation. The National Defense Act as it was originally submitted to Congress, he reminded Pershing, was designed to "perpetuate the Army that you commanded in France as an ever-living National institution" by including provisions for universal training. Congress had deleted this feature from the act of 1920, but the bill now under consideration, he explained, would help remedy that defect. Soon afterward Clark wired back, "Great work, wonderful" and he assured his elderly friend that his offer to testify at the expected congressional committee hearings on the proposed bill would be of "utmost importance."[30]

Here was a call to duty too pressing to delay. After nearly two weeks with the boys, Palmer was feeling younger than he had for years. Although Clark assured him his testimony on Capital Hill would not be required immediately, the general packed his grandsons off to finish the journey on their own, while he flew back East to prepare for the coming action.

47 The Draft Act of 1940

Palmer's decision to take an airplane to Washington in June 1940 was in many ways symbolic. If he was old in years, he was once again young in spirit. He was certain the army was on the verge of repeating the folly of previous mobilizations.

From news reports he had learned that a scheme was afoot to expand the Regular Army to a total strength of 750,000. Were the planners going to ignore history and use up the pitifully limited supply of trained officers in forming units for the Regular Army, leaving none for the more important task of training the great hordes of citizen soldiers? Were they forgetting the endless complications they would create with a postwar hump of regular officers? Admittedly, a vast expansion of the Regular forces would open up many opportunities for promotion; but was this a sufficient reason for abandoning the carefully wrought concepts of mobilization implicit in the Defense Act of 1920?

Even before his departure the general wrote ahead to question the proposed line of action. Characteristically, his letter was a model of humility. In the first place, he addressed it to Maj. Lewis B. Hershey rather than to his friend George Marshall "because I know that he is under tremendous pressure." Moreover, while indicating his opposition to an expansion of the Regular Army, he carefully qualified his stand as an opinion "subject to further enlightenment," since he was out of touch and would welcome coaching on current thinking.[1]

Was this a needless effacement, throwing away the trump card of ready access to the Chief of Staff? Or was it a shrewd maneuver to win the cooperation of the junior officers with whom he would have to work? After all, whatever his relations with Marshall, Palmer was not an officer on active duty; he was an elderly retired gentleman volunteering his services to help

Grenville Clark's hastily formed National Emergency Committee secure passage of a draft act.

Clark and his friends had already scored two important successes. The first of these was in securing sponsors on Capitol Hill for their committee's draft measure. Many of those favoring a draft regarded the bill as a hot potato in an election year. Republican Rep. James W. Wadsworth, now a member of the House of Representatives, agreed to introduce the bill, but a senatorial backer had been harder to find. Most of those approached seemed to agree with floor leader James F. Byrnes that compulsory training in peacetime didn't stand "a Chinaman's chance" of passing. Finally a lame-duck Democrat, Sen. Edward R. Burke of Nebraska, joined his colleague in the House, introducing the measure soon to be known as the Burke-Wadsworth bill.[2]

The very next day the members of the National Emergency Committee saw their second major endeavor crowned with success when President Roosevelt appointed Henry L. Stimson as Secretary of War. The President had been toying with the notion of giving a nonpartisan cast to his handling of national defense by bringing distinguished Republicans into his cabinet. He had already turned to Chicago publisher Frank Knox as Secretary of the Navy when Clark, through the good offices of Justice Felix Frankfurter, thrust forward Stimson as a candidate for the War Department post. Stimson, as an eminent Republican, suited the President's political needs almost perfectly. But for Clark and his groups it was Stimson's positive stand on compulsory military training that made his appointment so imperative. With an aggressive proponent of an immediate draft in control, full cooperation could be assured from the War Department.[3]

Little more than a month had passed since the group of private citizens had met at the Harvard Club in New York and resolved to save the nation by drafting an army. Their initiative had helped to overcome election-year paralysis, but it was too soon to celebrate. Serious opposition was to be expected from several directions, but the first note of dissent came from inside their own ranks.

The inside critic was Tompkins McIlvaine, Palmer's long-time friend and fellow collaborator in the Military Training Camps Association. After reading the Burke-Wadsworth bill, McIlvaine sent out a series of memos from his law offices in New York urging immediate amendment. As he saw it, the measure was a straddle between a long-range compulsory training bill and a bill for an immediate strengthening of the armed forces of the United States to meet a current danger. In attempting to meet two objectives at once, he argued, the Burke-Wadsworth bill did neither adequately.

There was considerable merit in McIlvaine's objections. The eight months of training prescribed by the bill would not be adequate, especially if the army expected to secure experience in maneuvers with larger formations such as divisions and corps. To permit the public to believe that eight months of training would provide genuine security, McIlvaine contended, would border on gross deception. He threatened to speak out in opposition when asked to testify before Congress. Still worse, he intimated that Elihu Root, Jr., and several others shared his feelings.[4]

Understandably enough, Palmer was annoyed at this development. Opposition from within the group favoring compulsory training was almost certain to harm the bill's chances of passing. As he wrote to Grenville Clark "I know McIlvaine of old. I acquired most of my grey hairs when I was on duty with the Senate Military Committee and he headed your association. I was always grateful when a day passed without some new amendment for the bill." Nonetheless, the criticisms McIlvaine leveled against the bill had much to be said for them. Therefore, with characteristic fair-mindedness, Palmer informed Clark, "As I have heard only one side of this controversy and have not seen the specific amendments that McIlvaine proposes, I am in no position to give any opinion on the merits." Then he telegraphed General Pershing, asking him to delay his public announcement in favor of the Burke-Wadsworth bill until the questions raised by the dissenters could be settled.[5]

In placating McIlvaine, as he and others eventually managed to do, Palmer was fulfilling the role Clark visualized for him. His tact, humor, and wide circle of friendships were important factors, but there was more to his effectiveness than personal charm and fair-mindedness. When the occasion required, he could be tough-minded even when dealing with his closest friends.

Just how hard hitting the general could be, Grenville Clark soon discovered when he criticized the Chief of Staff for his insistence upon recruiting officer candidates from the enlisted ranks of the army. Clark was pushing Stimson to establish a scheme of Plattsburg-style camps similar to those organized before World War I. Convinced that this alternative would recruit the cream of the nation's young business and professional men, without the delays of Selective Service or enlistment in the ranks, he regarded Marshall as "stubborn as a mule" for resisting his proposal. Marshall finally threatened to resign unless Secretary Stimson supported the stand officially promulgated by the War Department. Palmer's letter of admonishment to Clark is worth quoting at length because it reveals his character no less than the qualities of his mind.

In my opinion you are wrong in your controversy with General Marshall in this matter. I would not be a true friend to you or to the cause we both serve if I did not tell you this frankly and give you my reasons for thinking as I do.

The issue far transcends the merits of your September camp proposal. General Marshall is *responsible* to the Secretary of War, to the President, and to the country in a great military crisis while you are entirely free from that burden of responsibility. His position as Chief of Staff under Elihu Root's theory and under the law that he caused to be enacted, is tenable only so long as he enjoys the *full* and *complete* confidence of the Secretary. If I were in his position and the Secretary should take his advice from some outside source to the extent of deranging a carefully digested program that I had prepared for him, after prolonged study by my subordinates, I would tender my resignation—not from personal pique but because it would be contrary to the spirit of the General Staff law for me to continue to bear the burden of responsibility in such circumstances. Nor would I retain the respect and confidence of my subordinates if they felt that a project prepared by them and approved by me could be upset under the pressure of an outside influence—no matter how worthy the purport of that influence might be.

I am sure that you too would resign in such a situation. Or, suppose that you were my retained counsel in some important litigation and I should disregard your advice in some essential particular and take the contrary advice of some other person in that particular, would you not throw up your brief?

When you were in the Adjutant General's office in 1917, you ruptured the inhibitions of the hidebound War Department of that day and through your defiance of fuddy-duddy superiors you accomplished a great reform and performed a great public service. This naturally made you impatient of red-tape and narrow routine. But, in spite of my repeated assurances, you refuse to believe that the War Department of 1940 is entirely different from the War Department of 1917.

George Marshall is the first Chief of Staff who measures up to the full standard that Elihu Root had in mind when he conceived that the full efficiency of the General Staff must wait upon a long period of strictly professional education. He is not a mere talented and accomplished four-flusher such as Wood and his fellows were twenty-odd years ago. He is an educated and trained member of the General Staff profession in the same sense that you are an educated and trained member of the legal profession. He stands at the very head of his profession just as you stand at the head of yours.

After a year as deputy chief of staff and a year as Chief of Staff he is fully acquainted with all the details of the European situation and of the military problem that arises from it. In my opinion, he is by far the ablest officer in the army and after many years of intimate acquaintance with him, I know that his integrity and his disinterestedness are equal to his high abilities.

I am not familiar with all the details of your September camp proposal, but if Marshall opposes it, it is not from timidity or lack of imagination but because he believes that the War Department's limited resources can be used to better advantage in the present crisis—especially if our Selective Service bill passes. And I must confess that on the relative merits of his program and yours, the burden of proof is against you. He not only bears the burden of responsibility for the whole military program but his knowledge of the whole military situation is necessarily broader than yours.

When I first had news of Stimson's appointment my enthusiasm was unbounded. I immediately pictured to myself a great triumvirate—composed of three men who have my unbounded admiration, respect and affection—a great Secretary of War, aided by a great Chief of Staff and both supported by a great, dynamic and disinterested leader and organizer of public opinion. This is why I deplore the rift between you and Marshall. In comparison with this issue, I don't give a damn for the September camps one way or the other—that is a mere trifle.

If there is a rift, in my opinion, it is your fault. Imagine Marshall's relief when Stimson was appointed. After two years of uncertainty, indecision and political hypocrisy, he would now serve under a great statesman with previous experience in the State and War Departments. But before he can acquaint his new chief with the War Department program, he finds that he is already more or less committed to a proposal that tends to disrupt portions of a carefully contrived general plan.

As I understand it, you want to provide some extra training for mature reserve officers. That is a worthy project and one which Marshall would probably approve and be able to fit in with his plans to bring the regular army and the National Guard to full strength. But when you insist upon a particular method of accomplishing that object and propose to utilize resources and facilities that were to be used otherwise in a carefully prepared and more comprehensive plan, your effort must necessarily be disturbing—especially at a time when so much depends upon the fullest harmony and understanding between a new Secretary of War and his Chief of Staff.[6]

Resolving internal disagreements was only a small part of Palmer's effort. Somewhat more visible was his role in dealing with opposition in the press. One of the most serious attacks on the proposed measure came from the widely-read military commentator George Fielding Eliot, whose *New York Herald Tribune* column was syndicated in some forty newspapers. Eliot was also a regular contributor to *Life Magazine* and presented a nightly radio program for the Columbia Broadcasting System.

The Burke-Wadsworth bill, Eliot claimed, gave an illusion of strength that could lull the public into a false sense of security. A half-trained eight-month militia simply could not stand up to the test of modern war waged

by well-trained professionals. Far better for Congress to build up the Regular Army to its authorized strength by encouraging volunteers with greater
pay and allowances; then and only then might compulsion be used, to
accumulate a reserve force of draftees called up for not less than two
years.[7]

Here was a full-fledged attack on the very principles upon which the
Burke-Wadsworth bill was drawn. Moreover, Eliot's proposal seemed to call
for a major reorganization of the army in the midst of a national emergency,
the contingency Palmer had struggled so hard to avoid under the terms of the
Defense Act of 1920. What is more, the *Tribune* carried an editorial approving
Eliot's notions in principle.[8]

Julius Adler at the *Times* immediately sensed the difficulties that Eliot's
article might create, especially if the line taken by the *Tribune's* Republican
editors developed into a party issue during the presidential campaign. He
therefore urged Palmer to reply in a letter to the editors of the *Tribune*. This
the general did. The peacetime army, he argued, should be capable of orderly
expansion in time of emergency. Eliot's scheme would repeat the mistake
made at the outbreak of the Civil War, when an ill-considered expansion of
the Regular Army absorbed virtually all the professional officers and left few
to train the masses of citizen soldiers, upon whom the brunt of the fighting
eventually fell.[9]

Eliot's politically vulnerable suggestion that the National Guard should be
virtually reduced to a home guard, the general rejected in short order. He
agreed that the Guard lacked adequate training, but this was to be remedied
by the Burke-Wadsworth bill. Recruits enlisting in the Guard could receive
the same federal training as other inductees before returning to their local
units. That the eight months of training was too brief he cheerfully conceded.
Perhaps the journalist would join him in offering an "Eliot-Palmer amendment" to the bill's sponsors?[10]

A few days later Eliot replied in another long letter to the *Tribune*. He
graciously acknowledged his hesitation to criticize "so distinguished an officer
and so profound a military student." Recalling Palmer's central role in
drafting the Defense Act of 1920, he conceded that this statute had been "a
tremendous step forward" in its day. But times had changed; the present called
for fewer but better trained men, armed with the latest weapons of modern
technology.[11]

The general's first reaction was to write still another letter to the *Tribune*.
But a close reading of their exchanges revealed that they were not engaging
each other's arguments squarely; what they needed was a face-to-face confrontation. In a few minutes of conversation they could almost certainly find
large areas of agreement. To publicize these would far better serve the cause of
national defense.

The general wrote a personal note to Eliot suggesting that they get acquainted. Then he went on to point out, as tactfully as he could, what he believed to be the central weakness in Eliot's proposal.

> I have been greatly impressed by your brilliant books and articles, but I hope you will permit a much older man to say that, in his opinion, their author had not given full weight to the fact that sound military institutions are organic growths and not structures. A sound national defense system is not like a tower of brick and stone that can be built de novo on the surface of the ground. It is, rather, like a living tree with roots deep in the political tradition and history of a nation. It is the province of the military statesman, not to invent something new, but to improve a living thing that already exists.[12]

That military institutions are organic, animate, with roots in the past and complex implications for the future, is a conception often overlooked by those in the upper echelons of command. Armed with large authority, they have frequently displayed little memory of their institutional past. Among lawyers and legislators it is perhaps a commonplace that "new laws, like new boots, search out men's corns," which is to say, it is often better to amend an old law that is workable, tested in the courts, and perfected by administrative procedures than to embark upon a new and untried law. But military leaders, perhaps because they dwell less often upon past administrative experience, seldom seem to deal with their component organizations upon the same assumptions as their legal bretheren.

Whether Eliot recognized the significance of Palmer's insight or merely saw an opportunity to cultivate another useful contact, he responded with enthusiasm to the general's proposal for a meeting.[13] The encounter finally took place during one of the general's trips to New York. The two men hit it off well from the start. Although Eliot remained unhappy with several features of the Burke-Wadsworth bill, following his meeting with Palmer, he professed himself better pleased with the measure. This was a limited success, but a more or less neutral critic was better than an overtly hostile one. The importance of the general's personal intervention cannot be measured, but soon afterward, when Eliot participated in a panel discussion of the Burke-Wadsworth bill over a national hookup of the Columbia Broadcasting System, his treatment of the measure was substantially constructive.[14]

The one point on which the two men never could seem to agree was the composition of a suitable ready reserve for the Regular Army. Eliot wanted a reserve organized under the army clause of the Constitution; he would draft all eligible young men for two full years of active duty, followed by eight years in a standby reserve. Palmer had wanted much the same thing twenty years earlier. His experience on Capital Hill had convinced him, however, that it was politically more prudent to use an all-volunteer National Guard as the primary reserve of the army. Over the intervening years he had acquired increasing respect for the Guard, a respect Eliot did not share.

> I think this matter of a reserve for the Regular Army is of extreme importance, and I am afraid that it has been cut out due to National Guard pressure. The National Guard, as you know, have never wanted a first class Regular Army reserve, and I think the time has come for them to abandon this selfish dog-in-the-manger attitude.[15]

Remarks in this tenor only served to remind the general that here was yet another area where his services as a mediator were still required.

Both the Senate and the House committees conducting hearings on the bill invited Palmer to appear as a witness. He was introduced by Grenville Clark as "one of the most distinguished, if not the most distinguished authority on military policy in the United States."[16] As an experienced witness, Palmer knew how to maximize his effectiveness. He kept his testimony brief and resorted to homespun metaphors. Asking the army to plan for national defense on the uncertainties of volunteer enlistments, he suggested, was akin to asking an engineer to plan a bridge without knowing the quantity of steel available to him. He knew that congressional thinking is never far removed from the question of appropriations, so he adroitly linked the scheme of defense he advocated to budgetary economy by observing that most of the national debt was directly attributable to the country's unpreparedness in earlier crises.[17]

Many other witnesses, among them Clark and Marshall, spoke with telling effect in favor of the bill. Nonetheless, Palmer's presence among those sponsoring it helped in winning support. This became evident when Maj. Gen. Milton A. Reckord of the 29th Division, National Guard, took the stand.[18]

As a former president of the National Guard Association and as chairman of the association's legislative committee, General Reckord represented a formidable threat. Were he to oppose the Burke-Wadsworth bill, it was almost certain that most if not all of the elaborate machinery of the National Guard would be unlimbered in opposition also. And he stated his reservation unequivocally. While professing to be "thoroughly in accord with the principles" upon which the bill had been built, he objected pointedly to the failure of the text to clarify the role of the Guard. "Frankly, gentlemen, the bill will have to be amended in a number of instances before I would wish to give it my support and before, in my opinion, the National Guard as an institution would support it."[19]

What Reckord feared, of course, was just what George Fielding Eliot and others had been advocating. He did not want the Guard to lose its favored position within the framework of the Defense Act as the ready reserve of the Regular Army. Yet the proposed legislation gave no assurance on this point. "Except for the fact that we know the National Guard has friends in the group...responsible for this piece of legislation,...we might almost think the National Guard was being relegated to the status of a home guard."[20]

That General Reckord had not been invited to the initial discussions on the measure in May and June was a tactical error. The blunder clearly suggests the character of Palmer's participation in the whole affair; he was a willing worker, but the initiative was not his. As it turned out, however, Reckord's confidence in the friends of the Guard among the bill's sponsors was not entirely misplaced.

Palmer immediately entered into negotiations to get the bill amended to reassure the guardsmen. As an entirely voluntary force the Guard had much to commend it in contrast with a ready reserve of draftees.[21]

The negotiations with General Reckord were facilitated by the President's decision to call up the Guard for a year of active duty training as soon as he could secure authority from Congress. This decision, clearly reflecting the advice given by the Secretary of War and the Chief of Staff, seemed to offer ample assurance that the Guard would be used as a first-line reserve. But Reckord wanted statutory language to insure the Guard "its rightful place immediately behind the Regular Army," at some future time when the interpretation of the law would no longer rest with such friends as Stimson and Marshall. Palmer relayed Reckord's fears to his friends in the group pushing the Burke-Wadsworth bill. "He insists that there are some persons in and out of the army who still adhere to the old doctrine of an expansible standing army as opposed to the citizen army established by the National Defense Act."[22]

The obvious solution, Palmer suggested, was to include in the text of the bill a declaration of policy on the role of the National Guard. In the ensuing maneuvering Palmer served as mediator between General Reckord and the bill's sponsors, including not only Senator Burke and Congressman Wadsworth, but the members of Clark's group as well. Eventually both the Senate and the House committee gave the Guard something very close to an ironclad guarantee.

> It is essential that the strength and organization of the National Guard as an integral part of this nation be at all times maintained and assured. To this end it is the intent of Congress that whenever the Congress shall determine that troops are needed for the national security in excess of the Regular Army and those in active-training and service under [Selective Service], the National Guard...shall be ordered to active field service and continue therein so long as such emergency exists.[23]

Although Palmer was instrumental in securing the statutory assurances, he was no blind partisan of the National Guard. The President's decision to call up the Guard for a year of active duty training he regarded as a test. "If it makes good, its place in our military system will be secure in the future. If not, even its most ardent friends recognize that it must be replaced by something else." That the institution would meet the test he had little doubt. "I feel confident that it will make good, but if not, the sooner we know what it is really worth, the better it will be for the country and for the members of the Guard."[24]

The general found his role as a negotiator exciting but exhausting. Somewhat wistfully he hinted to his friends that while he was anxious to help all he could, he rather hoped it would not be necessary for him to make any more tiring trips to Washington.

There was, of course, much that could be accomplished from a remote hillside farm in New Hampshire. For the rest of the summer the general supported the Burke-Wadsworth bill at long range. When, for example, a large group of educators issued a public manifesto opposing the principle of a peacetime draft, he fired off a letter to the *New York Times* noting factual errors in their published statement. At Wadsworth's request he brought up quotations by George Washington in favor of universal training. With a reporter from the *Boston Post*, he helped prepare a full-page spread on just what a draft act would mean to the nation and the young men concerned.[25]

The general's most ambitious propaganda effort was a formal address in Bristol, New Hampshire. This was a widely advertised affair aimed particularly at the well-to-do and influential summer visitors who came to the Newfound Lake region from all over the United States. Palmer found the task a congenial one. As he told Wadsworth, "I am not much of an orator, but I have one hell of a good speech in me." The address received good coverage from the press. At best, however, an elderly retired general could scarcely expect to make more than a modest contribution to the total effort of Clark's National Emergency Committee.[26]

By mid-July the committee propaganda campaign had achieved the dream of every professional publicist: it had become front-page news. The appointment of Stimson and Knox to cabinet positions, which had been encouraged, if not entirely engineered, by the group, had helped provide the draft measure with additional publicity at a crucial time. And then by pushing the statements of General Pershing, Grenville Clark, James Conant, William Donovan, and Julius Ochs Adler, as well as those General Palmer made before the congressional hearings, the initial momentum had been carried along.

Newspaper opinions, as measured by a careful tabulation of news clippings and editorials, revealed some 87 percent in favor of a draft by the middle of July. Of the remaining 13 percent, some were in outspoken opposition, while others were more neutral. But the advocates of the bill were taking no chances;

they continued to distribute persuasive arguments where they would do the most good. Mailings went out to the editors of some 2,000 daily newspapers and 11,400 weeklies. Literature went to 595 members of Congress, 3,500 trade papers, 5,500 legion posts, 8,500 state committeemen and legislators, 2,000 chambers of commerce, 1,695 college presidents, 1,500 Rotary Clubs, 850 radio stations, and many others. In all, more than 52,000 mailings went out.[27]

The line of reasoning adopted in the propaganda by the National Emergency Committee affords an instructive contrast to the appeal made by General Palmer. His arguments tended to be historical. A peacetime draft was thoroughly acceptable because it dated back to George Washington. It would provide an orderly and equitable system for making manpower available to the armed forces. But Palmer never seemed to realize that by no means all of his audience shared his belief in the relevance of history or the desirability of an army based on citizen soldiers.

The committee propagandists took an entirely different line. They stuck to current facts and naked fear. They listed the pitifully inadequate resources of the armed forces in men, guns, tanks, and the like and garnished their reports with observations from recent headlines. One release capitalized on the tragedy of Poland by reporting a simple fact: "The Polish Army was much better equipped for mechanized warfare than is the U.S. Army."[28]

Palmer's share in the activities of Clark's committee reflected the effort one would expect in any attempt to ram through an important piece of national legislation. At the most obvious level, that of publicizing the issue for the voters at large, Palmer's efforts were probably least effective. More significant was his role in helping to define the issue. Because he had devoted years of his life to thinking about the problems of securing military manpower, he was able to provide the friends of a draft with counsel precisely when it was needed. And it was just as important to influence friends as to convert opponents. Public opinion was moving rapidly toward acceptance of massive and drastic steps for national defense; the real problem was to determine which steps to take, and to win acceptance for them. Here the general's clearly thought out conceptions, his skills as a negotiator, and his wide circle of friends made him extraordinarily useful.

As the summer of 1940 wore on, it became increasingly apparent that some sort of draft bill was almost certain to pass. The terrifying successes of Hitler's *blitzkrieg* in Europe continued to produce converts throughout a badly frightened nation. But Clark and his committee pursued their labors relentlessly. Fearing crippling last-minute amendments, they went on buttonholing congressmen and pushing their campaign throughout the country. The general made two brief trips to New York and Washington but largely confined himself to writing and to local speaking engagements.

To the immense satisfaction of all those who had worked so hard for it, a slightly amended but still thoroughly acceptable bill passed with the support of generous majorities in both houses. President Roosevelt signed the measure on 16 September 1940 and on the same day issued a proclamation calling for a massive registration of all males in the eligible age groups.[29]

For Palmer the occasion was one of infinite relief and no little pleasure. If he and his friends could not claim full credit for the new law, it was not unreasonable for them to assume that because of their efforts the draft had come sooner than it would have otherwise. Secretary Stimson was emphatic on this point when writing his thanks to Clark.

> If it had not been for you no such bill would have been enacted at this time. Of this I am certain. . . . The officers in the Department around me from General Marshall down agree that none of them expected that the passage of such a bill would be possible, and if it hadn't been for the efforts of you and your associates, they would have been right.[30]

No matter whose the credit, the nation had saved time by getting a selective service system in operation before war broke out. And time, in the desperate summer of 1940, was exceedingly precious. Even a single month of delay might spell the difference between security and disaster.

If Clark and his friends are to merit praise for their accomplishment, it may be useful to ask why they acted as they did. They were not a partisan group, although many of them happened to be Republicans. And while some of them were well-to-do, it could scarcely be claimed that they were frightened conservatives rushing to pledge other men's lives for their protection. Virtually all of them had risked their own lives when they had volunteered for military service in World War I, and their sons were doing the same in the current emergency. The sincerity of their recent effort was in some measure attested when they contributed from their own pockets a large share of the $90,000 raised to finance the propaganda drive sponsored by the National Emergency Committee, and by the days and even weeks of valuable time that so many of them gave to the cause.[31]

Although men's motives are seldom if ever knowable, the evidence suggests that Clark and his associates were lingering survivors of the Progressive tradition. They were gentlemen-amateurs who accepted the obligation to play a disinterested, if highly personal, role in the public life of the nation, something they regarded as far too important to be left to professional politicians and self-serving pressure groups.

To celebrate their triumph, McIlvaine arranged a testimonial dinner in honor of Clark, for his initiative and his leadership. Although Palmer was reluctant to make the long train ride, he simply could not decline. As it turned out, McIlvaine did himself proud in providing what the general later described as a "symphony of wines" to enhance the tribute. From the apértif, Amontillado 1865, they proceeded through an intriguing assortment of vintages, to Madeira 1797 and Cognac 1876 with the dessert and coffee.

There was no need for the heavy-handed and fulsome speeches to the guest of honor; the host had put it all quite simply in a single quotation on the menu. It read:

> To know him is to love him
> To name him is to praise.[32]

So instead of the conventional offering of laudatory rhetoric, Palmer led the way in a succession of hilarious anecdotes, which kept the company in such continuous laughter he nearly missed his train for home at one o'clock in the morning.

In celebrating Clark's leadership, the members of his committee were not unmindful of the supporting role played by Palmer. To express their regard, they sent him a check for $500 as a token of appreciation for "invaluable counsel and aid." The sum, Clark hastily assured him, was not intended as a measure of his worth but merely as a demonstration.[33] No less than other men, the general welcomed the approval of his friends and colleagues, but his pleasure did not keep him from seeing that the job was far from done.

As Palmer had reason to know from painful experience, putting a statute on the books did not mean the cause was won. On the very day the draft bill successfully emerged from the congressional hopper, he had written Grenny Clark of the work that yet remained. "We must build military strength into the democratic state without creating an exclusive samurai caste. We must have military power without militarism."[34] A draft concocted to meet an onrushing emergency was no substitute for more permanent legislation giving the nation a military establishment compatible with a democracy. This, Palmer indicated, was one of the pressing issues to which the Military Training Camps Association should now turn. For his part he would write a book; he would convert his memoirs into a living brief for an enduring military policy.

48   America in Arms

The general's decision to recast his memoirs into propaganda for a permanent scheme of universal military training was not a sudden inspiration. When he had first undertaken to write his memoirs, he had been thoroughly discouraged by the failure of his previous literary efforts to win converts to the military policy he advocated. He had, albeit reluctantly, accepted the advice of his editors that the public was far less interested in defense legislation than in colorful narrative about West Point and "the old army,"[1] so he had turned out a number of trial chapters and sent them off to the Yale Press and to several of his friends for criticism. Their replies had been most encouraging—"delightful; when can we expect more?" "Splendid anecdotes." "The pervading sense of humor is just right." "You are on the right track."[2]

What he wanted to do now was to weave "a serious public motif into a story of general human interest," using his own life as the narrative vehicle. When he discussed this idea with his friends at the Yale University Press, they came up with a counterproposal. Why not write a short book on the history of volunteering and conscription in the United States? Over the long haul, anecdotal recollections would almost certainly sell better than a serious work on defense policy, but at the moment the prospects were unusually good for a more serious work on conscription. By encouraging him to write two separate volumes, they could let Palmer eat his cake and have it too.[3]

Whatever their motives, the Yale editors finally persuaded the general to drop his memoirs for a few months in order to turn out a tract for the times. They invited him to discuss the project with Prof. Leonard W. Labaree, one of the highly respected historians on the Yale faculty. Palmer agreed, observing that Labaree might find his *Washington, Lincoln, Wilson; Three War Statesmen*, a useful point of departure.[4] But the Yale University library contained no copy of his book. Whether this was a measure of its insignificance or of the low esteem in which the scholarly world then held military studies, he never decided. The best he could do was to lend the professor his sole remaining personal copy.

After considerable reflection, Labaree urged the general to abandon his propagandistic approach. Instead of ringing the changes on what might have been with a "well regulated militia" such as Washington favored, Labaree suggested that the new book ask: What has been our national experience in organizing manpower for military purposes? From such a body of experience one might then offer informed insights on how best to provide "the most economical, effective, and democratic arrangements for the future."

For the professor the answers to these major questions of national policy were by no means as self-evident as they appeared to the general. Would universal military training in peace really preserve democratic institutions? Would the existence of a large trained force, either under arms or in a civilian reserve, become "a temptation to dictatorial or fascist-minded political leaders?" Would they, too, raid the treasury, as the organized veterans in the Grand Army of the Republic and American Legion had done? With these and other similarly probing queries, Labaree sought to expand the range and depth of the general's approach to compulsory military training.[5]

Labaree's ideas, provocative though they were, held little appeal for Palmer. What he had in mind was a condensation of his earlier work.

> The earlier book [Washington, Lincoln, Wilson] was an unsuccessful attempt to popularize our military problem at a time of complete public indifference and lethargy. The new book will be addressed to a thoroughly aroused public—a public sufficiently aroused to demand and secure legislation for conscription in time of peace—in spite of the reluctance of most Congressmen and Senators to handle any such political dynamite while they were candidates for re-election. When I published the earlier book in 1930, no sane man could have predicted that such a revolution could occur ten years later. The public of 1930 didn't give a damn about our military problem. The public of 1940 is interested and wants to know all about it. It also wants to know how America can arm adequately and still remain a democracy—without militarism and without national bankruptcy. In my opinion this public wants a concise and popular statement of the philosophy of military institutions appropriate for the modern democratic state. And this is what I want to write for them.[6]

There were no doubts in the general's mind. As he wrote to George Marshall when arranging for access to the latest developments in army organization, "the book, as I conceive it, will lay down the true philosophy of military institutions in a modern democratic state."[7]

This new mood of self-assurance was in marked contrast to his earlier discouragement. Now, belatedly, the tide seemed to be running strongly in his direction. He could perform an important public service with his pen, and in so doing there was even an off chance of reaping a financial return. Having borrowed against his insurance to buy his country home, he felt, as he explained to Grenville Clark, a gnawing obligation to seize this last opportunity "to earn Maude a nest egg." But by far his most powerful goad to action was the opportunity to fulfill the dream of his life: to help secure legislation creating a sound and enduring military establishment along democratic lines.[8]

He would write a short popular study of the nation's military institutions. He would explain how President Washington had proposed an ideal system of defense. He would explain how the failure to adopt this proposal had cost dearly of blood and treasure in one war after another until the people of the United States had belatedly adopted Washington's organization in the Defense Act of 1920 and finally, in 1940, accepted the principle of compulsory military training in peacetime. All that remained was to wage a campaign to wrap all these elements in a single comprehensive and permanent statute. As Palmer explained it to his brother, "I expect to lay down the principles underlying the campaign in the book that I am writing."[9]

The general was determined to let nothing whatever delay him. To a long series of letters from Tompkins McIlvaine filled with advice for Secretary Stimson, he replied, "It seems to me that we should concentrate on big things and that we should not waste energy on interference with the War Department in its solution of current problems." Looking back he recalled the "big things" that had been accomplished by the Military Training Camps Association in the previous quarter century. It had helped develop an intelligent public opinion on preparedness before World War I and had then helped mobilize the vote for the Draft Act of 1917. It had helped secure a nonpolitical means for recruiting officers. It had helped in obtaining the Defense Act of 1920 and more recently the new Draft Act of 1940. The proper role of the association, he believed, was to confine itself to the major problems of policy. Taking his own advice, he shut himself up in his study for an intensive effort to write just such a statement.[10]

The general completed his manuscript in three months. Little or no fresh research had been required, but the product was no pastepot patchwork. Because he was writing to convince, and because he was writing from conviction, he had poured into the task every ounce of artistic talent he possessed.

The resulting manuscript proved so felicitous that the editors of the Yale University Press readily agreed to accept it, under the title *America in Arms: The Experience of the United States with Military Organization.* Since it would be at least three or four months before the finished volume would reach the public, the author would just have to curb his fears and wait as patiently as he could for the reactions of readers and reviewers. Of one thing he was certain, humor was better than anger when replying to the criticism that was sure to come. This conviction he demonstrated in a little episode involving his friend Augustus L. Richards, owner of Baron von Steuben's estate, Sixty, who had been so helpful with the biography.

Richards had been infuriated by Kenneth Roberts's latest historical novel, *Oliver Wiswell*, a story of the American Revolution with a Tory hero. To express his agitation, he dashed off a pamphlet excoriating the author, ostensibly for the way he had represented patriotic rebels as the scum of the earth. But the real reason for this blast, Palmer suspected, lay elsewhere. His friend's full name was Augustus *Loring* Richards, which may have accounted for his anger at Roberts's treatment of the Mrs. Loring who was reputed to have been the American mistress of that royal soldier, General Howe.

In high good humor Palmer subsequently described the incident for his daughter.

The pamphlet delighted me with its vehemence which is so characteristic of my friend Augustus, and I was so pleased that I composed the following limerick.

There once was a lawyer named Rich
who filed a demurrer in which
He proved that the story
of Wiswell the Tory
was composed by a ...

You will note that my rhyming vocabulary gave out when I got to the last line, but I sent it incomplete as it was with the hope that he would be able to fill it out.[11]

Although the general hoped for the best possible treatment of his *America in Arms* by reviewers, he had no intention of leaving his fate entirely to them. To maximize his impact, he would have to see that his work reached a number of critically important people. This called for careful planning. To some he could send presentation copies himself; to others it would be more appropriate to have Grenny Clark or another of his friends do the honors. So he drew up a list of names, including such personalities as Wendell Willkie, Dorothy Thompson, Raymond Gram-Swing, Clarence Streit, Clare Booth Luce, and Mark Sullivan, as well as a dozen or more legislators, cabinet officers, and the like.[12]

The reaction to these prepublication copies was most heartening. Walter Lippman, for example, indicated that he expected to use some ideas from the book in a forthcoming article and actually did so not long afterward. Felix Frankfurter praised the lucidity and force of the volume, assuring the author that "to a mere lawyer you write with sense and persuasiveness." Although the Justice disclaimed any competence as a soldier, it was encouraging to know that one so influential with the President thought well of the book.[13]

One response that Palmer especially prized came from Lewis B. Hershey, recently promoted to brigadier general and currently serving as deputy director of the Selective Service. Hershey thought that every last regular should read the book. "I wish," he added, "it might be read and understood by every cadet before he becomes an officer of the United States Army."[14] Hershey, more than any other officer in the service, was to determine the spirit in which the draft of citizen soldiers was to be administered. If he really grasped the author's message that citizen soldiers should not be confined to the role of cannon fodder in an army run by professionals, then the book had already scored an important success.

Palmer could also exert his influence directly and personally. For example, when Walter Millis contributed the preface for a translation of Gen. Charles de Gaulle's passionate plea for greater emphasis on the professional soldier in the general's book, *The Army of the Future*, Palmer immediately engaged Millis in a friendly but critical correspondence. He admonished Millis not to forget that even de Gaulle backed his "career" army with large masses of citizen soldiers. In the dramatic success of Hitler's panzer divisions, Palmer reminded him, it would be fatally easy to overlook the fact that they were followed up by 200 conventional divisions filled with reservists. And the matter of their organization and training was a problem of military policy no less vital than the nurturing of regulars.[15]

The general fed ideas to others, notably George Fielding Eliot. His various exchanges with Eliot illustrate just how he set about trying to wield influence. Almost invariably he was complimentary, if not flattering. Moreover, he consistently brushed aside differences and discord to concentrate on broad areas of agreement, whether these were real or only apparent. For example, when Eliot somewhat noncommittally indicated that *America in Arms* had "opened up an entirely new point of view," the author's reply blandly assumed that Eliot really had isolated and identified the political dimension that was inescapably a part of all military institutions.

> I do not expect you to agree with me as to the application of this principle but if I have succeeded in turning your thoughts in that direction I feel that I have performed a real public service. I say this because, perhaps more than any other writer, you are exerting a powerful influence on military thought in this country. Last year when I first had the pleasure of meeting you, I felt that you were inclined to find a solution in building something new rather than in putting energy and vigor into existing institutions which are deeply rooted in our national tradition.

Political realism, he argued, made it imperative to advance by taking fully into account the strength of existing institutions.

> For example, the Selective Service Act was far from giving us a complete military system, but I think it went just about as far as was politically possible last summer. . . . One year's service was too short, as you urged then, but by building up an organization with the one year men we are . . . in a position to keep it alive because, now, public opinion is prepared for an extension of the period.
>
> There were also almost unanswerable objections, theoretically, against utilizing the National Guard. But an effort to displace it then would have aroused political opposition that might have blocked everything. In my opinion, the eventual solution will be a strictly federal citizen army entirely divorced from the militia, and if handled tactfully, the real leaders in the National Guard will support it. That solution could have been adopted before World War I, if we regulars had not stood rigidly for a military policy that could have no congenial place in our political system.[16]

Almost certainly Palmer overstated the case when in a note to George Marshall he referred to Eliot as "one of my disciples."[17] Nonetheless, even if Eliot and others like him did not receive his doctrines at face value, the fact remains that Palmer did play a useful role as a kind of intellectual middleman. Typical of the way he performed this function was the effort he made to bring Eliot and Clark together. Eliot had unparalleled outlets for radio, newspaper, and magazine publicity, and Clark enjoyed access to the inner circles of the Administration and a ready-made national organization in the Military Training Camps Association. These two performing as a team, Palmer realized, should be able to mount a most effective drive for permanent military legislation.[18]

The difficulty at the moment was that the MTCA seemed to have lost momentum. Its leaders were groping for a role, now that the Selective Service Act had been secured. Several committes had been organized to look into specific problem areas. The most important of these was one on military policy, headed by Howard C. Petersen, a vigorous young New York lawyer who had done yeoman service with Clark's National Emergency Committee. But Peterson had been called to Washington to help Robert P. Patterson, the new Assistant Secretary of War. Leadership of the policy committee reverted to Clark, who undertook a thorough reconsideration of his committee in relation to the association and its proper role in the current crisis.

There was general agreement within the association that the primary objective remained universal military training on a permanent basis. There had been some thought of undertaking a drive to recruit a large nationwide grassroots organization of some 30,000 individuals to buttress the influence of the National Emergency Committee. In March 1941 a gathering of nearly 150 representatives of the association from eight or more states discussed the problem of tactics at length. After much deliberation it was decided to defer the drive for mass support in favor of a more immediate goal of six to seven hundred individuals, selected for their influence in their home states.[19]

In choosing to rely on influential individuals rather than on a mass-membership organization, the committee leaders were undoubtedly making a realistic assessment of their resources. Among the members of the National Emergency Committee, for example, was Henry S. Hooker, who for many years had been associated with Franklin D. Roosevelt as a law partner and therefore enjoyed a familiar access to him. Hooker had visited the President and urged upon him the need for converting the draft into permanent legislation. Although Clark considered this move somewhat premature, the President actually dared to allude to the subject, albeit indirectly, in a press conference during April 1941, shortly after Hooker's visit.[20]

Roosevelt still did not feel free to speak out on the subject of compulsory military training. Instead, he hinted obliquely at the possibility of asking all young people to contribute a year of service to the government. With consummate political skill, the President had drawn his audience of newsmen into laughter; then, adroitly dodging a pointed question on a bill to retain the draftees already in uniform for more than a single year of training, he began to think aloud, "entirely off hand," as he put it, about the benefits to be derived from asking citizens to contribute a year of their lives. The emphasis was on the advantage to the participants themselves, with no mention whatever of military duty.

The President's cautious and hesitant approach was a revealing straw in the wind. Public opinion had made remarkable strides, but it was far from clear that the strategic moment had arrived to launch a concerted drive for permanent legislation. Grenville Clark recognized this difficulty and confessed himself uncertain as to the next move. Whether the National Emergency Committee continued to function or not, he knew there would be a need for numerous studies on the technical problems of compulsory military training in peacetime. So he invited Palmer to consider a position as a paid consultant and researcher for the committee.[21]

Although the general encouraged Clark to continue building his committee, the part he envisioned for himself was not at all what his friend proposed. He preferred to assign first priority to his own literary endeavors. His volume of memoirs would, he hoped, make an important contribution to the cause by its indirect approach.

> It may catch the general reader unawares for it will be the story of an
> old fellow who has had a varied life with many interesting contacts and
> experiences all over the world. But in the background it will also be an

inner history of our military system from pre-Spanish War days to the present world crisis. This story will be told, not dogmatically, but in the gradual evolution of a young soldier who eventually broke away from the narrow point of view of the old army in which he was bred. I think I can put this over in a story form to general readers who would not think of digging the same philosophy out of a serious book like *America in Arms*. If I succeed in this it will be a popular dose of national military policy in the form of a sugar-coated pill.[22]

If he were to undertake anything in addition, the general concluded, he might try writing a regular newspaper column specializing on the relation of military institutions to modern democracy. But before he had time to explore this idea, events on the national political front had swept on to a new crisis.

The problem this time was to help secure congressional authority to retain the draftees in the army beyond the twelve months specified in the original act. Although the President had skirted the issue in April, by June the situation had changed. The Nazi invasion of Russia and Japanese truculence in the far Pacific had done much to condition public opinion in the United States. By the middle of July 1941, the President was willing to come out boldly: unless Congress extended the tours of those already on duty, the army would face "disintegration." Figures released by the Chief of Staff clearly demonstrated how serious the impact would be. If the draftees were allowed to go home at the end of twelve months, some of the Regular Army divisions to which they had been assigned would lose up to 85 percent of their manpower. If the National Guard divisions recalled to active duty were released, the situation would be even worse.[23]

By any realistic appraisal of the nation's peril, it was imperative not to break up divisions just as their training reached the point where they were fit to hold maneuvers. Without such maneuvers the army would remain little more than an assemblage of lesser troop formations virtually incapable of aggressive action. The leaders of the MTCA must throw their resources into the campaign to persuade Congress not to dismantle the army.

Public opinion during the spring and summer of 1941 had begun to pull ahead of Congress. At the time, however, it was by no means clear that the voters would tolerate the "breach of faith" implied by keeping the draftees in uniform beyond the twelve months originally stipulated. As late as July even so shrewd a politician as Rep. Sam Rayburn of Texas, the influential speaker of the House, continued to oppose the idea.[24]

Although Clark and Palmer again appeared before the military committees of each house, it is doubtful whether their efforts changed many votes. The most persuasive arguments came from outside the committee hearings. Hitler's armies, at that very moment sweeping into Russia, seemed to give validity to a congressional declaration of emergency that would automatically authorize the President to retain the draftees in uniform. Even so, the outcome was a near thing. The Senate approved, 37 to 19, to extend the draftees' tour of duty. In the House, however, the measure carried by a single vote, giving rise to Winston Churchill's famous quip that the United States was the only great power in modern times that could scarcely decide on the very eve of war whether or not to have an army.[25]

For Palmer the hearings, especially the testimony of George Marshall, demonstrated the soundness of the doctrines he had been preaching for years. Improvisations in a crisis were detrimental to national defense. The obvious need was for some scheme to permit an orderly mobilization of whatever portion of the nation's manpower the situation required. Those who argued for a highly trained professional army seemed to ignore the question of expense. Moreover, to rely upon highly trained regular units hastily expanded in wartime with untrained draftees was a dubious gamble. Such a course assumed that the enemy would always delay its attack long enough for the citizen soldiers to be trained and assumed a willingness to squander lives by throwing untrained men into battle.

Machinery for an orderly mobilization was already available under the terms of the Defense Act of 1920. All that remained was to put universal military training in peacetime on a permanent basis. Universal training in peace would, he believed, assure a minimal level of military competence for virtually all the nation's usable manpower. Few if any of these trainees would be the equal of professionals, but if called up in an emergency they would be far more capable than raw draftees. And some trainees could be expected to remain involved in the reserve program on a voluntary basis. Citizen soldiers sufficiently interested to devote time and energy to further training could climb the ladder of promotion, in some instances even to the upper echelons of command. In this way the professional army, always the most expensive component, could be kept small. And the threat of a militaristic elite corps of professionals would be offset by heavy infusions of citizen soldiers, both in the ranks and in positions of command.

But ideas that were self-evident to Palmer were by no means so obvious to many of his contemporaries, including some influential commentators on national defense. Among those who differed most pointedly was Hanson W. Baldwin, whose position as military correspondent for the *New York Times* gave him a substantial leverage in shaping opinion. Baldwin had repeatedly contended that the old concepts of the mass army had been "invalidated to a considerable extent" by the lessons from the Nazi blitzkreig. In general he echoed the arguments of Hoffman Nickerson, in his book *The Armed Horde*, calling for a highly trained army of regulars "rather than hordes of hastily trained amateurs led by professionals."[26]

The problem, as Baldwin saw it, was one of "mass vs. mobility." A peacetime draft would delude the public with the "shadow of strength without the substance" by getting mass at the expense of mobility. To clinch his argument, he observed that a mass army of conscripts had failed to save France in the debacle of 1940.[27]

That the fate of French conscripts had influenced many students of military policy became evident when reviews of *America in Arms* finally began to appear.[28] The Nazi successes had given instant appeal to the advocates of a smaller professional army along the lines of the German *Reichswehr*. Nickerson was so anxious to attack Palmer's thesis that he wrote to several editors begging for an opportunity to review it.[29] Among those who actually did review the book was Baldwin in the *New York Times*.

Baldwin carefully avoided attacking the author head on. He identified Palmer as "one of the most capable and experienced of our contemporary students of military policy," one deserving respectful attention. "But," he continued, "one could have wished for a more comprehensive development of his thesis; what length of service, for instance, would he advocate for our trainees;... how large a standing professional army would supplement the citizen army?"[30] These vital questions, Baldwin charged, the author had slurred over, just as he had ignored the impact of permanent universal military training on the social structure of the nation.

Baldwin's criticisms were well founded; Palmer's prescriptions for a national military policy were, to put it bluntly, oversimplifications. Rather than engage in debate on the controversial issues, he glossed them over. His formulas for salvation won adherents, one suspects, more from the lucidity of their expression than from any willingness on his part to treat highly involved issues exhaustively. His handling of the National Guard question offers a case in point.

In *America in Arms*, Palmer had suggested that the National Guard might be more effectively employed if organized under the army clause of the Constitution. The general was not uninformed as to the relative merits of this ancient argument; he himself had studied it ever since 1916. Under the army clause, Guard officers could be promoted or discharged on the basis of merit, with but scant regard to state politics, and individual units could be transferred or reconstituted to conform to military need rather than to community desires. But the general knew perfectly well that one should reckon the probable costs. Would a National Guard organized under the army clause lose its base of support, now so firmly entrenched in statehouse and courthouse politics? Under the army clause, would the Guard become just another federal reserve? And if it did, would it suffer the same fate as the Organized Reserve in the between-war years, when Congress all but dismantled the politically impotent Organized Reserve while continuing to support the Guard, with its well-organized network of state lobbies. It might be possible to organize the Guard under the army clause in such a way as to retain its suport from the states. But would such an arrangement escape what the editors of the *Army and Navy Register* called "state chicanery"?[31]

These questions deserved close study before any permanent statutes were to be enacted, but Palmer ignored them. Indeed, as he blandly informed one student of the problem, the omission was deliberate; he had "carefully avoided" offering any opinion on the legal and constitutional problems implicit in the reforms he proposed. Insofar as he thought of himself as a scholar, this evasion was regrettable, but *America in Arms* was written as propaganda, not history. As a pamphleteer Palmer was probably right; the public wanted easy formulas for instant defense.[32]

To at least one segment of Palmer's audience, the book seemed eminently acceptable. Among those who wrote to express their appreciation of *America in Arms* was Maj. Gen. J. F. Williams, the chief of the National Guard Bureau in Washington. General Williams perceived what he wanted to: the book offered a strong rationale for retaining the Guard as the principal ready reserve of the army. With the whole subject of military organization certain to come up for thorough consideration in the years of crisis ahead, he was determined to see the interest of the Guard protected. To this end he wanted not only the officers of the Guard but all those in the citizen forces to be familiar with Palmer's book. As a start, he informed the author, he had already purchased fifty copies to distribute to division commanders, adjutants general, and others who had shown a "studious attitude."[33]

This was almost too good to be true, but General Williams went on to sharpen the author's anticipation still further. For years past, he observed, the Army ROTC had been turning out some 7,000 reserve officers annually. Every one of these young men had been indoctrinated with Upton's book and its contemptuous view of the militia. This, he believed, had prejudiced a whole generation against service in the Guard. By substituting Palmer for Upton, Williams suggested, this misfortune might be rectified.

Palmer's cup overflowed when he read the covering letter Williams had sent out with the copies of *America in Arms*. The bureau chief identified the author as the one officer "best qualified" to deal with the subject of military organization and credited him with political stature as well. "His prestige with Senators and Representatives in Congress is such that his opinions must be seriously considered even by those who do not agree with him." With the Secretary of War, the Chief of Staff, and now the Chief of the National Guard Bureau all believers, there might be some hope for his ideas after all.[34]

Palmer agreed with Williams that a postwar reorganization of the armed forces was inevitable. But it was imperative to avoid "the political compromise of practical views" that had marred so many attempted reforms in the past. Instead he looked for a "scientific solution." This could be achieved, he insisted, if a few professional soldiers would sit down with some representative citizen soldiers and one or two "constructive statesmen." If these gentlemen would work "with all the cards on the table," he was sure they could write an ideal statute, a permanent military policy for the United States, workable and acceptable to all.

What the general was proposing, of course, was a return to the mixed committees of regulars and reservists provided for in the Defense Act of 1920. Whether or not the results would be as "scientific" as he anticipated, the mixed committee formula had proven highly effective in the reorganizations under-taken after the passage of the Defense Act. Almost wistfully the general observed, "There would be no place for an old timer like me at such a table." Then he concluded, rather more artfully, "but you might let me sit in as a sort of 'friend of the court'."[35]

An elderly retired general on a hillside farm in New Hampshire might not be ideally situated for launching a major reform of the military organization, but this did not deter Palmer. He did not sit back and wait for the Guard Bureau to act; instead he wrote the next day to George Fielding Eliot, repeating his proposal for a mixed committee. And again he deprecatingly suggested that, while there might not be a place "for an old back number like me," he might usefully sit in a corner as *amicus curiae*. The general knew that Eliot was much concerned lest the War Department lose sight of postwar planning entirely. He also knew that George Marshall was consciously striving to build a unified military force without the frictions that had so often warped the relations of the Guard and the Regular Army. Palmer hoped that both Eliot and Marshall would be receptive to his proposal for a mixed committee to consider postwar military policy. As it turned out, these elaborate missionary efforts were probably unnecessary; the very first seed he had planted brought results.[36]

The response came in the form of a telephone call from General Williams at the National Guard Bureau. Would Palmer be willing to come down to the War Department to discuss the role of the Guard in relation to national military policy? A group of Guard officers studying the postwar problem at the bureau wanted him to share his wide experience with them. Delighted to be asked, he agreed to come, but only with the knowledge and consent of the Chief of Staff. Marshall, of course, promptly indicated that he not only had no objection but would appreciate Palmer's help. This informal conference was to be another turning point in Palmer's long and unorthodox military career.[37]

49

Military Elder
Statesman

The call for General Palmer grew out of one of those misunderstandings that so frequently marked the relations of the National Guard with the War Department. A committee of General Staff officers engaged in drawing up a long-range plan for the citizen forces had classified their study as confidential. This precaution against premature publicity aroused the guardsmen's suspicions. Actually, copies of the report had been shown to a number of Guard leaders, but the planners were anxious to avoid charges of bad faith if events on the international scene forced last-minute changes.[1]

Palmer had scarcely started when General Marshall began toying with the notion of recalling him to active duty so he would be continually available for such a role. Marshall's misgivings about Palmer's age and physical condition deterred him somewhat, but it seemed unfair not to reward the substantial services being rendered. He finally recalled his friend to duty, but instructed him to establish his headquarters in his usual study room at the Library of Congress. There he would be available for consultation and, more importantly, for contemplation, without being caught up in the daily turmoil at the War Department.[2] Palmer was elated. His devoted wife was fairly bursting with pride; at long last her beloved John was going to receive the recognition she knew he richly deserved.

The task before the general seemed to be a relatively simple one. The Chief of Staff had informed the officers of the National Guard Association and the Adjutants General Association of his action in recalling Palmer. Both groups had responded with expressions of genuine approval. For his part, the new mediator was careful to express himself with the utmost diffidence: "When we get together you must remember that I am somewhat in the position of Rip Van Winkle.... I will come with an open mind.... I also come without any instructions from my chief except to be as helpful as I can."[3] Getting together proved unexpectedly difficult, since many of the Guard officers were off on the army's fall maneuvers. Palmer tried to make the best of the delay. On Saturday, 6 December 1941, he mailed a brief note explaining the postponement to George Marshall and suggested that it might work out for the best, since after the maneuvers these busy men would have more time "to be patient with an old codger who does not think quite as fast as he used to."[4]

The explosion the next morning at Pearl Harbor banished all thought of long-range planning; not until a month later did the guardsmen consider the question of postwar organization, and then they recommended that definitive action be deferred until after the war; meanwhile, they urged the formation of a mixed committee of regulars and citizen soldiers to study the problem in depth. Palmer concurred, suggesting that his old friend Maj. Gen. Milton A. Reckord of the Maryland Guard would make a valuable contribution if appointed to such a group. But Marshall simply swept the proposal aside, promising in a stiffly formal letter to his elderly adviser to bring the matter up "at an appropriate time in the future." The tone and phraseology of the letter clearly revealed that someone else had written it. The cue to Palmer was unmistakable; now that the nation was at war, his relationship with the Chief of Staff was going to be different.[5]

The more the general reflected on his situation, the clearer it became that he could not wait for the Chief of Staff to call upon him. If he was going to be of value as an adviser on the citizen components, he must familiarize himself with the views of his chief's principal subordinates. There was, for example, Lt. Gen. Leslie J. McNair, the newly appointed commander of the Army Ground Forces. For a start, Palmer wrote "as your old West Point instructor," praising McNair's new triangular division as a brilliant piece of planning. McNair replied, giving most of the credit to Brig. Gen. Mark W. Clark. Palmer picked up this lead immediately, confessing that he had only just learned that Mark W. Clark was the Wayne Clark he had known as a boy at Leavenworth. From there on it was easy to pursue his interest naturally, by accepting Clark's invitation to come down and visit him at the Ground Forces headquarters.[6]

While Palmer was undoubtedly wise in taking the initiative by opening up such lines of communication, in one quarter, at least, this was unnecessary. George Marshall found time to keep in touch. For example, in 1942, when launching the major reorganization of the army that created the Army Ground Forces (AGF), and the Services of Supply (SOS), later redesignated the Army Service Forces (ASF), he wrote a long letter to his elderly friend explaining the move in detail. Effecting such major changes with a minimum of dissension from within the army and on the Hill required a high order of statesmanship and diplomacy. There were chiefs of Arms and Services whose positions were abolished while new and more powerful commands were created. Only by exquisite timing and maneuvering could the Chief of Staff carry out the shifts with a minimum of opposition and resentment. "I would be interested in your view of the reorganization," Marshall wrote, "if you can force yourself to write without reservation or fear of hurting feelings." Palmer was one of the few to whom the Chief of Staff could turn for an entirely candid reply.[7]

For Marshall his friend served as a military elder statesman, a phrase he coined to describe Palmer when writing to Secretary of War Stimson.[8] The Chief of Staff was acutely sensitive to the need for handling the citizen components, and especially the National Guard, with the utmost care. Few of his young staff officers recalled the bitter animosities that had marred the relations of the guardsmen and the Regulars during and after World War I. Marshall was determined to avoid any recurrence of this tragedy. Whatever its shortcomings, the Guard represented too valuable an asset to dissipate it in needless internal bickering. What he expected of Palmer was a long memory of the political clout wielded by the Guard and sympathy for the concept of the citizen soldier.[9]

Relations between the Guard and the Regulars were at low ebb in the winter of 1942. That the mobilization of the Guard during the summer would produce a great many strains and stresses was to be expected. Virtually all of the part-time soldiers were physically slack; many were woefully lacking in training, especially with the newer types of weapons and equipment. Forty-year-old captains were not uncommon. Impatient Regulars inveighed bitterly against the deficiencies of Guard leadership. Several division commanders were abruptly replaced. The guardsmen believed that the Regulars were trying to open the high-ranking positions for themselves, while the Regulars wrote off the dismissed guardsmen as incompetents and political appointees.[10] There was doubtlessly a measure of truth on both sides, but such internal feuding was destructive.[11]

That there were deficiences in the National Guard no one would deny, but to write off the institution as a whole because it fell short of perfection was to miss the point. As Palmer had tirelessly reiterated, to rest the national defense on citizen soldiers accepts in advance something less than the military ideal in return for a cost the taxpayers can be induced to accept. The remarkable thing about the mobilization of the National Guard in 1941 was not how faulty but how effective it was, in view of the limitations under which it had labored for twenty-odd years. If there were forty-year-old captains, whose fault was that? Surely those who had suffered the frustrations of slow promotion within rigidly imposed rank ceilings were not to be penalized for their loyalty. If senior officers, such as division commanders, were ill-trained, it was because they had begged in vain for funds to launch large-scale maneuvers. The National Guard brought into service more than a quarter of a million men in organized units. These units were admittedly neither ready nor fully trained, but as the Chief of Staff himself observed, they were not diluted with raw, untrained recruits to the same extent as the newly formed Regular Army divisions then being filled up with draftees and inexperienced ROTC graduates.[12]

Even though the Chief of Staff understood the positive case for the National Guard and usually acted accordingly, not all his principal subordinates shared his outlook. They tended to see only the current difficulties and disagreements. Thus, for example, when the Guard request for a joint committee to study the future status of the organization reached Maj. Gen. J. H. Hildring, the army G-1, he recommended that all such joint committees formed under Section 5 of the Defense Act be suspended and their current papers turned over to the Adjutant General.[13] Despite the fact that Palmer had heartily endorsed the Guard proposal, the Chief of Staff approved of Hildring's course, apparently moved by the G-1 contention that the new, smaller General Staff formed under the reorganization of March 1942 could no longer spare the manpower.

To the guardsmen the decision to suspend all Section 5 committees was a slap in the face. It was easy indeed to interpret this action as but the latest in a series of moves to squeeze the guardsmen out of the upper echelons of command. Only a month before they had learned that the National Guard Bureau had been dropped from its favored place on the General Staff, where it enjoyed ready access to the Chief of Staff and the civilian secretaries, to a subordinate status two echelons below in the Army Service Forces.[14]

The leaders of the Guard reacted in characteristic fashion. A meeting of the Adjutants General Association in Washington provided a ready-made occasion. As a matter of course they invited Palmer. Here was just the opportunity to play the kind of mediating role his chief expected of him. With this in mind he presented a brief historical sketch of the chaos in the Guard following the demobilization of 1919, stressing the importance of having a plan ready to avoid a painful repetition. The guardsmen should come up with a positive program of their own, a proposal outlining the permanent postwar organization they themselves wished to see established. By urging them to take the initiative, the general seemed to put himself in their camp. Had he stopped there, he would have retained his considerable influence in Guard circles, but he went on to say that the postwar organization he personally favored for the National Guard was one that rested upon the army clause of the Constitution rather than the militia clause.[15]

Nothing Palmer might have said could have aroused the fears of the Guard leaders more abruptly. This was heresy. To mention organizing under the army clause was to evoke memories of repeated attempts by the regulars to abolish the Guard, dating all the way back to the Continental Army scheme of Secretary Garrison in 1916. Appalled at the reaction, the general backed off hastily, observing that the view he expressed was only a personal opinion and did not represent an official War Department policy. But the damage was done.[16]

For the guardsmen Palmer's heresy was doubly galling; as a Regular who was a friend of the Guard, in espousing the army clause he seemed to confirm their worst fears. If our "friends" think this, what can we expect from our "enemies"? Since the general was known to have the confidence of the Chief of Staff, might this not indicate the probable drift of his opinion, too?

Although Palmer gave no sign that he realized the full significance of his gaffe, his effectiveness as a liaison agent was seriously compromised, at least for the time being. The episode was typical of the general: he was an idealist; if men would only put all their cards on the table face up, the most complicated problems could readily be solved. That views he regarded as partisan in others could be convictions no less honestly held than his own was sometimes difficult for him to grasp, but he was always willing to listen to those who differed with him. And when the guardsmen cited evidence of hostility on the part of the Regulars, he was forced to admit that he was out of touch with opinion in the War Department.

To be truly effective he would have to become more fully informed about the policies and opinions prevailing in General Staff circles. An opportunity for this came to him, albeit by a most indirect route. The 1942 graduation at West Point would mark the 50th anniversary of the Class of 1892. There was to be a gala reunion, of course, and C. P. Summerall wrote from his post as commandant at the Citadel in Charleston, South Carolina, rallying his classmates. Would Palmer write an ode for the occasion? The general made several attempts at composition but rejected each one in disgust. "I find that my muse . . . was a companion of my early youth and I cannot recall her." Besides, he had some doubts about the propriety of an officer on active duty taking leave for a reunion during wartime.[17]

As it turned out Palmer did attend the reunion, and despite his earlier fears and failures, his muse did return. In fact, the program turned out to be something of a Palmer literary festival; it included not only his "Ode to '92," a toast of his composition, and several of the songs he had composed years before, but also a delightful sketch of cadet days entitled "How Football Came to West Point," written only a week or two before the reunion.[18] But what really made the occasion notable was the opening it afforded for a long heart-to-heart talk with George Marshall, who had come up to the academy to give the graduation address. It was his first opportunity since the declaration of war to hold a serious conversation with his chief, and he explained how his isolation at the Library of Congress seriously impaired his effectiveness.

For Marshall it was a simple matter to issue an order creating a Postwar Planning Board to advise Palmer in formulating recommendations on the role of the citizen components in the peacetime establishment. As members of the board the Chief of Staff selected the G-1, the G-3, the executive for Reserve and ROTC affairs, the chief of the National Guard Bureau, and several subordinate General Staff officers. If anyone knew the drift of current opinion in the War Department, these men would. The scheme broke down almost immediately, however. How could a group of men already over their heads in work on the current war effort be expected to pay more than fleeting attention to an elderly general talking about a subject so remote as the postwar establishment?[19]

The general's difficulties in making use of the Postwar Planning Board were epitomized in his relations with one of its members, Col. Miller G. White. As a National Guard officer, White was living proof of George Marshall's determination not to repeat the mistakes of his predecessors in World War I. Just as President Roosevelt had appointed Republican Henry Stimson to the post of Secretary of War as a pledge that the war effort would be nonpartisan, so the Chief of Staff was to make White his G-1, where every guardsman could take comfort in having a presumably friendly eye watching over the promotion lists. But like all the other members of the board, White was coming to his office before dawn, working twelve hours at his desk, and carrying a bulging briefcase home at night.[20]

White and the other members of the board tried to enlighten the general on staff thinking, but at best they could give him only tag ends of their time. When he took to composing closely packed, single-spaced typewritten pages recalling the failures of the planners after World War I, they often went unread. The effort was not, however, entirely wasted. One of these rejected compositions, a rationale for a democratic military policy based on universal training, the general polished up and sent to the *Infantry Journal*, where it was published in the June 1942 issue under the title "Two Views of War."[21]

Palmer's old friend Congressman James W. Wadsworth read the article with satisfaction, and a few days later he included the text in the *Congressional Record*. Delighted, the general began sending Wadsworth copies of the papers he had been compiling to educate the members of the Postwar Planning Board.[22] This time the innoculation took, and soon afterward Wadsworth decided to draft a bill to establish the principle of postwar universal military training. A trial balloon launched in the *Washington Star* brought such a positive reaction that Wadsworth was convinced the political climate was favorable.[23]

Palmer promptly wrote to the Chief of Staff urging him to let Wadsworth sit down with the Postwar Planning Board to consider the bill he was drafting.[24] Then he drew up a paper on "Proposed Legislation for Universal Military Training" to outline the essentials of such a bill. The permanent establishment, he concluded, must rest upon Washington's democratic principle that "every citizen who enjoys the protection of a free government owes not only a portion of his property but even of his personal services to the defense of it." To this end all male citizens must be trained in the exercise of arms in early manhood. Congress should therefore enact a statute providing for universal military training. Insofar as possible, this statute should be confined to the principle of universal training, leaving to a "scientific determination" in the postwar period all the complex details as to just how the principle should be reduced to practice. After some hesitation Wadsworth decided to introduce his bill at the opening of the next session, in order to capitalize on the public determination never to be caught short again.[25]

Wadsworth's decision brought an immediate and favorable reaction from his friends in the Military Training Camps Association. With more than 5,000 names in its file of those who had pushed the Draft Act fight in 1940, the Association was in a position to render help at the grass roots. The experience in 1940 had revealed that there was considerable merit in getting started as soon as possible on the drive for universal training.[26] By sending out reprints of a *New York Times* account of Wadsworth's scheme[27] and inviting suggestions about the timing of the proposed bill, the association would publicize the drive for UMT while verifying its own address list and identifying its most concerned members.

American Legion officials also responded with enthusiasm. The chairman of the Legion's legislative committee visited Palmer and insisted on having him attend the annual Legion convention to make a pitch for UMT.[28] The general did go to the convention in Kansas City during September 1942, and he found it the "most serious and interesting" he had ever attended. His plea was well received, and the delegates endorsed a resolution calling for a year of universal military training in peacetime.[29] Well pleased, Palmer sat down to prepare a rough draft of the proposed statute. What he had in mind was a simple affirmation of principle; implementation would be left to the military authorities acting under the executive powers of the President.[30]

Although the drive for universal training seemed to be gathering impressive momentum, a few critical voices could be heard. Maj. Gen. J. F. Williams, the chief of the National Guard Bureau, was one such. Any proposal with a public impact on the scale anticipated from UMT, he argued, must have broad popular support. He urged that the guardsmen should be consulted in the preparation of any such legislation.[31] More bluntly, the *Army and Navy Register* warned that Wadsworth's scheme would remove the National Guard from the states altogether. Since this would provoke a three-cornered fight for dominance in the postwar army, the editors suggested that it might be wiser to forget UMT for the time being and concentrate on winning the war.[32] Undeterred, Palmer moved firmly ahead, drawing up a policy paper under which the Organized Reserve to be generated by UMT should be an unequivocably federal force, raised under the army clause of the Constitution. No force raised under the militia clause, he argued, could ever hope to produce a fully effective reserve for war.[33]

Congressman Wadsworth accepted Palmer's line of reasoning, and early in 1943, with the opening of the 78th Congress, introduced a universal training bill that closely resembled the measure he and Palmer had unsuccessfully offered in 1919. Sen. Chan Gurney of South Dakota submitted a parallel measure in the upper house. The text of the Gurney-Wadsworth bill made no concessions whatever to the National Guard.[34]

To forestall trouble, Palmer sent his friend Gen. John Williams at the Guard Bureau an advance copy of the bill. He admitted that he himself believed that a change in the constitutional status of the National Guard should be effected after the war. But any such change would require extensive congressional hearings, at which guardsmen who differed would be free to refute him. Meanwhile, the Gurney-Wadsworth bill would leave the Defense Act of 1920 in full force. Any reservists generated by UMT would be absorbed into the National Guard or the Organized Reserve, as currently authorized under the statute of 1920. Since the guardsmen professed to support the principle of UMT, how could they complain of a bill that proposed no change in the organization of the Guard as such?[35]

Palmer's argument was ingenious but quite missed the mark, as was soon revealed in his negotiations with his old friend Maj. Gen. Milton A. Reckord, now commanding the Army's 3rd Service District. In response to Reckord's suggestion that the bill should be amended, he argued that the all-important principle of UMT itself was liable to be lost in controversies over details. Nothing in the bill, he argued, would change the status of the National Guard. "I've always been frank with you and that's how it really is." Reckord was obviously reluctant to criticize a friend of so many years standing, so instead of going into particulars to spell out his objections, he contented himself with saying he could shoot the text full of holes were he not so entirely absorbed in war work.[36]

Wadsworth, when shown the general's response, revealed that he too was blind to the intensity of the guardsmen's fears. As to the notion that his bill would prove injurious to the Guard, he declared, "It just ain't so."[37] Insofar as intentions were concerned, this was entirely true. But between the sincerest intentions of the framers and the way the measure might work out in practice, there was ample room for the guardsmens' doubts. Palmer had seen his high hopes for the Defense Act of 1920 largely negated by those in command of the army. If such a fate were possible when his friend General Pershing was Chief of Staff, were the guardsmen entirely mistaken in fearing that a similar fate might be in store for their organization after the present war?

If the guardsmen were at fault, it was in failing to get down to details. When Palmer declined to consider amending the Gurney-Wadsworth bill, Reckord wrote to protest the "elimination" of the Guard from the whole scheme of national defense.[38] Although the authors of the bill regarded Reckord's fears of "elimination" as unwarranted, a strong case could be made for his view. If

UMT were enacted without statutory provisions to encourage reservists upon finishing their mandatory year of active duty training to enter the Guard, would they in fact do so? Or would they prefer to enter units of the Organized Reserve established in their home areas? The latter would be free of all irksome necessity to serve in labor disputes, civil uprisings, and other such unpopular state and local duties. Moreover, there was always the danger that the army, in its desire to build a reserve more amenable to centralized control, would find opportunities for active duty assignments and promotions for men in the Organized Reserve that might be denied to those in the Guard.

The apprehensions of the guardsmen finally came to a head at the annual meeting of the Adjutants General Association held in Harrisburg, Pennsylvania, early in April 1943. Many of their objections related to technical details that threatened to have a disproportionately large impact. For example, under the legislation of 1940 a trainee acquired a ten-year obligation in the Organized Reserves. But if he agreed to enroll in the Guard, he could clear this obligation in three years. By contrast, the Gurney-Wadsworth bill offered no such positive inducement. Palmer, as an invited guest of the association, agreed that an amendment providing such an inducement would not be unreasonable, but he held out for a bill authorizing UMT in principle without any encumbering compromises.[39]

General Reckord counterattacked vigorously; the guardsmen would resist the bill unless it were amended. Then he spelled out with remarkable candor the basis of his fears. How long, he asked, would Congress continue to support the National Guard once the army achieved a large and well-paid Organized Reserve under federal control? As a veteran lobbyist, Reckord could readily foresee what might happen when the Organized Reserve had fully manned, paid units scattered in communities across the nation. Who could say that the Organized Reserve, with better access to the benefits than the Guard had ever enjoyed, would not soon evolve into a highly efficient political machine. "It is bad legislation," declared Reckord. Then, when he turned and admonished Palmer to "go back and tell 'Senator' Wadsworth we are going to kill the bill," the assembled guardsmen broke into applause.[40]

General Palmer readily admitted that Reckord and his guardsmen could certainly kill the bill. But if you do, he warned, "it will be one of the great mistakes of your life." Then he attempted to mollify his opposition. Go ahead, he counseled, submit an amendment to Wadsworth, who might change his mind as to the merits of the case. Instead of taking up Palmer's belatedly conciliatory gesture, Reckord returned to the attack, protesting against the way the framers of the bill had managed to con the veterans in the American Legion into supporting their measure while the guardsmen were out fighting the war. For this last salvo Palmer had only himself to blame; he had conferred at great length with Legion officials while the bill was being drafted, without entering into parallel negotiations with either of the Guard associations.

To have the National Guard in open opposition was bad enough, but the guardsmen were not the only vested interest disturbed by the threat of universal military training; the members of the Association of Land Grant Colleges and Universities also felt threatened by the proposed legislation. Since the ROTC constituted an important drawing card in land grant schools, the leaders of the association reacted defensively to the proposed bill. What Palmer regarded as its virtue, the simplicity of its text touching upon principle alone, they saw as a menace. Would UMT undermine their local ROTC programs and cut enrollments?[41] The officers of the association invited Palmer to participate in their deliberations, but they ended up where the guardsmen had: they were willing to endorse UMT in principle but insisted upon guarantees that ROTC would be preserved.[42]

Neither the general nor his associates in the drive for UMT had anything but the highest regard for the ROTC program. Between 1920 and 1942 ROTC had turned out 127,000 officers from some 137 colleges.[43] In many of the recently mobilized tactical divisions, nearly half of all the officers currently on duty came from this source. But if the sponsors of the Gurney-Wadsworth bill agreed to an amendment insuring the retention of ROTC, they would open the door to requests for similar treatment from every other interest group and thus hopelessly prejudice their freedom of action when developing UMT after the war.[44]

The opposition of the National Guard and the land grant college interests, coming to a head in the winter of 1943, only served to confirm what had been increasingly evident for some months previously; the whole problem of post-war military organization was so complex and had so many ramifications that it would require far more intensive analysis than one elderly retired officer with flagging energies could hope to give. What was needed, Palmer realized, was a full-time staff within the War Department exclusively devoted to postwar planning.

To guide such an effort, Palmer devised a diagram he used to illustrate the problem facing the army. It is worth reproducing because it reflects so well the general's knack for reducing issues to lucid simplicity (see figure 2). The curve a-b represented the army's current buildup, with its dangerous delay in reaching full strength; b-c indicated the army fighting at maximum strength; c-d represented partial demobilization after victory; d-e reflected the troop strength required to insure stability during the period of postwar disorder or until "final world settlement," to use the general's own optimistic phrase; e-f-g represented the small peacetime army that would be required to support a very rapid mobilization of a large force from the onset of a crisis at f, providing the nation accepted UMT; and e-h-i represented the large peacetime army and the

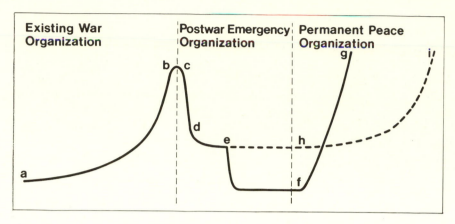

Figure 2

low rate of buildup, repeating the delays of 1939-41, that would result were UMT not accepted by the nation.[45]

The effectiveness of the diagram lay in its elegant simplicity. In a few pen strokes it illuminated two important theses. The first of these was exercising his historical memory, recalling how the need for retaining a relatively large force during demobilization to serve in the occupation of Germany had seriously prejudiced discussions on the whole question of permanent organization after World War I. By separating the immediate from the remote postwar era he hoped to overcome this difficulty. As he later described it, "The idea was to treat the two problems as separate as two dishes of poached eggs." In that way Congress would always be able to count the number of eggs in each dish. His second thesis, so readily evident when reduced to simple graphic form, was that the acceptance of UMT would provide the nation with a better defensive posture, with a smaller Regular Army and hence a lower cost, than would be possible without UMT.[46]

The Chief of Staff was not unreceptive to the need for a full-fledged postwar planning organization. His public relations staff, anxious not to be caught unawares by a sudden armistice as in 1918, had also been urging him to create an agency to think about the coming contingency.[47] But it was difficult for General Marshall to devote much thought to problems that seemed so distant, at a time when the war appeared to be going badly both in Africa and the Pacific, as bloody reverses at Guadalcanal were matched by checks in Tunisia. When Palmer suggested that Operations might be the proper place for demobilization studies, the G-3 begged off, saying the task was far too big for his overworked staff.[48] Finally, after the subject had been passed back and forth for nearly six months, the Chief of Staff set up a small group within the Army Service Forces to look into the question of organization for postwar planning.[49] The ASF team soon discovered what Palmer had long contended: To be effective, any agency dealing with the big questions of policy on postwar organization must have direct access to the highest echelons of authority for decisions and guidance.[50] The Secretary of War, the Under Secretary, and the Chief of Staff all agreed and during July 1943 created a new element in the War Department Special Staff known as the Special Planning Division.[51] The innocuous designation was deliberate; it was feared that any obvious reference to postwar planning might create an adverse public reaction at a time when the nation's forces were so far from success on the far-flung battle fronts.[52]

When the Chief of Staff selected Brig. Gen. William F. Tompkins to head the new division, Palmer was genuinely pleased; he had known Tompkins ever since the 1920s. He immediately established a close personal relationship with the head of the new division. Although he continued to make the Library of Congress his headquarters, he gladly accepted the desk Tompkins offered him within the division at the Pentagon. Here he was a sincerely welcomed visitor, for he brought a wealth of experience to the work of postwar planning that none of the newly assigned officers could hope to equal. This abrupt change in fortunes was highly gratifying to the general. No longer did he have to seek means of thrusting his schemes upon men too busy to listen; quite the reverse. If anything, Tompkins and his staff were almost too demanding. As Palmer himself put it, "At 73, even the most youthful old gentleman must remember that he is living on borrowed time."[53] Tompkins was fully aware of the valuable asset of an adviser who provided informal backdoor access to the Chief of Staff.[54] Access to the Chief of Staff was difficult, even for senior division directors, not because George Marshall was unapproachable but because of his overwhelming workload. Acutely conscious of this, Palmer leaned over backwards not to presume upon friendship and intrude unnecessarily. For his part, however, Marshall never allowed the man-killing loads he bore to become an excuse for neglecting his elderly friend.

Sometimes Marshall was able to combine solicitude for his friend with the requirements of the moment. One such occasion cropped up when he invited Palmer to act as a host and guide to Gen. F. E. Morgan and some other members of the British mission in Washington on a brief expedition to the historic battlefields in the Shenandoah Valley. Before the group set off, Lord Halifax, the British Ambassador, gave them a dinner at the embassy, where Palmer endeared himself to the company with an evening of Lincoln anecdotes he remembered from his grandfather. Although the old gentleman was careful to brush up on his history before departing for this new "Valley Campaign," he discovered that his guests were already very well informed, having "got more from Henderson than I ever had," as he subsequently reported to the chief.[55]

Marshall was ever mindful of the limits to an old man's strength. Annually, as the broiling summer heat mounted in Washington, he would issue orders for Palmer to repair to his farm in New Hampshire "for calm contemplation." On one occasion he insisted upon "deliberation on the bank of a trout stream." Then, to make certain he was taken seriously, he added, "My best thoughts regarding Army organization and operations have usually occurred while I was riding horseback." Even this affirmation, coupled with specific instructions not to return to Washington until the temperature dropped to 70 degrees, seemed to trouble the Palmer conscience. With his quaint but scrupulous rectitude, he refused to file any claim for mileage to reimburse himself for the expenses of his summer trips.[56]

As a matter of fact, General Marshall's consideration paid off handsomely; the summers of meditation proved most fruitful in ideas. As the old gentleman himself put it to a friend, "My special job as I conceive it is to formulate some general or axiomatic principles which should always govern the military establishment of a democratic state."[57]

The first fruits of the general's desire to formulate principles appeared in an article, "Our Future Military Policy," which he turned out for the August 1943 issue of the *Infantry Journal*. Taking as his text George Washington's contention that the nation must remain "respectable in the eyes of our friends and formidable to those who would otherwise be our enemies," he proceeded to an axiomatic conclusion: There can be no sound military policy that does not rest on the principle that every able-bodied American should be trained in youth to defend the nation. What he hoped to do, of course, was to get down to fundamentals, laying a strong foundation for universal military training that reached far beyond the expedient, and vulnerable, arguments usually put forward in its defense. But having done this, he went further and tacked on a proposal looking to the mechanics of implementing the fundamentals he identified. After his recent experiences with the National Guard, he was more than ever convinced that the various components of the military establishment would never rise above their ex parte claims for support. And after the war, with the Air Force joining the Army and Navy, there would be three services, each appearing before a separate committee of Congress. The best hope of reconciling all these conflicting claims, Palmer suggested in his article, was to create a commission made up of "able and broad-minded civilians including professional men, scientists, educators, and men of affairs. Such a commission, he believed, could present Congress with a coherent system of national defense rather than the combination of compromises arising from normal political brokerage.

Although the *Infantry Journal* article brought some gratifying responses, ranging from one by Justice Felix Frankfurter to a wide scattering of press notices,[58] it was, after all, only a seed; germination would take a long time. Much the same could be said of another literary project, a revised edition of the general's book, *America in Arms*. He had undertaken the task at the urging of Col. Joe Greene, his long-time friend, the highly respected editor of the *Infantry Journal*. Greene had recognized the potential value of Palmer's book as propaganda for UMT if a paperback edition were produced for wide distribution. Since the original version had come out before Pearl Harbor, it required some updating. The general welcomed this opportunity to sharpen his arguments. For example, when he first wrote, he had hardly dared do more than hint at the need for a unified department of defense; now public opinion had moved to the point where he felt he could push the idea vigorously.[59]

The reception encountered by the new edition of *America in Arms* was most encouraging. Even before the book rolled off the press, American Legion officials ordered a thousand copies, to put into the hands of every important national and departmental officer and committeeman.[60] Although this was preaching to the converted, there was much to be said for supplying a comprehensive historical argument to buttress the position of those who had hitherto relied largely upon opinion and personal experience; the same could be said of the hundreds of copies that found their way into the hands of officers throughout the military establishment. Palmer's facile pen was undeniably a significant asset to the advocates of UMT, but he was quite unwilling to coop himself up in his study to concentrate on writing. He much preferred the daily interchange with people and responded with enthusiasm to the opportunities that were thrust upon him regularly.[61]

In light of the general's advanced years and limited strength, he might have made more effective use of his energies had he been more cautious and more selective. But men of his temperament are seldom inclined to be either cold-bloodedly objective or nicely discriminating in choosing their fields of action. Although Palmer repeatedly spoke of the need for a "scientific" determination of major policy questions, he gave little evidence in his own life that he ever undertook any objective analysis, even of the crudest sort, before plunging into some new enterprise. Thus, for example, when the World Peace Foundation invited him to Boston to a conference on the enforcement of postwar military sanctions, he accepted without hesitation even though the whole affair required a good deal of tiresome travel, no little advance preparation, and a spate of time-consuming correspondence.[62] Similarly, when the U.S. Chamber of Commerce expressed an interest in taking a stand on UMT, it was Palmer who was called upon to draft a suitable resolution. Almost exactly the same kind of invitation came to him from the National Association of Manufacturers. Some invitations he could not refuse; when General Pershing asked him to prepare a rough draft for a personal endorsement of the Gurney-Wadsworth bill, loyalty no less than inclination led him to comply. But there were certainly many among the weekly calls upon his talents where he might wisely have exercised more restraint.[63]

So long as the general was playing the advocate, he could be remarkably convincing. On the defensive, however, he was far less persuasive. When, for example, Paul V. McNutt, the chairman of the War Manpower Commission, refused to support the Gurney-Wadsworth bill, Palmer undertook to draft a point-by-point rebuttal for Senator Gurney to use in reply. One of the major arguments adduced was that UMT could be financed "largely if not entirely" from the economies it would make possible from corresponding reductions in the size of the Regular Army. Characteristically, this sweeping claim rested on no close analysis of the facts. Indeed, scattered through the general's files were numerous bits of evidence suggesting that the cost of UMT might well prove far more than he contended. He did not suppress this evidence; he simply failed to see it. His arguments for the economies of UMT were more clearly acts of faith than products of objective study.[64]

Ardent and unselective as the general often was in the lavish way he poured out his limited strength, at times even he understood that inaction was the proper course when confronted with the barbs and misrepresentations of hostile critics. It was also sometimes best to remain silent when one's supporters marched out of step. Just such an occasion cropped up when Tompkins McIlvaine wrote a letter to the *New York Times* suggesting that the National Guard and the ROTC had no proper place in a military establishment incorporating universal training and should therefore no longer receive any federal subsidy. It would be difficult to think of any statement more exquisitely calculated to arouse the antipathies of the two groups best situated to hurt the chances of UMT in Congress. In a reprint of his letter McIlvaine had also identified not only his own role as a one-time official of the MTCA, but also his association with Palmer. The general knew that his only course was to sit in silence and squirm, hoping that the whole affair would blow over without too much damage.[65]

On the other hand, some critics had to be answered even when their attacks seemed to stoop to personal invective. When, for example, the monthly magazine *Free World* carried an article deploring all the current "loose thinking" about "conscription" and the "bristling postwar militarism" brought on by "Legionnaires, General Palmer and others of their kind" as dangerous to the prospects of a sound international organization after the war, Grenville Clark immediately wrote to Palmer underscoring how important it was to study ways and means of reconciling UMT with the currently evolving schemes for world order within the United Nations. There was much to be said for tying the case for UMT to the stance in favor of a strong international organization. As Clark observed, an effective United Nations would certainly require a peace-keeping force, and the United States would be called upon to contribute much of the muscle. How better to support the cause of internationalism than by a democratic force composed of citizen soldiers, trained under UMT? By recognizing this overlapping of interest, Clark implied, the general might be able to recruit useful allies for the cause of UMT from the many advocates of a new world order based on the United Nations. But there is no evidence whatever that Palmer ever did more than file Clark's constructive suggestion.[66]

During his long career the general had had many occasions to observe how often legislators tend to vote from interest rather than from principle. But in his campaign for universal military training, he repeatedly insisted that the vote should be on principle only, leaving the details until after the war for settlement. One after another of his friends wrote urging him to sit down and bargain with the various parties holding a stake in the issue. One such letter from a friend in the American Legion suggested that a simple amendment reaffirming the provisions of the Defense Act of 1920 regarding ROTC would promptly bring the powerful Association of Land Grant Colleges and Universities into line.[67] But the general refused this option as emphatically as he did a similar suggestion from a spokesman for the National Guard. "To me it is all very simple. The Gurney-Wadsworth bill ... is in no sense a military organization bill and should not be made a vehicle for anticipating any feature of the military organization which Congress must establish when the outlines of our future international relations can be determined." True, he admitted, the guardsmen had indeed threatened to fight the measure unless it were amended to their satisfaction.

I am inclined to think that if the National Guard and other special interest groups take this attitude they will have no difficulty in killing the bill. But I hope they will think better of it and prepare themselves to present their well-considered views to the Military Affairs Committees when after the war Congress takes up the problem of amending the National Defense Act to meet our military requirements in the postwar world. I hope that they will derive satisfaction from the fact that a law for universal military training is then on the Statute Books and that they helped to secure its passage.[68]

Was this a display of courageous and steadfast adherence to principle or one of incredible political naiveté? In light of the mounting evidence of a surge of popular support for the concept of universal training as a cornerstone of national defense, who could say with assurance that the general was mistaken when he held out against those he regarded as ill-informed partisans, men whose awareness of their short-run interests temporarily blinded them to the larger vistas of the national interest that he pointed out to them? A Gallup poll showing that approximately two-thirds of the nation's adults favored some form of UMT gave substantial support to Palmer's course of action. And several other less scientific samples published at about the same time seemed to confirm the notion that compromises might not be necessary.[69]

If, in retrospect, the general's insistence upon UMT without compromise seems only slightly less unrealistic than his espousal of a "civilian commission" as a panacea, it is only fair to recall that in November 1943 neither of these ideas appeared especially quixotic. No less an authority on practical politics than Congressman A. J. May, then in the full tide of his power and prestige and as yet untouched by the scandal that would retire him in disgrace, asked the general to draw up a bill embracing universal military training and a reserve force under the army clause of the Constitution. If the hard-bitten realist who served as chairman of the House Military Affairs Committee during the nation's greatest war was willing even to consider sponsoring such a bill, there was good reason for optimism about its chances on the part of a political observer far less acute.[70]

For the general, Congressman May's request for help came as most welcome evidence that the tide had turned. Looking back, he could identify the signs of progress since his return to active duty. The War Department had a full-time organization of able young officers working on postwar problems; they had already accepted universal military training as the basis of their planning. If there were partisan groups within the Guard and elsewhere who still seemed to obtrude their short-range interests, it certainly appeared that public opinion was finally coming around to support those who wanted universal training as the foundation of national defense.

The prospect was exciting; the war on the fighting front had at last turned dramatically toward victory. Buoyed by these successes, the general was increasingly confident that the coming triumph in arms would be matched by a political victory on the home front with the passage of legislation giving the nation a permanent military organization suited to the genius of a democratic people.

50   The Struggle for a Citizen Army

When success in the drive for a universal military training (UMT) statute at last seemed imminent, Palmer's long-time friend Archibald Thacher wrote from New York proffering the active support of the Military Training Camps Association whenever it was needed. "We recognize you," he assured the general, "as the leader in this movement."[1] Although Palmer himself was ever inclined to be modest about his active duty role, repeatedly emphasizing its advisory character, he was in fact far more of a leader, formulating proposals and initiating action, than his humility would suggest. But what kind of leadership did he provide, not just for his friends in the MTCA but for the men he encountered in his larger function as a senior adviser within the War Department? Did he point the way toward sound policies, or did he lead the War Department into a futile quest for a statute authorizing UMT in principle, while deliberately fending off compromises that might have given some expectation of success? Subsequent events were to show that his tactics were unsuccessful. It can only be said that if he was in error, he had substantial approval for the course he advocated. But to focus attention on the drive for UMT is to obscure the real character of General Palmer's leadership.

The full range of the general's statesmanship is evident only when one looks beyond the institutions he advocated and the tactics he urged in securing them. Far more than most of the men who surrounded him, he endeavored to ground his proposals on fundamental principles. His military colleagues suffered from one serious disadvantage when laying plans for a peacetime establishment; unlike Palmer, they had not devoted a lifetime of study to devising a military policy ideally suited to a democracy. Few of them, with the notable exception of George Marshall, understood so well the inherently political dimensions of most military institutions. And it was by striving at every turn to insure that those political dimensions remained unequivocally democratic that Palmer made his most significant contribution. It was his persistence in pursuing the ideal of a thoroughly democratic army that led George Marshall to describe him as "the civilian conscience of the U.S. Army."

Palmer had been striving for this goal throughout most of his professional career, but not until the spring and early summer of 1943, when General Marshall finally established a full-time staff for postwar planning, did the problem come clearly into focus. The director of the new organization, Brig. Gen. William F. Tompkins, invited his elderly adviser to give a lecture to all of the newly assigned officers in his division to share with them the fruits of his wide experience.

The resulting address was a descriptive sketch of the ideal postwar military establishment as the general visualized it. All the familiar ingredients were there. The essence of the scheme was that prior training of all able-bodied men would make it possible to mobilize all or any required portion of the nation's total usable manpower in sufficient time to reinforce the small professional army. By means of UMT, it would be possible to avoid the twelve or more months of delay inevitably incurred when levies of raw draftees had to be hastily assembled and formed into armies. But the full advantages of prior training could be realized only if the "graduates" of UMT were formed into a reserve army, into organized units under citizen officers capable of moving promptly up behind the regulars.[2]

The reserve army was simply a restatement of the scheme Palmer and Senator Wadsworth had proposed in 1919, a unified reserve organization formed under the army clause of the U.S. Constitution to free it from the inconveniences and inefficiencies resulting from state control. This goal had not been attained under the Defense Act of 1920. As the general blandly put it, the concept of a unified reserve had at that time been "modified through political influences," to establish a dual reserve, with the National Guard organized under the militia clause and the Organized Reserves under the army clause.

Although Palmer advocated abandonment of state control in the interests of efficiency, he recognized the many advantages that stemmed from local or territorial organization. Under a scheme of territorial units, the initial rate of mobilization would be vastly accelerated. More importantly from the point of view of an army suited to a democratic people, a reserve force composed of local or territorial units would provide opportunities for cultivating leadership by giving reservists frequent occasions to handle troops and exercise the responsibilities of command. And unless reservists enjoyed such opportunities, did it not follow that all of the more significant positions of army command would fall to a professional caste? This not only deprived the nation of that vast pool of talent for leadership dispersed throughout the citizenry, but incurred the political risk of assigning a virtual monopoly of military power to the regulars. Yet another political advantage the general attributed to a territorial reserve was its visibility in the eyes of Congress. Deficiencies in equipment or numbers would be immediately evident in the ranks of reservists formed into local units that could elicit popular support. As a final political argument, the general pointed out that territorial units were the traditional pattern of organization; therefore one could solicit congressional support for an attempt to improve them by modifications without assuming the burden of the massive campaign of education that would be required to effect any major departure from tradition.

Surprisingly enough, Palmer's proposed application of UMT raised no serious dissent. Although its adoption would involve a well-nigh revolutionary impact on American life, the postwar planners seemed preoccupied with other issues. Doubtlessly they were conditioned by the nation's peril, but their failure to subject this initial premise to searching scrutiny at the outset was to cost them dearly later on. At the moment the opposition to the general's proposals was almost entirely limited to opposition to his insistence upon organizing the graduates of the universal training program into territorial units.

The most articulate opponent of Palmer's notions of a territorial reserve was his friend Miller G. White, now a brigadier serving as G-1 on the War Department General Staff. Despite his background as a Guard officer—or perhaps because of it—White had become convinced by his wartime experience that a territorial organization, whether after the pattern of the National Guard or along the lines of the Organized Reserve under the 1920 Act, was no longer workable. In its place he proposed to put all graduates of UMT into an unassigned pool, from which each individual could be drawn in an emergency according to his talents, age, and level of training.[3] Palmer was horrified by this suggested solution. This was nothing less than a return to the heresies of old Emory Upton. If White's views were adopted, he feared, the reserve army would be transformed into a roster of rank fillers, instead of potential leaders whose talents had been cultivated by every available means.[4]

Months earlier, at the first inkling of their disagreement, Palmer had sought White out to be certain that he fully understood his position. Sensitive to the daily burdens White carried in G-1, he invited him to dinner at the Army-Navy Club so they could explore the problem at leisure. "My respect for your judgment, experience, and intellectual integrity is such that to know we differ on a fundamental question of policy makes me feel insecure."[5] They did meet but failed to arrive at any common ground. Palmer was fully conscious of his dangerously exposed flank: a hostile G-1. He therefore seized the initiative and wrote the following note to General Tompkins immediately after delivering his lecture.

In view of General White's wide experience in developing our present war army it seems to me that it would be of great benefit to our whole group if he could be invited to give us a brief outline of his alternative solution of the reserve program. Though at present my mind is pretty well made up, I am open to conviction and would like to know more about the alternative solution.[6]

General White accepted the challenge and made a formal presentation of his views. The problem was to put round pegs in round holes. The modern army required a vast array of technical skills unevenly distributed throughout the population. It was no longer a matter of assembling a company of riflemen for a few simple tactical drills; the new and ever more complicated weapons, vehicles, and other types of equipment demanded a high degree of specialized training not readily available to local units. By placing the graduates of UMT in the Corps Area pool from which they could be called up as individuals, technical skills acquired in civilian life could be exploited in a way quite impossible within the constraints of local units, with their prescribed Tables of Organization. For example, under the pool system an X-ray technician at a local hospital could, upon recall to duty in a crisis, be assigned to an appropriate medical unit where his skills were needed; under a scheme of territorial organization, if his local unit happened to be, say, a company of Engineers, the benefits of his civilian skills might well be lost.[7]

General White's presentation convinced Palmer that the territorial organization in the simple form proposed in 1919 would no longer do. But he had to be convinced that this traditional form could not be modified to meet present need. "An outmoded organization should not be retained solely because it is deeply grounded in national tradition," he told Tompkins, "but on the other hand, it is ... practical statesmanship to reform an ancient and well-known institution" wherever possible.[8]

A series of conferences with White and the G-3, Brig. Gen. R. E. Porter, further undermined Palmer's faith in the validity of a territorial organization. Ever conscious of how out of date he was in regard to the newer weapons and equipment of the army, he admitted to Tompkins that these encounters "jolted me rather brusquely out of some old preconceptions." Finally, after several weeks of deliberation, he capitulated entirely. Soon afterward General Tompkins sent the Chief of Staff an "Outline of a Postwar Permanent Military Establishment," seeking approval for planning purposes. Having brought Palmer into camp and well aware of the added weight this would have with General Marshall, he proudly noted that the paper had full staff concurrence.[9]

That General Palmer did indeed concur with the Special Planning Division "outline" is evidence of how far he had succumbed to the arguments of the younger officers around him. Although the outline itself did not say so in as many words, General Tompkins' covering letter flatly stated: "The National Guard, under the system of universal military training disappears." For the postwar planners, the only future contemplated for the Guard was in the status of an entirely nonfederal force organized as a home guard under the militia clause. As for the graduates of UMT, according to the outline they would, "based on experience during the present war," enter a manpower pool, "doing away with the territorial organization of reserve units." Interestingly enough, the reasons given in support of this action ignored completely the matter of technical training and dwelt upon the need for flexibility in assignment, on the uncertainty as to the kinds of units needed in future emergencies, on the morale problems encountered in a community when its local Guard unit suffers heavy casualties, and on the adverse economic impact when the mobilization of a local unit pulls a large number of young men out of a community all at once.[10]

If the members of the Special Planning Division thought that "full staff concurrence" would assure approval of their outline by the Chief of Staff, they were mistaken. General Marshall was especially disturbed by what he regarded as the unrealistic attitude the planners were taking toward the postwar years. "Any scheme which presupposes a large Regular Army . . . will be wholly impracticable." Recalling the fate of the nine regular divisions stipulated in the 1920 act, he warned the planners that they were "entirely wrong" in looking to regulars rather than reservists to carry most of the burden of training in the UMT program. Although he failed to comment directly on their proposed pool in lieu of a terrritorial organization for reservists, he made it clear that he had far more to say about the whole question of reserves specified in their outline and promised to take the matter up soon in person.[11]

In the meantime Palmer, having bowed to what he regarded as his better-informed younger colleagues, threw himself into the task of finding ways to win converts to the new scheme. Opposition in Congress, he warned Tompkins, was certain to materialize from the Guard, and it would be necessary to make a convincing case against the traditional policy. He was busily engaged in this effort when a letter arrived from his friend of long standing, Lt. Gen. Hugh A. Drum, now retired from the army and serving as commanding general of the New York National Guard. Drum explained that he was currently drawing up plans to establish the place of the National Guard in the postwar military establishment and solicited Palmer's suggestions.[12]

The opportunity opened up by Drum was alluring but not without pitfalls. An exceedingly able officer, Drum had suffered two traumatic frustrations at the peak of his career. The first was when President Roosevelt selected George Marshall rather that Hugh Drum as Chief of Staff. So certain had he been of receiving the nod, his wife had actually measured the windows in Quarters One at Fort Myer in the expectation of moving in.[13] Hardly had Drum digested this first disappointment when the administration again frustrated his ambitions. This time it was in awarding the China mission—if such a term as award can be applied to so thankless a task—to Gen. "Vinegar Joe"Stilwell rather than to him.[14] As a consequence, when he left the army to assume command of the New York Guard, there was at least some reason to anticipate that he might espouse the cause of his new affiliation with a vigor reflecting something of his disenchantment. Although Palmer readily agreed to a meeting with Drum, it proved difficult to arrange a mutually convenient date. Eventually Drum went ahead without waiting to see Palmer and drew up a plan to implement UMT largely through the use of local National Guard units.

There was a double irony in Drum's scheme, which was entitled "Considerations Relative to Proposed Training in Peace."[15] Just at the moment when Palmer, the lifelong advocate of a citizen army, seemed to be abandoning the cause. Drum, the epitome of the professional soldier, was concocting a thoroughly civilianized scheme of training. Even Drum's phrases seemed to reflect the tone of Palmer's earlier writings. Preserve the spirit of the acts of 1916 and 1920, Drum urged, and retain the threefold structure of the Army of the United States, with its National Guard, Organized Reserve, and Regular Army units. If it is "impracticable and undesirable to attempt a departure from this traditional system," because the people of the United States won't accept a change, then why not enact new laws to make the old system work. The failures in the past, he argued, resulted not from defects in conception but from faulty execution, notably the failure of the War Department to utilize its full powers when trying to build workable citizen components.

Drum's proposal, Palmer realized, would have great appeal in Congress. It retained the existing organizational structure, assigned a major role to the Guard, ostentatiously made full use of the ROTC, and offered a scheme of training that aimed at disturbing the citizen's normal life as little as possible. He knew of all these arguments. The more he reflected on the problem of persuading Congress to accept the rather different approach being concocted in the Special Planning Division, the more impossible it appeared. The only escape that he could see was to lift the issue out of the political area entirely. With this in mind he wrote a long letter for his friend Archie Thacher to share with their Military Training Camps Association crowd in New York. The letter merits quotation not only as an indication of the current state of his thought but also for what it reveals of his expectation that a civilian commission on military policy might somehow rise above the normal give and take of politics.

I have read General Drum's paper and find that it rests upon an assumption that I cannot accept. He believes that our postwar military organization should include a reserve component like our National

Guard having a dual state and federal status under the militia clause of the constitution. I cannot see that Gen. Drum supports this on any higher ground than the belief that such an organization now exists and that it will be politically impossible to displace it.

My own idea is that such an organization might have been justified, more or less, in the world situation as it appeared to exist after the last war. But I cannot see that it has any place in a world dominated as ours now is by the airplane. The old type organization based on the idea of defense against invasion by sea will not meet this new situation. If we are opposed by a nation or group of nations having command of the air they will not attack the seaboard. Their planes will carry bombs and para-troopers direct to the interior of the continent. Our mission will be to see to it that, with the aid of Russia, Britain and the other United Nations, no aggressive enemy with such command of the air can ever rise again. To carry out this mission we must be prepared to form expeditionary or task forces to act immediately in any part of the world. The reservists of our army must therefore be ready for immediate mobilization in a very great variety of situations and perhaps with a different tactical organiza-tion in each one of these situations. I do not think it will be possible to organize a citizen army reserve like this unless it is formed under the army clause of the constitution just as the regular army is. I do not see how a force organized like our old National Guard into conventional territorial divisions, under amateur divisional commanders and con-trolled in peacetime by forty-eight separate states can have any place in such a reserve system.

Most of those who favor such a system favor it not because they believe the National Guard would form a sound reserve under such conditions but because they believe it has a political power that cannot be defeated and that therefore we must just as well agree to surrender to it in the beginning.

If we assume that the matter is to be decided by normal committee action in Congress, as in the past, I am inclined to think that they are right. I am quite sure that I can state my case so as to convince any competent mind capable of making a scientific decision. But I do not think I would get very far with a committee of Congress whose members are subject to political pressure by [the] National Guard lobby.

In my opinion, the National Guard problem is one of many problems connected with our future military policy that simply cannot be solved correctly if they are thrown willy-nilly into the Congressional hopper in the old way. In other words, unless we can create and construct some means of submitting a coordinated solution to Congress it will be impossible to solve our postwar military problem in the scientific and economical manner. I believe, however, if Congress should authorize a

commission of able civilians to study the whole problem of national
defense and to submit its final conclusions to Congress it might be
possible in this way to arrive at a constructive solution.

Suppose that a commission composed of distinguished and disinterested civilians should be established and directed to report to Congress
on fundamental questions such as the following: 1. should we have a
single Department of War? 2. should we have a separate Air Force? 3.
should we have UMT? (But I hope that Congress will answer this
question in the affirmative in the immediate future without waiting for
the commission) 4. How should a system of UMT be coordinated with
our present educational and industrial systems? 5. What should be the
dimensions, missions and mutual relations of the Land, Sea, and Air
Force? (This would be the foundation of a scientific military budget.) 6.
How should our reserve forces be organized? 7. What is the future of the
National Guard in our system? Should it retain its present dual status?
Or should it be essentially a state force organized solely for internal
defense? In the day of the airplane there will be a demand for a nation-
wide force to insure our internal security and such a force might well be
raised under the militia clauses of the Constitution and made available to
the Federal Government only for the limited purposes covered by the
militia clauses. But it should form no part of a task force formed to
stamp out the recrudescence of militarism in Japan and Germany.

It seems to me that if a group of able civilians should cover the broad
outlines of the whole problem in this way, its conclusions would have a
weight that would appeal to the Congress and to the people at large. If I,
for example, should present my view of the National Guard to such a
commission I think that I could convince them. But I would not have
any show at all before a congressional committee composed of men,
most of whom have no knowledge of military policy except what is fed
to them by constituents who are members of the National Guard
Association.

As to the composition of the commission—it might have members
from the armed services as well as civilians but there is much to be said
for having it composed of civilians only. Representatives of the several
armed forces would appear before it as *ex parte* witnesses. The commission would arrive at the truth judicially by weighing the issues joined
between opposing experts in open court. The sea force expert would
present his case in the presence of the ground force expert and the air
force expert and be subject to open rebuttal by either or both of them. If
you and Sec. Root and Phil Carroll and Ken Budd and Grenny Clark
formed the panel for such a commission, it would be difficult for any of
us service partisans to put anything over on you. In some cases, however, you might find it useful to follow another judicial precedent by

calling in an old soldier occasionally to sit with you temporarily as a 'friend of the court.'

I did not intend to dictate such a long letter but when I started I had to get the whole story out of my system.[16]

Far from getting "the whole story" out of his system, the general's letter to Thacher only made him more painfully aware of the dilemma in which he found himself. He wanted to go along with his younger colleagues, but he was conscious of a nagging conviction that the policy paper taking shape in the Special Planning Division was lacking in several significant respects. If somebody would sit down and work out a concrete picture of just how the proposed reserve would take shape, it might be possible to come up with "something that we can sell" not only to reserve officers but also to the National Guard.[17]

After several weeks of sporadic effort he came up with a rather rambling paper, "The Place of the National Guard in the Post-War Reserve System." The new single reserve, under the army clause, would be based on areas of equal population. Each congressional district would constitute a reserve district within these areas, sending about 1,700 men for universal training each year. Assuming a five-year obligation and allowing for attrition, each district would have 6,000 reservists on tap, or approximately 2,500,000 men for the nation as a whole. Reserve officers in each district would keep the rosters up to date, note transfers, make vocational reclassifications, and so on. But how would it be possible to sustain interest among the reservists with such an arrangement? As if covertly trying to slip in a terrritorial organization by the back door, the general suggested that each district might assemble its reservists from time to time for "training."[18] But what kind of training did he have in mind? A mere pool of reservists would have no mission, no organization, no equipment, no functional cohesion, and only the most nominal sort of leadership from officers performing routine personnel administration. All of which led to the conclusion that the National Guard would have no future. The general's suggestion that the menace of aircraft and of assaults by parachute raised a new and important role for militia forces he left undeveloped; he had little expectation that the notion would find any takers among the guardsmen.

The paper, one of the poorest the general ever wrote, reflected his own confusion and loss of direction. The truth of the matter was that he had ceased to lead. Painfully aware of being out of his depth when it came to modern weaponry, and genuinely anxious to be a loyal member of the planning team, he honestly tried to go along with the majority view. But his doubts would not down, and over a period of several weeks his ideas once again changed course.

A number of factors combined to precipitate the drastic alteration in the general's thinking, and since they eventually led to what was probably his most significant achievement during the war years, the process is of no little interest as an example of policy formation at the staff level. In the first place, he was never really persuaded that the idea of a reserve pool was workable. He recognized the merit of the arguments advanced in support of the pool, but saw that the real defect was not in what the pool idea would accomplish but in what it would fail to do. How could it be trained or even develop and sustain enthusiasm for reserve duty? What opportunities would the pool offer to potential leaders? He was willing to concede that "amateur major generals," as he called them, might not be able to lead reserve divisions efficiently, but every time he tried to reincorporate some of the constructive features of territorial units, his fellow planners rejected his suggestions. Gradually it dawned on him that many of them simply did not share his fundamental faith in a citizen army. Their conception of the citizen soldier turned out to be Uptonian: citizen soldiers were useful to fill up the cadres officered by professionals.[19]

The other factors that changed the general's mind came from outside the division. Although he had endeavored to dismiss General Drum's proposals for using the National Guard in connection with UMT as political expediency, the scheme as outlined would do far more to foster a true citizen army than any of the pool ideas of the Special Planning Division. While still mulling over Drum's paper, he received an invitation from Maj. Gen. Ellard A. Walsh of Minnesota, the newly chosen president of the National Guard Association, to confer with him at the Guard Bureau.[20] Walsh left no doubt that the Guard would fight to the bitter end to retain its place as the principal federal reserve, but he also persuaded his elderly acquaintance that the guardsmen rested their case on something more than their political power. All they asked now was an opportunity to present their case on its merits. Palmer soon arranged for a conference, to be attended by representatives of the Special Planning Division, led by Tompkins and Palmer; by spokesmen for the Guard, led by Walsh and Drum; and by members of the Guard Bureau, represented by Maj. Gen. J. F. Williams.

The two-day conference, 28 and 29 February 1944, got off to a bad start. General Tompkins explained that universal military training was the primary objective and discussed some of the assumptions used by the planners. When General Walsh asked what assumptions had been made concerning the National Guard, he was told "none so far."[21] To be sure, the Chief of Staff had not formally approved the outline drafted by the division, but the answer was certainly less than candid; Tompkins himself had suggested to the Chief of Staff that under the division plan the Guard would "disappear." And only a few days earlier one of the officers present at the conference, Col. W. E. Carpenter, had protested that the "generally accepted" planning assumption calling for a single reserve component predicated "the elimination of the National Guard as now provided by law."[22]

General Tompkins was a man of integrity, a fair-minded officer, certainly not one known to be inherently hostile to the Guard. His answer to Walsh's question may best be understood as overly cautious; it reflected his fear of how the guardsmen might exploit his words politically. Walsh, especially, was noted for the violence of his speeches voicing mistrust of the Regular Army, so Tompkins had good reason for being circumspect. Nonetheless, the episode resembled independent nations forced into an unstable alliance. Each feared that the other might take unfair advantage of any concession or inadvertant admission. Because the National Guard Association did not yet maintain a permanent office in Washington, all attempts at finding common ground had to rely upon written communication or upon hurried encounters when association officers paid brief visits to the capital. Even a two-day conference was too short, but as Palmer had anticipated, this more protracted discussion did begin to produce results.

The guardsmen, as might have been predicted, insisted upon a policy statement, similar to the one they had secured in the Draft Act of 1940, assuring them a place in the federal reserve. But they also brought up various other points of importance. Maj. Gen. Edward Martin, who had recently given up his position as president of the National Guard Association to serve as governor of Pennsylvania, warned that it would be folly not to limit the scale of universal training to hold down the cost. As Martin and others put it, unconsciously echoing General Marshall's earlier arguments along the same line, economy and not foreign policy would determine the real character of the postwar establishment. Far from urging an ever-larger postwar organization for themselves, the guardsmen suggested that 300,000 men, the number mobilized in 1940, was far more than the states would be willing to finance without federal aid. If the Guard were to be used as the reserve vehicle for the graduates of UMT, the period of obligatory enrollment should be limited to two years. From long experience they understood that only volunteers made good guardsmen; if the period of obligatory membership were extended unduly, a majority of those enrolled would soon lack that *esprit* so indispensible to an effective organization. In short, instead of threatening the Regulars with their political power, the Guard spokesmen emphasized their limitations. They even went so far as to suggest giving Guard commissions to selected regular officers, who might then take over the command of Guard divisions and other larger units, thus undercutting much of the argument against "amateur major generals."[23]

Palmer was amazed to learn that the guardsmen had for some years sought the assignment of professionals only to be rebuffed by the War Department. "This almost makes it appear," he subsequently commented to General Drum, "that some of our narrow-minded regulars were frankly unwilling to permit the National Guard to become efficient." His own views were in striking contrast. Were he a governor, he declared, he would treat the National Guard as part of the educational system of the state. He would treat the senior officers of the Guard as educators and would select them with the same care employed in selecting professors at the state university. "I would not tolerate the idea that they must be limited to the state university's alumni or to nominees of the alumni association. In selecting a professor of geology, I would not hesitate to take a graduate of Yale or Rutgers if he were recognized among geologists as superior to any graduates of my own state university." The wisdom of comparable procedure in selecting brigade and division commanders for the state guard seemed manifest. If the guardsmen were willing to accept this, the general believed, they would go far toward "disarming their enemies and encouraging their friendly critics."[24] What impressed the regulars most, however, was the way the guardsmen insisted that the War Department already had authority under existing statutes to make the National Guard into a fully efficient federal reserve force while continuing it under the dual status and as a territorial organization. If the Guard had been inefficient, Walsh contended, it had been so because the War Department had failed to exercise the powers it already possessed.[25]

The results of the conference pleased Palmer, who wrote a long memo to Tompkins urging immediate action by the Judge Advocate to determine whether or not the powers of the War Department really did extend as far as the guardsmen claimed. If they did, the wise course might be to retain the Guard as an integral part of the postwar reserve. With UMT the Guard could probably be maintained in a greater state of readiness than had ever been possible before. At best, however, its real efficiency would largely depend upon "the development of a genuine sympathetic interest in the National Guard throughout the officer corps of the Regular Army."[26] Even with this somewhat utopian qualification, General Tompkins was inclined to go along, and a few days later he bucked Palmer's memo to the Chief of Staff, suggesting that its recommendations be approved as War Department policy.[27]

For Palmer, Tompkins's willingness to revise the basic statement of policy was a personal triumph. The position paper, or "Outline of a Post-war Military Establishment," concocted by the Special Planning Division might now be recast to include the territorial organization he had advocated in the first place. Although both G-3 and the Operations Division raised objections, the main criticism came from G-1. Once again G-1 urged a pool rather than territorial units for the graduates of UMT and suggested that all UMT training should be done by Regular Army units as part of their normal duties.[28]

Well aware that the tide was again flowing in his direction, Palmer plunged in to beat down the attack. He was 74 years old, always tired, and at the time intermittently confined to his quarters with a miserable winter cold. Nonetheless, his rejoinder comprised ten pages of single-spaced typescript.[29]

The G-1 proposal to let Regular Army units conduct UMT training Palmer set out to destroy in two passes. First, he suavely observed that such a scheme had a precedent in the plan that had been put forward by Chief of Staff Peyton C. March in 1919—that touch was almost certainly planted to catch George

Marshall's eye. Then he attacked the G-1 scheme on its merits, clinching his point with a quotation from Lord Macaulay's *History of England*: "It is an axiom in the science of organization, as in mechanics, that organizations or mechanisms designed to perform a double function rarely, if ever, perform either function satisfactorily." Tactical units of the Regular Army should concentrate on bringing themselves to a high state of readiness for combat; the training of recruits should be left to others for whom this would be a primary mission, in which there should be a large role for reservists.[30]

There was still another reason why the young men called up for UMT should not be put into Regular Army units: that would give substance to claims that UMT was only a disguised means of filling up the ranks of professional cadres—in short, conscription. If the distinction between universal *training* and universal *service* was to be maintained, it was decidedly unwise to assign the training function to Regular Army tactical units.

Contemptuously dismissing the whole concept of "an amorphous manpower pool," the general sketched out the compelling necessity for local reserve units. Even if a powerful organization of the United Nations were to make the probability of total war remote, he argued, the army must nevertheless develop plans for mobilizing the total manpower of the nation. And a pool of reservists designed to fill up Regular Army cadres would be of no use as a source of additional cadres, once the relatively small number of regular units had been fleshed out. Territorial units such as those of the National Guard and Organized Reserve, for all their shortcomings, had already demonstrated that they were able to provide important cadres in the time of crisis. More importantly, these units managed to elicit participation of many dedicated reservists in peacetime. We must continue to "awaken and sustain" the interest of reserve officers at the community level. "Only in this way can we hope to mobilize the brain as well as the brawn of the American people."[31]

Above all, Palmer sought a military establishment suited to the genius of a democratic people. During the first two years since his return to active duty, it had been the reservists, the ROTC interests, and especially the guardsmen who had seemed to be the obstacles. But during the past few months, in the latter half of 1943, as the general worked more closely with the regulars, he had found that they too could be myopic.

Palmer regarded his role as one of mediating to bring regulars and reservists into one coherent Army of the United States. By holding out for what he honestly believed to be the best possible solution, he ran the risk of being written off as politically naive. But he also understood, perhaps better than many of his more cynical contemporaries, that real leadership, sound statesmanship, involves a subtle admixture of the ideal and the practical.

The general's readiness to compromise when necessary was perhaps best exemplified in the issue of dual control for the Guard. He still believed that direct control under the army clause was to be preferred, but that it would be possible to live with dual control. If organizing under the army clause proved to be politically impossible, he assured General Drum, "the sensible thing for sensible men is to do the best they can with the powers that are available to them." The art of compromise, however, is in the timing.[32] As Palmer expressed it to his friend Kenneth P. Budd in the MTCA, "There is real merit in his plan when the time comes to compromise, but we have not reached that stage yet."[33]

One reason the general was so sure the time for compromise had not yet arrived was the high hopes he held for an independent civilian commission. His friend Jim Wadsworth was actively exploring the idea on Capitol Hill. The chilly reception it encountered there induced the congressman to back off in favor of a bipartisan joint committee from both houses. When this too was forestalled by parliamentary considerations, Wadsworth finally settled for a House select committee, an arrangement that won strong support from the House leaders.[34] As a consequence, when he formally introduced his resolution on 3 March 1944 to establish such a committee, it carried with ease.[35]

If the newly formed Select Committee on Postwar Military Policy was considerably less than Palmer had hoped for, it was a step in the right direction. This was to be a committee to formulate broad outlines of policy, not one concerned with the details of implementation. The House leaders selected Rep. Clifton Woodrum, a Democrat from Virginia, as chairman. In addition to Wadsworth, the twenty-three-man committee included Rep. A. J. May of the Military Affairs Committee, Rep. Carl Vinson of the Naval Affairs Committee, and a rising young New Deal congressman from Texas named Lyndon B. Johnson. At its first informal meeting, the chairman invited Palmer to sit in regularly with the committee as an adviser, much as he had done for Wadsworth's committee in 1919. Although Palmer protested that his advanced years made this impractical, he agreed to appear as the first witness at the forthcoming hearings. As he rather proudly reported to his daughter, "I feel this is one of the most important jobs ever assigned to me."[36]

When the hearings finally did begin late in March 1944, the general had to steer a middle course between the extreme demands of the guardsmen and those of the regulars. He tried to show that he was no tame spokesman for either faction. The postwar reserve, he argued, must be kept flexible, ready at all times to reinforce the army in a variety of situations, even if this required some departure from the old way of doing things.

It is obvious that a nation-wide organization of territorial divisions as in the plan of 1920 will not meet these conditions. To lock up all our trained reservists in a rigid territorial organization that will probably never be mobilized as such will serve no useful purpose and will seriously hamper the prompt employment of trained reserve officers and reservists when and where they are needed.[37]

Then, having served notice on his Guard friends that he was no blind tool of their demands, he turned to consider the other side of the equation.

The regulars, the general warned the listening congressmen, were all too prone to believe that they and only they understood the mysteries of military leadership. Then, knowing his audience, he resorted to an anecdote to make his point, recalling the tale of an Irish construction foreman who assigned the heavy pick and shovel jobs to "Eyetalians," while using Irishmen to trundle the loaded barrows downhill. When one of the benighted shovelers boldly sought to take over one of the wheelbarrows, the foreman knocked him flat, shouting, "What d'you Eyetalians know about machinery?" Pointing to the current strength figures of the General Staff, he observed that more than two-thirds of the officers serving there were reservists, a fact that seemed to suggest that citizen soldiers might just possibly know something about running the "machinery."

By way of peroration, the general urged the creation of a single Department of Defense to reconcile the conflicting claims of the several services. He illustrated this need, too, with an anecdote. Recalling an episode from his own experience after World War I, he told how the various branches of the army were instructed to estimate their manpower requirements within the 280,000 ceiling on regulars prescribed by the 1920 act; when the totals of their individual requests were finally compiled, they added up to no less than 1,500,000 men. All of which led him to recall the words of Robert Burns:

> But Och! Mankind are unco' weak
> And little to be trusted;
> If self the wavering balance shake
> It's rarely right adjusted.

If the general expected to produce the same kind of sensation he had in 1919, he was to be disappointed; even the press coverage on the hearings was scanty at best. He could scarcely expect more in competition with the war news. As an old hand at testifying before Congress, he understood that no small part of the purpose of the hearings was to develop evidence to educate individuals in key positions. So he distributed more than fifty copies of his testimony where he thought it would do the most good among his military colleagues, his friends in the MTCA, journalists, and members of Congress.[38]

There were some grounds for optimism; Woodrum and Wadsworth both indicated that there was already considerable support for universal military training within the committee. But the members all felt it would be wiser to shelve the highly controversial subject of UMT until the presidential elections were safely over.[39] As the general tactfully put it, they were afraid of "inconveniently unfavorable reactions from their constituents," most especially in the form of crippling amendments suggested by the ROTC people, the Guard, and other special interests.[40]

As it turned out, the guardsmen did take issue with the army. Although Palmer had been inclined to believe that some sort of accommodation would be worked out, he was abruptly disabused of any such notion when he read Walsh's statement to the committee. Although there was a good deal of exaggeration and superheated prose, Walsh built his case with no little skill. First he warned the regulars that Congress, "our refuge and our strength," had "never turned a deaf ear to our petitions." Then he went on to show how the Guard of the several states had justified this confidence, investing over $500 million in armories, spending over $25 million annually on upkeep, and mobilizing over 300,000 officers and men in eighteen divisions when the crisis arrived. Only 233 Guard officers, out of more than 20,000 called up, he proudly recalled, had failed to pass their physical examinations. To the charge that Guard leaders were ineffectual "political appointees," he offered the rejoinder that virtually all the senior commanders in the Guard were men who had combat experience in World War I and many of them had come up through the ranks.[41]

What rankled most, apparently, was the ruthless way in which Guard officers had been relieved when the old prewar square divisions were scaled down into triangular divisions. "By every conceivable stratagem and by completely ignoring the law our commanding officers have been relieved wholesale and replaced by young West Pointers with little or no experience." And when the War Department reactivated the old 42nd, or Rainbow, Division, one of the most famous Guard divisions of World War I, not a single Guard unit was included.

The regulars had indeed made mistakes in their realignment of state units. It was also true that some Guard units had suffered from what Palmer repeatedly described as "amateur generals assisted by amateur staff officers." The difference between Palmer and so many of his fellow regulars was that he was perfectly willing to let a citizen officer command a division if that officer could demonstrate his competence to do so; moreover, he insisted on creating a system of reserves that would provide opportunities for reservists to acquire such competence. The trouble with the professionals was that they looked to the failure of some reservists to measure up to the exceedingly complex tasks of commanding divisions and other large units, while ignoring the accomplishments of others. The tabulation Palmer secured from G-1 at the time of the Woodrum hearing strongly suggests that criticism by the regulars of senior leaders in the National Guard, however justified in particular instances, tended to obscure the real character of the problem.[42]

	Officers Commissioned			
	Regular Army	National Guard	Organized Reserve	Officers Holding Temporary War-Time Commissions
Percentage of total officer strength of army	2.3	2.9	27.2	67.7
Percentage of all general officers	91.5	6.1	1.8	.9
Percentage of all colonels	73.5	7.5	16.1	2.9

With Guard generals accounting for no more than a trifle over 6 percent of the total army strength in that category, in contrast to 91.5 percent for the regulars, the charge of amateurism appeared to be little more than a rationalization for those who wished to do away with the Guard altogether.

Although it is easy to write Walsh off as an intemperate partisan, his position deserves more careful analysis. Walsh did accuse the War Department of never overlooking an opportunity to "destroy the National Guard." And he did so after the February conference with the postwar planners, which had seemed to go far toward reconciling their differences. But while the Special Planning Division had shifted toward preserving the Guard in the postwar establishment, General Walsh had no knowledge of this change, and as president of the National Guard Association he occupied a difficult position. He had to play a political role, finding issues to focus the attention of the state contingents and win their support. A total capitulation by the War Department might strip him of vital support. Thus, at the very time when the regulars and the Guard seemed to be drawing toward a rapprochment, General Walsh found it tactically useful to keep up his barrage against the regulars.[43]

In Walsh's view, the Defense Act of 1920 should be retained as the cornerstone of defense policy. If the tripartite arrangement of the Army of the United States were perpetuated, with the Regular Army, the National Guard, and the Organized Reserve each continuing in its present status, he saw no great difficulty in accommodating to the introduction of universal military training. The 1920 statute, he reminded the congressmen, assured the civilian components a "positive voice" in all policies affecting their organization. Under the provisions contained in Section 5 of the act, such policies had to be submitted to joint committees of regulars and reservists, but the War Department had chosen to ignore this requirement of the law. When the National Guard Association protested this violation, the Special Planning Division had added one Guard officer to the planning group and then relegated him, Walsh charged, to "a decidedly inferior and inconsequential place." Under the circumstances, he urged the congressmen to defer action on UMT until after the war, when the guardsmen now in combat would be free to present their case.[44]

In a sense Walsh's blast actually strengthened Palmer's hand in the struggle to preserve the concept of a territorial organization. Palmer promptly drew up two long memos in which he canvassed the whole question for General Tompkins. He had previously surrendered to G-1 and G-3, he admitted, because as one long in retirement he thought it "presumptuous in me to contest the views of two such distinguished officers." When they had assured him that the old scheme of reserve divisions had no place in the postwar reestablishment, he had bowed to their judgment. But now, after studying the problem anew, he was convinced that his original stand had been correct. What is more, he was convinced that the Woodrum Committee, prodded along by the National Guard Association and the Reserve Officers' Association, would also take this view. So the Special Planning Division should come up with some scheme of organization that did not rest upon mere pools of reservists. And since there was "a strong probability" that the legislators would favor a solution along the lines suggested by General Drum, he urged that the planners try to perfect Drum's plans for postwar application.[45]

Palmer was now convinced that he had been on the right path when he insisted on an *organized* reserve formed into territorial or local units. Such units not only provided cadres for mobilization and visibility for grass-roots political support, but they also offered steps up which interested reservists could climb, acquiring both training and experience in command. Whether this reserve was to be provided by the National Guard under a dual state and federal status or by a single newly constituted Organized Reserve under the army clause was now an open question. The essential feature, in a democratic nation, was to preserve the concept of an organized territorial reserve of citizen soldiers. For some months past it had appeared that the National Guard solution would be adopted because it could muster the necessary votes. In a democracy that was an asset, for in the lean years of peace a capacity to rally political support for defense appropriations was not to be overlooked. If the professional soldiers on the General Staff continued to show Uptonian tendencies, there was something more to be said for the political power of the National Guard; it could at least preserve the basic concept of an organized reserve. But this left a big issue unresolved. If the National Guard were to be retained as the principal ready reserve, it would have to achieve a higher degree of efficiency. Even if universal military training greatly improved the general level of all who enlisted in the ranks of the Guard, this still left the serious problem of insuring effectiveness among the higher unit commanders.[46]

The difficulty, the general began to realize, was that everyone had been thinking of organizations. The human side of the equation had been missed.

He came to this realization while mulling over General Drum's suggestions. The primary problem was to get thoroughly competent commanders and staffs throughout the National Guard.[47] If this problem were not solved, then no amount of organizational rearrangement, whether under the army clause or the militia clause, would make the Guard efficient.

Why not, Palmer asked, set up a standard of performance to be met by all officers, regulars, and reservists alike, who aspire to command? Unconsciously, perhaps, he was reverting to the idea he had sketched out in an article in 1917.[48] Without going into details, he simply noted that a company commander might be certified as fit after a few hours of testing, while a candidate for division commander might be required to perform for a week. There were all manner of practical difficulties to be anticipated; the important point was that it moved the discussion from the legal or constitutional one of organization to the practical one of administration.

Palmer wrote Drum that he had decided to abandon his fight for a National Guard under the army clause. Instead of attempting the "politically impossible," he intended to work for improvement of the Guard from within the framework of the existing statutes.[49] And one of the strongest instruments within the existing statutes was Section 5 of the 1920 act, which called for joint committees of reservists and regulars to advise the Secretary of War on questions of organization and policy touching the civilian components. Now that General Walsh had accused the War Department of violating the law in not using Section 5 committees, the time was obviously ripe for a move to have them reconstituted. So he urged General Tompkins to ignore the offensive tone of Walsh's remarks, inasmuch as the Guard leader was substantially correct in his allegations, and give him the committees he sought.[50] Tompkins agreed, and the Chief of Staff added his approval.[51]

While waiting for the joint committees to get organized, Palmer turned back to his primary mission: drafting a statement of policy on the military institutions best suited to a democracy. As he explained the matter to Grenville Clark, he wanted to get high-level approval for an authoritative statement of fundamentals that would avoid the extremes of "those who want too big a Regular Army and those who want a wishy-washy and ineffective citizen army."[52] He used a long memo to Tompkins to clarify his thoughts and provoke a reaction. He was disturbed, he confessed, by the many papers currently being turned out within the War Department revealing "a distinct trend away from our traditional military policy." Most of the trouble, he suggested, grew out of disagreements over the proper place of reserve officers in the military establishment. If the guardsmen were unreasonable in contending for divisions led by amateur major generals, then so too were those regulars who suggested that no reserve officer should be promoted above the rank of captain in peacetime. With the Organized Reserve providing more than 16 percent of the full colonels and over 50 percent of the lieutenant colonels currently on active duty, exclusive of the Guard, one had only to ask where all this talent would be found in a future emergency.[53]

The wisest plan, the general argued, would be to have the Special Planning Division formulate a statement on the respective roles and missions of regulars and reserve officers and on the means for qualifying reserve officers in peacetime. If truly sound standards for promotion were established, it would be difficult for the guardsmen to seek anything less in Congress. The younger postwar planners were inclined to dismiss all this as mere detail. In Palmer's view the status of reserve officers was the crux of the whole problem. Since no one in the Special Planning Division seemed to agree with his assessment, he resolved to carry his case to George Marshall.

Although the time and energy of the Chief of Staff were carefully protected, his elderly advisor had no difficulty in securing entry. His companion of the "Valley Campaign," Col. Frank McCarthy, one of the guardians at Marshall's door, assured Palmer that "as a specimen citizen soldier, I concur heartily in every idea you have expressed" and said the chief would find the paper on his desk in the morning.[54] General Tompkins was less enthusiastic. So long as the flow of ideas conformed to the will of the division, there was a decided advantage in having backstairs access to the Chief of Staff through his elderly friend, but if Palmer began taking papers upstairs independently, the easy access might prove troublesome. He reminded Palmer that the division already had a statement of postwar policy approved by the War Department. Tompkins was not unfriendly to a major role for citizen soldiers in the postwar establishment, but he knew he must continue to deal with those regulars who disagreed and was therefore anxious not to proceed too rapidly.[55]

That General Tompkin's caution was not without merit was evident the day after Palmer sent up his memo. Lt. Gen. Leslie J. McNair wrote from his headquarters as Commanding General of the Army Ground Forces to the Chief of Staff, criticizing the National Guard in the harshest terms. "One of the great lessons of the present war, he declared, is that the National Guard as organized before the war contributed nothing to National Defense." Virtually every one of its general officers, he added, had lacked the competence to command in that grade; indeed, almost all the leaders, from colonel to major general, had had to be replaced before the Guard divisions could perform effectively, and even then they were, in his opinion, less sound than the new divisions created entirely from scratch. The Guard, he concluded, should be "dispensed with" as a component of the Army of the United States.[56]

The timing of General McNair's blast may have been coincidence, but it is difficult not to believe that someone, either among the postwar planners or in the chief's office, had tipped off McNair to Palmer's memo. McNair was notorious for his hostility to the Guard, and anyone sharing his views might have turned to him for support, especially some officer aware of how receptive the Chief of Staff was to the ideas presented by his old friend Palmer. A copy of McNair's letter was soon in Palmer's possession, apparently given to him by Marshall. The lack of any covering letter may be eloquent testimony to Marshall's skill in presiding over the Army of the United States. He could appreciate and make use of two such markedly different individuals as General McNair of the Army Ground Forces and General Walsh of the National Guard Association, using their strengths and ignoring their shortcomings. It was no small part of Palmer's service to Marshall that he helped to bridge the gap between these two symbolic figures. He did this most effectively by turning out that statement of fundamental policy he had so long visualized as his most important wartime task.

Early in August 1944, after nearly a month of writing and rewriting, he sent the Chief of Staff a fully developed statement along the lines of his earlier memo, carefully routing it through General Tompkins. His covering letter, which also bore evidence of no little literary polishing, reminded the chief that even the ablest soldiers do not always realize that there is a political as well as a professional aspect to military institutions.

> The wise military statesman must therefore consider both aspects of this problem and will generally be inclined to perfect or improve existing military institutions rather than to propose new or alien types. He will appreciate that an effective national institution is a living organism, like a growing tree, deeply rooted in the soil of national history and tradition. It can be pruned or guided or stimulated as it grows, but it cannot be replaced by a lifeless artificial structure such as a post or stake driven in the ground.[57]

The planners were going ahead to build the postwar establishment around the traditional components, but to be successful they would need the whole-hearted backing of the citizen soldiers themselves. A broad statement of general policy assuring the citizen components that their traditional role would be respected, Palmer argued, would win widespread support and vastly simplify the task of postwar planning.

The effort involved in turning out the policy statement took more out of Palmer than he cared to admit. As the summer wore on and Washington grew increasingly hotter, General Marshall had once again "ordered" him to New Hampshire, but the general begged off, instructing Colonel McCarthy to tell the chief of the project he had in hand. "In a sense it is the culmination of my life work and I hope it will be of great service to him and to the country." At last, however, he set out for his New Hampshire farm.[58]

The general desperately needed to rest. The death of his son-in-law, Norman Chandler, after a painful illness had cast a gloom over the family. He himself had been sick repeatedly. Ever since he joined the Special Planning Division, his load had grown enormously. His friends at the Library of Congress obligingly provided a cot in the dispensary for him to take a noontime nap; yet even so, he usually spent six full hours at his desk each day.[59]

One chore that had absorbed a great deal of his time and energy over many months was his effort to secure appointments to the U.S. Military Academy for his two grandsons. One obliging congressman from a western state, long an admirer of the general's, offered him an appointment when one of his constituents failed to qualify, complaisantly recording the replacement as a resident of his state. While the general was quite ready to accept favors from a "fibbable congressman" as he put it, he realized after some reflection that he was altogether unwilling to have any grandson of his certify falsely as to his place of residence. So his search continued.[60]

After many frustrations his luck finally changed when Governor Saltonstall of Massachusetts designated Sinclair Weeks for the place vacated by Sen. Henry Cabot Lodge, who had gone off to war. The general assured Weeks, a long-time family friend, that as an "unbiased grandfather" he could vouch for the qualifications of his kin, and soon afterward the interim senator assured him of an appointment. But which youngster should get the coveted position? Eventually the elder boy, Norman, Norry to the family, who was already in service, secured his commission at the Engineer Office Candidate School at Fort Belvoir, where his proud grandfather gave the graduation address. So the academy appointment went to the younger grandson, John, then in his third year at Harvard, where he stroked the crew and excelled in his studies.[61]

When the Palmers finally reached their farm in New Hampshire, they discovered that wartime rationing of gasoline kept their friends from visiting and that getting domestic help was next to impossible. Such routine tasks as opening the house and putting up screens were more tiring than they used to be, and since Follansbee's food store in the village could no longer deliver, one had to spend hours each week in fetching up provisions. In less than a month the Palmers were quite ready to return to the city.[62]

Although the weeks spent in New Hampshire turned out to be somewhat less than restful, in one respect they were most eventful. For it was there that the general received word that his great hope had been fulfilled: the Chief of Staff had approved the statement of principles he had toiled so long to produce.[63] General Marshall not only accepted the statement without change, but directed that it be issued for army-wide consumption as an official publication.[64]

The document, which appeared in War Department Circular No. 347 on 25 August 1944, read as follows:

MILITARY ESTABLISHMENT

1. Preliminary assumptions. It is assumed that for some time after the defeat of the Axis powers the United States will maintain such temporary military forces, in cooperation with its Allies, as may be necessary in order to lay the foundations for a peaceful world order. The plans for a permanent peace establishment, referred to in this circular, relate to a later period when the future world order can be envisaged.

It is also assumed, for the purpose of planning, that the Congress will enact (as the essential foundation of an effective national military organization), that every able-bodied young American shall be trained to defend his country; and that for a reasonable period after his training (unless he volunteers for service in the regular establishment of the armed forces) he shall be incorporated in a reserve, all, or part of which, shall be subject to active military duty in the event of an emergency requiring reinforcement of the Regular Army.

2. Types of military organization. There are two types of military organization through which the manpower of a nation may be developed.

a. One of these is the standing army type. In this type, the men of the nation are drawn into the army to serve in the lower grades. The function of the common citizen is ordinarily to be a private soldier or, at most, a noncommissioned officer in war. Reserve officers are drawn from the better educated classes but are generally employed in the lower grades and in subordinate capacities. Under this system, leadership in war and the control of military preparations and policy in peacetime are concentrated largely and necessarily in a special class or caste of professional soldiers.

This is the system of Germany and Japan. It produces highly efficient armies. But it is open to serious political objections. In a nation maintaining such a system, intelligent opinion as to military policy (and the international political policy associated therewith) is concentrated in a special class. Under such a system the people themselves are competent to exert only a limited intelligent influence on the issues of war and peace. Under such a system only the brawn of a people is prepared for war, there being no adequate provision for developing the latent military leadership and genius of the people as a whole. It, therefore, has no place among the institutions of a modern democratic state based upon the conception of government by the people.

b. The second type of military institution through which the national manpower can be developed is based upon the conception of a professional peace establishment (no larger than necessary to meet normal peacetime requirements) to be reinforced in time of emergency by organized units drawn from a citizen army reserve, effectively organized for this purpose in time of peace; with full opportunity for competent citizen soldiers to acquire practical experience through temporary active service and to rise by successive steps to any rank for which they can definitely qualify; and with specific facilities for such practical experience, qualification, and advancement definitely organized as essential and predominating characteristics of the peace establishment.

An army of this type has, among others, the following advantages:

First. — While, as in all effective military systems, the efficiency of this system depends primarily upon expert professional control, its leadership is not exclusively concentrated in a professional soldier class. All citizen soldiers after their initial training are encouraged to develop their capacity for leadership to such an extent as may be consistent with their abilities, their tastes, and their civil obligations.

Second. — As a great majority of the leaders of the war army are included in the civil population in time of peace, an intelligent and widespread public opinion is provided as the basis for the determination of all public questions relating to military affairs.

Third. — As with a properly organized citizen army reserve no officers or men need be maintained in the Regular Army to perform duties which can be performed effectively and in time by reserve officers and reservists, the dimensions and cost of the peace establishment, under such a system, are necessarily reduced to a determinable minimum.

And finally, as all our great wars have been fought in the main by citizen armies, the proposal for an organized citizen army reserve in time of peace is merely a proposal for perfecting a traditional national institution to meet modern requirements which no longer permit extemporization after the outbreak of the war. This is the type of army which President Washington proposed to the First Congress as one of the essential foundations of the new American Republic. This is the type of army which, in the absence of effective peacetime organization, had to be extemporized to meet our needs in World War I and World War II.

Details of military organization change with changes in weapons, modes of transportation, and international relations. But the *type* of our military institutions was determined in the beginning by the form of our government and has not changed since Washington's Administration. It will therefore be made the basic for all plans for a post-war peace establishment.

By order of the Secretary of War:

G. C. Marshall,
Chief of Staff

The popular reaction was emphatically favorable. The War Department Public Relations Bureau assembled clippings from papers all over the country giving the publication not only excellent coverage in their news columns, but also enthusiastic approval in their editorials. The reaction in Congress was no less favorable.[65] Even though War Department circulars scarcely rank as popular literary media, the message was, in its way, a best seller. It seemed to strike some inner chord, some deeply felt conviction in the popular mind. Although the National Guard was never mentioned in the statement, General Walsh called it "military statesmanship of the highest order." A less partisan observer, Howard C. Petersen, Palmer's friend from the Draft Act days of 1940, wrote from his post in the Under Secretary's office, sending a clutch of clippings with the comment, "Your wisdom in these matters is well proven by the popular acceptance of this pronouncement."[66]

Palmer was scrupulously careful to see that the statement was attributed to Marshall and not to himself.[67] When the Chief of Staff suggested that the real author should be credited, he was quick to decline. "This is not the time for such credit. The country has hailed the pronouncement as the 'Marshall Plan.' With your great prestige back of it, I hope to live to see the accomplishment of what I have worked for all my life. That is all I ask."

This modesty did produce some amusing results. For one, as Palmer delightedly reported to his chief, his own daughter Mary read the statement in the press and then commented to her father, "General Marshall's views are very similar to yours, aren't they!"[68] On the other hand, the *Army and Navy Journal* found sufficient internal evidence in the text to assure its readers that this was "General Marshall's own philosophy."[69]

Only one unhappy note marred the general's triumph. The statement, as it appeared in Circular 347, was buried in a mass of administrative trivia. What was needed was a convenient pamphlet with a title page that would be immediately self-evident. A reprint edition of uncluttered text was eventually run off on a mimeograph to meet requests for copies arriving in the chief's office; this proved to be of some help but still fell far short of what the general had in mind. So once again he had occasion to observe that the best of ideas may falter if presented in a defective format.[70]

The critical role of form in determining substance was an idea that cropped up again and again in Palmer's thinking. At the simplest and most obvious level, an important principle was likely to be communicated more effectively if conveyed in a handy pamphlet. At a higher level of complexity, the form or structure of a military unit, the territorial organization of a training unit for example, was of fundamental significance in determining the ultimate character of the reserves. In a community constituted the way an army is, where tours are short and members come and go continually, form or established procedures and organizations take on an inordinate importance. Although the general never expressed this thought in so many words, he gave it substance in

his actions, most notably in his original conception of the Section 5 committees in the Defense Act of 1920. It was an article of faith with him that the joint
regular and reserve committees established under Section 5 would by their
very make-up bring about the harmonization of views desired.

The progress being made by the newly reconstituted joint committees, one
for the Guard and one for the Organized Reserve, seemed to confirm the
general's fullest expectations from this type of military institution. At first,
just as he had predicted, there was a period of acrimonious dispute between
the citizen soldiers and the professionals. One of the regulars on the committee
refused to be budged from his view that the Guard should never be allowed to
organize divisions.[71] This stand infuriated General Walsh, who wrote Palmer
to see if he could have the offender replaced. "He has made no attempt to
disguise his hostility to everything connected with the National Guard," said
the association president, "and whatever his determinations may be, you may
rest assured that they will be influenced by his prejudices."[72]

Palmer, of course, regarded the recriminations as part of the necessary
educational process. Quoting Voltaire, he observed, "When there is prolonged
dispute, it signifies that both parties are wrong." To illustrate his point he
recalled one of the peacetime abuses practiced by the guardsmen, in connection with the so-called inactive reserve. Company commanders, perennially
short of competent cooks, were in the habit of enlisting such men just prior to
the two-week summer tour of active duty, with the promise that as soon as the
unit returned from the field they would be put into the inactive reserve, where
they could avoid all the inconvenience of military training until the following
summer.[73] The whole point of the committee exercise was to thrust such
problems out in the open and bring about a mutual understanding.[74]

By December 1944 Palmer could report to General Marshall that the joint
committees were producing "the rapprochement between the regular and
reserve points of view which was hoped for by the Senate Military Affairs
Committee when it incorporated Section 5 in the National Defense Act of
1920." But the preliminary committee recommendations were being studied
by the General Staff, and there was reason to believe they would encounter
opposition there.[75] This time G-3 took the lead, recommending that the word
"units" be abandoned in favor of "cadres." This looked much like an effort to
introduce the reserve pool concept by the back door. With cadres rather than
fully manned units, Palmer's conception of leadership training for reserve
officers would be gutted.[76]

Palmer wrote to the deputy chief of staff in the hope of winning yet another
ally. Praising the joint committee report, now happily unanimous, as "one of
the most highly constructive staff studies I have been privileged to see since I
was first called to the General Staff in 1911," he placed it "on a much higher
plane than an ordinary staff study." As one who participated in drafting the
provisions of Section 5 in the statute, he felt no hestitation in regarding

himself as qualified "to throw some light on the intent of Congress." And that intent, he insisted, was to put all the members of the joint committee on an equal footing. Therefore, he concluded, it would scarcely be "consistent with a due regard for the expressed purpose of the Congress to amend a unanimous joint report of such a committee except by formal order of the Secretary of War based upon specific recommendations by the Chief of Staff." This was an ingenious ploy, but in lifting the issue out of the hands of the staff, he might be accused of running away from the arguments presented.[77]

Far from running away from his opponents on the staff, however, he sought them out. But first he made sure that he held high cards in his hand. The mission for the reserve envisioned by the joint committee report was to provide *units* for mobilization, as many organized units as could be filled up with volunteers drawn from the graduates of universal training. The staff critics preferred to wait until the crisis arrived and then draw the graduates of UMT into newly constituted organizations. When G-1 and G-3 continued to reiterate this stand, the general's first reaction was to win them over by a direct personal appeal, but instead he wrote to General Marshall and described the problem, saying that he thought it improper for him to take the initiative. "I recalled how I felt as an active General Staff officer twenty-five years ago when General Carter and other retired officers intervened in my official work on military policy and organization." He would intervene, he declared, only if the Chief of Staff thought it might be useful to do so.[78] What he wanted, without quite asking for it, was a directive from General Marshall that would add weight to his arguments. And he got it in a "Dear John" letter instructing him to act at his earliest convenience.[79] So he did go to see the G-1 and G-3, but he went armed. With Circular 347, the official War Department policy, in one hand and a directive from the Chief of Staff to take the matter up with the recalcitrants in the other, there was little doubt of the outcome. Two days later the general was happily reporting that no basic differences remained unsettled.[80]

The popular success of Circular 347 produced a noticeable transformation in Palmer. His self-confidence improved markedly; the tone of his memos became bolder and more assured. He even went so far as to propose to the Chief of Staff that since some staff officers still had doubts about "your policy," it might be useful to suggest that they be referred to him for a bit of persuading. "The chances are that, in most cases, I would be able to tell them exactly what you would tell them if you were free." But then, having just volunteered himself as the chief's *alter ego,* he added a covering note to his friend Col. Frank McCarthy asking him to return the memo without showing it to General Marshall if it appeared to presume too much.[81]

Although Palmer spent a considerable amount of time and energy during the fall of 1944 in trying to assure the acceptance of Circular 347 within the army, he was more or less convinced the battle had been won. Having played a major role in establishing a sound policy for the army's civilian components, he now set out, at Marshall's request, to help sell that policy to the general public.[82]

As the first step in his propaganda campaign for a truly democratic army, the general turned out an article suitable for a popular magazine. On sending the manuscript to Marshall for approval, he explained his intentions: "My hope is that the wide spread and enthusiastic public opinion which acclaimed the publication of the circular will welcome a better understanding of its historical background."[83] The Chief of Staff promptly sent it off to the *Saturday Evening Post*, which then ranked among the top mass circulation magazines in the nation. Ben Hibbs, the editor of the *Post*, accepted it immediately and sent the author a check for $750.[84]

The unexpectedly large sum was more for a few days of effort than all Palmer's years on the Steuben biography had netted. In a characteristic gesture, he immediately went out and bought his devoted wife a fur coat, something he had wanted to do for years.[85] But he was soon to receive even greater, if less tangible, rewards from his journalistic success. The first of these came when General Marshall sent Hibbs a biographical sketch describing the author of the article as "the Army's leading authority on the subject of American military policy."[86] His pleasure from this compliment was reinforced when the galley proofs of the article were sent to General Marshall, who promptly dispatched the pages to the Special Planning Division with instructions to have them reproduced and circulated to all postwar planers as an explanatory supplement to his official policy laid down in Circular 347.[87]

When the piece finally appeared in the 23 December 1944 issue of the *Saturday Evening Post*, the general was delighted to find that it was the lead article and illustrated with a photograph of himself standing at General Marshall's elbow. Ben Hibbs had exercised the talent that made him so successful as an editor by changing the author's somewhat prosaic original title, "An Army of the People," to "General Marshall Wants a Citizen Army." Hibbs estimated that this simple alteration might boost the number of readers by as much as 50 percent, since Marshall's name was "magic" insofar as readership was concerned. And so it proved to be.[88]

The popular response to the *Post* article came as a considerable surprise even to Palmer.[89] The *New York Herald Tribune* commented favorably on the article in an editorial.[90] But he knew for certain that he was on target when Sen. Warren R. Austen of the Military Affairs Committee wrote to tell him the piece was a "great service to the country," which he had "read, re-read and marked up for use."[91] The general actually began to feel sorry for himself when the flood of correspondence got to be "more than the old man can take care of," as he told one well-wisher.[92]

One of the most rewarding of the letters from readers came from the general's colorful and crotchety friend Augustus L. Richards, the master of

"Sixty," the Steuben estate. He wrote, he said, from within sight of the old drillmaster's tomb, where the shade of the ancient hero prompted his pen.

> For so many years you have had this message on your tongue—going about like the Ancient Mariner, buttonholing people, repeating it over and over, and all to deaf ears. Then finally you retire—give it up—turn to something else—thinking it is all over, setting it down as a life's work thrown away. Then suddenly you find yourself in the spotlight— millions of faces turned to you. "The Army's leading authority" says General Marshall as he sits like a school boy while you point out to him the whys and wherefors of what has now become a topic in the very highest bracket of importance in America and perhaps in the world.
>
> Say, talk about your fairy tales and your Arabian Nights!... right now, John, you wouldn't change places with any five-starred general in the United States Army. I know I wouldn't if I were in your place.... Life for you has begun all over again.[93]

If there was a certain amount of hyperbole in this imagery, it was nonetheless true that a great many people were responding positively. By no means least among these was the President of the United States. Harry S. Hooker, Roosevelt's former law partner who was just then a house guest of the Roosevelts, reported to Palmer that the President had read his *Post* article with interest.[94] So had Eleanor Roosevelt, who expressed a desire to talk with the author, and sure enough, soon afterward the general was astonished to receive an invitation to lunch with the First Lady at the White House to discuss his proposals for a citizen army. After years in the Wilderness, the Promised Land was now at last in sight.[95]

51

The Drive for Universal Military Training

Palmer's career had reached its zenith. In December 1944 his personal prestige had never been higher and the outlook for UMT had never been better. A variety of polls had revealed a strong majority in the nation in favor of UMT: a Gallup study reported 63 percent favorable; a *Fortune* poll taken months later showed 69 percent in favor; and a study of enlisted men in service returned the same figure.[1] A *New York Times* reporter found one congressman after another accepting the notion that universal training would become the accepted way of life in the United States.[2]

The rising tide for compulsory training brought complications for the War Department. For many months those in authority had been reluctant to commit the army on the issue lest critics accuse the military of making rather than following public policy. But many, Palmer among them, believed the time had come for a clear statement of policy. Without such a statement even the friends of UMT would be groping in the dark, and might blunder into taking stands on the issue that could subsequently prove to be in conflict with the actual requirements of the army. Moreover, the organized opposition could work unopposed, free to persuade various national associations, professional groups, and other influential blocs of voters to take positions they would find it embarrassing to abandon at a later date.[3]

Although repeatedly prodded, the President squirmed and evaded, ever fearful of committing himself in advance of public opinion. During August 1944 he was finally persuaded to come out in favor of a compulsory year of training, but he deliberately obscured this with talk of vocational and other training "not necessarily military."[4] That his private views may have been somewhat more favorable, however, is indicated by his willingness to allow Secretary of War Stimson to issue a strong statement in favor of UMT.[5] The official statements not only seemed to strengthen the rising tide of opinion favorable to UMT, but gave the War Department the lead it had been waiting for.

The Chief of Staff established a special staff office under Maj. Gen. W. L. Weible to direct the information effort of the War Department in favor of UMT. One of Weible's first acts was to solicit Palmer's assistance in the form of speeches to off-the-record conferences to be held with representatives from interest groups such as organized labor, education, religion, and the farm bloc. The labor leaders were suspicious, fearing that the army would indoctrinate future trainees with antiunion views. To convince the union men that the training program would be thoroughly "civilianized" and not a "brass hat" operation, Palmer was an ideal choice, not only for his disarming personal charm but for his utter sincerity when speaking for a truly democratic army.[6]

During the previous summer Palmer, at the urging of his friends in the MTCA, had prepared a brief pamphlet, "Notes on Universal Military Training." The catchy subtitle: "Should We or Should We Not Give Effective Military Training to Every Able-bodied Young Man as the Foundation of Our Military System after the Present War?" clearly showed that Palmer had forgotten none of his debater's tricks. A hastily contrived Citizens Committee for Universal Military Training, largely made up of his MTCA friends, soon raised the necessary funds to publish several thousand copies of the pamphlet.[7]

The subsequent distribution of the general's "Notes" offers an instructive illustration of how the propaganda network functioned. *Army Officer* picked up the pamphlet and ran it as an article in its August 1944 issue with the author's picture on the cover. This carried the word to some 40,000 subscribers. Of course, this was preaching to the converted. A larger and more significant audience was tapped when the U.S. Chamber of Commerce made its mailing list of some 700,000 members available for a massive distribution sponsored by the American Legion.[8]

The national leaders of the American Legion not only used the general's "Notes" as propaganda but repeatedly sought his attendance at their planning sessions. "We look to you," wrote Col. S. Perry Brown, the chairman of the Legion's National Defense Committee, "for advise and counsel to keep our thinking and our planning on the right course."[9] Legion officials sent copies of Palmer's *America in Arms* to every department commander, adjutant, and executive committeeman, as well as to every member of Congress. But here again most of those reached may have favored UMT already.[10]

The general groped for a somewhat more uncertain audience when he agreed to present the case for UMT before such other groups as the Chamber of Commerce of the United States and the National Association of Manufacturers (NAM). The executive committee of the NAM was impressed with the general's pitch but finally decided not to take an official stand; an endorsement by "organized business" might prove more harmful than helpful.[11] The national leadership of the Chamber of Commerce made a conscientious effort to educate the membership in the complexities of the training issue by establishing "pro" and "con" committees to state the case for each side. When the members decided for themselves, they returned substantial majorities in favor of UMT.[12] That the general was called in to assist in preparing the "pro" case for the Chamber of Commerce commitee was characteristic of his approach. Virtually all of his efforts were affirmative, making the positive case for UMT. Far more difficult was the task of meeting the arguments of the opposition, but this he largely ignored.[13]

As the year 1944 drew to a close, the opponents of compulsory training became more articulate. In a phenomenon well understood by professional propagandists, the "bow wave effect," the very success enjoyed by the advocates of UMT stirred up a vigorous reaction. The General Staff news summary reported this reaction building up in November. By no means all of it was hostile to UMT in principle; many open-minded individuals and cautious organizations, unwilling to be rushed into so profound a commitment without exhaustive hearings, opposed any effort to ram legislation through Congress on a wave of wartime emotion.

The general's reactions were varied. When, for example, an American Friends Service committee published a pamphlet entitled "Conscription or Conscience," he found the arguments it offered "absolutely unrealistic" and "out of touch with everything in the world."[14] When a committee from the American Council on Education (ACE) circulated a resolution opposing "universal military service," the general was quick to point out that UMT called for a program of compulsory *training* but specifically excluded military *service* unless authorized in time of emergency by Congress. But the ACE resolution contained a number of other points that the general chose to ignore.[15] Even if he himself did not wish to enter into dispute, the points raised should have been met by someone within the War Department. There is no evidence that he regularly referred the arguments of opponents either to General Weible's shop or to some of his younger colleagues in the Special Planning Division. For hostile arguments he seldom if ever framed an answer, even for his own edification.[16]

On occasion Palmer did exchange ideas with critics and doubters, but even where they proposed potentially fruitful alternatives, he customarily reverted to his initial premises rather than explore the new ideas in depth. An interesting example of this pattern is afforded by the case of President Karl T. Compton of MIT. The support of President Compton, as a distinguished scientist and educator, would lend great strength to the advocates of universal training. But during 1944 the staff of the Special Planning Division learned that Compton was reluctant to come out for UMT unless provision could be made to exempt men in scientific training, on the grounds that such university graduates would be of more value to the nation for their brains than their brawn. The division staff members, including Palmer, desperately wanted Compton's support, but they finally insisted, on grounds of simple equity, that it would be unwise to make any exceptions. This firm stand was a tribute to the fundamentally egalitarian outlook Palmer had always insisted upon, but it took no heed of President Compton's concession that as a condition of exemption for university students, he was willing to require them to enroll in some kind of ROTC program. For the small privilege of exemption, he would lay on them a large obligation.[17]

One can only speculate on the profound consequences that might have been produced if Compton's idea had been applied to the workings of the draft in the decades of the 1950s and 1960s, when a far less equitable system of student exemptions was in effect. But Palmer did not pick up the idea and pursue it; instead he reverted to his first premises in simple terms and reiterated them. Universality of compulsory training might well be desirable, but it might have been sounder to arrive at such a conclusion only after exhaustive consideration of the alternatives raised by the opposition.

As one of the most articulate official spokesmen for UMT, the general became something of a symbol for the movement. His many friends and acquaintances in and out of uniform confirmed this by sending him all manner of suggestions for modifying the proposed training program. For example, Joe Greene, the editor of the *Infantry Journal*, wrote to suggest the need for baiting UMT with educational features. Compulsory military training will be hard to sell in peacetime, he warned, and harder still to resell as the years roll on, but an educational component in the training program might add just the fillip needed to make the measure acceptable. "If you have touch with Senator Wadsworth," Greene concluded, "for God's sake get to him with this idea."[18] Arguments pro and con could be raised to this proposal; their relative merits are of less interest here than the way the general responded. He filed it.

Another illustration is to be found in Palmer's dealings with Brig. Gen. E. W. Smith, the Executive for Reserve and ROTC Affairs, an office roughly comparable to the National Guard Bureau. General Smith greatly admired his elderly colleague and shared many of his convictions. His own work with educational institutions all over the country had led him to conclude that the educators would be reluctant to support UMT unless they were assured of substantial civilian control over the program. To forestall this potentially dangerous opposition, Smith suggested the creation of a new civilian "secretary for reserves," to rank equally with the secretaries of the army, navy, and air force.[19] Once again the old general made no effort to incorporate the idea into his thinking.

The point is not that Palmer was unwilling to make tactical concessions but that he tended to ignore the ideas of others if they did not conform to his prior conceptions. Nor was this simply a function of his advancing years, for the trait had been evident throughout much of his active career. He himself was imaginative and creative, but once he had built up a structure of ideas, challenges or even constructive amendments seemed to roll off his mind like rain from a dry window.

On the other hand, when it came to developing ideas that were already a part of his intellectual baggage, the general could be both eloquent and original. An example is to be seen in a second article he turned out for the *Saturday Evening Post*. Increasingly distressed by the way the politicians on the Hill succumbed to pressure groups when considering military legislation, he began to despair of ever securing a truly coherent national defense statute. "The existing committee machinery is no more qualified to write a coordinated military policy than it is to write an epic poem." The Select Committee on Postwar Military Policy, the Woodrum Committee, seemed to be a move in the right direction, but even its members went into their hearings with the lobbyists for powerful groups at their backs. In such a context, the general believed, the politicians were inclined to prejudge the issues; what was needed was some means for raising the process of deliberation above the cross currents and pressure groups. Palmer's goal was nothing less than a "scientific solution," as he phrased it, of the national defense problem.[20]

A "scientific solution" had been in Palmer's mind for many years, ever since he had watched Secretary Stimson adjudicate the claims of the rival components of the army back in 1912. He had fleshed out the idea in his *Infantry Journal* article in 1943, when he proposed an independent commission to do the same thing on a larger scale with all three military services. He had reiterated the plan in the revised edition of *America in Arms*, only to see it rejected on the Hill, where he had been forced to accept Woodrum's House Select Committee as the best that could be salvaged from his original proposal.

Why not take a precedent from the judiciary? In courts of equity the presiding judge sometimes finds it constructive to assign a complex case to a master in chancery, who can hear testimony, weigh the evidence, and present it in a form conducive to a sound decision. Each special pleader, each advocate for a particular interest, must present his or her case in open court and be subject to rebuttal by those with conflicting interests. What the general envisioned was an entirely coherent structure for national defense. It would be arrived at judicially rather than as a least common denominator of special interests. The master in chancery, as the appointee of Congress, would be able to come up with a result so eminently sound, so thoroughly integrated, and so free of political trade-offs that it would immediately commend itself to the legislators. Congress would still have to vote on the bill drafted by the master selected by the two houses, but the whole burden of proof would fall upon the individual congressman who advocated any changes or amendments.[21]

The master in chancery idea, as a variation of Stimson's open court procedure, had come to Palmer from his dealings with Newton D. Baker back in the twenties. In 1927, at the same time that Palmer and Baker were negotiating over the proposed volume of Baker-Pershing correspondence, the former secretary had been deeply engaged, as an attorney, in the famous Chicago Drainage Canal case. In that complex affair, the general recalled, the Supreme Court of the United States had appointed as special master Charles Evans Hughes, the former Secretary of State who would later be appointed Chief Justice. After months of hearings Hughes had presented the issues so succinctly that the Supreme Court was able to dispose of the case in two days. To refresh his memory Palmer resolved to call upon the now retired Chief Justice.[22]

The venerable jurist expressed considerable interest in Palmer's novel idea. He even agreed to help in writing the article. The Justice had read the general's Steuben, and he praised it extravagantly. Palmer in turn sent Hughes proof sheets of his first *Post* article, calling attention to General Marshall's endorsement of the author. It was, he said, a great honor to be so sponsored by "America's greatest soldier," but now he was delighted to get help from "America's greatest layman." Then he added an offhand comment that epitomized his fundamentally democratic convictions: "This is highly important for, after all, this is a layman's country."[23]

For the general a "layman's country" meant something more than mere pro forma subordination of the military to civilian control. It also involved an inner attitude of respect and restraint, if not outright humility, by those in uniform. His own life exemplified this. No small part of the charm that made him so disarming stemmed from his utter innocence of manner. When he first called on Justice Hughes, for example, he confessed that he had been somewhat at a loss on how to address his distinguished host. The old gentleman laughed and assured him that either "Mr. Chief Justice" or "Charlie" would be quite acceptable. The general later recalled his reply: "I told him I would exercise the first option but would pass the second on to my grandsons."[24]

The finished article finally appeared in the 27 January 1945 issue of the *Saturday Evening Post* under the caption "How to Solve our Postwar Defense Problem." It elucidated the mastery in chancery idea in the general's usual graceful style, worked in a plug for universal military training, and attempted to assure skeptics that the scheme would work by a humorous reference to Palmer's own experience in getting Congress to accept the single-list promotion bill following World War I. The success of this "promotion perturbation eliminator," as he called the single list, was, he suggested, but a token of what a special master could do for Congress in dealing with such controversial issues as UMT and the proposed department of defense.

Palmer's two *Post* articles circulated far beyond the 3.5 million regular *Post* subscribers. Sen. Chan Gurney had both articles reprinted in the *Congressional Record* and then reissued as a pamphlet, "The Postwar Defense Problem," for convenient distribution.[25] The Press Alliance secured reprint rights for a French translation, and the Office of War Information distributed copies to such far-flung outposts as Bombay, Chungking, Baghdad, and Beirut, as well as all the major capitals of western Europe. The H. W. Wilson Company requested permission to include the articles in its annual debater's handbook.[26]

For weeks after the articles appeared, Palmer was swamped with correspondence.[27] The sheer burden of answering mail became a painful chore. One correspondent, however, stood out from all the rest. This was Prof. Horace M. Kallen of the New School for Social Research. After reading the *Post* articles, Kallen sent the author one of his own articles, "The Place of War in the Education of Free men," from the *Journal of Legal and Political Sociology*. What he had to say so impressed Palmer that he sent a copy for General Marshall to share.[28]

The professor, who had never met the general, found it hard to believe he was dealing with an individual seventy-five years old. "You write like a vigorous young man," he assured his correspondent. Kallen put forward a number of interesting and challenging suggestions and criticisms, but the general often seemed not to be listening. When the professor quoted John Stuart Mill on the dangers that beset one in the "deep slumber of a decided opinion" and warned that truths untested and unexamined might "atrophy into dogmas,"[29] it apparently never occurred to the general that these caveats could apply to him.

One of Kallen's constructive notions was the suggestion that the Woodrum Committee should hold hearings not just in Washington but in various cities throughout the country. Such sessions, he contended, would serve as a point of departure for informed discussions by local citizens. The views of the War Department should be presented to the people "frequently and directly" and not merely to their legislative instruments. Kallen agreed wholeheartedly with the general that the nation would have to place its potential military resources "in negotiable form" if it wished to preserve the ideal of constitutional freedom. But the people of the United States will resist universal training and their resistance will be successful, he contended, unless they can be persuaded that such training is a necessary means of preserving democracy.[30]

There were, of course, a great many practical difficulties in the way of any scheme to convert a House hearing into a propaganda roadshow. But while technically the War Department was free to send out speakers and issue statements defining the official departmental position on UMT, that would make it difficult for the military men not to become advocates of a policy not yet formally accepted by the political authorities. There were certain limits within which officials of the department felt constrained to act. While never precisely prescribed, in practice these limits seemed to admit of exposition while stopping short of advocacy.[11]

The dilemma of the War Department in dealing with the UMT issue is evident in the efforts of the staff to formulate a position for presentation before the Woodrum Committee. While the department might incur criticism if it were to invest money and manpower prematurely in a series of propaganda roadshows at the grass roots, it would be well within its constitutional limits in preparing the best possible case for UMT in response to a congressional request. But even this passive role raised many difficulties, not the least of which was that such a course left the initiative and the timing largely to the politicians. On the other hand, the necessity of framing an official position forced the War Department to develop plans that could not be perfected until internal disagreements within the several staff sections could be resolved.

The Woodrum hearings had opened in March of 1944 but had been put off until after the elections in November. The chairman had expected that the sessions would resume when Congress reassembled, but the war in Europe intruded. The unexpected German breakout in the Battle of the Bulge sent shock waves through the military, as units still in the United States were stripped of every possible man, including many with but minimal training, to provide replacements for General Eisenhower's depleted armies. Robert P. Patterson, the Under Secretary of War, urged delay in the congressional hearings until after the flare-up had passed. Secretary Stimson concurred and secured the assent of Representative Woodrum.[32] But just as the Secretary acted to slow down the rush toward UMT, President Roosevelt moved in the opposite direction.

Roosevelt apparently regarded the sobering setback as an ideal moment to confront the nation with the heavy obligations it would have to shoulder in the postwar era and at last came out squarely for UMT in his message to Congress. "I am clear in my own mind that, as an essential factor in the maintenance of peace in the future, we must have universal military training after this war and I shall send a special message to Congress on this subject."[33] But for the moment Secretary Stimson had another order of priorities. Apparently fearing that a protracted public debate on compulsory training in peacetime would inhibit the war effort, he wrote the President urging him to hold back his promised message on UMT until the current manpower and production crisis had passed.[34]

In urging delay the Secretary may have unwittingly sealed the doom of universal training. He had no way of knowing that Roosevelt would be dead in three months and that, with the weight of his leadership gone, the whole political equation would have to be reckoned anew. But delay gained more time for the War Department to perfect its case. And as the formulation of the departmental brief proceeded, it became increasingly evident that there were a great many problems to overcome.

The effort of the staff to prepare the official War Department case for the Woodrum Committee reveal not only the incredible complexity of the process but also the continuing role played by Palmer. Whatever his other limitations, he can scarcely be faulted for laxity in the relentless way he pursued those who tried to inject heretical ideas into the presentation. Similarly, the other members of the Special Planning Division regarded their preparations for the Woodrum hearings as a major commitment. As one imaginative staff officer described the process,

> the Special Planning Division becomes the nozzle through which ideas relative to postwar military policy are to be sprayed upon the fertile ground of the Select Committee. Since the Committee is composed for the most part of individuals with little or no military background or experience, it follows that strong, healthy plants of sound policy will also need cultivation to keep down the weeds of pet theories and irrelevant ideas.[35]

To this end Palmer advocated encouraging the whole committee, and not just known friendly members such as Wadsworth, to rely upon the Special Planning Division for information. The division, he urged, should feed ideas to the members of the committee, letting them receive full credit with their constituents for the arguments presented. The effort at cultivation enjoyed considerable success; a scant four months after it had been introduced, Chairman Woodrum admitted privately that every member of his committee now favored UMT.[36]

A characteristic example of the obstacles to sound planning encountered by the division was the matter of securing meaningful statistics on public opinion. The army's pollsters scrupulously avoided asking questions that might violate the statute prohibiting attempts to influence pending legislation, but when they resorted to broad, general questions, they failed to elicit data on which sound generalizations could be erected. Moreover, when the planners tried to rely upon outside polls, these often lacked the precise focus desired. For example, when a Gallup poll asked: "After this war is over do you think every able-bodied young American should be required to serve one year in the Army or Navy?"[37] Palmer immediately registered a protest. The question as posed dealt with conscription and not universal training. He proposed rephrasing the question: Do you think every able-bodied young man should be trained to defend his country? Ever sensitive to the popular resentment of anything resembling military coercion, he suggested that the revised wording would come to Gallup with better grace from some civilian group, such as the MTCA. Subsequently the wording was revised along the line Palmer suggested and used repeatedly over many months.[38]

Some officers seemed unwilling to hazard a poll on what front-line combat troops actually thought about training in peacetime. They feared that men suffering in the mud and snow of a grim wartime winter might take a dim view of any peacetime role whatever. So soldiers in the Zone of the Interior were polled by the War Department, with results paralleling those produced by

Gallup and others. Indeed, the further one got from combat, the stronger the support for UMT seemed to grow. A survey of men leaving the service showed over 66 percent favoring UMT, while a similar check of veterans back in civilian life ran to 80 percent. With good reason Palmer was optimistic.[39]

Evidence of broad popular support was encouraging, but it would be a hollow victory if the public supported universal training only to find that the whole spirit of a citizen force had been subverted by the regulars. As the drafts of the statements to be presented before the Select Committee were circulated, Palmer was horrified at the backsliding he detected in them. An early version of the proposed testimony submitted by the G-3 envisioned the use of cadres of regulars to carry out the training of the Organized Reserve units formed of graduates from UMT. The distinct impression conveyed was that UMT would produce only privates, with no one promoted any higher unless he attended a Regular Army school. With Palmer at his elbow, the director of the Special Planning Division sent the proposed statement back to G-3 with the acid comment that such views would impair the prospects of getting a UMT statute out of Congress.[40]

For Palmer, there were three essential elements in the ideal democratic force of citizen soldiers: universal training, an Organized Reserve formed from the men completing their training, and opportunities for these reservists to climb through the ranks in their units. All three of these elements were carefully articulated in the draft statement prepared by G-1.[41] The general relished this victory in particular, in view of the sustained opposition he had encountered in G-1 to the whole idea of an organized reserve.

A few weeks later the general was busy admonishing the director of the division on the backsliding he detected in a statement being promulgated as the official army and navy view of UMT. The proposed text declared that the Regular Army would be "reinforced in time of emergency by units organized from a citizen reserve trained in peacetime." To most observers this might seem innocuous enough, but to Palmer it betrayed a gross violation of General Marshall's War Department Circular 347. The passages as originally worded had read: "reinforced in time of emergency by organized units drawn from a citizen army reserve, effectively organized for this purpose in time of peace." As the general saw it, the effect of the change would be to "vitiate the fundamental purpose of universal training—the avoidance of extemporization after the outbreak of war." Whether the change was in fact a deliberate effort to undercut the Organized Reserve or merely editorial is not clear. But the general remained highly suspicious of anything that smacked of the slightest departure from the principles articulated in Circular 347.[42]

For all his efforts, however, there seemed to be a tide running against him. He had finally vanquished the last advocates of an "inchoate manpower pool," but the Organized Reserve he did secure turned out to be a good deal less than he had originally anticipated. As the general had envisioned it, the young men graduating from their year of compulsory training would be enrolled for a period of years in units of the Organized Reserve in their home communities. Their skills would be developed, or at least maintained, and the small Regular Army would be assured of a large force trained, organized, and ready in an emergency—but only in an emergency officially declared as such by Congress. Although the legislators agreed to require one full year of compulsory training, there was reason to doubt that they would consent to impose an extended period of obligatory membership in a reserve unit and provided instead that all graduates of UMT would revert to a reserve roster under obligation for five years to answer the call in any congressionally approved emergency. Those who wished to volunteer for the Organized Reserves would be encouraged to do so, but no one would be required to enroll. As an inducement to enter the Reserves, the duration of the obligatory liability to duty would be reduced for all who volunteered.

The official compromise seriously undercut if it did not entirely destroy Palmer's claim that UMT in conjunction with an Organized Reserve would permit the orderly mobilization of "all or any necessary part" of the nation's manpower in an emergency. But the planners believed Congress would never approve UMT if it were coupled to enforced enrollment in the Organized Reserves. General Marshall himself was so convinced of this that he even questioned the advisability of requiring an obligatory five-year period "on call." Even the concept of "universal" training, Palmer discovered, had been transformed into something else; induction statistics from the wartime draft showed that as many as one-quarter or even one-third of the young men coming of age would be exempt from training on medical grounds. This was based on the assumption that the physical standards for UMT would be the same as those for admission into the military services. So something less than three quarters of the nation's eligible young men would receive training, and only the small fraction of these willing to volunteer for the Organized Reserve or the National Guard would actually be ready for action in time of need.[43]

General Marshall finally went along on the five-year obligation, but how could the army ever hope to keep track of the individuals supposedly "on call"? In the highly mobile population of the United States, a great deal of effort would be required to maintain a current locator file. To do this they proposed to carry all such individuals in nonfunctioning, nontactical paper units. But the objection was immediately raised that such units might be interpreted as a clandestine attempt to coerce the nonvolunteers.[44] This kind of problem and many others like it were but minor obstacles; nonetheless, as such minor obstacles piled up one after another, Palmer saw his grand scheme of national defense eroded.[45]

Far more serious as threats to the whole conception of UMT were the burgeoning cost estimates. One of the key arguments in the general's case for universal training was that it would be less costly than a large standing army.

In some exasperation Palmer complained to General Marshall that the planners were not following the spirit of Circular 347. Instead of using less expensive reservists, they were inflating the number of more expensive regulars. One proposal had called for a training cadre in which regulars made up 30 percent of the overhead, although only 6 percent of the men in the divisional training cadres in the current conflict had been regulars. All of which led Palmer to recall the "steel and concrete" metaphor he had used in testifying before Congress. Just as he had then predicted, here were the planners with a vested interest in professional "steel" enlarging the number of regulars at the expense of the reservist "concrete."[46]

"I don't know where to draw the line," Palmer admitted, "but of one thing I am certain: whenever we maintain a permanent professional to do something that can be done effectively by a part-time nonprofessional, we increase the cost of our establishment unduly."[47] This was an article of faith with him. But was his faith justified in fact? Were reservists actually so much cheaper than regulars?

Accurate cost figures were exceedingly difficult to come by. The War Department had no system of cost accounting that could produce the kind of figures required to support or confute Palmer's contention. Would a succession of short-tour reservists, including their travel pay, actually perform a given training function more cheaply than a single permanently assigned regular? Since personnel costs were dwarfed by materiel costs, would the savings claimed for the use of reservists actually loom as large as the general seemed to believe? The best the planners were able to do was come up with crude per capita costs derived by dividing the total number of men in uniform into the total annual departmental budget. This produced an estimated per capita figure of $4,500, but $1,200 of this was accounted for by the annual replacement cost of airplanes alone, so the figure was really almost meaningless.[48]

When the staff planners came up with an estimated annual cost of $1.5 billion for UMT with appoximately 630,000 trainees and 110,000 cadre, half regular and half reserve, Palmer was horrified. Even if the proportion of reservists in the cadre were increased substantially, this would not produce the economies required. He insisted that further study of the Swiss experience would produce significantly lower costs, but the only tangible suggestion he himself offered was to reduce the trainees' pay from $20 a month to no more than a small allowance for incidentals, since men performing a civic duty should require no pay incentive. The savings thus derived would scarcely be enough to cover the increases incurred by a proposal to lower the physical qualifications so that all but the totally unfit would participate in compulsory training under UMT.[49]

When all the costs were assessed as accurately as possible, the lower physical qualifications taken into account along with such factors as dependency allowances, the total annual estimate for UMT approached $2.75 billion. The painful contrast between what the general's spacious rhetoric had originally promised and what actually emerged in the War Department plan was more than enough to depress even the most confirmed optimist.[50]

If the staff planners in the War Department found it difficult to hammer out a workable program for UMT on which they themselves could agree, they encountered a whole new range of problems as soon as they tried to coordinate their plans with such natural allies as the American Legion and the MTCA. When the subject of universal training had first come up, it had been assumed on the staff that the Legion would serve as the primary agency for carrying the case for UMT to the people. To be sure, the Legion national convention had passed a resolution favoring universal training and a few Legion officials had given speeches in favor of the principle. But this was not the same thing as an organized drive that got every local post actively behind the program. Somewhat plaintively the director of the Special Planning Division remarked that it would be ideal if only the legionnaires were to put as much energy and enthusiasm into the drive for UMT as they had in pushing the GI Bill of Rights through the last Congress.[51] General Tompkins was learning what Palmer had discovered after World War I; the Legion seldom if ever gave defense legislation the same support it put behind veterans' benefits.

The Citizens Committee for Universal Military Training formed by the old Military Training Camps crowd in New York offered another convenient vehicle. With Howard Petersen in the Under Secretary's office and Palmer in the Special Planning Division, there was no great difficulty in establishing direct communication with the organization. Nonetheless, General Tompkins had some reservations as to how effective the committee would be in selling UMT. "While they are excellent people, I felt that there was not enough young blood in the organization, . . . it was too much of a 'silk stocking' group." His appraisal was sound; virtually all of the committee members were investment brokers, corporate officers, or members of prominent law firms in New York. While they were able to raise large sums quickly to finance propaganda pamphlets and could provide disinterested talent of a high order to staff committees or put prestigious witnesses before Congress, their ability to be persuasive at the grass roots had yet to be demonstrated.[52]

The failure of the Legion to organize a vigorous drive for UMT was a serious blow to the army planners, but an even worse development was to follow. While still professing to favor universal training, the Legion policy makers began casting about for something more palatable than one continuous year of training. The essence of their alternative was to require all able-bodied young men to take four months of training, June through September, and then choose one of four options: (1) train as a specialist in a college course, a military technical school, or with industry; (2) enlist in the

Regular Army; (3) enlist in the National Guard or the Organized Reserve; or (4) enroll in ROTC.

There was no denying that the Legion plan would enjoy a good deal of political appeal. Indeed, Congressman May indicated privately that he was going to introduce a revised version of his earlier UMT bill, which had roughly paralleled the War Department program, to conform to the wishes of the Legion. Since May was chairman of the House Military Affairs Committee, this brought consternation to the planners. An open break was temporarily avoided when the Secretary of War persuaded the Legion to defer any official statement on UMT that might divert public attention from the current drive to win the war.[53] This respite, however, only put off the real issue. The planners understood perfectly well that Gresham's law applied in politics as well as in economics: "soft" solutions that offer the voters an easy escape drive out "hard" solutions requiring significant sacrifice.

In a sense the Legion proposal marked a serious personal defeat for Palmer. The chief spokesman for the scheme was Col. Perry Brown, chairman of the Legion's National Defense Committee, who had told the general, "We look to you for guidance." But the general had been unsuccessful in deflecting Brown and his committee. In the best professional judgment of the army planners, the proposed summer training stint was entirely inadequate. A maneuver held in September after three months of basic training would be almost worthless. So too would Organized Reserve units built of men whose training had been limited to a single short summer tour. Moreover, the options offered for the remainder of the obligation were manifestly inequitable.[54]

The army planners had reason to believe that at least one factor behind the defection of the Legion could be found in the machinations of certain interests in the National Guard. In April 1945 Maj. Gen. Ellard Walsh published an elaborate plan to implement universal training entirely through the National Guard. In barest outline, his proposal would enlist trainees for three years in the Guard, with forty-eight drill periods each year, followed by active duty tours of twenty-eight days, twenty-one days, and fourteen days in each successive summer.[55]

After the cordial meetings of the previous winter, the War Department planners had assumed that the old controversies had been settled. As Tompkins observed, the War Department had agreed to "play all cards above the table." Now it appeared that the Guard leader felt under no obligation to reciprocate, since General Walsh had released his plan without the least effort to coordinate it with the planning staff. What was worse, he had not even shown it to the Guard representatives on the mixed committee organized under Section 5 of the Defense Act to consider postwar policy. This was particularly galling, because it had been Walsh himself who had criticized the Regulars for their failure to use the mechanism of the mixed committee. But

General Tompkins's real concern was that the guardsmen's proposal would appeal to members of Congress who lacked the professional skills to see its many defects.[56]

To the staff planners, Walsh's proposal was unworkable on its face. He left largely unexplained just how he would accommodate all those young men in communities where no Guard units existed. The irregular distribution of population would pose almost insurmountable training problems, quite apart from the matter of financing suitable armories. Nor did Walsh really cope with the problem of how trainees would ever master the intricacies of advanced fire-control systems and electronic communications equipment in one-night-a-week sessions undertaken by men who had already put in a day's work in their civilian callings.

The shortcomings of General Walsh's proposal were so evident that even his fellow guardsmen saw the need for substantial modification. In an effort to bridge the gap between Walsh's approach and the full-year training period advocated by the army, Lt. Gen. Hugh Drum once again sketched out a substitute. As a professional he recognized the merit of a sustained period of training under federal auspices, but as a leader of the New York Guard and a political realist, he also recognized the appeal of any scheme that would not remove young men from their home communities. His proposal was to provide for an initial four months in a federal training program under the control of the regulars. Thereafter trainees would be required to enter either their local National Guard or Organized Reserve unit for a period of two years and eight months, during which they would be expected to train three hours per week and attend two summer tours of active duty of two weeks each. Following this there would be two more years of obligatory membership in a reserve unit, but training would be reduced to two required hours per month and a single summer tour of active duty.[57]

Drum's plan was obviously superior to Walsh's; even if professionals regarded a four-month period as inadequate, at least it would insure a minimum uniform standard of basic training. When Palmer's views were solicited, however, he pointed out that Drum's solution would disrupt the life of the trainee far more than the army's one continuous year. By stretching the training over five years, it would become more rather than less burdensome. Moreover, Drum's four-month trainees would be less ready to perform than the army's twelve-month men if called to duty. The relative merits of the two plans were of far less significance, however, than the breach in the united front the army hoped to present when testifying before the Woodrum Committee.[58]

As it turned out, the panic engendered by the Battle of the Bulge was only the first in a series of delays that put off the hearings. Another postponement seemed advisable when a spate of criticism cropped up in Congress over the army's use of eighteen-year-old draftees as replacements in divisions on the battlefront after no more than fifteen weeks of training, although this episode might seem convincing proof of the need for a year-long period of training in peacetime, to avoid the necessity of putting half-prepared boys into battle. But the critics on the Hill needed a scapegoat, so the army was blamed. Scarcely had this storm subsided when the meeting at San Francisco to formulate a charter for the United Nations led to a demand from the advocates of world order to defer all talk of universal training as evidence of good faith on the part of the United States. So it was not until June 1945 that the long-delayed Woodrum hearings finally opened.[59]

Each day Palmer went to the Hill and followed the testimony in his role as tactician and liaison agent. He urged Congressman Wadsworth to let civilian witnesses carry the major burden and thus minimize any charges of militarism. Observing that many of the groups lined up to give evidence against UMT bore such titles as the National Council to Oppose Conscription or the Women's Committee to Oppose Conscription, he suggested that these witnesses be cross-examined closely to bring out the fact that the army plan called for training, not conscription. People who used the word conscription to describe the army plan were, he declared, either ignorant or dishonest, and "those who misuse the term dishonestly should be pilloried and exposed." The very word conscription tended to rouse an unreasoning opposition among those who had fled Europe to avoid this hated institution. Palmer also suggested exposure of those groups opposing UMT who had also fought against the draft in 1917 and in 1940. If cross-examination could show how their bad advice had left the nation critically undefended and unprepared, their credibility might be undermined.[60]

The general kept the Chief of Staff informed of developments. He was appalled at the ignorance of history betrayed by many of those offering hostile testimony, but as Wadsworth assured him, unreasonable opponents made some of the best witnesses in favor of UMT.[61] When a professor opposed to compulsory training cited the debates in the Constitutional Convention on the possibility of limiting the size of the army, Palmer was quick to point out that he was not telling the whole truth. To be sure, a delegate had suggested that the army be limited to some 2,000 men. Then George Washington had come down from the chair to offer a substitute motion—that no enemy be permitted to invade the United States with more than 2,000 men![62]

With a knowledge of history and a sense of humor, the general believed, one could do much for the cause. Sometimes, however, even his own gift of humor deserted him momentarily. For example, when recounting for Marshall the testimony of Charles G. Bolte of the American Veterans' Committee, the AVC, he remarked that the young veteran expressed views so similar to his own that he must have read the Palmer writings. Then in the next sentence he went on to describe Bolte as a "brilliant forceful young man who will have a voice in future plans."[63] It was undoubtedly a part of Marshall's greatness that he knew how to make use of the men around him—and when not to. His ties with Palmer were affectionate and close, almost brotherly, as Palmer once described their relationship, but this never obscured his judgment. Just prior to his appearance before the Woodrum Committee, he asked Palmer's advice on what to say. The latter replied at length, but the Chief of Staff had prepared his own testimony when he arrived at the witness table.[64]

Palmer's appearance before the committee was largely routine; he introduced no surprises, confining himself to a broad-brush description of just how UMT would provide the essential ingredient for national defense. He once again asserted that the proposed scheme would permit the orderly deployment of "all or any necessary part" of the nation's total manpower. Just how this would be accomplished if only limited and inadequate numbers of trainees voluntarily enrolled in the National Guard or the Organized Reserve after completing their training, he failed to explain. The listening congressmen were left to assume that the year-long training program—nine weeks of basic, nine weeks of specialist training, followed by thirteen weeks in small-unit work and thirteen weeks in large units, all terminating in one grand eight-week maneuver of all arms—would so raise the general level of proficiency that the citizen soldiers could quickly line up behind the Regular Army in a declared emergency. That this notion was entirely inconsistent with Palmer's earlier strictures against hastily extemporized forces, he seemed not to notice.[65]

After hearing more than a hundred witnesses, the Woodrum Committee report supported the position advanced by the army planners in virtually every respect. And for Palmer there was the added pleasure that in phrase after phrase the language of the committee findings reflected his own writings. The nation's position of power in the world must rest on a commensurate military power—on negotiable military assets. The only true course was the traditional one, a small Regular Army backed by a trained reserve of citizen soldiers. In the future, time would never be available to prepare adequate forces after an emergency appeared. Support for the United Nations and the needs of national defense required prior training. The notion that such training would militarize the people was rejected out of hand; the training should be "universal and democratic," and whatever program was adopted should be in the spirit of the Defense Act of 1920, which is to say, consistent with the preservation of the National Guard, the Organized Reserve, and the ROTC.[66]

The highly favorable report of the Woodrum Committee brought a good deal of elation to the army planners. Their reaction was widely seconded in the press. Arthur Krock felt that the report "disposed of all reasonable fears" that democracy would be endangered by compulsory training. There were, however, a number of ominous portents.[67] Six of the twenty-two members of the committee declined to sign the final report. They were not opposed to the findings; they simply refused to take a stand "at this time" on universal training.[68] No matter what the opinion polls might indicate about strong popular support for UMT, it was clear to political realists that the measure faced a long uphill road.

There was some question in Palmer's mind as to whether he would be allowed to participate in the coming struggle for UMT. Ever since V-E day the War Department had been relieving retired officers recalled to active duty for wartime service. General Marshall ended this uncertainty by issuing an order retaining his elderly adviser until personally relieved by the Chief of Staff.[69] Palmer was amused to recall a striking parallel between this episode in his life and one in the life of his grandfather and namesake. In 1863 Maj. Gen. John M. Palmer had resigned his commission after a dispute over policy with his military superiors, but President Lincoln had refused to accept the resignation.[70]

Sometime later there occurred still another parallel with the life of grandfather Palmer. The general had been in to confer with the Chief of Staff when the latter, to prolong their conversation, asked him to come sit beside him while he had his hair trimmed in a private barber shop, reserved, as Palmer put it, for the Secretary and "other grandees." The next day he remembered that his grandfather had told about a barber-chair conversation with President Lincoln, so he sat down and wrote Marshall a brief account of his recollection.

President Lincoln...summoned him to a personal conference in Washington. The Military Governor of Kentucky arrived at the White House at the time indicated and went to the President's anteroom feeling that as an old personal friend as well as a visitor on highly important business, he would be called in promptly. But the attendants called in everybody else and had not reached him when the proper functionary announced that the interviews were over for the day.

In those days there was no executive annex to the White House. So when my grandsire left, somewhat hot under the collar, he started to pass out through the main front door of the White House. Just as he approached the door he heard Mr. Lincoln's voice from upstairs saying, "Come up here Palmer, you are home folks. We can discuss things better up here."

The President, with his face covered with lather, met him at the head of the stairs and led him to his bedroom where he resumed his seat in a barber chair, from which point of vantage he conducted the business. After the business was concluded they exchanged views as to Illinois politics and then swapped a few stories for both of them were rare artists in that line. As my grandfather was about to leave after a highly satisfactory interview, he approached the barber chair and placing his hand on the President's shoulder said "Mr. Lincoln, I sometimes wonder if we had known this great war was coming, we should have gone to a one-horse town to make a one-horse lawyer President of the United States." To this Mr. Lincoln replied, "You know Palmer, I have wondered about that every day of my life. But Palmer, it is a good thing they did not elect a great man with a policy. The only policy that I ever had was to get through each day's problems as well as I could.[71]

Although personal friendship undoubtedly played some part in Marshall's decision to retain Palmer on active duty, he had more compelling reasons to keep the "civilian conscience" of the army at his elbow. Though his elderly adviser could be repetitious to the point of boredom, his historical perspectives continued to be valuable and his imaginative suggestions sometimes turned out to be highly constructive. For example, his appraisal of the testimony presented before the Woodrum Committee, sharpened by his exchanges with Professor Kallen, led him to realize that in seeking UMT the army was actually proposing "a revolutionary change in our whole national life." It would be foolish, he believed, not to expect parents, churchmen, educators, labor leaders, and others to approach such a change with great caution. "We may be sure they won't give us carte blanche as to the disposition of their sons for a whole year in peacetime." The people themselves should have a role in establishing the training program laid out under UMT. To this end he urged that the proposed statute authorizing universal training should include a clause establishing a commission of civilians chosen by the service secretaries "to participate fully and freely with selected army and navy officers to the end that the paramount demands of national security shall be harmoniously coordinated with all other aspects of the national life."[72]

The proposal was to bear substantial fruit many months later. It was characteristic of Palmer, however, that he was entirely willing to be self-effacing if the idea could be sponsored more effectively by others. It would be ideal, he suggested, if the substance of his thought could be incorporated as part of a presidential message sent to Congress in support of UMT.

There was only one difficulty; the unexpected death of President Roosevelt had undone the effort of many months in cultivating his support for UMT.[73] Although President Truman had given a number of informal indications that he favored universal training in principle, the planners had been distressed to hear that he was toying with the possibility of coming out for one of the watered-down versions, such as those propounded by Col. Perry Brown of the Legion and Gen. Ellard Walsh of the National Guard Association. The Special Planning Division set to work on a staff paper to put the army's case before the President as persuasively as possible.[74]

The briefing paper prepared for the President showed that the planners had learned a good deal from their sustained association with the Woodrum Committee. To begin with, they suggested that it would be prohibitively expensive to rely solely upon a Regular Army, even if a large army were not regarded as "inimical to those democratic principles on which our nation is founded." The only alternative way to provide adequate security under modern conditions, they argued, was to have the National Guard and the Organized Reserve fully ready to take their places behind the Regulars. But the existing structure of the Guard failed to provide enough training. If some variant scheme, such as the one calling for four summers of three months each, were adopted, the time consumed in processing in and out would reduce the actual training to some thirty-six weeks. By contrast, one continuous year in uniform would provide forty-nine weeks of actual training.[75]

Other compelling arguments were set before the President. It was easy to show that the facilities available to the Guard were inadequate for training nearly 750,000 men each year. The wide range of special skills required would involve not only a heavy investment in weapons and equipment but firing ranges and maneuver grounds as well. There was no way for local Guard units to offer the full spectrum of training opportunities that would normally be available under Regular Army auspices. The travel costs of assembling individual trainees over several years would add substantially to the total. Spreading universal training over four years would also destroy the new ROTC program, which was to be built on the assumption that every student admitted would already have completed his year of compulsory training. A full year of prior training would permit the ROTC courses to work on an advanced level far more appealing to the abler undergraduates the army hoped to attract as future officers. Moreover, if the trainees had to spend all summer in camp, this would impair their capacity to earn their way through college and thus in many cases deny the individual an opportunity to enter ROTC, the major source of army commissions.

After the planners had presented their case to the President, Palmer had other worries to absorb his attention. Not the least of these was a serious defection in the ranks of the MTCA coterie in New York. Through his friend Archie Thacher, he learned that Grenville Clark, of all people, had written to the Secretary of War urging him to defer the drive for UMT in order to concentrate on getting Congress to extend the existing draft law. Clark had a plausible case: Occupation forces in Germany and Japan might be needed for anywhere from fifteen to thirty years. In addition, the United Nations would certainly require a suitable police force to forestall instances of aggression. If the United States continued the draft, it would strengthen the United Nations. In Clark's view UMT was not compatible with these requirements of the cold war era and should be deferred in favor of the draft. Palmer was horrified; what Clark was proposing was nothing less than old-fashioned conscription, using the draft in peacetime to fill the ranks of the army.[76]

Then, with dramatic suddenness, the war came to an end. Palmer was immediately alert to the need for rethinking military problems in the light of the newly revealed nuclear weapons. The atomic bomb, he wrote to a fellow officer in the Special Planning Division, has given "new dimensions" to the question of postwar organization.[77] But having said this, he dropped the idea entirely and went on pushing for UMT in a form and character essentially unchanged.

To expect Palmer, or even the officers of the Special Planning Division, to come up with an immediate assessment of the implications of the Bomb for military policy would be unreasonable, but meanwhile, with the war over and the armed forces already demobilizing in understandable but unseemly haste, the time for a revised national defense statute was already at hand. Since the planners had repeatedly been warned that it would be unwise to delay the drive for UMT until after the war, the ideal moment had already passed. Nonetheless, if they moved at once and obtained a universal training statute, it could be amended later if experiments with nuclear weapons showed the need. If they delayed and the Bomb proved to be inadequate when standing alone as a vehicle for national security, they had good reason to fear that the voters might be reluctant to authorize the burdens of compulsory training. So the decision was made to go ahead. Or, more accurately, a decision was *not* made to defer the effort until the "new dimensions" of nuclear weapons could be thoroughly explored.[78]

Whatever momentary pessimism Palmer may have experienced in the late summer of 1945 was soon dispelled. The Gallup poll in October once again revealed strong popular support for UMT. Despite the predictions of the pundits, the returns continued to show support for compulsory training at 70 percent, with the opposition running at 24 percent, exactly what it had been for several months. Even the farmers gave a 68 percent return in support, and union members supported UMT at 78 percent, or well above the general average.[79]

Still another factor contributing to Palmer's sanguine outlook was the publication of the final report of the so-called Section 5 committee, officially designated as the General Staff Committee on National Guard and Reserve Policy. At the direction of the Chief of Staff, the two separate committees established earlier to deal with the National Guard and the Organized Reserve had been reconstituted as a single committee under the chairmanship of Palmer's old friend and sometime opponent, Maj. Gen. Milton A. Reckord. This mixed committee, with equal representation from the regulars and the citizen components, had haggled for months, sometimes with no little acrimony.[80] In the end the committee turned in a unanimous report, which was subsequently accepted not only by all the staff divisions but also by the chief of the National Guard Bureau, the executive for reserve and ROTC affairs, the Liaison and Legislative Division, and the Bureau of Public Relations. To top it all off, the officer presenting this impressive record of agreement to the Chief of Staff added the comment, "Reckord says Palmer heartily concurs."[81]

The Section 5 committee had produced a policy document that embodied not one but literally dozens of Palmer's fundamental ideas. Not only in its basic assumptions but in many of its details the report reflected his handiwork, albeit indirectly. The mixed committee had come up with a realistic specification for the future Army of the United States. Both regulars and reservists would be expected to yield for the common good. By way of illustration, the professionals were firmly reminded that no regular unit would be authorized when a comparable unit could be equipped, trained, and made ready in a suitable time by a citizen component. The citizen soldiers were equally held to the mark; for example, the old Inactive Guard, with all its abuses, was to be abolished.

Palmer was persuaded that a new and higher sense of professionalism was now to be expected from the citizen forces. Sometime earlier, while the Section 5 committee members were still deliberating, they had come up with a tentative recommendation that would have required all officers in the citizen forces of field grade and above to attend a Regular Army service school as a condition of promotion. General Marshall had objected that any such stipulation would be impractical. He may well have been correct, but Palmer saw the recommendation as evidence that the members had a keen appreciation for the limitations of the prewar Guard and were determined to put the Guard in condition to meet the larger and more demanding postwar mission.[82] That some elements of the Guard had a long way to go could scarcely be denied. There had been, for example, units in several states down to the eve of World War II that still indulged in the questionable practice of electing officers.[83] But in Palmer's eyes, the report of the mixed committee would sweep away all these abuses.

The general was so delighted with the report of General Reckord's committee that he sat right down and wrote a glowing letter to Marshall. "This highly constructive paper fully vindicates the wisdom of Congress in prescribing that in the determination of all policies affecting the citizen forces, citizen officers should participate equally with professional officers on the policy-making level."[84] Since he himself had written Section 5 into the Defense Act of 1920, this could be interpreted as self-serving, but Marshall knew that his old friend was simply expressing his lifelong faith in the citizen forces. Indeed, he even had a good word for General Walsh. When his friend Thacher wrote in some distress about a recent effusion by the president of the National Guard Association, depicting the Regular Army as a "military samurai," Palmer went out of his way to be conciliatory: "I know Walsh well. He is a rather explosive sort of fellow but like yeast he serves a very useful purpose.... He keeps things leavened." After all, it had been an earlier blast from Walsh that led to the reestablishment of the Section 5 committees, with obviously fruitful results![85]

The accord hammered out by the Section 5 committee under General Reckord's leadership was a significant milestone on the road to UMT. If the professionals and the citizen soldiers could establish common ground, they would be able to present a unified front to the public in selling the need for universal training. But this was not the same thing as a positive, affirmative stroke in favor of UMT. Something far more dramatic was clearly needed. General Marshall decided to use his final biennial report as a vehicle to this end. He could scarcely have expected to start a political landslide for UMT, but his personal prestige, which had probably never been higher, promised to endow even such a sober document as the Chief of Staff's final report with a unique significance.

Marshall's main argument for UMT was contained in a final chapter entitled "For the Common Defense." In it he rehearsed the case for universal training in terms calculated to appeal to the widest possible audience. He introduced his argument by warning against the dangers of a large standing army, ever subject to political abuse in the hands of adventurers and men on horseback. "The citizen soldier is the guarantee against such a misuse of power." The United States looked hopefully to the United Nations, he assured his readers, but would court disaster if it disarmed, since "peace can only be maintained by the strong." Surely, he urged, the nation would accept the trivial restrictions on individual freedom imposed by compulsory training rather than repeat the awful tragedies of the war just over.[86]

Marshall left no doubt whatever that he regarded the civilian in arms as the essential guardian of the nation's liberties. "Probably the most important mission of the Regular Army is . . . training the citizen soldier, upon whom, in my opinion, the future peace of the world largely depends." To support this contention he quoted President Washington: "If we desire to avoid insult we must be ready to repel it; if we desire to secure peace, one of the most powerful instruments of our rising prosperity, it must be known that we are at all times ready for war." And to this he added an admonishment of his own. "If this nation is to remain great it must bear in mind now and in the future that war is not the choice of those who wish passionately for peace. It is the choice of those who are willing to resort to violence for political advantage.

With his customary thoughtfulness Marshall sent Palmer a finely bound copy of the report. An inscription on the flyleaf offered his "personal and official thanks for helpful support and great wisdom in reaching many decisions." The gesture was gracious but quite unnecessary; he had already paid Palmer the highest possible compliment by adopting so many of his ideas. Palmer had already read the full text from a working draft and had reported to his chief that he found it entirely in accord with his own lifelong teachings. "I concur fully in every sentence. My final reaction is that you have at last stated the true military objective of American democracy in terms that the American people can no longer ignore. You have translated Washington's philosophy into the language and thought of the atomic age." The document, Palmer believed, would prove persuasive to the man in the street. "Your countrymen will trust your disinterested wisdom and heed your advice. They were not wise enough to accept the message from Washington, but I believe they have now matured enough through costly experience to accept it from you.[87]

After so much frustration and neglect, it was gratifying indeed, as Palmer explained to a well-wisher, to have Marshall "give his high sanction to the policy I have been working for nearly half a century."[88] When others, seeing the close parallels between what the Chief of Staff wrote and what Palmer had been advocating for years, congratulated the old general on the final report, he scrupulously denied having any part in drafting the document.[89] Even in the execution of such a routine chore as preparing his biennial report, Marshall insisted on doing the job personally. The general had learned this two years earlier upon reading the Chief of Staff's previous biennial report, covering the period from 1941 to 1943. At that time he had casually mentioned to General McNarney that the publication had "a literary unity and flavor of personal authorship" that created the illusion that it was written by Marshall rather than for him. General McNarney assured him that this was not illusion but fact.[90]

To maximize the impact of the Chief of Staff's report, with its special plea for UMT, the army's public relations people geared up a big campaign to obtain the widest possible dissemination. The MTCA printed thousands of copies of the concluding chapter, "For the Common Defense," in pamphlet form for mass distribution.[91] But it is doubtful if many votes were changed on Capitol Hill by this. Any expectation by the advocates of UMT that Marshall's great prestige might tip the scales and make the vital difference in the crucial vote seems to have been unwarranted. No matter what the opinion polls reported, on the Hill the issue was still very much in doubt. One political observer went so far as to declare flatly, "Compulsory military training is still a dead duck."[92] Something even more dramatic, more compelling, than the Marshall report would be needed to move Congress.

For over a month President Truman had been giving out indications of his intention to address Congress on the subject of military training. If the President were to come out strongly in favor, it just might make the necessary difference.[93] But would he? There were still rumors that he would seek some politically palatable or watered-down version. The military planners wanted no shams, no bogus alternatives; far better to have no compulsory training at all and use the funds thus saved to bolster an entirely voluntary citizen force.

When Truman finally did make up his mind, his decision could scarcely have been more gratifying to those who favored universal training. His message to Congress was a notable example of political courage: without equivocation or evasion he called for universal peacetime training, truly universal training with no exemptions whatever save for individuals totally disqualified for physical reasons. In his blunt, democratic way, the President called for the whole package.[94] Even the opponents of UMT were impressed with the forcefulness of the chief executive's message. On the other hand, those who agreed with him, while pleased with the stand he had taken, were guarded in their expectations. Representative Wadsworth called Truman's message "one of the most forthright and courageous . . . ever delivered to the Congress." Yet even he regarded its impact as "difficult to estimate."[95]

Palmer watched the varied fortunes of the training issue with intense interest. It was a heartbreaking business. In November 1945 the House Military Affairs Committee began hearings prior to framing a bill to put before Congress. Almost immediately, however, a determined group of opponents began to engage in a series of parliamentary tactics in an effort to put the measure off until the following year.[96] They hoped to entangle the issue with the coming elections and thus kill it.

Among the witnesses called before the committee was Dr. George F. Zook, president of the American Council on Education, with whom Palmer had crossed swords earlier over his misuse of the term compulsory service as a label for the army UMT scheme. From the general's point of view Zook was a shortsighted idealist who hoped to end compulsory participation in the military by international agreement. The dimensions of Zook's impracticality were most clearly manifested in his suggestion that the army establish its minimum manpower requirements for national security and then attempt to secure the number of men necessary entirely through the recruitment of volunteers. Just what the nation would do if an enemy attacked with more than the minimum number of trained volunteers, the witness left unexplained as he went on to urge the appointment of a national commission to study all aspects of the problem. Since the commission scheme was virtually identical with what Palmer had long advocated, it came as a painful surprise to find the idea now being used by those hostile to his goals. The *New York Times* reported, "Dr. Zook's recommendations had the effect of ranging his organization, including hundreds of educational associations, on the side of the opponents."[97]

Not long afterward both the American Legion and the Veterans of Foreign Wars came out officially for what they called "home training." In deference to army wishes, their sponsors had refrained for several months from publicizing their emasculated four-month substitutes for the official twelve-month plan, but they could not be bottled up indefinitely. These politically palatable alternatives set forth by the veterans' organizations only served to aggravate the split in Congress. When the Military Affairs Committee began its hearings in November 1945, political observers had regarded the prospects for compulsory training as merely doubtful. Scarcely a month later a veteran journalist was convinced that the legislators would now vote for nothing stronger than one of the much watered-down substitute measures.[98]

Palmer refused to be downhearted. On the contrary, he professed to find in the press and elsewhere "an unprecedented new demand for real national security as a first step toward a better world organization." "Intelligent people" wanted real training, not half measures. They would prefer the opinion of the President and General Marshall, he argued, to the "wishy-washy political compromise" of the American Legion. Palmer had fought successfully in the past against what seemed to be hopeless odds, so he saw no reason to throw in the sponge too soon this time. "We put over Selective Service on its merits, in 1940, in spite of timid politicians, pacifists, and half-educated crackpots. I feel sure that we will win the present campaign for universal training in the same way."[99] But who "put over" the Draft Act? The general was obviously thinking of Grenville Clark and his cohorts in the MTCA when he said "we"; he overlooked the swath of destruction cut through Europe by Hitler's *wehrmacht*.

With the end of the war, Palmer thought surely that his tour of active duty was coming to an end. To his surprise no retirement orders arrived, even when General Marshall gave way to General Eisenhower as Chief of Staff. Only later did he learn that the Special Planning Division had asked to retain his services until it went out of business. The planners wanted Palmer's counsel while UMT was still pending and also wished to show him that the need for their "elder statesman" had not expired just because General Marshall was leaving office.[100]

General Eisenhower approved the request from the Special Planning Division and responded to another request from General Marshall. More than a year earlier General Tompkins had formally recommended the Legion of Merit for Palmer in recognition of his services, especially in promulgating War Department Circular 347. "No greater contribution has been made to our military future," Tompkins declared. Marshall suggested deferring the matter until Palmer was about to go back into retirement. Later, just before he himself left office, he asked his successor to make an award appropriate to Palmer's achievements. Not long afterward a special courier summoned Gen. and Mrs. Palmer to the office of the Chief of Staff, where in a simple ceremony General Eisenhower pinned a Distinguished Service Medal on the old gentleman's blouse.[101]

The general was immensely pleased. In reporting the episode to George Marshall he tactfully ascribed all the pride to his wife, who was "greatly thrilled" to see her beloved husband receive his second DSM.[102] It was clear, however, that the formal and official recognition meant a great deal to the recipient himself. Only one doubtful prospect remained: the compulsory training bill had yet to secure congressional approval.

52　The End of the Line

The pleasure Palmer experienced when General Eisenhower pinned an oakleaf cluster on his blouse in token of a second Distinguished Service Medal did not last long. The new chief was personally charming; he even recalled their first meeting in General Pershing's office way back in 1919. But affability was not the same thing as fundamental agreement on principles. Many of the men around Eisenhower were the same ones who had served under Marshall, nevertheless, Palmer noticed almost at once that there had been a change in the prevailing climate.

The first indication of the new outlook in the chief's office was trivial. Early in January 1946, Palmer had drafted a memo urging Eisenhower to consider the merits of a civilian commission as an effective route to UMT. He was careful to avoid mentioning his own authorship of the idea, observing only that President Conant of Harvard had suggested it when testifying before the Woodrum Committee. In characteristic fashion, the new Chief of Staff referred the memo to the director of special planning. This post was no longer occupied by Palmer's friend W. F. Tompkins; now the director was Maj. Gen. R. E. Porter, the one-time G-3 with whom he had repeatedly crossed swords over the issue of an organized civilian reserve. Porter's negative reaction to a civilian commission, coupled with General Eisenhower's decision to hold the idea "in abeyance," were all Palmer needed to indicate his status in the new regime.[1]

Once convinced that his usefulness was over, Palmer determined to ask for orders returning him to retirement. Pleasant as it was to go on drawing full pay, he realized that would scarcely be "fair to Uncle Sam" if he were not to be permitted to do what he had been recalled to do. However, when he approached one of the staff with a request for terminal leave, he was surprised to learn that the chief had a big job in store for him. As the officer put it,

"When you see the paper Eisenhower is preparing for you, you'll no longer feel you are not earning your pay."[2]

When the paper finally arrived, Palmer was appalled. The Chief of Staff gave every evidence that he was not really attached to the principle of universal training. The root of the problem was money. A Regular Army of 891,000 and a National Guard of 572,000, or twenty divisions, with overhead and replacements, would cost nearly $4 billion a year. The best estimates on UMT indicated an annual cost of $1.75 billion. With the budget officer gloomily predicting that Congress would give the army no more than $3 billion in all, what was to be cut? Should the planned UMT training be reduced? Eisenhower wanted Palmer to study the problem, seeking ways and means to provide an adequate reserve without resorting to universal training.[3]

The Chief of Staff's request sounded like 1919 all over again. Rather than attempt a reply along the lines obviously expected, Palmer went directly to the heart of the matter. What Eisenhower was asking for was a fiscal expedient that evaded the real issues. Until the roles and missions of all the elements in the armed forces were authoritatively established, any estimates submitted by the army would necessarily be inadequate. To prevent overlapping defense budgets, Palmer urged a civilian commission along the lines of his earlier memo. Such a body would simply serve as a master in chancery, identifying the overlaps in the proposed military budgets while working from a perspective above the partisan interests of the individual branches and services. Until Congress voted for unification as the President wished, a civilian commission might well prove useful.[4]

Palmer's argument, in nine and one-half pages of single-spaced typescript, fared no better than his earlier memo. All the staff sections submitted comments offering doubts, warnings, and qualifications, after which the Chief of Staff referred the paper back to the author "for further study." This may have been just a polite way of getting the old gentleman off his back, but if so Palmer failed to take the hint. Now thoroughly aroused, he replied in a flood of memos, picking holes in the chief's line of approach.[5]

He first questioned the army's cost figures. With per capita charges for trainees under UMT estimated at more than $2,500, he was certain that some less expensive solution would have to be found. That was enough for a year in college, a thought that might lead the voters to favor education instead of defense. And why was so large an overhead necessary? "A Swiss officer would be amazed to learn that we propose to maintain an expensive corps of 136,900 professional officers and soldiers in order to conduct the training of 700,000."

Palmer readily admitted that he lacked the experience to do a detailed cost analysis. "My forte," he reminded the Chief of Staff, "is policy." Then he recalled at some length how his views on the role of citizen soldiers had been officially sanctioned in War Department Circular 347. With just a hint of asperity he suggested that "a closer adherence to the principles laid down in

Circular 347" would have produced the lower costs everyone desired. If compromises were unavoidable, then it might be necessary to cut federal training to six months, followed by an enlistment in the National Guard. All he asked was that officers from the Guard and the Organized Reserves be invited to sit in on the deliberations. After all, as he observed somewhat tartly, Section 5 of the Defense Act was still on the statute books.

For a man whose whole life was a model of humility, Palmer's rather brisk rapping of the Eisenhower knuckles may seem somewhat incongruous. But here was a man quietly infuriated at seeing the greatest work of his career melting before his eyes. Nor were his fears entirely groundless. A few days earlier he had tried to secure Eisenhower's formal reendorsement of Circular 347, to give it "renewed currency," but the attempt had failed. The drift of the wind was all too evident.[6]

The values and priorities of Eisenhower were not the same as those of his predecessor. The spirit of Circular 347 no longer dominated the General Staff, as Palmer discovered in a painful encounter with one of the newly arrived officers in the chief's coterie. This hapless soul, obviously unaware of the old gentleman's relationship to the previous chief or his authorship of Circular 347, suggested that now that Marshall was out of the way on his mission to China, it would be a good time to scuttle the "Marshall policy." Palmer retorted that the policy went all the way back to George Washington.[7] Three months later Eisenhower quietly rescinded Circular 347; fortunately the old general never learned of this action. He would have enjoyed hearing about the other side of the coin, however; years later, army officers were still quoting Circular 347 as if it were approved doctrine. A policy trumpeted with great fanfare to the four winds cannot be quietly undone. An idea once set free has a life of its own.[8]

The mounting evidence of the change in policy grew too obvious for Palmer to ignore. Why wear himself out on fruitless forays? As he later described the situation to his friend Archie Thacher, "the officers of the new regime treated me courteously as an amiable old gentleman with antiquated ideas but completely ignored any advice that I had to give." Finally, in April 1946, he wrote to the Chief of Staff asking for retirement. General Eisenhower immediately granted this request, adding a note of thanks for his "wise counsel"! Since none of his counsel had been accepted, it was difficult not to sense a certain hollowness in this tribute.[9]

Although the Chief of Staff's rather pro forma farewell left something to be desired, the War Department public relations people did much better, giving considerable play to the retirement of the "oldest Army officer on active service," the man whom Marshall had called his "military elder statesman."[10] The publicity triggered a flood of letters from old friends and acquaintances. One in particular, coming from a younger colonel on the staff, pleased the general no end, recalling his courage when testifying in 1919. "Had you failed to speak your convictions then," wrote the colonel, "the whole course of history since 1940 might have been vastly different. I hope that you will be able to speak again should the need arise." It was even more gratifying to learn that his contributions were not all forgotten or rejected: "Your authorship of Circular 347, which has been called the 'Charter of the Citizen Army' merely confirms your position as the father of the reserve system."[11]

Palmer was not really leaving the army; he was merely shifting back to the Library of Congress. The future and progress of the Army of the United States would still be his central preoccupation, but from now on he intended to put all his energy into the completion of his memoirs. The rejection of his philosophy that occasioned his departure from active duty still rankled, but he refused to let his frustration embitter him. He turned to the memoirs, he told Wadsworth, because no publisher would dare accept the book he really wanted to write, a volume entitled, "S.O.B.'s I Have Known." After a long career in the army he was a connoisseur of the species, but would gladly welcome a collaborator from Capitol Hill.[12]

Even before the general stepped down from active duty, the War Department withdrew the secretary who had served him throughout the war. The impact of this loss was offset somewhat when Grenville Clark and some of his friends arranged for a small grant from the Carnegie Corporation of New York to cover the general's typing costs. This was helpful, but not at all the same thing as having a secretary to handle his voluminous correspondence as well as the pencilled chapter drafts of his memoirs. He tried dictating without success. "What little wit there is in my writing comes out through the point of my pencil within six inches of an eraser."

By the general's calculations, if he worked only three hours each morning for five mornings a week, he could finish his manuscript within a year. The three-hour day was realistic, considering his age, but he had so much fun recalling his adventures that a single episode, such as the Boxer Rebellion, soon expanded beyond its 5,000-word quota to more than 12,000 words. But he was determined to make his book something more than an old gaffer's adventures. As he explained to his daughter, he wanted to finish before the next Congress because he had a message. "It will contain a gospel that our solons sorely need."[13] But this time he would not make the mistake he had in 1915, when he had asked permission from the War Department before publishing. As he explained in high good humor to Grenville Clark, "When the War Department calls me to account, my reply will simply be: 'I suggest a court martial.' If that suggestion is adopted, I will retain Grenny Clark, 'Sec' Root, Phil Carroll, Archie Thacher and other Plattsburg co-conspirators as counsel. Such a 'state trial' should be good advertising for the book."[14]

For all his determination to get in one last blow for a sound policy, there was still something of a Cincinnatus about the old general. A letter from Wadsworth on his farm in upstate New York provoked a nostalgic mood.

Palmer was intrigued by his friend's operations, cultivating thousands of acres in the Geneseo Valley, where he fattened steers shipped in by the trainload. But he confessed a preference for the kind of "farming" he himself practiced on fifty acres of New Hampshire hillside gradually going back to birch and spruce. The only livestock on the family acres were the deer feeding on Mrs. Palmer's flowers. "I'm so grateful to the deer for they have left me nothing to weed. I am not fond of the minutiae of gardening. In fact, I love wild flowers because God does all the gardening for them—and who am I to compete with Him?" He concluded his description of the family estate in a bantering tone. "I know you will want to swap farms with me when you read this. So right now I want to nip that hope in the bud. I will do anything else for you, Jim, but I positively won't swap this farm for any other farm in Christendom."[15]

The impression Palmer conveyed was one of serene old age, of an elderly gentleman who has put all battles and all bitterness behind him to enjoy a few years of well-earned repose. Yet even as he wrote he was deeply engaged in a struggle over policy. He might admonish a friend to heed Walt Whitman and learn to "loaf away your soul," but he drove himself relentlessly to finish his memoirs, so they could speak for him when he would no longer be able to do so.[16]

During 1946, the first postwar year, Palmer watched the progress of UMT with mounting dismay. Just as predicted, the issue had become hopelessly entangled with the measures required to demobilize combat soldiers. Even when the army lowered its physical standards to induct men hitherto classified as 4F or physically unfit, the Selective Service was unable to meet the demand. In an election year, the politicians were obviously reluctant to keep combat veterans in uniform; drafting the current crop of eighteen-year-old high school seniors was equally unacceptable. One senator, apparently innocent of any knowledge of Roman history, proposed to meet the need without affronting the voters by recruiting "non-resident aliens" from the Polish liberation forces in exile.[17] Congress finally passed a stopgap measure temporarily extending the wartime draft. Even this unsatisfactory concession, however, was secured only after the Administration agreed not to induct any more men for at least two months to avoid the fall elections.[18]

If UMT had been fully debated on its merits and voted down, even those who advocated compulsory training could have accepted the judgment and proceeded to alternatives. But the legislators left the military planners up in the air. The postwar goal of 681,000 men in the National Guard had been set on the assumption that after experiencing a year of universal training, large numbers of young men would be eager to enlist in the Guard. Without UMT, Guard recruiting was lagging. Even such a dedicated guardsman as Maj. Gen. Milton A. Reckord estimated that 300,000 would be the maximum number one could realistically expect to enlist voluntarily without UMT. As a consequence, the reserve of civilian components on which the planners had counted when they called for a small Regular Army was not available. Lacking a Guard of full-strength units, the nation had no ready reserve. If the Guard, with its paid armory drills and summer duty, was unable to meet the quota, the unpaid Organized Reserve was in even worse shape. Of 8,000-odd projected units, only some 2,500 had been activated by the spring of 1946, and not one of these had a full complement of officers and men.[19]

If the military planners gave up the fight for UMT and turned instead to a large, all-volunteer Regular Army, they could not be certain of getting the volunteers and would surely be damned as militarists for advocating a big Regular establishment. Then, too, they would be charged with lacking the courage of their convictions in dropping the drive for UMT just because there was opposition. On the other hand, Congress might even refuse to extend the draft long enough to provide the manpower required for occupation duties. In this quandry the army planners decided to compromise, and in September 1946, Secretary of War Robert P. Patterson formally presented a scheme similar to the one put forward by the American Legion during the previous year.[20]

In place of one continuous year of federal training, there would now be substituted six months under army auspices, followed by the equivalent of a second six months, spread out over the period of an enlistment in a reserve component. Under the old full-year plan, the trainee who graduated from UMT might enlist in a reserve unit if he wished to but was under no obligation to do so. He could be called up only when authorized by Congress. Under the six-month scheme, a trainee moving into the second phase of his training with, say, the Guard unit in his home town, would incur the same obligation as any other individual enlisting in the Guard; in short, he could be called to duty by a mere executive order; the distinction between "training" and "conscription" that Palmer had struggled so hard to maintain was entirely ignored. Had the old general still been on duty, this was precisely the kind of conceptual flaw to which he would have been sensitive. From outside the division he had no opportunity to forestall such a blunder. It is doubtful whether he even recognized the fundamental shift in philosophy implicit in Secretary Patterson's proposal as announced in the newspapers; if he did, he left no evidence of the fact.

While the army six-month plan departed from the ideal for which Plamer had struggled, it nonetheless reflected the acute necessities under which the Truman Administration labored. The large number of men needed by the Army—nominally for occupation troops but actually as a counterforce to the mounting Soviet threat—could only be secured by the continued operation of the draft. But Congress had already indicated an unwillingness to extend the draft indefinitely. Even if the legislators approved some form of UMT almost immediately, it would be some years before the system built up an adequate civilian component. It was patently impossible to operate the draft and

universal training at the same time while still maintaining any semblance of
equity. Therefore, by a kind of inexorable logic, the army was led to propose
the six-month plan. This new scheme would, its sponsors hoped, go a long way
toward making UMT acceptable while at the same time yielding a full-
strength ready reserve.

Secretary Patterson's announcement of the six-month training plan coincided with the annual American Legion convention in San Francisco. The
national elections were only a month away, but any expectations of political
advantage Truman may have had were shattered when the Republicans
captured the Congress in November. But the President believed in universal
training as a matter of principle; instead of dodging the issue, as so many
politicians on the Hill seemed to be doing, he faced up to it boldly. The
elections were scarcely over when he announced the formation of a nine-
member civilian commission as the next step in his continuing campaign for
adequate national defense.[21]

At last one of the ideas Palmer had been advocating in season and out was
coming to fruition. It was certainly true that others, including President
James. B. Conant of Harvard, had also proposed such a commission, but
credit for authorship was of little moment when there was new hope on the
horizon. And the eminence of the individuals appointed to the commission
gave every reason to believe that its findings would command widespread
respect. The chairman was Dr. Karl T. Compton, president of MIT; the other
members were Joseph E. Davies, former ambassador to Moscow; Dr. Harold
W. Dodds, president of Princeton; Truman Y. Gibson, a black, formerly a
civilian aide to the Secretary of War; the Rev. Dr. Daniel Poling, editor of the
Christian Herald; Anna Rosenberg, an eminent industrial relations consultant; Samuel I. Rosenman, former counsel and ghostwriter to President
Roosevelt, the Rev. Dr. Edmund A. Walsh, vice-president of Georgetown
University; and Charles E. Wilson, the president of General Electric and
wartime vice-chairman of the War Production Board.[22]

President Truman himself attended the first meeting of the commission and
laid out its charge. Significantly, he asked the members to remove the word
"military" from their announced designation as the President's Advisory
Commission on Universal Military Training. That the President felt such a
gesture desirable is strong evidence of the way he read the political climate.

Palmer was almost certain that he would be called to testify; nonetheless, he
thought it well to make his presence known by sending Compton a long
statement describing the historic background of the training issue in the
United States. About the same time, Congressman Wadsworth also wrote
Compton urging him to call Palmer as a witness. The chairman wrote back
saying that he had actually been reading Palmer's paper when Wadsworth's
letter arrived. Moreover, he added, "I had marked several passages from his

statement which seemed well adapted for quotation in a final report." He promised to bring Palmer's material to the attention of all the members but questioned the need to have the general testify in person since he had presented his case so effectively in writing.[23]

When Wadsworth passed this information along, his old friend took fire immediately. The material he had sent Compton was only background, he explained; if the members of the commission invited him to testify, he promised to hand them "an even bigger bombshell" than the one he had submitted to Congress in 1919. He could not in good grace invite himself to testify nor, he added, would that be suggested by "my friends in the War Department." This last may not have been justified, but it does indicate the sense of betrayal Palmer felt at the treatment he had received from the Chief of Staff.[24]

The general's feeling of neglect by the War Department was not entirely warranted. Two days later Lt. Gen. R. S. McLain of the Legislative and Liaison Division wrote to tell him that his name had been suggested as a witness, but since his views were so much in agreement with those of the members, the commission staff feared it might appear that he was being called to support conclusions already reached.[25] Meanwhile, Wadsworth had sent a second letter to Compton. In it, he recalled how Palmer had dared to speak out in 1919 against the official War Department line; if the official military spokesman once again made inadequate recommendations, Palmer could be counted on to come out boldly in opposition.[26]

Chairman Compton was sufficiently impressed to call Palmer to the stand. There the old general described in detail how the army planners had resisted his views on the importance of an organized reserve of citizen soldiers. Scathingly he denounced the professionals who had expected to use UMT only as a pool of fillers for the Regular Army: "They proposed, in effect, to solve the problem of a peacetime organized reserve by dispensing with it entirely." Then, in conclusion, he outlined the democratic military philosophy published by George Marshall in War Department Circular 347.[27]

The general's testimony obviously impressed the members of the commission. Thereafter, Compton's staff members consulted freely with him, even submitting drafts of their working materials for him to comment on.[28] Still convinced that much could be learned from a careful study of the Swiss militia at first hand, the general urged the commission to visit Switzerland, taking representatives of the Budget Bureau along to uncover some of the economies inherent in the system. "The militarist always opposes a careful study of the Swiss system," he concluded, "because he instinctively dreads it just as the devil dreads holy water—and for much the same reason."[29]

The Compton Commission report, published in June 1947, mirrored Palmer's views on virtually all points. He would have preferred a full year of training under army auspices but had long since come to accept the need for compromising on six months as the commission recommended. Beyond this the commission proposed a variety of options: (1) an additional six months of training with the army; (2) a normal enlistment in the army or navy for at least two years; (3) enrollment at one of the service academies; (4) enrollment in the National Guard or the Organized Reserve with obligatory drill periods for three years; or (5) enrollment either in an ROTC program or a technical training course approved by the armed services.[30] The general was especially pleased that the commission picked up his idea of a permanent supervisory committee of one military and two civilian members to serve as a kind of civilian conscience for the services, functioning as he himself had done for many years past. "I am convinced," he declared, "that the soldier will have much more to learn from his civilian brethren than they from him if our training system is to be in full harmony with the genius of democratic institutions."[31]

Although editorial opinion was generally favorable to the report itself, virtually all observers seemed to agree that there was no chance whatever of securing passage of a universal training measure in the current session of Congress. Even those legislators who spoke well of the commission findings asked not to be quoted by name. Despite the high degree of support for UMT that continued to be indicated by the professional pollsters, many congressmen were only too glad to put off a showdown vote. What is more, they had a valid excuse for delay; the members had been preoccupied with the pressing problem of unification for the armed forces, a measure finally enacted in July 1946.[32]

There was, however, a notable difference between the legislators in general and those who served on the military committees, now realigned into a single Committee on Armed Services in each house. Including the Woodrum hearings, the several hearings of the former Military Affairs Committees, and those of the Compton Commission, these representatives now had before them the testimony of nearly two hundred witnesses. The sheer weight of this prolonged exposure began to take effect. Finally, at the very end of the session, the House committee took the plunge and reported out a bill calling for universal training along the lines suggested by the Compton Commission. The unanimous vote on this action, 20 to 0, suggests that the urgency of the Compton report had been reinforced by the increasingly truculent tone of the Communist bloc.[33]

The bill was something of a landmark. None of the many universal training bills previously offered had successfully crossed the committee hurdle. But the session was over. The best the committee could do under the circumstances was to extract a promise from the House leaders to put the bill on the calendar for the next session in January 1948, an election year. Since even the most ardent friends of compulsory training conceded that nothing could be accomplished in an election year, it looked as if the issue once again were dead.[34]

For Palmer it was almost as if a malevolent fate had determined not to let the issue come to a fair debate and a final vote. It was so maddening he evidently determined to put the question out of his mind entirely. At the close of the session he wrote Wadsworth to congratulate him on his part in pushing the unification bill toward enactment, but pointedly avoided all comment on the subject that meant most to him.[35] But it was next to impossible for him to ignore universal training. Each day, as he worked away on his memoirs, he raked up recollections of old legislative battles lost and hopeful schemes shattered. And each one seemed to find its maddening echo in some more recent event in the long train of compromises and defective half measures that made up the nation's response to the problems of defense. It was, therefore, not in the least surprising that he once again allowed himself to be drawn into the struggle.

The occasion of Palmer's return to action—his last, as it proved—was the appointment of a Committee on Civilian Components by Secretary of Defense James Forrestal in November 1947. Behind the Secretary's move lay a complicated story, but at the heart of the matter was the long-standing rivalry between the National Guard and the Organized Reserve.[36] The unpaid and largely unsupported reserve officers were inclined to complain of the favored position enjoyed by the Guard. They were supported by those regulars who deplored the whole system of dual control, with all its political overtones for appointments and promotions in the Guard. Since the postwar Guard was woefully weak, having recruited fewer than 200,000 men against its quota of 681,000, the time seemed propitious to those proposing change. Maj. Gen. Harry H. Vaughan, military aide to President Truman and a reservist himself, led the attack with an article in *The Reserve Officer* advocating a merger of the Organized Reserve and the National Guard under federal auspices.[37] A war of words promptly erupted in the pages of their respective journals and in the daily press.

Forrestal's committee, chaired by Gordon Gray, who was then Assistant Secretary of the Army, was directed to investigate the whole reserve question. Although nothing in its charge explicitly stated that the committee was to consider removing the National Guard from state control, the hostile reaction of the Guard lobbyists was so prompt that Secretary Forrestal felt constrained to issue a denial that the committee had been formed to study General Vaughan's proposal.[38] Against this backdrop of contending interests, Palmer set aside his memoirs and began to prepare a statement, which he easily induced the committee to consider.

There were few new ideas in the presentation the general made before the committee early in 1948. Somewhat unfairly he characterized the proposals of the Special Planning Division during the war as "more frankly militaristic" than those offered by General March after World War I. Then he described how General Marshall had finally sanctioned his views by issuing War

Department Circular 347 as an official statement of policy. But even this high authentication, he explained, rested upon an unstable foundation once Marshall stepped down as Chief of Staff.

> It seems to me that one of the first duties of this Committee is to put an end to the conflict between two mutually antagonistic military policies.... Before making detailed plans for the house, the Committee should settle the style of architecture. It should, therefore, recommend that a statement of policy, in substance like that contained in Circular 347, should be given final and permanent sanction by Act of Congress.[39]

Even before the Gray committee submitted its final report calling for a single reserve component entirely under federal control, the guardsmen had stirred up enough opposition in Congress to assure themselves that the committee recommendations would be stillborn.[40]

The old general found it woefully depressing to march offstage while the major problem of national security was still unresolved. About the best he could hope for now was to make some small contribution with his memoirs.[41] Yet even this goal was threatened when cataracts began to form on both his eyes. He struggled on, sustained by the conviction that he had an important message for posterity. When Luther H. Evans, the Librarian of Congress, wrote on his eightieth birthday and enquired how the memoirs were progressing, he expressed his faith succinctly. "The story is one that should be told.... It will show how two world wars and the threat of a third are chargeable to the interrelations of an *un*educated citizenry and a *mis*educated soldier."[42] But even after he had put aside all thought of further involvement in political battles, his reserves of energy never seemed enough. As he explained the problem to a friend, "I find my working hours grow shorter even more rapidly than my leisure grows longer."[43]

Although the old general drove himself hard in the race to finish his writing before his eyesight dimmed beyond repair, there were many happy aspects to his second retirement. Living in Washington, the Palmers dined often at the Army-Navy Club, where they enjoyed a large circle of friends. These included not only their own contemporaries but many younger officers the general had come to know while on duty during the war.

To the great amusement of the younger set, the arrival of the Palmers at the rear or ladies entrance of the club was the occasion of a regular ritual. To the end of her days the general's lady never relented in her disapproval of drinking. With proper attention to military logistics, the general trained the barkeepers to have his favorite drink standing ready. Then, while his dear wife went to remove her wrap, he would pay a quick visit to the bar. The precision with which he executed this maneuver attracted quite an audience among the younger officers, and some would help the old gentlemen have a more leisurely glass by going out to distract "Aunt Maude" with friendly banter.

There were invitations now and then to official functions, especially after George Marshall became Secretary of State. The general would admit to a genuine feeling of pride as he watched his beloved wife being escorted in to a White House dinner on the arm of the Secretary of State. All in all, the elderly couple managed to find a great deal of fun in life even if the stairs did seem steeper than formerly.

Sometimes, of course, the official functions were of another kind. For example, on the occasion of General Pershing's death, Palmer learned that his old chief had expressed a wish to have him act as a pallbearer. He performed this last service with grim pride, marching for more than a mile behind the caisson bareheaded in the sun of a sweltering July day.[44] Yet even these evidences of mortality failed to daunt the general and his officer friends. One wit among them illustrated this trait to perfection; whenever he referred to the apartment hotel on Connecticut Avenue where the Palmers and many other retired service couples lived, he called it "Arlington prep."

One of the happiest episodes of the old general's declining years grew out of a birthday remembrance sent to him by a number of the old MTCA crowd in New York. It was a heavy sterling tray. Beneath the general's name appeared the words:

Soldier, Patriot, Historian of Military Policy
Discoverer in 1930 of the Washington Manuscript of 1783
"Sentiments on a Peace Establishment"

From his friends in Military Preparedness

The names that followed made up a roster of boon companions in a common cause:

Julius Ochs Adler	J. Lloyd Derby
Douglas Arant	Duncan G. Harris
Kenneth P. Budd	Alfred Roelker
Philip A. Carroll	Elihu Root, Jr.
Grenville Clark	Archibald G. Thacher
Arthur F. Cosby	James W. Wadsworth

Beneath the list of friends was this final inscription:

Each year to Ancient Friendship
Add a Ring as to an Oak!

Palmer was deeply moved by this token of affection and esteem from his friends. He may have failed in many of his struggles for national defense, but it was heartwarming to know that so many of his old friends appreciated his efforts. He sat right down to compose a letter of thanks, an essay on the enduring problem of military policy. "During all these years the superior civil authority has neglected to give an authoritative mandate to the inferior military authority. This is the real reason for our past unpreparedness and for today's enormous burden of debt and taxation."[45] Thoughtful men, he reminded his friends, fear that "a militarized America might also become a militaristic America," escaping external peril only to succumb to an internal peril. And in either event "government by the people would perish from the earth." The spirit of Circular 347, he concluded, must be made more permanent by act of Congress if the nation would escape these disasters.

After reading what he had just written, he decided not to send it after all. Why preach to the converted? Far better to devote his limited energies to composing his memoirs—while enjoying life with his circle of friends and watching his grandsons as they followed in his footsteps.

During the spring of 1949, the general's mind was very much occupied with his grandsons. The younger boy, John Palmer Chandler, was to graduate from the Military Academy in June. Feeble though he felt, the old general knew he had to be there; he desperately wanted to see "Old West Point" one more time.[46]

The superintendent graciously made quarters available near the center of activities and saw to it that a car was always at hand to serve the elderly couple. The evening of their arrival they had intended to retire early, but the strains of music from the cadet hop proved too tempting. So they walked over and watched the dancers from the side lines. The following morning the general and his lady were escorted to the superintendent's pew in the majestic academy chapel. That afternoon the general was filled with pride as he watched his tall young grandson, resplendent in white uniform, plumed shako, and the red sash betokening his status as an officer on the brigade staff. The doting grandfather later observed with a twinkle, "His grandmother considered him the most important figure in the ceremony, and I'm inclined to agree with her."[47]

In the days of Cadet Captain John M. Palmer the whole academy had comprised a battalion of four companies, less than three hundred souls in all. And now there was a full brigade, 2,400 strong. The graduating class alone was now larger than the entire academy had been. And if a young graduate could not even know all his contemporaries in the officer corps, the army was becoming a very different kind of institution from the one he himself had served so gladly.

How different, too, was the discipline. The cadets nowadays seemed very much like college boys everywhere. How would grandson Johnnie and his contemporaries have reacted if they had been subjected to the kind of supervision practiced before the turn of the century? They could go to the library and see for themselves. It was all there, recorded in copperplate hand in the "gig book," the Register of Discipline for each year. Some of the penalties charged against Cadet Palmer would seem perfectly familiar:

late for 7 a.m. drill	1 demerit
put on cap before leaving mess	1 demerit
barrel of rifle scratched	4 demerits
gunner at artillery drill; gave command "fire" without authority	5 demerits

On the other hand, a few of the entries would certainly provoke surprise:

odor of tobacco smoke in quarters	5 demerits
not taking bath during week ending 18 January 1889	2 demerits
overstaying time at bath, 3:10 to 3:45 p.m.	5 demerits[48]

As the ancient philosopher Democritus once observed, the world is divided into two groups: those who bathe too often and those who bathe not often enough. Those entrusted with the shaping of officers and gentlemen in Cadet Palmer's day apparently believed there was an attainable ideal between these two extremes that would produce just the kind of military leaders the nation required.

Alumni day found the general out on the parade gound early. He expected to be near the end of the line, but when it came time to fall in, he was surprised to discover just how near the end he actually was. There were only five or six men to the right of him. At the far right was Maj. Gen. Henry Clay Hodges of the class of 1881, the oldest graduate present—an honor he had enjoyed for some years.[49]

Graduation day was something of an anticlimax. To be sure, the Palmers were proud to see their grandson take his commission standing so near the top, 24 in a class of 572. As they watched his beaming mother, they felt that life had come full circle. Mary had been born on the academy grounds when her father was on duty as an instructor, and now her youngest was fairly launched on an army career. With graduation over, the old couple suddenly felt distressingly tired. They had been sustained by the excitement of the past few days, but now, abruptly, they were completely exhausted. They had to get away. As the automobile carrying them back to the city rolled out of the academy grounds, the old general looked back; he was never to see the academy again.

The visit to West Point marked the close of the general's career. Now all that remained was to wrap up the loose ends, most particularly the unfinished manuscript of his memoirs. He applied himself grimly to this task, but it moved ever more slowly. At last failing eyesight and flagging energy convinced him that he could no longer go on. With one last burst of will power, he arranged to transfer his papers to the custody of the Library of Congress, while launching a search for a younger man to carry on in his stead.[50] Yet even as he did so, he knew that any book by another hand would never be the same as the one he himself had planned. Even his legacy to the future was to be compromised. When Jim Wadsworth retired at the end of the current session of Congress, who would carry on the struggle for a military policy without militarism?[51]

Brig. Gen. John McAuley Palmer died 26 October 1955 after a long illness. He was buried on a hillside in Arlington National Cemetery with full military honors. The site selected was just below the grave of General Pershing, who had arranged many years before to have the officers close to him in life brought back to lie forever near him in death.

53 A Life in Retrospect

When General Marshall learned that his old comrade John Palmer was dead, he sat silent for a few moments and then observed somewhat wistfully to his wife, "He was the last of those who called me George." The remark aptly defined the place of his friend and fellow soldier in the march of history. John McAuley Palmer was never a household word, never a battlescarred folk hero known to every schoolboy. He was one of those figures who stand just outside the limelight, generating ideas, advising, drawing plans, wielding an influence difficult to assess but clearly out of all proportion to nominal rank or status.[1] For a long generation, from the time he was a young captain at Secretary Stimson's elbow in William Howard Taft's administration to his years of service as an elderly general called back to active duty in World War II, Palmer enjoyed a favored position as an intimate of the leading military men and their civilian superiors. Again and again his imagination, his integrity, and his dedication won him the support and enduring friendship of those in authority. Moreover, it was the role for which he was best fitted by temperament and personality.

George Marshall had never been blind to his friend's limitations, and he had never let his friendship distort his professional judgment. An example of this was his reaction to a suggestion by old Gen. John F. O'Ryan of the "Fighting 27th," long in retirement, that Palmer's contributions since his recall to duty in 1941 merited a promotion to major general. Marshall replied, confirming his high opinion of Palmer, "a source of strength to both the Army and me personally," but firmly rejected all thought of a promotion on grounds of age and discontinuous service. When O'Ryan showed this flattering exchange of correspondence to Palmer, Palmer characteristically observed that, while grateful for the intervention in his behalf, he only regretted that the chief's attention had been diverted from more important duties on his account.[2]

That Marshall's appraisal of Palmer was not just an accident of association is indicated by the latter's relationship to General Pershing two decades earlier. Just before Pershing retired, he rated Palmer officially, placing him sixteenth among the forty-two general officers of his peer group.[3] Since virtually all of these men had seen far more combat service than Palmer in World War I, it is evident that this rating reflected Pershing's estimate of Palmer's achievements as a staff officer and adviser on policy. After retirement he was to describe Palmer as "one of the best staff officers ever produced by our Army."[4] Although Pershing himself was never known as an original thinker, it was a mark of his stature that he willingly surrounded himself with highly imaginative men of Palmer's stamp.

While it is undoubtedly true that Palmer's greatest achievements were in the role of staff officer, he was also successful in combat in World War I as a brigade commander. Moreover, he attained the genuine affection of his men. As his division commander, Maj. Gen. Charles G. Morton, put it, "His men not only respected him but loved him."[5] It was precisely this capacity to win both respect and devotion that seems to have lain at the heart of Palmer's unusual qualities as a soldier. Appraising him many years after his death, General Lewis D. Hershey, the veteran director of Selective Service, expressed much the same thought. "He had a sympathetic nature that made him attractive, likeable. But this could fool you; underneath he was shrewd; he had an inner steel."[6]

Testimonials to Palmer's charming and remarkably attractive personality abound on every hand, but there is a vast difference between assertion and explanation. The elements of his magnetism were doubtlessly many and varied, yet at least one ingredient seems always to have been present: he remained humble. Close as he was to Pershing, Marshall, and others in high positions of authority, he retained an unfailing sense of humility. It is doubtful that this was a pose; humility suffused his whole personality and colored his way of life. Somewhere, very early in his career, he had learned the value of the indirect approach. Perhaps he learned this, unwittingly, as a small boy listening to his mother reading Joel Chandler Harris's narratives of that shrewd ex-slave, Uncle Remus.

Throughout his life Palmer employed the indirect approach with telling effect. He practiced a minor whimsy on his family for many years; whenever he had some difficult or especially unpleasant advice to give, he assumed the role of that delightful character out of A. A. Milne, Mr. Pim, and let Mr. Pim take the onus. In this way it was never the loving father who put aside his teenage daughter's pleas, nor was it the devoted grandfather who said no to grandsons bent on some devilment. With Mr. Pim's help the general preserved his role as fond companion, confidant, and ally against the erosion inevitable when a parent must speak out as disciplinarian and judge. When the grandsons were too young to savor the Pickwickian flavor of Mr. Pim, admonitory tales of

Br'er Fox and Br'er Rabbit served the same purpose. When they were older it was "orders from headquarters" that had to be obeyed by "Sergeant Norry" and "Corporal John." Palmer's charm was concocted from a blend of imagination, sensitivity, subtle shrewdness, and whimsical good humor.

Important as the general's attributes of personality undoubtedly were, in the long run it is the quality of his ideas that will count for most. For this reason it will be useful to consider the character of his mind before looking at his specific ideas.

An episode back in 1922 nicely illustrates the range of Palmer's learning and the originality of his thinking, while reflecting his characteristic self-doubt when asked to make a decision. The general's aunt, Jessie Palmer Weber, the librarian of the Illinois State Historical Library, reported to him that the statue of his illustrious grandfather and namesake, the Civil War general and governor of Illinois, then being erected by well-wishers in Springfield, was nearing completion. All that remained was the matter of a suitable inscription. She offered two extracts from the governor's speeches for consideration: "The rights of the people are safe with the people," and "As strong as the law and no stronger."[7] Palmer agreed they were both characteristic of his grandfather's political faith, but then he went on to weigh their relative merits.

The phrase "The Rights of the people are safe with the people" is complete in itself, but I am a little uncertain as to whether there is such a distinct flavor of originality about it. I do not mean to say that he got that precise language from any other source, but I have an impression, without recalling it exactly, that Lincoln said something very much like it. It is beautiful and is an actual text of his public life, and it has the further advantage that it is complete in itself. The casual observer will accept it without any comment and understand it and will not seek further enlightenment.

The second phrase "As strong as the law and no stronger" I think is more characteristic of the man and has more of a flavor of originality. On the other hand as I recall it, it is only half of a quotation, and in his speech was followed by the words "As weak as the law and no weaker."

I can imagine that an intelligent observer, seeing the second phrase on the pedestal, would ask himself: "What does that mean?" This might awaken a curiosity that could only be satisfied by going into the biography a little. No such question would be raised by the first phrase. Now it is just here where I can not quite make up my mind. I am not certain whether the suggestion of this inquiry is an advantage or a disadvantage. You will recall an instance of one of these vague, questioning inscriptions in Bible history. When St. Paul went to Athens, we find no record of the many statues he saw erected to Jupiter or Venus or Diana. It was the statue to the "Unknown God" that aroused his intellectual interest. This idea is in my mind. An intelligent visitor to the statue would accept the first phrase as obvious. If he looked at the second phrase he would ask "Just what does that mean?" and if his curiosity was strong enough it would impel him toward some inquiry as to the manner of man who used the phrase and how he came to use it.

I have analyzed it so far, but I must confess that I have not been able to make up my mind whether raising such an inquiry would be an advantage or not. The first phrase has the advantage of great simplicity, and I believe that the odds are generally in favor of that.[8]

Throughout his life Palmer was a reader. He had a wide-ranging familiarity not only with military studies and history in general but with the standard classics of English literature. His reading was, however, more extensive than profound. There were significant and rather surprising omissions. For example, despite his lifelong concern with citizen soldiers, he seems to have neglected entirely the experience of the ancients as well as of many moderns, even though a careful study of Greek practice might have forewarned him of many of the problems encountered in his own era. He left no indication of having read Machiavelli's *Art of War* or of having studied the experience of the citizen soldiery of the Italian city-states of the Renaissance, much of it disastrous for the militia. Still more surprising is the absence of any indication that he was familiar with the work of Lord Roberts, the ever popular "Sir Bobs," the great English advocate of citizen soldiers. Since Leonard Wood conferred with Lord Roberts extensively, it is inconceivable that Palmer could have been entirely unaware of the views of this famous contemporary.[9] Even more remarkable is the absence of evidence indicating any effort on the general's part to conduct a really thorough study of the literature on the Swiss experience with citizens in arms.

When tackling a problem, the general seems never to have planned an exhaustive program of reading that would expose him to the full range of thought on the subject. This defect probably reflects more or less accurately the shortcomings in his education. Little in the curriculum at the Military Academy in his day had been designed to foster critical thinking on nonscientific subjects or any very rigorous training in the systematic approach to problem solving or research. This weakness in method is all the more remarkable because it stands in sharp contrast to Palmer's frequently expressed desire to secure a "scientific solution" to the problems before him. When he employed the phrase he seems to have used it merely in the sense of an objective solution, without the emphasis on quantification implicit in present-day use of the term "scientific." What is more, he displayed only the vaguest notions of just how one actually goes about seeking a "scientific solution."

Typically, Palmer's reasoning was deductive rather than inductive. He reasoned down from principles or premises, which he accepted without searching scrutiny. His thinking thus seems more theological than scientific—

a metaphor that is further substantiated by his tendency to think in terms of "final solutions"—salvation! Again and again he seems to have believed that if only a certain law were passed or presidential directive issued, the matter in hand would be settled once and for all. For one who read widely in historical literature, he was strangely blind to the character of history as a process in which nothing is ever final. His was one of those optimistic minds of the Progressive Era: he had great faith in experts, who would use the "scientific method" to reach a "final solution." He expressed this faith in a half-humorous way on one occasion, when writing to a friend of his conviction that the voters of the nation would finally see the light and provide legislation for a sound scheme of defense: "My confidence is fortified by my religious belief— for though I do not retain all of the Methodist doctrine in which I was bred, I still retain the gist of it, that in the long run, God is against the sons of bitches—even though He is sometimes slow in taking appropriate action."[10]

If the general was unsystematic and unscientific in his approach to problems, he was nonetheless fair-minded. One suspects that this was as much a dimension of his personality as it was a conscious intellectual effort to hear the other side. But just because he let others present rival points of view was no assurance that he was listening. Repeatedly he simply filed criticisms or failed to appreciate the full value of criticism as a foil for the development of his own views. When, for example, a debate coach from a Topeka high school wrote asking for negative arguments on universal military training, he blandly replied, "During a life long study of our history and institutions I have never found one single valid argument against Washington's position that every young American should be trained to defend his country."[11]

The general not only read history but was himself a writer of history. His status as a scholar was greatly enhanced by his title as special consultant to the Library of Congress in Military History, an honor conferred on him after his discovery of Washington's "Sentiments on a Peace Establishment." But he lacked even the most rudimentary training in the techniques of historical scholarship, and his writings clearly reflected this fact. As his old friend and colleague Col. A. L. Conger observed when criticizing one of the general's earlier books, it was ironic that the one member of his class at Leavenworth who went on to write and publish extensively was precisely that individual who had been excused, for entirely transient reasons, from the course in historical method that formed part of the curriculum. What is more, the general did not significantly develop his methods even after writing several books. More than a decade after Conger had first questioned Palmer's technique, Yale historian Leonard Labaree felt constrained to suggest, tactfully, how the manuscript for *America In Arms* might be made more "historical."[12] In sum, the general was more publicist than historian.

Palmer's conception of historical research seems to have been one of finding evidence to support his preconceived ideas. He saw the position of Chief of Staff, when filled by General March who was hostile to his views, as that of a kind of academic departmental chairman, a first among equals. But when General Marshall, who was decidedly friendly to his views, occupied the office, Palmer showed a marked inclination to attribute something resembling the full authority of command to the incumbent.

Although Palmer was willing to use history flexibly, he was probably quite unconscious of doing any violence to the facts. On the contrary, he had great faith in the authority of history; he seemed to feel that if he could show historical sanction for a policy, the case was made beyond dispute. If George Washington favored it, what more could be said? He seems never to have heeded the admonition of Count Otto Von Moltke, in one of the books in his own library: "The testimony of one who is dead, as it concerns the needs of the living, can be admitted as decisive only in respect to their ethical, but not in respect to their material aspect."[13]

For one who had such faith in history and held such high expectations of achieving significant military reforms by means of published historical volumes, Palmer showed remarkably little interest in getting the Army to encourage historical research.[14] On two separate occasions he served as an intimate adviser to the Chief of Staff, yet he never suggested historical studies on subjects of interest to him, apart from vain attempts to send a commission to Switzerland to investigate universal training there. Those efforts were probably doomed at the outset on grounds of cost or diplomatic delicacy, but surely it would have been no great undertaking to foster a series of historical studies, for example, of the National Guard, the Organized Reserve, and their lobbies, all subjects on which sound historical evidence in usable form had long been wanting. Although he was fully aware of the significant role played by the historical section of the German General Staff, there is no hint in the record of his service as adviser with Pershing or Marshall that he made the slightest use of the historical facilities available within the staff at headquarters, let alone sought the cooperation of outside scholars.

If Palmer's academy education failed to provide him with suitable analytical and critical skills, it manifestly did succeed in imbuing him with those timeless values, Duty, Honor, Country, which have inspired generations of officers ever since the day of Washington and Jefferson, Palmer's idols. Less evident is the source of another aspect of the general's intellectual development. Whether it was from his family and home environment or from the modes of instruction he encountered at the Academy, he understood and was actively committed to self-education. And this commitment paid off. It was precisely because he was familiar with the historic past of the army and its political context that he was able to play such a creative role in bringing the institution out of the nineteenth century and into the twentieth. That the education that permitted him to do this was largely the result of his own self-directed life-long effort only makes his accomplishments the more noteworthy.

In view of the evident limitations in Palmer's scholarly training and his obvious deficiencies as a systematic thinker, George Marshall's description of him as "the Army's leading intellectual" may appear as unduly generous.[15] But Marshall was referring to the between-war years, the two decades from 1919 to 1939, a period when a very little serious thinking or writing was being done on the interrelationships of democracy and defense. It was a time when military history this side of the Civil War was at low ebb, if not actually out of favor in the scholarly world. And within the War Department the historical program that had flourished briefly during World War I was largely moribund. In this setting, Palmer's forays into military history and his provocative proposals for military reform may well have justified calling him the leading intellectual of the army.

One of Palmer's most appealing traits, which influenced the quality of his thought, was his unfailing sense of modesty. This, coupled with his personal charm, could be utterly disarming. Together these qualities sometimes appeared to win over those whose ideas were actually fundamentally opposed. This could and did on occasion lead to misunderstandings. But at a deeper level the general's modesty stands as a reminder to aspiring officers that the ideal involves not only a capacity for critical evaluation but also a prior commitment to openness, a willingness to be shown, and above all a desire to dig out the facts, to see for oneself. There was a further dimension to Palmer's modesty: he understood and practiced the art of compromise, something the arrogant find it difficult if not impossible to do.

Whatever his strengths and limitations, General Palmer did contribute significantly to military policy. His most direct and tangible contributions were the part he played in writing the Defense Act of 1920 and his authorship of War Department Circular 347 in 1944. If the latter never had the impact enjoyed by the 1920 act, it nonetheless put some of his most important ideas and values into a succinct form, in which they continued to circulate long after the document was officially rescinded as a statement of departmental policy. Less directly and less demonstrably influential but scarcely less significant were the contributions arising from the general's several books, especially, *Washington, Lincoln, Wilson: Three War Statesman* and its recast successor, *America in Arms*, the most widely read of all his writings.

While the Defense Act of 1920 and Circular 347 were undoubtedly the most important of Palmer's explicit contributions to official policy, he also played a leading part in many other pivotal improvements in army organization and procedure. Among these, perhaps none has been more influential than the introduction of the single promotion list, a major reform which is now so much a part of the army that it is taken for granted, and the baleful nature of the former regimental system of advancement is too easily forgotten. Similarly, Palmer played a leading role in the struggle to see that only properly trained staff officers received assignment to the General Staff. If he was less successful in this than with the single list, his writings nonetheless continue to provide a well of ideas with which to sustain the effort.

Less widely recognized but of profound importance was Palmer's insistence upon the distinction between universal *training* and universal *service*, or conscription. Many of his contemporaries failed to appreciate the subtle but far-reaching implications of this differentiation. Universal training, as conceived by Palmer, would make the citizen components available to the army, under the President or the Executive branch of government, *only* if specifically authorized by a majority of Congress, the popular or legislative branch. This provision, reflecting the founding fathers' fear of militarism and their reluctance to give the President too free a hand with the armed forces, reveals the breadth and depth of Palmer's understanding of the Clausewitzian dictum that war must be regarded as an extension of politics "by other means." He understood, as many of his younger contemporaries apparently did not, that the manpower of the nation should never be mobilized without first mobilizing the national will. The humiliating disaster in Vietnam stands as compelling evidence of the national failure to grasp this insight which suffused Palmer's thinking.

While one cannot fairly distill the ideas of a man's lifetime into a few sentences, it is perhaps easier to do this with Palmer than with other military writers of his era. The great central theme of all his thought was the task of keeping the military establishment democratic, or as he expressed it, of devising a system of defense suited to the genius of a democratic people. It was this core value that George Marshall sensed so perfectly when he conferred on Palmer the symbolic title of "civilian conscience of the Army." Although himself a U.S. Military Academy graduate and a regular, Palmer devoted his career to fostering the role of the citizen soldier because he was convinced that a strong civilian component in the military establishment was the surest safeguard against the abuse of military power. Subordination of the military to civilian control at the secretarial level he recognized as imperative but insufficient by itself to provide adequate defense without the risk of militarism. Only by suffusing the entire establishment with citizen soldiers, from raw recruit to division commander and even higher, he believed, could the nation be guaranteed against the threat of military adventurism. A peoples' army, he contended, would not only forestall caesarism at home but would, because of its essentially defensive character, resist involvement in agressive or imperial wars.

A second theme that ran through much of Palmer's writing touched on the need to insure a realistic relationship between the foreign and military policies of the nation. He was inclined to place the blame for failures to establish this necessary relationship upon the prevailing ignorance of most educated Americans concerning the evolution of the country's military institutions.[16] Military history, he complained, occupied itself almost exclusively with battles and heroes, to the scandalous neglect of military organization and procedures. He traced the national attitude back to the founding fathers and their reaction to Cromwell. Ever since then, he protested with no little asperity, our citizens have been "so suspicious of military efficiency they have never been willing to give any thought to it."[17]

The problem, then, as Palmer conceived it, was to keep the nation's military establishment geared to the demands of foreign policy while at the same time retaining a character appropriate for a free people. There was a curious paradox in this dual relationship, he believed. While the superiority of the civil to the military authority was well established as a general principle, the civil powers had never made their authority fully effective by defining the limits, functions, and character of the subordinate agency with sufficient precision.

In the general's view, the principal means for insuring a democratic military establishment was to keep the Regular Army small and place ultimate reliance upon citizen soldiers. He reached this conclusion from the assumption that while a professional force would always be required to develop doctrine and meet emergencies, the centralization it necessarily involved would ever remain a temptation to military adventurism. Just because the United States had never suffered a military takeover in the past was no guarantee that there was no need to fear men on horseback in the future. On the other side of the coin, citizen soldiers organized into territorial units across the land would diffuse the military power so broadly through so many political jurisdictions as to provide a built-in safeguard against the misuse of military might. It was the essense of Palmer's conception that he recognized the crucial importance of the political dimensions in the fundamental organizational questions confronting military men. His repeated insistence upon the organic character of military institutions was a reflection of this awareness. His favorite metaphor, likening a military institution to a living, growing tree, with roots in the soil of contemporary society and reaching deep into the historic traditions of the past, effectively expressed this idea. In using this figure of speech he clearly suggested how dangerous if not impossible it was to create new and allegedly more efficient military structures that failed to take into account the political dimension implicit in their relation to the surrounding community and its historic traditions.

When Palmer spoke out as the prophet of the citizen soldier, he had in mind a very particular kind of institutional arrangement. After all, even that archpriest of professionalism, Emory Upton, expected to employ the citizen in arms. But Upton, with his scathing contempt for that broken reed, the militia, would confine the citizen to the role of filler, cannon fodder in the ranks of a hastily expanded professional army led by regular officers in every rank above the most junior subalterns. By contrast, Palmer placed ultimate reliance on the citizen soldier organized, in peace, into local or territorial units. Such units would not only provide a vehicle for the orderly mobilization of all or any necessary part of the nation's military manpower but would also elicit powerful political support born of local pride and involvement. Above all, the general insisted these local units were to be led by local reserve officers. By affording opportunities for upward mobility, citizen soldiers with the inclination and ability could win promotions commensurate to their ever-widening experience. Palmer understood, as many of his fellow regulars other than George Marshall did not, that without opportunities for command, even at the level of corps and division, the citizen components would never attract and retain that abler class of individuals who had most to offer the army.

For Palmer the sine qua non for the whole scheme of a citizen soldiery lay in the twin values implicit in territorial units providing opportunities for upward mobility. In achieving these, however, grave difficulties were inevitable. The full-time professional soldiers would normally be more proficient than part-time citizen soldiers. Similarly, some of the very virtues of the civilian components—for example, their local character, providing valuable political support—left them vulnerable to political influence in the matter of appointments and preferments. So the enduring problem has been how to exploit the proficiencies of the career soldiers without giving them undue authority over the reservists, and how to exploit the civilian components without succumbing to the more egregious political abuses to which they have so often been subject. Palmer's outstanding contribution to the resolution of these traditional dilemmas, of course, was the scheme for mixed committees of regulars and reservists to advise on matters of policy affecting the civilian components. Embodied in Section 5 of the 1920 Defense Act, this ingenious administrative device proved highly effective in practice even though sometimes it was allowed to fall into disuse.

One of the more obvious shortcomings in the general's thinking was his lack of realism about costs. For him it was literally an article of faith that citizen soldiers were less expensive to maintain than professionals. Most of his allusions to the economy of civilian components stem from the Swiss example. But it is noteworthy that he never studied the Swiss experience very closely. His references all depict the Swiss army as it existed before World War I, when it consisted almost entirely of militia units, with only a minute cadre of full-time professionals. Even though his Swiss friend of Academy days, Colonel Le Comte, reported to him as early as 1938 on how the march of technology and the advent of ever more complex weapons was forcing the Swiss to extend the period of militia training substantially while adding a much larger cadre of regulars, the information seems to have made no impression.[18] Whether Palmer was right or wrong in regard to the economy of reservists is of less importance here than the fact that he did so little in the way of cost analysis.[19]

Palmer's preoccupation with manpower led him to neglect matters of materiel, the arming and equipping of the troops he talked about. Admittedly, he was fully capable of appreciating the impact that innovations in weapons would have on doctrine. His perceptive observations in 1916 on the implications of the airplane, for example, show that he could see the interrelations of arms and men with foresight. Such observations, however, were a separate intellectual problem. Whenever he wrote or thought about citizen soldiers, the image he had in mind was a stereotype infantry unit--almost invariably companies and battalions bearing a remarkable similarity to the National Guard units of the 29th Division that had served under him in France during World War I.

Palmer's tendency to think about citizen soldiers almost exclusively as infantry units had two far-reaching consequences. His lack of interest in the arming and equipping of these units not only led him to underestimate the costs involved but also induced him to neglect the mounting difficulty of conducting effective training with reservists, as weapons and equipment became more complex. The rapid pace of technological change at once imposes more frequent replacement of intricate and costly apparatus and demands far greater investments of training time to aquire and maintain the skills necessary to operate such apparatus. Moreover, the greater the complexity, the greater the overhead required to administer it. Because Palmer continued to think largely in terms of infantry units with arms and equipment conventional in World War I, he displayed little appreciation for the difficulties to be encountered in conducting a training program for, say, the advanced electronic equipment of a signal unit, on a one-night-a-week basis with realistic field exercises only at remote intervals. Nor did he give any indication that he was sensitive to the difficulties inescapable in running reserve units in a highly mobile society, in which the high rate of turnover in personnel would help to undermine some of the very values he regarded as intrinsic to a territorial reserve.

Still another significant shortcoming in the general's thinking was his tendency to conceive of the citizen components almost entirely in terms of the role they had played in World War I. With few exceptions, in his writings he saw reservists as responding to a mass mobilization, to reinforce the Regular Army in an all-out war into which the nation had presumably thrown itself with a high degree of political unanimity. He did, admittedly, foresee that there might be situations calling for less than total mobilization, but most of his discussions were built around the anticipation of a major war. It would be unfair to fault him for inability to foresee the future, but for all his interest in history, the general failed to study the national experience in using citizen soldiers for "limited wars," although one such war had occurred during his own time. The employment of National Guard units on the Mexican border in 1916 was a form of limited war without the prior mobilization of the national political will. As such, it offered a potentially instructive example of the limitations to be encountered in the sustained use of citizen components on unpopular duty without a full-fledged national commitment to the enterprise.

Nowhere in his writings did the general give the slightest indication that he understood the severe political limitations that sometimes operate to constrict the availability of reserve units, even if those units are in a high state of readiness. Although he repeatedly called attention to the political dimensions of military organization, he never really explored the implications of the strong temptation for an administration in power to do what is politically acceptable rather than what is militarily desirable. A clear example of this was the dilemma of the Truman administration when confronted with the Korean threat. After World War II the reserve units of the nation were almost entirely composed of combat veterans, who could have been used effectively with but a minimum of training. Nonetheless, the President was under heavy pressure not to muster the Organized Reserve into active service in Korea but to draft younger men instead, on the grounds that it was only fair to let others share the burdens.

In sum, then, there were many omissions and neglected areas in Palmer's thinking. Even his fundamental ideas were seldom if ever followed out to their further implications, certainly not in any systematic way. If the general is to be criticized for these omissions, however, much the same charge will lie against his successors, individuals in and out of uniform who have yet to follow up his many leads exhaustively.

One of the most baffling aspects of Palmer's thought was his vacillation on the question of whether to organize the civilian components under the army clause or the militia clause of the Constitution. Certainly it was not surprising that he came out for a single federal reserve under the army clause in his first book, *An Army of the People.* When he wrote that little volume, his experience had been largely confined to service with the Regular Army. His continued advocacy in 1919 of a single federal reserve is easily explained also. His personal experience with National Guard units in the 29th Division had been a happy one, giving him no cause to change his views. Moreover, his stand was considerably reinforced by the backing of Maj. Gen. John F. O'Ryan of the 27th Division. But O'Ryan's division had operated in the British sector, where O'Ryan had been singularly free from exacerbating contacts with hostile regulars. Thus, it was not until the guardsmen stirred up their violent reaction to the army clause in the congressional hearings of 1919-20 that Palmer began to appreciate the full scope of their grievances. He continued to prefer the army clause approach, but exposure to the complaints of the Guard enlarged his outlook considerably. Not until he was forced to compromise and the dual arrangement of National Guard (under the militia clause) and Organized Reserve (under the army clause) had been embodied in the Defense Act of 1920 did he profess to believe that there was an intrinsic advantage in having the Guard under the militia clause after all.

Of course, Palmer's conversion to acceptance of a Guard under state control may have been nothing more than a realistic acceptance of the political solution forced on him by the strength of the Guard lobby on the Hill. If so, he certainly masked his real feelings carefully, for he repeatedly expressed enthusiastic approval of the dual reserve arrangement. He came to see that there were real political advantages in having courthouse and state-house backing, especially, when it came to prying appropriations and favorable legislation out of Congress. In addition to this, however, his experiences as an adviser to Pershing in the 1920s proved to be somewhat disillusioning. When the drastic cutbacks were imposed by Congress, Palmer observed with distress that his fellow professionals were only too glad to eliminate or reduce the citizen components to save slots for regulars. Only then did he finally appreciate the full value of citizen soldiers and their political ties as a bulwark against the self-centered concerns of the regulars. The shock of this revelation was considerable, especially when General Pershing, the chief Palmer so greatly admired, decided to go along with the emasculation of the whole scheme for building the Regular Army around the functions to be performed in preparing the civilian components for war.

In light of Palmer's repeated expressions of belief in the dual reserve during the 1920s and 1930s, his renewed advocacy of a single federal reserve under the army clause, immediately after his return to active duty in the 1940's may appear inexplicable. Was his subsequent final reversion in 1943 to espousal of a dual reserve a sincere expression of respect for the merits of such an arrangement or only an expedient retreat forced upon him by the strength of the opposition? Given the personality of the man, his self-doubt, his inherent fair-mindedness, and his desire to accommodate those opposed to him, these gyrations on this issue are perhaps not so inexplicable after all. On grounds of sheer efficiency he wanted a reserve under the army clause, but after observing the manifest lack of faith in citizen soldiers displayed by so many of his fellow professionals, he appreciated the leverage provided by the dual status. His switches from one view to the other seem to reflect not so much intellectual vacillation as his point of vantage at the moment. Alone in his study, the abstract advantages of a single reserve under the army clause looked best; in daily collision with the army-centered views of many professionals and the realities of congressional politics, the dual status looked best.

In short, if the general seemed to gyrate, it was between being a dreamer and being a decidedly practical manipulator. That General March, long after his retirement, dismissed him as "a theorist" should occasion no surprise, but even some of his friends would agree with the judgment of his classmate George Van Horn Moseley as early as 1916, when Moseley observed. "John writes well, but in my opinion he is not a practical soldier.[20] There was a measure of validity in these judgments, but they were not the whole truth. In his writing Palmer did indeed sometimes reveal the impractical theorist, but when drawn into the day-to-day problems of operations and administration, he could be decidedly practical.

For a man as imaginative as the general undeniably was, he appears to have devoted remarkably little thought to the search for alternative means of disseminating his ideas. His faith in the published word was apparently inexhaustible. Despite repeated failures, he went on writing books. Even after bitter experience had taught him how few people will read, let alone buy, serious studies on military policy, to the end of his days he pursued this route to influence as his primary track. Although he occasionally exchanged ideas with younger officers, there is no evidence that he gave any sustained thought to the possibility of cultivating individual disciples within the ranks of the professionals to perpetuate his principles. Even more surprising is his almost total neglect of the military schools as vehicles for doctrinal reform.

One can only speculate on how much more effective the general might have been had he used his influence and his entrée, especially during those periods when Pershing and later Marshall were in power, to have his teachings established as official doctrine throughout the military school system. Had he invested more of his energies in attempting to shape the curriculum at the U.S. Military Academy, at the Army War College, and at the Command and General Staff College at Fort Leavenworth, not to mention the subordinate branch institutions such as the Infantry School at Fort Benning, his influence might well have acquired a greater survival value. Surely his facile pen could have produced highly readable training manuals. What is more, the necessity of thrusting and parrying ideas in personal confrontation with members of the faculty in the school system would have afforded a valuable impetus to his creative efforts.

In sum, the general manifestly violated one of the cardinal principles of war in the course of his lifelong campaign. He dissipated his forces in a one-man attempt to influence opinion at the grass roots, the public at large, rather than concentrate on a narrower front in military circles, where there was a greater degree of interest in military doctrine and where the probability of achieving a single-handed breakthrough was substantially greater. Thus, while it may be argued that Palmer never really claimed to be a scholar and should not be measured by the standards appropriate to that calling, even when judged by a military yardstick, his tactics were defective or at least inadequate.

The foregoing criticisms only serve to put the man into perspective as a human being. What is remarkable about General Palmer is not his limitations but how much he accomplished in spite of them. His effectiveness was impaired not only by shortcomings in formal education, which blunted the intellectual tools he so much needed but also by serious limitations of health. Cursed with a sense of inadequacy and self-doubt out of all proportion to his actual abilities, he repeatedly worried himself into a state of debilitating depression. Yet for all of this, he continued to perform over a long span of years at a pace even his younger contemporaries found remarkable. For all his shortcomings, Palmer was an authentic military intellectual. More profound and more important than Emory Upton, though less visible than Alfred Thayer Mahan, he shared with Clausewitz the belief that "war cannot be waged with distinction except by men of outstanding intellect," even in junior positions of command.[21]

What, then, is of enduring significance in the life of Gen. John McAuley Palmer? As a soldier among soldiers he was worthy of emulation. To an unusual degree he put service and nation ahead of his own career and prospects for promotion. This capacity for disinterested performance of duty stands as an inspiration for all to follow. But his bequest to the future was far more than an inspiring example of self-denial. Fame eluded him, but he never sought it, even though he might grumble privately that some of his most notable contributions were ignored by the public. His life's central, driving concern was to awaken his countrymen to the need for a military philosophy appropriate to a free people.

One of the great problems of statecraft has ever been to balance security with liberty, finding means to keep the military from running away with the nation. It has long been the pride and the boast of the United States that her armed forces have been domesticated, brought into effective subordination to the civil authorities. This was certainly true in the past, in the days of the young republic, when ocean barriers made possible the luxury of a negligible military establishment. But the new imperium, with its far-flung military commitments, had raised the issue in new and increasingly baffling forms. Chance placed John McAuley Palmer on the stage just as this transition was beginning.

The general's contributions were unquestionably significant, yet by their very nature ephemeral. Even such an epochal statute as the Defense Act of 1920 has been amended, revised, and in time largely superseded. The policies, regulations, and programs into which he poured his life, when administered by other and later hands, took on new directions at the very least and not infrequently were scuttled. Palmer had to endure the frustration and disappointment of seeing his proudest accomplishments misconstrued, compromised, distorted, and even destroyed or abandoned. He had scarcely left office when the work of defacing his monuments was begun. Clearly, his most enduring achievement was neither a law nor a program but an idea.

Gen. John McAuley Palmer's great contribution was a challenge to posterity. However much the particulars might change over time, he knew that one constant would remain: if the nation wished to stay free, it must contrive military institutions suited to the genius of a democratic people.

Notes

All items cited in the notes without specific file locations can be found in the chronological file of the Palmer manuscripts in the Library of Congress at the date given. Citations in the form "v. 4, p. 27" refer to Palmer's notebooks containing chapter drafts, all of which are in the Palmer manuscripts.

For interviews, the date of the interview but not the place is given in the note. The place is indicated in the list of interviews in the sources.

The following glossary identifies all abbreviations that may not be self-evident.

GLOSSARY OF ABBREVIATIONS
USED IN THE NOTES

AAF	Army Air Forces
AEF	American Expeditionary Force
AG	Adjutant General
AGO	Adjutant General's Office
Amb	Ambassador
ASF	Army Service Forces
AUS	Army of the United States
CG	Commanding General
C/S	Chief of Staff
Cong	Congress
Cy	Copy
DA	Department of Army
Div	Division
fn	footnote

GO	General Order
GPO	Government Printing Office
Hq	Headquarters
L/C	Library of Congress
Mss	Manuscripts
MTCA	Military Training Camps Association
NA	National Archives
NG	National Guard
OCMH	Office of Chief of Military History
OCS	Office of Chief of Staff
OPD	Operations Division, U.S. Army General Staff
OR	Organized Reserve
OUSW	Office of Under Secretary of War
OWI	Office of War Information
RG	Record Group
Rec	Record
S	Senate
Sess	Session
SO	Special Order
S/W	Secretary of War
TAG	The Adjutant General
teleg	telegram
UMT	Universal Military Training
USMA	U.S. Military Academy
USW	Under Secretary of War
WD	War Department
WDGS	War Department General Staff
WPD	War Plans Division

CHAPTER 25

1. Unless otherwise indicated, this chapter is based on materials in the notebook "chapter notes" (v. 8 p. 15ff) compiled by Palmer on the basis of his wartime "old red diary" and other personal sources, not all of which are extant. To these materials have been added information derived from the chronological file in the L/C Palmer Mss, as well as from published sources and extended conversations with General Palmer and interviews with others as indicated below.

2. *Army and Navy Journal,* 17 July 1948, pp. 1275-82.

3. For an account of de Chambrun, see T. B. Mott, *Twenty Years as Military Attaché* (New York, 1937), 293-94.

4. Palmer for J. Lloyd Derby, 6 November 1916, chronological file.

5. See, for example, Maj. Gen. J. G. Harbord, *Leaves from a War Diary* (New York, 1925), 50; Ruth Mitchell, *My Brother Bill* (New York, 1953), 183ff; I. D. Levine, *Mitchell, Pioneer of Air Power* (New York, 1943), 103ff; and A. F. Hurley, *Billy Mitchell: Crusader for Air Power* (New York, 1964), 28-32.

6. Bernard Serrigny, *Trente ans avec Pétain* (Paris, 1959), 134.

7. Maj. Gen. J. G. Harbord, *A Chief of Staff in the Theater of Operations* (New York, 1939), 24.

8. Interview with Brig. Gen. Sanford Wadhams, U.S. Army M.C., 18 June 1957.

9. V. 8, p. 22.

10. John M. Palmer, *Washington, Lincoln, Wilson: Three War Statesmen* (Garden City, N.Y., 1930), 335 ff.

11. See also, Lt. Gen. Robert Lee Bullard, *Personalities and Reminiscences of the War* (Garden City, N.Y., 1925,), 112.

12. Lt. Col. J. M. Palmer, Pres. of Board Considering Questions of Zone of the Army, 28 June 1917, in Historical Div., *United States Army in the World War, 1917-1919* (Washington, D. C.: GPO, 1948), v. 3, p. 240.

13. Palmer to Maude Laning Palmer, 3 December 1917, Mary Palmer Rockwell Mss.

14. Avery D. Andrews, *My Friend and Classmate, John J. Pershing* (Harrisburg, Pa., 1939), 172-74.

15. For the official version of this episode, see *United States Army in the World War, 1917-1919*, v. 1, pp. 107-114. See also pp. 55-89 for text of C. D. Baker's report.

16. For Harbord's recollection of this issue, see his Army War College lecture of 29 April 1933, *Cong Rec,* 79 Cong, 1 Sess, 1 May 1933, pp. 2617 ff.

17. Harbord, *A Chief of Staff in the Theater of Operations*, pp. 17 ff; and Maj. Fox Conner, "Divisional Organization," Ms for article in *Infantry Journal*, May 1933, in L/C Pershing Mss, F. Conner.

18. *United States Army in the World War, 1917-1919*, v. 1, p. 183. See also Frederick D. Palmer, *Newton D. Baker* (New York, 1931), I, 254 ff.

19. Lt. Gen. Tasker Bliss to Brig. Gen. R. K. Evans, 9 August 1917, L/C Bliss Mss; and N. D. Baker, S/W, to President Wilson, 28 June 1917, L/C Baker Mss, Box no. 4, 1917, W. Wilson.

20. See, for example, Palmer to Maude Laning Palmer, 25 June 1917, Mary Palmer Rockwell Mss.

21. *United States Army in the World War, 1917-1919*, v. 1, p. 113; Gen. J. J. Pershing to Bliss, 9 July 1917, L/C Bliss Mss; and Harbord, *A Chief of Staff in the Theater of Operations,* pp. 17 ff.

22. Pershing to Bliss, 9 July 1917, L/C Bliss Mss.

23. V. 8, p. 37.

CHAPTER 26

1. This chapter is based upon the material in notebook chapter notes, v. 8, p. 38 ff, supplemented by other sources, interviews, etc.

2. Maj. J. G. Harbord to Palmer, undated [18 July 1917?] chronological file.

3. Palmer to "Dearest Polly" [Mary Palmer Rockwell], [July 1917] Mary Palmer Rockwell Mss.

4. Palmer to Maude Laning Palmer, 12 August 1917, loc. cit.

5. Palmer to Maude Laning Palmer, 2 August 1917, loc. cit.

6. Palmer to Maude Laning Palmer, 1, 5, and 12 August 1917, loc. cit.

7. V. 8, p. 44.

8. Gen. J. J. Pershing for Harbord, 28 July 1917, L/C Harbord Mss, Pershing-Harbord letters.

9. Palmer to Maude Laning Palmer, 2 August, 1917, Mary Palmer Rockwell Mss.

10. Interview with Gen. George C. Marshall, 21 July 1953.

11. Gen. John J. Pershing, *My Experiences in the World War* (New York, 1931) v. 1, pp. 150 ff. and v. 2 p. 114. See also Lt. Gen. Robert Lee Bullard, *Personalities and Reminiscences of the War* (Garden City, N.Y., 1925), 102. For evidence of the extent to which French thought had set the pattern for the AEF before Pershing insisted upon his independence, see Maj. F. Parker to Chief, American Military Mission, 28 May 1917, in Historical Div., DA, United States Army in the World War, 1917-1919, (Washington, D.C.: GPO, 1948), v. 3, p. 238-40.

12. Palmer for Harbord, 8 August 1917, NA, RG 120, G-3 Gen'l Corresp., Political Military folder 1814, and "Notes on Operations Section, Organization and Duties," G-3, by F. Conner, (undated but prepared after 11 Nov. 1918), OCMH Historical file: War 9/2-AEF-8A, as well as J. G. Harbord, *The American Army in France* (Boston, 1936), 91-97.

13. Palmer for C/S, AEF, 15 August 1917, *United States Army in the World War, 1917-1919*, v. 2, p. 27.

14. V. 8, p. 53.

15. Palmer to Maude Laning Palmer, 21 August 1917, and Report of Official Journey, 18-21 August 1917, in v. 8, pp. 60-61. See Palmer's retrospective account in *Washington, Lincoln, Wilson: Three War Statesmen* (Garden City, N.Y., 1930) 335-37.

16. Diary entry for 18 August 1917, v. 8, p. 56. On the importance of language skills for officers, see also Lt. Gen. Hunter Liggett, *Commanding an American Army: Recollections of the World War* (New York, 1925), 263.

17. Palmer's awareness of Pershing's intent is evident in the contrast between the critical comments in his diary entry (v. 8, p. 58) and the laudatory tone in his official report on the 18-21 August trip, cited above.

18. See diary entry 18 August 1917, v. 8, p. 56 ff.

19. V. 8, p. 58 ff.

20. Report of Official Journey, 18-21 August 1917, pp. 4-5, v. 8, p. 61.

21. Palmer to Maude Laning Palmer, 12 August 1917, Mary Palmer Rockwell Mss.

22. Pershing, *My Experiences in the World War*, v. 1, p. 161.

23. Report of Official Journey, 18-21 August 1917, p. 5, v. 8, p. 61.

24. V. 8, p. 62.

CHAPTER 27

1. Gen. John J. Pershing, *My Experiences in the World War* (New York, 1931) v. 1, p. 125.

2. Palmer to Maude Laning Palmer, 27 August 1917, Mary Palmer Rockwell Mss. See also chapter notes prepared by Palmer with extracts from his diary, his letters to his wife, etc., notebook, v. 8, p. 68 ff., the main sources for this chapter.

3. Palmer to Maude Laning Palmer, 6 September 1917, Mary Palmer Rockwell Mss.

4. Palmer to Maude Laning Palmer, 27 August 1917, loc. cit.

5. Palmer to Maude Laning Palmer, 15 September 1917, loc. cit.

6. Palmer to Maude Laning Palmer, 6 October 1917, loc. cit.

7. Maj. J. G. Harbord to Palmer, 12 October 1917.

8. Palmer to Maude Laning Palmer, 11 September 1917, Mary Palmer Rockwell Mss.

9. Palmer to Maude Laning Palmer, 8 October 1917, loc. cit.

10. Palmer to Harbord, 22 November 1917, L/C Harbord Mss, personal letters.

11. *Cong Rec* 1 May 1933, 73 Cong, 1 Sess, p. 2617.

12. Ibid; see also Maj. Gen. James G. Harbord, *Leaves from a War Diary* (New York, 1925), 310.

13. C/S for S/W, 4 January 1917, L/C T. H. Bliss Mss.

14. Maj. Gen. T. H. Bliss for Brig. Gen. J. E. Kuhn, 26 and 27 July 1917; also Bliss memo for record, 29 August 1917, L/C Bliss Mss.

15. Bliss to Kuhn, 27 July 1917 and Bliss for TAG, 17 September 1917, loc. cit.

16. For the slow pace at which Pershing's subordinate commanders acquired self-confidence, no source is more revealing than the private diary of General Bullard. See especially entries prior to his assumption of division command, 14 December 1917. The full manuscript diary is in the Library of Congress. Less valuable but revealing extracts appear in Lt. Gen. Robert Lee Bullard, *Personalities and Reminiscences of the War* (Garden City, N.Y., 1925). For evidence of the role of the Hq, AEF, staff in shaping the corps of six divisions, see especially *United States Army in the World War, 1917-1919,* v. 1, pp. 93-94, reflecting French origins for the corps table of organization and the rationale behind it.

17. For revealing examples of Harbord in action, see two separate memos, Harbord for Pershing, both 8 March 1918, L/C Harbord Mss, Harbord-Pershing letters.

18. Harbord to Palmer, 7 September 1917.

19. Harbord to Palmer, 20 September 1917.

20. Palmer to Maude Laning Palmer, 4 November 1917, Mary Palmer Rockwell Mss; see also chapter notes, v. 8, p. 103 ff.

CHAPTER 28

1. Palmer to Maude Laning Palmer, 7 November 1917, original in v. 8, p. 104. See also chapter notes, diary entries, etc., prepared by Palmer, beginning v. 8, p. 105.

2. J. M. Palmer, *Washington, Lincoln, Wilson: Three War Statesmen* (Garden City, N.Y., 1930), 334.

3. Harbord's views on staff training are touched upon in his Army War College addresses of 6 April 1939, entitled "A Chief of Staff in the Theater of Operations," copy in OCMH War-9, 3-Har-4, and of 29 April 1933, entitled "Personalities and Personal Relationships in the AEF," the latter reprinted in *Cong Rec,* 1 May 1933, 79 Cong, 1 Sess, pp. 2617 ff, and also in *Army and Navy Journal,* 6 May 1933 and 3 June 1933. See also his "Report of Chief of Staff, AEF," 30 June 1919, in Historical Div., DA, *United States Army in the World War, 1917-1919,* (Washington, D.C.: GPO, 1948), v. 14, pp. 70 ff.; v. 12 (Reports, Part 1), pp. 90 ff.

4. For contemporary evidence on the defects of staff procedures, see Gen. J. J. Pershing for Maj. J. G. Harbord, 21 September 1917, L/C Harbord Mss, and Avery D. Andrews, *My Friend and Classmate, John J. Pershing* (Harrisburg, Pa., 1939), 92.

5. See Maj. M. B. Parsons to Maj. Gen. T. H. Bliss, 25 June 1917, L/C Bliss Mss.

6. Harbord reiterated the importance of common doctrine in his postwar book, J. G. Harbord, *The American Army in France* (Boston, 1936), 40. For a similar view, see T. B. Mott, *Twenty Years as Military Attaché* (New York, 1937), 223 ff.

7. *United States Army in the World War, 1917-1919*, v. 12, pp. 90-95.

8. On opposition to staff training, see Robert Lee Bullard, *Personalities and Reminiscences of the War* (Garden City N.Y., 1925), 101-2. See also, *United States Army in the World War, 1917-1919*, v. 14, pp. 297 ff.

9. *United States Army in the World War, 1917-1919*, v. 14, pp. 400 ff.

10. Ibid., v. 3, p. 456.

11. Ibid., v. 14, pp. 303 ff.

12. For significant clues on this inference, see undated notes by F. D. Palmer on 1st Division, L/C Pershing Mss; Box 153. See also Memo, Gen. H. P. Pétain for Pershing, 12 December 1917, in *United States Army in the World War, 1917-1919*, v. 3, pp. 457-58, and Bullard, *Personalities and Reminiscences*, 165, as well as J. G. Harbord, *Leaves from a War Diary* (New York, 1925), 206-07.

13. The great importance Pershing attached to the General Staff is well illustrated in Pershing to President Wilson, 26 December 1918, L/C Pershing Mss, Box 213, Wilson folder.

14. Palmer to Maude Laning Palmer, 13 November 1917, copy in v. 8 p. 107.

15. V. 8, p. 108.

16. Palmer to Maude Laning Palmer, 13 November 1917, v. 8, p. 107.

17. Palmer to Maude Laning Palmer, 17 November 1917, v. 8, p. 109.

18. "Instruction sur la creation des écoles d'infanterie Americaine à Langres," 18 November 1917, chronological file.

19. Palmer to Polly [Mary Palmer Rockwell], 25 November 1917, cy in v. 8, p. 111.

20. V. 9, 113.

21. Palmer to Polly, 25 November 1917, cy in v. 8, p. 111.

22. Clipping with photo from *Le Tableau d'Honneur*, undated, chronological file, December 1917, and v. 9, p. 114.

23. Palmer to Maude Laning Palmer, 29 November 1917, extract in v. 9, p. 114.

24. F. Foch, *Memoirs of Marshal Foch* (New York, 1931), xxxii.

25. Headquarters, Infantry Officers School, La Valbonne, Special Order No. 15, 6 December 1917.

26. Palmer to Maude Laning Palmer, 17 November 1917.

27. Harbord to Palmer, 9 December 1917, v. 9, p. 119.

28. V. 9, p. 123.

29. Palmer to Maude Laning Palmer, 18 December 1917, extract in v. 9, p. 124.

30. Palmer to Maude Laning Palmer, 5 January 1918, extract in v. 9, p. 130.

31. Palmer to Maude Laning Palmer, 24 and 25 December 1917, extract in v. 9, pp. 125 ff.

32. Palmer to Maude Laning Palmer, 30 December 1917, extract in v. 9, p. 128.

33. Maj. Gen. J. W. McAndrew, *The Great War* (Philadelphia, 1921), v. 5, pp. 395 ff.

34. See Lectures, Army General Staff Course, Langres, November 1917-March 1918, in NA, RG316, Pershing Papers, Box 23. See also NA, RG316 G-3 Training, Class Books, folder 2103A, as well as Herbert Croly, *Willard Straight* (New York, 1924), 489-510. For a British view of the AEF staff course, see Sir Thomas A. A. Montgomery-Cuninghame, *Dusty Measure* (London, 1939), 290 ff. Further details are given in *United States Army in the World War, 1917-1919*, v. 14, pp. 333, 426, as well as in E. E. Morison, *Turmoil and Tradition* (Boston, 1960), 235.

35. Palmer to Harbord, 22 January 1918, v. 7, p. 137, and Harbord, *American Army in France,* 149.

36. Palmer to Maude Laning Palmer, 30 January 198, extract in v. 9, p. 141.

37. On Bonham-Carter, see London *Times*, 22 October 1955, p. 9.

38. On the staff school problem, see Bullard, *Personalities and Reminiscences of the War*, 64-68.

39. Palmer to Maude Laning Palmer, 9 February 1918, extract in v. 9, p. 143.

CHAPTER 29

1. Palmer to Maude Laning Palmer, 17 February 1918, extracts in v. 9, p. 144. See also Teleg, Maj. J. G. Harbord to Gen. J. J. Pershing, 2 February 1918, and related correspondence, NA, RG120, AEF, Item 11951 et seq.

2. Brig. Gen. C. G. Treat, Report of American Mission to Italy, 9 May 1919, NA, RG 120, AEF G-3 file, Box 3120, folder 737A.

3. Gen. John J. Pershing, *My Experiences in the World War* (New York, 1931), v. 1, pp. 105-6.

4. Cy, Amb. T. N. Page to President Wilson, 15 December 1917, Page Mss, Duke Univ. Library.

5. Page to Pershing, 19 February 1918, loc. cit.

6. Pershing to Gen. T. H. Bliss, 4 October 1917, L/C, Pershing Mss., Bliss file.

7. Harbord to Palmer, 19 January 1918. See also Treat, Report of American Mission to Italy, 9 May 1919, NA, RG 120, AEF G-3 file, Box 3120, folder 737A.

8. Chapter notes, v. 9, pp. 145 ff.

9. Interview with Gen. George C. Marshall, 21 July 1953.

10. Ibid.

11. Cy, Palmer to Maude Laning Palmer, 20 February 1918, v. 9, p. 146, and interview with Eugene C. Pomeroy, 27 December 1960.

12. Palmer to Maude Laning Palmer, 25 February 1918, v. 9, pp. 148 ff.

13. Cy, Page to Wilson, 26 February 1918, Page Mss., Duke Univ. Library.

14. See Edgar Ansel Mowrer in *Chicago Daily News*, 23 February 1918, cy in chronological file.

15. For corroborative details, see, Page to Sec'y of State R. Lansing, 8 February 1918, and Page to Wilson, 21 May 1918, Page Mss., Duke Univ. Library.

16. Treat, Report of the American Mission to Italy, 9 May 1919, NA, RG 120, AEF G-3 file, Box 3120, folder 737A.

17. Palmer to Maude Laning Palmer, 6 April 1918, v. 9, pp. 167 ff.

18. V. 9, p. 151.

19. Palmer to Maude Laning Palmer, 3 March 1918, v. 9, p. 151a.

20. Interviews with Mary Palmer Rockwell, 15 August 1960, and Eugene C. Pomeroy, 27 December 1960.

21. Cy, Page to Rep. M. McCormick, 19 January 1918, Page Mss., Duke Univ. Library.

22. Archibald W. Butt, *Taft and Roosevelt: The Intimate Letters of Archie Butt,* (Garden City, 1930), 424.

23. Interviews with Mary Palmer Rockwell, 15 August 1960, and Maude Laning Palmer, 30 December 1958.

24. Interview with Eugene C. Pomeroy, 27 December 1960.

25. Ibid., and Col. E. F. Swift to author, 3 October 1961.

26. Palmer to Maude Laning Palmer, 31 March 1918, v. 9, p. 165; interview with Eugene C. Pomeroy, 27 December 1960.

27. Cy, Palmer to Maude Laning Palmer, 10 March 1918, v. 9, pp. 155 ff., and interview with Eugene C. Pomeroy, 27 December 1960. See also *Army and Navy Journal,* 9 February 1918, p. 877.

28. Palmer to Maude Laning Palmer, 14, 16, and 31 March 1918, v. 9, pp. 158 ff.

29. Palmer, report of a visit to the bridgehead of Cavazuccherina, 6 March 1918, NA, RG 120, AEF G-3 file, Box 3120, folder 737A.

30. Palmer to Maude Laning Palmer, 14 and 16 March 1918, v. 9, pp. 158 ff.

31. Col. E. G. Paules, "With the Military Mission to Italy," *Military Engineer* 24 (July-August 1932), 373-82.

32. Interview with Eugene C. Pomeroy, 27 December 1960.

33. Ibid., and Palmer to Maude Laning Palmer, 14 and 16 March 1918, v. 9, pp. 158 ff.

34. Interview with Eugene C. Pomeroy 27 December 1960.

35. Ibid.

36. Ibid.

37. Ibid.

38. Palmer to Maude Laning Palmer, 6 April 1918, v. 9, pp. 167 ff.

39. *Army and Navy Journal,* 2 March 1918, p. 991.

40. V. 9, pp. 164, 169.

41. Palmer to Maude Laning Palmer, 10 March 1918, v. 9, pp. 155 ff.

42. Palmer to Maude Laning Palmer, 17 April 1918, v. 9, pp. 170 ff.

43. Maj. Gen. L. Wood to Page, 4 March 1918, Page Mss., Duke Univ. Library.

44. Herman Hagedorn, *Leonard Wood, A Biography* (New York, 1931), 267-70.

45. Interview with Gen. George C. Marshall, 22 July 1953.

46. Pershing to Page, 19 February 1918, L/C, Pershing Mss., Box 152; Page to Lansing, 12 March 1918, Page Mss., Duke Univ. Library.

47. Thomas Nelson Page, *Italy and the World War* (New York, 1920), 350-57, and Page to H. Frazier, 5 November 1918, Page Mss., Duke Univ. Library.

48. Pershing to Page, 19 March 1918, Page Mss, Duke Univ. Library.

49. S/W N. D. Baker to Wilson, 1 and 8 May 1918, L/C Baker Mss., Box 8, 1918 Wilson folder; Pershing, *My Experiences in the World War,* v. 2, p. 37.

50. Pershing, *My Experiences in the World War,* v. 1, p. 358.

51. Col. T. B. Mott, reports to G-3, passim, 8 December 1917 to 19 March 1918, NA, RG 120, AEF G-3 file, Box 3120, folder 737B.

52. Interview with Eugene C. Pomeroy, 27 December 1960.

53. Memo for confidential cable, undated [c. January 1918] T. N. Page Mss., Duke Univ. Library, and T. B. Mott, *Twenty Years as Military Attaché* (New York, 1937), 214 ff.

54. Col. L. Eltinge, notes for F. Conner, "received 13 Jan. 1918," and Conner to Eltinge, 14 January 1918, NA, RG 120, G-3 file, Box 3120, folder 730, Liaison with French.

55. Mott, Final Report, 19 March 1918, NA, RG 120, G-3 file, Box 3120, folder 737B. See also Maj. Gen. W. Crozier to TAG, 1 May 1918, "Report of Trip to Italy," NA, RG 120, AGO file, item 16668.

56. Interview with Eugene C. Pomeroy, 27 December 1960.

57. Col. R. U. Patterson, Medical Corps, to Brig. Gen. J. G. Harbord, 1 and 24 April 1918, NA, RG 120, AGO file, item 13128-A-171.

58. Swift to Harbord, 24 April 1918, NA, RG 120, AGO file, item 13120-A-184.

CHAPTER 30

1. Cy, Maj. Gen. J. G. Harbord to Palmer, 5 May 1918, v. 9, 154.

2. Chapter notes, v. 10, p. 1.

3. This and the following paragraphs, unless otherwise indicated, are based on extracts from a diary kept by Palmer beginning 31 May 1918, v. 10, pp. 3 ff, as well as interviews with General Palmer.

4. See Palmer to Col. F. McCarthy, 12 October 1945, chronological file, as well as v. 10, p. 9.

5. Harbord to Palmer, 21 August 1918; cy Gen. J. J. Pershing to Palmer, 30 August 1918; Brig. Gen. E. E. Booth to Palmer, 31 August 1918; and Brig, Gen. C. P. Summerall to Palmer, 4 September 1918, v. 10, pp. 29-32.

6. Interview with Maude Laning Palmer, 3 July 1957. See also Frederick D. Palmer, *Newton D. Baker* (New York, 1931), v. 2, p. 410.

7. Palmer to Maude Laning Palmer, 22 September 1918, v. 10, p. 34.

8. Palmer to Maude Laning Palmer, 2 October 1918, v. 10, p. 37.

CHAPTER 31

1. Palmer to Maude Laning Palmer, 8 October 1918, v. 10, p. 39, and chapter notes pp. 38-40.

2. This passage is paraphrased from John M. Palmer, *Washington, Lincoln, Wilson: Three War Statesmen* (Garden City, N.Y., 1930), 340. See also chapter notes, v. 10, p. 44.

3. For general accounts of the 29th Division, see John A. Cutchins and G. S. Stewart, Jr., *History of the 29th Division, "Blue and Gray," 1917-1919* (Philadelphia, 1921); American Battle Monuments Commission, *29th Division: Summary of Operations in the World War* (Washington, D.C., GPO, 1944); John A. Cutchins, *An Amateur Diplomat in the World War* (Richmond, Va., 1938); Lt. Gen. Hunter Liggett, *Commanding an American Army: Recollections of the World War* (Boston, 1925);

and Arthur Kyle Davis, ed., *Publications of the Virginia War History Commission,* especially Vol. 5, *Virginia Military Organizations in the World War* (Richmond, Va., 1927).

4. Col. H. L. Opie, in *Virginia Military Organizations in the World War,* 23, 27.

5. See Historical Section, Army War College, *Order of Battle of the United States Land Forces in the World War, American Expeditionary Forces: Divisions* (Washington, D.C., GPO, 1931), 152.

6. Chapter notes, v. 10, p. 46.

7. Gen. J. J. Pershing's evaluation of Maj. Gen. C. G. Morton, 1 July 1922, NA, RG 316, Pershing, Box 6. See also William J. Reddan, *Other Men's Lives: 1917-1919* (Bloomfield, N.J., 1936), 14 ff.

8. John A. Cutchins, *A Famous Command: The Richmond Light Infantry Blues* (Richmond, Va., 1934), 239.

9. Ibid., 235 ff.

10. See Morton to Commanding General, V Corps, 10 August 1918, NA, RG 316, Box 27; Reddan, *Other Men's Lives,* 61-66, 103.

11. Chapter notes, v. 10, p. 46.

12. Morton to TAG, 18 January 1922, chronological file, 1918. See also Opie, in *Virginia Military Organization in the World War,* 33 ff.

13. Cutchins, *An Amateur Diplomat in the World War,* 77.

14. Cy in chronological file, October 1918.

15. American Battle Monuments Commission, *29th Division: Summary of Operations,* 30.

16. Palmer to Maude Laning Palmer, 18 October 1918, v. 10, p. 52, and Gen. John J. Pershing, *My Experiences in the World War,* (New York, 1931), v. 2, p. 299.

17. Interview with Maj. Gen. Milton A. Reckord, 28 December 1961, and chapter notes, v. 10, p. 46.

18. Chapter notes, v. 10, p. 47.

19. Opie, in *Virginia Military Organizations in the World War,* 12, 38; Frederick C. Reynolds, ed., *115th Infantry, U.S. Army, in the World War* (Baltimore, c. 1920).

20. Cutchins and Stewart, *History of the 29th Division,* 171-72.

21. Chapter notes, v. 10, p. 47.

22. For similar evaluations of Reckord, see Cutchins and Stewart, *History of the 29th Division,* 146, and Reddan, *Other Men's Lives,* 105 ff.

23. Interview with Maj. Gen. Milton A. Reckord, 28 December 1961.

24. Ibid.

25. Palmer to Maude Laning Palmer, 17 October 1918, v. 10, p. 52.

26. Ibid. See also chapter notes, v. 10, p. 53 ff.

27. Palmer to Maude Laning Palmer, 21 October 1918, v. 10, p. 58, and chapter notes p. 59.

28. 58th Brigade Field Order 24, 14 Oct. 1918, chronological file.

29. Opie, in *Virginia Military Organizations in the World War,* 42-47; Cutchins and Stewart, *History of the 29th Division,* 181 ff.

30. Interview with Maj. Gen. Milton A. Reckord, 28 December 1961.

31. See running account of 58th Brigade Command Post in Maj. W. S. Bowen [G-3, 29th Div.], "Operations of the 29th Division East of the Meuse River Oct. 8th to 30th,

1918," Coast Artillery Corps School, Ft. Monroe, Va., 1922, and "Operations Journal," in 29th Division Historical Papers, NA, RG 120, Box 2.

32. Opie, in *Virginia Military Organizations in the World War,* 46-47.

33. Cutchins and Stewart, *History of the 29th Division,* 186-88.

34. Chapter notes, v. 10, p. 48.

35. Cutchins and Stewart, *History of the 29th Division,* 187-88.

36. Ibid.

CHAPTER 32

1. H. L. Opie, in *Virginia Military Organizations in the World War,* 46-47, Vol. 5 in Arthur Kyle Davis, ed., *Publications of the Virginia War History Commission* (Richmond, Va., 1927). See also Mold [Hq. 58th Brig.] to Mockingbird [Hq. 29th Div], 16 October 1918, NA, RG 120, 29th Div., Hist. Box 2, Operational Journal.

2. V. 10, p. 50.

3. See, for example, comments on General C. G. Morton's use of praise as reflected in narrative of Ambulance Co. with 113th Regiment records, NA, RG 120, 29th Div. Historical Mss. of G. S. Stewart, Box 14, and History of Company L, 113th Inf., n.d., NA, RG 120, 29th Div. Hist. Mss. of G. S. Stewart, Jr., Box 11.

4. William J. Reddan, *Other Men's Lives: 1917-1919* (Bloomfield, N.J., 1936), 14 ff; interview with John A. Cutchins, 21 December 1961.

5. See Col. J. M. Palmer, Report of 58th Brigade, 23 December 1918, in Maj. W. S. Bowen, "Operations of the 29th Division East of the Meuse River Oct. 8th to 30th, 1918," mimio, CAC School, Ft. Monroe, Va., 1922, cy in NA, RG 120, 29th Div. Hist. Mss., Box 3, folder 229-233.2.

6. John A. Cutchins and G. H. Stewart, Jr., *History of the 29th Division, "Blue and Gray," 1917-1919,* (Philadelphia, 1921), 131-32.

7. See Palmer, Report of 58th Brigade, and Col. M. A. Reckord, Operational Report, 115th Infantry, 8-30 October 1918, prepared 7 November 1918, in Bowen, "Operations of the 29th Div."

8. Cutchins and Stewart, *History of the 29th Division,* 223-25.

9. Col. L. H. McKinlay to Palmer, 18 October 1918, chronological file.

10. Palmer to Maude Laning Palmer, 5 November 1918, v. 10, p. 73.

11. Chapter notes, v. 10, p. 64.

12. See notes on conference at command post of XVII Corps (French), 20 October 1918, by 29th Div. representative, NA, RG 120, 29th Div. Hist. Mss., Box 2, folder 229-32.

13. Chapter notes, v. 10, p. 54.

14. Ms. diary, Lt. Gen. R. L. Bullard, entry for 26 December 1917, L/C Bullard Mss.

15. Palmer to Maude Laning Palmer, 26 October 1918, v. 10, p. 62; chapter notes, v. 10, p. 57.

16. Cutchins and Stewart, *History of the 29th Division,* 194 ff; Palmer, Report of 58th Brigade, *loc. cit.*

17. 58th Brigade, Field Order 27, 21 October 1918; chapter notes, v. 10, p. 55.

18. Col. S. A. Cloman, C/S, 29th Div. Message No. 1, 21 October 1918, Chapter notes, v. 10, p. 56.

19. Palmer to Maude Laning Palmer, 26 October 1918, v. 10, pp. 59, 62.

20. "Operations of the 29th Division...," entries for 23 Oct. 1918. See note 5, above.

21. Cutchins and Stewart, *History of the 29th Division*, 196.

22. Reddan, *Other Men's Lives*, 256 ff.

23. See Lt. Col. C. C. Bankhead, Operational Report, 116th Infantry, 7 to 29 October 1918, in Bowen, "Operations of the 29th Division," pp. 225-26, *loc. cit.*

24. See 58th Brigade Field Order 29, 28 October 1918, chapter notes, v. 10, p. 63.

25. Chapter notes, v. 10, p. 65.

26. Chapter notes, v. 10, p. 74.

CHAPTER 33

1. "Billeting" folder, NA, RG 120, 29th Division Historical Mss., Box 1; Palmer to Maude Laning Palmer, 1 December 1918, v. 11, p. 84.

2. Ms. History, Company K, 116th Infantry, NA, RG 316, G. S. Stewart Mss. on 29th Div., Box 12.

3. Frederick C. Reynolds, ed., *115th Infantry, U.S. Army, in the World War* (Baltimore, c. 1920), 163.

4. American Battle Monuments Commission, *29th Division; Summary of Operations in the World War* (Washington, D.C., GPO, 1944), 28; chapter notes, v. 10, p. 72.

5. Col. H. L. Opie, in *Virginia Military Organizations in the World War*, Vol. 5 of Arthur Kyle Davis, ed., *Publications of the Virginia War History Commission* (Richmond, Va., 1927), 48.

6. Chapter notes, v. 10, p. 78.

7. John A. Cutchins, *An Amateur Diplomat in the World War* (Richmond, Va., 1933), 110.

8. Chapter notes, v. 10, p. 68.

9. Maj. Gen. C. G. Morton to TAG, Hq. AEF, in chapter notes, v. 10, p. 66.

10. Maj. Gen. J. W. McAndrew to Palmer, 10 November 1918, in chapter notes, v. 10, p. 77.

11. Chapter notes, v. 10, p. 78 ff.

12. John A. Cutchins and G. S. Stewart, Jr., *History of the 29th Division, "Blue and Gray," 1917-1919* (Philadelphia, 1921), 235 ff.

13. Palmer to Maude Laning Palmer, 12 November 1918, v. 11, p. 79.

14. See 58th Brigade Regimental Maneuver Problem, 14 November 1918, chronological file.

15. Cutchins, *History of 29th Division*, 238; chapter notes, v. 10, p. 78.

16. Palmer to Maude Laning Palmer, 17 November 1918, in chapter notes, v. 11, p. 80.

17. Palmer to Maude Laning Palmer, 24 November 1918, in chapter notes, v. 11, p. 81.

18. Palmer to Maude Laning Palmer, 1 December 1918, in chapter notes, v. 11, p. 84, and 5 December 1918, v. 11, p. 88.

19. Chapter notes, v. 11, pp. 79-80.

20. Palmer to Maude Laning Palmer, 24 November 1917, in chapter notes, v. 11, p. 81.

21. Capt. G. Henderson to author, 1 April 1962. Henderson was brigade adjutant during the period described.

22. Chapter notes, v. 11, p. 83.

23. William J. Reddan, *Other Men's Lives: 1917-1919* (Bloomfield, N.J., 1936), 289 ff.

24. Palmer to Maude Laning Palmer, 10 December 1918, in chapter notes, v. 11, p. 91.

25. Cutchins and Stewart, *History of the 29th Division*, Appendix R; Reddan, *Other Men's Lives*, 232-33; chapter notes, v. 11, p. 86.

26. Chapter notes, v. 11, p. 86.

27. Original in chronological file.

28. Palmer to Maude Laning Palmer, 1 December 1918, in chapter notes, v. 11, p. 84.

29. Palmer to Maude Laning Palmer, 24 November 1918, in chapter notes, v. 11, p. 81.

30. Palmer to Maude Laning Palmer, 16 December 1918, in chapter notes, v. 11, p. 94.

31. Ibid.

32. Ibid.

33. Chapter notes, v. 11, p. 85 ff.

34. See, for example, Capt. J. C. Gibson, History of 2nd Battalion, 116th Infantry Regiment, n.d., NA, RG 136, G. S. Stewart Mss., Box 12; Cutchins and Stewart, *History of 29th Division*, 61.

35. See 58th Brigade F.O. Y-3, 18 December 1918, chapter notes, v. 11, p. 98.

36. Reddan, *Other Men's Lives*, 296.

37. Chapter notes, v. 11, p. 97; Palmer to Maude Laning Palmer, 23 December 1918, in chapter notes, v. 11, pp. 100-103.

CHAPTER 34

1. Chapter notes, v. 11, p. 103-4; Palmer to Maude Laning Palmer 27 and 31 December 1918, in chapter notes, v. 11, p. 107 ff.

2. Palmer to Maude Laning Palmer, 27 December 1918, *loc. cit.* Maj. Gen. C. G. Morton to Palmer, 25 December 1918, in chapter notes v. 11, p. 106 ff.

3. Lt. P. D. la Rochelle to Palmer, 12 January 1919, chapter notes, v. 11, p. 116.

4. Palmer to Maude Laning Palmer, 1 January 1919, in chapter notes, v. 11, p. 109. See also GHQ, AEF, "Memorandum on Military Policy of the United States," 23 December 1918, mimeo; cy in chronological file.

5. See, for example, memo, Maj. Gen. E. Hinds for C/S, AEF, 12 December 1918, NA, RG 120, AEF, 20532.

6. Memo, Brig. Gen. H. B. Fiske, G-5, for C/S, AEF, 24 December 1918, NA, RG 316, Pershing Mss., Box 3, Army Reorganization folder; Fiske to C/S, 6 December

1918, NA, RG 120, AEF, 20532; "Memorandum on Military Policy of the United States," loc. cit.

7. Memo, Palmer for Fiske, G-5, 2 and 9 December 1918, chapter notes, v. 11, pp. 87, 89.

8. Brig. Gen. H. A. Drum, C/S, First Army, to Palmer, 14 January 1919, in Chapter notes, v. 11, p. 118.

9. Palmer to Fiske, 2 December 1918, chapter notes v. 11, p. 87.

10. Memo, Palmer for C/S, AEF, 4 January 1919, in chapter notes, v. 11, pp. 110 ff.

11. Ibid.

12. For the opinion of a contemporary who had reservations about Palmer's competence as a planner, see assessment by G. V. H. Moseley based on a conversation with Palmer at this time: "Unfortunately he has little experience here practically with the problems confronting us, and he still speaks from a theoretical standpoint." Quoted in Edward M. Coffman, *The Hilt of the Sword* (Madison, Wis., 1966), 499, fn 23.

13. "Memorandum on Military Policy of the United States."

14. Palmer to Fiske, 2 December 1918, chapter notes, v. 11, p. 87.

15. Memo, Palmer for C/S, AEF, 4 January 1919, in chapter notes v. 11, pp. 110 ff.

16. Palmer for C/S, AEF, 5 December 1918, NA, RG 120 AEF, 20532. [Apparently erroneous dating for 5 January 1919.]

17. "At Last, An American Military System," typescript draft of article by Palmer, chronological file, April-December 1919, p. 5.

18. Palmer to Maude Laning Palmer, 9 January 1918, in chapter notes v. 11, p. 114. See also p. 111.

19. Cy, TAG, AEF, to Palmer, 3 January 1919, in chapter notes, v. 11, p. 112.

20. Chapter notes, v. 11, p. 113.

21. "At Last, An American Military System," p. 5.

22. Ibid.

23. John M. Palmer, *America in Arms* (New Haven, 1941), 165; William Frye, *Marshall: Citizen Soldier* (Indianapolis, Ind., 1947), 195 ff, based on interview with Palmer. See also chapter notes, v. 11, p. 115 ff.

24. Memo, Brig. Gen. F. Conner, G-3, for Fiske, 14 December 1918, NA, RG 120, G-3, folder 630.

25. Memo, Conner, for C/S, 9 January 1919, NA, RG 120, AEF, 20532.

26. Memo, Gen. J. J. Pershing for C/S, 7 February 1919, NA. RG 120, G-3, folder 630.

27. S. Johnson to J. G. Harbord, 28 January 1919, L/C Harbord Mss., "Military Activities."

28. Harbord to Pershing, 10 March 1919, L/C, Harbord Mss. "Harbord-Pershing Letters."

CHAPTER 35

1. *Army and Navy Journal*, 8 February 1919. See also chapter notes v. 12, p. 2.

2. 65 Cong, 3 Sess.

3. For testimony on the War Department bill, see *Historical Documents Relating to the Reorganization Plans of the War Department* (Washington, D.C., GPO, 1927),

especially, pp. 251 ff. See also *Washington Post*, 22 February 1919. Also in House Military Affairs Com. *Hearings* on National Defense, March, 1927, p. 569 ff.

4. John M. Dickinson, *The Building of an Army* (New York, 1922), 330 ff. See also testimony of Gen. P. C. March in *Historical Documents*, 280 ff.

5. *Historical Documents*, pp. 253, 264-65, 299-300.

6. For background on attitudes of the Wilson administration, see R. S. Baker, *Woodrow Wilson and the World Settlement* (Garden City, N.Y., 1922), vol. 1, chapter 20. See also N.D. Baker to President Wilson 28 July 1918, L/C Baker Mss., Box 8, Wilson; Baker to Senator T. S. Martin, 24 November 1918, Box 10, M, 1919.

7. Quoted in memo, Brig. Gen. L. Brown, Director, WPD, for C/S, 8 March 1919, cy in chapter notes, v. 12, p. 11.

8. See mimeo instructions for use of the War Plans Division, 19 March 1919, signed by chief, War Plans Branch, chronological file.

9. Memo, Palmer for Brown, 13 March 1919, chapter notes, v. 12, p. 13.

10. Memo, Palmer for WPD officers, 18 March 1919, with attached concurrences, chapter notes, v. 12, p. 14 ff. See also *Historical Documents*, p. 303. That General March did have at least one strong backer on the General Staff appears to be indicated in Brig. Gen. H. Jervey to Palmer, 21 March 1919, NA, RG 165. Army 50, C/S, cited by Edward M. Coffman, *The Hilt of the Sword* (Madison, Wis., 1966), 554, fn 24. See also Col. R. D. Black to Palmer, 16 October 1919, in chapter notes, v. 13, p. 60.

11. Cy in chronological file.

12. Chapter notes, v. 12, pp. 22-23.

13. See, for example, L. L. Babcock to Palmer, 20 March 1919, chapter notes; v. 12, p. 17. See also Palmer for C/S, 1 April 1919, chronological file; Palmer, *America in Arms* (New Haven, 1941), 166.

14. Chapter notes, v. 12, p. 22, and Peyton C. March, *The Nation at War* (Garden City, N.Y., 1932), 330-32. See also S. 2715, 66 Cong, 1 Sess, 7 August 1918.

15. Draft memo by Palmer, S/W for Chairman, Senate Military Affairs committee, May 1919, chapter notes, v. 12, p. 31a.

16. *Army and Navy Journal* 18 January 1919, p. 720; 1 March 1919, p. 920; 29 March 1919, p. 1060.

17. *Cong Rec*, 65 Cong, 3 Sess, p. 3292.

18. *Army and Navy Journal*, 5 July 1919, p. 1544, and 26 July 1919, p. 1629.

19. Palmer to A. Ruhl, 11 May 1919, unsent draft in chapter notes, v. 12, p. 29.

20. G. Clark to Palmer, 1 March 1919, in chapter notes, v. 12, p. 8.

21. Cy T. McIlvaine to H. B. Clark, 10 July 1919, chapter notes, v. 12. p. 34.

22. Baker to Martin, 24 November 1918, L/C, Baker Mss., Box 10, M, 1919.

23. *Army and Navy Journal* 17 May 1919, p. 1298, and 1 February 1919, p. 777.

24. *New York Times*, 17 May 1919, 8:2, and 17 June 1919, 19:1.

25. G. Clark to Palmer, 16 April 1919, in chapter notes, v. 12, p. 24.

26. Draft reply, Palmer to G. Clark, 17 April 1919, in chapter notes v. 12, p. 25.

27. William Frye, *Marshall: Citizen Soldier* (Indianapolis, Ind., 1947), 175-76.

28. *Historical Documents*, p. 300. It is not without significance that Secretary Baker subsequently admitted he had not seen the bill March refused to accept. See Baker testimony, 18 August 1919, before Senate Military Affairs Committee on S. 2745, 66 Cong, 1 Sess, p. 179.

29. See Maj. Gen. W. H. Carter, "Army Reformers," *North American Review*, October 1918, pp. 548-57.

30. For a typical example of congressional concern, see Rep. S. O. Bland to S/W; 4 August 1919, NA, RG 165, OCS Box 119 N.G. See also H. L. Opie, *"Virginia Military Organizations in the World War,"* In Arthur K. Davis, ed., *Publications of the Virginia War History Commission* (Richmond, Va., 1927), 22; *Cong Rec,* 65 Cong, 3 Sess, 1 February 1919, pp. 2530 ff.

31. Babcock to Palmer, 20 March 1919, in chapter notes, v. 12, p. 17.

32. *Cong. Rec.,* 65 Cong, 3 Sess, 1 to 7 February 1919, p. 2527 ff.

33. *Army and Navy Journal,* 15 February 1919, p. 860.

34. *Army and Navy Journal,* 10 May 1919, p. 1266, and 24 May 1919, p. 1333. For an example of reactions to the association stand, see H. T. Johnson, AG, Vermont, to Rep. F. L. Greene, 27 August 1919, L/C Greene Mss., Box 32 UMT.

35. Interview with Maj. Gen. M. A. Reckord, NG, Maryland, 28 December 1961.

36. See, for example, Director, WPD, for C/S, 25 February 1919, NA, RG 165, OCS-NG, Box 119, and other items in this file, as well as interview with John A. Cutchins, 1 December 1961; John A. Cutchins, and G. S. Stewart, Jr., *History of the 29th Division, "Blue and Gray," 1917-1919* (Philadelphia, 1921), 59 ff.

37. Maj. Gen. J. F. O'Ryan to C/S, 6 June 1919, NA, RG 165, WPD 675.

38. Cy, O'Ryan to AG, Texas, 7 May 1919, chapter notes, v. 12. p. 32.

39. See cy of OCS staff paper on O'Ryan scheme, unsigned June 1919, NA, RG 165, OCS Box 15 Misc., cited in Coffman, *The Hilt of the Sword,* 504, and K. Walker to Palmer, 26 May 1919, with attached notes as well as memo, Palmer for Maj. Gen. W. G. Haan, 18 June 1919, in chapter notes, vo. 12, 32-33.

40. Ralph Barton Perry, *The Plattsburg Movement* (New York, 1921), 240-42.

41. Military Training Camps Assn. of the U.S., Annual Report of Executive Secretary (New York, 31 January 1919), 7, cy in chapter notes, v 12, p. 12.

42. *Army and Navy Journal,* 27 September 1919, p. 102.

43. Perry, *Plattsburg Movement,* 13, 216-17. For Guard lobbying see Carter, "Army Reformers," 555-56.

44. Interview with Grenville Clark, 18 August 1964.

45. S. 2691 and HR 8068 Cong, 1 Sess, 31 July 1919.

46. Memo, Palmer for Haan, 18 June 1919, in chapter notes, v. 12, p. 33.

47. Chapter notes, v. 12, pp. 35, 37. See also "At Last, An American Military System," typescript draft of article by Palmer, April-December 1919, in chronological file, pp. 7-8.

CHAPTER 36

1. *Army and Navy Journal,* 8 March 1919, p. 963. See also G. R. Brown article in Washington *Post,* 26 March 1919, p. 1.

2. Memo Maj. Gen. Henry Jervey, director of operations, for director, WPD, 19 August 1919, chapter notes, v. 12, p. 41.

3. T. McIlvaine to Palmer, 13 August 1919, and McIlvaine to Senator J. W. Wadsworth, 28 August 1919, in chapter notes, v. 12, pp. 40, 43.

4. See, for example, testimony of Maj. Gen. H. L. Rogers, pp. 543 ff, and Maj. Gen. M. W. Ireland, pp. 598 ff, in Senate Military Affairs Committee, Subcommittee

hearings, *Reorganization of the Army*, 66 Cong, 1 Sess, 1919, pp. 544, 598. See also *Army and Navy Journal*, 27 September 1919, p. 103.

5. General Staff College Lecture, 3 September 1919, Chief of Military History U.S. Army, Historical file, General Staff College Lectures 1919-20.

6. Brig. Gen. J. Hagood to C/S, 18 August, and reply 15 September 1919, NA, RG 165, OCS Legislation, Box, 91.

7. Maj. Gen. J. W. McAndrew, *Reorganization of the Army*, 128. See also *Army and Navy Journal*, 16 August 1919, p. 1738; Maj. Gen. Wood, *Reorganization of the Army*, 622; remarks of Sen. G. E. Chamberlain, ibid., 657.

8. Maj. Gen. J. F. O'Ryan, *Reorganization of the Army*, 511 ff., especially at 517.

9. Ibid., 518.

10. Ibid., 825 ff., especially at 834.

11. For a critique of the MTCA proposal, see *Army and Navy Journal*, 27 September 1919, p. 112.

12. *Reorganization of the Army*, 625.

13. Ibid., 48.

14. Ibid., 45 ff. For a detailed hostile criticism of the War Department bill, see also Senator George E. Chamberlain, *Army Reorganization Bill: Analytical and Exploratory Statement*, Senate Military Affairs Committee print, 5 September, 1919, 66 Cong, 1 Sess; *Army and Navy Journal*, 20 September 1919, p. 71.

15. Wadsworth to Palmer, 8 March 1940, in chapter notes, v. 13, p. 69.

16. Ibid. See also McIlvaine to Wadsworth, 28 August 1919, in chapter notes, v. 12, p. 43.

17. Chapter notes, v. 13, p. 49.

18. Ibid.

19. Wadsworth to Palmer, 8 March 1940, loc. cit.

20. *Reorganization of the Army*, 9 October 1919, pp. 1173 ff.

21. Ibid., 1174 ff.

22. Typescript draft of article by Palmer, "Inner History of the National Defense Act of 1920," chronological file, April 1919.

23. *Reorganization of the Army*, 1180 ff, 1192 ff.

24. See John M. Palmer, *Statesmanship or War* (Garden City, N.Y., 1927), introduction by James W. Wadsworth; Wadsworth to Palmer, 8 March 1940, chapter notes, v. 13.

25. *Reorganization of the Army*, 1182-83.

26. Ibid., 1183-84.

27. Ibid., 1186-88, 1209.

28. Ibid., 1196-97.

29. Ibid., 1190, 1198 ff.

30. Wadsworth to Palmer, 8 March 1940, chapter notes, v. 13.

31. *Reorganization of the Army*, 10 October 1919, pp. 1205 ff.

32. Ibid., 1211-14.

33. Ibid., 1220.

34. Ibid., 1218, 1220.

35. Ibid., 1214.

36. Ibid., 1220.

37. Ibid., 1225.

38. Ibid., 1223-24.
39. Ibid., 1224-25.
40. Ibid., 1225.
41. Chapter notes, v. 13, p. 53. See also "At Last An American Military System," typescript draft of article by Palmer, chronological file, April-December 1919, p. 10, for quoted remarks.
42. *New York Times,* 22 November 1919 editorial, 12:3, and *Washington Star,* 9 November 1919, in chapter notes, v. 13, p. 76.
43. Fries to Palmer, 23 October 1919, in chapter notes, v. 13, p. 64. Among other such letters received, see also Maj. Gen. C. M. Morton to Palmer, 11 December 1919, in v. 13, p. 104.
44. Col. J. R. M. Taylor to Palmer, 11 November 1919.
45. Col. C. D. Herron to Palmer, 24 October 1919, chronological file.
46. McIlvaine to Palmer, 28 October 1919, in chapter notes, v. 13, p. 72, and 3 December 1919, v. 13, p. 95. See also Grenville Clark to Palmer, chapter notes, v. 13, p. 25.
47. Chapter notes, v. 13, p. 54.
48. See especially Maj. Gen. William H. Carter to Palmer, 16 November 1919, in chapter notes, v. 14, p. 84, and Palmer to Joel E. Spingarn, Harcourt, Brace & Howe, 27 November 1919, v. 14, p. 92.
49. C. C. Jamieson to Palmer, 31 July 1919, with enclosures, chapter notes, v. 12, p. 34. See also unsigned contract, 29 October 1919, and Grenville Clark to Palmer, 21 November 1919, both in chronological file. See also Grenville Clark to Palmer, 14 October 1919, in chapter notes, v. 13, p. 58.
50. Cy Baker to Wadsworth, 18 October 1919, in chapter notes, v. 13, p. 61.
51. Typescript article draft, "Inner History of the National Defense Act of 1920," in chronological file, April 1919. See also chapter notes, v. 13, p. 63.
52. Wadsworth to Palmer, 8 March 1940, in chapter notes, v. 13, p. 69.
53. Baker to Wadsworth, 27 October 1919, chronological file; chapter notes, v. 13, p. 68.
54. Wadsworth to Palmer, 8 March 1940, chapter notes v. 13, p. 69; McIlvaine to Palmer, 28 August 1919, chronological file.
55. War Dept SO 25-Officers 423, 31 January 1920, and amended version SO 27-0, 2 February 1919, as well as SO 61-9, 13 March 1920, chronological file.
56. McIlvaine to Palmer, 8 February 1920, chronological file.
57. Typescript article draft, "Inner History of the National Defense Act of 1920," p. 5, chronological file, April 1919.

CHAPTER 37

1. Draft, Palmer to Sen. J. W. Wadsworth, undated, c. 1937, in chapter notes, v. 13, p. 57.
2. Ibid. See also Palmer to Wadsworth, 30 September 1937, chronological file.
3. Palmer to Wadsworth, 25 October 1919, and Palmer for Gen. J. J. Pershing, 6 November 1919, both in chapter notes, v. 13, pp. 67 and 75.

4. Maj. Gen. C. M. Saltzman, "Reminiscences of the Battle of Washington," *Army Industrial College* lecture, 26 November 1935, p. 7; memo, Brig. Gen. W. Mitchell for Palmer, 9 January 1920, chronological file.

5. "Inner History of the National Defense Act of 1920," typescript draft of article by Palmer, chronological file, April-December 1919.

6. Edward M. Coffman, *The Hilt of the Sword* (Madison, Wis., 1966), 352; Palmer to Wadsworth, 25 October 1919, in chapter notes, v. 13, p. 67.

7. *New York Times*, 6 August 1919, 15:8 and 7 August 1919, 6:1. See also J. L. Derby letter to editor, *New York Times*, 13 August 1919, 10:6, as well as T. McIlvaine statement, 9 August 1919, 9:4. *See also Army and Navy Journal*, 16 August 1919, p. 1737.

8. Wadsworth to Palmer, 8 March 1940, in chapter notes, v. 13, p. 69.

9. For evidence supporting this suspicion, see Maj. Gen. C. G. Morton to Palmer, 17 December 1919, in chapter notes, v. 14, p. 115, and Maj. Gen. J. T. Dickman to Maj. Gen. W. G. Haan, 7 October 1919, NA, RG 165, WPD 1825.

10. See, for example, Palmer to Col. M. A. Reckord, 12 November 1919, and to Col. G. W. Ball, 9 December 1919, among many others, in chapter notes, v. 14, pp. 90, 98.

11. Maj. A. W. Woodcock to Palmer, 7 December 1919, in chapter notes, v. 14, p. 96.

12. Woodcock to Palmer, 22 November 1919, chronological file. See also W. H. Bradley to Palmer, 14 December 1919, in chapter notes, v. 14, p. 110.

13. Chapter notes, v. 13, p. 74; *Army and Navy Journal*, 13 September 1919, p. 49.

14. Coffman, *The Hilt of the Sword*, 561, and Palmer to Pershing, 6 November 1919, in chapter notes, v. 13, p. 74-75. See also cy, Pershing to Rep. J. Kahn, 24 November 1919, NA, RG 120 AEF, folder 20532.

15. For Pershing's notes on these interviews see NA, RG 316, Box 6 Reorganization Interviews. See especially notes relating to Maj. Gen. J. F. O'Ryan, 30 October 1919.

16. Senate Military Affairs Committee, Subcommittee Hearings. *Reorganization of the Army*, 66 Cong, 1 Sess, 1919, pp. 1645 ff.

17. *Army and Navy Journal*, 15 March 1919, p. 1022, and 15 November 1919, p. 339. See also *New York Times*, 9 December 1919, p. 10:2, 16 December 13:2, and 28 December III, 1:1.

18. Markey to Palmer, 21 November 1919, in chapter notes, v. 14, p. 87.

19. Mimeo, MTCA, "Open Letter to the Committee of the American Legion Concerned with Military Policy," n.d. 1919, in chapter notes, v. 13, p. 79; McIlvaine to Palmer, 23 November 1919, v. 14, p. 88; *Committee Reports and Resolutions adopted at the First National Convention of the American Legion*, 10-12 November 1919, Minneapolis, Minn., n.p, n.d. cy in chapter notes, v. 14, p. 81. See also *Army and Navy Journal*, 29 April 1922, p. 822.

20. McIlvaine to Palmer, 23 November 1919, in chapter notes, v. 14, p. 88.

21. See S. 3412, 66 Cong, 1 Sess, and Palmer to McIlvaine, 19 and 26 November and 5 December 1919, in chapter notes, v. 14, pp. 85, 91, 96.

22. Quoted in *New York Times*, 28 December 1919, III, 1:1.

23. *New York Times*, 17 December 1919, 23:2.

24. For committee membership in full, see *Reorganization of the Army*, 1985 ff.

25. Palmer to G. Clark, 12 December 1919, and Palmer to D. M. Goodrich, 18 December 1919, in chapter notes, v. 14, pp. 107, 118.

26. *Reorganization of the Army*, 16 October 1919, p. 1249.

27. See chapter notes, v. 14, p. 116.

28. *Reorganization of the Army*, 1853 ff. 1857 ff, 1867 ff, 1891 ff, 1919 ff.

29. McIlvaine to Palmer, 13 December 1919, and replies 15, 19, and 23 December, chapter notes, v. 14, pp. 109, 112, 119, 124.

30. McIlvaine to Palmer, 13 and 16 December 1919, chapter notes, v. 14, pp. 109, 114.

31. Palmer to McIlvaine, 19 and 23 December 1919, chapter notes, v. 14, pp. 119, 124.

32. Palmer for Wadsworth, 22 December 1919, chapter notes, v. 14, p. 120.

33. Maj. R. Stockton to Col. E. E. Lewis OCS, 20 November 1919, enclosure in Stockton to Palmer, 9 December 1919, chapter notes, v. 14, p. 99.

CHAPTER 38

1. Memo, Palmer for Sen. J. W. Wadsworth, 22 December 1919, v. 14, p. 120.

2. *Army and Navy Journal*, 10 January 1920, p. 873.

3. H. H. Gross to Palmer, 1 December 1919 and 22 Dec. 1919, v. 14, p. 94 and p. 123.

4. T. McIlvaine to Wadsworth, 24 January 1920, in *Army and Navy Journal*, 31 January 1920, p. 68.

5. G. Clark to Palmer, 22 December 1919, v. 14, p. 122.

6. *Army and Navy Journal*, 10 January 1920, p. 580, and 17 January 1920, p. 608.

7. Palmer to Maj. Gen. J. F. O'Ryan, 20 January 1920.

8. Palmer to D. J. Markey, 5 February 1920.

9. See S-3688 and S-3792, 66 Cong, 2 Sess. See also S. Report 400, 28 January 1920, and S. Report 400, Part 2, 31 January 1920.

10. Palmer To Maj. Gen. M. A. Reckord, 17 Jan. 1920; Palmer to O'Ryan, 3 March 1920.

11. O'Ryan to Palmer, 14 January 1920.

12. Palmer to O'Ryan, 20 January 1920.

13. H. C. Stebbins to Palmer, 5 March 1920, and reply 6 March 1920.

14. Palmer to Markey, 5 February 1920; Markey to Palmer, 28 February 1920.

15. F. D'Olier, National Commander, American Legion, "Recommendations of the Military Policy Committee at Meeting Held 9 February 1920, National Headquarters, Indianapolis, Ind.," mimeo.

16. See *Reorganization of the Army*, Hearings, Subcommittee of Senate Military Affairs Committee, 66 Cong, 1 and 2 Sess, 1 March 1920, p. 1-34.

17. Palmer to Markey, 2 March 1920.

18. Palmer to Stebbins, 20 March 1920, with draft article and reply 6 April 1920.

19. S. Report 400, Part 2, on S-3792, 31 January 1920.

20. Stebbins to Palmer, 20 April 1920.

21. McIlvaine to Palmer, 10 March 1920, and reply, 17 March 1920, with draft article; Stebbins to Palmer, 23 March 1920, with reply, 27 March 1920.

22. *Army and Navy Journal*, 6 March 1920, p. 827.

23. Ibid., 7 February 1920, p. 693.

24. Palmer to Editor, *Army and Navy Journal*, 23 March 1920.

25. *Army and Navy Journal*, 3 April 1920, pp. 973, 975.

26. S. 3688 and its amended successor S-3792, 66 Cong, 2 Sess.

27. *Cong Rec*, 66 Cong, 2 Sess, pp. 5182-96.

28. "At Last, An American Military System," typescript draft of article by Palmer, chronological file, April-December 1919, pp. 16-17.

29. N. D. Baker to W. Wilson, 7 February 1920, L/C, Baker Mss, Box 13, 1919 W.

30. *New York Times,* 10 February 1920, 1:6, and *Army and Navy Journal,* 14 February 1920.

31. "At Last, An American Military System," 14 ff. See also J. M. Palmer, *America in Arms*, (New Haven, 1941), 179 ff. The two versions differ slightly. The book, written long after the event, credits Col. Thomas M. Spaulding, a War Department liaison officer with the House of Representatives Military Affairs Committee, with the redrafting, whereas the earlier article names Gulick as the draftsman.

32. *Army and Navy Journal*, 10 April 1920, p. 982; Palmer to H. B. Clark (of White Weld, & Co., N.Y., N.Y.), 9 April 1920.

33. McIlvaine to Executive Committee, MTCA, 14 April 1920.

34. *Army and Navy Journal*, 17 April 1920, p. 997.

35. See, for example, Rep. F. L. Greene, Vermont, to B.A. Robinson, 25 February 1920, L/C Greene Mss, Box 32 UMT.

36. McIlvaine to Exective Committee, MTCA, 14 April 1920.

37. *Army and Navy Journal*, 15 May 1920, p. 1136.

38. McIlvaine to Palmer 19 and 20 April 1920.

39. Palmer to Stebbins, 22 April 1920.

40. Palmer to G. Clark, 26 April 1920.

41. *Army and Navy Journal*, 19 July 1919, p. 1611; 15 November 1919, p. 337; and 13 December 1919, p. 458.

42. See especially Col. J. C. Gilmore chief, War Plans Branch, for director, WPD, 7 January 1920, NA, RG 165, WPD 3029, citing technical errors in the House version of the measure.

43. "At Last, An American Military System," pp. 13 ff.

44. *Army and Navy Journal*, 13 March 1920, pp. 852 ff; 20 March 1920, p. 888.

45. Ibid., 27 March 1920, p. 913.

46. See remarks of Rep. D. R. Anthony, *Cong Rec*, 66 Cong, 2 Sess, pp. 7263, 7305-6.

47. *Cong Rec,* 66 Cong, 2 Sess, p. 7331, 20 May 1920.

48. *Army and Navy Journal*, 22 May 1920, p. 1169.

49. "At Last, An American Military System," p. 18.

50. Ibid., p. 20.

51. Baker to Wilson, 3 and 4 June 1920, L/C Baker Mss, Box 13, W, 1920.

52. Cy, A. Page to Palmer, 17 April 1940, v. 13, p. 70.

53. See, for example, Lt. Gen. Hunter Liggett, *Commanding an American Army: Recollections of the World War* (New York, 1925), 154; Gilmore, War Plans Branch for Director, War Production Board, 2 June 1920, NA, RG 165, WPD 6166. Twenty

years later even General March saw the 1920 act in favorable terms. See Wadsworth to Palmer, 8 March 1940, v. 13, p. 69.

54. *Army and Navy Journal*, 29 May 1920, p. 1210.

55. Palmer to McIlvaine, 22 May 1920.

56. Maj. Gen. W. H. Carter to Palmer, 28 June 1920.

57. William Frye, *Marshall, Citizen Soldier* (Indianapolis, Ind., 1947), 177, which quotes Wadsworth as saying Palmer was "the real author of the act."

58. Palmer to Wadsworth, 20 and 28 May 1920, the latter enclosing a statement entitled "Intent of Congress relative to National Military Policy as Developed in the Army Reorganization Bill."

59. See J. M. Palmer, *Washington, Lincoln, Wilson: Three War Statesmen* (Garden City, N.Y., 1930), pp. 364-6.

60. For an example of fumbling by unfamiliar hands implementing the new legislation, see Col. G. Ordway for Director, WPD, 9 June 1920, and WPD committee (Col. Munson, Col. Smith, Col. Ordway), 16 August 1920, NA, RG 165, WPD 6377-81.

61. Palmer for Wadswoth, 27 May 1920.

62. Baker to Wadsworth, 12 June 1920.

63. Interview with Maude Laning Palmer, 3 July 1957.

CHAPTER 39

1. Palmer to Sen. J. W. Wadsworth, 7 July 1920.

2. Wadsworth to Palmer, 26 June 1920.

3. Palmer, chapter notes, v. 15, p. 16.

4. Wadsworth to Palmer, 26 June 1920. Wadsworth was apparently in error when attributing this plan to General March. The plan for twenty-one divisions of 16,000 men each had been concocted by the AEF Superior Board on Organization, whose report was approved June 1920 by Pershing. See Edward M. Coffman, *The Hilt of the Sword*, (Madison, Wis., 1966) 593 and fn. 39.

5. Chapter notes, v. 15, p. 6.

6. Palmer to G. Clark, 7 June 1920.

7. See Palmer's 201 file, DA, TAG, with letters from three senators and five representatives.

8. Wadsworth to Brig. Gen. F. W. Ward, AG, N.Y., 14 February 1927, L/C Wadsworth Mss, Box 18.

9. See, for example, Surgeon General M. W. Ireland to Palmer, 17 July 1920, v. 15, p. 16, and 1 December 1920, chronological file.

10. Chapter notes, v. 15, p. 13.

11. Ireland to Palmer, 17 July 1920, v. 15, p. 16; Brig Gen. G.V.H. Moseley to Palmer, 3 and 7 September 1920, chronological file; Col. G. C. Marshall to Palmer, 2 August 1920, v. 15, p. 20.

12. Chapter notes, v. 15, p. 14.

13. Chapter notes v. 15, pp. 17 ff.

14. Misc papers relating to Southard and the "Kennebago Tribe" in Palmer 1920-1921 chronological file.

15. "At Last, an American Military System," typescript of article by Palmer, chronological file, April-December 1919, p. 12.

16. For the problems involved in reorganizing historic units, see *Army and Navy Journal*, 13 August 1921, p. 1332.

17. Palmer for Director, WPD, 10 June 1920.

18. See comments on the work of the joint committees in N. D. Baker, Annual Report of the Secretary of War, 1920, p. 49, indicating that they had "control of the reorganization of the National Guard."

19. *Army and Navy Journal*, 6 November 1920, p. 275; *New York Times*, 5 November 1920, 5:4, and 4 March 1921, 3:4.

20. Chapter notes, v. 15, p. 40.

21. See Pershing Mss, NA, RG 136, Pershing, Box 3.

22. Palmer to Marshall, 17 April 1921, v. 15, p. 44.

23. Palmer to Gen. J. J. Pershing, 4 April 1921, v. 15, p. 41.

24. Palmer to Marshall, 17 April 1921, v. 15, p. 44.

25. Chapter notes, v. 15, p. 50.

26. See Pershing diary, 7 May 1921 et seq., L/C Pershing Mss.

27. *Army and Navy Journal*, 16 July 1921, p. 1229.

28. See Pershing to Maj. Gen. J. G. Harbord, 1 and 12 February 1921, and reply 20 March 1921, L/C Harbord Mss, Harbord-Pershing Correspondence, and Pershing to Brig. Gen. F. Conner, 15 December 1920, L/C Pershing Mss, Box 52, Conner, F.

29. *New York Times*, 29 January 1921, 4:6; 23 July 1921, 19:8; and 30 June 1921, 7:2.

30. Cy, Palmer for Harbord, 13 August 1921, v. 16, pp. 26 ff.

31. Ibid.

32. Harbord for Palmer, 12 December 1921, v. 16, p. 26 ff.

33. Joint Resolution 96, 5 August 1921.

34. *Army and Navy Journal*, 13 August 1921, pp. 1325, 1328.

35. Palmer for Pershing, 1 July 1921, v. 16, pp. 13 ff.

36. Palmer to Brig. Gen. F. Conner, 14 and 15 June 1921, v. 16, p. 10 ff.

37. Col. J. H. Parker to Palmer, 17 May 1921, v. 16, p. 5. See also Parker to Palmer, 14 April 1922, and reply, 17 April 1922, v. 18, pp. 144 ff.

38. Palmer to Col. A. W. Bjornstad, 2 August 1921, with undated endorsed reply, v. 16, p. 22.

39. Palmer to Conner, 15 June 1921, v. 16, p. 11.

40. Palmer to Wadsworth, 26 January 1921, v. 15, p. 33 ff; cy, Palmer to Wadsworth, 4 February 1921, v. 15, p. 35.

41. Palmer to Pershing, 14 May 1921, v. 16, p. 4.

42. Palmer for Pershing, 14 May 1921, and attached note, v. 16, p. 4.

43. War Dept. GO 31, 18 July 1921.

44. See, for example, Palmer to T. McIlvaine, 28 July 1921, v. 16, p. 20.

45. War Dept. SO 155-0, 7 July 1921. See also minutes in chronological file, 8 July 1921.

46. *Army and Navy Journal*, 20 August 1921, p. 1340 ff; and 27 August 1921, p. 1365.

47. Palmer for Harbord, 10 August 1921, v. 16, pp. 24 ff.

48. Pershing to Palmer, 15 August 1921, Palmer 201 file, DA, TAG.

49. Chapter notes, v. 16, pp. 29 ff.
50. Palmer to Brig. Gen. E. F. McGlachlin, Jr., 28 July 1921, v. 16, p. 21.
51. McIlvaine to Palmer, 12 September 1921, and reply 15 September 1921, v. 16, pp. 44-45.
52. War Dept. Bulletin No. 19, 3 October 1921. See also Army War College, 1921-22, Vol. 7, Misc. Lecture No. 5, 3 September 1921. Cy also in L/ C Pershing Mss., Palmer, J. M.
53. Palmer to Rep. F. L. Greene (Vermont), 24 September 1921.
54. War Dept. Bulletin No. 19, 3 October 1921.
55. Brig. Gen. L. S. Upton to Palmer, 14, Dec. 1921, v. 17, p. 71.
56. Chief, Militia Bureau, for C/S, 28 November 1921, DA, TAG, 352.02, cross-reference sheet from Palmer 201 file, DA, TAG. See also Palmer draft reply prepared for Harbord's signature, 4 December 1921, in Palmer chronological file.
57. Chapter notes, v. 17, passim.
58. Palmer for S/W Weeks, 22 April 1922, v. 17, p. 16; interview, Maude Laning Palmer, 3 July 1957.
59. Palmer to I. Tarbell, 14 May 1923, chronological file; J. B. Walker, editor of *Scientific American*, to Palmer, 19 June 1922, v. 19, p. 174.
60. Palmer to C. B. Laning, 18 February 1922, v. 18, p. 109.
61. Ibid.
62. Harbord to Pershing, 20 March 1921, L/C Harbord Mss, Harbord-Pershing Correspondence.
63. See "Data on Impending Pay Cuts" compiled for Pershing, 21 November 1921, NA, RG 316, Box 3, Army Reorganization, and NA, RG 165, WDGS subject index, 19 May 1920, file 6110.
64. Annual Report of the Secretary of War, 1922, pp. 129-30, 161. See also WD news releases of 29 March 1922 and 20 July 1922, NA, RG 136, Box 4, Pershing.
65. Palmer to Marshall, 7 March 1922, NA, RG 136, Box 4, Pershing.

CHAPTER 40

1. Palmer for Brig. Gen. J. G. Harbord, 13 October 1921.
2. Ibid.
3. Ibid.
4. Maj. Gen. W. M. Wright to Palmer, 9 January 1922, v. 17, p. 82.
5. Harbord for Gen. J. J. Pershing, 26 June 1921, L/C Pershing Mss, Box 88.
6. Gen. P. C. March to S/W J. Weeks, 1 June 1922, L/C March Mss, Letters 1918-32.
7. Palmer for Pershing, 1 February 1922, v. 18, p. 102. Copy of this fundamentally important memo also in NA, RG 316, Box 3, Army Reorganization folder.
8. Army War College lecture, "Military Policy of the United States and the Present State of the Military Forces Thereunder," 2 September 1922, Misc. No. 4., mimeo, v. 20, p. 197.
9. Palmer for Pershing, 20 February 1922, v. 18, p. 110.
10. Interview with Gen. G. C. Marshall, 21 July 1953.
11. Army War College lecture, 2 September 1922, chapter notes, v. 20, p. 197.

12. Memo, Sec'y of General Staff, Lt. Col. L. D. Gasser, 23 March 1922, v. 18, p. 137.

13. *Army and Navy Journal*, 3 December 1921, p. 319.

14. See *Washington Times*, 31 December 1921, and Palmer to Wright, 31 December 1921, v. 17, pp. 77-78.

15. Wright to Palmer, 9 January 1922, v. 17, p. 82.

16. G. Clark to Palmer, 9 August 1922, v. 20, p. 191.

17. T. McIlvaine to Palmer et al., 2 December 1921, v. 17, p. 68, and reply 6 December 1921, chronological file.

18. Lt. Co. D. J. Markey to Palmer, 26 May 1921, v. 16, p. 6; Palmer to Markey, 6 December 1921, chronological file.

19. Pershing to H. MacNider, 18 January 1922, v. 18, p. 90.

20. Palmer for Pershing, 7 February 1922, with attached undated clipping, v. 18. p. 105.

21. Palmer for Pershing, 14 July 1922, v. 19, p. 181.

22. B. C. Clark, President, NG Assn., to Palmer, 14 February 1922, in Palmer 201 file, DA, TAG.

23. *Army and Navy Journal*, 11 March 1922, p. 677; NG Convention proceedings, 27-28 February 1922, in *NG Journal*, April 1922, pp. 11-15.

24. Brig. Gen. W. A. Raupp, AG of Missouri, to Palmer, 14 September 1922, and reply 20 September 1922.

25. Palmer to Col. J. H. Parker, 17 April 1922, v. 18, pp. 144 ff.

26. Martha Derthick, *The National Guard in Politics* (Cambridge, Mass., 1965), 48, 90.

27. Palmer to Pershing, 28 February 1922, v. 18, p. 127.

28. *Army and Navy Journal*, 1 April 1922, p. 728, and 20 May 1922, p. 894.

29. Ibid., 22 April 1922, p. 798.

30. Ibid., 1 April 1922, p. 728.

31. Ibid., 3 June 1922, p. 945.

32. Palmer to Col. W. Uline, C/S 98th OR Div., 29 September 1922.

33. *Army and Navy Journal*, 24 June 1922, pp. 1035, 1037; 1 July 1922, p. 1063; 5 August 1922, p. 1205. See also Palmer to G. Clark, 19 September 1922, Palmer notes v. 20, p. 198, and *New York Times*, 4 October 1922, 25:1.

34. Palmer to G. Clark, 19 September 1922, Palmer notes, v. 20, p. 198; Palmer notes, v. 20, p. 200a. See also *New York Times*, 13 January 1923, 13:4.

35. Uline to Palmer, 27 September 1922, and reply 29 September 1922.

36. Ibid.

37. Derthick, *The National Guard in Politics,* 48.

38. See, for example, Palmer for Pershing, draft, 3 July 1923, NA, RG 136, Pershing Mss, Box 5, OR.

39. See Maj. Gen. G. B. Duncan, CG, VII Corps Area, to TAG, 24 August 1925; Col. T. Ross, C/S VII Corps Area, to Col. E. J. Williams, Office, Chief of Militia Bureau, 4 September 1925, and reply 28 September 1925.

40. Untitled ten-page typescript by Palmer, in 1919 chronological file but clearly relating to 1922-23. Only external identification is word "insert" at top of page one.

41. Palmer for Pershing, 28 June 1923, with enclosed draft for Pershing's signature, v. 21, p. 251a ff.

42. J. F. Weeks, Annual Report of S/W, 1921, pp. 7, 19-22.

43. Interview with Gen. George C. Marshall, 21 July 1953, and Weeks, Annual Report of S/W, 1922, pp. 13-17.

44. Palmer for Brig. Gen. W. Lassiter, 14 January 1922, v. 17, p. 89a; Palmer for Pershing, 16 January 1922, v. 18, p. 87.

45. Interview with Gen. George C. Marshall, 21 July 1953.

46. War Dept. Release 1, 11 May 1922, v. 19, p. 154.

47. Palmer for Pershing, 21 July 1922, v. 19, p. 183.

48. Palmer to Marshall, 27 September 1922, v. 20, p. 205.

49. Interview with Gen. George C. Marshall, 21 July 1953.

50. Palmer to Markey, 11 May 1922, v. 19, p. 156.

51. Maj. Gen. C. G. Morton to TAG, 18 January 1922; Pershing rating 30 June 1922; and Maj. Gen. J. F. O'Ryan to S/W, 19 January 1922, all in DA, TAG, Palmer 201 file.

52. Interview with Gen. George C. Marshall, 21 July 1953.

53. Marshall to Maj. Gen. C. H. Martin, 7 November 1934, DA, TAG, Marshall 201 file.

CHAPTER 41

1. *Army and Navy Journal*, 27 May 1922, p. 919; Palmer for S/W, 31 May 1922.

2. Maj. Gen. J. G. Harbord to N. D. Baker, 5 February 1923, L/C Harbord Mss, Harbord-Pershing letters.

3. T. McIlvaine to Palmer, 8 May 1922, v. 19, p. 153.

4. Palmer to Col. H. Le Comte, Swiss Army, 21 December 1921.

5. Herman Hagedorn, *Leonard Wood, A Biography* (New York, 1931), v. 1, pp. 398-99; E. E. Morison et al., eds., *The Letters of Theodore Roosevelt*, (Cambridge, Mass, 1951-54), 851, 1057.

6. See misc. correspondence of Palmer and Le Comte in 1922-23 v. 8, chronological file.

7. Palmer for Gen. J. J. Pershing, 23 February 1922, NA, RG 136, Box 4. See also Palmer for Pershing 14 February 1922, L/C Pershing Mss, Box 153, Palmer.

8. Palmer to Charles Scribner's Sons, 24 April 1924.

9. Ibid.

10. Palmer to I. Tarbell, 11 and 13 October 1922.

11. Palmer to G. P. Putnam Sons, 15 December 1922.

12. G. H. Putnam for G. P. Putnam Sons, 20 December 1922. See also Putnam to Palmer, 13 August 1923.

13. *New York Times*, 2 July 1923, 1:8.

14. Published by Scribner's (New York, 1924), E. E. Lape, ed.

15. E. E. Lape to Palmer, 29 February 1924.

16. See, for example, *New York Times*, 23 March 1924, IX, 1:7, and *Book Review Digest*, 1924, pp. 337-38.

17. H. Holt to Palmer, 5 September 1924.

18. L. Eltinge to Palmer, 10 September 1924. See also Brig. Gen. S. Heintzelman to Palmer, 9 May 1923, v. 21, p. 246.

19. J. Hagood to Palmer, 28 September 1922, v. 20, p. 207.

20. Interview with Gen. George C. Marshall, 21 July 1953.

21. Interview with Mary Palmer Rockwell, 15 August 1963.

22. Interview with Maude Laning Palmer, 5 July 1957; Mrs. Palmer to Pershing, undated (June 1923), L/C Pershing Mss, Box 153.

23. Interviews with Mary Palmer Rockwell, 12 August 1960 and 13 August 1963.

CHAPTER 42

1. Col. J. W. Gulick to Palmer, 15 August 1923.

2. Interview with Maude Laning Palmer, 3 July 1957.

3. Interviews with Gen. T. D. White, 8 April 1957 and 22 May 1964. See also Palmer to Bishop J. C. White, 31, August 1925, in Gen. T. D. White personal papers, Air Force Simpson Historical Research Center, Maxwell AFB, Alabama.

4. Ibid., and interview with Maj. Gen. Herbert M. Jones, 27 May 1964.

5. Interview with Mary Palmer Rockwell, 13 August 1963.

6. Interview with Maude Laning Palmer, 5 July 1957. See also Dixon Wector, *The Saga of American Society* (New York, 1937), 419.

7. Marshall to Palmer, 26 October 1923.

8. Marshall to Palmer, 11 January 1924.

9. Brig. Gen. B. H. Wells to Palmer, 1 December 1923; Palmer to B. P. Disque and A. A. Boyden, 29 January 1924.

10. *New York Times*, 2 January 1924, 19:8, and 16 January 1924, 1:4, and interviews with Gen. Thomas D. White, 22 May 1964, and Maj. Gen. Herbert M. Jones, 27 May 1964.

11. *New York Times*, 17 January 1924, 1:2; 18 January 1924, 1:3; "Joint Army-Navy Maneuver 1923-1924; Critique: Statement by Brig. Gen. J. M. Palmer Commanding General, Atlantic Subsector," chronological file, 1924.

12. Maj. Gen. R. L. Spragins to author, 22 June 1962.

13. Interview with Gen. Thomas D. White, 22 May 1964.

14. *Army and Navy Journal*, 26 January 1924, p. 501; *New York Times*, 25 January 1924, 1:6, and 4 Feb. 1924, 12:1.

15. Spragins to author, 16 July 1962.

16. "Joint Army-Navy Maneuver 1923-1924, Critique . . . ", p. 9.

17. Palmer to Gen. J. J. Pershing, 24 May 1924, L/C Pershing Mss, Box 153, Palmer folder, and interview with Maj. Gen. H. M. Jones, 27 May 1964.

18. Spragins to author, 22 June 1962.

19. Interview with Maude Laning Palmer, 30 December 1958.

20. Col. M. C. Kerth to Palmer, 23 January 1924, and reply 16 April 1924.

21. Brig. Gen. J. M. Palmer, CG, 19th Inf. Brig., to CG, Panama Canal Division, 30 April 1925, and related correspondence.

22. Ibid. See also interviews with Maude Laning Palmer and Maj. Gen. H. M. Jones 3 July 1958.

23. Palmer to Disque and Boyden, 29 January 1924, and Disque to Palmer, 15 December 1923; Boyden to Palmer, 12 February 1924; Charles Scribner's Sons to Palmer, 7 May 1924.

24. Interview with Maude Laning Palmer, 3 July 1957.

CHAPTER 43

1. The account that follows is largely based on three long, diary-like letters Palmer wrote to his wife between 9 July and 23 August 1925.

2. See undated outline, "A Virtue of Necessity," in Palmer chronological file, 1925 Algonquin Park.

3. See "Fishing Diary," 17-30 August 1925, chronological file.

4. Interview with Mary Palmer Rockwell, 12 April 1964.

5. Palmer to Maude Laning Palmer, 17 July 1925; interview with Maj. Gen. Herbert M. Jones, 27 May 1964.

6. *Army and Navy Journal*, 3 October 1925, p. 101.

7. Palmer to Adj. Gen. R. C. Davis, 25 July 1925; Palmer to Maude Laning Palmer, 7 August 1925.

8. J. W. Wadsworth to Palmer, 26 January 1926; M. A. Reckord to Palmer, 5 January 1926.

9. *Army and Navy Journal*, 13 June 1925, p. 2257, and 1 August 1925, p. 2425.

10. Ibid., 26 September 1925, p. 77.

11. Ibid., 25 August 1925, p. 2469.

12. Proceedings of retirement board, 16 October 1925, DA, TAG, Palmer 201 file.

13. H. W. Miller to Palmer, 20 October 1925.

14. Gen. G. C. Marshall to Palmer, 31 December 1925.

15. Maj Gen. W. Lassiter to Palmer, 9 November 1925.

CHAPTER 44

1. Palmer to Brig. Gen. H. Jervey, 30 August 1922.

2. Jessie Palmer Weber to Palmer, 30 November 1925.

3. Interview with Mary Palmer Rockwell, 13 August 1963; undated ms. of "The Organization of Peace" in her possession.

4. Interviews with Mary Palmer Rockwell, 13 August 1963; Gen. George C. Marshall, 21 July 1953; Lt. Gen. Stanley D. Embick, 8 July 1952.

5. Interview with Maj. Gen. Herbert M. Jones, 27 May 1964.

6. Palmer to Lt. T. D. White, 24 December 1927, White Mss, Palmer folder.

7. Palmer to White, 8 July 1929, loc. cit.

8. Charles Scribner's Sons to Palmer, 22 July 1926; A. W. Page to Palmer, 27 September 1926, chronological file, Doubleday folder.

9. Undated pencil draft of Palmer to Page. [November 1926], loc. cit.

10. Palmer to C. E. Hughes, 28 November 1926, Doubleday folder.

11. Palmer to Hughes, 10 December 1926, loc. cit.

12. Pencil draft, Palmer to Hughes, 6 February 1927, and reply, 11 February 1927, ibid.

13. Palmer to Page, 3 November 1926, loc. cit.

14. Palmer to B. Stowe, 9 March 1927.

15. Hughes to Palmer, 19 March 1927, chronological file, Doubleday folder.

16. Hughes to Palmer, 2 May 1927, loc. cit.

17. *New York Times*, 29 April 1927, 1:30, and editoral 20:1. See also *Memphis Commercial Appeal*, 29 May 1927, and *Baltimore Evening Sun*, 4 June 1927, for guardsman-oriented reviews.

18. "Inner History of the National Defense Act of 1920," typescript draft of article by Palmer, chronological file, April 1919, pp. 4-5, and pencil draft, Palmer to N. D. Baker, 24 December 1926.

19. Pencil draft, Palmer to Page, 28 November 1926, chronological file, Doubleday folder.

20. Doubleday, Page & Co., Memorandum of Agreement, 20 October 1926, chronological file, Doubleday folder.

21. Undated pencil draft Palmer to Page, [October 1926?] and Page to Palmer, 13 and 20 October 1926, loc. cit.

22. Palmer to N.D. Baker, 17 February 1927, and reply 18 February 1927; Palmer to Stowe, 1 March 1927.

23. Stowe to Palmer, 23 and 26 February 1927.

24. "Two War Presidents, Lincoln and Wilson: General Plan," attached to Doubleday, Page & Co., Memorandum of Agreement, 8 March 1927.

25. Palmer to Stowe, 1 March 1927.

26. Stowe to Palmer, 8 March 1927; C. E. McPherren to Palmer, 7 November 1927; W. H. Seward to Palmer, 25 April 1928; Palmer to Stowe, 7, 18 & 23 May 1927.

27. Marshall to Palmer, 26 August 1927; E. Root to Palmer, 2 September 1927.

28. H. L. Stimson to Palmer, 24 March 1927; Root to Palmer, 2 September 1927.

29. Palmer to Stowe, 19 July 1927; Le Comte to Palmer, 22 August 1927, and reply, 13 September 1927; Le Comte to Palmer, 14 October 1927.

30. Palmer to Marshall, 1 March 1928.

31. S. Miles to Palmer, 22 September 1927. See also Palmer to White, 29 November (1927?), White Mss.

32. Lt. Col. T. W. Hammond to Palmer, 18 July 1927, and reply, 20 July 1927.

33. Palmer to Stowe, 16 December 1927; Rep. S. W. Dempsey (N.Y.) to Palmer, 12 July 1927.

34. *Proc.* U.S. Naval Inst., July 1927, 820-22.

35. Le Comte to Palmer, 3 July 1927.

36. Col. A. L. Conger to Palmer, 21 August 1927, and reply 13 September 1927.

37. Jared Sparks, ed., *Writings of George Washington* (Boston, 1834); and Worthington C. Ford, ed., *Writings of George Washington* (New York, 1890).

38. Palmer to Stowe, 11 January 1928.

39. T. B. Wells to Palmer, 17 February and 23 March 1927, chronological file. Also 12 and 23 April, 1 and 14 May 1928, 1926 chronological file, Doubleday folder; Palmer to White, 13 May 1928, White Mss.

40. John M. Palmer, "America's Debt to a German Soldier: Baron Von Steuben and What He Taught Us," *Harper's*, September 1928; interview with Gen. Thomas D. White, 22 May 1964.

41. Palmer to White, 21 January 1928, White Mss.

42. Issue of December 1928, pp. 529-42.

43. Interview with Mary Palmer Rockwell, 18 August 1964; Palmer to O. L. Schmidt, 9 April 1930, and A. B. Hart to Palmer, 5 April 1930, 1930 chronological file, Schmidt folder.

44. Palmer to L. Hay, 10 December 1928, and reply, 15 December 1928.

45. Palmer to White, 13 September 1927, White Mss.

46. Palmer to J. R. Garfield, 19 May 1928, and reply, 28 May 1928, with enclosed copies of Upton and Sherman letters to President Garfield.

47. Palmer to Maude Laning Palmer, 4 November 1928, and reply, 18 November 1928; Palmer to Gen. C. R. Ballard, 4 November 1928, and reply, 26 January 1929.

48. Palmer to Hay, 11 and 26 May 1928, and Hay to Palmer, 14 May 1928.

49. Pencil draft, Palmer to Stowe, 21 July 1929, chronological file, Doubleday folder on *Washington, Lincoln, Wilson.*

50. Palmer to White, 30 September 1928, White Mss.

51. Palmer to Le Comte, 3 February 1928, 1928 chronological file; and pencil draft, Palmer to Stowe, 13 December 1928, 1926 chronological file, Doubleday folder.

52. Stowe to Palmer, 17 July 1929, chronological file, Doubleday folder.

53. Marshall to Palmer, 30 July 1929.

54. Cy, Marshall to Palmer, 17 September 1929, 1929 chronological file, Doubleday folder; Palmer to Marshall, 18 December 1929.

55. Tarbell to Palmer, 25 November 1929.

56. Palmer to Stowe, 21 July 1929, and reply, 24 July 1929; Palmer to Pershing, 20 September 1929, and reply, 21 October 1929; Palmer to Stowe, 24 and 29 November 1929, all in 1929 chronological file, Doubldeday folder; Palmer to Marshall, 18 December 1929, chronological file; Palmer to White, 21 December 1929, White Mss.

57. Stowe to Palmer, 14 November 1929, chronological file; Palmer to Stowe, 16 November 1929, and reply 1929, 20 November 1929, chronological file, Doubleday folder.

58. Stowe to Palmer, 18 October and 23 December 1929, chronological file, Doubleday folder.

59. Page to Palmer, 26 July 1929; Palmer to Stowe, 26 and 27 July 1929; Stowe to Palmer, 31 July 1929, loc. cit.

60. Palmer to Stowe, 26 July 1929, loc. cit.

61. Stowe to Palmer, 31 July 1929, and reply 9 August 1929, loc. cit.

62. Page to Palmer, 21 August 1929, loc. cit. Subsequently Palmer believed he had had some influence on President Hoover's National Guard policy. See Palmer to Stowe, 4 December 1929, loc. cit.

63. Page to Palmer, 10 August 1929, loc. cit.

64. Palmer to Maude Laning Palmer, 21 and 23 August 1929, chronological file.

65. Stowe to Palmer, 6 September 1929, and reply, 12 September 1929, as well as Stowe to Palmer, 12 September 1929, chronological file, Doubleday folder.

66. Baker to Stowe, 21 August, 16 and 27 September 1929, loc. cit.

67. Stowe to Palmer, 25 September 1929; 31 October 1929 office memo by Stowe; and T. Cooper to Palmer, 28 February 1930, loc. cit. See also Peyton C. March, *The Nation at War* (Garden City, N.Y., 1932) 342-43.

68. Stowe to Palmer, 10 January 1929, and reply 13 Jan. 1929, chronological file, Doubleday folder.

69. Palmer to J. Craig, 17 February 1930 and reply, 17 February 1930, loc cit.

70. L. L. Babcock to Palmer, 12 and 20 December 1929, and reply, 18 December 1929.

71. Stowe to Palmer, 23 December 1929, chronological file, Doubleday folder.

72. *N.Y. Herald Tribune Magazine*, 23 February 1930, and similar spreads in Worcester Telegram, Atlanta Sunday Constitution Magazine, and others. See also, *N.Y. Times Book Review*, 6 July 1930, p. 5.

73. *Cong Rec*, 71 Cong, 2 Sess, 13 February 1930, pp. 3630-31. See also Palmer to T. Cooper, 16 February 1930.

74. Le Comte to Palmer, 2 January 1930, and reply 31 January 1930; Le Comte to Palmer, 26 February 1930.

75. See *Bookman* 71 (August 1930): 562: *Christian Science Monitor*, 26 July 1929, p. 13. See also "Guide to Militarism," Evansville, (Ind.) Press, 12 March 1980; and *Trenton (N.J.) Times-Advertiser*, 19 March 1930.

76. *Am. Hist. Rev.* 35 (July 1930): 894.

77. Marshall to Palmer, 20 December 1928 and 17 January 1929.

78. Memo for record by Palmer, February 1930.

79. Marshall to Palmer, 21 March 1930, chronological file, 1930 Review WLW folder.

80. Col. T. B. Mott to Palmer, 6 March and 12 April; Maj. Gen. E. Swift to Palmer, 29 February.; Maj. Gen. H. Liggett to Brig. Gen. P. Pierce, 5 July 1930, loc. cit.

81. "The Military Policy of the United States," War College lecture, 21 September 1928.

82. Hammond to Palmer, 6 September 1929.

83. Palmer to Pierce, 18 April 1930, chronological file, 1930 Review WLW folder.

84. D. Fletcher to Palmer, 15 March 1930, loc. cit.

85. W. H. Morley to Palmer, 27 March 1930, and Doubleday Doran & Co. to Palmer, 1 November 1937, 1930 chronological file, Doubleday folder.

86. Pencil draft, Palmer to D. J. Markey, 1 April 1934, 1933-40 chronological file, Literary Projects folder.

87. Pencil draft, Palmer to B. Baumgarten, 1 April 1934, chronological file, Steuben Book 1933-36 folder.

CHAPTER 45

1. Palmer to Gen. T. D. White, 10 September 1928, White Ms.

2. Interview with Mary Palmer Rockwell, 14 August 1965; *N.Y. Times*, 21 August 1935, 19:5, and *National Cyclopedia of American Biography*, vol. 29, p. 190.

3. *Transactions of the Illinois State Historical Society*, 1927.

4. O. L. Schmidt to Palmer, 14 June and 6 December 1928, 5 June 1929; and Palmer to Schmidt, 2 August 1928, chronological file, O. L. Schmidt 1927-35 folder.

5. Palmer to Schmidt, 9 June 1929, and Schmidt to Palmer, 28 June 1929, loc. cit.

6. M. Baum to Palmer, 10 January 1935, loc. cit.

7. Palmer to Schmidt, 10 June 1929, and Schmidt to Palmer, 18 November 1929, loc. cit.

8. Palmer to Schmidt, 28 September and 14 October 1929, loc. cit.

9. Palmer to Schmidt, 2 July and 27 November 1929, loc. cit.

10. Palmer to Schmidt, 11 August 1929, loc cit.

11. Schmidt to Palmer, 5 June 1929, and J. Goebel to Palmer, 15 October 1929, loc. cit.

12. Palmer to Goebel, 29 January 1930, chronological file, O. L. Schmidt 1930-32 folder.

13. Goebel to Palmer, 15 November 1929, chronological file, O. L. Schmidt, 1927-35 folder; Palmer to Goebel, 20 January 1930, with attached correspondence, chronological file, O. L. Schmidt, 1930-32 folder.

14. Palmer to Schmidt, 8, 22, and 31 January 1930, chronological file, O. L. Schmidt, 1930-32 folder.

15. Palmer to Schmidt, 8 October 1929, and Schmidt to Palmer, 30 November 1929, chronological file, O. L. Schmidt 1927-35 folder; Palmer to Schmidt, 16 September 1930, chronological file, O. L. Schmidt, 1930-32 folder.

16. Palmer to Schmidt, 31 January, 1 March, and 9 May 1930, and Palmer to A. L. Richards, 30 March 1931, chronological file, O. L. Schmidt, 1930-32 folder.

17. Palmer to Schmidt, 9 May 1930, loc. cit.

18. Palmer to Schmidt, 31 January and 20 March 1930, Palmer to Goebel, 2 April 1930, and Palmer to Schmidt, 11 and 16 September and 24 December 1930, loc. cit.

19. Palmer to Schmidt, 25 September 1930, and Palmer to M. Kalkhorst, 16 December 1930, loc. cit.

20. Schmidt to Palmer, 27 December 1930, loc. cit.

21. Palmer to Schmidt, 5 and 29 November 1929, chronological file, O.L. Schmidt 1927-35 folder; Palmer to Goebel, 20 January 1930, with attached correspondence, chronological file.

22. Palmer to Schmidt, 24 November and 24 December 1930, chronological file, O.L. Schmidt 1930-32 folder.

23. Palmer to Schmidt, 3 January 1931, loc. cit.

24. *New York Times*, 17 November 1930, 9:2.

25. Baron Ludovic G. M. duBessy deContenson, *"Baron de Steuben and German Propaganda in the United States,"* Paris, n.d. [1931?], pamphlet.

26. Palmer to Schmidt, 24 November 1930, chronological file, O.L. Schmidt, 1930-32 folder.

27. K. F. Von Frank to mayor of Steuben, N.Y., 19 January 1931, and Palmer to Schmidt, 30 March 1931, with draft reply, loc cit.

28. Palmer to the German ambassador, 21 May 1930, chronological file. See also Palmer to Von Frank, 21 July, and reply, 12 September 1931, chronological file, O.L. Schmidt, 1930-32 folder.

29. R. Doblhoff to Palmer, 13 June 1931, chronological file, O. L. Schmidt 1930-32 folder.

30. Interview with Mary Palmer Rockwell, 18 August 1964; *New York Times*, 13 April 1931, 24:2; Doblhoff to Palmer, 9 February 1932, chronological file; Palmer to Schmidt, 25 April 1931, chronological file, O. L. Schmidt 1930-32 folder.

31. Palmer to Schmidt, 22 October and 21 November 1931, loc. cit.

32. Palmer to Schmidt, 22 October, and reply 26 October 1931, loc. cit.

33. Palmer to Schmidt, 21 November 1931, loc. cit.

34. The following paragraphs, except where otherwise indicated, are based on interviews with Mary Palmer Rockwell over a period of several years. See also Palmer to Maude Laning Palmer, 19, 26, and 29 August 1929.

35. Memo, "John" for "Tiss," 31 December 1931, chronological file, Edgewild 1931-33 folder.

36. H. Murdock to Palmer, 24 February, 1 March, and 18 April 1932.

37. Palmer to Murdock, 26 February 1932.

38. Murdock to Palmer, 24 February, and reply 26 February 1932.

39. Murdock to Palmer, 30 December 1932.

40. Ibid.

41. Palmer to Murdock, 17 December, and Palmer to G. C. Marshall, 12 November 1933.

42. "Spring Record" 1933-35, chronological file, Edgewild 1931-33 folder.

43. Palmer to Col. M. C. Kerth, 30 January 1930.

44. Palmer to Capt. N. B. Chandler, 24 January 1930.

45. Palmer to Z. Southard, 18 November 1931.

46. Southard to Palmer, 7 July 1931.

47. *Bristol (N.H.) Enterprise*, 31 January 1935, and Palmer to Murdock, 30 January 1935.

48. H. Putnam to Palmer, 14 March 1933 and 24 September 1935.

49. Palmer to Gen. J. J. Pershing, 13 July 1937.

50. Mary [Palmer Rockwell] to Palmer, 5 December 1928.

51. Palmer to Maude Laning Palmer, 25 November 1933.

52. Palmer to Murdock, 17 December 1933.

53. John M. Palmer, "Franklin's Patriotic Fib," *North American Review*, June 1932.

54. Palmer to Brandt & Brandt, 9 and 13 July 1932, and cy, T. B. Costain [*Saturday Evening Post*] to C. Brandt, 19 September 1932. See also miscellaneous correspondence in chronological file, Literary Projects 1933-40 folder.

55. Brandt to Palmer, 7 August 1933, chronological file, Literary Projects 1933-40 folder.

56. Palmer to Schmidt, 1 December 1931, chronological file, O. L. Schmidt 1927-35 folder, and Palmer to Brandt, 12 February 1934, chronological file, Steuben Book 1933-36 folder.

57. Undated memo [April 1934] Palmer to Brandt, marked "not sent," chronological file, Steuben Book 1933-36 folder.

58. Palmer to Murdock, 17 December 1933.

59. Palmer to Brandt, 12 February 1934, chronological file, Steuben Book 1933-36 folder.

60. B. Baumgarten to Palmer, 14 and 29 March 1934, loc. cit.

61. Palmer to Schmidt, 8 September 1934, chronological file, O. L. Schmidt 1927-35 folder.

62. A. C. Flick to Palmer, 3 August 1934, and Richards to Palmer, 19 December 1934, chronological file, Steuben Book 1933-36 folder.

63. M. Hearst to Palmer, 1 November 1934, loc. cit.

64. Palmer to Schmidt, 11 and 21 October 1934, chronological file, O. L. Schmidt 1927-35 folder.

65. Palmer to Marshall, 6 January 1935.

66. Palmer to Marshall, 26 March, and reply, 29 March 1935.

67. Palmer to J. W. Wadsworth, 31 March and 5 April 1935.

68. Palmer to Wadsworth, 3 May 1935; Palmer to Col. O. Johnson, 22 May 1935.

69. Johnson to Palmer, 20 May and 24 August 1935.

70. Palmer to Marshall, 31 October 1935, and undated reply [November 1935], chronological file. See also Marshall to Wadsworth, 2 October, and reply 7 October 1935, Marshall 201 file, DA, TAG.

71. N. V. Donaldson to Palmer, 27 October and 4 November 1937, chronological file, Steuben 1937-38 folder.

72. Palmer to Donaldson, 2 December 1937, loc. cit.

73. Donaldson to Palmer, 12 and 20 January 1938.

74. *Washington Post*, 13 March 1965, p. 2, and Palmer to Mary [Palmer Rockwell], 14 March 1945, Mary Palmer Rockwell Mss.

CHAPTER 46

1. Palmer to G. C. Marshall, 21 May 1938, Marshall 201 file, DA, TAG.

2. G. Palmer to Palmer, 8 September 1938; Palmer to E. A. Davidson, 13 September 1937.

3. J. W. Wadsworth to Palmer, 30 September 1937.

4. Palmer to Gen. T. D. White, 5 June 1928, White Mss.

5. Wadsworth to Palmer, 9 November 1939; Palmer to Wadsworth, 30 November and 11 December 1939.

6. Issue of 11 November 1939. See also John M. Palmer, "The Initial Protective Force," *Illinois Guardsman*, February 1940, pp. 14, 38.

7. Interview with Mary Palmer Rockwell, 14 August 1965.

8. Interview with John Palmer Chandler, 29 January 1964.

9. Palmer to G. Clark, 26 May 1941.

10. Interview with John Palmer Chandler, 29 January 1964.

11. Interviews with Mary Palmer Rockwell, 15 August 1960 and 14 August 1965.

12. Interview with John Palmer Chandler, 16 August 1962.

13. Interview with Maj. Gen. Milton A. Reckord, 26 December 1961. See also *New York Times*, 16 August 1939, p. 14.

14. G. Palmer to Palmer, 26 April 1940.

15. Interviews with Mary Palmer Rockwell, 12 April 1964 and 14 August 1965.

16. G. Palmer to Palmer, 16 January 1940.

17. G. Palmer to Palmer 26 April 1940.

18. Interview with Grenville Clark, 18 August 1964, and A. Roelker to Palmer, 10 May 1940, chronological file, Burke-Wadsworth Bill 1940 folder. See also Samuel R. Spencer, Jr., "A History of the Selective Training and Service Act of 1940 from Inception to Enactment," Ph.D. diss., Harvard University, 1951, passim.

19. G. Clark to Palmer, 17 May 1940, chronological file, Burke-Wadsworth Bill 1940 folder.

20. Typescript text, "Remarks of General John McAuley Palmer, U.S.A., Retired," 22 May 1940, loc. cit.

21. "Plattsburg Group Asks Conscription," *New York Times,* 23 May 1940, reprinted by MTCA for distribution, loc. cit.

22. Marshall testimony on S. 4164, Senate Military Affairs Committee Hearings, 76 Cong, 3 Sess, 3-12 July 1940, p. 340; interview with Grenville Clark, 18 August 1964.

23. G. Clark to Palmer, 25 May 1940, chronological file, Burke-Wadsworth Bill 1940 folder.

24. Marshall to Palmer, 27 May 1940, loc. cit.

25. MTCA, "Preliminary Report of Committee on Equal Universal Service," 29 May 1940, by A. G. Thacher, loc. cit. and interviews with Grenville Clark, 18 August 1954, and Lt. Gen. L. B. Hershey, 13 February 1967.

26. Palmer to Thacher, 4 June 1940, and Palmer to G. Clark, 4 June 1940, Burke-Wadsworth Bill 1940 folder.

27. Interviews with Mary Palmer Rockwell, 14 August 1965, and John Palmer Chandler, 29 January 1964.

28. Boone, "Progress Report," Department of Publicity [National Emergency Committee], 1 June to 19 July 1940, Burke-Wadsworth Bill 1940 folder; interview with Grenville Clark, 18 August 1964; Spencer, "History of the Selective Training and Service Act," 126-34

29. Teleg. G. Clark to Palmer, 14 June 1940, Burke-Wadsworth Bill 1940 folder.

30. Teleg., Palmer to G. Clark, 16 June 1940, and teleg in reply 17 June 1940, loc. cit.

CHAPTER 47

1. Palmer to Maj. L. B. Hershey, 26 June 1940, chronological file, Burke-Wadsworth Bill 1940 folder.

2. E. E. Morison, *Turmoil and Tradition* (Boston, 1960), 480. See also *New York Times*, 20 June 1940, 1:4, and 22 June 1940, 8:1, 2; H.R. 10132, 22 June 1940.

3. Harold L. Ickes, *Secret Diary of Harold L. Ickes* (New York, 1953), v. 3, pp 8, 93, 120, offers details on the Knox appointment. For the Stimson appointment, see Morison, *Turmoil and Tradition*, 478-81; H.L. Stimson and M. Bundy, *On Active Service in Peace and War* (New York, 1948), 318-31; M. W. Watson, *Chief of Staff: Prewar Plans and Preparations* (Washington, D.C., GPO, 1950), 189-92; E. S. Greenbaum, *A Lawyer's Job: In Court, in the Army, in Office* (New York, 1967), 126-28, with an appendix pp. 225-28 reproducing Grenville Clark's version of the appointment. For an excellent account of the Stimson appointment and the Burke-Wadsworth bill, see John G. Clifford, "Grenville Clark and the Origins of Selective Service," *Review of Politics* 35 (January 1973): 17-40.

4. T. McIlvaine to Palmer, 25 and 28 June 1940; McIlvaine to Maj. L.B. Hershey, 27 June 1940, McIlvaine to G. Clark, 2 July 1940, chronological file, Burke-Wadsworth Bill 1940 folder.

5. Palmer to G. Clark, 28 June 1940, and teleg, Palmer to Gen. J.J. Pershing, 27 June 1940, loc. cit.

6. Interview with Grenville Clark, 18 August 1964, and Palmer to G. Clark, 26 July 1940, loc. cit.

7. George Fielding Eliot, "Wanted—A Battle-worthy Army," *New York Herald Tribune*, 22 June 1940, 16:5.

8. *New York Herald Tribune,* editorial, "Universal Service Bill," 22 June 1940, p. 16.

9. P. Boone to Palmer, 24 June 1940, and reply 27 June 1940, with draft article, chronological file, Burke-Wadsworth Bill 1940 folder.

10. Palmer to *New York Herald Tribune,* 28 June 1940, p. 22.

11. Eliot to *New York Herald Tribune,* 2 July 1940, p. 24.

12. Palmer to Eliot, 15 July 1940.

13. Teleg, Eliot to Palmer, 19 July 1940.

14. Tape of CBS panel discussion of Burke-Wadsworth bill, broadcast 27 July 1940, in University of Washington phonoarchive. See also Palmer to Eliot 25 July 1940.

15. Eliot to Palmer, 28 July 1940.

16. Senate Military Affairs Committee, Hearings on S.4164, 3 July 1940, 76 Cong, 3 Sess, p. 8.

17. Ibid., 44 ff.

18. Ibid., 7-14, 335-40. See also H.R. Military Affairs Committee, *Hearings* on H.R. 10132, 10 July to 14 August 1940, 76 Cong, 3 Sess, pp. 44 ff.

19. Senate Military Affairs Committee, Hearings, on S. 4164, 3 July 1940, 76 Cong, 3 Sess, p. 57.

20. Ibid.

21. See M.A. Reckord's second appearance before the Senate Military Affairs Committee after conferring with sponsors of the Burke-Wadsworth bill, 12 July 1940, ibid., 386 ff. See also *New York Times,* 1 June 1940, 1:1 and 13 July 1940, 1:8.

22. Memo, Palmer for A.G. Thacher, 19 July 1940, and Reckord to Palmer, 23 July 1940, chronological file, Burke-Wadsworth Bill 1940 folder; Stimson and Bundy, *On Active Service,* 347.

23. Palmer to Reckord, 20 July; Palmer to Thacher, 20 July; Palmer to Hershey, 20 July; Reckord to Palmer, 23 July; Palmer to Reckord, 27 July 1940, chronological file, Burke-Wadsworth Bill 1940 folder; Public 783, Selective Training and Service Act, 16 September 1940 (54 U.S. Stat 885), Sect. c.

24. Palmer to McIlvaine, 25 July; Palmer to J.W. Wadsworth, 27 July 1940, chronological file, Burke-Wadsworth Bill 1940 folder.

25. Palmer to editor, *New York Times,* 18 July 1940, 18:6. See also Wadsworth to Palmer, 1 August 1940, chronological file, Burke-Wadsworth Bill 1940 folder; "Just What Conscription Means to You," *Boston Sunday Post,* 28 July 1940.

26. Palmer to Wadsworth, 15 July 1940, chronological file, Burke-Wadsworth Bill 1940 folder. See also *Bristol (N.H.) Enterprise,* 25 July; *Concord (N.H.) Daily Monitor,* 24 July; and *New York Times,* 24 July 1940, 11:5.

27. Boone, progress report, Publicity Department, 1 June to 19 July 1940, chronological file, Burke-Wadsworth Bill 1940 folder.

28. National Emergency Committee of MTCA pamphlet, "Why We Must Have Selective, Compulsory, Military Training and Service" [1 July 1940], loc. cit.

29. *Cong Rec,* 76 Cong, 3 Sess, pp. 12213-27, 12236, 12290; PL 783, 16 September 1940 (54 U.S. Stat 885).

30. G. Clark to Palmer, 1 November 1940, enclosed cy of Stimson to G. Clark, 17 September 1940. See also Samuel R. Spencer, Jr., "A History of the Selective Training and Service Act of 1940 from Inception to Enactment," Ph.D. diss., Harvard University, 1951, pp. 487 ff.

31. G. Clark memo for members of the Administrative Committee of the National Emergency Committee of the MTCA, 10 September 1940, and G. Clark to Palmer, 23 May 1941.

32. Palmer to G. Clark, 2 November 1940; Cy of handwritten menu in chronological file, 31 October 1940.

33. G. Clark to Palmer, 11 September 1940.

34. Palmer to G. Clark, 14 September 1940.

CHAPTER 48

1. G. Davidson, Yale University Press, to Palmer, 11 July 1938, chronological file, Doubleday . . . 1929-38 folder.

2. Davidson to Palmer, 12 September; B. Baumgarten to Palmer, 12 September 1940, chronological file, Literary Projects 1933-40 folder; J. W. Wadsworth to Palmer, 13 September 1940.

3. Palmer to G. Clark, 14 September; Palmer to Wadsworth, 18 September 1940.

4. Palmer to Davidson, 8 Oct. 1940.

5. L. W. Labaree to Palmer, 11 October 1940, chronological file, Doubleday 1929-38 folder.

6. Palmer to Labaree, 15 October 1940.

7. Palmer to G. C. Marshall, 12 October 1940.

8. Palmer to A. Burton, 27 September 1940; Palmer to G. Clark, 26 May 1941.

9. Palmer to G. Palmer, 31 October 1940.

10. T. McIlvaine to H. C. Peterson, 25 October; McIlvaine to H. L. Stimson, 22 October; Palmer to McIlvaine, 5 November; McIlvaine to Palmer, 14 November and reply 16 November 1940.

11. Palmer to Mary [Palmer Rockwell], 8 March 1941.

12. Palmer to N. V. Donaldson, 5 April 1941, chronological file, America in Arms . . . 1941 folder.

13. W. Lippmann to G. Clark, 8 May; Lippman to Palmer, 8 May, and reply 15 May; F. Frankfurter to Palmer, 14 May 1941, loc. cit. See also Lippman column, "The Army in the Hands of Congress," *New York Herald Tribune,* 17 July 1941, 17:1.

14. Brig, Gen. L. B. Hershey to Palmer, 27 May 1941, chronological file, "America in Arms 1941 folder.

15. Palmer to W. Millis, 21 April, and replies, 26 April and 26 May 1941, loc. cit.

16. Palmer to G. F. Eliot, 31 December 1940; Eliot to Palmer, 28 June, and reply, 31 July 1941.

17. Palmer to Marshall, 4 August 1941.

18. Palmer to G. Clark, 21 March, and Palmer to Eliot, 21 March 1941.

19. G. Clark to Palmer, 6 November 1940; memo, G. Clark for T. R. Wyles and R. H. Jamison, 24 April 1941; interview with Grenville Clark, 18 August 1964.

20. S. I. Rosenman, ed., *Public Papers and Addresses of F. D. Roosevelt* (New York, 1950), vol. 10, 15 April 1941 press conference, pp. 113-14.

21. G. Clark to Palmer, 21 May 1941.

22. Palmer to G. Clark, 26 May 1941.

23. *New York Times,* 16 July 1941, 1:1, and 18 July 1941, 10:5. See also Marshall testimony. Senate Military Affairs Committee, Hearings on Draft Extension, 77 Cong, 1 Sess, 9 July 1941, pp. 2-5.

24. *New York Times,* 10 July 1941, 13:4.

25. Ibid., 8 August 1941, 1:1, and 13 August 1941, 1:8. See also Senate Military Affairs Committee, Hearings on Draft Extension, 77 Cong, 1 Sess, 17-24 July 1941, passim; H.R. Military Affairs Committee Hearings, 77 Cong, 1 Sess, 22-28 July 1941, passim; *Cong Rec*, 77 Cong, 1 Sess, 12 August 1941, pp. 7076-77.

26. *New York Times*, 1 July 1941, 14:1; and H. W. Baldwin, "Military Lessons of the War," *Yale Review* 30 (June 1941): 657.

27. H. W. Baldwin, "New American Army," *Foreign Affairs*, October 1940, pp. 52-54.

28. T. H. Williams, *Mississippi Valley Historical Review,* (September 1941), 319; R. E. Runser, "Which Man's Army?" *Washington Post*, 11 May 1941, 12:1.

29. G. Clark to Palmer, 23 May, and reply, 26 May 1941.

30. *New York Times: Book Review*, 20 July 1941, p. 6.

31. *Army and Navy Register*, 24 May 1941.

32. Palmer to F. B. Wiener, 2 June 1941, chronological file, America in Arms, 1941 folder.

33. Maj. Gen. J. F. Williams to Palmer, 1 August 1941, loc, cit.

34. Ibid., attached covering letter, 1 August 1941.

35. Palmer to Maj. Gen. J. F. Williams, 7 Aug. 1941, loc. cit.

36. Eliot to Palmer, 2 August; Palmer to Eliot, 8 August, and reply, 23 August 1941.

37. Memo, Palmer for Marshall, 24 October 1941, chronological file, Return to Active Duty folder; Marshall to "dear John"[Palmer], 25 October 1941, chronological file.

CHAPTER 49

1. Gen. G. C. Marshall to Palmer, 25 October and 13 November 1941.

2. Palmer to G. H. McMaster, 31 October 1941; TAG to Palmer, 13 November 1941; interview with Gen. George C. Marshall, 22 July 1953.

3. Palmer to Maj. Gen. E. A. Walsh, 21 November 1941, chronological file, Return to Active Duty folder.

4. Palmer to Marshall, 6 December 1941, loc. cit.

5. Palmer to Marshall, 7 January, 1942, and reply 15 January 1942, loc. cit.

6. Palmer to Lt. Gen. L. McNair, 24 March, and Palmer to Brig. Gen. M. W. Clark, 24 March 1942.

7. Marshall to Palmer, 7 March and 12 March 1942.

8. Marshall to H. L. Stimson, 1 June 1942, xerox copy of buckslip, in Palmer Mss in possession of Mary Palmer Rockwell. See also Palmer to E. A. Davison, 13 May 1943, Yale University Press Correspondence folder.

9. Marshall interview, 22 July 1953.

10. For examples of such recriminations, see R. D. Keehn to Palmer, 24 April 1942, chronological file, but found in 1947-49 box. See also Marshall to Maj. Gen. F. Parker 21 August 1942.

11. For a résumé of pros and cons of AUS components, see Maj. Gen. J. E. Edmonds's comments on the plan of organization of AUS, 1 April 1942. Cy in chronological file.

12. Editorial, "Here's to the Citizen Soldier," *Army and Navy Register,* 14 March 1942, p. 8.

13. Maj. Gen. J. H. Hildring for Marshall, 12 April 1942, chronological file, World War II notebook, Vol. 1.

14. Martha Derthick, *The National Guard in Politics* (Cambridge, Mass., 1965), 60.

15. Transcript of Palmer's remarks, Adjutants General Assn. convention, Washington, D. C., 21 April 1942.

16. Interview with Maj. Gen. Milton A. Reckord, 28 December 1961.

17. Palmer to Gen. C. P. Summerall, 30 March and 14 May 1942.

18. See USMA, *Assembly,* June 1943.

19. TAG to G-1, WDGS, 24 June 1942.

20. Interview with Maj. Gen. Miller G. White, 18 August 1953.

21. Palmer to G-1, WDGS, 14 July 1942.

22. *Cong Rec,* 77 Cong, 1 Sess, 26 June 1942, p. A2476; Palmer to J. W. Wadsworth, 6 July 1942, chronological file, 1947-49.

23. See Gould Lincoln, "The Political Mill," *Washington Star,* 16 July 1942; Wadsworth to Palmer, 20 July 1942, chronological file, 1947-49.

24. Palmer to G-1, WDGS, 22 July 1942, and Palmer for C/S, 22 July 1942, chronological file, 1947-49.

25. Undated typescript, chronological file, 1942-43.

26. Col. A. Roelker, Secretary, MTCA, to Wadsworth, 21 July 1942, chronological file, 1947-49.

27. *New York Times,* 20 July 1940, 5:1.

28. M. F. Devine, Chairman, Legislative Committee, American Legion, to Brig. Gen. F. E. Lower, 28 August, and Devine to Palmer, 9 Sept. 1942, chronological file, 1947-49.

29. Palmer to Roelker, 28 September 1942.

30. Palmer to Wadsworth, 22 December 1942.

31. Maj. Gen. J. F. Williams to President, Postwar Planning Board, 13 July 1943.

32. *Army and Navy Register,* 25 July 1942.

33. Memo, Palmer for President, Postwar Planning Board, 24 November 1942.

34. 78 Cong, 1 Sess, H.R. 1806 and S. 701, 11 February 1943.

35. Palmer to Williams, 13 January 1943, chronological file, 1947-49.

36. Palmer to M. A. Reckord, 22 February, and reply 26 February 1943, loc. cit.

37. Wadsworth to Palmer, 29 March 1943, loc. cit.

38. Reckord to Palmer, 31 March 1943, loc. cit.

39. Extract from transcript of Adjutants General Association meeting, Harrisburg, Pa., 1-3 April 1943.

40. Ibid. Also interview with Maj. Gen. Milton A. Reckord, 28 December 1961.

41. Palmer to T. O. Walton, President, Texas A & M, 28 December, and Palmer to Maj. Gen. C. B. Hodges, USA ret., Pres. of Louisiana State Univeristy; with related correspondence, chronological file, 1947-49.

42. Committee on Military Organization and Policy, Association of Land Grant Colleges and Universities, Annual Report, 5 October 1943, loc. cit.

43. Brig. Gen. E. W. Smith, "An Analysis: The Reserve Components of the Army in Planning for a Permanent Peacetime Military Establishment," 15 October 1943.

44. Memo, Palmer for Brig. Gen. W. F. Tompkins, 20 July 1943, chronological file, Box 10, downgraded materials.

45. Palmer to Brig. Gen. M. G. White, 9 January, and Palmer to Marshall, 25 January 1943.

46. Memo for record by Palmer, 9 January 1948.

47. Memo, Palmer for President, Postwar Planning Board, 14 January 1943.

48. Memo, G-3 for C/S, 8 April 1943.

49. Memo, Marshall for Palmer, 25 May 1943. See also Marshall for Palmer, 4 April 1943, chronological file, Box 10, downgraded materials.

50. Tompkins, "Wartime Planning for Demobilization," Army War College lecture, 20 December 1950.

51. Memo, Director, Special Planning Div., for all officers of the division, 6 August 1943, chronological file, World War II notebook, Vol. 3.

52. Tompkins to Palmer, 21 May 1943, chronological file, Box 10, downgraded materials.

53. Palmer to Davidson, 13 May 1943.

54. Interview with Maj. Gen. William F. Tompkins, 18 August 1965.

55. Palmer to Marshall, 20 October, and reply, 21 October 1943, chronological file, Box 10, downgraded materials.

56. Marshall to Palmer, 1 July 1943 and 4 August 1944; Col. F. McCarthy to Palmer, 4 August 1944; Palmer to McCarthy, 4 July 1944.

57. Palmer to Maj. Gen. S. Miles, 16 August 1943.

58. F. Frankfurter to Palmer, 27 August 1943, and misc. clippings, especially *Washington Post* editorial, 17 August 1943.

59. Col. J. Greene to Palmer, 14 August 1943, chronological file, America in Arms folder. See also Palmer to N. Donaldson, 25 August 1943, Mary Palmer Rockwell Mss.

60. K. Burch, Sec'y to Exec. Dir., American Legion, to Palmer, 16 August 1943.

61. See, for example, McMaster to Palmer, 17 September 1943, McMaster read the book and then declared that Palmer rather than Upton was "America's foremost military philosopher."

62. L. M. Goodrich to Palmer, 25 May 1943.

63. Smith to Palmer, 4 October, and N. Sargeant, Sec'y of NAM, to Tompkins, 28 October 1943, both in chronological file for 1943. See also Palmer to Tompkins, 24 August 1943, chronological file for 1947-49.

64. Palmer to Wadsworth, with enclosures, 7 July 1943.

65. *New York Times,* 17 October 1943, 8:5, and cy, T. McIlvaine to Palmer, 1 October 1943, chronological file for 1947-49.

66. *Free World,* v 5, June 1943, pp. 511-14. See also G. Clark to Palmer, 21 August 1943.

67. Devine to Palmer, 27 August 1943.

68. Palmer to Col. S. P. Brown, National Defense Committee, American Legion, 22 October 1943, chronological file, 1947-49, Box 13.

69. Reported in *New York Times,* 28 November 1943, 26:1. See also editorial in *Collier's,* 27 November 1943, p. 291.

70. Palmer to Tompkins, Director, Special Planning Div., 9 November 1943.

CHAPTER 50

1. A. G. Thacher to Palmer, 27 January 1944.

2. Lecture, "Outlines of a Post-War Military Establishment," 29 June 1943, chronological file, Box 24, downgraded materials.

3. Brig. Gen. W. F. Tompkins for Brig. Gen. R. E. Porter, G-3, 15 July 1943, NA, RG 165, Special Planning Div., AG 353, Training.

4. Palmer for Tompkins, 12 July 1943, loc. cit.

5. Palmer to Brig. Gen. M. G. White, 18 July 1942.

6. Palmer for Tompkins, 29 June 1943, chronological file, Box 24, downgraded materials.

7. Interview with Maj. Gen. Miller G. White, 18 August 1953.

8. Palmer for Tompkins, 12 July 1943, See note 6, above.

9. Palmer for Tompkins, 19 July and 5 August 1943; Tompkins for C/S 18 August 1943, chronological file, box 24, downgraded materials.

10. Tompkins for C/S, 18 August 1943, loc. cit.

11. Gen. G. C. Marshall for Tompkins, 8 September 1943, loc. cit.

12. Lt. Gen. H. A. Drum to Palmer, 15 November 1943, chronological file, Box 24, misc.

13. Forrest Pogue, *George C. Marshall* (New York, 1963), v. 1, pp. 528-29. The story of the curtains was given to me by an army wife who declared the episode was a matter of common knowledge at the time. See also Noel F. Busch, "General Drum," *Life* 10 (16 June 1941): 82-96.

14. C. F. Romanus and R. Sunderland, *Stilwell's Mission to China* (Washington, GPO, 1953), 63-70.

15. Cy, dated December 1943, in Palmer, chronological file, Box 24, Misc.

16. Palmer to Thacher, 18 December 1943, chronological file, 1947-49, last folder.

17. Palmer to Brig. Gen. E. W. Smith, 23 December 1943, chronological file, Box 24, Misc.

18. Palmer to Tompkins, 23 February 1944, NA, RG 165, Special Planning Div., AG 325, NG.

19. See Palmer memo for record, 9 January 1948.

20. Tompkins for C/S, 31 January 1944.

21. "Notes on National Guard Conference," 28-29 February 1944, with related buckslips, NA, RG 163, Special Planning Div., AG 325, NG.

22. Col. W. E. Carpenter for Director, Special Planning Div., 3 January 1944, loc. cit.

23. "Notes on National Guard Conference," 28-29 Feb. 1944, loc. cit.

24. Ibid. See also Palmer to Drum, 16 March 1944, loc. cit.

25. Tompkins for Drum, 3 March 1944, loc. cit.

26. Palmer for Director, Special Planning Div., 3 March 1944, loc. cit.

27. Director, Special Planning Div., for C/S, 8 March 1944, loc. cit.

28. Palmer to Director, Special Planning Div., 10 March 1944, chronological file, Box 24, downgraded materials.

29. Palmer to Mrs. J. L. Price, Springfield, Ill., 16 November 1943, in 1944 file; Palmer to S. Miles, 29 January 1944.

30. Palmer for Director, Special Planning Div., 10 March 1944, chronological file, Box 24, downgraded materials.

31. Ibid.

32. Palmer to Drum, 15 March 1944, NA, RG 165, Special Planning Div., AG 325, NG. See also Palmer to Drum, 24 March 1944, chronological file.

33. Palmer to K. P. Budd, 15 May 1944, NA, RG 165, Special Planning Div., AG 353, Training.

34. Palmer to "dear George" [Marshall], 10 March 1944, NA, RG 165, Special Planning Div., AG 032.2, Woodrum.

35. H Resolution 465, 78 Cong, 2 Sess, 28 March 1941, Rep. J. W. Wadsworth.

36. Palmer to Polly [Mary Palmer Rockwell] 18 March 1944, chronological file, Box 13, downgraded materials. See also Tompkins for C/S, 10 March 1944, with buckslip and amendments on Palmer's proposed testimony, undated.

37. House Hearings, Select Committee on Postwar Military Policy, 78 Cong, 2 Sess, Proposal to Establish a Single Department of Armed Forces, 1944, Palmer's testimony, pp. 5-18, 28 March 1944.

38. Palmer to Polly, 25 April 1944, Mary Palmer Rockwell papers. See also Palmer to Rep. C. J. Bell, 25 April 1944, and fifty-four other recipients, chronological file, 1945-46.

39. Palmer to T. McIlvaine, 23 April 1944.

40. Palmer to Budd, 18 April 1944.

41. Walsh's statement is in House Hearings, Select Committee on Postwar Military Policy, 78 Cong, 2 Sess, Proposal to Establish a Single Department of Armed Forces, 1944, pp. 276-93, and also in a pamphlet, "Statement of Policy Submitted to House Select Committee on Postwar Military Organization," 18 May 1944, on behalf of the National Guard Association and the Adjutants General Association, cy in Palmer, chronological file.

42. Tabulation dated 30 April 1944, chronological file, Box 11.

43. General Walsh may have been shown a copy of Director, Special Planning Div., to Chief, National Guard Bureau, 28 April 1944, correspondence file, Box 15, downgraded materials, proposing studies on the future of the Guard, which could easily have been interpreted as reflecting an intention to reduce the Guard to the status of a home guard. For insights on the political role of the leader of the National Guard Association, see Martha Derthick, *The National Guard in Politics* (Cambridge, Mass., 1965), 69-71.

44. Maj. Gen. E. A. Walsh statement, House Hearings, Select Committee on Postwar Military Policy, 78 Cong, 2 Sess, Proposal to Establish a Single Department of Armed Forces, 1944, p. 288.

45. Palmer for Director, Special Planning Div., 23 May 1944, chronological file, Box 24, and 25 May 1944, correspondence file.

46. For the unreadiness of the Guard, see testimony of Marshall, House Hearings before the Select Committee on Postwar Military Policy, 79 Cong, 1 Sess, 16 June 1945, p. 576.

47. Palmer to Drum, 24 May 1944.

48. John M. Palmer, "The Tactical Measuring Rod," *National Service*, April 1917.

49. Palmer to Drum, 26 May 1944.

50. Palmer, typescript, "An Old Soldier's Memories" v. 2, pp. 396-97, chapter notes, Box 23.

51. Director, Special Planning Div., for C/S, 19 June 1944, and C/S for G-1, 2, 3, and 4 and OPD, 3 October 1944, Box 24, Misc. See also Director, Special Planning Div., for C/S, 5 August 1944, chronological file, World War II notebook, v. 4. Brig. Gen. E. W. Smith, Executive for Reserve and ROTC Affairs, apparently unaware that Marshall had already approved the Section 5 committees, wrote a long memo to the Chief of Staff, 4 Aug. 1944 urging their reconstitution, NA, RG 165, Special Planning Div., AG 334, AUS Committee on Reserve Policy. Clearly, not all the staff sections manifested opposition to a voice for the civilian components in policy making.

52. Palmer to G. Clark, 23 June 1944.

53. Palmer for Tompkins, 11 July 1944.

54. Col. F. McCarthy to Palmer, 11 July 1944.

55. Tompkins for Palmer, 22 July 1944.

56. Lt. Gen. L. J. McNair for C/S, 12 July 1944.

57. Palmer for C/S, 3 August 1944.

58. Palmer to McCarthy, 17 July 1944.

59. Palmer to Miles, 29 January 1944; Palmer to Tompkins, 6 March 1944.

60. Palmer to Polly, 14 February 1944, Mary Palmer Rockwell papers.

61. Palmer to Polly, 10 February 1944, and related correspondence through 2 November 1944, Mary Palmer Rockwell papers.

62. Mary [Polly] to Palmer, 23 May, 4 July, and 20 September 1944, and reply 12 September 1944, Mary Palmer Rockwell papers.

63. Director, Special Planning Div., for C/S, 8 August 1944, NA, RG 165, OCS, AG 370.1.

64. Smith to Palmer, 31 August 1944, chronological file, Box 24, Misc.

65. War Dept. Public Relations Bureau release, 23 September 1944. See, for example, *New York Times,* 3 September; *Boston Herald,* 10 September; and *Washington Daily News,* 4 September 1944.

66. *Army and Navy Journal,* 23 September 1944, p. 1. H. C. Petersen to Palmer, 15 September 1944, chronological file, Box 24, Misc.

67. Palmer to Woodrum, 7 September 1944.

68. Palmer to "Dear George" [Marshall] 14 September 1944, chronological file, Box 24, Misc.

69. *Army and Navy Journal,* 9 September 1944, p. 31.

70. Palmer to McCarthy, 22 November 1944, chronological file, and reply, 23 November 1944, NA, RG 165, OCS, AG 000.76.

71. Palmer to Maj. Gen. F. Parker, 18 October 1944.

72. Walsh to Palmer, 28 September 1944, chronological file, Box 24, Misc.

73. Palmer to Gen. T. T. Handy, 13 December 1945, chronological file, 1942-3.

74. Palmer to Parker, 18 October 1944.

75. Palmer for C/S, 1 December 1944.

76. Brig. Gen. E. A. Evans, Chairman, G/S Committee on Reserve Policy, for C/S, 22 December 1944, NA, RG 165, Special Planning Div., AG 334, General Staff Committee on Reserve Policy.

77. Palmer for Deputy C/S, 6 December 1944, loc. cit.

78. Palmer for C/S, 29 December 1944, loc. cit.

79. Marshall for Palmer, 30 December 1944, loc. cit.

80. Palmer for C/S, 1 January 1945, loc. cit.

81. Palmer to Marshall, 17 November, and Palmer to McCarthy, 17 November 1944.

82. Palmer to Polly, 22 September 1944, Mary Palmer Rockwell papers.

83. Palmer for C/S, 3 October 1944, chronological file, 1947-49.

84. Palmer to Polly, 25 October 1944, Mary Palmer Rockwell papers; B. Hibbs to Palmer, 25 October 1944, chronological file, *Saturday Evening Post* folder.

85. Palmer to Polly, 18 December 1944, Mary Palmer Rockwell papers.

86. Marshall to Hibbs, 22 October 1944, chronological file, *Saturday Evening Post* folder.

87. C/S for Director, Special Planning Div., 22 November 1944, chronological file, 1944; Palmer for C/S; 2 November 1944, chronological file, 1947-49.

88. Hibbs to Palmer, 6 November and 10 November 1944, chronological file, *Saturday Evening Post* folder.

89. See, for example, Palmer for Hibbs, 2 November 1944, loc. cit.

90. *New York Herald Tribune*, 22 December 1944, editorial.

91. Sen. W. R. Austin to Palmer, 30 December 1944.

92. Palmer to E. A. Davidson, 4 January 1945, Mary Palmer Rockwell papers, Yale Press folder.

93. A. Richards to Palmer, 26 December 1944.

94. Palmer to Polly, 7 January 1945, Mary Palmer Rockwell papers, G. C. Marshall folder.

95. For a note of cautious appraisal, see Palmer for Marshall, 9 January 1945, chronological file, 1947-49.

CHAPTER 51

1. Brig. Gen. W. F. Tompkins, statement before National Defense Committee of American Legion, Chicago, 18 September 1944.

2. *New York Times*, 10 September 1944, IV, 10:5, and 25 August 1944, 13:1.

3. Tompkins for Asst. S/W, 9 June 1944.

4. For the president's equivocation, see *New York Times*, 11 August 1944, 11:1; 19 August, 1:2; and 18 November, 1:3.

5. *New York Times*, 18 August 1944, 8:1; pamphlet by Citizens Committee for Universal Military Training, *"Declaration of Purposes: Statement of Hon. H. L. Stimson, Secretary of War,"* 24 August 1944.

6. Maj. Gen. W. L. Weible for Palmer, 28 December 1944.

7. H. C. Petersen for Tompkins, 13 July 1944, and K. P. Budd to Petersen, 17 August 1944, NA, RG 165, Special Planning Div., AG 353 Training.

8. Brig. Gen. E. W. Smith, Executive for Reserve and ROTC affairs, WD General Staff, to Col. S. P. Brown, American Legion Defense Committee, 15 August 1944, loc. cit.

9. Palmer for Tompkins, 6 May 1944; Palmer to M. D. Campbell, director, Div. of National Defense, American Legion, 24 August, and reply, 15 September, and Brown to Palmer, 2 September 1944.

10. F. M. Sullivan, executive director, American Legion, to Palmer, 2 October 1944.

11. N. Sargeant, Sec'y NAM, to Col. D. C. Clark, 12 May 1944, NA, RG 165, Special Planning Div., AG 353, Training.

12. *New York Times*, 6 November 1944, 13:1, and 15 June 1945, 3:5.

13. Palmer to A. G. Thacher, 23 October 1944, chronological file, 1947-49.

14. Palmer to Thacher, 17 Nov. 1944.

15. Text of resolution, 1 March 1944, in chronological file. For comments, see Palmer to Maj. Gen. C. B. Hodges, president, Louisiana State University, 29 April 1944.

16. See, for example, E. Angell, President, Council for Democracy, to Palmer, 27 September, and reply 16 October 1944, the latter covering six pages of single-spaced typescript which restate the affirmative case without meeting Angell's objections.

17. J. W. Farley to Budd, 30 June 1944; Director, Special Planning Div. for Petersen, OUSW, 22 July 1944, NA, RG 165, Special Planning Div., AG 353, Training.

18. Col. J. Greene to Palmer, 2 February 1944, loc cit.

19. Smith for Director, Special Planning Div., 7 June 1944. See also Smith to author, 23 September and 8 October 1957.

20. Palmer to Thacher, 17 September 1945, chronological file, 1947-49.

21. Palmer to Gen. G. C. Marshall, 13 November 1944, and Palmer to B. Hibbs, 11 November 1944, chronological file, 1947-49.

22. Palmer to C. E. Hughes, 13 November 1944, chronological file, 1947-49.

23. Palmer to Marshall, 18 November 1944, Hughes to Palmer, 11 December 1944, and Palmer to Hughes, 18 November 1944, chronological file, 1947-49.

24. Palmer to A. Richards, 2 December 1944, chronological file, 1947-49.

25. Palmer to Polly [Mary Palmer Rockwell], 14 February 1945, Mary Palmer Rockwell papers.

26. Palmer to Chief, News and Features Bureau, OWI, 28 March 1945, and J. E. Kramm, H. W. Wilson Co., to Palmer, 5 July 1945, chronological file, 1943-44; J. Begg, Information Liaison Office, OWI, to Palmer, 16 April 1945, chronological file, 1947-49.

27. For a favorable reaction, see Gen. M. W. Clark to Palmer, 2 February 1945. For a hostile reaction see editorial in John LaFarge, "Catholic Review of the Week," *America,* 13 January 1945.

28. Palmer for Weible, 19 April 1945; Horace M. Kallen, "The Place of War in the Education of Free Men," *Journal of Legal and Political Sociology,* v. 3, Fall 1944, pp. 5-33; Palmer to Kallen, 29 March 1945.

29. Kallen to Palmer, 29 March and 27 April 1945.

30. Kallen to Palmer, 17 May 1945.

31. See 58 Stat. 148, Public Law 277, 1 April 1944, Title V, Section 22.

32. R. P. Patterson, USW, for S/W, 4 January 1945, and endorsement by H. L. Stimson, NA, RG 165, Special Planning Div., AG 032.2, Woodrum.

33. Text of president's address, *New York Times*, 7 January 1945, 32:8.

34. Stimson for F. D. Roosevelt, 12 January 1945, NA, RG 165, Special Planning Div., AG 353, Training.

35. Col. W. E. Carpenter for Director, Special Planning Committee, 8 April 1944, NA, RG 165, Special Planning Div., AG 032.2, Woodrum.

36. Smith, Chief, Legislative and Liaison Div., WDGS, for Director, Special Planning Div., 7 August 1944, loc. cit.

37. Maj. Gen. F. H. Osborn, Director, Morale Services Div., For Director, Special Planning Div., 23 June 1944, loc. cit.

38. Palmer for Col. D. W. Wainhouse, 4 October 1944; Thacher to Tompkins, 23 October 1944, and George H. Gallup, *The Gallup Poll: Public Opinion, 1935-1971* (N.Y., 1972) I, pp. 483, 490, 495, 501, 509, 516.

39. Director, Special Planning Div., for CG, ASF, 10 February 1945, and Comment No. 2 on above, OPD for Special Planning Div., 24 February 1945. See also Maj. Huffman to Director, Special Planning Div., 6 December 1945, NA, RG 165, Special Planning Div., AG 353, Training.

40. Director, Special Planning Div., for Maj. Gen. R. E. Porter, G-3, 27 October, and reply 31 October 1944, NA, RG 165, Special Planning Div. AG 032.2, Woodrum.

41. Lt. Col. G. B. Walker for Director, Special Planning Div., 12 January 1945, loc. cit.

42. See unsigned memo, 24 April 1945, and Palmer for Director, Special Planning Div., 30 May 1945, chronological file, Box 24, Misc.

43. Col. G. E. Textor, Deputy Director, Special Planning Div., for Director, 12 May 1945, NA 165, Special Planning Div., AG 353, Training.

44. Col. F. S. Skinner for Director, Special Planning Div., 2 June 1945, NA, RG 165, Special Planning Div. AG 334, General Staff Committee on Reserves.

45. For some further examples, see Acting Chief of Staff, AAF, for Director, Special Planning Div., 2 March 1945, and Maj. Gen. I. H. Edwards, G-3, to Director, Special Planning Div., 16 March 1945, NA, RG 165, Special Planning Div., AG 353, Training; Col. R. B. Shuman for Director, Special Planning Div., 25 March 1944, chronological file, Box 11, downgraded materials.

46. Palmer to C/S 16 November 1944, chronological file, 1947-49.

47. Palmer to Col. R. M. Shaw, 21 October 1944, NA, RG 165, Special Planning Div., AG 353, Training.

48. Draft memo, Textor for C/S, 26 December 1944, NA, RG 165, Special Planning Div., AG 350.06, Military Problems.

49. Palmer for Acting Director, Special Planning Div., 18 December 1944, chronological file, Box 11, downgraded materials.

50. Wadsworth to Rep. L. H. Gavin, 1 December 1945.

51. Director, Special Planning Div., Director, Military Training Div., ASF, 19 January 1945, NA, RG 165, Special Planning Div., AG 353, Training.

52. Ibid.

53. Porter, Director, Special Planning Div., for C/S, 29 June 1945, and S/W to National Commander, American Legion, 11 January 1945, loc. cit.

54. Director, Special Planning Div., for C/S, 29 June 1945, loc. cit.

55. "A Plan for the Permanent Postwar Military Establishment Prepared and Presented to the Congress of the United States by the National Guard Association of the United States on behalf of the National Guard of the United States," 2 April 1945, NA, RG 165, Special Planning Div., AG 325, National Guard. This flamboyant title,

accurately mirroring General Walsh's style, appears not to have been approved by the association.

56. Tompkins, Disposition Form Comment No. 1, 20 April 1945, loc. cit.

57. Col. J. Cooke, President, Citizen's Committee for Universal Military Training, to Weible, 7 May 1945, NA, RG 163, Special Planning Div., AG 353, Training. See also Palmer to Director Special Planning Div., 16 May 1945.

58. Palmer for Director, Special Planning Div., 16 May 1945, loc. cit.

59. Maj. Gen. W. B. Persons, Chief, Legislative and Liaison Div., for Assistant Secretary of War, 12 March 1945, loc. cit. and *Cong Rec*, 79 Cong, 1 Sess, 31 May 1945, p. A2633.

60. Palmer to Rep. J. W. Wadsworth, 1 June 1945.

61. Palmer for C/S, 7 June 1945, chronological file, Box 24, Misc.

62. Palmer to Thacher, 6 June 1945, chronological file, 1943-44.

63. Palmer for C/S, 5 June 1945.

64. Palmer for C/S, 12 June 1945.

65. Hearings before the Select Committee on Postwar Military Policy, House of Representatives, 79 Cong, 1 Sess, 4-19 June 1945, pp. 489 ff (Woodrum Committee).

66. House Report 857, 79 Cong, 1 Sess, 5 July 1945, "Universal Military Training."

67. *New York Times*, 6 July 1945, 10:5.

68. *New York Times*, 6 July 1945, 1:5.

69. Palmer to G. Clark, 14 June 1945, chronological file, 1947-49.

70. Facsimile copy, E. Staunton to Mr. President, 12 December 1863; Lincoln's endorsement, 12 December 1863, Mary Palmer Rockwell papers, misc. file.

71. Palmer to Marshall, 5 December 1945, Mary Palmer Rockwell papers, Marshall file.

72. Palmer for C/S through Director, Special Planning Div., 2 July 1945.

73. Carpenter for Director, Special Planning Div., 15 August 1945, NA, RG 163, Special Planning Div. AG 353, Training; *New York Times*, 17 August 1945, 1:2.

74. Palmer to Thacher, 6 September 1945, chronological file, 1943-44.

75. Director, Special Planning Div., for C/S, 7 September 1945, and Special Planning Div., memo for the President, 21 September 1945, NA, RG 163, SPD, AG 353, Training.

76. Thacher to Stimson, 30 August 1945, and Palmer to Thacher, 6 September 1945, chronological file, 1943-44. See also Hanson W. Baldwin, *New York Times*, 29 August 1945, 12:2.

77. Palmer to Textor, 31 August 1945, NA, RG 165, Special Planning Div., AG 353, Training.

78. Interview with Maj. Gen. W. F. Tompkins, 18 August 1965.

79. *Cong Rec,* 79 Cong, 1 Sess, 15 November 1945, p. A 4890, and 20 November 1945, p. A 5068.

80. Palmer for C/S through Director, Special Planning Div., 2 July 1945.

81. "War Department Policies Relating to the Postwar National Guard," approved 13 October 1945, NA, RG 165, Special Planning Div., AG 334 General Staff Committee on National Guard and Reserve Policy. See also Brig. Gen. H. I. Hodes,

Asst. Deputy C/S, for C/S 28 September 1945, NA, RG 465, OCS, AG 325, National Guard.

82. Palmer for Director, Special Planning Div., 21 March 1945, chronological file, Box 15, downgraded materials.

83. Maj. Gen. J. F. Williams to National Guard Assn., 25 April 1945, NA 165, Special Planning Div., RG 325, National Guard.

84. Palmer for C/S, 28 September 1945.

85. Palmer to Thacher, 27 September 1945.

86. Biennial Report of the Chief of Staff of the U.S. Army, 1 July 1943 to 30 June 1945. Full text in *New York Times*, 10 October 1945, II.

87. Palmer to "Dear George," 24 September 1945, chronological file, Box 24, misc.

88. Palmer to Kallen, 16 October 1945.

89. Palmer to Thacher, 24 October 1945, chronological file, 1947-49.

90. Palmer to Marshall, 30 September 1943.

91. *New York Times*, 28 October 1945, IV, 10:1; Thacher to Palmer, 15 October 1945, chronological file, 1942-43.

92. *New York Times*, 14 October 1945, V, 5:7.

93. For some indications of Truman's tortured approach to the UMT issue, see *New York Times*, 17 August 1945, 1:2; 7 September, 17:3; 18 October, 11:1; 21 October, 15:3; 23 October, 8:8.

94. For a brief and inadequate account of the background of Truman's decision, see H. S. Truman, *Memoirs*, (Garden City, N.Y., 1955-56) v. 1, pp. 510-12. The full text of his address is in *New York Times*, 24 October 1945, 1:8.

95. Wadsworth to Thacher, 24 October 1945, chronological file, Box 31, misc.

96. For opposition tactics, see *New York Times*, 9 November 1945, 9:4; 15 November, 13:2; 18 November, 33:2.

97. *New York Times*, 21 November 1945, 5:7.

98. *Cong Digest*, November 1945, p. 258; *New York Times*, 9 December 1945, 10:8; *Cong Rec*, 77 Cong, 1 Sess, 27 November 1945, p. A5146.

99. Palmer to Thacher, 3 December 1945.

100. Deputy Director, Special Planning Div., for C/S, 20 December 1945; marked "O.K. D.E.," NA, RG 165, OCS, AG 381.

101. Director, Special Planning Div., To TAG, 22 September 1944, and Acting Sec'y, General Staff, for Tompkins, 23 September 1944, NA, RG 165, OCS, AG 201 P.

102. Palmer to "Dear George," 28 December 1945.

CHAPTER 52

1. Palmer for C/S, 7 January 1946; Maj. Gen. R. E. Porter, Director, Special Planning Div., for C/S, 9 January 1946; C/S for Palmer, 21 January 1946, chronological file, World War II, v. 6.

2. Palmer to Gen. G. C. Marshall, 25 February 1946.

3. Gen. D. D. Eisenhower for Palmer, 30 January 1946.

4. Palmer for C/S, 11 Feburary 1946, chronological file, Box 15, downgraded materials.

5. In addition to the memo of 11 February, see Palmer for C/S, 7 March and 19 March, as well as chief of staff for Palmer, 9 March 1946, loc. cit.

6. Palmer for Col. H. W. Kent, 15 February 1946.

7. Memorandum for the Committee on Civilian Components (Gray Board), 9 January 1948, cy in "An Old Soldier's Memories," typescript, v. 2, pp. 383 ff., Palmer Mss, Box 23.

8. Circular 347 of 25 August 1944 rescinded by W. D. Memo 310-20-1, 10 July 1946; interview with C. N. Macklin, AGO, 15 July 1969.

9. Palmer to A. G. Thacher, 26 November 1946; Palmer for C/S, 8 April, and reply, 12 April 1946, chronological file, 1947-49.

10. WD, Bureau of Public Relations release, 1 May 1946.

11. Lt. Col. R. M. Thurston, Office of Executive for Reserve and ROTC Affairs, to Palmer, 3 May 1946, chronological file, Box 24, Misc.

12. Palmer to J. W. Wadsworth, 3 May 1946.

13. Palmer to E. Davidson, 20 November 1946; Palmer to Polly [Mary Palmer Rockwell], 20 May 1946.

14. Palmer to G. Clark, 28 November 1947, chronological file, Box 2, 1916 folder.

15. Palmer to Wadsworth, 9 August 1945, chronological file, 1947-49.

16. Palmer to Col. F. McCarthy, 12 October 1945.

17. *Cong Rec,* 79 Cong, 2 Sess, 5 June 1946, p. 6335.

18. *New York Times,* 26 June 1946, 1:8.

19. H. W. Baldwin in *New York Times,* 23 March 1946, 24:2.

20. *New York Times,* 3 October 1946, 1:1, and 29 December 1946, IV, 7:1.

21. Memo for record, Lt. Col. A. Snyder, 9 May 1946, re commission proposed by J. Conant, offers insights on the background of the commission idea.

22. *New York Times,* 20 December 1946, 1:5, and 21 December, 1:4. See also *Army and Navy Journal,* 21 December 1946, p. 1.

23. K. T. Compton to Wadsworth, 18 January 1947.

24. Palmer to Wadsworth, 20 and 28 January 1947.

25. Lt. Gen. R. S. McLain to Palmer, 30 January 1947.

26. Wadsworth to Compton, 28 January 1947.

27. Palmer's testimony is in J. H. Ohly, Exec. Sec'y, Compton Commission, to Palmer, 17 February 1947.

28. W. J. Cohen, Director of Research, Compton Commission, to Palmer, 6 May 1947, and undated memo No. 2 [May 1947], Palmer for Compton Commission.

29. Palmer to Ohly, 14 June 1945.

30. *Army and Navy Journal,* 7 June 1947, p. 1055; *Time,* 9 June 1947, p. 19, and *New York Times,* 2 June 1947, 1:8.

31. Palmer to Ohly, 14 June 1947.

32. See roundup of press opinion in *Army and Navy Journal,* 7 June 1947, p. 1030, and *New York Times,* 27 June 1947, 5:1.

33. House Report 1107, 80 Cong. 1 Sess, 26 July 1947, to accompany HR 4278. See also *New York Times,* 26 July 1947, 11:3.

34. For a revealing insight on attitudes in Congress on UMT, see Wadsworth to E. A. Sumner, 26 January 1948, L/C, Wadsworth Mss, Box 31.

35. Palmer to Wadsworth, 28 July 1947, chronological file, 1945-46.

36. The episode may be traced in *New York Times*, 30 September 1947, 8:4; 2 October, 26:3; 7 November, 1:2; 8 November, 3:7; 13 February 1948, 17:2; 14 February 4:7; 15 February, 25:1; 25 February, 5:6.

37. "The National Guard and Reserve Must Be Unified", *Reserve Officer* 24 (Oct. 1947) 10-11.

38. *Army and Navy Journal*, 15 November 1947, p. 271, and 6 December 1947, p. 351.

39. Memorandum for the Committee on Civilian Components (Gray Board), 9 January 1948, cy in "An Old Soldier's Memories," typescript, v. 2, pp. 383 ff., Palmer Mss., Box 23.

40. *Army and Navy Journal*, 14 August, p. 1378, and 21 August 1948, p. 1411. See also Martha Derthick, *The National Guard in Politics* (Cambridge, Mass., 1965), 73, and mimeograph "Address to the Command and General Staff College by Maj. Gen. Ellard A. Walsh, President of the National Guard Assn. of the U.S.," Ft. Leavenworth, Kans., 10 February 1949, cy in chronological file.

41. Palmer to Wadsworth, 30 August 1948.

42. Palmer to L. H. Evans, 3 May 1950, chronological file, Box 24, misc.

43. Palmer to B. Baumgarten, 16 May 1949, Mary Palmer Rockwell Mss., Brandt and Brandt folder.

44. Palmer to Polly, undated [July 1948], Mary Palmer Rockwell Mss.

45. Palmer to "Dear Friend in Military Preparedness" no date [April 1947], not sent, chronological file, 1945-46.

46. Palmer to Maj. Gen. B. E. Moore, 15 March 1959.

47. "Account of a Journey from Washington to West Point Made by Maude and John Palmer, 3-7 June 1949," chronological file, Box 24, misc.

48. "Register of Delinquencies: 1888-1892," No. 26, 1888. USMA Archives.

49. *New York Times*, 7 June 1949, 22:2; interviews with Mary Palmer Rockwell, 13 August 1963 and 20 August 1968.

50. Palmer to R. M. Lester, Sec'y, Carnegie Corp., 11 February 1950, Mary Palmer Rockwell Mss, Brandt and Brandt folder.

51. Thacher to Palmer, 15 June 1950, chronological file, 1947-49.

CHAPTER 53

1. See, for example, Lt. Col. William Geffen, ed., *Command and Commanders in Modern Warfare*, proceedings of Second Military History Symposium, USAF Academy 2-3 May 1968 (Washington, D.C., Office of Air Force History, 1971), 65.

2. C/S to Maj. Gen. J. F. O'Ryan, 24 May; O'Ryan to Palmer, 26 May; and Palmer to O'Ryan 28 May 1944, Mary Palmer Rockwell Mss.

3. WD, TAG, Palmer 201 file, 23 June 1923.

4. Cy, Gen. J. J. Pershing to H. C. Lodge, 15 June 1942, L/C Pershing Mss, Palmer, J., folder.

5. Maj. Gen. C. G. Morton to WD, TAG, 18 January 1922, chronological file, 1918.

6. Interview with Gen. Lewis B. Hershey, 13 February 1967.

7. Jessie Palmer Weber to Palmer, 25 July 1922.

8. Palmer to Jessie Palmer Weber, 29 July 1922.

9. H. Hagedorn, *Leonard Wood* (New York, 1931), vol. 1, p. 398, and Frederick Sleigh, Lord Roberts, *Fallacies and Facts*, London, 1911.

10. Palmer to P. T. Bohan, 19 June 1944.

11. Palmer to P. B. Graves, 11 Dec. 1941; Palmer to D. Buzhardt, 12 May 1943, chronological file, 1941 America in Arms folder.

12. See above, chapter 44, text at note 36; L. W. Labaree to Palmer 11 Oct. 1940, chronological file 1930, Doubleday folder.

13. Count Otto Moltke, *Einst, Jetzt, Was Dann?* (Berlin: Beteuchtung der Militarvorlag, 1893), 22, quoted in Baron Hugo Von Freytag-Loringhoven, *A Nation Trained in Arms or a Militia?* (New York, 1918), 217.

14. For a minor exception to this generalization, see Palmer to A. G. Thacher, 26 April 1944.

15. Interview with Gen. George C. Marshall, 21 July 1953.

16. See, for example, Palmer to E. M. Earle, Institute for Advanced Study, 10 June 1943, chronological file, Box 24.

17. Palmer to Thacher, 19 February and 26 April 1944.

18. H. Le Comte to Palmer, 16 August 1938, chronological file.

19. For an example of an early warning on the hidden costs encountered in maintaining a reserve force, see N. Carothers for Palmer, 9 June 1919.

20. Document 178 1/2, comment on reverse, Brig. Gen. G. V. H. Moseley, Scrapbook, pp. 1899 ff, L/C, Moseley papers; E. M. Coffman to author, 7 March 1963, re Gen. P. C. March's comments on Palmer in Army War College lecture.

21. Karl von Clausewitz, *On War* (Princeton, N.J.: Princeton University Press, 1976), 110-111.

Sources

MAJOR REPOSITORIES OF MANUSCRIPTS

LIBRARY OF CONGRESS, MANUSCRIPTS DIVISION, WASHINGTON, D. C.

The most important body of source materials used in the preparation of this volume was the collection of personal papers assembled by General Palmer and deposited in the Manuscripts Division after his retirement. These consist of four broad categories: the first, comprising fifteen file boxes, is a chrono-logical file containing incoming correspondence, drafts or carbons of outgo-ing correspondence, article manuscripts, military staff studies, and miscellaneous clippings, pamphlets, working papers, reading notes, and so on, with the bulk of the materials falling between the years 1886 and 1947. Boxes 1 through 9 cover the years 1886 to 1941; Boxes 10 through 15 cover the period of Palmer's service during World War II. The second category, Boxes 16 through 21, contain "chapter notes" assembled by Palmer when planning his memoirs. Some of these consist of typed preliminary rough drafts of actual text written by him; some consist of typed copies of documents such as orders, diary entries, extracts from letters, and so on; and some consist of the original documents themselves. The third category, Box 22, consists of an annotated carbon copy of "An Old Soldier's Memories," Palmer's draft text for chapters 1 through 10, substantially as published in this volume. The fourth and final category, comprising Boxes 23-26, contains miscellaneous papers contributed by the Palmer family after the original accession, declassified materials that had been segregated from the mass of the general's World War II papers before being downgraded, and a group of papers relating to Palmer contri-buted by Anson Conger Goodyear of Buffalo, New York.

The Palmer papers constitute an unusually rich lode for a biographer for several reasons. Throughout his career the general methodically preserved not only the usual items of record but also working drafts of many of his outgoing holograph letters and a wide variety of pamphlets, military memoranda, and similar ephemera useful in providing a contemporary context for his own work. Further, when organizing his papers in retirement prior to writing his memoirs, the general dictated a number of memoranda or sketches to fill in blank spots in the record or to enrich the account of an episode not entirely self-evident from the remaining documents.

In addition to the Palmer papers, among the many collections consulted in the Manuscripts Division of the Library of Congress, the personal papers of the following individuals proved to be most helpful: Newton D. Baker, Gen. Tasker H. Bliss, Gen. Robert L. Bullard, Sen. F. L. Greene of Vermont, Rep. James Hay of Virginia, Gen. James G. Harbord, Gen. Peyton C. March, Gen. George Van Horn Moseley, Gen. John J. Pershing, Gen. Charles P. Summerall, and Rep. James W. Wadsworth of New York.

THE NATIONAL ARCHIVES, WASHINGTON, D.C.

Materials from the following Record Groups proved to be of particular value:

RG 94	Adjutant General's Office (AGO).
RG 111	World War Signal Corps Films, especially Film 111 M-29, Item 49, 29th Division Combat Operations (3 reels), and Film H 1486, Item 129, 29th Division, et al., Meuse-Argonne Offensive (1 reel).
RG 120	American Expeditionary Force (AEF) General Headquarters Files, 1917-21.
RG 129	29th Division Historical File; Historical Collections 27.7 and 32.7.
RG 165	War Department General Staff File, 1903-21. See subject and name index.
RG 165	War Department Special Planning Division Files. (World War II).
RG 316	29th Division Historical File of Col. George S. Stuart, Boxes 13-17.
RG 316	Army Reorganization File, Box 3.
RG 316	Pershing Papers.

CENTER FOR MILITARY HISTORY, DEPARTMENT OF ARMY, WASHINGTON, D.C.

The Center for Military History maintains a vertical file of a wide variety of items of interest to military historians. These resources can be located through an alphabetical subject and proper name index. There is a separate index for the files of the former Army War College Historical Section dating from the World War I period. Of particular value for this study were copies of Palmer's lectures at the Army War College not found in his own papers.

DUKE UNIVERSITY LIBRARY MANUSCRIPTS
DIVISION, DURHAM, N.C.

Especially useful among the resources of this collection were the papers of Thomas Nelson Page, U.S. Ambassador to Italy during the period of Palmer's mission to Italy.

UNITED STATES MILITARY ACADEMY,
WEST POINT, N.Y.

The Manuscripts Division of the USMA Library contains a scattering of items relating to Palmer's cadet days, and the files of the Association of Graduates contain a few items concerning his subsequent military career.

THE UNITED STATES ARMY MILITARY HISTORY
INSTITUTE, CARLISLE BARRACKS, PA.

This splendid collection includes among its holdings on the Army War College of the pre-1941 period a subject and proper-name card index maintained by the AWC library staff, which provides access to a wide range of military publications, many of them not indexed elsewhere. This finding aid proved to be highly valuable in the preparation of this volume.

INTERVIEWS CONDUCTED BY THE AUTHOR WITH
INDIVIDUALS WHO WERE ASSOCIATED WITH
JOHN M. PALMER

The most significant interviews undertaken by the author in the preparation of this volume were, understandably, those conducted with members of the Palmer family. Over a period of five years, when the author could find time from his teaching duties, he was most graciously and hospitably received by General and Mrs. Palmer into their home for many rewarding sessions devoted to uncovering the distant past. Any biographer who is privileged to know his subject from close association enjoys a priceless advantage. For this biographer the privilege was made doubly rewarding by the general's whimsical humor, his seemingly endless fund of anecdote, and his pervasive charm, all in addition to the manifest sincerity with which he articulated the convictions and articles of belief which underlay so much of his life's work.

No less important were the author's sessions over many years with the general's daughter, Mary Palmer Rockwell, whose devotion to her father's memory has in many ways made this volume possible. Having shared so many of the vicissitudes of the general's career, from his early days at rude western army posts and thatched huts in the Philippine jungles to Washington dinner tables with statesmen and military leaders, she has been able to supply the testimony of an eyewitness and participant at many critical points. Her generosity with time and hospitality to the author during the preparation of this volume have placed him forever in her debt. It is only fair to add, however, that the deep affection she feels for her father has not clouded her objectivity; she has respected the author's scholarly independence even when differing from his interpretations or judgments.

The author is also indebted to Col. John Palmer Chandler, U.S. Army, one of the General's grandsons, for sharing many of his childhood memories and for critical appraisals of appropriate portions of the manuscript, a process in which he was no less fair-minded than his mother.

All of the individuals listed alphabetically below, with the place and date of interview, shared their memories freely with the author, who only regrets that he cannot thank each of them individually for their contribution to the finished volume, since many of them are now deceased:

Mr. N. J. Anthony, May 1964, Washington, D.C.

Mr. Grenville Clark, July 1961 and August 1964, Dublin, N.H.

Col. Robert L. Clifford, January 1973, Durham, N.C.

Col. Arthur S. Cowan, July 1952, Washington, D.C.

Brig. Gen. John A. Cutchins, December 1961, Richmond, Va.

Dr. Wilbert C. Davison, January 1961, Durham, N.C.

Mr. John P. Eicher, July 1962, Washington, D.C.

Lt. Gen. Stanley D. Embick, July 1952, Washington, D.C.

Lt. Gen. Lewis B. Hershey, February 1967, Durham, N.C.

Maj. Gen. Herbert M. Jones, July 1958 and May 1964, Washington, D.C.

Adm. C. Barrett Laning, September 1966, Washington, D.C.

Gen. George C. Marshall, July 1953, Leesburg, Va.

Mr. Eugene C. Pomeroy, December 1960, Washington, D.C.

Mrs. M. W. Rogers, December 1958, Washington, D.C.

Maj. Gen. Milton A. Reckord, December 1961, Washington, D.C.

Maj. Gen. William F. Tompkins, August 1965, Wolfeboro, N.H.

Brig. Gen. Sanford Wadhams, June 1957, Torrington, Conn.

Miss Doris S. Whitney, July 1953, Washington, D.C.

Maj. Gen. Miller G. White, August 1953, Washington, D.C.

Gen. Thomas D. White, August 1958 and June 1964, Washington, D.C.

Brig. Gen. Willard Webb, July 1953, Washington, D.C.

The following individuals, whom the author was unable to interview in person, generously prepared written reminiscences of their association with General Palmer:

Judge George Henderson of Cumberland, Md.
Mr. E. Ormonde Hunter of Savannah, Ga.
Brig. Gen. D. John Markey of Frederick, Md.
Maj. Gen. R. L. Spragins of Huntsville, Ala.

Index

Senate bill, 466; urges Palmer promotion, 517, 707; MTCA role, 591; AEF experience of, 718
Ovenshine, Samuel, 273

pacifists, 500
pack mules. *See* mules.
Padua, Italy, 345; Cafe Pedrocchi, 352; Palazzo del Drago, 344; Stappato's restaurant, 358; Treves Palace, 345
Page, Arthur W.: reports Baker's views, 477; publishes Palmer's book, 547-48; plans Baker-Pershing book, 550; resigns as publisher, 550; promotes Palmer book, 561; summer home of, 561-62
Page, Thomas Nelson, 340, 344, 346, 350, 354
Page, Mrs. Walter Hines, 561
Palmer, Ellen Clark Robertson (mother), 6, 9; and reading, 23, 32; visits West Point, 49; relations with son, 51; moves to Chicago, 62; visits son, 68, 75, 100, 126
Palmer family, 5-6, 15-16
Palmer, Dr. George Thomas (brother), 7, 9, 32; relations with brother, 49, 68, 589; love of Illinois, 588; writes biography, 589
Palmer, Hannah Lamb Kimball ("Aunt Han") (step-grandmother), 34
Palmer, Isaac (great-great-grandfather), 5
Palmer, Jessie. *See* Weber, Jessie P.
Palmer, John McAuley (grandfather), 3-4; ancestry of, 5; education of, 5; marriage of, 13; governor of Illinois, 6, 12, 14, 31; U.S. Senator, 12, 70-71; Republican party founder, 13; principles of, 14; military service of, 9, 14, 31; XIV Corps commander, 7, 14, 30, 31, 63; views on U.S. Military Academy, 30, 31; gets appointment for grandson, 29; remarries, 34; state senator, 55-56; supports Cleveland, 63; presidential candidate, 70, 73; advice to

grandson, 71, 89, 95, 203; visits grandson, 72; visits great-grandson, 85; quotes Grant, 96; letter from Lincoln, 233; biography of, 545, 589; relations with Lincoln, 683-84; monument for, 709-10
Palmer, John McAuley
—as aide: to Gen. E. V. Sumner, 97; to Pres. McKinley, 97; to Gen. L. Wood, 215; to Secretary H. L. Stimson, 218; to Gen. J. J. Pershing, 492
—appraisals of: by Gen. Pershing, 517, 708; by Gen. Morton, 376, 402, 517, 708; by Gen. Hershey, 708; by Gen. Marshall, 713; by Gen. March, 719; by Gen. Moseley, 719, 736 n.12; by MTCA leaders, 703; by Col. Gulick, 527; by Secretary Baker, 477; by G. H. McMaster, 762 n.61
—character and personality: candor, 105-7, 226, 318-19, 624; charm, 338, 352-53, 412, 503, 556, 578; compassion, 114, 124, 165, 371; courage, 345, 347, 370; courtliness, 546; dedication, 331, 334, 534, 556; disinterestedness, 455, 533, 610, 652, 711; humor, 171, 319, 495, 515, 709; idealism, 226, 624; loyalty, 322, 324, 495, 516; modesty, 353, 371, 582, 707, 713; self-appraisal, 316, 566; self-confidence, 333, 557, 610, 663; self-delusion, 466, 495, 547, 576, 584; self-denial, 278, 334, 575, 595, 661, 671, 684, 708; self-doubt, 308-9, 318-20, 535; sensitivity, 402-3, 534; tactfulness, 196, 612-13; rectitude, 113-15, 632
—command experience: scouting patrol, 78-79; river junks, 122-25; company, 109, 117, 121, 194, 224-26; post, 126; battalion, 224, 228; qualifications, 224; brigade, 374-401, 528-29, 531-36
—contributions, 451, 713-16, 719-21
—education: childhood, 16, 18-21, 23-24; parental role, 23, 32, 712; high school, 29-30; West Point preparatory school, 30, 32; USMA, 34-61, 66, 710; on duty, 217; lack of historical training, 555,

Palmer, John McAuley (continued)
German Soldier," 556, 579; "Washington's Lost Legacy," 559; "Steuben as a Military Statesman," 569; "Franklin's Patriotic Fib," 579; "How Football Came to West Point," 624; "Two Views of War," 625; "Our Future Military Policy," 632; "General Marshall Wants a Civilian Army," 664; "How to Solve Our Postwar Defense Problem," 671
—works (books): *An Army of the People*, 230, 234-40, 252; *Ways to Peace* (chapter), 522; *The Organization of Peace*, 520-21, 545; *Statesmanship or War*, 547-50, 552-53, 560-61; *Washington, Lincoln, Wilson: Three War Statesmen*, 558, 560, 565-66, 608; *General von Steuben*, 567-68, 583-84; *America in Arms*, 608-9, 617-18
—works (pamphlets): *Infantry Journal* reprint of testimony before Senate subcommittee, 1919, 446; "Notes on Universal Military Training," 667; "The Postwar Defense Problem," 671
—works (staff studies): "The Organization of the Land Forces of the United States," 204, 209, 211; "War College memo report, 639-136, 20 Nov. 1916" (General Staff), 251-57; "Military Policies of the United States as Settled by Recent Law and Executive Orders," 492; "Proposed Legislation for Universal Military Training," 625; "The Place of the National Guard in the Postwar Reserve System," 645; "Military Establishment," War Department Circular 347, 658
—writing: verse, 50, 181-82, 611, 624; plans book on military policy, 124, 147, 223, 230, 397, 497, 519; for *N.Y. Sunday Herald*, 127; for *North American Review*, 134, 579; for *The Voter*, 137; for *McClure's* magazine, 135-36, 468; for *National Service* magazine, 186, 296; for *Infantry Journal*, 191-92, 200, 203, 231, 625, 632; for *Army and Navy*

Journal, 201, 204, 295, 469; for *Scribner's* magazine, 211, 579; for *American Legion Weekly*, 468; for *Revue Militaire Suisse*, 556; for *Harper's* magazine, 556, 579-80; for *N.Y. Herald Tribune*, 559, 563; for *German-American Historical Review*, 569; for *Army-Navy Register*, 586; for *Assembly*, 624; for *Saturday Evening Post*, 664, 667; for *Army Officer*, 667; for Chief of Staff, 204, 209, 211, 246-47, 256-57, 262, 266; criticized, 493, 523; method, 521; frustrations of, 535; on fishing, 539; plans biography of grandfather, 545; Doubleday contract, 551; lacks training in research, 555, 557; technique of, 557; publicist vs. historian, 557-58, 563, 711, 713; begins Steuben book, 567-68; attempts fiction, 539, 579; Yale contract, 580; for *Dictionary of American Biography*, 580; memoirs, 585, 608, 614-15, 695; form vs. substance, 661; translations of, 672; reprints, 446, 667, 671-72; faith in the power of, 720
Palmer, John McAuley (chronology)
—boyhood (1870-1888): Lincoln stories, 3-5; ancestry, 5-6; brothers, 7-9, 11; childhood, 3-5, 6-12, 15-21; early education, 16, 18-25; religious instruction, 17, 20; U.S. Army, first contact, 24; meets future wife, 24-25; appointment to U.S. Military Academy, 29-30; first sees West Point, 32; meets President Cleveland, 33. *See also* Palmer, John McAuley (grandfather); Robertson, Charles
—at U. S. Military Academy (1888-1892): hazed, 35; "beast," 37, 48; sworn in, 37; drilling, 38; guard mount, 39; roommates, 41, 43; promoted, 48, 50, 56; engagement, 51; July fourth speaker, 56
—at Fort Sheridan, Ill. (1892-1896): pay, 52, 62; proposes marriage, 51, 62; reflections on militia, 56-57; joins 15th Infantry, 62; drafts legislation, 66;

pay, 418, 496; attacked by disgruntled, 454; lack public support, 462, 496; morale of low, 496; as standing army, 437; as citizen army, 437; 1920 act defines role, 478, 494, 502, 504, 513; resists Palmer's views, 497, 719; costs, 501-2, 684; officers of not disinterested, 524, 649; Palmer's concept of role, 549; relations with National Guard, 423, 452-53, 617, 622, 652, 697; recruits dilute, 623; command monopoly, 639, 653; doctrinal role, 715; pros and cons, 716, 719. *See also* Army of the United States; American Expeditionary Force

Reilly, Henry J., Jr., 506, 511

Remond, Louis, 283

replacements, 270, 391, 680-81

Republican party, 3, 13, 471

Requin, Major Edouard J., 272, 283

Reserve Officer, 701

Reserve Officers Association, 511, 654

Reserve Officers Training Corps (ROTC), 85, 582, 623, 627, 685

reserves: organization of, 210; Continental Army scheme, 236; planning for peacetime, 399; Regular Army views on, 404; motivation of, 649; officers' role unclear, 655; officer standards, 656. *See also* citizen soldiers; civilian components; militia; National Guard; Organized Reserve; Regular Army, relation to reservists

retirement, 397, 419, 421, 538, 544, 694

reunions. *See* Class of 1892

reviews of Palmer books, 523, 552, 584, 617

Revue Militaire Suisse, 556

Rhodes, Charles D. ("Teddy"), 34, 36, 40, 183

Richards, Augustus L., 581, 611, 664

Richardson, C. E., 447

Richardson, Brig. Gen. Sir George L. R., 116

Rickards, George C., 494

rifle grenades, 309, 379, 385

rifles, 154, 161, 166, 226-27, 365. *See also* rifle grenades

Rinehart, Mary Roberts, 558-59

roads, 215

Robertson, Anna (aunt), 15, 17

Robertson, Charles (uncle), 15-20

Robertson, Edgar B., 109, 111, 113, 118

Robertson, Dr. Frederick McNaughton, 578

Robertson, Nancy Halliday (grandmother), 7, 16, 30, 85

Robertson, William (ancestor), 15

Robertson, William Addison (grandfather), 11, 15

Robertson College, Harrodsburg, Ky., 593

Rockwell, Mary. *See* Palmer, Mary

Roelker, Alfred, 590, 703

rolling kitchen. *See* field kitchens

Rome, Italy, 343

Roosevelt, Archibald, 591

Roosevelt, Eleanor, 665

Roosevelt, Franklin D.: on compulsory training, 591, 614, 666, 673; appoints Stimson secretary of war, 596; signs draft act, 606; death of curbs UMT, 684

Roosevelt, Theodore: Buffalo speech, 127; visits USMA, 131-32; on conservation, 215; fosters MTCS, 249; on compulsory training, 250-52, 520; on king of Italy, 346

Roosevelt, Theodore, Jr., 252

Root, Clark, Buckner and Ballantine, 249

Root, Elihu: visits West Point, 131-32; on Philippine railway, 134; founds War College, 182; on open court, 207; relations with Grenville Clark, 249; concept of General Staff, 443; Bok Peace Prize judge, 522; on Palmer's writing, 552, 562

Root, Elihu, Jr., 591, 695, 703

Rosenberg, Anna, 698

Ross, Tenney, 261

ROTC. *See* Reserve Officers Training Corps

ROTC Association of the United States, 582-83

Royal Navy, 227

Ruger, Thomas H., 131

About the Author

I. B. HOLLEY, JR. is Professor of History at Duke University in Durham, North Carolina. His previous books include *Ideas and Weapons*; *Buying Aircraft: Material Procurement for the Army Air Forces* (a volume in the Official History series, *The United States Army in World War II*); *The Transfer of Ideas* (with C. D. Goodwin); and *An Enduring Challenge: The Problem of Air Force Doctrine*. He retired from the Air Force Reserve as a Major General in 1981.